RIA Federal Tax Handbook Quick
2007 Income, Gift and Estate Taxes

Single Taxpayers

Taxable income	Amount of tax
Not over $ 7,825	10% of taxable income
Over $ 7,825 but not over $ 31,850	$ 782.50 plus 15% of the amount over $ 7,825
Over $ 31,850 but not over $ 77,100	$ 4,386.25 plus 25% of the amount over $ 31,850
Over $ 77,100 but not over $ 160,850	$ 15,698.75 plus 28% of the amount over $ 77,100
Over $ 160,850 but not over $ 349,700	$ 39,148.75 plus 33% of the amount over $ 160,850
Over $ 349,700	$ 101,469.25 plus 35% of the amount over $ 349,700

Married Taxpayers
Filing Joint Returns and Qualified Widows and Widowers

Taxable income	Amount of tax
Not over $ 15,650	10% of taxable income
Over $ 15,650 but not over $ 63,700	$ 1,565 plus 15% of the amount over $ 15,650
Over $ 63,700 but not over $ 128,500	$ 8,772.50 plus 25% of the amount over $ 63,700
Over $ 128,500 but not over $ 195,850	$ 24,972.50 plus 28% of the amount over $ 128,500
Over $ 195,850 but not over $ 349,700	$ 43,830.50 plus 33% of the amount over $ 195,850
Over $ 349,700	$ 94,601 plus 35% of the amount over $ 349,700

Married Taxpayers
Filing Separate Returns

Taxable income	Amount of tax
Not over $ 7,825	10% of taxable income
Over $ 7,825 but not over $ 31,850	$ 782.50 plus 15% of the amount over $ 7,825
Over $ 31,850 but not over $ 64,250	$ 4,386.25 plus 25% of the amount over $ 31,850
Over $ 64,250 but not over $ 97,925	$ 12,486.25 plus 28% of the amount over $ 64,250
Over $ 97,925 but not over $ 174,850	$ 21,915.25 plus 33% of the amount over $ 97,925
Over $ 174,850	$ 47,300.50 plus 35% of the amount over $ 174,850

Heads Of Household

Taxable income	Amount of tax
Not over $ 11,200	10% of taxable income
Over $ 11,200 but not over $ 42,650	$ 1,120 plus 15% of the amount over $ 11,200
Over $ 42,650 but not over $ 110,100	$ 5,837.50 plus 25% of the amount over $ 42,650
Over $ 110,100 but not over $ 178,350	$ 22,700 plus 28% of the amount over $ 110,100
Over $ 178,350 but not over $ 349,700	$ 41,810 plus 33% of the amount over $ 178,350
Over $ 349,700	$ 98,355.50 plus 35% of the amount over $ 349,700

Estates and Trusts

Taxable income	Amount of tax
Not over $ 2,150	15% of taxable income
Over $ 2,150 but not over $ 5,000	$ 322.50 plus 25% of the amount over $ 2,150
Over $ 5,000 but not over $ 7,650	$ 1,035 plus 28% of the amount over $ 5,000
Over $ 7,650 but not over $ 10,450	$ 1,777 plus 33% of the amount over $ 7,650
Over $ 10,450	$ 2,701 plus 35% of the amount over $ 10,450

Bankruptcy estates use the rate schedules for married taxpayers filing separate returns.

Capital Gains—
Individuals, Estates & Trusts and qualified dividend income*

Net short-term (held one year or less) capital gain is taxed at: Ordinary income rates

Long-term (more than one year) **capital gain** and **qualified dividend income*** are taxed at: 15% (5% for gain otherwise taxable at ordinary 10% or 15% rate)

Except the maximum tax on:

Unrecaptured section 1250 gain (attributable to real estate depreciation) is: 25%

Collectibles gain (on works of art, rugs, antiques, etc.) is: 28%

Section 1202 gain (from the sale of small business stock eligible for partial exclusion from gross income) is: 28%

* Equals dividends from domestic corporations and qualified foreign corporations that meet specified holding period requirements. Exclusions may apply.

Standard Deductions

Basic*

Single	$ 5,350
Married filing separate	$ 5,350
Married filing joint and surviving spouses	$ 10,700
Head of household	$ 7,850

Additional (for 65 or over and/or blind)

Unmarried (including head of household)	$ 1,300
Married or surviving spouse (whether or not joint return)	$ 1,050

* Limited to greater of $ 850 or the sum of $ 300 plus earned income for individuals who can be claimed as a dependent by another taxpayer.

Standard Mileage Rates

Business use of auto	48.5¢ a mile
Charitable	14¢
Medical	20¢
Moving expenses	20¢

[1]

RIA Federal Tax Handbook Quick Reference Card
2007 Income, Gift and Estate Tax Rates

Itemized Deductions
Percentage Limitations

Medical expenses	7.5% of adjusted gross income (AGI)—floor
Personal interest	0%
Net nonbusiness casualty losses	10% of AGI (after $100 per casualty limitation) -- floor
Charitable contributions	50%* of AGI—ceiling on deductible amount
Miscellaneous itemized deductions	2% of AGI—floor
Otherwise allowable itemized deductions**	Reduced if AGI exceeds $ 156,400 ($ 78,200 for marrieds filing separately)

* Other limits apply depending on type of gift and/or recipient.

** Medical expenses, investment interest, nonbusiness casualty and theft losses, and gambling losses aren't subject to the reduction. For 2007, reduction is ²/₃ of reduction that would otherwise apply. Reduction is applied after any other limitation on the allowance of an itemized deduction.

Personal Exemption

Exemption amount	$3,400

The exemption amount is reduced if AGI exceeds:

- $156,400 for single taxpayers
- $117,300 for marrieds filing separately
- $234,600 for marrieds filing jointly and qualified widows and widowers
- $195,500 for heads of household

For 2007, a taxpayer can lose no more than ²/₃ of exemption dollar amount.

Alternative Minimum Tax

AMT rates (on taxable excess – i.e., alternative minimum taxable income less exemption amount):

Individual, estate, trust:*	26% of taxable excess that doesn't exceed $175,000 ($87,500 for married filing separately)
	28% of taxable excess that exceeds $175,000 ($87,500 for married filing separately)
Corporation (other than an exempt small corporation):	20% of taxable excess

*Tax rate on net capital gain is the same as for regular tax.

AMT Exemption Amount

The AMT exemption amounts (before phaseout) are $22,500 for estates and trusts, and $40,000 for corporations. Pending legislation as we went to press would increase the AMT exemption amount for 2007 (before phaseout) to $44,350 for individuals and $66,250 for married taxpayers filing jointly. (AMT exemption for marrieds filing separately is half the joint filer amount.) Special calculations apply to child subject to kiddie tax. Check http://ria.thomson.com/federaltaxhandbook for the latest legislative news.

2007 Social Security Tax

FICA	Tax base	Rate	Maximum tax
Social Security	$ 97,500	6.2%	$ 6,045
Medicare	no limit	1.45%	no limit

2007 Self-Employment Tax

FICA	Tax base	Rate	Maximum tax
Social Security	$ 97,500	12.4%	$ 12,090
Medicare	no limit	2.9%	no limit

Corporations

Taxable income	Amount of tax
Not over $ 50,000	15% of taxable income
Over $ 50,000 but not over $ 75,000	$ 7,500 plus 25% of the amount over $ 50,000
Over $ 75,000 but not over $ 100,000	$ 13,750 plus 34% of the amount over $ 75,000
Over $ 100,000 but not over $ 335,000	$ 22,250 plus 39% of the amount over $ 100,000
Over $ 335,000 but not over $ 10,000,000	$ 113,900 plus 34% of the amount over $ 335,000
Over $ 10,000,000 but not over $ 15,000,000	$ 3,400,000 plus 35% of the amount over $ 10,000,000
Over $ 15,000,000 but not over $ 18,333,333.33	$ 5,150,000 plus 38% of the amount over $ 15,000,000
Over $ 18,333,333.33	$ 6,416,666.67 plus 35% of the amount over $ 18,333,333.33

Capital gains are taxable at regular corporate rates. The tax on qualified personal service corporations is 35% of taxable income.

2007 Unified Gift and Estate Tax Rates

Amount subject to tax	Amount of tax	Rate on excess
$ –	18% of amount transferred	
10,000	$1,800	20
20,000	3,800	22
40,000	8,200	24
60,000	13,000	26
80,000	18,200	28
100,000	23,800	30
150,000	38,800	32
250,000	70,800	34
500,000	155,800	37
750,000	248,300	39
1,000,000	345,800	41
1,250,000	448,300	43
1,500,000	555,800	45

Subject to unified credit of $ 780,800 to US citizens and residents for estate tax purposes, and a credit of $345,800 allowed to U.S. citizens and residents for gift tax purposes.

Generation-skipping taxes may also apply.

Lower rates apply to armed forces members dying in combat zone-related deaths, victims of certain terrorist attacks, and astronauts dying in the line of duty.

CPE & Training Solutions

from Thomson Tax & Accounting

800.231.1860

trainingcpe.thomson.com

Online Learning

MicroMash

A trusted provider of technology-based CPE and training for over 20 years. Choose from over 160 courses on hot topics that will help you stay on top of your field!

PASS Online

A CPE provider since 1990, PASS Online offers more than 240 electronic courses covering a variety of accounting and tax topics, including industry-leading state ethics training courses for accountants.

The Webinar Partnership Series

You'll find webinars on the latest developments in tax, accounting, auditing, finance and more!

Live Seminars & Conferences

Gear Up Live Seminars & Conferences

A leading provider of tax and accounting education for over 35 years, with nationwide seminars and exciting conferences! 2008 week-long conferences take place throughout the year in Las Vegas, Honolulu, Orlando, and—new!—Chicago.

Bell Learning

Bell Learning offers high quality regional instructor-led courses in seven states to meet your continuing professional education needs. Choose from a selection of one-day courses on key topics.

PPC Conferences

In 2008, PPC brings together authorities on topics such as Risk Assessment, Auditing, Tax Planning for High-Income Clients, and the popular PPC Users' Conference, for practical guidance and intensive learning at conferences nationwide.

In-House Training

PPC In-House Seminars

PPC offers affordable, on-site customized training on over 60 topics related to accounting and tax professions. This learning experience is custom-tailored to meet your needs, taught by highly rated instructors, features current, relevant course content. For more information call 800.323.8724, ext. 4274.

Self-Study Courses

Gear Up Self-Study

Gear Up offers standalone and seminar-based self-study courses in a variety of formats.

PPC Self-Study

Learn with the company that provides the industry-leading PPC Guides—more than 80 convenient self-study courses are available.

Quickfinder | Gear Up Self-Study CPE

Quickfinder's trusted content combined with Gear Up's 35-year+ history as a leader in tax & accounting professional education— a winning combination!

Also of interest...

Reqwired. Online CPE tracking and compliance for CPAs, with customized learning plans, self-service tools, and more!

Audit Risk Assessment CPE Solutions. A comprehensive offering of risk assessment CPE, including live conferences from PPC, In-House customized learning, Webinars, MicroMash online courses, and PPC self-study, in addition to our analysis and implementation tools.

For more CPE information on all of these solutions and products, visit: trainingcpe.thomson.com

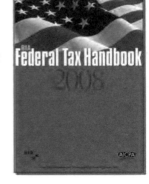

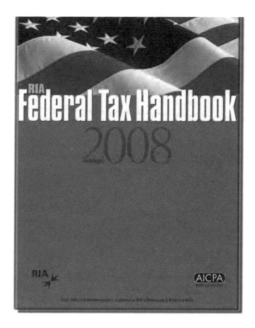

RIA
Federal Tax Handbook
2008

RIA

AICPA

More than 90% of the
Top 100 Accounting Firms
rely on RIA for their research needs.

▼ DETACH HERE AND MAIL. POSTAGE IS PAID ▼

NO POSTAGE
NECESSARY
IF MAILED
IN THE
UNITED STATES

BUSINESS REPLY MAIL
FIRST-CLASS MAIL   PERMIT NO. 50   VALHALLA, NY

POSTAGE WILL BE PAID BY ADDRESSEE

THOMSON TAX & ACCOUNTING
117 E STEVENS AVENUE
VALHALLA, NY 10595-9900

DETACH HERE AND MAIL. POSTAGE IS PAID

RIA Federal Tax Handbook

Information Products Staff

Steven A. Zelman
(LL.M., NY, NJ Bar)
Senior Vice President,
Publishing

Linda Scheffel
(LL.M., NY Bar)
Vice President
and Publisher

James A. Seidel
(LL.M., NY Bar)
Director,
Federal Taxes

Christine Carr
Director,
Data Management

Saryia Green
Product Coordinator

Kersten Behrens
(J.D., NY, NJ Bar)
Managing Editor

Cornell R. Fuerst
(J.D., NY Bar)
Managing Editor

Dennis P. McMahon
(LL.M., NY, MA Bar)
Managing Editor

Richard S. Nadler
(LL.M., NY Bar)
Managing Editor

Jeffrey N. Pretsfelder
(C.P.A.)
Managing Editor

Suzanne Baillie Schmitt
(LL.M., NY Bar)
Managing Editor

Robert Trinz
(M.A., M.S. (Tax))
Managing Editor

William E. Massey
(LL.M., NY Bar)
Manager

David Freid
(J.D., NY Bar)
Senior Editor

Carla M. Martin
(LL.M, AL, FL Bar)
Senior Editor

Frederick M. Stein
(LL.M., PA Bar)
Senior Editor

Laurie Asch
(LL.M., NY Bar)
Senior Project Editor

Stanley V. Baginski
(LL.M., NY Bar)
Senior Project Editor

Thomas Long
(LL.M., NY, NJ Bar)
Senior Project Editor

Betsy McKenny
(J.D., NY, NJ Bar)
Senior Project Editor

Rosemary Saldan-Pawson
(J.D., NY, KS Bar)
Senior Project Editor

Harris Abrams
(LL.M., PA, VA Bar)

Wendy C. Bicovny
(LL.M, C.P.A.,
NY, CA Bar)

Mary-Agnes Bornhoeft
(J.D., NY Bar)

Peter Brennan
(LL.M., NY, NJ,
DC Bar)

Gary S. Bronstein
(LL.M., CA, MA Bar)

Steve Brylski
(LL.M., NY Bar)

John G. Clark
(LL.M., NY Bar)

Sean Crooke
(J.D., CT Bar)

Gregory J. Evanella
(J.D., NJ Bar)

Rachel Glatt
(J.D., NY Bar)

Catherine Graf
(J.D., C.P.A.,
NY Bar)

Megan F. Landers
(J.D., NY Bar)

Michael A. Levin
(J.D., NY Bar)

Michael J. McGoffin
(LL.B., FL Bar)

Elizabeth McLeod
(J.D., NY Bar)

Catherine E. Murray
(J.D.)

Richard O'Donnell
(LL.M., NJ Bar)

Peter Ogrodnik
(LL.M., NJ Bar)

Michael E. Overton
(LL.M., NY, VA Bar)

Selva Ozelli
(J.D., MN Bar,
C.P.A., NY)

Max Rogel
(J.D., NY Bar)

Julie S. Rose
(J.D., CT Bar)

Marian Rosenberg
(LL.M., NY Bar)

Roger M. Ross
(LL.M., NY Bar)

E.H. Rubinsky
(LL.M., NY Bar)

Robert Rywick
(J.D., NY Bar)

Simon Schneebalg
(LL.M., NY Bar)

Sally P. Schreiber
(J.D., PA Bar)

Ralph M. Silberman
(J.D., VA, DC Bar)

Debrah M. Smith
(LL.M., NY,
NJ, PA Bar)

Kristina G. Smith
(J.D., NY, DC Bar)

Richard H. Sternberg
(LL.M., NY Bar)

Scott E. Weiner
(J.D., NY Bar)

Sidney Weinman
(J.D., NY, NJ Bar)

Data Management

Taji Mabra,
Manager

Joan Baselice,
Senior Data
Support Coordinator

Jonathan Thayer,
Senior Data
Support Coordinator

June Babb,
Supervisor

Charlene Brown
Michael Gonzalez
Timothy Marino
Angel Morales
Thalia Sirjue
Norine Wright

Ruby Charles,
Supervisor

Lourdes Acosta
Akinsheye Babb
Jon Benson
Nancy Golden
Richard Reicherter
Noel Rockwood
Dean Whang

Dan Danquah,
Supervisor

Craig Clark
Lenar Clark
Genevieve Gorta
Vijay Jagdeo
Benjamin Jahre
Anthony Kibort
Veronica Mason
Lisa Zolesi

Denise Donahue,
Supervisor

Dino Colacito
Denise Dockery
Anissa Esquina

Tushar Shetty,
Supervisor

Raymond AuYeung
Sydney Pokorny
Cindy Sotero
Christopher Stryshak

Kurt Coffman,
Manager

Andrew Glicklin,
Senior Data
Support Coordinator

Lisa Sarracino,
Senior Data
Support Coordinator

Melanie Thomas,
Senior Data
Support Coordinator

Judy Cosme,
Supervisor

Christopher Barbieri
Lisa Crater
Geneva Gittens
Robert Gleason
Xiomara Tejeda

Gregg Reed Harris,
Supervisor

Michelle Bell
Valerie Brown
Natalie Carrero
Kevin Ledig
Helen McFarlane
Marcia Sam
Dominic Smith

Marisa Swanson
Brett Whitmoyer

Marie Rivera,
Supervisor

Melissa Acquafredda
Sharon Alexander
Kathryn Grott
Esther Maclin
Eddie Rodriguez

Sue Ellen Sobel,
Supervisor

Alexis Brown
Adel Faltas
Amelia Massiah
Jennifer Stryshak

Data Analysts

Young Sone
Lisa Alcock

THOMSON

TAX & ACCOUNTING

2008 RIA Federal Tax Handbook

The 2008 edition of the RIA Federal Tax Handbook is designed to answer the tax questions and resolve the tax problems that arise in everyday business and personal transactions. The Handbook helps in preparing 2007 federal income tax returns, and provides specific guidance to tax consequences of transactions occurring in 2008. It is prepared by the same professional staff that prepares the comprehensive federal tax service, RIA's Federal Tax Coordinator 2d, and the complete income tax service, RIA's Analysis of Federal Taxes: Income, and is derived from these tax services and RIA's Tax Desk and Tax Guide. The 2008 RIA Federal Tax Handbook reflects federal tax legislation to the date of publication, including the Tax Relief and Health Care Act of 2006 (P.L. 109-432, 12/20/2006) and the Small Business and Work Opportunity Tax Act of 2007 (P.L. 110-28, 5/25/2007). It also reflects other key developments (such as new regulations, rulings and revenue procedures) and key rates and inflation-adjusted figures affecting the 2007 return and the 2008 tax year.

caution: Congress is considering a number of tax bills that could affect the 2007 return and the 2008 tax year, including retroactive alternative minimum tax relief to the beginning of 2007 and the extension of a number of tax provisions that will expire at the end of 2007. For highlights of later-enacted tax laws that affect the 2008 edition, consult the homepage dedicated to users of the RIA Federal Tax Handbook (http://ria.thomson.com/federaltaxhandbook).

The Handbook discusses and explains the common tax problems in clear, concise, nontechnical language. And, where appropriate, the Handbook includes:

illustration: To clarify the tax rules and problems discussed, with simple easy-to-follow illustrations.

caution: To warn of dangers that arise in particular tax situations and, where appropriate, to indicate what should be done.

recommendation: To provide specific, carefully studied guides to action which will keep taxes at a legal minimum.

observation: For professional analysis or commentary that is not part of cited authorities.

Forms to use: The Handbook explains which IRS forms to use to report transactions, pay taxes, make elections, etc. For a complete list of all official forms discussed, with references to the paragraph where they are discussed, see the "Forms" entry in the Topic Index.

References: The Handbook uses the following references:

. . . "Code Sec." references are to sections of the Internal Revenue Code.

. . . "Reg § " references are to sections of the federal tax regulations. "Prop Reg § " references are to proposed regulations, which are only cited in the text where IRS has indicated that "Taxpayers may rely" on them.

. . . Footnote references beginning with a single letter are to paragraphs in RIA's Federal Tax Coordinator 2d and RIA's Analysis of Federal Taxes: Income. However, RIA's Analysis of Federal Taxes: Income doesn't include coverage of estate, gift and excise taxes. Accordingly, references to ¶Q-1000 *et seq.* (gift tax), ¶R-1000 *et seq.* (estate tax), and ¶W-1000 *et seq.* (excise taxes) are only to paragraphs in RIA's Federal Tax Coordinator 2d. References beginning with numbers are to paragraphs in RIA's United States Tax Reporter. References beginning with the letters "TD" are to paragraphs in RIA's Tax Desk.

¶101. Highlights of the 2008 Edition.

The 2008 RIA Federal Tax Handbook reflects federal tax legislation to the date of publication, including the Tax Relief and Health Care Act of 2006 (P.L. 109-432, 12/20/2006) and the Small Business and Work Opportunity Tax Act of 2007 (P.L. 110-28, 5/25/2007). It also reflects other key developments (such as new regulations, rulings and revenue procedures) affecting the 2007 return and the 2008 tax year.

caution: Congress is considering a number of other tax bills that could affect the 2007 return and the 2008 tax year, including retroactive alternative minimum tax relief to the beginning of 2007 and the extension of a number of tax provisions that will expire at the end of 2007. For highlights of later-enacted tax laws that affect the 2008 edition, consult the homepage dedicated to users of the RIA Federal Tax Handbook (http://ria.thomson.com/federaltaxhandbook).

What's new in the 2008 Edition. The 2008 RIA Federal Tax Handbook includes the new tax developments listed below:

- "What's new on the 2007 IRS Form 1040." (¶105)
- 2007 and 2008 income tax rates for individuals and estates and trusts. (¶1100 *et seq.*)
- 2007 and 2008 wage bases and rates for Social Security and Medicare taxes, for employers, employees and self-employed taxpayers. (¶1107 *et seq.*)
- Revised gift and estate tax unified rate schedule for individuals dying and gifts made in 2007. (¶1113)
- For sales on or after Dec. 20, 2006, gross income doesn't include 25% of qualifying gain from conservation sales of qualifying mineral or geothermal interests. (¶1206)
- Several Circuit courts hold that income is recognized when stock options are exercised, not when margin loans are repaid. (¶1220)
- IRS agrees with the Tax Court's holding that payment under VA work therapy program is excludible from income. (¶1225)
- The maximum fair market value (FMV) for 2007 for which the fleet-average valuation method can be used is $20,100 for a passenger auto and $21,100 for a truck or van. (¶1234)
- The maximum FMV for 2007 for which the cents-per-mile valuation method can be used is $15,100 for a passenger auto and $16,100 for a truck or van. (¶1237)
- Higher monthly exclusion for parking and for combined value of transit passes and commuter highway vehicle transportation applies for 2007 and 2008. (¶1248)
- The 2007 exclusion for employer-provided adoption assistance is $11,390 ($11,650 for 2008), and the AGI-based phaseout ranges are increased. (¶1255)
- IRS explains how Code Sec. 409A nonqualified deferred compensation (NQDC) plan rules apply to split-dollar life insurance arrangements. (¶1267)
- New comprehensive proposed reliance regs clarify rules on cafeteria plans and FSAs. (¶1270)
- IRS issues final regs on Code Sec. 409A NQDC plan rules. But later relief provides that compliance with the final regs is generally extended to the end of 2008. (¶1276)
- The exception from the below market loans rules for certain continuing care facilities is made permanent. (¶1306)
- Higher 2007 and 2008 limits apply for the exclusion of benefits from long-term care insurance. (¶1379)
- "Covered employee" definition is revised for purposes of $1 million deduction limit on compensation. (¶1519)
- The inflation-indexed definition of a high deductible health plan and limit on contributions for 2007 and 2008 for MSA purposes (¶1528) and for HSA purposes. (¶1529)

- For tax years beginning after 2006, a taxpayer who is an eligible individual under the HSA rules for the last month of a tax year is "deemed eligible" for the entire year. (¶1529)
- After Dec. 20, 2006, and before Jan. 1, 2012, health FSA or HRA distributions may be rolled over via direct transfer to an HSA if several conditions are met. (¶1529)
- Employers may make larger HSA contributions for nonhighly compensated employees than for highly compensated employees and HSA comparability rules have been revised where the employer offers differing levels of family coverage. (¶1529)
- Mental health parity requirements apply through 2007. (¶1532)
- Under some circumstances, an accrual basis employer may treat payroll tax liability as incurred in the year before the year in which the deferred compensation is deductible. (¶1539)
- IRS intends to amend regs to provide that lodging costs not incurred in traveling away from home aren't deductible unless allowed under Code Sec. 162 or Code Sec. 217. Pending additional guidance, IRS won't apply disallowance of non-away-from-home lodging expenses to certain employee expenses. (¶1547)
- The list of countries treated as being in the North American area for deducting business convention expenses has been revised. (¶1550)
- For 2007, the business standard mileage rate is 48.5¢ per mile. (¶1561)
- Regs explain limits on employer deduction for entertainment expenses of "specified employees." (¶1573)
- Entire reimbursement for business meals and incidental expenses treated as paid under a nonaccountable plan if employer routinely doesn't track expenses or require employees to fully substantiate costs or return excess reimbursements. (¶1574)
- Simplified (high-low) per-diem rates changed for 2007 business travel. (¶1576, ¶1582)
- Updated and revised rules for the Code Sec. 199 domestic production activities deduction, including: only domestic production wages count for purposes of the deduction; revised wage limit for passthroughs; inclusion of Puerto Rico (pre-2008) in definition of U.S.; modified rules for qualified films eligible for the deduction; statistical sampling methods permitted for various computation purposes; and modified safe harbor test for determining if qualifying property is manufactured or produced in whole or in significant part within the U.S. (¶1614 *et seq.*)
- For purposes of the moving expenses deduction, a taxpayer using his own car to travel to the new home may deduct 20¢ per mile for 2007. (¶1647)
- Election to treat qualified environmental remediation expenses otherwise chargeable to capital account as deductible is available through 2007 (with petroleum products allowed to be treated as a hazardous substance). (¶1669)
- A deduction is allowed for mortgage insurance premiums paid or incurred for qualified residences in 2007, subject to a phaseout rule. (¶1736)
- The optional itemized deduction for state and local sales and use taxes instead of state and local income taxes is available through 2007. (¶1756)
- Vineyard trellising is property in the 7-year MACRS class. (¶1915)
- Placed-in-service deadline for 15-year MACRS classification for qualified leasehold improvement property and qualified restaurant property applies through 2007. (¶1917)
- Shorter depreciation periods for qualified Indian reservation property is available for property placed-in-service through 2007. (¶1924)
- IRS issues final regs on depreciation of property acquired in a like-kind exchange or involuntary conversion. (¶1930)
- Qualified cellulosic ethanol plant property placed in service before 2013 is eligible for bonus depreciation. (¶1935)

- Bonus depreciation for GO Zone property is available through 2010 (and sometimes 90 days beyond) for buildings in highly damaged areas. (¶1941)
- Boosted limit on Code Sec. 179 expensing deduction is available for tax years beginning before 2011 and increased to $125,000 for tax years beginning in 2007 ($128,000 for tax years beginning in 2008). (¶1944)
- Increased investment-based phaseout level for the Code Sec. 179 expensing deduction is available for tax years beginning before 2011 and increased to $500,000 for tax years beginning in 2007 ($510,000 for tax years beginning in 2008). (¶1944)
- Right to revoke or change without IRS consent an election to claim the Code Sec. 179 expensing deduction is available for tax years beginning before 2011. (¶1944)
- Additional Code Sec. 179 expensing for GO Zone property is available through 2008 for eligible property in highly damaged areas. (¶1946)
- Eligibility of off-the-shelf computer software for Code Sec. 179 expensing is available for tax years beginning before 2011. (¶1948)
- Autos, trucks and vans placed in service in 2007 are subject to revised luxury auto dollar caps. (¶1956)
- Revised income inclusion amounts apply to luxury autos, trucks and vans leased in 2007. (¶1961)
- Special expensing is made available for qualified advanced mine safety equipment placed in service before 2009. (¶1968)
- IRS issues temporary regs on the special expensing available for qualified film and television production costs. (¶1969)
- Deduction for energy efficient commercial building property is available through 2008. (¶1971)
- IRS issues guidance on the energy efficient commercial building deduction. (¶1971)
- Suspension of taxable income limitation on percentage depletion for marginal properties applies for tax years beginning before 2008. (¶1983)
- New rules on valuing donated clothing and household property clarified. (¶2103)
- Enhanced deduction for qualified computer contributions by corporations applies through 2007 for property constructed or assembled by the taxpayer. (¶2108)
- Guidance issued on the relaxed rules for qualified conservation contributions. (¶2124)
- IRS explains how payroll contributions to a charity can meet toughened substantiation rules. (¶2136)
- Maximum amounts of long-term care insurance premiums qualifying as deductible medical expenses are increased for 2007 and 2008. (¶2146)
- Tuition at school to treat learning disabilities such as dyslexia is deductible medical expense. (¶2147)
- The cents per mile deduction for medical-care-related use of an auto is 20¢ for 2007. (¶2149)
- For 2007 and 2008, the Hope scholarship credit increases and phases out over higher levels of modified AGI. (¶2202)
- For 2007 and 2008, the exclusion for education-related savings bond interest phases out over higher levels of modified AGI. (¶2220)
- For 2007 and 2008, the above-the-line deduction for qualified education loan interest phases out over higher levels of modified AGI. (¶2220)
- Above-the-line deduction for higher-education expenses applies through 2007. For 2007, the deduction is claimed on Form 8917. (¶2223)
- The up-to-$250 above-the-line deduction for teachers' out-of-pocket classroom-related expenses applies for 2007. (¶2232)

- A credit is provided for amounts paid or incurred in tax years beginning before 2009 for training mine rescue teams. (¶2302)
- For tax years beginning after 2006, the FICA tip credit and the work opportunity tax credit (WOTC) can offset 100% of alternative minimum tax (AMT) liability. (¶2303)
- The 30% credits for solar energy property and qualified fuel cell property and the 10% credit for qualified microturbine property is available for 2008. (¶2311)
- The WOTC is available up to Aug. 31, 2011. (¶2314) In addition, the welfare-to-work credit is repealed as a separate credit and consolidated with the WOTC after 2006; long-term family assistance recipients become a targeted group under the WOTC. (¶2314, ¶2315)
- For those who begin work after May 25, 2007, the amount of qualified first-year wages that can be taken into account for the WOTC for qualified veteran employees is increased to $12,000 (¶2314), and "high-risk youths" WOTC targeted group renamed as "designated community residents" with relaxed age and location requirements. (¶2315)
- For those who begin work after 2006, the deadline for submitting paperwork for certification of employees under the WOTC is extended to 28 days after the beginning of work. (¶2315)
- Research credit is available for amounts paid or incurred before 2008. (¶2318) For tax years ending after 2006, the rates for the elective alternative incremental research credit are increased (¶2318); and an alternative simplified credit can be elected for qualified research expenses. (¶2318)
- Monthly low-income housing credit percentages are updated. (¶2319)
- The placed-in-service date is extended through 2008 for certain qualified facilities for the credit for producing electricity from renewable resources. (¶2323)
- Credit for qualified zone academy bonds is available through 2007. (¶2326)
- The Indian employment credit is available for tax years beginning before 2008. (¶2327)
- For tips received for services performed after 2006, the FICA tip credit isn't reduced by any increase in the minimum wage. (¶2328)
- New markets tax credit is available for qualified equity investments through 2008. (¶2331)
- The energy efficient home credit for eligible contractors is available through 2008. (¶2337)
- The nonconventional source production credit for coke and coke gas isn't subject to a phase-out limitation, and the credit doesn't apply to a facility producing coke or coke gas from petroleum-based products. (¶2339)
- For 2007, the maximum earned income tax credit amount is increased; the maximum amount of "disqualified income" that may be received also is increased. (¶2341, ¶2344)
- The election to include combat pay as earned income for purposes of the earned income credit is available for 2007. (¶2342)
- The maximum credit for the adoption of a child (including a special-needs child) increases for 2007 and 2008, as do the AGI-based phaseout thresholds. (¶2356)
- The earned-income phaseout levels for the refundable child credit have been increased for 2007 and 2008. (¶2358)
- The residential energy efficient property credit is available for property placed in service before 2009, and IRS has clarified which property qualifies for the credit. (¶2361)
- A number of vehicles potentially qualify for the Code Sec. 30B alternative motor vehicle credit; Mazda joins the hybrid club; no credit applies for hybrids manufactured by Toyota purchased after Sept. 30, 2007; and a hydrogen-powered Honda vehicle qualifies for the qualified fuel cell vehicle credit. (¶2362)
- IRS details impact of AMT on hybrid car credit. (¶2362)

- The DC homebuyer credit applies for property bought before 2008. (¶2364)
- Under a new rule, for a tax year beginning before 2013, an individual's minimum tax credit can't be less than the "alternative minimum tax refundable credit amount." (¶2367)
- Clean renewable energy bonds (CREBs) may be issued through the end of 2008. (¶2368)
- The possessions tax credit for American Samoa applies through 2007 for existing claimants. (¶2369)
- For sales or exchanges after Dec. 20, 2006, and before 2011, an employee of the intelligence community may elect to suspend the 5-year period for measuring ownership and use during periods that he or his spouse serves on extended duty at a duty station located outside the U.S. (¶2442)
- The exclusion for the sale of a principal residence is allowed for the involuntary conversion of the residence as a result of its destruction only if it is totally destroyed. (¶2442)
- Capital gain treatment for certain self-created musical works is made permanent. (¶2622)
- The zero percent capital gains rate for capital gains from the sale of certain qualified DC Zone assets held for more than five years is available through 2012. (¶2652)
- One Circuit has held that a cash advance by a wholesaler to a retailer for a volume purchase commitment (advance trade discount) wasn't includible on receipt, but another Circuit reached a contrary conclusion for a similar supply agreement. A new revenue procedure provides an accounting method generally adopting the former result. (¶2826)
- A new revenue ruling concludes that for an accrual method taxpayer a liability for services is not fixed by the mere execution of a contract for the future provision of services. (¶2832)
- IRS guidance provides that prepaid services must be fully completed within 3-1/2 or 8-1/2 months (for recurring items) to be currently deductible under accrual accounting exceptions. (¶2833)
- New final regs treat most changes in computing depreciation (or amortization) as accounting method changes. (¶2839)
- IRS postpones transfer pricing regs on controlled service transactions to apply to tax years beginning after 2007. (¶2858)
- A revenue procedure provides a new safe harbor method of accounting to treat rotable spare parts as depreciable assets rather than as inventory. (¶2864)
- Sole owner of unincorporated business entity (e.g., LLC) not electing treatment as a corporation under the check-the-box rules is personally liable for withholding. (¶3001)
- For wages paid after 2008, disregarded entities must pay their own employment and excise taxes under final regs. (¶3001)
- Regs which no longer require employers to send IRS questionable employee Forms W-4S are made permanent. (¶3019)
- "Nanny tax" threshold is $1,500 for 2007 and $1,600 for 2008. (¶3029)
- The 2007 and 2008 standard deduction amounts are increased. (¶3112)
- For 2007 and 2008, the phaseout of itemized deductions begins at higher income levels. Additionally, for 2007, a taxpayer loses only ⅔ (⅓ for 2008) of the amount he would otherwise lose under the regular reduction computation. (¶3114)
- Personal exemption amounts are higher for 2007 and 2008. (¶3115)
- For 2007 and 2008, the personal exemption deduction phases out at higher AGI levels. For 2007, a taxpayer loses only ⅔ (⅓ for 2008) of the amount he would otherwise lose under the regular phaseout computation. (¶3117)
- 2007 and 2008 kiddie tax figures are reflected. (¶3134)
- After 2007, the kiddie tax applies to a child age 18 (age 19 - 23 if a full time student) if

the child's earned income doesn't exceed one-half of his support. (¶3135)

- Kiddie tax AMT exemption amounts for 2007 and 2008 are reflected. (¶3204)
- The Tax Court holds that a valid Code Sec. 83(b) election causes gain on incentive stock option (ISO) stock to be recognized for AMT purposes. (¶3208)
- The Tax Court has concluded that the difference between the regular tax basis and AMT basis on the exercise of an ISO isn't an adjustment and doesn't result in an alternative tax net operating deduction. (¶3211)
- Treasury shares are not counted for the personal service corporation ownership test. (¶3334)
- Special anti-avoidance rules aim to prevent consolidated groups from avoiding the loss suspension rule by reimporting certain losses to the group. (¶3343)
- Final regs address prohibition against using dual consolidated loss to reduce the taxable income of an affiliated group member. (¶3343)
- Estimated tax payment that is due in July, Aug. and Sept. 2012 by a corporation with assets of at least $1 billion increases to 115% of the amount otherwise due. (¶3349)
- For tax years beginning after 2006, the sale of an interest in a qualified subsidiary is treated as a taxable sale of a portion of the assets followed by a tax-free incorporation. (¶3355)
- Restricted bank director stock is not taken into account for the one class of stock S corporation eligibility requirement. (¶3358)
- S corporation capital gains are not treated as passive income. (¶3369)
- Pre-'83 S corporation E&P has been eliminated for post-'96 tax years for certain S corporations. (¶3376)
- The assumption of excess liabilities rule does not apply to certain transactions that qualify as both an acquisitive reorganization and a Code Sec. 351 exchange. (¶3515)
- Stock purchases, undertaken in connection with certain triangular reorganizations, are treated as taxable dividends. (¶3545)
- Certain transactions qualify as D reorganizations even though no stock and/or securities of the acquiring corporation are issued and distributed in the transaction. (¶3547)
- Long-term tax exempt rates are updated. (¶3567)
- Temporary regs provide that certain nonrecognition transactions (including asset reorganizations and nontaxable liquidations) will not trigger gain recognition under Code Sec. 367. (¶3586)
- For tax years beginning after 2006, where a qualified joint venture is conducted by a husband and wife who file a joint return for the tax year, the joint venture isn't treated as a partnership for tax purposes. (¶3701)
- Partnership has gain on distribution of property to partner in satisfaction of guaranteed payment. (¶3730)
- Partnership's purchase of home distributed to partner treated as distribution of the cash it used to buy the home. (¶3744)
- For tax years beginning after 2006, interest on debt used to acquire S corporation stock may be deducted by electing small business trusts (ESBTs). (¶3910)
- Supreme Court to decide how the 2% floor on miscellaneous itemized deductions applies to trust expenses. (¶3921)
- IRS guidance shows examples of prohibited and permissible political activities of tax-exempts. (¶4102)
- New safe harbor to establish reasonable cause for a political organization's failure to report contributor information. (¶4109)
- Interim guidance on public inspection of a charitable organization's unrelated business

income tax return. (¶4120)

- IRS has created Form 990-N for organizations exempted from filing information returns to use to meet their obligation to file annual notice with IRS. (¶4124)
- IRS has established a procedure for reclassifying supporting organizations. (¶4125)
- Final S Corp employee stock ownership plan (ESOP) regs are issued. (¶4314)
- New hardship distribution rules apply for 401(k) plans. (¶4317)
- 401(k) elective deferral limits is $15,500 for 2007 and 2008; those age 50 or older can make extra, catch-up contributions. (¶4317)
- New rules allow in-service distributions to be made to employees age 62 or older. (¶4319)
- The amount of an employee's annual compensation that a plan may take into account is $225,000 for 2007 ($230,000 for 2008). (¶4319)
- New normal retirement age rules apply for vesting purposes. (¶4321)
- Use of bifurcated vesting schedules for pre-2007 and post-2006 employer nonelective contributions is allowed. (¶4321)
- Elective deferral limits for 2007 and 2008 are reflected for plans covering self-employed persons. (¶4326)
- Overall limits on plan contributions and benefits updated to reflect 2007 and 2008 amount. (¶4327)
- Relief is provided from new diversification requirements for plans holding employer securities. (¶4332)
- AGI levels for 2007 and 2008 at which IRA deductions for active participants in employer sponsored retirement plans phase out are reflected. (¶4352)
- After 2006, eligible individuals can elect one-time tax-free rollover of IRA distribution into an HSA. (¶4364)
- Amendment date rules for prototype Roth IRAs accepting rollovers from designated Roth accounts. (¶4368)
- 2007 and 2008 AGI-based phaseout figures for Roth IRA contributions are reflected. (¶4369)
- The maximum deferral amount under a SIMPLE qualified salary reduction arrangement for 2007 and 2008 is reflected. (¶4384)
- New regs governing 403(b) plans narrow differences between 403(b) plans and 401(k) plans. (¶4388 *et seq.*)
- Maximum foreign income exclusion increases to $85,700 for 2007 and $87,600 for 2008. (¶4613).
- Maximum foreign housing cost exclusion is $11,998 for 2007 and $12,264 for 2008. (¶4614)
- The look-through treatment of payments between related controlled foreign corporations under the foreign personal holding company rules is modified. (¶4630)
- Average annual net income amount for triggering expatriation rules increases to $136,000 for 2007 ($139,000 for 2008). (¶4658)
- Threshold amount for reporting foreign gifts increases to $13,258 for 2007 ($13,561 for 2008). (¶4682)
- Individual return filing thresholds are increased for 2007 and 2008. (¶4701)
- Frivolous submissions in certain requests and applications are subject to IRS dismissal. (¶4723, ¶4826, ¶4904, ¶4910)
- Form 1120-A is eliminated for tax years beginning after 2006. (¶4727)
- Income tax return filing thresholds for bankruptcy estate of an individual have increased for 2007 and 2008. (¶4739)

- IRS may impose mortgage insurance premium reporting requirements. (¶4749)
- Material advisors must disclose reportable transactions on Form 8918. (¶4752)
- Taxpayers have to disclose their participation in transactions of interest (i.e., transactions of interest that are the same or substantially similar to transactions identified by IRS). (¶4753)
- For returns prepared after May 25, 2007, a tax return preparer includes preparers of estate, gift, employment and excise tax returns, and exempt organization returns. (¶4756)
- The District of Columbia's Emancipation Day is treated as a holiday under the timely filing/payment rule. (¶4761)
- A new program allows qualifying taxpayers to request IRS to examine specific issues relating to tax returns before they are filed. (¶4805)
- IRS guidance explains how IRS may impose monetary penalties on practitioners. (¶4809)
- Courts have reached contrary results on whether a basis overstatement is an omission for purposes of the six-year assessment period. (¶4832)
- The Tax Court has held that a preparer's fraud keeps an income tax return open indefinitely, even if the taxpayer had no intent to evade taxes. (¶4835)
- Overpayment (¶4853) and underpayment (¶4865) interest rates are updated.
- The Federal Circuit has held that the special refund limitations period rule for overpayments resulting from a capital loss carryback does not apply to a year to which a net capital loss is carried over. (¶4854)
- The Tax Court jurisdiction to review IRS's failure to abate interest is exclusive. (¶4858)
- The Tax Court has held that it could adjudicate a taxpayer's claim for spousal relief even though her former spouse intervened and later filed for bankruptcy, triggering an automatic stay. (¶4858)
- The Tax Court has held that the dollar limit for its small case procedures includes tax, interest and penalties and applies to the total owed for multiple years in a single proceeding. (¶4860)
- The dollar limit on recoveries of attorneys fees is $170 for 2007 and 2008. (¶4862)
- For notices after Nov. 25, 2007, IRS has 36 (up from 18) months to notify individuals of the basis for liability before it must suspend interest and penalties. (¶4870)
- Where an amended return (or other written document) is filed showing additional tax liability, the period for IRS to issue required notice of liability is restarted. (¶4870)
- For returns prepared after May 25, 2007, the scope of tax return preparer penalties is broadened, penalty amounts are increased and standards for avoiding penalties are modified. (¶4885)
- For claim filed after May 25, 2007, a new penalty applies to filing an erroneous refund claim. (¶4882)
- IRS procedures establish how to request rescission of the penalty for failure to report reportable transactions. (¶4890)
- Various information return penalties (¶4894) and civil penalties relating to information reporting (¶4895) are updated to reflect statutory changes.
- Levies issued after Sept. 21, 2007 to collect federal employment taxes are excepted from the pre-levy collection due process hearing requirement. (¶4904)
- The Supreme Court has held that Code Sec. 7426(a)(1) is the exclusive remedy for third-party levy claims. (¶4904)
- Top estate tax rate drops for individuals dying in 2007. (¶5000)
- For 2007 and 2008, indexing allows greater savings from estate-tax special use valuation. (¶5028)
- Annual per-donee gift tax exclusion is $12,000 for 2007 and 2008 (¶5037)
- For 2007 and 2008, larger amounts may be transferred to a noncitizen spouse free of gift tax. (¶5046)

¶105. What's New on the 2007 Form 1040?

Here are the changes with the greatest impact on the preparation of 2007 individual returns, cross-referenced to where they are discussed in the Handbook, and referenced to the appropriate lines on the draft versions of Form 1040 and related Schedules available at press-time.

⊘caution: For highlights of later-enacted tax laws that affect the 2007 return, consult the homepage dedicated to users of the RIA Federal Tax Handbook (http://ria.thomson.com/federaltaxhandbook).

FORM 1040, INDIVIDUAL INCOME TAX RETURN

Gross Income

Line 7. Elective salary deferrals.

The maximum amount that an individual can defer under all plans is generally limited to $15,500. The catch-up contribution limit is $5,000. (¶4317)

Adjusted Gross Income

Line 25. Health Savings Account deduction.

Beginning in 2007, (1) an individual can fund his HSA by making a one-time direct transfer from his IRA to his HSA; (2) qualifying health FSA or HRA distributions may be rolled over on a one-time-only basis via direct transfer to an HSA; (3) the maximum deductible contribution is no longer limited to the annual deductible under the high deductible plan; (4) for computing the annual HSA contribution, a taxpayer who is an eligible individual in the last month of a tax year is "deemed eligible" during every month of that year (he must remain eligible during a testing period); and (5) an individual is allowed a maximum HSA contribution of $2,850 for single coverage ($5,650 for family coverage). (¶1529)

Line 26. Moving expenses.

The deduction for moving expenses is 20 cents per mile. (¶1647)

Line 32. IRA deduction.

The IRA contribution limit is $4,000 ($5,000 if over 50 at the end of 2007). For 2007, the AGI phaseout ranges for making deductible contributions to regular IRAs by taxpayers that are active participants in an employer-sponsored retirement plan are higher (e.g., $83,000 to $103,000 for joint return filers). For 2007 (as well as 2008 and 2009), an individual may be able to deduct catch-up contributions of up to $3,000 each year to his IRA if he participated in a 401(k) plan of an employer that was a debtor in bankruptcy proceedings. (¶4352)

Line 35. Domestic production activities deduction.

The deduction rate increased to 6%. (¶1615)

Tax and Credits

Line 40. Standard deduction.	For 2007, the standard deduction is $5,350 for single filers and for married persons filing separately, $10,700 for joint filers and qualifying widow(er)s, and $7,850 for heads of household. (¶3112)
Line 42. Personal exemptions.	The exemption (¶3115) for 2007 is $3,400. Exemption starts to phase out (see ¶3117) if adjusted gross income exceeds: $156,400 for single filers, $117,300 for married persons filing separately, $234,600 for joint filers and qualifying widow(er)s, and $195,500 for heads of household. For 2007, a taxpayer loses only 2/3 of the amount he would otherwise lose under the regular phaseout computation.
Line 45. Alternative minimum tax.	As we went to press, Congress was considering legislation that would increase the 2007 AMT exemption amounts for individuals. See ¶3202.
Line 49. Education credits.	For 2007, the Hope and Lifetime credits phase out ratably for taxpayers with modified AGI of $47,000 to $57,000 ($94,000 to $114,000 for joint filers). Use Form 8863. (¶2202)
Line 54. Credits from certain forms.	This line is used to report the adoption credit from Form 8839. The maximum adoption credit for 2007 is $11,390, and begins to phase out when modified AGI exceeds $170,820. (¶2356)

Other Taxes

Line 58. Self-employment tax.	Maximum amount of self-employment income subject to FICA tax is $97,500; no ceiling on Medicare wage base (¶1107).

Payments

Line 67. Excess social security and RRTA tax withheld.	Maximum Social Security (OASDI) tax for 2007 is $6,045 (computed on the first $97,500 of wages) for purposes of credit for excess tax withheld. (¶1107)

Form 1040, SCHEDULE A ITEMIZED DEDUCTIONS 2007

Line 1. Medical and dental expenses.	The standard mileage rate for medically-related use of an auto is 20 cents per mile. (¶2149)
Line 13. Qualified mortgage insurance premiums.	A homeowner who obtains a qualified mortgage in 2007, and whose AGI is less than $110,000 ($55,000 if married filing separately), may be able to deduct some of the mortgage insurance premiums paid during the tax year (as if they were mortgage interest) as an itemized deduction. (¶1736)
Line 21. Unreimbursed employee expenses.	The standard mileage rate is 48.5 cents per mile for 2007. (¶1561).

| *Line 29. Total itemized deductions.* | The allowable amount of itemized deductions will be reduced if adjusted gross income in 2007 is more than $156,400 ($78,200 for married filing separately). For 2007, a taxpayer will lose only 2/3 of the amount he would otherwise lose under the regular reduction computation. (¶3114) |

FORM 1040, SCHEDULE B INTEREST AND DIVIDEND INCOME 2007

| *Line 1. Interest.* | Accrued interest on Series E or EE U.S. savings bonds issued in '67 or in '77 is taxable, (¶1334) |
| *Line 3. Excludable interest on Series EE or Series I U.S. savings bonds.* | The exclusion for education related savings bond interest phases out at higher income levels. For 2007, the phaseout begins at modified adjusted gross income above $65,600 ($98,400 on a joint return). (¶2220) |

FORM 1040, SCHEDULE C PROFIT OR LOSS FROM BUSINESS 2007

| *Line 9. Car and truck expenses.* | The standard mileage rate is 48.5 cents per mile for 2007. (¶1561) |
| *Line 13. Depreciation and section 179 expense.* | See entries for Form 4562, below. |

FORM 4562, DEPRECIATION AND AMORTIZATION

Part I. Election to expense certain tangible property under Sec. 179.	The amount that may be expensed under Code Sec. 179 in 2007 is $125,000, with investment-based phaseout beginning at $500,000. (¶1944) Maximum expensing amount is increased by $35,000 for enterprise zone, renewal property and New York Liberty Zone property (¶1945), and by up to $100,000 for Go Zone property (¶1946).
Part II. Special depreciation allowance.	Taxpayers may claim a 50% bonus depreciation deduction for qualified GO Zone property. (¶1941)
Part V. Listed property.	First-year luxury auto limits for vehicles first placed in service in 2007 are $3,060 for autos and $3,260 for light trucks or vans. (¶1956)

¶1000. Tax Calendar—2008 Due Dates.

2007 GENERAL TAX CALENDAR

This tax calendar has the due dates for 2007 that most taxpayers will need. Employers also should use the Employer's Tax Calendar.

FISCAL-YEAR TAXPAYERS.
If you file your income tax return for a fiscal year rather than the calendar year, you must change some of the dates in this calendar. These changes are described under Fiscal-Year Taxpayers at the end of this calendar.

FIRST QUARTER

The first quarter of a calendar year is made up of January, February, and March.

JANUARY 10

EMPLOYEES WHO WORK FOR TIPS. If you received $20 or more in tips during December, report them to your employer. You can use Form 4070, Employee's Report of Tips to Employer.

JANUARY 16

INDIVIDUALS. Make a payment of your estimated tax for 2006 if you did not pay your income tax for the year through withholding (or did not pay in enough tax that way). Use Form 1040-ES. This is the final installment date for 2006 estimated tax. However, you do not have to make this payment if you file your 2006 return (Form 1040) and pay any tax due by January 31, 2007.

FARMERS AND FISHERMEN. Pay your estimated tax for 2006 using Form 1040-ES. You have until April 17 to file your 2006 income tax return (Form 1040). If you do not pay your estimated tax by January 16, you must file your 2006 return and pay any tax due by March 1, 2007, to avoid an estimated tax penalty.

JANUARY 31

INDIVIDUALS WHO MUST MAKE ESTIMATED TAX PAYMENTS. If you did not pay your last installment of estimated tax by January 16, you may choose (but are not required) to file your income tax return (Form 1040) for 2006 by January 31. Filing your return and paying any tax due by January 31 prevents any penalty for late payment of the last installment. If you cannot file and pay your tax by January 31, file and pay your tax by April 17.

ALL BUSINESSES. Give annual information statements to recipients of certain payments you made during 2006. You can use the appropriate version of Form 1099 or other information return. Form 1099 can be issued electronically with the consent of the recipient. Payments that may be covered include the following.

  o Cash payments for fish (or other aquatic life) purchased from anyone engaged in the trade or business of catching fish.
  o Compensation for workers who are not considered employees (including fishing boat proceeds to crew members).
  o Dividends and other corporate distributions.
  o Interest.
  o Amounts paid in real estate transactions.
  o Rent.
  o Royalties.
  o Amounts paid in broker and barter exchange transactions.
  o Payments to attorneys.
  o Payments of Indian gaming profits to tribal members.
  o Profit-sharing distributions.
  o Retirement plan distributions.
  o Original issue discount.
  o Prizes and awards.
  o Medical and health care payments.
  o Debt cancellation (treated as payment to debtor).
  o Cash payments over $10,000. See the instructions for Form 8300, Report of Cash Payments Over $10,000 Received in a Trade or Business.

See the 2006 General Instructions for Forms 1099, 1098, 5498, and W-2G for information on what payments are covered, how much the payment must be before a statement is required, which form to use, when to file, and extensions of time to provide statements to the IRS.

FEBRUARY 12

Employees who work for tips. If you received $20 or more in tips during January, report them to your employer. You can use Form 4070.

FEBRUARY 15

INDIVIDUALS. If you claimed exemption from income tax withholding last year on the Form W-4 you gave your employer, you must file a new Form W-4 by this date to continue your exemption for another year.

FEBRUARY 28

ALL BUSINESSES. File information returns (Form 1099) for certain payments you made during 2006. These payments are described under January 31.

There are different forms for different types of payments. Use a separate Form 1096 to summarize and transmit the forms for each type of payment. See the 2006 General Instructions for Forms 1099, 1098, 5498, and W-2G for information on what payments are covered, how much the payment must be before a return is required, which form to use, and extensions of time to file.

If you file Forms 1098, 1099, or W-2G electronically (not by magnetic media), your due date for filing them with the IRS will be extended to April 2. The due date for giving the recipient these forms remains January 31.

MARCH 1

FARMERS AND FISHERMEN. File your 2006 income tax return (Form 1040) and pay any tax due. However, you have until April 17 to file if you paid your 2006 estimated tax by January 16, 2007.

MARCH 12

EMPLOYEES WHO WORK FOR TIPS. If you received $20 or more in tips during February, report them to your employer. You can use Form 4070.

MARCH 15

CORPORATIONS. File a 2006 calendar year income tax return (Form 1120 or 1120-A) and pay any tax due. If you want an automatic 6-month extension of time to file the return, file Form 7004 and deposit what you estimate you owe.

S CORPORATIONS. File a 2006 calendar year income tax return (Form 1120S) and pay any tax due. Provide each shareholder with a copy of Schedule K-1 (Form 1120S), Shareholder's Share of Income, Deductions, Credits, etc., or a substitute Schedule K-1. If you want an automatic 6-month extension of time to file the return, file Form 7004 and deposit what you estimate you owe.

S CORPORATION ELECTION. File Form 2553, Election by a Small Business Corporation, to choose to be treated as an S corporation beginning with calendar year 2007. If Form 2553 is filed late, S treatment will begin with calendar year 2008.

ELECTING LARGE PARTNERSHIPS. Provide each partner with a copy of Schedule K-1 (Form 1065-B), Partner's Share of Income (Loss) From an Electing Large Partnership, or a substitute Schedule K-1. This due date is effective for the first

March 15 following the close of the partnership's tax year. The due date of March 15 applies even if the partnership requests an extension of time to file the Form 1065-B by filing Form 7004.

SECOND QUARTER

The second quarter of a calendar year is made up of April, May, and June.

APRIL 2

ELECTRONIC FILING OF FORMS 1098, 1099, AND W-2G. File Forms 1098, 1099, or W-2G with the IRS. This due date applies only if you file electronically (not by magnetic media). Otherwise, see February 28. The due date for giving the recipient these forms remains January 31. For information about filing Forms 1098, 1099, or W-2G electronically, see Publication 1220, Specifications for Filing Forms 1098, 1099, 5498 and W-2G Electronically or Magnetically.

APRIL 10

Employees who work for tips. If you received $20 or more in tips during March, report them to your employer. You can use Form 4070.

APRIL 17

INDIVIDUALS. File a 2006 income tax return (Form 1040, 1040A, or 1040EZ) and pay any tax due. If you want an automatic 6-month extension of time to file the return, file Form 4868, Application for Automatic Extension of Time To File U.S. Individual Income Tax Return, or you can get an extension by phone or over the Internet. Then, file Form 1040, 1040A, or 1040EZ by October 15.

HOUSEHOLD EMPLOYERS. If you paid cash wages of $1,500 or more in 2006 to a household employee, you must file Schedule H. If you are required to file a federal income tax return (Form 1040), file Schedule H with the return and report any household employment taxes. Report any federal unemployment (FUTA) tax on Schedule H if you paid total cash wages of $1,000 or more in any calendar quarter of 2005 or 2006 to household employees. Also, report any income tax you withheld for your household employees. For more information, see Publication 926.

INDIVIDUALS. If you are not paying your 2007 income tax through withholding (or will not pay in enough tax during the year that way), pay the first installment of your 2007 estimated

tax. Use Form 1040-ES. For more information, see Publication 505.

PARTNERSHIPS. File a 2006 calendar year return (Form 1065). Provide each partner with a copy of Schedule K-1 (Form 1065), Partner's Share of Income, Deductions, Credits, etc., or a substitute Schedule K-1. If you want an automatic 6-month extension of time to file the return and provide Schedule K-1 or a substitute Schedule K-1, file Form 7004. Then, file Form 1065 by October 15.

ELECTING LARGE PARTNERSHIPS. File a 2006 calendar year return (Form 1065-B). If you want an automatic 6-month extension of time to file the return, file Form 7004. Then, file Form 1065-B by October 15. See March 15 for the due date for furnishing Schedules K-1 or substitute Schedules K-1 to the partners.

CORPORATIONS. Deposit the first installment of estimated income tax for 2007. A worksheet, Form 1120-W, is available to help you estimate your tax for the year.

MAY 10

EMPLOYEES WHO WORK FOR TIPS. If you received $20 or more in tips during April, report them to your employer. You can use Form 4070.

JUNE 11

Employees who work for tips. If you received $20 or more in tips during May, report them to your employer. You can use Form 4070.

JUNE 15

INDIVIDUALS. If you are a U.S. citizen or resident alien living and working (or on military duty) outside the United States and Puerto Rico, file Form 1040 and pay any tax, interest, and penalties due. Otherwise, see April 17. If you want additional time to file your return, file Form 4868 to obtain 4 additional months to file. Then, file Form 1040 by October 15. However, if you are a participant in a combat zone, you may be able to further extend the filing deadline. See Publication 3, Armed Forces' Tax Guide.

INDIVIDUALS. Make a payment of your 2007 estimated tax if you are not paying your income tax for the year through withholding (or will not pay in enough tax that way). Use Form 1040-ES. This is the second installment date for estimated tax in 2007. For more information, see Publication 505.

CORPORATIONS. Deposit the second installment of estimated income tax for 2007. A worksheet, Form 1120-W, is available to help you estimate your tax for the year.

THIRD QUARTER

The third quarter of a calendar year is made up of July, August, and September.

JULY 10

Employees who work for tips. If you received $20 or more in tips during June, report them to your employer. You can use Form 4070.

AUGUST 10

Employees who work for tips. If you received $20 or more in tips during July, report them to your employer. You can use Form 4070.

SEPTEMBER 10

Employees who work for tips. If you received $20 or more in tips during August, report them to your employer. You can use Form 4070.

SEPTEMBER 17

INDIVIDUALS. Make a payment of your 2007 estimated tax if you are not paying your income tax for the year through withholding (or will not pay in enough tax that way). Use Form 1040-ES. This is the third installment date for estimated tax in 2007. For more information, see Publication 505.

CORPORATIONS. File a 2006 calendar year income tax return (Form 1120 or 1120-A) and pay any tax, interest, and penalties due. This due date applies only if you timely requested an automatic 6-month extension. Otherwise, see March 15.

S CORPORATIONS. File a 2006 calendar year income tax return (Form 1120S) and pay any tax due. This due date applies only if you timely requested an automatic 6-month extension. Otherwise, see March 15. Provide each shareholder with a copy of Schedule K-1 (Form 1120S) or a substitute Schedule K-1.

CORPORATIONS. Deposit the third installment of estimated income tax for 2007. A worksheet, Form 1120-W, is available to help you estimate your tax for the year.

FOURTH QUARTER

The fourth quarter of a calendar year is made up of October, November, and December.

OCTOBER 10

EMPLOYEES WHO WORK FOR TIPS. If you received $20 or more in tips during September, report them to your employer. You can use Form 4070.

OCTOBER 15

INDIVIDUALS. If you have an automatic 6-month extension to file your income tax return for 2006, file Form 1040, 1040A, or 1040EZ and pay any tax, interest, and penalties due.

PARTNERSHIPS. File a 2006 calendar year return (Form 1065). This due date applies only if you were given an additional 6-month extension. Provide each partner with a copy of Schedule K-1 (Form 1065) or a substitute Schedule K-1.

ELECTING LARGE PARTNERSHIPS. File a 2006 calendar year return (Form 1065-B). This due date applies only if you were given an additional 6-month extension. See March 15 for the due date for furnishing Schedules K-1 or substitute Schedules K-1 to the partners.

NOVEMBER 13

Employees who work for tips If you received $20 or more in tips during October, report them to your employer. You can use Form 4070.

DECEMBER 10

Employees who work for tips. If you received $20 or more in tips during November, report them to your employer. You can use Form 4070.

DECEMBER 17

CORPORATIONS. Deposit the fourth installment of estimated income tax for 2007. A worksheet, Form 1120-W, is available to help you estimate your tax for the year.

FISCAL-YEAR TAXPAYERS

If you use a fiscal year (rather than the calendar year) as your tax year, you should change some of the dates in this calendar. Use the following general guidelines to make these changes.

TIP: The 3 months that make up each quarter of a fiscal year may be different from those of each calendar quarter,

depending on when the fiscal year begins.

INDIVIDUALS

FORM 1040. This form is due on the 15th day of the 4th month after the end of your tax year.

ESTIMATED TAX PAYMENTS (Form 1040-ES). Payments are due on the 15th day of the 4th, 6th, and 9th months of your tax year and on the 15th day of the 1st month after your tax year ends.

PARTNERSHIPS

FORM 1065. This form is due on the 15th day of the 4th month after the end of the partnership's tax year. Provide each partner with a copy of Schedule K-1 (Form 1065) or a substitute Schedule K-1.

FORM 1065-B (ELECTING LARGE PARTNERSHIPS). This form is due on the 15th day of the 4th month after the end of the partnership's tax year. Provide each partner with a copy of Schedule K-1 (Form 1065-B) or a substitute Schedule K-1 by the first March 15 following the close of the partnership's tax year.

CORPORATIONS AND S CORPORATIONS

FORM 1120 AND FORM 1120S (OR FORM 7004). These forms are due on the 15th day of the 3rd month after the end of the corporation's tax year.

S corporations must provide each shareholder with a copy of Schedule K-1 (Form 1120S) or a substitute Schedule K-1.

ESTIMATED TAX PAYMENTS. Payments are due on the 15th day of the 4th, 6th, 9th, and 12th months of the corporation's tax year.

FORM 2553. This form is used to choose S corporation treatment. It is due by the 15th day of the 3rd month of the first tax year to which the choice will apply or at any time during the preceding tax year.

2007 EMPLOYER'S TAX CALENDAR

This tax calendar covers various due dates of interest to employers. Principally, it covers the following federal taxes.

o Income tax you withhold from your employees' wages or from nonpayroll amounts you pay out.

o Social security and Medicare taxes (FICA taxes) you withhold from your employees' wages and the social security and Medicare taxes you must pay as an employer.
o Federal unemployment (FUTA) tax you must pay as an employer. The calendar lists due dates for filing returns and for making deposits of these three taxes throughout the year. Use this calendar with Publication 15 (Circular E), which gives the deposit rules.

FORMS YOU MAY NEED. The following is a list and description of the primary employment tax forms you may need.

1. Form 940, Employer's Annual Federal Unemployment (FUTA) Tax Return. This form is due 1 month after the calendar year ends. Use it to report the FUTA tax you paid.

2. Form 941, Employer's Quarterly Federal Tax Return. This form is due 1 month after the calendar quarter ends. Use it to report social security and Medicare taxes and withheld income taxes on wages if your employees are not farm workers.

3. Form 943, Employer's Annual Federal Tax Return for Agricultural Employees. This form is due 1 month after the calendar year ends. Use it to report social security and Medicare taxes and withheld income taxes on wages if your employees are farm workers.

4. Form 944, Employer's Annual Federal Tax Return. Due 1 month after calendar year ends. Starting with calendar year 2006, certain small employers must file Form 944 instead of Form 941.

5. Form 945, Annual Return of Withheld Federal Income Tax. This form is due 1 month after the calendar year ends. Use it to report income tax withheld on all nonpayroll items. Nonpayroll items include the following.

a. Backup withholding.

b. Withholding on pensions, annuities, IRAs, and gambling winnings.

c. Payments of Indian gaming profits to tribal members.

FISCAL-YEAR TAXPAYERS. The dates in this calendar apply whether you use a fiscal year or the calendar year as your tax year. The only exception is the date for filing Forms 5500 and 5500-EZ. These employee benefit plan forms are due by the last day of the seventh month after the plan year ends. See July 31, later.

EXTENDED DUE DATES. If you deposit in full and on time the tax you are required to report on Form 940, 941, 943, 944, or 945, you have an additional 10 days to file that form.

FIRST QUARTER

The first quarter of a calendar year is made up of January, February, and March.

DURING JANUARY

ALL EMPLOYERS. Give your employees their copies of Form W-2 for 2006 by January 31, 2007. If an employee agreed to receive Form W-2 electronically, post it on a website accessible to the employee and notify the employee of the posting by January 31.

JANUARY 1

EARNED INCOME CREDIT. Stop advance payments of the earned income credit for any employee who did not give you a new Form W-5 for 2007.

JANUARY 16

SOCIAL SECURITY, MEDICARE, AND WITHHELD INCOME TAX. If the monthly deposit rule applies, deposit the tax for payments in December 2006.

NONPAYROLL WITHHOLDING. If the monthly deposit rule applies, deposit the tax for payments in December 2006.

JANUARY 31

ALL EMPLOYERS. Give your employees their copies of Form W-2 for 2006. If an employee agreed to receive Form W-2 electronically, have it posted on a website and notify the employee of the posting.

PAYERS OF GAMBLING WINNINGS. If you either paid reportable gambling winnings or withheld income tax from gambling winnings, give the winners their copies of Form W-2G.

NONPAYROLL TAXES. File Form 945 to report income tax withheld for 2006 on all nonpayroll items, including backup withholding and withholding on pensions, annuities, IRAs, gambling winnings, and payments of Indian gaming profits to tribal members. Deposit any undeposited tax. (If your tax liability is less than $2,500, you can pay it in full with a timely filed return.) If you deposited the tax for the year in full and on time, you have until February 10 to file the return.

SOCIAL SECURITY, MEDICARE, AND WITHHELD INCOME TAX. File Form 941 for the fourth quarter of 2006 or, Form 944, if applicable, for 2006. Deposit any undeposited tax. (If your tax liability is less than $2,500, you can pay it in full with a timely filed return.) If you deposited the tax for the quarter in full and on time (or, for Form 944 filers, for the year), you have until February 12 to file the return.

FARM EMPLOYERS. File Form 943 to report social security and Medicare taxes and withheld income tax for 2006. Deposit any undeposited tax. (If your tax liability is less than $2,500, you can pay it in full with a timely filed return.) If you deposited the tax for the year in full and on time, you have until February 12 to file the return.

FEDERAL UNEMPLOYMENT TAX. File Form 940 for 2006. If your undeposited tax is $500 or less, you can either pay it with your return or deposit it. If it is more than $500, you must deposit it. However, if you deposited the tax for the year in full and on time, you have until February 12 to file the return.

FEBRUARY 12

NONPAYROLL TAXES. File Form 945 to report income tax withheld for 2006 on all nonpayroll items. This due date applies only if you deposited the tax for the year in full and on time.

SOCIAL SECURITY, MEDICARE, AND WITHHELD INCOME TAX. File Form 941 for the fourth quarter of 2006 or Form 944, if applicable, for 2006. This due date applies only if you deposited the tax for the quarter (or, for Form 944 filers, for the year) in full and on time.

FARM EMPLOYERS. File Form 943 to report social security and Medicare taxes and withheld income tax for 2006. This due date applies only if you deposited the tax for the year in full and on time.

FEDERAL UNEMPLOYMENT TAX. File Form 940 for 2006. This due date applies only if you deposited the tax for the year in full and on time.

FEBRUARY 15

SOCIAL SECURITY, MEDICARE, AND WITHHELD INCOME TAX. If the monthly deposit rule applies, deposit the tax for payments in January.

NONPAYROLL WITHHOLDING. If the monthly deposit rule applies, deposit the tax for payments in January.

FEBRUARY 16

ALL EMPLOYERS. Begin withholding income tax from the pay of any employee who claimed exemption from withholding in 2006, but did not give you a new Form W-4 to continue the exemption this year.

FEBRUARY 28

PAYERS OF GAMBLING WINNINGS. File Form 1096, Annual Summary and Transmittal of U.S. Information Returns, along with Copy A of all the Forms W-2G you issued for 2006.

If you file Forms W-2G electronically (not by magnetic media), your due date for filing them with the IRS will be extended to April 2. The due date for giving the recipient these forms remains January 31.

ALL EMPLOYERS. File Form W-3, Transmittal of Wage and Tax Statements, along with Copy A of all the Forms W-2 you issued for 2006.

If you file Forms W-2 electronically (not by magnetic media), your due date for filing them with the SSA will be extended to April 2. The due date for giving the recipient these forms remains January 31.

LARGE FOOD AND BEVERAGE ESTABLISHMENT EMPLOYERS. File Form 8027, Employer's Annual Information Return of Tip Income and Allocated Tips. Use Form 8027-T, Transmittal of Employer's Annual Information Return of Tip Income and Allocated Tips, to summarize and transmit Forms 8027 if you have more than one establishment. If you file Forms 8027 electronically (not by magnetic media), your due date for filing them with the IRS will be extended to April 2.

MARCH 15

SOCIAL SECURITY, MEDICARE, AND WITHHELD INCOME TAX. If the monthly deposit rule applies, deposit the tax for payments in February.

NONPAYROLL WITHHOLDING. If the monthly deposit rule applies, deposit the tax for payments in February.

SECOND QUARTER

The second quarter of a calendar year is made up of April, May, and June.

April 2

ELECTRONIC FILING OF FORMS W-2. File Copy A of all the Forms W-2 you issued for 2006. This due date applies only if you electronically file (not by magnetic media). Otherwise, see February 28. The due date for giving the recipient these forms remains January 31.

ELECTRONIC FILING OF FORMS W-2G. File copies of all the Forms W-2G you issued for 2006. This due date applies only if you electronically file (not by magnetic media). Otherwise, see February 28. The due date for giving the recipient these forms remains January 31. For information about filing Forms W-2G electronically, see Publication 1220, Specifications for Filing Forms 1098, 1099, 5498 and W-2G Electronically or Magnetically.

ELECTRONIC FILING OF FORMS 8027. File Forms 8027 for 2006. This due date applies only if you electronically file (not by magnetic media). Otherwise, see February 28.

April 17

SOCIAL SECURITY, MEDICARE, AND WITHHELD INCOME TAX. If the monthly deposit rule applies, deposit the tax for payments in March.

NONPAYROLL WITHHOLDING. If the monthly deposit rule applies, deposit the tax for payments in March.

HOUSEHOLD EMPLOYERS. If you paid cash wages of $1,500 or more in 2006 to a household employee, you must file Schedule H. If you are required to file a federal income tax return (Form 1040), file Schedule H with the return and report any household employment taxes. Report any federal unemployment (FUTA) tax on Schedule H if you paid total cash wages of $1,000 or more in any calendar quarter of 2005 or 2006 to household employees. Also, report any income tax you withheld for your household employees. For more information, see Publication 926.

APRIL 30

SOCIAL SECURITY, MEDICARE, AND WITHHELD INCOME TAX. File Form 941 for the first quarter of 2007. Deposit any undeposited tax. (If your tax liability is less than $2,500, you can pay it in full with a timely filed return.) If you deposited the tax for the quarter in full and on time, you have until May 10 to file the return.

FEDERAL UNEMPLOYMENT TAX. Deposit the tax owed through March if more than $500.

MAY 10

Social security, Medicare, and withheld income tax. File Form 941 for the first quarter of 2007. This due date applies only if you deposited the tax for the quarter in full and on time.

MAY 15

SOCIAL SECURITY, MEDICARE, AND WITHHELD INCOME TAX. If the monthly deposit rule applies, deposit the tax for payments in April.

NONPAYROLL WITHHOLDING. If the monthly deposit rule applies, deposit the tax for payments in April.

JUNE 15

SOCIAL SECURITY, MEDICARE, AND WITHHELD INCOME TAX. If the monthly deposit rule applies, deposit the tax for payments in May.

NONPAYROLL WITHHOLDING. If the monthly deposit rule applies, deposit the tax for payments in May.

THIRD QUARTER

The third quarter of a calendar year is made up of July, August, and September.

JULY 16

SOCIAL SECURITY, MEDICARE, AND WITHHELD INCOME TAX. If the monthly deposit rule applies, deposit the tax for payments in June.

NONPAYROLL WITHHOLDING. If the monthly deposit rule applies, deposit the tax for payments in June.

JULY 31

SOCIAL SECURITY, MEDICARE, AND WITHHELD INCOME TAX. File Form 941 for the second quarter of 2007. Deposit any undeposited tax. (If your tax liability is less than $2,500, you can pay it in full with a timely filed return.) If you deposited the tax for the quarter in full and on time, you have until August 10 to file the return.

FEDERAL UNEMPLOYMENT TAX. Deposit the tax owed through June if more than $500.

ALL EMPLOYERS. If you maintain an employee benefit plan, such as a pension, profit-sharing, or stock bonus plan, file

Form 5500 or 5500-EZ for calendar year 2006. If you use a fiscal year as your plan year, file the form by the last day of the seventh month after the plan year ends.

AUGUST 10

SOCIAL SECURITY, MEDICARE, AND WITHHELD INCOME TAX. File Form 941 for the second quarter of 2007. This due date applies only if you deposited the tax for the quarter in full and on time.

AUGUST 15

SOCIAL SECURITY, MEDICARE, AND WITHHELD INCOME TAX. If the monthly deposit rule applies, deposit the tax for payments in July.

NONPAYROLL WITHHOLDING. If the monthly deposit rule applies, deposit the tax for payments in July.

SEPTEMBER 17

SOCIAL SECURITY, MEDICARE, AND WITHHELD INCOME TAX. If the monthly deposit rule applies, deposit the tax for payments in August.

NONPAYROLL WITHHOLDING. If the monthly deposit rule applies, deposit the tax for payments in August.

FOURTH QUARTER

The fourth quarter of a calendar year is made up of October, November, and December.

OCTOBER 15

SOCIAL SECURITY, MEDICARE, AND WITHHELD INCOME TAX. If the monthly deposit rule applies, deposit the tax for payments in September.

NONPAYROLL WITHHOLDING. If the monthly deposit rule applies, deposit the tax for payments in September.

OCTOBER 31

SOCIAL SECURITY, MEDICARE, AND WITHHELD INCOME TAX. File Form 941 for the third quarter of 2007. Deposit any undeposited tax. (If your tax liability is less than $2,500, you can pay it in full with a timely filed return.) If you deposited the tax for the quarter in full and on time, you have until November 13 to file the return.

FEDERAL UNEMPLOYMENT TAX. Deposit the tax owed through September if more than $500.

DURING NOVEMBER

2008 RIA FEDERAL TAX HANDBOOK

Contents

Table of Contents—Main Topics

Chapter 1 Tax Rates and Tables

¶ 1100 Tax Rates and Tables

Federal tax rates for income, gift, estate, excise and other taxes are set forth in this Chapter. Also included are current income tax tables. The rate brackets for individuals and estates and trusts are adjusted annually for cost-of-living increases based on the average consumer price index (CPI) for the 12-month period ending the previous Aug. 31. Similar adjustments are made to other key figures.

¶ 1101 Income tax rates for individuals.

Different rates apply to:

. . . single taxpayers (¶1102);

. . . married persons filing joint returns and qualified widows and widowers (¶1103);

. . . married persons filing separate returns (¶1104); and

. . . heads of households (¶1105).

Bankruptcy estates of individuals compute their tax using the same rate schedule as married individuals filing separate tax returns.

Individuals with taxable income under a ceiling amount ($100,000) compute their tax using tax tables (Code Sec. 3), reproduced at ¶1110.

For capital gains rates, see ¶2600 *et seq.*

¶ 1102 Single individuals.

Taxpayers who aren't married *at year's end* and who don't qualify as surviving spouses or heads of household, and certain married taxpayers living apart compute their tax under the following tax rates for single persons if they can't use the tax tables.

The rates for 2007 are:

If taxable income is:	The tax is:
Not over $7,825	10% of taxable income
Over $7,825 but not over $31,850	$782.50 plus 15% of the excess over $7,825
Over $31,850 but not over $77,100	$4,386.25 plus 25% of the excess over $31,850
Over $77,100 but not over $160,850	$15,698.75 plus 28% of the excess over $77,100
Over $160,850 but not over $349,700	$39,148.75 plus 33% of the excess over $160,850
Over $349,700	$101,469.25 plus 35% of the excess over $349,700

The rates for 2008 are:

If taxable income is:	The tax is:
Not over $8,025	10% of taxable income
Over $8,025 but not over $32,550	$802.50 plus 15% of the excess over $8,025
Over $32,550 but not over $78,850	$4,481.25 plus 25% of the excess over $32,550

References beginning with a single letter are to paragraphs in RIA's Federal Tax Coordinator 2d and RIA's Analysis of Federal Taxes: Income. Those beginning with numbers are to paragraphs in RIA's United States Tax Reporter. Those beginning with TD are to paragraphs in RIA's Tax Desk.

Over $78,850 but not over $164,550	$16,056.25 plus 28% of the excess over $78,850
Over $164,550 but not over $357,700	$40,052.25 plus 33% of the excess over $164,550
Over $357,700	$103,791.75 plus 35% of the excess over $357,700

¶ 1103   Married filing joint returns and surviving spouses.

Married taxpayers filing joint returns and surviving spouses who can't use the tax tables compute their tax on the basis of the rates indicated below.

The rates for 2007 are:

If taxable income is:	The tax is:
Not over $15,650	10% of taxable income
Over $15,650 but not over $63,700	$1,565.00 plus 15% of the excess over $15,650
Over $63,700 but not over $128,500	$8,772.50 plus 25% of the excess over $63,700
Over $128,500 but not over $195,850	$24,972.50 plus 28% of the excess over $128,500
Over $195,850 but not over $349,700	$43,830.50 plus 33% of the excess over $195,850
Over $349,700	$94,601.00 plus 35% of the excess over $349,700

The rates for 2008 are:

If taxable income is:	The tax is:
Not over $16,050	10% of taxable income
Over $16,050 but not over $65,100	$1,605.00 plus 15% of the excess over $16,050
Over $65,100 but not over $131,450	$8,962.50 plus 25% of the excess over $65,100
Over $131,450 but not over $200,300	$25,550.00 plus 28% of the excess over $131,450
Over $200,300 but not over $357,700	$44,828.00 plus 33% of the excess over $200,300
Over $357,700	$96,770.00 plus 35% of the excess over $357,700

¶ 1104   Married filing separate returns.

Married taxpayers filing separate returns who can't use the tax tables compute their tax on the basis of the rates indicated below.

The rates for 2007 are:

If taxable income is:	The tax is:
Not over $7,825	10% of taxable income
Over $7,825 but not over $31,850	$782.50 plus 15% of the excess over $7,825
Over $31,850 but not over $64,250	$4,386.25 plus 25% of the excess over $31,850
Over $64,250 but not over $97,925	$12,486.25 plus 28% of the excess over $64,250

| Over $97,925 but not over $174,850 ..... | $21,915.25 plus 33% of the excess over $97,925 |
| Over $174,850 .... | $47,300.50 plus 35% of the excess over $174,850 |

The rates for 2008 are:

If taxable income is:	The tax is:
Not over $8,025	10% of taxable income
Over $8,025 but not over $32,550	$802.50 plus 15% of the excess over $8,025
Over $32,550 but not over $65,725	$4,481.25 plus 25% of the excess over $32,550
Over $65,725 but not over $100,150	$12,775.00 plus 28% of the excess over $65,725
Over $100,150 but not over $178,850	$22,414.00 plus 33% of the excess over $100,150
Over $178,850	$48,385.00 plus 35% of the excess over $178,850

¶ 1105   Head of household.

Unmarried persons maintaining households who can't use the tax tables compute their tax on the basis of the rates indicated below.

The rates for 2007 are:

If taxable income is:	The tax is:
Not over $11,200	10% of taxable income
Over $11,200 but not over $42,650	$1,120.00 plus 15% of the excess over $11,200
Over $42,650 but not over $110,100	$5,837.50 plus 25% of the excess over $42,650
Over $110,100 but not over $178,350	$22,700.00 plus 28% of the excess over $110,100
Over $178,350 but not over $349,700	$41,810.00 plus 33% of the excess over $178,350
Over $349,700	$98,355.50 plus 35% of the excess over $349,700

The rates for 2008 are:

If taxable income is:	The tax is:
Not over $11,450	10% of taxable income
Over $11,450 but not over $43,650	$1,145.00 plus 15% of the excess over $11,450
Over $43,650 but not over $112,650	$5,975.00 plus 25% of the excess over $43,650
Over $112,650 but not over $182,400	$23,225.00 plus 28% of the excess over $112,650
Over $182,400 but not over $357,700	$42,755.00 plus 33% of the excess over $182,400
Over $357,700	$100,604.00 plus 35% of the excess over $357,700

¶ 1106   Income tax rates for trusts and estates.

The income tax on trusts and decedent's estates is imposed at graduated rates on their taxable income. (Code Sec. 1(e)) For capital gains rates, see ¶2600.

The rates for 2007 are:

If taxable income is:	The tax is:
Not over $2,150	15% of taxable income
Over $2,150 but not over $5,000	$322.50 plus 25% of the excess over $2,150
Over $5,000 but not over $7,650	$1,035.00 plus 28% of the excess over $5,000
Over $7,650 but not over $10,450	$1,777.00 plus 33% of the excess over $7,650
Over $10,450	$2,701.00 plus 35% of the excess over $10,450

The rates for 2008 are:

If taxable income is:	The tax is:
Not over $2,200	15% of taxable income
Over $2,200 but not over $5,150	$330.00 plus 25% of the excess over $2,200
Over $5,150 but not over $7,850	$1,067.50 plus 28% of the excess over $5,150
Over $7,850 but not over $10,700	$1,823.50 plus 33% of the excess over $7,850
Over $10,700	$2,764.00 plus 35% of the excess over $10,700

¶ 1107 FICA (Social Security and Medicare) tax.

A 7.65% FICA tax for employers and employees is imposed: the 6.20% Social Security tax plus the 1.45% Medicare tax. (Code Sec. 3101(a), Code Sec. 3101(b); Code Sec. 3111(a), Code Sec. 3111(b))

For 2008 the 6.20% Social Security tax is computed on the first $102,000 of the employee's wages. Thus, the maximum Social Security tax for 2008 is $6,324 (6.20% of $102,000). The 1.45% Medicare tax is computed on the employee's total wages (no ceiling).

For 2007 the 6.20% Social Security tax was computed on the first $97,500 of the employee's wages. Thus, the maximum Social Security tax for 2007 was $6,045 (6.20% of $97,500). The 1.45% Medicare tax was computed on the employee's total wages (no ceiling).

¶ 1108 Self-employment tax.

A self-employment tax is imposed on self-employed people at a rate of 15.30%: a combination of a 12.40% Old Age, Survivors, and Disability Insurance tax (OASDI, the equivalent of the Social Security tax at ¶1107), and a 2.90% Medicare tax. (Code Sec. 1401(a), Code Sec. 1401(b))

For 2008, the 12.40% OASDI tax is computed on the first $102,000 of self-employment income. Thus, the maximum OASDI tax for 2008 is $12,648 (12.40% of $102,000). The 2.90% Medicare tax is computed on the entire self-employment income (no ceiling).

For 2007, the 12.40% OASDI tax was computed on the first $97,500 of self-employment income. Thus, the maximum OASDI tax for 2007 was $12,090 (12.40% of $97,500). The 2.90% Medicare tax was computed on the entire self-employment income (no ceiling).

RIA *observation:* Sole proprietors and partners are subject to the Medicare tax on their entire self-employment income even if the income isn't distributed (unlike shareholders in an S corporation, who aren't subject to the self-employment tax on their share of the corporation's net income, whether distributed or not, see ¶3140).

¶ 1109   Federal unemployment tax (FUTA).

The tax is 6.2% through 2007, and 6.0% for 2008 and after (Code Sec. 3301), of the first $7,000 paid each employee as wages during the calendar year. (Code Sec. 3306(b)) (Check http://ria.thomson.com/federaltaxhandbook for any new law changes.)

The employer gets a credit against FUTA tax for contributions paid into state unemployment funds. The credit can't exceed 5.4% of the first $7,000 of wages. (Code Sec. 3302)

¶ 1110   Tax Table for Individuals

2007
Tax Table

See the instructions for line 44 that begin on page 33 to see if you must use the Tax Table below to figure your tax.

Example. Mr. and Mrs. Brown are filing a joint return. Their taxable income on Form 1040, line 43, is $25,300. First, they find the $25,300–25,350 taxable income line. Next, they find the column for married filing jointly and read down the column. The amount shown where the taxable income line and filing status column meet is $3,016. This is the tax amount they should enter on Form 1040, line 44.

Sample Table

At least	But less than	Single	Married filing jointly *	Married filing separately	Head of a household
			Your tax is—		
25,200	25,250	3,393	3,001	3,393	3,224
25,250	25,300	3,400	3,009	3,400	3,231
25,300	25,350	3,408	(3,016)	3,408	3,239
25,350	25,400	3,415	3,024	3,415	3,246

If line 43 (taxable income) is— At least	But less than	Single	Married filing jointly *	Married filing separately	Head of a household
			Your tax is—		
0	5	0	0	0	0
5	15	1	1	1	1
15	25	2	2	2	2
25	50	4	4	4	4
50	75	6	6	6	6
75	100	9	9	9	9
100	125	11	11	11	11
125	150	14	14	14	14
150	175	16	16	16	16
175	200	19	19	19	19
200	225	21	21	21	21
225	250	24	24	24	24
250	275	26	26	26	26
275	300	29	29	29	29
300	325	31	31	31	31
325	350	34	34	34	34
350	375	36	36	36	36
375	400	39	39	39	39
400	425	41	41	41	41
425	450	44	44	44	44
450	475	46	46	46	46
475	500	49	49	49	49
500	525	51	51	51	51
525	550	54	54	54	54
550	575	56	56	56	56
575	600	59	59	59	59
600	625	61	61	61	61
625	650	64	64	64	64
650	675	66	66	66	66
675	700	69	69	69	69
700	725	71	71	71	71
725	750	74	74	74	74
750	775	76	76	76	76
775	800	79	79	79	79
800	825	81	81	81	81
825	850	84	84	84	84
850	875	86	86	86	86
875	900	89	89	89	89
900	925	91	91	91	91
925	950	94	94	94	94
950	975	96	96	96	96
975	1,000	99	99	99	99

1,000

At least	But less than	Single	Married filing jointly *	Married filing separately	Head of a household
1,000	1,025	101	101	101	101
1,025	1,050	104	104	104	104
1,050	1,075	106	106	106	106
1,075	1,100	109	109	109	109
1,100	1,125	111	111	111	111
1,125	1,150	114	114	114	114
1,150	1,175	116	116	116	116
1,175	1,200	119	119	119	119
1,200	1,225	121	121	121	121
1,225	1,250	124	124	124	124
1,250	1,275	126	126	126	126
1,275	1,300	129	129	129	129

If line 43 (taxable income) is— At least	But less than	Single	Married filing jointly *	Married filing separately	Head of a household
			Your tax is—		
1,300	1,325	131	131	131	131
1,325	1,350	134	134	134	134
1,350	1,375	136	136	136	136
1,375	1,400	139	139	139	139
1,400	1,425	141	141	141	141
1,425	1,450	144	144	144	144
1,450	1,475	146	146	146	146
1,475	1,500	149	149	149	149
1,500	1,525	151	151	151	151
1,525	1,550	154	154	154	154
1,550	1,575	156	156	156	156
1,575	1,600	159	159	159	159
1,600	1,625	161	161	161	161
1,625	1,650	164	164	164	164
1,650	1,675	166	166	166	166
1,675	1,700	169	169	169	169
1,700	1,725	171	171	171	171
1,725	1,750	174	174	174	174
1,750	1,775	176	176	176	176
1,775	1,800	179	179	179	179
1,800	1,825	181	181	181	181
1,825	1,850	184	184	184	184
1,850	1,875	186	186	186	186
1,875	1,900	189	189	189	189
1,900	1,925	191	191	191	191
1,925	1,950	194	194	194	194
1,950	1,975	196	196	196	196
1,975	2,000	199	199	199	199

2,000

At least	But less than	Single	Married filing jointly *	Married filing separately	Head of a household
2,000	2,025	201	201	201	201
2,025	2,050	204	204	204	204
2,050	2,075	206	206	206	206
2,075	2,100	209	209	209	209
2,100	2,125	211	211	211	211
2,125	2,150	214	214	214	214
2,150	2,175	216	216	216	216
2,175	2,200	219	219	219	219
2,200	2,225	221	221	221	221
2,225	2,250	224	224	224	224
2,250	2,275	226	226	226	226
2,275	2,300	229	229	229	229
2,300	2,325	231	231	231	231
2,325	2,350	234	234	234	234
2,350	2,375	236	236	236	236
2,375	2,400	239	239	239	239
2,400	2,425	241	241	241	241
2,425	2,450	244	244	244	244
2,450	2,475	246	246	246	246
2,475	2,500	249	249	249	249
2,500	2,525	251	251	251	251
2,525	2,550	254	254	254	254
2,550	2,575	256	256	256	256
2,575	2,600	259	259	259	259
2,600	2,625	261	261	261	261
2,625	2,650	264	264	264	264
2,650	2,675	266	266	266	266
2,675	2,700	269	269	269	269

If line 43 (taxable income) is— At least	But less than	Single	Married filing jointly *	Married filing separately	Head of a household
			Your tax is—		
2,700	2,725	271	271	271	271
2,725	2,750	274	274	274	274
2,750	2,775	276	276	276	276
2,775	2,800	279	279	279	279
2,800	2,825	281	281	281	281
2,825	2,850	284	284	284	284
2,850	2,875	286	286	286	286
2,875	2,900	289	289	289	289
2,900	2,925	291	291	291	291
2,925	2,950	294	294	294	294
2,950	2,975	296	296	296	296
2,975	3,000	299	299	299	299

3,000

At least	But less than	Single	Married filing jointly *	Married filing separately	Head of a household
3,000	3,050	303	303	303	303
3,050	3,100	308	308	308	308
3,100	3,150	313	313	313	313
3,150	3,200	318	318	318	318
3,200	3,250	323	323	323	323
3,250	3,300	328	328	328	328
3,300	3,350	333	333	333	333
3,350	3,400	338	338	338	338
3,400	3,450	343	343	343	343
3,450	3,500	348	348	348	348
3,500	3,550	353	353	353	353
3,550	3,600	358	358	358	358
3,600	3,650	363	363	363	363
3,650	3,700	368	368	368	368
3,700	3,750	373	373	373	373
3,750	3,800	378	378	378	378
3,800	3,850	383	383	383	383
3,850	3,900	388	388	388	388
3,900	3,950	393	393	393	393
3,950	4,000	398	398	398	398

4,000

At least	But less than	Single	Married filing jointly *	Married filing separately	Head of a household
4,000	4,050	403	403	403	403
4,050	4,100	408	408	408	408
4,100	4,150	413	413	413	413
4,150	4,200	418	418	418	418
4,200	4,250	423	423	423	423
4,250	4,300	428	428	428	428
4,300	4,350	433	433	433	433
4,350	4,400	438	438	438	438
4,400	4,450	443	443	443	443
4,450	4,500	448	448	448	448
4,500	4,550	453	453	453	453
4,550	4,600	458	458	458	458
4,600	4,650	463	463	463	463
4,650	4,700	468	468	468	468
4,700	4,750	473	473	473	473
4,750	4,800	478	478	478	478
4,800	4,850	483	483	483	483
4,850	4,900	488	488	488	488
4,900	4,950	493	493	493	493
4,950	5,000	498	498	498	498

* This column must also be used by a qualifying widow(er).

2007 Tax Table–*Continued*

5,000

At least	But less than	Single	Married filing jointly *	Married filing separately	Head of a household
			Your tax is—		
5,000	5,050	503	503	503	503
5,050	5,100	508	508	508	508
5,100	5,150	513	513	513	513
5,150	5,200	518	518	518	518
5,200	5,250	523	523	523	523
5,250	5,300	528	528	528	528
5,300	5,350	533	533	533	533
5,350	5,400	538	538	538	538
5,400	5,450	543	543	543	543
5,450	5,500	548	548	548	548
5,500	5,550	553	553	553	553
5,550	5,600	558	558	558	558
5,600	5,650	563	563	563	563
5,650	5,700	568	568	568	568
5,700	5,750	573	573	573	573
5,750	5,800	578	578	578	578
5,800	5,850	583	583	583	583
5,850	5,900	588	588	588	588
5,900	5,950	593	593	593	593
5,950	6,000	598	598	598	598

6,000

At least	But less than	Single	Married filing jointly *	Married filing separately	Head of a household
6,000	6,050	603	603	603	603
6,050	6,100	608	608	608	608
6,100	6,150	613	613	613	613
6,150	6,200	618	618	618	618
6,200	6,250	623	623	623	623
6,250	6,300	628	628	628	628
6,300	6,350	633	633	633	633
6,350	6,400	638	638	638	638
6,400	6,450	643	643	643	643
6,450	6,500	648	648	648	648
6,500	6,550	653	653	653	653
6,550	6,600	658	658	658	658
6,600	6,650	663	663	663	663
6,650	6,700	668	668	668	668
6,700	6,750	673	673	673	673
6,750	6,800	678	678	678	678
6,800	6,850	683	683	683	683
6,850	6,900	688	688	688	688
6,900	6,950	693	693	693	693
6,950	7,000	698	698	698	698

7,000

At least	But less than	Single	Married filing jointly *	Married filing separately	Head of a household
7,000	7,050	703	703	703	703
7,050	7,100	708	708	708	708
7,100	7,150	713	713	713	713
7,150	7,200	718	718	718	718
7,200	7,250	723	723	723	723
7,250	7,300	728	728	728	728
7,300	7,350	733	733	733	733
7,350	7,400	738	738	738	738
7,400	7,450	743	743	743	743
7,450	7,500	748	748	748	748
7,500	7,550	753	753	753	753
7,550	7,600	758	758	758	758
7,600	7,650	763	763	763	763
7,650	7,700	768	768	768	768
7,700	7,750	773	773	773	773
7,750	7,800	778	778	778	778
7,800	7,850	783	783	783	783
7,850	7,900	790	788	790	788
7,900	7,950	798	793	798	793
7,950	8,000	805	798	805	798

8,000

At least	But less than	Single	Married filing jointly *	Married filing separately	Head of a household
			Your tax is—		
8,000	8,050	813	803	813	803
8,050	8,100	820	808	820	808
8,100	8,150	828	813	828	813
8,150	8,200	835	818	835	818
8,200	8,250	843	823	843	823
8,250	8,300	850	828	850	828
8,300	8,350	858	833	858	833
8,350	8,400	865	838	865	838
8,400	8,450	873	843	873	843
8,450	8,500	880	848	880	848
8,500	8,550	888	853	888	853
8,550	8,600	895	858	895	858
8,600	8,650	903	863	903	863
8,650	8,700	910	868	910	868
8,700	8,750	918	873	918	873
8,750	8,800	925	878	925	878
8,800	8,850	933	883	933	883
8,850	8,900	940	888	940	888
8,900	8,950	948	893	948	893
8,950	9,000	955	898	955	898

9,000

At least	But less than	Single	Married filing jointly *	Married filing separately	Head of a household
9,000	9,050	963	903	963	903
9,050	9,100	970	908	970	908
9,100	9,150	978	913	978	913
9,150	9,200	985	918	985	918
9,200	9,250	993	923	993	923
9,250	9,300	1,000	928	1,000	928
9,300	9,350	1,008	933	1,008	933
9,350	9,400	1,015	938	1,015	938
9,400	9,450	1,023	943	1,023	943
9,450	9,500	1,030	948	1,030	948
9,500	9,550	1,038	953	1,038	953
9,550	9,600	1,045	958	1,045	958
9,600	9,650	1,053	963	1,053	963
9,650	9,700	1,060	968	1,060	968
9,700	9,750	1,068	973	1,068	973
9,750	9,800	1,075	978	1,075	978
9,800	9,850	1,083	983	1,083	983
9,850	9,900	1,090	988	1,090	988
9,900	9,950	1,098	993	1,098	993
9,950	10,000	1,105	998	1,105	998

10,000

At least	But less than	Single	Married filing jointly *	Married filing separately	Head of a household
10,000	10,050	1,113	1,003	1,113	1,003
10,050	10,100	1,120	1,008	1,120	1,008
10,100	10,150	1,128	1,013	1,128	1,013
10,150	10,200	1,135	1,018	1,135	1,018
10,200	10,250	1,143	1,023	1,143	1,023
10,250	10,300	1,150	1,028	1,150	1,028
10,300	10,350	1,158	1,033	1,158	1,033
10,350	10,400	1,165	1,038	1,165	1,038
10,400	10,450	1,173	1,043	1,173	1,043
10,450	10,500	1,180	1,048	1,180	1,048
10,500	10,550	1,188	1,053	1,188	1,053
10,550	10,600	1,195	1,058	1,195	1,058
10,600	10,650	1,203	1,063	1,203	1,063
10,650	10,700	1,210	1,068	1,210	1,068
10,700	10,750	1,218	1,073	1,218	1,073
10,750	10,800	1,225	1,078	1,225	1,078
10,800	10,850	1,233	1,083	1,233	1,083
10,850	10,900	1,240	1,088	1,240	1,088
10,900	10,950	1,248	1,093	1,248	1,093
10,950	11,000	1,255	1,098	1,255	1,098

11,000

At least	But less than	Single	Married filing jointly *	Married filing separately	Head of a household
			Your tax is—		
11,000	11,050	1,263	1,103	1,263	1,103
11,050	11,100	1,270	1,108	1,270	1,108
11,100	11,150	1,278	1,113	1,278	1,113
11,150	11,200	1,285	1,118	1,285	1,118
11,200	11,250	1,293	1,123	1,293	1,124
11,250	11,300	1,300	1,128	1,300	1,131
11,300	11,350	1,308	1,133	1,308	1,139
11,350	11,400	1,315	1,138	1,315	1,146
11,400	11,450	1,323	1,143	1,323	1,154
11,450	11,500	1,330	1,148	1,330	1,161
11,500	11,550	1,338	1,153	1,338	1,169
11,550	11,600	1,345	1,158	1,345	1,176
11,600	11,650	1,353	1,163	1,353	1,184
11,650	11,700	1,360	1,168	1,360	1,191
11,700	11,750	1,368	1,173	1,368	1,199
11,750	11,800	1,375	1,178	1,375	1,206
11,800	11,850	1,383	1,183	1,383	1,214
11,850	11,900	1,390	1,188	1,390	1,221
11,900	11,950	1,398	1,193	1,398	1,229
11,950	12,000	1,405	1,198	1,405	1,236

12,000

At least	But less than	Single	Married filing jointly *	Married filing separately	Head of a household
12,000	12,050	1,413	1,203	1,413	1,244
12,050	12,100	1,420	1,208	1,420	1,251
12,100	12,150	1,428	1,213	1,428	1,259
12,150	12,200	1,435	1,218	1,435	1,266
12,200	12,250	1,443	1,223	1,443	1,274
12,250	12,300	1,450	1,228	1,450	1,281
12,300	12,350	1,458	1,233	1,458	1,289
12,350	12,400	1,465	1,238	1,465	1,296
12,400	12,450	1,473	1,243	1,473	1,304
12,450	12,500	1,480	1,248	1,480	1,311
12,500	12,550	1,488	1,253	1,488	1,319
12,550	12,600	1,495	1,258	1,495	1,326
12,600	12,650	1,503	1,263	1,503	1,334
12,650	12,700	1,510	1,268	1,510	1,341
12,700	12,750	1,518	1,273	1,518	1,349
12,750	12,800	1,525	1,278	1,525	1,356
12,800	12,850	1,533	1,283	1,533	1,364
12,850	12,900	1,540	1,288	1,540	1,371
12,900	12,950	1,548	1,293	1,548	1,379
12,950	13,000	1,555	1,298	1,555	1,386

13,000

At least	But less than	Single	Married filing jointly *	Married filing separately	Head of a household
13,000	13,050	1,563	1,303	1,563	1,394
13,050	13,100	1,570	1,308	1,570	1,401
13,100	13,150	1,578	1,313	1,578	1,409
13,150	13,200	1,585	1,318	1,585	1,416
13,200	13,250	1,593	1,323	1,593	1,424
13,250	13,300	1,600	1,328	1,600	1,431
13,300	13,350	1,608	1,333	1,608	1,439
13,350	13,400	1,615	1,338	1,615	1,446
13,400	13,450	1,623	1,343	1,623	1,454
13,450	13,500	1,630	1,348	1,630	1,461
13,500	13,550	1,638	1,353	1,638	1,469
13,550	13,600	1,645	1,358	1,645	1,476
13,600	13,650	1,653	1,363	1,653	1,484
13,650	13,700	1,660	1,368	1,660	1,491
13,700	13,750	1,668	1,373	1,668	1,499
13,750	13,800	1,675	1,378	1,675	1,506
13,800	13,850	1,683	1,383	1,683	1,514
13,850	13,900	1,690	1,388	1,690	1,521
13,900	13,950	1,698	1,393	1,698	1,529
13,950	14,000	1,705	1,398	1,705	1,536

* This column must also be used by a qualifying widow(er).

2007 Tax Table–*Continued*

If line 43 (taxable income) is— At least	But less than	And you are— Single	Married filing jointly*	Married filing separately	Head of a household
		Your tax is—			
14,000					
14,000	14,050	1,713	1,403	1,713	1,544
14,050	14,100	1,720	1,408	1,720	1,551
14,100	14,150	1,728	1,413	1,728	1,559
14,150	14,200	1,735	1,418	1,735	1,566
14,200	14,250	1,743	1,423	1,743	1,574
14,250	14,300	1,750	1,428	1,750	1,581
14,300	14,350	1,758	1,433	1,758	1,589
14,350	14,400	1,765	1,438	1,765	1,596
14,400	14,450	1,773	1,443	1,773	1,604
14,450	14,500	1,780	1,448	1,780	1,611
14,500	14,550	1,788	1,453	1,788	1,619
14,550	14,600	1,795	1,458	1,795	1,626
14,600	14,650	1,803	1,463	1,803	1,634
14,650	14,700	1,810	1,468	1,810	1,641
14,700	14,750	1,818	1,473	1,818	1,649
14,750	14,800	1,825	1,478	1,825	1,656
14,800	14,850	1,833	1,483	1,833	1,664
14,850	14,900	1,840	1,488	1,840	1,671
14,900	14,950	1,848	1,493	1,848	1,679
14,950	15,000	1,855	1,498	1,855	1,686
15,000					
15,000	15,050	1,863	1,503	1,863	1,694
15,050	15,100	1,870	1,508	1,870	1,701
15,100	15,150	1,878	1,513	1,878	1,709
15,150	15,200	1,885	1,518	1,885	1,716
15,200	15,250	1,893	1,523	1,893	1,724
15,250	15,300	1,900	1,528	1,900	1,731
15,300	15,350	1,908	1,533	1,908	1,739
15,350	15,400	1,915	1,538	1,915	1,746
15,400	15,450	1,923	1,543	1,923	1,754
15,450	15,500	1,930	1,548	1,930	1,761
15,500	15,550	1,938	1,553	1,938	1,769
15,550	15,600	1,945	1,558	1,945	1,776
15,600	15,650	1,953	1,563	1,953	1,784
15,650	15,700	1,960	1,569	1,960	1,791
15,700	15,750	1,968	1,576	1,968	1,799
15,750	15,800	1,975	1,584	1,975	1,806
15,800	15,850	1,983	1,591	1,983	1,814
15,850	15,900	1,990	1,599	1,990	1,821
15,900	15,950	1,998	1,606	1,998	1,829
15,950	16,000	2,005	1,614	2,005	1,836
16,000					
16,000	16,050	2,013	1,621	2,013	1,844
16,050	16,100	2,020	1,629	2,020	1,851
16,100	16,150	2,028	1,636	2,028	1,859
16,150	16,200	2,035	1,644	2,035	1,866
16,200	16,250	2,043	1,651	2,043	1,874
16,250	16,300	2,050	1,659	2,050	1,881
16,300	16,350	2,058	1,666	2,058	1,889
16,350	16,400	2,065	1,674	2,065	1,896
16,400	16,450	2,073	1,681	2,073	1,904
16,450	16,500	2,080	1,689	2,080	1,911
16,500	16,550	2,088	1,696	2,088	1,919
16,550	16,600	2,095	1,704	2,095	1,926
16,600	16,650	2,103	1,711	2,103	1,934
16,650	16,700	2,110	1,719	2,110	1,941
16,700	16,750	2,118	1,726	2,118	1,949
16,750	16,800	2,125	1,734	2,125	1,956
16,800	16,850	2,133	1,741	2,133	1,964
16,850	16,900	2,140	1,749	2,140	1,971
16,900	16,950	2,148	1,756	2,148	1,979
16,950	17,000	2,155	1,764	2,155	1,986

If line 43 (taxable income) is— At least	But less than	And you are— Single	Married filing jointly*	Married filing separately	Head of a household
		Your tax is—			
17,000					
17,000	17,050	2,163	1,771	2,163	1,994
17,050	17,100	2,170	1,779	2,170	2,001
17,100	17,150	2,178	1,786	2,178	2,009
17,150	17,200	2,185	1,794	2,185	2,016
17,200	17,250	2,193	1,801	2,193	2,024
17,250	17,300	2,200	1,809	2,200	2,031
17,300	17,350	2,208	1,816	2,208	2,039
17,350	17,400	2,215	1,824	2,215	2,046
17,400	17,450	2,223	1,831	2,223	2,054
17,450	17,500	2,230	1,839	2,230	2,061
17,500	17,550	2,238	1,846	2,238	2,069
17,550	17,600	2,245	1,854	2,245	2,076
17,600	17,650	2,253	1,861	2,253	2,084
17,650	17,700	2,260	1,869	2,260	2,091
17,700	17,750	2,268	1,876	2,268	2,099
17,750	17,800	2,275	1,884	2,275	2,106
17,800	17,850	2,283	1,891	2,283	2,114
17,850	17,900	2,290	1,899	2,290	2,121
17,900	17,950	2,298	1,906	2,298	2,129
17,950	18,000	2,305	1,914	2,305	2,136
18,000					
18,000	18,050	2,313	1,921	2,313	2,144
18,050	18,100	2,320	1,929	2,320	2,151
18,100	18,150	2,328	1,936	2,328	2,159
18,150	18,200	2,335	1,944	2,335	2,166
18,200	18,250	2,343	1,951	2,343	2,174
18,250	18,300	2,350	1,959	2,350	2,181
18,300	18,350	2,358	1,966	2,358	2,189
18,350	18,400	2,365	1,974	2,365	2,196
18,400	18,450	2,373	1,981	2,373	2,204
18,450	18,500	2,380	1,989	2,380	2,211
18,500	18,550	2,388	1,996	2,388	2,219
18,550	18,600	2,395	2,004	2,395	2,226
18,600	18,650	2,403	2,011	2,403	2,234
18,650	18,700	2,410	2,019	2,410	2,241
18,700	18,750	2,418	2,026	2,418	2,249
18,750	18,800	2,425	2,034	2,425	2,256
18,800	18,850	2,433	2,041	2,433	2,264
18,850	18,900	2,440	2,049	2,440	2,271
18,900	18,950	2,448	2,056	2,448	2,279
18,950	19,000	2,455	2,064	2,455	2,286
19,000					
19,000	19,050	2,463	2,071	2,463	2,294
19,050	19,100	2,470	2,079	2,470	2,301
19,100	19,150	2,478	2,086	2,478	2,309
19,150	19,200	2,485	2,094	2,485	2,316
19,200	19,250	2,493	2,101	2,493	2,324
19,250	19,300	2,500	2,109	2,500	2,331
19,300	19,350	2,508	2,116	2,508	2,339
19,350	19,400	2,515	2,124	2,515	2,346
19,400	19,450	2,523	2,131	2,523	2,354
19,450	19,500	2,530	2,139	2,530	2,361
19,500	19,550	2,538	2,146	2,538	2,369
19,550	19,600	2,545	2,154	2,545	2,376
19,600	19,650	2,553	2,161	2,553	2,384
19,650	19,700	2,560	2,169	2,560	2,391
19,700	19,750	2,568	2,176	2,568	2,399
19,750	19,800	2,575	2,184	2,575	2,406
19,800	19,850	2,583	2,191	2,583	2,414
19,850	19,900	2,590	2,199	2,590	2,421
19,900	19,950	2,598	2,206	2,598	2,429
19,950	20,000	2,605	2,214	2,605	2,436

If line 43 (taxable income) is— At least	But less than	And you are— Single	Married filing jointly*	Married filing separately	Head of a household
		Your tax is—			
20,000					
20,000	20,050	2,613	2,221	2,613	2,444
20,050	20,100	2,620	2,229	2,620	2,451
20,100	20,150	2,628	2,236	2,628	2,459
20,150	20,200	2,635	2,244	2,635	2,466
20,200	20,250	2,643	2,251	2,643	2,474
20,250	20,300	2,650	2,259	2,650	2,481
20,300	20,350	2,658	2,266	2,658	2,489
20,350	20,400	2,665	2,274	2,665	2,496
20,400	20,450	2,673	2,281	2,673	2,504
20,450	20,500	2,680	2,289	2,680	2,511
20,500	20,550	2,688	2,296	2,688	2,519
20,550	20,600	2,695	2,304	2,695	2,526
20,600	20,650	2,703	2,311	2,703	2,534
20,650	20,700	2,710	2,319	2,710	2,541
20,700	20,750	2,718	2,326	2,718	2,549
20,750	20,800	2,725	2,334	2,725	2,556
20,800	20,850	2,733	2,341	2,733	2,564
20,850	20,900	2,740	2,349	2,740	2,571
20,900	20,950	2,748	2,356	2,748	2,579
20,950	21,000	2,755	2,364	2,755	2,586
21,000					
21,000	21,050	2,763	2,371	2,763	2,594
21,050	21,100	2,770	2,379	2,770	2,601
21,100	21,150	2,778	2,386	2,778	2,609
21,150	21,200	2,785	2,394	2,785	2,616
21,200	21,250	2,793	2,401	2,793	2,624
21,250	21,300	2,800	2,409	2,800	2,631
21,300	21,350	2,808	2,416	2,808	2,639
21,350	21,400	2,815	2,424	2,815	2,646
21,400	21,450	2,823	2,431	2,823	2,654
21,450	21,500	2,830	2,439	2,830	2,661
21,500	21,550	2,838	2,446	2,838	2,669
21,550	21,600	2,845	2,454	2,845	2,676
21,600	21,650	2,853	2,461	2,853	2,684
21,650	21,700	2,860	2,469	2,860	2,691
21,700	21,750	2,868	2,476	2,868	2,699
21,750	21,800	2,875	2,484	2,875	2,706
21,800	21,850	2,883	2,491	2,883	2,714
21,850	21,900	2,890	2,499	2,890	2,721
21,900	21,950	2,898	2,506	2,898	2,729
21,950	22,000	2,905	2,514	2,905	2,736
22,000					
22,000	22,050	2,913	2,521	2,913	2,744
22,050	22,100	2,920	2,529	2,920	2,751
22,100	22,150	2,928	2,536	2,928	2,759
22,150	22,200	2,935	2,544	2,935	2,766
22,200	22,250	2,943	2,551	2,943	2,774
22,250	22,300	2,950	2,559	2,950	2,781
22,300	22,350	2,958	2,566	2,958	2,789
22,350	22,400	2,965	2,574	2,965	2,796
22,400	22,450	2,973	2,581	2,973	2,804
22,450	22,500	2,980	2,589	2,980	2,811
22,500	22,550	2,988	2,596	2,988	2,819
22,550	22,600	2,995	2,604	2,995	2,826
22,600	22,650	3,003	2,611	3,003	2,834
22,650	22,700	3,010	2,619	3,010	2,841
22,700	22,750	3,018	2,626	3,018	2,849
22,750	22,800	3,025	2,634	3,025	2,856
22,800	22,850	3,033	2,641	3,033	2,864
22,850	22,900	3,040	2,649	3,040	2,871
22,900	22,950	3,048	2,656	3,048	2,879
22,950	23,000	3,055	2,664	3,055	2,886

* This column must also be used by a qualifying widow(er).

2007 Tax Table–*Continued*

At least	But less than	Single	Married filing jointly *	Married filing separately	Head of a household
23,000					
23,000	23,050	3,063	2,671	3,063	2,894
23,050	23,100	3,070	2,679	3,070	2,901
23,100	23,150	3,078	2,686	3,078	2,909
23,150	23,200	3,085	2,694	3,085	2,916
23,200	23,250	3,093	2,701	3,093	2,924
23,250	23,300	3,100	2,709	3,100	2,931
23,300	23,350	3,108	2,716	3,108	2,939
23,350	23,400	3,115	2,724	3,115	2,946
23,400	23,450	3,123	2,731	3,123	2,954
23,450	23,500	3,130	2,739	3,130	2,961
23,500	23,550	3,138	2,746	3,138	2,969
23,550	23,600	3,145	2,754	3,145	2,976
23,600	23,650	3,153	2,761	3,153	2,984
23,650	23,700	3,160	2,769	3,160	2,991
23,700	23,750	3,168	2,776	3,168	2,999
23,750	23,800	3,175	2,784	3,175	3,006
23,800	23,850	3,183	2,791	3,183	3,014
23,850	23,900	3,190	2,799	3,190	3,021
23,900	23,950	3,198	2,806	3,198	3,029
23,950	24,000	3,205	2,814	3,205	3,036
24,000					
24,000	24,050	3,213	2,821	3,213	3,044
24,050	24,100	3,220	2,829	3,220	3,051
24,100	24,150	3,228	2,836	3,228	3,059
24,150	24,200	3,235	2,844	3,235	3,066
24,200	24,250	3,243	2,851	3,243	3,074
24,250	24,300	3,250	2,859	3,250	3,081
24,300	24,350	3,258	2,866	3,258	3,089
24,350	24,400	3,265	2,874	3,265	3,096
24,400	24,450	3,273	2,881	3,273	3,104
24,450	24,500	3,280	2,889	3,280	3,111
24,500	24,550	3,288	2,896	3,288	3,119
24,550	24,600	3,295	2,904	3,295	3,126
24,600	24,650	3,303	2,911	3,303	3,134
24,650	24,700	3,310	2,919	3,310	3,141
24,700	24,750	3,318	2,926	3,318	3,149
24,750	24,800	3,325	2,934	3,325	3,156
24,800	24,850	3,333	2,941	3,333	3,164
24,850	24,900	3,340	2,949	3,340	3,171
24,900	24,950	3,348	2,956	3,348	3,179
24,950	25,000	3,355	2,964	3,355	3,186
25,000					
25,000	25,050	3,363	2,971	3,363	3,194
25,050	25,100	3,370	2,979	3,370	3,201
25,100	25,150	3,378	2,986	3,378	3,209
25,150	25,200	3,385	2,994	3,385	3,216
25,200	25,250	3,393	3,001	3,393	3,224
25,250	25,300	3,400	3,009	3,400	3,231
25,300	25,350	3,408	3,016	3,408	3,239
25,350	25,400	3,415	3,024	3,415	3,246
25,400	25,450	3,423	3,031	3,423	3,254
25,450	25,500	3,430	3,039	3,430	3,261
25,500	25,550	3,438	3,046	3,438	3,269
25,550	25,600	3,445	3,054	3,445	3,276
25,600	25,650	3,453	3,061	3,453	3,284
25,650	25,700	3,460	3,069	3,460	3,291
25,700	25,750	3,468	3,076	3,468	3,299
25,750	25,800	3,475	3,084	3,475	3,306
25,800	25,850	3,483	3,091	3,483	3,314
25,850	25,900	3,490	3,099	3,490	3,321
25,900	25,950	3,498	3,106	3,498	3,329
25,950	26,000	3,505	3,114	3,505	3,336

At least	But less than	Single	Married filing jointly *	Married filing separately	Head of a household
26,000					
26,000	26,050	3,513	3,121	3,513	3,344
26,050	26,100	3,520	3,129	3,520	3,351
26,100	26,150	3,528	3,136	3,528	3,359
26,150	26,200	3,535	3,144	3,535	3,366
26,200	26,250	3,543	3,151	3,543	3,374
26,250	26,300	3,550	3,159	3,550	3,381
26,300	26,350	3,558	3,166	3,558	3,389
26,350	26,400	3,565	3,174	3,565	3,396
26,400	26,450	3,573	3,181	3,573	3,404
26,450	26,500	3,580	3,189	3,580	3,411
26,500	26,550	3,588	3,196	3,588	3,419
26,550	26,600	3,595	3,204	3,595	3,426
26,600	26,650	3,603	3,211	3,603	3,434
26,650	26,700	3,610	3,219	3,610	3,441
26,700	26,750	3,618	3,226	3,618	3,449
26,750	26,800	3,625	3,234	3,625	3,456
26,800	26,850	3,633	3,241	3,633	3,464
26,850	26,900	3,640	3,249	3,640	3,471
26,900	26,950	3,648	3,256	3,648	3,479
26,950	27,000	3,655	3,264	3,655	3,486
27,000					
27,000	27,050	3,663	3,271	3,663	3,494
27,050	27,100	3,670	3,279	3,670	3,501
27,100	27,150	3,678	3,286	3,678	3,509
27,150	27,200	3,685	3,294	3,685	3,516
27,200	27,250	3,693	3,301	3,693	3,524
27,250	27,300	3,700	3,309	3,700	3,531
27,300	27,350	3,708	3,316	3,708	3,539
27,350	27,400	3,715	3,324	3,715	3,546
27,400	27,450	3,723	3,331	3,723	3,554
27,450	27,500	3,730	3,339	3,730	3,561
27,500	27,550	3,738	3,346	3,738	3,569
27,550	27,600	3,745	3,354	3,745	3,576
27,600	27,650	3,753	3,361	3,753	3,584
27,650	27,700	3,760	3,369	3,760	3,591
27,700	27,750	3,768	3,376	3,768	3,599
27,750	27,800	3,775	3,384	3,775	3,606
27,800	27,850	3,783	3,391	3,783	3,614
27,850	27,900	3,790	3,399	3,790	3,621
27,900	27,950	3,798	3,406	3,798	3,629
27,950	28,000	3,805	3,414	3,805	3,636
28,000					
28,000	28,050	3,813	3,421	3,813	3,644
28,050	28,100	3,820	3,429	3,820	3,651
28,100	28,150	3,828	3,436	3,828	3,659
28,150	28,200	3,835	3,444	3,835	3,666
28,200	28,250	3,843	3,451	3,843	3,674
28,250	28,300	3,850	3,459	3,850	3,681
28,300	28,350	3,858	3,466	3,858	3,689
28,350	28,400	3,865	3,474	3,865	3,696
28,400	28,450	3,873	3,481	3,873	3,704
28,450	28,500	3,880	3,489	3,880	3,711
28,500	28,550	3,888	3,496	3,888	3,719
28,550	28,600	3,895	3,504	3,895	3,726
28,600	28,650	3,903	3,511	3,903	3,734
28,650	28,700	3,910	3,519	3,910	3,741
28,700	28,750	3,918	3,526	3,918	3,749
28,750	28,800	3,925	3,534	3,925	3,756
28,800	28,850	3,933	3,541	3,933	3,764
28,850	28,900	3,940	3,549	3,940	3,771
28,900	28,950	3,948	3,556	3,948	3,779
28,950	29,000	3,955	3,564	3,955	3,786

At least	But less than	Single	Married filing jointly *	Married filing separately	Head of a household
29,000					
29,000	29,050	3,963	3,571	3,963	3,794
29,050	29,100	3,970	3,579	3,970	3,801
29,100	29,150	3,978	3,586	3,978	3,809
29,150	29,200	3,985	3,594	3,985	3,816
29,200	29,250	3,993	3,601	3,993	3,824
29,250	29,300	4,000	3,609	4,000	3,831
29,300	29,350	4,008	3,616	4,008	3,839
29,350	29,400	4,015	3,624	4,015	3,846
29,400	29,450	4,023	3,631	4,023	3,854
29,450	29,500	4,030	3,639	4,030	3,861
29,500	29,550	4,038	3,646	4,038	3,869
29,550	29,600	4,045	3,654	4,045	3,876
29,600	29,650	4,053	3,661	4,053	3,884
29,650	29,700	4,060	3,669	4,060	3,891
29,700	29,750	4,068	3,676	4,068	3,899
29,750	29,800	4,075	3,684	4,075	3,906
29,800	29,850	4,083	3,691	4,083	3,914
29,850	29,900	4,090	3,699	4,090	3,921
29,900	29,950	4,098	3,706	4,098	3,929
29,950	30,000	4,105	3,714	4,105	3,936
30,000					
30,000	30,050	4,113	3,721	4,113	3,944
30,050	30,100	4,120	3,729	4,120	3,951
30,100	30,150	4,128	3,736	4,128	3,959
30,150	30,200	4,135	3,744	4,135	3,966
30,200	30,250	4,143	3,751	4,143	3,974
30,250	30,300	4,150	3,759	4,150	3,981
30,300	30,350	4,158	3,766	4,158	3,989
30,350	30,400	4,165	3,774	4,165	3,996
30,400	30,450	4,173	3,781	4,173	4,004
30,450	30,500	4,180	3,789	4,180	4,011
30,500	30,550	4,188	3,796	4,188	4,019
30,550	30,600	4,195	3,804	4,195	4,026
30,600	30,650	4,203	3,811	4,203	4,034
30,650	30,700	4,210	3,819	4,210	4,041
30,700	30,750	4,218	3,826	4,218	4,049
30,750	30,800	4,225	3,834	4,225	4,056
30,800	30,850	4,233	3,841	4,233	4,064
30,850	30,900	4,240	3,849	4,240	4,071
30,900	30,950	4,248	3,856	4,248	4,079
30,950	31,000	4,255	3,864	4,255	4,086
31,000					
31,000	31,050	4,263	3,871	4,263	4,094
31,050	31,100	4,270	3,879	4,270	4,101
31,100	31,150	4,278	3,886	4,278	4,109
31,150	31,200	4,285	3,894	4,285	4,116
31,200	31,250	4,293	3,901	4,293	4,124
31,250	31,300	4,300	3,909	4,300	4,131
31,300	31,350	4,308	3,916	4,308	4,139
31,350	31,400	4,315	3,924	4,315	4,146
31,400	31,450	4,323	3,931	4,323	4,154
31,450	31,500	4,330	3,939	4,330	4,161
31,500	31,550	4,338	3,946	4,338	4,169
31,550	31,600	4,345	3,954	4,345	4,176
31,600	31,650	4,353	3,961	4,353	4,184
31,650	31,700	4,360	3,969	4,360	4,191
31,700	31,750	4,368	3,976	4,368	4,199
31,750	31,800	4,375	3,984	4,375	4,206
31,800	31,850	4,383	3,991	4,383	4,214
31,850	31,900	4,393	3,999	4,393	4,221
31,900	31,950	4,405	4,006	4,405	4,229
31,950	32,000	4,418	4,014	4,418	4,236

* This column must also be used by a qualifying widow(er).

2007 Tax Table—*Continued*

If line 43 (taxable income) is— At least	But less than	Single	Married filing jointly *	Married filing separately	Head of a household
32,000					
32,000	32,050	4,430	4,021	4,430	4,244
32,050	32,100	4,443	4,029	4,443	4,251
32,100	32,150	4,455	4,036	4,455	4,259
32,150	32,200	4,468	4,044	4,468	4,266
32,200	32,250	4,480	4,051	4,480	4,274
32,250	32,300	4,493	4,059	4,493	4,281
32,300	32,350	4,505	4,066	4,505	4,289
32,350	32,400	4,518	4,074	4,518	4,296
32,400	32,450	4,530	4,081	4,530	4,304
32,450	32,500	4,543	4,089	4,543	4,311
32,500	32,550	4,555	4,096	4,555	4,319
32,550	32,600	4,568	4,104	4,568	4,326
32,600	32,650	4,580	4,111	4,580	4,334
32,650	32,700	4,593	4,119	4,593	4,341
32,700	32,750	4,605	4,126	4,605	4,349
32,750	32,800	4,618	4,134	4,618	4,356
32,800	32,850	4,630	4,141	4,630	4,364
32,850	32,900	4,643	4,149	4,643	4,371
32,900	32,950	4,655	4,156	4,655	4,379
32,950	33,000	4,668	4,164	4,668	4,386
33,000					
33,000	33,050	4,680	4,171	4,680	4,394
33,050	33,100	4,693	4,179	4,693	4,401
33,100	33,150	4,705	4,186	4,705	4,409
33,150	33,200	4,718	4,194	4,718	4,416
33,200	33,250	4,730	4,201	4,730	4,424
33,250	33,300	4,743	4,209	4,743	4,431
33,300	33,350	4,755	4,216	4,755	4,439
33,350	33,400	4,768	4,224	4,768	4,446
33,400	33,450	4,780	4,231	4,780	4,454
33,450	33,500	4,793	4,239	4,793	4,461
33,500	33,550	4,805	4,246	4,805	4,469
33,550	33,600	4,818	4,254	4,818	4,476
33,600	33,650	4,830	4,261	4,830	4,484
33,650	33,700	4,843	4,269	4,843	4,491
33,700	33,750	4,855	4,276	4,855	4,499
33,750	33,800	4,868	4,284	4,868	4,506
33,800	33,850	4,880	4,291	4,880	4,514
33,850	33,900	4,893	4,299	4,893	4,521
33,900	33,950	4,905	4,306	4,905	4,529
33,950	34,000	4,918	4,314	4,918	4,536
34,000					
34,000	34,050	4,930	4,321	4,930	4,544
34,050	34,100	4,943	4,329	4,943	4,551
34,100	34,150	4,955	4,336	4,955	4,559
34,150	34,200	4,968	4,344	4,968	4,566
34,200	34,250	4,980	4,351	4,980	4,574
34,250	34,300	4,993	4,359	4,993	4,581
34,300	34,350	5,005	4,366	5,005	4,589
34,350	34,400	5,018	4,374	5,018	4,596
34,400	34,450	5,030	4,381	5,030	4,604
34,450	34,500	5,043	4,389	5,043	4,611
34,500	34,550	5,055	4,396	5,055	4,619
34,550	34,600	5,068	4,404	5,068	4,626
34,600	34,650	5,080	4,411	5,080	4,634
34,650	34,700	5,093	4,419	5,093	4,641
34,700	34,750	5,105	4,426	5,105	4,649
34,750	34,800	5,118	4,434	5,118	4,656
34,800	34,850	5,130	4,441	5,130	4,664
34,850	34,900	5,143	4,449	5,143	4,671
34,900	34,950	5,155	4,456	5,155	4,679
34,950	35,000	5,168	4,464	5,168	4,686

If line 43 (taxable income) is— At least	But less than	Single	Married filing jointly *	Married filing separately	Head of a household
35,000					
35,000	35,050	5,180	4,471	5,180	4,694
35,050	35,100	5,193	4,479	5,193	4,701
35,100	35,150	5,205	4,486	5,205	4,709
35,150	35,200	5,218	4,494	5,218	4,716
35,200	35,250	5,230	4,501	5,230	4,724
35,250	35,300	5,243	4,509	5,243	4,731
35,300	35,350	5,255	4,516	5,255	4,739
35,350	35,400	5,268	4,524	5,268	4,746
35,400	35,450	5,280	4,531	5,280	4,754
35,450	35,500	5,293	4,539	5,293	4,761
35,500	35,550	5,305	4,546	5,305	4,769
35,550	35,600	5,318	4,554	5,318	4,776
35,600	35,650	5,330	4,561	5,330	4,784
35,650	35,700	5,343	4,569	5,343	4,791
35,700	35,750	5,355	4,576	5,355	4,799
35,750	35,800	5,368	4,584	5,368	4,806
35,800	35,850	5,380	4,591	5,380	4,814
35,850	35,900	5,393	4,599	5,393	4,821
35,900	35,950	5,405	4,606	5,405	4,829
35,950	36,000	5,418	4,614	5,418	4,836
36,000					
36,000	36,050	5,430	4,621	5,430	4,844
36,050	36,100	5,443	4,629	5,443	4,851
36,100	36,150	5,455	4,636	5,455	4,859
36,150	36,200	5,468	4,644	5,468	4,866
36,200	36,250	5,480	4,651	5,480	4,874
36,250	36,300	5,493	4,659	5,493	4,881
36,300	36,350	5,505	4,666	5,505	4,889
36,350	36,400	5,518	4,674	5,518	4,896
36,400	36,450	5,530	4,681	5,530	4,904
36,450	36,500	5,543	4,689	5,543	4,911
36,500	36,550	5,555	4,696	5,555	4,919
36,550	36,600	5,568	4,704	5,568	4,926
36,600	36,650	5,580	4,711	5,580	4,934
36,650	36,700	5,593	4,719	5,593	4,941
36,700	36,750	5,605	4,726	5,605	4,949
36,750	36,800	5,618	4,734	5,618	4,956
36,800	36,850	5,630	4,741	5,630	4,964
36,850	36,900	5,643	4,749	5,643	4,971
36,900	36,950	5,655	4,756	5,655	4,979
36,950	37,000	5,668	4,764	5,668	4,986
37,000					
37,000	37,050	5,680	4,771	5,680	4,994
37,050	37,100	5,693	4,779	5,693	5,001
37,100	37,150	5,705	4,786	5,705	5,009
37,150	37,200	5,718	4,794	5,718	5,016
37,200	37,250	5,730	4,801	5,730	5,024
37,250	37,300	5,743	4,809	5,743	5,031
37,300	37,350	5,755	4,816	5,755	5,039
37,350	37,400	5,768	4,824	5,768	5,046
37,400	37,450	5,780	4,831	5,780	5,054
37,450	37,500	5,793	4,839	5,793	5,061
37,500	37,550	5,805	4,846	5,805	5,069
37,550	37,600	5,818	4,854	5,818	5,076
37,600	37,650	5,830	4,861	5,830	5,084
37,650	37,700	5,843	4,869	5,843	5,091
37,700	37,750	5,855	4,876	5,855	5,099
37,750	37,800	5,868	4,884	5,868	5,106
37,800	37,850	5,880	4,891	5,880	5,114
37,850	37,900	5,893	4,899	5,893	5,121
37,900	37,950	5,905	4,906	5,905	5,129
37,950	38,000	5,918	4,914	5,918	5,136

If line 43 (taxable income) is— At least	But less than	Single	Married filing jointly *	Married filing separately	Head of a household
38,000					
38,000	38,050	5,930	4,921	5,930	5,144
38,050	38,100	5,943	4,929	5,943	5,151
38,100	38,150	5,955	4,936	5,955	5,159
38,150	38,200	5,968	4,944	5,968	5,166
38,200	38,250	5,980	4,951	5,980	5,174
38,250	38,300	5,993	4,959	5,993	5,181
38,300	38,350	6,005	4,966	6,005	5,189
38,350	38,400	6,018	4,974	6,018	5,196
38,400	38,450	6,030	4,981	6,030	5,204
38,450	38,500	6,043	4,989	6,043	5,211
38,500	38,550	6,055	4,996	6,055	5,219
38,550	38,600	6,068	5,004	6,068	5,226
38,600	38,650	6,080	5,011	6,080	5,234
38,650	38,700	6,093	5,019	6,093	5,241
38,700	38,750	6,105	5,026	6,105	5,249
38,750	38,800	6,118	5,034	6,118	5,256
38,800	38,850	6,130	5,041	6,130	5,264
38,850	38,900	6,143	5,049	6,143	5,271
38,900	38,950	6,155	5,056	6,155	5,279
38,950	39,000	6,168	5,064	6,168	5,286
39,000					
39,000	39,050	6,180	5,071	6,180	5,294
39,050	39,100	6,193	5,079	6,193	5,301
39,100	39,150	6,205	5,086	6,205	5,309
39,150	39,200	6,218	5,094	6,218	5,316
39,200	39,250	6,230	5,101	6,230	5,324
39,250	39,300	6,243	5,109	6,243	5,331
39,300	39,350	6,255	5,116	6,255	5,339
39,350	39,400	6,268	5,124	6,268	5,346
39,400	39,450	6,280	5,131	6,280	5,354
39,450	39,500	6,293	5,139	6,293	5,361
39,500	39,550	6,305	5,146	6,305	5,369
39,550	39,600	6,318	5,154	6,318	5,376
39,600	39,650	6,330	5,161	6,330	5,384
39,650	39,700	6,343	5,169	6,343	5,391
39,700	39,750	6,355	5,176	6,355	5,399
39,750	39,800	6,368	5,184	6,368	5,406
39,800	39,850	6,380	5,191	6,380	5,414
39,850	39,900	6,393	5,199	6,393	5,421
39,900	39,950	6,405	5,206	6,405	5,429
39,950	40,000	6,418	5,214	6,418	5,436
40,000					
40,000	40,050	6,430	5,221	6,430	5,444
40,050	40,100	6,443	5,229	6,443	5,451
40,100	40,150	6,455	5,236	6,455	5,459
40,150	40,200	6,468	5,244	6,468	5,466
40,200	40,250	6,480	5,251	6,480	5,474
40,250	40,300	6,493	5,259	6,493	5,481
40,300	40,350	6,505	5,266	6,505	5,489
40,350	40,400	6,518	5,274	6,518	5,496
40,400	40,450	6,530	5,281	6,530	5,504
40,450	40,500	6,543	5,289	6,543	5,511
40,500	40,550	6,555	5,296	6,555	5,519
40,550	40,600	6,568	5,304	6,568	5,526
40,600	40,650	6,580	5,311	6,580	5,534
40,650	40,700	6,593	5,319	6,593	5,541
40,700	40,750	6,605	5,326	6,605	5,549
40,750	40,800	6,618	5,334	6,618	5,556
40,800	40,850	6,630	5,341	6,630	5,564
40,850	40,900	6,643	5,349	6,643	5,571
40,900	40,950	6,655	5,356	6,655	5,579
40,950	41,000	6,668	5,364	6,668	5,586

* This column must also be used by a qualifying widow(er).

2007 Tax Table—*Continued*

If line 43 (taxable income) is— At least	But less than	Single	Married filing jointly *	Married filing separately	Head of a household
41,000					
41,000	41,050	6,680	5,371	6,680	5,594
41,050	41,100	6,693	5,379	6,693	5,601
41,100	41,150	6,705	5,386	6,705	5,609
41,150	41,200	6,718	5,394	6,718	5,616
41,200	41,250	6,730	5,401	6,730	5,624
41,250	41,300	6,743	5,409	6,743	5,631
41,300	41,350	6,755	5,416	6,755	5,639
41,350	41,400	6,768	5,424	6,768	5,646
41,400	41,450	6,780	5,431	6,780	5,654
41,450	41,500	6,793	5,439	6,793	5,661
41,500	41,550	6,805	5,446	6,805	5,669
41,550	41,600	6,818	5,454	6,818	5,676
41,600	41,650	6,830	5,461	6,830	5,684
41,650	41,700	6,843	5,469	6,843	5,691
41,700	41,750	6,855	5,476	6,855	5,699
41,750	41,800	6,868	5,484	6,868	5,706
41,800	41,850	6,880	5,491	6,880	5,714
41,850	41,900	6,893	5,499	6,893	5,721
41,900	41,950	6,905	5,506	6,905	5,729
41,950	42,000	6,918	5,514	6,918	5,736
42,000					
42,000	42,050	6,930	5,521	6,930	5,744
42,050	42,100	6,943	5,529	6,943	5,751
42,100	42,150	6,955	5,536	6,955	5,759
42,150	42,200	6,968	5,544	6,968	5,766
42,200	42,250	6,980	5,551	6,980	5,774
42,250	42,300	6,993	5,559	6,993	5,781
42,300	42,350	7,005	5,566	7,005	5,789
42,350	42,400	7,018	5,574	7,018	5,796
42,400	42,450	7,030	5,581	7,030	5,804
42,450	42,500	7,043	5,589	7,043	5,811
42,500	42,550	7,055	5,596	7,055	5,819
42,550	42,600	7,068	5,604	7,068	5,826
42,600	42,650	7,080	5,611	7,080	5,834
42,650	42,700	7,093	5,619	7,093	5,844
42,700	42,750	7,105	5,626	7,105	5,856
42,750	42,800	7,118	5,634	7,118	5,869
42,800	42,850	7,130	5,641	7,130	5,881
42,850	42,900	7,143	5,649	7,143	5,894
42,900	42,950	7,155	5,656	7,155	5,906
42,950	43,000	7,168	5,664	7,168	5,919
43,000					
43,000	43,050	7,180	5,671	7,180	5,931
43,050	43,100	7,193	5,679	7,193	5,944
43,100	43,150	7,205	5,686	7,205	5,956
43,150	43,200	7,218	5,694	7,218	5,969
43,200	43,250	7,230	5,701	7,230	5,981
43,250	43,300	7,243	5,709	7,243	5,994
43,300	43,350	7,255	5,716	7,255	6,006
43,350	43,400	7,268	5,724	7,268	6,019
43,400	43,450	7,280	5,731	7,280	6,031
43,450	43,500	7,293	5,739	7,293	6,044
43,500	43,550	7,305	5,746	7,305	6,056
43,550	43,600	7,318	5,754	7,318	6,069
43,600	43,650	7,330	5,761	7,330	6,081
43,650	43,700	7,343	5,769	7,343	6,094
43,700	43,750	7,355	5,776	7,355	6,106
43,750	43,800	7,368	5,784	7,368	6,119
43,800	43,850	7,380	5,791	7,380	6,131
43,850	43,900	7,393	5,799	7,393	6,144
43,900	43,950	7,405	5,806	7,405	6,156
43,950	44,000	7,418	5,814	7,418	6,169

If line 43 (taxable income) is— At least	But less than	Single	Married filing jointly *	Married filing separately	Head of a household
44,000					
44,000	44,050	7,430	5,821	7,430	6,181
44,050	44,100	7,443	5,829	7,443	6,194
44,100	44,150	7,455	5,836	7,455	6,206
44,150	44,200	7,468	5,844	7,468	6,219
44,200	44,250	7,480	5,851	7,480	6,231
44,250	44,300	7,493	5,859	7,493	6,244
44,300	44,350	7,505	5,866	7,505	6,256
44,350	44,400	7,518	5,874	7,518	6,269
44,400	44,450	7,530	5,881	7,530	6,281
44,450	44,500	7,543	5,889	7,543	6,294
44,500	44,550	7,555	5,896	7,555	6,306
44,550	44,600	7,568	5,904	7,568	6,319
44,600	44,650	7,580	5,911	7,580	6,331
44,650	44,700	7,593	5,919	7,593	6,344
44,700	44,750	7,605	5,926	7,605	6,356
44,750	44,800	7,618	5,934	7,618	6,369
44,800	44,850	7,630	5,941	7,630	6,381
44,850	44,900	7,643	5,949	7,643	6,394
44,900	44,950	7,655	5,956	7,655	6,406
44,950	45,000	7,668	5,964	7,668	6,419
45,000					
45,000	45,050	7,680	5,971	7,680	6,431
45,050	45,100	7,693	5,979	7,693	6,444
45,100	45,150	7,705	5,986	7,705	6,456
45,150	45,200	7,718	5,994	7,718	6,469
45,200	45,250	7,730	6,001	7,730	6,481
45,250	45,300	7,743	6,009	7,743	6,494
45,300	45,350	7,755	6,016	7,755	6,506
45,350	45,400	7,768	6,024	7,768	6,519
45,400	45,450	7,780	6,031	7,780	6,531
45,450	45,500	7,793	6,039	7,793	6,544
45,500	45,550	7,805	6,046	7,805	6,556
45,550	45,600	7,818	6,054	7,818	6,569
45,600	45,650	7,830	6,061	7,830	6,581
45,650	45,700	7,843	6,069	7,843	6,594
45,700	45,750	7,855	6,076	7,855	6,606
45,750	45,800	7,868	6,084	7,868	6,619
45,800	45,850	7,880	6,091	7,880	6,631
45,850	45,900	7,893	6,099	7,893	6,644
45,900	45,950	7,905	6,106	7,905	6,656
45,950	46,000	7,918	6,114	7,918	6,669
46,000					
46,000	46,050	7,930	6,121	7,930	6,681
46,050	46,100	7,943	6,129	7,943	6,694
46,100	46,150	7,955	6,136	7,955	6,706
46,150	46,200	7,968	6,144	7,968	6,719
46,200	46,250	7,980	6,151	7,980	6,731
46,250	46,300	7,993	6,159	7,993	6,744
46,300	46,350	8,005	6,166	8,005	6,756
46,350	46,400	8,018	6,174	8,018	6,769
46,400	46,450	8,030	6,181	8,030	6,781
46,450	46,500	8,043	6,189	8,043	6,794
46,500	46,550	8,055	6,196	8,055	6,806
46,550	46,600	8,068	6,204	8,068	6,819
46,600	46,650	8,080	6,211	8,080	6,831
46,650	46,700	8,093	6,219	8,093	6,844
46,700	46,750	8,105	6,226	8,105	6,856
46,750	46,800	8,118	6,234	8,118	6,869
46,800	46,850	8,130	6,241	8,130	6,881
46,850	46,900	8,143	6,249	8,143	6,894
46,900	46,950	8,155	6,256	8,155	6,906
46,950	47,000	8,168	6,264	8,168	6,919

If line 43 (taxable income) is— At least	But less than	Single	Married filing jointly *	Married filing separately	Head of a household
47,000					
47,000	47,050	8,180	6,271	8,180	6,931
47,050	47,100	8,193	6,279	8,193	6,944
47,100	47,150	8,205	6,286	8,205	6,956
47,150	47,200	8,218	6,294	8,218	6,969
47,200	47,250	8,230	6,301	8,230	6,981
47,250	47,300	8,243	6,309	8,243	6,994
47,300	47,350	8,255	6,316	8,255	7,006
47,350	47,400	8,268	6,324	8,268	7,019
47,400	47,450	8,280	6,331	8,280	7,031
47,450	47,500	8,293	6,339	8,293	7,044
47,500	47,550	8,305	6,346	8,305	7,056
47,550	47,600	8,318	6,354	8,318	7,069
47,600	47,650	8,330	6,361	8,330	7,081
47,650	47,700	8,343	6,369	8,343	7,094
47,700	47,750	8,355	6,376	8,355	7,106
47,750	47,800	8,368	6,384	8,368	7,119
47,800	47,850	8,380	6,391	8,380	7,131
47,850	47,900	8,393	6,399	8,393	7,144
47,900	47,950	8,405	6,406	8,405	7,156
47,950	48,000	8,418	6,414	8,418	7,169
48,000					
48,000	48,050	8,430	6,421	8,430	7,181
48,050	48,100	8,443	6,429	8,443	7,194
48,100	48,150	8,455	6,436	8,455	7,206
48,150	48,200	8,468	6,444	8,468	7,219
48,200	48,250	8,480	6,451	8,480	7,231
48,250	48,300	8,493	6,459	8,493	7,244
48,300	48,350	8,505	6,466	8,505	7,256
48,350	48,400	8,518	6,474	8,518	7,269
48,400	48,450	8,530	6,481	8,530	7,281
48,450	48,500	8,543	6,489	8,543	7,294
48,500	48,550	8,555	6,496	8,555	7,306
48,550	48,600	8,568	6,504	8,568	7,319
48,600	48,650	8,580	6,511	8,580	7,331
48,650	48,700	8,593	6,519	8,593	7,344
48,700	48,750	8,605	6,526	8,605	7,356
48,750	48,800	8,618	6,534	8,618	7,369
48,800	48,850	8,630	6,541	8,630	7,381
48,850	48,900	8,643	6,549	8,643	7,394
48,900	48,950	8,655	6,556	8,655	7,406
48,950	49,000	8,668	6,564	8,668	7,419
49,000					
49,000	49,050	8,680	6,571	8,680	7,431
49,050	49,100	8,693	6,579	8,693	7,444
49,100	49,150	8,705	6,586	8,705	7,456
49,150	49,200	8,718	6,594	8,718	7,469
49,200	49,250	8,730	6,601	8,730	7,481
49,250	49,300	8,743	6,609	8,743	7,494
49,300	49,350	8,755	6,616	8,755	7,506
49,350	49,400	8,768	6,624	8,768	7,519
49,400	49,450	8,780	6,631	8,780	7,531
49,450	49,500	8,793	6,639	8,793	7,544
49,500	49,550	8,805	6,646	8,805	7,556
49,550	49,600	8,818	6,654	8,818	7,569
49,600	49,650	8,830	6,661	8,830	7,581
49,650	49,700	8,843	6,669	8,843	7,594
49,700	49,750	8,855	6,676	8,855	7,606
49,750	49,800	8,868	6,684	8,868	7,619
49,800	49,850	8,880	6,691	8,880	7,631
49,850	49,900	8,893	6,699	8,893	7,644
49,900	49,950	8,905	6,706	8,905	7,656
49,950	50,000	8,918	6,714	8,918	7,669

* This column must also be used by a qualifying widow(er).

2007 Tax Table–*Continued*

50,000

If line 43 (taxable income) is— At least	But less than	And you are— Single	Married filing jointly *	Married filing separately	Head of a household
		Your tax is—			
50,000	50,050	8,930	6,721	8,930	7,681
50,050	50,100	8,943	6,729	8,943	7,694
50,100	50,150	8,955	6,736	8,955	7,706
50,150	50,200	8,968	6,744	8,968	7,719
50,200	50,250	8,980	6,751	8,980	7,731
50,250	50,300	8,993	6,759	8,993	7,744
50,300	50,350	9,005	6,766	9,005	7,756
50,350	50,400	9,018	6,774	9,018	7,769
50,400	50,450	9,030	6,781	9,030	7,781
50,450	50,500	9,043	6,789	9,043	7,794
50,500	50,550	9,055	6,796	9,055	7,806
50,550	50,600	9,068	6,804	9,068	7,819
50,600	50,650	9,080	6,811	9,080	7,831
50,650	50,700	9,093	6,819	9,093	7,844
50,700	50,750	9,105	6,826	9,105	7,856
50,750	50,800	9,118	6,834	9,118	7,869
50,800	50,850	9,130	6,841	9,130	7,881
50,850	50,900	9,143	6,849	9,143	7,894
50,900	50,950	9,155	6,856	9,155	7,906
50,950	51,000	9,168	6,864	9,168	7,919

51,000

At least	But less than	Single	Married filing jointly *	Married filing separately	Head of a household
51,000	51,050	9,180	6,871	9,180	7,931
51,050	51,100	9,193	6,879	9,193	7,944
51,100	51,150	9,205	6,886	9,205	7,956
51,150	51,200	9,218	6,894	9,218	7,969
51,200	51,250	9,230	6,901	9,230	7,981
51,250	51,300	9,243	6,909	9,243	7,994
51,300	51,350	9,255	6,916	9,255	8,006
51,350	51,400	9,268	6,924	9,268	8,019
51,400	51,450	9,280	6,931	9,280	8,031
51,450	51,500	9,293	6,939	9,293	8,044
51,500	51,550	9,305	6,946	9,305	8,056
51,550	51,600	9,318	6,954	9,318	8,069
51,600	51,650	9,330	6,961	9,330	8,081
51,650	51,700	9,343	6,969	9,343	8,094
51,700	51,750	9,355	6,976	9,355	8,106
51,750	51,800	9,368	6,984	9,368	8,119
51,800	51,850	9,380	6,991	9,380	8,131
51,850	51,900	9,393	6,999	9,393	8,144
51,900	51,950	9,405	7,006	9,405	8,156
51,950	52,000	9,418	7,014	9,418	8,169

52,000

At least	But less than	Single	Married filing jointly *	Married filing separately	Head of a household
52,000	52,050	9,430	7,021	9,430	8,181
52,050	52,100	9,443	7,029	9,443	8,194
52,100	52,150	9,455	7,036	9,455	8,206
52,150	52,200	9,468	7,044	9,468	8,219
52,200	52,250	9,480	7,051	9,480	8,231
52,250	52,300	9,493	7,059	9,493	8,244
52,300	52,350	9,505	7,066	9,505	8,256
52,350	52,400	9,518	7,074	9,518	8,269
52,400	52,450	9,530	7,081	9,530	8,281
52,450	52,500	9,543	7,089	9,543	8,294
52,500	52,550	9,555	7,096	9,555	8,306
52,550	52,600	9,568	7,104	9,568	8,319
52,600	52,650	9,580	7,111	9,580	8,331
52,650	52,700	9,593	7,119	9,593	8,344
52,700	52,750	9,605	7,126	9,605	8,356
52,750	52,800	9,618	7,134	9,618	8,369
52,800	52,850	9,630	7,141	9,630	8,381
52,850	52,900	9,643	7,149	9,643	8,394
52,900	52,950	9,655	7,156	9,655	8,406
52,950	53,000	9,668	7,164	9,668	8,419

53,000

At least	But less than	Single	Married filing jointly *	Married filing separately	Head of a household
53,000	53,050	9,680	7,171	9,680	8,431
53,050	53,100	9,693	7,179	9,693	8,444
53,100	53,150	9,705	7,186	9,705	8,456
53,150	53,200	9,718	7,194	9,718	8,469
53,200	53,250	9,730	7,201	9,730	8,481
53,250	53,300	9,743	7,209	9,743	8,494
53,300	53,350	9,755	7,216	9,755	8,506
53,350	53,400	9,768	7,224	9,768	8,519
53,400	53,450	9,780	7,231	9,780	8,531
53,450	53,500	9,793	7,239	9,793	8,544
53,500	53,550	9,805	7,246	9,805	8,556
53,550	53,600	9,818	7,254	9,818	8,569
53,600	53,650	9,830	7,261	9,830	8,581
53,650	53,700	9,843	7,269	9,843	8,594
53,700	53,750	9,855	7,276	9,855	8,606
53,750	53,800	9,868	7,284	9,868	8,619
53,800	53,850	9,880	7,291	9,880	8,631
53,850	53,900	9,893	7,299	9,893	8,644
53,900	53,950	9,905	7,306	9,905	8,656
53,950	54,000	9,918	7,314	9,918	8,669

54,000

At least	But less than	Single	Married filing jointly *	Married filing separately	Head of a household
54,000	54,050	9,930	7,321	9,930	8,681
54,050	54,100	9,943	7,329	9,943	8,694
54,100	54,150	9,955	7,336	9,955	8,706
54,150	54,200	9,968	7,344	9,968	8,719
54,200	54,250	9,980	7,351	9,980	8,731
54,250	54,300	9,993	7,359	9,993	8,744
54,300	54,350	10,005	7,366	10,005	8,756
54,350	54,400	10,018	7,374	10,018	8,769
54,400	54,450	10,030	7,381	10,030	8,781
54,450	54,500	10,043	7,389	10,043	8,794
54,500	54,550	10,055	7,396	10,055	8,806
54,550	54,600	10,068	7,404	10,068	8,819
54,600	54,650	10,080	7,411	10,080	8,831
54,650	54,700	10,093	7,419	10,093	8,844
54,700	54,750	10,105	7,426	10,105	8,856
54,750	54,800	10,118	7,434	10,118	8,869
54,800	54,850	10,130	7,441	10,130	8,881
54,850	54,900	10,143	7,449	10,143	8,894
54,900	54,950	10,155	7,456	10,155	8,906
54,950	55,000	10,168	7,464	10,168	8,919

55,000

At least	But less than	Single	Married filing jointly *	Married filing separately	Head of a household
55,000	55,050	10,180	7,471	10,180	8,931
55,050	55,100	10,193	7,479	10,193	8,944
55,100	55,150	10,205	7,486	10,205	8,956
55,150	55,200	10,218	7,494	10,218	8,969
55,200	55,250	10,230	7,501	10,230	8,981
55,250	55,300	10,243	7,509	10,243	8,994
55,300	55,350	10,255	7,516	10,255	9,006
55,350	55,400	10,268	7,524	10,268	9,019
55,400	55,450	10,280	7,531	10,280	9,031
55,450	55,500	10,293	7,539	10,293	9,044
55,500	55,550	10,305	7,546	10,305	9,056
55,550	55,600	10,318	7,554	10,318	9,069
55,600	55,650	10,330	7,561	10,330	9,081
55,650	55,700	10,343	7,569	10,343	9,094
55,700	55,750	10,355	7,576	10,355	9,106
55,750	55,800	10,368	7,584	10,368	9,119
55,800	55,850	10,380	7,591	10,380	9,131
55,850	55,900	10,393	7,599	10,393	9,144
55,900	55,950	10,405	7,606	10,405	9,156
55,950	56,000	10,418	7,614	10,418	9,169

56,000

At least	But less than	Single	Married filing jointly *	Married filing separately	Head of a household
56,000	56,050	10,430	7,621	10,430	9,181
56,050	56,100	10,443	7,629	10,443	9,194
56,100	56,150	10,455	7,636	10,455	9,206
56,150	56,200	10,468	7,644	10,468	9,219
56,200	56,250	10,480	7,651	10,480	9,231
56,250	56,300	10,493	7,659	10,493	9,244
56,300	56,350	10,505	7,666	10,505	9,256
56,350	56,400	10,518	7,674	10,518	9,269
56,400	56,450	10,530	7,681	10,530	9,281
56,450	56,500	10,543	7,689	10,543	9,294
56,500	56,550	10,555	7,696	10,555	9,306
56,550	56,600	10,568	7,704	10,568	9,319
56,600	56,650	10,580	7,711	10,580	9,331
56,650	56,700	10,593	7,719	10,593	9,344
56,700	56,750	10,605	7,726	10,605	9,356
56,750	56,800	10,618	7,734	10,618	9,369
56,800	56,850	10,630	7,741	10,630	9,381
56,850	56,900	10,643	7,749	10,643	9,394
56,900	56,950	10,655	7,756	10,655	9,406
56,950	57,000	10,668	7,764	10,668	9,419

57,000

At least	But less than	Single	Married filing jointly *	Married filing separately	Head of a household
57,000	57,050	10,680	7,771	10,680	9,431
57,050	57,100	10,693	7,779	10,693	9,444
57,100	57,150	10,705	7,786	10,705	9,456
57,150	57,200	10,718	7,794	10,718	9,469
57,200	57,250	10,730	7,801	10,730	9,481
57,250	57,300	10,743	7,809	10,743	9,494
57,300	57,350	10,755	7,816	10,755	9,506
57,350	57,400	10,768	7,824	10,768	9,519
57,400	57,450	10,780	7,831	10,780	9,531
57,450	57,500	10,793	7,839	10,793	9,544
57,500	57,550	10,805	7,846	10,805	9,556
57,550	57,600	10,818	7,854	10,818	9,569
57,600	57,650	10,830	7,861	10,830	9,581
57,650	57,700	10,843	7,869	10,843	9,594
57,700	57,750	10,855	7,876	10,855	9,606
57,750	57,800	10,868	7,884	10,868	9,619
57,800	57,850	10,880	7,891	10,880	9,631
57,850	57,900	10,893	7,899	10,893	9,644
57,900	57,950	10,905	7,906	10,905	9,656
57,950	58,000	10,918	7,914	10,918	9,669

58,000

At least	But less than	Single	Married filing jointly *	Married filing separately	Head of a household
58,000	58,050	10,930	7,921	10,930	9,681
58,050	58,100	10,943	7,929	10,943	9,694
58,100	58,150	10,955	7,936	10,955	9,706
58,150	58,200	10,968	7,944	10,968	9,719
58,200	58,250	10,980	7,951	10,980	9,731
58,250	58,300	10,993	7,959	10,993	9,744
58,300	58,350	11,005	7,966	11,005	9,756
58,350	58,400	11,018	7,974	11,018	9,769
58,400	58,450	11,030	7,981	11,030	9,781
58,450	58,500	11,043	7,989	11,043	9,794
58,500	58,550	11,055	7,996	11,055	9,806
58,550	58,600	11,068	8,004	11,068	9,819
58,600	58,650	11,080	8,011	11,080	9,831
58,650	58,700	11,093	8,019	11,093	9,844
58,700	58,750	11,105	8,026	11,105	9,856
58,750	58,800	11,118	8,034	11,118	9,869
58,800	58,850	11,130	8,041	11,130	9,881
58,850	58,900	11,143	8,049	11,143	9,894
58,900	58,950	11,155	8,056	11,155	9,906
58,950	59,000	11,168	8,064	11,168	9,919

* This column must also be used by a qualifying widow(er).

2007 Tax Table—*Continued*

59,000 – 62,000 – 65,000

At least	But less than	Single	Married filing jointly*	Married filing separately	Head of a household
59,000					
59,000	59,050	11,180	8,071	11,180	9,931
59,050	59,100	11,193	8,079	11,193	9,944
59,100	59,150	11,205	8,086	11,205	9,956
59,150	59,200	11,218	8,094	11,218	9,969
59,200	59,250	11,230	8,101	11,230	9,981
59,250	59,300	11,243	8,109	11,243	9,994
59,300	59,350	11,255	8,116	11,255	10,006
59,350	59,400	11,268	8,124	11,268	10,019
59,400	59,450	11,280	8,131	11,280	10,031
59,450	59,500	11,293	8,139	11,293	10,044
59,500	59,550	11,305	8,146	11,305	10,056
59,550	59,600	11,318	8,154	11,318	10,069
59,600	59,650	11,330	8,161	11,330	10,081
59,650	59,700	11,343	8,169	11,343	10,094
59,700	59,750	11,355	8,176	11,355	10,106
59,750	59,800	11,368	8,184	11,368	10,119
59,800	59,850	11,380	8,191	11,380	10,131
59,850	59,900	11,393	8,199	11,393	10,144
59,900	59,950	11,405	8,206	11,405	10,156
59,950	60,000	11,418	8,214	11,418	10,169
60,000					
60,000	60,050	11,430	8,221	11,430	10,181
60,050	60,100	11,443	8,229	11,443	10,194
60,100	60,150	11,455	8,236	11,455	10,206
60,150	60,200	11,468	8,244	11,468	10,219
60,200	60,250	11,480	8,251	11,480	10,231
60,250	60,300	11,493	8,259	11,493	10,244
60,300	60,350	11,505	8,266	11,505	10,256
60,350	60,400	11,518	8,274	11,518	10,269
60,400	60,450	11,530	8,281	11,530	10,281
60,450	60,500	11,543	8,289	11,543	10,294
60,500	60,550	11,555	8,296	11,555	10,306
60,550	60,600	11,568	8,304	11,568	10,319
60,600	60,650	11,580	8,311	11,580	10,331
60,650	60,700	11,593	8,319	11,593	10,344
60,700	60,750	11,605	8,326	11,605	10,356
60,750	60,800	11,618	8,334	11,618	10,369
60,800	60,850	11,630	8,341	11,630	10,381
60,850	60,900	11,643	8,349	11,643	10,394
60,900	60,950	11,655	8,356	11,655	10,406
60,950	61,000	11,668	8,364	11,668	10,419
61,000					
61,000	61,050	11,680	8,371	11,680	10,431
61,050	61,100	11,693	8,379	11,693	10,444
61,100	61,150	11,705	8,386	11,705	10,456
61,150	61,200	11,718	8,394	11,718	10,469
61,200	61,250	11,730	8,401	11,730	10,481
61,250	61,300	11,743	8,409	11,743	10,494
61,300	61,350	11,755	8,416	11,755	10,506
61,350	61,400	11,768	8,424	11,768	10,519
61,400	61,450	11,780	8,431	11,780	10,531
61,450	61,500	11,793	8,439	11,793	10,544
61,500	61,550	11,805	8,446	11,805	10,556
61,550	61,600	11,818	8,454	11,818	10,569
61,600	61,650	11,830	8,461	11,830	10,581
61,650	61,700	11,843	8,469	11,843	10,594
61,700	61,750	11,855	8,476	11,855	10,606
61,750	61,800	11,868	8,484	11,868	10,619
61,800	61,850	11,880	8,491	11,880	10,631
61,850	61,900	11,893	8,499	11,893	10,644
61,900	61,950	11,905	8,506	11,905	10,656
61,950	62,000	11,918	8,514	11,918	10,669
62,000					
62,000	62,050	11,930	8,521	11,930	10,681
62,050	62,100	11,943	8,529	11,943	10,694
62,100	62,150	11,955	8,536	11,955	10,706
62,150	62,200	11,968	8,544	11,968	10,719
62,200	62,250	11,980	8,551	11,980	10,731
62,250	62,300	11,993	8,559	11,993	10,744
62,300	62,350	12,005	8,566	12,005	10,756
62,350	62,400	12,018	8,574	12,018	10,769
62,400	62,450	12,030	8,581	12,030	10,781
62,450	62,500	12,043	8,589	12,043	10,794
62,500	62,550	12,055	8,596	12,055	10,806
62,550	62,600	12,068	8,604	12,068	10,819
62,600	62,650	12,080	8,611	12,080	10,831
62,650	62,700	12,093	8,619	12,093	10,844
62,700	62,750	12,105	8,626	12,105	10,856
62,750	62,800	12,118	8,634	12,118	10,869
62,800	62,850	12,130	8,641	12,130	10,881
62,850	62,900	12,143	8,649	12,143	10,894
62,900	62,950	12,155	8,656	12,155	10,906
62,950	63,000	12,168	8,664	12,168	10,919
63,000					
63,000	63,050	12,180	8,671	12,180	10,931
63,050	63,100	12,193	8,679	12,193	10,944
63,100	63,150	12,205	8,686	12,205	10,956
63,150	63,200	12,218	8,694	12,218	10,969
63,200	63,250	12,230	8,701	12,230	10,981
63,250	63,300	12,243	8,709	12,243	10,994
63,300	63,350	12,255	8,716	12,255	11,006
63,350	63,400	12,268	8,724	12,268	11,019
63,400	63,450	12,280	8,731	12,280	11,031
63,450	63,500	12,293	8,739	12,293	11,044
63,500	63,550	12,305	8,746	12,305	11,056
63,550	63,600	12,318	8,754	12,318	11,069
63,600	63,650	12,330	8,761	12,330	11,081
63,650	63,700	12,343	8,769	12,343	11,094
63,700	63,750	12,355	8,779	12,355	11,106
63,750	63,800	12,368	8,791	12,368	11,119
63,800	63,850	12,380	8,804	12,380	11,131
63,850	63,900	12,393	8,816	12,393	11,144
63,900	63,950	12,405	8,829	12,405	11,156
63,950	64,000	12,418	8,841	12,418	11,169
64,000					
64,000	64,050	12,430	8,854	12,430	11,181
64,050	64,100	12,443	8,866	12,443	11,194
64,100	64,150	12,455	8,879	12,455	11,206
64,150	64,200	12,468	8,891	12,468	11,219
64,200	64,250	12,480	8,904	12,480	11,231
64,250	64,300	12,493	8,916	12,493	11,244
64,300	64,350	12,505	8,929	12,507	11,256
64,350	64,400	12,518	8,941	12,521	11,269
64,400	64,450	12,530	8,954	12,535	11,281
64,450	64,500	12,543	8,966	12,549	11,294
64,500	64,550	12,555	8,979	12,563	11,306
64,550	64,600	12,568	8,991	12,577	11,319
64,600	64,650	12,580	9,004	12,591	11,331
64,650	64,700	12,593	9,016	12,605	11,344
64,700	64,750	12,605	9,029	12,619	11,356
64,750	64,800	12,618	9,041	12,633	11,369
64,800	64,850	12,630	9,054	12,647	11,381
64,850	64,900	12,643	9,066	12,661	11,394
64,900	64,950	12,655	9,079	12,675	11,406
64,950	65,000	12,668	9,091	12,689	11,419
65,000					
65,000	65,050	12,680	9,104	12,703	11,431
65,050	65,100	12,693	9,116	12,717	11,444
65,100	65,150	12,705	9,129	12,731	11,456
65,150	65,200	12,718	9,141	12,745	11,469
65,200	65,250	12,730	9,154	12,759	11,481
65,250	65,300	12,743	9,166	12,773	11,494
65,300	65,350	12,755	9,179	12,787	11,506
65,350	65,400	12,768	9,191	12,801	11,519
65,400	65,450	12,780	9,204	12,815	11,531
65,450	65,500	12,793	9,216	12,829	11,544
65,500	65,550	12,805	9,229	12,843	11,556
65,550	65,600	12,818	9,241	12,857	11,569
65,600	65,650	12,830	9,254	12,871	11,581
65,650	65,700	12,843	9,266	12,885	11,594
65,700	65,750	12,855	9,279	12,899	11,606
65,750	65,800	12,868	9,291	12,913	11,619
65,800	65,850	12,880	9,304	12,927	11,631
65,850	65,900	12,893	9,316	12,941	11,644
65,900	65,950	12,905	9,329	12,955	11,656
65,950	66,000	12,918	9,341	12,969	11,669
66,000					
66,000	66,050	12,930	9,354	12,983	11,681
66,050	66,100	12,943	9,366	12,997	11,694
66,100	66,150	12,955	9,379	13,011	11,706
66,150	66,200	12,968	9,391	13,025	11,719
66,200	66,250	12,980	9,404	13,039	11,731
66,250	66,300	12,993	9,416	13,053	11,744
66,300	66,350	13,005	9,429	13,067	11,756
66,350	66,400	13,018	9,441	13,081	11,769
66,400	66,450	13,030	9,454	13,095	11,781
66,450	66,500	13,043	9,466	13,109	11,794
66,500	66,550	13,055	9,479	13,123	11,806
66,550	66,600	13,068	9,491	13,137	11,819
66,600	66,650	13,080	9,504	13,151	11,831
66,650	66,700	13,093	9,516	13,165	11,844
66,700	66,750	13,105	9,529	13,179	11,856
66,750	66,800	13,118	9,541	13,193	11,869
66,800	66,850	13,130	9,554	13,207	11,881
66,850	66,900	13,143	9,566	13,221	11,894
66,900	66,950	13,155	9,579	13,235	11,906
66,950	67,000	13,168	9,591	13,249	11,919
67,000					
67,000	67,050	13,180	9,604	13,263	11,931
67,050	67,100	13,193	9,616	13,277	11,944
67,100	67,150	13,205	9,629	13,291	11,956
67,150	67,200	13,218	9,641	13,305	11,969
67,200	67,250	13,230	9,654	13,319	11,981
67,250	67,300	13,243	9,666	13,333	11,994
67,300	67,350	13,255	9,679	13,347	12,006
67,350	67,400	13,268	9,691	13,361	12,019
67,400	67,450	13,280	9,704	13,375	12,031
67,450	67,500	13,293	9,716	13,389	12,044
67,500	67,550	13,305	9,729	13,403	12,056
67,550	67,600	13,318	9,741	13,417	12,069
67,600	67,650	13,330	9,754	13,431	12,081
67,650	67,700	13,343	9,766	13,445	12,094
67,700	67,750	13,355	9,779	13,459	12,106
67,750	67,800	13,368	9,791	13,473	12,119
67,800	67,850	13,380	9,804	13,487	12,131
67,850	67,900	13,393	9,816	13,501	12,144
67,900	67,950	13,405	9,829	13,515	12,156
67,950	68,000	13,418	9,841	13,529	12,169

* This column must also be used by a qualifying widow(er).

If line 43 (taxable income) is— At least	But less than	And you are— Single	Married filing jointly *	Married filing separately	Head of a household
68,000					
68,000	68,050	13,430	9,854	13,543	12,181
68,050	68,100	13,443	9,866	13,557	12,194
68,100	68,150	13,455	9,879	13,571	12,206
68,150	68,200	13,468	9,891	13,585	12,219
68,200	68,250	13,480	9,904	13,599	12,231
68,250	68,300	13,493	9,916	13,613	12,244
68,300	68,350	13,505	9,929	13,627	12,256
68,350	68,400	13,518	9,941	13,641	12,269
68,400	68,450	13,530	9,954	13,655	12,281
68,450	68,500	13,543	9,966	13,669	12,294
68,500	68,550	13,555	9,979	13,683	12,306
68,550	68,600	13,568	9,991	13,697	12,319
68,600	68,650	13,580	10,004	13,711	12,331
68,650	68,700	13,593	10,016	13,725	12,344
68,700	68,750	13,605	10,029	13,739	12,356
68,750	68,800	13,618	10,041	13,753	12,369
68,800	68,850	13,630	10,054	13,767	12,381
68,850	68,900	13,643	10,066	13,781	12,394
68,900	68,950	13,655	10,079	13,795	12,406
68,950	69,000	13,668	10,091	13,809	12,419
69,000					
69,000	69,050	13,680	10,104	13,823	12,431
69,050	69,100	13,693	10,116	13,837	12,444
69,100	69,150	13,705	10,129	13,851	12,456
69,150	69,200	13,718	10,141	13,865	12,469
69,200	69,250	13,730	10,154	13,879	12,481
69,250	69,300	13,743	10,166	13,893	12,494
69,300	69,350	13,755	10,179	13,907	12,506
69,350	69,400	13,768	10,191	13,921	12,519
69,400	69,450	13,780	10,204	13,935	12,531
69,450	69,500	13,793	10,216	13,949	12,544
69,500	69,550	13,805	10,229	13,963	12,556
69,550	69,600	13,818	10,241	13,977	12,569
69,600	69,650	13,830	10,254	13,991	12,581
69,650	69,700	13,843	10,266	14,005	12,594
69,700	69,750	13,855	10,279	14,019	12,606
69,750	69,800	13,868	10,291	14,033	12,619
69,800	69,850	13,880	10,304	14,047	12,631
69,850	69,900	13,893	10,316	14,061	12,644
69,900	69,950	13,905	10,329	14,075	12,656
69,950	70,000	13,918	10,341	14,089	12,669
70,000					
70,000	70,050	13,930	10,354	14,103	12,681
70,050	70,100	13,943	10,366	14,117	12,694
70,100	70,150	13,955	10,379	14,131	12,706
70,150	70,200	13,968	10,391	14,145	12,719
70,200	70,250	13,980	10,404	14,159	12,731
70,250	70,300	13,993	10,416	14,173	12,744
70,300	70,350	14,005	10,429	14,187	12,756
70,350	70,400	14,018	10,441	14,201	12,769
70,400	70,450	14,030	10,454	14,215	12,781
70,450	70,500	14,043	10,466	14,229	12,794
70,500	70,550	14,055	10,479	14,243	12,806
70,550	70,600	14,068	10,491	14,257	12,819
70,600	70,650	14,080	10,504	14,271	12,831
70,650	70,700	14,093	10,516	14,285	12,844
70,700	70,750	14,105	10,529	14,299	12,856
70,750	70,800	14,118	10,541	14,313	12,869
70,800	70,850	14,130	10,554	14,327	12,881
70,850	70,900	14,143	10,566	14,341	12,894
70,900	70,950	14,155	10,579	14,355	12,906
70,950	71,000	14,168	10,591	14,369	12,919

If line 43 (taxable income) is— At least	But less than	And you are— Single	Married filing jointly *	Married filing separately	Head of a household
71,000					
71,000	71,050	14,180	10,604	14,383	12,931
71,050	71,100	14,193	10,616	14,397	12,944
71,100	71,150	14,205	10,629	14,411	12,956
71,150	71,200	14,218	10,641	14,425	12,969
71,200	71,250	14,230	10,654	14,439	12,981
71,250	71,300	14,243	10,666	14,453	12,994
71,300	71,350	14,255	10,679	14,467	13,006
71,350	71,400	14,268	10,691	14,481	13,019
71,400	71,450	14,280	10,704	14,495	13,031
71,450	71,500	14,293	10,716	14,509	13,044
71,500	71,550	14,305	10,729	14,523	13,056
71,550	71,600	14,318	10,741	14,537	13,069
71,600	71,650	14,330	10,754	14,551	13,081
71,650	71,700	14,343	10,766	14,565	13,094
71,700	71,750	14,355	10,779	14,579	13,106
71,750	71,800	14,368	10,791	14,593	13,119
71,800	71,850	14,380	10,804	14,607	13,131
71,850	71,900	14,393	10,816	14,621	13,144
71,900	71,950	14,405	10,829	14,635	13,156
71,950	72,000	14,418	10,841	14,649	13,169
72,000					
72,000	72,050	14,430	10,854	14,663	13,181
72,050	72,100	14,443	10,866	14,677	13,194
72,100	72,150	14,455	10,879	14,691	13,206
72,150	72,200	14,468	10,891	14,705	13,219
72,200	72,250	14,480	10,904	14,719	13,231
72,250	72,300	14,493	10,916	14,733	13,244
72,300	72,350	14,505	10,929	14,747	13,256
72,350	72,400	14,518	10,941	14,761	13,269
72,400	72,450	14,530	10,954	14,775	13,281
72,450	72,500	14,543	10,966	14,789	13,294
72,500	72,550	14,555	10,979	14,803	13,306
72,550	72,600	14,568	10,991	14,817	13,319
72,600	72,650	14,580	11,004	14,831	13,331
72,650	72,700	14,593	11,016	14,845	13,344
72,700	72,750	14,605	11,029	14,859	13,356
72,750	72,800	14,618	11,041	14,873	13,369
72,800	72,850	14,630	11,054	14,887	13,381
72,850	72,900	14,643	11,066	14,901	13,394
72,900	72,950	14,655	11,079	14,915	13,406
72,950	73,000	14,668	11,091	14,929	13,419
73,000					
73,000	73,050	14,680	11,104	14,943	13,431
73,050	73,100	14,693	11,116	14,957	13,444
73,100	73,150	14,705	11,129	14,971	13,456
73,150	73,200	14,718	11,141	14,985	13,469
73,200	73,250	14,730	11,154	14,999	13,481
73,250	73,300	14,743	11,166	15,013	13,494
73,300	73,350	14,755	11,179	15,027	13,506
73,350	73,400	14,768	11,191	15,041	13,519
73,400	73,450	14,780	11,204	15,055	13,531
73,450	73,500	14,793	11,216	15,069	13,544
73,500	73,550	14,805	11,229	15,083	13,556
73,550	73,600	14,818	11,241	15,097	13,569
73,600	73,650	14,830	11,254	15,111	13,581
73,650	73,700	14,843	11,266	15,125	13,594
73,700	73,750	14,855	11,279	15,139	13,606
73,750	73,800	14,868	11,291	15,153	13,619
73,800	73,850	14,880	11,304	15,167	13,631
73,850	73,900	14,893	11,316	15,181	13,644
73,900	73,950	14,905	11,329	15,195	13,656
73,950	74,000	14,918	11,341	15,209	13,669

If line 43 (taxable income) is— At least	But less than	And you are— Single	Married filing jointly *	Married filing separately	Head of a household
74,000					
74,000	74,050	14,930	11,354	15,223	13,681
74,050	74,100	14,943	11,366	15,237	13,694
74,100	74,150	14,955	11,379	15,251	13,706
74,150	74,200	14,968	11,391	15,265	13,719
74,200	74,250	14,980	11,404	15,279	13,731
74,250	74,300	14,993	11,416	15,293	13,744
74,300	74,350	15,005	11,429	15,307	13,756
74,350	74,400	15,018	11,441	15,321	13,769
74,400	74,450	15,030	11,454	15,335	13,781
74,450	74,500	15,043	11,466	15,349	13,794
74,500	74,550	15,055	11,479	15,363	13,806
74,550	74,600	15,068	11,491	15,377	13,819
74,600	74,650	15,080	11,504	15,391	13,831
74,650	74,700	15,093	11,516	15,405	13,844
74,700	74,750	15,105	11,529	15,419	13,856
74,750	74,800	15,118	11,541	15,433	13,869
74,800	74,850	15,130	11,554	15,447	13,881
74,850	74,900	15,143	11,566	15,461	13,894
74,900	74,950	15,155	11,579	15,475	13,906
74,950	75,000	15,168	11,591	15,489	13,919
75,000					
75,000	75,050	15,180	11,604	15,503	13,931
75,050	75,100	15,193	11,616	15,517	13,944
75,100	75,150	15,205	11,629	15,531	13,956
75,150	75,200	15,218	11,641	15,545	13,969
75,200	75,250	15,230	11,654	15,559	13,981
75,250	75,300	15,243	11,666	15,573	13,994
75,300	75,350	15,255	11,679	15,587	14,006
75,350	75,400	15,268	11,691	15,601	14,019
75,400	75,450	15,280	11,704	15,615	14,031
75,450	75,500	15,293	11,716	15,629	14,044
75,500	75,550	15,305	11,729	15,643	14,056
75,550	75,600	15,318	11,741	15,657	14,069
75,600	75,650	15,330	11,754	15,671	14,081
75,650	75,700	15,343	11,766	15,685	14,094
75,700	75,750	15,355	11,779	15,699	14,106
75,750	75,800	15,368	11,791	15,713	14,119
75,800	75,850	15,380	11,804	15,727	14,131
75,850	75,900	15,393	11,816	15,741	14,144
75,900	75,950	15,405	11,829	15,755	14,156
75,950	76,000	15,418	11,841	15,769	14,169
76,000					
76,000	76,050	15,430	11,854	15,783	14,181
76,050	76,100	15,443	11,866	15,797	14,194
76,100	76,150	15,455	11,879	15,811	14,206
76,150	76,200	15,468	11,891	15,825	14,219
76,200	76,250	15,480	11,904	15,839	14,231
76,250	76,300	15,493	11,916	15,853	14,244
76,300	76,350	15,505	11,929	15,867	14,256
76,350	76,400	15,518	11,941	15,881	14,269
76,400	76,450	15,530	11,954	15,895	14,281
76,450	76,500	15,543	11,966	15,909	14,294
76,500	76,550	15,555	11,979	15,923	14,306
76,550	76,600	15,568	11,991	15,937	14,319
76,600	76,650	15,580	12,004	15,951	14,331
76,650	76,700	15,593	12,016	15,965	14,344
76,700	76,750	15,605	12,029	15,979	14,356
76,750	76,800	15,618	12,041	15,993	14,369
76,800	76,850	15,630	12,054	16,007	14,381
76,850	76,900	15,643	12,066	16,021	14,394
76,900	76,950	15,655	12,079	16,035	14,406
76,950	77,000	15,668	12,091	16,049	14,419

* This column must also be used by a qualifying widow(er).

2007 Tax Table—*Continued*

If line 43 (taxable income) is—		And you are—			
At least	But less than	Single	Married filing jointly *	Married filing sepa-rately	Head of a house-hold
		Your tax is—			
77,000					
77,000	77,050	15,680	12,104	16,063	14,431
77,050	77,100	15,693	12,116	16,077	14,444
77,100	77,150	15,706	12,129	16,091	14,456
77,150	77,200	15,720	12,141	16,105	14,469
77,200	77,250	15,734	12,154	16,119	14,481
77,250	77,300	15,748	12,166	16,133	14,494
77,300	77,350	15,762	12,179	16,147	14,506
77,350	77,400	15,776	12,191	16,161	14,519
77,400	77,450	15,790	12,204	16,175	14,531
77,450	77,500	15,804	12,216	16,189	14,544
77,500	77,550	15,818	12,229	16,203	14,556
77,550	77,600	15,832	12,241	16,217	14,569
77,600	77,650	15,846	12,254	16,231	14,581
77,650	77,700	15,860	12,266	16,245	14,594
77,700	77,750	15,874	12,279	16,259	14,606
77,750	77,800	15,888	12,291	16,273	14,619
77,800	77,850	15,902	12,304	16,287	14,631
77,850	77,900	15,916	12,316	16,301	14,644
77,900	77,950	15,930	12,329	16,315	14,656
77,950	78,000	15,944	12,341	16,329	14,669
78,000					
78,000	78,050	15,958	12,354	16,343	14,681
78,050	78,100	15,972	12,366	16,357	14,694
78,100	78,150	15,986	12,379	16,371	14,706
78,150	78,200	16,000	12,391	16,385	14,719
78,200	78,250	16,014	12,404	16,399	14,731
78,250	78,300	16,028	12,416	16,413	14,744
78,300	78,350	16,042	12,429	16,427	14,756
78,350	78,400	16,056	12,441	16,441	14,769
78,400	78,450	16,070	12,454	16,455	14,781
78,450	78,500	16,084	12,466	16,469	14,794
78,500	78,550	16,098	12,479	16,483	14,806
78,550	78,600	16,112	12,491	16,497	14,819
78,600	78,650	16,126	12,504	16,511	14,831
78,650	78,700	16,140	12,516	16,525	14,844
78,700	78,750	16,154	12,529	16,539	14,856
78,750	78,800	16,168	12,541	16,553	14,869
78,800	78,850	16,182	12,554	16,567	14,881
78,850	78,900	16,196	12,566	16,581	14,894
78,900	78,950	16,210	12,579	16,595	14,906
78,950	79,000	16,224	12,591	16,609	14,919
79,000					
79,000	79,050	16,238	12,604	16,623	14,931
79,050	79,100	16,252	12,616	16,637	14,944
79,100	79,150	16,266	12,629	16,651	14,956
79,150	79,200	16,280	12,641	16,665	14,969
79,200	79,250	16,294	12,654	16,679	14,981
79,250	79,300	16,308	12,666	16,693	14,994
79,300	79,350	16,322	12,679	16,707	15,006
79,350	79,400	16,336	12,691	16,721	15,019
79,400	79,450	16,350	12,704	16,735	15,031
79,450	79,500	16,364	12,716	16,749	15,044
79,500	79,550	16,378	12,729	16,763	15,056
79,550	79,600	16,392	12,741	16,777	15,069
79,600	79,650	16,406	12,754	16,791	15,081
79,650	79,700	16,420	12,766	16,805	15,094
79,700	79,750	16,434	12,779	16,819	15,106
79,750	79,800	16,448	12,791	16,833	15,119
79,800	79,850	16,462	12,804	16,847	15,131
79,850	79,900	16,476	12,816	16,861	15,144
79,900	79,950	16,490	12,829	16,875	15,156
79,950	80,000	16,504	12,841	16,889	15,169

If line 43 (taxable income) is—		And you are—			
At least	But less than	Single	Married filing jointly *	Married filing sepa-rately	Head of a house-hold
		Your tax is—			
80,000					
80,000	80,050	16,518	12,854	16,903	15,181
80,050	80,100	16,532	12,866	16,917	15,194
80,100	80,150	16,546	12,879	16,931	15,206
80,150	80,200	16,560	12,891	16,945	15,219
80,200	80,250	16,574	12,904	16,959	15,231
80,250	80,300	16,588	12,916	16,973	15,244
80,300	80,350	16,602	12,929	16,987	15,256
80,350	80,400	16,616	12,941	17,001	15,269
80,400	80,450	16,630	12,954	17,015	15,281
80,450	80,500	16,644	12,966	17,029	15,294
80,500	80,550	16,658	12,979	17,043	15,306
80,550	80,600	16,672	12,991	17,057	15,319
80,600	80,650	16,686	13,004	17,071	15,331
80,650	80,700	16,700	13,016	17,085	15,344
80,700	80,750	16,714	13,029	17,099	15,356
80,750	80,800	16,728	13,041	17,113	15,369
80,800	80,850	16,742	13,054	17,127	15,381
80,850	80,900	16,756	13,066	17,141	15,394
80,900	80,950	16,770	13,079	17,155	15,406
80,950	81,000	16,784	13,091	17,169	15,419
81,000					
81,000	81,050	16,798	13,104	17,183	15,431
81,050	81,100	16,812	13,116	17,197	15,444
81,100	81,150	16,826	13,129	17,211	15,456
81,150	81,200	16,840	13,141	17,225	15,469
81,200	81,250	16,854	13,154	17,239	15,481
81,250	81,300	16,868	13,166	17,253	15,494
81,300	81,350	16,882	13,179	17,267	15,506
81,350	81,400	16,896	13,191	17,281	15,519
81,400	81,450	16,910	13,204	17,295	15,531
81,450	81,500	16,924	13,216	17,309	15,544
81,500	81,550	16,938	13,229	17,323	15,556
81,550	81,600	16,952	13,241	17,337	15,569
81,600	81,650	16,966	13,254	17,351	15,581
81,650	81,700	16,980	13,266	17,365	15,594
81,700	81,750	16,994	13,279	17,379	15,606
81,750	81,800	17,008	13,291	17,393	15,619
81,800	81,850	17,022	13,304	17,407	15,631
81,850	81,900	17,036	13,316	17,421	15,644
81,900	81,950	17,050	13,329	17,435	15,656
81,950	82,000	17,064	13,341	17,449	15,669
82,000					
82,000	82,050	17,078	13,354	17,463	15,681
82,050	82,100	17,092	13,366	17,477	15,694
82,100	82,150	17,106	13,379	17,491	15,706
82,150	82,200	17,120	13,391	17,505	15,719
82,200	82,250	17,134	13,404	17,519	15,731
82,250	82,300	17,148	13,416	17,533	15,744
82,300	82,350	17,162	13,429	17,547	15,756
82,350	82,400	17,176	13,441	17,561	15,769
82,400	82,450	17,190	13,454	17,575	15,781
82,450	82,500	17,204	13,466	17,589	15,794
82,500	82,550	17,218	13,479	17,603	15,806
82,550	82,600	17,232	13,491	17,617	15,819
82,600	82,650	17,246	13,504	17,631	15,831
82,650	82,700	17,260	13,516	17,645	15,844
82,700	82,750	17,274	13,529	17,659	15,856
82,750	82,800	17,288	13,541	17,673	15,869
82,800	82,850	17,302	13,554	17,687	15,881
82,850	82,900	17,316	13,566	17,701	15,894
82,900	82,950	17,330	13,579	17,715	15,906
82,950	83,000	17,344	13,591	17,729	15,919

If line 43 (taxable income) is—		And you are—			
At least	But less than	Single	Married filing jointly *	Married filing sepa-rately	Head of a house-hold
		Your tax is—			
83,000					
83,000	83,050	17,358	13,604	17,743	15,931
83,050	83,100	17,372	13,616	17,757	15,944
83,100	83,150	17,386	13,629	17,771	15,956
83,150	83,200	17,400	13,641	17,785	15,969
83,200	83,250	17,414	13,654	17,799	15,981
83,250	83,300	17,428	13,666	17,813	15,994
83,300	83,350	17,442	13,679	17,827	16,006
83,350	83,400	17,456	13,691	17,841	16,019
83,400	83,450	17,470	13,704	17,855	16,031
83,450	83,500	17,484	13,716	17,869	16,044
83,500	83,550	17,498	13,729	17,883	16,056
83,550	83,600	17,512	13,741	17,897	16,069
83,600	83,650	17,526	13,754	17,911	16,081
83,650	83,700	17,540	13,766	17,925	16,094
83,700	83,750	17,554	13,779	17,939	16,106
83,750	83,800	17,568	13,791	17,953	16,119
83,800	83,850	17,582	13,804	17,967	16,131
83,850	83,900	17,596	13,816	17,981	16,144
83,900	83,950	17,610	13,829	17,995	16,156
83,950	84,000	17,624	13,841	18,009	16,169
84,000					
84,000	84,050	17,638	13,854	18,023	16,181
84,050	84,100	17,652	13,866	18,037	16,194
84,100	84,150	17,666	13,879	18,051	16,206
84,150	84,200	17,680	13,891	18,065	16,219
84,200	84,250	17,694	13,904	18,079	16,231
84,250	84,300	17,708	13,916	18,093	16,244
84,300	84,350	17,722	13,929	18,107	16,256
84,350	84,400	17,736	13,941	18,121	16,269
84,400	84,450	17,750	13,954	18,135	16,281
84,450	84,500	17,764	13,966	18,149	16,294
84,500	84,550	17,778	13,979	18,163	16,306
84,550	84,600	17,792	13,991	18,177	16,319
84,600	84,650	17,806	14,004	18,191	16,331
84,650	84,700	17,820	14,016	18,205	16,344
84,700	84,750	17,834	14,029	18,219	16,356
84,750	84,800	17,848	14,041	18,233	16,369
84,800	84,850	17,862	14,054	18,247	16,381
84,850	84,900	17,876	14,066	18,261	16,394
84,900	84,950	17,890	14,079	18,275	16,406
84,950	85,000	17,904	14,091	18,289	16,419
85,000					
85,000	85,050	17,918	14,104	18,303	16,431
85,050	85,100	17,932	14,116	18,317	16,444
85,100	85,150	17,946	14,129	18,331	16,456
85,150	85,200	17,960	14,141	18,345	16,469
85,200	85,250	17,974	14,154	18,359	16,481
85,250	85,300	17,988	14,166	18,373	16,494
85,300	85,350	18,002	14,179	18,387	16,506
85,350	85,400	18,016	14,191	18,401	16,519
85,400	85,450	18,030	14,204	18,415	16,531
85,450	85,500	18,044	14,216	18,429	16,544
85,500	85,550	18,058	14,229	18,443	16,556
85,550	85,600	18,072	14,241	18,457	16,569
85,600	85,650	18,086	14,254	18,471	16,581
85,650	85,700	18,100	14,266	18,485	16,594
85,700	85,750	18,114	14,279	18,499	16,606
85,750	85,800	18,128	14,291	18,513	16,619
85,800	85,850	18,142	14,304	18,527	16,631
85,850	85,900	18,156	14,316	18,541	16,644
85,900	85,950	18,170	14,329	18,555	16,656
85,950	86,000	18,184	14,341	18,569	16,669

* This column must also be used by a qualifying widow(er).

2007 Tax Table–*Continued*

86,000

If line 43 (taxable income) is— At least	But less than	Single	Married filing jointly *	Married filing separately	Head of a household
86,000	86,050	18,198	14,354	18,583	16,681
86,050	86,100	18,212	14,366	18,597	16,694
86,100	86,150	18,226	14,379	18,611	16,706
86,150	86,200	18,240	14,391	18,625	16,719
86,200	86,250	18,254	14,404	18,639	16,731
86,250	86,300	18,268	14,416	18,653	16,744
86,300	86,350	18,282	14,429	18,667	16,756
86,350	86,400	18,296	14,441	18,681	16,769
86,400	86,450	18,310	14,454	18,695	16,781
86,450	86,500	18,324	14,466	18,709	16,794
86,500	86,550	18,338	14,479	18,723	16,806
86,550	86,600	18,352	14,491	18,737	16,819
86,600	86,650	18,366	14,504	18,751	16,831
86,650	86,700	18,380	14,516	18,765	16,844
86,700	86,750	18,394	14,529	18,779	16,856
86,750	86,800	18,408	14,541	18,793	16,869
86,800	86,850	18,422	14,554	18,807	16,881
86,850	86,900	18,436	14,566	18,821	16,894
86,900	86,950	18,450	14,579	18,835	16,906
86,950	87,000	18,464	14,591	18,849	16,919

87,000

At least	But less than	Single	Married filing jointly *	Married filing separately	Head of a household
87,000	87,050	18,478	14,604	18,863	16,931
87,050	87,100	18,492	14,616	18,877	16,944
87,100	87,150	18,506	14,629	18,891	16,956
87,150	87,200	18,520	14,641	18,905	16,969
87,200	87,250	18,534	14,654	18,919	16,981
87,250	87,300	18,548	14,666	18,933	16,994
87,300	87,350	18,562	14,679	18,947	17,006
87,350	87,400	18,576	14,691	18,961	17,019
87,400	87,450	18,590	14,704	18,975	17,031
87,450	87,500	18,604	14,716	18,989	17,044
87,500	87,550	18,618	14,729	19,003	17,056
87,550	87,600	18,632	14,741	19,017	17,069
87,600	87,650	18,646	14,754	19,031	17,081
87,650	87,700	18,660	14,766	19,045	17,094
87,700	87,750	18,674	14,779	19,059	17,106
87,750	87,800	18,688	14,791	19,073	17,119
87,800	87,850	18,702	14,804	19,087	17,131
87,850	87,900	18,716	14,816	19,101	17,144
87,900	87,950	18,730	14,829	19,115	17,156
87,950	88,000	18,744	14,841	19,129	17,169

88,000

At least	But less than	Single	Married filing jointly *	Married filing separately	Head of a household
88,000	88,050	18,758	14,854	19,143	17,181
88,050	88,100	18,772	14,866	19,157	17,194
88,100	88,150	18,786	14,879	19,171	17,206
88,150	88,200	18,800	14,891	19,185	17,219
88,200	88,250	18,814	14,904	19,199	17,231
88,250	88,300	18,828	14,916	19,213	17,244
88,300	88,350	18,842	14,929	19,227	17,256
88,350	88,400	18,856	14,941	19,241	17,269
88,400	88,450	18,870	14,954	19,255	17,281
88,450	88,500	18,884	14,966	19,269	17,294
88,500	88,550	18,898	14,979	19,283	17,306
88,550	88,600	18,912	14,991	19,297	17,319
88,600	88,650	18,926	15,004	19,311	17,331
88,650	88,700	18,940	15,016	19,325	17,344
88,700	88,750	18,954	15,029	19,339	17,356
88,750	88,800	18,968	15,041	19,353	17,369
88,800	88,850	18,982	15,054	19,367	17,381
88,850	88,900	18,996	15,066	19,381	17,394
88,900	88,950	19,010	15,079	19,395	17,406
88,950	89,000	19,024	15,091	19,409	17,419

89,000

At least	But less than	Single	Married filing jointly *	Married filing separately	Head of a household
89,000	89,050	19,038	15,104	19,423	17,431
89,050	89,100	19,052	15,116	19,437	17,444
89,100	89,150	19,066	15,129	19,451	17,456
89,150	89,200	19,080	15,141	19,465	17,469
89,200	89,250	19,094	15,154	19,479	17,481
89,250	89,300	19,108	15,166	19,493	17,494
89,300	89,350	19,122	15,179	19,507	17,506
89,350	89,400	19,136	15,191	19,521	17,519
89,400	89,450	19,150	15,204	19,535	17,531
89,450	89,500	19,164	15,216	19,549	17,544
89,500	89,550	19,178	15,229	19,563	17,556
89,550	89,600	19,192	15,241	19,577	17,569
89,600	89,650	19,206	15,254	19,591	17,581
89,650	89,700	19,220	15,266	19,605	17,594
89,700	89,750	19,234	15,279	19,619	17,606
89,750	89,800	19,248	15,291	19,633	17,619
89,800	89,850	19,262	15,304	19,647	17,631
89,850	89,900	19,276	15,316	19,661	17,644
89,900	89,950	19,290	15,329	19,675	17,656
89,950	90,000	19,304	15,341	19,689	17,669

90,000

At least	But less than	Single	Married filing jointly *	Married filing separately	Head of a household
90,000	90,050	19,318	15,354	19,703	17,681
90,050	90,100	19,332	15,366	19,717	17,694
90,100	90,150	19,346	15,379	19,731	17,706
90,150	90,200	19,360	15,391	19,745	17,719
90,200	90,250	19,374	15,404	19,759	17,731
90,250	90,300	19,388	15,416	19,773	17,744
90,300	90,350	19,402	15,429	19,787	17,756
90,350	90,400	19,416	15,441	19,801	17,769
90,400	90,450	19,430	15,454	19,815	17,781
90,450	90,500	19,444	15,466	19,829	17,794
90,500	90,550	19,458	15,479	19,843	17,806
90,550	90,600	19,472	15,491	19,857	17,819
90,600	90,650	19,486	15,504	19,871	17,831
90,650	90,700	19,500	15,516	19,885	17,844
90,700	90,750	19,514	15,529	19,899	17,856
90,750	90,800	19,528	15,541	19,913	17,869
90,800	90,850	19,542	15,554	19,927	17,881
90,850	90,900	19,556	15,566	19,941	17,894
90,900	90,950	19,570	15,579	19,955	17,906
90,950	91,000	19,584	15,591	19,969	17,919

91,000

At least	But less than	Single	Married filing jointly *	Married filing separately	Head of a household
91,000	91,050	19,598	15,604	19,983	17,931
91,050	91,100	19,612	15,616	19,997	17,944
91,100	91,150	19,626	15,629	20,011	17,956
91,150	91,200	19,640	15,641	20,025	17,969
91,200	91,250	19,654	15,654	20,039	17,981
91,250	91,300	19,668	15,666	20,053	17,994
91,300	91,350	19,682	15,679	20,067	18,006
91,350	91,400	19,696	15,691	20,081	18,019
91,400	91,450	19,710	15,704	20,095	18,031
91,450	91,500	19,724	15,716	20,109	18,044
91,500	91,550	19,738	15,729	20,123	18,056
91,550	91,600	19,752	15,741	20,137	18,069
91,600	91,650	19,766	15,754	20,151	18,081
91,650	91,700	19,780	15,766	20,165	18,094
91,700	91,750	19,794	15,779	20,179	18,106
91,750	91,800	19,808	15,791	20,193	18,119
91,800	91,850	19,822	15,804	20,207	18,131
91,850	91,900	19,836	15,816	20,221	18,144
91,900	91,950	19,850	15,829	20,235	18,156
91,950	92,000	19,864	15,841	20,249	18,169

92,000

At least	But less than	Single	Married filing jointly *	Married filing separately	Head of a household
92,000	92,050	19,878	15,854	20,263	18,181
92,050	92,100	19,892	15,866	20,277	18,194
92,100	92,150	19,906	15,879	20,291	18,206
92,150	92,200	19,920	15,891	20,305	18,219
92,200	92,250	19,934	15,904	20,319	18,231
92,250	92,300	19,948	15,916	20,333	18,244
92,300	92,350	19,962	15,929	20,347	18,256
92,350	92,400	19,976	15,941	20,361	18,269
92,400	92,450	19,990	15,954	20,375	18,281
92,450	92,500	20,004	15,966	20,389	18,294
92,500	92,550	20,018	15,979	20,403	18,306
92,550	92,600	20,032	15,991	20,417	18,319
92,600	92,650	20,046	16,004	20,431	18,331
92,650	92,700	20,060	16,016	20,445	18,344
92,700	92,750	20,074	16,029	20,459	18,356
92,750	92,800	20,088	16,041	20,473	18,369
92,800	92,850	20,102	16,054	20,487	18,381
92,850	92,900	20,116	16,066	20,501	18,394
92,900	92,950	20,130	16,079	20,515	18,406
92,950	93,000	20,144	16,091	20,529	18,419

93,000

At least	But less than	Single	Married filing jointly *	Married filing separately	Head of a household
93,000	93,050	20,158	16,104	20,543	18,431
93,050	93,100	20,172	16,116	20,557	18,444
93,100	93,150	20,186	16,129	20,571	18,456
93,150	93,200	20,200	16,141	20,585	18,469
93,200	93,250	20,214	16,154	20,599	18,481
93,250	93,300	20,228	16,166	20,613	18,494
93,300	93,350	20,242	16,179	20,627	18,506
93,350	93,400	20,256	16,191	20,641	18,519
93,400	93,450	20,270	16,204	20,655	18,531
93,450	93,500	20,284	16,216	20,669	18,544
93,500	93,550	20,298	16,229	20,683	18,556
93,550	93,600	20,312	16,241	20,697	18,569
93,600	93,650	20,326	16,254	20,711	18,581
93,650	93,700	20,340	16,266	20,725	18,594
93,700	93,750	20,354	16,279	20,739	18,606
93,750	93,800	20,368	16,291	20,753	18,619
93,800	93,850	20,382	16,304	20,767	18,631
93,850	93,900	20,396	16,316	20,781	18,644
93,900	93,950	20,410	16,329	20,795	18,656
93,950	94,000	20,424	16,341	20,809	18,669

94,000

At least	But less than	Single	Married filing jointly *	Married filing separately	Head of a household
94,000	94,050	20,438	16,354	20,823	18,681
94,050	94,100	20,452	16,366	20,837	18,694
94,100	94,150	20,466	16,379	20,851	18,706
94,150	94,200	20,480	16,391	20,865	18,719
94,200	94,250	20,494	16,404	20,879	18,731
94,250	94,300	20,508	16,416	20,893	18,744
94,300	94,350	20,522	16,429	20,907	18,756
94,350	94,400	20,536	16,441	20,921	18,769
94,400	94,450	20,550	16,454	20,935	18,781
94,450	94,500	20,564	16,466	20,949	18,794
94,500	94,550	20,578	16,479	20,963	18,806
94,550	94,600	20,592	16,491	20,977	18,819
94,600	94,650	20,606	16,504	20,991	18,831
94,650	94,700	20,620	16,516	21,005	18,844
94,700	94,750	20,634	16,529	21,019	18,856
94,750	94,800	20,648	16,541	21,033	18,869
94,800	94,850	20,662	16,554	21,047	18,881
94,850	94,900	20,676	16,566	21,061	18,894
94,900	94,950	20,690	16,579	21,075	18,906
94,950	95,000	20,704	16,591	21,089	18,919

* This column must also be used by a qualifying widow(er).

2007 Tax Table–*Continued*

If line 43 (taxable income) is— At least	But less than	Single	Married filing jointly*	Married filing separately	Head of a household
95,000					
95,000	95,050	20,718	16,604	21,103	18,931
95,050	95,100	20,732	16,616	21,117	18,944
95,100	95,150	20,746	16,629	21,131	18,956
95,150	95,200	20,760	16,641	21,145	18,969
95,200	95,250	20,774	16,654	21,159	18,981
95,250	95,300	20,788	16,666	21,173	18,994
95,300	95,350	20,802	16,679	21,187	19,006
95,350	95,400	20,816	16,691	21,201	19,019
95,400	95,450	20,830	16,704	21,215	19,031
95,450	95,500	20,844	16,716	21,229	19,044
95,500	95,550	20,858	16,729	21,243	19,056
95,550	95,600	20,872	16,741	21,257	19,069
95,600	95,650	20,886	16,754	21,271	19,081
95,650	95,700	20,900	16,766	21,285	19,094
95,700	95,750	20,914	16,779	21,299	19,106
95,750	95,800	20,928	16,791	21,313	19,119
95,800	95,850	20,942	16,804	21,327	19,131
95,850	95,900	20,956	16,816	21,341	19,144
95,900	95,950	20,970	16,829	21,355	19,156
95,950	96,000	20,984	16,841	21,369	19,169
96,000					
96,000	96,050	20,998	16,854	21,383	19,181
96,050	96,100	21,012	16,866	21,397	19,194
96,100	96,150	21,026	16,879	21,411	19,206
96,150	96,200	21,040	16,891	21,425	19,219
96,200	96,250	21,054	16,904	21,439	19,231
96,250	96,300	21,068	16,916	21,453	19,244
96,300	96,350	21,082	16,929	21,467	19,256
96,350	96,400	21,096	16,941	21,481	19,269
96,400	96,450	21,110	16,954	21,495	19,281
96,450	96,500	21,124	16,966	21,509	19,294
96,500	96,550	21,138	16,979	21,523	19,306
96,550	96,600	21,152	16,991	21,537	19,319
96,600	96,650	21,166	17,004	21,551	19,331
96,650	96,700	21,180	17,016	21,565	19,344
96,700	96,750	21,194	17,029	21,579	19,356
96,750	96,800	21,208	17,041	21,593	19,369
96,800	96,850	21,222	17,054	21,607	19,381
96,850	96,900	21,236	17,066	21,621	19,394
96,900	96,950	21,250	17,079	21,635	19,406
96,950	97,000	21,264	17,091	21,649	19,419
97,000					
97,000	97,050	21,278	17,104	21,663	19,431
97,050	97,100	21,292	17,116	21,677	19,444
97,100	97,150	21,306	17,129	21,691	19,456
97,150	97,200	21,320	17,141	21,705	19,469
97,200	97,250	21,334	17,154	21,719	19,481
97,250	97,300	21,348	17,166	21,733	19,494
97,300	97,350	21,362	17,179	21,747	19,506
97,350	97,400	21,376	17,191	21,761	19,519
97,400	97,450	21,390	17,204	21,775	19,531
97,450	97,500	21,404	17,216	21,789	19,544
97,500	97,550	21,418	17,229	21,803	19,556
97,550	97,600	21,432	17,241	21,817	19,569
97,600	97,650	21,446	17,254	21,831	19,581
97,650	97,700	21,460	17,266	21,845	19,594
97,700	97,750	21,474	17,279	21,859	19,606
97,750	97,800	21,488	17,291	21,873	19,619
97,800	97,850	21,502	17,304	21,887	19,631
97,850	97,900	21,516	17,316	21,901	19,644
97,900	97,950	21,530	17,329	21,915	19,656
97,950	98,000	21,544	17,341	21,932	19,669
98,000					
98,000	98,050	21,558	17,354	21,948	19,681
98,050	98,100	21,572	17,366	21,965	19,694
98,100	98,150	21,586	17,379	21,981	19,706
98,150	98,200	21,600	17,391	21,998	19,719
98,200	98,250	21,614	17,404	22,014	19,731
98,250	98,300	21,628	17,416	22,031	19,744
98,300	98,350	21,642	17,429	22,047	19,756
98,350	98,400	21,656	17,441	22,064	19,769
98,400	98,450	21,670	17,454	22,080	19,781
98,450	98,500	21,684	17,466	22,097	19,794
98,500	98,550	21,698	17,479	22,113	19,806
98,550	98,600	21,712	17,491	22,130	19,819
98,600	98,650	21,726	17,504	22,146	19,831
98,650	98,700	21,740	17,516	22,163	19,844
98,700	98,750	21,754	17,529	22,179	19,856
98,750	98,800	21,768	17,541	22,196	19,869
98,800	98,850	21,782	17,554	22,212	19,881
98,850	98,900	21,796	17,566	22,229	19,894
98,900	98,950	21,810	17,579	22,245	19,906
98,950	99,000	21,824	17,591	22,262	19,919
99,000					
99,000	99,050	21,838	17,604	22,278	19,931
99,050	99,100	21,852	17,616	22,295	19,944
99,100	99,150	21,866	17,629	22,311	19,956
99,150	99,200	21,880	17,641	22,328	19,969
99,200	99,250	21,894	17,654	22,344	19,981
99,250	99,300	21,908	17,666	22,361	19,994
99,300	99,350	21,922	17,679	22,377	20,006
99,350	99,400	21,936	17,691	22,394	20,019
99,400	99,450	21,950	17,704	22,410	20,031
99,450	99,500	21,964	17,716	22,427	20,044
99,500	99,550	21,978	17,729	22,443	20,056
99,550	99,600	21,992	17,741	22,460	20,069
99,600	99,650	22,006	17,754	22,476	20,081
99,650	99,700	22,020	17,766	22,493	20,094
99,700	99,750	22,034	17,779	22,509	20,106
99,750	99,800	22,048	17,791	22,526	20,119
99,800	99,850	22,062	17,804	22,542	20,131
99,850	99,900	22,076	17,816	22,559	20,144
99,900	99,950	22,090	17,829	22,575	20,156
99,950	100,000	22,104	17,841	22,592	20,169

$100,000 or over — use the Tax Computation Worksheet

* This column must also be used by a qualifying widow(er)

¶ 1111   Earned Income Credit Table

2007 Earned Income Credit (EIC) Table
Caution. This is **not** a tax table.

1. To find your credit, read down the "At least - But less than" columns and find the line that includes the amount you were told to look up from your EIC Worksheet.

2. Then, go to the column that includes your filing status and the number of qualifying children you have. Enter the credit from that column on your EIC Worksheet.

Example. If your filing status is single, you have one qualifying child, and the amount you are looking up from your EIC Worksheet is $2,455, you would enter $842.

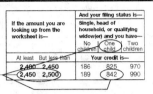

If the amount you are looking up from the worksheet is—	And your filing status is— Single, head of household, or qualifying widow(er) and you have—		
At least But less than	No children	One child	Two children
	Your credit is—		
2,400 2,450	186	825	970
2,450 2,500	189	842	990

If the amount you are looking up from the worksheet is—	Single, head of household, or qualifying widow(er) and you have—			Married filing jointly and you have—		
	No children	One child	Two children	No children	One child	Two children
At least But less than	Your credit is—			Your credit is—		
$1 $50	$2	$9	$10	$2	$9	$10
50 100	6	26	30	6	26	30
100 150	10	43	50	10	43	50
150 200	13	60	70	13	60	70
200 250	17	77	90	17	77	90
250 300	21	94	110	21	94	110
300 350	25	111	130	25	111	130
350 400	29	128	150	29	128	150
400 450	33	145	170	33	145	170
450 500	36	162	190	36	162	190
500 550	40	179	210	40	179	210
550 600	44	196	230	44	196	230
600 650	48	213	250	48	213	250
650 700	52	230	270	52	230	270
700 750	55	247	290	55	247	290
750 800	59	264	310	59	264	310
800 850	63	281	330	63	281	330
850 900	67	298	350	67	298	350
900 950	71	315	370	71	315	370
950 1,000	75	332	390	75	332	390
1,000 1,050	78	349	410	78	349	410
1,050 1,100	82	366	430	82	366	430
1,100 1,150	86	383	450	86	383	450
1,150 1,200	90	400	470	90	400	470
1,200 1,250	94	417	490	94	417	490
1,250 1,300	98	434	510	98	434	510
1,300 1,350	101	451	530	101	451	530
1,350 1,400	105	468	550	105	468	550
1,400 1,450	109	485	570	109	485	570
1,450 1,500	113	502	590	113	502	590
1,500 1,550	117	519	610	117	519	610
1,550 1,600	120	536	630	120	536	630
1,600 1,650	124	553	650	124	553	650
1,650 1,700	128	570	670	128	570	670
1,700 1,750	132	587	690	132	587	690
1,750 1,800	136	604	710	136	604	710
1,800 1,850	140	621	730	140	621	730
1,850 1,900	143	638	750	143	638	750
1,900 1,950	147	655	770	147	655	770
1,950 2,000	151	672	790	151	672	790
2,000 2,050	155	689	810	155	689	810
2,050 2,100	159	706	830	159	706	830
2,100 2,150	163	723	850	163	723	850
2,150 2,200	166	740	870	166	740	870
2,200 2,250	170	757	890	170	757	890
2,250 2,300	174	774	910	174	774	910
2,300 2,350	178	791	930	178	791	930
2,350 2,400	182	808	950	182	808	950
2,400 2,450	186	825	970	186	825	970
2,450 2,500	189	842	990	189	842	990

If the amount you are looking up from the worksheet is—	Single, head of household, or qualifying widow(er) and you have—			Married filing jointly and you have—		
	No children	One child	Two children	No children	One child	Two children
At least But less than	Your credit is—			Your credit is—		
2,500 2,550	193	859	1,010	193	859	1,010
2,550 2,600	197	876	1,030	197	876	1,030
2,600 2,650	201	893	1,050	201	893	1,050
2,650 2,700	205	910	1,070	205	910	1,070
2,700 2,750	208	927	1,090	208	927	1,090
2,750 2,800	212	944	1,110	212	944	1,110
2,800 2,850	216	961	1,130	216	961	1,130
2,850 2,900	220	978	1,150	220	978	1,150
2,900 2,950	224	995	1,170	224	995	1,170
2,950 3,000	228	1,012	1,190	228	1,012	1,190
3,000 3,050	231	1,029	1,210	231	1,029	1,210
3,050 3,100	235	1,046	1,230	235	1,046	1,230
3,100 3,150	239	1,063	1,250	239	1,063	1,250
3,150 3,200	243	1,080	1,270	243	1,080	1,270
3,200 3,250	247	1,097	1,290	247	1,097	1,290
3,250 3,300	251	1,114	1,310	251	1,114	1,310
3,300 3,350	254	1,131	1,330	254	1,131	1,330
3,350 3,400	258	1,148	1,350	258	1,148	1,350
3,400 3,450	262	1,165	1,370	262	1,165	1,370
3,450 3,500	266	1,182	1,390	266	1,182	1,390
3,500 3,550	270	1,199	1,410	270	1,199	1,410
3,550 3,600	273	1,216	1,430	273	1,216	1,430
3,600 3,650	277	1,233	1,450	277	1,233	1,450
3,650 3,700	281	1,250	1,470	281	1,250	1,470
3,700 3,750	285	1,267	1,490	285	1,267	1,490
3,750 3,800	289	1,284	1,510	289	1,284	1,510
3,800 3,850	293	1,301	1,530	293	1,301	1,530
3,850 3,900	296	1,318	1,550	296	1,318	1,550
3,900 3,950	300	1,335	1,570	300	1,335	1,570
3,950 4,000	304	1,352	1,590	304	1,352	1,590
4,000 4,050	308	1,369	1,610	308	1,369	1,610
4,050 4,100	312	1,386	1,630	312	1,386	1,630
4,100 4,150	316	1,403	1,650	316	1,403	1,650
4,150 4,200	319	1,420	1,670	319	1,420	1,670
4,200 4,250	323	1,437	1,690	323	1,437	1,690
4,250 4,300	327	1,454	1,710	327	1,454	1,710
4,300 4,350	331	1,471	1,730	331	1,471	1,730
4,350 4,400	335	1,488	1,750	335	1,488	1,750
4,400 4,450	339	1,505	1,770	339	1,505	1,770
4,450 4,500	342	1,522	1,790	342	1,522	1,790
4,500 4,550	346	1,539	1,810	346	1,539	1,810
4,550 4,600	350	1,556	1,830	350	1,556	1,830
4,600 4,650	354	1,573	1,850	354	1,573	1,850
4,650 4,700	358	1,590	1,870	358	1,590	1,870
4,700 4,750	361	1,607	1,890	361	1,607	1,890
4,750 4,800	365	1,624	1,910	365	1,624	1,910
4,800 4,850	369	1,641	1,930	369	1,641	1,930
4,850 4,900	373	1,658	1,950	373	1,658	1,950
4,900 4,950	377	1,675	1,970	377	1,675	1,970
4,950 5,000	381	1,692	1,990	381	1,692	1,990

2007 Earned Income Credit (EIC) Table—*Continued*   (**Caution.** This is **not** a tax table.)

If the amount you are looking up from the worksheet is—		Single, head of household, or qualifying widow(er) and you have—			Married filing jointly and you have—		
At least	But less than	No children	One child	Two children	No children	One child	Two children
		Your credit is—			Your credit is—		
5,000	5,050	384	1,709	2,010	384	1,709	2,010
5,050	5,100	388	1,726	2,030	388	1,726	2,030
5,100	5,150	392	1,743	2,050	392	1,743	2,050
5,150	5,200	396	1,760	2,070	396	1,760	2,070
5,200	5,250	400	1,777	2,090	400	1,777	2,090
5,250	5,300	404	1,794	2,110	404	1,794	2,110
5,300	5,350	407	1,811	2,130	407	1,811	2,130
5,350	5,400	411	1,828	2,150	411	1,828	2,150
5,400	5,450	415	1,845	2,170	415	1,845	2,170
5,450	5,500	419	1,862	2,190	419	1,862	2,190
5,500	5,550	423	1,879	2,210	423	1,879	2,210
5,550	5,600	428	1,896	2,230	428	1,896	2,230
5,600	5,650	428	1,913	2,250	428	1,913	2,250
5,650	5,700	428	1,930	2,270	428	1,930	2,270
5,700	5,750	428	1,947	2,290	428	1,947	2,290
5,750	5,800	428	1,964	2,310	428	1,964	2,310
5,800	5,850	428	1,981	2,330	428	1,981	2,330
5,850	5,900	428	1,998	2,350	428	1,998	2,350
5,900	5,950	428	2,015	2,370	428	2,015	2,370
5,950	6,000	428	2,032	2,390	428	2,032	2,390
6,000	6,050	428	2,049	2,410	428	2,049	2,410
6,050	6,100	428	2,066	2,430	428	2,066	2,430
6,100	6,150	428	2,083	2,450	428	2,083	2,450
6,150	6,200	428	2,100	2,470	428	2,100	2,470
6,200	6,250	428	2,117	2,490	428	2,117	2,490
6,250	6,300	428	2,134	2,510	428	2,134	2,510
6,300	6,350	428	2,151	2,530	428	2,151	2,530
6,350	6,400	428	2,168	2,550	428	2,168	2,550
6,400	6,450	428	2,185	2,570	428	2,185	2,570
6,450	6,500	428	2,202	2,590	428	2,202	2,590
6,500	6,550	428	2,219	2,610	428	2,219	2,610
6,550	6,600	428	2,236	2,630	428	2,236	2,630
6,600	6,650	428	2,253	2,650	428	2,253	2,650
6,650	6,700	428	2,270	2,670	428	2,270	2,670
6,700	6,750	428	2,287	2,690	428	2,287	2,690
6,750	6,800	428	2,304	2,710	428	2,304	2,710
6,800	6,850	428	2,321	2,730	428	2,321	2,730
6,850	6,900	428	2,338	2,750	428	2,338	2,750
6,900	6,950	428	2,355	2,770	428	2,355	2,770
6,950	7,000	428	2,372	2,790	428	2,372	2,790
7,000	7,050	426	2,389	2,810	428	2,389	2,810
7,050	7,100	422	2,406	2,830	428	2,406	2,830
7,100	7,150	418	2,423	2,850	428	2,423	2,850
7,150	7,200	414	2,440	2,870	428	2,440	2,870
7,200	7,250	410	2,457	2,890	428	2,457	2,890
7,250	7,300	407	2,474	2,910	428	2,474	2,910
7,300	7,350	403	2,491	2,930	428	2,491	2,930
7,350	7,400	399	2,508	2,950	428	2,508	2,950
7,400	7,450	395	2,525	2,970	428	2,525	2,970
7,450	7,500	391	2,542	2,990	428	2,542	2,990
7,500	7,550	387	2,559	3,010	428	2,559	3,010
7,550	7,600	384	2,576	3,030	428	2,576	3,030
7,600	7,650	380	2,593	3,050	428	2,593	3,050
7,650	7,700	376	2,610	3,070	428	2,610	3,070
7,700	7,750	372	2,627	3,090	428	2,627	3,090
7,750	7,800	368	2,644	3,110	428	2,644	3,110
7,800	7,850	365	2,661	3,130	428	2,661	3,130
7,850	7,900	361	2,678	3,150	428	2,678	3,150
7,900	7,950	357	2,695	3,170	428	2,695	3,170
7,950	8,000	353	2,712	3,190	428	2,712	3,190

If the amount you are looking up from the worksheet is—		Single, head of household, or qualifying widow(er) and you have—			Married filing jointly and you have—		
At least	But less than	No children	One child	Two children	No children	One child	Two children
		Your credit is—			Your credit is—		
8,000	8,050	349	2,729	3,210	428	2,729	3,210
8,050	8,100	345	2,746	3,230	428	2,746	3,230
8,100	8,150	342	2,763	3,250	428	2,763	3,250
8,150	8,200	338	2,780	3,270	428	2,780	3,270
8,200	8,250	334	2,797	3,290	428	2,797	3,290
8,250	8,300	330	2,814	3,310	428	2,814	3,310
8,300	8,350	326	2,831	3,330	428	2,831	3,330
8,350	8,400	322	2,853	3,350	428	2,853	3,350
8,400	8,450	319	2,853	3,370	428	2,853	3,370
8,450	8,500	315	2,853	3,390	428	2,853	3,390
8,500	8,550	311	2,853	3,410	428	2,853	3,410
8,550	8,600	307	2,853	3,430	428	2,853	3,430
8,600	8,650	303	2,853	3,450	428	2,853	3,450
8,650	8,700	299	2,853	3,470	428	2,853	3,470
8,700	8,750	296	2,853	3,490	428	2,853	3,490
8,750	8,800	292	2,853	3,510	428	2,853	3,510
8,800	8,850	288	2,853	3,530	428	2,853	3,530
8,850	8,900	284	2,853	3,550	428	2,853	3,550
8,900	8,950	280	2,853	3,570	428	2,853	3,570
8,950	9,000	277	2,853	3,590	428	2,853	3,590
9,000	9,050	273	2,853	3,610	426	2,853	3,610
9,050	9,100	269	2,853	3,630	422	2,853	3,630
9,100	9,150	265	2,853	3,650	418	2,853	3,650
9,150	9,200	261	2,853	3,670	414	2,853	3,670
9,200	9,250	257	2,853	3,690	410	2,853	3,690
9,250	9,300	254	2,853	3,710	407	2,853	3,710
9,300	9,350	250	2,853	3,730	403	2,853	3,730
9,350	9,400	246	2,853	3,750	399	2,853	3,750
9,400	9,450	242	2,853	3,770	395	2,853	3,770
9,450	9,500	238	2,853	3,790	391	2,853	3,790
9,500	9,550	234	2,853	3,810	387	2,853	3,810
9,550	9,600	231	2,853	3,830	384	2,853	3,830
9,600	9,650	227	2,853	3,850	380	2,853	3,850
9,650	9,700	223	2,853	3,870	376	2,853	3,870
9,700	9,750	219	2,853	3,890	372	2,853	3,890
9,750	9,800	215	2,853	3,910	368	2,853	3,910
9,800	9,850	212	2,853	3,930	365	2,853	3,930
9,850	9,900	208	2,853	3,950	361	2,853	3,950
9,900	9,950	204	2,853	3,970	357	2,853	3,970
9,950	10,000	200	2,853	3,990	353	2,853	3,990
10,000	10,050	196	2,853	4,010	349	2,853	4,010
10,050	10,100	192	2,853	4,030	345	2,853	4,030
10,100	10,150	189	2,853	4,050	342	2,853	4,050
10,150	10,200	185	2,853	4,070	338	2,853	4,070
10,200	10,250	181	2,853	4,090	334	2,853	4,090
10,250	10,300	177	2,853	4,110	330	2,853	4,110
10,300	10,350	173	2,853	4,130	326	2,853	4,130
10,350	10,400	169	2,853	4,150	322	2,853	4,150
10,400	10,450	166	2,853	4,170	319	2,853	4,170
10,450	10,500	162	2,853	4,190	315	2,853	4,190
10,500	10,550	158	2,853	4,210	311	2,853	4,210
10,550	10,600	154	2,853	4,230	307	2,853	4,230
10,600	10,650	150	2,853	4,250	303	2,853	4,250
10,650	10,700	146	2,853	4,270	299	2,853	4,270
10,700	10,750	143	2,853	4,290	296	2,853	4,290
10,750	10,800	139	2,853	4,310	292	2,853	4,310
10,800	10,850	135	2,853	4,330	288	2,853	4,330
10,850	10,900	131	2,853	4,350	284	2,853	4,350
10,900	10,950	127	2,853	4,370	280	2,853	4,370
10,950	11,000	124	2,853	4,390	277	2,853	4,390

2007 Earned Income Credit (EIC) Table—*Continued* (**Caution.** This is **not** a tax table.)

If the amount you are looking up from the worksheet is—		Single, head of household, or qualifying widow(er) and you have—			Married filing jointly and you have—		
At least	But less than	No children	One child	Two children	No children	One child	Two children
		Your credit is—			Your credit is—		
11,000	11,050	120	2,853	4,410	273	2,853	4,410
11,050	11,100	116	2,853	4,430	269	2,853	4,430
11,100	11,150	112	2,853	4,450	265	2,853	4,450
11,150	11,200	108	2,853	4,470	261	2,853	4,470
11,200	11,250	104	2,853	4,490	257	2,853	4,490
11,250	11,300	101	2,853	4,510	254	2,853	4,510
11,300	11,350	97	2,853	4,530	250	2,853	4,530
11,350	11,400	93	2,853	4,550	246	2,853	4,550
11,400	11,450	89	2,853	4,570	242	2,853	4,570
11,450	11,500	85	2,853	4,590	238	2,853	4,590
11,500	11,550	81	2,853	4,610	234	2,853	4,610
11,550	11,600	78	2,853	4,630	231	2,853	4,630
11,600	11,650	74	2,853	4,650	227	2,853	4,650
11,650	11,700	70	2,853	4,670	223	2,853	4,670
11,700	11,750	66	2,853	4,690	219	2,853	4,690
11,750	11,800	62	2,853	4,716	215	2,853	4,716
11,800	11,850	59	2,853	4,716	212	2,853	4,716
11,850	11,900	55	2,853	4,716	208	2,853	4,716
11,900	11,950	51	2,853	4,716	204	2,853	4,716
11,950	12,000	47	2,853	4,716	200	2,853	4,716
12,000	12,050	43	2,853	4,716	196	2,853	4,716
12,050	12,100	39	2,853	4,716	192	2,853	4,716
12,100	12,150	36	2,853	4,716	189	2,853	4,716
12,150	12,200	32	2,853	4,716	185	2,853	4,716
12,200	12,250	28	2,853	4,716	181	2,853	4,716
12,250	12,300	24	2,853	4,716	177	2,853	4,716
12,300	12,350	20	2,853	4,716	173	2,853	4,716
12,350	12,400	16	2,853	4,716	169	2,853	4,716
12,400	12,450	13	2,853	4,716	166	2,853	4,716
12,450	12,500	9	2,853	4,716	162	2,853	4,716
12,500	12,550	5	2,853	4,716	158	2,853	4,716
12,550	12,600	*	2,853	4,716	154	2,853	4,716
12,600	12,650	0	2,853	4,716	150	2,853	4,716
12,650	12,700	0	2,853	4,716	146	2,853	4,716
12,700	12,750	0	2,853	4,716	143	2,853	4,716
12,750	12,800	0	2,853	4,716	139	2,853	4,716
12,800	12,850	0	2,853	4,716	135	2,853	4,716
12,850	12,900	0	2,853	4,716	131	2,853	4,716
12,900	12,950	0	2,853	4,716	127	2,853	4,716
12,950	13,000	0	2,853	4,716	124	2,853	4,716
13,000	13,050	0	2,853	4,716	120	2,853	4,716
13,050	13,100	0	2,853	4,716	116	2,853	4,716
13,100	13,150	0	2,853	4,716	112	2,853	4,716
13,150	13,200	0	2,853	4,716	108	2,853	4,716
13,200	13,250	0	2,853	4,716	104	2,853	4,716
13,250	13,300	0	2,853	4,716	101	2,853	4,716
13,300	13,350	0	2,853	4,716	97	2,853	4,716
13,350	13,400	0	2,853	4,716	93	2,853	4,716
13,400	13,450	0	2,853	4,716	89	2,853	4,716
13,450	13,500	0	2,853	4,716	85	2,853	4,716
13,500	13,550	0	2,853	4,716	81	2,853	4,716
13,550	13,600	0	2,853	4,716	78	2,853	4,716
13,600	13,650	0	2,853	4,716	74	2,853	4,716
13,650	13,700	0	2,853	4,716	70	2,853	4,716
13,700	13,750	0	2,853	4,716	66	2,853	4,716
13,750	13,800	0	2,853	4,716	62	2,853	4,716
13,800	13,850	0	2,853	4,716	59	2,853	4,716
13,850	13,900	0	2,853	4,716	55	2,853	4,716
13,900	13,950	0	2,853	4,716	51	2,853	4,716
13,950	14,000	0	2,853	4,716	47	2,853	4,716
14,000	14,050	0	2,853	4,716	43	2,853	4,716
14,050	14,100	0	2,853	4,716	39	2,853	4,716
14,100	14,150	0	2,853	4,716	36	2,853	4,716
14,150	14,200	0	2,853	4,716	32	2,853	4,716
14,200	14,250	0	2,853	4,716	28	2,853	4,716
14,250	14,300	0	2,853	4,716	24	2,853	4,716
14,300	14,350	0	2,853	4,716	20	2,853	4,716
14,350	14,400	0	2,853	4,716	16	2,853	4,716
14,400	14,450	0	2,853	4,716	13	2,853	4,716
14,450	14,500	0	2,853	4,716	9	2,853	4,716
14,500	14,550	0	2,853	4,716	5	2,853	4,716
14,550	14,600	0	2,853	4,716	*	2,853	4,716
14,600	14,650	0	2,853	4,716	0	2,853	4,716
14,650	14,700	0	2,853	4,716	0	2,853	4,716
14,700	14,750	0	2,853	4,716	0	2,853	4,716
14,750	14,800	0	2,853	4,716	0	2,853	4,716
14,800	14,850	0	2,853	4,716	0	2,853	4,716
14,850	14,900	0	2,853	4,716	0	2,853	4,716
14,900	14,950	0	2,853	4,716	0	2,853	4,716
14,950	15,000	0	2,853	4,716	0	2,853	4,716
15,000	15,050	0	2,853	4,716	0	2,853	4,716
15,050	15,100	0	2,853	4,716	0	2,853	4,716
15,100	15,150	0	2,853	4,716	0	2,853	4,716
15,150	15,200	0	2,853	4,716	0	2,853	4,716
15,200	15,250	0	2,853	4,716	0	2,853	4,716
15,250	15,300	0	2,853	4,716	0	2,853	4,716
15,300	15,350	0	2,853	4,716	0	2,853	4,716
15,350	15,400	0	2,853	4,716	0	2,853	4,716
15,400	15,450	0	2,847	4,709	0	2,853	4,716
15,450	15,500	0	2,839	4,698	0	2,853	4,716
15,500	15,550	0	2,831	4,688	0	2,853	4,716
15,550	15,600	0	2,823	4,677	0	2,853	4,716
15,600	15,650	0	2,815	4,667	0	2,853	4,716
15,650	15,700	0	2,807	4,656	0	2,853	4,716
15,700	15,750	0	2,799	4,645	0	2,853	4,716
15,750	15,800	0	2,791	4,635	0	2,853	4,716
15,800	15,850	0	2,783	4,624	0	2,853	4,716
15,850	15,900	0	2,775	4,614	0	2,853	4,716
15,900	15,950	0	2,767	4,603	0	2,853	4,716
15,950	16,000	0	2,759	4,593	0	2,853	4,716

*If the amount you are looking up from the worksheet is at least $12,550 ($14,550 if married filing jointly) but less than $12,590 ($14,590 if married filing jointly), your credit is $2. Otherwise, you cannot take the credit.

2007 Earned Income Credit (EIC) Table—*Continued*　　　(**Caution.** This is **not** a tax table.)

If the amount you are looking up from the worksheet is—		Single, head of household, or qualifying widow(er) and you have—			Married filing jointly and you have—		
At least	But less than	No children	One child	Two children	No children	One child	Two children
		Your credit is—			Your credit is—		
16,000	16,050	0	2,751	4,582	0	2,853	4,716
16,050	16,100	0	2,743	4,572	0	2,853	4,716
16,100	16,150	0	2,735	4,561	0	2,853	4,716
16,150	16,200	0	2,727	4,551	0	2,853	4,716
16,200	16,250	0	2,719	4,540	0	2,853	4,716
16,250	16,300	0	2,711	4,530	0	2,853	4,716
16,300	16,350	0	2,703	4,519	0	2,853	4,716
16,350	16,400	0	2,695	4,509	0	2,853	4,716
16,400	16,450	0	2,687	4,498	0	2,853	4,716
16,450	16,500	0	2,679	4,487	0	2,853	4,716
16,500	16,550	0	2,671	4,477	0	2,853	4,716
16,550	16,600	0	2,663	4,466	0	2,853	4,716
16,600	16,650	0	2,655	4,456	0	2,853	4,716
16,650	16,700	0	2,647	4,445	0	2,853	4,716
16,700	16,750	0	2,639	4,435	0	2,853	4,716
16,750	16,800	0	2,631	4,424	0	2,853	4,716
16,800	16,850	0	2,623	4,414	0	2,853	4,716
16,850	16,900	0	2,615	4,403	0	2,853	4,716
16,900	16,950	0	2,607	4,393	0	2,853	4,716
16,950	17,000	0	2,599	4,382	0	2,853	4,716
17,000	17,050	0	2,591	4,372	0	2,853	4,716
17,050	17,100	0	2,583	4,361	0	2,853	4,716
17,100	17,150	0	2,575	4,351	0	2,853	4,716
17,150	17,200	0	2,567	4,340	0	2,853	4,716
17,200	17,250	0	2,559	4,330	0	2,853	4,716
17,250	17,300	0	2,551	4,319	0	2,853	4,716
17,300	17,350	0	2,543	4,308	0	2,853	4,716
17,350	17,400	0	2,535	4,298	0	2,853	4,716
17,400	17,450	0	2,527	4,287	0	2,847	4,709
17,450	17,500	0	2,519	4,277	0	2,839	4,698
17,500	17,550	0	2,511	4,266	0	2,831	4,688
17,550	17,600	0	2,503	4,256	0	2,823	4,677
17,600	17,650	0	2,495	4,245	0	2,815	4,667
17,650	17,700	0	2,487	4,235	0	2,807	4,656
17,700	17,750	0	2,479	4,224	0	2,799	4,645
17,750	17,800	0	2,471	4,214	0	2,791	4,635
17,800	17,850	0	2,463	4,203	0	2,783	4,624
17,850	17,900	0	2,455	4,193	0	2,775	4,614
17,900	17,950	0	2,448	4,182	0	2,767	4,603
17,950	18,000	0	2,440	4,172	0	2,759	4,593
18,000	18,050	0	2,432	4,161	0	2,751	4,582
18,050	18,100	0	2,424	4,151	0	2,743	4,572
18,100	18,150	0	2,416	4,140	0	2,735	4,561
18,150	18,200	0	2,408	4,129	0	2,727	4,551
18,200	18,250	0	2,400	4,119	0	2,719	4,540
18,250	18,300	0	2,392	4,108	0	2,711	4,530
18,300	18,350	0	2,384	4,098	0	2,703	4,519
18,350	18,400	0	2,376	4,087	0	2,695	4,509
18,400	18,450	0	2,368	4,077	0	2,687	4,498
18,450	18,500	0	2,360	4,066	0	2,679	4,487
18,500	18,550	0	2,352	4,056	0	2,671	4,477
18,550	18,600	0	2,344	4,045	0	2,663	4,466
18,600	18,650	0	2,336	4,035	0	2,655	4,456
18,650	18,700	0	2,328	4,024	0	2,647	4,445
18,700	18,750	0	2,320	4,014	0	2,639	4,435
18,750	18,800	0	2,312	4,003	0	2,631	4,424
18,800	18,850	0	2,304	3,993	0	2,623	4,414
18,850	18,900	0	2,296	3,982	0	2,615	4,403
18,900	18,950	0	2,288	3,972	0	2,607	4,393
18,950	19,000	0	2,280	3,961	0	2,599	4,382

If the amount you are looking up from the worksheet is—		Single, head of household, or qualifying widow(er) and you have—			Married filing jointly and you have—		
At least	But less than	No children	One child	Two children	No children	One child	Two children
		Your credit is—			Your credit is—		
19,000	19,050	0	2,272	3,950	0	2,591	4,372
19,050	19,100	0	2,264	3,940	0	2,583	4,361
19,100	19,150	0	2,256	3,929	0	2,575	4,351
19,150	19,200	0	2,248	3,919	0	2,567	4,340
19,200	19,250	0	2,240	3,908	0	2,559	4,330
19,250	19,300	0	2,232	3,898	0	2,551	4,319
19,300	19,350	0	2,224	3,887	0	2,543	4,308
19,350	19,400	0	2,216	3,877	0	2,535	4,298
19,400	19,450	0	2,208	3,866	0	2,527	4,287
19,450	19,500	0	2,200	3,856	0	2,519	4,277
19,500	19,550	0	2,192	3,845	0	2,511	4,266
19,550	19,600	0	2,184	3,835	0	2,503	4,256
19,600	19,650	0	2,176	3,824	0	2,495	4,245
19,650	19,700	0	2,168	3,814	0	2,487	4,235
19,700	19,750	0	2,160	3,803	0	2,479	4,224
19,750	19,800	0	2,152	3,793	0	2,471	4,214
19,800	19,850	0	2,144	3,782	0	2,463	4,203
19,850	19,900	0	2,136	3,771	0	2,455	4,193
19,900	19,950	0	2,128	3,761	0	2,448	4,182
19,950	20,000	0	2,120	3,750	0	2,440	4,172
20,000	20,050	0	2,112	3,740	0	2,432	4,161
20,050	20,100	0	2,104	3,729	0	2,424	4,151
20,100	20,150	0	2,096	3,719	0	2,416	4,140
20,150	20,200	0	2,088	3,708	0	2,408	4,129
20,200	20,250	0	2,080	3,698	0	2,400	4,119
20,250	20,300	0	2,072	3,687	0	2,392	4,108
20,300	20,350	0	2,064	3,677	0	2,384	4,098
20,350	20,400	0	2,056	3,666	0	2,376	4,087
20,400	20,450	0	2,048	3,656	0	2,368	4,077
20,450	20,500	0	2,040	3,645	0	2,360	4,066
20,500	20,550	0	2,032	3,635	0	2,352	4,056
20,550	20,600	0	2,024	3,624	0	2,344	4,045
20,600	20,650	0	2,016	3,614	0	2,336	4,035
20,650	20,700	0	2,008	3,603	0	2,328	4,024
20,700	20,750	0	2,000	3,592	0	2,320	4,014
20,750	20,800	0	1,992	3,582	0	2,312	4,003
20,800	20,850	0	1,984	3,571	0	2,304	3,993
20,850	20,900	0	1,976	3,561	0	2,296	3,982
20,900	20,950	0	1,968	3,550	0	2,288	3,972
20,950	21,000	0	1,960	3,540	0	2,280	3,961
21,000	21,050	0	1,952	3,529	0	2,272	3,950
21,050	21,100	0	1,944	3,519	0	2,264	3,940
21,100	21,150	0	1,936	3,508	0	2,256	3,929
21,150	21,200	0	1,928	3,498	0	2,248	3,919
21,200	21,250	0	1,920	3,487	0	2,240	3,908
21,250	21,300	0	1,912	3,477	0	2,232	3,898
21,300	21,350	0	1,904	3,466	0	2,224	3,887
21,350	21,400	0	1,896	3,456	0	2,216	3,877
21,400	21,450	0	1,888	3,445	0	2,208	3,866
21,450	21,500	0	1,880	3,434	0	2,200	3,856
21,500	21,550	0	1,872	3,424	0	2,192	3,845
21,550	21,600	0	1,864	3,413	0	2,184	3,835
21,600	21,650	0	1,856	3,403	0	2,176	3,824
21,650	21,700	0	1,848	3,392	0	2,168	3,814
21,700	21,750	0	1,840	3,382	0	2,160	3,803
21,750	21,800	0	1,832	3,371	0	2,152	3,793
21,800	21,850	0	1,824	3,361	0	2,144	3,782
21,850	21,900	0	1,816	3,350	0	2,136	3,771
21,900	21,950	0	1,808	3,340	0	2,128	3,761
21,950	22,000	0	1,800	3,329	0	2,120	3,750

2007 Earned Income Credit (EIC) Table—*Continued* (Caution. This is **not** a tax table.)

If the amount you are looking up from the worksheet is—		Single, head of household, or qualifying widow(er) and you have—			Married filing jointly and you have—		
At least	But less than	No children	One child	Two children	No children	One child	Two children
22,000	22,050	0	1,792	3,319	0	2,112	3,740
22,050	22,100	0	1,784	3,308	0	2,104	3,729
22,100	22,150	0	1,776	3,298	0	2,096	3,719
22,150	22,200	0	1,768	3,287	0	2,088	3,708
22,200	22,250	0	1,760	3,277	0	2,080	3,698
22,250	22,300	0	1,752	3,266	0	2,072	3,687
22,300	22,350	0	1,744	3,255	0	2,064	3,677
22,350	22,400	0	1,736	3,245	0	2,056	3,666
22,400	22,450	0	1,728	3,234	0	2,048	3,656
22,450	22,500	0	1,720	3,224	0	2,040	3,645
22,500	22,550	0	1,712	3,213	0	2,032	3,635
22,550	22,600	0	1,704	3,203	0	2,024	3,624
22,600	22,650	0	1,696	3,192	0	2,016	3,614
22,650	22,700	0	1,688	3,182	0	2,008	3,603
22,700	22,750	0	1,680	3,171	0	2,000	3,592
22,750	22,800	0	1,672	3,161	0	1,992	3,582
22,800	22,850	0	1,664	3,150	0	1,984	3,571
22,850	22,900	0	1,656	3,140	0	1,976	3,561
22,900	22,950	0	1,649	3,129	0	1,968	3,550
22,950	23,000	0	1,641	3,119	0	1,960	3,540
23,000	23,050	0	1,633	3,108	0	1,952	3,529
23,050	23,100	0	1,625	3,098	0	1,944	3,519
23,100	23,150	0	1,617	3,087	0	1,936	3,508
23,150	23,200	0	1,609	3,076	0	1,928	3,498
23,200	23,250	0	1,601	3,066	0	1,920	3,487
23,250	23,300	0	1,593	3,055	0	1,912	3,477
23,300	23,350	0	1,585	3,045	0	1,904	3,466
23,350	23,400	0	1,577	3,034	0	1,896	3,456
23,400	23,450	0	1,569	3,024	0	1,888	3,445
23,450	23,500	0	1,561	3,013	0	1,880	3,434
23,500	23,550	0	1,553	3,003	0	1,872	3,424
23,550	23,600	0	1,545	2,992	0	1,864	3,413
23,600	23,650	0	1,537	2,982	0	1,856	3,403
23,650	23,700	0	1,529	2,971	0	1,848	3,392
23,700	23,750	0	1,521	2,961	0	1,840	3,382
23,750	23,800	0	1,513	2,950	0	1,832	3,371
23,800	23,850	0	1,505	2,940	0	1,824	3,361
23,850	23,900	0	1,497	2,929	0	1,816	3,350
23,900	23,950	0	1,489	2,919	0	1,808	3,340
23,950	24,000	0	1,481	2,908	0	1,800	3,329
24,000	24,050	0	1,473	2,897	0	1,792	3,319
24,050	24,100	0	1,465	2,887	0	1,784	3,308
24,100	24,150	0	1,457	2,876	0	1,776	3,298
24,150	24,200	0	1,449	2,866	0	1,768	3,287
24,200	24,250	0	1,441	2,855	0	1,760	3,277
24,250	24,300	0	1,433	2,845	0	1,752	3,266
24,300	24,350	0	1,425	2,834	0	1,744	3,255
24,350	24,400	0	1,417	2,824	0	1,736	3,245
24,400	24,450	0	1,409	2,813	0	1,728	3,234
24,450	24,500	0	1,401	2,803	0	1,720	3,224
24,500	24,550	0	1,393	2,792	0	1,712	3,213
24,550	24,600	0	1,385	2,782	0	1,704	3,203
24,600	24,650	0	1,377	2,771	0	1,696	3,192
24,650	24,700	0	1,369	2,761	0	1,688	3,182
24,700	24,750	0	1,361	2,750	0	1,680	3,171
24,750	24,800	0	1,353	2,740	0	1,672	3,161
24,800	24,850	0	1,345	2,729	0	1,664	3,150
24,850	24,900	0	1,337	2,718	0	1,656	3,140
24,900	24,950	0	1,329	2,708	0	1,649	3,129
24,950	25,000	0	1,321	2,697	0	1,641	3,119
25,000	25,050	0	1,313	2,687	0	1,633	3,108
25,050	25,100	0	1,305	2,676	0	1,625	3,098
25,100	25,150	0	1,297	2,666	0	1,617	3,087
25,150	25,200	0	1,289	2,655	0	1,609	3,076
25,200	25,250	0	1,281	2,645	0	1,601	3,066
25,250	25,300	0	1,273	2,634	0	1,593	3,055
25,300	25,350	0	1,265	2,624	0	1,585	3,045
25,350	25,400	0	1,257	2,613	0	1,577	3,034
25,400	25,450	0	1,249	2,603	0	1,569	3,024
25,450	25,500	0	1,241	2,592	0	1,561	3,013
25,500	25,550	0	1,233	2,582	0	1,553	3,003
25,550	25,600	0	1,225	2,571	0	1,545	2,992
25,600	25,650	0	1,217	2,561	0	1,537	2,982
25,650	25,700	0	1,209	2,550	0	1,529	2,971
25,700	25,750	0	1,201	2,539	0	1,521	2,961
25,750	25,800	0	1,193	2,529	0	1,513	2,950
25,800	25,850	0	1,185	2,518	0	1,505	2,940
25,850	25,900	0	1,177	2,508	0	1,497	2,929
25,900	25,950	0	1,169	2,497	0	1,489	2,919
25,950	26,000	0	1,161	2,487	0	1,481	2,908
26,000	26,050	0	1,153	2,476	0	1,473	2,897
26,050	26,100	0	1,145	2,466	0	1,465	2,887
26,100	26,150	0	1,137	2,455	0	1,457	2,876
26,150	26,200	0	1,129	2,445	0	1,449	2,866
26,200	26,250	0	1,121	2,434	0	1,441	2,855
26,250	26,300	0	1,113	2,424	0	1,433	2,845
26,300	26,350	0	1,105	2,413	0	1,425	2,834
26,350	26,400	0	1,097	2,403	0	1,417	2,824
26,400	26,450	0	1,089	2,392	0	1,409	2,813
26,450	26,500	0	1,081	2,381	0	1,401	2,803
26,500	26,550	0	1,073	2,371	0	1,393	2,792
26,550	26,600	0	1,065	2,360	0	1,385	2,782
26,600	26,650	0	1,057	2,350	0	1,377	2,771
26,650	26,700	0	1,049	2,339	0	1,369	2,761
26,700	26,750	0	1,041	2,329	0	1,361	2,750
26,750	26,800	0	1,033	2,318	0	1,353	2,740
26,800	26,850	0	1,025	2,308	0	1,345	2,729
26,850	26,900	0	1,017	2,297	0	1,337	2,718
26,900	26,950	0	1,009	2,287	0	1,329	2,708
26,950	27,000	0	1,001	2,276	0	1,321	2,697
27,000	27,050	0	993	2,266	0	1,313	2,687
27,050	27,100	0	985	2,255	0	1,305	2,676
27,100	27,150	0	977	2,245	0	1,297	2,666
27,150	27,200	0	969	2,234	0	1,289	2,655
27,200	27,250	0	961	2,224	0	1,281	2,645
27,250	27,300	0	953	2,213	0	1,273	2,634
27,300	27,350	0	945	2,202	0	1,265	2,624
27,350	27,400	0	937	2,192	0	1,257	2,613
27,400	27,450	0	929	2,181	0	1,249	2,603
27,450	27,500	0	921	2,171	0	1,241	2,592
27,500	27,550	0	913	2,160	0	1,233	2,582
27,550	27,600	0	905	2,150	0	1,225	2,571
27,600	27,650	0	897	2,139	0	1,217	2,561
27,650	27,700	0	889	2,129	0	1,209	2,550
27,700	27,750	0	881	2,118	0	1,201	2,539
27,750	27,800	0	873	2,108	0	1,193	2,529
27,800	27,850	0	865	2,097	0	1,185	2,518
27,850	27,900	0	857	2,087	0	1,177	2,508
27,900	27,950	0	850	2,076	0	1,169	2,497
27,950	28,000	0	842	2,066	0	1,161	2,487

2007 Earned Income Credit (EIC) Table—*Continued*   (**Caution.** This is **not** a tax table.)

If the amount you are looking up from the worksheet is—		Single, head of household, or qualifying widow(er) and you have—			Married filing jointly and you have—		
At least	But less than	No children	One child	Two children	No children	One child	Two children
		Your credit is—			Your credit is—		
28,000	28,050	0	834	2,055	0	1,153	2,476
28,050	28,100	0	826	2,045	0	1,145	2,466
28,100	28,150	0	818	2,034	0	1,137	2,455
28,150	28,200	0	810	2,023	0	1,129	2,445
28,200	28,250	0	802	2,013	0	1,121	2,434
28,250	28,300	0	794	2,002	0	1,113	2,424
28,300	28,350	0	786	1,992	0	1,105	2,413
28,350	28,400	0	778	1,981	0	1,097	2,403
28,400	28,450	0	770	1,971	0	1,089	2,392
28,450	28,500	0	762	1,960	0	1,081	2,381
28,500	28,550	0	754	1,950	0	1,073	2,371
28,550	28,600	0	746	1,939	0	1,065	2,360
28,600	28,650	0	738	1,929	0	1,057	2,350
28,650	28,700	0	730	1,918	0	1,049	2,339
28,700	28,750	0	722	1,908	0	1,041	2,329
28,750	28,800	0	714	1,897	0	1,033	2,318
28,800	28,850	0	706	1,887	0	1,025	2,308
28,850	28,900	0	698	1,876	0	1,017	2,297
28,900	28,950	0	690	1,866	0	1,009	2,287
28,950	29,000	0	682	1,855	0	1,001	2,276
29,000	29,050	0	674	1,844	0	993	2,266
29,050	29,100	0	666	1,834	0	985	2,255
29,100	29,150	0	658	1,823	0	977	2,245
29,150	29,200	0	650	1,813	0	969	2,234
29,200	29,250	0	642	1,802	0	961	2,224
29,250	29,300	0	634	1,792	0	953	2,213
29,300	29,350	0	626	1,781	0	945	2,202
29,350	29,400	0	618	1,771	0	937	2,192
29,400	29,450	0	610	1,760	0	929	2,181
29,450	29,500	0	602	1,750	0	921	2,171
29,500	29,550	0	594	1,739	0	913	2,160
29,550	29,600	0	586	1,729	0	905	2,150
29,600	29,650	0	578	1,718	0	897	2,139
29,650	29,700	0	570	1,708	0	889	2,129
29,700	29,750	0	562	1,697	0	881	2,118
29,750	29,800	0	554	1,687	0	873	2,108
29,800	29,850	0	546	1,676	0	865	2,097
29,850	29,900	0	538	1,665	0	857	2,087
29,900	29,950	0	530	1,655	0	850	2,076
29,950	30,000	0	522	1,644	0	842	2,066
30,000	30,050	0	514	1,634	0	834	2,055
30,050	30,100	0	506	1,623	0	826	2,045
30,100	30,150	0	498	1,613	0	818	2,034
30,150	30,200	0	490	1,602	0	810	2,023
30,200	30,250	0	482	1,592	0	802	2,013
30,250	30,300	0	474	1,581	0	794	2,002
30,300	30,350	0	466	1,571	0	786	1,992
30,350	30,400	0	458	1,560	0	778	1,981
30,400	30,450	0	450	1,550	0	770	1,971
30,450	30,500	0	442	1,539	0	762	1,960

If the amount you are looking up from the worksheet is—		Single, head of household, or qualifying widow(er) and you have—			Married filing jointly and you have—		
At least	But less than	No children	One child	Two children	No children	One child	Two children
		Your credit is—			Your credit is—		
30,500	30,550	0	434	1,529	0	754	1,950
30,550	30,600	0	426	1,518	0	746	1,939
30,600	30,650	0	418	1,508	0	738	1,929
30,650	30,700	0	410	1,497	0	730	1,918
30,700	30,750	0	402	1,486	0	722	1,908
30,750	30,800	0	394	1,476	0	714	1,897
30,800	30,850	0	386	1,465	0	706	1,887
30,850	30,900	0	378	1,455	0	698	1,876
30,900	30,950	0	370	1,444	0	690	1,866
30,950	31,000	0	362	1,434	0	682	1,855
31,000	31,050	0	354	1,423	0	674	1,844
31,050	31,100	0	346	1,413	0	666	1,834
31,100	31,150	0	338	1,402	0	658	1,823
31,150	31,200	0	330	1,392	0	650	1,813
31,200	31,250	0	322	1,381	0	642	1,802
31,250	31,300	0	314	1,371	0	634	1,792
31,300	31,350	0	306	1,360	0	626	1,781
31,350	31,400	0	298	1,350	0	618	1,771
31,400	31,450	0	290	1,339	0	610	1,760
31,450	31,500	0	282	1,328	0	602	1,750
31,500	31,550	0	274	1,318	0	594	1,739
31,550	31,600	0	266	1,307	0	586	1,729
31,600	31,650	0	258	1,297	0	578	1,718
31,650	31,700	0	250	1,286	0	570	1,708
31,700	31,750	0	242	1,276	0	562	1,697
31,750	31,800	0	234	1,265	0	554	1,687
31,800	31,850	0	226	1,255	0	546	1,676
31,850	31,900	0	218	1,244	0	538	1,665
31,900	31,950	0	210	1,234	0	530	1,655
31,950	32,000	0	202	1,223	0	522	1,644
32,000	32,050	0	194	1,213	0	514	1,634
32,050	32,100	0	186	1,202	0	506	1,623
32,100	32,150	0	178	1,192	0	498	1,613
32,150	32,200	0	170	1,181	0	490	1,602
32,200	32,250	0	162	1,171	0	482	1,592
32,250	32,300	0	154	1,160	0	474	1,581
32,300	32,350	0	146	1,149	0	466	1,571
32,350	32,400	0	138	1,139	0	458	1,560
32,400	32,450	0	130	1,128	0	450	1,550
32,450	32,500	0	122	1,118	0	442	1,539
32,500	32,550	0	114	1,107	0	434	1,529
32,550	32,600	0	106	1,097	0	426	1,518
32,600	32,650	0	98	1,086	0	418	1,508
32,650	32,700	0	90	1,076	0	410	1,497
32,700	32,750	0	82	1,065	0	402	1,486
32,750	32,800	0	74	1,055	0	394	1,476
32,800	32,850	0	66	1,044	0	386	1,465
32,850	32,900	0	58	1,034	0	378	1,455
32,900	32,950	0	51	1,023	0	370	1,444
32,950	33,000	0	43	1,013	0	362	1,434

2007 Earned Income Credit (EIC) Table—*Continued*   (**Caution.** This is **not** a tax table.)

If the amount you are looking up from the worksheet is—		Single, head of household, or qualifying widow(er) and you have—			Married filing jointly and you have—		
At least	But less than	No children	One child	Two children	No children	One child	Two children
		Your credit is—			Your credit is—		
33,000	33,050	0	35	1,002	0	354	1,423
33,050	33,100	0	27	992	0	346	1,413
33,100	33,150	0	19	981	0	338	1,402
33,150	33,200	0	11	970	0	330	1,392
33,200	33,250	0	*	960	0	322	1,381
33,250	33,300	0	0	949	0	314	1,371
33,300	33,350	0	0	939	0	306	1,360
33,350	33,400	0	0	928	0	298	1,350
33,400	33,450	0	0	918	0	290	1,339
33,450	33,500	0	0	907	0	282	1,328
33,500	33,550	0	0	897	0	274	1,318
33,550	33,600	0	0	886	0	266	1,307
33,600	33,650	0	0	876	0	258	1,297
33,650	33,700	0	0	865	0	250	1,286
33,700	33,750	0	0	855	0	242	1,276
33,750	33,800	0	0	844	0	234	1,265
33,800	33,850	0	0	834	0	226	1,255
33,850	33,900	0	0	823	0	218	1,244
33,900	33,950	0	0	813	0	210	1,234
33,950	34,000	0	0	802	0	202	1,223
34,000	34,050	0	0	791	0	194	1,213
34,050	34,100	0	0	781	0	186	1,202
34,100	34,150	0	0	770	0	178	1,192
34,150	34,200	0	0	760	0	170	1,181
34,200	34,250	0	0	749	0	162	1,171
34,250	34,300	0	0	739	0	154	1,160
34,300	34,350	0	0	728	0	146	1,149
34,350	34,400	0	0	718	0	138	1,139
34,400	34,450	0	0	707	0	130	1,128
34,450	34,500	0	0	697	0	122	1,118
34,500	34,550	0	0	686	0	114	1,107
34,550	34,600	0	0	676	0	106	1,097
34,600	34,650	0	0	665	0	98	1,086
34,650	34,700	0	0	655	0	90	1,076
34,700	34,750	0	0	644	0	82	1,065
34,750	34,800	0	0	634	0	74	1,055
34,800	34,850	0	0	623	0	66	1,044
34,850	34,900	0	0	612	0	58	1,034
34,900	34,950	0	0	602	0	51	1,023
34,950	35,000	0	0	591	0	43	1,013
35,000	35,050	0	0	581	0	35	1,002
35,050	35,100	0	0	570	0	27	992
35,100	35,150	0	0	560	0	19	981
35,150	35,200	0	0	549	0	11	970
35,200	35,250	0	0	539	0	*	960
35,250	35,300	0	0	528	0	0	949
35,300	35,350	0	0	518	0	0	939
35,350	35,400	0	0	507	0	0	928
35,400	35,450	0	0	497	0	0	918
35,450	35,500	0	0	486	0	0	907
35,500	35,550	0	0	476	0	0	897
35,550	35,600	0	0	465	0	0	886
35,600	35,650	0	0	455	0	0	876
35,650	35,700	0	0	444	0	0	865
35,700	35,750	0	0	433	0	0	855
35,750	35,800	0	0	423	0	0	844
35,800	35,850	0	0	412	0	0	834
35,850	35,900	0	0	402	0	0	823
35,900	35,950	0	0	391	0	0	813
35,950	36,000	0	0	381	0	0	802
36,000	36,050	0	0	370	0	0	791
36,050	36,100	0	0	360	0	0	781
36,100	36,150	0	0	349	0	0	770
36,150	36,200	0	0	339	0	0	760
36,200	36,250	0	0	328	0	0	749
36,250	36,300	0	0	318	0	0	739
36,300	36,350	0	0	307	0	0	728
36,350	36,400	0	0	297	0	0	718
36,400	36,450	0	0	286	0	0	707
36,450	36,500	0	0	275	0	0	697
36,500	36,550	0	0	265	0	0	686
36,550	36,600	0	0	254	0	0	676
36,600	36,650	0	0	244	0	0	665
36,650	36,700	0	0	233	0	0	655
36,700	36,750	0	0	223	0	0	644
36,750	36,800	0	0	212	0	0	634
36,800	36,850	0	0	202	0	0	623
36,850	36,900	0	0	191	0	0	612
36,900	36,950	0	0	181	0	0	602
36,950	37,000	0	0	170	0	0	591
37,000	37,050	0	0	160	0	0	581
37,050	37,100	0	0	149	0	0	570
37,100	37,150	0	0	139	0	0	560
37,150	37,200	0	0	128	0	0	549
37,200	37,250	0	0	118	0	0	539
37,250	37,300	0	0	107	0	0	528
37,300	37,350	0	0	96	0	0	518
37,350	37,400	0	0	86	0	0	507
37,400	37,450	0	0	75	0	0	497
37,450	37,500	0	0	65	0	0	486
37,500	37,550	0	0	54	0	0	476
37,550	37,600	0	0	44	0	0	465
37,600	37,650	0	0	33	0	0	455
37,650	37,700	0	0	23	0	0	444
37,700	37,750	0	0	12	0	0	433
37,750	37,800	0	0	**	0	0	423
37,800	37,850	0	0	0	0	0	412
37,850	37,900	0	0	0	0	0	402
37,900	37,950	0	0	0	0	0	391
37,950	38,000	0	0	0	0	0	381

*If the amount you are looking up from the worksheet is at least $33,200 ($35,200 if married filing jointly) but less than $33,241 ($35,241 if married filing jointly), your credit is $3. Otherwise, you cannot take the credit.

**If the amount you are looking up from the worksheet is at least $37,750 but less than $37,783, your credit is $4. Otherwise, you cannot take the credit.

2007 Earned Income Credit (EIC) Table–*Continued*   (**Caution.** This is **not** a tax table.)

If the amount you are looking up from the worksheet is–		Single, head of household, or qualifying widow(er) and you have–			Married filing jointly and you have–		
At least	But less than	No children	One child	Two children	No children	One child	Two children
		Your credit is–			Your credit is–		
38,000	38,050	0	0	0	0	0	370
38,050	38,100	0	0	0	0	0	360
38,100	38,150	0	0	0	0	0	349
38,150	38,200	0	0	0	0	0	339
38,200	38,250	0	0	0	0	0	328
38,250	38,300	0	0	0	0	0	318
38,300	38,350	0	0	0	0	0	307
38,350	38,400	0	0	0	0	0	297
38,400	38,450	0	0	0	0	0	286
38,450	38,500	0	0	0	0	0	275
38,500	38,550	0	0	0	0	0	265
38,550	38,600	0	0	0	0	0	254
38,600	38,650	0	0	0	0	0	244
38,650	38,700	0	0	0	0	0	233
38,700	38,750	0	0	0	0	0	223
38,750	38,800	0	0	0	0	0	212
38,800	38,850	0	0	0	0	0	202
38,850	38,900	0	0	0	0	0	191
38,900	38,950	0	0	0	0	0	181
38,950	39,000	0	0	0	0	0	170

If the amount you are looking up from the worksheet is–		Single, head of household, or qualifying widow(er) and you have–			Married filing jointly and you have–		
At least	But less than	No children	One child	Two children	No children	One child	Two children
		Your credit is–			Your credit is–		
39,000	39,050	0	0	0	0	0	160
39,050	39,100	0	0	0	0	0	149
39,100	39,150	0	0	0	0	0	139
39,150	39,200	0	0	0	0	0	128
39,200	39,250	0	0	0	0	0	118
39,250	39,300	0	0	0	0	0	107
39,300	39,350	0	0	0	0	0	96
39,350	39,400	0	0	0	0	0	86
39,400	39,450	0	0	0	0	0	75
39,450	39,500	0	0	0	0	0	65
39,500	39,550	0	0	0	0	0	54
39,550	39,600	0	0	0	0	0	44
39,600	39,650	0	0	0	0	0	33
39,650	39,700	0	0	0	0	0	23
39,700	39,750	0	0	0	0	0	12
39,750	39,783	0	0	0	0	0	4

¶ 1112   Corporate income tax rates.

The rates for domestic corporations (other than qualified personal service corporations) are: (Code Sec. 11(b))[1]

Taxable income over—	But not over—	The tax is:	Of the amount over—
0	$ 50,000	15%	0
$ 50,000	75,000	$ 7,500 + 25%	$ 50,000
75,000	100,000	13,750 + 34%	75,000
100,000	335,000	22,250 + 39%	100,000
335,000	10,000,000	113,900 + 34%	335,000
10,000,000	15,000,000	3,400,000 + 35%	10,000,000
15,000,000	18,333,333	5,150,000 + 38%	15,000,000
18,333,333	—	35%	0

A qualified personal service corporation (as defined in Code Sec. 448(d)(2)) is taxed at a flat 35% of its taxable income. (Code Sec. 11(b)(2))[2]

Special taxes or rates on corporations include the alternative minimum tax, see ¶3200 *et seq.*; the accumulated earnings tax, see ¶3316 ; and the personal holding company tax, see ¶3324.

For tax rates on foreign corporations, see ¶4644 *et seq.*

¶ 1113   Gift and estate tax rates (unified rate schedule).

The estate tax is imposed on the decedent's taxable estate (gross estate less deductions). For credits against the estate tax, see ¶5029 *et seq.* The gift tax is based on the cumulative value of current and prior gifts (after a specified exclusion) after specified deductions, see ¶5037 *et seq.* (Code Sec. 2001, Code Sec. 2501)[3]

For individuals dying and gifts made in 2007, the unified rate schedule is as follows:

Unified Rate Schedule

(A)		(B)	(C) Tax on amount in Column A*	(D) Tax rate on excess over amounts in Column A*
Amount subject to tentative tax				
exceeding		but not exceeding		Percent
$ —		$ 10,000	$ —	18
10,000		20,000	1,800	20
20,000		40,000	3,800	22
40,000		60,000	8,200	24
60,000		80,000	13,000	26
80,000		100,000	18,200	28
100,000		150,000	23,800	30
150,000		250,000	38,800	32
250,000		500,000	70,800	34
500,000		750,000	155,800	37

---

1. ¶D-1003; ¶114.01; TD ¶600,503
2. ¶D-1006; ¶114.02; TD ¶600,901

3. ¶s Q-8003 *et seq.*, R-7000 *et seq.*; ¶20,014 *et seq.*, ¶25,024 *et seq.* (Estate & Gift); TD ¶s 751,000, 744,002

750,000	1,000,000	248,300	39
1,000,000	1,250,000	345,800	41
1,250,000	1,500,000	448,300	43
1,500,000	—	555,800	45

* Before credits.

The top estate and gift tax rate (and the GST tax rate) remains at 45% through 2009. The top gift tax rate for gifts made in 2010 will be 35%. For estate tax and GST tax repeal after 2009, see ¶5000.

For the estate tax on nonincome distributions from a qualified domestic trust for a surviving spouse who isn't a U.S. citizen, see ¶5025.

For the unified credit against estate tax, see ¶5029. For the credit against estate tax imposed on estates of nonresident aliens, see ¶5036.

For post-2010 sunset provisions, see ¶1114.

¶ 1114 Post-2010 sunset provisions.

The provisions of the Economic Growth and Tax Relief Reconciliation Act of 2001 (PL 107-16), other than those made permanent or extended by subsequent legislation, sunset and won't apply to tax or limitation years beginning after 2010. In the case of Title V of PL 107-16, relating to estate, gift and generation skipping transfer taxes, the provisions of PL 107-16 sunset and won't apply to estates of decedents dying, gifts made, or generation skipping transfers, after 2010. (Sec. 901(a) of PL 107-16) The Internal Revenue Code of '86 will be applied and administered to tax or limitation years beginning after 2010, and to estates of decedents dying, gifts made, or generation skipping transfers, after 2010 as if the provisions of, and amendments made by, PL 107-16 had never been enacted. (Sec. 901(b) of PL 107-16)

observation: Thus, upon sunset of PL 107-16, the Code would revert to its status before the enactment of PL 107-16, except for those provisions made permanent or extended by subsequent legislation. For example, the tax rates for individuals and estates and trusts would revert to their pre-2001 Act levels (e.g., the top tax rate would be 39.6%, and for individuals the 10% rate would disappear) and the repeal of the estate tax (see ¶5000) and generation skipping transfer tax (see ¶5055) would be effective only in 2010, i.e., for just one year.

observation: The Pension Protection Act of 2006 (PL 109-280) repealed the sunset provisions of PL 107-16 as they relate to pension and IRA provisions and qualified tuition plans. Other sunset provisions in PL 107-16 may be substantially changed or repealed before they go into effect.

¶ 1115 Excise tax rates (nonpenalty).

Here are selected "nonpenalty" excise tax rates.[4] For penalty-type excise taxes, see the entries under "Excise taxes" in the Topic Index.

Retail excise taxes

Trucks, trailers, etc.

- auto truck chassis and bodies (for vehicles weighing more than 33,000 lbs),   12% of first retail sale amount. Tax scheduled to expire after 9/30/2011.

---

4. ¶s W-3100 *et seq.*, W-1500 *et seq.*, W-2000 *et seq.*; ¶s 40,009.05   *et seq.*, 40,609 *et seq.* (Excise)

- truck trailer and semi-trailer chassis and bodies (for vehicles weighing more than 26,000 lbs)

- tractors used chiefly for highway transportation, in combination with a trailer or semi-trailer (for tractors weighing more than 19,500 lbs and in combination with trailer or semi-trailer weighing more than 33,000 lbs)

- accessories sold with one of the above or installed within 6 months after one of the above is placed in service

Transportation fuel taxes

Gasoline other than aviation gasoline; gasohol	Through 9/30/2011, on removal at terminal: 18.4¢ per gal. After 9/30/2011: 4.3¢ per gal.
Aviation gasoline [1]	Through 9/30/2007, on removal at terminal: 19.4¢ per gal. 10/1/2007-9/30/2011, 4.4¢ per gal. After 9/30/2011: 4.3¢ per gal.
Diesel fuel[2]; diesohol	Through 9/30/2011, on removal at terminal or retail sale: 24.4¢ per gal. After 9/30/2011: 4.3¢ per gal.
• Diesel-water fuel emulsion	Through 9/30/2011, on removal at terminal: 19.8¢ per gal. After 9/30/2011, see diesel fuel rate above
• Dyed diesel fuel, other than for export	Through 9/30/2011, on removal at terminal or retail sale: .1¢ per gal.
Kerosene	Through 9/30/2011, on removal at terminal or retail sale, generally: 24.4¢ per gal. After 9/30/2011: 4.3¢ per gal.
• Noncommercial aviation use —on removal directly into noncommercial aircraft's fuel tank[1]	Through 9/30/2007: 21.9¢ per gal. 10/1/2007-9/30/2011: 4.4¢ per gal. After 9/30/2011: 4.3¢ per gal.
• Commercial aviation use —on removal directly into commercial aircraft's fuel tank	Through 9/30/2011: 4.4¢ per gal. After 9/30/2011: 4.3¢ per gal.
• Retail sale for aviation use (where fuel not previously taxed)	Through 9/30/2011, for noncommercial aviation: 21.9¢ per gal.; for commercial aviation: 4.4¢ per gal. After 9/30/2011: 21.8¢ per gal. and 4.3¢ per gal., respectively
• Dyed kerosene, other than for export	Through 9/30/2011, on removal at terminal or retail sale: .1¢ per gal.
Alternative fuels	
• Special motor fuels (other than LPG and LNG)	Through 9/30/2011, on retail sale or use, for motor vehicle or motorboat use: 18.4¢ per gal. After 9/30/2011: 4.3¢ per gal.
• Liquefied petroleum gas (LPG) (e.g., propane, butane)	18.3¢ per gal.

• Liquefied natural gas (LNG)	24.3¢ per gal.
• Liquid fuel derived from biomass (other than ethanol or methanol) derived from coal, liquid hydrocarbons derived from biomass	Through 9/30/2011: 24.4¢ per gal. After 9/30/2011: 24.3¢ per gal.
• Partially exempt ethanol and methanol	Through 9/30/2011, for retail sale or use, of: partially exempt ethanol, 11.4¢ per gal.; partially exempt methanol, 9.25¢ per gal. After 9/30/2011, for partially exempt ethanol, 4.3¢ per gal.; for partially exempt methanol, 2.15¢ per gal.
Compressed natural gas (CNG)	18.3¢ per energy equivalent of a gal. of gasoline
Fuel used in commercial transportation on inland waterways	Through 9/30/2011, 20.1¢ per gal. After 9/30/2011, 20¢ per gal.

[1] The rates reflected are those in effect as of Oct 1, 2007. However, proposed legislation would extend the pre-Oct. 1, 2007 rates through Dec. 31, 2007, and other proposed legislation would thereafter increase the rates. Check http://ria.thomson.com/federaltaxhandbook for legislative developments.

[2] Special rates apply to diesel fuel used in certain buses and trains.

Selected Manufacturers excise taxes

Coal (except lignite)	
• From underground mines	Lower of $1.10 per ton or 4.4% of selling price
• From surface mines	Lower of 55¢ per ton or 4.4% of selling price
Tires (of type used in highway vehicles, wholly or in part made of rubber)	9.45¢ (4.725¢ for biasply or super single tires) for each 10 lbs. the tire's maximum rated load capacity exceeds 3,500 lbs. Tax scheduled to expire after 9/30/2011.
Sport fishing equipment	10% of mfrs. price of specified sport fishing equipment (up to max. of $10 on fishing rods and poles); 3% for electric outboard motors and fishing tackle boxes

Gas guzzling passenger autos, as follows:

If the fuel economy of the model type in which the automobile falls is:	*The tax is:*
At least 22.5	0
At least 21.5 but less than 22.5	$1,000
At least 20.5 but less than 21.5	1,300
At least 19.5 but less than 20.5	1,700
At least 18.5 but less than 19.5	2,100
At least 17.5 but less than 18.5	2,600
At least 16.5 but less than 17.5	3,000
At least 15.5 but less than 16.5	3,700
At least 14.5 but less than 15.5	4,500
At least 13.5 but less than 14.5	5,400
At least 12.5 but less than 13.5	6,400
Less than 12.5	7,700

¶ 1116 Applicable Federal Rates.

The IRS tables below show the Applicable one-month Federal Rates (AFRs). The tables provide short-term (obligations not exceeding three years), mid-term (over three years but not over nine years) and long-term (over nine years) rates (in percentages) based on annual, semiannual, quarterly and monthly compounding assumptions.[5]

Applicable Federal Rate	Annual	Semiannual	Quarterly	Monthly
November 2007				
Short-Term				
AFR	4.11%	4.07%	4.05%	4.04%
110% AFR	4.53%	4.48%	4.46%	4.44%
120% AFR	4.94%	4.88%	4.85%	4.83%
130% AFR	5.36%	5.29%	5.26%	5.23%
Mid-Term				
AFR	4.39%	4.34%	4.32%	4.30%
110% AFR	4.83%	4.77%	4.74%	4.72%
120% AFR	5.28%	5.21%	5.18%	5.15%
130% AFR	5.72%	5.64%	5.60%	5.57%
150% AFR	6.62%	6.51%	6.46%	6.42%
175% AFR	7.74%	7.60%	7.53%	7.48%
Long-Term				
AFR	4.89%	4.83%	4.80%	4.78%
110% AFR	5.38%	5.31%	5.28%	5.25%
120% AFR	5.88%	5.80%	5.76%	5.73%
130% AFR	6.38%	6.28%	6.23%	6.20%
October 2007				
Short-Term				
AFR	4.19%	4.15%	4.13%	4.11%
110% AFR	4.62%	4.57%	4.54%	4.53%
120% AFR	5.04%	4.98%	4.95%	4.93%
130% AFR	5.47%	5.40%	5.36%	5.34%
Mid-Term				
AFR	4.35%	4.30%	4.28%	4.26%
110% AFR	4.79%	4.73%	4.70%	4.68%
120% AFR	5.23%	5.16%	5.13%	5.11%
130% AFR	5.67%	5.59%	5.55%	5.53%
150% AFR	6.55%	6.45%	6.40%	6.36%
175% AFR	7.67%	7.53%	7.46%	7.41%
Long-Term				
AFR	4.88%	4.82%	4.79%	4.77%
110% AFR	5.37%	5.30%	5.27%	5.24%
120% AFR	5.86%	5.78%	5.74%	5.71%
130% AFR	6.37%	6.27%	6.22%	6.19%
September 2007				
Short-Term				
AFR	4.82%	4.76%	4.73%	4.71%
110% AFR	5.31%	5.24%	5.21%	5.18%
120% AFR	5.79%	5.71%	5.67%	5.64%
130% AFR	6.29%	6.19%	6.14%	6.11%
Mid-Term				
AFR	4.79%	4.73%	4.70%	4.68%
110% AFR	5.27%	5.20%	5.17%	5.14%
120% AFR	5.76%	5.68%	5.64%	5.61%
130% AFR	6.24%	6.15%	6.10%	6.07%
150% AFR	7.23%	7.10%	7.04%	7.00%
175% AFR	8.45%	8.28%	8.20%	8.14%

Applicable Federal Rate	Annual	Semiannual	Quarterly	Monthly
Long-Term				
AFR	5.09%	5.03%	5.00%	4.98%
110% AFR	5.61%	5.53%	5.49%	5.47%
120% AFR	6.13%	6.04%	6.00%	5.97%
130% AFR	6.65%	6.54%	6.49%	6.45%
August 2007				
Short-Term				
AFR	5.00%	4.94%	4.91%	4.89%
110% AFR	5.50%	5.43%	5.39%	5.37%
120% AFR	6.02%	5.93%	5.89%	5.86%
130% AFR	6.52%	6.42%	6.37%	6.34%
Mid-Term				
AFR	5.09%	5.03%	5.00%	4.98%
110% AFR	5.61%	5.53%	5.49%	5.47%
120% AFR	6.13%	6.04%	6.00%	5.97%
130% AFR	6.65%	6.54%	6.49%	6.45%
150% AFR	7.69%	7.55%	7.48%	7.43%
175% AFR	8.99%	8.80%	8.71%	8.64%
Long-Term				
AFR	5.31%	5.24%	5.21%	5.18%
110% AFR	5.84%	5.76%	5.72%	5.69%
120% AFR	6.39%	6.29%	6.24%	6.21%
130% AFR	6.93%	6.81%	6.75%	6.72%
July 2007				
Short-Term				
AFR	4.97%	4.91%	4.88%	4.86%
110% AFR	5.47%	5.40%	5.36%	5.34%
120% AFR	5.98%	5.89%	5.85%	5.82%
130% AFR	6.48%	6.38%	6.33%	6.30%
Mid-Term				
AFR	4.95%	4.89%	4.86%	4.84%
110% AFR	5.45%	5.38%	5.34%	5.32%
120% AFR	5.96%	5.87%	5.83%	5.80%
130% AFR	6.46%	6.36%	6.31%	6.28%
150% AFR	7.47%	7.34%	7.27%	7.23%
175% AFR	8.74%	8.56%	8.47%	8.41%
Long-Term				
AFR	5.15%	5.09%	5.06%	5.04%
110% AFR	5.68%	5.60%	5.56%	5.54%
120% AFR	6.20%	6.11%	6.06%	6.03%
130% AFR	6.73%	6.62%	6.57%	6.53%
June 2007				
Short-Term				
AFR	4.84%	4.78%	4.75%	4.73%
110% AFR	5.33%	5.26%	5.23%	5.20%
120% AFR	5.82%	5.74%	5.70%	5.67%
130% AFR	6.31%	6.21%	6.16%	6.13%
Mid-Term				
AFR	4.64%	4.59%	4.56%	4.55%
110% AFR	5.11%	5.05%	5.02%	5.00%
120% AFR	5.59%	5.51%	5.47%	5.45%

5. ¶J-4192; ¶12,714.01; TD ¶153,030

Applicable Federal Rate	Annual	Semiannual	Quarterly	Monthly
130% AFR	6.06%	5.97%	5.93%	5.90%
150% AFR	7.01%	6.89%	6.83%	6.79%
175% AFR	8.19%	8.03%	7.95%	7.90%
Long-Term				
AFR	4.91%	4.85%	4.82%	4.80%
110% AFR	5.41%	5.34%	5.30%	5.28%
120% AFR	5.90%	5.82%	5.78%	5.75%
130% AFR	6.41%	6.31%	6.26%	6.23%

May 2007
Short-Term

	Annual	Semiannual	Quarterly	Monthly
AFR	4.85%	4.79%	4.76%	4.74%
110% AFR	5.34%	5.27%	5.24%	5.21%
120% AFR	5.83%	5.75%	5.71%	5.68%
130% AFR	6.33%	6.23%	6.18%	6.15%
Mid-Term				
AFR	4.62%	4.57%	4.54%	4.53%
110% AFR	5.09%	5.03%	5.00%	4.98%
120% AFR	5.56%	5.48%	5.44%	5.42%
130% AFR	6.03%	5.94%	5.90%	5.87%
150% AFR	6.98%	6.86%	6.80%	6.76%
175% AFR	8.16%	8.00%	7.92%	7.87%
Long-Term				
AFR	4.90%	4.84%	4.81%	4.79%
110% AFR	5.39%	5.32%	5.29%	5.26%
120% AFR	5.89%	5.81%	5.77%	5.74%
130% AFR	6.39%	6.29%	6.24%	6.21%

April 2007
Short-Term

	Annual	Semiannual	Quarterly	Monthly
AFR	4.90%	4.84%	4.81%	4.79%
110% AFR	5.39%	5.32%	5.29%	5.26%
120% AFR	5.89%	5.81%	5.77%	5.74%
130% AFR	6.39%	6.29%	6.24%	6.21%
Mid-Term				
AFR	4.61%	4.56%	4.53%	4.52%
110% AFR	5.08%	5.02%	4.99%	4.97%
120% AFR	5.54%	5.47%	5.43%	5.41%
130% AFR	6.02%	5.93%	5.89%	5.86%
150% AFR	6.96%	6.84%	6.78%	6.74%
175% AFR	8.14%	7.98%	7.90%	7.85%
Long-Term				
AFR	4.81%	4.75%	4.72%	4.70%
110% AFR	5.30%	5.23%	5.20%	5.17%
120% AFR	5.78%	5.70%	5.66%	5.63%
130% AFR	6.28%	6.18%	6.13%	6.10%

March 2007
Short-Term

	Annual	Semiannual	Quarterly	Monthly
AFR	5.06%	5.00%	4.97%	4.95%
110% AFR	5.58%	5.50%	5.46%	5.44%
120% AFR	6.09%	6.00%	5.96%	5.93%
130% AFR	6.61%	6.50%	6.45%	6.41%
Mid-Term				
AFR	4.86%	4.80%	4.77%	4.75%
110% AFR	5.35%	5.28%	5.25%	5.22%
120% AFR	5.84%	5.76%	5.72%	5.69%
130% AFR	6.34%	6.24%	6.19%	6.16%
150% AFR	7.33%	7.20%	7.14%	7.09%
175% AFR	8.58%	8.40%	8.31%	8.26%
Long-Term				
AFR	5.01%	4.95%	4.92%	4.90%
110% AFR	5.52%	5.45%	5.41%	5.39%

Applicable Federal Rate	Annual	Semiannual	Quarterly	Monthly
120% AFR	6.03%	5.94%	5.90%	5.87%
130% AFR	6.54%	6.44%	6.39%	6.36%

February 2007
Short-Term

	Annual	Semiannual	Quarterly	Monthly
AFR	4.93%	4.87%	4.84%	4.82%
110% AFR	5.43%	5.36%	5.32%	5.30%
120% AFR	5.93%	5.84%	5.80%	5.77%
130% AFR	6.43%	6.33%	6.28%	6.25%
Mid-Term				
AFR	4.69%	4.64%	4.61%	4.60%
110% AFR	5.17%	5.10%	5.07%	5.05%
120% AFR	5.65%	5.57%	5.53%	5.51%
130% AFR	6.12%	6.03%	5.99%	5.96%
150% AFR	7.08%	6.96%	6.90%	6.86%
175% AFR	8.28%	8.12%	8.04%	7.99%
Long-Term				
AFR	4.86%	4.80%	4.77%	4.75%
110% AFR	5.35%	5.28%	5.25%	5.22%
120% AFR	5.84%	5.76%	5.72%	5.69%
130% AFR	6.34%	6.24%	6.19%	6.16%

January 2007
Short-Term

	Annual	Semiannual	Quarterly	Monthly
AFR	4.88%	4.82%	4.79%	4.77%
110% AFR	5.37%	5.30%	5.27%	5.24%
120% AFR	5.86%	5.78%	5.74%	5.71%
130% AFR	6.37%	6.27%	6.22%	6.19%
Mid-Term				
AFR	4.58%	4.53%	4.50%	4.49%
110% AFR	5.04%	4.98%	4.95%	4.93%
120% AFR	5.51%	5.44%	5.40%	5.38%
130% AFR	5.98%	5.89%	5.85%	5.82%
150% AFR	6.92%	6.80%	6.74%	6.71%
175% AFR	8.09%	7.93%	7.85%	7.80%
Long-Term				
AFR	4.73%	4.68%	4.65%	4.64%
110% AFR	5.22%	5.15%	5.12%	5.10%
120% AFR	5.70%	5.62%	5.58%	5.56%
130% AFR	6.17%	6.08%	6.03%	6.00%

December 2006
Short-Term

	Annual	Semiannual	Quarterly	Monthly
AFR	4.97%	4.91%	4.88%	4.86%
110% AFR	5.47%	5.40%	5.36%	5.34%
120% AFR	5.98%	5.89%	5.85%	5.82%
130% AFR	6.48%	6.38%	6.33%	6.30%
Mid-Term				
AFR	4.73%	4.68%	4.65%	4.64%
110% AFR	5.22%	5.15%	5.12%	5.10%
120% AFR	5.70%	5.62%	5.58%	5.56%
130% AFR	6.17%	6.08%	6.03%	6.00%
150% AFR	7.14%	7.02%	6.96%	6.92%
175% AFR	8.36%	8.19%	8.11%	8.05%
Long-Term				
AFR	4.90%	4.84%	4.81%	4.79%
110% AFR	5.39%	5.32%	5.29%	5.26%
120% AFR	5.89%	5.81%	5.77%	5.74%
130% AFR	6.39%	6.29%	6.24%	6.21%

¶ 1117   MACRS Tables. ■

Here are MACRS depreciation (cost recovery) tables.

The tables reproduced are the MACRS tables (general depreciation as well as alternative depreciation system (ADS)), plus the listed property tables used to determine income inclusion amounts by lessees of listed property other than automobiles. The depreciation amounts for automobiles under the luxury auto restrictions are carried at ¶1956; the income inclusion amounts for lessees of automobiles carried at ¶1118 are explained at ¶1961 *et seq.*

Under the general depreciation system (GDS) of MACRS, the table rates are based on: (1) the 200% declining balance method for 3-, 5-, 7-, and 10-year personal property; (2) the 150% declining balance method for 15-, and 20-year personal property; and (3) the straight-line method for residential and nonresidential realty. Under the alternative depreciation system (ADS) of MACRS, the table rates for personal and real property are based on the straight-line method. The use of the tables is discussed in ¶1911. (IRS alternative minimum tax tables and the tables for straight line depreciation under the midquarter convention are not reproduced in this Handbook. For those tables, see the Appendix to Federal Tax Coordinator 2d Chapter L-7400.)

Table 1

General Depreciation System
Applicable Depreciation Method: 200 or 150 Percent
Declining Balance Switching to Straight Line
Applicable Recovery Periods: 3, 5, 7, 10, 15, 20 years
Applicable Convention: Half-year

If the Recovery Year is:	and the Recovery Period is:					
	3-year	5-year	7-year	10-year	15-year	20-year
			the Depreciation Rate is:			
1	33.33	20.00	14.29	10.00	5.00	3.750
2	44.45	32.00	24.49	18.00	9.50	7.219
3	14.81	19.20	17.49	14.40	8.55	6.677
4	7.41	11.52	12.49	11.52	7.70	6.177
5		11.52	8.93	9.22	6.93	5.713
6		5.76	8.92	7.37	6.23	5.285
7			8.93	6.55	5.90	4.888
8			4.46	6.55	5.90	4.522
9				6.56	5.91	4.462
10				6.55	5.90	4.461
11				3.28	5.91	4.462
12					5.90	4.461
13					5.91	4.462
14					5.90	4.461
15					5.91	4.462
16					2.95	4.461
17						4.462
18						4.461
19						4.462
20						4.461
21						2.231

Table 2

General Depreciation System
Applicable Depreciation Method: 200 or 150 Percent
Declining Balance Switching to Straight Line
Applicable Recovery Periods: 3, 5, 7, 10, 15, 20 years
Applicable Convention: Mid-quarter
(property placed in service in first quarter)

If the Recovery Year is:	and the Recovery Period is:					
	3-year	5-year	7-year	10-year	15-year	20-year
			the Depreciation Rate is:			
1	58.33	35.00	25.00	17.50	8.75	6.563
2	27.78	26.00	21.43	16.50	9.13	7.000
3	12.35	15.60	15.31	13.20	8.21	6.482
4	1.54	11.01	10.93	10.56	7.39	5.996
5		11.01	8.75	8.45	6.65	5.546
6		1.38	8.74	6.76	5.99	5.130
7			8.75	6.55	5.90	4.746
8			1.09	6.55	5.91	4.459
9				6.56	5.90	4.459
10				6.55	5.91	4.459
11				0.82	5.90	4.459
12					5.91	4.460
13					5.90	4.459
14					5.91	4.460
15					5.90	4.459
16					0.74	4.460
17						4.459
18						4.460
19						4.459
20						4.460
21						0.557

Table 3

General Depreciation System
Applicable Depreciation Method: 200 or 150 Percent
Declining Balance Switching to Straight Line
Applicable Recovery Periods: 3, 5, 7, 10, 15, 20 years
Applicable Convention: Mid-quarter
(property placed in service in second quarter)

If the Recovery Year is:	and the Recovery Period is:					
	3-year	5-year	7-year	10-year	15-year	20-year
			the Depreciation Rate is:			
1	41.67	25.00	17.85	12.50	6.25	4.688
2	38.89	30.00	23.47	17.50	9.38	7.148
3	14.14	18.00	16.76	14.00	8.44	6.612
4	5.30	11.37	11.97	11.20	7.59	6.116
5		11.37	8.87	8.96	6.83	5.658
6		4.26	8.87	7.17	6.15	5.233
7			8.87	6.55	5.91	4.841
8			3.33	6.55	5.90	4.478
9				6.56	5.91	4.463
10				6.55	5.90	4.463
11				2.46	5.91	4.463
12					5.90	4.463
13					5.91	4.463
14					5.90	4.463
15					5.91	4.462
16					2.21	4.463
17						4.462
18						4.463
19						4.462
20						4.463
21						1.673

Table 4

General Depreciation System
Applicable Depreciation Method: 200 or 150 Percent
Declining Balance Switching to Straight Line
Applicable Recovery Periods: 3, 5, 7, 10, 15, 20 years
Applicable Convention: Mid-quarter
(property placed in service in third quarter)

If the Recovery Year is:	and the Recovery Period is:					
	3-year	5-year	7-year	10-year	15-year	20-year
			the Depreciation Rate is:			
1	25.00	15.00	10.71	7.50	3.75	2.813
2	50.00	34.00	25.51	18.50	9.63	7.289
3	16.67	20.40	18.22	14.80	8.66	6.742
4	8.33	12.24	13.02	11.84	7.80	6.237
5		11.30	9.30	9.47	7.02	5.769
6		7.06	8.85	7.58	6.31	5.336
7			8.86	6.55	5.90	4.936
8			5.53	6.55	5.90	4.566
9				6.56	5.91	4.460
10				6.55	5.90	4.460
11				4.10	5.91	4.460
12					5.90	4.460
13					5.91	4.461
14					5.90	4.460
15					5.91	4.461
16					3.69	4.460
17						4.461
18						4.460
19						4.461
20						4.460
21						2.788

Table 5

General Depreciation System
Applicable Depreciation Method: 200 or 150 Percent
Declining Balance Switching to Straight Line
Applicable Recovery Periods: 3, 5, 7, 10, 15, 20 years
Applicable Convention: Mid-quarter
(property placed in service in fourth quarter)

If the Recovery Year is:	and the Recovery Period is:					
	3-year	5-year	7-year	10-year	15-year	20-year
			the Depreciation Rate is:			
1	8.33	5.00	3.57	2.50	1.25	0.938
2	61.11	38.00	27.55	19.50	9.88	7.430
3	20.37	22.80	19.68	15.60	8.89	6.872
4	10.19	13.68	14.06	12.48	8.00	6.357
5		10.94	10.04	9.98	7.20	5.880
6		9.58	8.73	7.99	6.48	5.439
7			8.73	6.55	5.90	5.031
8			7.64	6.55	5.90	4.654
9				6.56	5.90	4.458
10				6.55	5.91	4.458
11				5.74	5.90	4.458
12					5.91	4.458
13					5.90	4.458
14					5.91	4.458
15					5.90	4.458
16					5.17	4.458
17						4.458
18						4.459
19						4.458
20						4.459
21						3.901

Table 6

General Depreciation System
Applicable Depreciation Method: Straight Line
Applicable Recovery Period: 27.5 years
Applicable Convention: Mid-month

If the Recovery Year is:	And the Month in the First Recovery Year the Property is Placed in Service is:											
	1	2	3	4	5	6	7	8	9	10	11	12
						the Depreciation Rate is:						
1	3.485	3.182	2.879	2.576	2.273	1.970	1.667	1.364	1.061	0.758	0.455	0.152
2-9	3.636	3.636	3.636	3.636	3.636	3.636	3.636	3.636	3.636	3.636	3.636	3.636
10	3.637	3.637	3.637	3.637	3.637	3.637	3.636	3.636	3.636	3.636	3.636	3.636
11	3.636	3.636	3.636	3.636	3.636	3.636	3.637	3.637	3.637	3.637	3.637	3.637
12	3.637	3.637	3.637	3.637	3.637	3.637	3.636	3.636	3.636	3.636	3.636	3.636
13	3.636	3.636	3.636	3.636	3.636	3.636	3.637	3.637	3.637	3.637	3.637	3.637
14	3.637	3.637	3.637	3.637	3.637	3.637	3.636	3.636	3.636	3.636	3.636	3.636
15	3.636	3.636	3.636	3.636	3.636	3.636	3.637	3.637	3.637	3.637	3.637	3.637
16	3.637	3.637	3.637	3.637	3.637	3.637	3.636	3.636	3.636	3.636	3.636	3.636
17	3.636	3.636	3.636	3.636	3.636	3.636	3.637	3.637	3.637	3.637	3.637	3.637
18	3.637	3.637	3.637	3.637	3.637	3.637	3.636	3.636	3.636	3.636	3.636	3.636
19	3.636	3.636	3.636	3.636	3.636	3.636	3.637	3.637	3.637	3.637	3.637	3.637
20	3.637	3.637	3.637	3.637	3.637	3.637	3.636	3.636	3.636	3.636	3.636	3.636
21	3.636	3.636	3.636	3.636	3.636	3.636	3.637	3.637	3.637	3.637	3.637	3.637
22	3.637	3.637	3.637	3.637	3.637	3.637	3.636	3.636	3.636	3.636	3.636	3.636
23	3.636	3.636	3.636	3.636	3.636	3.636	3.637	3.637	3.637	3.637	3.637	3.637
24	3.637	3.637	3.637	3.637	3.637	3.637	3.636	3.636	3.636	3.636	3.636	3.636
25	3.636	3.636	3.636	3.636	3.636	3.636	3.637	3.637	3.637	3.637	3.637	3.637
26	3.637	3.637	3.637	3.637	3.637	3.637	3.636	3.636	3.636	3.636	3.636	3.636
27	3.636	3.636	3.636	3.636	3.636	3.636	3.637	3.637	3.637	3.637	3.637	3.637
28	1.970	2.273	2.576	2.879	3.182	3.485	3.636	3.636	3.636	3.636	3.636	3.636
29	0.000	0.000	0.000	0.000	0.000	0.000	0.152	0.455	0.758	1.061	1.364	1.667

Table 7

General Depreciation System
Applicable Depreciation Method: Straight Line
Applicable Recovery Period: 31.5 years
Applicable Convention: Mid-month

If the Recovery Year is:	And the Month in the First Recovery Year the Property is Placed in Service is:											
	1	2	3	4	5	6	7	8	9	10	11	12
	the Depreciation Rate is:											
1	3.042	2.778	2.513	2.249	1.984	1.720	1.455	1.190	0.926	0.661	0.397	0.132
2-7	3.175	3.175	3.175	3.175	3.175	3.175	3.175	3.175	3.175	3.175	3.175	3.175
8	3.175	3.174	3.175	3.174	3.175	3.174	3.175	3.175	3.175	3.175	3.175	3.175
9	3.174	3.175	3.174	3.175	3.174	3.175	3.174	3.175	3.174	3.175	3.174	3.175
10	3.175	3.174	3.175	3.174	3.175	3.174	3.175	3.174	3.175	3.174	3.175	3.174
11	3.174	3.175	3.174	3.175	3.174	3.175	3.174	3.175	3.174	3.175	3.174	3.175
12	3.175	3.174	3.175	3.174	3.175	3.174	3.175	3.174	3.175	3.174	3.175	3.174
13	3.174	3.175	3.174	3.175	3.174	3.175	3.174	3.175	3.174	3.175	3.174	3.175
14	3.175	3.174	3.175	3.174	3.175	3.174	3.175	3.174	3.175	3.174	3.175	3.174
15	3.174	3.175	3.174	3.175	3.174	3.175	3.174	3.175	3.174	3.175	3.174	3.175
16	3.175	3.174	3.175	3.174	3.175	3.174	3.175	3.174	3.175	3.174	3.175	3.174
17	3.174	3.175	3.174	3.175	3.174	3.175	3.174	3.175	3.174	3.175	3.174	3.175
18	3.175	3.174	3.175	3.174	3.175	3.174	3.175	3.174	3.175	3.174	3.175	3.174
19	3.174	3.175	3.174	3.175	3.174	3.175	3.174	3.175	3.174	3.175	3.174	3.175
20	3.175	3.174	3.175	3.174	3.175	3.174	3.175	3.174	3.175	3.174	3.175	3.174
21	3.174	3.175	3.174	3.175	3.174	3.175	3.174	3.175	3.174	3.175	3.174	3.175
22	3.175	3.174	3.175	3.174	3.175	3.174	3.175	3.174	3.175	3.174	3.175	3.174
23	3.174	3.175	3.174	3.175	3.174	3.175	3.174	3.175	3.174	3.175	3.174	3.175
24	3.175	3.174	3.175	3.174	3.175	3.174	3.175	3.174	3.175	3.174	3.175	3.174
25	3.174	3.175	3.174	3.175	3.174	3.175	3.174	3.175	3.174	3.175	3.174	3.175
26	3.175	3.174	3.175	3.174	3.175	3.174	3.175	3.174	3.175	3.174	3.175	3.174
27	3.174	3.175	3.174	3.175	3.174	3.175	3.174	3.175	3.174	3.175	3.174	3.175
28	3.175	3.174	3.175	3.174	3.175	3.174	3.175	3.174	3.175	3.174	3.175	3.174
29	3.174	3.175	3.174	3.175	3.174	3.175	3.174	3.175	3.174	3.175	3.174	3.175
30	3.175	3.174	3.175	3.174	3.175	3.174	3.175	3.174	3.175	3.174	3.175	3.174
31	3.174	3.175	3.174	3.175	3.174	3.175	3.174	3.175	3.174	3.175	3.174	3.175
32	1.720	1.984	2.249	2.513	2.778	3.042	3.175	3.174	3.175	3.174	3.175	3.174
33	0.000	0.000	0.000	0.000	0.000	0.000	0.132	0.397	0.661	0.926	1.190	1.455

Table 7a

General Depreciation System
Applicable Depreciation Method: Straight Line
Applicable Recovery Period: 39 years
Applicable Convention: Mid-month

Year	Month property placed in service											
	1	2	3	4	5	6	7	8	9	10	11	12
1	2.461%	2.247%	2.033%	1.819%	1.605%	1.391%	1.177%	0.963%	0.749%	0.535%	0.321%	0.107%
2-39	2.564	2.564	2.564	2.564	2.564	2.564	2.564	2.564	2.564	2.564	2.564	2.564
40	0.107	0.321	0.535	0.749	0.963	1.177	1.391	1.605	1.819	2.033	2.247	2.461

Table 8

General and Alternative Depreciation Systems
Applicable Depreciation Method: Straight Line
Applicable Recovery Periods: 2.5-50 years
Applicable Convention: Half-year

If the Recovery Year is:	and the Recovery Period is: the Depreciation Rate is:															
	2.5	3.0	3.5	4.0	4.5	5.0	5.5	6.0	6.5	7.0	7.5	8.0	8.5	9.0	9.5	10.0
1	20.00	16.67	14.29	12.50	11.11	10.00	9.09	8.33	7.69	7.14	6.67	6.25	5.88	5.56	5.26	5.00
2	40.00	33.33	28.57	25.00	22.22	20.00	18.18	16.67	15.39	14.29	13.33	12.50	11.77	11.11	10.53	10.00
3	40.00	33.33	28.57	25.00	22.22	20.00	18.18	16.67	15.38	14.29	13.33	12.50	11.76	11.11	10.53	10.00
4		16.67	28.57	25.00	22.23	20.00	18.18	16.67	15.39	14.29	13.33	12.50	11.77	11.11	10.53	10.00
5				12.50	22.22	20.00	18.19	16.66	15.38	14.29	13.34	12.50	11.76	11.11	10.52	10.00
6						10.00	18.18	16.67	15.39	14.28	13.33	12.50	11.77	11.11	10.53	10.00
7							8.33	15.38	14.29	13.34	12.50	11.76	11.11	10.52	10.00	
8								7.14	13.33	12.50	11.77	11.11	10.53	10.00		
9									6.25	11.76	11.11	10.52	10.00			
10										5.56	10.53	10.00				
11											5.00					

If the Recovery Year is:	and the Recovery Period is: the Depreciation Rate is:															
	10.5	11.0	11.5	12.0	12.5	13.0	13.5	14.0	14.5	15.0	15.5	16.0	16.5	17.0	17.5	18.0
1	4.76	4.55	4.35	4.17	4.00	3.85	3.70	3.57	3.45	3.33	3.23	3.13	3.03	2.94	2.86	2.78
2	9.52	9.09	8.70	8.33	8.00	7.69	7.41	7.14	6.90	6.67	6.45	6.25	6.06	5.88	5.71	5.56
3	9.52	9.09	8.70	8.33	8.00	7.69	7.41	7.14	6.90	6.67	6.45	6.25	6.06	5.88	5.71	5.56
4	9.53	9.09	8.69	8.33	8.00	7.69	7.41	7.14	6.90	6.67	6.45	6.25	6.06	5.88	5.71	5.55
5	9.52	9.09	8.70	8.33	8.00	7.69	7.41	7.14	6.90	6.67	6.45	6.25	6.06	5.88	5.72	5.56
6	9.53	9.09	8.69	8.33	8.00	7.69	7.41	7.14	6.89	6.67	6.45	6.25	6.06	5.88	5.71	5.55
7	9.52	9.09	8.70	8.34	8.00	7.69	7.41	7.14	6.90	6.67	6.45	6.25	6.06	5.88	5.72	5.56
8	9.53	9.09	8.69	8.33	8.00	7.69	7.41	7.15	6.89	6.66	6.45	6.25	6.06	5.88	5.71	5.55
9	9.52	9.09	8.70	8.34	8.00	7.69	7.41	7.14	6.90	6.67	6.45	6.25	6.06	5.88	5.72	5.56
10	9.53	9.09	8.69	8.33	8.00	7.70	7.40	7.15	6.89	6.66	6.45	6.25	6.06	5.88	5.71	5.55
11	9.52	9.09	8.70	8.34	8.00	7.69	7.41	7.14	6.90	6.67	6.45	6.25	6.06	5.89	5.72	5.56
12		4.55	8.69	8.33	8.00	7.70	7.40	7.15	6.89	6.66	6.45	6.25	6.06	5.88	5.71	5.55
13				4.17	8.00	7.69	7.41	7.14	6.90	6.67	6.45	6.25	6.06	5.89	5.72	5.56
14						3.85	7.40	7.15	6.89	6.66	6.46	6.25	6.06	5.88	5.71	5.55
15								3.57	6.90	6.67	6.45	6.25	6.06	5.89	5.72	5.56
16										3.33	6.46	6.25	6.06	5.88	5.71	5.55
17												3.12	6.07	5.89	5.72	5.56
18														2.94	5.71	5.55
19																2.78

Table 8
General and Alternative Depreciation Systems
Applicable Depreciation Method: Straight Line
Applicable Recovery Periods: 2.5-50 years
Applicable Convention: Half-year
(continued)

If the Recovery Year is:	18.5	19.0	19.5	20.0	20.5	21.0	21.5	22.0	22.5	23.0	23.5	24.0	24.5	25.0	25.5	26.0
							and the Recovery Period is: the Depreciation Rate is:									
1	2.70	2.63	2.56	2.500	2.439	2.381	2.326	2.273	2.222	2.174	2.128	2.083	2.041	2.000	1.961	1.923
2	5.41	5.26	5.13	5.000	4.878	4.762	4.651	4.545	4.444	4.348	4.255	4.167	4.082	4.000	3.922	3.846
3	5.41	5.26	5.13	5.000	4.878	4.762	4.651	4.545	4.444	4.348	4.255	4.167	4.082	4.000	3.922	3.846
4	5.41	5.26	5.13	5.000	4.878	4.762	4.651	4.545	4.445	4.348	4.255	4.167	4.082	4.000	3.922	3.846
5	5.40	5.26	5.13	5.000	4.878	4.762	4.651	4.546	4.444	4.348	4.255	4.167	4.082	4.000	3.922	3.846
6	5.41	5.26	5.13	5.000	4.878	4.762	4.651	4.545	4.445	4.348	4.255	4.167	4.082	4.000	3.921	3.846
7	5.40	5.26	5.13	5.000	4.878	4.762	4.651	4.546	4.444	4.348	4.255	4.167	4.082	4.000	3.922	3.846
8	5.41	5.26	5.13	5.000	4.878	4.762	4.651	4.545	4.445	4.348	4.255	4.167	4.082	4.000	3.921	3.846
9	5.40	5.27	5.13	5.000	4.878	4.762	4.651	4.546	4.444	4.348	4.255	4.167	4.081	4.000	3.922	3.846
10	5.41	5.26	5.13	5.000	4.878	4.762	4.651	4.545	4.445	4.348	4.255	4.167	4.082	4.000	3.921	3.846
11	5.40	5.27	5.13	5.000	4.878	4.762	4.651	4.546	4.444	4.348	4.256	4.166	4.081	4.000	3.922	3.846
12	5.41	5.26	5.13	5.000	4.878	4.762	4.651	4.545	4.445	4.348	4.255	4.167	4.082	4.000	3.921	3.846
13	5.40	5.27	5.13	5.000	4.878	4.762	4.651	4.546	4.444	4.348	4.256	4.166	4.081	4.000	3.922	3.846
14	5.41	5.26	5.13	5.000	4.878	4.762	4.651	4.545	4.445	4.348	4.255	4.167	4.082	4.000	3.921	3.846
15	5.40	5.27	5.13	5.000	4.878	4.762	4.651	4.546	4.444	4.348	4.256	4.166	4.081	4.000	3.922	3.846
16	5.41	5.26	5.12	5.000	4.878	4.762	4.651	4.545	4.445	4.348	4.255	4.167	4.082	4.000	3.921	3.846
17	5.40	5.27	5.13	5.000	4.878	4.762	4.652	4.546	4.444	4.347	4.256	4.166	4.081	4.000	3.922	3.846
18	5.41	5.26	5.12	5.000	4.878	4.762	4.651	4.545	4.445	4.348	4.255	4.167	4.082	4.000	3.921	3.846
19	5.40	5.27	5.13	5.000	4.878	4.761	4.652	4.546	4.444	4.347	4.256	4.166	4.081	4.000	3.922	3.846
20		2.63	5.12	5.000	4.879	4.762	4.651	4.545	4.445	4.348	4.255	4.167	4.082	4.000	3.921	3.847
21				2.500	4.878	4.761	4.652	4.546	4.444	4.347	4.256	4.166	4.081	4.000	3.922	3.846
22						2.381	4.651	4.545	4.445	4.348	4.255	4.167	4.082	4.000	3.921	3.847
23								2.273	4.444	4.347	4.256	4.166	4.081	4.000	3.922	3.846
24										2.174	4.255	4.167	4.082	4.000	3.921	3.847
25												2.083	4.081	4.000	3.922	3.846
26														2.000	3.921	3.847
27																1.923

If the Recovery Year is:	26.5	27.0	27.5	28.0	28.5	29.0	29.5	30.0	30.5	31.0	31.5	32.0	32.5	33.0	33.5	34.0
							and the Recovery Period is: the Depreciation Rate is:									
1	1.887	1.852	1.818	1.786	1.754	1.724	1.695	1.667	1.639	1.613	1.587	1.563	1.538	1.515	1.493	1.471
2-6	3.774	3.704	3.636	3.571	3.509	3.448	3.390	3.333	3.279	3.226	3.175	3.125	3.077	3.030	2.985	2.941
7	3.773	3.704	3.636	3.572	3.509	3.448	3.390	3.333	3.279	3.226	3.175	3.125	3.077	3.030	2.985	2.941
8	3.774	3.704	3.636	3.571	3.509	3.448	3.390	3.333	3.279	3.226	3.175	3.125	3.077	3.030	2.985	2.941
9	3.773	3.704	3.637	3.572	3.509	3.448	3.390	3.333	3.279	3.226	3.175	3.125	3.077	3.030	2.985	2.941
10	3.774	3.704	3.636	3.571	3.509	3.448	3.390	3.333	3.279	3.226	3.174	3.125	3.077	3.030	2.985	2.941
11	3.773	3.704	3.637	3.572	3.509	3.448	3.390	3.333	3.279	3.226	3.175	3.125	3.077	3.030	2.985	2.941
12	3.774	3.704	3.636	3.571	3.509	3.448	3.390	3.333	3.279	3.226	3.174	3.125	3.077	3.030	2.985	2.941
13	3.773	3.703	3.637	3.572	3.509	3.448	3.390	3.334	3.279	3.226	3.175	3.125	3.077	3.030	2.985	2.941
14	3.773	3.704	3.636	3.571	3.509	3.448	3.390	3.333	3.279	3.226	3.174	3.125	3.077	3.030	2.985	2.941
15	3.774	3.703	3.637	3.572	3.509	3.449	3.390	3.334	3.278	3.226	3.175	3.125	3.077	3.031	2.985	2.941
16	3.773	3.704	3.636	3.571	3.509	3.448	3.390	3.333	3.279	3.226	3.174	3.125	3.077	3.030	2.985	2.941
17	3.774	3.703	3.637	3.572	3.509	3.449	3.390	3.334	3.278	3.226	3.175	3.125	3.077	3.031	2.985	2.941
18	3.773	3.704	3.636	3.571	3.508	3.448	3.390	3.333	3.279	3.226	3.174	3.125	3.077	3.030	2.985	2.941
19	3.774	3.703	3.637	3.572	3.509	3.449	3.390	3.334	3.278	3.226	3.175	3.125	3.077	3.031	2.985	2.941
20	3.773	3.704	3.636	3.571	3.508	3.448	3.390	3.333	3.279	3.226	3.174	3.125	3.077	3.030	2.985	2.941
21	3.774	3.703	3.637	3.572	3.509	3.449	3.389	3.334	3.278	3.225	3.175	3.125	3.077	3.031	2.985	2.941
22	3.773	3.704	3.636	3.571	3.508	3.448	3.390	3.333	3.279	3.226	3.174	3.125	3.077	3.030	2.985	2.941
23	3.774	3.703	3.637	3.572	3.509	3.449	3.389	3.334	3.278	3.225	3.175	3.125	3.077	3.031	2.985	2.941
24	3.773	3.704	3.636	3.571	3.508	3.448	3.390	3.333	3.279	3.226	3.174	3.125	3.077	3.030	2.985	2.941
25	3.774	3.703	3.637	3.572	3.509	3.449	3.389	3.334	3.278	3.225	3.175	3.125	3.077	3.031	2.985	2.942
26	3.773	3.704	3.636	3.571	3.508	3.448	3.390	3.333	3.279	3.226	3.174	3.125	3.077	3.030	2.985	2.942
27	3.774	3.703	3.637	3.572	3.509	3.449	3.389	3.334	3.278	3.225	3.175	3.125	3.077	3.031	2.985	2.942
28		1.852	3.636	3.571	3.508	3.448	3.390	3.333	3.279	3.226	3.174	3.125	3.077	3.030	2.985	2.941
29				1.786	3.509	3.449	3.389	3.334	3.278	3.225	3.175	3.125	3.077	3.031	2.985	2.942
30						1.724	3.390	3.333	3.279	3.226	3.174	3.125	3.077	3.030	2.985	2.941
31								1.667	3.278	3.225	3.175	3.125	3.076	3.031	2.986	2.942
32										1.613	3.174	3.125	3.077	3.030	2.985	2.941

Table 8

General and Alternative Depreciation Systems
Applicable Depreciation Method: Straight Line
Applicable Recovery Periods: 2.5-50 years
Applicable Convention: Half-year
(continued)

Recovery Year	34.5	35.0	35.5	36.0	36.5	37.0	37.5	38.0	38.5	39.0	39.5	40.0	40.5	41.0	41.5	42.0
33												1.562	3.076	3.031	2.986	2.942
34														1.515	2.985	2.941
35																1.471

If the Recovery Year is:	and the Recovery Period is:															
	34.5	35.0	35.5	36.0	36.5	37.0	37.5	38.0	38.5	39.0	39.5	40.0	40.5	41.0	41.5	42.0
	the Depreciation Rate is:															
1	1.449	1.429	1.408	1.389	1.370	1.351	1.333	1.316	1.299	1.282	1.266	1.250	1.235	1.220	1.205	1.190
2	2.899	2.857	2.817	2.778	2.740	2.703	2.667	2.632	2.597	2.564	2.532	2.500	2.469	2.439	2.410	2.381
3	2.899	2.857	2.817	2.778	2.740	2.703	2.667	2.632	2.597	2.564	2.532	2.500	2.469	2.439	2.410	2.381
4	2.899	2.857	2.817	2.778	2.740	2.703	2.667	2.632	2.597	2.564	2.532	2.500	2.469	2.439	2.410	2.381
5	2.899	2.857	2.817	2.778	2.740	2.703	2.667	2.632	2.597	2.564	2.532	2.500	2.469	2.439	2.410	2.381
6	2.899	2.857	2.817	2.778	2.740	2.703	2.667	2.632	2.597	2.564	2.532	2.500	2.469	2.439	2.410	2.381
7	2.898	2.857	2.817	2.778	2.740	2.703	2.667	2.632	2.597	2.564	2.532	2.500	2.469	2.439	2.410	2.381
8	2.899	2.857	2.817	2.778	2.740	2.703	2.667	2.631	2.597	2.564	2.532	2.500	2.469	2.439	2.410	2.381
9	2.898	2.857	2.817	2.778	2.740	2.703	2.667	2.632	2.597	2.564	2.532	2.500	2.469	2.439	2.410	2.381
10	2.899	2.857	2.817	2.778	2.740	2.703	2.667	2.631	2.598	2.564	2.532	2.500	2.469	2.439	2.410	2.381
11	2.898	2.857	2.817	2.778	2.740	2.703	2.667	2.632	2.597	2.564	2.532	2.500	2.469	2.439	2.410	2.381
12	2.899	2.857	2.817	2.778	2.740	2.703	2.667	2.631	2.598	2.564	2.532	2.500	2.469	2.439	2.410	2.381
13	2.898	2.857	2.817	2.778	2.740	2.703	2.667	2.632	2.597	2.564	2.532	2.500	2.469	2.439	2.410	2.381
14	2.899	2.857	2.817	2.778	2.740	2.703	2.667	2.631	2.598	2.564	2.531	2.500	2.469	2.439	2.409	2.381
15	2.898	2.857	2.817	2.778	2.740	2.703	2.666	2.632	2.597	2.564	2.532	2.500	2.469	2.439	2.410	2.381
16	2.899	2.857	2.817	2.778	2.740	2.703	2.667	2.631	2.598	2.564	2.531	2.500	2.469	2.439	2.409	2.381
17	2.898	2.857	2.817	2.778	2.740	2.703	2.666	2.632	2.597	2.564	2.532	2.500	2.469	2.439	2.410	2.381
18	2.899	2.857	2.817	2.778	2.740	2.702	2.667	2.631	2.598	2.564	2.531	2.500	2.469	2.439	2.409	2.381
19	2.898	2.857	2.817	2.778	2.739	2.703	2.666	2.632	2.597	2.564	2.532	2.500	2.469	2.439	2.410	2.381
20	2.898	2.857	2.817	2.778	2.740	2.702	2.667	2.631	2.598	2.564	2.531	2.500	2.469	2.439	2.409	2.381
21	2.899	2.857	2.817	2.778	2.739	2.703	2.666	2.632	2.597	2.564	2.532	2.500	2.469	2.439	2.410	2.381
22	2.898	2.857	2.817	2.777	2.740	2.702	2.667	2.631	2.598	2.564	2.531	2.500	2.469	2.439	2.409	2.381
23	2.899	2.857	2.817	2.778	2.739	2.703	2.666	2.632	2.597	2.564	2.532	2.500	2.469	2.439	2.410	2.381
24	2.898	2.857	2.817	2.777	2.740	2.702	2.667	2.631	2.598	2.564	2.531	2.500	2.469	2.439	2.409	2.381
25	2.899	2.857	2.817	2.778	2.739	2.703	2.666	2.632	2.597	2.564	2.532	2.500	2.469	2.439	2.410	2.381
26	2.898	2.857	2.817	2.777	2.740	2.702	2.667	2.631	2.598	2.564	2.531	2.500	2.469	2.439	2.409	2.381
27	2.899	2.857	2.817	2.778	2.739	2.703	2.666	2.632	2.597	2.564	2.532	2.500	2.469	2.439	2.410	2.381
28	2.898	2.858	2.817	2.777	2.740	2.702	2.667	2.631	2.598	2.564	2.531	2.500	2.469	2.439	2.409	2.381
29	2.899	2.857	2.817	2.778	2.739	2.703	2.666	2.632	2.597	2.564	2.532	2.500	2.469	2.439	2.410	2.381
30	2.898	2.858	2.817	2.777	2.740	2.702	2.667	2.631	2.598	2.564	2.531	2.500	2.469	2.439	2.409	2.381
31	2.899	2.857	2.817	2.778	2.739	2.703	2.666	2.632	2.597	2.564	2.532	2.500	2.469	2.439	2.410	2.381
32	2.898	2.858	2.816	2.777	2.740	2.702	2.667	2.631	2.598	2.564	2.531	2.500	2.470	2.439	2.409	2.381
33	2.899	2.857	2.817	2.778	2.739	2.703	2.666	2.632	2.597	2.565	2.532	2.500	2.469	2.439	2.410	2.381
34	2.898	2.858	2.816	2.777	2.740	2.702	2.667	2.631	2.598	2.564	2.531	2.500	2.470	2.439	2.409	2.381
35	2.899	2.857	2.817	2.778	2.739	2.703	2.666	2.632	2.597	2.565	2.532	2.500	2.469	2.439	2.410	2.381
36		1.429	2.816	2.777	2.740	2.702	2.667	2.631	2.598	2.564	2.531	2.500	2.470	2.439	2.409	2.381
37				1.389	2.739	2.703	2.666	2.632	2.597	2.565	2.532	2.500	2.469	2.439	2.410	2.381
38						1.351	2.667	2.631	2.598	2.564	2.531	2.500	2.469	2.439	2.410	2.381
39								1.316	2.597	2.565	2.532	2.500	2.469	2.439	2.410	2.381
40										1.282	2.531	2.500	2.470	2.439	2.409	2.381
41												1.250	2.469	2.439	2.410	2.380
42														1.220	2.409	2.381
43																1.190

Table 8

General and Alternative Depreciation Systems
Applicable Depreciation Method: Straight Line
Applicable Recovery Periods: 2.5-50 years
Applicable Convention: Half-year
(continued)

If the Recovery Year is:	and the Recovery Period is:																
	42.5	43.0	43.5	44.0	44.5	45.0	45.5	46.0	46.5	47.0	47.5	48.0	48.5	49.0	49.5	50.0
	the Depreciation Rate is:															
1	1.176	1.163	1.149	1.136	1.124	1.111	1.099	1.087	1.075	1.064	1.053	1.042	1.031	1.020	1.010	1.000
2	2.353	2.326	2.299	2.273	2.247	2.222	2.198	2.174	2.151	2.128	2.105	2.083	2.062	2.041	2.020	2.000
3	2.353	2.326	2.299	2.273	2.247	2.222	2.198	2.174	2.151	2.128	2.105	2.083	2.062	2.041	2.020	2.000
4	2.353	2.326	2.299	2.273	2.247	2.222	2.198	2.174	2.151	2.128	2.105	2.083	2.062	2.041	2.020	2.000
5	2.353	2.326	2.299	2.273	2.247	2.222	2.198	2.174	2.151	2.128	2.105	2.083	2.062	2.041	2.020	2.000
6	2.353	2.326	2.299	2.273	2.247	2.222	2.198	2.174	2.151	2.128	2.105	2.083	2.062	2.041	2.020	2.000
7	2.353	2.326	2.299	2.273	2.247	2.222	2.198	2.174	2.150	2.128	2.105	2.083	2.062	2.041	2.020	2.000
8	2.353	2.326	2.299	2.273	2.247	2.222	2.198	2.174	2.151	2.128	2.105	2.083	2.062	2.041	2.020	2.000
9	2.353	2.325	2.299	2.273	2.247	2.222	2.198	2.174	2.150	2.128	2.105	2.083	2.062	2.041	2.020	2.000
10	2.353	2.326	2.299	2.273	2.247	2.222	2.198	2.174	2.151	2.128	2.105	2.083	2.062	2.041	2.020	2.000
11	2.353	2.325	2.299	2.273	2.247	2.222	2.198	2.174	2.150	2.128	2.105	2.083	2.062	2.041	2.020	2.000
12	2.353	2.326	2.299	2.273	2.247	2.222	2.198	2.174	2.151	2.128	2.105	2.083	2.062	2.041	2.020	2.000
13	2.353	2.325	2.299	2.273	2.247	2.222	2.198	2.174	2.150	2.128	2.105	2.083	2.062	2.041	2.020	2.000
14	2.353	2.326	2.299	2.273	2.247	2.222	2.198	2.174	2.151	2.128	2.105	2.083	2.062	2.041	2.020	2.000
15	2.353	2.325	2.299	2.273	2.247	2.222	2.198	2.174	2.150	2.128	2.105	2.083	2.062	2.041	2.020	2.000
16	2.353	2.326	2.299	2.273	2.247	2.222	2.198	2.174	2.151	2.128	2.105	2.083	2.062	2.041	2.020	2.000
17	2.353	2.325	2.299	2.273	2.247	2.222	2.198	2.174	2.150	2.127	2.105	2.083	2.062	2.041	2.020	2.000
18	2.353	2.326	2.299	2.273	2.247	2.222	2.198	2.174	2.151	2.128	2.105	2.083	2.062	2.041	2.020	2.000
19	2.353	2.325	2.299	2.273	2.247	2.222	2.198	2.174	2.150	2.127	2.105	2.084	2.062	2.041	2.020	2.000
20	2.353	2.326	2.299	2.273	2.247	2.222	2.198	2.174	2.151	2.128	2.105	2.083	2.062	2.041	2.020	2.000
21	2.353	2.325	2.299	2.273	2.247	2.222	2.198	2.174	2.150	2.127	2.105	2.084	2.062	2.041	2.020	2.000
22	2.353	2.326	2.299	2.273	2.247	2.222	2.198	2.174	2.151	2.128	2.105	2.083	2.062	2.041	2.020	2.000
23	2.353	2.325	2.299	2.272	2.247	2.222	2.198	2.174	2.150	2.127	2.105	2.084	2.062	2.041	2.020	2.000
24	2.353	2.326	2.299	2.273	2.247	2.222	2.198	2.174	2.151	2.128	2.105	2.083	2.062	2.041	2.020	2.000
25	2.353	2.325	2.299	2.272	2.247	2.222	2.198	2.174	2.150	2.127	2.105	2.084	2.062	2.041	2.020	2.000
26	2.353	2.326	2.299	2.273	2.247	2.222	2.198	2.174	2.151	2.128	2.106	2.083	2.062	2.041	2.020	2.000
27	2.353	2.325	2.299	2.272	2.247	2.223	2.198	2.174	2.150	2.127	2.105	2.084	2.062	2.041	2.020	2.000
28	2.353	2.326	2.299	2.273	2.247	2.222	2.198	2.174	2.151	2.128	2.106	2.083	2.062	2.041	2.020	2.000
29	2.353	2.325	2.299	2.272	2.247	2.223	2.198	2.174	2.150	2.127	2.105	2.084	2.062	2.041	2.020	2.000
30	2.353	2.326	2.299	2.272	2.248	2.222	2.197	2.174	2.151	2.128	2.106	2.083	2.062	2.041	2.020	2.000
31	2.353	2.325	2.299	2.272	2.247	2.223	2.198	2.174	2.150	2.127	2.105	2.084	2.062	2.041	2.021	2.000
32	2.353	2.326	2.299	2.273	2.248	2.222	2.197	2.174	2.151	2.128	2.106	2.083	2.062	2.041	2.020	2.000
33	2.353	2.325	2.298	2.272	2.247	2.223	2.198	2.174	2.150	2.127	2.105	2.084	2.062	2.041	2.021	2.000
34	2.353	2.326	2.299	2.273	2.248	2.222	2.197	2.174	2.151	2.128	2.106	2.083	2.062	2.041	2.020	2.000
35	2.353	2.325	2.298	2.272	2.247	2.223	2.198	2.174	2.150	2.127	2.105	2.084	2.062	2.041	2.021	2.000
36	2.353	2.326	2.299	2.273	2.248	2.222	2.197	2.174	2.151	2.128	2.106	2.083	2.062	2.040	2.020	2.000
37	2.353	2.325	2.298	2.272	2.247	2.223	2.198	2.174	2.150	2.127	2.105	2.084	2.061	2.041	2.021	2.000
38	2.353	2.326	2.299	2.273	2.248	2.222	2.197	2.174	2.151	2.128	2.106	2.083	2.062	2.040	2.020	2.000
39	2.353	2.325	2.298	2.272	2.247	2.223	2.198	2.174	2.150	2.127	2.105	2.084	2.061	2.041	2.021	2.000
40	2.353	2.326	2.299	2.273	2.248	2.222	2.197	2.173	2.151	2.128	2.106	2.083	2.062	2.040	2.020	2.000
41	2.352	2.325	2.298	2.272	2.247	2.223	2.198	2.174	2.150	2.127	2.105	2.084	2.061	2.041	2.021	2.000
42	2.353	2.326	2.299	2.273	2.248	2.222	2.197	2.173	2.151	2.128	2.106	2.083	2.062	2.040	2.020	2.000
43	2.352	2.325	2.298	2.272	2.247	2.223	2.198	2.174	2.150	2.127	2.105	2.084	2.061	2.041	2.021	2.000
44		1.163	2.299	2.273	2.248	2.222	2.197	2.173	2.151	2.128	2.106	2.083	2.062	2.040	2.020	2.000
45				1.136	2.247	2.223	2.198	2.174	2.150	2.127	2.105	2.084	2.061	2.041	2.021	2.000
46						1.111	2.197	2.173	2.151	2.128	2.106	2.083	2.062	2.040	2.020	2.000
47								1.087	2.150	2.127	2.105	2.084	2.061	2.041	2.021	2.000
48										1.064	2.106	2.083	2.062	2.040	2.020	2.000
49												1.042	2.061	2.041	2.021	2.000
50														1.020	2.020	2.000
51																1.000

Table 9

Alternative Depreciation System
Applicable Depreciation Method: Straight Line
Applicable Recovery Period: 40 years
Applicable Convention: Mid-month

If the Recovery Year is:	And the Month in the First Recovery Year the Property is Placed in Service is:											
	1	2	3	4	5	6	7	8	9	10	11	12
	the Depreciation Rate is:											
1	2.396	2.188	1.979	1.771	1.563	1.354	1.146	0.938	0.729	0.521	0.313	0.104
2 to 40	2.500	2.500	2.500	2.500	2.500	2.500	2.500	2.500	2.500	2.500	2.500	2.500
41	0.104	0.312	0.521	0.729	0.937	1.146	1.354	1.562	1.771	1.979	2.187	2.396

Table I
Leased MACRS Business Listed Property

Income Inclusion Amounts — Step (1) Computation Rates — for
Business Listed Property (Except Autos) Leased After '86
(Reg §1.280F-7T(b)(2)(i)(C))

Type of Property	First Taxable Year During Lease in Which Business Use Percentage is 50% or Less											
	1	2	3	4	5	6	7	8	9	10	11	12 & Later
Property with a Recovery Period of Less Than 7 Years under the Alternative Depreciation System (Such as Computers, Trucks and Airplanes)	0.0%	10.0%	22.0%	21.2%	12.7%	12.7%	12.7%	12.7%	12.7%	12.7%	12.7%	12.7%
Property with a 7- to 10-Year Recovery Period under the Alternative Depreciation System (Such as Recreation Property)	0.0%	9.3%	23.8%	31.3%	33.8%	32.7%	31.6%	30.5%	25.0%	15.0%	15.0%	15.0%
Property with Recovery Period of more Than 10 Years under the Alternative Depreciation System (Such as Certain Property with No Class Life)	0.0%	10.1%	26.3%	35.4%	39.6%	40.2%	40.8%	41.4%	37.5%	29.2%	20.8%	12.5%

Table II
Leased MACRS Business Listed Property

Income Inclusion Amounts — Step (2) Computation Rates — for
Business Listed Property (Except Autos) Leased After '86
(Reg §1.280F-7T(b)(2)(i)(C))

Type of Property	First Taxable Year During Lease in Which Business Use Percentage is 50% or Less											
	1	2	3	4	5	6	7	8	9	10	11	12 & Later
Property with a Recovery Period of Less Than 7 Years under Alternative Depreciation System (Such as Computers, Trucks and Airplanes)	2.1%	−7.2%	−19.8%	−20.1%	−12.4%	−12.4%	−12.4%	−12.4%	−12.4%	−12.4%	−12.4%	−12.4%
Property with a 7- to 10-Year Recovery Period under the Alternative Depreciation System (Such as Recreation Property)	3.9%	−3.8%	−17.7%	−25.1%	−27.8%	−27.2%	−27.1%	−27.6%	−23.7%	−14.7%	−14.7%	−14.7%
Property with a Recovery Period of More Than 10 Years under the Alternative Depreciation System (Such as Certain Property with No Class Life)	6.6%	−1.6%	−16.9%	−25.6%	−29.9%	−31.1%	−32.8%	−35.1%	−33.3%	−26.7%	−19.7%	−12.2%

¶ 1118   Income Inclusion Amounts for Autos, Trucks and Vans ▣

REV. PROC. 2007-30 TABLE 3

DOLLAR AMOUNTS FOR PASSENGER AUTOMOBILES
(THAT ARE NOT TRUCKS OR VANS)
WITH A LEASE TERM BEGINNING IN CALENDAR YEAR 2007

Fair Market Value of Passenger Automobile		Tax Year During Lease				
Over	Not Over	1st	2nd	3rd	4th	5th & later
$15,500	$15,800	2	5	11	11	13
15,800	16,100	4	10	17	19	22
16,100	16,400	6	14	24	28	31
16,400	16,700	9	18	31	35	41
16,700	17,000	11	23	37	43	50
17,000	17,500	13	29	46	54	62
17,500	18,000	17	37	56	68	77
18,000	18,500	20	44	68	81	93
18,500	19,000	24	51	80	94	108
19,000	19,500	27	59	90	108	124
19,500	20,000	30	67	101	121	139
20,000	20,500	34	74	113	134	154
20,500	21,000	37	82	123	148	170
21,000	21,500	41	89	135	161	185
21,500	22,000	44	97	146	174	201
22,000	23,000	49	108	163	194	224
23,000	24,000	56	123	185	221	255
24,000	25,000	63	138	207	248	285
25,000	26,000	70	153	229	275	316
26,000	27,000	77	168	251	302	347
27,000	28,000	83	183	274	328	378
28,000	29,000	90	198	296	355	409
29,000	30,000	97	213	318	382	439
30,000	31,000	104	228	341	408	470
31,000	32,000	111	243	363	435	501
32,000	33,000	118	258	385	461	532
33,000	34,000	125	273	407	488	563
34,000	35,000	131	288	430	515	593
35,000	36,000	138	303	452	542	624
36,000	37,000	145	318	474	568	656
37,000	38,000	152	333	496	595	686
38,000	39,000	159	348	519	621	717
39,000	40,000	166	363	541	648	748
40,000	41,000	172	378	564	674	779
41,000	42,000	179	393	586	701	810
42,000	43,000	186	408	608	728	840
43,000	44,000	193	423	630	755	871
44,000	45,000	200	438	652	782	902
45,000	46,000	207	453	674	809	933
46,000	47,000	213	468	697	835	964
47,000	48,000	220	483	719	862	995
48,000	49,000	227	498	742	888	1,025
49,000	50,000	234	513	764	915	1,056
50,000	51,000	241	528	786	942	1,087
51,000	52,000	248	543	808	969	1,117
52,000	53,000	254	558	831	995	1,148

53,000	54,000	261	573	853	1,022	1,179
54,000	55,000	268	588	875	1,049	1,210
55,000	56,000	275	603	897	1,076	1,241
56,000	57,000	282	618	920	1,102	1,271
57,000	58,000	289	633	942	1,128	1,303
58,000	59,000	296	648	964	1,155	1,334
59,000	60,000	302	663	987	1,182	1,364
60,000	62,000	313	685	1,020	1,222	1,411
62,000	64,000	326	716	1,064	1,276	1,472
64,000	66,000	340	746	1,108	1,329	1,534
66,000	68,000	354	775	1,154	1,382	1,595
68,000	70,000	367	806	1,198	1,435	1,657
70,000	72,000	381	836	1,242	1,489	1,719
72,000	74,000	395	865	1,287	1,543	1,780
74,000	76,000	408	896	1,331	1,596	1,842
76,000	78,000	422	926	1,376	1,649	1,903
78,000	80,000	436	955	1,421	1,703	1,965
80,000	85,000	460	1,008	1,498	1,796	2,074
85,000	90,000	494	1,083	1,610	1,929	2,228
90,000	95,000	528	1,158	1,721	2,063	2,382
95,000	100,000	562	1,233	1,833	2,196	2,536
100,000	110,000	614	1,346	1,999	2,396	2,767
110,000	120,000	682	1,496	2,222	2,663	3,075
120,000	130,000	750	1,646	2,444	2,931	3,383
130,000	140,000	819	1,796	2,667	3,197	3,692
140,000	150,000	887	1,946	2,890	3,464	4,000
150,000	160,000	956	2,096	3,112	3,731	4,308
160,000	170,000	1,024	2,246	3,335	3,998	4,616
170,000	180,000	1,093	2,396	3,557	4,266	4,924
180,000	190,000	1,161	2,546	3,780	4,532	5,233
190,000	200,000	1,229	2,696	4,003	4,799	5,541
200,000	210,000	1,298	2,846	4,225	5,067	5,848
210,000	220,000	1,366	2,996	4,448	5,333	6,157
220,000	230,000	1,435	3,146	4,671	5,600	6,465
230,000	240,000	1,503	3,296	4,893	5,867	6,774
240,000	and up	1,571	3,446	5,116	6,134	7,082

REV. PROC. 2007-30 TABLE 4

DOLLAR AMOUNTS FOR TRUCKS AND VANS
WITH A LEASE TERM BEGINNING IN CALENDAR YEAR 2007

Fair Market Value of Passenger Automobile		Tax Year During Lease				
Over	Not Over	1st	2nd	3rd	4th	5th & later
$16,400	$16,700	2	4	8	10	11
16,700	17,000	4	9	15	17	21
17,000	17,500	6	15	24	28	33
17,500	18,000	10	22	35	42	48
18,000	18,500	13	30	46	55	64
18,500	19,000	17	37	57	69	79
19,000	19,500	20	45	68	82	94
19,500	20,000	24	52	80	95	109
20,000	20,500	27	60	90	109	125
20,500	21,000	30	67	102	122	141
21,000	21,500	34	75	113	135	156
21,500	22,000	37	82	124	149	171
22,000	23,000	42	94	140	169	194
23,000	24,000	49	109	163	195	225
24,000	25,000	56	123	186	222	256
25,000	26,000	63	138	208	249	286
26,000	27,000	70	153	230	276	317
27,000	28,000	77	168	252	302	349
28,000	29,000	83	184	274	329	379
29,000	30,000	90	199	296	356	410
30,000	31,000	97	214	318	383	440
31,000	32,000	104	228	342	408	472
32,000	33,000	111	243	364	435	503
33,000	34,000	118	258	386	462	534
34,000	35,000	125	273	408	489	564
35,000	36,000	131	289	430	515	595
36,000	37,000	138	304	452	542	626
37,000	38,000	145	318	475	569	657
38,000	39,000	152	333	497	596	688
39,000	40,000	159	348	520	622	718
40,000	41,000	166	363	542	649	749
41,000	42,000	172	379	563	676	780
42,000	43,000	179	394	586	702	811
43,000	44,000	186	409	608	729	842
44,000	45,000	193	423	631	756	872
45,000	46,000	200	438	653	783	903
46,000	47,000	207	453	675	810	934
47,000	48,000	213	469	697	836	965
48,000	49,000	220	484	719	863	996
49,000	50,000	227	499	741	890	1,026
50,000	51,000	234	514	764	916	1,057
51,000	52,000	241	528	787	943	1,088
52,000	53,000	248	543	809	969	1,119
53,000	54,000	254	559	831	996	1,150
54,000	55,000	261	574	853	1,023	1,180
55,000	56,000	268	589	875	1,050	1,211
56,000	57,000	275	604	897	1,076	1,243
57,000	58,000	282	618	920	1,103	1,273
58,000	59,000	289	633	943	1,129	1,304
59,000	60,000	296	648	965	1,156	1,335

60,000	62,000	306	671	998	1,196	1,381
62,000	64,000	319	701	1,043	1,249	1,443
64,000	66,000	333	731	1,087	1,303	1,504
66,000	68,000	347	761	1,131	1,357	1,566
68,000	70,000	361	791	1,176	1,410	1,627
70,000	72,000	374	821	1,221	1,463	1,689
72,000	74,000	388	851	1,265	1,517	1,751
74,000	76,000	402	881	1,309	1,570	1,813
76,000	78,000	415	911	1,354	1,624	1,874
78,000	80,000	429	941	1,399	1,676	1,936
80,000	85,000	453	994	1,476	1,770	2,044
85,000	90,000	487	1,069	1,587	1,904	2,198
90,000	95,000	521	1,144	1,699	2,037	2,352
95,000	100,000	555	1,219	1,810	2,171	2,506
100,000	110,000	607	1,331	1,977	2,371	2,737
110,000	120,000	675	1,481	2,200	2,638	3,045
120,000	130,000	744	1,631	2,423	2,904	3,354
130,000	140,000	812	1,781	2,646	3,171	3,662
140,000	150,000	880	1,932	2,867	3,439	3,970
150,000	160,000	949	2,081	3,091	3,705	4,279
160,000	170,000	1,017	2,232	3,313	3,972	4,586
170,000	180,000	1,086	2,381	3,536	4,239	4,895
180,000	190,000	1,154	2,532	3,758	4,506	5,203
190,000	200,000	1,222	2,682	3,981	4,773	5,511
200,000	210,000	1,291	2,831	4,204	5,040	5,820
210,000	220,000	1,359	2,982	4,426	5,307	6,128
220,000	230,000	1,428	3,131	4,649	5,575	6,435
230,000	240,000	1,496	3,282	4,871	5,841	6,744
240,000	and up	1,565	3,431	5,095	6,108	7,052

Chapter 2   Income—Taxable and Exempt

¶ 1200   Gross Income. ▆▆▆▆▆▆▆▆▆▆▆▆▆▆▆▆▆▆▆▆▆▆▆▆▆▆▆▆▆▆▆▆▆▆▆▆

Gross income consists of all income, from all sources, such as compensation for services, business income, interest, rents, dividends and gains from the sale of property. Only items specifically exempt may be excluded.

Gross income is the starting point in determining tax liability and is broadly defined. (Code Sec. 61)[1]

¶ 1201   Assignment of income.

The person who earns and is entitled to receive income is taxed on it. He can't avoid tax on it by assigning it to another.[2] But if a taxpayer assigns or transfers income-producing *property* before the income is earned, the assignee will be taxed on the income.[3]

¶ 1202   Income from co-owned property—joint tenancies, etc.

In a tenancy in common (co-owners without survivorship), each co-owner is taxable on that part of the income attributable to his share.[4] Co-owners who are joint tenants (with survivorship) split income from their property according to their ownership interests.[5]

Similarly, any gain (or loss) from sale of jointly-owned property is divided among the co-owners unless the joint ownership was created to save taxes on the sale, in which case the original owner is taxed on the full amount of the gain.[6]

Co-owners who are husband and wife and file joint returns report their combined income, gains and losses from the jointly-owned property. If they file separately, the income, etc., from the property is split equally if they so share it under state law.[7]

¶ 1203   Community property and income.

Federal tax law recognizes the principle of community income in community property states (AZ, CA, ID, LA, NV, NM, TX, WA and WI) or countries, which treats half of community income and expenses as belonging to each spouse.[8] Community income is all the income from community property (including business property) and salaries, etc., for the services of either or both spouses. Income from separate property during marriage is community income only in ID, LA, TX and WI.[9] IRS has said that CA domestic partners aren't subject to these rules.

If one spouse acts as if he's solely entitled to the community income and fails to notify his spouse of the nature and amount of the income before the return due date (with extensions), IRS may deny him any community property benefit. (Code Sec. 66(b))[10]

Community property income for a calendar year is taxed to the spouse who earned it if in that year the couple lived apart for the entire year, filed separate returns *and* one or both spouses had earned income no part of which was transferred between them. (Code Sec. 66(a), Code Sec. 66(d)(1))[11]

A divorced individual who resided in a community property state was not taxable on

1. ¶s J-1000 *et seq.*; ¶614; TD ¶101,000
2. ¶J-8151 *et seq.*; ¶s 614.185, 614.192; TD ¶201,001
3. ¶J-8172 *et seq.*; ¶s 614.192, 1024; TD ¶201,001
4. ¶J-8103; ¶614.202; TD ¶204,003
5. ¶s J-8101, J-8102; ¶614.202; TD ¶204,002
6. ¶J-8107; ¶614.202; TD ¶204,007

7. ¶J-8100 *et seq.*; ¶614.202; TD ¶204,005
8. ¶A-5001; ¶79,006.51; TD ¶573,501
9. ¶A-5008; TD ¶573,506
10. ¶A-5026; ¶664; TD ¶573,512
11. ¶A-5022; ¶664; TD ¶573,514

References beginning with a single letter are to paragraphs in RIA's Federal Tax Coordinator 2d and RIA's Analysis of Federal Taxes: Income. Those beginning with numbers are to paragraphs in RIA's United States Tax Reporter. Those beginning with TD are to paragraphs in RIA's Tax Desk.

amounts he paid from his wages to his ex-spouse as ordered by a state court. [12]

Relief for separate return liability. A spouse who did not file a joint return for the tax year for which he seeks relief and omits from gross income his share of community income (¶1203) is relieved from tax liability on that omitted income if he establishes lack of knowledge or reason to know of the omitted item and, under all the facts and circumstances, it's inequitable to include the omitted item in his gross income ("traditional relief"). (Code Sec. 66(c); Reg § 1.66-4(a)(1))[13]

IRS may grant equitable relief to a separately-filing spouse from liability attributable to a community income item for which relief isn't available under the above provision ("equitable relief"). (Code Sec. 66(c); Reg § 1.66-4(b))

Traditional relief applies only to deficiencies arising out of items of omitted income but equitable relief includes relief for underpayments of tax or any deficiency, including those arising from disallowed deductions or credits. (Reg § 1.66-4(c))

A spouse requesting relief under the above provisions does so by filing Form 8857. (Reg § 1.66-4(j)(1))[14] For joint filers, see ¶4711.

¶ 1204   Claim of right.

Income received without restriction—income the taxpayer has dominion and control over—must be reported in the year received, even if there's a possibility it may have to be repaid in a later year. [15] For deduction in the repayment year, see ¶2860 *et seq.*

¶ 1205   The "tax benefit rule"—recoveries attributable to an earlier year's deduction or credit.

The recovery of an amount deducted or credited in an earlier tax year is included in a taxpayer's income in the current (recovery) year, except to the extent the deduction or credit *didn't* reduce federal income tax (or alternative minimum tax, but not the accumulated earnings or personal holding company "penalty" taxes (Code Sec. 111(d)(1))[16] imposed in the earlier year. (Code Sec. 111(a))[17]

Similarly, if there's a downward price adjustment (e.g., price reduction) during the tax year that affects an amount paid or incurred on which a credit (other than the investment credit or the foreign tax credit) was allowed in an earlier year, taxpayer's tax for the adjustment year is increased by the amount of credit attributable to the adjustment, to the extent it reduced his tax in the earlier year. (Code Sec. 111(b))[18]

This "tax benefit rule" applies to recoveries of both itemized deductions (i.e., taxes, medical expenses and other items deductible on Form 1040, Schedule A) and non-itemized deductions (e.g., bad debts). The taxable amount is limited to the itemized deduction amount that reduced the tax in the earlier year. A taxpayer who recovers an amount he deducted in an earlier year as an itemized deduction is taxed on the *lesser* of the amount recovered, or the amount deducted on Schedule A. A taxpayer who wasn't required to itemize deductions in the earlier year is taxed on the *lesser* of his itemized deduction recoveries or the amount by which his itemized deductions exceeded the standard deduction. [19]

Illustration: B's itemized deductions on his Year 1 return were $6,250. The standard deduction B could have claimed for that year was $5,150. In Year 2, B recovers $2,400 of his Year 1 itemized deductions. B must include $1,100 of the recoveries in his Year 2 income, since that's the smaller of his itemized deduction recoveries ($2,400) or the excess of his itemized

12. ¶A-5013; TD ¶573,513
13. ¶A-5029; ¶664; TD ¶573,609
14. ¶A-5034; ¶664; TD ¶573,613
15. ¶J-8001 *et seq.*; ¶4514.069 *et seq.*; TD ¶203,001

16. ¶J-5526, ¶J-5527; ¶1114; TD ¶181,004
17. ¶J-5500 *et seq.*; ¶1114 *et seq.*; TD ¶181,001
18. ¶J-5511; ¶1114.02; TD ¶181,001
19. ¶J-5512; ¶1114.02; TD ¶181,020

70

deductions over the standard deduction ($6,250 − $5,150 = $1,100).[20]

If taxpayer had negative taxable income for the year the items were deducted, the otherwise includable amount of the recovery is reduced by the negative amount. [21]

The tax benefit rule applies to state income taxes deducted in an earlier year where there's a refund or credit of taxes paid or the cancellation of taxes accrued. [22]

If an earlier year's itemized deductions were reduced under the 3%/80% rule (see ¶3114), a later recovery of previously deducted amounts is generally fully includible in gross income. Specifically, the taxpayer is taxed on the difference between the earlier year's reduced itemized deductions, and his reduced itemized deductions (or standard deduction, if greater) had he paid the proper amount in the earlier year and not received the recovery. [23]

The increase of a carryover that hasn't expired as of the start of the tax year of the recovery (deduction) or adjustment (credit item) is treated as a reduction of tax imposed. (Code Sec. 111(c))[24]

The tax rates for the recovery (or adjustment) year are used to compute the tax on the portion that isn't excludible. [25] A recovery of amounts, e.g., bad debts, deducted in more than one tax year must be allocated pro rata between those years. (Reg § 1.111-1(a)(3))[26]

To claim any part of a recovery is tax-free, attach a schedule to the return showing the right to the exclusion. (Reg § 1.111-1(b)(1))[27]

¶ 1206 Miscellaneous taxable and exempt income.

Here is the taxable or exempt status of items not covered elsewhere in this Handbook:

. . . Alcohol fuel credit. Includable in gross income. (Code Sec. 87)[28]

. . . Barter, or the swapping of goods and services, results in gross income to each party to the swap to the extent of the fair market value of the goods or services received. The dollar value of barter "credits" received by members of barter clubs for goods or services rendered to other members is taxable. [29] For information returns of barter exchanges, see ¶4750.

. . . Car pool expenses reimbursed by fellow members. Nontaxable unless received as part of a trade or business of transporting workers. [30] For exclusion as a qualified transportation fringe benefit, see ¶1248.

. . . Damages recovered for faulty home construction are tax free to the extent of basis. They reduce basis and are taxable to the extent they exceed basis. [31]

. . . Employer-provided death benefits of specified victims of terrorism and astronauts who die in the line of duty. Excludable from gross income. (Code Sec. 101(i)(1))[32]

. . . Energy conservation subsidies provided (directly or indirectly) by a public utility to customers for buying or installing "energy conservation measures" for dwelling units are not taxable. (Code Sec. 136)[33]

. . . Escrow funds or property, and the income from them. Not taxable to the stakeholder but may be taxable to the ultimate recipient when paid to him. [34]

. . . Executor's or administrator's fees or commissions that are waived. Not taxed to executor, etc., who files a formal waiver within six months after appointment, or whose conduct amounts to an implied waiver. [35]

20. ¶J-5512; ¶1114.02; TD ¶181,020
21. ¶J-5512; TD ¶181,020
22. ¶J-5701 *et seq.*; ¶1114; TD ¶183,001
23. ¶J-5513; ¶1114.02; TD ¶181,022
24. ¶J-5524; ¶1114; TD ¶181,008
25. ¶J-5530; ¶1114.02; TD ¶181,030
26. ¶J-5603; ¶1114.02; TD ¶181,017
27. ¶J-5528; TD ¶181,003

28. ¶L-17505; ¶874
29. ¶s J-1010, J-1012; TD ¶112,003
30. ¶J-1398; TD ¶196,003
31. ¶J-5820; TD ¶182,011
32. ¶C-9674; ¶1014.10; TD ¶579,624
33. ¶J-1401 *et seq.*; ¶1364; TD ¶198,510
34. ¶J-1371; ¶4514.087
35. ¶J-1419; ¶4514.042; TD ¶198,511

. . . Financial counseling fees paid by employer to family members of terminally ill employees (taxable to employees) and survivors of deceased employees (taxable to survivors). [36]

. . . Foster care payments by state or licensed/certified placement agency to individual foster care provider. Not taxable, if payments are for caring for qualified foster individual (child or adult) in care provider's home (where provider resides), or are "difficulty-of-care payments." (Code Sec. 131)[37]

. . . Frequent flyer miles earned or received in connection with business travel are not included in taxable income. [38]

. . . Grants to homeowners under a city program to preserve old neighborhoods. Taxable. [39]

. . . 25% of qualifying gain from conservation sales of qualifying mineral or geothermal interests. Excludable from gross income. (TRHCA § 403(c)(1)(Div. C, Title IV)) [40]

. . . Illegal income. Taxable whether from an illegal business, an actual crime, or immoral or unethical practices, e.g., embezzlement. (Repayment is an itemized deduction.) [41]

. . . "Insider's" short-term stock sale profits which SEC requires be turned over to corporation. Taxable to corporation on receipt. [42]

. . . Insurance reimbursement for living expenses incurred due to the loss of use of (or government's denial of access to) principal residence (owned or rented) resulting from a fire, storm or other casualty. Nontaxable, to extent it covers additional living expenses (but balance of reimbursement is taxable). (Code Sec. 123; Reg § 1.123-1)[43] Use and occupancy insurance reimbursements for loss of profits if business is suspended are taxable. [44]

. . . Leave-donor who deposits leave in an employer-sponsored leave bank under a major disaster leave-sharing plan. Nontaxable, if plan treats payments made by the employer to leave recipients as wages. [45]

. . . Leaves under employer-sponsored leave-sharing plan which permits employees with a medical emergency to receive leave that other employees surrender or deposit into a leave bank. Taxable to recipient-employee as compensation. [46]

. . . Medicare (Part A and Part B). Not taxable (except for Part B amounts attributable to medical deductions taken in an earlier year). [47]

. . . Mortgage assistance payments by a federal agency to a mortgagee on mortgagor's behalf. Not taxable to the mortgagor unless *not* made for the general welfare (e.g., interest reduction payments to mortgagee). [48]

. . . Property tax rebates are taxable to the extent they exceed the property tax paid. Rebates received after the year of payment are subject to the tax benefit rule, see ¶1205. Rebates received in the year of payment reduce the amount of tax paid for that year. Where the tax was paid over two years, the rebate is apportioned over the two years. [49]

. . . Rate reduction or nonrefundable credit provided by utility to customer for participation in energy conservation program. Not taxable. [50]

. . . Rebates of part of purchase price by auto companies to retail customers. Not taxable. [1]

. . . Relocation payments and similar government subsidies for moving expenses and actual direct losses of property because of displacement from personal residences, as a result of urban renewal projects. Not taxable, to extent payments are made by government to compensate for (and are actually so used for) these expenses. [2] Taxable, to extent payments are made by nongovernmental landlords as part of co-op or condo conversion. [3]

36. ¶H-1701
37. ¶J-1500 *et seq.*; ¶s 1314.01, 1314.02; TD ¶196,501
38. ¶J-1393; TD ¶134,600
39. ¶J-1480
40. ¶I-8851; TD ¶229,901
41. ¶J-1600 *et seq.*; ¶614.176; TD ¶197,501
42. ¶J-5829; TD ¶182,018
43. ¶J-1311 *et seq.*; ¶1234; TD ¶195,501
44. ¶J-5830; ¶614.167; TD ¶182,019

45. ¶H-1013A
46. ¶H-1013; TD ¶198,521
47. ¶J-1307; TD ¶194,506
48. ¶J-1489
49. ¶J-1394.1
50. ¶J-1431; TD ¶198,522
1. ¶J-1391; TD ¶196,005
2. ¶J-1492; ¶614.006
3. ¶J-1492; TD ¶198,521

... Restitution (generally, money or property received as a result of an individual's persecution by the Nazis) received by Holocaust survivors or their heirs is excludable. [4]

... Security deposits received. If purpose is to guarantee performance of an obligation, not taxable where repayment is required if the obligation is performed. Taxed to the recipient when he becomes entitled to retain them because of a default. [5] If purpose is to protect taxpayer's interest in property and not to secure payment, it's not taxable. [6]

... Subsidies received from Social Security by sponsors of qualified retiree prescription drug plans under the Medicare Prescription Drug Act of 2003 for covered retiree drug costs between $250 and $5,000 are not taxable. [7]

¶ 1207   Exclusion for qualified disaster relief or mitigation payments.

A qualified disaster relief payment isn't included in gross income. It also isn't earnings for self-employment tax purposes or wages for employment tax purposes. (Code Sec. 139) The exclusion doesn't apply to amounts received for the sale or disposition of property, but the involuntary conversion rules may apply to such amounts, see ¶2430.[8]

A qualified disaster relief payment is any amount (to the extent not compensated by insurance or otherwise) paid to or for the benefit of an individual:

(1) to reimburse or pay reasonable and necessary personal, family, living, or funeral expenses incurred as a result of a qualified disaster (defined below),

(2) to reimburse or pay reasonable and necessary expenses incurred to repair or rehabilitate a personal residence (including a rented residence) or repair or replace its contents to the extent that the need for the work results from a qualified disaster,

(3) by a person who provides or sells transportation as a common carrier because of the death or personal physical injuries arising from a qualified disaster, or

(4) if the amount is paid by a federal, state, or local government, or an agency or instrumentality of those governments, in connection with a qualified disaster in order to promote the general welfare (but not if payments are made to businesses or for income replacement or unemployment compensation).

A qualified disaster is a disaster which results from a terroristic or military action, a Presidentially declared disaster, a disaster resulting from an accident involving a common carrier, or from any other event, that is determined by IRS to be of a catastrophic nature, or for payments by a federal, state, or local government, or an agency or instrumentality of those governments, a disaster that is determined by the appropriate governmental authority (as determined by IRS) to warrant assistance from the governmental authority. [9]

Qualified disaster mitigation payments are excluded from gross income. (Code Sec. 139(g)) These include payments under the Flood Mitigation Assistance Program, Pre-Disaster Mitigation Program, and Hazard Mitigation Grant Program. The exclusion does not apply to amounts received for the sale or disposition of property, but the involuntary conversion rules may apply to such amounts, see ¶2430.[10]

¶ 1208   Compensation Income. ▆▆▆▆▆▆▆▆▆▆▆▆▆▆▆▆▆▆

All forms of compensation received for personal services are included in gross income.

4. ¶J-1476; ¶614.0065
5. ¶J-1371; ¶4514.166; TD ¶121,008
6. ¶G-2490; ¶4514.166; TD ¶121,008
7. ¶J-1480.2; ¶139A4

8. ¶J-1296; ¶1394; TD ¶193,600
9. ¶J-1290 *et seq.*; TD ¶193,601
10. ¶J-1296; ¶1394; TD ¶193,600

¶ 1209   Compensation includible in gross income.

Gross income includes compensation for services including: wages, salaries, fees, tips (¶1211), salesperson's commissions (including on sales to self or family), percentage of profits paid as compensation, commissions on insurance premiums, bonuses (including Christmas bonuses, see ¶1213), termination or severance pay, golden parachute payments (excess golden parachute payments subject the recipient to a 20% excise tax (Code Sec. 4999(a)),[11] rewards, jury duty fees (Code Sec. 61(a)(1); Reg § 1.61-2(a)(1)),[12] and fringe benefits not excluded by statute (see ¶1229 *et seq.*). (Code Sec. 61(a)(1)) Vacation pay also is taxable. [13]

Pension or retirement allowances to employees (reported to recipients on Form 1099-R) generally are taxable to the recipient, see ¶4337 *et seq.* (Reg § 1.61-11(a))[14] For rules for certain military pensions, see ¶1284.

Amounts withheld from an employee's pay by his employer for income and social security taxes, savings bonds, union dues, etc., represent compensation constructively received by the employee and must be included in his income for the year in which withheld. [15]

The employee is taxed even if the employer can't deduct part or all of the compensation because it's "unreasonable." (¶1517). (Reg § 1.162-8)[16]

¶ 1210   Reporting compensation and self-employment income.

The amount of wages, salaries, tips, etc., that's includible in income (¶1209), which should be shown on a Form W-2 issued by the employer, is reported on Form 1040. [17]

Income (or loss) subject to self-employment tax (¶3138) from a business operated, or a profession practiced, as a sole proprietor is reported on Form 1040, Schedule C or C-EZ. If an individual operates more than one business as a sole proprietor, a separate Schedule C or C-EZ must be prepared for each business. An individual can't report his income on Schedule C or C-EZ if he earns it as an "employee." [18] For farm income, see ¶4501.

¶ 1211   Tips and similar payments.

Tips and similar payments for special services are income. (Reg § 1.61-2(a)(1)) But a waiter may deduct the portion of tips that he turns over to assistants. [19] A tipped employee must maintain sufficient evidence to establish the amount of tip income he receives in a tax year. (Reg § 31.6053-4(a))[20]

¶ 1212   Compensation distinguished from gift.

Although gifts are generally excluded from the recipient's gross income (¶1371), transfer by or for an employer to or for the benefit of an employee can't be excluded as a gift. (Code Sec. 102(c)(1)) Extraordinary transfers to the natural objects of an employer's bounty (e.g., an employee who is the employer's son) aren't transfers to or for the benefit of the employee if he can show the transfer wasn't made in recognition of his employment. [21] For holiday gifts of nominal value, see ¶1213. For de minimis fringe benefits, see ¶1247.

11. ¶H-3003; ¶49,994; TD ¶132,504
12. ¶H-1001 *et seq.*; ¶614.007; TD ¶111,002
13. ¶s H-1001, H-1012; TD ¶130,505
14. ¶H-3245; ¶s 614.007, 4014; TD ¶141,000
15. ¶H-2152; TD ¶141,000
16. ¶H-1021; ¶614.014; TD ¶130,513

17. ¶H-1001.1; TD ¶102,002
18. ¶H-1001.1; TD ¶102,002
19. ¶s H-1009, H-4342; TD ¶131,006
20. ¶H-4343; ¶60,534; TD ¶131,003
21. ¶H-1027.1 *et seq.*; ¶s 614.016, 1024; TD ¶132,010

¶ 1213   Holiday gifts.

If, as a means of promoting goodwill, an employer makes a general distribution to employees of hams, turkeys and other merchandise of nominal value at Christmas or a comparable holiday, the value of the gifts isn't included in the employees' income. But if an employer distributes cash, gift certificates or similar items of readily convertible cash value, the value of the gifts is additional wages or salary, *regardless* of the value.[22]

¶ 1214   Below-market interest rate loans from employer.

An employee or independent contractor who receives a below-market (¶1306) compensation-related loan (except certain de minimis loans), recognizes compensation income equal to:

. . . on a compensation-related demand loan, the forgone interest (interest at the applicable federal rate (¶1116) over actual interest payable), and

. . . on any other compensation-related loan, the excess of the amount borrowed over the present value of all payments required to be made under the terms of the loan. (Code Sec. 7872(a)(1), Code Sec. 7872(b)(1))[23]

Certain employee-relocation loans are exempt from these rules. (Reg §   1.7872-5T(b)(6))[24]

¶ 1215   Vacation trips for salespersons; other noncash compensation.

If services rendered by the taxpayer are paid for in property or services rather than money, the fair market value (FMV) of the property or services must be included in income. For example, if a vacation trip is awarded to salespersons as a prize, the FMV of the trip is income. Where a price has been specified for the services being rendered, that price is considered the FMV of the property or services received if there's no evidence showing a different value. (Code Sec. 83; Reg §   1.61-2(d))[25]

¶ 1216   Notes receivable as compensation.

Notes and other evidences of indebtedness received in payment for services or in settlement of a claim for compensation are taxable as compensation in the amount of their fair market value when received. When a taxpayer receives as compensation a non-interest-bearing note regarded as good for its face value at maturity, he treats as income its fair discounted value computed at the prevailing rate. As note payments are received, he includes in income that portion of each payment representing the proportionate part of the discount originally taken on the entire note. (Reg §   1.61-2(d)(4))[26]

¶ 1217   Bargain purchase from employer.

If property, including stock, is transferred by an employer to an employee for less than its fair market value, the difference is compensation. (Code Sec. 83(a); Reg §   1.83-1(a))[27] For stock options, see ¶1220 *et seq.*

If an employee pays with a recourse note for stock acquired from his employer under a nonqualified stock option, and the employer later reduces the amount due on the note, the debt reduction is treated as compensation income. [28]

---

22. ¶H-1033; ¶1324.06; TD ¶132,002
23. ¶s H-2002, H-2004; ¶78,724.14; TD ¶136,503
24. ¶H-2014; ¶78,724.20; TD ¶136,512
25. ¶H-2500 *et seq.*; ¶s 614.007, 614.027; TD ¶136,001

26. ¶H-2513; ¶614.034; TD ¶136,003
27. ¶H-2509; ¶614.030; TD ¶136,005
28. ¶H-2535

¶ 1218   Restricted stock or other property—Section 83 rules.

A person receiving a beneficial interest in stock or other property for his services has compensation income equal to the value of that property at the time of receipt. But if his interest in the property is subject to substantial risk of forfeiture (is "restricted") and can't be transferred free of that risk, then income is deferred until the interest in the property either: (1) is no longer subject to that risk, *or* (2) becomes transferable free of the risk, whichever occurs earlier. (Code Sec. 83)[29] For election not to defer income, see ¶1219.

But the employee (or other owner of the property) has income if he sells or disposes of the property before (1) or (2), above. (Code Sec. 83(a))[30]

The amount included in income (in the year in which (1) or (2) occurs) is the excess of: the fair market value of the property in that year (figured without regard to restrictions other than those that by their terms will never lapse), over the amount, if any, paid for the property. (Code Sec. 83(a))[31]

A substantial risk of forfeiture exists if a person's rights to full enjoyment of the property are conditioned, directly or indirectly, upon the future performance (or refraining from performance) of substantial services by any individual. (Code Sec. 83(c)(1); Reg § 1.83-3(c)(1)) Examples: a requirement that the property be returned to the employer if total earnings don't increase (Reg § 1.83-3(c)(2)),[32] and SEC restrictions, such as the "short swing" rule (insider must pay over profits if stock is sold within six months of receipt). (Code Sec. 83(c)(3))[33] The six-month period under the short swing rule is measured from the date a nonstatutory option to acquire the stock is granted, and not from the date of exercise. [34]

¶ 1219   Election not to defer income from restricted stock or other property.

An employee or other person who receives restricted stock or other property (¶1218) may elect to recognize the income immediately instead of deferring it. (Code Sec. 83(b)(1))[35]

The amount of compensation income included in the year the property is received is the excess of: the fair market value of the property at receipt (without regard to restrictions other than those that by their terms will never lapse), over the amount, if any, paid for the property. (Code Sec. 83(b)(1))[36]

recommendation: Elect if the income taxed at grant would be negligible. This defers tax on any post-grant appreciation until sale, makes it eligible for capital gain rates, and may eliminate additional income tax completely if the property is held until death.

If the stock or other property is forfeited after the election is made, the employee can't get a deduction or refund of tax previously paid on income reported. (Code Sec. 83(b)(1))[37] The employee will have capital loss at the time of forfeiture. (Reg § 1.83-2(a))[38]

Elect within 30 days after the property is transferred to the employee. (Code Sec. 83(b)(2)) To elect, file a statement (specified in the regs) with the IRS office where the person who performs the services files his return. Attach a copy of the statement to the return for the year the property was transferred. (Reg § 1.83-2(c))[39]

IRS will consent to a revocation if the election was filed under a mistake of fact in the underlying transaction and the revocation is requested within 60 days of discovering the mistake of fact. Request to revoke the election within the 30 day period for making the

29. ¶s H-2500, H-2517 *et seq.*; ¶834 *et seq.*; TD ¶136,006
30. ¶H-2547 *et seq.*; ¶834.01; TD ¶136,006
31. ¶H-2532 *et seq.*; ¶834.01; TD ¶136,007
32. ¶H-2521; ¶834.02; TD ¶135,014
33. ¶s H-2530, H-2531; ¶834.02; TD ¶135,018
34. ¶H-2530

35. ¶H-2540; ¶834.03; TD ¶135,016
36. ¶H-2541; ¶834.03; TD ¶135,016
37. ¶M-3503; ¶834.03; TD ¶135,016
38. ¶I-1020; ¶834.03; TD ¶135,016
39. ¶H-2542 *et seq.*; ¶834.03; TD ¶135,016

election will generally be granted. [40]

¶ 1220 Nonstatutory stock options.

An option—other than an option under an employee stock purchase plan (see ¶1221) or an incentive stock option (ISO, see ¶1222)—which is granted in connection with the performance of services, to buy stock at a bargain, results in compensation income to the employee (or independent contractor) grantee. (Code Sec. 83) If the option has a readily ascertainable fair market value (FMV) at grant, it's subject to the restricted property rules of Code Sec. 83 (¶1218 *et seq.*) when the option is granted. (Code Sec. 83; Reg § 1.83-7(a))[41]

An option "ordinarily" has a readily ascertainable FMV only if it (or a substantially identical option) is actively traded on an established market. If not so traded, it has value only if certain conditions specified in the regs exist. (Reg § 1.83-7(b))[42]

If the option doesn't have a readily ascertainable FMV when granted, the employee doesn't realize compensation until the optioned property is transferred at exercise. The amount of compensation is the FMV of the property at transfer less any amount paid for the property. (Reg § 1.83-7(a))[43] (For the employer's compensation deduction, see ¶1525.)

The above treatment for nonstatutory options without a readily ascertainable FMV doesn't apply where the option is transferred before exercise to a "related person." (Reg § 1.83-7(a))[44]

Under an exception, the exercise of an option is treated as the grant of another option, instead of a transfer of shares, where the amount paid for the exercise is a debt secured by the shares on which there is no personal liability. (Reg § 1.83-3(a)(2)) However, this exception doesn't apply simply because options are exercised through a margin loan, and income will be realized on the exercise of options without a readily ascertainable FMV. [45]

¶ 1221 Employee stock purchase plan options.

These are options issued to employees under an employer plan to buy stock in the employer. The employee pays no tax on the option or the stock until he disposes of the stock. If the option price at least equals the stock's fair market value (FMV) at grant, gain is capital gain. But gain is ordinary compensation income (to the extent of the spread between option price and FMV of stock when option is exercised) if the stock is sold within two years after the option was granted or within one year after its exercise. (Code Sec. 423(a), Code Sec. 423(c))[46]

If the option price is less than 100% (but at least 85%) of the stock's FMV at grant, and the above holding period is met, the amount treated as ordinary income (rather than capital gain) is the *lesser* of: (1) the FMV of the stock when the option was granted, minus the option price, or (2) the excess of the FMV at the time of disposition or optionee's death, over the amount paid for the share under the option. (Code Sec. 423(c); Reg § 1.423-2(k))[47]

An executive branch federal employee (or spouse or dependent child) who acquired stock through the exercise of an employee stock purchase plan option and sells the stock in order to comply with Code Sec. 1043 federal conflict-of-interest requirements is deemed to satisfy the Code Sec. 423(a)(1) holding period requirement. (Code Sec. 421(d))

The plan must be nondiscriminatory, i.e., available to all employees (with certain exceptions). (Code Sec. 423(b)(4))[48]

---

40. ¶H-2545
41. ¶s H-2853, H-2857; ¶s 834.07, 4214.03; TD ¶135,202
42. ¶H-2872; ¶834.07; TD ¶135,203
43. ¶H-2861; ¶834.07; TD ¶135,206
44. ¶H-2864.1; ¶834.07; TD ¶135,207

45. ¶H-2508.1; TD ¶135,012
46. ¶H-2952 *et seq.*; ¶4234.01; TD ¶136,101
47. ¶H-2953; ¶4234.01; TD ¶136,101
48. ¶H-2972; ¶4234.02; TD ¶136,103

¶ 1222   Incentive stock options (ISOs).

An ISO is granted to an employee by an employer corporation (or its parent or sub) to buy stock or ownership interests in one of those corporations (a term that takes in S corporations, foreign corporations, and limited liability companies treated as corporations for federal tax purposes). (Reg § 1.421-1(d)(3), Reg § 1.421-1(i)(1)) There are no regular income tax consequences when an ISO is granted or exercised; the employee has capital gain when the stock is sold at a gain. (Code Sec. 421(a))[49] To qualify, an ISO must meet various requirements. (Code Sec. 422(b))[50]

Stock acquired through the exercise of an ISO generally can't be disposed of within two years after the option is granted or one year after the stock is transferred to the employee. (Code Sec. 422(a)(1)) Also, for the entire time from the date an ISO is granted until three months (one year in case of total and permanent disability) before its exercise, the option holder must be an employee of the option grantor (or its parent or sub or certain successor corporations). (Code Sec. 422(a)(2), Code Sec. 422(c)(6))[1]

An executive branch federal employee (or spouse or dependent child) who acquired stock through the exercise of an ISO and sells the stock in order to comply with Code Sec. 1043 federal conflict-of-interest requirements is deemed to satisfy the Code Sec. 422(a)(1) holding period requirement. (Code Sec. 421(d))

If there is a disqualifying disposition of a share of stock, Code Sec. 421 does not apply to the transfer of the share. Instead, the exercise of the option is governed by Code Sec. 83 and its regs. Thus, in the tax year in which the disqualifying disposition occurs, the individual recognizes compensation income (and gets a basis increase) equal to the FMV of the stock on the date the stock is transferred less the exercise price (determined without reduction for any brokerage fees or other disposition costs). (Reg § 1.421-2(b)) If the disqualifying disposition would trigger an allowable loss (e.g., not a sale to a related taxpayer), then the amount includible in the employee's income (and deductible by the employer, see ¶1525) as a result of that disqualifying disposition can't be more than the amount realized on the sale, minus the employee's adjusted basis in the stock. (Code Sec. 422(c)(2); Reg § 1.422-1(b)(2)(i))[2]

caution: For alternative minimum tax treatment, see ¶3208.

¶ 1223   Sale or cancellation of employment contract.

Proceeds from an employee's sale of rights under an employment contract to be performed are ordinary income. The same is true of amounts received from an employer in cancellation of an employment contract.[3]

¶ 1224   Members of Armed Forces.

The pay of Armed Forces members is taxable (Reg § 1.61-2(a)(1)), with exceptions:[4]

Gross income doesn't include any "qualified military benefit." (Code Sec. 134(a)) A "qualified military benefit" is any allowance or in-kind benefit (other than personal use of an automobile) received by a member or former member of the uniformed services of the U.S., or his dependent, and which was excludable from gross income on Sept. 9, '86 under any provision of law, reg or administrative practice (other than the Code) in effect on that date. (Code Sec. 134(b)(1)) Excludable allowances include (within certain limitations): veteran's benefits (¶1225), medical benefits, disability benefits, dependent care assistance program

---

49. ¶H-2750; ¶4224.01; TD ¶136,001
50. ¶H-2767; ¶4224.02; TD ¶136,004
1. ¶H-2795 *et seq.*; ¶4224.01; TD ¶136,006

2. ¶H-2799; ¶4224.01; TD ¶136,008
3. ¶H-1048 *et seq.*; TD ¶182,009
4. ¶H-3101; ¶614.040; TD ¶138,001

benefits, professional education, moving and storage, group-term life insurance, survivor and retirement protection plan premiums, subsistence, uniform, housing, overseas cost-of-living, evacuation, family separation allowances, death gratuities, interment allowance, various travel allowances and dependent benefits. [5] Specifically, dislocation allowances, temporary lodging allowances and expenses and move-in housing allowances provided in connection with permanent changes of station are excludible from income. (Reg § 1.61-2(b)(2))[6] For treatment of retirement pay, see ¶1284. A "qualified military base realignment and closure" fringe benefit isn't included in gross income and isn't subject to FICA. This benefit is a payment (subject to a maximum allowance) received under the Homeowner's Assistance Program (HAP) (Code Sec. 132(a)(8)).[7]

The recipient of a tax-free military housing allowance isn't thereby prevented from deducting mortgage interest or real estate taxes on a personal residence. (Code Sec. 265(a)(6)(A))[8]

The Code also excludes combat-zone compensation (limited, for commissioned officers, to the maximum enlisted amount). (Code Sec. 112; Reg § 1.112-1) Areas designated as combat zones include: the Afghanistan area; the Kosovo area; Serbia/Montenegro; Albania; the Adriatic Sea; the Ionian Sea (north of the 39th parallel); the Persian Gulf area; the Red Sea; the Gulf of Oman; parts of the Arabian Sea; the Gulf of Aden; the total land areas of Iraq, Kuwait, Saudi Arabia, Oman, Bahrain, Qatar, and the United Arab Emirates. Qualified hazardous duty areas (treated as combat zones) include Bosnia and Herzegovina; Croatia; and Macedonia. [9]

For various deadline extensions for a member of the Armed Forces serving in a designated "combat zone," see ¶4720. For tax relief for military and civilian employees of the U.S. dying in combat or terrorist attacks, see ¶4716.

¶ 1225 VA and state benefits to veterans.

Benefits under any law, regulation, or practice in effect on Sept. 9, '86 and administered by the Department of Veterans' Affairs are excludable from the recipient's gross income. (Code Sec. 140(a)(3)) This includes interest earned on dividends left on deposit with the VA and amounts received under a VA administered work therapy program. [10] State bonuses to veterans for service rendered to the U.S. are also exempt. [11]

¶ 1226 Government employees' compensation.

Federal, state and municipal employees, including federal judges, are taxable on their salary, wages and other compensation the same as other employees. [12] Payments under the Civil Service Retirement System are taxed like annuities, see ¶1355 *et seq.* [13] For tax relief for military and civilian employees of the U.S. dying in combat or terrorist attacks, see ¶4716.

¶ 1227 Members of clergy.

Members of the clergy are taxable on the salaries and fees they receive, and on any offerings they receive for marriages, funerals, masses, etc., *but not* on offerings made to the religious institution. (Reg § 1.61-2(a))[14]

A member of the clergy who is a "minister of the gospel" [15] can exclude from gross income:

. . . the rental value of a home (parsonage), including utilities, furnished to him as part of

---

5. ¶H-3102; ¶1344; TD ¶138,002
6. ¶H-3103; TD ¶138,003
7. ¶H-3104; ¶1324.11 ; TD ¶138,003.5
8. ¶K-9009; ¶2654
9. ¶H-3106 *et seq.*; ¶1124.01; TD ¶138,005
10. ¶H-3128; ¶614.041; TD ¶138,029

11. ¶H-3129; TD ¶138,030
12. ¶H-3130; ¶614.036; TD ¶138,031
13. ¶J-5052; ¶724.26; TD ¶141,006
14. ¶H-3151; ¶614.007; TD ¶138,501
15. ¶H-3163; ¶1074.02; TD ¶138,511

his compensation; (Code Sec. 107(1); Reg § 1.107-1(a)) or

... the rental allowance (parsonage allowance) paid to him as compensation, to the extent it's used in the year received to rent or provide a home and to the extent it does not exceed the fair rental value of the home, including furnishings and appurtenances such as a garage, plus the cost of utilities. (Code Sec. 107(2)) The employer church or organization must designate the payment as a rental allowance before the payment is made. (Reg § 1.107-1(b))[16]

A retired member of the clergy is entitled to the exclusion. The retiree's widow is not. [17]

The rental allowance exclusion doesn't prevent a minister from deducting mortgage interest or real estate taxes on a personal residence. (Code Sec. 265(a)(6)(B))[18]

¶ 1228   Compensation of minors.

The income of a minor from compensation earned by him or received in respect of his services is income to him, even if received by the parent. (Code Sec. 73(a))[19]

observation: If the child is subject to the kiddie tax rules, the rate of tax on his unearned income may depend on the parent's tax rate, see ¶3134.

¶ 1229   Fringe Benefits.

Fringe benefits received by an employee are taxable unless specifically excluded.

¶ 1230   Taxation of fringe benefits.

A fringe benefit provided to any person in connection with the performance of services is treated as compensation for those services. (Reg § 1.61-21(a)(3))[20] Unless it's specifically excluded (¶1243), the benefit is includible in the gross income of the person performing the services, even if it's furnished to someone else. (Code Sec. 61(a)(1); Reg § 1.61-21(a)(4))[21]

¶ 1231   Valuation of taxable fringe benefits—general rule.

An employee who is taxed on a fringe benefit (¶1230) must include in gross income the fair market value (FMV) of the benefit minus: (1) any payment for the benefit, and (2) any amount specifically excluded by a Code provision. (Reg § 1.61-21(b)(1))[22] The FMV of a fringe benefit generally is the amount that an individual would have to pay for the particular benefit in an arm's-length transaction. (Reg § 1.61-21(b)(2))[23]

Unless a special valuation rule (¶1233) applies, an employer-provided vehicle is valued at the comparable lease cost (¶1234) (Reg § 1.61-21(b)(4)),[24] and flights on an employer-provided aircraft at comparable charter or lease cost. (Reg § 1.61-21(b)(6), Reg § 1.61-21(b)(7))[25]

Chauffeur services are valued separately from vehicle availability, at comparable arm's-length transaction costs or by reference to the chauffeur's compensation (including any non-taxable lodging, see ¶1268). (Reg § 1.61-21(b)(5))[26]

¶ 1232   Transportation furnished because of unsafe conditions.

Transportation or reimbursement for such (e.g., cab fare) furnished by an employer under a written policy solely because of unsafe conditions for employee commuting is valued at

---

16. ¶H-3153 *et seq.*; ¶1074; TD ¶138,502 *et seq.*
17. ¶H-3161; TD ¶138,509
18. ¶H-3160; ¶s 1074.03, 2654; TD ¶138,505
19. ¶H-3180; ¶734.01; TD ¶836,009
20. ¶H-1051; ¶614.027; TD ¶134,002
21. ¶H-1051; ¶H-1053; ¶614.027; TD ¶134,001; TD ¶134,002

22. ¶H-1055; ¶614.027; TD ¶134,003
23. ¶H-1056; ¶614.027; TD ¶134,003
24. ¶H-2232; ¶614.027; TD ¶134,502
25. ¶H-2302 *et seq.*; ¶614.027; TD ¶134,570
26. ¶H-2289 *et seq.*; ¶614.027

$1.50 per one-way commute (i.e., from home to work, or work to home) for each qualifying employee. (Reg § 1.61-21(k)(3))[27]

¶ 1233 Special valuation rules for autos, other vehicles and airflights.

Special valuation rules may be used under certain circumstances for certain commonly provided fringe benefits (e.g., automobiles, noncommercial flights, commuting). (Reg § 1.61-21(b), Reg § 1.61-21(c)(1), Reg § 1.61-21(c)(3))[28] Where the special rules aren't used, either by choice or because they aren't permitted, or where they're improperly applied, the value of the fringe benefit must be determined under the general valuation principles at ¶1231. (Reg § 1.61-21(c)(5))[29]

An employee can't use a special valuation rule to value a fringe benefit unless the employer uses the same rule to value it. (Reg § 1.61-21(c)(2))[30]

¶ 1234 Annual lease value method for automobiles—use of IRS table.

To compute an auto's annual lease value, first determine fair market value (FMV) as of the first date it is made available to *any* employee for personal use. Under safe harbor rules, where the auto is bought at arm's length by the employer, the FMV is the cost, including sales tax, title fees and other purchase expenses. Where leased, it's the suggested retail price less 8%, the retail value as reported in a nationally recognized publication that regularly reports such values (Reg § 1.61-21(d)(5)), or the manufacturer's invoice price plus 4%. [31] Then, find the dollar range in column (1) of the table below that includes the auto's FMV. The corresponding amount in column (2) is its annual lease value. (Reg § 1.61-21(d)(2)(iii))

Automobile fair market value (1)	Annual lease value (2)	Automobile fair market value (1)	Annual lease value (2)
$0 to 999	$600	22,000 to 22,999	6,100
1,000 to 1,999	850	23,000 to 23,999	6,350
2,000 to 2,999	1,100	24,000 to 24,999	6,600
3,000 to 3,999	1,350	25,000 to 25,999	6,850
4,000 to 4,999	1,600	26,000 to 27,999	7,250
5,000 to 5,999	1,850	28,000 to 29,999	7,750
6,000 to 6,999	2,100	30,000 to 31,999	8,250
7,000 to 7,999	2,350	32,000 to 33,999	8,750
8,000 to 8,999	2,600	34,000 to 35,999	9,250
9,000 to 9,999	2,850	36,000 to 37,999	9,750
10,000 to 10,999	3,100	38,000 to 39,999	10,250
11,000 to 11,999	3,350	40,000 to 41,999	10,750
12,000 to 12,999	3,600	42,000 to 43,999	11,250
13,000 to 13,999	3,850	44,000 to 45,999	11,750
14,000 to 14,999	4,100	46,000 to 47,999	12,250
15,000 to 15,999	4,350	48,000 to 49,999	12,750
16,000 to 16,999	4,600	50,000 to 51,999	13,250
17,000 to 17,999	4,850	52,000 to 53,999	13,750
18,000 to 18,999	5,100	54,000 to 55,999	14,250
19,000 to 19,999	5,350	56,000 to 57,999	14,750
20,000 to 20,999	5,600	58,000 to 59,999	15,250
21,000 to 21,999	5,850		

27. ¶H-2201 *et seq.*; TD ¶134,606
28. ¶s H-1056 *et seq.*, H-2200 *et seq.*, H-2300 *et seq.*; ¶614.027; TD ¶134,500
29. ¶H-1057; ¶614.027; TD ¶134,502
30. ¶H-1060; ¶614.027; TD ¶134,555
31. ¶H-2240; ¶614.027; TD ¶134,510

For autos with a FMV in excess of $59,999, the annual lease value equals: (.25 × auto FMV) + $500.[32]

illustration: On Jan. 1, of Year 1, X Co. provides a car worth $20,500 free to its employee E. None of the fringe benefit exclusions applies. The annual lease value (see chart above) is $5,600. This is the value of E's benefit for Year 1. E must include $5,600 in income.

This method takes into account the value of insuring and maintaining the auto, but not the value of fuel, which if provided in kind can be valued based on all facts and circumstances, or alternatively at 5½¢ per mile for all miles driven (in the U.S., Canada or Mexico) by the employee. (Reg § 1.61-21(d)(3))[33]

The annual lease values computed above are determined on the basis of an assumed four-year lease term (beginning on the first date this method is used and ending on Dec. 31 of the following fourth full calendar year). The annual lease value for each next four-year period is determined on the basis of the FMV on the Jan. 1 after the preceding period, using the lease valuation table. (Reg § 1.61-21(d)(2)(iv))[34]

Subject to certain restrictions, an employer with a fleet of 20 or more autos may determine the annual lease value of each auto in the fleet as if its FMV were equal to the "fleet-average value." (Reg § 1.61-21(d)(5)) This method can't be used for autos with a FMV greater than $20,100 for 2007 ($21,100 for trucks or vans). [35]

¶ 1235   Prorated annual lease value.

Where an employer-provided auto is continuously available to the employee for periods of 30 or more days, but less than an entire calendar year, the value of the availability of the auto is the prorated annual lease value, computed by multiplying the annual lease value (¶1235) by a fraction: the numerator is the number of days of availability, and the denominator is 365. (Reg § 1.61-21(d)(4))[36]

¶ 1236   Daily lease value.

Where an employer-provided auto is continuously available to the employee for at least one but less than 30 days, the value of the use of the auto is its daily lease value, calculated by multiplying the auto's annual lease value (¶1235) by a fraction: the numerator is four times the number of days of the auto's availability, and the denominator is 365. A 30-day period may be used even if availability is less than 30 days if this produces a lower valuation. (Reg § 1.61-21(d)(4))[37]

¶ 1237   Cents-per-mile valuation method.

Under this method, the value of an employer-provided auto equals the total number of miles the employee drove it for personal purposes in the tax year times the optional standard mileage rate, see ¶1561.[38] This method takes into account the value of insuring and maintaining the vehicle, and the value of fuel provided by the employer. If fuel isn't provided, the cents-per-mile rate may be reduced by no more than 5.5¢ per mile. (Reg § 1.61-21(e)(3))[39] The cents-per-mile method can't be used if the auto's fair market value, as of the date it's first made available to any employee for personal use, exceeds an annually-adjusted amount, $15,100 for 2007 ($16,100 for a truck or van). [40]

---

32. ¶s H-2238, H-2239; TD ¶134,508
33. ¶H-2253; ¶614.027; TD ¶134,521
34. ¶H-2246; ¶614.027; TD ¶134,516
35. ¶H-2260; ¶614.027; TD ¶134,527
36. ¶H-2243; ¶614.027; TD ¶134,513

37. ¶H-2245; ¶614.027; TD ¶134,515
38. ¶H-2268; ¶614.027; TD ¶134,536
39. ¶H-2277 *et seq.*; ¶614.027; TD ¶134,543
40. ¶H-2272; ¶614.027; TD ¶134,540

¶ 1238 Commuting value method—$1.50 per one-way commute.

Under this method, the value of an employee's use of a vehicle, including an automobile, for commuting purposes only is computed as $1.50 per one-way commute (e.g., from home to work, or work to home). If there's more than one employee who commutes in a single vehicle, the commuting benefit is still $1.50 per one way commute for each employee. (Reg § 1.61-21(f)(3))[41] Various requirements must be satisfied. For example, the employee must be required to commute in the auto for bona-fide noncompensatory business reasons. The method can't be used for "control employees" (certain owner-employees, higher-paid employees, and directors) (Reg § 1.61-21(f)(1)), or to value the commuting use of any chauffeur-driven vehicle, except for the commuting use by the chauffeur. (Reg § 1.61-21(f)(2))[42]

¶ 1239 Employer-provided airflights.

Airflights provided by an employer for an employee's personal purposes are fringe benefits includible in the employee's gross income. (Reg § 1.61-21(a)(1))[43]

Special valuation methods are available to value noncommercial flights on employer-provided aircraft (¶1240 *et seq.*), and "space available" flights on commercial aircraft (¶1242). Use of a special method is optional. But if an employer uses either special rule, he must generally use it to value all flights taken by employees in a calendar year. (Reg § 1.61-21(g)(14)(i), Reg § 1.61-21(h)(5)(i))[44]

If an employee takes a trip on an employer-provided aircraft primarily for his employer's business which includes both personal flights and business flights, the value of the personal flights is a taxable fringe benefit. The value of the benefit equals the excess of the value of all the flights comprising the trip, over the value of the flights the employee would have taken had he travelled only for business. If the employee combines personal and business flights on a trip that's primarily personal, the amount includible is the value of the personal flights that would have been taken had there been only personal flights. The value of all these flights may be computed under the special valuation rules (¶1240 *et seq.*). (Reg § 1.61-21(g)(4))[45]

¶ 1240 SIFL formula for noncommercial flights.

Value is determined by multiplying the "base aircraft valuation formula"—also known as the Standard Industry Fair Level (SIFL) formula (cents-per-mile rates that are revised semi-annually)—in effect at the time of the flight by the "aircraft multiple" (based on the takeoff weight of the plane) and adding the applicable "terminal charge." (Reg § 1.61-21(g)(5))[46]

¶ 1241 "Seating capacity" (zero inclusion) rule for noncommercial flights.

The "seating capacity" rule is available for noncommercial flights on employer-provided aircraft where at least half of the aircraft's passenger seating capacity is occupied by employees whose flights are primarily for the employer's business (and whose flights are excludable as a working condition fringe, see ¶1246). In this situation, the includible value of the flight taken by the employee for personal purposes is zero. (Reg § 1.61-21(g)(12))[47]

¶ 1242 "Space-available" rule for commercial flights.

If an employer provides an employee (as specially defined at Reg § 1.132-1(b)(1)) with a flight on a commercial aircraft for the employee's personal purposes, the flight is a taxable

41. ¶H-2282; ¶614.027; TD ¶134,549
42. ¶H-2283; ¶614.027; TD ¶134,550
43. ¶H-2301; ¶614.027; TD ¶134,570
44. ¶H-2301 *et seq.*; ¶614.027; TD ¶134,570

45. ¶s H-2314, H-2315; ¶614.027
46. ¶s H-2304, H-2307 *et seq.*; ¶614.027; TD ¶134,570
47. ¶H-2319; ¶614.027; TD ¶134,570

fringe benefit whose value must be included in the employee's gross income (¶1239). If the flight is a "space-available flight" on a commercial airline, its value for certain current or former airline employees may be computed under a special rule: 25% of the actual carrier's highest unrestricted coach fare for the flight taken. (Reg § 1.61-21(h)(1))[48]

¶ 1243 Excludable fringe benefits.

A fringe benefit isn't included in gross income if it's excluded under a specific Code Section (see below) (Code Sec. 61(a)), or qualifies as one of the following: (Code Sec. 132(a))[49]

. . . no additional cost service (¶1244);

. . . qualified employee discount (¶1245);

. . . working condition fringe (¶1246);

. . . de minimis fringe (¶1247);

. . . qualified transportation fringe (¶1248);

. . . qualified moving expense reimbursement (¶1249);

. . . employer-provided retirement advice (¶1251).

A fringe benefit that's expressly provided for in any other Code Section can't be excluded from gross income under the Code Sec. 132 rules, except as a de minimis fringe or as a qualified moving expense reimbursement. (Code Sec. 132(l))[50] Fringe benefits excluded under a specific Code Section include: holiday and other gifts of nominal value (¶1213); stock options (¶1220); clergy member's home ("parsonage allowance," ¶1227); employee achievement awards (¶1252); on-premises athletic facilities (¶1253); adoption assistance (¶1255); educational assistance (¶2215); medical care coverage, including accident and health insurance (¶1256 *et seq.*); group-term life insurance (¶1263); meals and lodging (¶1268); qualified campus lodging (¶1269); cafeteria (flexible benefit) plans (¶1270); dependent care assistance programs (¶1271); scholarships (¶2216); and cost of living allowances to certain U.S. government employees (¶4624).[1]

¶ 1244 No-additional-cost services.

No-additional-cost services are excluded from an employee's gross income (see ¶1243). (Code Sec. 132(a)(1))[2] These are services provided by an employer to an employee for personal use by the employee, his spouse or dependent children, if:

(1) the services are ordinarily offered for sale to nonemployee customers in the ordinary course of the line of business in which the employee works,

(2) the employer incurs no substantial additional cost (including foregone revenue) in providing the services to the employee —computed without regard to any amounts paid by the employee for the services (Code Sec. 132(b)),[3] and

(3) special nondiscrimination rules are satisfied. (Code Sec. 132(j)(1))[4]

No-additional-cost services include services that would remain unused if the employee customers didn't use them, e.g., hotel accommodations, transportation by air, train, bus, subway or cruise line, and telephone services. (Reg § 1.132-2(a)(2))[5]

---

48. ¶H-2337; ¶614.027; TD ¶134,570
49. ¶H-1051; ¶1324; TD ¶134,001
50. ¶H-1052; ¶1324; TD ¶134,001
1. ¶H-1052; ¶614.027; TD ¶134,018

2. ¶H-1871; ¶1324.03; TD ¶134,004
3. ¶H-1871; ¶1324.03; TD ¶134,004
4. ¶H-1930 *et seq.*; ¶1324.01; TD ¶134,007
5. ¶H-1872; ¶1324.03

¶ 1245   Qualified employee discounts.

Qualified employee discounts are excluded from an employee's gross income (see ¶1243). (Code Sec. 132(a)(2))[6] A "qualified employee discount" is an "employee discount" allowed with respect to "qualified property or services" provided by an employer to an employee, his spouse or dependent children, to the extent the discount doesn't exceed the limits described below. (Code Sec. 132(c)(1))[7]

An "employee discount" is the excess of:

(1) the price at which property or services are offered by an employer for sale to nonemployee customers, over

(2) the price at which the employer offers the same property or services to employees for use by those employees. (Code Sec. 132(c)(3))[8]

"Qualified property or services" means any property (other than real property, or personal property of a kind held for investment) or services that are offered for sale to nonemployee customers in the ordinary course of the employer's line of business in which the employee works. (Code Sec. 132(c)(4), Code Sec. 132(k))[9]

Limitations. The excludable amount of a qualified employee discount with respect to property is limited to the gross profit percentage of the price at which that property is offered by the employer to customers. (Code Sec. 132(c)(1)(A)) Gross profit percentage equals the aggregate sales price of the property sold by the employer to all customers, whether employees or nonemployees (Reg § 1.132-3(c)(1)(i)), over the aggregate cost of the property (Code Sec. 132(c)(2)(A)(i)), divided by the aggregate sales price. (Code Sec. 132(c)(2)(A)(ii))[10]

The excludable amount for services is limited to 20% of the price at which the employer offers the service to nonemployee customers. (Code Sec. 132(c)(1)(B), Code Sec. 132(k))[11]

¶ 1246   Working condition fringes.

Working condition fringes are excluded from the employee's gross income (see ¶1243). (Code Sec. 132(a)(3))[12] A "working condition fringe" is any property or services provided to an employee by the employer to the extent the cost of the property or services would have been deductible by the employee under either Code Sec. 162 (as trade or business expenses) or Code Sec. 167 (as depreciation expenses) if the employee had paid for the property or services himself. (Code Sec. 132(d))[13] Examples are: employer-paid business travel and the use of employer-provided vehicles for business purposes. [14]

Certain benefits qualify as working condition fringes only if special requirements are satisfied. These include: the use of consumer goods manufactured for sale to nonemployee customers and provided to employees for product testing and evaluation outside the employer's work place (Reg § 1.132-5(n)(1));[15] the personal use of vehicles otherwise used in connection with the business of farming (Reg § 1.132-5(g));[16] job placement assistance; [17] employer-paid club dues (Reg § 1.132-5(s));[18] employer-paid expenses of a companion on a business trip (Reg § 1.132-5(t));[19] "qualified automobile demonstration use" by automobile salespersons (Code Sec. 132(j)(3); Reg § 1.132-5(o));[20] the use of employer-owned aircraft for business travel (Reg § 1.132-5(k));[21] certain forms of transportation and other employer-provided

6. ¶H-1901; ¶1324.04; TD ¶134,008
7. ¶H-1902; ¶1324.04; TD ¶134,009
8. ¶H-1904; ¶1324.04
9. ¶H-1903; ¶1324.04; TD ¶134,008
10. ¶H-1909; ¶1324.04; TD ¶134,009
11. ¶H-1914; ¶1324.04; TD ¶134,009
12. ¶H-1701; ¶1324.05; TD ¶134,010
13. ¶H-1701; ¶1324.05; TD ¶134,010

14. ¶H-1701; ¶1324.05; TD ¶134,012
15. ¶H-1712; ¶1324.05; TD ¶134,012
16. ¶H-2370; ¶1324.05; TD ¶134,012
17. ¶H-1711; ¶1324.05; TD ¶134,012
18. ¶H-2153.1; TD ¶136,529
19. ¶H-2153.2; TD ¶136,530
20. ¶H-2364; ¶1324.05; TD ¶134,568
21. ¶H-2351; ¶1324.05; TD ¶134,012

security measures provided because of bona fide business-oriented security concerns (Reg § 1.132-5(m));[22] and the use of "qualified nonpersonal use vehicles." (Reg § 1.132-5(h))[23]

If an employer provides the use of a vehicle and includes the entire amount in the employee's income (without excluding any working condition fringe benefit amount), the employee can deduct the value multiplied by the percentage of business use as a miscellaneous itemized deduction (subject to the 2% floor, see ¶3110). This deduction can't be computed under a cents-per-mile method. (Reg § 1.162-25(b))[24]

¶ 1247   De minimis fringe benefits.

De minimis fringe benefits are excluded from the recipient's gross income (see ¶1243). (Code Sec. 132(a)(4)) A de minimis fringe is any property or service whose value is so small that accounting for it is unreasonable or administratively impracticable, taking into account the frequency with which similar fringe benefits are provided by the employer to its employees. (Code Sec. 132(e)(1))

Examples of de minimis fringes include: occasional meals, supper money, or local transportation provided because of overtime work (Reg § 1.132-6(d)(2)); meals at employer-operated eating facilities (see below); transportation (e.g., taxi fare) where other available means of transportation are unsafe, in excess of value over $1.50 per each one-way commute (¶1232) (Reg § 1.132-6(d)(2)); occasional cocktail parties or picnics; traditional holiday gifts of property (not cash) with a low FMV; flowers, fruit, etc., provided under special circumstances, such as sickness or outstanding performance; (Reg § 1.132-6(e)(1)) and electronically filing the employee's income tax return (but not paying someone to prepare his return). [25]

No qualified transportation fringe benefit (¶1248) (including amounts in excess of the dollar limit) may be excluded as a de minimis fringe benefit. (Code Sec. 132(f)(7))[26] However, partners, 2% S corporation shareholders and independent contractors (but not employees) can exclude transit passes, tokens and fare cards if not in excess of $21 per month. [27]

Meals at employer-operated eating facilities are de minimis fringes if the facility's annual revenues normally equal or exceed its direct operating costs and certain nondiscrimination rules are met. Employees who are entitled (under the rules at ¶1268) to exclude the value of a meal provided at the facility are treated as having paid an amount for the meal equal to the direct operating costs of the facility attributable to the meal. (Code Sec. 132(e)(2); Reg § 1.132-7(a)(2), Reg § 1.132-7(c))[28] Direct operating costs are the costs of the food and beverages served and the labor for related services performed primarily on the facility's premises. (Reg § 1.132-7(b)(1))[29]

¶ 1248   Qualified transportation fringe benefits.

An employee (other than a self-employed person) may exclude from income qualified transportation fringe benefits up to specified dollar amounts (below). (Code Sec. 132(a)(5), Code Sec. 132(f)(5)) These benefits include:

(1) Transportation in a commuter highway vehicle (van pool), if in connection with travel between the employee's residence and place of employment. A commuter highway vehicle has a seating capacity of 6 adults (excluding the driver) for which 80% of the mileage must be reasonably expected to be for employee commuting and to be for trips where the vehicle is half full (excluding the driver).

---

22. ¶H-2373 *et seq.*; ¶1324.05; TD ¶134,012
23. ¶H-2354; ¶1324.05; TD ¶134,012
24. ¶s H-2363, L-1912; ¶s 1624.283, 2744.17; TD ¶293,019
25. ¶H-1802 *et seq.*; ¶1324.06; TD ¶134,013

26. ¶H-2202; ¶1324.08; TD ¶134,596
27. ¶H-1806; TD ¶134,014
28. ¶H-1821; ¶1324.06; TD ¶131,510
29. ¶H-1823; ¶1324.06; TD ¶131,510

(2) Transit passes for use on a mass transit facility (e.g., rail, bus or ferry) or a commuter highway vehicle.

(3) Qualified parking at or near the employer's business premises or a location from which the employee commutes to work by mass transit or hired commuter vehicle. Any parking at or near the employee's residence isn't qualified parking. (Code Sec. 132(f)(1), Code Sec. 132(f)(5); Reg § 1.132-9(b))[30]

For 2007, up to $215 ($220 for 2008) a month of qualified parking and up to $110 a month ($115 for 2008) of the combined value of transit passes and vanpools may be excluded. (Code Sec. 132(f)(2))[31]

Cash reimbursements (but *not* cash advances) are excludable. But reimbursements for transit passes are excludable only where vouchers, etc. (which may be exchanged only for transit passes) aren't readily available for direct distribution by the employer to the employee. (Code Sec. 132(f)(3); Reg § 1.132-9(b))[32]

No amount is included in an employee's gross income solely because he may choose between any qualified transportation fringe and otherwise includible compensation. (Code Sec. 132(f)(4)) But if he chooses cash instead of a qualified transportation fringe, he will be taxed.[33] If he elects fringes rather than cash, he won't be taxed on any exchanged cash if requirements are met. (Reg § 1.132-9(b))[34]

The qualified transportation fringe exclusion doesn't apply to any arrangement that results in the reimbursement of an expense the employee hasn't actually incurred, e.g., where the employee is reimbursed for an item he paid for through a tax-free salary reduction. [35]

Partners, 2% S corporation shareholders and independent contractors can't exclude qualified transportation fringes. (Code Sec. 132(f)(5)(E))[36]

¶ 1249 Qualified moving expense reimbursement.

A taxpayer excludes from gross income any qualified moving expense reimbursement. (Code Sec. 132(a)(6))[37] A qualified moving expense reimbursement is any amount received (directly or indirectly) by the taxpayer from an employer as a payment of (or reimbursement for) moving expenses that would have been deductible had the taxpayer paid them directly (for employee's moving expense deduction, see ¶1645 *et seq.*). Expenses aren't excludable if the taxpayer actually deducted them in an earlier year. (Code Sec. 132(g))[38] Otherwise an employer's payment or reimbursement is income to the employee. (Code Sec. 82)[39] The employer reports moving expense reimbursements (but not qualifying payments to third parties or qualifying services furnished in kind) to the employee on Form W-2. [40]

¶ 1250 Reimbursement of employee in connection with sale of his home.

An employer's reimbursement for an employee's loss on sale of the employee's home is income to the employee.[41] However, if the employer buys the employee's home at its fair market value (FMV), the employee has no income other than gain on the sale. Where, as an alternative to reimbursing an employee for the loss, the employer buys the home for more than its FMV, that *excess* is taxable to the employee. [42]

30. ¶H-2205; ¶1324.08; TD ¶134,016
31. ¶H-2217.1; ¶1324.08; TD ¶134,591
32. ¶H-2212, H-2216; ¶1324.08; TD ¶134,578
33. ¶H-2216.1; ¶1324.08; TD ¶134,016
34. ¶H-2216.1; ¶1324.08; TD ¶134,584 *et seq.*
35. ¶H-2216
36. ¶H-2206; ¶1324.08; TD ¶134,572

37. ¶H-1971; ¶1324.09; TD ¶136,541
38. ¶H-1971; ¶1324.09; TD ¶136,541
39. ¶H-4418; ¶824; TD ¶136,535
40. ¶S-3170; ¶60,514; TD ¶812,012
41. ¶s H-2161, H-2162; ¶824.01; TD ¶136,536
42. ¶H-2162; TD ¶136,536

¶ 1251   Employer-provided retirement advice.

Qualified retirement planning services are excluded from the income of the employee receiving the services. (Code Sec. 132(a)(7)) Qualified retirement planning services are any retirement planning services provided to an employee and his spouse by an employer maintaining a qualified employer plan (as defined in Code Sec. 219(g)(5)). (Code Sec. 132(m))[43]

¶ 1252   Employee achievement awards.

Employee achievement awards are excludable only to the extent the employer can deduct the cost of the award—generally limited to $400 for any one employee, or $1,600 for a "qualified plan award," see ¶1591. (Code Sec. 74(c)(2))[44]

¶ 1253   On-premises athletic facilities.

The value of an on-premises athletic facility provided by an employer is excluded from an employee's gross income. (Code Sec. 132(j)(4)(A))[45]

¶ 1254   Employer payment of employee's personal expenses.

Where an employer pays the debts or personal expenses of an employee, or reimburses the employee's payment, the employee must include the employer's payment or reimbursement in his (employee's) income.[46] For medical expenses, see ¶1256.

An employer's payment of an employee's income taxes (federal or state) or other taxes is income to the employee. Pyramiding of income, and of tax, results where the employer agrees to pay all the employee's tax. (Reg § 1.61-14)[47]

¶ 1255   Employer-provided adoption assistance.

An employee may exclude amounts paid or expenses incurred by his employer for qualified adoption expenses (¶2356) connected with the employee's adoption of a child, if the amounts are furnished under an adoption assistance program in existence (and known to the employee) before the expenses are incurred. For 2007, the total amount excludable per child is limited to $11,390 ($11,650 for 2008). In the case of an adoption of a child with special needs the exclusion applies regardless of whether the employee has qualified adoption expenses. (Code Sec. 137(a), Code Sec. 137(b), Code Sec. 137(f))[48]

The excludable amount is phased out for taxpayers with adjusted gross income (AGI, as specially computed) over $170,820 in 2007 ($174,730 in 2008) (adjusted for inflation annually) and is fully eliminated when AGI reaches $210,820 in 2007 ($214,730 in 2008). (Code Sec. 137(b)(2), Code Sec. 137(f)) To compute the excluded employer-provided adoption benefits, use Form 8839.[49]

Amounts are excludable in the year in which the employer pays for qualified adoption expenses of an eligible child who is a U.S. citizen or resident when the adoption commenced. If the eligible child isn't a U.S. citizen or resident, the exclusion is available only for adoptions that become final, and only in the year that they are finalized. Where expenses of a foreign eligible child are paid in a year before the adoption becomes final, the employee includes the employer's assistance in income for that year, and claims the otherwise available exclusion in the year the adoption becomes final. A taxpayer may claim both an adoption

---

43. ¶H-1980; ¶1324.10
44. ¶L-2317 *et seq.*; ¶744.03; TD ¶132,007
45. ¶H-1951; ¶1324.07; TD ¶134,017
46. ¶H-2151; ¶s 614.007, 614.146; TD ¶136,527

47. ¶H-2157; ¶614.147; TD ¶198,506
48. ¶H-1450 et seq.; ¶1374; TD ¶133,600 et seq.
49. ¶H-1453; ¶1374; TD ¶133,603

expense credit (see ¶2356) and an exclusion for the adoption of an eligible child, but cannot claim a credit and an exclusion for the same expense. [50]

¶ 1256 Employee's medical expenses reimbursed or insured by employer.

An employee can exclude from gross income amounts received from his employer, directly or indirectly, as reimbursement for expenses for the medical care of himself, his spouse, and his dependents. (These amounts are excludable even where a sole proprietor employer is the employee's spouse, and the amounts received are for the employer-spouse's medical care.) [1] However, reimbursement is includible in the employee's income to the extent it exceeds medical expenses or it's attributable to medical expense deductions he took in a previous year. (Code Sec. 105(b); Reg § 1.105-2)[2]

An employee also excludes from gross income the cost (i.e., premiums paid) of employer-provided *coverage* under an accident or health plan. (Code Sec. 106)[3] However, if the employer-provided policy, trust, etc., provides other benefits, only the portion of the employer contributions for the accident and health coverage is excludable. (Reg § 1.106-1)[4]

Where a plan allows reimbursements of a nonqualifying beneficiary's medical expense, no payment from the plan during the year to any person —including the employee, his spouse or dependents—is excluded from income. IRS will apply this rule for plans with such provisions in them before Aug. 15, 2006, only for plan years beginning after 2008. [5]

Insurance premiums paid for partners and more-than-2% S corporation shareholders (who are treated as partners) are not excludable. [6]

Highly compensated individuals (as defined in Code Sec. 105(h)(5)) who benefit from an employer's "self-insured" medical reimbursement plan that discriminates in their favor must include "excess reimbursements" (reimbursements for benefits not available to other plan participants) in income. (Code Sec. 105(h))[7]

¶ 1257 Employer contributions to Archer medical savings account (Archer MSA).

Small-employer contributions to an employee's Archer medical savings account (Archer MSA) are treated as excludable employer-provided coverage for medical expenses under an accident or health plan (¶1256) to the extent the amounts don't exceed the applicable statutory limits (see ¶1528). (Code Sec. 106(b)(1))[8] Generally, small employers are those that employed on average no more than 50 employees during either of the two preceding years. An employer that grows past the 50-employee limit in a succeeding year may continue MSA contributions until the year after the first year in which it has more than 200 employees. (Code Sec. 220(c)(4))[9] For treatment of Archer MSA distributions, see ¶1380. Employer Archer MSA contributions aren't excludable if made at the employee's election under a salary reduction arrangement under a cafeteria plan. (Code Sec. 125(f))

Employers that provide high deductible health plan coverage plus an MSA and make employer contributions must make available a comparable contribution on behalf of all employees with comparable coverage during the same period. A 35% penalty applies for noncompliance. (Code Sec. 4980E)[10]

For the cutoff date for Archer MSA contributions, see ¶1528.

50. ¶H-1451 *et seq.*, ¶1374, TD ¶133,602; 133,608
1. ¶H-1110; TD ¶133,036
2. ¶H-1110 *et seq.*; ¶1054.01; TD ¶133,036
3. ¶H-1102; ¶1064; TD ¶133,032
4. ¶H-1106; ¶1064; TD ¶133,034
5. ¶H-1349.3

6. ¶H-1126; ¶1064; TD ¶133,026
7. ¶H-1138 *et seq.*; ¶1054.05; TD ¶133,013
8. ¶H-1101.1 et seq., ¶1064, TD ¶133,040
9. ¶s H-1333, H-1333.1; ¶2204.01; TD ¶288,102
10. ¶H-1336.3; ¶4980E4; TD ¶288,104

¶ 1258 Employer contributions to health savings accounts (HSA).

Employer contributions to a health savings account (HSA) of the employee are treated as employer-provided coverage for medical expenses under an accident or health plan (¶1256) to the extent the amounts don't exceed the statutory limits (see ¶1529) applicable to the employee for the tax year, and are deductible by the employer in the year they are paid. (Code Sec. 106(d)(2)) Employer contributions to an HSA on behalf of an eligible individual are excludable from income.[11] Employer contributions to an HSA must be reported on the employee's Form W-2, Box 12.[12] For HSA distributions, see ¶1381

There is no constructive receipt of income solely because the employee may choose between employer contributions to an HSA and to another health plan. (Code Sec. 106(d)(2)) Employer contributions to an HSA are excludable if made at the employee's election under a salary reduction arrangement in a cafeteria plan (see ¶1270). (Code Sec. 125(d)(2))

¶ 1259 Employer's payments for employee's loss of limb, disfigurement, etc.

Lump sum or installment amounts received under an employer's plan as payment for permanent loss or loss of use of a member or function of the body, or permanent disfigurement, of the employee, his spouse or his dependent are tax-free, but only if the payment is based on the nature of the injury without regard to the period the employee is absent from work. (Code Sec. 105(c))[13]

¶ 1260 Worker's compensation.

Amounts received under a worker's compensation act or similar law for personal injuries or sickness are excludable from the employee's (or survivor's) income. But worker's compensation is includible in income to the extent it's attributable to medical expense deductions taken in an earlier year. (Code Sec. 104(a)(1)); Reg § 1.104-1(b))[14]

¶ 1261 Annuities paid to survivors of public safety officers killed in line of duty.

Survivor annuity benefits paid on account of the death of a public safety officer (including law enforcement officers, firefighters, rescue squad workers and ambulance crew members) killed in the line of duty are excluded regardless of when the officer died if: (1) the annuity is provided under a governmental plan which meets the requirements of Code Sec. 401(a) to the officer's spouse, former spouse, or child; and (2) to the extent the annuity is attributable to the officer's service as a public safety officer. (Code Sec. 101(h)(1)) The exclusion doesn't apply under certain circumstances (e.g., if the death was caused by the officer's intentional misconduct). (Code Sec. 101(h)(2))[15]

¶ 1262 Employer-paid individual life insurance policies.

Premiums paid by an employer for policies on the life of an employee are taxable to the employee if the proceeds are payable to the employee's beneficiary (except for group-term insurance, see ¶1263) but not where the employer is the beneficiary. (Reg § 1.61-2(d)(2))[16]

¶ 1263 Group-term life insurance premiums.

An employee isn't taxed on premiums paid by the employer on insurance covering the employee's life under a group-term life insurance policy, if the employee's total coverage

---

11. ¶H-1101.5; ¶1064; TD ¶133,051
12. ¶S-3152; ¶60,514; TD ¶812,002
13. ¶H-1201; ¶1054.02; TD ¶133,048

14. ¶H-1351, ¶1044.01, TD ¶133,049
15. ¶H-1650 *et seq.*; ¶1014.09; TD ¶141,090
16. ¶H-1501 *et seq.*; ¶614.031; TD ¶137,000

under all such plans of all his employers doesn't exceed $50,000. If his total coverage does exceed $50,000, he's taxed on the "cost" (¶1264) of coverage over $50,000 minus the amount he paid. (Code Sec. 79(a))[17] For coverage of employee's spouse and dependents, see ¶1265.

An employee whose total coverage exceeds $50,000 for only part of the year includes the employer's payments for that part of the year coverage, even if his average coverage for the year is under this ceiling. (Code Sec. 79(a))[18]

A disabled terminated employee isn't taxable on group term coverage even if it exceeds $50,000. (Code Sec. 79(b)(1))[19]

Retired employees (except certain employees who reached 55 or retired before Jan. 2, '84) are treated the same as other employees. (Code Sec. 79(e))[20]

The exclusion doesn't apply to any insurance protection in excess of the maximum allowed by state law for employee group insurance. (Reg § 1.79-1(e))[21]

The exclusion is available to a key employee only if the plan doesn't discriminate in favor of key employees (at any time in the key employee's tax year) (Reg § 1.79-4T, Q&A-11) as to eligibility to participate and in the type and amount of benefits available. (Code Sec. 79(d))[22] If the plan is discriminatory, each key employee must include the *greater of* (a) the actual cost of the insurance (determined by apportioning the net premium allocable to the group-term coverage during the key employee's tax year among the covered employees (Reg § 1.79-4T, Q&A-6(b)), *or* (b) the cost determined from IRS's premium table. (Code Sec. 79(d)(1)(B))[23]

¶ 1264   "Cost" of taxable group-term insurance—IRS uniform premium table.

The employer must compute the "cost" of taxable group-term coverage (¶1263) and notify the employee on Form W-2 of the amount included in his income. The employee computes the cost only where he has two or more employers who provide him with coverage.

The cost of group-term life insurance is determined on the basis of uniform premiums (computed on the basis of five-year age brackets) prescribed by IRS. (Code Sec. 79(c)) The cost for each month of coverage is the number of thousands of dollars of coverage over $50,000 (to the nearest tenth) times the amount in IRS's table below for the employee's attained age on the last day of the employee's tax year. (Reg § 1.79-3(d)(2))[24] Under the IRS table, the cost per $1,000 of protection per month is 5¢ for under age 25; 6¢ for 25 through 29; 8¢ for 30 through 34; 9¢ for 35 through 39; 10¢ for 40 through 44; 15¢ for 45 through 49; 23¢ for 50 through 54; 43¢ for 55 through 59; 66¢ for 60 through 64; $1.27 for 65 through 69; and $2.06 for 70 and older.

If the employee contributes to the plan, all his contributions for the tax year are considered made for that part of his coverage over $50,000. (Code Sec. 79(a)(2))[25]

⦿*illustration:* J, a 57-year-old employee, is provided with a $250,000 group-term life insurance policy by his employer for the year. For this coverage, J contributes 20¢ per $1,000 of coverage per month. The amount included in J's income for the $200,000 excess coverage ($250,000 – $50,000) is $432 —the cost of the insurance above the excludable amount (43¢ monthly cost from the IRS table × 12 months × 200 [excess insurance]) less J's employee contribution (20¢ × 12 × 250 total insurance).

17. ¶H-1518; ¶794; TD ¶137,007
18. ¶H-1520; ¶794.01; TD ¶137,009
19. ¶H-1552; ¶794.03; TD ¶137,041
20. ¶s H-1555, H-1556; ¶794.06; TD ¶137,043
21. ¶H-1537

22. ¶H-1564; ¶794.05; TD ¶137,024
23. ¶H-1565; ¶794.05; TD ¶137,023; 137,025
24. ¶H-1521; ¶794.01; TD ¶137,010
25. ¶H-1522; ¶794.01; TD ¶137,011

¶ 1265 Group-term coverage of employee's spouse and dependents.

The cost (as determined at ¶1264) of group-term life insurance on the life of an individual other than an employee (e.g., the employee's spouse or dependent) provided in connection with the performance of services by the employee is includible in the employee's gross income. (Reg § 1.61-2(d)(2)(ii)(b)) If, however, the face amount of employer-provided group-term insurance payable on the death of an employee's spouse or dependent doesn't exceed $2,000, it's an excludable de minimis fringe (¶1247).[26]

¶ 1266 Group-permanent insurance premiums.

Group-permanent insurance premiums that an employer pays on an employee's life are included in the employee's income. Where a group term policy provides permanent benefits, the amount included in income for the permanent benefits is computed under a complex formula. (Reg § 1.79-1(d))[27]

¶ 1267 Split-dollar life insurance.

Under a "split-dollar" insurance arrangement, the employer pays part of the premium for a life insurance policy on the life of the employee (to the extent of the annual increase in cash surrender value) and the employee pays the rest. Out of the insurance proceeds, the employer gets either the cash surrender value or the amount it paid; the employee can designate the beneficiary of the balance.[28] For arrangements entered into (or materially modified) after Sept. 17, 2003, there are two mutually exclusive regimes for taxing split-dollar life insurance arrangements.

Under the economic benefit regime, the policy owner is treated as providing economic benefits to the non-owner (as valued in the regs). This regime governs the taxation of what are known as endorsement split-dollar arrangements (e.g., employer owns the policy and employee's rights are derived from the employer's endorsement in the contract of those rights to him). This regime automatically applies if the arrangement is (1) entered into in connection with the performance of services, and the employee or other service provider is not the contract owner, or (2) a gift situation, and the donee is not the contract owner. (Reg § 1.61-22)

Under the loan regime, the non-owner of the life insurance contract is treated as loaning premium payments to the contract owner. Unless specifically excepted, the loan regime applies to any split-dollar loan. The loan regime also governs what are known as collateral assignment split-dollar life insurance arrangements (e.g., employee owns the policy, which is used as collateral for employer's right to recover the premiums it pays). (Reg § 1.7872-15)

The employer (or donor in a gift arrangement) is treated as the owner of a split-dollar life insurance contract if the only economic benefit that the employee (or donee) has under the arrangement is current life insurance protection. (Reg § 1.61-22(c)(1))

Unless the non-owner's payments are made in consideration of economic benefits, then general income, employment, and gift tax principles apply to the arrangement. For example, if an employee/contract owner's repayment obligation to an employer were waived or cancelled, both parties have to account for the amount as compensation. (Reg § 1.61-22(b)(6))

In a split-dollar life insurance arrangement taxed under the economic benefit regime, the policy owner is treated as providing economic benefits to the non-owner, and those benefits have to be accounted for fully and consistently by both the owner and the non-owner. The

---

26. ¶H-1560 *et seq.*; ¶s 614.031, 1324.06; TD ¶137,044   28. ¶H-1601; ¶614.033; TD ¶137,030
27. ¶H-1545; ¶794.04; TD ¶137,016

value of the economic benefits, less any consideration paid by the non-owner, is treated as transferred from the owner to the non-owner. The tax consequences of that transfer depend on the relationship between the owner and the non-owner. Thus, depending on the circumstances, it might be treated as compensation, a dividend, or a gift. (Reg § 1.61-22(d)(1))

A payment made under a split-dollar life insurance arrangement is a split-dollar loan, and the policy owner and non-owner are treated, respectively, as borrower and lender, if: the payment is made directly or indirectly by the non-owner to the owner; the payment either is a loan under general tax law principles or if a reasonable person would expect the payment to be repaid in full to the non-owner; and repayment is to be made from, or secured by, the policy's death benefit or cash surrender value, or both. (Reg § 1.7872-15(a)(2))

Because split-dollar life insurance arrangements typically provide for deferred compensation, Code Sec. 409A (¶1276) generally applies. But Code Sec. 409A doesn't apply for earnings on amounts deferred under a split-dollar life insurance arrangement in tax years beginning before 2005 (unless the plan is materially modified after Oct. 3, 2004), including increases in the policy cash value —but not including increases attributable to continued services performed, compensation earned, or premium payments or other contributions made on or after 2005.[29]

For arrangements entered into before Sept. 18, 2003 and not materially modified on or after that date (unless rules similar to the above rules are relied on by taxpayers), an employee is taxed on the value of the insurance protection he receives, less any premium he paid; the taxable amount is determined under IRS's Table 2001 (reproduced below), and *not* under the group-term table at ¶1264), plus cash dividends or other benefits received, reduced by any part of the premiums he paid. (But in some cases, an insurer's published gross premium rates for initial-issue standard-risk insurance can be used for policies issued by that insurer, or, for certain pre-Jan. 28, 2002 arrangements, the PS 58 rates may be used). Insurance proceeds received by the employer and the employee's beneficiaries are tax-free. [30]

The Table 2001 rates per $1,000 of current life insurance protection are: [31]

Age	Rate	Age	Rate	Age	Rate	Age	Rate	Age	Rate
0	$ 0.70	21	$ 0.62	41	$ 1.13	61	$ 7.11	81	$ 60.51
1	$ 0.41	22	$ 0.64	42	$ 1.20	62	$ 7.96	82	$ 66.74
2	$ 0.27	23	$ 0.66	43	$ 1.29	63	$ 9.08	83	$ 73.07
3	$ 0.19	24	$ 0.68	44	$ 1.40	64	$ 10.41	84	$ 80.35
4	$ 0.13	25	$ 0.71	45	$ 1.53	65	$ 11.90	85	$ 88.76
5	$ 0.13	26	$ 0.73	46	$ 1.67	66	$ 13.51	86	$ 99.16
6	$ 0.14	27	$ 0.76	47	$ 1.83	67	$ 15.20	87	$110.40
7	$ 0.15	28	$ 0.80	48	$ 1.98	68	$ 16.92	88	$121.85
8	$ 0.16	29	$ 0.83	49	$ 2.13	69	$ 18.70	89	$133.40
9	$ 0.16	30	$ 0.87	50	$ 2.30	70	$ 20.62	90	$144.30
10	$ 0.16	31	$ 0.90	51	$ 2.52	71	$ 22.72	91	$155.80
11	$ 0.19	32	$ 0.93	52	$ 2.81	72	$ 25.07	92	$168.75
12	$ 0.24	33	$ 0.96	53	$ 3.20	73	$ 27.57	93	$186.44
13	$ 0.28	34	$ 0.98	54	$ 3.65	74	$ 30.18	94	$206.70
14	$ 0.33	35	$ 0.99	55	$ 4.15	75	$ 33.05	95	$228.35
15	$ 0.38	36	$ 1.01	56	$ 4.68	76	$ 36.33	96	$250.01
16	$ 0.52	37	$ 1.04	57	$ 5.20	77	$ 40.17	97	$265.09
17	$ 0.57	38	$ 1.06	58	$ 5.66	78	$ 44.33	98	$270.11
18	$ 0.59	39	$ 1.07	59	$ 6.06	79	$ 49.23	99	$281.05
19	$ 0.61	40	$ 1.10	60	$ 6.51	80	$ 54.56		
20	$ 0.62								

29. ¶H-3200.6; ¶409A4.01; TD ¶135,504.1
30. ¶H-1647 *et seq.*; ¶614.033; TD ¶137,031

31. ¶H-1647 *et seq.*; ¶614.033; TD ¶137,031

For split-dollar life insurance arrangements entered into before Jan. 28, 2002 under which an employer has made premium payments and has received, or is entitled to receive, full repayment of all of its payments, IRS won't assert that there has been a taxable transfer of property to a benefited person upon termination of the arrangement if for all periods beginning on or after Jan.1, 2004, all payments by the employer from inception of the arrangement (less any repayments) are treated as loans for tax purposes, and the parties report the tax treatment consistently with this loan treatment. Any payments by the employer not previously treated as loans must be treated as loans entered into at the beginning of that first year in which the payments are treated as loans. [32]

¶ 1268   Meals and lodging furnished by or on behalf of employer.

Meals or lodging (including utilities) furnished to an employee and his family (spouse and dependents) is nontaxable to the employee if (Code Sec. 119):

(1) the meals and lodging are furnished by or on behalf of the employer for the convenience of the employer (e.g., meals supplied because eating places near work are scarce, or because employees must for valid business reasons remain on-premises until their shifts end) (Reg § 1.119-1(a)(2)), and

(2) (a) in the case of *meals,* they are furnished on the employer's business premises, or (b) in the case of *lodging,* the employee is required to accept the lodging as a condition of his employment (i.e., to properly perform his duties). (Reg § 1.119-1(b))[33] This means the employee's presence must be required from a business standpoint —e.g., ranches, hotels, motels and resorts. [34] For faculty housing, see ¶1269.

The value (not the cost) of meals or lodging that fails to meet these tests generally is income to the employee. (Reg § 1.61-2(d)(3), Reg § 1.119-1(a)(1))[35] However, all meals furnished on the employer's business premises to its employees are treated as furnished for the employer's convenience —and so are excludable from the employees' income —if *more than half* of the employees to whom the meals are furnished on the premises are furnished the meals for the convenience of the employer. (Code Sec. 119(b)(4))[36]

⌅ᴿᴵᴬ*observation:* In other words, if the more-than-half test is met, all employees may exclude the value of meals provided on premises, even those who weren't supplied the meals for the convenience of the employer.

Cash allowances for meals are taxable. [37] If the employee can take either cash, or meals or lodging furnished in kind, the value of meals or lodging furnished is income. But occasional "supper money" paid to overtime employees is excludable as a de minimis fringe, see ¶1247.[38]

For meals and lodging furnished at a "camp" in a foreign country, see ¶4620.

¶ 1269   Faculty housing—qualified campus lodging.

The value of qualified campus lodging furnished to an employee of an educational institution is excludable (with limits, below) from his gross income. (Code Sec. 119(d))[39]

Qualified campus lodging is lodging that isn't eligible for the exclusion at ¶1268, that's located on or near a campus of a tax-exempt educational institution (or a qualifying academic health center), and that's furnished by the institution to an employee, his spouse, and his dependents for use as a residence. (Code Sec. 119(d)(3), Code Sec. 119(d)(4))[40]

---

32. ¶H-1647.10
33. ¶H-1751; ¶1194.01; TD ¶131,501
34. ¶H-1776; ¶1194.02; TD ¶131,511
35. ¶s H-1751, H-1785; ¶s 614.027, 1194 *et seq.*; TD ¶131,511
36. ¶H-1754; ¶1194.02

37. ¶H-1790; ¶1194.03; TD ¶131,506
38. ¶H-1791; ¶1324.06; TD ¶131,507
39. ¶H-1797; ¶1194.06; TD ¶131,525
40. ¶H-1799; ¶1194.06; TD ¶131,525

The exclusion isn't a total one. The employee must include the excess of: (1) the lesser of (a) 5% of the appraised value (as of the close of the tax year) of the qualified campus lodging, or (b) the average of the rentals paid by individuals other than employees or students for comparable lodging provided by the institution; over (2) the rent paid by the employee. (Code Sec. 119(d)(2))[41]

¶ 1270 Cafeteria plans (including flexible spending accounts).

No amount is included in the gross income of the participant in a cafeteria plan solely because, under the plan, the participant may choose among the benefits of the plan. (Code Sec. 125(a))[42] Cafeteria plans are generally the sole method of employers providing nontaxable benefits where employees can elect between taxable compensation and nontaxable benefits. (Prop Reg. § 1.125-1(b)(1) ["Taxpayers may rely"])

🅡🅘🅐 *observation:* The cafeteria plan proposed regs are generally effective when finalized for plan years beginning on or after Jan. 1, 2009, but taxpayers may rely on them until final regs are issued. They generally provide rules similar to the rules in previous proposed reliance regs (which have been withdrawn) and other guidance.

A "cafeteria plan" (also referred to as a flexible benefit plan) is a written plan under which participants (all employees) may choose their own "menu" of benefits consisting of "cash" and 'qualified benefits". (Code Sec. 125(d))[43] For this purpose, cash means cash from current compensation (including salary reduction), payment for annual leave, sick leave, or other paid time off, severance pay, property, and certain after-tax employee contributions; distributions from qualified retirement plans are not cash. (Prop Reg. § 1.125-1(a)(2) ["Taxpayers may rely"]) A qualified benefit, which generally must be excludible from employees' gross income under a specific Code section —and must not defer compensation (with some exceptions) (Code Sec. 125(d)(2))—includes: group-term life insurance on an employee's life (up to the excludable $50,000 amount, see ¶1263); employer-provided accident and health plans (¶1256) (including health flexible spending arrangements, and accidental death and dismemberment policies); a dependent care assistance program (¶1271); an adoption assistance program (¶1255); contributions to a Code Sec. 401(k) plan (¶4317); contributions to certain plans maintained by educational organizations, contributions to Health Savings Accounts (HSAs, see ¶1258); and long-term and short-term disability coverage. (Code Sec. 125(f), Prop Reg. § 1.125-1(a)(3) ["Taxpayers may rely"]) [44]

A cafeteria plan can provide an optional grace period immediately following the end of each plan year, extending the period for incurring expenses for qualified benefits to the 15th day of the third month after the end of the plan year. It may apply to one or more qualified benefits but can't apply to paid time off or elective contributions to Code Sec. 401(k) plans. Unused benefits or contributions for one qualified benefit may only be used to reimburse expenses incurred during the grace period for that same qualified benefit. Benefits or contributions not used as of the end of the grace period are forfeited. (Prop Reg. § 1.125-1(e) ["Taxpayers may rely"])[45]

In the case of a "highly compensated participant," the exclusion won't apply to any benefit attributable to a plan year for which the plan discriminates in favor of highly compensated participants as to contributions, benefits or eligibility to participate. (Code Sec. 125(b)(1))[46] An individual is a "highly compensated participant" if he is an officer or more-than-5% shareholder of the employer, a highly compensated employee or a spouse or dependent of such a person. (Code Sec. 125(e)(1))[47]

---

41. ¶H-1797; ¶1194.06; TD ¶131,525
42. ¶H-2401; ¶1254; TD ¶133,045
43. ¶H-2405; ¶1254.01; TD ¶133,042
44. ¶H-2413 *et seq.*; ¶1254.01; TD ¶133,042

45. ¶H-2417.1; TD ¶133,045.1
46. ¶H-2450; ¶1254.06; TD ¶133,045.
47. ¶H-2455; ¶1254.06

In the case of a key employee (defined in Code Sec. 416(i)(1)), the exclusion won't apply to any plan year if the qualified benefits provided to key employees under the plan exceed 25% of the total of such benefits provided for all employees under the plan. (Code Sec. 125(b)(2))[48]

FSAs. A cafeteria plan also can include one or more "flexible spending accounts" (FSAs). An FSA is a benefit designed to reimburse employees for expenses incurred for certain qualified benefits, up to a maximum amount not substantially in excess of the salary reduction and employer flex-credits allocated for the benefit. The maximum amount of reimbursement reasonably available must be less than five times the value of the coverage. (Prop Reg. § 1.125-5(a) ["Taxpayers may rely"]) Employer flex-credits are non-elective contributions that an employer makes available for every employee eligible to participate in the cafeteria plan, to be used at the employee's election only for one or more qualified benefits (but not as cash or other taxable benefits). (Prop Reg. § 1.125-5(b) ["Taxpayers may rely"]) The three types of FSAs are dependent care assistance, adoption assistance and medical care reimbursements (health FSA).

A health FSA may be limited to a subset of permitted Code Sec. 213(d) medical expenses, or it may be a health saving account (HSA) compatible limited-purpose health FSA or post-deductible health FSA. (Prop Reg. § 1.125-5(m) ["Taxpayers may rely"]) A health FSA may not reimburse premiums for accident and health insurance or long-term care insurance. (Code Sec. 125(f))

Under a new optional rule in the 2007 proposed regs, an employer may reimburse a terminated employee's qualified dependent care expenses incurred after termination through a dependent care FSA, if all other Code Sec. 129 requirements are otherwise satisfied. (Prop Reg. § 1.125-6(a)(4)(v) ["Taxpayers may rely"]) [49]

¶ 1271   Dependent care assistance payments.

Payments incurred by an employer for dependent care assistance under a written plan are excluded from an employee's gross income. (Code Sec. 129(a)(1))[50]

The amount an employee can exclude (computed on Form 2441 with Form 1040 or Form 1040A) can't exceed the employee's earned income (excluding employer dependent care assistance payments) or, for married employees, the earned income of the lower earning spouse. (Code Sec. 129(b))[1] The aggregate exclusion is further limited to $5,000 ($2,500 for a married individual filing separately). (Code Sec. 129(a)(2)(A)) Any excess is includible in the tax year the dependent care services are provided. (Code Sec. 129(a)(2)(B))[2]

Dependent care assistance is the payment for or provision of services that if paid for by the employee would be considered employment-related expenses under the child care credit rules (see ¶2353). (Code Sec. 129(e)(1))[3] For eligible dependents, see ¶2352. An employee includes a self-employed individual who can be covered under a self-employed retirement plan. An individual who owns the entire interest in an unincorporated trade or business is treated as his own employer. A partnership is treated as the employer of each partner who is eligible to be included in a self-employed retirement plan. (Code Sec. 129(e)(3), Code Sec. 129(e)(4))[4]

No amount is excludable unless the name, address and (except in the case of a tax-exempt service-provider) taxpayer identifying number (TIN) of the person providing the dependent care services are included on the employee's return. The employee can use Form W-10 to ask for this information from the service provider. Failure to provide this information is excused if the employee exercised due diligence in trying to do so. (Code Sec. 129(e)(9))[5]

The plan must satisfy specific nondiscrimination rules and certain other requirements.

---

48. ¶H-2456; ¶1254.06; TD ¶133,045
49. ¶H-2459 *et seq.*; ¶1254.05; TD ¶133,044
50. ¶H-1401; ¶1294 *et seq.*; TD ¶133,504
1. ¶H-1402; ¶1294; TD ¶133,505

2. ¶H-1402 *et seq.*; ¶1294; TD ¶133,503
3. ¶H-1419; ¶1294.02; TD ¶133,516
4. ¶H-1413 *et seq.*; ¶1294.02; TD ¶133,504
5. ¶H-1406 *et seq.*; ¶1294.03; TD ¶133,501

(Code Sec. 129(d))[6] If an otherwise qualified program fails to meet these requirements, the program will be a dependent care assistance program under which expenses are still excludable for nonhighly compensated employees. (Code Sec. 129(d)(1))[7]

For how excludable dependent care assistance affects the dependent care credit, see ¶2351.

¶ 1272 Time for Reporting Compensation.

Compensation income is reported according to the recipient's accounting method, subject to constructive receipt, repaid income and deferred income rules.

¶ 1273 Cash basis taxpayers.

Cash basis taxpayers report compensation for the tax year they actually receive it. [8]

Compensation paid by check is reported for the year the check is received, even if the check covers past or future services, or isn't cashed until the following year. [9]

Compensation income must be reported for the year it's constructively received (see ¶2822), even though it's not actually received until a later year. Income is constructively received for the year it's credited to the taxpayer's account, set apart for him, or otherwise made available so he can draw upon it at any time, or could have drawn upon it during the tax year if he had given notice of intention to withdraw. (Reg § 1.451-2(a))[10] For advances, see ¶1275.

¶ 1274 Accrual basis taxpayers.

Accrual basis taxpayers report compensation for the tax year in which it accrues. Compensation accrues when all events have occurred that fix the right to receive the income and its amount can be determined with reasonable accuracy. (Reg § 1.451-1(a))[11]

If the right to compensation for services or its amount can't be determined until the services are completed, the amount of compensation ordinarily isn't reported until the tax year the services are completed and the determination can be made. (Reg § 1.451-1(a))[12]

¶ 1275 Advances and drawing accounts.

A cash basis taxpayer who receives advances against commissions that haven't been earned reports the advances as income for the year they are received, if he isn't required to repay the amounts received in excess of commissions. If he must repay the excess drawings, those amounts aren't income until offset by a credit for commissions earned. [13]

¶ 1276 Deferred compensation plans.

All amounts deferred under a nonqualified deferred compensation (NQDC) plan for all tax years are currently includible in gross income to the extent not subject to a substantial risk of forfeiture and not previously included in gross income, unless the plan:

... meets specified distribution, acceleration of benefit, and election requirements; and

... is operated in accordance with these requirements. (Code Sec. 409A(a)(1)(A)(i))[14]

If a NQDC plan doesn't comply with the Code Sec. 409A rules, all amounts deferred under the plan for the tax year and all prior tax years, by any participant to whom the failure relates, are included in income for that year to the extent not subject to a substantial risk of

6. ¶H-1428 *et seq.*; ¶1294.01; TD ¶133,518
7. ¶H-1418; ¶1294.01; TD ¶133,515
8. ¶H-3501; ¶s 614.023, 4514.003; TD ¶130,526
9. ¶H-3502; ¶s 614.023, 4514.004; TD ¶130,527
10. ¶H-3508; ¶4514.036; TD ¶130,531

11. ¶G-2471; ¶4514.011; TD ¶441,701
12. ¶H-3526; ¶4514.011; TD ¶441,702
13. ¶H-3515; ¶614.023; TD ¶130,518
14. ¶H-3200; ¶409A4.01; TD ¶135,508

forfeiture and not previously included in income. This amount is also subject to: (1) interest (at the underpayment rate plus one percentage point) on the tax underpayments that would have occurred had the amount been included in income for the tax year when first deferred, or if later, when not subject to a substantial risk of forfeiture; and (2) a penalty of 20% of the compensation required to be included in income. (Code Sec. 409A(a)(1)(B))

Compensation is subject to a substantial risk of forfeiture if entitlement to it is conditioned on a person's performance of substantial future services or the occurrence of a condition related to the compensation's purpose (e.g., an amount conditioned on involuntary separation from service without cause), and the possibility of forfeiture is substantial. An amount isn't subject to a substantial risk of forfeiture merely because the right to the amount is conditioned upon the refraining from performance of services, such as a noncompete clause. (Prop Reg. § 1.409A-1(d) ["Taxpayers may rely"], Reg § 1.409A-1(d)(1))[15]

observation: For tax years beginning before Jan. 1, 2008, the final regs aren't generally applicable, but taxpayers may rely on the final regs, the proposed regs, or specified guidance.

A NQDC plan is any plan that provides for the deferral of compensation, other than (1) a qualified employer plan (a qualified retirement plan, tax-deferred annuity, simplified employee pension, SIMPLE plan, qualified governmental excess benefit arrangement under Code Sec. 415(m), or eligible deferred compensation plan under Code Sec. 457(b)), and (2) any bona fide vacation leave, sick leave, compensatory time, disability pay, or death benefit plan. (Code Sec. 409A(d)) It also doesn't include annual bonuses, or other annual compensation amounts, paid within 2 ½ months after the later of a service recipient's or service provider's tax year. (Prop Reg. § 1.409A-1(b)(4) ["Taxpayers may rely"], Reg § 1.409A-1(b)(4))[16]

Incentive stock options (ISOs) and options granted under an employee stock purchase plan (ESPP) aren't subject to Code Sec. 409A. Nonqualified stock options and stock appreciation rights (SARs) are similarly excepted if the exercise price may never be less than the fair market value (FMV) of the underlying stock when the option or right is granted, the number of shares subject to the option are fixed on the grant date, and there is no other deferral feature; in addition, the receipt, transfer or exercise of the stock option must be subject to tax under Code Sec. 83, and only the service recipient's stock may be delivered upon a SAR's exercise. (Prop Reg. § 1.409A-1(b)(5) ["Taxpayers may rely"], Reg § 1.409A-1(b)(5))[17]

The distribution requirement is met if a NQDC plan provides that compensation deferred under the plan cannot be distributed earlier than (1) the participant's separation from service; (2) the date the participant becomes disabled; (3) the participant's death; (4) a time specified, or a schedule fixed, under the plan as of the date of the deferral of the compensation (amounts payable on the occurrence of an event are not treated as payable at a specified time); (5) a change in the ownership or effective control of the corporation, or in the ownership of a substantial portion of the assets of the corporation; or (6) the occurrence of an unforeseeable emergency such as a severe financial hardship resulting from illness, casualty loss, etc. (Code Sec. 409A(a)(2); Prop Reg. § 1.409A-3(a) ["Taxpayers may rely"], Reg § 1.409A-3(a))[18]

The acceleration of benefits requirement is met if a NQDC plan doesn't allow the acceleration of the time or schedule of any payment under the plan, except as provided in IRS regs. (Code Sec. 409A(a)(3)) Changes in the form of distribution that accelerate payments generally are subject to this rule. But payments made in accordance with plan provisions for acceleration in the event of a service provider's separation from service, death or disability, or in the event of a change in control do not violate these rules. [19] Nor do payments under a domestic

---

15. ¶H-3200.50; ¶409A4.01; TD ¶135,511

16. ¶H-3200.27; ¶409A4.01; TD ¶135,508.1

17. ¶H-3200.28 *et seq.*; ¶409A4.01; TD ¶135,520

18. ¶H-3200.56; ¶409A4.01; TD ¶135,514

19. ¶H-3200.66; ¶409A4.01; TD ¶135,513.1

relations order, [20] or to comply with a certificate of divestiture for a conflict-of-interest, [21] or de minimis nonelective payments to terminate a participant's entire interest in the plan ($10,000 or less under the proposed regs; $15,500 or less for 2007 under the final regs). [22] (Prop Reg. § 1.409A-3(h) ["Taxpayers may rely"], Reg § 1.409A-3(j))

The election requirements are met if the plan provides that compensation for services performed during a tax year can be deferred at the participant's election only if the initial deferral election is made (1) not later than the close of the preceding tax year; or (2) at another time provided in IRS regs. For performance-based compensation (e.g., bonuses), based on services performed over a period of at least 12 months, the initial deferral election must be made no later than six months before the end of the period. The time and form of distributions have to be specified at the time of initial deferral. An election made after the initial election (a redeferral election) generally must not take effect until at least 12 months after the date on which the election is made and must require deferral for a period of not less than five years from the date on which payment would otherwise have been made. (Code Sec. 409A(a)(4))[23]

Effective dates and transitional relief. Generally, the Code Sec. 409A rules apply for amounts deferred in tax years beginning after 2004, and amounts deferred in tax years beginning before 2005 if the NQDC plan is materially modified after Oct. 3, 2004.

However, under transitional relief, a plan adopted before 2008 will not be treated as violating the Code Sec. 409A distribution, acceleration of benefit, and election requirements before 2009 if it is operated through Dec. 31, 2008 in compliance with Code Sec. 409A and any other pre-2009 guidance, and it is amended on or before Dec. 31, 2008 to conform to Code Sec. 409A and its final regs.

If an election or amendment to change a time and form of payment is made after 2006 and before 2008, it can apply only to amounts that would not otherwise be payable in 2007, and it can't cause an amount not otherwise payable to be paid in 2007. If such an election or amendment is made after 2007 and before 2009, it can only apply to amounts that would not otherwise be payable in 2008, and it can't cause an amount not otherwise payable to be paid in 2008.

If an election or amendment to change a time and form of payment is made after 2007 and before 2009, it can only apply to amounts that would not otherwise be payable in 2008, and it can't cause an amount not otherwise payable to be paid in 2008. If such an election or amendment is made after 2006 and before 2008, it can apply only to amounts that would not otherwise be payable in 2007, and it can't cause an amount not otherwise payable to be paid in 2007; if such an election or amendment is made after 2005 and before 2007, it can apply only to amounts that would not otherwise be payable in 2006, and it can't cause an amount otherwise not payable to be paid in 2006

Except for certain discounted stock rights, an outstanding stock right that provides for a deferral of compensation under Code Sec. 409A may be amended to provide for fixed payment terms consistent with Code Sec. 409A, or to allow holders of such rights to elect such fixed payment terms, without being treated as a change in the time and form of payment or an payment acceleration, if the option or right is amended and elections are made before 2009.

¶ 1277 Rabbi trusts and funding triggers.

Amounts deferred under nonqualified deferred compensation (NQDC) plans (¶1276) generally are not includible in income if the deferred compensation is payable from general corporate funds that are subject to the claims of general creditors. Arrangements known as "rabbi

---

20. ¶H-3200.67
21. ¶H-3200.68
22. ¶H-3200.69
23. ¶H-3200.72 *et seq.*; ¶409A4.01; TD ¶135,515

trusts" generally are irrevocable and don't permit the employer to use the assets for purposes other than payment of deferred compensation. However, the trust assets are subject to the claims of the employer's creditors in the case of insolvency or bankruptcy. Because of this feature, rabbi trusts are not considered to be funded and so compensation is deferred.

Assets directly or indirectly set aside in a trust for purposes of paying nonqualified deferred compensation are treated, for Code Sec. 83 purposes, as property transferred in connection with the performance of services (see ¶1218), whether or not the assets are available to satisfy claims of general creditors (1) at the time set aside, if the assets are located outside of the U.S.; or (2) at the time transferred, if the assets are later transferred outside of the U.S. (Code Sec. 409A(b)(1))

There is also a transfer of property, for Code Sec. 83 purposes, as of the earlier of (1) the date on which a NQDC plan first provides that assets will become restricted to the provision of benefits under the plan in connection with a change in the employer's financial health; or (2) the date on which assets are so restricted. (Code Sec. 409A(b)(2)) [24]

Interest and a 20% penalty apply with regard to the off-shore rabbi trust and financial trigger rules.

For assets set aside, transferred or restricted before Mar. 22, 2006, taxpayers aren't subject to income inclusion or penalties if, before 2008, the NQDC plan is brought into conformity with Code Sec. 409A(b) (see ¶1276) and any guidance issued before that date. [25]

¶ 1278 Social Security, Unemployment and Certain Disability Payments. ▮▮▮▮

Social security benefits may be partly taxable. Unemployment benefits are fully taxable. Payments under military and government disability pensions may be excludible from income.

For voluntary withholding on social security and certain other federal payments, and on unemployment compensation payments, see ¶3009.

¶ 1279 Social security payments—the Tier I and Tier II taxes.

A taxpayer whose "provisional income"—i.e., modified adjusted gross income (modified AGI, see below) plus one half of the social security benefits (including Tier 1 Railroad Retirement benefits) received—for a tax year exceeds either of two threshold amounts is taxed on a portion of social security benefits received that year, as follows:

Tier I: If provisional income exceeds a "base amount," include in gross income the *lesser* of:

. . . 50% of the social security benefits received that year; (Code Sec. 86(a)(1)(A)) or

. . . 50% of the excess of provisional income over the "base amount." (Code Sec. 86(a)(1)(B))[26]

"Modified AGI" means AGI: (1) determined without regard to the social security benefits; the deduction for qualified education loan interest (¶2225); the pre-2008 deduction for higher-education expenses (¶2224); the exclusions for foreign earned income and housing costs (¶4612 *et seq.*), savings bond proceeds for education expenses (¶2220), employer-provided adoption assistance (¶1255), and income from sources within U.S. possessions and Puerto Rico, and (2) increased by the amount of tax-exempt interest received or accrued by taxpayer during the tax year. (Code Sec. 86(b)(2))[27]

The "base amount" is $32,000 for married individuals filing a joint return; zero for a married individual filing a separate return who doesn't live apart from his spouse for the entire tax year; and $25,000 for all other individuals (Code Sec. 86(c)(1)), such as those filing

---

24. ¶H-3233; ¶409A4.20; TD ¶135,507   26. ¶J-1456; ¶864.04; TD ¶146,001
25. ¶H-2503.2   27. ¶J-1459; ¶864.02; TD ¶146,004

as single, head of household or qualifying widow(er). [28]

⚫️*illustration:* G's modified AGI for the tax year consists of pension income of $15,000 and $3,000 of taxable interest and dividends. His social security benefit is $12,000. He's married and files a joint return. His wife has no income. The sum of their modified AGI ($18,000) plus one-half of his social security benefit ($6,000) is $24,000. This is less than their base amount ($32,000), so no part of his social security benefit is taxable.

Tier II: If provisional income exceeds an "adjusted base amount," include in gross income the *lesser* of:

. . . 85% of the social security benefits received that year; or

. . . the sum of: (a) the amount included under the above 50% rule or, if less, one-half of the difference between taxpayer's "adjusted base amount" and "base amount," plus (b) 85% of the excess of provisional income over the "adjusted base amount." (Code Sec. 86(a)(2))

The "adjusted base amount" is $44,000 for married individuals filing jointly; zero for a married individual filing separately who doesn't live apart from his spouse for the entire tax year); and $34,000 for all other individuals. (Code Sec. 86(c)(2))

⚫️*caution:* Any spike in income, e.g., from the sale of stock or a mutual fund, or a retirement plan distribution, may subject a taxpayer to an unexpected tax on his social security benefits, if the extra income causes him to exceed his base or adjusted base amount.

Benefits a taxpayer repays during a tax year reduce the benefits taxed that year, whether the repayment is for overpayments received that repayment year or any earlier year. (Code Sec. 86(d)(2)(A))[29]

If any portion of a lump-sum social security benefit received during a tax year is attributable to an earlier year, the taxpayer can elect (write "LSE" on the return) to include in gross income with respect to that portion, the sum of the increases in gross income that would have resulted had the portion been paid in the earlier year. (Code Sec. 86(e)(1))[30]

¶ 1280 Railroad Retirement Act benefits other than Tier 1 benefits.

Railroad Retirement Act benefits (other than Tier 1 benefits, see ¶1279) are treated as benefits provided under an employer plan that meets the requirements of Code Sec. 401(a) (a "qualified plan," see ¶4319 *et seq.*). (Code Sec. 72(r)(1), Code Sec. 72(r)(3)) Lump-sum termination (early retirement) payments have been held to be taxable under these rules. [31]

¶ 1281 Unemployment compensation.

Unemployment compensation (reported to recipients on Form 1099-G) is fully taxable. (Code Sec. 85(a)) It includes any amount received under a law of the U.S. or a state that's in the nature of unemployment compensation. (Code Sec. 85(b)) It also includes disability benefits paid under federal or state law as a substitute for unemployment benefits to those who are ineligible for unemployment benefits because they're disabled. [32]

¶ 1282 Unemployment benefits paid by employers.

Unemployment benefits (not described at ¶1281) paid directly by an employer are includible in the employee's income. Amounts received by an employee from an employer under a "guaranteed annual wage plan" during periods of unemployment are taxable as wages. [33]

---

28. ¶J-1457; ¶864.03; TD ¶146,002
29. ¶J-1467; ¶864.05; TD ¶146,011
30. ¶J-1469; ¶864.08; TD ¶146,012

31. ¶J-1471; ¶724.26; TD ¶146,014
32. ¶H-3007 *et seq.*; ¶854.01; TD ¶132,506
33. ¶H-3005; ¶854.01; TD ¶132,501

¶ 1283   Strike and lockout benefits.

Strike and lockout benefits paid to an employee by a union, from union dues, including both cash and the fair market value of goods received, are included in the employee's income unless the facts clearly show they're intended as a gift. To be excluded, at a minimum, the union must inquire into the recipient's personal needs and make payments accordingly. [34]

¶ 1284   Certain military and government disability pensions.

Eligible members of the armed forces of any country, the National Oceanic and Atmospheric Administration, or the Public Health Service, and individuals who receive a disability annuity under section 808 of the Foreign Service Act of 1980, exclude from gross income amounts received as pension, annuity or similar allowance for personal injuries or sickness resulting from active service. Those eligible are primarily individuals with combat-related injuries or sickness or entitled to disability compensation from the Department of Veterans Affairs. (Code Sec. 104(a)(4))[35] While armed forces retirement pay based on length of service is taxable, that pay is excludible to the extent it could be received as a disability pension. [36]

¶ 1285   Dividends. ████████████████████████

When a corporation distributes its earnings to its shareholders, the distribution is usually a dividend. If the dividend is "qualified" it is taxable at rates that apply to net capital gain; otherwise it is taxable as ordinary income. But not all corporate distributions are dividends. And some transactions that don't appear to be dividends may be taxed as constructive dividends.

For stock redemptions, see ¶3526 *et seq.* For liquidations, see ¶3572 *et seq.*

¶ 1286   How dividends are taxed to shareholders.

Dividends (defined at ¶1287) are taxable to the person who has the present, enforceable right to receive them, whether or not he's the owner of the underlying stock. [37] Dividends received by an agent are taxable to his principal. [38] If the stock is sold before a dividend is declared and paid, or between the declaration and record (or "ex dividend") dates, the dividends are taxed to the buyer. Dividends on stock sold on or after the record date are taxed to the seller. (Reg § 1.61-9(c))[39]

Dividends are taxable in the year received or unqualifiedly made subject to the shareholder's demand. This applies to both cash and accrual shareholders. Thus, if a corporation pays a dividend on Dec. 30 last year, and the shareholder receives the check on Jan. 2 this year, the shareholder reports it on this year's return. (Reg § 1.301-1(b))[40] For RIC (mutual fund) dividends, see ¶1298. For REIT dividends, see ¶1299

Dividends received before 2011 are taxed to shareholders at the rates that apply to net capital gain (i.e., for 2007, 15% or 5%, and after 2007, 15% or 0% , see ¶2604) if they constitute "qualified dividend income" (¶1288) paid to noncorporate shareholders (Code Sec. 1(h)(11)) and otherwise at ordinary income rates, to the extent the distributing corporation has earnings and profits (E&P, ¶3522). (Code Sec. 301(c)(1)) The part of a distribution in excess of E&P is treated as a tax-free return of capital and is applied against (reduces) the shareholder's basis in the stock. (Code Sec. 301(c)(2)) Any remaining excess (once basis is reduced to zero) is treated as payment for the stock, i.e., as capital gain if the stock is a

---

34. ¶H-3009; TD ¶132,509
35. ¶H-3120; ¶s 614.041, 1044.04; TD ¶138,020
36. ¶H-3123; ¶s 614.040, 1044.04; TD ¶138,023
37. ¶J-2401; ¶3014.05; TD ¶172,013

38. ¶J-2405; ¶3014.05; TD ¶172,014
39. ¶J-2406; ¶3014.05; TD ¶172,021
40. ¶J-2451; ¶s 3014.07, 4514.036; TD ¶172,005

capital asset in the shareholder's hands. (Code Sec. 301(c)(3))[41]

¶ 1287 Dividend defined.

A dividend is a distribution of property by a corporation to its shareholders with respect to its stock, out of accumulated or current earnings and profits (E&P, see ¶3522). (Code Sec. 316(a)) The distribution must be made in the ordinary course of the corporation's business, but it may be extraordinary in amount. (Reg § 1.316-1(a)(1))[42]

A dividend needn't be proportionate [43] and needn't be formally declared. [44]

"Property" includes money, securities and any other property (except the corporation's own stock or rights to that stock, see ¶1295). (Code Sec. 317(a)) Property also includes any economic benefit the corporation gives its shareholders, in whatever form (Reg § 1.317-1), e.g., paying their debts (see ¶1289).[45]

¶ 1288 Qualified dividend income defined.

For dividends received before 2011, qualified dividend income is dividend income received from domestic corporations and qualified foreign corporations (U.S. possession corporations and corporations eligible for benefits of a comprehensive income tax treaty with the U.S. that includes an exchange of information program, but not passive foreign investment companies.) (Code Sec. 1(h)(11)(B)(i)) Dividends paid by other foreign corporations also are qualified if paid on stock or ADRs readily tradable on an established U.S. securities market. (Code Sec. 1(h)(11)(C)

IRS has provided guidance on the extent to which distributions, inclusions and other amounts received by, or included in the income of, individual shareholders as ordinary income from foreign corporations subject to certain "anti-deferral regimes" may be treated as qualified dividend income. [46]

Qualified dividend income does not include: (1) dividends paid on stock unless the stock has been held for more than 60 days during the 121 day period beginning 60 days before the ex-dividend date (more than 90 days during the 181 day period beginning 90 days before the ex-dividend date for preferred stock dividends attributable to a period of more than 366 days) (Code Sec. 1(h)(11)(B)(iii)(I)); (2) dividends on stock to the extent that the taxpayer is under an obligation to make related payments with respect to positions in substantially similar or related property (Code Sec. 1(h)(11)(B)(iii)(II)); (3) any amount that the taxpayer elects to treat as investment income to support an investment interest deduction (Code Sec. 1(h)(11)(D)(i)) (see ¶1729; (4) dividends from corporations that for the distribution year or the preceding year are exempt from tax under Code Sec. 501 (see ¶4100) or Code Sec. 521 (exempt farmers' cooperatives, see ¶4206 *et seq.*) (Code Sec. 1(h)(11)(B)(ii)(I)); (5) dividends deductible under Code Sec. 591 by mutual savings banks (Code Sec. 1(h)(11)(B)(ii)(II)); and (6) dividends paid on employer securities owned by an employee stock ownership plan (ESOP), which are deductible under Code Sec. 404(k). (Code Sec. 1(h)(11)(B)(ii)(III))[47]

Qualified dividend income does not include payments in lieu of dividends (typically made to owners of stock that has been lent in connection with a short sale). However, if a payment in lieu of dividends is reported as dividend income on a Form 1099-DIV, the recipient may treat the payment for tax purposes as a dividend, and not as a payment in lieu of dividends, unless he knows, or has reason to know, of the actual character of the payment. [48]

If an individual, trust, or estate receives extraordinary dividends (within the meaning of

---

41. ¶J-2350 *et seq.*; ¶3014; TD ¶172,001
42. ¶J-2356; ¶3164 *et seq.*; TD ¶171,001
43. ¶J-2366; ¶3014; TD ¶171,001
44. ¶J-2360; ¶3014.01; TD ¶171,001

45. ¶s J-2357, J-2365; ¶s 3014.01, 3174; TD ¶171,002
46. ¶I-5115.5
47. ¶I-5115; ¶14.085; TD ¶223,345
48. ¶I-5115.4; TD ¶223,349

Code Sec. 1059(c)) that are qualified dividend income before 2011, any loss on the dividend-paying stock is a long-term capital loss to the extent of the extraordinary dividends. (Code Sec. 1(h)(11)(D)(ii))[49]

For dividends from RICs, see ¶1298. For dividends from REITs, see ¶1299.

¶ 1289 Constructive or disguised dividends.

When a corporation pays excessive or unreasonably large amounts to a shareholder or a member of his family as salary (Reg § 1.162-7(b)(1)) or rent,[50] or for a purchase price,[1] the excess is a constructive dividend (assuming sufficient E&P, see ¶3522)). Similarly, constructive dividends include a corporation's payments of a shareholder's debts[2] or personal expenses.[3] A dividend may also result without a direct payment to the shareholder, if the corporation makes a payment to a third party that's for the shareholder's benefit and made with respect to his stock.[4]

¶ 1290 Loan vs. dividend.

A shareholder may borrow money from the corporation with or without interest, and with or without security. If the agreement and the genuine intent (at withdrawal) is that the amount be repaid to the corporation, and there's persuasive evidence of both that intent *and* the shareholder's ability to carry it out, the amount received is treated as a loan (i.e., nontaxable), and not as a dividend[5] (unless a below-market interest rate is involved, see ¶1291.

¶ 1291 Dividends from below-market loans between corporation and shareholder.

For any below-market interest rate loan (¶1306) (directly or indirectly) between a corporation and a shareholder, the corporation/lender is treated as having paid a dividend, equal to the amount of the foregone interest, that's includible in the shareholder/borrower's income. De minimis ($10,000 or less) and certain other loans are excepted. (Code Sec. 7872(a))[6]

¶ 1292 Determining the amount of a dividend (cash and in-kind).

The amount of a dividend is the sum of the cash plus the fair market value (FMV), at distribution, of any other property received (Code Sec. 301(b)(1), Code Sec. 301(b)(3)), reduced (but not below zero) by the amount of any liability of the corporation that the shareholder assumes in connection with the distribution, or to which the property is subject. (Code Sec. 301(b)(2))[7] But the amount taxable as a dividend in kind can't exceed the distributing corporation's E&P (¶3522). (Reg § 1.316-1(a)(2))[8]

A dividend consisting of the corporation's obligations equals the FMV of the notes. (Reg § 1.301-1(d)) For stock dividends, see ¶1296.

These rules apply to both corporate (U.S. or foreign) and noncorporate shareholders[9] (but a corporate shareholder may get a dividends-received deduction, see ¶3306 *et seq.*), and to dividends from a foreign corporation to its U.S. corporate shareholder. (Code Sec. 301(b)(1))[10]

¶ 1293 Basis of distributed property to shareholder-distributee.

The basis to the shareholder (corporate or individual) for property received as a dividend (¶1287) is the property's fair market value at distribution (Code Sec. 301(d)), i.e., the amount

---

49. ¶I-5104.1; ¶14.087; TD ¶223,304.1
50. ¶J-2726; ¶3014.09 *et seq.* TD ¶175,052
1. ¶J-2730; ¶3014.11; TD ¶175,044
2. ¶J-2749; ¶3014.14; TD ¶175,038
3. ¶J-2757; ¶3014.13; TD ¶175,007
4. ¶J-2700 *et seq.*; ¶3014.14; TD ¶175,002

5. ¶J-2707 *et seq.*; ¶3014.14; TD ¶175,014
6. ¶J-2721 *et seq.*; ¶78,724.16; TD ¶172,011
7. ¶J-2482; ¶3014.02; TD ¶173,503
8. ¶J-2361; ¶3164.01; TD ¶173,501
9. ¶J-2482; ¶s 3014, 3014.02
10. ¶3014.02

treated as a dividend (see ¶1292), but without the reduction for liabilities. [11]

¶ 1294　Holding period for property received as a taxable dividend.

The shareholder's holding period for property received as a taxable dividend begins on the date of receipt (actual or constructive). (Code Sec. 1223(2))[12]

¶ 1295　Distributions of stock or rights to stock.

With certain exceptions (see ¶1296), a stock dividend —i.e., a corporation's distribution of its *own* stock, or rights (e.g., options or warrants) to buy its stock, that's made to shareholders with respect to their stock (i.e., not as compensation) —isn't taxable to the shareholder. (Code Sec. 305) But a corporation's distribution of stock, or rights to buy stock, in *another* corporation (even if affiliated) is a regular dividend in kind, taxed under the rules at　¶1286 *et seq.* [13]

Stock splits are treated as stock dividends if identical stock is distributed on stock held. 　[14]

For stock (rights) received in connection with corporate organizations, reorganizations or divisions, see ¶3552.

¶ 1296　Taxable stock (or rights) dividends.

Where a stock (or rights) dividend is taxable, the dividend amount is the fair market value (FMV) at distribution of the stock (rights), under the "regular" dividend-in-kind rules, see ¶1292.[15] Where the dividend is taxable because of a cash election, the "dividend" equals: (1) the cash received, for shareholders electing cash, and (2) the FMV of the stock (rights) at distribution, for those receiving stock (rights). (Reg §　1.305-1(b))[16]

These stock (or rights) dividends are *not* tax-free (for taxable amount:

(1) A distribution in which *any* shareholder has the option to take cash or other property instead of the stock (or rights); (Code Sec. 305(b)(1); Reg § 1.305-2)[17]

(2) A "disproportionate" distribution that results in the receipt of property by some shareholders and, for others, an increase in their proportionate interests in the corporation's assets or earnings and profits; (Code Sec. 305(b)(2); Reg § 1.305-3)[18]

(3) A distribution that results in the receipt of preferred stock by some common shareholders and the receipt of common stock by others; (Code Sec. 305(b)(3); Reg § 1.305-4)[19]

(4) Any distributions on preferred stock, including a redemption premium treated as a distribution (for preferred stock issued after Oct. 9, '90, the premium is included as OID, see ¶1314 *et seq.*), *other than* an increase in the conversion ratio of convertible preferred stock made solely to take into account a stock dividend or stock split with respect to the stock into which the preferred is convertible; (Code Sec. 305(b)(4); Reg § 1.305-5)[20]

(5) Any distribution of convertible preferred stock unless IRS is satisfied it won't have the result in (2), above; (Code Sec. 305(b)(5); Reg § 1.305-6)[21]

(6) A constructive stock distribution, e.g., a change in conversion ratio or redemption price, or a redemption premium (difference between redemption price and issue price). (Code Sec. 305(c); Reg § 1.305-5(b); Reg § 1.305-7)[22]

---

11. ¶P-5401; ¶3014.03; TD ¶217,501
12. ¶s I-8903, I-8918; TD ¶223,508
13. ¶J-2478; ¶3054.01; TD ¶174,009
14. ¶J-2501; ¶3054.02; TD ¶174,001
15. ¶J-2504, J-2506; ¶3054.02; TD ¶173,501
16. ¶J-2507; ¶3054.02; TD ¶174,006

17. ¶s J-2508 *et seq.*, J-2501; ¶3054.02; TD ¶174,017
18. ¶J-2510 *et seq.*, ¶3054.02; TD ¶174,020
19. ¶J-2515; ¶3054.02; TD ¶174,024
20. ¶J-2501, J-2516 *et seq.*; ¶3054.02; TD ¶174,025
21. ¶s J-2501, J-2526; ¶3054.02; TD ¶174,027
22. ¶s J-2501, J-2527 *et seq.*; ¶3054.02; TD ¶174,013

¶ 1297   Cash for fractional shares.

Where a corporation's purpose in distributing cash (instead of scrip or fractional shares) in a distribution that otherwise qualifies as a nontaxable stock dividend (¶1295) is to save trouble, expense and inconvenience, and not to give any shareholder(s) an increased interest, the distribution is treated as if the fractional shares had been issued and then redeemed by the corporation. (Reg § 1.305-3(c)) The cash received is treated as an amount realized on the sale of a fractional share. Gain or loss is the cash received minus the basis of the share sold. (Reg § 1.305-3(c)(2))[23]

¶ 1298   Dividends from regulated investment companies (mutual funds).

Ordinary dividends a regulated investment company (RIC or mutual fund, see ¶4201) distributes to its shareholders generally are taxed to them just like other corporate dividends (¶1286; ¶1292). (Code Sec. 852; Reg § 1.852-4(a))[24] However, if the amount of dividends eligible for qualified dividend income treatment (i.e., taxable at the capital gain rates) (¶1286) received by a RIC for a tax year is less than 95% of its gross income (as specially computed) then only the amount of qualified dividend income received by the RIC for the tax year may be distributed to its shareholders as qualified dividend income. (Code Sec. 1(h)(11)(D)(iii), Code Sec. 854(b)(1)(B)) But capital gain dividends, which the RIC need not actually distribute, result in capital gain income (see ¶4201) (Code Sec. 852(b)(3)(D)),[25] and exempt-interest dividends are treated as tax-exempt interest (¶1331). (Code Sec. 852(b)(5)(B))[26] Capital gain dividends are not treated as qualified dividend income (¶1288). (Code Sec. 854(a)) The amount of RIC dividends that are qualifying dividend income must be reported to RIC shareholders within 60 days after the close of the RIC's tax year. (Code Sec. 854(b)(2))

A dividend the RIC pays after the close of its tax year generally is treated as received by the shareholder in the year actually paid, even if the RIC elects to treat it as paid in the preceding year (see ¶4203). (Code Sec. 855(b))[27] But dividends the RIC declares in Oct., Nov. or Dec. are treated as received by the shareholder on Dec. 31 if the RIC actually pays them during the following Jan. (Code Sec. 852(b)(7))[28]

🅡*caution:* Since dividends paid in Jan. may have to be picked up in the preceding year's income, that year's Form 1099, and not the RIC's monthly statements, should be used to determine the dividends to report for that year.

A RIC can designate a dividend as a capital gain dividend and additionally designate it as a 15%-rate gain distribution (or other class). Limitations apply, e.g., the additional designation cannot exceed the maximum distributable amount in that class. In general, a RIC determines the maximum amounts that may be designated in each class of capital gain dividends by performing the maximum capital gain rate computation of Code Sec. 1(h) (see ¶1288) as if the entity were an individual whose ordinary income is subject to a marginal tax rate of 28%, with modifications. [29]

Qualified dividend income is calculated without any reduction for expenses. In addition, where a RIC has several types of income that must be specially designated, the RIC may designate the maximum amount that may be designated in each category even if the aggregate of all the amounts so designated exceeds the total amount of the RIC's dividend distributions. Each shareholder may then apply these designations to the dividends he receives up to his share of these amounts, even though his designations differ from the designations applied by other shareholders. [30]

---

23. ¶J-2514; ¶3054.01; TD ¶174,014
24. ¶E-6150 *et seq.*; ¶8524.02; TD ¶172,005
25. ¶E-6152; ¶8524.02
26. ¶E-6160; ¶8524.02

27. ¶E-6201; ¶8554.01
28. ¶E-6202; ¶8554.01; TD ¶172,005
29. ¶E-6153.1; ¶8524.02; TD ¶173,000.1
30. ¶E-6163.1

¶ 1299 Dividends from real estate investment trusts (REITs).

Real estate investment trusts (REITs, see ¶4202) distribute ordinary dividends and capital gain dividends which (as with RICs, see ¶1298) the beneficiaries or shareholders (investors) treat, respectively, as ordinary income (except there's no dividends-received deduction) (Code Sec. 857(c)) and capital gain. (Code Sec. 857(b)(3)(B))[31] The only REIT dividends that are eligible for qualified dividend income treatment (i.e., taxable at the capital gain rate) (¶1286) are those that the REIT received as qualified dividend income, such as dividends paid to the REIT from a taxable REIT subsidiary. (Code Sec. 1(h)(11)(D)(iii), Code Sec. 857(c)(2)) For undistributed capital gains of REITs, see ¶4202. A deficiency dividend the REIT pays for any year is taxed to the shareholder in the year it's paid, not the year *for which* it's paid. (Reg § 1.860-2(a)(3)(i))[32] But any dividend declared by the REIT in Oct., Nov. or Dec. and payable to shareholders of record on a specified date in that month is considered received by the shareholder on Dec. 31 if the REIT actually pays it the next Jan. (Code Sec. 857(b)(8)(A))[33]

REITs are subject to the same capital gain designation rules as RICs (see ¶1298).[34]

¶ 1300 Dividends to co-op patrons; patronage dividends.

Distributions made by a co-op (¶4206) on its stock or other proprietary interests are taxed under the "regular" dividend rules (see ¶1292), but the dividends-received deduction doesn't apply if the co-op is exempt. (Code Sec. 246(a)(1))[35]

Patronage dividends and per-unit retain allocations (¶4207) received in money are included in income by the patron in the year received. Qualified written notices of allocation and qualified per-unit retain certificates (¶4207) are included in income at their stated dollar amount when received. Other property (but not nonqualified allocations or nonqualified per-unit retain certificates) is included at its fair market value when received. (Code Sec. 1385)[36]

But the amount of any patronage dividend isn't included in income to the extent it is: (1) properly taken into account as an adjustment to basis of property, or (2) attributable to personal, living or family items. (Code Sec. 1385(b))[37]

¶ 1301 Interest Income.

Whatever the name given to the amounts or the form of the transaction, the receipt or accrual of interest is taxable as ordinary income, unless specifically exempt.

¶ 1302 Taxation of interest.

Unless specifically exempt, any interest received by or credited to a taxpayer is taxable as ordinary income. (Code Sec. 61(a)(4); Reg § 1.61-7(a))[38] The interest is taxable even if it's usurious unless applicable state law automatically converts the illegal portion into a payment of principal. (Reg § 1.61-7(a))[39]

¶ 1303 What is interest?

Interest is the price paid for the use of another's money or for the right to defer payment of money owed to another, regardless of the form of the transaction. [40] Interest generally includes the FMV of gifts or services received for opening or adding to accounts in financial institutions, but not if it's a de minimis premium (for a deposit of less than $5,000, the

---

31. ¶E-6616; ¶8574.02; TD ¶173,006
32. ¶E-6304; ¶8604
33. ¶E-6704; ¶8574.02; TD ¶172,005
34. ¶E-6617.1; ¶8574.02; TD ¶173,000.1
35. ¶J-2608; ¶2434.04; TD ¶600,513

36. ¶J-2609 *et seq.*; ¶13,814.13; TD ¶171,042
37. ¶J-2612; ¶13,814.13
38. ¶J-2801; ¶614.067; TD ¶151,001
39. ¶J-2814; ¶614.068; TD ¶151,010
40. ¶J-2802 *et seq.*; TD ¶151,002

premium costs the bank $10 or less; for a deposit of $5,000 or more, it costs $20 or less). [41]

To be interest, generally a payment must be made with respect to a bona fide debt. [42] But other "interest" payments imposed by law, e.g., on judgments, tax refunds, installment sales, etc., are also interest. [43] And IRS may use the Code Sec. 482 allocation rules (¶2858) to "create" interest. [44]

¶ 1304   Interest on defaulted mortgage.

Amounts paid to a mortgagee as a result of the sale of property on foreclosure (or voluntary conveyance in lieu of foreclosure) of the mortgage, that represent accrued interest due on the mortgage, are taxable interest. [45] For mortgagee's gain or loss, see ¶1787.

For mortgage interest recipient's reporting requirements, see ¶4748.

¶ 1305   "Points" and other loan-related fees.

Payments made to a bank or other lender to get a loan are interest, to the extent they are made for the use or forbearance of money rather than for services rendered. Thus, "points" (i.e., charges connected with mortgages that the borrower pays in addition to the stated interest) are interest, while commitment and service fees (for escrow, recording, credit inspection, appraisal) aren't. [46] For recipient's reporting requirements, see ¶4748.

¶ 1306   Below-market interest-rate loans.

The forgone interest on a "below-market" loan is taxed to the lender as interest income. (Code Sec. 7872)[47] A "below-market" loan is:

. . . *a demand loan* where interest is payable on the loan at a rate less than the applicable federal rate (AFR, see ¶1310), (Code Sec. 7872(e)(1)(A))[48] or

. . . *a term loan* where the amount loaned exceeds the present value of all payments due under the loan. (Code Sec. 7872(e)(1)(B))[49]

For a below-market demand loan, the "interest" for any period is the excess of: (1) the interest that would have been payable on the loan if it accrued annually at the AFR, over (2) any interest payable on the loan and properly allocable to the period. (Code Sec. 7872(e)(2)) For below-market term loans, the "interest" (treated as original issue discount (OID), see ¶1313 *et seq.*) is the excess of: (a) the amount loaned, over (b) the present value of all payments required to be made under the loan. (Code Sec. 7872(b)(2)(B))[50]

These rules don't apply to certain de minimis ($10,000 or less) loans (Code Sec. 7872(c)(2), Code Sec. 7872(c)(3)),[1] amounts treated as "unstated interest" (see ¶1307) (Code Sec. 7872(f)(8)),[2] or certain loans under a written continuing care contract to a qualified continuing care facility. (Code Sec. 7872(g))[3]

¶ 1307   Unstated (imputed) interest on deferred payment sales.

For certain deferred payment or installment sales (¶1308) where the sales contract fails to provide for interest at a minimum rate specified by the Code or by IRS, part of the payments received is treated as interest ("unstated interest") that's taxable to the seller despite any

---

41. ¶J-2820; TD ¶811,513
42. ¶J-2803; ¶614.068; TD ¶151,003
43. ¶J-2834 *et seq.*; ¶614.068 *et seq.*; TD ¶151,030
44. ¶J-2817; ¶s 4824, 614.148;
45. ¶J-2819; ¶614.083
46. ¶J-2818; ¶1634.005; TD ¶151,013
47. ¶J-2900; ¶78,724 *et seq.*; TD ¶151,504

48. ¶J-2939 *et seq.*; ¶78,724.04; TD ¶155,010
49. ¶J-2947 *et seq.*; ¶78,724.06; TD ¶155,015
50. ¶s J-2902, J-2904; ¶s 78,724.04, 78,724.06; TD ¶155,004
1. ¶J-2961; ¶78,724.12 *et seq.*; TD ¶155,027
2. ¶J-2918; ¶78,724.20; TD ¶155,021
3. ¶J-2988; ¶78,724.20; TD ¶155,056

contrary intention of the parties. (Code Sec. 483)[4]

¶ 1308 Payments subject to unstated interest rules.

With certain exceptions (¶1312), the unstated interest rules (¶1307) apply to any payment where *all* the following requirements are met:

(1) The payment must be made on account of the sale or exchange of property.

(2) The payment must be part of the sales price under the contract.

(3) The "sales price" (determined at the time of sale) must be more than $3,000. "Sales price" includes the amount of any down payment, any liability encumbering the property and any amount treated as unstated interest under these rules, but not any *stated* interest payments.

(4) The payment must be due (under the contract) more than six months after the date of the sale or exchange.

(5) At least one payment under the contract must be due more than one year after the date of the sale or exchange.

(6) There must be total unstated interest (¶1309) under the contract. (Code Sec. 483(c)(1), Code Sec. 483(d)(2); Reg § 1.483-1(b)(1))[5]

A debt instrument of the buyer given in exchange for property isn't itself treated as a payment. Rather, any payment due under the instrument is treated as due under the sales contract. (Code Sec. 483(c)(2))[6]

¶ 1309 What is "total unstated interest"?

There's "total unstated interest" under the contract (see ¶1308) if the sum of all payments (other than *stated* interest payments) due under it more than six months after the date of the sale or exchange exceeds the sum of: (1) the present value of all those payments, plus (2) the present value of all interest payments due under the contract (regardless of when due). The total unstated interest equals the excess, if any. (Code Sec. 483(b))[7]

The present value of a payment is determined as of the date of the sale, etc., using a "test" rate prescribed by IRS. This test rate, which depends on the type of property sold, is a discount rate equal to the then applicable federal rate (AFR, see ¶1310), compounded semiannually. (Code Sec. 483(b), Code Sec. 1274(b)(2))[8]

These discount rates are used to determine the amount of unstated interest the seller must report as interest income:

(1) For sales or exchanges of property (not described below), the discount rate may not exceed 9% compounded semiannually if the stated principal amount of the debt instrument doesn't exceed a specified amount, as adjusted for inflation ($4,800,800 for sales and exchanges in 2007). If the stated principal amount is over the specified amount, the discount rate is 100% of the AFR, compounded semiannually. (Code Sec. 483(b), Code Sec. 1274A(a))[9]

(2) For sales or exchanges of new investment credit property, the discount rate is 100% of the AFR, compounded semiannually. (Code Sec. 483(b))[10]

(3) For sales or exchanges where part of the sold property is leased back to the seller, the discount rate is 110% of the AFR, compounded semiannually. (Code Sec. 1274(e))[11]

(4) For sales, etc., of land between family members where the aggregate sales price for all land sales between those individuals in that calendar year isn't over $500,000, the discount

---

4. ¶J-3750 *et seq.*; ¶4834; TD ¶152,001

5. ¶J-3800 *et seq.*; ¶s 4834, 4834.01; TD ¶152,221

6. ¶J-3806; ¶4834.01; TD ¶152,226

7. ¶J-3814; ¶4834; TD ¶152,233

8. ¶J-3814 *et seq.*; ¶4834.01; TD ¶152,234

9. ¶J-3816 *et seq.*; ¶4834.01; TD ¶152,234

10. ¶J-3818; ¶4834.01; TD ¶152,234

11. ¶J-3819; ¶12,714.03; TD ¶152,234

rate can't exceed 6% compounded semiannually. (Code Sec. 483(e))[12]

¶ 1310   Applicable federal rate (AFR).

IRS issues monthly tables (reproduced at ¶1116 for the most recent 12 months available as we went to press) showing the AFRs to be used in determining whether there is unstated interest (¶1309) (or OID in some cases, see ¶1318) on a sale or exchange of property, and if there is, the amount of that unstated interest. [13] The rate to use on a particular sale or exchange depends on the term over which the payments are to be made. If the term is three years or less, use the short-term rate (from the tables). If it's more than three years but not more than nine years, use the mid-term rate. If it's more than nine years, use the long-term rate. (Code Sec. 1274(d)(1)(A))[14] The rate to use also depends on when the contract was made. (Code Sec. 1274(d)(2))[15]

¶ 1311   Allocating total unstated interest.

For any payment subject to the unstated interest rules (¶1307), that part of the total unstated interest under the contract (¶1309) which is properly allocable to that payment is treated as interest. This "interest" amount is determined in a manner consistent with the method used to compute the amount of currently includible OID (¶1321) (Code Sec. 483(a)) so that unstated interest income must be reported on an economic accrual basis. [16]

¶ 1312   Exceptions to unstated interest rules.

Even if all the requirements listed at ¶1308 are met, there's no unstated interest on:

(1) sales or exchanges where the sales price (¶1308) is $3,000 or less; (Code Sec. 483(d)(2))[17]

(2) any debt instrument (given in connection with a sale or exchange of property) whose issue price is figured under the OID rules (¶1313 *et seq.*); (Code Sec. 483(d)(1))[18]

(3) any amount received on the sale of patent rights described in Code Sec. 1235(a) that's contingent on the productivity, use or disposition of those rights; (Code Sec. 483(d)(4))[19]

(4) amounts received under certain annuity contracts; [20]

(5) lump-sum divorce payments and property settlements payable in installments; [21] and

(6) certain acquisitions of amortizable section 197 intangibles (¶1977). (Reg § 1.197-2(f)(3)(iv)(B)(3))[22]

(7) payments under options to buy or sell property (Reg § 1.483-1(c)(3)(v)).[23]

(8) assumptions of debt in connection with sales or exchanges and acquisitions of property subject to debt (Code Sec. 1274(c)(4)).[24]

(9) below-market interest rate loans (¶1306) (Code Sec. 7872(f)(8)).[25]

¶ 1313   Current inclusion of original issue discount (OID) as interest income.

If a debt instrument is acquired from an issuer for an amount less than what the issuer will have to pay the holder when the instrument matures, the difference is original issue discount (OID, see ¶1314). No matter which method of accounting the holder uses, he must report part of the OID as interest income in each tax year the debt instrument is held

12. ¶J-3820; ¶4834.01; TD ¶152,234
13. ¶J-4181 *et seq.*; ¶4834.01; TD ¶153,030
14. ¶J-4181; ¶4834.01; TD ¶153,030
15. ¶J-4190 *et seq.*; ¶12,714.03; TD ¶153,030
16. ¶J-3951; ¶s 4834.01, 4464.01; TD ¶152,010
17. ¶J-3901; ¶4834.01; TD ¶152,005
18. ¶J-3902; ¶4834.01; TD ¶152,005

19. ¶J-3903; ¶4834.01; TD ¶152,005
20. ¶J-3905; ¶4834.01; TD ¶152,005
21. ¶J-3906; ¶4834.01; TD ¶152,005
22. ¶J-3903.1
23. ¶J-3904; ¶4834.01
24. ¶J-3909; ¶4834.01
25. ¶J-3910; ¶4834.01

(¶1321), even though the OID won't be paid until maturity. (Code Sec. 1272)[26]

The OID current inclusion rules apply to all debt instruments issued with OID (Code Sec. 1272)[27] *other than:*

(1) Tax-exempt obligations (unless stripped). (Code Sec. 1272(a)(2)(A), Code Sec. 1286(d))

(2) U.S. savings bonds. (Code Sec. 1272(a)(2)(B))

(3) Short-term obligations (i.e., with a fixed maturity date not more than one year from the date of issue). (Code Sec. 1272(a)(2)(C))

(4) Debt instruments issued by natural persons before Mar. 2, '84. (Code Sec. 1272(a)(2)(D))

(5) Certain nonbusiness loans of $10,000 or less between natural persons. (Code Sec. 1272(a)(2)(E))[28]

"Debt instruments" are bonds, debentures, notes, certificates or other instruments or contractual arrangements that are "indebtedness" under tax law principles, e.g., certificates of deposit or loans (Code Sec. 1275(a)(1); Reg § 1.1275-1(d)),[29] and REMIC interests and some similar instruments where payment may be accelerated. (Code Sec. 1272(a)(6)(C))[30] A debt instrument doesn't include a life annuity, or certain annuities issued by insurance companies. (Code Sec. 1275(a)(1)(B); Reg § 1.1275-1(j))[31]

The OID current inclusion rules also apply to bonds, and preferred stock bought (after being stripped) after Apr. 30, '93. (Code Sec. 305(e); Code Sec. 1286(a))[32]

The OID current inclusion rules don't apply to a holder who buys a debt instrument at a premium (Code Sec. 1272(c)(1))[33] (except as described at ¶1323).

¶ 1314   OID defined.

OID (see ¶1313) is the excess (if any) of: (1) a debt instrument's stated redemption price at maturity (¶1316) over (2) its issue price (¶1317). (Code Sec. 1273(a)(1))[34]

But the OID is treated as zero if that excess is less than: 0.25% of the stated redemption price at maturity, times the number of years to maturity. (Code Sec. 1273(a)(3)) In this case, all stated interest (including amounts that would otherwise be OID) is treated as "qualified stated interest" (¶1315). (Reg § 1.1273-1(d)(1))[35]

¶ 1315   "Qualified stated interest" defined.

"Qualified stated interest" is stated interest that's unconditionally payable in cash or property (other than the issuer's debt instruments), or will be constructively received under Code Sec. 451 (¶2822) at least annually at a single fixed rate. (Reg § 1.1273-1(c)(1))[36]

¶ 1316   Stated redemption price at maturity.

For OID purposes, an instrument's *stated redemption price at maturity* is usually its face value. It includes interest payable at maturity *but not* interest payable at a fixed rate at periodic intervals of a year or less during the entire term of the instrument (Code Sec. 1273(a)(2)), or "qualified stated interest" (¶1315). (Reg § 1.1273-1(b))[37]

26. ¶J-4000 *et seq.*; ¶12,714 *et seq.*; TD ¶153,001
27. ¶J-4051; ¶s 12,714, 12,714.01; TD ¶153,003
28. ¶J-4060 *et seq.*; ¶12,714.01; TD ¶153,003
29. ¶s J-4054, J-4055; ¶12,714; TD ¶153,002
30. ¶J-4343; ¶12,714.01; TD ¶153,010
31. ¶J-4057; ¶12,714; TD ¶153,002

32. ¶J-4400 *et seq.*; ¶12,864; TD ¶153,501
33. ¶J-4005; ¶12714.01; TD ¶153,001
34. ¶J-4100 *et seq.*; ¶12,714; TD ¶153,004
35. ¶J-4102; ¶12,714.01; TD ¶153,004
36. ¶J-4112; TD ¶153,006
37. ¶J-4111; TD ¶153,005

¶ 1317   Issue price.

A debt instrument's issue price depends on whether it's issued for cash or property, and if issued for property, whether the instrument or property is publicly traded, as follows:

. . . For a *publicly offered debt instrument issued for money,* the issue price is the initial offering price to the public at which a substantial amount of the instruments is sold. (Code Sec. 1273(b)(1); Reg § 1.1232-3(b)(2)(i))[38]

. . . For a *privately offered debt instrument issued for money,* the issue price is the price paid by the first buyer of that instrument (Code Sec. 1273(b)(2)) or the first price at which a substantial amount of instruments in the issue is sold. (Reg § 1.1273-2(a)(1))[39]

. . . For a *debt instrument issued for property where there's public trading,* the issue price is the instrument's fair market value (FMV) as of the issue date, if it's publicly traded. If the instrument itself isn't publicly traded but is issued for property (i.e., stock or securities) that is, its issue price is the FMV of that property. (Code Sec. 1273(b)(3); Reg § 1.1232-3(b)(2)(iii), Reg § 1.1273-2(b)(1))[40]

. . . For a *nonpublicly traded debt instrument issued for nonpublicly traded property,* the issue price is its stated principal amount (total payments due under the instrument, less stated interest payments or payments designated as interest or points) if the instrument pays adequate stated interest (¶1318), or its imputed principal amount (¶1319) if it doesn't. (Code Sec. 1274(a); Reg § 1.1274-2(b)(1))[41] For exceptions, see ¶1320.

. . . For *Treasury securities,* the issue price is the average price of the securities sold (price sold at auction, if sold before Mar. 13, 2001). (Reg § 1.1275-2(d))[42]

. . . For a *debt instrument that provides for one or more contingent payments,* issued after Aug. 12, '96, the issue price is the lesser of the instrument's noncontingent principal payments, or the sum of the present values of the noncontingent payments. (Reg § 1.1274-2(g))[43]

. . . For a *tax-exempt obligation* issued after Aug. 12, '96, the issue price is (a) the greater of the obligation's FMV or its stated principal amount, or (b) for contingent obligations, its FMV. (Reg § 1.1274-2(j))[44]

The issue price of a debt instrument issued in a potentially abusive situation (e.g., a tax shelter) is the FMV of the property received in exchange for the instrument, reduced by the sum of the money plus the FMV of any property or rights (other than the instrument) that are given for the sale or exchange. (Reg § 1.1274-2(b)(3))[45]

¶ 1318   Adequate stated interest.

There's adequate stated interest for a debt instrument if the sum of the present values (using the discount rate at ¶1309) of all payments of principal and interest due under it equals or exceeds its stated principal amount (¶1317) (Code Sec. 1274(c)(2)), or if the instrument has a single fixed rate of interest that's paid or compounded at least annually and is at least equal to the test rate. (Reg § 1.1274-2(c))[46]

¶ 1319   Imputed principal amount.

The imputed principal amount is the sum of the present values of all payments of principal and interest due under a debt instrument, computed as of the date of the sale or exchange

38. ¶J-4130; TD ¶153,021
39. ¶J-4138; TD ¶153,023
40. ¶J-4140; TD ¶153,024
41. ¶J-4151; ¶12,714.03; TD ¶153,025
42. ¶J-4131; TD ¶153,022

43. ¶J-4151.2; ¶12,714.037; TD ¶153,026
44. ¶J-4151.3, J-4151.4
45. ¶J-4151.5; TD ¶152,235
46. ¶J-4153 *et seq.*; ¶12,714.03; TD ¶153,027

using the discount rates at ¶1309. (Code Sec. 1274(b)(2); Reg § 1.1274-2(c)(1))[47]

The imputed principal amount of a variable rate debt instrument that provides for stated interest at a qualified floating rate(s) generally is determined by assuming that the instrument provides for a fixed rate of interest for each accrual period to which a qualified floating rate applies. (Reg § 1.1274-2(f)(1)(i))[48]

In a potentially abusive situation (e.g., tax shelter), the imputed principal amount of an instrument received in exchange for property is the property's fair market value, adjusted for other considerations in the transaction. (Code Sec. 1274(b)(3)(A); Reg § 1.1274-3(a))[49]

¶ 1320 Exceptions to OID rules for nonpublicly traded debt instruments.

The issue price of a nonpublicly traded debt instrument issued for nonpublicly traded property is its stated redemption price at maturity (so there's no OID, see ¶1314), instead of the amount determined under the rules at ¶1317, in these cases: (Code Sec. 1273(b)(4))[50]

(1) sales or exchanges involving total payments of $250,000 or less; (Code Sec. 1274(c)(3)(C))

(2) sales or exchanges by an individual of his principal residence; (Code Sec. 1274(c)(3)(B))

(3) sales or exchanges of certain farms where the sales price cannot exceed $1,000,000; (Code Sec. 1274(c)(3)(A))

(4) certain sales of patents; (Code Sec. 1274(c)(3)(E))

(5) certain transfers of land between family members where the total price for all land sales between them for the year is not more than $500,000; (Code Sec. 1274(c)(3)(F))

(6) sales or exchanges where, in exchange for property, a nonaccrual method buyer (other than a dealer) issues a "cash method debt instrument" —i.e., a debt instrument whose principal amount doesn't exceed a specified amount ($3,429,100 for sales and exchanges in 2007), if the "regular" issue price rules otherwise would apply *and* buyer and seller jointly elect cash method treatment for the instrument; (Code Sec. 1274A(c))[1]

(7) sales or exchanges of personal use property (to the issuer) that evidence a below-market loan (¶1306); (Reg § 1.1274-1(b)(3)(i))[2]

(8) transactions involving "demand" below-market loans; (Reg § 1.1274-1(b)(3)(ii))[3] or

(9) transfers between spouses or incident to divorce. (Reg § 1.1274-1(b)(3)(iii))[4]

Ⓡ *observation:* Even if there's no OID, there may be unstated interest (see ¶1307).

¶ 1321 Determining amount of currently includible OID.

A holder of a debt instrument issued with OID (¶1314) who is required to include part of the OID in gross income currently must include in gross income for his tax year, an amount equal to the sum of the daily portions of the OID for each day he held the instrument during that year. (Code Sec. 1272(a)(1))[5] For accrual under the constant yield method, see ¶1322.

To determine the daily OID portion, allocate to each day in any "accrual period" (below) that day's ratable portion of the increase (during that period) in the instrument's adjusted issue price (below). This increase equals the excess of: (1) the adjusted issue price at the start of the accrual period times the yield to maturity (based on compounding at the end of each accrual period), over (2) the sum of the amounts payable as interest on the instrument during that accrual period. (Code Sec. 1272(a)(3))[6]

47. ¶J-4154 *et seq.*; ¶12,714.03; TD ¶153,028
48. ¶J-4157
49. ¶J-4173 *et seq.*; ¶12,714.03; TD ¶153,029
50. ¶J-4196; ¶12,714.03; TD ¶153,031
1. ¶J-4207

2. ¶J-4202; ¶12,714.03; TD ¶153,031
3. ¶J-4203; ¶12,714.03; TD ¶153,031
4. ¶J-4204; ¶12,714.03; TD ¶153,031
5. ¶J-4301; ¶12,714.01; TD ¶153,008
6. ¶J-4301; ¶12,714.01; TD ¶153,008

The adjusted issue price of a debt instrument at the start of any accrual period is the sum of its issue price (¶1317), plus all adjustments (i.e., OID inclusions) in that issue price for all earlier accrual periods. (Code Sec. 1272(a)(4))[7]

Accrual period generally means a six-month period (or shorter period from date of issuance) ending on a day in the calendar year corresponding to the debt instrument's maturity date, or a date six months before that date. (Code Sec. 1272(a)(5))[8]

For *inflation-indexed debt instruments,* OID is computed using the coupon bond method or the discount bond method (see ¶1333). (Reg § 1.1275-7(a))[9]

¶ 1322   Accrual of OID using constant yield method.

Under the constant yield method, the amount of OID includible in the holder's income for a tax year (¶1321) is determined as follows:

(1) Determine the instrument's yield to maturity. This is the discount rate that, when used to compute the present value of all payments under the instrument, produces an amount equal to the instrument's issue price. The yield must be constant over the instrument's term and must be calculated to at least two decimal places. (Reg § 1.1272-1(b)(1)(i))

(2) Determine the accrual period, which may be any length (based on any reasonable accounting convention), but can't exceed one year. Each scheduled payment must occur either on the first or last day of an accrual period. The simplest OID computation is where the accrual periods correspond to the intervals between payment dates set forth by the instrument. (Reg § 1.1272-1(b)(1)(ii))

(3) Determine the OID allocable to each accrual period. This is the instrument's adjusted issue price at the start of the accrual period, times the instrument's yield, less the "qualified stated interest" (¶1315) allocable to the period. (Reg § 1.1272-1(b)(1)(iii))

(4) Determine the daily portions of OID, by allocating to each day in an accrual period the ratable portion of the OID allocable to that period. The holder includes in income the daily portions of OID for each day in the tax year on which he held the instrument. (Reg § 1.1272-1(b)(1)(iv))[10]

The constant yield method may not be used for certain interests held by a REMIC, certain instruments with payments subject to acceleration or that provide for contingent payments, or certain variable rate instruments. (Reg § 1.1272-1(b)(2))[11]

¶ 1323   OID inclusion reduced where holder paid acquisition premium.

If the holder of a debt instrument bought it from someone other than the original issuer, paying an acquisition premium (i.e., an amount in excess of the original issue price plus all OID required to be included in the gross income of earlier holders), the holder's current OID inclusion (¶1321) is reduced. This is done by reducing each daily includible OID portion by this constant fraction: the acquisition premium, divided by the total OID (before reduction) allocable to the days after the purchase date and ending on the date of maturity. However, the reduction applies only to the OID inclusion and isn't taken into account in computing the instrument's adjusted issue price at the start of an accrual period. (Code Sec. 1272(a)(7))[12]

¶ 1324   Accrued market discount on disposition of "market discount bonds."

Gain on the disposition of a market discount bond (¶1326) is ordinary income to the extent of the accrued market discount on the bond (Code Sec. 1276(a)(1)) (unless the holder elects to

---

7. ¶J-4324; ¶12,714.01; TD ¶153,008
8. ¶J-4301; TD ¶153,008
9. ¶J-4379 *et seq.*; ¶12,714.037; TD ¶153,043 *et seq.*

10. ¶J-4302; ¶12,714.01; TD ¶153,009
11. ¶J-4303; ¶12,714.01; TD ¶153,010
12. ¶J-4349; ¶12,714.01; TD ¶153,019

include the discount currently, see ¶1327). This ordinary income is treated as interest income, with exceptions. (Code Sec. 1276(a)(4))[13] For partial principal payments, see ¶1325.

The accrued market discount interest is computed under a ratable accrual method or, at taxpayer's election, a constant interest rate method. (Code Sec. 1276(b))[14]

Dispositions by gift and transfers to controlled corporations also can result in interest income under this rule. (Code Sec. 1276(d)(1)(A))[15] If the disposition is other than by sale, exchange or involuntary conversion, the amount realized is equal to the bond's fair market value. (Code Sec. 1276(a)(2))[16]

Interest treatment applies even if the gain wouldn't otherwise be recognized. Regs may allow nonrecognition in certain nontaxable transactions. (Code Sec. 1276(a)(1), Code Sec. 1276(d)(1))[17]

¶ 1325 Accrued market discount when partial principal payments are made.

If the principal on a market discount bond (¶1326) (acquired after Oct. 22, '86) is paid in more than one installment, any partial principal payment is included as ordinary income to the extent of the accrued market discount on the bond (Code Sec. 1276(a)(3)(A))[18] (unless the holder elects to include the discount currently, see ¶1327).

Any amount that has been included in gross income under this rule reduces the amount of any accrued market discount that's included on any later disposition of (¶1324), or further partial principal payments on, the bond. (Code Sec. 1276(a)(3)(B))[19]

If bond principal can be paid in two or more payments, the accrued market discount is to be determined under regs. (Code Sec. 1276(b)(3))[20]

¶ 1326 What are market discount bonds.

Market discount bonds are any "bonds" having a market discount *other than* short-term obligations (one year or less), tax-exempt obligations bought before May, 1, '93, U.S. savings bonds and certain installment obligations. (Code Sec. 1278(a)(1)(A), Code Sec. 1278(a)(1)(B))[21]

Market discount is the excess (if any) of the bond's stated redemption price at maturity (¶1316) over taxpayer's basis for the bond immediately after acquiring it. (Code Sec. 1278(a)(2))[22] The market discount is zero if it's less than 0.25% of the bond's stated redemption price at maturity times the number of years to maturity after the taxpayer acquires the bond. (Code Sec. 1278(a)(2)(C))[23]

Special rules determine the stated redemption price at maturity for this purpose if the bond was issued with OID. (Code Sec. 1278(a)(4))[24]

¶ 1327 Election to include accrued market discount in income currently.

Instead of including a bond's accrued market discount on disposition (¶1324) or partial payment of principal (¶1325), taxpayer may elect to include the discount as interest income for the tax years to which it is attributable, i.e., currently. Taxpayer may use either the ratable accrual method or the constant interest rate method. (Code Sec. 1278(b)(1))[25]

Elect by attaching to a timely filed income tax return, a statement that market discount has been included in gross income under Code Sec. 1278(b), describing the method used to

13. ¶J-4551; ¶12,764 *et seq.*; TD ¶154,001
14. ¶J-4560; ¶12,764.01; TD ¶154,004
15. ¶J-4570; ¶12,764.01; TD ¶154,007
16. ¶J-4551; ¶12,764.01; TD ¶154,001
17. ¶s J-4551, J-4569; ¶12,764.01; TD ¶154,007
18. ¶J-4566; ¶12,764.01; TD ¶154,006
19. ¶J-4567; ¶12,764.01; TD ¶154,006

20. ¶J-4568; TD ¶154,006
21. ¶s J-4552, J-4556; ¶12,764.01; TD ¶154,002
22. ¶J-4553; ¶12,764.01; TD ¶154,003
23. ¶J-4554; ¶12,764.01; TD ¶154,003
24. ¶J-4553; ¶12,764.01; TD ¶154,003
25. ¶J-4573; ¶12,764.02; TD ¶154,005

determine the amount attributable to that tax year. [26]

¶ 1328 Acquisition discount on short-term obligations—mandatory accrual.

Certain holders (below) of short-term obligations (not more than one year) are currently taxed on their daily portions of the "acquisition discount" (for government obligations, or nongovernment obligations if the holder so elects) or OID (for nongovernment obligations), for each day during the year that they hold the obligation. (Code Sec. 1281(a)(1), Code Sec. 1283(c)) Any other interest payable on the obligation also must be taken into account as it accrues. (Code Sec. 1281(a)(2))[27]

An obligation's "acquisition discount" is the excess of its stated redemption price at maturity (¶1316) over taxpayer's basis in it. (Code Sec. 1283(a)(2))[28]

The daily portion of the acquisition discount is computed using the ratable accrual method or, if taxpayer so elects, the constant interest method. (Code Sec. 1283(b))[29]

This mandatory accrual rule applies only to these holders of short-term obligations:

(1) Accrual basis taxpayers;

(2) Taxpayers who hold the obligations primarily for sale to customers in the ordinary course of their trade or business. (Code Sec. 1281(b)(1))[30] This doesn't include banks that make short-term loans to customers in the ordinary course of business; [31]

(3) Regulated investment companies (mutual funds, ¶4201) or common trust funds (¶4210);

(4) Taxpayers who identify the obligations as part of a Code Sec. 1256 hedging transaction;

(5) Taxpayers whose short-term obligations are stripped bonds or stripped coupons that taxpayer stripped. (Code Sec. 1281(b)(1))[32]

The mandatory accrual rules doesn't apply to the ordinary investor. [33]

observation: The mandatory accrual rule doesn't apply to a cash basis holder who isn't a dealer in these obligations and isn't subject to the Code Sec. 1256 hedging rules.

Special rules apply to obligations held by pass-through entities. (Code Sec. 1281(b)(2))[34]

¶ 1329 Interest on bonds sold between interest dates.

When fixed-interest bonds (not in default) are sold between interest dates, the amount the buyer pays that represents interest accrued as of the sale date is taxable interest to the seller. (Reg § 1.61-7(d)) Interest accrued after the sale date is taxable to the buyer on receipt. [35]

Bonds in default are usually traded "flat" (no part of the selling price is allocated between interest and principal). If there's accrued interest, the part of the selling price that represents interest accrued before the sale isn't taxable to the buyer until it exceeds the buyer's basis. [36]

¶ 1330 Interest credited to frozen deposits.

Interest credited to a frozen deposit (i.e., in a bankrupt or insolvent (actual or threatened) financial institution) during a calendar year, that's includible in the depositor's income for the year, can't exceed the sum of the net withdrawals during the year plus the amount withdrawable at the end of the year. (Code Sec. 451(g)(1))[37]

26. ¶J-4574; ¶12,764.02; TD ¶154,005
27. ¶s J-4501, J-4506; ¶12,814; TD ¶153,801
28. ¶J-4501; ¶12,814.01; TD ¶153,803
29. ¶J-4500; ¶12,814.01; TD ¶153,804
30. ¶J-4502; ¶12,814; TD ¶153,802
31. ¶J-4501; TD ¶153,802

32. ¶J-4502; ¶12,814; TD ¶153,802
33. ¶J-4502
34. ¶J-4502; ¶12,814; TD ¶153,802
35. ¶J-2827; ¶614.080; TD ¶151,020
36. ¶J-2828 *et seq.*; ¶614.081; TD ¶151,021
37. ¶J-3711; ¶4514.185; TD ¶151,507

¶ 1331   Tax-exempt interest.

Interest on state and local bonds (i.e., obligations of a state, the District of Columbia, a U.S. possession, certain Indian tribal governments or any political subdivision of the foregoing) is exempt from federal income tax (Code Sec. 103(a), Code Sec. 103(c); Code Sec. 7871(a)(4))[38] (with certain exceptions, see ¶1332). For "educational expense" exclusion for certain U.S. savings bonds, see ¶2220 *et seq.*

observation: Even if interest isn't subject to federal income tax, it may have to be taken into account, e.g., in calculating the taxable portion of social security benefits (¶1279), for alternative minimum tax purposes for certain bonds (¶3207), in calculating earnings and profits (¶3525), and for certain other purposes.

caution: There's also a bar against deducting interest on debt incurred or continued to buy or carry tax-exempt bonds (¶1723).

Every person required to file a return must report on it all tax-exempt interest received or accrued during the tax year. (Code Sec. 6012(d))[39]

¶ 1332   Taxable interest from private activity bonds, hedge bonds, arbitrage bonds.

Private activity bonds aren't eligible for the interest exemption described at ¶1331 unless the bond meets detailed requirements *and* is one of seven specified types of bonds (exempt facility, mortgage, veterans' mortgage, small issue, scholarship funding, redevelopment, or Code Sec. 501(c)(3) bonds). (Code Sec. 103(b)(1), Code Sec. 141(e))[40] Pre-Aug. 16, '86 industrial development bonds are subject to similar "qualification" rules. [41]

Hedge bonds (i.e., issued to "hedge" another bond) aren't exempt unless 85% of the bond's spendable proceeds (i.e., net of issuance expenses and certain reserves) are reasonably expected to be spent within specified periods, and at least 95% of the issuance costs (which can't be contingent) are paid within 180 days after issuance. (Code Sec. 149(g))[42]

Arbitrage bonds aren't exempt. (Code Sec. 103(b)(2)) This means a bond forming part of an issue any part of whose proceeds is reasonably expected to be used, directly or indirectly, to acquire (or refinance) nontemporary investments with a materially higher yield (more than ⅛ of 1 percentage point) than the bond itself, unless a required rebate is paid. (Code Sec. 148(a), Code Sec. 148(f); Reg § 1.148-2(d)(2)) If an issuer enters a transaction for a principal purpose of getting a material financial advantage based on the difference between tax-exempt and taxable rates, IRS has discretion to clearly reflect the economic substance of the transaction. (Reg § 1.148-10(e)) An issuer can't avoid having a bond treated as an arbitrage bond by giving away the prohibited arbitrage bond profit, e.g., by buying investments at other than fair market value ("yield burning").[43]

¶ 1333   Inflation-indexed debt instruments; Treasury Inflation-Indexed Securities.

There are two methods of accounting for stated interest and inflation adjustments on inflation-indexed debt instruments (issued after Jan. 1, '97). Inflation-indexed debt instruments are issued for cash, indexed for inflation and deflation using a general price or wage index, and are not otherwise contingent payment debt instruments. (Reg § 1.1275-7(c)(1), Reg § 1.1275-7(h)) These rules apply to Treasury Inflation-Indexed Securities (TIPS), but not certain debt instruments, e.g., U.S. savings bonds and bonds issued by qualified tuition

---

38. ¶J-3000; ¶1034; TD ¶158,001
39. ¶J-3001.1; ¶60,124; TD ¶158,003
40. ¶s J-3000 *et seq.*, J-3100, J-3252 *et seq.*, J-3600; ¶1414 *et seq.*; TD ¶158,009

41. ¶s J-3153 *et seq.*, J-3227 *et seq.*, J-3251; ¶1034.01; TD ¶158,009
42. ¶J-3667 *et seq.*; ¶1494.06; TD ¶158,001
43. ¶J-3400 *et seq.*; ¶1484 *et seq.*; TD ¶158,001

programs. (Reg § 1.1275-7(b))[44]

(1) The coupon bond method is a simplified method that applies if (a) the debt instrument is issued at par, and (b) all stated interest on it is qualified stated interest (i.e., it's unconditionally payable in cash at least annually, see ¶1315). The coupon bond method applies to TIPS that aren't stripped. Under this method, the stated interest is taxable to the holder when received or accrued, in accordance with his accounting method. Any increase in the inflation-adjusted principal amount is treated as OID (¶1314) for the period in which it occurs. (Reg § 1.1275-7(d))[45]

observation: Assuming there's some inflation and principal continues to be adjusted upward, holders will have to include amounts not yet realized as interest income.

A decrease in a bond's inflation-indexed principal first reduces the interest income attributable to the interest payments for the year of the adjustment. If the decrease exceeds that income, the excess generally is an ordinary deduction to the extent taxpayer previously included interest from the bond in income. Any remaining decrease is carried forward to reduce interest income in future years. A taxpayer generally has a capital loss if he sells the bond, or it matures, before he has used all the decrease. (Reg § 1.1275-7(f)(1), Reg § 1.1275-7(d)(4))[46]

(2) The discount bond method is used if the instrument doesn't qualify for the coupon bond method (e.g., because it is issued at a discount). Under this method, taxpayers make current adjustments to their OID accruals to account for changes in the inflation-adjusted principal amount. If the daily portions for an accrual period are positive amounts, they are taken into account under Code Sec. 1272 by the holder (¶1313). If the daily portions are negative, they are taken into account under the rules for deflation adjustments described above. (Reg § 1.1275-7(e)) The discount bond method applies to TIPS that are stripped under the Treasury's STRIPS program. (Reg § 1.1286-2)[47]

¶ 1334 Interest on U.S. savings bonds.

Interest on U.S. savings bonds now being issued is earned in three ways: On Series HH "face amount" bonds (not issued after Aug. 31, 2004), it's paid semiannually by check. On Series EE "discount" bonds, it's reflected as an increase in the bond's value over stated periods. On Series I inflation-indexed face amount bonds, it's credited monthly (at a fixed rate for the 30-year life of the bond and a semiannual variable inflation rate) and paid when the bond is cashed. The interest on these bonds (and on any unmatured or extended Series E and Series H bonds now outstanding) is fully taxable unless the exclusion at ¶2219 applies. [48]

Cash basis taxpayers report the interest on Series HH (or H) bonds in the year received. [49]

A cash basis owner of Series EE bonds (and outstanding Series E bonds) and Series I bonds may either: (1) defer reporting any interest (i.e., the bond's increase in value) until the year of final maturity, redemption, or other disposition, whichever is earlier, or (2) elect to report the annual increase in value in each year's return. [50]

Some Series E bonds can, at the owner's option, be held up to 30 years beyond their original maturity ("final maturity"). A cash basis owner who hasn't elected to report the interest on a Series E bond annually (under (2), above) must report all of the interest on the bond in the year in which the bond is redeemed or disposed of or, if earlier, the year in which it reaches "final maturity." (Code Sec. 454(a); Reg § 1.454-1(a)(1))[1]

observation: Series E bonds issued before Dec., '65 reach final maturity 40 years after

---

44. ¶J-4056.1, J-4379.1 *et seq.*; ¶12,714.037; TD ¶153,043 *et seq.*
45. ¶J-4379.1 *et seq.*; ¶12,714.037; TD ¶153,044
46. ¶J-4379.1 *et seq.*; ¶12,714.037; TD ¶153,044
47. ¶J-4379.5; ¶12,714.037; TD ¶153,045

48. ¶s J-3014, J-3719 *et seq.*; ¶4544.01; TD ¶156,001
49. ¶s J-3720, J-3721; ¶4544.01; TD ¶156,008
50. ¶J-3719; ¶4544 *et seq.*; TD ¶156,003
1. ¶s J-3721, J-3722; ¶4544 *et seq.*; TD ¶156,003

their issue date. Series E bonds issued after Nov., '65, and all Series EE bonds, reach final maturity 30 years after their issue dates. This means that any accrued interest on Series E or EE bonds issued in '77 is taxable in 2007.

Accrual basis taxpayers include the interest on the above bonds as it accrues. [2]

For the exclusion of income earned on qualified U.S. savings bonds by a payor of higher education expenses, see ¶2219 *et seq.*

¶ 1335   When to report interest income (other than OID).

Cash basis taxpayers report interest in the tax year it's actually or constructively received, regardless of when the interest is accrued on the debtor's books. [3] Generally, interest isn't constructively received if taxpayer's control of its receipt is subject to substantial limits or restrictions. (Reg § 1.451-2(a))[4] Thus, interest on a six-month certificate that isn't credited or made available before maturity without penalty isn't taxable until the certificate is redeemed or matures.[5]

Savings institution interest, or interest on life insurance dividends left to accumulate, is considered received when credited to the depositor's (policyholder's) account and subject to his withdrawal. [6]

Where a bank charges a penalty for premature withdrawals from a time savings account, the gross amount of interest paid or credited during the withdrawal year is reported as interest that year, even if the penalty partially or completely offsets the interest. [7] For deduction of forfeited interest, see ¶2171.

Matured interest coupons are constructively received in the year they mature unless it can be shown that there are no funds available for payment of the interest during the year. [8]

Accrual basis taxpayers report interest in the tax year in which the right to receive the interest becomes fixed, regardless of when it is received. [9] But if it appears reasonably certain the interest won't be paid because the debtor is insolvent, the creditor can delay reporting the interest until its collection appears reasonably certain. [10]

For cash and accrual taxpayers, there are special rules on when to include "interest" on below-market rate loans (¶1306), (Code Sec. 7872(a)(2), Code Sec. 7872(b)(2)(A))[11] "points" (¶1336), and unstated interest (¶1337).

caution: These rules don't apply to debt issued with original issue discount (¶1313).

¶ 1336   When "points" are included in income.

"Points" (¶1305) in the form of discount are taken into account under the "principal-reduction method" — i.e., as stated principal payments on the loan are made. "Points" paid out of funds not from the lender are included on receipt. [12]

¶ 1337   When to report unstated interest income.

A cash method seller includes unstated interest allocated to a payment (¶1307) as interest income in the tax year the payment is received. An accrual method seller includes the unstated interest in the tax year the payment is due. (Reg § 1.483-2(a)(1)(ii))[13]

---

2. ¶J-3719 *et seq.*; ¶4544.01; TD ¶156,008
3. ¶J-3703; ¶614.067; TD ¶151,501
4. ¶J-3706; ¶s 4514.036, 4514.053; TD ¶441,005
5. ¶J-3710; ¶4514.053; TD ¶151,015
6. ¶s J-3709, J-3717; ¶s 4514.036, 4514.053; TD ¶151,501
7. ¶J-2822; TD ¶151,501

8. ¶J-3715; ¶4514.053; TD ¶151,501
9. ¶J-3701; ¶4514.011; TD ¶151,502
10. ¶J-3702; ¶4514.023; TD ¶151,502
11. ¶J-3708; ¶78,724 *et seq.*; TD ¶155,000
12. ¶E-3004 *et seq.*; ¶4614.75; TD ¶151,503
13. ¶J-3758; ¶4834.01; TD ¶152,007

¶ 1338 Rents and Royalties. ▆▆▆▆▆▆▆▆▆▆▆▆▆▆▆

Rent is the payment for the use of real or tangible personal property. Royalties are payments for the use of certain rights, e.g., intangible rights such as patents. Both are includible in gross income.

¶ 1339 Rents.

Rents are includible in gross income, whether paid in cash or property. (Code Sec. 61(a)(5); Reg § 1.61-1(a)) If paid in property, the property's fair market value (at receipt) is the amount taxed as rent. [14]

Rents are reported by cash basis taxpayers when received, and by accrual basis taxpayers when due unless they're considered uncollectible. [15] For advance rentals, see ¶1341.

¶ 1340 Bonuses; lease cancellation payments.

A bonus or extra payment by the tenant to the lessor or sublessor on the execution of the lease is taxable as rent to the lessor or sublessor. [16]

If the tenant pays the landlord for permission to cancel the lease, the payments are rent to the landlord (whether cash or accrual basis) in the year received. (Reg § 1.61-8(a)) Payments to the landlord for modifying a lease or consenting to a sublease are also considered rent. [17] Where the lessor pays the tenant to cancel the lease, see ¶1598.

¶ 1341 Advance rentals and security deposits.

An advance rental is currently taxable (Reg § 1.61-8(b)), even if it's refundable or can be applied against the purchase price. [18] But a security deposit (¶1206) isn't taxable rent. [19]

¶ 1342 Deferred rentals.

Where the rules on deferred payment leases over $250,000 apply (see ¶1600), the lessor has a "constant accrual" of rental income in the same way that rental expenses are deductible by the lessee. (Code Sec. 467)[20]

¶ 1343 Tenant's payment of landlord's expenses.

Where a tenant is required under the lease to pay interest, property taxes, mortgage principal, etc., thus satisfying the *landlord's* own payment obligation, the payments are treated as rent paid by the tenant to the landlord. (Reg § 1.61-8(c))[21]

¶ 1344 Tenant's improvements to the leased property; construction allowances from lessor.

Where a tenant erects a building or makes other improvements to leased property, the resulting increase in the property's value isn't income to the landlord either at the time the improvements are made or at the end of the lease term. (Code Sec. 109) But the landlord does have rental income if the improvements are made as rent substitutes. [22]

A lessee may exclude any amount received in cash (or as a rent reduction) from a lessor

---

14. ¶J-2200 *et seq.*; ¶614.084 *et seq.*; TD ¶121,000
15. ¶J-2276; ¶s 4514.001, 4514.023; TD ¶121,002
16. ¶J-2278; TD ¶121,004
17. ¶J-2215 *et seq.*; ¶4514.022; TD ¶121,005
18. ¶J-2218; ¶4514.193; TD ¶121,003

19. ¶J-2277; ¶4514.194; TD ¶121,008
20. ¶L-6800 *et seq.*; ¶4674; TD ¶261,001
21. ¶J-2210 *et seq.*; ¶614.094; TD ¶121,007
22. ¶J-2250 *et seq.*; ¶1094.01 *et seq.*; TD ¶121,013

under a short-term lease (15 years or less) of retail space, that's for the purpose of the lessee's constructing or improving qualified long-term real property for use in the lessee's trade or business at the leased space. The construction allowance is excludible to the extent the lessee uses it for that purpose, within 8 ½ months after the end of the tax year it was received. Qualified long-term real property is nonresidential real property which is part of or otherwise present at the retail space and reverts to the lessor at lease termination. The lessor treats any qualified long-term real property that's constructed or improved with an allowance excluded under these rules as its own nonresidential real property (¶1923). (Code Sec. 110, Reg § 1.110-1)[23]

¶ 1345 Royalties.

Royalties (payments received for the use of copyrights, patents, trademarks, secret processes and similar intangibles, and for the right to exploit mineral or other natural resources) are taxable as ordinary income (Code Sec. 61(a)(6)), regardless of the name given to them by the parties or the form of payment (e.g., lump sum or property such as stock). [24]

Royalties are included by cash basis taxpayers on receipt (actual or constructive), and by accrual basis taxpayers when their rights to them are fixed. [25]

¶ 1346 Life Insurance Proceeds. ▬▬▬▬▬▬

Life insurance proceeds payable by reason of the insured's death are fully excludable or, if paid later than death under an interest option or in installments, partially excludable, from the recipient's gross income. All or part of the exclusion may be lost if the contract is transferred during the insured's life. Certain accelerated death benefits received by terminally or chronically ill insureds are excludable. Special requirements apply for employer-owned life insurance.

¶ 1347 How life insurance proceeds are taxed.

Amounts received under a "life insurance contract" (¶1348), that are paid by reason of the insured's death aren't included in the gross income of the recipient (i.e., beneficiary) (Code Sec. 101(a)) (unless the policy was transferred for value, see ¶1353). The exclusion applies to lump sum payments made at the time of the insured's death, and to amounts paid later to the extent the payment doesn't exceed the amount payable at death. (Reg § 1.101-1(a)(1))[26] For dividends and other lifetime payments, see ¶1351. For accelerated death benefits, see ¶1352.

For life insurance contracts that don't qualify, the exclusion is limited to the excess of the death benefits over the contract's net surrender value (i.e., value on surrender). (Code Sec. 7702(g)(2)) The net surrender value is treated as an annuity payment (¶1355 *et seq.*). Also, the owner of the contract is taxed (in the year it fails to qualify) on the income earned on it. This income equals the excess, for the year, of: (1) the sum of the net surrender value increase plus the cost of life insurance protection provided, over (2) premiums paid. (Code Sec. 7702(g)(1)(B))[27]

¶ 1348 Life insurance contract defined.

To qualify as a life insurance contract, a contract must be a life insurance (or endowment) contract under local law *and* satisfy either (a) a cash value accumulation test, or (b) a combined guideline premium requirement/cash value corridor test. (Code Sec. 101(f), Code Sec. 7702(a), Code Sec. 7702(h))[28] Pre-'85 contracts must entail risk shifting and risk

---

23. ¶J-2261 *et seq.*; ¶1104
24. ¶J-2300 *et seq.*; ¶614.084 *et seq.*; TD ¶122,001
25. ¶s J-2305, J-2306; ¶4514.001; TD ¶122,003
26. ¶J-4700 *et seq.*; ¶1014; TD ¶148,501
27. ¶J-4900 *et seq.*; ¶s 1014, 77,024.07; TD ¶148,504
28. ¶J-4800 *et seq.*; ¶s 1014, 77,024; TD ¶149,001

distribution.[29]

¶ 1349 Proceeds paid in installments.

If the life insurance proceeds payable on the insured's death are paid in installments or for life, only part (below) of each payment is excluded. Any amount that exceeds the excluded portion is taxable when received. But if the amount of the total anticipated payments can't exceed the total amount payable at the insured's death, then each payment is fully excludable, whenever it's made. (Code Sec. 101(d)(1); Reg § 1.101-4(a)(1)(i))[30]

The excludable portion of each payment is: (1) the excludable amount held by the insurer with respect to the particular beneficiary, divided by (2) the number of payments to be made or, if payments are for life, the number of payments anticipated over the life expectancy of the beneficiary. This same prorated amount of each payment is excludable, regardless of how many payments are made (Reg § 1.101-4) (i.e., even if the beneficiary exceeds his anticipated life expectancy). The excludable amount is the present value to the beneficiary (as of the date of death) of the settlement.[31]

A beneficiary who is the spouse of an insured who died before Oct. 23, '86, may exclude an *additional* $1,000 each year of amounts received by reason of the insured's death. [32]

¶ 1350 Proceeds left at interest.

Where excludable life insurance proceeds are held by the insurer under an agreement to pay interest, the interest is taxable to the recipient, whether the interest option was chosen by the insured or by his beneficiaries or estate. No part of this interest may be excluded under the proration rules (¶1349). (Code Sec. 101(c); Reg § 1.101-3(a))[33]

¶ 1351 Proceeds paid before death of insured—loans, refunds, dividends.

Payments made under life insurance or endowment contracts before the death of the insured (e.g., loans, refunds, dividends) generally are treated as amounts "not received" under an annuity contract (¶1367). (Code Sec. 72(a))[34] For accelerated death benefits received by terminally or chronically ill individuals, see ¶1352.

¶ 1352 Accelerated death benefits—terminally or chronically ill insureds—viatical settlements.

Amounts received under a life insurance contract on the life of individuals who are certified terminally or chronically ill are excluded from gross income as amounts paid by reason of the death of an insured (¶1347). (Code Sec. 101(g)(1)) A similar exclusion applies to amounts received for the sale or assignment of any portion of a death benefit under a life insurance contract to a viatical settlement provider (one that regularly buys or takes assignments of life insurance contracts on the lives of the terminally ill and meets detailed standards) if the insured under the life insurance contract is either terminally or chronically ill. (Code Sec. 101(g)(2)(A))[35] In the case of chronically ill individuals, the exclusions apply only if detailed requirements are met. (Code Sec. 101(g)(3))[36]

---

29. ¶J-4950 *et seq.*; ¶1014; TD ¶149,001
30. ¶J-4718; ¶1014.04; TD ¶148,505
31. ¶J-4720; ¶1014.04; TD ¶148,505
32. ¶J-4719; ¶1014.05; TD ¶148,505

33. ¶J-4717; ¶1014.03; TD ¶148,503
34. ¶J-5055 *et seq.*; ¶724 *et seq.*; TD ¶148,900 *et seq.*
35. ¶J-4750 *et seq.*; ¶J-4818; ¶1014.015; TD ¶148,900 *et seq.*
36. ¶J-4754 *et seq.*; ¶1014.015; TD ¶148,905 *et seq.*

¶ 1353 Death benefits exclusion where contract was transferred.

If a life insurance contract is transferred for valuable consideration, e.g., by sale, during the insured's lifetime, the transferee's exclusion for the life insurance proceeds he receives under the contract by reason of the insured's death (¶1347) is limited to the value of the consideration he paid for the contract, plus the net premiums and "other amounts" he paid later. (Code Sec. 101(a)(2))[37] For contracts issued after June 8, '97, "other amounts" includes interest paid or accrued by the transferee on debt with respect to a life insurance contract (or to an interest in one) that was transferred for valuable consideration, if the interest is disallowed under Code Sec. 264(a)(4) (see ¶1718). (Code Sec. 101(a)(2)) For the sale or assignment of any portion of the death benefit to a viatical settlement provider, see ¶1352.

If only an interest in the contract is transferred, the limit applies only to the part of the proceeds attributable to the transferred interest. [38]

This limitation doesn't apply if:

. . . the transfer is to the insured, his partner, his partnership or a corporation in which he is a shareholder or officer; (Code Sec. 101(a)(2)(B)) or

. . . the transferee's basis for the contract (or interest) is determined in whole or in part by reference to the transferor's basis (Code Sec. 101(a)(2)(A))[39] as in a tax-free reorganization. (Reg § 1.101-1(b)(5), Ex 2)[40]

Where the transfer is gratuitous, i.e., a gift, the above limitation doesn't apply. The full death benefits exclusion is preserved. (Reg § 1.101-1(b)(2))[41]

¶ 1354 Employer-owned life insurance.

For contracts issued after Aug. 17, 2006 (except for tax-free Code Sec. 1035 exchanges), an employer in a trade or businesses treats proceeds payable to it from an employer-owned life insurance contract on an employee as income, excluding as a death benefit only the premiums and other amounts it paid for the contract. (Code Sec. 101(j)(1))[42] This rule doesn't apply for a contract for which notice and consent requirements are met, if:

(1) the insured was an individual who was an employee within 12 months of his death;

(2) at the time the contract was issued, the insured was a director; a "highly compensated employee," i.e., a more-than-5% owner or employee who for the preceding year received in excess of $100,000 (for 2007; $105,000 for 2008) (¶4325); or a "highly compensated individual," i.e., one of the 5 highest paid officers, a shareholder owning more than 10%, or anyone else in the top 35% of employees ranked by pay;

(3) the amount is paid to: a family member of the insured (under Code Sec. 267(c)(4)), an individual who is a designated beneficiary under the contract (other than the policyholder), a trust established for either the family member's or beneficiary's benefit, or the insured's estate; or

(4) the amount is used to buy an equity (or partnership capital or profits) interest in the policyholder from the family member, beneficiary, trust or estate. (Code Sec. 101(j)(2)) It's intended that this amount be paid or used by the due date of the tax return for the policyholder's tax year in which the proceeds are received as a death benefit under the insurance contract, so that who is paid and what purchases are made with proceeds are known in the tax year in which the exception from the income inclusion rule is claimed. [43]

37. ¶J-4729; ¶1014.02; TD ¶148,528
38. ¶J-4731; ¶1014.02; TD ¶148,528
39. ¶J-4730; ¶1014.02; TD ¶148,528
40. ¶J-4742; ¶1014.02; TD ¶148,530

41. ¶J-4732; ¶1014.02; TD ¶148,529
42. ¶J-4744; ¶1014.11; TD ¶148,536
43. ¶J-4744; ¶1014.11; TD ¶148,536

The notice and consent requirements are met if, before the issuance of the contract, the employee is notified (and consents) in writing to the employer insuring him with the employer as a beneficiary. The employee must be told the maximum face amount of the life insurance and if coverage continues after his termination. (Code Sec. 101(j)(4))[44] Annual reporting and recordkeeping by policyholders that own one or more employer-owned life insurance contracts is also required. (Code Sec. 6039I)

¶ 1355   Taxation of Annuity Payments.

Annuity payments consist generally of two parts: nontaxable return of investment (based on an exclusion ratio), and taxable interest. Other amounts (e.g., withdrawals, dividends) are taxable to the extent they exceed the contract's cost.

¶ 1356   How annuities are taxed.

Gross income includes any amount received "as an annuity" that's paid under an annuity, life insurance or endowment contract. (Code Sec. 72(a))[45] For exclusion under the "annuity rule," see ¶1357. For "nonannuity" payments under the contract (e.g., loans, dividends), see ¶1367. For private annuities, see ¶1370. For annuities paid to survivors of certain public safety officers, see ¶1261.

¶ 1357   The annuity rule—"exclusion ratio" for amounts received "as an annuity."

If a payment under an annuity, life insurance or endowment contract is received "as an annuity" (i.e., a sum of money (or property) payable at regular intervals over a period of more than one full year from the starting date (¶1364) (Reg § 1.72-2(b)), all or part of it may be tax-free (for "natural person" holders, see ¶1358). The part of each "annuity" payment that represents return of investment (e.g., premiums paid) is excludable from the recipient's income until the entire investment is recovered. Excess receipts are fully taxable. (Code Sec. 72(b)(1); Reg § 1.72-4(a))[46]

The excludable portion is computed by multiplying each payment received by an "exclusion ratio," determined by dividing the investment in the contract (¶1362) by the contract's expected return (¶1363), as of the annuity starting date, and rounding to the nearest tenth. (Code Sec. 72(b); Reg § 1.72-4(a)) But the excludable portion of any payment can't exceed the amount of investment in the contract that is unrecovered immediately before the payment is received. (Code Sec. 72(b)(2))[47] (For employee annuities, see ¶1365 and ¶1366.)

Once computed, the exclusion ratio is applied to each "annuity" payment received under the contract, until the total investment has been recovered tax-free. (Code Sec. 72(b); Reg § 1.72-4(a))[48] But the ratio must be recomputed if the contract is transferred for valuable consideration, matures, is surrendered, or is exchanged. (Reg § 1.72-4(a)(4))[49]

If there was no investment in the contract, all payments are taxable in full. If investment exceeds total expected return, all payments are tax-free. (Reg § 1.72-4(d))[50]

Where the annuitant's death causes the annuity payments (starting after Jan. 1, '86) to stop, the amount of any investment in the contract that the annuitant hasn't yet recovered tax-free may be deducted on his final income tax return. (Code Sec. 72(b)(3)(A))[1] For after-death distribution requirements, see ¶1359.

For annuities that started before '87, the exclusion ratio, once computed, applies to all

---

44. ¶J-4744; ¶1014.11; TD ¶148,536
45. ¶J-5001; ¶724 *et seq.*; TD ¶146,501
46. ¶J-5100 *et seq.*; ¶724; TD ¶146,541
47. ¶J-5105; ¶724.06; TD ¶146,545

48. ¶J-5104; ¶724.06; TD ¶146,545
49. ¶J-5106; ¶724.06; TD ¶146,547
50. ¶J-5104; ¶724.06; TD ¶146,545
1. ¶J-5109; ¶s 724, 724.06; TD ¶146,551

payments no matter how long the annuitant lives (unless the contract is modified or exchanged). (Reg § 1.72-4(a))[2]

¶ 1358 Annuity rule exclusion available only to natural persons.

If an annuity contract is held by a person who isn't a natural person, the annuity rule (¶1357) doesn't apply. The income on the contract (for the holder's tax year) must be treated as ordinary income received or accrued by the holder during that year. (Code Sec. 72(u)(1))[3] A natural person doesn't include a trust or corporation. But holding by a trust, etc., *as agent* for a natural person is disregarded. (Code Sec. 72(u)(1))[4]

However, an *employer* that's the nominal owner (agent) of an annuity contract whose beneficial owners are (the employer's) employees is considered to hold the contract. [5]

The natural person rule *doesn't apply* to contracts: acquired by an estate by reason of the decedent's death; held by a qualified plan or IRA; that are "qualified funding assets" (¶1385); bought by an employer on termination of a qualified plan and held until all amounts under the contract are distributed to the employee (or his beneficiary) for whom the contract was bought; or that are immediate annuities. (Code Sec. 72(u)(3))[6]

¶ 1359 After-death distribution requirements for annuity contracts.

Payments under a contract aren't entitled to the partial exclusion under the annuity rule *unless* the contract provides that: (1) if any holder ("primary annuitant" for contracts not held by an individual) dies on or after the annuity starting date (¶1364) (and before the entire interest in the contract has been distributed), the balance will be distributed at least as rapidly as it was at the date of death, and (2) if any holder dies before the starting date, the entire interest must be distributed within five years of his death. (Code Sec. 72(s)(1))[7]

However, distributions that are payable to (or for) a designated beneficiary can be made for the beneficiary's life or a period not ending past his life expectancy. As long as the payments begin within one year of the holder's death, they'll be considered distributed on that starting date. (Code Sec. 72(s)(2)) A beneficiary who is the holder's surviving spouse will be considered the holder. (Code Sec. 72(s)(3))[8]

observation: Treating the surviving spouse/beneficiary as the holder means that the after-death distribution provisions must be satisfied with respect to the *spouse's* death.

The after-death distribution rules *don't apply to:* contracts provided under qualified pension, profit-sharing, stock bonus or annuity plans; tax-sheltered annuities; individual retirement annuities (or contracts provided under IRAs); qualified funding assets (¶1385), regardless of any qualified assignment (Code Sec. 72(s)(5))[9] or contracts issued before Jan. 19, '85. [10]

¶ 1360 Variable annuities.

A variable annuity contract is one where the amount paid varies depending on investment experience, cost of living indexes, market fluctuations, etc. The excludable portion of each payment is computed by dividing the investment in the contract (¶1362) by the total number of anticipated payments. (Reg § 1.72-2(b)(3), Reg § 1.72-4(d)(3))[11]

The excludable amount stays the same regardless of changes in the amount received. (Reg § 1.72-2(b)(3))[12] But if the amount received in a tax year is *less* than the excludable

---

2. ¶J-5104; ¶724.06; TD ¶146,541
3. ¶s J-5005; J-5006; ¶724.25; TD ¶146,506
4. ¶J-5005; ¶724.25; TD ¶146,506
5. ¶J-5005; ¶724.25; TD ¶146,506
6. ¶J-5007; ¶724.25; TD ¶146,508
7. ¶s J-5014, J-5015; ¶724.01; TD ¶146,515

8. ¶J-5014; ¶724.01; TD ¶146,515
9. ¶J-5016; ¶724.01; TD ¶146,515
10. ¶J-5014; ¶724.01; TD ¶146,517
11. ¶J-5143; ¶724.08; TD ¶146,582
12. ¶J-5143; ¶724.08; TD ¶146,582

amount, taxpayer may elect (attach a specified statement to the return) to recompute the exclusion ratio for later years' payments. (Reg § 1.72-4(d)(3)(ii), Reg § 1.72-4(d)(3)(iv))[13]

¶ 1361 Joint and survivor annuity contracts.

Under a joint and survivor annuity contract, payments are made during the lives of two annuitants and, after the death of one, during the life of the survivor. A single exclusion ratio (¶1357), based on the aggregate expected return to both annuitants, is applied to the payments received by both annuitants. (Reg § 1.72-2(a)(2))[14]

¶ 1362 Investment in the contract.

For annuity rule purposes (¶1357), the "investment in the contract" is, in general, the net cost of the contract as of the annuity starting date (¶1364) or, if later, the date of the first contract payment. It equals the aggregate amount of premiums and other consideration paid (as of that date) for the contract, minus the aggregate amount previously received under the contract that was excluded from income. (Code Sec. 72(c)(1))[15] It must also be reduced to account for any refund feature. (Code Sec. 72(c)(2))[16] Separate computations may be required for pre-July '86 and post-June '86 investments. (Reg § 1.72-6(d))[17]

For an employee annuity, investment in the contract includes certain employer contributions that were taxable to the owner (employee). (Reg § 1.72-8(a))[18] Where the annuity began after Nov. 18, '96 (¶1365), or the safe-harbor method is elected for annuities beginning before Nov. 19, '96 (¶1366), no refund feature adjustment is required. [19]

For an employee annuity where the decedent died before Aug. 21, '96, the survivor-annuitant's investment in the contract also includes prior law's $5,000 death benefit exclusion, if applicable. (Reg § 1.72-8(b))[20]

¶ 1363 Expected return from the contract.

For annuity rule purposes (¶1357), the "expected return from the contract" is the total amount to be received (or estimated to be received) under the contract. It is computed as of the annuity starting date (¶1364) (Code Sec. 72(b)(1)) and doesn't take into account any amount for dividends or other payments *not* received as an annuity (¶1367). (Code Sec. 72(c)(3); Reg § 1.72-7(a))[21]

If the annuity is for a fixed term and doesn't depend on any life expectancy, the expected return is the amount of the payment specified for each period multiplied by the number of periods. (Reg § 1.72-5(c))[22]

If the annuity is payable for life or joint lives, the expected return is the amount of the *annual* payment multiplied by the number of years of life expectancy using IRS actuarial tables. (Code Sec. 72(c)(3)(A); Reg § 1.72-5(a))[23]

If the annuity is for an amount certain payable in periodic installments, the expected return is the total amount guaranteed. (Reg § 1.72-5(d))[24]

¶ 1364 Annuity starting date.

The "annuity starting date" is the first day of the first period for which an amount is received *as an annuity* (¶1357) under the contract. This is the date the contractual obligation

---

13. ¶J-5145; ¶724.08; TD ¶146,584
14. ¶J-5132 *et seq.*; ¶724.15; TD ¶146,572
15. ¶J-5113; ¶724.10; TD ¶141,033
16. ¶J-5122; ¶724.12; TD ¶141,038
17. ¶J-5117 *et seq.*; ¶724.10; TD ¶146,558
18. ¶H-11032 *et seq.*; ¶724.11; TD ¶141,034

19. ¶H-11047; ¶4024.02
20. ¶H-11037; ¶724.12; TD ¶141,034
21. ¶J-5124 *et seq.*; ¶724.14; TD ¶146,564
22. ¶J-5130; ¶724.14; TD ¶146,570
23. ¶J-5126 *et seq.*; ¶724.14; TD ¶146,564
24. ¶J-5131; ¶724.14; TD ¶146,571

becomes fixed or, if later, the first day of the period (year, quarter, etc., depending on whether the payments are to be made annually, quarterly, etc.) that ends on the date of the first annuity payment. (Code Sec. 72(c)(4); Reg § 1.72-4(b)(1))[25] Special rules apply if the contract is transferred or exchanged. (Code Sec. 72(g)(3))[26]

¶ 1365   Employee annuities—simplified method for computing nontaxable portion.

The nontaxable portion of amounts received as an annuity (¶1357) under a Code Sec. 401(a) qualified employee plan, a Code Sec. 403(a) qualified employee annuity or a Code Sec. 403(b) tax-sheltered annuity is computed under a simplified method, by dividing the investment in the contract (¶1362) as of the annuity starting date (¶1364) by a designated number of monthly payments. (Code Sec. 72(d)(1)(B))

For an annuity payable over the life of a single individual, the number of payments is 360 if the age of the annuitant on the annuity starting date is not more than 55; 310 payments if the age is more than 55 but not more than 60; 260 payments if more than 60 but not more than 65; 210 payments if more than 65 but not more than 70; and 160 payments if more than 70. (Code Sec. 72(d)(1)(B)(iii))[27]

For an annuity payable over the lives of more than one individual, the number of payments is 410 if the combined age of the annuitants on the annuity starting date is not more than 110; 360 payments if more than 110 but not more than 120; 310 payments if more than 120 but not more than 130; 260 payments if more than 130 but not more than 140; and 210 payments if more than 140. (Code Sec. 72(d)(1)(B)(iv))[28]

Appropriate adjustments must be made if payments are not made on a monthly basis. (Code Sec. 72(d)(1)(F))[29]

The simplified method doesn't apply if the primary annuitant is 75 or older on the annuity starting date, unless there are fewer than 5 years of guaranteed payments under the annuity. (Code Sec. 72(d)(1)(E))[30]

A lump-sum payment received in connection with the start of annuity payments is taxable under Code Sec. 72(e) as if received before the annuity starting date (see ¶1367), and the investment in the contract is determined by taking into consideration the receipt of this lump-sum payment. (Code Sec. 72(d)(1)(D))[31]

For annuity starting dates before Jan. 1, '98 and after Nov. 18, '96, the designated number of payments is based on the age of the primary annuitant, and there is no separate table for annuities based on the life of more than one individual. [32]

For annuity starting dates before Nov. 19, '96, the regular annuity rules apply (¶1355 *et seq.*) unless the employee elects a simplified safe-harbor method (¶1366).[33]

¶ 1366   Safe-harbor exclusion ratio for pre-Nov. 19, '96 employee annuities.

For annuities with starting dates (¶1364) before Nov. 19, '96, a distributee who either: (1) was less than 75 when the payments start, or (2) was 75 or older and had less than five years of guaranteed payments, [34] could have elected a simplified safe harbor method to determine the taxable and tax-free portions of annuity payments that: (a) started after July 1, '86, (b) are made under a Code Sec. 401(a) qualified employee plan, a Code Sec. 403(a) qualified

25. ¶J-5110; ¶724.09; TD ¶141,019
26. ¶J-5112; ¶724.09; TD ¶146,553
27. ¶H-11012; ¶4024.02; TD ¶141,016
28. ¶H-11012; ¶4024.02; TD ¶141,016
29. ¶H-11012; ¶4024.02; TD ¶141,016

30. ¶H-11012; ¶4024.02; TD ¶141,016
31. ¶H-11012; ¶4024.02; TD ¶141,016
32. ¶H-11012; ¶4024.02; TD ¶141,016
33. ¶H-11012 *et seq.*; ¶724.07; TD ¶146,595
34. ¶s H-11016, H-11017; ¶4024.02; TD ¶141,021

employee annuity or a Code Sec. 403(b) tax-sheltered annuity, and (c) depend on the distributee's life or joint lives of the distributee and beneficiary. [35]

The excludable portion of each monthly payment is a level dollar amount, determined by dividing the investment in the contract (¶1362) by the number of expected annuity payments (see table below). This same amount is excluded even if the payment amount changes (e.g., for cost of living increases or a reduced survivor annuity). [36] If annuity payments are to be made to multiple beneficiaries, the total excluded amount is found by reference to the age of the oldest beneficiary. Each beneficiary excludes a portion of this total excludable amount from each annuity payment received, based on the ratio his monthly annuity bears to the total amount of the monthly annuity payments to all beneficiaries. [37]

The total number of monthly payments expected to be received (whether under a single life annuity or a joint and survivor one) is based on the distributee's age as of the birthday preceding the annuity starting date. The number of payments is 300 for a distributee age 55 and under; 260 for age 56 to 60; 240 for age 61 to 65; 170 for age 66 to 70; and 120 for age 71 and over.[38]

¶ 1367   Amounts "not" received as an annuity—cash withdrawals, dividends, etc.

Payments under life insurance, endowment and annuity contracts (other than modified endowment contracts, see ¶1369) that aren't "annuities" (e.g., cash withdrawals, loans, dividends, etc.) are fully taxable if received *on or after* the annuity starting date (¶1364). (Code Sec. 72(e)(2)(A), Code Sec. 72(e)(3)(A))[39]

"Nonannuity" amounts received *before* the annuity starting date are: (1) *not taxable,* to the extent that, as of the date of distribution, they don't exceed the cost of the contract (i.e., accumulated net premiums paid) and (2) *taxable,* to the extent allocable to income (i.e., excess of the contract's cash value over the owner's investment) at that time. (Code Sec. 72(e)(2)(B), Code Sec. 72(e)(3)(B))[40] (Veteran's insurance dividends are tax-free, regardless of cost.) [41]

🅡🄸🄰/caution: The pre-annuity starting date withdrawal may be subject to the premature distribution penalty (¶1368).

Receipts less than on insurance or endowment contract's cost don't give rise to a deductible loss.[42]

The contract's cost is reduced by the nontaxable amount of the dividend, etc., for purposes of computing the taxable portion of later payments. (Code Sec. 72(e)(6)(B))[43]

For these purposes, all contracts (other than immediate annuities or qualified plan annuities) issued by the same company (or its affiliates) to the same policyholder during any one calendar year are treated as a single contract. (Code Sec. 72(e)(11))[44]

For contracts entered into before Aug. 14, '82, and amounts allocable to investment made in contracts before that date, different rules apply. [45]

¶ 1368   10% penalty on premature distributions from annuity contracts.

A penalty is imposed (except as noted below) on a person who receives any nonannuity distribution (¶1367) before the annuity starting date (¶1364) in the tax year the distribution is received. The penalty equals 10% of the taxable portion of the distribution. (Code

35. ¶H-11012, H-11018; ¶4024.02; TD ¶141,022
36. ¶H-11019; ¶4024.02; TD ¶141,023
37. ¶H-11021; ¶4024.02; TD ¶141,025
38. ¶H-11023; ¶4024.02; TD ¶141,027
39. ¶J-5053; ¶724.17; TD ¶146,523
40. ¶724.17; TD ¶146,523

41. ¶J-5055; TD ¶146,525
42. ¶J-5308; TD ¶146,626
43. ¶J-5063; ¶724.10; TD ¶146,533
44. ¶J-5064; ¶724.17; TD ¶146,534
45. ¶J-5062; ¶724.17; TD ¶146,523

Sec. 72(q)(1))[46] Calculate and pay the penalty on Form 5329. [47]

This 10% penalty *doesn't apply* to any distribution:

(1) made on or after the date taxpayer (recipient) reaches age 59 ½;

(2) made on or after the death of the holder (or the primary annuitant, where the holder isn't an individual);

(3) attributable to recipient's total and indefinite disability;

(4) that's part of a series of substantially equal periodic payments (not less frequently than annually) made for the life (or life expectancy) of taxpayer or the joint lives (or joint life expectancies) of taxpayer and his designated beneficiary;

(5) made from a Code Sec. 401(a) qualified employee plan, a Code Sec. 403(a) qualified annuity plan, a Code Sec. 403(b) tax-sheltered annuity plan or a Code Sec. 818(a)(3) retirement plan for life insurance company employees (but for the separate penalty on premature distributions from these plans, see ¶4344);

(6) made from an individual retirement account or annuity (but for the separate penalty on premature distributions from these plans, see ¶4344);

(7) made under an annuity contract which is purchased by an employer on termination of a qualified plan (bonus, pension, profit-sharing or annuity) and which is held by the employer until the employee separates from service;

(8) under an immediate annuity;

(9) under a "qualified funding asset" (¶1385), regardless of any qualified assignment;

(10) to which the Code Sec. 72(t) tax on premature distributions from qualified plans applies (without regard to the Code Sec. 72(t)(2) exceptions), see ¶4344;

(11) allocable to pre-Aug. 14, '82 investment in the contract. (Code Sec. 72(q)(2))[48]

¶ 1369 Modified endowment contracts.

A modified endowment contract is a life insurance contract (entered into after June 20, '88) that fails to meet a "7-pay test" (or that is exchanged for such a contract). The test is failed if the accumulated amount paid under the contract during the first seven years exceeds the net level premiums that would have been paid as paid-up future benefits. (Code Sec. 7702A(a), Code Sec. 7702(b))[49]

Payments under a modified endowment contract that are received before the annuity starting date (¶1364) are includible in gross income to the extent allocable to income on the contract, as described at ¶1367. (Code Sec. 72(e)(10)(A)(i))[50] This applies to any amount received as a loan, or assigned or pledged on the value of the contract, unless the loan, etc., is made solely to cover burial expenses or prearranged funeral expenses where the maximum death benefit under the contract doesn't exceed $25,000. (Code Sec. 72(e)(10)(B)) However, taxpayer's investment in the contract (¶1362) is increased by the amount taxed to him (as a loan or assignment). (Code Sec. 72(e)(4)(A))[1]

Certain amounts received under a modified endowment contract that are includible in income are subject to a 10% penalty tax (Code Sec. 72(v)(1), Code Sec. 72(v)(2))[2] (use Form 5329).[3]

---

46. ¶J-5017; ¶724.21; TD ¶146,518
47. ¶S-2510; TD ¶146,519
48. ¶J-5018; ¶724.21; TD ¶146,520
49. ¶J-5066 *et seq.*; ¶s 724.17, 77,02A4; TD ¶146,536

50. ¶J-5065; ¶724.17; TD ¶146,535
1. ¶J-5063; ¶724.17; TD ¶146,529
2. ¶J-5076; ¶724.17; TD ¶146,540
3. ¶S-2510; TD ¶146,519

¶ 1370   Private annuities.

A private annuity generally involves the transfer of money or property to an individual or organization in exchange for the transferee's promise to make lifetime payments to the transferor. These transfers typically are made: to family members, controlled entities, or unrelated purchasers; to charitable organizations; and in settlement of a will contest. [4]

Transfer of an "unsecured" private annuity arrangement doesn't result in immediate taxable gain (or loss). Instead, any gain is reportable ratably over the lifetime of the transferor (i.e., annuitant). The gain equals the excess of the present value of the annuity (determined under regs) over the transferor's adjusted basis in the transferred property. Any loss may be disallowed if the arrangement is between related parties (¶2446 *et seq.*).[5]

If the arrangement is "secured" (i.e., the property transferred also is collateral for the payments), it's taxed (except for gift tax aspects) under the rules for commercial annuities, (¶1355 *et seq.*).[6] In applying those rules, the annuitant's basis in the property he transferred for the annuity is used as his investment in the contract. [7]

The value of annuities issued by charities is determined under IRS tables. [8]

¶ 1371   Gifts and Inheritances.

Property received as a gift, bequest, devise or inheritance is exempt from income tax.

¶ 1372   Gifts of property.

A gift of property isn't taxable to a recipient (Code Sec. 102; Reg § 1.102-1)[9] other than an employee, see ¶1212. For gifts of income, see ¶1374. For employee awards, see ¶1252. For gift tax, see ¶5037 *et seq.*

¶ 1373   Inheritances.

Tax-free bequests, devises and inheritances are money and any property that pass on the death of a person by his will or under intestacy, including amounts received in settlement of a will contest.[10] For bequests of income, see ¶1374. For estate tax, see ¶5000 *et seq.*

¶ 1374   Gifts and bequests of income.

Gifts and bequests of *income,* and the income from property that is received as a gift or bequest, are taxable to the recipient, whether paid periodically or in a lump sum. (Code Sec. 102(b); Reg § 1.102-1(c))[11] For an exception for income paid or credited as a gift or bequest of specific property or money, see ¶3950.

¶ 1375   Prizes and Awards.

Prizes and awards generally are taxable.

¶ 1376   Prizes and awards.

All prizes and awards (with exceptions for qualified scholarships, see ¶2216) are includible in gross income (Code Sec. 74(a); Reg § 1.74-1(b)) *unless:* the prize is primarily for religious, charitable, scientific, educational, artistic, literary, etc., achievement; the recipient was selected without any action on his part, and thus isn't required to render substantial future

---

4. ¶J-5252; ¶724.01; TD ¶146,601
5. ¶J-5256 *et seq.*; ¶724.05; TD ¶146,602
6. ¶J-5257; TD ¶146,606
7. ¶J-5254; ¶724.05; TD ¶146,603

8. ¶P-6615, P-6674 *et seq.*; TD ¶146,612
9. ¶J-6000 *et seq.*; ¶1024; TD ¶178,001
10. ¶J-6000 *et seq.*; ¶1024.02; TD ¶178,010
11. ¶J-6004, ¶J-6005; ¶1024; TD ¶178,004

services; *and* it's transferred by the payor to a governmental unit or charity the recipient designated (Code Sec. 74(b))[12] before getting any benefit from it.[13] IRS specifies the requirements of the designation (including model language).[14] For employee awards, see ¶1252.

For a prize paid in property or services, the taxable amount is the prize's current fair market (resale) value. (Reg § 1.74-1(a)(2))[15]

Under the principle of constructive receipt (¶2822), the winner of a contest (e.g., a lottery, jackpot) who is given the option of receiving either a lump sum or an annuity has to include the value of the award in gross income, even if he or she takes the annuity. However, in the case of a cash basis individual, a "qualified prize option" (to choose either cash or an annuity not later than 60 days after becoming entitled to the prize) is disregarded in determining the tax year for which any portion of a "qualified prize" (one payable over at least 10 years and that meets other requirements) is included in income. (Code Sec. 451(h)) That is, the individual doesn't have to include the value of the prize in income immediately merely by having had the option to choose cash.[16]

¶ 1377 Accident and Health Insurance Benefits. ▰▰▰▰▰▰▰▰▰▰▰▰▰▰▰

Benefits received from accident and health insurance are excluded from gross income, unless the benefits compensate for medical expense deductions from an earlier year. Benefits from long-term care insurance policies are subject to special rules.

¶ 1378 Exclusion for benefits received through accident or health insurance.

Amounts received through accident or health insurance (or through an arrangement having the effect of accident or health insurance) for personal injuries or sickness are generally excluded from income, except to the extent attributable to medical expenses that were deducted in a previous year. This exclusion doesn't apply to amounts received by an employee to the extent the amounts are (1) attributable to employer contributions that weren't includible in the employee's gross income, or (2) are paid by the employer. (Code Sec. 104(a)(3))[17]

Where an employer-provided disability plan allows employees to elect annually to pay for coverage out of pre- or post-tax dollars, disability benefits paid to an employee who elected the post-tax option for the plan year in which he became disabled are excludable from gross income.[18]

¶ 1379 Exclusion for benefits from long-term care insurance—per diem limit.

Qualified long-term care insurance contracts (see ¶2146) issued after '96 are treated as accident and health insurance contracts (Code Sec. 7702B(a)(1)). Pre-'97 contracts that met applicable state long-term care insurance requirements also qualify. (Reg § 1.7702B-2)[19] Amounts (other than policyholder dividends, as defined in Code Sec. 808 or premium refunds) received from such contracts are treated as amounts received for personal injury or sickness and as reimbursement for expenses actually incurred for medical care, and are excludable (see ¶1378), subject to a per diem limit, below.[20]

If the total of (1) the periodic payments received for any period under all qualified long-term care insurance contracts treated as made for qualified long-term care services for an insured and (2) the periodic payments received for the period which are treated under Code Sec. 101(g) (see ¶1352) as paid by reason of the death of the insured, exceeds the per diem limit for the period, the excess is includible in gross income. A payment isn't taken into

12. ¶J-1201 *et seq.*; ¶744; TD ¶194,001
13. ¶J-1208; ¶744.01; TD ¶194,006
14. ¶J-1210; ¶744.01; TD ¶194,008
15. ¶J-1223; ¶744.04; TD ¶194,019
16. ¶G-2424.2; ¶4514.043; TD ¶441,012

17. ¶J-1301; ¶1044.03; TD ¶194,501
18. ¶H-1115 *et seq.*; ¶1044.03; TD ¶194,501
19. ¶K-2141.6; ¶77,02B4; TD ¶346,304
20. ¶J-1308; ¶7702B4.04; TD ¶194,507

account under (2) if the insured is a terminally ill individual at the time the payment is received. (Code Sec. 7702B(d)(1))[21]

The per diem limit for any period is the excess (if any) of: (a) the greater of (i) $260 per day for 2007 ($270 per day for 2008), or the equivalent amount when payments are made on another periodic basis, or (ii) the costs incurred for qualified long-term care services provided for the insured for the period, over (b) the total payments received as reimbursement (by insurance or otherwise) for qualified long-term care services provided for the insured during the period. (Code Sec. 7702B(d)(2)) If payments exceed this limit, the excess is excludible only to the extent of actual costs incurred for long-term care services; amounts with respect to which no such actual costs are incurred are fully includible. [22]

¶ 1380 Exclusion for Archer medical savings account (MSA) distributions.

Distributions from an Archer medical savings account (MSA, see ¶1528 for limitations) are excludable from gross income if used exclusively to pay the qualified medical expenses of the individual (account holder) or his spouse or dependents. (Code Sec. 220(f)(1))[23] Otherwise, they are (1) included in gross income (Code Sec. 220(f)(2)) and (2) subject to an additional tax of 15% (use Form 8853) unless made after the individual attains age 65, dies, or becomes disabled. (Code Sec. 220(f)(4))[24]

Qualified medical expenses are for medical care as defined under the medical expense deduction rules (see ¶2145), but only to the extent not reimbursed by insurance or otherwise. (Code Sec. 220(d)(2)(A)) Qualified medical expenses don't include insurance premiums other than premiums for qualified long-term care insurance (¶2146), health care continuation coverage (COBRA), and coverage while receiving unemployment compensation. (Code Sec. 220(d)(2)(B))[25]

In any year for which an MSA contribution is made, distributions from that MSA to pay medical expenses are included in gross income if, for the month in which the expense was incurred, the individual for whom the expense was incurred wasn't covered under a "high deductible health plan" or had ineligible coverage. (Code Sec. 220(d)(2)(C))[26]

¶ 1381 Exclusion for health savings account (HSA) distributions.

Distributions from a health savings account (HSA) (see ¶1529) that are used exclusively to pay the qualified medical expenses of an eligible individual (account holder) or his spouse or dependents are excludable from gross income. (Code Sec. 223(f)) For this purpose, an individual may qualify as a dependent without regard to whether he: (1) is subject to the general rule that a dependent of a taxpayer shall be treated as himself having no dependents; (2) is married and files a joint return; and (3) has gross income that exceeds an otherwise applicable gross income limitation. (Code Sec. 223(d)(2)(A))

Qualified medical expenses are expenses paid for medical care as defined under the medical expense deduction rules (see ¶2145), but only to the extent they're not reimbursed by insurance or otherwise. (Code Sec. 223(d)(2)) Qualified medical expenses, which must be incurred after the HSA is established, don't include insurance premiums other than premiums for qualified long-term care insurance (¶2146), health care continuation coverage (COBRA) (see ¶1531), and coverage while the eligible individual is receiving unemployment compensation. (Code Sec. 223(d)(2)(B))[27]

Distributions not used for qualified medical expenses are subject to tax, they also are subject to an additional 10% tax (use Form 8853) unless made after the individual attains age

---

21. ¶J-1308; ¶7702B4.04; TD ¶194,507
22. ¶J-1308; ¶7702B4.04; TD ¶194,507
23. ¶H-1337 *et seq.*; ¶2204.01; TD ¶288,101 *et seq.*
24. ¶H-1338 *et seq.*; ¶2204.01; TD ¶288,101 *et seq.*
25. ¶H-1337.1 *et seq.*; ¶2204.01; TD ¶288,101 *et seq.*
26. ¶H-1337.2; ¶2204.01
27. ¶H-1350.1 *et seq.*; ¶2234; TD ¶289,103 *et seq.*

65, dies, or becomes disabled. (Code Sec. 223(f))[28]

Contributions for a year exceeding the deduction limit (see ¶1529) can be withdrawn tax-free if the distribution is: (1) completed by the extended tax return due date; and (2) accompanied by the net income (includible in the individual's income) attributable to the excess contribution. (Code Sec. 223(f)(3)(A))[29]

¶ 1382 Exclusion for benefits received through health reimbursement arrangements (HRAs).

Amounts received by an employee under a health reimbursement arrangement (HRA) are excluded from gross income as amounts received under an accident and health plan (¶1378). An HRA is a type of employee benefit plan reimbursing employees for medical expenses not covered by other forms of insurance. Benefits are paid up to a specific dollar amount from funds provided exclusively by the employer (and not through a salary reduction or otherwise under a cafeteria plan (¶1270)). Balances remaining in the employee's account at the end of a coverage period may be carried forward if the plan so provides. An HRA may use debit cards, credit cards, or other electronic media to support and document the tax-free reimbursement of an employee's claimed medical or dental expenses if proper safeguards and substantiation methods are used.[30]

¶ 1383 Damages.

Compensatory damages received on account of personal physical injuries or personal physical sickness are tax-free (but punitive damages generally are not excludable).

¶ 1384 Nonbusiness damages—personal physical injury or sickness.

Damages other than punitive damages received (by suit or agreement, in a lump-sum or as periodic payments) as compensation for personal *physical* injury or personal *physical* sickness are excluded from income (Code Sec. 104(a)(2)) If an action has its origin in a physical injury or physical sickness, then all nonpunitive damages from that injury or sickness are excluded, whether or not the recipient is the injured party. Emotional distress is not considered a physical injury or physical sickness, but the exclusion does apply to damages received up to the amount paid for medical care attributable to emotional distress. (Code Sec. 104(a)) Thus, the exclusion doesn't apply to damages (other than for medical expenses attributable to emotional distress) based on a claim of employment discrimination or injury to reputation accompanied by a claim of emotional distress and does apply to nonpunitive damages received based on a claim of emotional distress, that are attributable to a physical injury or physical sickness.[31] The exclusion does not apply to "delay damages," i.e., damages awarded due to the delay in payment, which have been held to be in the nature of interest. [32]

Punitive damages generally are taxable, regardless of the nature of the claim. (Code Sec. 104(a)(2)) But under an exception, punitive damages received in connection with a physical injury or sickness are tax-free if received in a civil wrongful death action, and under applicable state law (as in effect on Sept. 13, '95, and without regard to later modification) which provides (or has been construed by a court to provide) that only punitive damages may be awarded in the action. (Code Sec. 104(c))[33]

Where a lump-sum award is specifically allocated by the parties between compensatory and punitive damages, or between personal and business injury, that allocation generally controls. But if no allocation is made, the courts look to the nature of the claims (e.g., primary

---

28. ¶H-1350.11 *et seq.*; ¶2234.01; TD ¶289,111 *et seq.*
29. ¶H-1350.10; ¶2234.04; TD ¶289,110
30. ¶H-1349 *et seq.*; TD ¶289,000

31. ¶J-5801; ¶1044.02; TD ¶182,001
32. ¶J-5817; ¶1044.02; TD ¶151,027
33. ¶J-5816.1 *et seq.*; TD ¶182,006

nature of the harm inflicted) and the payor's intent. [34]

¶ 1385   Amounts received for accepting assignment of personal injury liability.

Amounts received by an assignee (e.g., insurance company) for accepting assignment of a liability to make periodic payments as damages for personal injury or sickness (in a case involving *physical* injury or sickness), including a liability to pay workers' compensation, are excludable from the assignee's gross income, up to the aggregate cost of any "qualified funding asset" used to satisfy the liability. A "qualified funding asset" is a commercial annuity contract, or a U.S. obligation, having payment periods corresponding to those of the liability, which the assignee: (1) purchased within 60 days before or after the date of the assignment, and (2) uses to satisfy that liability. (Code Sec. 130(c))[35]

¶ 1386   Business damages.

Damages received for injury to business that represent compensation for lost profits (including business interruption insurance proceeds) are taxable as ordinary income. This applies to awards for breach of a contract of sale and for business slander. Amounts received for injury to capital (e.g., injury to good will, fraudulent stock sale) are tax-free to the extent of basis; any excess is capital gain. [36] Punitive damages (e.g., insiders' profits, treble damages under antitrust laws) are taxable. (Reg § 1.61-14(a))[37]

There is a special deduction for certain expired net operating losses that resulted from the same injury. (Code Sec. 186(d))[38]

¶ 1387   Attorney's fees payable out of judgment.

Except as provided below, the full amount of the judgment or settlement awarded to the taxpayer belongs to him (and is therefore includable in his gross income), and attorney's fees payable from the award are deductible only as a miscellaneous itemized deduction regardless of whether the fees are contingent or noncontingent. [39]

🅡*observation:* Since miscellaneous itemized deductions are not deductible for AMT purposes (see ¶3208), attorney's fees not allowable as an above-the-line deduction under Code Sec. 62(a)(19) cannot be deducted in computing AMT.

But attorney fees and court costs paid in connection with the following are deductible from gross income to determine adjusted gross income: (1) a claim of unlawful discrimination; (2) a claim of a violation of subchapter III of chapter 37 of title 31, United States Code (Claims Against the U.S. Government); or (3) a claim made under section 1862(b)(3)(A) of the Social Security Act (42 U.S.C. 1395y(b)(3)(A)) (private cause of action under the Medicare Secondary Payer statute). (Code Sec. 62(a)(19))[40]

🅡*observation:* The deduction applies whether or not eligible legal fees are paid on a contingency basis.

¶ 1388   Income Realized on Discharge or Cancellation of Indebtedness. ▬▬▬▬▬

Gross income includes income from discharge of indebtedness.

For information reporting by banks, etc., that discharge indebtedness, see ¶4750.

---

34. ¶J-5810; ¶1044.02; TD ¶182,004
35. ¶J-5833 *et seq.*; ¶s 1304, 1304.01; TD ¶182,008
36. ¶J-5819 *et seq.*; ¶614.170 *et seq.*; TD ¶182,013
37. ¶J-5829; ¶614.168; TD ¶182,018

38. ¶K-8501 *et seq.*; ¶1864 *et seq.*
39. ¶J-8258; TD ¶201,086
40. ¶A-2628; ¶624.04; TD ¶560,715.2

¶ 1389   Debtor has income on discharge of debt—COD income.

Reduction or cancellation of debt (recourse or nonrecourse) is income to the debtor. (Code Sec. 61(a)(12))[41] Cancellation of debt (COD) income thus can result where a creditor accepts less than full payment as a complete discharge of the debt, or where events or circumstances make its collection unlikely. [42] But if the debtor's payment of the liability would have given rise to a deduction, the debtor won't have income from the discharge. (Code Sec. 108(e)(2))[43]

¶ 1390   Cancellation of debt under student loan programs.

There is no income (COD income, see ¶1389) from the cancellation of all or part of certain government student loans (or certain loans made by tax-exempt educational organizations), or loans made by exempt educational organizations or other exempt organizations to refinance any student loan, if the debtor is required to perform public service work for a period of time in certain professions for any of a broad range of employers. (Code Sec. 108(f)(1))[44]

Nor does gross income include any amount received under Sec. 338B(g) of the Public Health Service Act—relating to the National Health Service Corps Loan Repayment Program —or under a state program described in Sec. 338I of that Act. (Code Sec. 108(f)(4))[45]

¶ 1391   Discharge of indebtedness of solvent debtors outside bankruptcy.

Any discharge of indebtedness of a debtor, other than in a bankruptcy case (¶1393), or where the debtor is insolvent (¶1392), results in the current (i.e., year of discharge) recognition of income (COD income, see ¶1389) in the amount of the discharge (Reg § 1.61-12(a))[46] except for certain farm (¶1394) or real property (¶1395) indebtedness.

¶ 1392   Insolvent debtor outside bankruptcy—"insolvency exception"—Form 982

If the indebtedness is discharged when the debtor is insolvent (but not in a bankruptcy case), the discharge is excluded from the debtor's gross income up to the amount of the insolvency. (Code Sec. 108(a)(1)(B), Code Sec. 108(a)(2)(A), Code Sec. 108(a)(3))[47]

The amount excluded under this "insolvency exception" must be applied to reduce the debtor's tax attributes such as loss or credit carryovers or basis in assets. (Credit carryovers are reduced 33 ⅓¢ per dollar of debt discharge amount; other tax attributes are reduced dollar for dollar.) (Code Sec. 108(b)(3)) (Use Form 982 to report the reduction of tax attributes.) Or the debtor can elect (on Form 982) to apply any or all of the excluded amount *first* to reduce his basis in *depreciable* assets (or real property held as inventory). (Code Sec. 108(b)(5)(A), Code Sec. 1017(b)(3); Reg § 1.108-4(b))[48]

Any balance of the discharged debt (excess over the amount the debtor is insolvent) is COD income, as for a wholly solvent debtor (¶1391). (Code Sec. 108(a)(2)(B), Code Sec. 108(a)(3))[49]

A debtor is insolvent for this purpose if, immediately before the debt is discharged, his liabilities exceed the fair market value of his assets. (Code Sec. 108(d)(3))[50]

If a reorganization or other transaction described in Code Sec. 381(a) ends a year in which the distributor or transferor corporation excludes COD income under Code Sec. 108(a), any tax attributes to which the acquiring corporation succeeds and the basis of property acquired by the acquiring corporation must reflect the reductions required by Code Sec. 108 and Code

41. ¶J-7001; ¶614.114; TD ¶186,001
42. ¶J-7001 *et seq.*; ¶614.114; TD ¶186,015
43. ¶J-7504; ¶1084.04; TD ¶188,003
44. ¶J-7508; ¶1084.04; TD ¶188,006
45. ¶J-7510.1; ¶1084.04; TD ¶188,008.1

46. ¶s J-7001, J-7200 *et seq.* ¶s 1084, 1084.01; TD ¶188,011
47. ¶J-7401; ¶1084.01; TD ¶188,011
48. ¶J-7404; ¶1084.02; TD ¶188,011
49. ¶J-7401; ¶1084.01; TD ¶188,014
50. ¶J-7403; ¶1084.01; TD ¶188,014

Sec. 1017. (Reg § 1.108-7(c), Reg § 1.1017-1(b)(4))

For partners and S corporations, see ¶1396.

¶ 1393 Discharge of indebtedness of bankrupt debtor—Form 982.

No amount is included in a debtor's gross income by reason of a discharge of indebtedness in a bankruptcy case (Code Sec. 108(a)(1)(A)), even if the debtor is solvent after the discharge. (Code Sec. 108(a)(2))[1]

The amount of discharged debt that is excluded under this rule must be applied to reduce certain of the debtor's tax attributes (Code Sec. 108(b)(1)) (use Form 982) unless the debtor elects (on Form 982) to apply any or all of the excluded amount *first* to reduce his basis in depreciable assets (or real property held as inventory). (Code Sec. 108(b)(5)(A), Code Sec. 1017(b)(3); Reg § 1.1017-1(c))[2] For partners and S corporations, see ¶1396.

¶ 1394 Discharge of "qualified farm indebtedness" of solvent farmers.

A solvent taxpayer whose "qualified farm indebtedness" is discharged (outside bankruptcy) by certain unrelated lenders doesn't have COD income (see ¶1389), to the extent the discharge doesn't exceed the sum of his adjusted tax attributes plus the aggregate adjusted bases (as of the start of the year after discharge) of his business or income-producing property. (Code Sec. 108(a)(1)(C), Code Sec. 108(g)(1), Code Sec. 108(g)(3)) Any excess is COD income (but the insolvency (¶1392) or bankruptcy (¶1393) rules have precedence). (Code Sec. 108(a)(2))[3]

"Qualified farm indebtedness" is debt incurred directly in connection with taxpayer's farm business if at least 50% of taxpayer's total gross receipts for the three tax years preceding the tax year of the discharge is attributable to farming. (Code Sec. 108(g)(2))[4] For partners and S corporations, see ¶1396.

¶ 1395 Discharge of "qualified real property business indebtedness"—Form 982.

A solvent taxpayer other than a C corporation whose "qualified real property business indebtedness" (QRPBI) is discharged (outside bankruptcy) can elect to exclude the discharged amount from income, to the extent of the excess (if any) of (1) the outstanding principal amount of the QRPBI immediately before the discharge over (2) the fair market value (at discharge) of the property securing the QRPBI less the outstanding principal amount of any other QRPBI secured by the property at that time. (Code Sec. 108(a)(1)(D), Code Sec. 108(c)(2)(A), Code Sec. 108(c)(3)(C); Reg § 1.108-6(a))[5] The excluded amount must be applied (on Form 982) to reduce the basis of taxpayer's depreciable real property. (Code Sec. 108(c)(1)(A))[6]

QRPBI is indebtedness (other than qualified farm indebtedness, ¶1394) incurred or assumed by taxpayer in connection with real property used in a trade or business and secured by the real property (Code Sec. 108(c)(3)(A)) that:

. . . if incurred or assumed by the taxpayer after '92, is "qualified acquisition indebtedness" (Code Sec. 108(c)(3)(B))—i.e., indebtedness incurred or assumed to acquire, construct, reconstruct, or substantially improve the property (Code Sec. 108(c)(4)); *and*

. . . taxpayer elects to treat as "qualified real property business indebtedness" (Code Sec. 108(c)(3)(C))[7] on Form 982 attached to the return for the tax year of discharge. (Code Sec. 108(d)(9)(A); Reg § 1.108-5)[8]

---

1. ¶J-7402; ¶1084.01; TD ¶188,013
2. ¶J-7404; ¶1084.02; TD ¶188,016
3. ¶J-7405 *et seq.*; ¶1084.01; TD ¶188,018
4. ¶J-7406; ¶1084.01; TD ¶188,019

5. ¶J-7409; ¶1084.01; TD ¶188,022
6. ¶J-7411; ¶1084.01; TD ¶188,024
7. ¶J-7410; ¶1084.01; TD ¶188,023
8. ¶J-7412; ¶1084.01; TD ¶188,025

QRPBI also includes indebtedness incurred to refinance QRPBI, but only to the extent it doesn't exceed the amount of the indebtedness being refinanced. (Code Sec. 108(c)(3))[9]

¶ 1396 How COD income exclusions apply to partnership or S corporation debt.

For partnership debt, the insolvency (¶1392), bankruptcy (¶1393), qualified farm indebtedness (¶1394), and qualified real property indebtedness (¶1395) exclusions are applied at the partner level, not at the partnership level. (Code Sec. 108(d)(6))[10] For an S corporation's debt, the exclusions are applied at the corporate level, not at the shareholder level. (Code Sec. 108(d)(7)(A))[11]

¶ 1397 Discounted purchase of debtor's own obligations.

When a debtor buys or otherwise acquires his own obligations for less than face value (i.e., at a discount), he usually realizes taxable income to the extent of the discount. (Reg § 1.61-12(a))[12] This also applies if a party related to the debtor acquires the debtor's indebtedness from an unrelated party. (Code Sec. 108(e)(4)(A); Reg § 1.108-2)[13]

A corporation that repurchases its own bonds (directly or indirectly) has COD income (¶1389) to the extent of the excess of the adjusted issue price over the repurchase price. (Reg § 1.61-12(c)(2))[14]

For the debtor to be taxed, the obligation must require the unconditional payment of a fixed amount. If the obligation really represents an equity interest, a corporate debtor will be, in effect, acquiring its own stock and thus won't be taxed on the "discount." [15]

¶ 1398 Satisfaction of debt with property or services (including "stock for debt").

If a debtor transfers property (other than debt) to, or performs services for, a creditor (or third party) in full satisfaction of the debt, and the property or services are worth the amount owed, there's no *cancellation* of the debt since it was actually paid. But a debtor who satisfies debt with services has taxable *compensation* equal to the debt. (Reg § 1.61-12(a))[16]

A debtor who transfers property (other than debt) in satisfaction of the debt has gain (or loss) to the extent the fair market value (FMV) of the property transferred exceeds (or is less than) his basis in it. The type of gain (or loss), or whether any loss is deductible, is determined under the regular sale or exchange rules (¶2400 *et seq.*). If the property transferred is worth less than the face amount of the debt, the difference is cancellation of debt (COD) income to the debtor.[17]

If a debtor corporation transfers stock, or a debtor partnership transfers a capital or profits interest in that partnership, to a creditor in satisfaction of its recourse or nonrecourse debt, the corporation or partnership is treated as having satisfied the debt with an amount of money equal to the FMV of the stock or the interest. In the case of a partnership, any discharge of debt income recognized under this rule is included in the distributive shares of taxpayers that were partners in the partnership immediately before the discharge. (Code Sec. 108(e)(8)) So the debtor has taxable income to the extent the principal of the debt exceeds the value of the stock or interest.[18]

9. ¶J-7410; ¶1084.01; TD ¶188,023
10. ¶J-7415; ¶1084.03; TD ¶188,027
11. ¶J-7416; ¶1084.03; TD ¶188,028
12. ¶J-7011; ¶614.114; TD ¶186,020
13. ¶J-7016 *et seq.*; ¶1084.04; TD ¶186,024

14. ¶J-7204.1; ¶614.136; TD ¶186,003
15. ¶J-7007; TD ¶186,014
16. ¶J-7040; ¶614.114; TD ¶186,033
17. ¶J-7206; ¶10,014.76; TD ¶221,401
18. ¶J-7015; ¶1084.04; TD ¶186,021

¶ 1399   Debt-for-debt exchanges.

A debtor may satisfy an outstanding "old" debt by issuing a "new" debt. The old debt is treated as having been satisfied with an amount of money equal to the issue price of the new debt. (Code Sec. 108(e)(10)(A)) The excess (if any) of the "old" adjusted issue price over the "new" issue price is COD income (¶1389) to the debtor.[19]

For this purpose, "issue price" is determined under the OID rules (¶1317). (Code Sec. 108(e)(10)(B)) However, if the Code Sec. 483 unstated interest rules (¶1307 *et seq.*) (rather than the OID rules) apply, the new debt's issue price is its stated redemption price at maturity (¶1316) less the unstated interest. [20]

---

19. ¶J-7205; ¶1084.04; TD ¶186,004   20. ¶J-7205; ¶1084.04; TD ¶186,004

Chapter 3   Deductions—Expenses of a Business

¶ 1500   Start-Up Expenditures.

Start-up expenditures must be capitalized, unless a taxpayer elects to expense up to $5,000 of the cost and amortize the balance over a 180-month period.

¶ 1501   Tax treatment of start-up expenditures.

Start-up expenditures must be amortized and can't be deducted unless the taxpayer elects (¶1502) to expense up to $5,000 of these costs (the $5,000 cap is reduced by the excess of total start-up expenditures over $50,000) in the tax year in which the trade or business begins. The remainder of the start-up expenditures may be amortized (deducted ratably) over a 15-year period.(Code Sec. 195(a); Code Sec. 195(b)(1))[1]

Start-up expenditures are amounts paid or incurred in connection with:

. . . investigating the creation, acquisition, or establishment of an active trade or business, (Code Sec. 195(c)(1)(A)(i)) but not costs incurred after a taxpayer decides whether to enter a new business, and which new business it will enter or acquire; [2]

. . . creating an active trade or business (Code Sec. 195(c)(1)(A)(ii)); or

. . . any activity engaged in for profit and for the production of income before the day the active trade or business begins, in anticipation of that activity becoming an active trade or business. (Code Sec. 195(c)(1)(A)(iii))

The expenditure must be one that, if paid or incurred in connection with the operation of an existing active trade or business (in the same field as the taxpayer's new business), would be deductible for the year in which paid or incurred. (Code Sec. 195(c)(1)(B))[3]

Start-up expenses don't include any amounts deductible under Code Sec. 163(a) (i.e., as interest expenses); Code Sec. 164 (i.e., as taxes); or Code Sec. 174 (i.e., as research and experimental expenses). (Code Sec. 195(c)(1))[4]

¶ 1502   Election to expense/amortize start-up expenditures—Form 4562.

A taxpayer elects to deduct start-up costs (¶1501) by attaching Form 4562 with a statement to his return (filed by the due date including extensions) for the tax year in which the active trade or business begins. (Code Sec. 195(d)(1)) If a timely filed return for the year is made without the election, a taxpayer can still elect by filing an amended return within 6 months of the return's due date (excluding extensions). The statement should:

(1)   describe the trade or business to which it relates with enough detail so that the expenses can be identified properly;

(2)   include the number of months over which the expenses are to be amortized; and

(3)   include, to the extent known when the statement is filed, a description of each start-up expense incurred and the month in which the active trade or business began (or was acquired). (Reg § 1.195-1(c))

¶ 1503   Treatment of deferred start-up expenses on disposition of business.

If the trade or business is disposed of before the end of the amortization period, any deferred expenses not yet deducted may be deducted to the extent the disposition results in a

---

1. ¶L-5001; ¶1954; TD ¶301,001
2. ¶L-5013; ¶1954.01; TD ¶301,009
3. ¶L-5011; ¶s 1954, 1954.01; TD ¶301,012
4. ¶L-5011; ¶1954.01; TD ¶301,008

References beginning with a single letter are to paragraphs in RIA's Federal Tax Coordinator 2d and RIA's Analysis of Federal Taxes: Income. Those beginning with numbers are to paragraphs in RIA's United States Tax Reporter. Those beginning with TD are to paragraphs in RIA's Tax Desk.

loss under Code Sec. 165. (Code Sec. 195(b)(2))[5]

¶ 1504 Fruitless searches for new ventures.

A corporation that makes expenditures in fruitlessly searching for or investigating a new venture may deduct them as a loss when it abandons the effort. [6] A noncorporate taxpayer not engaged in the business of locating or promoting new ventures can't deduct expenditures made in fruitlessly searching for or investigating a new venture. However, once a taxpayer has focused on the acquisition of a specific business or investment, unsuccessful start-up expenses that are related to an attempt to acquire that business or investment are deductible as business or investment losses under Code Sec. 165 (¶1773).[7]

¶ 1505 Expanding an existing business.

A taxpayer can deduct expenditures made to expand an existing business. The taxpayer must show that the business contemplated and the one already conducted are closely related or "intramural," *and* that the expenditures are ordinary and necessary expenses of the business conducted when the expenses were incurred, and not capital expenditures.

Expansion costs must be capitalized if they provide the taxpayer with long-term benefits, or create separate and distinct assets, or relate to a change in the nature of the taxpayer's activities (e.g., wholesaler opening retail outlet). [8]

¶ 1506 Ordinary and Necessary Business Expenses. ▰▰▰▰▰

Individuals, corporations and other taxpayers generally can deduct ordinary and necessary expenses paid or incurred during the tax year in carrying on any trade or business. Various limits (e.g., percentage limit on meal and entertainment deductions, see ¶1570) may apply.

¶ 1507 "Ordinary and necessary" requirement.

A deductible business expense must be both ordinary and necessary in relation to the taxpayer's industry. (Code Sec. 162(a))[9]

An expense is *ordinary* if it's customary or usual in the taxpayer's business. [10] But an unusual expense may be ordinary if it's reasonably related to the taxpayer's trade or business.[11] A *necessary* expense is one that's appropriate and helpful in developing and maintaining the taxpayer's business. It need not be essential or indispensable. Usually the taxpayer's judgment as to what's necessary will be accepted. [12] Expenditures are deductible as ordinary and necessary even if they are unwise. [13]

Some courts have held that to be deductible under Code Sec. 162, an expense must not only be ordinary and necessary, but also reasonable in amount and reasonable in relation to its purpose.[14] It has been held that depreciation deductions are not to be considered in assessing if business expenses are reasonable under Code Sec. 162. [15]

¶ 1508 Connection to taxpayer's trade or business.

To be deductible as a business expense, an item must be directly connected with or pertain to a trade or business carried on by the taxpayer. (Code Sec. 162(a); Reg § 1.162-1(a))[16]

5. ¶L-5023; ¶1954.04; TD ¶301,015
6. ¶L-5019; ¶1954; TD ¶301,013
7. ¶L-5020; ¶1954; TD ¶301,014
8. ¶L-5101; ¶1624 *et seq.*; TD ¶301,016
9. ¶L-1200 *et seq.*; ¶1624.012; TD ¶255,512
10. ¶L-1201; ¶1624.012; TD ¶255,512

11. ¶s L-1201, L-1209; ¶1624.012; TD ¶255,512
12. ¶L-1201; ¶1624.012; TD ¶255,512
13. ¶L-1210; TD ¶255,522
14. ¶L-1202; ¶1624.013; TD ¶255,513
15. ¶L-1211
16. ¶L-1002; ¶1624; TD ¶256,001

Serving as an employee is a business (see ¶1628 for deduction limitations). [17] A trade or business need not be the taxpayer's principal occupation; a sideline can qualify. [18]

¶ 1509 Expense must benefit person claiming deduction.

A deductible expense must be an expense of *the taxpayer's* business. Expenses incurred on another's behalf aren't deductible. [19]

A corporation's payment of the personal expenses of its shareholders isn't deductible. [20] Payment by a corporation of the personal expenses of its officers and employees isn't deductible, except to the extent the payment represents reasonable compensation (¶1517) or is made for business reasons to provide benefits to employees in general. [21]

A corporate officer can't deduct an expenditure he makes to pay an expense of the corporation.[22]

If a taxpayer pays the debts or other obligations of another, the payment may sometimes qualify as a business expense. [23] Deductions have been allowed where such a payment is made for a good business reason, e.g., preserve sales-force morale and customer goodwill; reestablish or protect credit standing; avoid loss of business patronage, etc. [24]

¶ 1510 Right to deduction—*Cohan* rule.

Where a taxpayer's records or other proof aren't adequate to substantiate expense deductions, he may be allowed to deduct an estimated amount under the *Cohan* rule. But a court may allow a much smaller deduction than claimed, bearing heavily against a taxpayer whose inexactitude is of his own making. [25] The *Cohan* rule doesn't apply to travel or entertainment expenses, listed property, or business gifts, see ¶1580.

¶ 1511 Expenses of membership organizations.

Organizations that aren't exempt from tax under the rules discussed at ¶ 4100 *et seq.*, which are operated primarily to furnish services or goods to members, can deduct expenses of furnishing services, insurance, goods, or other items to members only to the extent of income derived during the year from members or transactions with members. (Code Sec. 277(a))[26] Any excess of expenses over income isn't deductible, but may be carried over to the following tax year. (Code Sec. 277(a))[27]

¶ 1512 Advertising and business promotion costs.

Advertising and business promotion costs relating to an existing business can be deducted currently, even though the business benefit they generate may extend over a period beyond the year they are incurred or paid. [28]

Production costs of a business catalog that will remain unchanged for several years must be capitalized according to IRS, but some courts disagree. [29] Display equipment (cabinets, signs, etc.) must be capitalized if it has a useful life beyond the tax year. [30] IRS says that package design costs (e.g., physical construction of a package containing a consumer product) must be capitalized. A court has held that graphic design costs making up the overall visual display of a product may be deducted currently as advertising expenses, but IRS disagrees. [31]

17. ¶L-3900; ¶1624; TD ¶256,005
18. ¶L-1100 *et seq.*; ¶1624.002
19. ¶L-4400; ¶1624.104; TD ¶256,500
20. ¶L-1214; ¶1624.104; TD ¶256,517
21. ¶L-4414; ¶1624.205; TD ¶256,517
22. ¶L-4405; ¶1624.009; TD ¶256,505
23. ¶L-1214; ¶1624.104; TD ¶256,500
24. ¶L-1214 *et seq.*; ¶s 1624.015, 1624.026; TD ¶255,515

25. ¶L-4509 *et seq.*; ¶1624.014; TD ¶257,007
26. ¶L-4301; ¶2774; TD ¶307,724
27. ¶L-4301; ¶2774; TD ¶307,727
28. ¶L-2201; ¶1624.355; TD ¶300,500
29. ¶L-2205; ¶1624.355; TD ¶300,510
30. ¶L-2206; ¶1624.355; TD ¶300,511
31. ¶L-5629

¶ 1513   Costs of determining or contesting tax liability.

Costs relating to tax matters that are ordinary and necessary in the course of the conduct of taxpayer's trade or business, including costs of tax advice, are deductible. The deduction applies to expenses incurred in: (1) preparing tax returns, (2) determining tax liability, (3) contesting tax liability, (4) securing tax counsel. (Code Sec. 62(a)(1); Reg § 1.62-1T(d)) This includes expenses incurred by an individual taxpayer in: [32]

- preparing that portion of the individual's tax return that relates to the taxpayer's business as sole proprietor,

- preparing schedules relating to income or loss from rentals or royalties, or farm income and expenses, and

- resolving asserted tax deficiencies relating to a business, to rental or royalty income, or to a farm.

For deduction of nonbusiness tax determination costs as miscellaneous itemized deductions subject to the 2%-of-AGI floor, see ¶3110. For deductibility of interest on taxes, see ¶1708.

¶ 1514   Other deductible costs of carrying on a trade or business.

These include: [33]

. . . cost of materials and supplies not consumed in the process of manufacturing; [34]

. . . annual license and regulatory fees; [35]

. . . amounts paid to cancel burdensome contracts; [36]

. . . cost of moving business equipment and machinery; [37]

. . . current membership fees (but not admission fees), dues (but for social club dues, see ¶1569) and assessments paid for business association, etc.; [38]

. . . restaurant's cost of smallware (glassware, flatware, etc.); [39]

. . . training costs; and [40]

. . . education expenses, see ¶2228 *et seq.*

¶ 1515   Compensation Deduction.

Reasonable amounts that are paid or incurred in connection with a trade or business as compensation for personal services actually rendered are deductible, subject to a limit for top officers. Payments for fringe benefits are deductible as compensation, subject to some limits.

¶ 1516   Compensation paid for personal services.

Compensation (including severance pay) [41] paid or incurred for personal services rendered is deductible as a trade or business expense. (Code Sec. 162(a)(1)) Deductible compensation includes amounts paid to independent contractors, as well as employees. [42]

A parent can deduct reasonable wages he pays his unemancipated minor child for personal services actually rendered as a bona fide employee in the business. [43]

---

32. ¶L-3000 *et seq.*; ¶2124.14; TD ¶307,201
33. ¶L-4200 *et seq.*; ¶1624.404; TD ¶307,700 *et seq.*
34. ¶L-4207 *et seq.*; TD ¶307,718
35. ¶L-4216 *et seq.*; TD ¶307,717
36. ¶L-4213 *et seq.*; TD ¶307,714
37. ¶L-4209 *et seq.*; ¶1624.052; TD ¶307,711

38. ¶L-4231; ¶1624.061; TD ¶307,721
39. ¶L-4207.1; ¶4465.22(5)
40. ¶L-4232.3; TD ¶256,201
41. ¶H-3600 *et seq.*; ¶1624.205; TD ¶276,000 *et seq.*
42. ¶H-3600 *et seq.*; ¶1624.205; TD ¶276,000
43. ¶H-3755; ¶1624.212; TD ¶276,045

For deductibility of amounts paid for fringe benefits, see ¶1524 *et seq.* For when compensation can be deducted, see ¶1538 *et seq.*

¶ 1517 Reasonableness of compensation.

Compensation is deductible only to the extent it's *reasonable*. Compensation paid to employee-shareholders also must be paid purely for services, or have a purely compensatory purpose, in order to be deductible. (Code Sec. 162(a)(1))[44] The question of reasonableness rarely arises unless the payments are made to a person "related" to the taxpayer —that is, to the members of an employer's family, or to stockholders of the employer, or to members of a stockholder's family.[45]

The unreasonable portion of compensation is nondeductible. If the recipient is a shareholder, the unreasonable portion may be treated as a dividend. (Reg § 1.162-7(b)(1))[46]

¶ 1518 Factors determining reasonableness.

Reasonable compensation is the amount that would ordinarily be paid for like services by like enterprises under like circumstances. (Reg § 1.162-7(b)(3))[47] Other factors determining reasonableness include: (1) duties performed by the employee; (2) character and amount of responsibility; (3) amount of time required; (4) ability and achievements of the employee; (5) volume of business handled by the employee; (6) complexities of the business; (7) relationship of compensation to gross and net income of the business; (8) living conditions in locality; (9) compensation history of the employee; and (10) salary policy as to all employees. [48]

The Seventh Circuit applies a single independent-investor test in evaluating if a stockholder-employee's pay is reasonable (i.e., would an outside investor have paid the compensation amount based on performance). Other courts employ the independent-investor test in conjunction with an analysis of the above factors. [49]

The test of whether compensation is reasonable is normally applied to the compensation paid to the particular individual and not to the total compensation paid to a group of employees.[50] Services rendered in earlier years can be taken into account in determining the reasonableness of compensation paid during the current year. [1] Reasonableness of compensation for part-time services is determined under the usual reasonableness rules. Generally, salaries that are reasonable for an employee's full-time services aren't reasonable for his part-time services.[2]

¶ 1519 Deduction limit for compensation over $1,000,000 paid to top officers.

A publicly held corporation can't deduct applicable employee remuneration (defined below) in excess of $1,000,000 per year paid to a covered employee (Code Sec. 162(m)(1))[3] —the principal executive officer (or someone acting in that capacity) and the three highest paid officers (other than the principal executive officer or principal financial officer). (Code Sec. 162(m)(3); Reg § 1.162-27(c)(2))[4] The $1 million limit is reduced (but not below zero) by the amount, if any, paid to the executive but not deductible under the golden parachute rules (¶1536). (Code Sec. 162(m)(4)(F); Reg § 1.162-27(g))[5]

Applicable employee remuneration means a covered employee's aggregate remuneration for services performed (either during the deduction year or during another tax year) which would be deductible entirely for the tax year if the $1 million limit didn't apply. (Code

44. ¶1624.229; TD ¶276,022
45. ¶s H-3725 *et seq.*, H-3752 *et seq.*; ¶1624.229; TD ¶276,044
46. ¶H-3607; ¶1624.268; TD ¶276,009
47. ¶H-3701; ¶1624.229; TD ¶276,023
48. ¶H-3706; ¶1624.229; TD ¶276,041
49. ¶H-3721; TD ¶276,027

50. ¶H-3705; ¶1624.229; TD ¶276,026
1. ¶H-3745; ¶1624.229; TD ¶276,062
2. ¶H-3715; ¶1624.229; TD ¶276,036
3. ¶H-3776; ¶1624.009; TD ¶276,001.1
4. ¶H-3780; ¶1624.009; TD ¶276,001.1
5. ¶H-3809; ¶1624.009; TD ¶276,001.1

Sec. 162(m)(4)(A)) But it doesn't include commissions generated directly by the executive's performance (Code Sec. 162(m)(4)(B); Reg § 1.162-27(d)), certain other performance-based compensation (Code Sec. 162(m)(4)(C); Reg § 1.162-27(e)), qualified plan contributions and certain excludable employee fringe benefits. (Code Sec. 162(m)(4)(E); Reg § 1.162-27(c)(3)(ii))[6]

¶ 1520   Services rendered to another.

A taxpayer can't deduct payments for services rendered to someone other than the taxpayer — for example, payments by a shareholder to employees of the corporation for services to the corporation, or by a corporation to its officers for services to subsidiaries and related corporations, or by a corporation to employees of a sub. But salary paid by a parent corporation to its own executives for supervising the operations of a sub is deductible by the parent as an expense of the parent's business. [7]

¶ 1521   Payment of employee debts or expenses.

An employer's payment of an employee's debts or personal expenses is deductible by the employer as compensation paid (if reasonable, see ¶1517), just as if the employee had been paid directly and he had used the money to pay his debts or expenses. [8]

¶ 1522   Contingent compensation.

An employer can deduct contingent compensation, where it's freely bargained for between the employer and the individual before the services are rendered, and not influenced by any consideration on the part of the employer other than that of securing the individual's services on fair and advantageous terms. This is so even though the arrangement results in higher compensation than would otherwise be allowed as a deduction. The reasonableness of the amount is determined by the circumstances at the date the contract for services is made, not when the contract is questioned. (Reg § 1.162-7(b)(2), Reg § 1.162-7(b)(3))[9]

¶ 1523   Payment in property other than cash.

The deduction for compensation paid in property, including a bargain sale and including restricted property, is the amount included in the income of the person who performed the services, to the extent the compensation is reasonable. (Code Sec. 83(h))[10] The "amount included" in income is the amount reported by the service provider on an original or amended return, or included in income as a result of an IRS audit. It includes excluded group-term life insurance and foreign income. (Reg § 1.83-6(a)(1))

Under a "deemed inclusion rule," however, a deduction may be taken by an employer (service recipient) if he timely complies with the applicable information reporting requirements. Thus, an employee is *deemed* to have included the property received in income, and a deduction can be claimed by the employer if he timely satisfies the Code Sec. 6041 or Code Sec. 6041A reporting requirements (Reg § 1.83-6(a)(2)), i.e., by timely reporting the transaction to the service provider and federal government on Form W-2 or Form 1099-MISC, whichever applies. If this rule isn't satisfied, an employer must demonstrate that the compensation amount deducted was actually included in the service provider's income. [11]

The deemed inclusion rule can be used where the service provider is a corporation by issuing Form 1099-MISC even though there would otherwise be a general reporting exemption for a service provider that's a corporation. (Reg § 1.83-6(a)(2))

If a transfer is less than $600 in any tax year (in which case the reporting requirements

---

6. ¶H-3781 *et seq.*; ¶1624.009; TD ¶276,001.1
7. ¶H-3613; ¶1624.104; TD ¶276,001
8. ¶H-4014; ¶1624.273; TD ¶136,527

9. ¶H-3732; ¶1624.229; TD ¶276,053
10. ¶H-3650 *et seq.*; ¶s 834.04, 1624.273; TD ¶277,001
11. ¶H-3650 *et seq.*; ¶s 834.04, 1624.273, TD ¶277,003

don't apply), or if the transfer is eligible for any other reporting exemption (applicable to a noncorporate service provider), no Form 1099 reporting is required in order for the service recipient to rely on the deemed inclusion rule. [12]

In addition, to be deductible a transfer can't be a capital expenditure, a deferred expense, or part of inventory. (Reg § 1.83-6(a)(4))[13]

If payment is in employer stock, no gain or loss results. (Code Sec. 1032)[14] If payment is in property other than the employer's stock, and the value of the property exceeds the employer's basis for the property, the excess is income to the employer (capital gain or ordinary income, depending on the character of the property used). (Reg § 1.83-6(b)) The employer has a loss deduction where the basis of the property exceeds its fair market value [15] (subject to related-taxpayer restrictions on losses). [16]

The deduction is allowed for the tax year of the employer in which, or with which, the employee's tax year ends. (Code Sec. 83(h))[17]

illustration: Corporation X, which is on a Sept. 30 fiscal year, pays calendar year employee J in stock on July 1, Year 1. J reports the income on his return for Year 1. X deducts the payment on its return for the year ending Sept. 30, Year 2, because that is X's tax year in which the tax year of J, in which the amounts are included in income, ends.

For restricted property, see ¶1218; for noncash fringe benefits, see ¶1524.

¶ 1524   Compensation paid as noncash fringe benefits.

If an employer furnishes a noncash fringe benefit to an employee as compensation, the employer may deduct only the costs it incurs in providing the property to its employees, not the property's value. The employer may claim a depreciation deduction if it owns the property or a deduction for leasing costs if it rents the property. (Reg § 1.162-25T(a))[18]

Furnishing property to an employee for his personal use is additional compensation to him and gives rise to a deduction by the employer. For example, the employer can deduct depreciation and maintenance expenses it pays on a car, house, etc., furnished for an employee's personal use and treated by the employer as compensation. (Code Sec. 274(e)(2))[19]

For deduction limits on entertainment expenses of officers, directors, and 10%-or-more owners, see ¶1573.

¶ 1525   Stock options.

With respect to a nonstatutory stock option, the employer's deduction is determined under the Code Sec. 83 payment-in-property rules at ¶1523 (and thus, the employer would deduct the amount the employee must include in income on exercise of the option, where the option has no readily ascertainable value at grant, see ¶1220).[20] The employer isn't allowed a compensation deduction for stock transferred under an incentive stock option or an employee stock purchase plan, unless the employee has income by reason of a disqualified (premature) disposition of the stock (¶1221 *et seq.*). (Code Sec. 421(a), Code Sec. 421(b))[21]

¶ 1526   Premiums on company-owned life insurance, endowment or annuity contracts.

A taxpayer can't deduct premiums on any life insurance policy, or endowment or annuity

---

12. ¶H-3654; ¶834.04; TD ¶277,003
13. ¶H-3650 *et seq.*; ¶s 834.04, 1624.273; TD ¶277,008
14. ¶H-3659; ¶10,324; TD ¶277,010
15. ¶H-3659; TD ¶277,010
16. ¶H-3659; TD ¶277,010

17. ¶H-3653; ¶834.04; TD ¶277,002
18. ¶H-4002; ¶1624.283; TD ¶278,303
19. ¶s H-2150 *et seq.*, H-2160; ¶1624.283; TD ¶277,000 *et seq.*
20. ¶H-2883
21. ¶H-2960; ¶4214.01 *et seq.*; TD ¶136,102

contract if it is directly or indirectly a beneficiary under the policy or contract. (Code Sec. 264(a)(1)) However, this rule doesn't apply to Code Sec. 72(s)(5) annuity contracts (certain qualified pension plans, retirement annuities, individual retirement annuities and qualified funding assets) or to any annuity contract to which Code Sec. 72(u) (annuity contracts held by other than natural persons) applies. (Code Sec. 264(b)(2)) Premiums are deductible as a noncash fringe benefit where only the insured employee or his beneficiaries will get the proceeds. For contracts issued before June 9, '97, the deduction disallowance only applies to premiums on the life of an officer, employee or any person financially interested in any trade or business carried on by the taxpayer if the taxpayer is directly or indirectly a beneficiary of any part of the policy. [22]

Premiums on group term life insurance are deductible (if the employer isn't directly or indirectly a beneficiary) even though the employee isn't taxed (¶1263) on group term coverage of $50,000 or less. [23]

For interest on business life insurance loans, see ¶1718.

¶ 1527 Health and accident insurance premiums and direct payment or reimbursement of medical expenses under a plan for employees.

The employer's payment of health and accident insurance premiums for employees and their families, or the employer's direct payment or reimbursement of actual expenses if under a plan, is deductible. (Reg § 1.162-10(a))[24] Reimbursements are deductible even where the employee is the spouse of a sole proprietor, and the medical expenses incurred on behalf of the employee's family include those of the sole proprietor (as the employee's spouse). [25] IRS treats these amounts as additional compensation deductible by the employer to the extent that it, when added to other compensation, is reasonable. [26]

¶ 1528 Contributions to Archer medical savings account (MSA)—Form 8853.

Eligible small employers (see ¶1257), their employees, and self-employed individuals may deduct contributions to an Archer medical savings account (MSA). (Code Sec. 106, Code Sec. 220) An eligible self-employed claims deductions for MSAs above the line, to arrive at adjusted gross income. (Code Sec. 62(a)(16)) After 2007, no new contributions can be made to MSAs, except by or for individuals who previously had MSA contributions and employees who are employed by a participating employer. (Code Sec. 220(i))[27]

caution: Check http://ria.thomson.com/federaltaxhandbook to see if this provision has been extended.

MSAs are available to employees covered under a high deductible health plan (HDHP) of a small employer (¶1257) and to self-employed individuals covered by a HDHP. An individual isn't eligible for an MSA if he's entitled to benefits under Medicare or covered under any other health plan, unless the other coverage is permitted insurance (e.g., insurance for a specified disease or illness, or fixed payment for hospitalization) or coverage for accidents, disability, dental care, vision care, or long-term care. For employees, contributions can be made by the employee or the employer, but not by both for the same year. An MSA is a tax-exempt entity but is subject to the tax on unrelated business income. (Code Sec. 220(c), Code Sec. 220(d))[28]

For 2007, a HDHP is a health plan with an annual deductible of at least $1,900 and no more than $2,850 for individual coverage ($3,750 and $5,650 for family coverage); in addition,

---

22. ¶H-4031; ¶2644; TD ¶278,505
23. ¶H-4037; ¶s 614.031, 794; TD ¶278,507
24. ¶s H-4071, H-4073; ¶1624.277; TD ¶278,901
25. ¶L-3510; TD ¶278,902

26. ¶L-3509; ¶1624.229; TD ¶278,901
27. ¶H-1326 *et seq.*; ¶2204 *et seq.*; TD ¶288,100 *et seq.*
28. ¶H-1331.1 *et seq.*, ¶H-1335.4; ¶2204.01; TD ¶288,108

the maximum out-of-pocket expenses can't exceed $3,750 for individual coverage ($6,900 for family coverage). For 2008, a HDHP is a health plan with an annual deductible of at least $1,950 and no more than $2,900 for individual coverage ($3,850 and $5,800 for family coverage); in addition, the maximum out-of-pocket expenses can't exceed $3,850 for individual coverage ($7,050 for family coverage). (Code Sec. 220(c)(2))[29]

The maximum annual contribution for individual coverage is 65% of the HDHP (75% for family coverage). The annual contribution limit is the sum of the limits determined separately for each month the individual is MSA-eligible. (Code Sec. 220(b)(1))[30] A self-employed's deduction for contributions to an MSA can't exceed his earned income from the trade or business that established the HDHP (Code Sec. 220(b)(4)(B)),[31] and an employee's contributions to an MSA can't exceed his compensation from the employer that set up the plan. (Code Sec. 220(b)(4)(A))[32] Contributions can be made until the tax return due date (without extensions). Excess contributions are subject to a 6% penalty tax (on Form 5329). (Code Sec. 4973(a)(2), Code Sec. 4973(d))[33]

For treatment of MSA distributions, see ¶1380.

¶ 1529 Contributions to health savings accounts (HSAs).

Eligible individuals may, subject to statutory limits, make deductible contributions to a health savings account (HSA). Other persons (e.g., family members) also may contribute on behalf of eligible individuals, as may employers (see ¶1258). (Code Sec. 106, Code Sec. 223) An account holder may deduct contributions to his HSA even if another (e.g., family member) makes the contributions. (Code Sec. 62(a)(19)) An HSA is a tax-exempt entity but is subject to the tax on unrelated business income. (Code Sec. 223(e)(1))

For tax-free distributions for qualifying medical expenses see ¶1381.

Eligible individuals. These are individuals who are covered under a high deductible health plan (HDHP) (see below) and are not covered under any other health plan which is not a HDHP, unless the other coverage is permitted insurance (for worker's compensation, torts, ownership and use of property such as auto insurance, insurance for a specified disease or illness, or providing a fixed payment for hospitalization) or coverage for accidents, disability, dental care, vision care, or long-term care. (Code Sec. 223(c))[34] HSA contributions for an individual aren't deductible if he is claimed as a dependent by another taxpayer for the year. (Code Sec. 223(b)(6)). There's no deduction for an HSA contribution for any month an individual is eligible for and enrolled in Medicare. (Code Sec. 223(b)(7))

HDHP. For 2007, a HDHP is a health plan with an annual deductible of at least $1,100 for individual coverage ($2,200 for family coverage) and maximum out-of-pocket expenses of $5,500 for individual coverage ($11,000 for family coverage). For 2008, a HDHP is a health plan with an annual deductible that is not less than $1,100 for individual coverage ($2,200 for family coverage), and maximum out-of-pocket expenses of $5,600 for individual coverage ($11,200 for family coverage). (Code Sec. 223(c)(2))[35] However, an HDHP may have a zero preventive care deductible or a preventive care deductible below the minimum annual deductible. (Code Sec. 223(c)(2)(C)) Preventive care does not generally include any service or benefit intended to treat an existing illness, injury, or condition.

Other coverage. Health flexible spending accounts (FSAs, see ¶1270) and health reimbursement arrangements (HRAs, see ¶1382) are "other coverage" that will generally preclude HSA eligibility. However, exceptions apply for limited purpose FSAs and HRAs (those providing only certain benefits, e.g., dental and vision); suspended HRAs (where the employee elects to

---

29. ¶H-1332; ¶2204.01; TD ¶288,103
30. ¶s H-1335, H-1335.1; ¶2204.01; TD ¶288,101
31. ¶H-1335.3; ¶2204.01; TD ¶288,101
32. ¶H-1335.3; ¶2204.01; TD ¶288,101

33. ¶H-1336.1 *et seq.*; ¶2204.01; TD ¶288,101
34. ¶H-1350.3 *et seq.*; ¶2204.01; TD ¶288,103
35. ¶H-1350.6; ¶2234.02; TD ¶289,106

forgo reimbursements); FSAs and HRAs imposing annual deductibles, and HRAs providing benefits only after retirement.[36] Coverage under a health FSA during the "grace period" (i.e., the period immediately following the end of a plan year during which unused benefits or contributions remaining may be paid or reimbursed to plan participants for qualified expenses) is disregarded coverage for HSA purposes if: (1) the balance in the health FSA at the end of the plan year is zero; or (2) the remaining balance in the health FSA at the end of the plan year is contributed to an HSA under the one-time rollover rule (see below). (Code Sec. 223(c)(1))

Limit on contributions. For 2007, the maximum annual deductible HSA contribution is $2,850 for self-only coverage and $5,650 for family coverage. For 2008, the maximum annual deductible HSA contribution is $2,900 for self-only coverage and $5,800 for family coverage. (Code Sec. 223(b)(2)) Additionally, an individual (and his covered spouse) who has attained age 55 before the close of the tax year may make an additional $800 "catch-up" contribution for the tax year beginning in 2007 ($900 in 2008; and $1,000 in 2009 and afterwards). There is no requirement that the individual have earnings. (Code Sec. 223(b))[37] Contributions for a year can be made until the account holder's tax return due date (without extensions) for that year. Excess contributions are subject to a 6% penalty tax (on Form 5329). (Code Sec. 4973(a)(5), Code Sec. 223(f)(3))[38] Maximum annual HSA contributions are reduced by Archer MSA (¶1528) contributions for that year. (Code Sec. 223(b)(4))

For computing the annual HSA contribution, a taxpayer who is an eligible individual in the last month of a tax year is "deemed eligible" during every month of that year. (Code Sec. 223(b)(8)) Thus, he can make contributions for months before he was enrolled in a HDHP. But if he contributes under the "deemed eligible" rule and does not remain an eligible individual (except because of disability) during the testing period (which begins with the last month of the tax year and ends on the last day of the 12th month following that month), contributions for months in which he was "deemed eligible" are includible in gross income and subject to a 10% penalty tax. The amount is includible for the tax year of the first day during the testing period that the taxpayer is not an eligible individual. (Code Sec. 223(b)(8)(B))

HSA rollovers and carryover of HSA funds. Amounts in an HSA can be rolled over tax free from an HSA, or from an Archer MSA, to an HSA. The rollover must be completed within 60 days after the date on which the account holder receives the amounts from the HSA or Archer MSA. These rollover amounts are not taken into account in determining the annual contribution limits for the recipient HSA. Only one tax-free rollover into an HSA is permitted per one year period. (Code Sec. 223(f)(5), Code Sec. 220(f)(5))[39]

One-time rollovers from health FSAs or HRAs. After Dec. 20, 2006 and before Jan. 1, 2012, health FSA or HRA distributions may be rolled over via direct transfer to an HSA. (Code Sec. 106(e)) The amount transferred can't exceed the lesser of the balance in the health FSA or HRA: (1) as of Sept. 21, 2006; or (2) as of the date of the distribution. An individual is allowed only one rollover from each of his health FSAs or HRAs. (Code Sec. 106(e)(2)) Amounts rolled over to an HSA up to the maximum amount are: excludable from income; not subject to employment tax; disregarded in applying the maximum deduction limit for other HSA contributions; and are not deductible. An employer allowing direct transfers from a health FSA or HRA to an HSA must permit all employees covered under its HDHP to make such transfers; a 35% excise tax applies for noncompliance. (Code Sec. 106(e)(5)(B)) A rollover can't be made for an individual who was not covered by a health FSA or HRA on Sept. 21, 2006.

For one-time rollovers from IRAs, see ¶4364.

---

36. ¶H-1350.4A
37. ¶H-1350, H-1350.7; ¶2234.02; TD ¶289,107

38. ¶H-1350.20; ¶49,734; TD ¶289,118
39. ¶H-1350.9; ¶2234; TD ¶289,101

Comparability rule for employer contributions. In general, employer contributions to employee HSAs must be the same amount or the same percentage of the HDHP deductible for all employees with the same category of HDHP coverage (self-only, or family coverage, i.e., any coverage other than self-only). But employers may make larger HSA contributions for nonhighly compensated employees than for highly compensated employees (as defined in Code Sec. 414(q), see ¶4325). (Code Sec. 4980G(d)) Employers that provide self + 1, self + 2 and self + 3 family coverage apply the comparability rules separately to each category. The comparability rules apply separately to full time, part-time, and former employees (except for former employees under COBRA continuation coverage). An employer that fails the comparability rule is subject to a 35% penalty tax. The comparability rules do not apply to HSA contributions made through a cafeteria plan. Instead, the Code Sec. 125 discrimination rules apply. (Code Sec. 4980G, Reg § 54.4980G-1 - Reg § 54.4980G-5)

¶ 1530 Medicare Advantage Medical Savings Accounts.

Individuals eligible for Medicare can choose either the traditional Medicare program or a Medicare Advantage MSA (formerly called Medicare +Choice Archer MSA), which is a medical savings account as defined in Code Sec. 220(d), (¶1528) but which is designated as a Medicare Advantage MSA by the individual account holder. (Code Sec. 138(b)(1)) A Medicare Advantage MSA is a tax-exempt trust (or a custodial account), similar to an IRA, created exclusively to pay qualified medical expenses of the account holder. The Health and Human Services Dept. makes contributions directly to the Medicare Advantage MSA designated by the account holder (the only other type of allowed contribution allowed is a trustee-to-trustee transfer from another Medicare Advantage MSA). Contributions and earnings on amounts held in a Medicare Advantage MSA aren't currently includible in income. (Code Sec. 138(a))

Distributions from a Medicare Advantage MSA for purposes other than qualified medical expenses are included in income, and subject to a 50% penalty (except if made because of the account holder's disability or death). (Code Sec. 138(c)(2)) Qualified medical expenses don't include amounts paid for the medical expenses of anyone other than the account holder, and distributions that are excludable from gross income can't be taken as a medical expense deduction. (Code Sec. 138(c)(1)) The 15% penalty on the amount includible in gross income for non-qualified distributions from regular Archer MSAs (¶1528) doesn't apply to any payment or distribution from a Medicare Advantage MSA. (Code Sec. 138(c)(2)(A))[40]

¶ 1531 Group-health plan continuation coverage (COBRA).

A group health plan (of or contributed to by an employer) must provide that each qualified beneficiary who would lose coverage under the plan because of a qualifying event may elect continuation coverage under the plan within a specified at-least-60-day election period. (Code Sec. 4980B(f)(1))[41]

"Qualified beneficiaries" are the covered employee, his spouse or dependent child, a deceased employee's surviving spouse in certain cases, and a child born to or placed for adoption with the covered employee during the COBRA coverage period. (Code Sec. 4980B(g)(1))[42]

"Qualifying events" include: death of the covered employee; termination or reduction of hours of his employment; divorce or legal separation from the covered employee; cessation of a child's dependency; and the employee's entitlement to certain Medicare benefits. (Code Sec. 4980B(f)(3))[43]

Continuation coverage must be identical to coverage provided under the plan to similarly

---

40. ¶H-1348; ¶1384; TD ¶288,500
41. ¶H-1250 *et seq.*; ¶49,80B4

42. ¶H-1266; ¶49,80B4
43. ¶H-1303; ¶49,80B4

situated beneficiaries who haven't had a qualifying event. (Code Sec. 4980B(f)(2)(A))[44] Coverage for a qualified beneficiary must begin on the date of the qualifying event and end not earlier than: a statutory maximum period, the end of the plan, the failure to pay a premium, or the eligibility for group health plan coverage or Medicare. [45] Coverage of the cost of pediatric vaccines can't be reduced below the coverage provided by the plan as of May 1, '93. (Code Sec. 4980B(f)(1))[46]

Employers (or for a multiemployer plan, the plan) and certain responsible persons are liable for an excise tax (Code Sec. 4980B(e))[47] if, with certain exceptions, a group health plan fails to provide the above coverage. (Code Sec. 4980B(a))[48]

¶ 1532   Group-health plan portability, access, renewability, and parity rules.

Group health plans must satisfy requirements regarding (1) portability, through limits on pre-existing condition exclusions (Code Sec. 9801, Reg § 54.9801-1), (2) prohibitions on excluding individuals from coverage based on health status (Code Sec. 9802, Reg § 54.9802-1), (3) guaranteed renewability of health insurance coverage. (Code Sec. 9803)[49] A tax is imposed on any failure to meet these requirements, (Code Sec. 4980D)[50] and (4) for services before 2008, parity between (a) medical and surgical benefits and (b) mental health benefits. (Code Sec. 9812) (Check http://ria.thomson.com/federaltaxhandbook to see if this provision has been extended.)

¶ 1533   Self-employed individual's health insurance deduction

A self-employed individual (or a partner or a more-than-2%-shareholder of an S corporation) can deduct as a business expense 100% of the amount paid during the tax year for medical insurance on himself, his spouse and his dependents. (Code Sec. 162(l)(1)(B))

No deduction is allowed to the extent the deduction exceeds the individual's earned income as defined in Code Sec. 401(c) (net earnings from self-employment) derived from the trade or business for which the plan providing the coverage is established. (Code Sec. 162(l)(2)(A))[1] For purposes of applying the earned income limit to the deduction of a more-than-2% S corporation shareholder, that shareholder's wages from the S corporation are treated as his earned income. (Code Sec. 162(l)(5)(A))[2]

No individual who's eligible to participate in any subsidized health plan maintained by any employer of the individual *or of the individual's spouse* is entitled to the deduction. This test for eligibility is made for each calendar month. This rule is applied separately to (1) plans that provide coverage for qualified long-term care services (¶2145), or are qualified long-term care insurance contracts (¶2146) and (2) plans which don't include such coverage and aren't such contracts. (Code Sec. 162(l)(2)(B)) Thus, an individual eligible for employer-subsidized health insurance may still be able to deduct long-term care insurance premiums, so long as he isn't eligible for employer-subsidized long-term care insurance. [3]

¶ 1534   Contributions to funded welfare benefit plans.

An employer's contribution to a "welfare benefit fund" is deductible only for the tax year paid, and only to the extent the contribution doesn't exceed the "qualified cost" of the plan for its tax year that relates to (ends with or within) the employer's tax year. (Code Sec. 419(a), Code Sec. 419(b))[4] Contributions for independent contractors are also subject to

---

44. ¶H-1272; ¶49,80B4
45. ¶H-1294; ¶49,80B4
46. ¶H-1250 *et seq.*; ¶49,80B4
47. ¶H-1316; ¶49,80B4
48. ¶H-1315; ¶49,80B4
49. ¶H-1325 *et seq.*; ¶98,014 *et seq.*

50. ¶H-1325.34 *et seq.*; ¶98,014, ¶4980D4
1. ¶L-3510; ¶1624.403; TD ¶304,420
2. ¶L-3512; ¶1624.403; TD ¶304,421
3. ¶L-3510; ¶1624.403; TD ¶304,420
4. ¶s H-4101, H-4113 *et seq.*; ¶4194 *et seq.*; TD ¶278,001

this rule. (Code Sec. 419(g))[5] The rule, however, doesn't apply to a ten-or-more employer plan if no employer (or related employer) normally contributes more than 10% of total contributions, unless the plan uses experience ratings to determine each employer's contribution. (Code Sec. 419A(f)(6), Reg § 1.419A(f)(6)-1(b)(1))[6]

A welfare benefit fund is a fund that is part of an employer's plan through which the employer provides welfare benefits to employees or their beneficiaries, but doesn't include amounts held under certain kinds of insurance contracts. (Code Sec. 419(e), Reg § 1.419A(f)(6)-1(b)(4))[7]

¶ 1535 Death benefits to employee's beneficiaries.

Payments to the widow or other beneficiaries of a deceased employee, i.e., continuing the decedent's salary for a reasonable period, are deductible by the employer to the extent they qualify as a business expense. A benefit paid as a gift based on the beneficiary's need doesn't qualify as a business expense. (Reg § 1.404(a)-12(b)(2))[8]

¶ 1536 "Golden parachute" payments.

No deduction is allowed for an excess parachute payment. (Code Sec. 280G)[9] An excess parachute payment is the amount by which a parachute payment (below) exceeds the base amount (below) allocated to it. (Code Sec. 280G(b)(1)) If there's only one parachute payment the entire base amount is allocated to it. [10]

A parachute payment is any payment in the nature of compensation to (or for the benefit of) a disqualified individual (described below) *if*:

(1) the payment is contingent on a change (a) in the ownership or effective control of the corporation, *or* (b) in the ownership of a substantial part of the corporation's assets, *and*

(2) the aggregate present value of all such contingent compensation payments equals, or exceeds, three times the base amount. (Code Sec. 280G(b))[11] This base amount is the average annualized compensation income includible in a disqualified individual's gross income in the five-tax-year period preceding the tax year in which the change of ownership or control of the corporation occurs. (Code Sec. 280G(b), Code Sec. 280G(d))[12]

A disqualified individual is any individual who is: (1) an employee, independent contractor, or other person specified in regs to be issued who performs personal services for a corporation, *and* (2) is an officer, shareholder or highly compensated individual. (Code Sec. 280G(c); Reg § 1.280G-1, Q&As 15 to 20)[13] Highly compensated individual means a member of the highest paid 1% of employees or, if less, the highest paid 250 employees. (Code Sec. 280G(c))[14]

A parachute payment doesn't include an amount that the taxpayer can establish, by clear and convincing evidence, is reasonable compensation for services to be rendered on, or after, the date of change in ownership or control. (Code Sec. 280G(b)(4)(A)) The amount of an excess parachute payment can be reduced to the extent that the taxpayer can establish by clear and convincing evidence that the payment is reasonable compensation for personal services actually rendered before the date of change of ownership or control. (Code Sec. 280G(b)(4)(B))[15]

The parachute payment rules don't apply to a corporation (1) that was (immediately before the change in control or assets) a "small business corporation," without regard to whether it has a nonresident alien shareholder (¶3354) or (2) whose stock isn't readily tradeable if

5. ¶H-4104; ¶4194.01 *et seq.*
6. ¶H-4154; ¶419A4.02; TD ¶278,005
7. ¶H-4105 *et seq.*; ¶4194.02; TD ¶278,003
8. ¶H-4051 *et seq.*; ¶1624.277; TD ¶278,703
9. ¶H-3826; ¶280G4; TD ¶279,001
10. ¶H-3874; ¶280G4; TD ¶279,014

11. ¶H-3830; ¶280G4; TD ¶279,002
12. ¶H-3864; ¶280G4; TD ¶279,016
13. ¶H-3840; ¶280G4; TD ¶279,011
14. ¶H-3843; ¶280G4; TD ¶279,011
15. ¶H-3876; ¶280G4; TD ¶279,019

shareholder approval has been obtained. (Code Sec. 280G(b)(5)) A corporation that meets the requirements to elect to be treated as an S corporation, but does not elect S status, may nevertheless use the small business exemption. (Reg § 1.280G-1, Q&A 6(a)(1))[16]

Payments to or from a qualified pension or profit-sharing plan, Code Sec. 403(a) annuity, simplified employee pension or SIMPLE plan (¶4382 *et seq.*) aren't parachute payments. (Code Sec. 280G(b)(6); Reg § 1.280G-1, Q&A 8)[17]

¶ 1537　Compensation payments as capital outlays.

Compensation payments that result in the acquisition of business property generally must be added to the property's basis. [18]

Payments otherwise designated as compensation may actually be payments for property. For example, where a partnership sells out to a corporation and the former partners agree to continue to work for the corporation, the salaries of the former partners may be in part payment for the transfer of their business. (Reg § 1.162-7(b)(1))[19]

¶ 1538　Year for deducting compensation.

An employer deducts compensation in the year allowed under its accounting method (¶2816 *et seq.*) with special rules for compensation in property and bargain sales (¶1215 *et seq.*), deferred compensation (¶1539), and contributions to employee benefit plans (¶4333).

If salary is paid or accrued in one year for services to be rendered in a later year, the deduction is allowed only over the period during which the services are rendered. This applies to both cash and accrual-basis employers. [20]

For limitations on accrual-basis taxpayers' deductions for compensation paid to related cash-basis taxpayers, see ¶2836.

¶ 1539　When to deduct deferred compensation.

An employer's contributions to a nonqualified deferred compensation plan are deductible in the tax year in which an amount attributable to the contribution is includible in the gross income of employees participating in the plan (Code Sec. 404(a)(5)), even if the employer is an accrual basis taxpayer. [21]

Benefits provided under a welfare benefit fund (Code Sec. 404(b)(2)(B)), and payments of bonuses or other amounts within 2½ months after the close of the tax year in which significant services required for payment have been performed (Reg § 1.404(b)-1T, Q&A-2(c)), aren't treated as deferred compensation. [22]

To determine if compensation is deferred compensation, and when deferred compensation is paid, no amount is treated as paid or received until it's actually received by the employee. (Code Sec. 404(a)(11))[23]

If the all events test (¶2832) and recurring item exception (¶2833) are otherwise met, an accrual basis taxpayer may treat its payroll tax liability as incurred in Year 1, regardless of whether the compensation to which the liability relates is deferred compensation deductible under Code Sec. 404 in Year 2. [24]

---

16. ¶H-3835; ¶280G4; TD ¶279,006
17. ¶H-3839; ¶280G4; TD ¶279,010
18. ¶H-3603; ¶1624.081; TD ¶276,006
19. ¶H-3604; ¶1624.205; TD ¶276,006
20. ¶H-3934; ¶1624.205; TD ¶279,520

21. ¶H-3677; ¶4044.16; TD ¶277,500
22. ¶s H-3673, H-3674; TD ¶277,503
23. ¶H-3674; ¶4044.16
24. ¶H-3670; TD ¶279,504

¶ 1540   When to deduct bonuses paid to employees.

A cash basis employer deducts bonuses only for the year in which the bonuses are actually paid (¶1539).[25]

Bonuses by an accrual basis taxpayer are deductible in the tax year when all the events have occurred that establish the fact of liability to pay the bonus, the amount can be determined with reasonable accuracy, and economic performance has occurred for the liability (¶2833). (Reg § 1.461-1(a)(2)(i))[26]

To deduct a year-end bonus in the accrual year rather than the actual payment year an employer must pay the bonus within a brief period of time after the close of the employer's tax year. If an employer pays bonuses within 2 ½ months after the close of the tax year, then a deduction for the bonuses won't be subject to the deferred compensation rules (¶1539), which would bar the deduction until the bonus is included in the employee's income. (Reg § 1.404(b)-1T)[27] Payment after 2 ½ months is presumed to be deferred compensation, and that presumption can only be rebutted by showing that: (1) it was either administratively or economically impossible to avoid a later payment, and (2) as of the end of the employer's tax year, the impracticability was unforeseeable. (Reg § 1.404(b)-1T)[28]

For limitations on accrual-basis taxpayers' deductions for compensation paid to related cash-basis taxpayers, see ¶2836.

¶ 1541   When to deduct vacation pay.

Cash basis employers take a deduction when the vacation pay is paid (¶1539) in accordance with the general rules for cash basis employers. [29]

For an accrual basis employer, vacation pay earned during any tax year but not paid on or before 2½ months after the end of the tax year is deductible for the tax year of the employer in which it's paid. (Code Sec. 404(a)(5))[30]

¶ 1542   Travel Expenses. ██

The costs of away-from-home business travel can qualify as deductible expenses.

¶ 1543   Deduction for away-from-home travel costs.

Ordinary and necessary expenses incurred while traveling "away from home" in pursuit of a trade or business are deductible. Those expenses include amounts (other than amounts that are lavish or extravagant) paid for meals (subject to a percentage limit, see ¶1570) and lodging. (Code Sec. 162(a)(2))[31]

A taxpayer isn't away from home unless he is away *overnight*, or at least long enough to require rest or sleep. [32] He need not be away from his tax home for an entire 24-hour day or throughout the hours from dusk to dawn if his relief from duty is long enough to get necessary sleep. A layover sufficient only for a short rest and to get a meal isn't "overnight." [33]

Deductible business travel expenses include baggage charges, air, rail and bus fares, cost of transporting sample cases or display materials, expenses for sample rooms, cost of maintaining or operating a car, house trailer or airplane, telephone and telegraph expenses, laundry and dry cleaning costs, taxi fares, etc., from the airport or station to the hotel and back, from one customer to another, transportation from where meals and lodging are obtained to the

25. ¶H-3901, H-3916; ¶1624.218; TD ¶279,500
26. ¶H-3916; TD ¶279,503
27. ¶H-3919; TD ¶279,511
28. ¶H-3919; TD ¶279,512
29. ¶H-3922; ¶4614.01; TD ¶279,513

30. ¶H-3922; ¶4614.15; TD ¶279,513
31. ¶L-1701; ¶1624.114; TD ¶291,002
32. ¶L-1710; ¶1624.147
33. ¶L-1710; ¶1624.147

temporary work assignment, and reasonable tips for any of these expenses. (Reg § 1.162-2(a))[34] Travel expenses don't include expenses of the taxpayer's own entertainment. [35]

¶ 1544   Home defined for travel expense purposes.

A taxpayer's home for travel expense purposes is his "tax home" —his principal place of business, employment station, or post of duty, regardless of where his family lives. [36]

Where an individual has no principal place of business or employment but continually changes work locations (e.g., a traveling salesperson), his regular residence is his tax "home."[37] If such a taxpayer has no regular place of abode in a real and substantial sense, he has no "home" and can't deduct travel expenses. [38]

If a taxpayer regularly works at two or more separate locations, his tax home is the general area where his *principal* employment or business is, determined on the facts of the particular case. Important factors are: (1) time spent, (2) business activity, and (3) financial return. Income is the most significant factor.[39] In rare situations, a taxpayer may have two tax homes.[40]

Costs of traveling to and from the minor place of employment, 50% of the cost of meals (but see ¶1570), and the cost of lodging at the minor post are deductible travel expenses. [41]

Certain state legislators may elect to treat their residence in their legislative district (instead of the state capitol) as their tax home. (Code Sec. 162(h))[42]

¶ 1545   Temporary (one year or less) assignment away from home.

A temporary assignment away from home —an assignment whose termination can be foreseen within a fixed and reasonably short period —doesn't shift the "tax home." Therefore, a taxpayer may deduct the necessary traveling expenses in getting to his temporary assignment and also for the return trip to his tax home after the temporary assignment is completed, and his expenses for lodging and 50% of the cost of meals while he is in the place to which he is temporarily assigned. [43] If he returns home on his nonworking days, he may deduct his travel expenses to his home, but his travel expenses deduction is limited to the amount he would have spent to stay at his temporary location. [44]

A taxpayer isn't treated as being temporarily away from home if his period of employment exceeds one year (certain federal employees on crime investigations are exempt from this rule). (Code Sec. 162(a)). The one-year rule generally isn't triggered by short intermittent assignments that span more than one year. [45] Employment away from home at a single location for less than one year is treated as temporary, in the absence of facts and circumstances indicating otherwise. If employment away from home in a single location initially is realistically expected to last for one year or less, but later is realistically expected to exceed one year, then the employment will be treated as temporary (in the absence of facts and circumstances indicating otherwise) until the date that the taxpayer's realistic expectation changes (at which point the employment will no longer be "temporary"). [46]

¶ 1546   Indefinite assignment away from home.

An indefinite assignment away from home shifts the "tax home" and taxpayer can't deduct the expenses of travel, meals and lodging while in the location of the "indefinite"

---

34. ¶L-1705; ¶1624.114; TD ¶291,005
35. ¶L-1713; TD ¶291,007
36. ¶L-1801; ¶1624.125; TD ¶292,001
37. ¶L-1802; ¶1624.125; TD ¶292,002
38. ¶L-2025; ¶1624.125
39. ¶L-1807; ¶1624.141; TD ¶292,005
40. ¶L-1808

41. ¶s L-1805, L-2135; ¶1624.141; TD ¶292,005
42. ¶L-2026; ¶1624.141; TD ¶292,520
43. ¶s L-1810, L-2135; ¶1624.130; TD ¶292,009
44. ¶L-1813; TD ¶292,011
45. ¶L-1811; ¶1624.130
46. ¶L-1812; ¶1624.130; TD ¶292,009

assignment.[47] Employment is indefinite if it lasts for more than one year, or there is no realistic expectation that the employment will last for one year or less. [48]

¶ 1547   Meals and lodging when not away from home.

The cost of a taxpayer's meals not incurred in traveling away from home aren't deductible unless allowed under Code Sec. 162 (business expenses), Code Sec. 212 (expenses for production of income), or Code Sec. 217 (moving expenses). Lodging costs not incurred in traveling away from home aren't deductible unless allowed under Code Sec. 217. (Reg § 1.262-1(b)(5)) IRS intends to amend these rules to provide that lodging costs not incurred in traveling away from home aren't deductible unless allowed under Code Sec. 162 or Code Sec. 217.

Pending additional guidance, IRS won't apply Reg § 1.262-1(b)(5) to an employee's non-away-from-home lodging his employer provides to him, or requires him to obtain, if: the lodging is on a temporary basis and is necessary for him to participate in or be available for a bona fide business meeting or function of the employer; and the expenses are otherwise deductible by the employee, or would be deductible if paid by him, under Code Sec. 162(a).[49]

¶ 1548   U.S. travel for both business and pleasure.

Transportation costs to and from the destination are deductible only if the trip is related primarily to the taxpayer's business. Expenses at the destination allocable to the taxpayer's business are deductible even if the round-trip travel expenses are disallowed because the trip was primarily for pleasure. [50] If the trip is primarily for business, but the taxpayer extends his stay for personal reasons, makes side trips, or engages in other nonbusiness activities, he may deduct only the expenses, such as lodging and 50% of the cost of meals, that he would have incurred if the trip had been totally for business. But no allocation is required for travel costs to and from the business destination. (Reg § 1.162-2(b)(1))[1]

¶ 1549   Foreign travel for both business and pleasure.

If travel is primarily for pleasure, the rules at ¶1548 apply, so that only the amount directly allocable to business is deductible. But under special rules for foreign travel, even where travel is primarily for business, a portion of the transportation cost is nondeductible if the travel has a pleasure element. The nondeductible part is computed on a time ratio, usually in the proportion of nonbusiness days to all travel days.

This allocation and denial of deduction isn't made if: (1) travel is for one week or less; or (2) less than 25% of the time is spent on nonbusiness activity; or (3) the individual traveling had no substantial control over the arranging of the trip; or (4) a personal vacation wasn't a major consideration in making the trip. (Code Sec. 274(c); Reg § 1.162-2(b), Reg § 1.274-4(f)(5))[2] For foreign conventions, see ¶1550.

¶ 1550   Convention expenses.

Travel expenses incurred in attending a domestic convention are subject to the regular business trip rules if attendance will benefit or advance the taxpayer's business or the employee's responsibilities as distinguished from serving some social, political, or other nonbusiness function. (Reg § 1.162-2(d))[3]

No business expense deduction is allowed for expenses allocable to a convention, seminar, or similar meeting held outside the North American area (defined below) unless the taxpayer

47. ¶L-1814; ¶1624.130; TD ¶292,012
48. ¶L-1811; ¶1624.130; TD ¶292,013
49. ¶L-1709; ¶1624.114; TD ¶291,000
50. ¶s L-1702, L-2135; ¶1624.119; TD ¶291,004

1. ¶L-1702; ¶1624.119; TD ¶291,004
2. ¶L-1726 *et seq.*; ¶2744.04; TD ¶291,507
3. ¶L-1716; ¶1624.119; TD ¶291,014

establishes that the meeting is directly related to the active conduct of his trade or business, or to an activity relating to the production of income, and that after taking specified factors into account, it's as reasonable for the meeting to be held outside the North American area as within it. (Code Sec. 274(h)(1))

North American area means the U.S., its possessions, the Trust Territory of the Pacific Islands, Canada and Mexico. (Code Sec. 274(h)(3)(A)) U.S. possessions include Puerto Rico and the U.S. Virgin Islands. [4] "North American area" also includes Aruba, Antigua, Bahamas, Barbados, Barbuda, Bermuda, Costa Rica, Dominica, the Dominican Republic, Grenada, Guyana, Honduras, Jamaica, the Netherlands Antilles, Trinidad and Tobago. [5]

¶ 1551   Cruise ship convention—$2,000 deduction limit.

A deduction of up to $2,000 per individual per year is allowed for attending business conventions, etc., held aboard a cruise ship, but only if the ship is registered in the U.S. and all ports of call of the cruise ship are located in the U.S. or its possessions. (Code Sec. 274(h)(2)) A married couple filing a joint return can deduct $4,000 if each spent at least $2,000 for attending an otherwise deductible business-related cruise ship convention. [6] A taxpayer claiming the deduction must attach to his return two specified written substantiation statements (including one signed by the sponsor). (Code Sec. 274(h)(5)) [7]

¶ 1552   Travel expense deduction for a companion.

No deduction is allowed (other than under Code Sec. 217, moving expenses) for travel expenses paid or incurred for a spouse, dependent, or other individual accompanying the taxpayer (or an officer or employee of the taxpayer) unless: (1) the spouse, etc., is an employee of the taxpayer; (2) the travel of the spouse, etc., is for a bona fide business purpose; and (3) the expenses would otherwise be deductible by the spouse, etc. (Code Sec. 274(m)(3)) [8]

The limits on deductions for travel companions don't apply to a companion who (1) is a business associate (¶1563), (2) comes along for a bona-fide business purpose, and (3) could otherwise deduct the expense if he incurred it. (Reg § 1.274-2(g))

If a wife accompanies her husband on a business trip and her expenses aren't deductible, the deductible expense for transportation and lodging is the single rate cost of similar accommodations for the husband. But the full rental for a car in which both spouses travel is deductible, since no part of the expense is attributable to the "extra" spouse. [9]

¶ 1553   Deduction for luxury water travel is limited.

The deduction allowed for travel by ocean liner, cruise ship, or other form of "luxury" water transportation is limited to twice the highest domestic per diem allowance of executive branch U.S. government employees (other than high-ranking executive personnel) multiplied by the number of days of luxury water travel. (Code Sec. 274(m)(1)(A)) If the cost includes separately stated amounts for meals and entertainment, these amounts must be reduced by 50% (¶1570). The per diem rule doesn't apply to expenses of a cruise-ship convention or seminar to which the rules at ¶1551 apply (Code Sec. 274(m)(1)(B)(i)), or to:

. . . expenses treated as compensation paid to an employee or otherwise included in the gross income of the recipient;

. . . reimbursed, accounted-for expenses of the taxpayer where the services are performed for someone else, and if performed for an employer, the reimbursement hasn't been treated as compensation;

4. ¶s L-1744, L-1745; ¶2744.04; TD ¶291,515
5. ¶L-1746; ¶2744.04; TD ¶291,516
6. ¶L-1721; ¶2744.04; TD ¶291,018

7. ¶L-1722; ¶2744.04; TD ¶291,019
8. ¶L-1739; ¶2744.035; TD ¶291,023
9. ¶L-1740 et seq.; ¶1624.119

. . . expenses for recreational or social activities primarily for the benefit of employees;

. . . services and facilities made available by the taxpayer to the general public; and

. . . services and facilities sold to customers. (Code Sec. 274(m)(1)(B)(ii))[10]

¶ 1554 Above-the-line deduction for overnight travel of reservists.

A member of the Armed Forces reserves who travels over 100 miles from home for an overnight stay connected with the performance of services (e.g., to attend meetings), can deduct travel expenses as an above-the-line adjustment to gross income. The amount deductible is limited to the regular federal per diem rate for lodging, meals, and incidental expenses, and the standard mileage rate for car expenses plus parking fees and tolls. (Code Sec. 62(a)(2)(E)) Expenses in excess of these limits, or for overnight travel not over 100 miles from home, are deductible as miscellaneous itemized expenses subject to the 2%-of-AGI floor (¶3110).[11]

¶ 1555 Transportation Expenses. ▬▬▬▬▬▬▬

Costs of local transportation (including the cost of operating and maintaining a car directly attributable to the conduct of a trade or business) can qualify as deductible expenses.

¶ 1556 Transportation expenses other than commuting expenses.

Transportation expenses (but not commuting expenses, see ¶1557) directly attributable to the conduct of the taxpayer's business are deductible even though he isn't away from home overnight. (Reg § 1.162-1(a)) These expenses (sometimes called local travel expenses) include air, train, bus and cab fares and costs of operating automobiles. [12] If a taxpayer works at two or more places each day, he can deduct the cost of getting from one to the other. [13]

¶ 1557 Expenses of daily transportation between home and work site.

Expenses of commuting between a taxpayer's residence and his regular business location, wherever situated, aren't deductible (Reg § 1.162-2(e), Reg § 1.162-2(f)), even to a remote area where there's no residential area nearby and no public transportation. [14]

A taxpayer may deduct daily transportation expenses incurred in going between the taxpayer's residence and a temporary (¶1558) work location *outside* the metropolitan area where the taxpayer lives and normally works. [15]

Daily transportation expenses incurred in going between the taxpayer's residence and a temporary (¶1558) work location *within* the same metropolitan area is business transportation if: (1) the taxpayer has one or more regular work locations away from his residence; or (2) the taxpayer's residence is his principal place of business (¶1636 *et seq.*).[16]

¶ 1558 One-year temporary workplace rule.

A work location is "temporary" for purposes of deducting daily transportation costs (¶1557) if employment at the location is realistically expected to last (and in fact does last) for one year or less. If the employment initially is realistically expected to last for one year or less, but at some later date it is realistically expected to exceed one year, that employment is temporary (absent facts and circumstances indicating otherwise) until the date that the

---

10. ¶L-1708; ¶2744.05; TD ¶291,009
11. ¶A-2611.4; ¶624.02; TD ¶560,706.3
12. ¶L-1601; ¶1624.150; TD ¶290,501
13. ¶L-1602; ¶1624.153; TD ¶290,504

14. ¶L-1608 *et seq.*; ¶1624.151; TD ¶290,512
15. ¶L-1605; ¶1624.130; TD ¶290,506
16. ¶L-1605; ¶1624.151; TD ¶290,505

taxpayer's realistic expectation changes, and is treated as not temporary after that date.

Where an assignment at a work location is expected to last for more than one year, but the taxpayer is realistically expected to be present at that location *for no more than 35 workdays (partial or complete)* during each of the calendar years in that period, the location is temporary for a calendar year in which he actually works there for no more than 35 partial or complete workdays.

⭕*illustration:* A taxpayer who normally works in an office building works at an offsite location on an assignment lasting 36 months, but he is at the offsite location for only 30 days each year. The offsite location is "temporary," and his round-trip transportation costs between home and that location are deductible. [17]

¶ 1559   Automobile expenses.

The expenses of operating and maintaining a car used for business purposes, such as gasoline, oil, repairs, insurance, depreciation, interest to buy the car, taxes, licenses, garage rent, parking, fees, tolls, etc., are deductible. [18] If a taxpayer makes both personal and business use of his car, he must apportion his expenses between business (deductible) and personal (nondeductible) transportation. [19] Report business auto expenses on Form 2106 or Form 2106-EZ (employees) or on Form 1040, Schedule C or Form 1040, Schedule C-EZ (self-employeds). [20]

⭕*caution:* An employee who uses a car for his job is subject to the 2%-of-AGI floor on deducting the *un*reimbursed auto expenses he incurs, see ¶3104, and can't deduct interest on a car loan (¶1715).

¶ 1560   Transporting tools to work.

A taxpayer may deduct only *additional* expenses incurred because of the need to transport tools, etc., to work *and* only if the additional expenses can be determined accurately. The deduction is only for that portion of the cost of transporting the tools, etc., that exceeds the cost of commuting *by the same mode of transportation* without the tools, etc. [21]

¶ 1561   Business standard mileage rate.

Employees or self-employed individuals can use the optional business standard mileage rate in computing the deductible costs of operating passenger automobiles owned or leased by them (including vans and pickup or panel trucks) for business purposes.

For 2007, a taxpayer who uses this method multiplies the number of business miles by a rate of 48.5¢ per mile. [22]

A deduction using the standard mileage rate is in lieu of deducting operating and fixed costs. A taxpayer who uses the standard mileage rate forgoes deductions for depreciation (or leasing costs), maintenance and repairs, tires, gasoline (including taxes), oil, insurance, and registration fees. But deductions for parking fees and tolls are still available. [23]

Use of the standard mileage rate isn't available where taxpayer's auto is used for hire (e.g., as a taxi) or for five or more autos that are used simultaneously, such as in fleet operations, nor is it available for a purchased car if it has previously been depreciated using any method other than the straight-line method, or if Code Sec. 179 additional first-year depreciation has been claimed. The standard mileage rate may generally be used for a leased auto only if the

17. ¶L-1606; ¶1624.151; TD ¶290,507
18. ¶L-1902; ¶1624.150; TD ¶293,000
19. ¶L-1907; ¶1624.157; TD ¶293,014
20. ¶L-1901; ¶1624.157; TD ¶293,002

21. ¶L-1611; ¶1624.152; TD ¶290,515
22. ¶L-1903; ¶1624.157; TD ¶293,005
23. ¶L-1905; ¶1624.157; TD ¶293,009

taxpayer uses this method (or a fixed and variable rate (FAVR) allowance, see ¶1576) for the entire lease period (including renewals). [24]

Rural mail carriers receiving qualified reimbursements (equipment maintenance allowance) don't report them in income even if they exceed the amount of their expenses. (Code Sec. 162(o)(1)) However, if the expenses exceed the amount of the qualified reimbursement, the mail carrier can take the excess into account in computing miscellaneous itemized deductions under Code Sec. 67. (Code Sec. 162(o)(2))[25]

A taxpayer may use the optional business standard mileage rate in substantiating reimbursed expenses paid by another. [26] For consequences if the reimbursement is made under an accountable plan, or under a nonaccountable plan, see ¶3104.

¶ 1562 Entertainment Expenses. ▬▬▬▬▬▬▬▬▬

Costs incurred for entertainment must meet strict tests in order to be deductible. A 50% rule also limits otherwise-allowable deductions for meals and entertainment.

Entertainment expenses, except as limited by the rules in ¶1570 (percentage limit) and ¶1572 (other restrictions), are deductible if they are ordinary and necessary expenses of carrying on a trade or business. (Code Sec. 274(a), Code Sec. 274(e); Reg § 1.162-1(a)) Strict substantiation requirements must be met (¶1580). But no deduction is allowed unless the taxpayer can show that the entertainment expenses are: (1) "directly related" to the active conduct of a trade or business (¶1565), or (2) "associated with" the active conduct of a trade or business (¶1566), or (3) covered by one of the exceptions at ¶1567. (Code Sec. 274(a))[27]

"Entertainment" includes any activity generally considered to be entertainment, amusement or recreation. This covers entertaining guests at night clubs, theaters, sporting events, and at entertainment facilities such as yachts, country clubs, hunting lodges, etc. If the expense involves the use of an entertainment facility, see ¶1568. (Reg § 1.274-2(b)(1)) It doesn't include: supper money furnished to an employee working overtime, a hotel room maintained by an employer and furnished to employees while traveling on business, or an auto used for business even though used for commuting to and from work. [28]

Expenses of entertaining customers or clients at the taxpayer's home may be ordinary and necessary. But only the *extra* expense incurred because they are present is deductible. Failure to show a business purpose for entertaining bars a deduction. [29]

¶ 1563 Who may be entertained?

A "business associate" who may be entertained is a person with whom the taxpayer could reasonably expect to engage or deal with in the active conduct of his trade or business. Examples are customers, suppliers, clients, employees, agents, partners, or professional advisors, *whether established or prospective.* (Reg § 1.274-2(b)(2)(iii))[30] For spouses, see ¶1564.

¶ 1564 Entertainment expenses allocable to spouse.

A taxpayer can deduct the cost of entertaining taxpayer's spouse or the spouse of a business customer if taxpayer can show a clear business purpose rather than a personal or social purpose for incurring the expenses. For example, a customer's spouse may join the party for the entertainment because it's impracticable, under the circumstances, to entertain the customer without the spouse. And if the taxpayer's spouse joins the party because the customer's spouse is present, the cost of the entertainment allocable to the taxpayer's spouse is also deductible. (Reg § 1.274-2(d)(2), Reg § 1.274-2(d)(4))[31]

---

24. ¶L-1903 *et seq.*; ¶1624.157; TD ¶293,006
25. ¶L-1911; ¶1624.157; TD ¶293,018
26. ¶L-4715; ¶2744.17; TD ¶293,011
27. ¶L-2101; ¶2744.01; TD ¶294,001

28. ¶L-2102; TD ¶294,003
29. ¶L-2108 *et seq.*; ¶2744.01; TD ¶294,009
30. ¶L-2103; ¶2744.10; TD ¶294,007
31. ¶L-2104 *et seq.*; ¶2744.01; TD ¶294,008

¶ 1565   "Directly related" test for deducting costs of entertainment.

Amounts paid for entertainment are deductible if they are directly related to the active conduct of the taxpayer's trade or business. This test is met if the entertainment: (1) involved an active discussion aimed at getting immediate revenue; (2) occurred in a clear business setting such as a hospitality room; or (3) must be reported as compensation for services performed by an individual other than an employee. (Reg § 1.274-2(c)(1))[32] Costs generally aren't "directly related" if entertainment occurs where there's little or no possibility of engaging in the active conduct of business, e.g., at night clubs, theaters, or sporting events, but they may be deductible under the "associated with" rule (¶1566). (Reg § 1.274-2(c)(7))[33]

¶ 1566   "Associated with" test for deducting costs of entertainment.

Entertainment expenses that fail the directly related test but are associated with the active conduct of the taxpayer's business are deductible if the entertainment directly precedes or follows a substantial and bona fide business discussion. (Reg § 1.274-2(d)(1))[34] An entertainment expense is generally associated with the active conduct of a taxpayer's business if he can show a clear business purpose in incurring the expenditure. (Reg § 1.274-2(d)(2))[35]

The portion of an otherwise deductible expense allocable to the spouse of a person who engaged in the discussion is ordinarily considered associated with the active conduct of the business (Reg § 1.274-2(d)(4)),[36] see ¶1564.

Whether a business discussion is substantial depends on all the facts of each case. The taxpayer must show that he or his representative actively engaged in a discussion, meeting, negotiation, or other bona fide business transaction (other than entertainment) in order to get a specific business benefit. The meeting doesn't have to be for any specific length of time, but the business discussion must be substantial in relation to the entertainment. Nor does more time have to be devoted to business than entertainment. (Reg § 1.274-2(d)(3)(i))[37]

¶ 1567   Expenses to which "directly related" and "associated" tests don't apply.

Certain ordinary and necessary entertainment expenses are deductible even if they aren't "directly related" to or "associated with" the active conduct of the taxpayer's trade or business. But they are subject to the strict substantiation requirements (¶1580) that apply to other entertainment expenses. The exceptions are:

(1) Food and beverages furnished on the taxpayer's business premises primarily for the taxpayer's employees. [38]

(2) The expense (other than club dues, see ¶1569) of providing recreational, social, or similar activities primarily for the benefit of the taxpayer's employees, other than highly-compensated employees (defined at ¶4325).[39]

(3) Goods, services, and the use of a facility, if treated as compensation and as wages by the employer for withholding tax purposes. [40]

(4) Expenses connected with meetings of directors, shareholders, employees or trade associations. [41]

(5) Cost of providing entertainment or recreational facilities to the general public as a means of advertising or promoting good will in the community. [42]

---

32. ¶L-2112; ¶2744.01; TD ¶294,013
33. ¶L-2116; ¶2744.01; TD ¶294,017
34. ¶L-2118; ¶2744.01; TD ¶294,019
35. ¶L-2118; ¶2744.01; TD ¶294,020
36. ¶L-2104; ¶2744.01; TD ¶294,008
37. ¶L-2119; ¶2744.01; TD ¶294,020

38. ¶L-2122; ¶2744.01; TD ¶294,025
39. ¶L-2125; ¶2744.01; TD ¶294,029
40. ¶L-2123; ¶2744.01; TD ¶294,026
41. ¶L-2129; ¶2744.01; TD ¶294,031
42. ¶L-2131; ¶2744.01; TD ¶294,033

(6) Expense of providing entertainment, goods, and services, or use of facilities, that are sold to the public in a bona fide transaction for adequate and full consideration. [43]

(7) Reimbursed and substantiated expenses or allowances of employees where the employer hasn't treated the expenses as wages subject to withholding, and reimbursed, accounted-for entertainment expenses of self-employeds reimbursed or covered with an allowance by the client or customer. (Code Sec. 274(e); Reg § 1.274-2(f)(2)) In these situations, the "directly related" and "associated with" tests apply to the payor. [44]

¶ 1568 Entertainment facilities.

No deduction is allowed for any expense paid or incurred for an entertainment facility used in conjunction with any activity that is generally considered to be entertainment, amusement or recreation. (Code Sec. 274(a)(1)(B))[45] Entertainment facilities include yachts, hunting lodges, fishing camps, swimming pools, tennis courts, and bowling alleys. Facilities also may include airplanes, automobiles, hotel suites, apartments, and houses located in recreational areas (e.g., beach cottages and ski lodges). However, a facility isn't an entertainment facility unless it's actually used at least in part for entertainment. Expenses of an automobile or an airplane used on business trips are allowed. (Reg § 1.274-2(e)(2))[46]

The following expenditures aren't subject to the entertainment facility rules:

... Interest, taxes, and casualty losses on entertainment facilities; these are deductible subject to the regular rules that apply to these items.

... Out-of-pocket expenses for such items as food and beverages, or expenses for catering furnished during entertainment at a facility, are subject to the general entertainment deduction rules.

... Actual business (as opposed to entertainment) use of a facility, such as using a plane or car for business transportation or chartering a yacht to an unrelated person. (Reg § 1.274-2(e)(3)(iii), Reg § 1.274-6)[47]

¶ 1569 Club dues.

Deductions are generally barred for the cost of membership in any club organized for business, pleasure, recreation or other social purpose (Code Sec. 274(a)(3)), such as country clubs, golf and athletic clubs, airline clubs, hotel clubs, and business luncheon clubs. (Reg § 1.274-2(a)(2)(iii)(a)) However, a deduction is allowed to the extent dues are treated as compensation income to an employee. (Reg § 1.132-5(s)) Dues for membership in professional and trade associations and civic or public service organizations (e.g., Rotary, Kiwanis) are deductible. (Reg § 1.274-2(a)(2)(iii)(b))[48]

¶ 1570 Meal and entertainment deduction limits—the 50% rule.

The amount of an otherwise allowable deduction for meal or entertainment expenses (including meals while on business travel status, ¶1542) is reduced by 50%. This reduction applies to any expense for food or beverages, and any item for entertainment, amusement, or recreation, or for a facility used for such an activity. (Code Sec. 274(n)(1))

The 50% limit doesn't apply to:

... Expenses treated as compensation paid to an employee or otherwise included in the gross income of the recipient of the meal or entertainment. (Code Sec. 274(n)(2)(A))

---

43. ¶L-2132; ¶2744.01; TD ¶294,034
44. ¶L-2124; ¶2744.01; TD ¶294,028
45. ¶L-2149; ¶2744.02; TD ¶295,001

46. ¶L-2150; ¶2744.02; TD ¶295,002
47. ¶L-2152 *et seq.*; ¶2744.02; TD ¶295,004
48. ¶L-2181 *et seq.*; ¶2744.03; TD ¶295,201

... Meals and entertainment expenses that are reimbursed. (Code Sec. 274(n)(2)(A)) Instead, the percentage limit applies to the person making the reimbursement.

... Traditional recreational expenses for employees. (Code Sec. 274(n)(2)(A))

... Services and facilities made available by the taxpayer to the general public. (Code Sec. 274(n)(2)(A))

... Expenses of goods, services, or use of facilities, sold by the taxpayer in a bona fide transaction (entertainment sold to customers). (Code Sec. 274(n)(2)(A))

... Food or beverage expenses that are excludable from the gross income of the recipient under the de minimis fringe benefit rules. (Code Sec. 274(n)(2)(B))[1]

... An expense that is part of a package that includes a ticket to attend certain charitable sporting events. (Code Sec. 274(n)(2)(C)) The event must: (1) be organized for the primary purpose of benefiting a tax-exempt charitable organization, (2) contribute 100% of the net proceeds to the charity, and (3) use volunteers for substantially all work performed in carrying out the event. (Code Sec. 274(l)(1)(B))

... Food or beverage expenses of crews of certain drilling rigs and crews of certain commercial vessels. (Code Sec. 274(n)(2)(E))[49]

Where an employee's deduction of unreimbursed employee business expenses is subject to the 2%-of-AGI floor discussed at ¶3110, the 50% limit is applied before the 2% floor. [50]

The deductible percentage of meals for certain transport workers (e.g., air transport employees, truck and bus drivers, railroad employees) while away from home during or incident to the period of duty subject to the hours of service limitations of the Dept. of Transportation is: 75% for 2007 and 80% for 2008 or later years. (Code Sec. 274(n)(3))[1]

¶ 1571   Limits on deductions for skyboxes.

Where a skybox or other private luxury box is leased for more than one sporting event, the amount allowable as a deduction for business-related entertainment use is limited to the face value of nonluxury box seat tickets for the seats in the box covered by the lease. (Code Sec. 274(l)(2)) This is reduced by 50% to determine the deduction. (Code Sec. 274(n))[2]

¶ 1572   Other restrictions on meal and entertainment deductions.

No deduction is allowed for any food or beverage expense unless —

(1) the expense isn't lavish or extravagant under the circumstances, and

(2) the taxpayer (or one of taxpayer's employees) is present when the food or beverages are furnished (Code Sec. 274(k)(1)), and

(3) the taxpayer establishes that the expenditure was directly related (¶1565) to the active conduct of taxpayer's business or, for an expenditure directly preceding or following a substantial and bona fide business discussion, was associated with the active conduct of the taxpayer's business (¶1566). (Code Sec. 274(a), Code Sec. 274(k))[3]

Neither the lavish or extravagant limit nor the presence test applies to any expense that is excepted from the percentage limit under ¶1570, above. (Code Sec. 274(k)(2))[4]

In determining the deduction for the cost of a ticket to an entertainment or recreation activity, the amount taken into account can't exceed the face value of the ticket (including any ticket tax). But the face value limit doesn't apply to a ticket to a charitable sporting event

49. ¶L-2138 *et seq.*; ¶2744.01; TD ¶294,507 *et seq.*
50. ¶L-2135; ¶2744.01; TD ¶294,506
1. ¶L-2145.1; ¶2744.01

2. ¶L-2146 *et seq.*; ¶2744.01; TD ¶294,519
3. ¶s L-2133 *et seq.*, L-2112, L-2118; ¶2744.01; TD ¶294,503 *et seq.*
4. ¶L-2134; ¶2744.12; TD ¶294,503 *et seq.*

that's excepted from the percentage limit (¶1570). (Code Sec. 274(l)(1))[5]

¶ 1573 Deduction limit on entertainment expenses of officers, directors, and 10%-or-more owners.

For costs to provide entertainment-, amusement-, or recreation-related goods, services or facilities to "specified individuals" (e.g., an officer, director, or 10%-or-more owner of the entity, or a related entity) and their relatives or friends, an employer's deduction is limited to the amount of the costs which were treated by the employer as compensation on the employer's income tax return and as wages (or nonemployee compensation) to the qualified recipient. (Code Sec. 274(e)(2)(B), Code Sec. 274(e)(9), Prop Reg. § 1.274-9(b) ["Taxpayers may rely])[6]

Detailed rules apply for allocating plane costs between usage for entertainment of specified individuals and expenses for all other users (but in making this allocation, expenses of bona fide charters to third parties aren't counted). The deduction limitation applies to all expenses of maintaining and operating a plane (e.g., fuel, crew's salaries, take-off, landing and hangar fees, insurance, depreciation or lease payments, and amounts expensed under Code Sec. 179).[7] Where a specified individual's flight includes a business segment and entertainment segment, the entertainment cost subject to the limitation is the excess of the total cost of the flights over the cost of the flights that would have been taken without the entertainment segment or segments.[8] The deduction limitation doesn't apply to business entertainment air travel or personal travel that can't be characterized as "entertainment" (e.g., flight to attend family member's funeral). (Prop Reg. § 1.274-10(b) ["Taxpayers may rely"])[9]

¶ 1574 Expense Reimbursements. ▬▬▬▬▬▬▬▬

An employee doesn't pay tax on an advance, reimbursement or other expense allowance received under an "accountable plan." The tax treatment of an advance or reimbursement to an independent contractor depends on whether he accounts to his principal for the expense.

An employee doesn't pay tax on an advance, reimbursement or other expense allowance received from his employer (or from a third party) under an "accountable plan." (Reg § 1.62-2(c)(4)) By contrast, an advance, etc., made under a "nonaccountable plan," is fully taxable to the employee and subject to FICA and income tax withholding. (Reg § 1.62-2(c)(5))[10]

An advance, etc., is treated as made under an "accountable plan" if:

(1) the employee receives the advance, etc., for a deductible business expense that he paid or incurred while performing services as an employee of his employer (¶1575),

(2) the employee must adequately account to his employer for the expense within a reasonable period of time (¶1576), and

(3) the employee must return any excess reimbursement or allowance within a reasonable period of time (¶1577).

An advance, etc., that doesn't satisfy all three conditions is treated as paid under a nonaccountable plan—it is taxed to the employee and is subject to FICA and income tax withholding. (Code Sec. 62(c); Reg § 1.62-2(c)(5)) A per-hour or per-day reimbursement by pipeline industry employers for certain employee-provided equipment is made under a nonaccountable plan, but a limited amount of payments meeting safe harbor requirements are made under an accountable plan.[11] Similarly, auto mechanics' tool allowances relying on estimated actual

5. ¶L-2145; ¶2744.01; TD ¶294,516
6. ¶L-2123; ¶2744.01; TD ¶294,026
7. ¶L-2123.2; TD ¶294,026.2
8. ¶L-2123.7

9. ¶L-2101.1; TD ¶294,001.1
10. ¶J-1050; TD ¶296,006.
11. ¶S-3672

expenses failed to qualify under the accountable plan rules. But IRS has set the criteria it would consider in allowing deemed-substantiation safe-harbors with industries that demonstrate they can't comply with the existing accountable plan rules.

If an employee does not timely return advances or reimbursements in excess of those that are substantiated, only the excess is treated as made under a nonaccountable plan. (Reg § 1.62-2(c)(3)(ii))[12]

An arrangement that would in part be an accountable plan and in part be a nonaccountable plan if both parts were viewed separately is treated as two expense allowance arrangements—one an accountable plan, and the other a nonaccountable plan. [13] But the entire reimbursement for business-travel meals and incidental expenses (M&IE) is deemed paid under a nonaccountable plan if an employer routinely doesn't track expenses and doesn't require employees either to substantiate actual expenses or pay back amounts exceeding the deemed substantiated amount (¶1576).[14]

¶ 1575 Business connection requirement for employee business expenses.

An arrangement satisfies the "business connection" requirement if it provides advances, allowances (including per diem or mileage allowances, or allowances for meals and incidental expenses only), or reimbursements only for business expenses that are allowable as deductions, and that are paid or incurred by the employee in connection with performing services as an employee. (Reg § 1.62-2(d))[15] For example, a reimbursement for an employee's meal eaten while he was away from home overnight on employer business (¶1543) satisfies the business connection requirement, but a reimbursement for an employee's (non-business-entertainment) meal eaten during a non-overnight trip (¶1543) on employer business wouldn't satisfy the requirement. An advance, reimbursement or allowance that would be treated as made partially under a nonaccountable plan solely because the expense is subject to the 50% deduction limit for business meals and entertainment (¶1570) is treated as made under an accountable plan. (Reg § 1.62-2(h)(1))[16]

¶ 1576 Accounting to employer for expenses.

To the extent an employee business expense such as travel or entertainment isn't deductible unless the substantiation requirements of Code Sec. 274(d) are met (¶1580 et seq.), the employee must meet those requirements within a reasonable period of time (¶1577), i.e., submit to the payor information sufficient to substantiate the requisite elements of each expense or use.

For all other business expenses, sufficient information must be submitted to enable the one making the reimbursement to identify the specific nature of each expense and to conclude that the expense is attributable to the employer's business activities. (Reg § 1.62-2(e)(3))

The following simplified substantiation rules apply to per diem or mileage allowances paid under an arrangement that otherwise qualifies as an accountable plan (¶1574):

. . . Per diem allowance. If a payor (i.e., the employer, its agent, or a third party) pays a per diem allowance in lieu of reimbursing actual expenses for lodging, meal and incidental expenses (M&IE) incurred or to be incurred by an employee for travel away from home, the amount of the expenses that is treated as substantiated for each calendar day (or part of that day) is the lesser of the per diem allowance or the amount computed at the federal per diem rate for the locality of travel for that day (or part of that day). [17] An employee who is "related" to his employer (¶1580) isn't considered to have accounted to his employer for the

---

12. ¶L-4703; TD ¶296,009
13. ¶L-4744; TD ¶296,007
14. ¶L-4704

15. ¶L-4703.1; TD ¶561,009
16. ¶L-4703.1; TD ¶532,004
17. ¶L-4717; ¶2744.18; TD ¶296,019

full federal per diem allowances for lodging and M&IE, and must substantiate any deductions he claims, but he may use the meals-only per diem (¶1582) and the business standard mileage rate (¶1561).[18]

. . . Simplified (high-low) method for substantiating travel allowances. A simplified method can be used for per diem amounts paid for lodging plus M&IE during travel within the continental U.S. If the regular federal per diem option isn't used, for post-Sept. 30, 2006 travel, he may reimburse up to $246 for high-cost localities ($188 for lodging and $58 for M&IE) and $148 for other localities ($103 for lodging and $45 for M&IE). For post-Sept. 30, 2007 travel, he may reimburse up to $237 for high-cost localities ($179 for lodging and $58 for M&IE) and $152 for other localities ($107 for lodging and $45 for M&IE). For travel outside the continental U.S., a separate lodging expense rate and M&IE rate is available for each locality outside the continental U.S. [19]

. . . Mileage allowance. An employee who receives a fixed mileage allowance of not more than the optional business standard mileage rate (¶1561) to cover transportation expenses while traveling away from home or for transportation expenses, is considered to have made an adequate accounting to his employer if the elements of time, place, and business purpose of the travel are substantiated. (Reg § 1.274-5T(f))[20]

. . . Fixed and variable rate (FAVR) allowances for autos. Where an employer provides a mileage allowance under a reimbursement or other expense allowance arrangement for an employee owned or leased car, the substantiation requirement is satisfied as to the amount if the employer reimburses in accordance with a fixed and variable rate (FAVR) allowance. A FAVR allowance is periodic fixed payments to cover fixed costs such as depreciation, coupled with periodic variable payments to cover operating costs such as gasoline. Among other things, a FAVR allowance may be paid only to an employee who substantiates at least 5,000 miles driven in connection with the performance of services as an employee, and at least ten employees must be covered by the FAVR allowance. [21]

¶ 1577 Returning amounts in excess of expenses; when to substantiate.

Under an accountable plan, an employee must be required to return to the payor within a reasonable period of time any reimbursement in excess of substantiated business expenses. (Reg § 1.62-2(f)(1)) The definition of reasonable period of time depends on the facts and circumstances. However, under a safe-harbor rule, (1) an advance within 30 days of the time the employee has the expense, (2) an expense adequately accounted for within 60 days after it was paid or incurred, or (3) an amount returned to the employer within 120 days after the expense was paid or incurred will be treated as having occurred within a reasonable period of time. (Reg § 1.62-2(g)(2)(i)) If the employee is given a periodic statement (at least quarterly) that asks him to either return or adequately account for outstanding reimbursements and he complies within 120 days of the statement, the amount is adequately accounted for or returned within a reasonable period of time. (Reg § 1.62-2(g)(2))[22]

¶ 1578 Reporting reimbursed business expenses.

If an employee's expenses equal advances or reimbursements made under an accountable plan, he reports no income from the expenses and claims no deductions. However, if the employee's actual business expenses exceed nontaxable accountable-plan advances or reimbursements, and he wishes to deduct the excess, he can do so under the rules that follow for deductions under nonaccountable plan reimbursements.

---

18. ¶L-4713; TD ¶296,014
19. ¶L-4718; ¶2744.18; TD ¶296,020
20. ¶L-4715; ¶2744.18; TD ¶296,016

21. ¶L-4725 *et seq.*; ¶2744.18; TD ¶296,029
22. ¶L-4746; TD ¶296,047

An employee who pays for employment-related business expenses but receives a nonaccountable plan advance or reimbursement (e.g., he isn't required to account to the employer) reports the advance or reimbursement as income and claims otherwise allowable deductions on Form 2106 or Form 2106EZ, and on Form 1040, Schedule A as miscellaneous itemized deductions. The employee's meal and entertainment expenses are subject to the 50% limit (¶1570), and total miscellaneous itemized deductions are subject to the 2%-of-adjusted-gross-income limit (¶3110). The employee must provide the information required for listed property as discussed at ¶1584, and must also be able to substantiate each element of his business expenditures. (Reg § 1.274-5T(f)(3))[23]

¶ 1579   Reimbursed expenses of a self-employed person.

Expenses of a self-employed person incurred on behalf of and reimbursed by a client or customer aren't included in the self-employed's gross income if the self-employed substantiates the expenses to his principal under the rules at ¶1580. But if he doesn't substantiate those reimbursed expenses to his principal, he must include the reimbursements in gross income and may deduct the expenses, subject to the usual limitations (e.g., 50% limit on business meals and entertainment), if he has kept the necessary records and receipts. (Reg § 1.274-5T(h)(1), Reg § 1.274-5T(h)(2))[24]

The client or customer must substantiate business travel or entertainment expenses (and is subject to the 50% limit) if a self-employed person accounts for those expenses to the client or customer and is reimbursed. However, if the self-employed person doesn't account for the expenses, the client or customer doesn't have to substantiate reimbursed expenses (and isn't subject to the 50% limit). (Reg § 1.274-5T(h)(2), Reg § 1.274-5T(h)(4))[25]

¶ 1580   Substantiating T&E and "Listed Property" Expenses. ▂▂▂▂▂▂▂▂

In order to deduct travel and entertainment (T&E) expenses, each expense must be substantiated. With respect to listed property, certain elements of each expenditure or business use must be proved.

Taxpayers must substantiate each element of every T&E expense for which a deduction is claimed. (Code Sec. 274(d)(1), Code Sec. 274(d)(2), Code Sec. 274(d)(3)) The elements of away from home travel expenses are explained at ¶1581; entertainment expenses, at ¶1583; and business gifts, at ¶1592.

Taxpayers can't claim deductions or credits for "listed property" unless they substantiate every element of each expenditure and use of the listed property (¶1584) for business or investment purposes. (Code Sec. 274(d)(4)) "Listed property" is passenger automobiles and other property used as a means of transportation —for example, taxicabs, airplanes, trucks, boats, etc.—certain computers, and property used for entertainment, recreation or amusement. For depreciation of "listed property," see ¶1950 et seq.

Generally, proper substantiation requires "adequate records" (¶1585 et seq.), or a taxpayer statement supported by sufficient corroborating evidence (¶1587), plus documentary evidence where required (¶1586). (Code Sec. 274(d))[26] Approximations or estimates aren't sufficient. (Reg § 1.274-5T(a))[27] However, statistical sampling may be used in some cases to establish the amount of meal and entertainment expenses that isn't subject to the 50% limit (¶1570).[28] All elements of an expenditure or use must be proved. Failure to prove any one will bar the deduction. (Reg § 1.274-5T(c)(1))[29]

In the usual instance, an employee who substantiates expenses to the employer need not

---

23. ¶L-4710; ¶2744.16; TD ¶296,012
24. ¶L-4757; ¶2744.16; TD ¶296,056
25. ¶L-4758; ¶2744.16; TD ¶296,057
26. ¶L-4600 et seq.; ¶2744.10; TD ¶295,301

27. ¶L-4601; ¶2744.10; TD ¶295,301
28. ¶L-4641; ¶2744.10
29. ¶s L-4644, L-4608; ¶2744.10; TD ¶295,302

account for them to the IRS. However, an employee who is "related" to his employer (certain close relatives of an individual employer, or a more than 10% shareholder of a corporate employer) may be asked by IRS to substantiate his expense accounts even though he has accounted to his employer. (Reg § 1.274-5T(f)(5)(ii))[30]

Simplified substantiation procedures apply to expenses of certain federal employees. [31]

¶ 1581 Proving travel and transportation expenses.

The taxpayer must prove all of the following elements by adequate records or by a sufficiently corroborated statement:

(1) The amount of each separate expenditure for traveling away from home, such as the cost of transportation or lodging. The daily cost of breakfast, lunch, and dinner and other incidental travel elements may be aggregated if they are set forth in reasonable categories, such as for meals, oil and gas, taxi fares, etc.

(2) The dates of the departure and return home for each trip, and the number of days spent on business away from home.

(3) The destinations or locality of the travel.

(4) The business reason for the travel or the nature of the business benefit derived or expected to be derived as a result of the travel. (Reg § 1.274-5T(b)(2))[32]

Incidental travel expenses, e.g., tips, aren't subject to these rules. Where records are incomplete and documentary proof is unavailable, the taxpayer may establish the amount of incidental travel expenses by reasonable approximations. (Reg § 1.162-17(d)(3))[33]

¶ 1582 Substantiation by use of optional meal or incidental expenses allowance.

Employees and self-employeds who are away from home on business travel may use standard per diem amounts to compute meal expense deductions (and in some instances to claim deductions for incidental expenses) instead of keeping records to substantiate the actual amount of the expense. [34]

Employees or self-employeds whose work directly involves moving people or goods (e.g., by plane, bus, truck, ship) and regularly involves travel to different localities with different meal and incidental expense (M&IE) rates may for 2007 travel treat $52 as the federal M&IE (meals and incidental expenses) rate for any locality in the continental U.S. and $58 as the M&IE rate for any nonforeign locality outside the continental U.S. This method also can be used by payors of a per diem allowance only for M&IE away-from-home expenses to an employee in the transportation industry, if the payment qualifies as a regular meals-only allowance under the rules below. [35]

Employees and self-employed individuals who don't pay or incur meal expenses for a calendar day (or partial day) of 2007 travel away from home may deduct $3 per day for each away-from-home calendar (or partial) day. [36]

If a payor (employer, its agent, or third party) pays a per diem allowance only for meals and incidental expenses in lieu of reimbursing these actual expenses incurred for travel away from home, the amount that's deemed substantiated is the lesser of the per diem allowance or the amount computed at the federal M&IE rate (¶1576) for the locality of travel for each calendar day (or part of a day) the employee is away from home. [37]

30. ¶L-4713; ¶2744.16; TD ¶296,014
31. ¶L-4700; ¶624.02
32. ¶L-4630; ¶2744.10; TD ¶295,324
33. ¶L-4633; TD ¶295,326

34. ¶L-4632; ¶2744.10; TD ¶294,502
35. ¶L-4721; ¶2744.17; TD ¶296,026
36. ¶L-4632.1; ¶2744.17; TD ¶295,325.1
37. ¶s L-4632, L-4717; ¶2744.10; TD ¶296,019

Using standard per diem amounts only releases the taxpayer from the duty of substantiating the actual amount. *Time, place and business purpose must still be substantiated.*

An employee who is out of pocket for M&IE or is reimbursed under a nonaccountable plan may deduct an amount computed under this method only as an itemized deduction (subject to the percentage limit on meal and entertainment expenses, ¶1570, and then to the 2%-of-AGI floor on miscellaneous itemized deductions, ¶3110). A self-employed individual deducts the amount in determining adjusted gross income. This deduction is subject to the percentage limit on meal and entertainment expenses. [38]

¶ 1583 Proving entertainment expenses.

For entertainment expenses, all these elements must be proved:

(1) The amount of each separate expenditure, except that incidental items like cab fares and telephone calls may be aggregated on a separate basis.

(2) The date the entertainment took place.

(3) The name (if any), address or location, and the type of entertainment, such as dinner or theater, if that information isn't clear from the location.

(4) The reason for entertaining, or the nature of the business benefit derived or expected to be derived, and the nature of any business discussion or activity that took place. If deducting entertainment "associated with" the active conduct of business (¶1566), the date, duration, place and nature of the business discussion, the persons entertained who participated in the business discussion, and the business reason for the entertainment or the nature of business benefit derived or expected to be derived as the result of entertaining.

(5) The occupation or other information about the person or persons entertained, including name, title or other designation, sufficient to establish his business relationship to the taxpayer. (Reg § 1.274-5T(b)(4), Reg § 1.274-5T(b)(3))[39]

¶ 1584 Substantiating costs of listed property.

For listed property, all the relevant elements from the following list must be proved for each expenditure or business use of the property:

(1) The amount and date of each separate expenditure (for example, the cost and date of acquisition or leasing, the cost and date of maintenance and repairs, etc.).

(2) The amount and date of each use of the item of listed property for business or investment, based on an appropriate measure (mileage for automobiles and other property used for transportation, time for other types of property, unless IRS approves an alternative method), and the total use of the item of listed property for the tax period.

(3) The business purpose for each expenditure or use with respect to the listed property. (Reg § 1.274-5T(b)(6))[40]

For optional business standard mileage rate, see ¶1561.

¶ 1585 Adequate records of T&E expenses and listed-property expenses.

Adequate records of T&E expenses and of listed property expenditures and uses consist of a currently maintained account book, diary, log, statement of expenses, trip sheet, or similar record and, where necessary (¶1586), documentary evidence such as receipts and paid bills, which together are sufficient to establish each element of every expenditure or use that must be substantiated. Information reflected on a receipt need not be duplicated in an account book

---

38. ¶L-4632; ¶2744.18; TD ¶294,502
39. ¶L-4635; ¶2744.10; TD ¶295,327

40. ¶L-4644; ¶2744.10; TD ¶295,333

or other record so long as the account book or other record and the receipt complement each other in an orderly fashion. (Reg § 1.274-5T(c)(2)(i))[41] Both written and computer records are adequate records. (Reg § 1.274-5T(c)(2)(ii)(C)(2))[42]

Where the business purpose of an expenditure is evident from the surrounding facts and circumstances, a written explanation isn't required. (Reg § 1.274-5T(c)(2)(ii)(B))[43]

¶ 1586 Adequate documentary evidence to support lodging expenditures and other expenditures of $75 or more.

Documentary evidence, such as receipts or bills marked paid is required to support all expenditures for (1) lodging while away from home and (2) for any other expenses of $75 or more (except for transportation charges for which documentary evidence is not readily available). (Reg § 1.274-5(c)(2)(iii))[44]

Documentary evidence is ordinarily considered adequate to support an expenditure if it discloses the amount, date, place, and essential character of the expenditure. For example, a hotel receipt is sufficient to support expenditures for business travel if it contains the name and location of the hotel, the date or dates taxpayer stayed there, and separate amounts for charges such as for lodging, meals, and telephone. A restaurant receipt is sufficient to support an expenditure for a business meal if it contains the name and location of the restaurant, the date and amount of the expenditure, and an indication that a charge (if any) is made for an item other than meals and beverages. A canceled check, together with a bill from the payee, ordinarily will establish the cost but may not alone show business purpose. (Reg § 1.274-5(c)(2)(iii)[45] Documentary evidence need not be in the form of original documents. Faxes, copies, or printouts of e-mail (if they contain the necessary information) may also qualify. [46]

¶ 1587 Sufficiently corroborated statements used to substantiate expenses.

Taxpayers may substantiate the elements of their expenditures and uses not only by adequate records, but also by their own statements, written or oral, if those statements are supported by sufficient corroborating evidence. (Code Sec. 274(d))[47]

Corroborating evidence may be oral, but if so, should be from a disinterested, unrelated party who has knowledge of the expenditure or use in question. Written evidence has greater probative value, and its probative value increases if set down close to the time of the expenditure or use in question. (Reg § 1.274-5T(c)(1)) A taxpayer's written or oral statement must contain specific, detailed information about the element being substantiated, and the taxpayer must present other corroborative evidence sufficient to establish that element. (Reg § 1.274-5T(c)(3)(i))[48]

¶ 1588 Inadequate substantiation—remedies.

If a taxpayer hasn't fully substantiated a particular element of an expenditure or use, but does establish to IRS's satisfaction that he has substantially complied with the adequate records requirements, IRS may permit the taxpayer to establish the missing element by other evidence that it considers adequate. (Reg § 1.274-5T(c)(2)(v))

Where a taxpayer establishes that, by reason of "the inherent nature of the situation," he was unable to get either fully adequate records, or fully sufficient corroborating evidence in support of his own statement, he will be treated as satisfying the substantiation requirements if he presents other evidence that possesses the highest degree of probative value under the

41. ¶L-4616 *et seq.*; ¶2744.13; TD ¶295,311
42. ¶L-4616; ¶2744.13; TD ¶295,312
43. ¶L-4609; ¶2744.13; TD ¶295,307
44. ¶s L-4603, L-4619; ¶2744.13; TD ¶295,316

45. ¶L-4619; ¶2744.13; TD ¶295,316
46. ¶L-4616; ¶2744.13; TD ¶295,316
47. ¶L-4626 *et seq.*; ¶2744.14; TD ¶295,323
48. ¶L-4626; ¶2744.14; TD ¶295,323

circumstances. (Reg § 1.274-5T(c)(4))[49]

Where a taxpayer establishes that he has maintained adequate records of an expenditure or use, but can't produce them because they have been lost through circumstances beyond his control (e.g., damage by fire, flood, earthquake or other casualty), he may prove his entitlement to a deduction by a reasonable reconstruction of the expenditure or use in question. (Reg § 1.274-5T(c)(5))[50] Destruction of records in marital disputes has been held to fall within this rule.[1]

¶ 1589 Business Gifts and Employee Awards. ▬▬▬▬▬▬

The costs of ordinary and necessary business gifts to individuals other than employees are deductible, subject to a $25 per-year per-person limit. Gifts to employees aren't deductible as gifts, but may be deductible as compensation. Certain noncash awards to employees are deductible.

¶ 1590 Business gifts.

The cost of ordinary and necessary business gifts may be deducted up to $25 a year to any one individual. Gift means any item excludable from gross income by the recipient under Code Sec. 102 (¶1212), but not excludable under any other Code income tax provision. (Code Sec. 274(b))[2] However, any item for general distribution having a cost of not more than $4 and on which the giver's name is clearly and permanently imprinted, and signs, display racks, or other promotional material donated to a retailer to be used on his business premises, aren't classified as gifts. (Code Sec. 274(b)(1); Reg § 1.274-3(b)(2))[3]

Since no amount transferred by or for an employer to or for the benefit of an employee is excludable as a gift (under Code Sec. 102) no such amount is deductible as a gift, though it may be deductible under other rules (e.g., as compensation).[4]

¶ 1591 Employee achievement awards.

An employer can deduct the cost of employee achievement awards (defined below). (Code Sec. 274(j)) The maximum deduction for awards made to one employee is $400 per year ($1,600 if the award is a qualified plan award, including the cost of awards that aren't qualified plan awards). (Code Sec. 274(j)(2)) The award must be given as part of a meaningful presentation under conditions and circumstances that don't create a likelihood that the payment is disguised compensation. (Code Sec. 274(j)(3))

An employee achievement award is an item of tangible personal property awarded to an employee because of length of service achievement, or safety achievement. (Code Sec. 274(j)(3))[5] Tangible personal property doesn't include cash or any gift certificate other than a nonnegotiable gift certificate conferring only the right to receive tangible personal property. (Reg § 1.274-3(b)(2)(iv))

A qualified plan award is an item awarded as part of a permanent, written, nondiscriminatory plan of the employer. (Code Sec. 274(j)(3)(B); Reg § 1.274-3(d))

A length-of-service award won't qualify for deduction under these rules if given during an employee's first five years of employment, or if a length-of-service award was given to the same employee during the same year or any of the earlier four years. (Code Sec. 274(j)(4)(B))

Safety achievement awards don't qualify if given to managerial, administrative, professional or clerical employees, or if such awards previously have been given to more than 10% of

---

49. ¶L-4628; ¶2744.15; TD ¶295,310
50. ¶L-4623; ¶2744.15; TD ¶295,320
1. ¶L-4624; TD ¶295,321
2. ¶L-2306; ¶2744.08; TD ¶303,005

3. ¶L-2306; ¶2744.08; TD ¶303,007
4. ¶H-4009; ¶1624.363; TD ¶278,309
5. ¶L-2313; ¶2744.09; TD ¶303,012

other employees during the year. (Code Sec. 274(j)(4)(C))[6]

No deduction is allowed for an employee achievement award (under the normal Code Sec. 162 ordinary and necessary rules or the Code Sec. 212 production of income rules) except under the above rules. (Code Sec. 274(j)(1))[7]

¶ 1592 Substantiating business gift expenses.

To substantiate business gift expenses adequate records or a sufficiently corroborated statement must show: (1) a description of the gift, (2) the taxpayer's cost, (3) when the gift was made, (4) the occupation or other information about the gift's recipient, including his name, title, or other designation sufficient to establish his business relationship to the taxpayer, and (5) the reason for making the gift or the nature of business benefit derived or expected. (Reg § 1.274-5T(b)(5))[8]

¶ 1593 Rent Expense.

Rent is deductible if paid for the use of property used in whole or in part in the taxpayer's trade, business, or profession, or for the production of income.

Rent for the use of real or personal property in the taxpayer's trade, business, or profession, is deductible. (Code Sec. 162(a)(3)) But rent for personal-use property isn't. (Code Sec. 262(a); Reg § 1.262-1(b)(3))[9]

Besides normal cash rent payable periodically, rent includes a lump sum paid as advance rental, bonus, etc.; a percentage of the tenant's receipts or profits; the tenant's payment of the expenses of maintaining the rented property (taxes, insurance, etc.), and payment in property other than money (deductible to the extent of the property's fair market value). [10]

¶ 1594 Rent paid to related lessor.

Rentals paid between parties who are related either as members of a family or by stock ownership may not be deductible to the extent that they exceed the rent that would have been paid in an arm's-length transaction.

A corporation may deduct fair and reasonable rentals paid to corporate shareholders or their relatives. But excessive rentals can be treated as nondeductible dividends. [11] Reasonable rental payments by a shareholder for use of corporate property are deductible. [12]

¶ 1595 Rent under leaseback arrangements.

A transfer by sale or gift coupled with a leaseback may be more advantageous than a mortgage loan and can create tax benefits for the transferor. Tax advantages (including rent deduction) of a sale and leaseback arrangement may be lost if IRS treats it as a mortgage loan, a tax-free exchange, or a sham transaction. [13]

A gift in trust with a leaseback of the property to the grantor will generally be upheld as a valid rental or royalty arrangement by the courts if: (1) the transfer is complete and irrevocable, (2) the trustee is independent, and (3) the rental is reasonable. Reasonableness of rent and the independence of the trustee are questions of fact. [14]

6. ¶L-2315; ¶2744.09; TD ¶303,014
7. ¶L-2313 *et seq.*; ¶2744.09; TD ¶303,012
8. ¶L-4643; ¶2744.10; TD ¶295,332
9. ¶L-6604; ¶1624.285; TD ¶260,501
10. ¶L-6605 *et seq.*; ¶1624.285; TD ¶260,505

11. ¶L-6702; ¶1624.299; TD ¶260,522
12. ¶L-6710; ¶1624.299 TD ¶260,522
13. ¶L-6300 *et seq.*; ¶1624.299; TD ¶262,500
14. ¶L-6317; TD ¶262,510

¶ 1596   Rent or purchase; lease with purchase options.

A payment is deductible as rent only if the taxpayer-lessee hasn't taken or isn't taking title to the property and has no equity interest in it. (Code Sec. 162(a)(3)) Thus, payments made under conditional sales contracts aren't deductible as rent. [15]

A lease that contains an option permitting the lessee to buy the property may be construed as a sale so that none of the payments is deductible as rent. Whether the lease is considered to be a sale depends essentially upon the intent of the parties, as shown in the agreement, read in light of the facts and circumstances existing at the time the agreement was made. [16] Important factors indicating sale instead of lease include nominal option price, excessive rent, designating part of the payment as interest, rental plus option price equal to the property's value plus interest, and application of rent payments to the lessee's equity in the property. [17]

¶ 1597   Lease acquisition costs.

Payments made by a lessee to get a business lease aren't currently deductible but must be amortized over the period specified below. (Reg § 1.162-11(a)) This rule applies whether the tenant is on the cash or accrual basis and even though he has an option to buy the property. [18]

If the lease isn't renewable, lease acquisition costs are amortized over the unexpired term of the lease. [19] If the lease is renewable any renewal period must be taken into account in determining the amortization period, if less than 75% of the lease cost is attributable to the portion of the lease (exclusive of the renewal period) remaining on the date of acquisition of the lease. [20]

¶ 1598   Lessor's costs.

Costs incurred by a lessor in leasing his property, or by a lessee in subletting, aren't currently deductible but must be amortized ratably over the term of the lease. [21] For tax treatment of construction allowances, see ¶1344.

The cost of MACRS improvements made by lessors are recoverable over the cost recovery period applicable to the leasehold improvements —regardless of the period of time the property is leased. (Code Sec. 168(i)(8))[22]

A lessor's payments for cancellation of a lease must be amortized and deducted over the remaining term of the *cancelled* lease, [23] except that if the payment is made in order to enter a lease with a new tenant, the payment must be amortized over the term of the *new* lease. [24]

¶ 1599   Year of deduction for rent.

The tax year in which the rent is paid by a cash basis taxpayer or incurred by an accrual basis taxpayer is generally the proper year for deduction. [25] But advance rentals must be apportioned and deducted over the term of the lease or other rental period. [26]

¶ 1600   Deferred payments for the use of property or services.

Rent and interest attributable to a deferred rental agreement must be both reported and deducted as if both parties are accrual basis taxpayers. This rule applies to leases of over

---

15. ¶L-6209; ¶1624.284; TD ¶260,502
16. ¶L-6222 *et seq.*; ¶1624.305; TD ¶260,502
17. ¶L-6200 *et seq.*; ¶1624.305; TD ¶260,502
18. ¶L-6501; ¶1624.323; TD ¶261,501
19. ¶s L-6501, L-6504; ¶1624.323; TD ¶261,505
20. ¶L-6504 *et seq.*; ¶1624.323; TD ¶261,504

21. ¶L-6401; ¶1624.081; TD ¶262,001
22. ¶L-6404; ¶1674.023; TD ¶262,004
23. ¶L-6405; ¶1624.081; TD ¶262,005
24. ¶L-6407; ¶1624.081; TD ¶262,006
25. ¶L-6616; ¶1624.285; TD ¶260,536
26. ¶L-6617; ¶s 1624.081, 1624.285; TD ¶260,537

$250,000 that require either: (1) at least one payment for the use of property to be paid after the close of the calendar year following the calendar year of the use of the property, or (2) increases (or decreases) in the amounts to be paid as rent. (Code Sec. 467)[27]

For lessees, the deductible rental amount for the tax year is the sum of:

(1) rent deemed accrued by allocating rents in accordance with the rental agreement, taking into account the present value of rent to be paid after the close of the period, and

(2) interest for the year on amounts taken into account for earlier tax years (under (1), above), but which are as yet unpaid. (Code Sec. 467(b)(1))[28]

Present value and interest are computed using a rate equal to 110% of the applicable federal rate (¶1116). (Code Sec. 467(e)(4))[29]

If the agreement is silent as to rent allocation or the agreement is a disqualified leaseback or long-term agreement, then constant rental accrual applies. (Code Sec. 467(b)(2), Code Sec. 467(b)(3)) The constant rental amount is an amount paid as of the close of each lease period which would result in a total present value equal to the present value of the total payments required under the lease. (Code Sec. 467(e)(1))[30]

A rental agreement is a disqualified leaseback or long-term agreement if:

(1) it is part of a leaseback transaction to any person who had an interest in the leased property within two years before the leaseback (Code Sec. 467(e)(2)), or the term of the agreement exceeds 75% of a prescribed recovery period (Code Sec. 467(b)(4)), *and*

(2) a principal purpose of the increased rents provided in the agreement is tax avoidance. (Code Sec. 467(b)(4))[31]

An agreement isn't a disqualified leaseback or long-term agreement if it qualifies for any of the various safe harbors, including the uneven rent test, which is met if the rent allocated to each calendar year does not vary from the average rent allocated to all calendar years by more than 10%. (Reg § 1.467-3(c))

Under regs to be issued, similar rules will apply to certain deferred payments for services. (Code Sec. 467(g))[32]

A reasonable rent holiday won't cause an agreement to be treated as a disqualified leaseback or long-term agreement. (Code Sec. 467(b)(5)) A rent holiday of 3 months or less at the beginning of the lease term is disregarded in determining if the rental agreement has increasing or decreasing rent. (Reg § 1.467-1(c)(2)(i)(B)) A lessor's granting of an 11.5 month zero rent period in a 25-year lease was held to be a reasonable rent holiday in an area where such inducements were needed to attract lessees. [33]

¶ 1601   Research and Experimental Expenditures. ▮▮▮▮▮▮▮▮▮▮▮

Taxpayers can choose whether to immediately deduct or to capitalize research and experimental (R&E) expenditures. In some cases, they also have the option of writing off the expenditures over several years.

¶ 1602   Deduct or capitalize research & experimental expenditures.

Taxpayers can choose whether to immediately deduct or to capitalize research and experimental (R&E) expenditures. (Code Sec. 174(a)(1)) If the taxpayer adopts current expense treatment, he must use it for all qualifying expenses for the year he adopts it and for all later years, unless he gets IRS permission to switch. (Code Sec. 174(a)(3))[34]

27. ¶s L-6800, L-6801.13; ¶4674; TD ¶261,001
28. ¶L-6803; ¶4674; TD ¶261,035
29. ¶L-6804
30. ¶L-6805; ¶4674; TD ¶261,043

31. ¶L-6808; ¶4674; TD ¶261,050
32. ¶G-3451; ¶4674; TD ¶446,801
33. ¶L-6812; ¶4674; TD ¶261,053
34. ¶L-3117; ¶1744; TD ¶306,508

For R&E expenditures that aren't chargeable to depreciable or depletable property, instead of current deduction or capitalizing the taxpayer can elect (use Form 4562) to deduct the expenditures ratably over 60 months or longer, beginning with the month the taxpayer first realized benefits from the expenditures. (Code Sec. 174(b)(1); Reg § 1.174-4(b)(1))[35]

In general, expenditures that qualify as R&E costs are research and development costs in the experimental or laboratory sense. This includes all costs incident to the development or improvement of a product, including a pilot model, process, formula, invention, technique, patent or similar property. (Reg § 1.174-2(a))[36]

All taxpayers, including partners and S corporation shareholders, may elect to deduct all or any portion of these costs ratably over ten years. (Code Sec. 59(e)(1); Reg § 1.59-1)[37]

For limitations on deductions for R&E expenses that also qualify for the research credit or the orphan drug credit, see ¶ 2318 and ¶2329. For alternative minimum tax treatment of research and experimentation expenditures, see ¶ 3208.

¶ 1603 Legal and Accounting Expenses. ▬▬▬▬▬▬▬▬▬▬▬▬▬▬▬▬▬▬▬▬▬▬▬▬▬▬

Legal expenses and accounting and related expenses may be deductible.

For expenses of determining or contesting tax liability, see ¶1513.

¶ 1604 Legal expenses.

Attorney's fees, court costs and other legal expenses can qualify as deductible business expenses. Legal expenses aren't deductible if they are either capital expenditures or a personal expense of the taxpayer. (Code Sec. 162, Code Sec. 262(a), Code Sec. 263)[38] Qualified legal expenses can include expenses incurred in litigation, for legal advice, and for the drafting of instruments,[39] but not to acquire, perfect or defend title to property. (Reg § 1.212-1(k))[40] A legal retainer must be capitalized if it is applied to legal expenses associated with the acquisition of a business. [41]

¶ 1605 Accounting and related expenses.

Fees for bookkeeping and accounting work incurred in the operation of the taxpayer's business are deductible. [42]

¶ 1606 Insurance Premiums. ▬▬▬▬▬▬▬▬▬▬▬▬▬▬▬▬▬▬▬▬▬▬▬▬▬▬▬▬

Certain premiums that qualify as trade or business expenses, or as investment expenses, are deductible.

¶ 1607 Insurance premiums on nonlife policies.

Premiums for insurance against various types of risks, such as property damage, are generally deductible as business expenses (Code Sec. 162; Reg § 1.162-1(a)), but premiums on policies on taxpayer's residence, or for other personal use, aren't. (Code Sec. 262(a); Reg § 1.262-1(b))[43] Payments to an insurance company to assume capped costs certain to be incurred in the future isn't insurance for tax purposes. [44]

Self-insurance reserve funds aren't deductible even if taxpayer can't get business insurance

---

35. ¶L-3121 *et seq.*; ¶1744; TD ¶306,512
36. ¶L-3117; ¶1744; TD ¶306,505
37. ¶A-8194; ¶594; TD ¶695,503
38. ¶s L-2901, L-2969; ¶1624.040; TD ¶305,004
39. ¶L-2902; ¶1624.040; TD ¶305,004

40. ¶L-2908; ¶2634.01; TD ¶305,010
41. ¶L-2901.1; TD ¶305,002
42. ¶L-2959; TD ¶305,061
43. ¶L-3500 *et seq.*; ¶1624.032; TD ¶304,404
44. ¶L-3517

coverage for certain business risks. [45] Neither are payments to "captive" insurance subsidiaries or other similar arrangements where there's no true risk-shifting. [46] But a limited deduction is allowed for certain payments made to a medical malpractice self-insurance pool. [47]

Premiums are nondeductible capital expenditures where paid for property insurance during construction. So are premiums for title insurance and for public liability and worker's compensation insurance paid in connection with the construction of a building. [48]

¶ 1608   Life insurance premiums.

Life insurance premiums aren't deductible if the taxpayer is directly or indirectly a beneficiary. (Code Sec. 264(a)(1); Reg § 1.264-1) See ¶1526. For example, the cost of a corporation's key person insurance isn't deductible. [49] Premiums paid by an individual for personal life insurance aren't deductible. (Reg § 1.262-1(b)(1))[50] For group-term premiums, see ¶1526.

¶ 1609   Time for deducting insurance premiums.

If a cash basis taxpayer pays an otherwise deductible premium for one year's coverage which applies in part to the following tax year, the entire premium is deductible in the year paid. But if premiums for several years are paid in advance, IRS and most courts require the premium to be amortized and deducted over the life of the policy, though one court has allowed a full deduction to a cash basis taxpayer in the year of payment where the taxpayer had consistently deducted premiums in the year of payment.

For an accrual basis taxpayer, deductibility of an accrued liability for insurance expense is determined under the economic performance rules —that is, when the premium is paid. But where prepaid premiums cover more than one year, an accrual basis taxpayer must prorate the premium paid in advance over the life of the policy. [1]

For the "12-month rule" exception to capitalization of certain intangibles, see ¶1671.

¶ 1610   Bribes, Kickbacks, Fines and Penalties. ▬▬▬▬▬▬

Certain illegal bribes, kickbacks, rebates and other payments aren't deductible. Nor are fines and penalties for violation of a law, including tax penalties.

Public policy isn't a ground for denying deduction. Unless a payment is nondeductible by law, it's deductible if ordinary and necessary. (Reg § 1.162-1)[2]

¶ 1611   Bribes and other illegal payments.

No deduction is allowed for any illegal bribe, kickback or other illegal payment under any law of the U.S., or of a state (if the state law is generally enforced), that subjects the payor to a criminal penalty or the loss of license or privilege to engage in business, whether or not that penalty or loss of license actually occurs. A kickback includes a payment in consideration of the referral of a client, patient, or customer. (Code Sec. 162(c)(2))[3]

No deduction is allowed for any kickback, rebate, or bribe made by any provider of services, supplier, physician, or other person who furnishes Medicare or Medicaid items or services, if made in connection with the furnishing of such items or services or the making or receiving of such payments. A kickback includes a payment for the referral of a client, patient, or customer. For these payments, deduction is denied regardless of legality. (Code Sec. 162(c)(3))[4]

No business expense deduction is allowed for any illegal bribe or kickback made directly or

45. ¶L-3518; ¶1624.032; TD ¶304,423
46. ¶L-3520; ¶1624.032; TD ¶304,425
47. ¶L-3515; TD ¶304,413
48. ¶L-3530; TD ¶304,429
49. ¶L-3407; ¶2644; TD ¶304,006

50. ¶L-3401; ¶2644; TD ¶304,001
1. ¶L-3526 *et seq.*; ¶1624.081; TD ¶304,430 *et seq.*
2. ¶L-2609; ¶1624.377; TD ¶304,804
3. ¶L-2606; ¶1624.384; TD ¶304,801
4. ¶L-2608; ¶1624.384; TD ¶304,807

indirectly to any federal, state, or local public official or employee. If the payment is to an official or an employee of a foreign government, no deduction is allowed if the payment violates the U.S. Foreign Corrupt Practices Act. (Code Sec. 162(c)(1))[5]

Business kickbacks, fee-splitting, etc., that aren't specifically disallowed are deductible if they qualify as ordinary and necessary. [6]

¶ 1612   Illegal businesses and drug trafficking.

The ordinary and necessary expenses incurred in operating an illegal business are deductible, even though payment of the expense and the acts performed by the employees of the business are illegal (e.g., a bookmaker's expenses). [7] But there's no deduction or credit for amounts paid or incurred in illegal drug trafficking (Code Sec. 280E), although gross receipts may be adjusted for cost of goods sold. [8]

¶ 1613   Fines and penalties.

No business expense deduction is allowed for fines or similar penalties paid to a government for the violation of any law. (Code Sec. 162(f))[9] For example, state law penalties on public school teachers for striking aren't deductible. Similarly, penalties paid for violating federal environmental protection laws aren't deductible. [10]

Also, penalties paid in connection with federal, state, and local taxes are generally not deductible—for example, penalties for negligence, delinquency, or fraud relating to federal taxes (Reg § 1.162-21(b)), and for failure to withhold federal payroll taxes. [11]

¶ 1614   Domestic Production Activities Deduction. ■■■■■■■■■

Taxpayers are allowed a domestic production activities deduction (DPAD) under Code Sec. 199 equal to the specified percentage for the tax year of the taxpayer's qualified production activities income for the tax year, subject to certain limits.

¶ 1615   Deduction for manufacturing and production activities—Form 8903.

Taxpayers may claim a deduction on Form 8903 generally equal to 6% (for tax years beginning in 2007-2009, 9% for later years) of the lesser of: (1) the taxpayer's "qualified production activities income" (¶1616) for the tax year or (2) taxable income (modified adjusted gross income, for individual taxpayers) without regard to this deduction, for the tax year. (Code Sec. 199(a); Reg § 1.199-1(a))

The deduction as computed above is limited to 50% of the W-2 wages of the employer for the tax year. W-2 wages are the sum of the aggregate amounts that must be included on the employees' Forms W-2 under Code Sec. 6051(a)(3) (i.e., wages subject to withholding) and Code Sec. 6051(a)(8) (elective deferrals), that are made by the taxpayer during the calendar year that ends in the tax year. (Code Sec. 199(b); Reg § 1.199-1(a))[12] W-2 wages are the wages of employees including common-law employees and officers of a corporate employer which are properly included in a return filed with the Social Security Administration on or before the 60th day after the due date (including extensions) for that return. For tax years beginning after May 17, 2006, W-2 wages only include amounts that are properly allocable to domestic production gross receipts (¶1616). (Code Sec. 199(b)(2), Reg § 1.199-2(a)(1)) This allocation may be made using any reasonable method that satisfies IRS based on all facts and circumstances. (Reg § 1.199-2T) IRS has provided three alternative methods for calculating

5. ¶L-2601; ¶1624.384; TD ¶304,801
6. ¶L-2601; ¶1624.384; TD ¶304,804
7. ¶L-2631; ¶1624.382; TD ¶304,815
8. ¶L-2632; ¶280E4; TD ¶304,815

9. ¶L-2701 *et seq.*; ¶1624.388; TD ¶302,501
10. ¶L-2701; ¶1624.388; TD ¶302,501
11. ¶L-2709; ¶1624.388; TD ¶302,507
12. ¶L-4325; ¶1994; TD ¶307,800

W-2 wages. [13]

The deduction is directly available to all taxpayers except pass-through entities (partnerships, S corporations, trusts and estates) and is available to owners of pass-through entities. (Code Sec. 199(d)) The deduction for partnerships and S corporations is determined at the partner or shareholder level. For tax years beginning after May 17, 2006, partners or shareholders are treated as having W-2 wages equal to their allocable share of the partnership's or S corporation's W-2 wages for the tax year. (Code Sec. 199(d)(1)(A))

For treatment of the deduction for alternative minimum tax, see ¶3201.

¶ 1616   Qualified production activities income defined.

"Qualified production activities income" is equal to domestic production gross receipts (DPGR), reduced by the sum of: (1) the costs of goods sold that are allocable to the receipts; (2) other deductions, expenses, or losses that are allocable to these receipts; and (3) a ratable portion of other deductions, expenses, and losses that are not directly allocable to the receipts or to another class of income. (Code Sec. 199(c))[14]

DPGR is the taxpayer's gross receipts derived from:

. . . any lease, rental, license, sale, exchange or other disposition of qualifying production property—i.e., tangible personal property, many types of computer software and certain sound recordings (Code Sec. 199(c)(5))[15]—that was manufactured, produced, grown or extracted by the taxpayer in whole or in significant part within the U.S. (Code Sec. 199(c)(4)(A)(i)(I)),[16] Gross receipts from providing computer software to customers for their direct use while connected to the Internet may be treated as DPGR if certain conditions are met. (Reg § 1.199-3(i)(6)(iii))

. . . any lease, rental, license, sale, exchange or other disposition of qualified films produced by the taxpayer. (Code Sec. 199(c)(4)(A)(i)(II)) The taxpayer's production of the qualified film must be substantial in nature, taking into account all the facts and circumstances. (Prop Reg. § 1.199-3(k)(6), "Taxpayers may rely") A qualified film is one for which 50% of the total compensation for production of the film is for services performed in the U.S. by actors, production personnel, directors and producers, and which does not depict certain sexually explicit conduct. (Code Sec. 199(c)(6))[17]

. . . any sale, exchange or other disposition of electricity, natural gas, or potable water produced by the taxpayer in the U.S. (Code Sec. 199(c)(4)(A)(i)(III))

. . . construction of real property performed in the U.S. by a taxpayer engaged in the active conduct of a construction trade or business in the ordinary course of that trade or business (Code Sec. 199(c)(4)(A)(ii)),[18] including construction and substantial renovation of residential and commercial buildings and infrastructure, such as roads, power lines, water systems, and communications facilities. A taxpayer qualifies for the deduction even if it doesn't own the property being constructed, and more than one taxpayer may qualify for the same construction project.[19] Gross receipts from the rental of real property that the taxpayer builds are not derived from construction and are not eligible for the deduction.[20] Generally, for tax years beginning after May 31, 2006, construction includes certain grading, demolition (including under Code Sec. 280B (¶1783)), clearing, excavating, and other activities that physically transform the land. (Reg § 1.199-3(m)(2)(iii), Reg § 1.199-3(m))

. . . engineering or architectural services with respect to the construction of real property in the U.S. performed in the U.S. by a taxpayer engaged in the active conduct of an engineering or architectural services trade or business in the ordinary course of that trade or

13. ¶L-4385.1; ¶1994.010; TD ¶307,803
14. ¶L-4367; ¶1994.084; TD ¶307,804
15. ¶L-4352; ¶1994.064; TD ¶307,805
16. ¶L-4327.1 ¶1994.036; TD ¶307,805

17. ¶L-4356; ¶1994.070; TD ¶307,805
18. ¶L-4340; ¶1994.036; TD ¶307,805
19. ¶L-4335; ¶1994.036; TD ¶307,805
20. ¶L-4350; ¶1994.036; TD ¶307,805

business. (Code Sec. 199(c)(4)(A)(iii))[21]

Various de minimis rules are available for the computation of DPGR. (Reg § 1.199-1(d), Reg § 1.199-3)[22] Statistical sampling methods may be used if detailed conditions are met. [23] For a taxpayer's first two tax years beginning after 2005 and before 2008, Puerto Rico is included in the term "U.S." in determining DPGR. (Code Sec. 199(d)(8))

Qualifying production property is treated as manufactured, produced, grown or extracted in whole or in significant part within the U.S. if, based on all of the facts and circumstances, the manufacturing, production, etc., activity performed in the U.S. is substantial in nature, or, under a safe harbor, if the direct labor and overhead costs incurred by the taxpayer in the U.S. for the manufacture, production, growth, or extraction of the property are at least 20% of the taxpayer's (1) total cost for the property, or (2) unadjusted basis in the property, in a transaction without cost of goods sold (e.g., a lease). (Reg § 1.199-3(g)(3)(i))[24]

DPGR does not include gross receipts derived from:

. . . the sale of food or beverages prepared by the taxpayer at a retail establishment (Code Sec. 199(c)(4)(B)(i)), i.e., tangible property used in the trade or business of selling food or beverages to the public if retail (rather than wholesale) sales occur at the facility. A facility won't be treated as a retail establishment if less than 5% of total gross receipts for the tax year derived from the sale of food or beverages prepared at the facility are for retail sales. If a facility is a retail establishment, but food or beverages are prepared there and sold at wholesale, the taxpayer may allocate its gross receipts. [25]

. . . the transmission or distribution of electricity, natural gas, or potable water. (Code Sec. 199(c)(4)(B)(ii))[26]

. . . the lease, rental, license, sale, exchange, or other disposition of land. (Code Sec. 199(c)(4)(B)(iii))[27]

. . . property leased, licensed, or rented by the taxpayer for use by any related person (defined in Code Sec. 199(c)(7)(B)). (Code Sec. 199(c)(7)(A))[28]

In computing qualified production activities income, taxpayers may allocate cost of goods sold, and other expenses, deductions, etc., between DPGR and other gross receipts under any reasonable method. However, if the taxpayer has the necessary information readily available, and can do so without undue burden and expense, the taxpayer must make these allocations using a specific identification method under the regs. (Reg § 1.199-1(d)(2))[29]

¶ 1617   Miscellaneous Business Expenses. ▬▬▬▬▬▬▬▬▬▬▬▬▬▬▬

Royalty payments, circulation costs, mine exploration and development costs, and other miscellaneous costs of carrying on a business are deductible subject to certain conditions and limits.

¶ 1618   Royalty payments.

Royalty payments made for the right to use patents, copyrights and similar rights are deductible.[30] Payments to acquire the property itself are capital expenditures. [31]

21. ¶L-4338; ¶1994.036; TD ¶307,805
22. ¶L-4338, ¶1994.034, TD ¶307,853
23. ¶L-4336.4, ¶1994.129; TD ¶307,821.1
24. ¶L-4330; ¶1994.036; TD ¶307,805
25. ¶L-4330; ¶1994.036; TD ¶307,805
26. ¶L-4334; ¶1994.036; TD ¶307,805

27. ¶L-4350; ¶1994.074 *et seq.*; TD ¶307,805
28. ¶L-4346; ¶1994.038; TD ¶307,805
29. ¶L-4367.1; ¶1994.084; TD ¶307,804
30. ¶L-3201; ¶1624.284; TD ¶307,501
31. ¶L-3203; ¶1624.284; TD ¶307,505

¶ 1619   Circulation costs.

Publishers of periodicals can deduct currently their expenditures to establish, maintain and increase circulation. (Code Sec. 173)[32] Or, instead, they may elect to capitalize those costs. (Reg § 1.173-1(c))[33] A taxpayer may elect (use Form 4562) to amortize circulation costs over three years beginning with the year the expenditure is made. (Code Sec. 59(e)(1); Reg § 1.59-1) For alternative minimum tax treatment of circulation costs, see ¶3209.

¶ 1620   Serial contingent payments for franchises, trademarks, or trade names.

In the case of a transfer of a franchise, trademark or trade name, a deduction is allowed to the transferee for serial payments contingent on the productivity, use, or disposition of the franchise, trademark or trade name transferred. (Code Sec. 1253(d)(1))[34]

¶ 1621   Stock reacquisition expenses.

No deduction is allowed for any amount paid or incurred by a corporation in connection with the reacquisition of its stock (e.g., greenmail) or of the stock of any related person as specially defined in Code Sec. 465(b)(3)(C). Amounts deductible as interest under Code Sec. 163 or as dividends paid under Code Sec. 561 are among expenses not subject to this rule. (Code Sec. 162(k)) The no-deduction rule doesn't apply to deductions for amounts properly allocable to indebtedness (e.g., loan commitment fees) and amortized over the term of the indebtedness. (Code Sec. 162(k)(2)(A)(ii))[35]

¶ 1622   Co-op housing maintenance and lease expenses.

Cooperative housing maintenance and lease expenses are deductible if the cooperative unit is used in a trade or business or for the production of income. However, no deduction is allowed to the co-op stockholder for any payment to the co-op (in excess of the stockholder's share of taxes and interest) to the extent the payment is properly allocable to amounts chargeable to the co-op's capital account. The basis of the stockholder's stock is increased by the amount of any deduction disallowed under this rule. (Code Sec. 216(d))[36]

¶ 1623   Mine exploration costs.

Domestic mine exploration costs incurred before a mine has reached the development stage are nondeductible capital expenditures. However, taxpayers may elect to deduct mining exploration expenditures for minerals (other than oil and gas) that qualify for percentage depletion (Code Sec. 617).[37]

Deducted exploration costs are subject to recapture when the mine reaches the producing stage, when taxpayer receives a bonus or royalty, or when he disposes of all or part of the property, whichever happens first (except where IRS allows recapture to be postponed on disposition of a *part* interest). (Code Sec. 617(b)(1); Code Sec. 1254(a)(1); Reg § 1.1254-1(b))[38]

All taxpayers, including partners and S corporation shareholders, may elect (use Form 4562) to deduct all or any portion of their deductible mine exploration costs ratably over ten years. (Code Sec. 59(e); Reg § 1.59-1)[39]

Corporations' deductions for exploration costs are cut back 30% if they elect to write off the costs in the year they are incurred. (Code Sec. 291(b)(1)) The amount cut back is amortized

---

32. ¶L-2213; ¶1734.01; TD ¶300,515
33. ¶L-2215 *et seq.*; ¶1734; TD ¶300,516
34. ¶I-8415 *et seq.*; ¶12534.01
35. ¶s L-5305, L-5411; ¶1624.402; TD ¶301,033

36. ¶K-5900 *et seq.*; ¶2164.01; TD ¶213,014
37. ¶N-3103; ¶6174
38. ¶N-3601 *et seq.*; ¶6174.01
39. ¶N-3114; ¶594

over 60 months. (Code Sec. 291(b))[40]

¶ 1624 Mine development costs.

A taxpayer who incurs expenditures to develop minerals other than oil or gas may: (1) deduct those expenditures in the year they were paid or incurred (Code Sec. 616(a));[41] (2) elect to treat them as deferred expenses and deduct them ratably as the units of produced minerals benefited by the expense are sold (Code Sec. 616(b); Reg § 1.616-2(a));[42] or (3) treat them as deferred expenses and elect (use Form 4562) to amortize them ratably over ten years. (Code Sec. 59(e); Reg § 1.59-1)[43]

Corporations' deductions for mine development costs are cut back 30% if the corporation elects to write off the costs in the year incurred. (Code Sec. 291(b)(1)(B)) The amount cut-back is amortized over 60 months. (Code Sec. 291(b))[44]

Deducted mine development costs are recaptured (on Form 4797) as ordinary income on disposition of the property. (Code Sec. 1254(a)(1); Reg § 1.1254-1(b))[45]

¶ 1625 Intangible oil and gas and geothermal well drilling and development costs.

Geological and geophysical costs incurred in exploring for oil and gas are capital expenditures.[46] Taxpayers, however, may capitalize, amortize (over 60 months) or expense the so-called intangible drilling and development costs (IDCs) of oil, gas and geothermal wells. (Code Sec. 59(e); Reg § 1.59-1; Code Sec. 263(c); Reg § 1.612-4, Reg § 1.612-5)[47] In general, such intangible costs include only those costs that in themselves don't have a salvage value, such as labor and fuel.[48] For alternative minimum tax treatment of IDCs, see ¶3207.

Deducted IDCs are recaptured (on Form 4797) as ordinary income on disposition of the oil or gas wells. (Code Sec. 1254(a)(1)(A); Reg § 1.1254-1(b))[49]

¶ 1626 Lobbying costs, influencing public on legislation.

Deductible business expenses don't include:

. . . any amount paid or incurred (1) in influencing legislation; (2) in connection with participation in or intervention in any political campaign or any attempt to influence the general public with respect to elections, legislative matters, or referendums; or (3) in communicating directly with a covered executive branch official on official matters (Code Sec. 162(e)(1)),

. . . the portion of dues paid to a tax-exempt organization allocable to lobbying by the organization for which no deduction is allowed, if the organization informs taxpayer of the nondeductible portion. (Code Sec. 162(e)(3))

Taxpayers must allocate their costs between legislative-branch lobbying and executive-branch lobbying in determining the nondeductible amount by consistently using a reasonable method. (Reg § 1.162-28(a)(1), Reg § 1.162-29(c)(2))[50]

In-house expenditures of $2,000 or less per year aren't subject to these rules. (Code Sec. 162(e)(5)(B)(i))

The disallowance concerning influencing legislation, above, doesn't apply to legislation of a local government. (Code Sec. 162(e)(2)(A))[1]

---

40. ¶N-3104; ¶2914; TD ¶600,502
41. ¶N-3116; ¶6164; TD ¶213,512
42. ¶N-3123; ¶6164
43. ¶N-3124; ¶6164.04; TD ¶695,503
44. ¶N-3104; ¶2914
45. ¶N-3309 *et seq.*

46. ¶N-3201; ¶6124.001; TD ¶695,503
47. ¶N-3202 *et seq.*; ¶6124.008
48. ¶N-3206; ¶6124.009
49. ¶N-3406; ¶12,544 *et seq.*
50. ¶L-2400 *et seq.* ¶1624.395; TD ¶306,000 *et seq.*
1. ¶L-2401 *et seq.*; ¶1624.395; TD ¶306,012

¶ 1627 Civil damages.

Civil damages paid under judgments and out-of-court settlements arising out of normal business operations are deductible as business expenses [2] if the litigation is directly connected with the taxpayer's business. [3]

No deduction is allowed for two-thirds of treble damage or settlement payments to private parties where the taxpayer (payor) in a criminal proceeding for violation of federal anti-trust law is convicted or pleads guilty or no contest. (Code Sec. 162(g); Reg § 1.162-22)[4]

¶ 1628 Employee Business Expenses. ■■■■■■■■■■■■■■■■■■■■■■

Employees are engaged in the trade or business of being employees and thus can deduct certain employment-connected business expenses, such as travel expenses, union dues, work clothes, etc., as described in the following paragraphs.

Unreimbursed employee business expenses are generally deductible only as miscellaneous itemized deductions subject to the 2%-of-AGI floor, see ¶3110. (Reg § 1.67-1T(a)(1)(i))[5] For unreimbursed moving expenses, see ¶1645 *et seq.* For travel expenses of reservists more than 100 miles from home, see ¶1554.

¶ 1629 Cost of seeking and securing employment.

An employee can deduct the expenses of seeking new employment in his same trade or business, whether or not he gets the new job. Any local transportation expenses and travel expenses away from home and costs such as typing, printing and postage are deductible.

An employee can't deduct the cost of seeking employment in a different trade or business even if he gets the job. If an unemployed person is seeking a job and no substantial lack of continuity occurred between the time of the past employment and the seeking of the new employment, his trade or business is the services performed for his past employer. Where there's no continuity, or where a person looks for a job for the first time, the expenses aren't deductible, even if a job results.

If an individual travels to a destination where he both seeks new employment in his present trade or business and engages in personal activities, his round-trip travel expenses are deductible only if the trip is primarily related to seeking the new employment. Expenses allocable to seeking the job at the destination are deductible even if the travel expenses aren't.[6]

¶ 1630 Labor union dues, fees, and assessments.

Deduction has been permitted for dues, fines paid to remain in the union, strike funds, compulsory payments for unemployment benefits, and a mandatory service charge paid to a union by a nonmember. Deductions were denied for noncompulsory unemployment benefit fund payments, assessments for sick, accident, or death benefits, and other payments in exchange for valuable benefits. [7]

¶ 1631 Uniforms and special work clothes.

Deduction for the cost and maintenance of clothing is allowed if: (1) the employee's occupation is one that specifically requires special apparel or equipment as a condition of employment; and (2) the special apparel or equipment isn't adaptable to general or continued usage

---

2. ¶L-2500 *et seq.*; ¶1624.040; TD ¶303,500
3. ¶L-2502; ¶1624.040; TD ¶303,501
4. ¶L-2714; ¶1624.391; TD ¶303,511

5. ¶L-3900 *et seq.*; ¶1624.067; TD ¶561,603
6. ¶L-3850 *et seq.*; ¶1624.067; TD ¶351,503
7. ¶s L-3908, L-3910; ¶1624.067; TD ¶351,508

so as to take the place of ordinary clothing.

Thus, protective clothing, such as safety shoes, helmets, fishermen's boots, work gloves, oil clothes, etc., are deductible if required for the job. But work clothing and standard work shoes aren't deductible even if the worker's union requires them. [8] Clothes ruined on the job aren't deductible unless the above tests are met. [9]

¶ 1632   Other deductible employee expenses.

These include:

. . . membership dues in professional or business societies, [10]

. . . small tools and supplies, [11]

. . . salesman's briefcase used in business, [12]

. . . salesman's commissions paid to a third party who made the sales, [13]

. . . expenses incurred by a securities analyst for a stock brokerage firm in seeking to get new business for the employer and by so doing increase his own salary, [14]

. . . expenses of business use of home, see ¶1635 *et seq.*, and

. . . qualifying education expenses, see ¶2229.

¶ 1633   Deductions for expenses of professional individuals.

Costs of entering a profession or securing the right to practice are nondeductible. (Reg § 1.212-1(f))[15]

Individuals can deduct the expenses of their business or profession, such as supplies, rent, transportation, business, travel, telephone, etc., if they are self-employed. But a professional who is an employee may deduct only expenses allowed to employees.

Professionals, whether or not employees, can also deduct expenses peculiar to their professions such as dues to professional organizations, continuing professional education, subscriptions to professional journals, malpractice insurance and payments to assistants. The cost of professional books, furniture, instruments and equipment are deductible if their useful lives are short. (Reg § 1.162-6) But expenses incurred by business or professional people to build up their reputations are capital expenditures to develop or enhance goodwill, unless the expenses can be tied directly to the production of added income. [16] The following material highlights the rules on deductions for professionals, etc.:

Accountants can't deduct costs of a CPA review course or the CPA exam. [17]

Lawyers have been allowed to deduct bar association dues, but not costs of securing admission to practice (including bar examination fees, expenses to be admitted to second state bar, travel) (Reg § 1.162-5, Reg § 1.212-1(f)) which must be amortized over taxpayer's remaining life expectancy. The cost of bar review courses can't be amortized. [18]

Doctors and dentists can't deduct costs of securing the right to practice, fees on their initial licensing, etc. (Reg § 1.212-1(f))[19] Fees paid to a hospital for staff privileges are amortizable over taxpayer's useful life, or the useful life of the hospital privilege if shorter. [20] Compensation paid for services rendered by assistants is deductible. (Reg § 1.162-6)[21]

Teachers can deduct the cost of membership in professional societies, educational journals,

---

8. ¶L-3801; ¶1624.067; TD ¶351,001
9. ¶L-3805; ¶1624.067; TD ¶351,005
10. ¶s L-3918, L-4100; ¶1624.195; TD ¶307,721
11. ¶L-3918; TD ¶351,517
12. ¶L-3918; TD ¶351,517
13. ¶L-4237
14. ¶L-4416

15. ¶L-4101; ¶1624.193; TD ¶307,702
16. ¶L-4100 *et seq.*; ¶1624.191; TD ¶307,702
17. ¶L-3719; ¶1624.193; TD ¶302,019
18. ¶L-4102; ¶s 1624.193, 1624.195; TD ¶256,202
19. ¶s L-4100, L-4101; ¶1624.193; TD ¶307,702
20. ¶L-4107; TD ¶307,705
21. ¶L-4101; ¶1624.191; TD ¶307,702

and travel to teachers' conventions and similar events. Professors may deduct the costs of research, writing, or lecturing that the college or university expects, even though they receive no payment or extra compensation. Deductible costs may include travel and research costs. [22]

A financial analyst couldn't deduct the cost of a master's in management (equivalent of an MBA) because it was a minimum educational requirement to qualify for position of associate (investment banker) with her employer. [23]

¶ 1634 Impairment-related work expenses.

Impairment-related work expenses are deductible (on Form 2106 or Form 2106-EZ). They are ordinary and necessary expenses, including attendant care services (e.g., a blind tax-payer's use of a reader) at the place of employment, to enable an individual who has a handicap to work. (Code Sec. 67(d)) Impairment-related work expenses are itemized deductions but aren't subject to the 2%-of-AGI floor. (Code Sec. 67(b)(7))[24]

¶ 1635 Residence Used in Part for Business—Home Office Deduction. ▬▬▬▬

Employees and self-employed individuals may take office-at-home deductions if tough tests are met.

The general rule is that no deduction is allowed for the business use of a dwelling unit that's also used by the taxpayer as a residence during the tax year. But exceptions, discussed below, allow deductions under certain circumstances. (Code Sec. 280A(a)) The disallowance rule applies to individuals, trusts, estates, partnerships, and S corporations. However, disallowance doesn't apply to any deduction allowable without regard to its connection with either a business or income-producing activity. (Code Sec. 280A(b)) For example, the deductions allowed under Code Sec. 163 for interest, Code Sec. 164 for certain taxes, and Code Sec. 165 for casualty losses may be claimed without regard to their connection with the taxpayer's trade or business or income-producing activities. In effect, this means that the disallowance applies only to otherwise deductible business expenses (Code Sec. 162) and depreciation. [25]

The home office deduction isn't allowed for expenses of an income-producing activity, unless the activity is a trade or business. [26]

Allowable home-office expenses are deducted on Form 1040, Schedule A (employees), Form 1040, Schedule C (most self-employed persons, who must also attach Form 8829), and Form 1040, Schedule F (farmers).

In situations in the following paragraphs, otherwise allowable business expenses are deductible (subject to the limits discussed at ¶1641 and ¶1642) even though they are incurred in connection with the business use of a portion of a taxpayer's residence. In addition, the cost of capital improvements made to the entire residence may be recovered through depreciation to the extent allocable to the portion of the residence used for the taxpayer's business. [27]

An employee gets a deduction (subject to the 2%-of-AGI floor on miscellaneous itemized deductions, see ¶3110) only if the exclusive business use of a portion of his residence is for the convenience of his employer. (Code Sec. 280A(c)(1))[28]

Charges (including taxes) for basic local telephone services for the first telephone line for any residence is treated as a personal expense. (Code Sec. 262(b))[29]

---

22. ¶L-4108; ¶s 1624.191, 1624.195; TD ¶302,035
23. ¶L-3713
24. ¶L-3906 *et seq.*; ¶674; TD ¶351,506
25. ¶L-1301 *et seq.*; ¶280A4 *et seq.*; TD ¶258,001 *et seq.*

26. ¶L-1305; ¶280A4.013; TD ¶258,002
27. ¶L-1306 *et seq.*; ¶280A4.04; TD ¶258,039
28. ¶L-1348 *et seq.*; ¶280A4.018; TD ¶258,021
29. ¶L-1307 *et seq.*; ¶2624; TD ¶258,035

¶ 1636 Residence used as principal place of business.

Deduction is allowed to the extent allocable to a portion of a residence *used exclusively* and *on a regular basis* (¶1641) as the taxpayer's principal place of business for *any* trade or business of the taxpayer. (Code Sec. 280A(c)(1)(A))[30]

Following are the two ways to meet the principal place of business requirement:

(1) Under the statutory administrative/management activities test, the principal place of business test is met if a portion of the home is used for the administrative or management activities of any trade or business of the taxpayer, but only if there is no other fixed location where the taxpayer conducts substantial administrative or management activities of that trade or business. (Code Sec. 280A(c)(1)) Examples of administrative or management activities are: billing customers, clients or patients; keeping books and records; ordering supplies; setting up appointments; and forwarding orders or writing reports. The fact that a taxpayer also carries out administrative or management activities at sites that aren't fixed locations of the business, such as a car or hotel room, won't affect his ability to claim a home office deduction under the above rules. Moreover, if a taxpayer conducts some administrative or management activities at a fixed location of the business outside the home, he can still claim a home-office deduction as long as those activities aren't substantial (e.g., the taxpayer occasionally does minimal paperwork at another fixed location of the business). A taxpayer's eligibility to claim a home office deduction under the above rules won't be affected by the fact that he conducts substantial non-administrative or non-management business activities at a fixed location outside the home (e.g., meeting with, or providing services to, customers, clients, or patients at a fixed location outside of his home). [31]

illustration: Most of a self-employed plumber's time is spent at customers' homes and offices installing and repairing plumbing. His sole office is in his home and he uses it exclusively and regularly for the administrative or management details of his business (phoning customers, ordering supplies, and keeping his books). The plumber's home office qualifies as a principal place of business.

(2) Under the comparative analysis test, set forth under the Supreme Court's *Soliman* decision, the determination of a taxpayer's principal place of business requires a comparative analysis of: (1) the relative importance of the activities performed at each business location, and (2) the time spent at each place, i.e., the amount of time spent at the home compared with the amount of time spent in each of the other places where business activities occur. If the nature of the trade or profession requires the taxpayer to meet or confer with clients or patients or to deliver goods or services to a customer, the place where that contact occurs, particularly where that place is a facility with unique or special characteristics, is often important.[32]

¶ 1637 Residence used to meet clients.

Deduction is allowed to the extent allocable to a portion of a residence that's *used exclusively* and *on a regular basis* (¶1641) as a place of business (even if not a principal place of business) that is used by patients, clients, or customers in meeting or dealing with the taxpayer in the normal course of his trade or business. (Code Sec. 280A(c)(1)(B)) This permits a doctor, lawyer, sales rep, insurance agent, claims adjuster, etc., to deduct office-at-home expenses even though he operates his business or profession primarily from an office away from his residence. Telephone conversations alone aren't enough; patients, customers, etc., must be physically present for deductions to be claimed under this rule. [33]

30. ¶s L-1317, L-1324; ¶280A4.014; TD ¶s 258,005, 258,007
31. ¶L-1335; ¶280A4.014; TD ¶258,009

32. ¶L-1330 *et seq.*; ¶280A4.014; TD ¶258,010
33. ¶L-1344 *et seq.*; ¶280A4.016; TD ¶258,019

¶ 1638 Separate structure not attached to residence.

A deduction is allowed for costs allocable to a portion of a separate structure not attached to the residence if it's used *exclusively* and *on a regular basis* (¶1641) in connection with the taxpayer's business. (Code Sec. 280A(c)(1)(C)) For example, an artist's studio in a structure next to but not attached to his residence qualified under this rule. [34]

¶ 1639 Residence used by wholesaler or retailer for storage of inventory and product samples.

Deduction is allowed to the extent allocable to space within the residence that the taxpayer uses *on a regular basis* to store inventory and/or product samples in his business of selling products at retail or wholesale, if the residence is the sole fixed location of the trade or business. (Code Sec. 280A(c)(2)) The space in the residence doesn't have to be used *exclusively* for permissible storage purposes, but must be so used on a regular basis and must be a separately identifiable space suitable for storage. [35]

¶ 1640 Nonexclusive use of home as day-care facility.

A deduction is allowed if a residence is used to provide day-care services for compensation on a regular basis to children, physically or mentally handicapped individuals, or persons 65 or over. If there is only part-time use of a portion of the residence, allocation must be made first on the basis of the proportion of total space used to furnish services and then on the basis of the amount of time that space is used for those services compared to the total time the space is available for all uses. The deduction is allowed only if the day-care services aren't primarily educational and comply with any applicable state licensing, certification, or approval requirements. (Code Sec. 280A(c)(4))[36]

¶ 1641 "Exclusive" use on a "regular" basis.

For purposes of ¶1636 through ¶1640, a taxpayer is required to use a portion of his residence (or separate structure) for business on a regular basis; ¶1636 through ¶1638 require that portion to be used exclusively as a place of business.

Exclusive use means that the taxpayer must use a specific portion of a residence or detached structure for carrying on his business. For example, a taxpayer who uses a den to write legal briefs and prepare tax returns as well as for personal purposes doesn't meet the exclusive use test. [37] A portion of a room used exclusively for business can qualify for the deduction, even though the room isn't divided. [38] Expenses attributable to the exclusive but incidental or occasional trade or business use of a portion of a dwelling unit aren't deductible because the space isn't used on a regular basis. [39]

¶ 1642 Gross income limit on home office deduction.

The deduction is limited to the activity's gross income reduced by all other deductible expenses that are allowable regardless of qualified use and by the business deductions that aren't allocable to the use of the home itself. (Code Sec. 280A(c)(5)(A), Code Sec. 280A(c)(5)(B)) Expenses disallowed solely because they exceed business income can be carried forward (Code Sec. 280A(c)(5)), subject to the gross income limitation in the later year.[40]

34. ¶L-1347; ¶280A4.017; TD ¶258,020
35. ¶L-1355 *et seq.*; ¶280A4.02; TD ¶258,023
36. ¶L-1359; ¶280A4.03; TD ¶258,024 *et seq.*
37. ¶L-1317 *et seq.*; ¶280A4.011; TD ¶258,005

38. ¶L-1317; ¶280A4; TD ¶258,005
39. ¶L-1324; ¶280A4.012; TD ¶258,007
40. ¶L-1365 *et seq.*; ¶280A4.060; TD ¶258,027

¶ 1643   Allocation of home office expenses.

Allocation of expenses and depreciation on a house is generally based on a comparison of space used for business and personal purposes. [41]

¶ 1644   Rental by employer of space in employee's home.

No home-office deduction is allowed for expenses attributable to the rental by an employee of all or part of his home to his employer if the employee uses the rented portion to perform services as an employee of the employer. (Code Sec. 280A(c)(6))[42]

¶ 1645   Moving Expenses. ▪▪▪▪▪▪▪▪▪▪▪▪▪▪▪▪▪▪▪▪▪▪▪▪▪▪▪▪▪▪▪▪▪▪▪

An employee or self-employed individual may deduct certain expenses of moving to a new home if the move results from a change in the individual's principal place of work and if distance and time (working at the new location) tests are met. Exceptions apply to members of the armed forces.

¶ 1646   Claiming a moving expense deduction.

Form 3903 is filed by taxpayers, whether employed or self-employed, who claim moving expenses. [43] The deduction is ordinarily claimed on the return for the year in which the expenses were paid or incurred, see ¶1652. But in certain circumstances, taxpayers may elect to claim the deduction before satisfying the time tests, see ¶1649.

¶ 1647   Deductible above-the-line expenses.

An employee or self-employed individual who moves his residence because of a change in his principal place of work may deduct the reasonable expenses of (Code Sec. 217(b)(1)): (1) moving household goods and personal effects from the old residence to the new place of residence; and (2) traveling (including lodging but not meals) from the old residence to the new place of residence. [44]

If a taxpayer uses his auto to travel to the new home, he may deduct actual expenses (e.g., gas and oil) or for 2007, 20¢ per mile. [45]

Moving expenses are "above-the-line" deductions; that is, they are deductible from gross income in arriving at adjusted gross income. (Code Sec. 62(a)(15))[46]

In the case of any individual other than the taxpayer, the expenses above are deductible only if the individual has both the former residence and the new residence as his principal place of abode and is a member of the taxpayer's household. (Code Sec. 217(b)(2)) [47]

Ⓡobservation: There are no dollar limits on the amount of deductible moving expenses.

Moving expenses aren't deductible to the extent they are reimbursed by the employer and the reimbursements are excludable from the taxpayer's income (¶1249).

¶ 1648   50-mile distance test.

The new job site must be at least 50 miles farther from the taxpayer's old principal residence than was the old principal job site. If he didn't have a full-time job before the move, the new job site must be at least 50 miles from his old residence. (Code Sec. 217(c)(1))[48]

---

41. ¶L-1310 *et seq.*; ¶280A4.041; TD ¶258,041
42. ¶L-1354; ¶280A4.019; TD ¶258,003
43. ¶L-3601; TD ¶350,501
44. ¶L-3602 *et seq.*; ¶2174; TD ¶350,512
45. ¶L-3615; TD ¶350,515
46. ¶L-3602; ¶2174; TD ¶350,501
47. ¶L-3602; ¶2174; TD ¶350,502
48. ¶L-3619; ¶2174.01; TD ¶350,519

¶ 1649   39-week/78-week time tests.

A 39-week or 78-week test must be met: (Code Sec. 217(c)(2))

. . . 39-week test: An employee must be employed full-time in the general location of his new principal place of work for at least 39 weeks during the 12-month period immediately following his arrival in the new area. (Code Sec. 217(c)(2)(A))

. . . 78-week test: The taxpayer must be a "full time employee" or must "perform services as a self-employed individual on a full time basis" in the general location of his new principal place of work for at least 78 weeks during the 24-month period immediately following his arrival there. Thirty-nine of the 78 weeks must be during the 12-month period above. (Code Sec. 217(c)(2)(B))

Joint filers qualify for the deduction if either spouse satisfies the 39-week or 78-week test. But weeks worked by one spouse can't be added to weeks worked by the other. (Reg § 1.217-2(c)(4)(v), Reg § 1.217-1(c)(4))

Failure to meet the 39- or 78-week test doesn't bar deduction if the failure was caused by: (1) death or disability, or (2) involuntary separation from employment (other than for willful misconduct), or re-transfer for the benefit of the employer (*not* initiated by the employee), after getting full-time employment in which the taxpayer could reasonably have been expected to meet the test. (Code Sec. 217(d)(1))[49]

¶ 1650   Foreign moves (from the U.S.).

Expenses of moving from the U.S. or its possessions to a new principal place of work outside the U.S. or its possessions include the reasonable expenses (no dollar ceiling) of moving household goods and personal effects to and from storage, and of storing these items while the new place of work is the taxpayer's principal place of work. (Code Sec. 217(h)) [50]

Moving expenses aren't deductible to the extent allocable to exempt foreign-source earned income. In the absence of evidence to the contrary, reimbursement of expenses to move to a foreign country is attributed to future services to be performed at the new place of work. (Reg § 1.911-3(e)(5)(i))[1]

¶ 1651   Moving to U.S. not connected with employment.

Moving expense deductions under special rules are allowed for persons who worked abroad and move to the U.S. (or its possessions) on retirement, and for the spouse or dependent who moves to the U.S. following the death of a person who worked abroad. (Code Sec. 217(i))[2]

¶ 1652   When to deduct moving expenses.

A taxpayer may:

- deduct moving expenses in the year the expenses were paid or incurred even though the 39- or 78-week condition isn't satisfied before the due date for filing (including extensions) (Code Sec. 217(d)(2); Reg § 1.217-2(a)(2)), or

- wait until the applicable condition is satisfied; then file an amended return claiming the deduction for the tax year the moving expense was paid or incurred. (Reg § 1.217-2(d))[3]

---

49. ¶L-3620 *et seq.*; ¶2174.01; TD ¶350,520 *et seq.*
50. ¶L-3610; ¶2174.03; TD ¶350,533
1. ¶L-3635; ¶9114.11; TD ¶350,535

2. ¶L-3632; ¶L-3633; ¶2174.03; TD ¶350,533
3. ¶L-3637; ¶2174; TD ¶350,537

¶ 1653   Moving expenses of members of the armed forces.

A move by an active duty member of the armed forces under a military order and incident to a permanent change of station can qualify for deduction regardless of the distance moved or the length of time worked at the new station. Cash reimbursements or allowances are excludable to the extent of moving and storage expenses actually paid or incurred, as are all in-kind moving and storage services provided by the military. This exclusion also applies to a spouse and dependents when they don't accompany an armed forces member and move to a location different from that *to* which he moves or different from that *from* which he moves. Where the military moves the member and the member's family to or from separate locations and they incur unreimbursed expenses, their moves are treated as a single move to the member's new principal place of work. (Code Sec. 217(g)) No deduction is permitted for any moving or storage expense reimbursed by an allowance that's excluded from income. (Reg § 1.217-2(g)(6))[4]

¶ 1654   Capital Expenditures. ■■■■■■■■■■■■■■■■■■■■■■■■■■■■■■■■■

Capital expenditures generally can't be deducted except through depreciation, expensing, depletion, or amortization deductions.

These rules apply only to the extent they don't conflict with the uniform capitalization rules (¶1660 *et seq.*). Taxpayers can elect to capitalize interest under Code Sec. 266 only after applying the uniform capitalization rules for interest under Code Sec. 263A (¶1662).

A capital expenditure differs from a deductible expense because the anticipated benefit of the capital expenditure extends beyond the tax year. Capital expenditures include amounts paid or incurred to add to the value, or to substantially extend the useful life, of property owned by the taxpayer. (Code Sec. 263; Reg § 1.263(a)-1)[5] (For repairs and maintenance of property, see ¶1668.)

Examples of capital expenditures include:

. . . Original cost of getting a business license that's good or renewable for an indefinite period.[6]

. . . Initiation fees or initial admission fees paid for business association, etc., memberships. [7]

. . . Costs incurred by a corporation related to the issuance, redemption and sale of its stock.[8]

. . . Installation costs of purchased machinery, equipment, etc., including labor, material and freight charges to the extent that these expenses don't conflict with the uniform capitalization rules (¶1660).[9] But costs of retiring and removing old depreciable assets in connection with the installation or production of replacement assets don't have to be capitalized. [10]

. . . Costs other than interest incurred to borrow funds and other finance costs are capital expenditures to be amortized over the life of the loan. (For capitalization of interest on produced property, see ¶1662.) This applies to commissions and other fees paid to get a loan, cost of issuing bonds, including legal fees and printing costs and finder's fees and commissions paid by a lender to get borrowers. [11]

. . . Payments made to get the goodwill of a business, including payments for the use of an individual's name in a business bought from him; the cost of acquiring a dealer's franchise;[12] cost of acquiring customer lists. [13]

---

4. ¶L-3630; ¶2174.02; TD ¶350,530
5. ¶L-5601; ¶2634; TD ¶308,010
6. ¶L-4216; TD ¶307,717
7. ¶L-4230; TD ¶307,720
8. ¶L-5300 *et seq.*; TD ¶301,029

9. ¶L-5811; ¶2634.16; TD ¶308,010
10. ¶L-5811.1; TD ¶256,216
11. ¶L-6001 *et seq.*; ¶1624.081
12. ¶L-5711; ¶2634.10; TD ¶229,501
13. ¶L-5712; ¶2634.10

For amortization of "Code Sec. 197 intangibles," see ¶1977.

¶ 1655   Costs of acquisition, construction or erection of property.

Costs of acquisition, construction or erection of property are included in inventory if allocable to inventory, and capitalized if allocable to other property. (Code Sec. 263A(a))[14] These rules apply to real or tangible personal property that taxpayers produce and inventory that taxpayers acquire for resale. (Code Sec. 263A(b)(2)(A))[15] See ¶1660 *et seq.*

¶ 1656   Taxes, interest, and carrying charges—election to capitalize.

Some taxes and carrying charges that would normally be deducted currently or amortized may be capitalized if the taxpayer so elects. [16] For depreciable property this has the effect of deferring the deduction to later years as depreciation. For nondepreciable property, such as unimproved real estate, the capitalized expenses increase basis and serve to reduce gain (or increase loss) on a later sale of the property. (Code Sec. 266; Reg § 1.212-1(n), Reg § 1.266-1)[17]

¶ 1657   Annual election for unimproved and unproductive real estate.

A taxpayer can elect to capitalize taxes, mortgage interest (subject to the interest capitalization rules at ¶1662) and deductible carrying charges on unimproved and unproductive real property. (Reg § 1.266-1(b))[18]

¶ 1658   Election for expenditures on real estate improvement project.

A taxpayer engaged in the development of real estate or the construction of an improvement to real estate can elect to capitalize the following items relating to the project:

. . . interest on loans,

. . . taxes measured by compensation paid to employees and taxes imposed on the purchase of materials, or on the storage, use, or other consumption of materials,

. . . other necessary charges, including fire insurance premiums. (Reg § 1.266-1(b)(1))[19]

¶ 1659   Capitalizing taxes, interest, etc., before installing or using personal property.

The election to capitalize deductible items also applies to interest on a loan to finance the purchase, transportation and installation of machinery and other assets, state and local taxes imposed on the taxpayer, transportation, storage, use or other consumption of the property, and state and local taxes, including sales and use taxes, and state and federal unemployment taxes and the taxpayer's share of federal social security taxes on the wages of employees engaged in transportation and installation of the assets. (Reg § 1.266-1)[20]

¶ 1660   Uniform capitalization rules.

A taxpayer must (1) include in inventory costs the "allocable costs" (defined below) of "property" (also defined below) that is inventory; (Code Sec. 263A(a)(1)(A)) and (2) capitalize the allocable costs of any other property. (Code Sec. 263A(a)(2)(B)) The *allocable costs* are:

. . . the direct costs of the property (Code Sec. 263A(a)(2)(A));

---

14. ¶G-5452; ¶263A4; TD ¶456,003
15. ¶s G-5461 *et seq.*, G-5476 *et seq.*; ¶263A4; TD ¶456,003
16. ¶L-5901; ¶2664; TD ¶256,221
17. ¶L-5901; ¶2664; TD ¶256,221
18. ¶L-5901; ¶2664; TD ¶256,223
19. ¶L-5904; ¶2664; TD ¶256,222
20. ¶s L-5901, L-5905; ¶2664; TD ¶256,224

. . . the indirect costs, to the extent of the property's proper share of that part (or all) of the costs allocable to that property. (Code Sec. 263A(a)(2)(B))

Allocable costs include all depreciation deductions for the taxpayer's assets, and interest, but only where the underlying debt was incurred or continued to finance certain produced property, see ¶1662. Taxes are allocable indirect costs. (Code Sec. 263A(a)(2)(B)) Environmental remediation costs incurred by a manufacturer (e.g., to clean land it contaminated with hazardous waste) must be included in inventory costs under these rules. [21]

Allocable costs don't include:

. . . selling, marketing, advertising and distribution expenses (Reg § 1.263A-1(e)(3)(iii)(A));

. . . any amounts allowable as a deduction under Code Sec. 174 for research and experimental expenditures (Code Sec. 263A(c)(2));

. . . any cost to the extent allowable as a deduction under Code Sec. 263(c) (intangible drilling and development costs), Code Sec. 616(a) (mining development expenses) or Code Sec. 617(a) (mining exploration expenses) (Code Sec. 263A(c)(3));

. . . any qualified creative expense incurred by a "writer," "photographer" or "artist" that would otherwise be deductible. Expenses related to printing photographic plates, motion picture films, video tapes or similar items aren't qualified creative expenses (Code Sec. 263A(h));

. . . "deductible service costs." (Reg § 1.263A-1(e)(3)(iii)(K))

What is property? A taxpayer must include in inventory or capitalize the allocable costs for:

. . . real or tangible personal property (defined below) that the taxpayer *produced* (defined below) (Code Sec. 263A(b)(1));

. . . real or personal Code Sec. 1221(a)(1) property —inventory and property held primarily for sale to customers in the ordinary course of the taxpayer's trade or business —that the taxpayer acquired for resale. (Code Sec. 263A(b)(2)(A))

Tangible personal property includes a film, sound recording, video tape, book or similar property. (Code Sec. 263A(b))

A taxpayer "produces" tangible property if he constructs, builds, installs, manufactures, develops or improves it. (Code Sec. 263A(g)(1)) Where a taxpayer makes progress or advance payments to a contractor, the taxpayer is treated as producing any property the contractor produces for the taxpayer under the contract, to the extent of those payments (whether paid or incurred by the taxpayer under the contract or otherwise). (Code Sec. 263A(g)(2))

Property acquired for resale includes intangible as well as tangible property.

"Property" doesn't include(and so allocable costs don't have to be capitalized for):

. . . Any property produced by the taxpayer for use by the taxpayer other than in a trade or business or an activity conducted for profit. (Code Sec. 263A(c)(1))

. . . Any property produced by the taxpayer under a long-term contract (Code Sec. 263A(c)(4)) except for certain home construction contracts. (Code Sec. 460(e)(1))

. . . Timber and certain ornamental trees. (Code Sec. 263A(c)(5)(A))

. . . Personal property acquired for resale by certain taxpayers with average annual gross receipts of $10,000,000 or less. (Code Sec. 263A(b)(2)(B))[22]

Taxpayers who acquire and hold property for resale (such as retailers and wholesalers) may elect a simplified resale method to determine the additional costs properly allocable to the

21. ¶G-5500.1; ¶263A4 *et seq.*; TD ¶456,000 *et seq.*   TD ¶456,000
22. ¶G-5451 *et seq.*; ¶s 263A4 *et seq.*, 263A4.06 *et seq.*;

resale property. (Reg § 1.263A-3(d))[23]

For the application of the uniform capitalization rules to farmers and ranchers, see ¶4518.

¶ 1661 How to allocate costs to property.

Allocable costs (¶1660) must be allocated to inventory or capitalized as follows:

. . . Direct labor costs are generally allocated by using a specific identification ("tracing") method (Reg § 1.263A-1(g)(2)), but any reasonable method may be used. (Reg § 1.263A-1(f)(4))

. . . Indirect costs should be allocated to particular production, resale, etc., activities using either a specific identification ("tracing") method, the standard cost method, or a method using burden rates, such as ratios based on direct costs, hours, or other items, or similar formulas, so long as the method employed reasonably allocates indirect costs among production, resale, etc., activities. (Reg § 1.263A-1(g)(3)) Taxpayers may be able to use simplified methods such as the simplified production method (Reg § 1.263A-2) and the simplified resale method (Reg § 1.263A-3)[24]

¶ 1662 Interest capitalization rules.

A taxpayer must capitalize interest he pays or incurs during a production period that is allocable to property he produces if that property (1) has a long useful life (it is real property or property with a class life of 20 years or more); (2) has an estimated production period exceeding two years; or (3) has an estimated production period exceeding one year and a cost exceeding $1,000,000. (Code Sec. 263A(f)(1); Reg § 1.263A-8(b)(1))[25]

The taxpayer must also capitalize any interest on debt allocable to an asset needed to produce the above property. (Code Sec. 263A(f)(3); Reg § 1.263A-8(a)(2)) A taxpayer must capitalize interest whether he produces the property for his own use or for sale.

The "production period" for any property begins on the date production of the property begins and ends on the date it is ready to be placed in service or is ready to be held for sale. (Code Sec. 263A(f)(4)(B))[26]

Interest isn't capitalized for real or personal property acquired solely for resale.

A taxpayer doesn't capitalize interest allocable to property that's not subject to the capitalization rules, such as property produced under a long-term contract (see the discussion of this and other exceptions at ¶1660). (Reg § 1.263A-8(d)(2)(v)(A)) Thus, a taxpayer who produces property under a long term contract capitalizes interest only to the extent he doesn't report income under the percentage of completion method. [27]

Allocating interest to produced property. Interest is allocable to property a taxpayer produces if the taxpayer incurred or continued the underlying debt to finance the construction or production of the property.

A taxpayer is treated as having incurred or continued debt to finance the production of income: (1) where the debt can be specifically traced to production expenditures, and (2) where the debt can't be so traced, but where production or construction expenditures exceed the debt that is directly traceable. (Reg § 1.263A-9(a)(2))

The interest on the debt incurred or continued to finance production is allocated to the property produced as follows: [28]

(1) interest (other than qualified residence interest) on a debt that is directly attributable

---

23. ¶G-5452 *et seq.*; ¶263A4.09; TD ¶456,011
24. ¶G-5458; ¶263A4.06; TD ¶456,006
25. ¶L-5920;¶263A4.11; TD ¶456,017 *et seq.*

26. ¶L-5932; ¶263A4.11; TD ¶456,023
27. ¶L-5918; ¶263A4.03; TD ¶456,017
28. ¶L-5926; ¶263A4.11; TD ¶456,021

to production expenditures for the produced property is assigned to that property; (Code Sec. 263A(f)(2)(A)(i); Reg § 1.263A-9(a)(2)(i)(A)), and

(2) interest on any other debt is assigned to the produced property to the extent that the taxpayer's interest costs could have been reduced if production expenditures (not attributable to the debt in (1), above) had not been incurred (Code Sec. 263A(f)(2)(A)(ii); Reg § 1.263A-9(a)(2)(i)(B)) (that is, had the expenditures that were incurred for construction been used instead to repay the debt).

¶ 1663   Computer software for own use.

A buyer's treatment of software depends on how it is billed by the seller:

. . . If a charge for computer software is included in the price of the hardware (i.e., the computer) without a separate identification of the charge for software, then the buyer capitalizes and depreciates the cost along with the cost of the hardware. (Reg § 1.167(a)-14(b)(2))

. . . If the charge for the software is separately stated, it can be amortized over 36 months using the straight-line method. This rule *doesn't* apply to any software that's a Code Sec. 197 intangible. (Reg § 1.167(a)-14(b)(1))[29]

The cost of software licensed for a specific period of time (unless properly chargeable to capital account) is deducted over that term, in the same way that a business tenant may under Reg § 1.162-11 deduct the cost of acquiring a leasehold over the lease term. (Reg § 1.167(a)-14(b)(2))[30] Rental payments for leased software are deducted just like any other rentals.[31]

caution: Code Sec. 197 intangibles include software acquired in connection with the acquisition of a business. For 15-year amortization of such software, see ¶1979 *et seq.*

¶ 1664   Costs of developing computer software.

Costs of developing computer software (other than software that is a Code Sec. 197 intangible (¶1979)) can be either: (1) consistently expensed currently under Code Sec. 174(a), or (2) consistently treated as capital expenditures recoverable through deductions for ratable amortization over a period of 60 months from the date of completion of the development under Code Sec. 174(b) or over 36 months from the date the software is placed in service under Code Sec. 167(f)(1).[32] Costs of developing software may also qualify as research and experimental expenditures under Code Sec. 174 [33] (for deductions under Code Sec. 174, see ¶1601). If costs for developing computer software that the taxpayer elected to treat as deferred expenses under Code Sec. 174(b) (¶1601) result in the development of property subject to depreciation, the 36 month amortization rule applies to the unrecovered costs. (Reg § 1.167(a)-14(b)(1))[34]

¶ 1665   Commissions paid upon transfer of property.

Commissions paid for the *purchase* of real estate or other property aren't deductible as expenses but must be capitalized and added to the cost of the property, whether or not the taxpayer is engaged in the real estate business. [35]

A partnership or S corporation producing property to which the interest capitalization rules apply must first capitalize interest as described above. The remaining production expenditures must be allocated to the partners or shareholders based on respective shares. The

---

29. ¶L-7935; ¶1674.033; TD ¶265,434
30. ¶L-5621; ¶1674.033; TD ¶265,434
31. ¶L-5615 *et seq.*; ¶1674.033; TD ¶265,434
32. ¶L-5616; ¶1674.033; TD ¶256,236

33. ¶L-5615; ¶1674.033; TD ¶256,234
34. ¶L-7935; ¶1674.033; TD ¶265,434
35. ¶I-2536

owners are then subject to the interest capitalization rules. [36]

Commissions paid for the *sale* of real estate or other property by a taxpayer who is not engaged in the real estate business must be offset against the selling price to determine the gain or loss realized on the sale. If the seller is engaged in the real estate business, the commissions on property sales are deductible business expenses. [37]

¶ 1666 Interest and carrying charges relating to straddles.

The interest and carrying charges properly allocable to personal property that is part of a straddle (¶2653) aren't deductible, but must be charged to the capital account of the property for which they were paid or incurred. (Code Sec. 263(g)(1)) However this requirement doesn't apply to any identified hedging transactions (¶2660). (Code Sec. 263(g)(3))[38]

"Interest and carrying charges" means the excess of:

. . . the sum of interest on indebtedness incurred or continued to buy or carry personal property that is part of a straddle, and amounts paid or incurred to insure, store, or transport that personal property, *over*

. . . the sum of: (1) the amount of interest income, including original issue discount, from the property includible in gross income for the taxable year, (2) any amount treated as ordinary income under Code Secs. 1271(a)(3)(A), 1281(a), (dealing with acquisition discount on short-term government and nongovernment obligations), or Code Sec. 1278 (dealing with market discount bonds), (3) the excess of any dividends includible in income over the dividends received deductions allowable for those dividends under Code Secs. 243, 244, 245, and (4) any payment for a security loan that's included in gross income for the tax year. (Code Sec. 263(g)(2)) Also, the term "interest" includes amounts paid or incurred in connection with personal property used in a short sale. [39]

¶ 1667 Architectural and transportation barrier removal expenses.

A taxpayer can elect to treat up to $15,000 of qualified architectural and transportation barrier removal expenses as a deduction rather than as a charge to capital account. (Code Sec. 190(a), Code Sec. 190(c)) To elect, claim the deduction as a separate item identified as such on the timely filed (including extension) return for the tax year for which the election is to apply. (Reg § 1.190-3(a))[40] For the credit for eligible access expenditures, see ¶2322.

¶ 1668 Repairs.

The cost of repairing business property of the taxpayer is deductible currently as a business expense, while an improvement that materially adds to the value or utility of the property or appreciably prolongs its useful life must be capitalized. (Reg § 1.162-4)[41]

Expenditures as part of a general plan of reconditioning, renovating, improving or altering property must be capitalized even though certain portions of the work standing alone might properly be classifiable as repairs. [42]

¶ 1669 Environmental cleanup costs; expensing election.

If a taxpayer acquires property in clean condition and contaminates it in the course of its everyday business operations, the cost of restoring the property to its approximate condition at the time of acquisition doesn't result in a permanent improvement that increases the

36. ¶L-5963 *et seq.*; TD ¶456,037
37. ¶I-2537; ¶2634.05; TD ¶222,023
38. ¶L-5985; ¶2634; TD ¶228,715
39. ¶L-5985 *et seq.*; ¶2634

40. ¶L-3151 *et seq.*; ¶1904 *et seq.*; TD ¶256,219
41. ¶L-6101; ¶1624.171; TD ¶308,001
42. ¶L-6108; ¶1624.183; TD ¶308,010

property's value and the restoration costs are deductible. IRS has privately ruled that the cost a business incurs to remove mold from a building it owns and leases out is currently deductible. One court has held that the "restoration principle" doesn't apply to asbestos removal undertaken as part of a major remodeling project, and another court has allowed a current deduction for removing/encapsulating deteriorating asbestos taxpayer had installed because the work wasn't done to refurbish the building or prepare it for a new use and the cost represented only a small fraction of the building's value. The restoration principle doesn't apply where the taxpayer acquires property that's already in a contaminated state. The cleanup expenses must be capitalized if the remediation results in permanent improvement or betterment of the property that increases its value, prolongs its useful life or adapts it to a new or different use. The cost of replacing a company's existing underground storage tanks (removing, cleaning, and discarding old tanks, and buying, installing, and filling new tanks with waste by-products, as well as cost of monitoring new tanks) is currently deductible where new tanks, after being filled with waste and sealed, have no salvage value and no remaining useful life, and are used to facilitate permanent disposal of waste by-product. [43]

For expenses paid or incurred before 2008, taxpayers may elect to treat qualified environmental remediation expenses that would otherwise be chargeable to a capital account as deductible in the year paid or incurred. To be deductible currently, such expense has to be paid or incurred in connection with the abatement or control of hazardous substances (including petroleum products) at a qualified contaminated site. (Code Sec. 198) Special rules apply to expenses for depreciable property. (Code Sec. 198(b)(2)) Expensed qualified environmental remediation costs are subject to recapture upon the sale or other disposition of the property. (Code Sec. 198(e))[44]

caution: Check http://ria.thomson.com/federaltaxhandbook to see if this provision has been extended.

¶ 1670 Capitalization rules for costs associated with intangible assets.

Taxpayers are required to capitalize amounts paid or incurred to (i) acquire or create an intangible asset, (ii) create or enhance a separate, distinct intangible asset, (iii) create or enhance a "future benefit" identified in published guidance as capitalizable, or (iv) "facilitate" the acquisition or creation of an intangible in (i) through (iii) (e.g., transaction costs). (Reg § 1.263(a)-4(b)(1)) Capitalizable costs cannot be deducted and are generally added to the basis of the intangible. (Reg § 1.263(a)-4)[45] These rules do not affect the treatment of amounts specifically provided for in a Code Section other than Code Sec. 162 or Code Sec. 212 (e.g., Code Sec. 174 research expenses). (Reg § 1.263(a)-4(b)(4))

observation: Capitalized costs may be amortizable (e.g., payment to a departing employee for a 3-year noncompete covenant may be deducted ratably over the 3 years).

For the "12-month" and de minimis exceptions to these requirements, see ¶1671. For 15-year amortization of certain intangibles, see ¶1903.

¶ 1671 De minimis and 12-month rule exceptions to capitalization rules for intangibles.

The following are exceptions to the capitalization rules for intangibles discussed at ¶1670.

De minimis costs, — i.e., costs that don't exceed $5,000 — paid to another party to create, originate, enter into, renew, or renegotiate an agreement (Reg § 1.263(a)-4(d)(6)(v)), or paid in the process of investigating a transaction (Reg § 1.263(a)-4(e)(4)(iii)) don't have to be

---

43. ¶L-6154; TD ¶308,011
44. ¶L-6150.1; ¶1984

45. ¶L-5751; ¶2634; TD ¶256,300

capitalized even if they facilitate a capital transaction and otherwise would be subject to the capitalization rules. Payments made in the form of property are valued at fair market value at the time of payment. The de minimis rule applies on a transaction-by-transaction basis. If transaction costs (other than compensation and overhead) exceed $5,000, none of the costs are treated as de minimis. A pooling method may be used for de minimis transaction costs. Commissions paid to facilitate the acquisition of an intangible aren't treated as de minimis costs (and therefore must be capitalized). [46]

12-month rule. Capitalization is not required for amounts paid to create or facilitate the creation of any right or benefit that does not extend beyond the earlier of (1) 12 months after the first date on which the taxpayer realizes the right or benefit; or (2) the end of the tax year following the tax year in which the payment is made. (Reg § 1.263(a)-4(f)) Amounts paid to terminate an agreement before its expiration date create a benefit for the taxpayer that lasts for the unexpired term of the agreement immediately before the termination date. (Reg § 1.263(a)-4(f)(2)) The 12-month rule doesn't apply to amounts paid to create (or facilitate the creation of) financial interests or amortizable Code Sec. 197 intangibles or to amounts paid to create or enhance a right of indefinite duration. (Reg § 1.263(a)-4(f)(3), Reg § 1.263(a)-4(f)(4)) The 12-month rule does not affect the determination of whether a liability is incurred during the tax year, including the determination of whether economic performance has occurred. (Reg § 1.263(a)-4(f)(6))[47]

---

46. ¶L-5757.1, ¶L-5760.2; ¶2634; TD ¶256,317

47. ¶L-5760.5 *et seq.*; ¶2634; TD ¶256,320

Chapter 4 Interest Expense—Taxes—Losses—Bad Debts

¶ 1700 Deduction for Interest.

Generally, interest paid or accrued during the tax year is deductible whether or not it is incurred in a trade or business. It must be incurred with respect to a valid debt and be actually paid or accrued during the tax year.

To be deductible, interest must be paid or incurred with respect to a valid debt. [1] And the amount of interest must be definitely ascertainable. [2] But, to be deductible, interest need not be reasonable, [3] and may even be usurious. [4]

There's no deduction for interest incurred in most personal transactions and on certain kinds of debt (¶1715 et seq.). The amount of interest that's deductible on certain other kinds of debt is limited (for example, investment interest, see ¶1726 et seq.; qualified residence interest, see ¶1730 et seq.; interest incurred in a passive activity, see ¶1810 et seq.; and qualified education loan interest, see ¶2225 et seq.). For interest expenses that must be included in inventory or capitalized, see ¶1654 et seq.

¶ 1701 Interest is payment for the use or forbearance of money.

Interest includes the amount paid: (1) for the borrower's *use* of money during the term of a loan, or (2) for his *detention* of money after the due date for repayment. Merely designating a payment as "interest" won't make it deductible. [5] Nor does the fact that the payment is taxable interest to the lender make it deductible by the payor-borrower. [6]

These forms of "interest" are true interest for federal tax purposes:

. . . Interest and similar charges (¶1704) (including "points," ¶1703, but not fees for services) paid to lenders. [7]

. . . Bonuses and premiums the borrower is required to pay the lender to get the loan. [8]

. . . Discounts (including original issue discount (OID), see ¶1751)—i.e., where the borrower receives less than the face amount of the loan but is required to repay the full face amount, the difference is interest. [9]

. . . Foregone interest on below-market loans that the borrower is "deemed" to have paid to the lender (¶1306). [10]

. . . Interest paid by banks or other financial institutions on deposits, certificates or other evidences of indebtedness. [11] For amounts forfeited on premature withdrawal of a bank deposit, see ¶2171.

. . . Payments of redeemable ground rents. (Code Sec. 163(c)) [12]

. . . Interest on deposits, down payments, etc., where the seller defers delivery of a purchased item [13] (for unstated interest, see ¶1707). For installment sale interest, see ¶1706.

. . . Interest on judgment debts. [14]

. . . Interest on declared but unpaid dividends. [15]

. . . Interest on deferred payments of legacies. [16]

1. ¶K-5060 et seq.; ¶1634; TD ¶311,502
2. ¶K-5024; ¶1634.025
3. ¶K-5001; ¶1634; TD ¶311,002
4. ¶K-5002; ¶1634.021; TD ¶311,002
5. ¶K-5020 et seq.; ¶1634; TD ¶311,501
6. ¶K-5020; ¶1634
7. ¶K-5026, K-5030; ¶1634; TD ¶311,503, 311,526
8. ¶K-5028; ¶s 1634.001, 1634.005; TD ¶318,705

9. ¶K-5028; ¶s 1634.001, 1634.051; TD ¶311,503
10. ¶K-5039; ¶78,724 et seq.; TD ¶319,504
11. ¶E-3105, ¶E-3107; ¶4614.51
12. ¶K-5044; ¶1634; TD ¶311,523
13. ¶K-5045; TD ¶311,515
14. ¶K-5050; TD ¶311,518
15. ¶K-5051; ¶1635.014(75); TD ¶311,519
16. ¶K-5052; TD ¶311,520

References beginning with a single letter are to paragraphs in RIA's Federal Tax Coordinator 2d and RIA's Analysis of Federal Taxes: Income. Those beginning with numbers are to paragraphs in RIA's United States Tax Reporter. Those beginning with TD are to paragraphs in RIA's Tax Desk.

¶ 1702 Mortgage interest.

Interest on a mortgage on real property (including a condominium or co-op, ¶1714) generally is deductible. (Reg § 1.163-1(b))[17] For "points," see ¶1703. For prepayment penalties and late payment charges, see ¶1705. For who deducts mortgage interest, see ¶1713.

🅡🅘🅐*caution:* Interest on a home mortgage must be "qualified residence interest" (¶1730 *et seq.*) to be deductible.

¶ 1703 "Points."

"Points" (loan origination fees, loan processing fees, loan discount fees, etc., that are a specified percentage of the amount borrowed) a borrower pays, out of his own funds, to a lender in order to get a loan are deductible as interest *only* if they are *solely* for the use or forbearance of money and not a charge for services. This includes "points" on a VA or FHA home mortgage. But points paid for services of the lender *in lieu of* specific service charges (e.g., a one-point charge for appraisal, etc.) aren't deductible as interest. Nor is a "commitment fee" charged for the lender's agreement to make a future loan. [18]

Points paid by the *seller* aren't deductible as interest (except by certain cash basis buyers, see ¶1746). Rather, they are included in the seller's selling expenses, reducing the amount realized on sale. But a seller in the business of building and selling houses was allowed a *business* expense deduction for these payments. [19]

For when to deduct points, see ¶1745; home mortgage points, see ¶1746; and refinancing points, see ¶1747.

¶ 1704 Finance charges and credit card fees.

The amount of finance charges imposed on the unpaid balances of revolving charge accounts or budget charge accounts of retail stores, or on the unpaid balances of bank and oil company credit cards, is deductible as interest (subject to the bar on personal interest deductions, see ¶1715), as are credit card fees imposed for cash, check, or overdraft advances, but only to the extent the payment isn't a service charge, etc. [20]

¶ 1705 Prepayment penalties and late payment charges.

A penalty paid for prepaying a debt (including a mortgage) is deductible as interest, [21] as is a late payment charge (that isn't a service charge). [22]

¶ 1706 Interest and carrying charges on installment purchases and deferred tuition; 6% rule.

Interest on installment purchases that's separately stated or definitely determinable and provable is deductible as interest, subject to the rules for credit cards (¶1704).[23] For deduction of "unstated interest," see ¶1707.

If carrying charges (including finance charges, service charges, etc.) on an installment purchase of personal property or educational services are *separately stated* but the amount of *interest* included in the charges can't be ascertained, the installment payments are considered to include a 6% interest charge based on the average unpaid balance under the contract

---

17. ¶K-5043; ¶s 1634.050, 1634.052; TD ¶311,504
18. ¶K-5026; ¶1634.005; TD ¶311,506, 311,527
19. ¶I-2531, K-5027; TD ¶337,011
20. ¶K-5029, ¶K-5031; ¶1634.050; TD ¶311,507

21. ¶K-5034; ¶1634; TD ¶311,512
22. ¶K-5032, K-5033; TD ¶311,510, 311,511
23. ¶K-5029 *et seq.*; ¶1634.050; TD ¶311,507

during the tax year. (Code Sec. 163(b); Reg § 1.163-2)[24]

¶ 1707   Unstated interest on deferred payment sales.

On certain deferred payment sales, part of each payment is treated as interest ("unstated interest") that's treated by the buyer as interest expense. The amount of this "unstated interest" attributed to the buyer is determined under the rules governing the unstated interest that's taxed to the seller (¶1307 *et seq.*). (Code Sec. 483(a); Reg § 1.483-1)[25]

These rules *don't apply* to buyers of: (1) personal use property (Code Sec. 1275(b)(1)); or (2) personal property on installment where payments include separately stated carrying charges otherwise treated as interest (¶1706). (Code Sec. 483(d)(3))[26]

¶ 1708   Interest on taxes.

Interest on delinquent tax payments may be deducted, to the extent it's otherwise deductible.[27] So, interest on sales, excise and similar taxes incurred in connection with taxpayer's business or investment activities may be deducted. But interest paid by an individual (or a trust, S corporation or other pass-through entity) on income tax underpayments, or on debt used to pay those taxes, is nondeductible personal interest (¶1715). (Reg § 1.163-9T(b)(2)) And interest on an income tax deficiency arising from an unincorporated business is also nondeductible personal interest that can't be deducted as a business expense. [28]

A corporation can't deduct interest paid on an understatement with respect to certain listed or reportable transactions that have a potential for tax avoidance or evasion, and that it didn't adequately disclose under Code Sec. 6664(d)(2)(A). (Code Sec. 163(m))[29]

¶ 1709   Corporate debt or equity; "thin" capitalization.

Corporations may favor heavy debt capitalization because interest paid on debt is deductible, while dividends paid on stock aren't. But a corporation's debt obligations may be treated as equity (stock), making the "interest" paid on them a nondeductible dividend. Also, repayment of a debt isn't taxable to the lender (corporation), while a stock redemption may be taxable, as a dividend, to the shareholders (¶3526 *et seq.*).[30] For disallowed deductions for interest on corporate debt payable in the issuer's stock, see ¶1710.

The corporate issuer's characterization (at issuance) of a corporate instrument (issued after 10/24/92) as stock or debt is binding on the issuer and all holders (unless the holder discloses inconsistent treatment on his return), but not on IRS. (Code Sec. 385(c))[31]

A number of key factors are relevant in whether purported corporate debt will be treated as debt for federal tax purposes. No single factor is controlling. They include:

* the names given to the certificates evidencing the "debt";
* the presence or absence of a fixed interest, maturity date and payment schedule;
* the right to enforce payment of principal and interest and the source of payments;
* any resulting participation in management;
* whether the "debt" is subordinate to the corporation's other debt and whether it is convertible into stock;
* whether there is a high ratio of debt to equity;
* identity of interest between creditor and shareholder;
* the corporation's ability to get loans from outside lenders;

---

24. ¶K-5151; ¶1634.050; TD ¶319,502
25. ¶K-5280 *et seq.*; ¶4834; TD ¶319,500 *et seq.*
26. ¶s K-5281, K-5282; ¶4834.01; TD ¶319,501
27. ¶K-5048; ¶1634.013; TD ¶311,509

28. ¶K-5513; TD ¶314,002
29. ¶K-5506.1; ¶1634.013; TD ¶311,509.1
30. ¶K-5790 *et seq.*; ¶3854 *et seq.*; TD ¶313,501
31. ¶K-5791 *et seq.*; ¶3854.01; TD ¶313,501

- the extent to which the advance was used to acquire capital assets and the security, if any, for the advances;
- the "debtor's" failure to repay on time or to seek a postponement; and
- the economic realities and business purpose of the transaction, as well as the intent of the parties.[32]

¶ 1710 No deduction for interest on corporate debt payable in issuer's stock.

No deduction is allowed for interest paid or accrued on a disqualified debt instrument (Code Sec. 163(l)(1)), or OID (¶1751) on such an instrument.[33] A disqualified debt instrument is any corporate debt (or debt issued by a partnership to the extent of its corporate partners) that's payable in (1) equity (i.e., stock) of the issuer or a related party (under Code Sec. 267(b), see ¶2448, or Code Sec. 707(b), see ¶3731), and, (2) for debt instruments issued after Oct. 3, 2004, equity held by the issuer or any related party in any other person (basis in the equity is increased by the disallowed deduction). (Code Sec. 163(l)(2); Code Sec. 163(l)(6))[34] But it doesn't include certain debt issued by dealers in securities. (Code Sec. 163(l)(5))[35]

Debt is treated as payable in equity of the issuer or a related party only if:

(1) a substantial amount of the principal or interest is required to be paid or converted, or at the option of the issuer or related party, is payable in or convertible into, the equity,

(2) a substantial amount of the principal or interest is required to be, or at the option of the issuer or related party is, determined by reference to the value of the equity, or

(3) the debt is part of an arrangement that is reasonably expected to result in a transaction described in (1) or (2) (Code Sec. 163(l)(3)), such as in the case of certain issuances of a forward contract in connection with the issuance of debt, nonrecourse debt secured principally by stock, or certain debt instruments that are convertible at the holder's option when it's substantially certain that the right will be exercised. [36]

For these purposes, principal or interest is treated as required to be so paid, converted, or determined if it may be required at the option of the holder or a related party and there's a substantial certainty that the option will be exercised. (Code Sec. 163(l)(3))[37]

These rules deal only with the deduction by the issuer, generally for debt instruments issued after June 8, '97. They don't affect the treatment of a holder of an instrument. [38]

¶ 1711 Who may deduct interest?

With some exceptions (¶1712, ¶1713), a taxpayer's interest deduction is limited to interest he pays or accrues on his *own* indebtedness, and not for interest on debts of others.[39] But for joint obligors—i.e., persons who are jointly and severally liable for a debt —each obligor may deduct the amount of interest he actually pays on the debt. [40]

A person who is only secondarily liable for the debt, e.g., as endorser or guarantor, generally can't deduct interest on the debt. But if he actually pays all or part of the debt, he may be allowed to deduct the interest (or take a bad debt deduction, see ¶1851 *et seq.*).[41]

¶ 1712 Interest paid by another.

In certain cases where a person other than taxpayer pays or accrues the interest on taxpayer's debt, the payments are treated as made by taxpayer so he can deduct the interest.

32. ¶K-5801 *et seq.*; ¶1634.057; TD ¶313,501
33. ¶K-5507; ¶1634.059; TD ¶313,502
34. ¶K-5508; ¶1634.059; TD ¶313,502
35. ¶K-5509; ¶1634.059; TD ¶313,502.2
36. ¶K-5507 *et seq.*; ¶1634.059; TD ¶313,502

37. ¶K-5507; ¶1634.059; TD ¶313,502
38. ¶K-5507; ¶1634.059; TD ¶313,502
39. ¶K-5120 *et seq.*; ¶1634.015; TD ¶318,401
40. ¶K-5130; ¶1634.015; TD ¶318,405
41. ¶K-5133; ¶1664.450; TD ¶318,407

This occurs when the interest payor is acting (or is treated as acting) merely as taxpayer's agent (e.g., where a tenant pays the interest on his landlord's mortgage), or where taxpayer has given some consideration for the payor's payment. [42]

¶ 1713   Who deducts mortgage interest (and points).

A taxpayer who is personally liable for a mortgage debt may deduct the otherwise deductible mortgage interest (¶1702) (and points) he actually pays out of his own funds even if, when he makes the payments, he no longer owns the property subject to the mortgage (for points on seller-financed mortgages, see ¶1703; for co-ops, see ¶1714). But where a conveyance of mortgaged property would, under state law, automatically relieve the transferor of personal liability on the mortgage, he can't deduct the payments he makes after the transfer. [43]

A taxpayer who *isn't* personally liable for a mortgage debt may deduct the mortgage interest he actually pays *only* if he's the legal or equitable owner (solely or jointly with others) of the mortgaged property.[44] Home buyers whose occupancy of the residence gave them equitable (but not legal) title to it could deduct interest they paid on the builder's construction loan. [45]

Where the joint owners of mortgaged property are also jointly liable on the mortgage, each owner may deduct the mortgage interest he actually pays out of his own funds. [46]

☝caution: Mortgage interest that's deductible *solely* because it's "qualified residence interest" may be deducted *only* by the person who owns the property, see ¶1730.

¶ 1714   Cooperative housing corporation's (co-op's) mortgage payments.

Tenant-stockholders of cooperative housing corporations (co-ops) deduct their share of the co-op's mortgage interest payments (subject to the "qualified residence interest" limits, see ¶1730). (Code Sec. 216)[47]

¶ 1715   No deduction for personal interest.

Noncorporate taxpayers can't deduct "personal interest." (Code Sec. 163(h)(1))[48] Personal interest is all interest *other than*: (1) interest properly allocable to trade or business debt (other than the trade or business of being an employee); (2) interest paid on qualified education loans (¶2225 *et seq.*); (3) qualified residence interest (¶1730 *et seq.*); (4) interest considered in computing income or loss from a passive activity (¶1810 *et seq.*); (5) investment interest (¶1728); (6) interest payable under Code Sec. 6601 on unpaid estate tax during the time there is a Code Sec. 6163 extension of time for paying the tax because of a remainder or reversionary interest (see ¶5035). (Code Sec. 163(h)(2))[49]

But no deduction is allowed for any interest payable under Code Sec. 6601 on any unpaid estate tax for the period when a Code Sec. 6166 payment extension (for estate tax attributable to certain closely held business interests) is in effect. (Code Sec. 163(k))[50]

¶ 1716   Net direct interest expense—market discount bonds.

Taxpayer's "net direct interest expense" with respect to any taxable market discount bond (¶1326) is deductible in a tax year only to the extent the expense exceeds the market discount allocable to the days during the year the bond was held by taxpayer. (Code Sec. 1277(a); Code Sec. 1278(a)(1)(C))[1] (For tax-exempt bonds, see ¶1723.)

---

42. ¶K-5129; ¶1634.018; TD ¶318,409
43. ¶K-5135, ¶K-5136; TD ¶318,601
44. ¶K-5136; ¶1634.015; TD ¶318,602
45. ¶K-5136; TD ¶318,602
46. ¶K-5138; TD ¶318,604

47. ¶K-5140; ¶K-5900 *et seq.*; ¶2164.01; TD ¶314,511
48. ¶K-5510; ¶1634.054; TD ¶314,000
49. ¶K-5511; ¶1634.054; TD ¶314,001
50. ¶K-5513; ¶1634.013; TD ¶314,002
1. ¶K-5341; ¶12,764.02; TD ¶316,501

"Net direct interest expense" is any excess of: (1) interest paid or accrued on debt incurred or continued to buy or carry a market discount bond, over (2) interest (including OID, ¶1314) includible in income for the tax year with respect to the bond. (Code Sec. 1277(c))[2]

The disallowed interest expenses are deductible in the year the bond is disposed of (Code Sec. 1277(b)(2)(A)) or, if taxpayer so elects (bond-by-bond), in an earlier year when (but only to the extent that) taxpayer has net interest income from the bond. (Code Sec. 1277(b)(1))[3]

¶ 1717 Net direct interest expense—short-term government obligations.

The "net direct interest expense" (¶1716) with respect to a short-term government obligation is deductible in a tax year only to the extent the expense exceeds the total of: (1) the daily portions of the acquisition discount for each day during the year that taxpayer held the obligation, plus (2) the amount of any other (stated) interest payable on the obligation that accrues during the tax year while taxpayer held the obligation and that, because of taxpayer's accounting method, wasn't included in his gross income. (Code Sec. 1282(a))[4]

Deduction of disallowed interest expense generally is deferred until (as with market discount bonds, see ¶1716) taxpayer disposes of the obligation or makes the special election. (Code Sec. 1282(c))[5]

¶ 1718 Interest on business life insurance, annuity or endowment contract loans.

No deduction is allowed (for exception, see below) for any interest paid or accrued on any debt with respect to one or more life insurance policies owned by the taxpayer covering the life of any individual, or any annuity or endowment contract owned by the taxpayer covering any individual. (Code Sec. 264(a)(4))

For contracts issued before June 9, '97, the interest disallowance rule applies only if the covered individual is or was either an officer or employee of, or financially interested in, any trade or business currently or formerly carried on by the taxpayer. For policies purchased before June 21, '86, the disallowance rule generally didn't apply. [6]

A taxpayer *may* deduct a limited amount of interest (assuming it isn't barred by the rules at ¶1719 and ¶1720), subject to certain rate limitations, paid or accrued with respect to policies or contracts covering a "key person" (an officer or 20% owner) to the extent that the aggregate amount of the debt with respect to policies and contracts covering that person doesn't exceed $50,000. (Code Sec. 264(e)(1)) This exception applies only to a limited number of key persons (not more than the greater of: (1) 5 individuals, or (2) the lesser of 5% of total officers and employees, or 20 individuals). (Code Sec. 264(e)(3))[7]

¶ 1719 Single premium life insurance, endowment and annuity contracts.

No deduction is allowed for interest on debt incurred or continued to buy or carry single premium life insurance, endowment or annuity contracts. (Code Sec. 264(a)(2); Reg § 1.264-2) A contract is "single premium" if "substantially all" the premiums are paid within four years from the purchase date, or if an amount is deposited with the insurer for payment of a "substantial" number of future premiums on the contract. (Code Sec. 264(c); Reg § 1.264-3)[8]

¶ 1720 "Plan of purchase" borrowing against life insurance contracts.

No deduction is allowed for interest on debt incurred or continued to buy or carry a life insurance, endowment or annuity contract under a plan of purchase (borrowing for more than

2. ¶K-5342; ¶12,764.02; TD ¶316,502
3. ¶K-5343; ¶12,764.02; TD ¶316,503
4. ¶K-5344; ¶12,814.02; TD ¶316,504
5. ¶K-5343; ¶12,814.02; TD ¶316,505

6. ¶K-5351; ¶2644; TD ¶316,801
7. ¶K-5352; ¶2644; TD ¶316,802
8. ¶K-5570 *et seq.*; ¶2644; TD ¶317,200 *et seq.*

3 years is presumed to be a plan (Reg § 1.264-4(d)(2))) contemplating systematic direct or indirect borrowing of part or all of the increases in the contract's cash value. The deduction is barred whether the lender is the insurer or another party (e.g., a bank). (Code Sec. 264(a)(3))[9]

But even if the borrowing is under a "systematic plan," the interest is deductible (subject to the other bars and limits on interest deductions) if:

(1) at least four of the first seven annual premiums are paid without *any* borrowing (the "4-out-of-7 rule"); or

(2) the total interest paid or accrued that year with respect to the "plan of purchase" is not over $100 (otherwise entire interest deduction is disallowed); or

(3) the borrowing was incurred because of an unforeseen loss of income or substantial increase in financial obligations; or

(4) the borrowing was in connection with taxpayer's business. (Code Sec. 264(d); Reg § 1.264-4(d))[10]

¶ 1721   No deduction for interest allocable to unborrowed policy cash values ("inside buildup") on life insurance, annuity and endowment contracts.

Except as discussed below, no deduction is allowed for that portion of the taxpayer's interest expense that's allocable to unborrowed policy cash values —i.e., with respect to any life insurance policy, annuity, or endowment contract, the excess of (a) the cash surrender value of the policy or contract determined without regard to any surrender charge (or, if (a) does not reasonably approximate the policy's, etc. actual value, a statutorily-defined amount), over (b) the amount of any loan with respect to the policy or contract. (Code Sec. 264(f))[11] This rule must be applied before the Code Sec. 263A uniform capitalization rules (¶1660). (Code Sec. 264(f)(6)(B))[12]

observation: Unless an exception (see below) applies, if a taxpayer owns a life insurance policy, etc., with "inside buildup" —i.e., the policy's cash surrender value exceeds the amount of any loans taken out with respect to it —the taxpayer will lose an allocable portion of any interest deduction to which he would otherwise be entitled.

The portion of the interest expense that's allocable to unborrowed policy cash values is an amount that bears the same ratio to that interest expense as (1) average unborrowed policy cash values of life insurance policies, and annuity and endowment contracts, issued after June 8, '97, bears to (2) the sum of: (i) for assets that are life insurance policies or annuity or endowment contracts, the average unborrowed policy cash values of the policies and contracts; and (ii) for assets that aren't described in (i), the average adjusted bases (under Code Sec. 1016) of those assets. (Code Sec. 264(f)(2))[13]

The disallowance rule doesn't apply to any of the following:

(1) Any policy or contract owned by an entity engaged in a trade or business if the policy or contract covers only one individual and if that individual is (at the time first covered by the policy or contract) a 20% owner of the entity, or an individual (who isn't a 20% owner) who is an officer, director, or employee of the trade or business. (Code Sec. 264(f)(4)(A))[14]

(2) Any annuity contract to which Code Sec. 72(u) applies (i.e., annuity contracts subject to the natural-person-as-holder requirement, ¶1358). (Code Sec. 264(f)(4)(B))[15]

(3) Any policy or contract held by a natural person. But, if a trade or business is directly or indirectly the beneficiary, the policy or contract is treated as held by the trade or business

---

9. ¶K-5584; ¶2644; TD ¶317,500
10. ¶K-5584 *et seq.*; ¶2644; TD ¶317,505
11. ¶K-5601; ¶2644.01; TD ¶317,601
12. ¶K-5601; ¶2644.01; TD ¶317,601

13. ¶K-5604; ¶2644.01; TD ¶317,603
14. ¶K-5606; ¶2644.01; TD ¶317,605
15. ¶K-5606.1; ¶2644.01; TD ¶317,605

and not by a natural person, but this doesn't apply to any trade or business carried on as a sole proprietorship, or to any trade or business of performing services as an employee. (Code Sec. 264(f)(5)(A))[16]

(4) Certain insurance companies. (Code Sec. 264(f)(8)(B))[17]

(5) Any policy or contract issued before June 9, '97. [18]

For purposes of exception (1), above: (a) a policy or contract covering a 20% owner of an entity isn't treated as failing to meet the requirements because it covers the joint lives of the 20% owner and the owner's spouse (Code Sec. 264(f)(4)); and (b) if coverage for each insured individual under a master contract is treated as a separate contract for purposes of Code Sec. 817(h), Code Sec. 7702, and Code Sec. 7702A (technical insurance, annuity and modified endowment contract rules), then coverage for each such insured is treated as a separate contract. (Code Sec. 264(f)(4)(E)) A "master contract" doesn't include any group life insurance contract (as defined in Code Sec. 848(e)(2)).[19]

In applying the above rules, all members of a controlled group generally are treated as one taxpayer (Code Sec. 264(f)(8)(A)),[20] and in the case of partnerships and S corporations, the rules apply at the entity level. (Code Sec. 264(f)(5)(B))[21]

¶ 1722   Loans from qualified employer plans.

No deduction is allowed for interest on any loan from a qualified employer plan that isn't treated as a distribution, for the period: (1) on or after the first day the individual to whom the loan is made is a key employee (defined in Code Sec. 416(i)), or (2) during which the loan is secured by amounts attributable to elective deferrals under a Code Sec. 401(k) plan (¶4317) or a Code Sec. 403(b) annuity (¶4388 *et seq.*). (Code Sec. 72(p)(3))[22]

¶ 1723   Loans to buy or carry tax-exempt securities.

No deduction is allowed for interest on debt incurred or continued to buy or carry tax-exempt securities (e.g., state or local bonds, see ¶1331) (Code Sec. 265(a)(2)), or stock of a mutual fund ¶4201) distributing exempt interest. (Code Sec. 265(a)(4))[23]

¶ 1724   Registration-required obligations.

No deduction is allowed for interest on "registration-required obligations" (defined in Code Sec. 163(f)(2)) that aren't in registered form. (Code Sec. 163(f)(1))[24]

¶ 1725   Interest on corporate acquisition indebtedness.

The deduction allowed to a corporation for the interest it pays or accrues during a tax year on certain "corporate acquisition indebtedness" can't exceed $5,000,000. But all or part of the excess may not be subject to disallowance if specified tests (acquisition purpose, subordination, convertibility, and debt-equity) are met. (Code Sec. 279)[25]

¶ 1726   Investment Interest Deduction Limitations. ▰▰▰▰▰

Noncorporate taxpayers can deduct investment interest only to the extent of net investment income.

16. ¶K-5606.2; ¶2644.01; TD ¶317,605
17. ¶K-5606.3; ¶2644.01; TD ¶317,605
18. ¶K-5601; ¶2644.01; TD ¶317,601
19. ¶K-5606; ¶2644.01
20. ¶K-5602

21. ¶K-5603; ¶2644.01; TD ¶317,602
22. ¶K-5506, H-11065 *et seq.* ; ¶724.23; TD ¶317,000
23. ¶K-5520 *et seq.* ; ¶K-5546; ¶2654; TD ¶316,001
24. ¶K-5550 *et seq.* ; ¶1634
25. ¶K-5405 *et seq.* ; ¶s 1634, 2794

¶ 1727   Investment interest deductions of noncorporate taxpayers—Form 4952.

The amount of investment interest (¶1728) that may be deducted in any tax year by a noncorporate taxpayer generally is limited to taxpayer's "net investment income" (¶1729) for the year. (Code Sec. 163(d)(1)) Form 4952 is used to compute the limitation. [26]

Interest that's disallowed because of this limit can be carried over and deducted in later years, subject to the later year's investment income limit. (Code Sec. 163(d)(2))[27]

¶ 1728   "Investment interest."

"Investment interest" is interest paid or accrued on indebtedness properly allocable to property held for investment. (Code Sec. 163(d)(3)(A))[28] But the deduction limit on investment interest (¶1727) doesn't apply to interest expense that must be capitalized (e.g., construction interest), or that's disallowed under Code Sec. 265 (¶1723).[29]

Property held for investment is: (1) any property that produces income properly allocable to portfolio income under the passive activity rules —e.g., interest, dividends (but stock is "held for investment" even if it doesn't pay dividends), royalties, annuities, see ¶1820; (Code Sec. 163(d)(5)(A)(i))[30] and (2) any interest in an activity involving a trade or business in which taxpayer doesn't materially participate, if that activity isn't "passive" under the passive activity rules (¶1824). (Code Sec. 163(d)(5)(A)(ii))[31]

Investment interest includes interest on a home mortgage (other than "qualified residence interest," see below) if its purpose is to acquire investment property. [32] It also includes any amount allowable as a deduction in connection with personal property used in a short sale. (Code Sec. 163(d)(3)(C))[33]

Investment interest *doesn't include* interest on funds borrowed in connection with a trade or business, or any interest that is: (1) taken into account in determining taxpayer's income or loss from a passive activity, (2) qualified residence interest (¶1732) (Code Sec. 163(d)(3)(B)), or (3) properly allocable to a rental real estate activity in which, under the passive activity rules (¶1837), taxpayer actively participates. [34]

¶ 1729   "Net investment income" defined.

Taxpayer's "net investment income" for a tax year is the excess of "investment income" over "investment expenses" for the year. (Code Sec. 163(d)(4)(A))[35] (For the definition of net investment interest for alternative minimum tax purposes, see ¶3208.)

"Investment income" is the sum of: (1) gross income from property held for investment (¶1728); (2) any excess of *net gain* attributable to the disposition of investment property over *net capital gain* determined by only taking into account gains and losses from these dispositions; (3) so much of taxpayer's *net capital gain* (or *net gain,* if less) described in (2), as he elects (on Form 4952) to include in investment income (for the effect of such an election on net capital gain, see ¶2604); plus (4) so much of taxpayer's qualified dividend income (dividends received from domestic and qualified foreign corporations that are taxable at net capital gains rates, see ¶1286 *et seq.*), as he elects (on Form 4952) to include in investment income. (For the effect of such an election on qualified dividend income, see ¶1288.) (Code Sec. 163(d)(4)(B); Reg § 1.163(d)-1)[36]

---

26. ¶K-5310 *et seq.*; ¶1634.053; TD ¶315,011
27. ¶K-5321, ¶1634.053; TD ¶315,021
28. ¶K-5312; ¶1634.053; TD ¶315,012
29. ¶K-5312; TD ¶315,012
30. ¶K-5322; ¶1634.053; TD ¶315,022
31. ¶K-5322; ¶1634.053; TD ¶315,018

32. ¶K-5313; TD ¶315,013
33. ¶K-5312; TD ¶315,012
34. ¶K-5312 *et seq.*; ¶1634.053; TD ¶315,012
35. ¶K-5311; ¶1634.053; TD ¶315,015
36. ¶K-5315 *et seq.*; ¶1634.053; TD ¶315,015 *et seq.*

"Investment expenses" are deductible expenses *other than interest* that are directly connected with the production of investment income (Code Sec. 163(d)(4)(C)), but limited to the amount allowed after the 2%-of-AGI floor (¶3110). Nonbusiness bad debts (¶1856) directly connected with the production of income are taken into account to the extent they are currently deductible. [37]

Investment income and expenses don't include any amounts taken into account in computing income or loss from a passive activity (¶1810 *et seq.*). (Code Sec. 163(d)(4)(D))[38]

¶ 1730 Qualified Residence Interest.

Taxpayers may claim itemized deductions for "qualified residence interest" —i.e., interest on (1) up to $1,000,000 of acquisition debt and (2) up to $100,000 of home-equity debt. The debt must be secured by taxpayer's "qualified residence."

¶ 1731 Deduction of "qualified residence interest."

"Qualified residence interest" (¶1732) is not subject to these limits and special rules:

- personal interest deduction bar (¶1715) (Code Sec. 163(h)(2)(D); Reg § 1.163-10T(b));

observation: In other words, qualified residence interest is not subject to the prohibition on the deduction of personal interest, and may be deducted under the general rule allowing the deduction of interest, discussed at ¶1700 *et seq.*

- investment interest limitations (¶1728) (Code Sec. 163(d)(3)(B)(i); Reg § 1.163-10T(b));

- passive activity interest limitations (¶1815); (Code Sec. 469(j)(7); Reg § 1.163-10T(b))

- uniform capitalization rules (¶1660). (Reg § 1.163-10T(b))[39]

But qualified residence interest is subject to the interest bars and limits in connection with: single premium insurance (¶1719); tax-exempt income (¶1723); related-party transactions (¶2836); the "at-risk" rules (¶1803 *et seq.*); accrued market discount (¶1716); and straddle interest (¶2653 *et seq.*). (Reg § 1.163-10T(b))[40]

For how the interest allocation rules apply to qualified residence interest, see ¶1741.

caution: For the treatment of residence interest for alternative minimum tax purposes, see ¶3208.

¶ 1732 What is "qualified residence interest"?

"Qualified residence interest" (see ¶1731) is any interest paid or accrued during the tax year on acquisition indebtedness (¶1733) or home equity indebtedness (¶1734) with respect to any property that, at the time the interest is accrued, is taxpayer's "qualified residence" (¶1735), but only to the extent the interest is paid or accrued while the debt is secured by the residence. (Code Sec. 163(h)(3)(A); Reg § 1.163-10T(j)(1)) For a cash basis taxpayer, it also includes certain "points" paid on debt incurred in connection with his principal residence. (Reg § 1.163-10T(j)(2)(i))[41] For treatment of certain mortgage insurance premiums as qualified residence interest, see ¶1736

A debt may be part acquisition indebtedness and part home equity indebtedness. [42]

---

37. ¶K-5320; ¶1634.053; TD ¶315,020
38. ¶s K-5315, K-5320; ¶1634.053; TD ¶315,020
39. ¶K-5473; ¶1634.052; TD ¶314,501

40. ¶K-5473 *et seq.*; TD ¶314,501
41. ¶K-5471; ¶1634.052; TD ¶314,502
42. ¶K-5491; TD ¶314,521

¶ 1733   Acquisition indebtedness.

Acquisition indebtedness (interest on which is deductible qualified residence interest, see ¶1731) is debt that: (1) meets the dollar limitation described below; (2) is incurred in acquiring, constructing or substantially improving taxpayer's "qualified residence" (¶1735) (or adjoining land) and (3) is secured by the residence. (Code Sec. 163(h)(3)(B)(i)) In general, acquisition debt must be an obligation of the taxpayer. [43] New debt a taxpayer incurs to refinance his acquisition indebtedness also qualifies, but only up to the amount of the refinanced debt. (Code Sec. 163(h)(3)(B)(i))[44] Debt is treated as incurred in acquiring, etc., a residence if the debt proceeds can be traced to payment of the costs of the acquisition, etc. [45]

The aggregate amount of debt that may be treated as acquisition indebtedness for any period can't exceed $1,000,000 ($500,000 for a married individual filing a separate return). (Code Sec. 163(h)(3)(B)(ii)) These dollar amounts are reduced (not below zero) by the aggregate amount of outstanding (including refinanced) "pre-Oct. 13, '87 indebtedness." (Code Sec. 163(h)(3)(D))[46] For where debt exceeds these limits, see ¶1741.

¶ 1734   Home equity indebtedness.

Home equity indebtedness (interest on which is deductible qualified residence interest, see ¶1731) is any debt (other than acquisition indebtedness, see ¶1733) secured by taxpayer's qualified residence (¶1735), to the extent the aggregate amount of the debt doesn't exceed the fair market value of the residence (as reduced by the amount of acquisition indebtedness on it). (Code Sec. 163(h)(3)(C)(i)) Unlike acquisition debt (¶1733), home equity debt generally may be used for any purpose without affecting its deductibility, see ¶1741. The aggregate amount treated as home equity indebtedness for any period may not exceed $100,000 ($50,000 for a married individual filing a separate return). (Code Sec. 163(h)(3)(C)(ii))[47] For debt that exceeds these limits, see ¶1741.

observation: In other words, home equity indebtedness is limited to the taxpayer's net equity in the residence, with a $100,000 ($50,000) ceiling.

¶ 1735   Qualified residence.

A qualified residence (see ¶1732) is: (1) taxpayer's principal residence (i.e., one that would qualify for exclusion of gain under Code Sec. 121 (¶2442) (Code Sec. 163(h)(4)(A)(i)(I)) and/or (2) any other residence (second residence) taxpayer properly elects to treat as qualified for the tax year, even if he didn't use it as a residence that year. But a second residence that taxpayer rents out to others during the year can't qualify unless he also uses it as a residence (i.e., uses it for personal purposes during the year for more than the greater of 14 days or 10% of the number of days it is rented out for a fair rental). (Code Sec. 163(h)(4)(A)(i)(II), Code Sec. 163(h)(4)(A)(iii); Reg § 1.163-10T(p)(3)(iii)) A taxpayer who has more than one residence that meets these tests may elect each year which to treat as the second (qualified) residence. (Code Sec. 163(h)(4)(A)(i); Reg § 1.163-10T(p)(3)(iv))[48]

A residence for this purpose includes a condominium or cooperative housing corporation (co-op). Any indebtedness secured by stock in a co-op is treated as secured by the house or apartment taxpayer is entitled to occupy. Even if local restrictions prohibit using the stock as security, it will be treated as securing the debt if taxpayer can show the debt was incurred to acquire the stock. (Code Sec. 163(h)(4)(B); Reg § 1.163-10T(p)(3))[49] A time-share can also

---

43. ¶K-5484; ¶1634.052; TD ¶314,515
44. ¶K-5488; ¶1634.052; TD ¶314,519
45. ¶K-5487; TD ¶318,001
46. ¶s K-5485, K-5489; ¶1634.052; TD ¶314,516

47. ¶K-5490; ¶1634.052; TD ¶314,520
48. ¶K-5474 et seq.; ¶1634.052; TD ¶314,504
49. ¶K-5481; ¶1634.052; TD ¶314,511

qualify if it satisfies the above tests for rental property. (Reg § 1.163-10T(p)(6))[50]

A residence under construction may be treated as a qualified residence for a period of up to 24 months, but only if it otherwise qualifies as of the time it's ready for occupancy. (Reg § 1.163-10T(p)(5))[1]

For married taxpayers filing jointly, the second residence may be owned and/or used by either spouse. For spouses filing separately, each may have only one qualified residence (unless the other spouse gives written consent otherwise). (Code Sec. 163(h)(4)(A))[2]

¶ 1736 Mortgage insurance premiums paid or incurred in 2007 for acquisition indebtedness on qualified residence treated as qualified residence interest.

Premiums paid or accrued by a taxpayer during the tax year for qualified mortgage insurance in connection with acquisition indebtedness (see ¶1733) with respect to a qualified residence of the taxpayer are treated as qualified residence interest (Code Sec. 163(h)(3)(E)(i)), subject to a phase-out based on the taxpayer's adjusted gross income (AGI) (below).[3]

◆/caution: Check http://ria.thomson.com/federaltaxhandbook to see if this provision has been extended.

◆/observation: To be deductible under the above rule, premiums for qualified mortgage insurance must be paid or accrued in connection with acquisition indebtedness. But, qualified mortgage insurance isn't a category of acquisition indebtedness, but rather a separate category of qualified residence interest. So, qualified mortgage insurance isn't subject to the amount limitations on acquisition indebtedness, and doesn't affect the amount of indebtedness that may qualify as acquisition indebtedness under those limitations, see ¶1733.

Qualified mortgage insurance means mortgage insurance provided by the Veterans Administration (VA), the Federal Housing Administration (FHA), or the Rural Housing Administration (RHA), and private mortgage insurance, as defined by Sec. 2 of the Homeowners Protection Act of '98 (12 U.S.C. 4901), as in effect on Dec. 20, 2006. (Code Sec. 163(h)(4)(E)(ii))

Except for amounts paid for qualified mortgage insurance provided by the VA or the RHA, any amounts paid by the taxpayer for qualified mortgage insurance that is properly allocable to any mortgage the payment of which extends to periods that are after the close of the tax year in which that amount is paid are chargeable to capital account and must be treated as paid in those periods to which they are allocated.

But, no deduction is allowed for the unamortized balance of premiums that have been capitalized if the mortgage is satisfied before the end of its term. (Code Sec. 163(h)(4)(F))

The rules treating qualified mortgage insurance premiums as deductible qualified residence interest apply only if the amounts: (1) are paid or accrued before Jan. 1, 2008; (2) aren't properly allocable to any period after Dec. 31, 2007; and (3) are paid or accrued with respect to a mortgage insurance contract issued after Dec. 31, 2006. (Code Sec. 163(h)(3)(E))

The amount of mortgage insurance premiums otherwise treated as qualified residence interest under the rule above must be reduced (but not below zero) by: (a) for taxpayers other than married persons filing separately, 10% of the amount of qualified mortgage insurance for each $1,000 (or fraction thereof) that the taxpayer's AGI for the tax year exceeds $100,000, and (b) for married persons filing separately, 10% of the amount of qualified mortgage insurance for each $500 (or fraction thereof) that the taxpayer's AGI for the tax year exceeds $50,000. (Code Sec. 163(h)(3)(E)(i))

50. ¶K-5482; TD ¶314,512
1. ¶K-5483; TD ¶314,513

2. ¶K-5480; ¶1634.052; TD ¶314,510
3. ¶K-5493.1; ¶1634.052; TD ¶314,519.1

¶ 1737   Allocation Rules for Interest and Debt. ▆▆▆▆▆▆

Debt proceeds may be used in ways that trigger more than one interest deduction limitations. To determine which limit applies (personal interest, ¶1715, investment interest, ¶1727, or passive activity interest, ¶1815), the interest and underlying debt must be properly allocated, generally by tracing the use of the borrowed money.

¶ 1738   Interest deduction limits require allocation of interest expense.

For certain taxpayers (see ¶1739), where the proceeds of a single debt are used for multiple purposes—e.g., to make investments *and* to buy "personal" items—the debt must be allocated among the various expenditures. (Reg § 1.163-8T)[4]

Interest expense is allocated the same way as the debt with respect to which the interest accrues, by tracing disbursements of the debt proceeds to specific expenditures. (Reg § 1.163-8T(a)(3), Reg § 1.163-8T(c)(1)) Except for qualified residence interest (¶1732), the nature of any property securing the debt isn't relevant. (Reg § 1.163-8T(c)(1))[5]

The interest, as allocated, is subject to the appropriate deduction limit, as follows:

. . . Interest allocated to a passive activity expenditure (current or former) is subject to the passive activity limitations (¶1815).

. . . Interest allocated to an investment expenditure is subject to the investment interest limitations (¶1727).

. . . Interest allocated to a personal expenditure is treated as personal interest (i.e., it's not deductible, see ¶1715).

. . . Interest allocated to a trade or business expenditure is treated as trade or business interest (i.e., it's not subject to the personal or investment interest limits). (Code Sec. 469(l)(4); Reg § 1.163-8T(a)(4)(i))[6]

The interest expense allocation rules don't control the allocation of interest for any purpose other than those listed above. [7]

¶ 1739   Taxpayers who must allocate interest.

The interest expense allocation rules (¶1738) apply to all taxpayers *other than* widely-held C corporations. So, the rules apply to a pass-through entity (e.g., partnership or S corporation) that borrows money to make distributions to its owners (partners or shareholders), or whose debt is allocated to those distributions. Repayments of a pass-through entity's debt that is allocated partly to a distribution to its owners and partly to other expenditures are treated first as a repayment of the portion of the debt allocated to the distribution. [8]

¶ 1740   Time for allocation of debt and interest expense

Debt is allocated to an expenditure for the period: (1) beginning on the date the proceeds of the debt are used or treated as used to make the expenditure, and (2) ending on the date the debt is repaid or reallocated (¶1742), whichever is earlier. (Reg § 1.163-8T(c)(2)(i))[9]

Generally, interest expense that accrues on a debt is allocated in the same manner as the debt is allocated from time to time, regardless of when the interest is actually paid. (Reg § 1.163-8T(c)(2)(ii)(A))[10]

---

4. ¶K-5231 *et seq.*; ¶1634.055; TD ¶318,001
5. ¶K-5231; ¶1634.055; TD ¶318,001
6. ¶K-5232; ¶1634.055; TD ¶318,000 *et seq.*
7. ¶K-5234; TD ¶318,002

8. ¶K-5259 *et seq.*; ¶1634.056; TD ¶318,033
9. ¶K-5233; ¶1634.055; TD ¶318,008
10. ¶K-5233; ¶1634.055; TD ¶318,008

¶ 1741 Qualified residence interest as "allocable" interest.

Qualified residence interest (¶1730 *et seq.*) is deductible without regard to how that interest expense (or the underlying debt) is allocated. (Reg §   1.163-8T(m)(3))[11]

Illustration: E borrows $20,000. The loan is secured by a residence. E uses the loan proceeds to buy a car strictly for personal use. The debt and the interest are allocable to personal expenditures, so the interest would normally be subject to the personal interest limits (¶1715). But, if the interest is qualified residence interest (i.e., home equity debt, see ¶1735), it's not personal interest and would be fully deductible. (Reg §   1.163-8T(m)(3))[12]

But, where the debt exceeds the qualified residence interest limits (¶1733, ¶1734), allocation is required for the "excess." (Reg §   1.163-10T(e))[13]

¶ 1742 Reallocation of interest

Where the use of debt proceeds, or of assets bought with debt proceeds, changes, the interest on the debt must be reallocated to the new use. The interest, as so reallocated, will be subject to any appropriate deduction limits (see ¶1738). (Reg § 1.163-8T(j)(1))[14]

¶ 1743 When Interest May Be Deducted. ▄▄▄▄▄▄▄▄▄▄▄▄

The proper time for deducting interest is generally determined by the taxpayer's method of accounting. Special rules govern when mortgage "points," unstated interest and original issue (OID) discount must be deducted.

¶ 1744 Cash method taxpayer's interest deduction.

A cash method taxpayer may deduct interest only if it is actually *paid* during the tax year. (Code Sec. 163(a)) (For accrual taxpayers, see ¶1748.) The payment can be with funds borrowed from another creditor, but not with funds borrowed from the same creditor, or by giving a note for the interest or adding the unpaid interest to principal. [15]

Contested interest (where the debtor claims he doesn't owe it) isn't deductible. But if a cash basis taxpayer transfers money or other property to provide for the satisfaction of the asserted (and otherwise deductible) interest, it's deductible in the year of the transfer. (Code Sec. 461(f))[16] For prepaid interest (including "points"), see ¶1745.

¶ 1745 Prepaid interest (including "points").

Interest that is prepaid, including "points" (except certain home mortgage points, see ¶1746), is deductible only in the tax year to which, and to the extent that, the interest is allocable —i.e., as it accrues. (Code Sec. 461(g)(1)) Cash method taxpayers thus generally deduct points ratably over the term of the loan (for refinancings, see ¶1747).[17]

A taxpayer who "pays" points by receiving discounted loan proceeds gets no current deduction (except certain mortgage points, ¶1746).[18] Instead, the discount is treated as OID, deductible by the borrower under the OID rules (¶1751). Discounts *not* subject to the OID rules may be deducted ratably as the underlying debt is repaid. [19]

If the mortgage ends early, e.g., because of a prepayment, refinancing, foreclosure or similar event, taxpayer may deduct the remaining balance of points in the year it ends. [20]

---

11. ¶K-5238; ¶1634.055; TD ¶318,005
12. ¶K-5238; ¶1634.055; TD ¶318,005
13. ¶K-5499; TD ¶314,530
14. ¶K-5254 *et seq.*; ¶1634.055; TD ¶318,023
15. ¶K-5170 *et seq.*; ¶s 1634.030, 1634.031; TD ¶318,700 *et seq.*

16. ¶G-2442 *et seq.*; ¶4614.56 *et seq.*; TD ¶319,004, 319,005
17. ¶K-5177; ¶s 1634.005, 1634.032, 4614.75; TD ¶318,707
18. ¶K-5178; ¶4614.75; TD ¶319,201
19. ¶K-5176; ¶4614.75; TD ¶318,706
20. ¶K-5183; TD ¶319,206

¶ 1746 "Points" on a home mortgage—cash method taxpayer's deduction in year of payment.

A cash method taxpayer may (but doesn't have to) deduct points paid on indebtedness incurred in connection with the purchase or improvement of (and secured by) his principal residence, in the tax year of actual payment —i.e., in advance, not ratably (see ¶1745) (for refinancings, see ¶1747). The charging of points must reflect an established business practice in the geographical area where the loan is made, and the deduction allowed can't exceed the number of points generally charged there. (Code Sec. 461(g)(2)) For loans used to improve the residence, the points must be paid with funds other than those borrowed from the lender or mortgage broker.[21]

For loans used to acquire the residence, cash basis taxpayers may currently deduct amounts that meet the above tests *and* are: (1) clearly designated (on Form HUD-1) as points incurred in connection with the debt (including "points" on VA and FHA loans) —i.e., they aren't paid in lieu of nondeductible amounts that are ordinarily stated separately, e.g., appraisal fees; (2) computed as a percentage of the stated principal amount of the debt; *and* (3) paid directly by taxpayer to the lender (or mortgage broker). Condition (3) is met where taxpayer provides, from funds that haven't been borrowed for this purpose as part of the overall transaction, an amount at least equal to what is required to be applied as points at closing (even if the amount so provided is used for down payments, escrow deposits, etc., actually paid at closing).[22]

Points paid by (or charged to) the seller in connection with a loan to the buyer (taxpayer) also are deductible by the buyer if he subtracts them from the purchase price in computing the basis of the residence.[23]

¶ 1747 "Points" on refinancing.

Points paid to *refinance* an existing mortgage generally are deductible only ratably over the loan term (see ¶1745). But where the refinancing is incurred for home improvements, points paid from separate funds may be deducted currently.[24]

¶ 1748 Accrual method taxpayer's interest deduction.

Accrual method taxpayers deduct interest when all the events have occurred that fix the fact of the liability, the amount of the liability can be determined with reasonable accuracy, and economic performance (¶2832 *et seq.*) has occurred.[25] (For cash method, see ¶1744.)

The interest is deductible only in the year it accrues, without regard to when the (accrual basis) taxpayer pays it. For these purposes, interest (including prepaid interest) accrues ratably over the life of a loan. But interest that's contingent on events other than the creditor's demand for payment doesn't accrue until the contingency happens.[26]

Contested interest (where the debtor claims he doesn't owe it) isn't accruable or deductible. But if the accrual basis taxpayer transfers money or other property to provide for the satisfaction of the asserted interest, it's deductible in the year of the transfer. (Code Sec. 461(f))[27]

---

21. ¶K-5178 *et seq.*; ¶s 1634.005, 4614.75; TD ¶319,201
22. ¶K-5179; ¶4614.75; TD ¶319,202
23. ¶K-5179; ¶4614.75; TD ¶318,606
24. ¶K-5180; ¶s 1634.005, 4614.75; TD ¶319,203

25. ¶K-5200 *et seq.*; ¶1634.035 *et seq.*; TD ¶319,000 *et seq.*
26. ¶s K-5200, K-5201; ¶s 1634.035, 1634.036; TD ¶319,001
27. ¶G-2643*et seq.*; ¶4614.56 *et seq.*; TD ¶319,004, 319,005

¶ 1749 Interest under the "Rule of 78s" method.

The Rule of 78s method can't be used to compute interest. Interest so computed must be recomputed under an economic accrual method for federal income tax purposes. [28]

¶ 1750 When to deduct "unstated interest."

The unstated interest allocated to a payment in a deferred payment sale (¶1707) is deducted by cash method buyers in the year the payment is made, and by accrual method buyers in the year the payment is due. (Reg § 1.483-2(a)(1)(ii))[29] But both cash and accrual taxpayers use the cash method rules to deduct interest on cash method debt instruments (¶1320). (Code Sec. 1274A(c)(1)(B))[30]

¶ 1751 Original issue discount (OID).

The issuer of a debt instrument issued with OID (see ¶1313 *et seq.*) may (with some exceptions, ¶1753) deduct part of the OID (¶1752) in each tax year the instrument is outstanding, even though the OID isn't paid until maturity. (Code Sec. 163(e)(1); Reg § 1.163-3(a)(1), Reg § 1.163-4(a)(1)) This current deduction rule applies regardless of the method of accounting used by the issuer. [31] But a cash method obligor of a short-term obligation can only deduct OID (and other interest) when it is paid. (Code Sec. 163(e)(2)(C))[32]

An issuer may deduct OID only to the extent the issuer is primarily liable on the debt instrument. (Reg § 1.163-7(a))[33]

OID for this purpose has the same meaning as for purposes of requiring the holder to include OID in gross income currently (see ¶1314) *except*:

. . . The de minimis exception doesn't apply. (Code Sec. 163(e)(2)(B))[34] But an issuer with de minimis OID may elect to deduct the OID at maturity. (Reg § 1.163-7(b)(2))[35]

. . . A nonpublicly traded debt instrument issued to a seller in exchange for personal use property isn't treated as issued with OID that the buyer (issuer) can deduct currently. (Code Sec. 1275(b)(1))[36]

¶ 1752 Amount of OID deductible currently.

The amount of OID the issuer of a debt instrument deducts currently (¶1751) is determined in the same way as the amount of OID the holder includes in gross income currently (using the constant yield method, see ¶1321), but without regard to (1) the reduction for any acquisition premium paid by the holder and (2) the treatment of stated interest as "qualified stated interest" where OID is de minimis. (Code Sec. 163(e)(2)(B); Reg § 1.163-7(a))[37]

¶ 1753 Limits on OID deduction for certain high yield OID obligations.

For certain high yield OID obligations (at least five percentage points over the applicable federal rate for month of issue) issued after July 10, '89, a C corporation can't deduct (or otherwise take into account) any part of the OID until actually paid. In some cases, the deduction may be barred for all or part of the OID, depending on the obligation's yield, maturity date and amount of OID. (Code Sec. 163(e)(5))[38]

28. ¶K-5153; ¶1634.030
29. ¶K-5283; ¶1634; TD ¶319,503
30. ¶K-5283; TD ¶319,503
31. ¶K-5700 *et seq.*; ¶1634.051; TD ¶319,701
32. ¶K-5712; ¶1634.032, 1634.051; TD ¶319,710
33. ¶K-5745; ¶1634.051; TD ¶319,714

34. ¶K-5727; ¶1634.051; TD ¶319,719
35. ¶K-5748; ¶1634.051; TD ¶319,725
36. ¶K-5724; TD ¶319,717
37. ¶K-5745 *et seq.*; ¶1634.051; TD ¶319,725 *et seq.*
38. ¶K-5754 *et seq.*; ¶1634.051

¶ 1754   Deduction for Taxes. ■■■■■■■

Certain state, local, U.S. possessions and foreign taxes are deductible whether or not connected with a trade or business; so are some federal taxes (not income tax).

Only payments that are really taxes (regardless of what they are called) are deductible as taxes (see ¶1757). Taxes are charges imposed on persons or property by governmental authority to raise funds for the support of government or for public purposes. The mere fact that a levy is called a "tax" isn't conclusive. [39] Fees imposed primarily as charges for government services, e.g., fees for a driver's license or car inspection, or passport fees, aren't deductible as taxes. [40] Penalties paid to a government for violation of a law aren't taxes. (Code Sec. 162(f))[41]

¶ 1755   Which taxes are deductible?

Deductible *state, local and foreign taxes* are:

. . . state, local and foreign income, war profits and excess profits taxes (but a taxpayer can deduct state and local sales taxes instead of income taxes, see ¶1756);

. . . state, local and foreign real property taxes;

. . . state and local personal property taxes (see ¶1760); and

. . . other state, local and foreign taxes (e.g., occupational taxes) paid or accrued in business or for the production of income unless incurred in connection with an acquisition or disposition of property (e.g., sales taxes, see ¶1756). (Code Sec. 164(a)(1), Code Sec. 164(a)(3))[42]

For state unemployment and disability taxes, see ¶1758.

These *federal taxes* are deductible as taxes:

• Federal (and state) generation-skipping transfer (GST) tax imposed on income distributions (¶5055 *et seq.*) (Code Sec. 164(a)(4), Code Sec. 164(b)(4));[43]

• Estate tax attributable to income in respect of a decedent (¶3971);

• Self-employment taxes (¶3138 *et seq.*) are one-half deductible. (Code Sec. 164(f))[44]

caution: For the deductibility of taxes for alternative minimum tax purposes, see ¶3208.

Taxes not included above (e.g., gasoline, diesel and other motor fuel taxes, Social Security (FICA) and unemployment (FUTA) taxes on employers, motor vehicle registration fees) aren't deductible as *taxes* (although some motor vehicle fees may qualify as personal property taxes), but may be deductible as *business expenses* or *expenses for the production of income* (¶1506 *et seq.*). (Reg § 1.164-2(f))[45]

For deduction of taxes by individuals who don't itemize, see ¶1757.

These taxes aren't deductible as taxes, expenses or otherwise:

(1) Federal income taxes, including amounts withheld from wages, interest, etc.

(2) Alternative minimum tax.

(3) Social Security (FICA) tax on employees, and Railroad Retirement tax on employees and employee representatives. (Code Sec. 275(a)(1); Reg § 1.164-2(a))

(4) Federal war profits and excess profits taxes. (Code Sec. 275(a)(2); Reg § 1.164-2(b))

(5) Estate, inheritance, legacy, succession and gift taxes (Code Sec. 275(a)(3); Reg § 1.164-2(c)) except as noted above, whether state, federal or foreign.

(6) Income, war profits and excess profits taxes of any foreign country or U.S. possession if

---

39. ¶K-4003; ¶1644; TD ¶326,011
40. ¶K-4003 *et seq.*; ¶1644; TD ¶326,011
41. ¶K-4009; ¶1644; TD ¶326,008
42. ¶K-4001; ¶1644.03; TD ¶326,008

43. ¶K-4403 *et seq.*; ¶1644.06; TD ¶326,004
44. ¶K-4401; ¶1644.07; TD ¶326,002
45. ¶K-4000, L-2350*et seq.*; ¶1644; TD ¶327,001 *et seq.*

taxpayer takes the foreign tax credit for them (¶2369 *et seq.*). (Code Sec. 275(a)(4); Reg § 1.164-2(d)) But deduction is allowed for any tax that isn't allowable as a foreign tax credit because of Code Sec. 901(j) (which denies the credit for taxes paid to certain foreign countries, see ¶2371) (Code Sec. 901(j)(3)), or because of Code Sec. 901(k) (relating to minimum holding period requirements for certain taxes, see ¶2377).

(7) Excise taxes imposed on: charities' excess expenditures to influence legislation; private foundations; qualified pension, etc., plans; certain investment entities (REITs and RICs); excess golden parachute payments; greenmail (Code Sec. 275(a)(6)) and charitable split-dollar insurance transactions (¶2115). (Code Sec. 170(f)(10)(F)(iv))[46]

¶ 1756 Sales and use taxes.

Taxpayers may elect (on Schedule A of Form 1040) to deduct state and local *general sales and use* taxes instead of state and local *income* taxes, for tax years beginning before 2008. With limited exceptions, a sales or use tax is general if imposed at one rate with respect to the retail sale of a broad range of classes of items. (Code Sec. 164(b)(5); Reg § 1.164-3)[47]

caution: Check http://ria.thomson.com/federaltaxhandbook to see if this provision has been extended.

Electing taxpayers may deduct either:

(1) the amount of state and local general sales taxes paid, by accumulating receipts; or

(2) the amount determined under IRS tables (see below), plus the actual amount of sales taxes paid on motor vehicles, boats and other IRS-specified items (e.g., aircraft, homes). (Code Sec. 164(b)(5)(H))[48]

The IRS tables (in IRS Pub. 600) provide an amount of sales taxes paid based on the taxpayer's state of residence, total available income, and number of exemptions. Taxpayers living in more than one state during the year must prorate the table amounts based on the number of days lived in each state. For married taxpayers (¶1762), use of the tables depends on whether they file jointly or separately, and whether they live in the same state. [49]

The elective sales tax deduction doesn't apply to sales taxes paid on items used in a taxpayer's trade or business. [50]

If the election is not made, state and local sales or use taxes are deductible only to the following extent: State or local sales or use taxes paid or incurred in connection with the acquisition or disposition of property, and taxes on the transfer of property (e.g., securities, real estate), aren't deductible (buyer treats them as part of the cost, seller as a reduction in the amount realized). Other sales taxes are deductible only if paid or incurred in a trade or business or for the production of income. (Code Sec. 164(a))[1]

¶ 1757 Limitations on deduction for taxes if individual doesn't itemize.

An individual generally may deduct taxes only if he itemizes (on Schedule A of Form 1040). (Code Sec. 63(d))[2]

For an individual who doesn't itemize, the deduction is limited to these taxes that are deductible "above the line" (i.e., from gross income in arriving at AGI, ¶3102): taxes attributable to a trade or business (including taxes on real property) (Code Sec. 62(a)(1)), or to property held for the production of rents or royalties (Code Sec. 62(a)(4)), and one-half of any

46. ¶L-2358; ¶1644; TD ¶327,003
47. ¶K-4510 *et seq.*; ¶1644.03; TD ¶326,019.1 *et seq.*
48. ¶K-4511; ¶1644.03; TD ¶326,019.2
49. ¶K-4511 *et seq.*; TD ¶326,019.2 *et seq.*

50. ¶K-4510 *et seq.*; ¶1644.03; TD ¶326,019.1 *et seq.*
1. ¶I-2502, ¶K-4500 *et seq.*, ¶L-2352.1, ¶P-1174.1; ¶1644.03, ¶1644.09; TD ¶326,006, TD ¶327,001
2. ¶A-2701; ¶634; TD ¶561,201

self-employment taxes imposed on him. (Code Sec. 164(f))[3]

¶ 1758   State unemployment and disability taxes.

Employers' contributions to state unemployment insurance funds are deductible as taxes if the state so classifies them. Whether an employee's contributions to a state unemployment insurance fund or disability plan are deductible as taxes similarly is determined on a state-by-state basis. [4]

¶ 1759   Local benefit assessments.

Assessments that tend to increase the value of the assessed property (whether or not the value does increase) aren't deductible as taxes (but may be capitalized, see ¶1654 *et seq.*). But deduction *is* allowed, to the extent taxpayer shows the assessment is properly allocable to maintenance or interest charges. (Code Sec. 164(c)(1); Reg § 1.164-4(b)(1))[5]

¶ 1760   Personal property taxes.

Personal property taxes imposed by a state or local government are deductible. (Code Sec. 164(a)(2)) The tax must be imposed annually on personal property, on an ad valorem basis (i.e., based on the value of the personal property). (Code Sec. 164(b)(1))[6]

¶ 1761   Who deducts the tax?

Taxes generally are deductible only by the person on whom they are imposed. (Reg § 1.164-1(a))[7]

One who voluntarily pays a tax imposed on another isn't entitled to a deduction. So, a shareholder can't deduct his payment of the corporation's taxes, or vice versa. [8]

Property taxes are ordinarily imposed on, and so are deductible by, the property owner. (For the year of sale, see ¶1770.) A person who owns a beneficial interest in property may deduct property taxes he pays to protect that interest. [9]

Taxes on property that's leased are deductible by the landlord, even if it's the tenant who makes the payment (which tenant treats as additional rent expense, see ¶1593). (Reg § 1.162-11(a)) But a tenant deducts taxes paid on improvements the tenant makes where the useful life of the improvements will terminate before the end of the lease. [10]

¶ 1762   Married couple's deduction of taxes.

Spouses filing joint federal returns may deduct on that return all deductible taxes paid by either spouse, whether or not they file joint *state* returns.[11]

If the spouses file separate federal and separate state returns, each spouse may deduct only the state income taxes imposed on and actually paid by that spouse. If a joint state return was filed, then for federal tax purposes, that joint state tax is prorated according to each spouse's gross income, but not to exceed the amount actually paid by the spouse. [12]

---

3. ¶L-2351; ¶624; TD ¶327,002
4. ¶K-4003 *et seq.*; ¶L-2353 *et seq.*; ¶1644.03; TD ¶327,006
5. ¶K-4600 *et seq.*; TD ¶326,020
6. ¶K-4502; ¶1644.03; TD ¶326,014
7. ¶K-4101 *et seq.*; ¶1644.01; TD ¶328,001

8. ¶K-4103, ¶K-4114; ¶1644.01; TD ¶328,021
9. ¶K-4103; ¶1644.01; TD ¶328,002
10. ¶K-4104; TD ¶328,004
11. ¶s K-4105, K-4107; ¶1644.01; TD ¶328,011
12. ¶s K-4106, K-4108; ¶1644.01; TD ¶328,010

¶ 1763   Property taxes on co-owned property.

An individual's deduction for taxes on property he owns with other persons as tenants-in-common may be limited to his pro rata part of the taxes, i.e., the amount attributable to his interest, even if he pays *all* the taxes on the property. This pro rata share limit applies where the tenant is only assessed for his share, where he has a right to contribution from the other tenants, or where his share won't be subject to sale on their default. [13]

Tenants by the entirety (i.e., spouses) and joint tenants with right of survivorship are entitled to deduct in full the taxes they pay on the jointly-owned property. [14]

¶ 1764   Cooperative and condominium housing realty taxes.

Tenant-stockholders of cooperative housing corporations (co-ops) deduct their share of the co-op's real property taxes. (Code Sec. 216)[15] Condominium owners deduct the real property taxes on their individual interests. [16]

¶ 1765   When cash basis taxpayers deduct taxes.

A cash basis taxpayer's taxes are deductible for the tax year he pays them. State and local taxes withheld from the taxpayer's wages are deductible in the year they are withheld. [17] (For accrual taxpayers, see ¶1767.) For prepaid taxes, see ¶1766.

The tax is deductible in the year of payment even if taxpayer contests the liability and seeks to recover the payment (see ¶1768).[18] For estimated tax payments, see ¶1766.

¶ 1766   Prepaid taxes and estimated tax payments.

A cash basis taxpayer may deduct an advance payment of tax in the year of payment as long as it's an actual good faith payment and not a mere deposit. But the advance payment of state taxes that are later refunded won't be deductible unless taxpayer had a reasonable basis, at the time of payment, for believing he owed the taxes. [19]

Deduction in the year of payment also is allowed for advance estimated tax payments made under a pay-as-you-go tax collection system. [20]

¶ 1767   When accrual basis taxpayers deduct taxes.

An accrual basis taxpayer deducts a tax liability in his tax year in which all events have occurred which determine that he is liable for the tax and fix the amount of that liability, and economic performance (¶2833) has occurred—i.e., the tax is paid. (Code Sec. 461(h); Reg § 1.461-1(a)(2), Reg § 1.461-4(g)(6))[21] (For cash basis taxpayers, see ¶1765.) For ratable accrual of real property taxes, see ¶1769. For construction period taxes, see ¶1656.

An accrual basis taxpayer who pays an additional tax without protest or appeal deducts that additional tax in the year the tax was originally due, and not when it's later assessed or paid. [22] For contested tax, see ¶1768.

---

13. ¶K-4112; ¶1644.01; TD ¶328,017
14. ¶K-4112; ¶1644.01; TD ¶328,016
15. ¶K-5900 *et seq.*; ¶2164.01.
16. ¶K-4103; TD ¶328,002
17. ¶K-4201 *et seq.*; ¶1644.02; TD ¶329,001

18. ¶K-4201; ¶4614.56; TD ¶329,001
19. ¶K-4203; ¶1644.02; TD ¶329,005
20. ¶K-4204; ¶1644.02; TD ¶329,006
21. ¶G-2673, K-4300 *et seq.*; ¶4614.75; TD ¶329,007
22. ¶K-4320; TD ¶329,015

¶ 1768   When to deduct contested tax.

An accrual basis taxpayer who contests (through an overt act of protest or suit) an assessment can't deduct the contested portion of the tax until the contest is ended and the amount determined.[23]

A taxpayer (cash or accrual) who, by transferring sufficient cash or property, pays the contested liability without giving up the contest may deduct the tax in the year of payment, if otherwise deductible in that (or an earlier) year. But the contest must have existed at the time of transfer. (Code Sec. 461(f))[24] But foreign or U.S. possession income, war profits and excess profits tax can't be deducted until the contest is finally determined. (Code Sec. 461(f))[25]

¶ 1769   Election by accrual method taxpayers to accrue realty taxes ratably—Form 3115.

An accrual basis taxpayer may elect to accrue real property taxes that relate to a definite period of time ratably over that period. (Code Sec. 461(c)(1); Reg § 1.461-1(c)(1))[26]

IRS consent isn't required for an election made for the first tax year taxpayer incurs real property taxes. The election must be made by the return due date (with extensions) for that first year. In all other cases, the election may be made at any time, but requires IRS consent. (Code Sec. 461(c)(2)) Application for IRS's consent must be made in writing (on Form 3115) within 90 days (or 180 days, if taxpayer applies for an automatic extension) after the start of the first tax year to which the election applies.[27] The election is binding unless IRS consents to its revocation. (Reg § 1.461-1(c)(4))[28]

¶ 1770   Apportionment of real property taxes between seller and buyer.

For both cash and accrual taxpayers (Code Sec. 164(d)(2)), the real property tax on property that's sold during the tax year is considered to be imposed:

. . . *on the seller* to the extent properly allocable to that part of the real property tax year (period to which the tax relates) ending on the day before the date of sale; and

. . . *on the buyer* to the extent properly allocable to that part of the real property tax year beginning on the date of sale. (Code Sec. 164(d)(1); Reg § 1.164-6)[29]

For when the seller or buyer deducts the sale year realty tax, see ¶1771. For where seller took excessive deduction, see ¶1772.

¶ 1771   When seller or buyer deducts real property tax.

An *accrual basis* seller or buyer deducts his share of sale year realty tax (as apportioned, ¶1770) in his income tax year in which the accrual date (date of sale) falls. If an election to accrue realty taxes ratably (¶1769) is in effect for that year, his share of the tax is deductible in the year it accrues under the election. (Code Sec. 164(d)(2)(B); Reg § 1.164-6(d)(6))[30]

A *cash basis* seller or buyer deducts his portion of the sale year realty tax in the income tax year he pays it. But where the tax isn't payable until after the sale date, or where the buyer is liable for the tax under local law, the *seller* may, at his option, deduct the tax either in the year of sale (whether or not he actually paid it) or in the year of payment, if later. So, the seller can deduct a tax paid by the buyer. (Reg § 1.164-6(d)(1)(ii))[31]

---

23. ¶K-4319 *et seq.*; ¶4614.56; TD ¶329,017
24. ¶s G-2445, G-2645; ¶s 1644.02, 4614.56; TD ¶329,017
25. ¶K-4322; TD ¶329,019
26. ¶K-4327 *et seq.*; ¶s 1644.02, 4614.45; TD ¶329,025
27. ¶s K-4329, K-4330; ¶4614.45; TD ¶329,026

28. ¶K-4334; ¶4614.45; TD ¶329,028
29. ¶K-4117; ¶1644.01; TD ¶328,005
30. ¶s K-4129, K-4130; ¶1644.01; TD ¶329,024
31. ¶K-4124 *et seq.*; ¶1644.01; TD ¶329,004

¶ 1772   Excessive deduction of real property tax before sale.

If the seller (cash or accrual) deducted more than his share of realty taxes on property he sells in a later year, and that "excess" tax payment is allocable to and deductible by the buyer (see ¶1770), the seller is treated as receiving a recovery in the sale year. The seller must include this "recovery" in gross income for the sale year, to the extent he got a tax benefit (i.e., his excess deduction) in that earlier year (see ¶1205). (Reg § 1.164-6(d)(5))[32]

¶ 1773   Deduction for Losses. ■■■■■■■■■■■■■

Taxpayers may sustain a loss when their property is transferred, stolen, destroyed, confiscated, abandoned, taken by foreclosure or becomes worthless, and they receive less than adequate compensation for it. This loss may be deductible.

Subject to the limits discussed in the following paragraphs, the at-risk rules (¶1803 *et seq.*) and the passive loss rules (¶1810 *et seq.*), taxpayers may deduct losses they sustain that aren't compensated for by insurance or otherwise. (Code Sec. 165(a))[33]

For losses from a sale or exchange, see ¶ 2400 *et seq.*

¶ 1774   What is a deductible loss?

A deductible loss arises when a taxpayer loses or gives up money, property or rights, or when these items lose value as a result of an identifiable event. It must be shown that taxpayer sustained a loss of a type that's deductible and that the loss was sustained in the tax year; the amount of the loss also must be shown. [34]

To be deductible, a loss must be evidenced by a closed and completed transaction fixed by identifiable events (Reg § 1.165-1(b)), such as a sale, exchange, foreclosure, stock redemption, casualty, theft, abandonment, governmental condemnation or seizure. Mere fluctuations in an asset's value don't result in deductible losses. [35]

¶ 1775   How much loss is deductible?

The amount of a loss sustained on disposition of property is the adjusted basis of the property, minus the amount of any money and the fair market value of any property received in exchange. (Code Sec. 165(b); Reg § 1.165-1(c))[36] No loss is deductible to the extent taxpayer was reimbursed or compensated for it (¶1791, ¶1796). (Code Sec. 165(a))[37] Deduction isn't allowed to the extent that property has salvage value. (Reg § 1.165-1(c))[38] For limit on tax-exempt use losses, see ¶1782. For casualty and theft losses, see ¶1793 *et seq.* and ¶1799 *et seq.*

¶ 1776   Limits on losses of individuals.

Individuals may deduct losses only if they're from a trade or business (¶1777) (Code Sec. 165(c)(1)),[39] a transaction entered into for profit (¶1778) (Code Sec. 165(c)(2)),[40] or a casualty (¶1793) or theft (¶1799). (Code Sec. 165(c)(3))[41]

An individual's losses on personal transactions are deductible only if they qualify as casualty or theft losses. (Code Sec. 165(c)(3))[42] So, no loss deduction is allowed for a loss on

32. ¶K-4131; TD ¶328,009
33. ¶M-1000; ¶1654; TD ¶360,501
34. ¶M-1000 *et seq.*; ¶1654.020 *et seq.*; TD ¶360,500 *et seq.*
35. ¶M-1101; ¶M-1305 *et seq.*; ¶1654.020 *et seq.*; TD ¶361,001 *et seq.*
36. ¶M-1401; TD ¶363,001
37. ¶M-1408; ¶1654.304; TD ¶363,008

38. ¶M-1401; TD ¶363,001
39. ¶M-1501; ¶s 1654, 1654.060 *et seq.*; TD ¶421,000
40. ¶M-1510; ¶s 1654, 1654.060 *et seq.*; TD ¶421,000
41. ¶s M-1600, M-2100; ¶1654.300 *et seq.*, ¶1654.350 *et seq.*; TD ¶421,000
42. ¶M-1500; ¶1654; TD ¶361,508

taxpayer's residence or car (if used only for personal purposes) unless the loss is from casualty or theft. These rules also apply to losses of estates and trusts. [43]

Property that taxpayer holds partly for personal use and partly for business or income-producing use is treated as two properties: one personal, one business (or income-producing). Loss on the personal part (except by casualty or theft) isn't deductible. [44]

¶ 1777   What is a trade or business?

A trade or business is a pursuit or occupation carried on for profit (¶1778), whether or not profit actually results. An isolated transaction isn't a business. Taxpayer may engage in one business, in more than one business, or in no business. [45]

¶ 1778   Transactions for profit defined.

A transaction is entered into for profit if taxpayer intends to receive income from it overall. For a transaction involving property, taxpayer must intend to receive income from it or to profit from disposing of it. [46]

Profit must be the primary motive, not merely incidental. A loss deduction is possible where a secondary nonprofit motive exists, as long as the profit motive predominates. [47]

An activity is presumed to be engaged in for profit for a tax year if it shows a profit for any three or more out of five consecutive years ending in that tax year (or two out of seven years, for breeding, showing or racing of horses). (Code Sec. 183(d); Reg § 1.183-1(c))[48] A taxpayer who hasn't engaged in an activity for more than five years (seven, for horse breeding, etc.) can elect (on Form 5213) to postpone the determination as to whether these presumptions apply until the close of the fourth tax year (sixth, for horse breeding, etc.) after the tax year taxpayer first engages in the activity. (Code Sec. 183(e); Reg § 12.9)[49]

Whether the activities of an S corporation are "engaged in for profit" is determined at the entity level (Reg § 1.183-1(f)), as it is for partnerships. [50]

¶ 1779   Hobby (not-for-profit) losses.

For individuals, partnerships, estates, trusts and S corporations, deductions attributable to an activity not engaged in for profit (¶1778) (Code Sec. 183(a); Reg § 1.183-1(a))[1] are allowed only as follows:

(1) The full amount of deductions (e.g., state and local property taxes) otherwise allowable for the tax year without regard to whether the activity is engaged in for profit (Code Sec. 183(b)(1); Reg § 1.183-1(b)(1)(i))—referred to as Category 1 deductions.

(2) Amounts allowable as deductions only if the activity were engaged in for profit, but only if the allowance *doesn't* result in a basis adjustment, *and only* to the extent the gross income from the activity exceeds the deductions in (1), above (Code Sec. 183(b)(2); Reg § 1.183-1(b)(1)(ii))—Category 2 deductions.

(3) Amounts allowable as deductions only if the activity were engaged in for profit, that if allowed *would* result in a basis adjustment (e.g., depreciation), *but only* to the extent the gross income from the activity exceeds deductions allowed or allowable under (1) and (2) (Code Sec. 183(b)(2); Reg § 1.183-1(b)(1)(iii), Reg § 1.183-1(b)(3))—Category 3 deductions. [2]

In other words, deductions attributable to the "not for profit" activity are allowed to the

43. ¶M-1524, C-2215, C-7214; TD ¶361,508
44. ¶M-1420; ¶s 1654.061, 1654.430; TD ¶363,020
45. ¶L-1100 *et seq.*; ¶1654.060 *et seq.*; TD ¶256,001
46. ¶M-1510; ¶1654.062; TD ¶422,005
47. ¶M-1512; ¶1654.062; TD ¶422,024

48. ¶M-5818; ¶1834.02; TD ¶422,017
49. ¶M-5821; ¶1834.02; TD ¶422,020
50. ¶M-5802; TD ¶422,002
1. ¶M-5802; ¶1834 *et seq.*; TD ¶422,001
2. ¶M-5804 *et seq.*; ¶1834; TD ¶422,001 *et seq.*

extent of income from it, or for the full amount of related deductions allowable regardless of profit-seeking, *whichever is larger.*[3]

But, the deductions allowable under these rules are subject to the 2%-of-AGI floor (¶3110) on miscellaneous itemized deductions. (Reg §   1.67-1T(a)(1)(iv))[4]

¶ 1780   Vacation home expenses.

Where an individual, trust, estate, partnership or S corporation owns a vacation home or a dwelling unit (below) and uses it for both personal and rental purposes, deduction of expenses is limited (Code Sec. 280A(a)),[5] except for those expenses which are deductible without regard to business use of the property —e.g., mortgage interest, property taxes and casualty losses. (Code Sec. 280A(b))[6]

The owner's personal use of the home (or portion of it) for even one day in the tax year triggers these "vacation home" limits. (Code Sec. 280A(e)(1))[7]

For any tax year in which the owner uses the (rented) vacation home or other dwelling unit for personal purposes, or rents it out for less than a fair rental, the owner's deduction for maintenance, utilities, depreciation, etc., can't exceed the percentage of those total expenses for the year "attributable" to the rental period. (Code Sec. 280A(e)(1))[8] If a taxpayer who rents out a dwelling unit also uses it as a residence (see below), the deductions attributable to rental use are *further* limited to no more than the gross income derived from rental use for that year, *minus* the sum of (1) the deductions allocable to rental use that are allowable whether or not the unit (or portion of it) was used for rental (e.g., interest and taxes), and (2) deductions allocable to the business or rental activity but which aren't allocable to the use of the home itself. Excess rental expenses may be carried forward to later years. (Code Sec. 280A(c)(5))[9]

The proper ratio for allocating interest and taxes to the rental period is: (1) number of days for which the property is rented, to (2) number of days of total use (according to IRS, but not according to some courts: they would use "number of days in the year"). [10]

A home is used as a residence in any tax year in which the owner's use of the unit (or a portion of it) for personal purposes exceeds the longer of: (1) 14 days, or (2) 10% of the period of rental use. (Code Sec. 280A(d)(1))[11]

For purposes of applying the rules limiting rent-related deductions for a dwelling unit used as a residence, personal-use days don't include days the taxpayer used a dwelling unit as his principal residence (1) before or after a rental (or attempted rental) period of 12 or more consecutive months beginning or ending in the tax year, or (2) before a consecutive rental (or attempted rental) period of less than 12 months beginning in the tax year, at the end of which the residence is sold or exchanged. A fair rental rate must be charged. (Code Sec. 280A(d)(4))[12]

If a home is rented for less than 15 days a year, the owner can't deduct *any* of the rental expenses, but isn't taxed on any of the rental income. (Code Sec. 280A(g))[13]

¶ 1781   Worthless stock or securities.

A taxpayer may deduct a loss from worthlessness of stock or other securities (i.e., a bond, debenture, note, certificate or other evidence of indebtedness issued by a corporation or a government (or its political subdivision) with interest coupons or in registered form). (Code

---

3. ¶M-5804; ¶1834; TD ¶422,001
4. ¶A-2710; ¶674; TD ¶422,003
5. ¶M-6001 *et seq.*; ¶280A4; TD ¶423,001 *et seq.*
6. ¶M-6001; ¶280A4; TD ¶423,001
7. ¶M-6005; ¶280A4; TD ¶423,021
8. ¶M-6005, ¶M-6028 *et seq.*; ¶280A4.060 *et seq.*, ¶280A4.072;

TD ¶423,008 *et seq.*, TD ¶423,021
9. ¶M-6018, M-6022; ¶280A4.060 *et seq.*; TD ¶423,023, 423,026
10. ¶M-6006; ¶280A4.065; TD ¶423,021
11. ¶M-6024; ¶280A4.062, 280A4.064; TD ¶423,007
12. ¶M-6038; ¶280A4.067; TD ¶423,027
13. ¶M-6023; ¶280A4.064; TD ¶423,020

Sec. 165(a), Code Sec. 165(g)(1))[14]

Taxpayer must show that the security had value at the end of the year preceding the deduction year and that an identifiable event caused a loss in the deduction year. [15]

The amount of the loss is, to extent not compensated for (e.g., by insurance), the security's adjusted basis for determining loss on sale (¶ 2474). (Code Sec. 165(b); Reg § 1.165-1(c))[16]

The deduction is a capital loss if the security is a capital asset to taxpayer. (Code Sec. 165(g)(1)) An ordinary loss deduction is allowed if the security is:

. . . not a capital asset (Reg § 1.165-5(b));

. . . Code Sec. 1244 stock (¶ 2644 *et seq.*);

. . . for corporate taxpayers, stock in an "affiliated" corporation (at least 80%-owned by taxpayer), where more than 90% of the affiliate's gross receipts has been from sources other than passive income (royalties, dividends, etc.). (Code Sec. 165(g)(3))[17]

Certain losses by, or on stock of, small business investment companies also are ordinary losses. (Code Sec. 1242, Code Sec. 1243)[18]

Total worthlessness of the security is required for the deduction. No loss deduction is allowed for partial worthlessness or (except for dealers who inventory securities [19]) for mere decline in value. (Reg § 1.165-4, Reg § 1.165-5)[20]

No loss deduction is allowed on a shareholder's surrender of stock to the corporation, whether or not the surrender is pro rata. Instead, the shareholder's basis for stock surrendered is added to his basis for stock retained. [21]

¶ 1782   Limits on "tax-exempt use losses."

For leases entered into (and in the case of property treated as tax-exempt use property other than by reason of a lease, for property acquired) after Mar. 12, 2004, [22] a "tax-exempt-use loss" for any tax year isn't allowed. (Code Sec. 470(a)) (For exceptions, see below.)[23]

A tax-exempt use loss is the amount by which the total deductions allocable to a "tax-exempt use property" exceed the total income from the property, for the tax year. (Code Sec. 470(c)(1)) Tax-exempt use property is Code Sec. 168(h) property (generally, property subject to leases, or certain other arrangements, involving governments, tax-exempts, or foreign persons or entities), with certain modifications. (Code Sec. 470(c)(2))[24]

A tax-exempt use loss in excess of gross income may be carried forward to the next tax year, subject to that year's limit. (Code Sec. 470(b)) A special loss carryforward limit applies for "former tax-exempt use property." (Code Sec. 470(e)(1))[25]

If, during the tax year, a taxpayer disposes of its entire interest in tax-exempt use property (or former tax-exempt use property), rules similar to the Code Sec. 469(g) disallowed passive activity loss and credit rules (¶1840) apply. (Code Sec. 470(e)(2))[26]

The limit on "tax-exempt use losses" doesn't apply to any lease (an "excepted lease") which meets the requirements of Code Sec. 470(d). [27]

14. ¶M-3301; ¶1654.200 *et seq.*; TD ¶372,001
15. ¶M-3300 *et seq.*, ¶M-3400 *et seq.*; ¶1654.210; TD ¶372,010
16. ¶M-3305; ¶1654.205; TD ¶372,004
17. ¶M-3310 *et seq.*; ¶1654.203; TD ¶372,021
18. ¶M-3308; ¶1654.203; TD ¶372,006
19. ¶G-5021; TD ¶228,718.1
20. ¶M-3304; ¶1654.200 *et seq.*; TD ¶372,009 *et seq.*

21. ¶M-3501; TD ¶373,001
22. ¶L-6901; ¶4704; TD ¶261,202
23. ¶L-6901 *et seq.*; ¶4704; TD ¶261,201 *et seq.*
24. ¶L-6901 *et seq.*; ¶4704; TD ¶261,201 *et seq.*
25. ¶L-6902; L-6903; ¶4704; TD ¶261,202; 261,203
26. ¶L-6904; ¶4704; TD ¶261,204
27. ¶L-6906 *et seq.*; ¶4704; TD ¶261,206 *et seq.*

¶ 1783   Demolition losses.

Except as noted below, no deduction is allowed to the owner or lessee of a building for any loss on demolition of the building, or for any of the demolition expenses. (Code Sec. 280B(1)) The loss or expenses must be capitalized and added to the basis of the land. (Code Sec. 280B(2))[28] But, the Tax Court held that a loss sustained before a building's demolition as a result of its abnormal retirement from a taxpayer's business because of a casualty to or an extraordinary obsolescence of the building isn't treated as sustained on account of the demolition.[29]

For amounts paid or incurred after Aug. 27, 2005, and before 2008, 50% of otherwise capitalized costs relating to site cleanup and demolition of structures are deductible. The expenses must relate to real property in the GO Zone (¶2308) and the property must be held by the taxpayer for use in a trade or business or for production of income, or be inventory held primarily for sale to customers in the ordinary course of business. (Code Sec. 1400N(f))[30]

¶ 1784   Abandonment loss.

A loss deduction is allowed for loss of usefulness or for obsolescence of nondepreciable property, both tangible and intangible (e.g., land, a contract), *if*: (1) the loss is incurred in business or a transaction entered into for profit; (2) it arises from the sudden termination of usefulness in the business or transaction; *and* (3) the property is permanently discarded from use, or the business or transaction is discontinued. (Reg § 1.165-2) The taxpayer must be able to establish specifically which property has been abandoned. [31]

The loss is an ordinary loss not subject to capital loss limitations. (Reg § 1.165-2(b))[32] The loss can't exceed the adjusted basis of the property for determining loss on a disposition (¶ 2474). (Reg § 1.165-1(c))[33]

For losses on mortgaged property, see ¶1787 and ¶1788.

¶ 1785   Costs of unsuccessful investigation of proposed venture.

A corporation that pays or incurs expenses in *unsuccessfully* searching for or investigating a new venture may deduct those costs as a business loss, when it abandons the search or investigation (see ¶1504). But for a noncorporate taxpayer, these expenses are personal and nondeductible.[34] For expenses of a *successful* investigation, see ¶ 1500 *et seq.*

¶ 1786   Gambling losses.

Taxpayer may deduct gambling losses suffered in the tax year, but only to the extent of that year's gambling gains. (Code Sec. 165(d); Reg § 1.165-10) "Gains" include "comps" (complimentary goods and services taxpayer receives from a casino). Losses from one kind of gambling (e.g., horse bets) are deductible against gains from another kind (e.g., keno). [35] Individuals not engaged in the gambling business deduct gambling losses (to extent of gambling gains) only as miscellaneous itemized deductions (but not subject to the 2%-of-AGI floor),[36] and must report gambling gains even if they are exceeded by gambling losses. [37]

28. ¶M-2200 *et seq.*; ¶s 1654.180, 280B4; TD ¶376,019
29. ¶M-2201; ¶s 1654.180, 280B4; TD ¶376,019
30. ¶L-4232.3; ¶14,00N4.03; TD ¶307,733
31. ¶M-2301; ¶1654.150 *et seq.*; TD ¶376,001
32. ¶M-2353; TD ¶376,005

33. ¶M-2351; TD ¶376,004
34. ¶L-5018 *et seq.*; TD ¶301,013
35. ¶M-6100 *et seq.*; ¶s 1654.500, 1654.501; TD ¶424,001
36. ¶M-6105; TD ¶424,003
37. ¶J-1651; TD ¶197,001

¶ 1787   Mortgagee's loss (or gain) on mortgaged property.

The mortgagee (mortgage lender) treats a loss on mortgaged property as follows:

A loss on *compromise or settlement* of the debt of an insolvent debtor is treated as a bad debt (¶1851 *et seq.*).[38]

A lender to whom mortgaged or pledged property is surrendered has a bad debt deduction if the fair market value (FMV) of the property received is less than the debt. (The mortgagee has a gain if the FMV of the surrendered property is greater than the debt's basis.) [39] For where the surrender is a repossession by the seller, see ¶ 2467.

A loss on a *mortgage foreclosure* is treated as a bad debt (see ¶1851) equal to the sum of: (1) the excess of the debt's basis over the net proceeds from the property foreclosure; (2) accrued interest previously reported as income; plus (3) legal and other expenses. This is true whether the price is paid by the mortgagee (by applying the debt to the price) or someone else. (Reg § 1.166-6(a))[40]

A mortgagee that bids on the property at the foreclosure sale *also* realizes a loss to the extent the debt applied to the bid exceeds the property's FMV. He realizes a taxable gain to the extent FMV exceeds the amount of the debt so applied. FMV is assumed to equal the bid price, absent convincing proof to the contrary. (Reg § 1.166-6(b))[41]

¶ 1788   Owner's loss on foreclosure, surrender or abandonment of mortgaged property.

The owner of mortgaged property, whether or not he's the mortgagor and whether or not he's personally liable for the mortgage debt, realizes a loss (occasionally a gain) on foreclosure of the mortgage or surrender of the property. The foreclosure (or surrender) is considered a sale or exchange. [42] The owner-borrower's gain or loss is the difference between adjusted basis of the transferred property and the amount realized. If the owner-borrower isn't personally liable for repaying the debt secured by the transferred property, the amount realized includes the full amount of the debt canceled by the transfer. If the borrower is personally liable, the amount realized doesn't include any cancellation of debt income (¶1388) arising from the debt. But if the FMV of the property is less than the canceled debt, the amount realized includes canceled debt up to the FMV. [43]

Abandonment is generally treated as a sale or exchange. [44] For tax sales, see ¶1789.

¶ 1789   Loss on tax sale.

The tax treatment of an owner whose property is sold for delinquent taxes is similar to that for foreclosure (¶1788). The tax sale is a sale or exchange. [45]

¶ 1790   When to deduct loss.

A loss is deductible only for the tax year it's sustained. (Code Sec. 165(a)) This is the year the loss occurs, as evidenced by closed and completed transactions and as fixed by identifiable events in that year. (Reg § 1.165-1(d))[46] For casualty or theft losses, see ¶1797 and ¶1801.

---

38. ¶M-3709; ¶1664.350 *et seq.*; TD ¶371,021
39. ¶M-3710; ¶1664.353; TD ¶371,022
40. ¶M-3701; ¶1664.353 *et seq.*; TD ¶371,016
41. ¶M-3704; ¶1664.352; TD ¶371,019
42. ¶M-3801; ¶1654.451; TD ¶371,001

43. ¶M-3803; TD ¶371,001, 371,006
44. ¶M-3808; ¶1654.155; TD ¶371,003
45. ¶M-3806; ¶1654.155, 1654.451; TD ¶371,001
46. ¶M-1301; ¶s 1654.090, 1654.111; TD ¶362,001

¶ 1791 Deducting reimbursable losses.

If taxpayer has a claim for reimbursement on which there's a reasonable prospect of recovery, that "reimbursable" loss can't be deducted until it's reasonably certain the reimbursement will or won't be made. This may be ascertained by, among other things, settlement, adjudication or abandonment of the claim. (Code Sec. 165(a); Reg § 1.165-1(d))[47]

¶ 1792 Casualty, Disaster, and Theft Losses. ▬▬▬▬▬▬▬▬

Losses from fire, storm, auto accident or other casualty, and losses from theft, are deductible, regardless of whether the loss is sustained in a business or for-profit transaction. An early deduction for disaster losses is available. An individual can elect to treat a loss on a frozen bank deposit as a casualty or theft loss.

¶ 1793 Casualty losses—Form 4684.

A deduction is allowed (report on Form 4684) for losses arising from a casualty (¶1794; for amount, see ¶1795) where taxpayer actually sustains a loss *and* the loss is on *property*. (Code Sec. 165(c)(3)) The property must suffer physical damage and not just a decline in value, even if that decline results from being in or near an area where casualties have occurred and might occur again.[48]

¶ 1794 "Casualty" defined.

A casualty is the complete or partial destruction of property resulting from an identifiable event of a sudden, unexpected or unusual nature such as a fire, storm, shipwreck, car crash, or similar event. Progressive deterioration from a steadily operating cause isn't a casualty. [49]

¶ 1795 Amount of casualty loss.

The amount treated as a loss from a casualty depends on whether taxpayer held the property for personal or for business purposes, as follows:

For property held for personal use, the amount of the casualty loss is the *lesser* of: (1) the property's adjusted basis (i.e., its basis for determining loss on disposition, see ¶2474), or (2) its decline in value (i.e., its fair market value (FMV) immediately before the casualty *minus* its FMV immediately afterward). This applies whether the property is totally destroyed or merely damaged. (Reg § 1.165-7(b)) The loss is reduced for any salvage value, insurance or other compensation received (¶1796). (Reg § 1.165-1(c)(4))[50]

For property used in business or held for the production of income, the amount of the casualty loss is determined under the same rules as for personal-use property (above), except that if the property is *totally* destroyed, the amount of the loss is the property's adjusted basis in all cases. (Reg § 1.165-7(b)(1))[1]

The decline in a property's value should be ascertained by competent appraisal where possible.[2] IRS may issue guidance permitting the use of an appraisal made for the purpose of getting a federal loan or federal loan guarantee as a result of a Presidentially-declared disaster (¶1798), to establish the amount deductible as a disaster loss. (Code Sec. 165(i)(4))[3]

Costs of repairing, replacing, or cleaning up property after a casualty can be used to measure the amount of the loss (decline in value) if: the repair, etc., is necessary to restore

47. ¶M-2136; ¶1654.304; TD ¶362,001
48. ¶M-1601; ¶M-2132¶1654.300 *et seq.*; TD ¶366,000; 366,001
49. ¶M-1701; ¶1654.301; TD ¶366,008
50. ¶M-1801 *et seq.*; ¶1654.304; TD ¶368,001

1. ¶M-1802; ¶1654.304; TD ¶368,001
2. ¶M-1809; ¶1654.304; TD ¶368,008
3. ¶M-2008.1, ¶1654.520; TD ¶369,011

the property to its pre-casualty condition; the amount spent isn't excessive; the repairs do no more than take care of the damage suffered; and the post-repair value is no greater than the pre-casualty value. (Reg § 1.165-7(a)(2))[4]

Except for individuals' casualty losses on personal-use property, the amount of a casualty loss, as determined above, is deductible in full. See ¶1774 *et seq.* A taxpayer may deduct a casualty loss on property not used in business or held for production of income only to the extent that: (1) the casualty loss exceeds $100 ("$100 floor"), and (2) all of taxpayer's casualty losses for the tax year exceed 10% of AGI for the year ("10%-of-AGI limit") (Code Sec. 165(h)),[5] as described below.

$100 floor. Each personal-use property casualty is subject to a separate $100 floor to determine the extent it's deductible. But events closely related in origin give rise to a single casualty. So, one storm's damage to taxpayer's house and car is a single casualty, so only the total damage has to exceed $100 to be deductible. (Code Sec. 165(h)(1); Reg § 1.165-7(b)(4)(ii))[6] A single $100 floor applies where one casualty causes loss to joint filers, whether the loss is to property jointly or separately owned. But separate $100 floors apply to each spouse if they file separately, even if the property is jointly owned. (Code Sec. 165(h)(4)(B); Reg § 1.165-7(b)(4)(iii))[7]

10%-of-AGI floor. In addition to (and after applying) the $100 per casualty "floor" (above), personal-use property casualties are then subject to this other limit: If personal casualty losses for a tax year exceed personal casualty gains for that tax year, taxpayer may deduct those losses for that year, but only to the extent of the sum of:

(1) the amount of the personal casualty gains for the year, plus

(2) the amount by which (a) the excess of personal casualty losses over gains ((1) above), exceeds (b) 10% of taxpayer's adjusted gross income (AGI, ¶3102) (computed without regard to casualty gains). (Code Sec. 165(h)(2)(A))[8]

In determining a taxpayer's personal casualty gains and losses, the amount of any recognized loss is subject to the $100 floor before netting. (Code Sec. 165(h)(3)(B))[9]

If the personal casualty losses for a tax year exceed the personal casualty gains for that year, the deduction for personal casualty losses is allowable in computing AGI, to the extent of those gains. (Code Sec. 165(h)(4)(A))[10]

If the personal casualty gains for any tax year exceed the personal casualty losses for that year, all these gains and losses are treated as capital gains and losses (Code Sec. 165(h)(2)(B)) not subject to the 10% floor.[11]

Where property is held for both business (or profit) and personal purposes (e.g., a home office, ¶1635), these limits apply only to the personal part of the loss. (Reg § 1.165-7(b)(4)(iv))[12]

¶ 1796   Insurance or other compensation for casualty loss.

The casualty loss deduction isn't allowed to the extent the loss is compensated by insurance or otherwise (see ¶1795). (Code Sec. 165(a)) But, costs incurred in collecting the compensation reduce the recovery so as to increase the loss deduction. [13]

Where an individual's casualty and theft losses aren't attributable to a business or for-profit transaction, a loss covered by insurance is taken into account only if taxpayer files a

---

4. ¶M-1815; ¶1654.304; TD ¶368,013
5. ¶M-1900 *et seq.*; ¶1654.304; TD ¶368,501
6. ¶s M-1901; M-1902; ¶1654.304; TD ¶368,502; 368,503
7. ¶M-1904 *et seq.*; ¶1654.304; TD ¶368,506
8. ¶M-1907, M-1911; ¶1654.304; TD ¶368,508
9. ¶M-1911; ¶1654.304; TD ¶368,512

10. ¶M-1908; TD ¶368,508
11. ¶M-1910; ¶1654.304; TD ¶368,509
12. ¶M-1906, M-1908.1; ¶1654.304, 280A4.044; TD ¶368,507, 368,511
13. ¶M-1408, M-1421; ¶1654.304; TD ¶368,016, 363,019

timely insurance claim. (Code Sec. 165(h)(4)(E)) But, this limit applies only to the extent the insurance policy would have provided reimbursement had the claim been filed. [14]

Compensation includes property insurance, damage recoveries, debt forgiveness, cash or property received from taxpayer's employer or from disaster relief agencies to rehabilitate the property (e.g., qualified disaster relief payments, see ¶1207), and condemnation awards. Compensation doesn't include disaster relief such as food, medical supplies, and other forms of assistance, unless they are replacements for lost or destroyed property. Nor does it include use and occupancy insurance reimbursements for lost business profits. [15]

A casualty loss to inventory is automatically reflected in cost of goods sold (¶2869). It isn't separately deducted as a loss unless adjustments are made to inventory. [16]

¶ 1797 When to deduct casualty losses.

A casualty loss (like other losses, see ¶1781) is considered "sustained" (and deductible) only during the tax year the loss occurs, as fixed by identifiable events occurring in that year. (Code Sec. 165(a); Reg § 1.165-1(d)(1)) A loss may be sustained in the tax year even though repairs or replacements aren't made until a later year. And a loss may be sustained in a year *after* the casualty occurs, as when trees died a year after the year a blizzard damaged them. [17] For election to deduct disaster losses early, see ¶1798.

¶ 1798 Early deduction election for disaster losses.

A taxpayer may *elect* to deduct a disaster loss (defined below) for the tax year *before* the year the loss occurred, instead of for the year the loss occurred (¶1797). (Code Sec. 165(i))[18]

RIA *observation:* Claiming a disaster loss on the earlier year's return can save taxes immediately, without waiting until the end of the year the loss was sustained. In some cases, it may result in a net operating loss that will bring a refund through a carryback to an earlier year (¶4850). But deduction for the later loss year may save taxes where taxpayer expects to be in a higher bracket that year. Those weighing the value of an early disaster loss deduction also must consider the relative amounts of AGI they have or expect to have for the current and earlier tax years, and any other casualty losses incurred in those years.

Individuals who incur a disaster loss with respect to nonbusiness property are subject to the regular $100/10%-of-AGI floors (¶1795). (Code Sec. 165(i))[19]

A disaster loss is a loss that's attributable to a disaster occurring in an area the President later says is entitled to federal disaster assistance. (Code Sec. 165(i)(1))[20] Also, the loss must be *otherwise* deductible as a loss. (Reg § 1.165-11(b)(3)) A taxpayer whose residence is located in a Presidentially declared disaster area may deduct any loss attributable to the disaster as a casualty loss if the residence is rendered unsafe by the disaster, and he is ordered (within 120 days after the disaster designation) by the state or local government to demolish or relocate the residence. (Code Sec. 165(k))[21] A non-casualty loss may be a disaster loss if incurred in the course of a trade or business or profit-seeking transaction. For example, a farmer might deduct a loss from a drought disaster, even though loss from drought is ordinarily not deductible as a casualty loss. [22]

The early deduction is elected on the return (original or amended) for the previous year, or on a refund claim. Elect by the later of: (1) the due date for the disaster year return (without

---

14. ¶M-1914; ¶1654.304

15. ¶M-1411 *et seq.*; ¶1654.304; TD ¶363,011 *et seq.*

16. ¶M-1808; ¶s 1654.302, 4714.21; TD ¶368,007

17. ¶M-1610; ¶1654.111; TD ¶366,066

18. ¶M-2001; ¶1654.520; TD ¶369,002

19. ¶M-2009; ¶1654.304; TD ¶369,012

20. ¶M-2002; ¶1654.520; TD ¶369,001

21. ¶M-2010; ¶1654.302; TD ¶369,008

22. ¶M-2004; ¶1654.520; TD ¶369,009

regard to extensions), or (2) the due date for the previous year return *with* permitted extensions. Once made, the election becomes irrevocable after 90 days. (Reg § 1.165-11(e))[23]

For involuntary conversion of a principal residence damaged in a Presidentially declared disaster, see ¶2433.

¶ 1799 Theft losses—Form 4684.

Theft losses (reported on Form 4684) are deductible (for amount, see ¶1800) under rules that closely follow those for casualty losses, including the $100/10%-of-AGI floors (¶1793 *et seq.*). (Code Sec. 165(a), Code Sec. 165(h)(1), Code Sec. 165(h)(2)) A theft is the unlawful taking and removing of money or property with the intent to deprive the owner of it, and includes larceny, robbery, embezzlement (Reg § 1.165-8(d)), burglary, extortion, kidnapping for ransom, blackmail and false representation. [24]

A theft loss deduction is not allowed for the decline in market value of stock purchased on the open market, where the decline is caused by the disclosure of accounting fraud or other illegal conduct on the part of officers or directors of the corporation that issued the stock. [25]

A taking by a person known to have a claim to the property (e.g., spouse, joint owner) isn't a theft unless there's evidence of criminal intent. [26]

¶ 1800 Amount of theft loss.

For theft of business or investment property, the *deductible loss* is the adjusted basis of the property minus insurance or other compensation received or recoverable (¶1796). (Reg § 1.165-8(c))[27]

For theft of personal-use property, the *loss* is: (1) the lesser of the property's fair market value (FMV) immediately before theft or its adjusted basis, reduced by (2) insurance or other compensation received or recoverable. (Reg § 1.165-8(c) The $100/10%-of-AGI floors (¶1795) are then applied to determine the amount of the loss that is *deductible*. (Code Sec. 165(c)(3))[28]

If stolen personal-use property is recovered in the deduction year, the loss is the lesser of: (1) the property's adjusted basis, or (2) the decline in its FMV between theft and recovery. If it's recovered after the deduction year, the excess of the earlier deduction over the loss determined as above is included in income (under the tax benefit rule, see ¶1205), to the extent the earlier loss deduction decreased taxpayer's tax. [29]

¶ 1801 When to deduct theft loss.

A theft loss (¶1799) is deductible in the year the loss is *discovered,* regardless of when the theft actually occurred. But the deduction is postponed to the extent taxpayer, in the year of discovery, had a reimbursement claim on which there was a reasonable prospect of recovery. (Code Sec. 165(e); Reg § 1.165-8(a))[30]

¶ 1802 Elections to treat frozen bank deposits as losses from casualty or from transaction entered into for profit.

If a "qualified individual" (other than the institution's officers, 1% owners, or those related to either)[31]) has a loss on a deposit in a bankrupt or insolvent qualified financial institution, and that loss may be reasonably estimated, the loss may be treated, at taxpayer's election:

---

23. ¶M-2011 *et seq.*; ¶1654.520; TD ¶369,003 *et seq.*
24. ¶M-2100 *et seq.*; ¶1654.351 *et seq.*; TD ¶367,001
25. ¶M-2111; ¶1654.351; TD ¶367,009
26. ¶M-2104; TD ¶367,003
27. ¶M-2125; ¶1654.370; TD ¶367,023

28. ¶M-2126; ¶1654.370; TD ¶367,025
29. ¶M-2129; TD ¶367,027
30. ¶M-2132; ¶1654.380; TD ¶367,036
31. ¶M-1762; ¶1654.530; TD ¶366,073

(10 as a casualty or theft loss (¶1793, ¶1799) instead of as a nonbusiness bad debt (¶1857) (Code Sec. 165(l)(1)),[32] or (2) as an ordinary loss incurred in a transaction entered into for profit, up to $20,000 ($10,000 for marrieds filing separately) of loss. (Code Sec. 165(l)(5))[33]

Elect by claiming the loss (casualty or ordinary) on the return (or timely amended return) for the tax year in which a reasonable estimate of the loss can be made. [34]

¶ 1803 At-Risk Limitations.

For certain taxpayers, deductions from specified leveraged investment activities are limited to the aggregate amount the taxpayer-investor has "at risk."

¶ 1804 Taxpayers subject to "at-risk" rules.

The at-risk rules (¶1806) apply to: (1) individuals, (2) C corporations but only if more than 50% in value of the corporation's stock is owned by not more than five individuals at any time during the last half of its tax year (Code Sec. 465(a)(1)),[35] and (3) estates and trusts. [36] But even if the stock ownership test is met, the at-risk rules *don't apply* to:

... certain active businesses ("qualifying businesses") carried on by a qualified C corporation (i.e., *not* a personal holding company, or personal service corporation determined by substituting 5% for 10% in Code Sec. 269A(b)(2)), (Code Sec. 465(c)(7))[37] or

... the activity of equipment leasing. (Code Sec. 465(c)(4))[38]

💡*observation:* Even though the at-risk rules don't apply to pass-through entities such as S corporations and partnerships, they *do* apply to determine whether a person with an interest in any of those entities may deduct items of loss, etc., passed through.

¶ 1805 "At-risk" activities.

The at-risk rules (¶1806) apply to:

... certain specified activities: (1) holding, producing or distributing motion pictures or video tapes, (2) farming, (3) equipment leasing, (4) exploring for, or exploiting, oil and gas resources, (5) exploring for, or exploiting, geothermal resources; (Code Sec. 465(c)(1)) and

... a "catch-all" group of activities that taxpayer engages in, in carrying on a trade or business or in the production of income, other than those above (Code Sec. 465(c)(3)),[39] e.g., real estate activities (see ¶1809).

In applying the at-risk rules to the specified activities, taxpayer's activity with respect to each property (e.g., each film in (1), above) is treated as a separate activity. (Code Sec. 465(c)(2)(A)) Activities in the "catch-all" group are treated as one activity ("aggregated") if either: (A) taxpayer actively participates in the management of the trade or business, or (B) the trade or business is carried on by a partnership or S corporation *and* 65% or more of the losses for the tax year is allocable to persons who actively participate in its management. (Code Sec. 465(c)(3)(B))[40]

¶ 1806 How the at-risk rules work—Form 6198.

For a taxpayer (¶1804) engaged in an at-risk activity (¶1805), any loss from the activity for the tax year is deductible in that year only to the extent that taxpayer is at risk (¶1807) with respect to the activity at the end of the year. (Code Sec. 465(a)) The losses so limited are the

32. ¶M-1761; ¶1654.530; TD ¶366,071
33. ¶M-1765, M-1766; ¶1654.530; TD ¶366,076, 366,077
34. ¶M-1771; ¶1654.530; TD ¶366,072
35. ¶M-4511, M-4515; ¶4654; TD ¶402,001
36. ¶M-4512; TD ¶402,002

37. ¶M-4516 *et seq.*; ¶4654; TD ¶402,006 *et seq.*
38. ¶M-4529; ¶4654; TD ¶403,009
39. ¶M-4521; ¶4654; TD ¶403,001
40. ¶M-4522 *et seq.*; ¶4654; TD ¶403,002

excess of the deductions allocable to the activity that otherwise would be allowed for the year, over the income (other than recapture, see ¶1808) received or accrued by taxpayer during the year from that same activity. (Code Sec. 465(d))[41]

Any loss thus disallowed is treated as allocable to the same activity in the next tax year, and may be deducted in the later year subject to that year's at-risk limit for the activity. (Code Sec. 465(a)(2)) So, a current year's "loss" may include "suspended" loss accounts from earlier years. (Code Sec. 465(d))[42]

⊘caution: In addition to the at-risk rules, losses and credits from an activity may also be subject to the passive activity rules, discussed at ¶1810 *et seq.*

Form 6198 is used to compute the deductible loss from an at-risk activity. [43]

For the at-risk rules otherwise applicable to real property, see ¶1809.

¶ 1807   Amounts considered "at risk."

A taxpayer is considered at risk for an activity to the extent of:

(1) the amount of money and the adjusted basis of other property taxpayer contributed to the activity (Code Sec. 465(b)(1)), plus

(2) amounts borrowed with respect to the activity to the extent taxpayer is personally liable for the repayment of or has pledged property, other than property used in the activity, as security for the borrowed amount. The borrowings can't exceed the fair market value of taxpayer's interest in the pledged property. No property is treated as security if it is directly or indirectly financed by indebtedness secured by property in (1), above. (Code Sec. 465(b)(1), Code Sec. 465(b)(2))[44]

Amounts borrowed "at risk" ((2) above) don't include borrowings from any person who has an interest in the activity other than as a creditor, or from a related person as specially defined. A corporation is at risk with respect to amounts it borrowed from a shareholder. (Code Sec. 465(b)(3))[45]

Any amounts, even equity capital contributed by taxpayer, aren't treated as at risk if the amounts are protected against loss through nonrecourse financing, guarantees, stop loss agreements or similar arrangements. (Code Sec. 465(b)(4))[46]

In determining the amount at risk for any tax year, the amount for that year is reduced by any losses allowed under these limitations in an earlier year. (Code Sec. 465(b)(5))[47]

¶ 1808   Recapture of losses where amount at-risk is less than zero.

If taxpayer's amount at risk (¶1807) is less than zero (e.g., by distributions to taxpayer or by debt changing from recourse to nonrecourse), taxpayer recognizes income to the extent of that negative amount. (Code Sec. 465(e)(1)(A)) But, the amount recaptured is limited to the excess of the losses previously allowed in that activity over any amounts previously recaptured. (Code Sec. 465(e)(2)) The amount added to income under this recapture rule is treated as a deduction allocable to the activity in the first succeeding year, and is allowed if and to the extent taxpayer's at-risk basis is increased. (Code Sec. 465(e)(1)(B))[48]

---

41. ¶M-4502; ¶4654; TD ¶401,001
42. ¶M-4502; ¶4564; TD ¶401,006
43. ¶M-4501; ¶4654; TD ¶401,001
44. ¶M-4541 *et seq.*; ¶4654; TD ¶404,001, 404,008

45. ¶M-4557 *et seq.*; ¶4654; TD ¶404,017, 404,018
46. ¶M-4568 *et seq.*; ¶4654; TD ¶404,028
47. ¶M-4507; ¶4654; TD ¶401,007
48. ¶M-4509; ¶4654; TD ¶401,009

¶ 1809 At-risk rules for real property.

A taxpayer engaged in the activity of holding real property is subject to the at-risk rules, for losses on property placed in service after '86. The at-risk rules also apply to a taxpayer's losses from real estate attributable to an interest in a pass-through entity that is acquired after '86, regardless of when the entity acquired the real property. [49]

Taxpayer is considered at risk for his share of any "qualified nonrecourse financing" secured by the real property. (Code Sec. 465(b)(6)(A)) This means financing: (1) borrowed by taxpayer with respect to the activity of holding real property (as specially defined); (2) borrowed by taxpayer from a qualified person (as specially defined) or from any federal, state, or local government or instrumentality or that is guaranteed by any federal, state or local government; (3) except as regs provide, on which no one is personally liable for repayment (if there is personal liability for repayment of a portion of a refinancing, the portion for which no person is personally liable may be qualified nonrecourse financing; (4) personal liability of partnerships is disregarded if certain conditions are met; and (5) that isn't convertible debt. (Code Sec. 465(b)(6)(B); Reg § 1.465-27(b))[50]

¶ 1810 "Passive Activity" Losses and Credits. ▬▬▬▬▬

Losses from passive activities —activities in which the taxpayer doesn't materially participate, and most rental activities —may only be used to offset passive activity income (which doesn't include portfolio income); thus they can't be used to offset income from, for example, compensation, interest or dividends. Any losses that are unused in a tax year because of this rule are carried forward to the following year(s) until used, or until taxpayer disposes of the interest in the activity (or substantially all of the activity) in a taxable transaction. Passive activity credits may be used only to offset tax on income from passive activities, with a carryover of any unused credits. But, individuals who actively participate in rental real estate activities may use up to $25,000 of losses from those activities to offset nonpassive income; and those activities are not automatically passive for real estate professionals.

caution: For passive activity losses for alternative minimum tax purposes, see ¶3209.

¶ 1811 Disallowance of passive activity losses and credits—Form 8582; Form 8582-CR; Form 8810.

A taxpayer specified at ¶1812 may not deduct a passive activity loss (i.e., the excess of aggregate losses from passive activities over aggregate income from those activities, see ¶1814) (Code Sec. 469(a)(1)(A)) or use a passive activity credit (i.e, the excess of specified credits attributable to passive activities over the regular tax liability allocable to those activities, see ¶1823) (Code Sec. 469(a)(1)(B)), except with respect to certain rental real estate activities (¶1834 *et seq.*). (Reg § 1.469-1T(a)(2))[1] For carryover of suspended losses and credits, see ¶1839. For deduction of suspended losses on disposition of the activity, see ¶1840.

A passive activity deduction disallowed for a tax year under these rules isn't taken into account as a deduction in computing taxable income (or self-employment income). (Reg § 1.469-1T(d)(3)) And a passive activity deduction that *is* allowed under these rules may still be disallowed under the Code Sec. 613A limit on percentage depletion of oil and gas wells, or the Code Sec. 1211 limit on capital losses. (Reg § 1.469-1(d)(2))[2]

Whether a loss is disallowed under these rules is determined *after* the application of the at-risk rules (¶1803 *et seq.*), and the interest deduction limitations (¶1726 *et seq.*), as well as

49. ¶M-4533; TD ¶403,013
50. ¶M-4534 *et seq.*; ¶4654; TD ¶403,014 *et seq.*

1. ¶M-4600 *et seq.*; ¶4694 *et seq.*; TD ¶411,001 *et seq.*
2. ¶M-4603; ¶4694.47; TD ¶411,002, 411,004

other provisions measuring taxable income. (Reg § 1.469-2(d)(6), Reg § 1.469-1T(d))[3]

Where taxpayer's disallowed passive activity losses are derived from more than one activity, a ratable portion of the loss (if any) from each passive activity, in general, is disallowed. (Reg § 1.469-1T(f)(2)(i))[4] Any loss so disallowed is then generally allocated ratably among all passive activity deductions (¶1815) from the activity for the year. (Reg § 1.469-1T(f)(2)(ii))[5] If all or any portion of a passive activity credit is disallowed, a ratable portion of each credit from each passive activity, in general, is disallowed. (Reg § 1.469-1T(f)(3)(i))[6]

The passive activity limits are calculated on Form 8582 (individuals, estates, and trusts), Form 8582-CR (credits for individuals, estates, and trusts), or Form 8810 (closely held corporations and personal service corporations). [7]

¶ 1812   Who is subject to the passive activity rules?

The passive activity limits (¶1811) apply to any individual, estate, trust (Code Sec. 469(a)(2)(A)) (other than a trust, or portion of a trust, which is a grantor trust) (Reg § 1.469-1T(b)(2)), personal service corporation (PSC) as specially defined (Code Sec. 469(a)(2)(C), Code Sec. 469(j)(2)) and closely held C corporation (except as described at ¶1814 and ¶1815) as specially defined. (Code Sec. 469(a)(2)(B), Code Sec. 469(j)(1))[8] For pass-through entities, see ¶1813.

Spouses filing a joint return are treated as one taxpayer, with certain exceptions. (Reg § 1.469-1T(j)(1))[9]

The passive activity rules don't apply, except as regs may provide, to any corporation that isn't a PSC or a closely held corporation for the tax year. (Reg § 1.469-1T(g)(1))[10] But the rules *do* apply to any of the corporation's losses or credits that arose during a tax year when it *was* a PSC or closely held C corporation. (Code Sec. 469(f)(2))[11]

The passive activity rules apply to an affiliated group of corporations that files a consolidated return, but only if the consolidated group as a whole is properly treated as a PSC or closely held C corporation. (Code Sec. 469(j)(11), Reg § 1.469-1(h))[12]

¶ 1813   Pass-through entities subject to the passive activity rules.

Partnerships (unless publicly traded, see below) and S corporations aren't subject to the passive activity rules (¶1811). (Code Sec. 469(a)(2)) But the rules *do* apply to the losses and credits passed through to the partners and shareholders. [13]

The passive activity rules apply to publicly traded partnerships (PTPs, defined below) that aren't treated as corporations (¶3302). The rules are applied separately with respect to items attributable to each PTP (except in certain situations involving the low-income housing and rehabilitation credits). (Code Sec. 469(k)(1)) A partner's net passive income for a tax year from a PTP can't be offset by losses from other passive activities. [14]

A PTP is a partnership the interests of which are traded on an established securities market (national or local exchange, or an over-the-counter market) or are readily tradable on a secondary market (or the substantial equivalent). (Code Sec. 469(k)(2), Reg § 1.469-10(b))[15]

3. ¶M-4603 *et seq.*; ¶4694.30, 4694.31, 4694.47; TD ¶411,004 *et seq.*
4. ¶M-5501; ¶4694.40; TD ¶416,502
5. ¶M-5502; ¶4694.42; TD ¶416,503
6. ¶M-5604; ¶4694.44; TD ¶417,006
7. ¶M-5200; ¶4694, 4694.36; TD ¶411,001
8. ¶M-4700 *et seq.*; ¶4694; TD ¶411,500 *et seq.*

9. ¶M-4702; ¶4694.70; TD ¶411,502
10. ¶M-4705; ¶4694; TD ¶411,504
11. ¶M-4705; TD ¶411,504
12. ¶M-4708; ¶4694.75; TD ¶411,507
13. ¶s M-4709, M-5302; ¶4694.80; TD ¶411,508
14. ¶M-4710; ¶4694.85; TD ¶411,509
15. ¶M-4710; ¶4694.85; TD ¶411,510

¶ 1814   Passive activity loss defined.

A passive activity loss for a tax year is the amount, if any, by which the aggregate losses from all passive activities (¶1824) for the tax year exceed the aggregate income from all passive activities for that year —i.e., the excess of "passive activity deductions" (¶1815) over "passive activity gross income" (¶1817) for the year. (Code Sec. 469(d)(1); Reg § 1.469-2T(b)(1))[16]

For a closely held C corporation, the passive activity loss is the excess of passive activity deductions over the sum of passive activity gross income *plus* the corporation's net active (but not portfolio) income for the tax year. (Code Sec. 469(e)(2)(A); Reg § 1.469-1T(g)(4))[17]

For how passive loss characterization affects other Code provisions, see ¶1811.

¶ 1815   What is a passive activity deduction?

A deduction is a "passive activity deduction" for a tax year only if it: (1) arises in connection with the conduct of an activity that is a passive activity for that year (¶1824), or (2) is carried over as a passive activity deduction from an earlier tax year (¶1839). (Reg § 1.469-2T(d)(1)) A deduction "arises" in the tax year the item would be deductible under taxpayer's method of accounting if taxable income for all tax years were determined without regard to the passive loss rules, the Code Sec. 613A(d) rules denying percentage depletion for oil and gas wells, and the Code Sec. 1211 capital loss limitation rules. (Reg § 1.469-2(d)(8))[18]

The character (as a passive activity deduction) of an item allocated to taxpayer by a partnership or S corporation is determined, in any case in which participation is relevant, by taxpayer's participation in the activity that generated the item for the entity's tax year. (Reg § 1.469-2T(e))[19]

For when loss on the sale or other disposition of an interest in property is a passive activity deduction, see ¶1816.

Passive activity deductions *don't include* (Reg § 1.469-2(d)(2); Reg § 1.469-2T(d)(2)) (and thus the passive loss limits don't restrict the deductibility of): (1) interest expense properly allocable to portfolio income (Code Sec. 469(e)(1)(A)(i)(III));[20] (2) an expense (other than interest) clearly and directly allocable to portfolio income (Code Sec. 469(e)(1)(A)(i)(II)); (3) state, local, or foreign income, war profits, or excess profits taxes; (4) a deduction allowed for a charitable contribution; (5) miscellaneous itemized deductions subject to the 2%-of-AGI floor (see ¶3110), but without regard to any amount disallowed because of that floor; (6) a dividends-received deduction with respect to any dividend that's not included in passive activity gross income (¶1817); (7) a loss that's carried to the tax year under Code Sec. 172(a) (net operating losses, ¶1842), Code Sec. 613A(d) (limit on depletion deductions, ¶1984), Code Sec. 1212(a) (corporate capital loss carrybacks and carryovers, ¶2615), and Code Sec. 1212(b) (noncorporate capital loss carryovers, ¶2612); (8) nonrecurring casualty and theft losses; or (9) a deduction or loss allocable to business or rental use of a dwelling unit for any tax year to which the Code Sec. 280A(c)(5) limits (¶1780) apply. [21]

Deductions in excess of a partner's (or shareholder's) basis, or in excess of the at-risk limits, aren't passive activity deductions for the tax year. (Reg § 1.469-2T(d)(6))[22]

---

16. ¶M-4601; ¶4694; TD ¶411,001
17. ¶M-5507 *et seq.*; ¶4694.36; TD ¶416,509
18. ¶M-5401; ¶4694.30; TD ¶416,001
19. ¶M-5402; ¶4694.80; TD ¶416,005

20. ¶M-5416 *et seq.*; ¶s 4694.23, 4694.31; TD ¶416,013 *et seq.*
21. ¶M-5421; ¶4694.31; TD ¶416,018
22. ¶M-4606; ¶4694.30; TD ¶411,007

¶ 1816   Loss on sale, exchange or other disposition as passive activity deduction.

Passive activity deductions (¶1815) include any loss recognized on the sale, exchange or other disposition of an interest in property used in an activity at the time of disposition, and any deduction allowed on account of the abandonment or worthlessness of the interest, *if and only if* the activity was a passive activity (¶1824) of taxpayer for the tax year of disposition (or other event giving rise to the deduction). (Reg § 1.469-2T(d)(5)(i))[23]

If the interest in property disposed of was used in more than one activity during the 12-month period ending on the date of disposition, the amount realized from the disposition (as well as the adjusted basis of the interest) must be allocated among the activities (with a de minimis exception) on a basis that reasonably reflects those uses. (Reg § 1.469-2(d)(5)(iii), Reg § 1.469-2T(d)(5)(i), Reg § 1.469-2T(d)(5)(ii))[24]

Passive activity deductions don't include: (1) a loss from the disposition of property that produces portfolio income (¶1820) (Reg § 1.469-2T(d)(2)(iv)), or (2) a deduction for a disposition of an entire interest in a passive activity if, under the rules for those dispositions (¶1840), the deduction isn't treated as a passive activity deduction. (Reg § 1.469-2T(d)(2)(v))[25]

¶ 1817   Passive activity gross income.

Passive activity gross income is, in general, gross income from a passive activity (¶1824). (Reg § 1.469-2T(c)(1))[26] The character (as passive activity gross income) of a partner's or S corporation shareholder's allocable items of gross income is determined, in general, by reference to the partner's or shareholder's participation in the activity(ies) that generated the items for the entity's tax year. (Reg § 1.469-2T(e)(1))[27] For when gain on disposition of a property interest is passive activity gross income, see ¶1818.

Passive activity gross income doesn't include portfolio income (¶1820) (Code Sec. 469(e)(1)(A)(i)(I); Reg § 1.469-2T(c)(3)(i)), or compensation for personal services (as specially defined). (Code Sec. 469(e)(3); Reg § 1.469-2T(c)(4))[28]

Other items specifically excluded are gross income:

. . . from intangible property (e.g., a patent) if taxpayer's personal efforts contributed significantly to the property's creation;

. . . attributable to a tax refund;

. . . from an oil or gas property, if any loss from a working interest in the property for any earlier tax year was treated as a loss not from a passive activity; (Code Sec. 469(c)(3)(B); Reg § 1.469-2(c)(6))[29]

. . . of an individual from a covenant not to compete;

. . . that is treated as not from a passive activity under the regs;

. . . attributable to the reimbursement of a casualty or theft loss if: the reimbursement is included in gross income, the loss was deducted in an earlier year, and the loss deduction wasn't a passive activity deduction. (Reg § 1.469-2(c)(7))[30]

¶ 1818   Gain on sale, exchange, or other disposition of interest in passive activity.

Gain recognized on the sale, exchange or other disposition of an interest in property generally is treated as passive activity gross income (¶1817) for the year the gain is recognized, if the activity in which the property was used was a passive activity (¶1824) for the

---

23. ¶M-5406; ¶4694.32; TD ¶416,004
24. ¶M-5406; ¶4694.32; TD ¶416,004
25. ¶M-5421; ¶4694.31; TD ¶416,018
26. ¶M-5301; ¶4694.21; TD ¶415,001

27. ¶M-5302; ¶4694.80; TD ¶415,019
28. ¶M-5325, M-5332; ¶4694.22; TD ¶415,022, 415,023
29. ¶M-5333 *et seq.*; ¶4694.66; TD ¶415,028 *et seq.*
30. ¶M-5334; ¶4694.22; TD ¶415,031

year of disposition. (Reg § 1.469-2T(c)(2)(i)(A))[31]

But gain from the disposition of an interest in property that is substantially appreciated (fair market value exceeds 120% of adjusted basis) is treated as *not* from a passive activity unless the interest was used in a passive activity for either 20% of the period taxpayer held the interest or the entire 24-month period ending on the date of disposition. (Reg § 1.469-2(c)(2)(iii))[32]

If the property disposed of was used in more than one activity in the 12-month period before disposition, the amount realized on disposition (as well as the adjusted basis of the interest in the property) must be allocated among those activities (with a de minimis exception) on a basis that reasonably reflects those uses. (Reg § 1.469-2T(c)(2)(ii))[33]

If taxpayer acquires an interest in property in a taxable transaction (i.e., not a Code Sec. 7701(a)(45) nonrecognition transaction), the ownership and use of the interest before the transaction isn't taken into account in applying these rules to taxpayer's later disposition of it. (Reg § 1.469-2(c)(2)(iv))[34] In certain instances, property held in a "dealing activity" (i.e., for sale to customers in the ordinary course of business) is treated as being held in the last nondealing activity in which it was used before its sale. (Reg § 1.469-2(c)(2)(v)(A))[35]

For disposition of *entire* interest in (or substantially all of) a passive activity, see ¶1840.

¶ 1819 Disposition of interest in partnership or S corporation.

Where there's a disposition of a partnership interest or S corporation stock, a ratable portion of the net gain is treated as gain from the disposition of an interest in each trade or business, rental, or investment activity in which the entity owns an interest. (Reg § 1.469-2T(e)(3)(ii)(A))[36] But, gain attributable to certain substantially appreciated property (¶1818) isn't passive activity gross income (¶1817) if that gain exceeds 10% of the gain allocated to the activity. (Reg § 1.469-2T(e)(3)(iii))[37]

Similarly, a ratable portion of the loss is treated as loss from the disposition of an interest in each trade or business, etc., in which the entity owns an interest. (Reg § 1.469-2T(e)(3)(ii)(A))[38]

¶ 1820 Portfolio income.

Portfolio income (treated as not passive activity gross income, see ¶1817) includes all gross income, *other than* income derived in the ordinary course of a trade or business (¶1821), attributable to:

... interest;

... dividends from a C corporation or an S corporation's accumulated earnings and profits;

... annuities;

... royalties;

... net income from publicly traded partnerships (PTPs, ¶1813);

... income (including dividends) from a RIC (¶4201), REIT (¶4202), REMIC (¶4204), Code Sec. 1381(a) cooperative (¶4205), common trust fund (¶4208), controlled foreign corporation (¶4629) or qualified electing fund (¶4636);

... gain (loss) from the disposition of property that produces portfolio income;

... gain (loss) from the disposition of property held for investment (¶1728) (Code Sec. 469(e)(1)(A); Reg § 1.469-2T(c)(3)(i));

31. ¶M-5304; ¶4694.28; TD ¶415,002
32. ¶M-5306; ¶4694.28; TD ¶415,004
33. ¶M-5305; ¶4694.28; TD ¶415,003
34. ¶M-5307; ¶4694.28; TD ¶415,005

35. ¶M-5308; ¶4694.28; TD ¶415,006
36. ¶M-5708; ¶4694.82; TD ¶417,512
37. ¶M-5342; ¶4694.82; TD ¶415,045
38. ¶M-5708; ¶4694.82; TD ¶417,512

. . . income, gain or loss from investment of working capital (¶1821).[39]

¶ 1821 When is income derived in the ordinary course of a trade or business?

Income that otherwise would be portfolio income (¶1820) is treated as derived in the ordinary course of a trade or business —i.e., *not* portfolio income—only if derived from the trade or business of lending money, from trade accounts receivable, or in certain other limited situations specified in the regs or by IRS. (Reg § 1.469-2T(c)(3)(ii), Reg § 1.469-2T(c)(3)(iii))[40]

Any income, gain or loss attributable to an investment of working capital (defined as current assets minus current liabilities [41]) is treated as *not* derived in the ordinary course of business (i.e., it's portfolio income, ¶1820). (Code Sec. 469(e)(1)(B))[42]

A dealer's income or gain from property isn't derived in the ordinary course of a trade or business if the dealer held the property for investment at any time before the income or gain is recognized. (Reg § 1.469-2T(e)(3)(iii)(A))[43]

¶ 1822 Recharacterization of passive income as nonpassive income.

Certain income is treated as income that *isn't* from a passive activity, i.e., income from: significant participation activities (in which the taxpayer participates for more than 100 hours during the tax year, but doesn't materially participate); rental of nondepreciable property; net interest income from an equity-financed lending activity or certain rental property; and certain royalty income. (Reg § 1.469-2T(f)(1))[44]

¶ 1823 Passive activity credit defined.

A "passive activity credit" is the amount (if any) by which: (1) the sum of all credits from passive activities ("passive credits," see below) allowable for the tax year, exceeds (2) taxpayer's regular tax liability for the year allocable to all passive activities. (Code Sec. 469(d)(2)) This includes a credit attributable to the tax year arising in connection with the conduct of an activity that is "passive" (¶1824) for the year, as well as a credit carried over (¶1839) from an earlier tax year when it was disallowed under the passive activity rules. (Reg § 1.469-3T(b)(1))[45]

The regular tax liability allocable to all passive activities ((2) above) is the excess of taxpayer's regular tax liability for the tax year, over the regular tax liability determined by reducing taxpayer's taxable income by the excess (if any) of his passive activity gross income (¶1817) over his passive activity deductions (¶1815), for the year. (Reg § 1.469-3T(d)(1))[46]

Where taxpayer is a closely held corporation, the passive activity credit for the tax year is reduced by its net active income tax liability. (Code Sec. 469(e)(2); Reg § 1.469-1T(g)(5))[47]

"Passive credits" include the credits for orphan drug clinical testing, alcohol fuels, low income housing, research, enhanced oil recovery, nonconventional source fuel production, qualified electric vehicles and the rehabilitation credit. (Code Sec. 469(d)(2)(A); Reg § 1.469-3T(b))[48] For discussion of credits, see ¶2300 *et seq.*

Where the activity that gives rise to taxpayer's credit is conducted by a partnership or S corporation, whether the credit is "passive" is based on taxpayer's participation in the activity (if participation is relevant) for the entity's tax year. (Reg § 1.469-3T(b)(3))[49]

---

39. ¶M-5325 *et seq.*; ¶4694.23; TD ¶415,023
40. ¶M-5329 *et seq.*; ¶4694.23; TD ¶415,025
41. ¶D-2842
42. ¶M-5329; ¶4694.23; TD ¶415,025
43. ¶M-5329; TD ¶415,025
44. ¶M-5335; ¶4694.25; TD ¶415,035

45. ¶M-5601; ¶4694.35; TD ¶417,002
46. ¶M-5603; TD ¶417,005
47. ¶M-5607; ¶4694.36; TD ¶417,010
48. ¶M-5601; ¶4694.35; TD ¶417,002
49. ¶M-5602; ¶4694.35; TD ¶417,004

¶ 1824   What is a passive activity?

A passive activity is any activity (¶1826) involving the conduct of any trade or business (¶1825) in which taxpayer doesn't materially participate (¶1828). (Code Sec. 469(c)(1)) For rental activities, see ¶1834.

A working interest in an oil or gas well *isn't* a passive activity (Code Sec. 469(c)(3)), whether or not taxpayer materially participated in the activity. (Code Sec. 469(c)(4)) The working interest must be held directly or through an entity that doesn't limit taxpayer's liability (i.e., general partnership interest in a partnership). (Reg § 1.469-1T(e)(4))[50]

¶ 1825   Trade or business activities under passive activity rules.

A trade or business that can be a passive activity (¶1824) includes any activity:

. . . in connection with a trade or business (under Code Sec. 162);

. . . with respect to which expenses are allowable as a deduction under Code Sec. 212 (for the production, etc., of income) (Code Sec. 469(c)(6));[1] and

. . . involving research or experimentation (under the Code Sec. 174 rules for deducting business-related research, etc., expenditures, see ¶1601). (Code Sec. 469(c)(5))[2]

For rules for grouping activities, see ¶1826.

Trade or business activities do not include rental activities (although rental activities generally are treated as passive activities, see ¶1834) or activities that are (under Reg § 1.469-1T(e)(3)(vi)(B)) incidental to an activity of holding property for investment. (Reg § 1.469-1(e)(2), Reg § 1.469-4(b)(1))[3]

Trade or business activities thus include activities (other than the rental, etc., activities described above) that involve the conduct of a trade or business, are conducted in anticipation of starting a trade or business, or involve research or experimental expenditures that are (or would be) deductible under Code Sec. 174. (Reg § 1.469-4(b)(1))[4]

¶ 1826   Rules for grouping "activities" for passive activity rule purposes.

A taxpayer may treat one or more trade or business activities (¶1825) or rental activities (¶1834) as a single activity if the activities are an appropriate economic unit for measuring gain or loss for Code Sec. 469 purposes (the "passive activity" rules) (Reg § 1.469-4(c)(1)), based on all the relevant facts and circumstances. A taxpayer may use any reasonable method of applying the relevant facts and circumstances in grouping activities. These factors are given the greatest weight: similarities and differences in types of trades or businesses, the extent of common control, the extent of common ownership, geographical location, and interdependencies among the activities. (Reg § 1.469-4(c)(2))[5]

A rental activity (as defined in Reg § 1.469-1T(e)(3)) (Reg § 1.469-4(b)(2)) can't be grouped with a trade or business activity unless the activities being grouped together are an appropriate economic unit *and:*

. . . the rental activity is insubstantial in relation to the trade or business activity; or

. . . the trade or business activity is insubstantial in relation to the rental activity; or

. . . each owner of the trade or business activity has the same proportionate ownership interest in the rental activity. In that case the part of the rental activity that involves the rental of items of property for use in the trade or business may be grouped with the trade or

---

50. ¶M-4813; ¶4694.65; TD ¶412,014
1. ¶M-4801 *et seq.*; ¶s 4694.01, 4694.02; TD ¶412,001 *et seq.*
2. ¶M-4802; ¶4694.02; TD ¶412,002

3. ¶M-4802; ¶4694.02; TD ¶412,002
4. ¶M-4802; ¶4694.02; TD ¶412,002
5. ¶M-4803, M-4804; ¶4694.10; TD ¶412,003, 412,004

business activity. (Reg § 1.469-4(d)(1))[6]

Real property rentals and personal property rentals (other than personal property rentals provided in connection with the real property, or vice versa) can't be grouped together. (Reg § 1.469-4(d)(2))[7]

Once the taxpayer has grouped activities, the taxpayer can't re-group them in later years. If a material change occurs that makes the original grouping clearly inappropriate, the taxpayer must regroup the activities. IRS may regroup activities to prevent tax avoidance. (Reg § 1.469-4(e), Reg § 1.469-4(f))[8]

In a year when there's a disposition of substantially all of an activity, taxpayer may under specified conditions treat the part disposed of as a separate activity. (Reg §   1.469-4(g))[9]

¶ 1827   Activities conducted through PSCs, closely-held corporations, S corporations and partnerships.

For purposes of the passive activity rules (¶1810 *et seq.*), a taxpayer's activities include those conducted through personal service corporations (PSCs), closely-held C corporations, S corporations, and partnerships. (Reg § 1.469-4(a))[10]

A PSC, closely-held C corporation, S corporation or partnership must group its activities under the rules described at ¶1826. Once the entity groups its activities, a shareholder or partner must group those activities with each other, with activities conducted directly by the shareholder or partner, and with activities conducted through other such entities. A shareholder or partner may not treat activities grouped together by one of these entities as a separate activity. (Reg § 1.469-4(d)(5)) Particular limits apply to grouping by limited partners and limited entrepreneurs. (Reg § 1.469-4(d)(3))[11]

¶ 1828   What is "material participation"?

A taxpayer materially participates in an activity only if he's involved in the activity's operations on a regular, continuous and substantial basis (¶1829 *et seq.*). (Code Sec. 469(h)) A trust materially participates in an activity if a fiduciary, in his capacity as such, so participates.[12] A closely held C corporation or personal service corporation materially participates, in general, only if one or more of its shareholders who own more than 50% of its stock (by value) themselves materially participate. (Code Sec. 469(h)(4)(A))[13]

¶ 1829   Material participation by individuals.

An individual materially participates in an activity for a tax year *if and only if* the individual meets at least *one* of the following tests:

(1) The individual participates (as defined at ¶1832) in it for more than 500 hours during the year. (Reg § 1.469-5T(a)(1))

(2) The individual's participation in the activity for the tax year is substantially all of the participation in it by all individuals (including nonowner individuals) for the year. (Reg § 1.469-5T(a)(2))

(3) The individual participates in the activity for more than 100 hours during the tax year and that isn't less than that of any other individual (including nonowners) for that year. (Reg § 1.469-5T(a)(3))

6. ¶M-4805; ¶4694.10; TD ¶412,005

7. ¶M-4806; ¶4694.10; TD ¶412,006

8. ¶M-4809; ¶4694.10; TD ¶412,013

9. ¶M-5701.3; ¶4694.50; TD ¶412,001 *et seq.*

10. ¶M-4807.2; ¶4694.10; TD ¶412,009

11. ¶M-4807.2; ¶4694.10; TD ¶412,009

12. ¶M-5005; TD ¶413,024.

13. ¶M-4901 *et seq.*; ¶M-5006; ¶4694.06; TD ¶413,002 *et seq.*

(4) The activity is a "significant participation activity" for the tax year, and the individual's aggregate participation in all significant participation activities that year exceeds 500 hours. A "significant participation activity" is a trade or business in which the individual significantly participates (for more than 100 hours), but in which he doesn't otherwise materially participate. (Reg § 1.469-5T(a)(4), Reg § 1.469-5T(c))

(5) The individual materially participated in the activity for any five tax years (consecutive or not) during the 10 immediately preceding tax years. (Reg § 1.469-5T(a)(5))

(6) The activity is a personal service activity, and the individual materially participated in the activity for any three tax years (consecutive or not) before the tax year. (Reg § 1.469-5T(a)(6), Reg § 1.469-5T(d))

(7) The individual meets a facts and circumstances test (¶1830). (Reg § 1.469-5T(a)(7))[14]

For purposes of (5) and (6), above, taxpayer materially participated in an activity for an earlier tax year if that activity included significant Code Sec. 469 activities that are substantially the same as significant Code Sec. 469 activities that were included in an activity in which taxpayer materially participated (without regard to (5)) for that preceding year. (Reg § 1.469-5(j)(1))[15]

The extent of an individual's material participation in an activity may be established by any reasonable means, including, but not limited to, appointment books, calendars, or narrative summaries, contemporaneous daily time reports or logs, but not the taxpayer's oral testimony, standing alone. Reg § 1.469-5T(f)(4)[16]

For participation by the individual's spouse, see ¶1833.

¶ 1830 Facts and circumstances test for material participation.

An individual materially participates (¶1829) in an activity if he participates on a regular, continuous and substantial basis during the year, based on all the facts and circumstances. (Reg § 1.469-5T(a)(7)) An individual who participates in the activity for 100 hours or less during the year doesn't meet this test. (Reg § 1.469-5T(b)(2)(iii))[17]

The fact that the individual (except for certain retirees and surviving spouses, in the case of farming activities) satisfies participation standards under other Code provisions isn't taken into account for this purpose. (Reg § 1.469-5T(b)(2)(i)) Nor is the individual's participation in the management of the activity, unless there's no other paid manager, and no other individual performs management services that exceed (by hours) those performed by the individual. (Reg § 1.469-5T(b)(2)(ii))[18]

¶ 1831 Limited partner's material participation.

An individual limited partner is not treated as materially participating (¶1828) in any activity of a limited partnership with respect to his interest in that partnership (or to any gain or loss from the activity recognized on a sale or exchange of that interest) *unless* the individual would be treated as materially participating under the 500-hour, five-tax-years-out-of-ten, or three-year-personal-service-activity tests at ¶1829 (items (1), (5) or (6), respectively), if he weren't a limited partner. (Code Sec. 469(h)(2); Reg § 1.469-5T(e)(2))[19]

An individual's partnership interest *isn't* treated as a limited partnership interest if the individual is a general partner in the partnership at all times during the partnership's tax year ending with or within the individual's tax year. (Reg § 1.469-5T(e)(3)(ii))[20]

---

14. ¶M-4901 *et seq.*; ¶4694.06; TD ¶413,002 *et seq.*
15. ¶M-4911; ¶4694.06; TD ¶413,011
16. ¶M-4904; ¶4694.06; TD ¶413,004
17. ¶M-4912; ¶4694.06; TD ¶413,012

18. ¶M-4913, ¶M-4917, ¶M-4918; ¶4694.06; TD ¶413,013, 413,016, 413,017
19. ¶M-5003 *et seq.*; ¶4694.06; TD ¶413,022
20. ¶M-5003; ¶4694.06; TD ¶413,022

¶ 1832 Participation defined.

Any work done by an individual (without regard to the capacity in which he does the work) in connection with the activity, where the individual owns (directly or indirectly) an interest in the activity at the time the work is done, is treated as participation by that individual in the activity, except as otherwise provided. (Reg § 1.469-5(f)(1))[21]

Work not of a type customarily done by an owner isn't treated as participation if one of its principal purposes is to avoid the passive loss rules. (Reg § 1.469-5T(f)(2)(i))[22]

An individual's work as an investor is not participation unless the individual is directly involved in day-to-day management or operations. (Reg § 1.469-5T(f)(2)(ii))[23]

¶ 1833 Spouse's material participation.

In determining whether a married taxpayer materially participates in an activity, the participation of taxpayer's spouse is taken into account (Code Sec. 469(h)(5)), without regard to whether the spouse owns an interest in the activity, or whether the spouses file a joint return for the year. (Reg § 1.469-5T(f)(3))[24]

¶ 1834 Rental activities as passive activities.

For purposes of the passive activity rules (¶1810 *et seq.*), all rental activities are treated as passive activities (Code Sec. 469(c)(2)), except for (a) individuals who actively participate in rental real estate activities (¶1835) and (b) certain real estate professionals (¶1838).[25]

A rental activity is any activity where payments are principally for the use of tangible property (Code Sec. 469(j)(8)), without regard to whether a lease, service contract, or other arrangement is involved. (Reg § 1.469-1T(e)(3)(i)(B)) But, a rental activity doesn't include an activity involving the use of tangible property if:

(1) The average period the customer uses the property is: 7 days or less (Reg § 1.469-1T(e)(3)(ii)(A)), or 30 days or less, and the owner (or someone on the owner's behalf) provides significant personal services (as defined in the regs). (Reg § 1.469-1T(e)(3)(ii)(B))

(2) The owner (or someone on the owner's behalf) provides extraordinary personal services (as defined in the regs), without regard to the average period the customer uses the property. (Reg § 1.469-1T(e)(3)(ii)(C))

(3) The rental of the tangible property is incidental to a nonrental activity of taxpayer (Reg § 1.469-1T(e)(3)(ii)(D)) (as measured by certain percentage and other tests). (Reg § 1.469-1T(e)(3)(vi))

(4) Taxpayer customarily makes the property available during defined business hours for nonexclusive use by various customers (Reg § 1.469-1T(e)(3)(ii)(E)) (e.g., a golf course).

(5) The property is provided for use in a nonrental activity of a partnership, joint venture, or S corporation in which taxpayer owns an interest, where taxpayer provided the property in his capacity as owner of that interest (Reg § 1.469-1T(e)(3)(ii)(F)) (not as a renter of the property to the partnership, etc.). [26]

¶ 1835 Individuals' active participation rental real estate losses up to $25,000 may be used against nonpassive income.

A natural person who: (1) has at least a 10% interest in any rental real estate activity

---

21. ¶M-4902; ¶4694.06; TD ¶413,002
22. ¶M-4903; ¶4694.06; TD ¶413,003
23. ¶M-4903; ¶4694.06; TD ¶413,003

24. ¶M-4902; ¶4694.06; TD ¶413,002
25. ¶M-5100 *et seq.*; ¶s 4694.01, 4694.60, 4694.63; TD ¶413,501
26. ¶M-5101 *et seq.*; ¶4694.03; TD ¶413,502

(¶1836), and (2) otherwise "actively participates" in that activity (¶1837), may offset up to $25,000 of nonpassive income with that portion of the passive activity loss, or of the deduction equivalent of the passive activity credit, attributable to that activity. (Code Sec. 469(i)(1), Code Sec. 469(i)(2), Code Sec. 469(j)(5))[27]

For a married person filing a separate return, the allowance is $12,500 if he lives apart from his spouse at all times during the tax year (Code Sec. 469(i)(5)(A)(i)), and zero if he does not live apart from his spouse at all times during the tax year. (Code Sec. 469(i)(5)(B))[28]

The $25,000 allowance ($12,500 for marrieds filing separately) is reduced (but not below zero) by 50% of the amount by which taxpayer's adjusted gross income (AGI) as specially computed exceeds (1) $100,000 ($50,000 for marrieds filing separately), or (2) $200,000 ($100,000 for marrieds filing separately) in the case of rehabilitation investment credits (¶2308). There's no AGI-based phaseout of the $25,000 ($12,500) offset for low-income housing credits (¶2319) or the commercial revitalization deduction (¶1976). (Code Sec. 469(i)(3), Code Sec. 469(i)(5))[29]

¶ 1836   Who is a 10%-or-more owner entitled to rental real estate allowance?

An individual is a 10%-or-more owner (for the allowance at ¶1835) with respect to any interest in any rental real estate activity (¶1834) for any period only if *at all times* during that period (i.e., the tax year or shorter period the individual held the interest) his interest was at least 10% (by value) of all interests in that activity. The individual's interest includes any interest of his spouse. (Code Sec. 469(i)(6)(A))[30]

¶ 1837   What is "active participation"?

Taxpayer must participate (¶1832) in an activity in a significant and bona fide sense to actively participate in it. Taxpayer participates if he makes management decisions, e.g., approves new tenants, decides on rental terms, approves capital or repair expenditures or arranges for others to provide services (such as repairs). He need not have regular, continuous and substantial involvement in operations. But, a merely formal and nominal participation in management, without a genuine exercise of independent discretion and judgment, is insufficient.[31] The active participation test is less stringent than the material participation requirement (¶1828). Active participation isn't required to take low-income housing (¶2319) or rehabilitation investment credits (¶2308), or the commercial revitalization deduction (¶1976). (Code Sec. 469(i)(6)(B))[32]

In determining whether taxpayer actively participates, the participation of taxpayer's spouse is taken into account. (Code Sec. 469(i)(6)(D))[33]

A taxpayer isn't treated as actively participating (except as regs may provide) with respect to any interest as a limited partner. (Code Sec. 469(i)(6)(C))[34]

¶ 1838   Rental real estate activities of real estate professionals not treated as automatically passive .

For any tax year in which the taxpayer is a "qualifying taxpayer" (usually known as a real estate professional), the rule treating all rental activities as passive activities (¶1834) doesn't apply to any rental real estate activity of the taxpayer. (Code Sec. 469(c)(7)(A)(i)) Instead, that activity is a passive activity unless the taxpayer materially participates (¶1828).

---

27. ¶M-5131; ¶4694.60; TD ¶413,601
28. ¶M-5131; ¶4694.60; TD ¶413,601
29. ¶M-5142 *et seq.*; ¶4694.60; TD ¶413,612 *et seq.*
30. ¶M-5139; TD ¶413,609

31. ¶M-5138; ¶4694.60; TD ¶413,608
32. ¶M-5141; ¶4694.60; TD ¶413,611
33. ¶M-5138; ¶4694.70; TD ¶413,608
34. ¶M-5140; ¶4694.60; TD ¶413,610

(Reg § 1.469-9(e)(1))[35]

⊘*observation:* So, real estate professionals who materially participate in a rental real estate activity may use losses or credits from the activity to offset other, non-passive income.

A taxpayer is a qualifying taxpayer (i.e., real estate professional) for a particular tax year if: (1) more than half of the personal services (see below) the taxpayer performs during that year are performed in real property trades or businesses (see below) in which the taxpayer materially participates (¶1828) (Code Sec. 469(c)(7)(B)(i)), and (2) the taxpayer performs more than 750 hours of services during that year in real property trades or businesses in which he materially participates. (Code Sec. 469(c)(7)(B)(ii)) [36]

A taxpayer who owns at least one interest in rental real estate and who meets the above tests is a real estate professional. (Reg § 1.469-9(b)(6))[37]

In determining whether a taxpayer is a real estate professional, each of his interests in rental real estate is treated as a separate activity, unless he elects (by filing a specified statement with his original income tax return) to treat all interests in rental real estate as one activity. (Code Sec. 469(c)(7)(A); Reg § 1.469-9(g))[38] The election is binding for the tax year it's made and for all future years in which the taxpayer qualifies. Failure to elect in one year doesn't bar the election in a later year. (Reg § 1.469-9(g)(1)).[39]

Spouses filing a joint return qualify as real estate professionals only if one spouse separately satisfies the above tests (Code Sec. 469(c)(7)(B), Reg § 1.469-9(c)(4)), without regard to the other spouse's services. [40]

A closely-held C corporation qualifies as a real estate professional if more than 50% of its gross receipts for the tax year are derived from real property trades or businesses in which it materially participates. (Code Sec. 469(c)(7)(D)(i)) [41]

A real property trade or business is any real property development, redevelopment, construction, reconstruction, acquisition, conversion, rental, operation, management, leasing or brokerage trade or business. (Code Sec. 469(c)(7)(C)) The determination of a taxpayer's real property trades or businesses is based on all relevant facts and circumstances. Once a taxpayer determines the real property trades or businesses in which personal services are provided, he can't redetermine them later unless the original determination was clearly erroneous or there's been a material change of facts and circumstances. (Reg § 1.469-9(d)(1))[42]

Personal services means any work performed by an individual in connection with a trade or business, but not as an investor. (Reg § 1.469-9(b)(4)) Services performed as an employee don't count, unless he is a more-than-5%-owner of the employer. (Code Sec. 469(c)(7)(D)) [43]

¶ 1839   Carryover of suspended losses and credits.

Any deduction (or credit) from a passive activity (¶1824) that's disallowed under the passive loss rules (¶1810 *et seq.*) for a tax year is allocated among taxpayer's activities for the next tax year in a manner that reasonably reflects the extent each activity continues the business and rental operations that made up the loss activity. As so allocated, it is treated as a deduction (or credit) from that activity for that next year. (Code Sec. 469(b); Reg § 1.469-1(f)(4)(i))[44]

---

35. ¶M-5161; ¶4694.63; TD ¶413,801
36. ¶M-5168; ¶4694.63; TD ¶413,808
37. ¶M-5168; ¶4694.63; TD ¶413,808
38. ¶M-5163; ¶4694.63; TD ¶413,803, 413,804
39. ¶M-5163; ¶4694.63; TD ¶413,803

40. ¶M-5171; ¶4694.63; TD ¶413,811
41. ¶M-5172; ¶4694.63; TD ¶413,812
42. ¶M-5175; ¶4694.63; TD ¶413,815
43. ¶M-5169, M-5170 *et seq.*; ¶4694.63; TD ¶413,809, 413,810
44. ¶M-5504; ¶M-5604; ¶4694.45; TD ¶416,505, 417,006

¶ 1840 Disposition of taxpayer's entire interest in passive activity or substantially all of passive activity.

If a taxpayer disposes of his entire interest in a passive activity (or former passive activity), and all gain or loss realized on the disposition is recognized, the excess of: (1) any loss from the activity for the tax year of disposition (including losses carried over from earlier years, ¶1839), over (2) any net income or gain for that year from all other passive activities (including loss carryovers), is treated as loss *not* from a passive activity. (Code Sec. 469(g)(1)(A)) Loss from the activity under (1) is computed by taking into account all income, gain, and loss, including gain and loss recognized on the disposition. [45]

A taxpayer that disposes of *substantially all* of an activity may treat the part disposed of as a separate activity, if the taxpayer can establish with reasonable certainty: (A) the deductions and credits allocable to the part of the activity for the tax year under Reg § 1.469-1(f)(4) (relating to carryover of disallowed deductions and credits, see ¶1839), and (B) the gross income and any other deductions and credits allocable to that part of the activity for the tax year in which the disposition occurs. (Reg § 1.469-4(g)(2))[46]

⦿*observation:* This permits a taxpayer to treat the part of the activity disposed of as a complete disposition on which suspended losses are allowed.

Passive loss carryforwards ("suspended losses") are allowed against all the taxpayer's income (Code Sec. 469(g)(1)(A)), but carryforwards of passive activity credits ("suspended credits") aren't.[47]

Where the disposition is by installment sale, the amount treated as a nonpassive loss is the portion of the losses from each tax year that bears the same ratio to all these losses as the gain recognized on the sale bears to the gross profit from the sale. (Code Sec. 469(g)(3))[48]

Special rules apply where a disposition is to a related party (Code Sec. 469(g)(1)(B)), where the interest in the activity is transferred by reason of death (Code Sec. 469(g)(2)), or where the disposition is by gift. (Code Sec. 469(j)(6))[49]

¶ 1841 Net Operating Losses (NOLs).

An NOL sustained in one year may be used to reduce the taxable income for another year. It may be carried back to earlier years and yield tax refunds. If not exhausted in earlier years (or if taxpayer elects not to use the carryback), it may be carried forward to later years and reduce the tax for those years.

¶ 1842 NOL defined.

An NOL is the excess of business deductions (computed with certain modifications) over gross income in a particular tax year. A deduction is allowed for that loss, through an NOL carryback or carryover, in some other tax year(s) (see ¶1843) in which gross income exceeds business deductions. (Code Sec. 172(a); Reg § 1.172-1(a))[50]

An NOL deduction is allowed to individuals, corporations (Code Sec. 172), estates and trusts (Code Sec. 642(d)) (and charitable organizations with respect to the unrelated business income tax. (Code Sec. 512(b)(6))) It isn't allowed to partnerships (Code Sec. 703(a)(2)(D)), common trust funds (Code Sec. 584(g)) (but the deduction is allowed to the partners and beneficiaries), regulated investment companies (Code Sec. 852(b)(2)(B)), or S corporations (losses are passed through to shareholders). (Code Sec. 1366(a))[1]

---

45. ¶M-5701; ¶4694.50; TD ¶417,501
46. ¶s M-5701, M-5701.3; ¶4694.50; TD ¶417,504
47. ¶M-5701; ¶4694.50; TD ¶417,501
48. ¶M-5701.2; ¶4694.50; TD ¶417,503

49. ¶M-5704 *et seq.*; ¶4694.50; TD ¶417,507 *et seq.*
50. ¶M-4001 *et seq.*; ¶1724; TD ¶354,001
1. ¶M-4003; ¶1724.02; TD ¶354,003

¶ 1843   NOL carryover and carryback periods.

Except as noted below (or taxpayer elects to forgo carryback, ¶1845), an NOL for any tax year may be carried back two years and forward 20 years (for NOLs for tax years beginning before Aug. 6, '97, carried back three years and forward 15 years). (Code Sec. 172(b)(1)(A))[2] A decedent's NOL can be carried back, but not forward. [3] For refunds based on NOL carrybacks, see ¶4850.

A three-year carryback period applies to the following (other than farming losses, including certain GO Zone Act reforestation losses, for which a five-year carryback applies, see ¶4503):

... NOLs arising from property losses of individuals due to fire, storm, shipwreck, or other casualty, or from theft.

... For a small business, or a taxpayer engaged in the trade or business of farming, NOLs attributable to Presidentially declared disasters (¶1798). A small business is one whose average annual gross receipts (under Code Sec. 448(c)) are $5 million or less. (Code Sec. 172(b)(1)(F))[4]

An NOL attributable to a "specified liability loss" (SLL) —i.e., a product liability loss and/or losses attributable to certain deferred statutory liabilities —may be carried back 10 years. (Code Sec. 172(b)(1)(C), Code Sec. 172(f)) The carry*forward* is the usual 20 years (15 years for NOLs for tax years beginning before Aug. 6, '97). (Code Sec. 172(b)(1)(A)(ii)) (The 10-year carryback isn't precluded by making the election at ¶1845 to forgo the carryback.) (Reg § 1.172-13(c)(4)) To carry back the loss under the regular two-year/20-year (three-year/15-year for NOLs for tax years beginning before Aug. 6, '97) rules, taxpayer must so elect. (Code Sec. 172(f)(6))[5]

The SLL for a tax year can't exceed the amount of the NOL for that year. (Code Sec. 172(f)(2)) The Supreme Court has held that for consolidated groups, this "NOL limitation rule" applies at the group level (the single-entity approach); the product liability expenses of all members are combined and the resulting product liability loss is limited only by the amount of the group's consolidated net operating loss (CNOL). [6]

For the five-year carryback period for a qualified GO Zone loss, see ¶1844.

Electric utility companies may elect a five-year carryback period for a portion of their NOLs for tax years ending in 2003, 2004, and 2005, if they invest in electric transmission equipment or pollution control facilities before 2008. The election can be made in any tax year ending before 2009. (Code Sec. 172(b)(1)(I))[7]

Taxpayers with certain casualty losses associated with public utility property caused by Hurricane Katrina may elect a 10-year NOL carryback. (Code Sec. 1400N(j)(1))[8]

Other carryback or carryover periods apply to banks, small business investment companies, and REITs. (Code Sec. 172(b)(1))[9] Special rules limit the carryback of losses attributable to interest allocable to a corporate equity reduction transaction (CERT). (Code Sec. 172(b)(1)(E), Code Sec. 172(h))[10]

An NOL from the short tax year that results from an accounting year change generally can't be carried back unless it's: (a) $50,000 or less, or (b) less than the NOL for the 12-month period beginning with the first day of the short period. So, if the NOL is more than $50,000, the taxpayer must wait until the end of the 12-month period described in (b) to determine

---

2. ¶M-4301; ¶1724.31; TD ¶356,001
3. ¶M-4004; ¶1724.02; TD ¶354,004
4. ¶M-4305.1, M-4305.2; ¶1724.434, 1724.436; TD ¶356,010, 356,011
5. ¶M-4322 *et seq.*; ¶1724.40; TD ¶356,006 *et seq.*

6. ¶E-9055.2, M-4322; TD ¶606,001
7. ¶M-4325 *et seq.*; ¶1724.37
8. ¶M-4334.1; ¶14,00N4.055; TD ¶356,009
9. ¶M-4321 *et seq.*; ¶1724.38, 1724.39
10. ¶M-4306; ¶1724.35; TD ¶356,005

whether it can be carried back. [11]

Any portion of an NOL that is attributable to any of the following losses is considered to be a separate NOL and is applied as a carryover after the remainder of the NOL for that year is applied: (1) an SLL, (2) a CERT loss, (3) an individual's NOL attributable to a casualty or disaster, and an NOL of a farm or small business that's attributable to a Presidentially-declared disaster, (4) a farming loss (¶4503), or (5) a 2003, 2004, or 2005 utility company's NOL that's carried back five years. (Code Sec. 172(f)(5); Code Sec. 172(h)(4)(B); Code Sec. 172(b)(1)(F)(iv); Code Sec. 172(i)(2); Code Sec. 172(b)(1)(I)(iii))[12]

¶ 1844   Five-year carryback period for qualified GO Zone loss.

For losses paid or incurred after Aug. 27, 2005, a 5-year carryback period applies for a qualified Gulf Opportunity (GO) Zone loss —which is the lesser of (1) the excess of the taxpayer's net operating loss for the tax year, over the specified liability loss for the tax year to which a 10-year carryback applies (¶1843), (Code Sec. 1400N(k)(2)(A)) or (2) the aggregate amount of the following deductions: (1) qualified GO Zone casualty losses (as defined in Code Sec. 1400N(k)(3)(A)); (2) certain moving and temporary housing expenses paid or incurred before Jan. 1, 2008; (3) depreciation or amortization deductions for qualified GO Zone property (¶1941) for the tax year the property is placed in service; and (4) deductions for certain repair expenses resulting from Hurricane Katrina paid or incurred before Jan. 1, 2008. (Code Sec. 1400N(k)(2)(B))[13]

The 5-year NOL carryback for casualty losses, and depreciation or amortization, doesn't apply to property ineligible under Code Sec. 1400N(p)(3) (i.e., property which is also ineligible for GO Zone bonus depreciation, see ¶1941). (Code Sec. 1400N(p)(1), Code Sec. 1400N(p)(2)) Among other limits, the amount of qualified GO Zone casualty loss is reduced by the amount of any gain recognized by the taxpayer from involuntary conversions of property located in the GO Zone caused by Hurricane Katrina. Electing taxpayers can't treat the loss as having occurred in any prior tax year under Code Sec. 165(i) (¶1798). (Code Sec. 1400N(k)(3))[14]

A taxpayer can irrevocably elect not to apply the 5-year loss carryback for any tax year. (Code Sec. 1400N(k)(4))

¶ 1845   Election to forgo NOL carryback.

A taxpayer may elect not to use the carryback period (¶1843) and instead only carry over the NOL for the allowed *carryforward* period. Once the election is made for any tax year (on a statement attached to the return or amended return), it's irrevocable for that year. (Code Sec. 172(b)(3); Reg § 301.9100-12T(d)) (The election also applies to alternative minimum tax NOLs (ATNOLs, see ¶3211.)[15]

¶ 1846   How the NOL deduction works.

Assume an NOL is sustained for a tax year beginning in 2007, and that the usual two-year carryback and 20-year carryover apply:

STEP (1). Compute the NOL. Note some deductions aren't allowed (¶1847 *et seq.*).

STEP (2). Find the earliest year to which this loss can be carried (here 2005).

STEP (3). Add this loss to all other NOLs carried to the year (2005), and deduct the total as an *NOL deduction*. Note that the 2007 loss is fully absorbed if 2005 taxable income (before NOL deduction) exceeds the sum of 2007 loss, plus pre-2007 losses, carried to 2004. File for

---

11. ¶G-1827 *et seq.*; ¶4424; TD ¶439,027 *et seq.*
12. ¶M-4333; ¶1724.49; TD ¶356,009
13. ¶M-4342 *et seq.*; ¶14,00N4.06; TD ¶356,014 *et seq.*
14. ¶M-4342 *et seq.*; ¶14,00N4.06; TD ¶356,014 *et seq.*
15. ¶M-4303; ¶1724.33; TD ¶356,003

refund if applicable.

STEP (4). To the extent the 2007 loss isn't deducted in 2005, it's carried to the next earliest year to which it may be carried (2006). Note that the amount carried to 2006 is reduced by "intervening years' modifications" (¶1850).

STEP (5). Repeat step (3)—that is, add the 2007 loss that may be carried to the next year (2006) to all other NOLs carried to that year, and deduct the total as an NOL deduction.

LATER STEPS. Repeat the process described in steps (3) and (4) for the first year after the loss year (2008 in our example) and then in order to each of the 19 following years or until the full amount of the NOL is absorbed, whichever happens first. If the loss is not absorbed by the 20th year succeeding the loss year, any further benefit is lost. [16]

¶ 1847   Computing the NOL for noncorporate taxpayers.

NOL for a noncorporate taxpayer (which may be carried to another year) is the deficit in taxable income for the year, with certain modifications: NOL carryback or carryover deduction from other years; personal exemptions; exclusion of gain from qualified small business stock (¶2648); and the Code Sec. 199 deduction for domestic production activities (¶1614) are not allowed; and deductions for capital losses and nonbusiness deductions are only allowed to a limited extent. (Code Sec. 172(d); Reg § 1.172-3(a))[17]

¶ 1848   Computing the NOL for corporate taxpayers.

A corporation's NOL is figured the same as its taxable income. But in computing the NOL for the year: (1) NOL carrybacks and carryovers from other years aren't deducted; (2) the deduction for dividends received is taken without limiting it by a percentage of the corporation's taxable income; (3) the deduction for dividends paid on certain preferred stock of public utilities is computed without limiting it to the year's taxable income; and (4) the Code Sec. 199 deduction for domestic production activities (¶1614) isn't allowed. (Code Sec. 172(d); Reg § 1.172-2(a))[18]

¶ 1849   Amount of NOL deduction.

The NOL deduction in any year is the sum of all NOL carrybacks and carryovers to that year. (Code Sec. 172(a))[19] For refunds based on NOL carrybacks, see ¶4850.

Where a husband and wife who make a joint return for the deduction year made a joint return for all other tax years involved in computing the NOL deduction, that deduction is computed on the basis of their joint NOLs and combined taxable incomes. (Reg § 1.172-7(c)) Special rules apply if they didn't make joint returns for all applicable years. (Reg § 1.172-7)[20]

🅡🅘🅐/*caution:* For limits on the NOL deduction for alternative minimum tax purposes, see ¶3211.

¶ 1850   NOL exceeds income in year to which carried; "intervening year."

If the NOL carried to an earlier tax year exceeds the taxable income for that year, modifications must be made in that year's taxable income, in computing the unused portion of the NOL that can be carried to the next year. These "intervening year modifications" apply only in computing NOL carryovers, and don't affect taxable income for other purposes. (Code Sec. 172(b)(2); Reg § 1.172-5)[21] Deductions for intervening years which are based on, or limited to, a percentage of adjusted gross income (AGI, ¶3102) or taxable income must be

---

16. ¶M-4402; ¶1724.10; TD ¶354,002

17. ¶M-4109 *et seq.*; ¶1724.12; TD ¶355,008 *et seq.*

18. ¶M-4105 *et seq.*; ¶1724.11; TD ¶355,007

19. ¶M-4401; ¶1724.01; TD ¶354,001

20. ¶M-4405 *et seq.*; ¶1724.13; TD ¶354,006, 354,007

21. ¶M-4202 *et seq.*; ¶1724, 1724.20 *et seq.*; TD ¶357,002 *et seq.*

recomputed, based on AGI or taxable income as modified. (Reg § 1.172-5(a)(2)(ii))[22]

¶ 1851 Deduction for Bad Debts.

Bad debts are deductible whether or not connected with taxpayer's business. Deduction is allowed for total worthlessness and, in some cases, for partial worthlessness.

Business bad debts are deductible as ordinary deductions. They are deductible if partially worthless as well as when wholly worthless. Nonbusiness bad debts are deducted only as short-term capital losses, and only when wholly worthless (¶1856).[23] An item can't be deductible both as a bad debt and as a loss. If it could be treated as either, it must be treated as a bad debt.[24]

But, a worthless debt that is evidenced by a security, and is owed by a corporation or a government, is a loss (see ¶1781), and not a bad debt, unless owed to a bank. (Code Sec. 165(g), Code Sec. 166(e), Code Sec. 582(a))[25]

¶ 1852 Bad debts of guarantors.

If taxpayer makes a guarantee agreement in the course of his trade or business, he's entitled to a business bad debt deduction for any payment he makes as guarantor, of principal or interest. (Reg § 1.166-9(a))[26]

If taxpayer makes a guarantee agreement in a transaction for profit (but not in the course of his business), and makes a payment of principal or interest, he's entitled to a nonbusiness bad debt deduction in the year his right of subrogation becomes totally worthless. (Reg § 1.166-9(b), Reg § 1.166-9(e)(2))[27] For general timing rules, see ¶1853.

¶ 1853 Time for deducting worthless debt.

Deduction is allowed for the tax year the debt becomes wholly worthless. (Code Sec. 166(a)(1))[28] (For *partial* worthlessness of *business* debts, see ¶1855.) Taxpayer must show the debt had value at the beginning of the year and no value at the end, and that the worthlessness occurred in the particular tax year claimed. [29] Worthlessness is a question of fact requiring consideration of all pertinent evidence, including the debtor's financial condition and the value of any security. (Reg § 1.166-2(a))[30]

¶ 1854 Amount of bad debt deduction.

The amount deductible for a wholly worthless debt (¶1853) is its adjusted basis for determining loss on a sale or exchange (¶2400 *et seq.*), regardless of its face value. (Code Sec. 166(b); Reg § 1.166-1(d))[31] The adjustments used to figure adjusted basis are generally the debtor's payments on the debt. But a deduction allowed for a debt's partial worthlessness reduces the debt's basis to that extent, whether or not taxpayer got a tax benefit from the deduction.[32]

If the creditor (taxpayer) has no basis in the debt, there's no deduction. [33] So there's no deduction for wages, rents, alimony, etc., that were never received, unless these items were included in income. (Reg § 1.166-1(e))[34] Where taxpayer reports receivables at fair market value (FMV) rather than face, the deduction can't exceed FMV. (Reg § 1.166-1(d)(2))[35]

---

22. ¶M-4207; ¶1724.20 *et seq.*; TD ¶357,007
23. ¶M-2801 *et seq.*, ¶M-2901 *et seq.*; ¶1664; TD ¶320,501 *et seq.*, TD ¶323,001 *et seq.*
24. ¶M-2503; ¶1654.040; TD ¶320,508
25. ¶s M-3301, M-3309; ¶1664.160; TD ¶320,501, 372,001
26. ¶M-3207; ¶1664.450; TD ¶324,007
27. ¶M-3210, M-3214; ¶1664.450; TD ¶324,011, 324,014
28. ¶M-2401; ¶1664; TD ¶320,501

29. ¶M-2701; ¶1664.220; TD ¶322,001
30. ¶M-2702; ¶1664.220; TD ¶322,002
31. ¶M-2402; ¶1664.210; TD ¶320,502
32. ¶s M-2406; M-2407; TD ¶320,504
33. ¶M-2404; ¶1664.210; TD ¶320,502
34. ¶M-2506; ¶1664.210; TD ¶320,503
35. ¶M-2402; TD ¶320,502

Where taxpayer fails to prove a debt's exact basis, it may be estimated by a court if taxpayer proves his right to *some* deduction.[36]

If a debt is compromised because of inability to pay the full amount, taxpayer deducts the debt's adjusted basis minus any cash and the value of any property received. If the debt is compromised for some other reason, taxpayer doesn't have a bad debt (but may have a loss). [37]

¶ 1855   Deduction for partially worthless business debts.

A deduction is allowed for partially worthless debts (Code Sec. 166(a)(2)) *only if*: (1) the debt is a business debt (see ¶1856); (2) IRS is satisfied that the specific debt is recoverable only in part; (3) the amount deducted was *charged off* on the books during the tax year; *and* (4) the debt is not evidenced by a security. (Code Sec. 166(d)(1), Code Sec. 166(e); Reg § 1.166-5(b))[38] (For deductibility of "worthless securities" as a loss, see ¶1781.)

Taxpayer may charge off and deduct a debt for partial worthlessness as it occurs. Or he can defer charge-off and deduction to a later year when partial worthlessness is greater, thus deducting several years' partial worthlessness in one year. Or he can defer deduction until total worthlessness (but not beyond the year of total worthlessness (Reg § 1.166-3(b)).[39]

¶ 1856   Effect of classification as business or nonbusiness bad debt.

The need to determine whether a debt is a business or nonbusiness debt (¶1857) arises only for noncorporate taxpayers. A corporation's debts are always business debts. (Code Sec. 166(d))[40]

Business bad debts are fully deductible against income (Code Sec. 166(a)), while nonbusiness bad debts are short-term capital losses of limited deductibility. (Code Sec. 166(d)(1)(B))[41] Business and nonbusiness debts are deductible when wholly worthless (see ¶1853), but only business debts are deductible when partly worthless (see ¶1855). (Code Sec. 166(a), Code Sec. 166(d)(1)(A))[42]

¶ 1857   Business and nonbusiness debts defined.

A *business debt* is either: (1) a debt created or acquired in the course of taxpayer's trade or business (whether or not it was related to that business when it became worthless, see ¶1853); or (2) a debt the loss from whose worthlessness is incurred in taxpayer's trade or business. This applies if the loss is proximately related to taxpayer's business when the debt becomes worthless. A bad debt is proximately related to business if business is the dominant motivation for the debt. (Reg § 1.166-5(b))[43]

A *nonbusiness debt* (for noncorporate taxpayers, see ¶1856) is a debt other than a business debt. (Code Sec. 166(d)(2); Reg § 1.166-5(b), Reg § 1.166-5(d))[44]

¶ 1858   Shareholders' loans or guarantees for their corporations as business debts.

A shareholder in a corporation can't treat the corporation's business as his business even if he's the sole shareholder. So, an individual shareholder's loan to his corporation isn't a business debt (¶1857) unless he shows the debt is related to his own business. [45] Devoting one's time and energies to a corporation's affairs isn't of itself a trade or business. But a

---

36. ¶M-2405; TD ¶320,502
37. ¶M-2408; TD ¶320,504
38. ¶M-2801 *et seq.*; ¶1664.270 *et seq.*; TD ¶322,501 *et seq.*
39. ¶M-2801; ¶1664.271; TD ¶322,502
40. ¶M-2800; ¶s 1664, 1664.300; TD ¶323,001
41. ¶s M-2401; M-2901; ¶s 1664, 1664.300; TD ¶320,501

42. ¶s M-2401; M-2800; ¶s 1664.210, 1664.270, 1664.300; TD ¶322,501
43. ¶M-2902; ¶1664.301; TD ¶323,003
44. ¶M-2902; ¶1664.301; TD ¶323,003
45. ¶M-2904; ¶1664.303; TD ¶323,010

shareholder's loan to his corporation can be a business debt if he's in the business of promoting, financing, and selling corporations. He must be seeking other than a mere investor's return, since investing isn't a business. [46]

If the shareholder is also an officer or other employee of the corporation, he may claim his loan, guarantee, or indemnity was made to protect his job (i.e., his business of being an employee). Business debt status is allowed if his dominant motive (not just a significant motive) for the loan, etc., was to protect his job. Which motive is dominant is determined by several factors, especially the amount of salary as compared to the amount invested. These principles also apply to a shareholder-employee who claims that his loan or guarantee for another corporation (e.g., his corporation's customer) was to protect his job. [47]

---

46. ¶M-2911; ¶1664.302; TD ¶323,006

47. ¶M-2914 *et seq.*; ¶1664.309; TD ¶323,011

Chapter 5 MACRS, ACRS, Depreciation, Amortization of Intangibles, Depletion

¶ 1900   The Depreciation Allowance. ▮▮▮▮▮▮▮▮▮▮▮▮▮▮

The Code allows an annual deduction of a portion of the cost or other basis of capital assets used during the year in a trade or business or held for the production of income. This annual deduction may be depreciation under the Modified Accelerated Cost Recovery System (MACRS) or under pre-'87 ACRS, or useful-life depreciation (for property outside of MACRS or ACRS and for pre-'81 depreciable property). For certain property amortization or depletion is allowed instead of depreciation.

Except where expensing under Code Sec. 179 or under specialized provisions applies (¶1944 *et seq.*, ¶1968 *et seq.*), a taxpayer who buys business or income-producing property with a useful life of more than one year cannot deduct its full cost as an expense for that year. (Code Sec. 263(a); Reg § 1.263(a)-2(a)) Instead, the cost of that property must be recovered over more than one year.

No depreciation deduction is allowed for property placed in service and disposed of in the same year. (Reg § 1.168(d)-1(b)(3)(ii))

¶ 1901   Claiming the depreciation deduction—Form 4562.

Form 4562 is used to claim the deduction for depreciation. Individuals and other noncorporate taxpayers (including S corporations) don't have to complete or attach Form 4562 if (1) the only depreciation (or amortization) claimed is for assets (other than listed property, see ¶1950) placed in service before the tax year, (2) no Code Sec. 179 expense deduction is claimed, and (3) deductions are not claimed for a vehicle reported on a form other than Schedule C or C-EZ.[1] For how employees, self-employeds and farmers claim depreciation on a car or truck, see ¶1958.

Failure to take a depreciation deduction in one year doesn't allow a taxpayer to take a larger deduction in later years, (Reg § 1.167(a)-10(a)) unless the taxpayer treats the failure as an impermissible method of accounting, correctable by filing a Form 3115 and otherwise following the procedures for changing to a permissible method of accounting in a later year. For changes in computing depreciation or amortization as changes in method of accounting, see ¶2839. An amended return can be used to correct depreciation if the error (1) is a mathematical or posting error, or (2) involves property for which the taxpayer has yet to file a return for any year after the year that the property was placed in service.[2]

¶ 1902   What property is depreciable?

Real property (except land), personal property and certain intangibles (as explained at ¶1903) are depreciable if the property:

. . . is used in a trade or business, or held for the production of income (Code Sec. 167(a));[3]

. . . has an exhaustible useful-life that can be determined with reasonable accuracy (Reg § 1.167(a)-1(b));[4] and

. . . isn't inventory or stock in trade (Reg § 1.167(a)-2).[5]

Some courts have held that property can be depreciated under MACRS or ACRS even if it

---

1. ¶L-7500; ¶1674.001; TD ¶264,500
2. ¶G-2103, ¶G-2106.1, ¶G-2207.1; ¶1674.112, ¶4464.227, ¶4464.25; TD ¶264,503, TD ¶442,404, TD ¶442,407, TD ¶442,608

3. ¶L-7900 *et seq.*; ¶1674.006 *et seq.*; TD ¶265,401
4. ¶L-7901 *et seq.*; ¶1674.006 *et seq.*; TD ¶265,407
5. ¶L-7905; ¶1674.006 *et seq.*; TD ¶265,401

References beginning with a single letter are to paragraphs in RIA's Federal Tax Coordinator 2d and RIA's Analysis of Federal Taxes: Income. Those beginning with numbers are to paragraphs in RIA's United States Tax Reporter. Those beginning with TD are to paragraphs in RIA's Tax Desk.

doesn't have a determinable useful life, but IRS disagrees. [6]

Property isn't depreciable if it isn't exhaustible or subject to wear and tear, such as land (Reg § 1.167(a)-2) or radium. [7] Natural resources such as oil, gas or minerals in the ground (Reg § 1.167(a)-2) qualify for *depletion* (¶1981 *et seq.*), not depreciation. [8]

The mere fact that property diminishes in value doesn't mean that it's depreciable, if the decrease isn't the result of exhaustion, wear and tear, or obsolescence. (Reg § 1.167(a)-1(a)) [9]

Property used solely for personal purposes isn't depreciable. (Reg § 1.167(a)-2) Where the same property is used both for personal and for business or income-producing purposes, depreciation is deductible only to the extent of nonpersonal usage. [10] For limits on depreciation where luxury automobiles and "listed property" are used partly for personal purposes, see ¶1950 *et seq.* For property acquired for personal use but later converted to business or income-production, see ¶1929.

¶ 1903 When intangible assets are depreciable.

An intangible asset is depreciable (but can't be depreciated under MACRS, Code Sec. 168(a)) if it's used in a trade or business or production of income, has a limited, ascertainable useful life, and the taxpayer can show the cost of that asset. (Reg § 1.167(a)-3(a)) [11] Effective for intangible assets created on or after Dec. 31, 2003, for purposes of the preceding rule, taxpayers may treat an intangible asset as having a useful life of 15 years unless:

. . . an amortization period or useful life for the intangible asset is specifically prescribed or prohibited by other rules (e.g., 15-year amortization under Code Sec. 197, see ¶1977);

. . . the intangible asset is described in Reg § 1.263(a)-4(c) (intangibles acquired from another person in a purchase or similar transaction) or Reg § 1.263(a)-4(d)(2) (relating to created financial interests);

. . . the useful life of the intangible asset can be estimated with reasonable accuracy; or

. . . the intangible asset is described in Reg § 1.263(a)-4(d)(8) (relating to certain benefits arising from the provision, production, or improvement of realty), in which case the taxpayer may treat the intangible asset as having a useful life equal to 25 years solely for purposes of Reg § 1.167(a)-3(a). (Reg § 1.167(a)-3(b)(1))

The above useful life safe harbor doesn't apply to amounts that must be capitalized by Reg § 1.263(a)-5 (amounts paid to facilitate an acquisition of a trade or business, a change in the capital structure of a business entity, and certain other transactions). (Reg § 1.167(a)-3(b)(2)) Under the safe harbor, the basis of the intangible (determined without regard to salvage value) is amortized ratably over 15 or 25 years beginning on the first day of the month in which the intangible asset is placed in service by the taxpayer. The intangible asset is not eligible for amortization in the month of disposition. (Reg § 1.167(a)-3(b)(3))

¶ 1904 Who is entitled to depreciation deductions?

Ordinarily the owner of depreciable property is the person entitled to deduct depreciation. [12] This is the equitable owner, and not the owner of bare legal title. [13]

A *lessor* (landlord) deducts depreciation on property that is already on the leased premises when he leases out the property and on any improvements he constructs during the term of the lease. (Reg § 1.167(a)-4) But he can't deduct depreciation where the lease requires the lessee to replace property at the lessee's expense because the lessor suffers no "depreciable"

---

6. ¶L-8201, ¶L-10901.1; TD ¶266,001, TD ¶268,103

7. ¶L-7902, L-7912; TD ¶265,414

8. ¶s L-7929, N-2250 *et seq.*; ¶6114 *et seq.*; TD ¶265,430

9. ¶L-7501; TD ¶264,501

10. ¶L-7908; ¶1674.006; TD ¶265,409

11. ¶L-8001 *et seq.*; ¶1674.013; TD ¶269,000

12. ¶L-7802; ¶1674.002; TD ¶265,001

13. ¶L-7803 *et seq.*; ¶1674.002; TD ¶265,002

loss, i.e., wear and tear, etc. [14] For the rules that apply to lessor-financed construction allowances on retail property, see ¶1344 and ¶1923.

A *lessee* (tenant) ordinarily depreciates the cost of improvements he makes, but the costs of acquiring a lease are amortizable, not depreciable, [15] see ¶1922.

If a life tenancy is in depreciable property, the life tenant deducts depreciation as if he were the absolute owner of the property. (Code Sec. 167(d)) After the life tenant's death, the depreciation deduction, if any, is allowed to the remainderman. (Reg § 1.167(h)-1)[16]

A tenant-stockholder of a cooperative housing corporation who uses his proprietary lease in a trade or business or for the production of income, depreciates the portion of the cost of his stock allocable to depreciable property. (Code Sec. 216(c)(1)) The allowance for depreciation is limited to the adjusted basis of the stock. But depreciation in excess of adjusted basis may be carried over to later years. (Code Sec. 216(c)(2))[17]

¶ 1905   When depreciation begins and ends.

The depreciation period generally begins when an asset is placed in service (Reg § 1.167(a)-10(b)), namely when it's in a condition or state of readiness and availability for a specifically defined function. [18] The depreciation period ends when the asset is retired from service, or its cost or other basis is fully recovered, or it's sold or disposed of —whichever occurs first. (Code Sec. 167, Code Sec. 168(d); Reg § 1.167(a)-10(b), Reg § 1.167(b)-0(a)) However, under MACRS these rules are subject to the depreciation conventions discussed at ¶1927 *et seq.*

Where no depreciation convention is adopted for useful-life depreciable property (¶1964 *et seq.*), a proportionate part of one year's depreciation is allowed for that part of the first year during which the asset was placed in service. (Reg § 1.167(a)-10(b))

¶ 1906   The Modified Accelerated Cost Recovery System (MACRS). ■■■■■■■■

MACRS depreciation is determined under one of two methods: (1) the general depreciation system (GDS) or (2) the alternative depreciation system (ADS), which is mandatory for some MACRS property (and elective for all other MACRS property, see ¶1931 *et seq.*). For the availability of "bonus depreciation" for certain property, see ¶1935 *et seq.*

In both cases, the depreciation deduction is determined by applying the depreciation method (¶1925) to the depreciable basis (¶1921) of the property (¶1907 *et seq.*), over the applicable recovery period (¶1924), and subject to the applicable placed-in-service conventions (¶1927 *et seq.*).[19] For use of optional IRS MACRS depreciation tables (reproduced at ¶1117) instead of making the above computation, see ¶1911.

MACRS elections (e.g., straight-line) are made on the return for the year the property is placed in service. Once made, they are irrevocable. (Code Sec. 168(b)(5); Reg § 301.9100-7T(a)(4)(i))

¶ 1907   MACRS property.

Subject to the exceptions discussed in ¶1908 (and the expensing and amortization rules discussed at ¶1944 *et seq.* and ¶1968 *et seq.*), most depreciable property (as described at ¶1902) must be depreciated under MACRS. (Code Sec. 168(a))[20]

---

14. ¶L-7808; ¶1674.023; TD ¶265,007

15. ¶L-7809, L-8013; ¶1674.023; TD ¶267,020

16. ¶L-7830; ¶1674.117; TD ¶265,022

17. ¶s K-5921 *et seq.*, L-7828, L-8013; ¶2164.01; TD ¶265,019

18. ¶L-7602; ¶1674.085; TD ¶264,506

19. ¶L-8100 *et seq.*; ¶1684 *et seq.*; TD ¶266,001

20. ¶L-8201 *et seq.*; ¶1674.006 *et seq.*, ¶1684; TD ¶266,008

¶ 1908 Property excluded from MACRS.

The following property isn't depreciable under MACRS: intangible property, see ¶1903 (Code Sec. 168(a));[21] property ineligible for MACRS under "antichurning" rules; property which the taxpayer elects to depreciate under a method not expressed in a term of years, e.g., the income-forecast method (¶1963)); public utility property for which the taxpayer doesn't use the MACRS normalization method of accounting; motion picture films or video tapes, including videocassettes;[22] and master sound recordings. (Code Sec. 168(f))

¶ 1909 General asset and vintage accounts for property under MACRS.

Taxpayers can elect to maintain one or more general asset (i.e., "vintage") accounts for eligible MACRS property. (Code Sec. 168(i)(4)) The election is made (on Form 4562) on a timely filed return (including extensions) for the tax year in which the assets are placed in service. For partnerships and S corporations, the election is made at the entity level. (Reg § 1.168(i)-1(k))[23]

A general asset account may include assets that are placed in service in the same tax year and have the same applicable depreciation method, recovery period, and depreciation convention. However, business automobiles subject to the listed property limitations (¶1955) may be grouped only in their own general asset account. Only recovery property with the same asset class (i.e., the same class life) may be placed in the same general asset account. (Reg § 1.168(i)-1(c)(2)) Assets either used in a personal activity (Reg § 1.168(i)-1(c)(1), Reg § 1.168(i)-1(h)(1)) or for which a credit or deduction recapture event has occurred (Reg § 1.168(i)-1(j)) can't be included in a general asset account (or if included, must be removed).[24]

The depreciation allowance for each account, determined by using the applicable depreciation method, recovery period, and depreciation convention for the assets in the account, is recorded in a depreciation reserve account for each account. (Reg § 1.168(i)-1(d)(1))

For a disposition of an asset from an account (Reg § 1.168(i)-1(e)(2)):

(1) The amount realized is recognized as ordinary income. (Code Sec. 168(i)(4)) The excess of (a) the unadjusted depreciable basis (i.e., generally cost) of the general asset account plus any expensed costs for assets in the account, over (b) any amounts previously recognized as ordinary income at the time of disposition of other assets in the account, is treated as ordinary income. Any remaining amount is recognized as income under other applicable Code sections, other than the Code Sec. 1245 and Code Sec. 1250 depreciation recapture rules. (Reg § 1.168(i)-1(b)(4), Reg § 1.168(i)-1(e)(2))

If an asset disposition is a "qualifying disposition" (i.e., is of less than all assets in the account and occurs due to a casualty, charitable contribution, cessation of business, etc.) and the taxpayer wants to end general asset account treatment for the asset(s) as of the first day of the tax year in which the disposition occurs, the gain, loss, or other deduction for the asset(s) takes into account the adjusted basis (i.e., unadjusted depreciable basis of the asset or assets, less depreciation allowed or allowable). (Reg § 1.168(i)-1(e)(3))

(2) Except for a "qualifying disposition," the unadjusted depreciable basis of the general asset account and the depreciation reserve of the general asset account aren't affected (i.e., reduced). (Reg § 1.168(i)-1(e)(2))

(3) Except when an account ends, no loss is realized upon the disposition of an asset, since the asset is treated as having an adjusted basis of zero. (Reg § 1.168(i)-1(e)(2)(i)) On a disposition of all remaining assets, the taxpayer at his option may treat the account as

21. ¶L-8200 *et seq.*; ¶1674.013; TD ¶266,008
22. ¶L-8212; ¶1684; TD ¶266,009
23. ¶L-8931; TD ¶266,215
24. ¶L-8922, ¶L-8925.1; TD ¶266,215

ended (by reporting the gain, loss or other deduction on the timely filed, including extensions, return for the disposition year) or as not ended. (Reg § 1.168(i)-1(e)(3))[25]

¶ 1910   "Step into the shoes" rule for certain carryover-basis property.

Where depreciable property is acquired in certain nontaxable transfers, the transferee-recipient must "step into the shoes" of the transferor with respect to the depreciation period and method of the transferred property. This applies to the extent that the basis of such property in the hands of the transferee equals the transferor's adjusted basis. The following nontaxable transfers are subject to the above rule: Code Sec. 332 (¶3575), Code Sec. 351 (¶3510), Code Sec. 361 (¶3560), Code Sec. 721 (¶3710), Code Sec. 731 (¶3742), and transfers of depreciable property between members of the same affiliated group of corporations during any tax year for which a consolidated return is filed. The "step into the shoes" rule doesn't apply to the termination of a partnership under Code Sec. 708(b)(1). (Code Sec. 168(i)(7)(B), Code Sec. 168(i)(7)(C))[26]

¶ 1911   IRS optional MACRS rate tables.

Instead of making the MACRS computations described at ¶1906 for either the general or alternate depreciation systems, a taxpayer can instead rely on tables provided by IRS (reproduced at ¶1117), subject to the following rules:

(1) All the tables' rates (accelerated or straight-line) are applied to the property's *unadjusted depreciable basis.* For that purpose, unadjusted depreciable basis is the basis for determining gain or loss, not reduced by prior depreciation, and reflecting reductions in basis for: (a) personal-use percentage of the asset for the tax year; (b) any portion of the asset that is expensed under Code Sec. 179 (¶1944); and (c) other initial basis adjustments—e.g., for the Code Sec. 44 disabled-access credit (¶2322), or, unless the taxpayer "elected out," for bonus depreciation if the asset is qualified property (¶1935) or qualified New York Liberty Zone property (¶1942). (Reg § 1.168(b)-1(a)(3))

(2) No special notice is filed with IRS to use the optional MACRS tables.

(3) The taxpayer must use the tables to compute the annual depreciation allowances for the entire recovery period of the property. However, a taxpayer may not continue to use the tables if there are any adjustments to the basis of the property for reasons other than: (a) depreciation allowed or allowable, or (b) an addition or an improvement to such property that is subject to depreciation as a separate item of property.

(4) Use of the tables is denied for a short tax year and for later tax years with respect to MACRS personal property not fully depreciated by the end of the short tax year (¶1926).[27]

illustration: T bought an item of used 7-year property for $10,000 and placed it in service on Aug. 11, Year 1. T used the item exclusively in his business. Also, T didn't expense the item under Code Sec. 179, and no other Code provisions requiring initial basis adjustments applied to the item. The unadjusted depreciable basis of the property is $10,000. The percentages for 7-year property using the 200% declining balance method and the half-year convention are found in Table 1, see ¶1117. Each year of the recovery period, multiply $10,000 by the percentages for 7-year property in Table 1. The depreciation deduction each year of the recovery period is as follows: [28]

---

25. ¶L-8923 *et seq.*; TD ¶266,215
26. ¶L-10401; ¶1684.04; TD ¶266,508

27. ¶L-8602, ¶L-8904 *et seq.*; ¶1684; TD ¶267,008
28. ¶L-8910

Year	Basis	Percentage	Deduction
1	$10,000	14.29%	$1,429
2	10,000	24.49%	2,449
3	10,000	17.49%	1,749
4	10,000	12.49%	1,249
5	10,000	8.93%	893
6	10,000	8.92%	892
7	10,000	8.93%	893
8	10,000	4.46%	446

¶ 1912 Determining the MACRS recovery class for an asset.

The assignment of MACRS property to a recovery class is generally made by reference to that property's class life as of Jan. 1, '86. (Code Sec. 168(i)(1)) The class life of many types of assets is carried in Rev Proc 87-56, 1987-2 CB 674. The assignment to a MACRS recovery class is determined as follows (Code Sec. 168(e)(1)):

MACRS Recovery Class	Property With a Class Life (in Years) of:
3-Year	4 or less
5-Year	More than 4 but less than 10
7-Year	10 or more but less than 16
10-Year	16 or more but less than 20
15-Year	20 or more but less than 25
20-Year	25 or more

In addition, MACRS assigns certain property specific classes as follows (and as described at ¶1913 *et seq.*): certain water utility property is in the 25-year class; residential rental property is in the 27.5-year class; nonresidential real property placed in service before May 13, '93 is in the 31.5-year class; nonresidential real property placed in service after May 12, '93 is in the 39-year class; and any railroad grading and tunnel bore is in the 50-year class. (Code Sec. 168(c))[29]

¶ 1913 The three-year MACRS class.

This class includes:

... Depreciable personal property with a class life of four years or less (Code Sec. 168(e)(1)), such as: tractor units for use over-the-road; breeding hogs; special handling devices used in the manufacture of food and beverages; and special tools used in the manufacture of rubber products, finished plastic products, and motor vehicles.

... Race horses more than two years old when placed in service and other horses more than 12 when placed in service. (Code Sec. 168(e)(3)(A))

... Qualified rent-to-own (RTO). (Code Sec. 168(e)(3)(A)(iii)) In essence, qualified RTO property is consumer durable property (see ¶1914) rented by a RTO dealer under a RTO contract that meets detailed requirements. (Code Sec. 168(i)(14))[30]

---

29. ¶L-8202; ¶1684; TD ¶266,202   30. ¶L-8204; ¶1684.01; TD ¶266,203

¶ 1914   The five-year MACRS class.

This class includes:

... Depreciable personal property with a class life of more than four years and less than ten years (Code Sec. 168(e)(1)), such as: information systems (computers); heavy general purpose trucks; trailers and trailer-mounted containers; breeding or dairy cattle; and certain assets used in the drilling of oil and gas wells, construction, the manufacture of textile yarns, apparel, and other finished goods, and the cutting of timber. [31]

... Any automobiles or light-general purpose trucks (Code Sec. 168(e)(3)(B)(i));

... Semiconductor manufacturing equipment (Code Sec. 168(e)(3)(B)(ii)) in ADR class 36.0;

... Computer-based   telephone   central   office   switching   equipment   (Code Sec. 168(e)(3)(B)(iii));

... Qualified technological equipment (Code Sec. 168(e)(3)(B)(iv));[32]

... Code Sec. 1245 property used in connection with research and experimentation (Code Sec. 168(e)(3)(B)(v));

... Gas station pump canopies (but not the concrete footings used to anchor the canopies); [33]

... Equipment used to produce, distribute, or use electrical energy derived from a geothermal deposit;[34] equipment that uses exclusively and directly solar or wind energy to generate electricity; certain equipment that converts biomass into energy, and, for periods after Dec. 31, 2005 and before Jan. 1, 2008, certain other solar-powered property, qualified fuel cell property and qualified microturbine property. (Code Sec. 168(e)(3)(B)(vi), Code Sec. 48(a)(3)(A));

⊘*caution:* Check http://ria.thomson.com/federaltaxhandbook to see if the provision discussed above has been extended.

... Qualified New York Liberty Zone leasehold improvement property (unless the taxpayer elects out of 5-year MACRS). This is property that is: (1) qualified leasehold improvement property as defined for the Code Sec. 168(k) bonus depreciation allowance (¶1936); (2) located in the Liberty Zone (¶1942); and (3) placed in service after Sept. 10, 2001 (not pursuant to a binding written agreement in effect before Sept. 11, 2001), and before 2007. Such property is depreciated via straight line only. (Code Sec. 1400L(c))

Consumer durable property (such as tangible personal property used in the home) subject to rent-to-own contracts is also 5-year property if it isn't qualified rent-to-own property (see ¶1913).[35]

¶ 1915   The seven-year MACRS class.

This class includes:

... Property with a class life of 10 years or more, but less than 16 years (Code Sec. 168(e)(1)), such as: office furniture, fixtures, and equipment; machinery and equipment used in agriculture (including vineyard trellising); certain assets (except helicopters) used in air transport; certain assets used in exploration for and production of petroleum and natural gas products, the manufacture of wood products and furniture, and theme and amusement parks and recreation facilities (e.g., bowling alleys).

... Property that doesn't have a class life and isn't specifically assigned to any other MACRS class. (Code Sec. 168(e)(3)(C)(v))

---

31. ¶L-8205; ¶1684.01; TD ¶266,205
32. ¶L-9619; ¶1684.01; TD ¶266,205
33. ¶L-8205; TD ¶266,205

34. ¶L-16426 *et seq.*; ¶1684.01; TD ¶266,205
35. ¶L-8205; ¶1684.01; TD ¶266,205

. . . Breeding and work horses, 12 years or younger when placed in service, and any horse not in any other category.

. . . Railroad tracks (Code Sec. 168(e)(3)(C)(i)).[36]

. . . Motorsports entertainment complexes, as defined in Code Sec. 168(i)(15), placed in service after Oct. 22, 2004 and before 2008. (Code Sec. 168(e)(3)(C)(ii))[37]

⬤*caution:* Check http://ria.thomson.com/federaltaxhandbook to see if the provision discussed above has been extended.

. . . Alaska natural gas pipeline property placed in service after calendar year 2013, or treated, by election, as placed in service after 2013 if placed in service after 2004 and before 2013.[38]

. . . Effective for property placed in service after Apr. 11, 2005, "natural gas gathering lines" the original use of which begins with the taxpayer. (Code Sec. 168(e)(3)(C)(iv)) Property won't qualify if the taxpayer or a related person (1) entered into a binding contract for the property's construction before Apr. 12, 2005 or (2) began to construct the property before Apr. 12, 2005. There is no AMT depreciation adjustment (¶3206) for the entire recovery period of natural gas gathering lines. (Code Sec. 56(a)(1)(B))[39]

¶ 1916   The ten-year MACRS class.

This class includes:

. . . Property with a class life of 16 years or more but less than 20 (Code Sec. 168(e)(1)), such as: water transport equipment not used in marine construction; assets used in petroleum refining, manufacture of grain and grain mill products, sugar and sugar products, and vegetable oils and vegetable oil products. [40]

. . . A single purpose agricultural or horticultural structure (Code Sec. 168(e)(3)(D)(i)).

. . . Any tree or vine bearing fruit or nuts (Code Sec. 168(e)(3)(D)(ii)).[41]

¶ 1917   The 15-year MACRS class.

This class includes:

(1) Property with a class life of 20 years or more but less than 25 years (Code Sec. 168(e)(1)), such as: land improvements (e.g., sidewalks and roads) that aren't explicitly included in another class and aren't buildings or structural improvements; "modern" golf-course greens; assets such as service-station and car-wash buildings; and concrete footings used to anchor gas station pump canopies.

(2) Municipal wastewater treatment plants (Code Sec. 168(e)(3)(E)(i));

(3) Telephone distribution plants and comparable equipment used for two-way exchange of voice and data communications. (Code Sec. 168(e)(3)(E)(ii))

(4) Any Code Sec. 1250 property (generally, depreciable real property) which is a retail motor fuels outlet (generally, a gas station) whether or not food or other convenience items are sold there (effective for property placed in service on or after Aug. 20, '96, or, electively, qualified property placed in service before that date). (Code Sec. 168(e)(3)(E)(iii))[42]

(5) Qualified leasehold improvement property and qualified restaurant placed in service after Oct. 22, 2004 and before 2008. Qualified leasehold improvement property is defined as it is for bonus first-year depreciation (¶1936), except that if a lessor makes an improvement that is a qualified leasehold improvement, it can't be qualified leasehold improvement

36. ¶L-8206; ¶1684.01; TD ¶266,206
37. ¶L-8206.3; ¶1684.01; TD ¶266,206
38. ¶L-8206.2; ¶1684.01
39. ¶L-8206.1; ¶1684.01; TD ¶266,206

40. ¶L-8207; ¶1684.01; TD ¶266,207
41. ¶L-8207; ¶1684.01; TD ¶266,207
42. ¶L-8208, ¶L-8804.1; ¶1684.02; TD ¶266,213

property to any subsequent owner, subject to exceptions for non-recognition and death transfers. Qualified restaurant property is any improvement to a building if the improvement is placed in service more than three years after the date the building was first placed in service and more than 50% of the building's square footage is devoted to the preparation of, and seating for, on-premises consumption of prepared meals. These types of property must be depreciated via the straight-line method. (Code Sec. 168(e)(3)(E), Code Sec. 168(b)(3), Code Sec. 168(e)(6)) Code Sec. 168(e)(7))[43]

⊘caution: Check http://ria.thomson.com/federaltaxhandbook to see if the provision discussed above has been extended.

(6) Effective for property placed in service after Oct. 22, 2004, initial clearing and grading land improvements relating to gas utility property. (Code Sec. 168(e)(3)(E)(vi))[44]

(7) Certain electrical transmission property, generally placed in service after Apr. 11, 2005, (Code Sec. 168(e)(3)(E)(vii)), and "natural gas distribution lines," generally placed in service after Apr. 11, 2005 and before Jan. 1, 2011. (Code Sec. 168(e)(3)(E)(viii)) The original use of both types of property must begin with the taxpayer. [45]

¶ 1918 The 20-year MACRS class.

This class includes property with a class life of 25 years or more (Code Sec. 168(e)(1)), such as farm buildings (other than single purpose agricultural or horticultural structures) and gas utility distribution facilities. [46]

¶ 1919 Residential and nonresidential buildings under MACRS.

A 27.5-year class is specifically assigned to residential rental property (Code Sec. 168(c)), including manufactured homes that are residential rental property, and elevators and escalators in that type of property. A 39-year class life is specifically assigned to nonresidential real property (Code Sec. 168(c)), and to elevators and escalators in that type of property. Nonresidential real property placed in service before May 13, '93, had a 31.5-year class. [47] The above recovery periods apply to buildings and their structural components. [48]

Whether equipment or fixtures are part of the building —and, thus, depreciated over a longer period than if they were treated as separate assets —may depend on whether the assets in question would have qualified as tangible personal property for purposes of prior law's investment tax credit. [49]

¶ 1920 Additions or improvements to real property.

The depreciation for any additions to, or improvement of, any real property (whether or not recovery property) is determined in the same manner as the depreciation deduction for the real property would be determined if the real property were placed in service at the same time as the addition or improvement. (Code Sec. 168(i)(6)(A))[50]

⊘illustration: In '95, a calendar year taxpayer bought and placed in service a residential apartment complex. In the current year, taxpayer made additions and improvements to the property. The additions and improvements are 27.5-year class property. If the property was a factory, then the additions and improvements to it would be 39-year class property.

---

43. ¶L-8208.1, ¶L-8208.2; ¶1684.02; TD ¶266,208.1, TD ¶266,208.2
44. ¶L-8208; ¶1684.01
45. ¶L-8208.3, ¶L-8208.4; ¶1684.01
46. ¶L-8209; ¶1684.01; TD ¶266,209

47. ¶L-8210; ¶1684.02; TD ¶266,211
48. ¶L-9105; TD ¶266,006
49. ¶L-8210; TD ¶266,211
50. ¶L-9105; TD ¶266,006

¶ 1921   Basis of recovery property for computing MACRS depreciation deductions.

If the taxpayer doesn't choose to apply the optional IRS depreciation tables (¶1911), MACRS depreciation deductions are computed on the property's adjusted basis (also referred to by IRS as the "unrecovered basis"), except that salvage value is considered to be zero, i.e., disregarded. (Code Sec. 168(b)(4)) This "unrecovered basis" is adjusted (i.e., ordinarily reduced) by depreciation previously allowed or allowable. [1]

For the basis used if the optional IRS depreciation tables are applied, see ¶1911. For mixed-use property, see ¶1902.

¶ 1922   Depreciation of leasehold improvements and amortization of lease acquisition costs by lessees.

Lessees are treated as any other owner-taxpayer for purposes of determining MACRS deductions for lessees' improvements subject to MACRS rules. Thus, a lessee's deductions for the property are determined without regard to the lease term. (Code Sec. 168(i)(8))

Where the lease ends or terminates before the end of the MACRS recovery period of the lessee's improvement, and the lessee doesn't retain the improvement, the lessee has a gain or loss for the remaining unrecovered basis of the property. [2]

⊘ observation: The remaining basis of unamortized leasehold improvements that are left behind when a lease terminates is deductible as a loss. A gain would arise if, for example, the tenant is paid to terminate the lease and the payment exceeds the basis of the leasehold improvements (and lease acquisition costs, if any).

For amortization of lease acquisition costs, see ¶1597.

¶ 1923   Leasehold improvements by lessor.

A lessor is entitled to recover the cost of depreciable leasehold improvements that it makes. If such improvements are made for the lessee (e.g., to customize the space for the lessee) and are irrevocably disposed of or abandoned by the lessor at the termination of the lease by the lessee, then for purposes of determining gain or loss, the improvement is treated as disposed of by the lessor at that time. (Code Sec. 168(i)(8)(B))[3]

A lessor may advance construction funds to the lessee to help the lessee pay for retail leasehold improvements. If, under the rules explained at ¶1344, a lessee excludes the funds from income, the lessor treats the improvements as its own nonresidential real property, including for purposes of the disposition-of-improvements rule (see above). (Code Sec. 110(b))[4]

¶ 1924   MACRS depreciation periods.

For the 3-year, 5-year, 7-year, 10-year, 15-year and 20-year MACRS classes, the depreciation period is the same as the name of the class (e.g., 5 years for 5-year property). The depreciation period is 25 years for the water utility property class, 27.5 years for the residential rental property class, 39 years for the nonresidential real property class (but 31.5 years if the property is placed in service before May 13, '93) and 50 years for the railroad grading or tunnel bore class. (Code Sec. 168(c))[5]

Where the 150% declining balance method is elected for MACRS property eligible for the 200% declining balance method, the applicable recovery period is as follows (Code

---

1. ¶L-8601; ¶1684; TD ¶266,003
2. ¶L-9106; ¶1684.02; TD ¶267,020
3. ¶L-9106; ¶1684.02; TD ¶267,020

4. ¶J-2265; ¶1104; TD ¶123,005
5. ¶L-8802; ¶s 1684.01, 1684.02; TD ¶267,004

Sec. 168(b)(2)): for property placed in service before '99, the recovery period provided under the "Alternative Depreciation System" (ADS) discussed at ¶¶1931 *et seq.*; for property placed in service after '98, the regular MACRS recovery periods described above. [6]

Shorter depreciation periods apply for "qualified Indian reservation property" placed in service after '93 and before 2008. (Code Sec. 168(j))[7]

caution: Check http://ria.thomson.com/federaltaxhandbook to see if the provision discussed above has been extended.

¶ 1925   MACRS depreciation methods.

There are three depreciation methods used for MACRS property: the 200% and 150% declining balance methods with an appropriate switch to straight-line to maximize deductions, and the straight-line method. (Code Sec. 168(b)) Under the declining balance methods, the depreciation rate (in percentage terms) generally is determined by dividing the declining balance percentage (200% or 150%) by the applicable recovery period. For example, the 200% declining balance method applied to property with a 5-year recovery period results in a depreciation rate of 40% (i.e., 200% ÷ 5). This 40% rate remains constant for each tax year in which the 200% declining balance method is used. [8]

The 200% declining balance method can be used for MACRS property in the three-, five-, seven-, and ten-year recovery classes except for any tree or vine bearing fruit or nuts, in the ten-year class, see below. (Code Sec. 168(b)(1))

The 150% declining balance method can used for MACRS property in the 15-year class (except for qualified leasehold improvements and qualified restaurant property, see ¶1917) and the 20-year class (Code Sec. 168(b)(2)(A)), any property (placed in service after '88) used in a farming business (Code Sec. 168(b)(2)(B)), and, if the taxpayer elects, any other property (other than that for which straight-line must be used). (Code Sec. 168(b)(2)(C))

The straight-line method must be used for all residential rental property in the 27.5-year class; for all nonresidential real property in the 39-year class (31.5-year class before May 13, '93); for qualified Liberty Zone leasehold improvement property; for any railroad grading or tunnel bore; for any tree or vine bearing fruit or nuts placed in service after '88; and for water utility property. (Code Sec. 168(b)(3))[9]

For property not required to use the straight-line method, a taxpayer can elect straight-line depreciation only over the same recovery period listed at ¶1924 in which the property belongs. This election must be for all property within a recovery class, but can be made for any or all classes. But once made, it's irrevocable for that year. (Code Sec. 168(b)(3), Code Sec. 168(b)(5))[10]

observation: Also, an alternative depreciation system election will often change the depreciation method from accelerated to straight-line, see ¶1931 *et seq.*

For computation of depreciation under IRS optional MACRS rate tables (reproduced at ¶1117), see ¶1911.

For the effect of depreciation methods on first-year and last-year depreciation, see ¶1927 *et seq.*

For the depreciation methods that must be used for alternative minimum tax purposes, see ¶3206 *et seq.*

6. ¶L-8103; ¶1684.01; TD ¶267,017
7. ¶L-8806; ¶1684.01; TD ¶267,007
8. ¶L-8902 *et seq.*; ¶1684.01; TD ¶266,004

9. ¶L-8917; ¶s 1684.01, 1684.02; TD ¶267,018
10. ¶L-8920 *et seq.*; ¶1684.01; TD ¶267,018

¶ 1926   Effect of short tax years on MACRS depreciation.

The depreciation allowance for MACRS personal property placed in service or disposed of in a short year can't be determined by using the IRS optional MACRS rate tables. The depreciation allowance for the short tax year is instead determined by: (1) multiplying the property's depreciable basis by the applicable depreciation rate, and (2) multiplying the product obtained in step (1) by a fraction, the numerator of which is the number of months (including fractions of months) the property is deemed in service during the short year under the applicable convention, and the denominator of which is 12. [11] The depreciation allowance for any tax year following the short tax year is determined by consistently using either the "allocation method" or the "simplified method," as described in a revenue procedure issued by IRS. [12]

Rules are provided for how the half-year and mid-quarter conventions for MACRS personal property apply where property is placed in service or disposed of in a short tax year. [13]

When a taxpayer has a short tax year other than the first year in the recovery period, the MACRS depreciation allowance for that short year must account for the difference between recovery years and tax years. [14]

MACRS depreciation deductions for real property for the year it is placed in service, or disposed of, is based on the mid-month convention and on the number of months the property is in service, see ¶1927, regardless of the length of the taxpayer's tax year. [15]

¶ 1927   Mid-month convention for MACRS realty.

The mid-month depreciation convention applies in determining MACRS depreciation deductions for the year real property in the 27.5 or 39-year class (31.5-year class before May 13, '93) is placed in service or is disposed of. Under this rule, all realty placed in service (or disposed of) during any month is treated as placed in service (or disposed of) at the mid-point of that month in computing MACRS depreciation deductions for the acquisition and disposition years. The mid-month convention also applies to property in the 50-year class. (Code Sec. 168(d)(2), Code Sec. 168(d)(4)(B))[16]

¶ 1928   Half-year and mid-quarter conventions for MACRS personal property.

In the case of "personal" property (that is, property other than residential rental or nonresidential real property and railroad gradings and tunnel bores), the half-year depreciation convention generally applies for the acquisition and disposition year. The half-year convention treats all property placed in service or disposed of during a tax year as placed in service or disposed of on the mid-point of that tax year. (Code Sec. 168(d)(1), Code Sec. 168(d)(4)(A))

With the exclusions noted below, the mid-quarter convention applies to all "personal" property placed in service during a tax year if more than 40% of the total basis of all "personal" property placed in service during that year is placed in service during the last three months of the year. (Code Sec. 168(d)(3) The mid-quarter convention applies only to personal property depreciable under MACRS. [17] Under the mid-quarter convention, property is treated as placed in service or disposed of on the mid-point of the applicable quarter. (Code Sec. 168(d)(4)(C))

illustration: A calendar year taxpayer actually placed in service a computer on Jan. 2, Year 1. If the half-year convention applies, the deemed placed in service date is July 1, Year

---

11. ¶L-9002; ¶1684.01; TD ¶267,301
12. ¶L-9003 *et seq.*; ¶1684.01; TD ¶267,302
13. ¶L-8705, ¶L-8712; ¶1684.01; TD ¶266,705, TD ¶266,712
14. ¶L-9007; ¶1684.01; TD ¶267,301
15. ¶L-9104; ¶1684.01; TD ¶267,301
16. ¶L-8713; ¶1684.01, ¶1684.02; TD ¶266,713
17. ¶L-8103; ¶1684.01; TD ¶266,707

1—thus, only a half-year depreciation is allowed for the computer for Year 1. If the mid-quarter convention applies, the deemed placed in service date for the computer is mid-Feb. of Year 1—thus, only 10.5 months of depreciation is allowed for Year 1.

When determining if the mid-quarter convention applies, the taxpayer excludes:

. . . That portion of the basis of property that is expensed under Code Sec. 179; see ¶1944. (Reg § 1.168(d)-1(b)(4)(i)).

. . . Nonresidential real property, residential rental property, and any railroad grading or tunnel bore. (Code Sec. 168(d)(3)(B)(i))

. . . Property placed in service and disposed of in the same tax year. (Code Sec. 168(d)(3)(B)(ii))

. . . Property excluded from MACRS under Code Sec. 168(f) (Reg § 1.168(d)-1(b)(1)), such as films, videotapes and sound recordings.

. . . The basis of a business car, if the taxpayer elects for the placed-in-service year to claim deductions using the standard mileage allowance method (¶1561).

. . . That portion of basis attributable to the personal-use portion of mixed-use assets (e.g., a self-employed's car used for both business and personal use). (Reg § 1.168(d)-1(b)(4)(iii))

The mid-quarter convention is the only applicable convention for MACRS personal property placed in service in a tax year of three months or less. [18]

A taxpayer could elect not to apply the mid-quarter convention, and instead apply the half-year convention, if the *third or fourth quarter* of a tax year included Sept. 11, 2001. [19]

¶ 1929   MACRS deductions for property after use change.

Effective generally for changes in the use of MACRS property in the hands of its owner in a tax year ending after June 16, 2004, the following rules apply.

Personal-use property converted to business or income-producing use (e.g., personal residence converted to rental property) is treated as placed in service on the conversion date, and is subject to the Code Sec. 168 depreciation method, recovery period, and placed-in-service convention applicable to the property beginning in the tax year of the conversion. The property's depreciable basis in the change year is the lesser of its fair market value or adjusted depreciable basis when it is converted. This rule doesn't apply when another rule (e.g., listed property rules under Code Sec. 280F(b)(2)(A)) prescribes the depreciation treatment for a change to business use. (Reg § 1.168(i)-4(b))

MACRS property converted from business or income-producing use to personal use generally is treated as a disposition, with depreciation for the conversion year computed by applying the applicable convention (¶1927 *et seq.*). However, the conversion doesn't result in gain, loss, or depreciation recapture. (Reg § 1.168(i)-4(c))

For use changes after placed-in-service year, where the asset continues to be MACRS property in the taxpayer's hands (e.g., commercial property converted to residential rental property), MACRS depreciation for the change year is determined as though the change occurred on the first day of that year. (Reg § 1.168(i)-4(d)(2)(iii))

If a use-change results in:

. . . A shorter recovery period and/or a faster depreciation method (e.g., property ceases to be used outside the U.S.), the property's adjusted depreciable basis as of the beginning of the change year is depreciated over the shorter recovery period and/or by the faster depreciation method beginning with the year of change as though the property were first placed in service in that year. (Reg § 1.168(i)-4(d)(3)) Taxpayers may elect to continue to depreciate

18. ¶L-8706 *et seq.*; ¶1684.01; TD ¶266,706 *et seq.*   19. ¶L-8705.1; ¶1684.01; TD ¶266,705.1 *et seq.*

the property as though the change in use had not occurred. (Reg §   1.168(i)-4(d)(3)(ii))

. . . A longer recovery period and/or slower depreciation method (e.g., property begins to be used predominantly outside the U.S.), the property's adjusted depreciable basis is depreciated over the longer recovery period and/or by the slower depreciation method beginning with the year of change as if the property had been originally placed in service with the longer recovery period and/or slower depreciation method. (Reg §   1.168(i)-4(d)(4))

Where use changes during placed-in-service year, the depreciation allowance generally is established by the primary use of the property during that tax year, determined in any reasonable manner that is consistently applied. However, in determining whether MACRS property is used within or outside the U.S. during the placed-in-service year, the predominant use of the property governs. (Reg §   1.168(i)-4(e))

General asset accounts. A change in use doesn't cause or permit the revocation of the election to account for the property in a general asset account (¶1909), but the property generally is removed from its existing general asset account and placed in a separate general asset account. (Reg §   1.168(i)-1(h)(2))[20]

¶ 1930   Depreciating MACRS property acquired in a like-kind exchange or involuntary conversion.

MACRS property may be acquired (1) in exchange for MACRS property in a Code Sec.   1031 like-kind property exchange (¶2418 *et seq.*) or (2) to replace involuntarily converted MACRS property in a Code Sec. 1033 involuntary conversion (¶2342 *et seq.*). (Reg § 1.168(i)-6(c)(1)) The replacement property is for depreciation purposes divided into the depreciable exchanged basis (i.e., remaining basis of the relinquished property carried over to the replacement property), and the depreciable excess basis (i.e., additional consideration to acquire the replacement property). Where the properties share the same recovery class and depreciation method, the depreciable exchanged basis is written off over what's left of the relinquished property's recovery period; and the depreciable excess basis is in effect treated as a separate property with a recovery period that begins anew. (Reg §   1.168(i)-6(c)(3)(ii))[21]

> **illustration:** In 2005, ABX Corp. bought a used refrigerator truck (5-year MACRS property, ¶1914) for $100,000 and placed it in service that year. In 2007, ABX acquires a newer truck by trading in the older truck and paying $50,000 cash. ABX uses the optional rate tables (¶1911) to compute depreciation and is subject to the half-year convention (¶1928) in 2005 and 2007. ABC claimed $20,000 of depreciation in 2005 (20%), and $32,000 in 2006 (32%). For 2007, ABX may claim a depreciation deduction of $9,600 for the relinquished truck ($100,000 × .192 [recovery year 3 table percentage for 5-year property] × 6/12 [half-year convention applies]). The remaining depreciable basis of the exchanged truck (i.e., the depreciable exchanged basis) is $38,400 ($100,000 cost – $20,000 – $32,000 – $9,600), which is depreciated over 2007—2010 (what's left of the original recovery period). ABX's depreciable excess basis in the replacement truck is $50,000, the cash it pays to acquire it. Per the table percentages, the depreciation allowance for this excess basis is $10,000 for 2007 (20%), $16,000 for 2008 (32%), $9,600 for 2009 (19.2%), $5,760 for 2010 and 2011(11.52%), and $2,880 (5.76%) for 2012.

Complex rules apply where the relinquished and replacement properties do not have the same recovery period and use the same depreciation method. (Reg §   1.168(i)-6(c)(3)(iii), Reg § 1.168(i)-6(c)(4))[22]

Election out. A taxpayer may elect not to apply the "split basis" approach explained above

---

20. ¶L-8108; TD ¶266,010
21. ¶L-10600 *et seq.*; TD ¶269,400 *et seq.*

22. ¶L-10601.2A; TD ¶269,403

to the relinquished and replacement properties in a Code Sec. 1031 or Code Sec. 1033 exchange. If the election is made, the exchanged basis and excess basis, if any, in the replacement property are treated as placed in service at the time of replacement and the adjusted depreciable basis of the relinquished MACRS property is treated as being disposed. (Reg § 1.168(i)-6(i)) The election is made on Form 4562.[23]

¶ 1931   The straight-line "alternative depreciation system" (ADS) of MACRS.

The alternative depreciation system (ADS) is a straight-line depreciation system, with generally longer depreciation periods than under the general depreciation system. (Code Sec. 168(g)(2)(C), Code Sec. 168(g)(3)(B)) ADS uses the same depreciation conventions as MACRS (Code Sec. 168(g)(2)(B)), see ¶1927 *et seq.*, and like MACRS, disregards salvage value. (Code Sec. 168(g)(2)(A))

Depreciation deductions must be computed under ADS only for certain specified properties, see ¶1932. However, ADS must be used for all properties including properties depreciated under MACRS for purpose of computing earnings and profits of corporations (Code Sec. 312(k)(3)(A)). ADS also applies for purposes of computing the depreciation tax preference for certain property under the alternative minimum tax, under the rules explained at ¶3206.[24] ADS may be elected for all other properties — on a class by class basis for personal property and on an individual basis for residential rental and nonresidential real properties. (Code Sec. 168(g)(7)(A))

An ADS election is an irrevocable year-by-year election. (Code Sec. 168(g)(7)(B)) This election is in addition to the straight-line MACRS election (¶1925).

Property excluded from MACRS because a depreciation method not measured in term of years is elected (¶1908) is also excluded from ADS. (Code Sec. 168(f)(1))

¶ 1932   MACRS property required to be depreciated under ADS.

The following MACRS property must be depreciated under ADS:

. . . "Luxury" automobiles and other "listed" (i.e., mixed-use) property used 50% or more for personal purposes, see ¶1952. (Code Sec. 280F(b)(1))

. . . Properties used predominantly outside the U.S.[25] (Code Sec. 168(g)(1)(A)), except certain properties listed in the Code.[26] (Code Sec. 168(g)(4))

. . . Tax-exempt use property (generally, certain property leased to tax-exempt organizations, governmental units or foreign persons or entities, see Code Sec. 168(h)(3)).[27] (Code Sec. 168(g)(1)(B))

. . . Tax-exempt bond financed property (¶1934).[28] (Code Sec. 168(g)(1)(C))

. . . Imported business equipment from countries that discriminate against U.S. goods from the date the equipment is placed on a restricted list by Presidential Executive Order. (Code Sec. 168(g)(6))[29]

. . . Pre-production costs of farming property excluded from the inventory-capitalization rule of Code Sec. 263A (discussed in ¶1660 *et seq.*).[30]

. . . Intermodal cargo containers not used predominantly in the direct transportation of property to or from the U.S.[31]

23. ¶L-10601.8; TD ¶269,413
24. ¶A-8220; ¶s 564.01, 1684.03; TD ¶267,501
25. ¶L-9406; ¶s 280F4, 1684.03; TD ¶267,502
26. ¶L-9406; ¶1684.03; TD ¶267,504
27. ¶L-9600 *et seq.*; ¶s 1684.03, 1684.06; TD ¶267,502

28. ¶L-9500 *et seq.*; ¶1684.03; TD ¶267,502
29. ¶L-9405; ¶1684.03; TD ¶267,502
30. ¶L-9402; ¶s 263A4, 263A4.15, 1684.03; TD ¶267,502
31. ¶s L-9402, L-9407; TD ¶267,502

¶ 1933　ADS depreciation periods.

The prescribed ADS straight-line periods are:

. . . except as discussed below, the property's "class-life" (¶1912). (Code Sec. 168(g)(3)(B))

. . . four years—for qualified rent-to-own property (¶1913). (Code Sec. 168(g)(3)(B))[32]

. . . five years—for automobiles, light-purpose trucks (Code Sec. 168(g)(3)(D)) and qualified technological equipment.[33] (Code Sec. 168(g)(3)(C))

. . . nine years—for qualified Liberty Zone leasehold improvement property (¶1914). (Code Sec. 1400L(c))

. . . 12 years—for personal property with no class life and not governed by any other rule discussed in this list. (Code Sec. 168(g)(2)(C))

. . . 14 years—for "natural gas gathering lines" the original use of which begins with the taxpayer (¶1915) and which are placed in service after Apr. 11, 2005; property is disqualified if a binding contract was in existence, or construction began, before Apr. 12, 2005. [34]

. . . 20 years—for any Code Sec. 1250 property (generally depreciable real property) which is a retail motor fuels outlet. (Code Sec. 168(g)(3)(B))

. . . 20 years—for initial clearing and grading land improvements relating to gas utility property, effective for property placed in service after Oct. 22, 2004 (¶1917). (Code Sec. 168(g)(3)(B))

. . . 22 years—for Alaska natural gas pipeline property placed in service after 2004 (¶1915). (Code Sec. 168(g)(3)(B))

. . . 30 years—for certain electrical transmission property the original use of which begins with the taxpayer (¶1917) (Code Sec. 168(g)(3)(B)) and which is placed in service after Apr. 11, 2005; property is disqualified if a binding contract was in existence, or construction began, before Apr. 12, 2005. [35]

. . . 35 years—for "natural gas distribution lines" the original use of which begins with the taxpayer (¶1917) (Code Sec. 168(g)(3)(B)) and which are placed into service after Apr. 11, 2005 and before Jan. 1, 2011; property is disqualified if a binding contract was in existence, or construction began, before Apr. 12, 2005. [36]

. . . 39 years—for qualified leasehold improvement property and qualified restaurant property placed in service after Oct. 22, 2004 and before 2008 (¶1917). (Code Sec. 168(g)(3)(B))

. . . 40 years—for nonresidential real property and for residential rental property other than low or moderate income housing qualifying for the 27.5-year period (Code Sec. 168(g)(2)(C)) and any Code Sec. 1245 real property with no class life. (Code Sec. 168(g)(3)(E))

Also, the ADS depreciation period is 5 years for semiconductor manufacturing equipment, 9.5 years for computer-based telephone central office switching equipment, 10 years for railroad tracks, 15 years for single-purpose agricultural or horticultural structures, 20 years for trees or vines bearing fruit or nuts, 24 years for a municipal wastewater treatment plant or for telephone distribution plant equipment and 50 years for railroad gradings, tunnel bores, or water utility property. (Code Sec. 168(g)(2)(C), Code Sec. 168(g)(3)(B))[37]

For "tax-exempt use property" (¶1932) subject to a lease, the above depreciation periods can't be less than 125% of the lease term. (Code Sec. 168(g)(1)(B), Code Sec. 168(g)(3)(A))[38]

---

32. ¶L-9403; ¶1684; TD ¶267,503　　　　36. ¶L-8208.4; ¶1684.01
33. ¶L-9403 *et seq.*; ¶1684.03; TD ¶267,503　　37. ¶L-9403; ¶1684.03; TD ¶267,503
34. ¶L-8206.1; ¶1684.01　　　　　　　　38. ¶L-9602; ¶1684.06
35. ¶L-8208.3; ¶1684.01

¶ 1934   ADS depreciation for MACRS property financed with tax-exempt bonds.

Subject to narrow exceptions, the portion of the cost of depreciable assets directly or indirectly financed with tax-exempt obligations issued after Mar. 1, '86, is depreciable only under straight-line ADS. (Code Sec. 168(g)(1)(C), Code Sec. 168(g)(5)(A))[39]

¶ 1935   30% or 50% bonus first-year depreciation allowance.

A bonus first-year depreciation allowance applies to "qualified property" (¶1936). The allowance, which is claimed in the first year that the property is placed in service by the taxpayer for use in its trade or business or for the production of income, is equal to the following percentage of the unadjusted depreciable basis (see ¶1911) of the property: (Reg § 1.168(k)-1(d)(1))

. . . 30%, if acquired after Sept. 10, 2001, and before May 6, 2003, and (Code Sec. 168(k)(1))

. . . 50%, if acquired after May 5, 2003 and before Jan. 1, 2005. (Code Sec. 168(k)(4))

50% bonus first-year depreciation also applies for new qualified cellulosic ethanol plant property bought after Dec. 20, 2006 and placed in service before 2013. (Code Sec. 168(l)) For the bonus depreciation available for "qualified GO Zone property," see ¶1941, and for "qualified New York Liberty Zone property," see ¶1942.

The adjusted basis of the property is reduced by the bonus depreciation before computing the amount otherwise allowable as a depreciation deduction for the tax year and any later tax year. (Code Sec. 168(k)(1)(B)) There is no AMT depreciation adjustment (¶3206) for the entire recovery period of qualified property. (Code Sec. 168(k)(2)(G); Reg § 1.168(k)-1(d)(2)(ii))[40]

¶ 1936   "Qualified property" eligible for bonus first-year depreciation allowance.

"Qualified property" eligible for bonus first-year depreciation (¶1935) includes most tangible personal property, "qualified leasehold improvement property" (i.e. certain interior improvements to nonresidential buildings), and most computer software. (Code Sec. 168(k)(2)(A)(i))[41] In addition to being of a qualifying type, the property must meet original use (¶1937), timely acquisition (¶1938), and timely placed-in-service (¶1939) requirements. (Reg § 1.168(k)-1(b)(1))

Property is ineligible for a bonus first-year depreciation allowance if it must be depreciated under the alternative depreciation system, see ¶1932 and ¶1952, or is qualified New York Liberty Zone leasehold improvement property, see ¶1914. (Code Sec. 168(k)(2)(D))[42]

¶ 1937   Original-use requirement for bonus first-year depreciation allowance.

The original use of qualified property must begin with the taxpayer after Sept. 10, 2001 (to be eligible for 30% bonus first-year depreciation), or after May 5, 2003 (to be eligible for 50% bonus first-year depreciation), see ¶1935. For "qualified GO Zone property," see ¶1941, and for "qualified New York Liberty Zone property," see ¶1942.

"Original use" is the first use, whether or not that use is *by the taxpayer* .(Code Sec. 168(k)(2)(A)(ii), Code Sec. 168(k)(4)(B)(i); Reg § 1.168(k)-1(b)(3)(i)) However, new property initially used by a taxpayer for personal use or as inventory and then later used by the taxpayer in a trade or business meets the original-use requirement. (Reg § 1.168(k)-

---

39. ¶L-9500 *et seq.*; TD ¶267,502
40. ¶L-9310 *et seq.*, ¶L-9320 *et seq.*; ¶1684.025 *et seq.*; TD ¶269,340 *et seq.*, TD ¶269,350 *et seq.*
41. ¶L-9312, ¶L-9322; ¶1684.026, ¶1684.028; TD ¶269,342,

TD ¶269,352
42. ¶L-9313, ¶L-9323; ¶1684.026, ¶1684.028; TD ¶269,343, TD ¶269,353

1(b)(3)(ii)) There are special rules for reconditioned or rebuilt property, sale-leasebacks, syndication transactions and fractional interests. (Code Sec. 168(k)(2)(E)(ii), Code Sec. 168(k)(2)(E)(iii); Reg § 1.168(k)-1(b)(3))[43]

¶ 1938 Acquisition requirement for bonus first-year depreciation allowance.

To be "qualified property" for purposes of the *30% bonus first-year depreciation allowance* (¶1935), otherwise eligible property must be:

(A) acquired by the taxpayer after Sept. 10, 2001, and before Jan. 1, 2005, but only if no written binding contract for the acquisition was in effect before Sept. 11, 2001, or

(B) acquired by the taxpayer under a written binding contract which was entered into after Sept. 10, 2001, and before Jan. 1, 2005. (Code Sec. 168(k)(2)(A)(iii))

For the bonus depreciation available for "qualified GO Zone property," see ¶1941, and for "qualified New York Liberty Zone property," see ¶1942.

To be "qualified property" for purposes of the *50% bonus first-year depreciation allowance* (¶1935), otherwise eligible property must be acquired by the taxpayer after May 5, 2003, and before Jan. 1, 2005, but only if no written binding contract for the acquisition was in effect before May 6, 2003. (Code Sec. 168(k)(4)(B)(ii))

Special rules apply to property manufactured, constructed or produced by or for the taxpayer, and to certain property purchased under a contract entered into by, or certain property constructed for or by, (1) users of the property and (2) persons related to the taxpayer or to users of the property. (Code Sec. 168(k)(2)(E), Code Sec. 168(k)(4)(C); Reg § 1.168(k)-1(b)(4))[44]

¶ 1939 Placed-in-service requirement for bonus first-year depreciation allowance.

To be "qualified property" for purposes of the bonus first-year depreciation allowance (¶1935), otherwise eligible property generally must be placed in service by the taxpayer before Jan. 1, 2005. (Code Sec. 168(k)(2)(A)(iv), Code Sec. 168(k)(4)(B)(iii)) However, a Dec. 31, 2005 deadline applies to certain aircraft, transportation property and long-lived property. That deadline may be extended to Dec. 31, 2006 for certain property placed in service or manufactured in the GO Zone, Rita GO Zone or Wilma GO Zone (¶2308, ¶2309). (Code Sec. 168(k)(2)(B), Code Sec. 168(k)(2)(C), Code Sec. 168(k)(4)(C); GO Zone Act § 105)[45]

Also, there are special rules for sale-leasebacks, syndication transactions and certain partnership terminations and non-recognition transactions. (Reg § 1.168(k)-1(b)(5))[46]

¶ 1940 Election not to claim bonus first-year depreciation allowance or to claim it at reduced rate.

With respect to property eligible for 50% bonus first-year depreciation (¶1935), the taxpayer may elect to claim bonus first-year depreciation at a 30% rate (instead of 50%) or elect not to claim bonus first-year depreciation. Either election may be made for any class of property (e.g., 5-year property) for any tax year and applies only to all property in that class that is eligible for 50% bonus first-year depreciation and is placed in service during that tax year. (Code Sec. 168(k)(2)(D)(iii), Code Sec. 168(k)(4)(E); Reg § 1.168(k)-1(e)(1)(ii))

With respect to property eligible only for 30% bonus first-year depreciation (¶1935), the taxpayer may elect not to claim bonus first-year depreciation. This election-out may be made for any class of property for any tax year, and does not affect qualified property in that class

43. ¶L-9314, ¶L-9325; ¶1684.026, ¶1684.028; TD ¶269,344, TD ¶269,355

44. ¶L-9315 *et seq.*, ¶L-9326 *et seq.*; ¶1684.026, ¶1684.028; TD ¶269,345 *et seq.*, TD ¶269,354 *et seq.*

45. ¶L-9316 *et seq.*, ¶L-9327 *et seq.*; ¶1684.027; TD ¶269,346 *et seq.*, TD ¶269,357 *et seq.*

46. ¶L-9316 *et seq.*, ¶L-9327 *et seq.*; ¶1684.026, ¶1684.027, ¶1684.028; TD ¶269,346 *et seq.*, TD ¶269,357 *et seq.*

that is eligible for 50% bonus first-year depreciation (unless the taxpayer elects-out for the latter property as well). (Code Sec. 168(k)(2)(D)(iii); Reg § 1.168(k)-1(e)(1))

A taxpayer that elects to claim no bonus depreciation also loses its exemption (discussed at ¶1935) from AMT depreciation adjustments for the elected-for property. (Reg § 1.168(k)-1(e)(6))

Rules are provided for the time and manner of making the above elections. (Reg § 1.168(k)-1(e)(3)) An election-out can be revoked only with IRS consent, except that if the election was made on a timely filed return, the taxpayer can revoke the election by filing an amended return within 6 months of the original return's due date. (Reg § 1.168(k)-1(e)(7))[47]

¶ 1941   50% bonus first-year depreciation allowance for qualified GO Zone property.

Taxpayers can claim a bonus first-year depreciation allowance equal to 50% of the adjusted basis of qualified Gulf Opportunity Zone (GO Zone) property. If claimed, the property's adjusted basis is reduced by the amount of that deduction before computing otherwise allowable depreciation for the tax year and any later tax year. (Code Sec. 1400N(d)(1))[48]

In general, qualified Zone property (property described at ¶1936 and nonresidential real property or residential rental property) must meet detailed use requirements and must be placed in service by the taxpayer before 2008 (before 2009 for nonresidential real property or residential rental property). But under an exception for specified GO Zone extension property—property in IRS-identified areas in which 2005 hurricanes damaged more than 60% (in the aggregate) of the occupied housing units—nonresidential real property or residential rental property can be placed in service before 2011 (but bonus depreciation is limited to the adjusted basis attributable to manufacture, construction or production before 2010) and certain property in those buildings can be placed in service 90 days after that. (Code Sec. 1400N(d)(2)(A)(v), (Code Sec. 1400N(d)(6))[49]

Taxpayers may elect out of bonus first-year depreciation for any class of GO Zone property for any tax year. (Code Sec. 1400N(d)(2)(B)(iv))[50]

Recapture rules apply similar to those under Code Sec. 179(d)(10), see ¶1949. (Code Sec. 1400N(d)(5)) Also, there is no AMT depreciation adjustment for qualified GO Zone property.(Code Sec. 1400N(d)(4))[1]

¶ 1942   30% bonus first-year depreciation allowance for qualified New York Liberty Zone property.

A 30% bonus first-year depreciation allowance applies to "qualified New York Liberty Zone property"—i.e., certain property used in the New York Liberty Zone (an area of southern-most Manhattan described in Code Sec. 1400L(h)).[2]

One of the requirements for being qualified New York Liberty Zone property is that the property be placed in service before Jan 1, 2007 (before Jan 1, 2010 for certain qualifying nonresidential real property and certain residential rental property, see above). [3]

There is no AMT depreciation adjustment for property that qualifies for the 30% allowance. (Code Sec. 1400L(b)(2)(E)) The 30% allowance reduces the asset's basis before computing regular depreciation deductions for the placed-in-service year and later years. (Code Sec. 1400L(b)(1)(B)) The taxpayer may elect out of the allowance for any class of property for

47. ¶L-9318 *et seq.*, ¶L-9329 *et seq.*; ¶1684.0291; TD ¶269,348.1 *et seq.*, TD ¶269,358
48. ¶L-9336 *et seq.*; ¶14,00N4.02 *et seq.*; TD ¶269,331 *et seq.*
49. ¶L-9337.7 *et seq.*; ¶14,00N4.021; TD ¶269,332 *et seq.*
50. ¶L-9338, ¶14,00N4.023; TD ¶269,334

1. ¶A-8221.1, ¶L-9339; ¶14,00N4.02, ¶14,00N4.023, ¶14,00N4.024; TD ¶269,335, TD ¶696,514
2. ¶L-9340 *et seq.*; ¶1400L4.05 *et seq.*; TD ¶267,700 *et seq.*
3. ¶L-9342; ¶14,00N4.06; TD ¶267,702

any tax year. (Code Sec. 1400L(b)(2)(C)(iv))

¶ 1943   The Pre-'87 Accelerated Cost Recovery System (ACRS). ▬▬▬▬▬▬▬

Under pre-'87 ACRS, virtually all tangible property placed in service after '80 and before '87 (and post-'86 transitional property) is depreciated by using a statutory rate and recovery period. Alternatively, the straight-line rate could have been elected over certain specified "optional recovery periods." [4]

Special recovery periods or rates applied to ACRS property leased to tax-exempt entities ("tax-exempt use property"), [5] financed by tax-exempt industrial development bonds (IDBs), [6] used predominantly outside the U.S. [7] or subject to the "luxury" auto and "listed property" rules, see ¶1950 *et seq.*

¶ 1944   Sec. 179 Expense Election. ▬▬▬▬▬▬▬

Many taxpayers are eligible to deduct (in lieu of depreciation) the cost (subject to dollar limits) of most tangible property (other than buildings and land improvements) and non-customized software used in the active conduct of a trade or business.

Taxpayers, except trusts, estates and certain noncorporate lessors (Code Sec. 179(d)(4), Code Sec. 179(d)(5)), can elect on Form 4562 to expense (deduct in lieu of depreciation) the cost (subject to the dollar limits discussed below) of "section 179 property" (see ¶1948). (Code Sec. 179(b)(1))

The maximum amount that may be expensed annually is $125,000 for tax years beginning after 2006 and before 2011 (inflation-adjusted for tax years beginning after 2007). The maximum expensing amount is $128,000 for tax years beginning in 2008. For tax years beginning after 2010, the maximum amount is $25,000. (Code Sec. 179(b)(1), Code Sec. 179(b)(5)) For special dollar limits for certain types of property, see ¶1945 *et seq.*

For tax years beginning after 2006 and before 2011, the maximum annual expensing amount generally is reduced dollar-for-dollar by the amount of section 179 property placed in service during the tax year in excess of $500,000 (inflation-adjusted for tax years beginning after 2007). The investment ceiling limit is $510,000 for tax years beginning in 2008. For tax years beginning after 2010, the investment ceiling limit is $200,000. (Code Sec. 179(b)(2))

The amount of deduction is further limited to the amount of taxable income from any of taxpayer's active trades or businesses. Taxable income, for this purpose, is computed without regard to the cost of any qualified expense property, the deduction for one-half of self-employment tax, any net operating loss carryback or carryforward, and any deductions suspended under other Code sections (Code Sec. 179(b)(3); Reg § 1.179-2(c)(1)), e.g., the passive activity rules. Employees are considered to be engaged in the active conduct of the trade or business of their employment. (Reg § 1.179-2(c)(6)(iv))

An amount that can't be deducted because of the taxable income limit is carried over indefinitely until it can be deducted. (Code Sec. 179(b)(3)(B))[8]

Where an expense election deduction is allocated to a taxpayer from a partnership or an S corporation, the deduction limitation, the investment limitation, and the "taxable income" limitation are applied at both the partnership (or S corporation) level and the taxpayer level. (Code Sec. 179(d)(8); Reg § 1.179-2(c)) However, for purposes of the investment limitation, the cost of qualifying property that the partnership or S corporation placed in service isn't attributed and allocated to the partner or shareholder. (Reg § 1.179-2(b)(3))[9]

---

4. ¶L-10900 *et seq.*, ¶L-10912 *et seq.*; ¶1684.05, ¶1688.400; TD ¶268,101, TD ¶268,102

5. ¶L-9600, ¶L-9602; ¶1684.06; TD ¶267,001

6. ¶L-9700 *et seq.*

7. ¶L-11500 *et seq.*; ¶1688.407; TD ¶268,108

8. ¶L-9900 *et seq.*; ¶1794 *et seq.*; TD ¶268,400 *et seq.*

9. ¶L-9909 *et seq.*; ¶1794.01; TD ¶268,414

Rules are provided for applying the annual dollar limitation to a controlled group of corporations. (Code Sec. 179(d)(7); Reg § 1.179-2(b)(1))[10]

Married taxpayers filing jointly are treated as one taxpayer in applying the expense deduction limit. (Reg § 1.179-2(b)(5)) Married taxpayers filing separately may elect other than a 50-50 allocation of the expense deduction. Absent the election, the 50-50 allocation applies. (Code Sec. 179(b)(4); Reg § 1.179-2(b)(6))[11]

For tax years beginning before 2011, an expensing election or specification of property to be expensed may be revoked without IRS's consent, but, if revoked, can't be re-elected. (Code Sec. 179(c)(2)) A taxpayer may make or revoke an expensing election on an amended return filed within the time prescribed by law for filing an amended return for the tax year for which the election is made. (Reg § 1.179-5(c)(1)) A taxpayer that elected to expense only part of the cost basis of property for a particular tax year (or didn't make any expensing election) may file an amended return and expense any part of the cost basis of property that was not expensed under a prior Code Sec. 179 election. Any such increase in the expensed amount is not treated as a revocation of the prior election for that particular tax year. (Reg § 1.179-5(c)(2))[12]

¶ 1945   Increase in expense amount for enterprise zone property, renewal property, and New York Liberty Zone property.

The maximum regular Code Sec. 179 expense election amount (e.g., $125,000 for tax years beginning in 2007, see ¶1944) is increased by $35,000 for:

. . . "qualified zone property" of an enterprise zone business; (Code Sec. 1397A(a)(1))[13]

. . . "qualified renewal property" acquired after 2001 before 2010, and placed in service in a renewal community; and (Code Sec. 1400J)[14]

. . . "qualified New York Liberty Zone property" placed in service before 2007 (¶1942)

Only 50% of expensing-eligible enterprise zone, qualified renewal property, and qualified New York Liberty Zone property is taken into account before subtracting the Code Sec. 179 phaseout amount (e.g., $500,000 for 2007, see ¶1944). (Code Sec. 1397A(a)(2); Code Sec. 1400J(a); Code Sec. 1400L(f))[15] Recapture (¶1949) applies if the above types of property cease to qualify during their normal recovery periods. (Code Sec. 1397A(b), Code Sec. 1400J(a), Code Sec. 1400L(f)(3))[16]

Qualified zone property or qualified renewal property generally is depreciable tangible personal property meeting these tests (buildings don't qualify for expensing):

(1) it is purchased (with the Code Sec. 179(d)(2) exceptions noted at ¶1948) by the taxpayer after the empowerment zone or renewal community designation took effect,

(2) the original use of the property in an empowerment zone or renewal community commences with the taxpayer, and

(3) 85% or more of the use of the property is in an empowerment zone (certain designated distressed areas) or renewal community (i.e., communities designated as such by the Housing and Urban Development Secretary) and in the active conduct of a qualified business by the taxpayer in the empowerment zone or renewal community. (Code Sec. 1397D(a)(1), Code Sec. 1400J(a))[17]

Requirements (1) and (2) are treated as satisfied if the taxpayer substantially renovates the

10. ¶L-9908; ¶1794.01; TD ¶268,411
11. ¶L-9907; ¶1794.01; TD ¶268,412
12. ¶L-9933; ¶1794.04; TD ¶268,409
13. ¶L-9951; ¶1397A4; TD ¶268,402
14. ¶L-9985; ¶14,00J4; TD ¶268,701

15. ¶1397A4; ¶14,00J4; TD ¶268,413, TD ¶268,704
16. ¶L-9964, ¶L-9989; ¶1397A4, ¶14,00J4; TD ¶268,428; TD ¶268,705
17. ¶L-9953, ¶L-9985; ¶1397A4, ¶14,00J4; TD ¶268,430, TD ¶268,701

property (during any 24-month period beginning after the zone or community renewal designation took effect, additions to the taxpayer's basis exceed the greater of (a) his adjusted basis at the beginning of the 24-month period, or (b) $5,000). (Code Sec. 1397D(a)(2), Code Sec. 1400J(b)) There's no expensing election increase for qualified zone property substantially all the use of which is in certain parcels described in Code Sec. 1391(g)(3)(A)(iii). (Code Sec. 1397A(c))[18]

¶ 1946   Increased expensing election for qualified Code Sec. 179 GO Zone property.

The maximum regular Code Sec. 179 expensing allowance (¶1944) is increased by the lesser of (1) $100,000 (not indexed for inflation), or (2) the cost of qualified Code Sec. 179 Gulf Opportunity (GO) Zone property placed in service during the tax year. In addition, the regular phaseout level for the amount of expensing-eligible property placed in service during the year (¶1944) is increased by the lesser of (1) $600,000 (not indexed for inflation) or (2) the cost of qualified Code Sec. 179 GO Zone property placed in service during the tax year. (Code Sec. 1400N(e)(1))[19]

observation: Thus, for tax years that begin in 2007, the maximum expensing allowance for Code Sec. 179 GO Zone property is $225,000 ($125,000 regular maximum expensing amount + $100,000)); and (2) the investment ceiling limit is $1,100,000 (regular $500,000 phaseout amount + $600,000). Similarly, for tax years that begin in 2008, the maximum allowance and ceiling limit are, respectively, $228,000 and $1,110,000 (see   ¶1944).

Qualified Code Sec. 179 GO Zone property is property that qualifies for expensing under Code Sec. 179(d) (¶1948) that is also qualified GO Zone property as defined for 50% bonus first year depreciation purposes (see ¶1941). However, in determining what is qualified GO Zone property for this purpose, the rules for "specified GO Zone extension property" don't apply (see ¶1941). For tax years beginning after May 25, 2007, qualified Code Sec. 179 GO Zone property that is placed in service in "specified portions of the GO Zone" (i.e., certain highly damaged portions of the GO Zone) includes property placed in service before 2009. (Code Sec. 1400N(e)(2))[20]

observation: The definition of qualified Code Sec. 179 GO Zone property includes the requirement that the property be qualified GO Zone property, determined without regard to the rules for "specified GO Zone extension property". Thus, qualified Code Sec. 179 GO Zone property generally must be placed in service by Dec. 31, 2007 (see   ¶1941), except for property that is subject to a Dec. 31, 2008 deadline under the rule for "specified portions of the GO Zone."

A taxpayer buying property qualifying for either the increased expensing for GO Zone property, or the increased expensing for qualified zone property (¶1945) or qualified renewal property (¶1945), may elect either, but not both, for the property. (Code Sec. 1400N(e)(3)) Expensing of GO Zone property is subject to recapture rules similar to those under Code Sec. 179(d)(10), see ¶1949. (Code Sec. 1400N(e)(4))[21]

¶ 1947   Restricted expensing deduction for heavy SUVs.

No more than $25,000 of the cost of a heavy SUV (sport utility vehicle) may be expensed under Code Sec. 179. (Code Sec. 179(b)(6)) The $25,000 expensing limit applies to any 4-wheeled vehicle which:

(1) is primarily designed (or can be used) to carry passengers on public streets, roads and

---

18. ¶L-9953, ¶L-9985; ¶1397A4, ¶14,00J4; TD ¶268,430, TD ¶268,701

19. ¶L-9996, ¶L-9996.1; ¶14,00N4.025; TD ¶268,601, TD ¶268,602

20. ¶L-9997, ¶L-9997.1; ¶14,00N4.025; TD ¶268,601, TD ¶268,601.1

21. ¶L-9998, ¶L-9999; ¶14,00N4.025; TD ¶268,603, TD ¶268,604

highways (except for rail vehicles), and

(2) has a GVWR (gross, or loaded, vehicle weight rating) of more than 6,000 pounds but not more than 14,000 pounds. (Code Sec. 179(b)(6)(B)(i))

⊘ *illustration:* In 2007 a calendar year taxpayer acquires and places in service a heavy SUV that costs $50,000. It is used entirely for business driving. The taxpayer may elect to expense $25,000 of the SUV's cost (if he is otherwise eligible to do so) and depreciate the $25,000 balance of the cost over the 5-year MACRS recovery period (¶1914) *without regard to* the depreciation dollar caps for luxury autos (¶1955).

A vehicle is *not* subject to the $25,000 expensing limit if it:

. . . is designed for more than nine individuals in seating rearward of the driver's seat;

. . . is equipped with an open cargo area, or a covered box not readily accessible from the passenger compartment, of at least six feet in interior length; or

. . . has an integral enclosure, fully enclosing the driver compartment and load carrying device, does not have seating rearward of the drivers seat, and has no body section protruding more than 30 inches ahead of the leading edge of the windshield. (Code Sec. 179(b)(6)(B)(ii))[22]

¶ 1948   Property eligible and ineligible for expense election.

Property eligible for the expense election consists of the following assets, if "purchased" for use in the active trade or business of the taxpayer:

. . . tangible recovery property that's Code Sec. 1245 property (most depreciable property other than buildings and other land improvements), and,

. . . if placed in service in a tax year beginning before 2011, off-the-shelf computer software. (Code Sec. 179(d)(1))

Code Sec. 179 property *does not include* property used in the production of income (Code Sec. 212 property), air conditioning and heating units, property used for lodging, property used outside the U.S., property used by certain tax-exempt organizations, and property used by governmental units or foreign persons or entities. (Code Sec. 179(d)(1)) The election isn't available for the portion of the property's basis that's determined by reference to the basis of other property held at any time by the purchaser (e.g., trade-ins). [23]

Purchase is any acquisition of property *except*

(1) property acquired from any person whose relationship to the purchaser would cause the disallowance of losses under Code Sec. 267 or Code Sec. 707(b) —this includes (a) family members (but *only* spouses, ancestors and lineal descendants), (b) 50%-owned corporations, (c) grantors, fiduciaries and beneficiaries of trusts, and (d) 50%-owned partnerships;

(2) property acquired by one member from another member of the same controlled group;

(3) property (a) whose basis is determined by reference to the adjusted basis of the person from whom acquired (e.g., gifts), or (b) that's acquired from a decedent. (Code Sec. 179(d)(2); Reg § 1.179-3(d))[24]

¶ 1949   Recapture of amount expensed under Code Sec. 179—Form 4797.

A Code Sec. 179 recapture is triggered when the business use of property placed in service in an earlier year is reduced to 50% or less during the recapture period.

---

22. ¶L-9907.2; ¶1794.015; TD ¶268,411.1   24. ¶L-9925; ¶1794.02; TD ¶268,427
23. ¶s L-9903, L-9922; ¶1794.02; TD ¶268,424

The recapture period of the expense election is the entire recovery period of the qualifying Section 179 property. (Code Sec. 179(d)(10))

The recapture amount (report on Form 4797) equals the expense deduction taken minus the MACRS depreciation amount that would have been allowed on the expensed amount from the time the property was placed in service up to and including the year of recapture. (Reg § 1.179-1(e)(1))[25] For depreciation recapture, see ¶2692 *et seq.*

¶ 1950 "Luxury" Automobiles and "Listed Property." ▬▬▬▬▬▬

MACRS depreciation deductions and the Code Sec. 179 expense election are limited for "luxury" business autos and other "listed property." Lessees of such property are subject to special rules.

The following restrictions on depreciation (and the Code Sec. 179 expense election) apply to listed property (defined at ¶1951):

. . . Property may be depreciated under the accelerated MACRS rates, and is eligible for the special first-year depreciation allowance, only if it is used more than 50% for business, see ¶1952 *et seq.* and ¶1936.

. . . Depreciation of passenger autos ("luxury autos") is subject to maximum ceiling limitations, see ¶1955.

. . . An employee may depreciate listed property only if its use is for the convenience of his employer and as a condition of employment, see ¶1959 *et seq.*

. . . A taxpayer who leases a "luxury" auto for business must add into income an "inclusion amount," see ¶1960 *et seq.*

. . . A taxpayer who leases listed property, other than a luxury auto, must take into income an "inclusion amount" when the property is no longer used more than 50% for business, see ¶1962.

. . . Specific recapture rules apply to listed property, see ¶2700.

. . . Strict substantiation rules apply to listed property expenses, see ¶1580 and ¶1584.

Lessors of listed property who are regularly engaged in the business of leasing that property aren't subject to the limitations applicable to owners for any listed property they lease or hold for leasing. (Code Sec. 280F(c)(1))[26]

¶ 1951 "Listed property" defined.

"Listed property" consists of:

. . . any passenger auto (except for ambulances or hearses used directly in a trade or business, taxis and other vehicles used directly for transporting people or property for pay, and trucks or vans specified by IRS regs);

. . . any other property used as a means of transportation (e.g., trucks, buses, trains, boats, airplanes), except for vehicles that, by reason of their nature, aren't likely to be used more than a de minimis amount for personal purposes;

. . . any property of a type generally used for entertainment, recreation or amusement, including photographic, phonographic, communication and video recording equipment, except if that property is used either exclusively at the taxpayer's regular business establishment, or in connection with the taxpayer's principal trade or business;

. . . any computer or peripheral equipment except those owned or leased by the taxpayer, and used exclusively at the taxpayer's regular business establishment;

. . . any cellular telephone or other similar telecommunications equipment; and

---

25. ¶L-9935; ¶1794.03; TD ¶268,428   26. ¶L-10201; ¶280F4; TD ¶267,630

. . . any other property specified by regs. (Code Sec. 280F(d)(4), Code Sec. 280F(d)(5); Reg § 1.280F-6(b)(1))[27]

¶ 1952   Depreciating listed property used more than 50% for business.

For the year listed property (including autos) is placed in service, an accelerated depreciation deduction (including the Section 179 expense election deduction, if available), and the bonus first-year depreciation allowance, is allowed for the property only if it is predominantly used in a qualified business use —as defined at ¶1953—for that year. If, for the acquisition year, the listed property is used 50% or less in a qualified business use (i.e., it isn't used predominantly on an annual basis in a qualified business use), it: (1) doesn't qualify for the expense election (¶1944) (Reg § 1.280F-3T(c)(1)), (2) is depreciable only under straight-line and the "ADS" recovery periods (¶1933), and (3) is ineligible for the bonus first-year depreciation allowance (¶1935). (Code Sec. 168(k)(2)(E), Code Sec. 280F(b)(1))[28]

ℝ𝕀𝔸 *observation:* Under Code Sec. 280F(b)(1), if qualified business use for listed property starts out by being 50% or less of total use, the straight-line ADS deduction method is required for that property for that year and for all later years.

In addition, depreciation of "luxury" autos is subject to annual maximum deduction limits, see ¶1955.

The actual deduction amount, however, is computed by using the "business/investment use" percentage (defined at ¶1954) and not by the qualified business use percentage. (Reg § 1.280F-6(d)(3)(i))[29]

The disallowed MACRS depreciation and Code Sec. 179 expense election deduction (if any) for the current and earlier years allocable to personal use is lost for all later years. (Code Sec. 280F(d)(2); Reg § 1.280F-4T(a)(1))[30]

When the more-than-50% qualified business use requirement isn't met in a post-acquisition year (during the property's normal recovery period), the listed property becomes, retroactively to the year of acquisition, straight-line ADS property. (Reg § 1.280F-3T(c)(2))[31] Depreciation in excess of straight-line (including the expensing election, ¶1944, and the bonus first-year depreciation allowance, ¶1935) previously taken is recaptured (report on Form 4797). (Code Sec. 280F(b)(2)(A); Reg § 1.280F-3T(b)(2), Reg § 1.280F-3T(d)(2))[32]

¶ 1953   "Qualified business use" for listed property defined.

Which depreciation method to use for listed property (¶1952), whether depreciation recapture applies (¶2700), and, for listed property other than autos, whether an inclusion amount is included in income (¶1962), depends on whether the qualified business use of the property is more than 50%.

"Qualified business use" generally is any use in a trade or business of the taxpayer. (Code Sec. 280F(d)(6)(B))[33] However, this term doesn't include Code Sec. 212 production-of-income use. (Reg § 1.280F-6(d)(2))[34]

Qualified business use doesn't include:

(1) Leasing property to any 5% owner of the taxpayer or to any person related to the taxpayer. Leasing aircraft to such persons, however, is qualified business use if business use, without counting the lease use, is at least 25% of the aircraft's total use.

(2) The use of listed property as compensation for services by a 5% owner or a related

27. ¶s L-10002, L-10003; ¶s 1684.01, 1794.02, 280F4; TD ¶267,616
28. ¶L-10018; ¶280F4; TD ¶267,615
29. ¶L-10029; ¶280F4; TD ¶267,622
30. ¶L-10019; ¶280F4; TD ¶267,617

31. ¶L-10021; ¶280F4; TD ¶267,625
32. ¶s L-10021, L-10032; ¶280F4; TD ¶267,625
33. ¶L-10025 *et seq.*; ¶280F4; TD ¶267,621
34. ¶L-10024; ¶280F4; TD ¶267,621

person.

(3) The use of listed property as compensation for services by any person other than a 5% owner or a related person, unless the provider of the property includes the value of the compensation in the recipient's gross income, properly reports it and, where necessary, treats it as wages subject to withholding. (Code Sec. 280F(d)(6)(C))[35]

¶ 1954   "Business/investment use" for listed property defined.

The amount of the allowable depreciation deduction (or the equivalent inclusion amount for leased listed property (¶1961)) is computed by using the business/investment use percentage. (Reg § 1.280F-6(d)(3)(i))[36]

The term "business/investment use" means the total of business use and investment use of any listed property for the tax year. Whether a particular use is business or investment use (with an important exception applicable to automobiles, explained below) is determined under the normal rules of Code Sec. 162 and Code Sec. 212. (Reg § 1.280F-6(d)(3)(i)) For example, if an item of listed property is used 70% in a trade or business and 20% for the production of income, the taxpayer may claim, if the property otherwise qualifies, accelerated depreciation deductions (including the expense election deduction) based on 90% business/investment use. (Reg § 1.280F-6(d)(5), Ex 2)[37]

The use of a taxpayer's automobile by another person (even if that other person is a 5% owner or a related person) is treated as business/investment use of the taxpayer if:

(1) its use is directly connected with the taxpayer's business,

(2) the value of that use is properly reported by the taxpayer as income to the other person, and where required, tax is withheld on that income, or

(3) the use of the taxpayer's automobile by that other person results in payment of fair market rent. (Reg § 1.280F-6(d)(3)(iv))

¶ 1955   Depreciation of business automobiles—"luxury" auto dollar caps.

Purchased autos used in a trade or business normally are depreciated as 5-year MACRS property. (Code Sec. 168(b)(1); Code Sec. 168(e)(3)(B)) However, the deduction normally obtained for an auto by applying the MACRS rules for 5-year property, the bonus first-year depreciation allowance (¶1935), and the Code Sec. 179 expensing rules (¶1944), is limited by the so-called "luxury auto dollar caps" of Code Sec. 280F. The dollar caps are periodically adjusted for inflation and vary with the placed-in-service year of the auto and the depreciation year. Thus, the maximum annual depreciation/expensing deduction for a business auto is the lesser of the otherwise allowable depreciation/expensing allowance or the applicable luxury auto dollar cap.

The Code Sec. 280F "luxury auto" dollar caps apply to a passenger auto, defined as any four-wheeled vehicle which is manufactured primarily for use on public streets, roads, and highways, and is rated at an unloaded gross vehicle weight of 6,000 pounds or less. In the case of a truck or van, the above 6,000-pound weight test is applied to the truck's or van's gross (loaded) vehicle weight rather than its unloaded gross vehicle weight. (Code Sec. 280F(d)(5)(A); Reg § 1.280F-6(c)(1))[38] Special vehicles (such as ambulances, hearses and autos used as taxis and limos) are excepted from the luxury auto rules, as are trucks or vans that are qualified nonpersonal use vehicles (one which, by reason of its nature is not likely to be used more than a de minimis amount for personal use) and are placed in service after July 6, 2003. (Reg § 1.280F-6(f)(1)).

---

35. ¶s L-10025, L-10027; ¶280F4; TD ¶267,621
36. ¶L-10029; ¶280F4; TD ¶267,622

37. ¶L-10029; ¶280F4; TD ¶267,622
38. ¶L-10003; ¶280F4; TD ¶267,603

observation: Sport-utility vehicles (SUVs) are trucks. Thus, SUVs that are rated at more than 6,000 pounds gross (loaded) vehicle weight are exempt from the luxury-auto dollar caps because they fall outside of the Code Sec. 280F(d)(5) definition of a passenger auto.

More generous first-year dollar caps were available for certain vehicles eligible for bonus depreciation (see ¶1935). (Code Sec. 168(k)(2)(F), Code Sec. 168(k)(4)(D))[39]

For the restricted expensing deduction for heavy SUVs, see ¶1947. For the luxury-auto dollar cap amounts, see ¶1956.

¶ 1956   Luxury" auto depreciation dollar cap amounts.

The annual depreciation dollar caps for (1) autos, and (2) trucks or vans (passenger autos built on a truck chassis, including minivans and sport-utility vehicles (SUVs) built on a truck chassis) first placed in service in 2007, are subject to the luxury auto dollar limits, and are used 100% for business are as follows: [40]

. . . for the placed-in-service year, $3,060 for autos, $3,260 for trucks and vans;

. . . for the second tax year, $4,900 for autos, $5,200 for trucks and vans;

. . . for the third tax year, $2,850 for autos and $3,050 for trucks and vans; and

. . . for each succeeding year, $1,775 for autos and $1,875 for trucks and vans.

observation: For rented (i.e., leased) automobiles and other listed property, income "inclusion amounts" apply instead of the above deduction limits, see ¶1960 *et seq.*

Where the "business/investment use percentage" (defined at ¶1954) is less than 100%, the caps are reduced proportionally to correspond to the taxpayer's business/investment use percentage. (Code Sec. 280F(a)(2))[41] Moreover, depreciation after the normal 5-year recovery period (actually six years because of the operation of the applicable convention) is based on unrecovered basis, i.e., adjusted basis determined as if the auto had been used 100% for business, so that the disallowed MACRS depreciation for the earlier years allocable to personal use is lost forever. (Code Sec. 280F(a)(1)(B), Code Sec. 280F(d)(8))

illustration: In June of 2007 a calendar year taxpayer bought and placed in service a $20,000 passenger car. The car is used 100% for business for 2007 and 2008, and 80% for all later years. Here are the MACRS depreciation deductions for each of the first four tax years assuming that the taxpayer uses regular 200% declining balance depreciation, doesn't make a Code Sec. 179 expense election for the car, and uses the half-year depreciation convention (¶1928) for 2007.

Year	MACRS Deductions
2007 (20% of $20,000 is $4,000 but limited to $3,060. 100% of $3,060)	$ 3,060
2008 (32% of $20,000 is $6,400 but limited to $4,900. 100% of $4,900)	4,900
2009 (19.20% of $20,000 is $3,840 but limited to $2,850. 80% of $2,850)	2,280
2010 (11.52% of $20,000 is $2,304 but limited to $1,775. 80% of $1,775)	1,420
Total 2007 through 2010 MACRS deductions	$11,660

If the vehicle purchased in the above illustration is a truck or van subject to the auto dollar limits, the dollar limits would be higher. For example, the deduction would be $3,260 for 2007 and $5,200 for 2008.

---

39. ¶L-10004.2, ¶L-10004.3; ¶1684.0281; TD ¶267,602.1,   40. ¶L-10004 *et seq.*; ¶280F4; TD ¶267,601
    TD ¶267,602.2   41. ¶L-10004; ¶280F4; TD ¶267,601

Where a vehicle isn't "predominantly used in a qualified business use" (as defined at ¶1953) only straight-line depreciation is available and neither the bonus first-year depreciation allowance nor the Code Sec. 179 expense election can be claimed for it, as explained at ¶1952.

A taxpayer that uses the IRS standard mileage allowance method (discussed at ¶1561) for a tax year isn't subject to the above limitations for that year. [42]

For vehicles placed in service in 2006, the dollar caps for cars were: for the 1st tax year, $2,960 for autos, $3,260 for trucks and vans; for the 2d tax year, $4,800 for autos, $5,200 for trucks and vans; for the 3rd tax year, $2,850 for autos and $3,150 for trucks and vans; and for each succeeding year, $1,775 for autos and $1,875 for trucks and vans.

For vehicles placed in service in 2005, the dollar caps for cars were: for the 1st tax year, $2,960 for autos, $3,260 for trucks and vans; for the 2d tax year, $4,700 for autos, $5,200 for trucks and vans; for the 3rd tax year, $2,850 for autos and $3,150 for trucks and vans; and for each succeeding year, $1,675 for autos and $1,875 for trucks and vans.

For vehicles placed in service in 2004, the dollar caps for cars were: for the 1st tax year, $2,960 for autos, $3,260 for trucks and vans; for the 2d tax year, $4,800 for autos, $5,300 for trucks and vans; for the 3rd tax year, $2,850 for autos and $3,150 for trucks and vans; and for each succeeding year, $1,675 for autos and $1,875 for trucks and vans.

For vehicles placed in service in 2003, the dollar caps for cars were: for the 1st tax year, $3,060 for autos, $3,360 for trucks and vans; for the 2d tax year, $4,900 for autos, $5,400 for trucks and vans; for the 3rd tax year, $2,950 for autos and $3,250 for trucks and vans; and for each succeeding year, $1,775 for autos and $1,975 for trucks and vans.

¶ 1957 Clean fuel vehicles placed in service before 2006 and electric vehicles placed in service before 2007.

For qualified clean fuel vehicle property placed in service before 2006 (and after Aug. 5, '97), the dollar limits on depreciation deductions for autos (¶1955) don't apply. Qualified clean fuel vehicle property is property installed on an auto which is propelled by a non-clean-burning fuel where the purpose of the installation is to permit the auto to be propelled by a clean-burning fuel (e.g., natural gas or electricity). (Code Sec. 280F(a)(1)(C)(i), Code Sec. 179A(c)(1)(A), Code Sec. 179A(f))[43]

For purpose-built passenger vehicles placed in service before 2007 (and after Aug. 5, '97), the auto depreciation dollar limits are approximately tripled (figures are adjusted annually). Purpose-built passenger vehicles are autos produced by an original equipment manufacturer and designed to run primarily on electricity. (Code Sec. 280F(a)(1)(C)(ii))

¶ 1958 Claiming auto depreciation (Form 2106, Form 2106-EZ, Form 4562, etc.).

Self-employeds and sole proprietors report their vehicle expenses on Form 1040, Schedule C (Form 1040, Schedule C-EZ for certain small businesses) or if they are farmers on Form 1040, Schedule F with Form 4562 attached. Employees deduct employee business expenses (including depreciation) on Form 2106. But if an employee is reimbursed for business related car expenses under an accountable plan (¶1574) and the expenses don't exceed the reimbursements, Form 2106 doesn't have to be filed. Form 2106-EZ can be used by an employee if (1) he isn't reimbursed by his employer for any expenses (amounts included in Box 1 of Form W-2 aren't considered reimbursements), and (2) if he claims vehicle expenses, he is using the standard mileage rate (and if he owns the vehicle, also used the standard mileage rate in the year the auto was first placed in service). [44] Otherwise, depreciation is reported on Form 4562, see ¶1901.

42. ¶L-10013 *et seq.*; ¶280F4; TD ¶267,612
43. ¶L-10003.1; ¶179A4, ¶280F4; TD ¶267,604
44. ¶L-10004; TD ¶267,601

¶ 1959   Requirements for "listed property" deductions by employees.

Listed property that an individual owns and uses in connection with his employment is eligible for MACRS deductions only if the property is required for the convenience of the employer and as a condition of employment. "Convenience of the employer," and "condition of employment" are defined as used in determining the exclusion from gross income for lodging furnished to an employee, see ¶1268 *et seq.*

To satisfy the condition-of-employment requirement, the property must be required for the employee to properly perform the duties of his or her employment. This requirement isn't satisfied merely by an employer's statement that the property is required as a condition of employment. (Code Sec. 280F(d)(3))[45]

A computer at home, even if used exclusively for the employer's work, is listed property if the taxpayer-employee doesn't qualify under the "office-at-home" requirements of Code Sec. 280A(c)(1), discussed in ¶1635 *et seq.*[46] If a home computer is listed property, the employee gets no depreciation or other deduction, as discussed at ¶1959, unless he proves the computer is: (1) for the convenience of the employer, and (2) required as a condition of employment. (Reg § 1.280F-6(a)).[47]

¶ 1960   Lessees' limitations on listed property.

Lessees of business automobiles and other listed property under leases of 30 days or more are subject to the MACRS limitations discussed in the preceding paragraphs, although indirectly. (Code Sec. 280F(c)(2), Code Sec. 280F(c)(3))[48]

Deductions for rental payments aren't limited. Instead, during every lease year, lessees of "luxury" autos must include in gross income an "inclusion amount," figured from IRS's tables, as discussed at ¶1961 *et seq.*

The "inclusion amount" for business automobiles is based on the fair market value of the automobile and the lessee's business/investment use. An amount must be included in the lessee's gross income for each year the automobile is leased, whether or not it's used 100% for business/investment purposes. (Reg § 1.280F-5T(d), Reg § 1.280F-5T(e))[49]

For listed property other than business automobiles, there's no annual "inclusion amount." The lessee must, however, take an "inclusion amount" into income for the first year the property ceases to be used predominantly in a qualified business use, (Reg § 1.280F-5T(f)) as explained at ¶1962.[50]

The fair market value of the property is equal to its fair market value on the first day of the lease term. If, however, the capitalized cost of the leased property is specified in the lease, that amount is its fair market value. (Reg § 1.280F-5T(h)(2))[1]

¶ 1961   "Inclusion amount" for leased business autos, trucks, and vans.

For passenger autos, trucks, and vans that are subject to the luxury auto limits (¶1955) and are first leased in 2007, the inclusion amount (see ¶1960) for each tax year of the lease is computed as follows: (Reg § 1.280F-7(a)(2))[2]

(1) Find the line from the appropriate table at ¶1118, which includes the fair market value of the leased auto, truck or van.

(2) Prorate the dollar amount for the number of days in the lease term included in the tax

---

45. ¶L-10022; ¶280F4; TD ¶267,618
46. ¶L-10023; TD ¶267,619
47. ¶L-10023; ¶280F4; TD ¶267,619
48. ¶L-10200 *et seq.*; ¶280F4; TD ¶267,629

49. ¶L-10202; ¶280F4; TD ¶267,631
50. ¶L-10205; ¶280F4; TD ¶267,631
1. ¶L-10203; ¶280F4; TD ¶267,632
2. ¶L-10204, ¶L-10204.2; ¶280F4; TD ¶267,632, TD ¶267,633

year at issue.

(3) Multiply the prorated dollar amount by the business/investment use percentage for the auto, truck or van for that tax year. The resulting amount is the inclusion amount.

For the last tax year of the lease, the dollar amount for the preceding year is used.

illustration: On Apr. 1, 2007, a calendar year taxpayer leased and placed in service an auto (not a truck or van) with a FMV of $31,500. The lease is for three years and the business/investment use is 100% in each year. The taxpayer must include the following "inclusion amounts" (from Table at ¶1118) in gross income: for 2007, $83.63 ($111 inclusion amount times 275/365); for 2008, $243 (full inclusion amount); for 2009, $363 (full inclusion amount); and for 2010 it's $90.50 ($363 inclusion amount times 91/365). (Reg § 1.280F-7(a)(2)(i))

For autos first leased in 2007, there's no inclusion amount unless the fair market value of the car exceeds $15,500 ($16,400 for trucks and vans). [3]

Separate income inclusion tables apply for electric autos (see ¶1957) leased before 2007 for trade or business use. [4]

Income inclusion amounts for business autos leased before 2007 are carried in earlier (pre-2008) issues of the RIA Federal Tax Handbook.

¶ 1962 Inclusion amount for MACRS leased listed property other than automobiles.

A lessee of listed property other than automobiles must include in gross income an inclusion amount in the first tax year in which the leased property isn't used predominantly —i.e., more than 50%—in a qualified business use, see ¶1953. (Reg § 1.280F-5T(f)(1))

The inclusion amount for MACRS listed property other than automobiles is the sum of the amount computed under Step (1) and Step (2), below. (Reg § 1.280F-7(b)(2))

STEP (1): Multiply the following three items: (a) the fair market value of the property, (b) the business/investment use of the property for the year that use is 50% or less, and (c) the applicable percentage from Table II reproduced at ¶1117. (Reg § 1.280F-7(b)(2)(i))

STEP (2): Multiply the following three items: (a) the fair market value of the property, (b) the average of the business/investment use for all tax years (in which the property is leased) that precede the year the business/investment use is 50% or less, and (c) the applicable percentage from Table I reproduced at ¶1117. (Reg § 1.280F-7(b)(2)(ii))

Special computation rules apply when a lease term for listed property begins within nine months of the end of the lessee's tax year, or when the lease term is less than one year. (Reg § 1.280F-5T(g))[5]

¶ 1963 Depreciation Deduction Under the Income Forecast Method. ████████

For property placed in service after Sept. 13, '95, depreciation deductions under the income forecast method are figured by multiplying the cost of the property (but only amounts that satisfy the Code Sec. 461(h) economic performance standard, ¶2833) less estimated salvage value, by a fraction, the numerator of which is the year's income generated by the property, and the denominator of which is all income earned before the close of the tenth tax year following the year in which the property was placed in service.

Under the income forecast method, the depreciation deduction for the tenth tax year after

---

3. ¶L-10204, ¶L-10204.2; ¶280F4; TD ¶267,632, TD ¶267,633   5. ¶L-10206 *et seq.*; ¶280F4; TD ¶267,634
4. ¶L-10204.1; ¶280F4; TD ¶267,632

the tax year in which the property was placed in service is equal to the taxpayer's entire remaining basis in the property. (Code Sec. 167(g)(1)(C)) Taxpayers using the income forecast method pay (or receive) interest in recomputation years (generally in the third and tenth years after the property was placed in service, unless income earned by the property is within 10% of original estimates; use Form 8866 to compute) based on the recalculation of depreciation under a look-back method (but there's no look-back for property that had a cost basis of $100,000 or less). (Code Sec. 167(g))[6] (For 15-year amortization for films, sound recordings, video tapes, etc., see ¶1979.)

For property placed in service after Aug. 5, '97, the income forecast method (or any similar method) can be used only for: (1) Motion picture films, video tapes, and sound recordings; (2) copyrights; (3) books; (4) patents; and (5) any other property to be specified in regulations. The income forecast method or any similar method cannot be used to depreciate amortizable section 197 intangibles (see ¶1978). (Code Sec. 167(g)(6))[7]

For property placed in service after Oct. 22, 2004:

. . . for computing income-forecast depreciation deductions, "participations and residuals" may, by election, be included in the adjusted basis of the property beginning in the year the property is placed in service, but only if they relate to income to be derived from the property before the close of the 10th tax year following the year the property is placed in service. "Participations and residuals" are costs the amount of which, by contract, varies with the amount of income earned in connection with the property. (Code Sec. 167(g)(7))[8]

. . . rather than accounting for participations and residuals as a cost of the property under the income forecast method, the taxpayer may deduct these payments as they are made. This may be done on a property-by-property basis and must be applied consistently for a given property thereafter. (Code Sec. 167(g)(7))

. . . the income from the property to be taken into account under the income forecast method is the gross income from the property. (Code Sec. 167(g)(5)(E))[9]

Special rules apply for making either election if it was not made, or not properly made, on a return filed before June 15, 2006. [10]

¶ 1964 Depreciation Deduction Under the "Useful-Life" Rules. ▬▬▬▬▬

Property not depreciable under MACRS or ACRS (see ¶1900, ¶1908 and ¶1943) may be depreciable under the useful-life rules, under which available depreciation methods are prescribed, but the depreciation periods are determined either under: (1) the period specified in Code Sec. 167(f) (see ¶1966), or (2) the period during which a depreciable asset, or group of similar assets, may reasonably be expected to be useful to the taxpayer in his trade or business or in income production. [11] In general, unless a method is prescribed by Code Sec. 167, a taxpayer may use any method of depreciation for nonrecovery property as long as it results in a reasonable allowance. (Code Sec. 167(a); Reg § 1.167(b)-0)[12]

Useful-life property generally can't be depreciated below salvage value. (Reg § 1.167(a)-1(c), Reg § 1.167(b)-2(a))[13]

¶ 1965 Basis for depreciation.

The basis on which depreciation is taken is the adjusted basis under Code Sec. 1011 for the purpose of gain or loss on a sale or other disposition. (Code Sec. 167(c)(1)) For property acquired after Aug. 10, '93, if property is acquired subject to a lease, no portion of the adjusted basis can be allocated to the leasehold interest, and the entire adjusted basis is

---

6. ¶L-10704; ¶1674.100; TD ¶268,004
7. ¶L-10704A; ¶1674.100; TD ¶268,004
8. ¶L-10707.1, ¶L-10707.1A; ¶1674.100
9. ¶L-10705, ¶L-10707; ¶1674.100

10. ¶L-10707.1B; ¶1674.100
11. ¶L-11800 *et seq.*; ¶1674.040 *et seq.*; TD ¶268,122
12. ¶L-11901; ¶1674.100; TD ¶268,001
13. ¶L-11711; ¶1674.044; TD ¶268,123

taken into account in determining any depreciation for the property subject to the lease. (Code Sec. 167(c)(2)) The no-allocation rule also applies to leases that terminate immediately after the acquisition. [14]

¶ 1966   Intangibles excluded from 15-year amortization.

For property acquired after Aug. 10, '93, certain property excluded from 15-year amortization, ¶¶1977 *et seq.*, is also depreciated under the useful-life rules, as follows:

(1) Computer software, in those situations in which it is excluded from 15-year amortization (see ¶1980), generally is depreciated using the straight-line method with a useful life of 36 months, beginning on the first day of the month that it is placed in service; see ¶1663 for exceptions. (Code Sec. 167(f)(1); Reg § 1.167(a)-14(b)(1))

(2) Rights to service debts secured by residential realty are depreciated using the straight-line method with a useful life of 108 months. (Code Sec. 167(f)(3); Reg § 1.167(a)-14(d)(1))

(3) Amortization of a right (other than one acquired as part of the purchase of a trade or business) to receive a fixed amount of tangible property or services under a contract or from a governmental unit is found by dividing its basis by a fraction (amount of tangible property or services received during the year divided by total amount of tangible property or services received or to be received). The cost or other basis of a right to receive an unspecified amount of tangible property or services over a fixed period is amortized ratably over the period of the right. The basis of a right to an unspecified amount over a fixed duration of less than 15 years is amortized over the term of the right. (Code Sec. 167(f)(2); Reg § 1.167(a)-14(c))

(4) If the purchase price of an interest in a patent or copyright (other than one acquired as part of a purchase of a trade or business) is payable at least annually either as a fixed amount per use or as a fixed percentage of revenue derived, the depreciation deduction is equal to the amount of the purchase price paid or incurred during the year. Otherwise, basis is depreciated either ratably over its remaining useful life or under the income forecast method (¶1963). (Code Sec. 167(f)(2); Reg § 1.167(a)-14(c)(4))

Effective for leases entered into after Mar. 12, 2004, the useful life of property described at items (1), (3) or (4) on the above list that, if it were tangible property, would be "tax-exempt use property" (see ¶1932), can't be less than 125% of the lease term. (Code Sec. 167(f)(1)(C), Code Sec. 167(f)(2))[15]

¶ 1967   Specialized "useful-life" depreciation methods.

These include:

. . . operating day method used for equipment affected chiefly by wear and tear rather than obsolescence, such as rotary oil drills; [16]

. . . sinking fund method (Reg § 1.167(b)-4(a));[17]

. . . unit-of-production method used for property, the usefulness of which is closely related to its use in production or to a source of supply or similar factor. (Reg § 1.167(b)-0(b), Reg § 1.611-5(a), Reg § 1.611-5(b)(2))[18]

¶ 1968   Special Expensing and Amortization Provisions. ■■■■■■■■■■■■■■■■■■■■■■

Instead of being subject to the ordinary depreciation or expensing rules, certain property is expensed or amortized as described at ¶¶1969 through ¶1980.

---

14. ¶L-7911.1; ¶1784; TD ¶265,413
15. ¶L-7935, ¶L-8018, ¶L-8025, ¶L-8030; ¶1674.013, ¶1674.025, ¶1674.033; TD ¶265,434, TD ¶269,025, TD ¶269,026
16. ¶L-10709; ¶1674.100; TD ¶268,015
17. ¶L-10711
18. ¶L-10702; ¶1674.100; TD ¶268,001

For example, taxpayers can elect to expense 50% of the cost of qualified advanced mine safety equipment property placed in service after Dec. 20, 2006 and before 2009. (Code Sec. 179E) Research and experimental expenditures connected with a trade or business may be amortized over a 60-month period (¶1601). Also, startup expenditures (¶1501), organization costs of a corporation (¶3520) and organization costs of a partnership (¶3707) may be amortized over a 180-month period. Bond premium or discount (¶2172 *et seq.*) and lease acquisition costs are also amortized (¶1597).

¶ 1969   Expensing election for costs of film and TV production

For qualified film and television (TV) productions commencing after Oct. 22, 2004 and before Jan. 1, 2009, taxpayers may elect to deduct production costs in the year the costs are incurred (i.e., to expense them) instead of capitalizing the costs and recovering them through depreciation allowances. (Code Sec. 181(a)(1))[19] In general, expensing doesn't apply to any film or TV production the aggregate cost of which exceeds $15 million for each qualifying production. The threshold is $20 million if production expenses are "significantly incurred" in areas (1) eligible for designation as a low-income community or (2) eligible for designation by the Delta Regional Authority (a federal-state partnership covering parts of certain states) as a low-income community or isolated area of distress. (Code Sec. 181(a)(2))[20]

A qualified film or TV production generally is any production of a motion picture or video tape if at least 75% of the total compensation expended on the production is "qualified compensation." Qualified compensation (but not participations and residuals, as defined by Code Sec. 167(g)(7)(B)) is compensation for services performed in the U.S. by actors, directors, producers, and other relevant production personnel. For property which is one or more episodes in a television series, only the first 44 episodes qualify. Sexually explicit productions, as defined by section 2257 of title 18 of the U.S. Code, do not qualify. (Code Sec. 181(d))[21]

Temporary regs explain how and when to make the election, including special rules for making the election if it was not made, or not properly made, on a return filed before Mar 12, 2007. (Reg § 1.181-2T) The election can be revoked only with prior consent of IRS (Code Sec. 181(c)(2))[22]

Recapture of the benefits of the expensing is required if a production no longer qualifies for expensing in tax years after the year for which the expensing election is made. (Reg § 1.181-4T(a))[23]

¶ 1970   Expensing elections for refining costs.

Under Code Sec. 179B, small business refiners may elect to expense 75% of "qualified capital costs" paid or incurred after 2002 to comply with certain EPA diesel fuel sulfur control requirements. Among the requirements for being qualified capital costs is that the costs be incurred no later than the earlier of (1) Dec. 31, 2009 or (2) the date one year after the date that the taxpayer must comply with the sulfur control requirements. [24]

Special rules apply for making the election if it was not made, or not properly made, on a return filed before June 15, 2006. The election can be revoked only with prior consent of IRS.[25]

Also, under Code Sec. 179C refiners (whether or not they are small business refiners) can elect to expense 50% of the costs of "qualified refinery property" placed in service after Aug. 8, 2005. Among the requirements for being "qualified refinery property" is that (1) no written binding contract for construction of the property be in effect before June 15, 2005 and (2) the

---

19. ¶L-3140 *et seq.*; ¶1814 *et seq.*; TD ¶269,451 *et seq.*
20. ¶L-3144 *et seq.*; ¶1814.01; TD ¶269,453 *et seq.*
21. ¶L-3142 *et seq.*; ¶1814.07 *et seq.*; TD ¶269,452
22. ¶L-3146 *et seq.*; ¶1814.05, ¶1814.13; TD ¶269,455

23. ¶L-3147; ¶1814.15
24. ¶L-3161 *et seq.*; ¶179B4; TD ¶307,101 *et seq.*
25. ¶L-3161; ¶179B4; TD ¶307,101

property be either (a) placed in service before Jan. 1, 2008 or (b) be placed in service before Jan. 1, 2012 and be either (i) subject to a written binding construction contract entered into before Jan. 1, 2008 or (2) if self-constructed, be property the construction of which began before Jan. 1, 2008 and after June 14, 2005. [26]

¶ 1971 Expensing for costs of making commercial buildings energy efficient.

Taxpayers may expense the cost of "energy efficient commercial building property" placed in service in calendar years 2006, 2007 or 2008. (Code Sec. 179D(a)) The deduction for any building for any tax year can't be more than the excess (if any) of (1) $1.80 × the square footage of the building over (2) the deductions allowed under Code Sec. 179D(a) for earlier years. (Code Sec. 179D(b))

"Energy efficient commercial building property" is property that is (1) depreciable or amortizable), (2) installed on or in a building located in the U.S. and (3) certified as being installed as part of a plan that will meet a 50% energy use reduction test described in Code Sec. 179D(c). In some situations in which the 50% test isn't satisfied, a partial deduction is permitted. (Code Sec. 179D(d)(1)

For property installed on government property, the person primarily responsible for designing the property is treated as the taxpayer. (Code Sec. 179D(d)(4))[27]

¶ 1972 Amortization elections for pollution control facilities.

A taxpayer may elect to amortize, over 60 months, part or all of the cost of new identifiable pollution control treatment facilities used in connection with a plant or other property in operation before '76. (Code Sec. 169(a), Code Sec. 169(d)) MACRS depreciation may be taken on any portion that doesn't qualify. (Code Sec. 169(g))

Also, a taxpayer may elect to amortize over an 84-month period *air* pollution control facilities used in connection with an electric generation plant or other property that is primarily coal fired. The election is available only for facilities that are both (1) placed in service in connection with a plant or other property placed in operation after Dec. 31, '75 and (2) placed in service after Apr. 11, 2005. (Code Sec. 169(d)(5))

For both 60 month amortization and 84 month amortization, limits on amortization apply to a facility with a useful life of more than 15 years (Code Sec. 169(f)) Also, amortization for a C corporation is reduced by 20%. (Code Sec. 291(a)(5)) (The 20% reduction rule of Code Sec. 291 applies to an S corporation only if it was formerly a C corporation and only for the first three tax years after a C tax year.) (Code Sec. 1363(b)(4))[28]

¶ 1973 Amortization election for expenses for creating or acquiring music.

For any tax year beginning after Dec. 31, 2005 and before Jan. 1, 2011, a taxpayer may elect to amortize over a 5-year period expenses that are both (1) paid or incurred to create or acquire a musical composition (including words), or a copyright to such property, and (2) otherwise properly capitalizable. The 5-year period begins with the month in which the composition or copyright is placed in service. The election doesn't apply to expenses that are Code Sec. 263A(h) qualified creative expenses (¶1660), subject to a specified simplified amortization procedure, amortizable section 197 intangibles (¶1979) or not otherwise allowable as a deduction. The election is to be made in the time and manner specified by IRS, and it applies to all musical property placed in service in the tax year. If the election isn't made for property eligible for the election, the costs of the property may be recovered under any allowable method, including the income forecast method (¶1963). (Code Sec. 167(g)(8))[29]

¶ 1974   Expensing and amortization of reforestation expenditures—Form 4562.

Effective for expenses paid or incurred after Oct. 22, 2004, taxpayers other than trusts may elect to deduct up to $10,000 ($5,000 if married filing separately) of reforestation costs, and taxpayers (including estates and trusts) may elect to amortize the balance of reforestation costs over 84 months. (Code Sec. 194) Use Form 4562.

For expenses paid or incurred before Oct. 23, 2004, taxpayers other than trusts may elect to amortize, over a seven-year period, up to $10,000 of reforestation expenditures in connection with qualified timber property. [30]

An individual need not itemize to claim deductions under Code Sec. 194. (Code Sec. 62(a)(11))[31] Reforestation costs expensed or amortized under Code Sec. 194 are subject to recapture as ordinary income (to the extent of gain) where there's a disposition of the timber property within ten years. (Code Sec. 1245(a)(2)(C))[32]

Taxpayers making either election must create and maintain separate accounts for each qualified timber property. Any property subject to either election may not be included in any other timber account (e.g., a depletion block) for which depletion is allowed under Code Sec. 611 (¶1981 *et seq.*). And, at no time may an amortizable timber account become part of a depletable account for purposes of deduction under Code Sec. 165(a). [33]

IRS consent to revoke the election is granted only in rare and unusual circumstances. Special rules apply for making an election if it was not made, or not properly made, on a return filed before June 15, 2006. [34]

The maximum reforestation amount that a taxpayer may elect to expense for qualified timber property, any portion of which is located in the GO Zone, Rita GO Zone or Wilma GO Zone (¶2308, ¶2309), is increased by the lesser of: (a) $10,000 ($5,000 if married filing separately); or (b) the amount of reforestation expenses paid or incurred by the taxpayer for qualified timber property during the specified portion of the tax year. (Code Sec. 1400N(i)(1))

The specified portion of the tax year is defined by reference to the property's location:

(1)   For any portion of qualified timber property located in the GO Zone, it's that part of the tax year after Aug. 27, 2005, and before Jan. 1, 2008;

(2) For any portion of qualified timber property (other than property described in (1)) located in the Rita GO Zone, it's that part of the tax year after Sept. 22, 2005, and before Jan. 1, 2008; and

(3) For any portion of qualified timber (other than property described in (1) or (2)) located in the Wilma GO Zone, it's that part of the tax year after Oct. 22, 2005, and before Jan. 1, 2008. (Code Sec. 1400N(i)(5))

caution: Check http://ria.thomson.com/federaltaxhandbook to see if the provision discussed above has been extended.

The increased expensing isn't available for publicly traded corporations or real estate investment trusts. Also excluded are taxpayers that hold more than 500 acres of qualified timber property at any time during the tax year. (Code Sec. 1400N(i)(3), Code Sec. 1400N(i)(4))[35]

---

30. ¶N-6301 *et seq.*; ¶1944 *et seq.*; TD ¶272,001 *et seq.*
31. ¶A-2601, ¶N-6301; ¶624.04; TD ¶560,702
32. ¶N-3704; ¶12,454.03; TD ¶299,026

33. ¶N-6301, ¶N-6310; ¶1944; TD ¶272,001, TD ¶272,009
34. ¶N-6301; ¶1944; TD ¶272,001
35. ¶N-6304.1; ¶14,00N4.045; TD ¶272,001

¶ 1975   24-month amortization for certain oil or gas costs; 5-year amortization for major integrated oil companies.

Geological and geophysical expenses paid or incurred, after Aug. 8, 2005, in connection with exploring or developing oil or gas within the U.S (as defined in Code Sec. 638) are amortized over the 24-month period beginning on the date that the expenses are paid or incurred. In calculating the amortization deductions, a half-year convention applies. (Code Sec. 167(h)(1), Code Sec. 167(h)(2))

RIA *observation:* Because of the half-year convention, one quarter of the expenditures are deducted in the year that they are paid or incurred (Year 1), one half are deducted in Year 2, and one-quarter are deducted in Year 3.

Geological and geophysical expenses of a major integrated oil company paid or incurred after May 17, 2006 are amortizable over a 5-year period. (Code Sec. 167(h)(5))

Amortization continues over the full 24-month period (5-year period for a major integrated oil company) even if the underlying property is abandoned or retired. (Code Sec. 167(h)(4), Code Sec. 167(h)(5))[36]

¶ 1976   50% expensing or 120-month amortization for qualified commercial revitalization expenditures.

A taxpayer that places into service a qualified revitalization building in a renewal community (communities designated as such by the Housing and Urban Development Secretary) after 2001 but before 2010 may elect to write off qualified revitalization expenses by either (Code Sec. 1400I(a)):

. . . deducting *one-half* of qualified revitalization expenses for any qualified revitalization building for the tax year in which the building is placed in service (50% expensing alternative); or

. . . amortizing *all* such expenses *over a 120-month period* beginning with the month in which the building is placed in service (the 120-month amortization alternative).

The total amount of eligible expenses per building can't exceed the lesser of $10,000,000, or the commercial revitalization expense amount allocated to the building by the commercial revitalization agency for the state in which the building is located. (Code Sec. 1400I(c)(2))

A qualified revitalization building is any building (and its structural components) if : (1) it is placed in service by the taxpayer in a renewal community and its original use begins with the taxpayer; or (2) it is substantially rehabilitated (within the meaning of Code Sec. 47(c)(1)(C), see ¶2309), and is placed in service by the taxpayer after the rehabilitation in a renewal community. (Code Sec. 1400I(b)(1))

A qualified revitalization expense is any amount properly chargeable to capital account for depreciable property which is nonresidential real property (or section 1250 property (¶2694) which is functionally related and subordinate to nonresidential real property). (Code Sec. 1400I(b)(2)(A))

Qualified revitalization expenses don't include (Code Sec. 1400I(b)(2)(B)):

. . . the cost of buying a building (or an interest in one) substantially rehabilitated by the taxpayer to the extent that those costs exceed 30% of the total qualified revitalization expenses for the building (not counting the cost of acquiring it or an interest in it), or

. . . any expense which the taxpayer takes into account in computing any credit allowed

---

36. ¶N-3201; ¶1674.126, TD ¶271,701

under the Code, unless he elects to take the expense into account only for purposes of the commercial revitalization deduction. [37]

¶ 1977   Amortization of Intangibles. ████████████████████████████████████

The cost of most acquired intangible assets, including goodwill and going concern value, is amortized ratably over a 15-year period.

¶ 1978   Fifteen-year amortization of intangibles—Form 4562.

Taxpayers claim deductions on Form 4562 for "amortizable section 197 intangibles" (¶1979) by amortizing the adjusted basis (for purposes of determining gain) of that intangible ratably over a 15-year period beginning on the *later* of: the first day of the month in which the intangible is acquired, or, for property held in connection with the conduct of a trade or business or a production-of-income activity, the first day of the month in which the conduct of the trade or business or the activity begins. (Code Sec. 197(a); Reg § 1.197-2(f)(1)(i)) No other depreciation or amortization deduction is permitted for any amortizable section 197 intangible. (Code Sec. 197(b))[38]

No loss deduction is permitted on the disposition of an amortizable section 197 intangible if the taxpayer retains one or more other intangibles acquired in the same transaction or series of related transactions along with the intangible disposed of. (Code Sec. 197(f)(1)(A)) On the disposition of the intangible, the bases of the other intangibles acquired in the same transaction or series of related transactions is increased by the amount of the loss barred. (Code Sec. 197(f)(1)(A)(ii)) The basis of each retained section 197 intangible is increased by the product of (1) the amount of the loss not recognized solely by reason of this rule, and (2) a fraction consisting of the basis of the intangible over the total bases of all such retained section 197 intangibles. [39]

Anti-churning rules keep taxpayers from converting existing intangibles for which a depreciation or amortization deduction isn't allowable under prior law into amortizable section 197 intangibles. (Code Sec. 197(f)(9))[40]

Effective for leases entered into after Mar. 12, 2004, the amortization period of Code Sec. 197 property that, if it were tangible property, would be "tax-exempt use property" (see ¶1932), can't be less than 125% of the lease term. (Code Sec. 197(f)(10))[41]

If, after Aug. 8, 2005, more than one amortizable section 197 intangible is disposed of in one transaction, or a series of related transactions, all of the amortizable section 197 intangibles in the transaction (or transactions) —except for any amortizable section 197 intangible with an adjusted basis greater than its fair market value —are treated as a single asset for Code Sec. 1245 recapture purposes (see ¶2695). (Code Sec. 1245(b)(8))[42]

For depreciation of intangibles that aren't section 197 intangibles, see ¶1903.

For property acquired before Aug. 11, '93, (except for certain elections), the 15-year amortization provisions didn't apply. [43]

¶ 1979   Amortizable section 197 intangible.

An amortizable section 197 intangible is any section 197 intangible acquired (after Aug. 10, '93) and held in connection with the conduct of a trade or business or a Code Sec. 212 production-of-income activity. (Code Sec. 197(c)(1)) An acquisition may be made in the form of

---

37. ¶L-12700; ¶14,00I4; TD ¶269,300
38. ¶L-7951; ¶1974; TD ¶269,002
39. ¶L-7977; ¶1974; TD ¶269,015
40. ¶L-7983 *et seq.*; ¶1974; TD ¶269,010

41. ¶L-7951; ¶1974; TD ¶269,002
42. ¶I-10219.1; ¶12,454.05
43. ¶L-7951; ¶1974; TD ¶269,002

a stock acquisition or redemption. [44] Amortizable section 197 intangibles include: [45]

. . . goodwill (Code Sec. 197(d)(1)(A); Reg § 1.197-2(b)(1)),[46]

. . . going concern value (Code Sec. 197(d)(1)(B); Reg § 1.197-2(b)(2)),[47]

. . . workforce in place (Code Sec. 197(d)(1)(C)(i); Reg § 1.197-2(b)(3)),[48]

. . . business books and records, operating systems, or any other information base (including lists or other information with respect to current or prospective customers) (Code Sec. 197(d)(1)(C)(ii); Reg § 1.197-2(b)(4)),[49]

. . . any patent, copyright, formula, process, design, pattern, know-how, format or similar item (Code Sec. 197(d)(1)(C)(iii); Reg § 1.197-2(b)(5)),[50]

. . . customer-based intangibles (Code Sec. 197(d)(1)(C)(iv); Reg § 1.197-2(b)(6)), including the deposit base and any similar asset of a financial institution. (Code Sec. 197(d)(2)(B)) Customer based intangibles are the composition of market, share, and any other value resulting from the future provision of goods or services out of relationships with customers (contractual or otherwise) in the ordinary course of business (Code Sec. 197(d)(2)(A)),[1]

. . . supplier-based intangibles. (Code Sec. 197(d)(1)(C)(v)) Supplier-based intangibles are the value resulting from the future acquisitions of goods or services out of relationships (contractual or otherwise) in the ordinary course of business with suppliers of goods or services to be used or sold by the taxpayer (Code Sec. 197(d)(3); Reg § 1.197-2(b)(7)),[2]

. . . government granted licenses, permits or other right (Code Sec. 197(d)(1)(D); Reg § 1.197-2(b)(8)),[3] and

. . . franchises, trademarks and trade names. (Code Sec. 197(d)(1)(F); Reg § 1.197-2(b)(10))[4]

⚡ caution: Certain patents, copyrights, and government granted rights (above) qualify only if acquired with the acquisition of a business, see below.

Section 197 intangibles also include any other item that is similar to workforce in place, information base, know-how, customer-based intangibles or supplier-based intangibles. (Code Sec. 197(d)(1)(C)(vi))[5]

The following intangibles are treated as section 197 intangibles only if acquired in connection with the acquisition of a business: [6]

. . . Covenant not to compete or similar arrangements. (Code Sec. 197(d)(1)(E); Reg § 1.197-2(b)(9))[7]

. . . Computer software (generally, programs designed to cause a computer to perform a desired function). (Code Sec. 197(e)(3)(B)) (For computer software excluded from 15-year amortization, see ¶1980. For software developed by the taxpayer, see ¶1664.)

. . . Films, sound recordings, video tapes and books. (Code Sec. 197(e)(4)(A); Reg § 1.197-2(c)(4))[8]

. . . Copyrights and patents. (Code Sec. 197(e)(4)(C))

. . . Rights to receive tangible property or services under a contract granted by the government. (Code Sec. 197(e)(4)(B))

. . . Contract rights and government grants if the right has a fixed duration of less than 15 years, or is fixed in amount and, without regard to Code Sec. 197 would be recoverable under a method similar to the unit of production method. (Code Sec. 197(e)(4)(D);

---

44. ¶L-7966; ¶1974; TD ¶269,002
45. ¶L-7952 *et seq.*; ¶1974; TD ¶269,002
46. ¶L-7953; ¶1974; TD ¶269,004
47. ¶L-7953; ¶1974; TD ¶269,004
48. ¶L-7954; ¶1974; TD ¶269,004
49. ¶L-7955; ¶1974; TD ¶269,004
50. ¶L-7957; ¶1974; TD ¶269,004
1. ¶L-7961; ¶1974; TD ¶269,004

2. ¶L-7964; ¶1974; TD ¶269,004
3. ¶L-7967; ¶1974; TD ¶269,004
4. ¶L-7968; ¶1974; TD ¶269,004
5. ¶L-7952; ¶1974; TD ¶269,004
6. ¶L-7952; ¶1974; TD ¶269,004
7. ¶L-7966; ¶1974; TD ¶269,004
8. ¶L-7958.3; ¶1974; TD ¶269,014

Reg § 1.197-2(c)(13))[9]

¶ 1980 Intangibles excluded from section 197 intangibles.

The following are never treated as section 197 intangibles regardless of how acquired: [10]

... interests in corporations, partnerships, trusts and estates (Code Sec. 197(e)(1)(A)),

... computer software that's readily available for purchase by the general public, is subject to a non-exclusive license, and hasn't been substantially modified. (Code Sec. 197(e)(3)(A)) For 36-month straight line depreciation see ¶1966.

... futures, foreign currency contracts and notional principal contracts (Code Sec. 197(e)(1)(B)),

... land (Code Sec. 197(e)(2)),

... leases of tangible property (Code Sec. 197(e)(5)(A)),

... debt instruments, except for deposit bases and similar items (Code Sec. 197(e)(5)(B)),

... mortgage servicing rights secured by residential real property. (Code Sec. 197(e)(6))

... sports franchises, if acquired before Oct. 23, 2004. (Former IRC § 197(e)(6))

... any fees for professional services or transaction costs incurred by parties to a transaction with respect to which any part of the gain or loss isn't recognized under the rules in Code Secs. 351 through 368 that govern corporate organizations and reorganizations (Code Sec. 197(e)(7)), and

... accounts receivable. (Reg § 1.197-2(b)(6))

Also, intangibles created by the taxpayer (or for the taxpayer by contract) aren't subject to 15-year amortization if they are (1) not (a) certain rights granted by a governmental unit, (b) covenants not to compete made in connection with acquisition of an interest in a trade or business, or (c) franchises, trademarks and trade names, and (2) not created in connection with a transaction (or a series of related transactions) that involves the acquisition of assets which constitute all, or a substantial portion of, a trade or business. (Code Sec. 197(c)(2); Reg § 1.197-2(d)(2))[11]

¶ 1981 Depletion Deduction. ■■■■■■■■■■■■■■■■■■■■■■■■■■■■■■

All exhaustible natural deposits and timber qualify for deduction of a reasonable allowance for depletion based on the taxpayer's cost or other basis of the resources — cost depletion. For mines and certain interests in oil or gas wells, the depletion deductions may be computed as a specified percentage of gross income if that is greater than cost depletion.

A taxpayer can claim percentage depletion on one property and cost depletion on another, or claim, on the same property, cost depletion for one year and percentage for another. [12]

Where the property is entitled to either cost or percentage depletion, the allowable deduction is the greater of the two. (Code Sec. 613)[13] Percentage depletion for oil and gas wells (except for gas from certain domestic geothermal deposits or geopressured brine) is limited to "independent producers and royalty owners," see ¶1984. The allowable deduction is never less than cost depletion. (Code Sec. 611, Code Sec. 612, Code Sec. 613) There's no official form for computing depletion, but Form T must be attached to the income tax return if a deduction for depletion of timber is taken.[14] The basis of the property must be reduced by the depletion deduction allowed or allowable, whichever is larger. [15]

---

9. ¶L-7967; ¶1974; TD ¶269,004
10. ¶L-7952.1, L-7968 *et seq.*; ¶1974; TD ¶269,010
11. ¶L-7975; ¶1974; TD ¶269,013
12. ¶N-2004, N-2250 *et seq.*; ¶6114; TD ¶270,501

13. ¶N-2004; ¶6114; TD ¶270,501
14. ¶N-3101 *et seq.*, ¶N-6107; ¶6114.027; TD ¶270,503
15. ¶N-3009; ¶6124.001; TD ¶214,000

A taxpayer may take a depletion deduction only if he owns an "economic interest" in the mineral deposit or the timber. Owners of an economic interest include: (1) owner-operators; [16] (2) lessors and lessees, [17] even where the lessee has an economic interest under a lease terminable without cause on short notice; [18] (3) owner of a royalty interest, or retained net profits interest; [19] and (4) owners of a production payment to the extent it isn't treated as a mortgage loan. (Reg § 1.611-1(b))

¶ 1982 Cost depletion.

This deduction is based on the property's adjusted basis, the number of recoverable units of mineral at the beginning of the year and the number of units sold or for which payment is received during the year. (Reg § 1.611-2(a)) An elective safe harbor may be used to determine recoverable oil and gas reserves. [20] Taxpayer's total cost depletion deductions can't exceed his basis for the mineral property. [21]

Basis for cost depletion and gain or loss is its cost or other basis plus or minus basis adjustments. (Code Sec. 612) It doesn't include the basis of nonmineral property, such as amounts recoverable through depreciation, or the residual value of land and improvements at the end of operations. (Reg § 1.612-1(b)(1)) [22] Additional basis adjustments also apply to natural resources. (Code Sec. 1016(a))

¶ 1983 Percentage depletion.

This is a specified percentage of the "gross income from the property" for the tax year. It can never exceed 50% (100% for oil and gas properties) of taxable income from the property before deducting depletion. (Code Sec. 613(a)) For this purpose, taxable income from the property is the excess of gross income from the property over the allowable deductions (exclusive of depletion) attributable to the mining processes (including mining transportation) on which depletion is claimed. (Reg § 1.613-5(a)) [23]

The 100%-of-taxable-income limit doesn't apply to so much of the depletion allowance as is determined under the rules relating to oil and gas produced from marginal properties (¶1984) for any tax year beginning before 2008. (Code Sec. 613A(c)(6)(H))

caution: Check http://ria.thomson.com/federaltaxhandbook to see if the provision discussed above has been extended.

Percentage depletion, like cost depletion, reduces basis. But percentage depletion continues to be deductible as long as there is gross income from the property even after taxpayer's basis for the property has been reduced to zero. Cost depletion is to be used where higher than percentage depletion. (Code Sec. 613(a)) [24]

A corporation's deductible depletion allowance for iron ore or coal (including lignite) is cut back by 20% of the otherwise allowable percentage depletion deduction in excess of the adjusted basis of the property at the close of the tax year (determined without regard to the depletion deduction for the tax year). (Code Sec. 291(a)(2)) For when the cutback applies to an S corporation, see ¶1972.

The minerals listed below qualify for percentage depletion at the rates shown. (Code Sec. 613(b); Reg § 1.613-2(b)) [25]

---

16. ¶N-2056; ¶6114; TD ¶270,504
17. ¶N-2058 *et seq.*; ¶6114.018; TD ¶270,506
18. ¶N-2058 *et seq.*; ¶6114.018
19. ¶N-2055; ¶6114.007; TD ¶270,504
20. ¶N-2255.2; TD ¶270,701

21. ¶N-2250 *et seq.*; ¶6114.020 *et seq.*; TD ¶270,701
22. ¶N-3000 *et seq.*; ¶s 6124, 6124.001; TD ¶270,703
23. ¶N-2702; ¶6134.009 *et seq.*; TD ¶271,013
24. ¶N-2300 *et seq.*; ¶6114; TD ¶271,000 *et seq.*
25. ¶N-2311; ¶s 2914, 6134 *et seq.*; TD ¶271,002

	Rate (%)
Oil and gas	(See ¶1984)
Sulphur and uranium	22
U.S. deposits of: anorthosite, clay, laterite, and nephelite syenite (to the extent that alumina and aluminum compounds are extracted therefrom), asbestos, bauxite, celestite, chromite, corundum, fluorspar, graphite, ilmenite, kyanite, mica, olivine, quartz crystals (radio grade), rutile, block steatite talc and zircon	22
U.S. deposits of ores of antimony, beryllium, bismuth, cadmium, cobalt, columbium, lead, lithium, manganese, mercury, molybdenum, nickel, platinum and platinum group metals, tantalum, thorium, tin, titanium, tungsten, vanadium and zinc	22
U.S. deposits of: gold, silver, copper, and iron ore and oil shale	15
Geothermal deposits in U.S. or its possessions	15
Metal mines that don't qualify for 22% or 15% rate, above	14
Rock asphalt and vermiculite	14
Ball clay, bentonite, china clay, sagger clay, and refractory clay exclusive of clay entitled to the 22% rate, above, or to 7½% or 5% rates	14
Asbestos (not entitled to 22% rate above), brucite, coal, lignite, perlite, sodium chloride and wollastonite	10
Natural gas from geopressurized brine from U.S. wells drilled after Sept. '78 and before '84	10
Clay and shale used or sold for use in the manufacture of sewer pipe or brick, and clay, shale, and slate used or sold for use as sintered or burned lightweight aggregates	7½
Clay used or sold for use, in the manufacture of drainage and roofing tile, flower pots and kindred products	5
Gravel, peat, pumice, sand, scoria, shale (other than shale entitled to 15% or 7 ½% rates, above) and stone (other than dimension and ornamental stone)	5
Bromine, calcium chloride and magnesium chloride (if from brine wells)	5
Other minerals: 14%, except generally 5% if used or sold as rip rap, ballast, road material, rubble, concrete aggregates or for similar purposes.	

Natural resources that don't qualify for percentage depletion include timber (Reg § 1.611-1(a)), minerals from sea water and other inexhaustible sources. (Code Sec. 613(b)(7)) Coal or iron ore disposed of with a retained economic interest that qualifies for capital gain-ordinary loss treatment doesn't qualify for percentage depletion. (Reg § 1.611-1(b)(2))[26] For the treatment of percentage depletion for alternative minimum tax purposes, see ¶3207.

¶ 1984　　Oil, gas and geothermal deposits percentage depletion.

Percentage depletion applies to oil and gas only in the following cases: [27]

• *Crude oil and natural gas production of independent producers and royalty owners.* 15% depletion is allowed a taxpayer who isn't a retailer or refiner for so much of his "average daily production" of domestic crude oil and domestic natural gas as doesn't exceed his "depletable oil quantity" or "depletable natural gas quantity." "Marginal production" may qualify for a higher percentage depletion rate (not to exceed 25%; for 2007, the percentage is 15%)[28] if the price of domestic crude oil is below $20 for the calendar year preceding the calendar year in which the tax year in question begins. (Code Sec. 613A(c)(6))

---

26. ¶N-2314; ¶s 6114.023, 6314.04; TD ¶271,003　　　　28. ¶N-2425; ¶613A4; TD ¶271,018
27. ¶N-2400 *et seq.*; ¶613A4; TD ¶271,014

The maximum depletable amount is 1,000 barrels of oil or 6,000,000 cubic feet of gas per day. A taxpayer who has both crude oil and natural gas production allocates the maximum depletable amount between oil and gas at the rate of 6,000 cubic feet of gas per barrel of oil. Over-ceiling production isn't entitled to any depletion. (Code Sec. 613(d), Code Sec. 613A)

The deduction can't exceed 65% of the taxpayer's taxable income from all sources. (Code Sec. 613A(d)) Also, the deduction for any costs for which taxpayer claims the 15% enhanced oil recovery credit (¶2321) must be reduced by that credit amount. (Code Sec. 43(d)(1))

• *Production of natural heat from geothermal deposits and natural gas production from geopressured brine* located in the U.S. or its possession. (Code Sec. 613(e), Code Sec. 613A(b)(2))[29]

Percentage depletion isn't available with respect to any lease bonus, advance royalty or other amount payable without regard to production from any oil, gas or geothermal property. (Code Sec. 613(e)(3), Code Sec. 613A(d)(5))[30] The restriction on the use of percentage depletion applies only to oil and natural gas; other minerals from oil and gas wells can qualify. [31] Partnerships (¶3717) and S corporations (¶3362) aren't allowed depletion deductions. [32]

¶ 1985   Related and commonly controlled producers.

The depletable ceiling amounts applicable to oil or gas production of independent producers or royalty owners who are related or are under common control is allocated among them. Allocation is required among corporations that are part of a controlled group; corporations, trusts and estates owned by the same or related persons; and an individual and his spouse and minor children. (Code Sec. 613A(c)(8))[33]

¶ 1986   Aggregation and division of depletable property.

Cost or percentage depletion must be computed separately for each property. (Code Sec. 612, Code Sec. 613)[34] A "property" is each separate interest owned by the taxpayer in each separate tract or parcel of land. (Code Sec. 614(a)) "Interest" means economic interest. It includes working or operating interests, royalties, overriding royalties and net profits interests. It also includes production payments to the extent they aren't treated as loans. (Reg § 1.614-1(a)(2)) Separate properties may be aggregated and treated as a single property. (Code Sec. 614(b), Code Sec. 614(c), Code Sec. 614(e)) A single interest in a "mine" may be treated as two or more separate properties, at the taxpayer's election. (Code Sec. 614(c)(2); Reg § 1.614-3(b))

29. ¶N-2316; ¶s 6134.001, 613A4; TD ¶271,014
30. ¶N-2105 *et seq.*; ¶613A4.02; TD ¶271,010
31. ¶N-2400 *et seq.*; TD ¶271,014

32. ¶N-2431, ¶N-2440; ¶613A4
33. ¶N-2420; ¶613A4; TD ¶271,026
34. ¶N-2901; ¶6114 *et seq.*; TD ¶271,027

Chapter 6 Charitable Contributions—Medical Expenses— Alimony—Other Nonbusiness Deductions

¶ 2100 Charitable Contribution Deduction. ▬▬▬▬▬▬▬▬▬▬▬

An individual who itemizes can deduct charitable contributions up to 50%, 30% or 20% of his adjusted gross income, depending on the type of property contributed and the type of donee. A corporation generally can deduct charitable contributions up to 10% of its taxable income. Amounts that exceed the ceilings can be carried forward for five years. The deduction allowed for property contributions is usually the property's fair market value, but the deduction is reduced for gifts of certain types of property.

For individuals, charitable contributions are deductible only as an itemized deduction on Schedule A (Form 1040). (Reg § 1.170A-1(a))[1]

⚡caution: The itemized deduction for charitable contributions is subject to reduction if adjusted gross income exceeds specified amounts, see ¶3114.

For the charity's requirement to disclose the deductibility of contributions to it, see ¶4118.

¶ 2101 What is a deductible charitable contribution?

A deductible charitable contribution generally is one that:

. . . is to or for the use of a qualified charitable organization (¶2102) (Code Sec. 170(c));

. . . is paid within the taxpayer's tax year, regardless of the taxpayer's accounting method (¶2133) (except for certain accrual basis corporations, see ¶2134) (Code Sec. 170(a));

. . . is within the applicable statutory ceilings for individuals (¶2124 et seq.), and corporations (¶2132) (Code Sec. 170(b)); and

. . . meets certain substantiation requirements (¶2135 et seq.). (Reg § 1.170A-13)[2]

¶ 2102 Qualified charitable organizations.

A qualified charitable organization is one that fits into one of the categories specified in the law and which IRS has ruled (or the donor establishes) is eligible to receive deductible charitable contributions.[3] IRS Pub. No. 78, "Cumulative List of Organizations described in Section 170(c)," lists qualified charitable organizations, but isn't exhaustive. [4]

Qualified charitable organizations include:

. . . a corporation, trust, community chest, fund or foundation (including a private foundation) that is organized and operated exclusively for charitable, religious, educational, scientific or literary purposes, or for the prevention of cruelty to children or animals, or to foster and conduct national or international amateur sports competition (but only if none of the activities involves providing athletic facilities or equipment); and that is organized or created in the U.S. or its possessions, or under their laws; and none of whose net earnings inures to the benefit of any private shareholder or individual. Corporate contributions to noncorporate donees must be used in the U.S. or its possessions (Code Sec. 170(c)(2));[5]

. . . U.S. states or possessions, their political subdivisions, the U.S., and the District of Columbia, but only if the gift is exclusively for public purposes (Code Sec. 170(c)(1));[6]

---

1. ¶A-2701; ¶1704.01; TD ¶330,201
2. ¶K-2803; ¶1704 et seq.; TD ¶330,202
3. ¶K-2850 et seq.; ¶1704.20; TD ¶330,265

4. ¶K-2945; ¶1704.21; TD ¶330,279
5. ¶K-2862 et seq.; ¶1704.20 et seq.; TD ¶330,269
6. ¶K-2899; ¶1704.25; TD ¶330,274

References beginning with a single letter are to paragraphs in RIA's Federal Tax Coordinator 2d and RIA's Analysis of Federal Taxes: Income. Those beginning with numbers are to paragraphs in RIA's United States Tax Reporter. Those beginning with TD are to paragraphs in RIA's Tax Desk.

. . . certain war veterans' organizations, (Code Sec. 170(c)(3));[7] certain domestic fraternal societies, orders or associations, (Code Sec. 170(c)(4))[8]; and certain nonprofit cemetery companies. (Code Sec. 170(c)(5))[9]

¶ 2103 Charitable deductions barred for certain contributions.

No charitable deduction is allowed for the following types of contributions:

. . . A contribution to a charity that conducts lobbying activities on matters of direct financial interest to the donor's trade or business, if a principal purpose of the contribution was to avoid federal income tax by getting a charitable deduction for lobbying expenses for which a business expense deduction would be disallowed (¶1626) if the donor had conducted the activities directly. (Code Sec. 170(f)(9))[10]

. . . A contribution to an organization which is disqualified from tax exemption because a substantial part of its activities is lobbying, or if it participates in any political campaign. (Reg § 1.170A-1(j)(5))[11]

. . . A contribution made to or for an individual (except for certain students, see ¶2123), unless made to the individual as an agent for a qualified organization (¶2102).[12]

. . . A transfer to charity to the extent the donor derives an economic benefit (for exception, see (¶2104). Thus, no charitable deduction is allowed for: tuition (or required "donation" of excess "tuition" payment) even for parochial school; or[13] a payment in connection with a person's admission to an old age or retirement home operated by a charity, to the extent allocable to care to be given (may be partly a *medical* expense, see ¶2147) or the privilege of being admitted. [14]

. . . vacation, sick, or personal leave given up by an employee in exchange for his employer's contributions of amounts to a charity under a leave-sharing program. [15]

. . . Contributions of clothing and household items that are not in good used condition or better (but deduction may be allowed if amount claimed for the item exceeds $500 and the taxpayer includes a qualified appraisal of the item with his return). Household items include furniture, furnishings, electronics, appliances, linens, and similar items, but don't include food, paintings, antiques, and other art objects, jewelry, gems, or collections. IRS may also deny a deduction for any contribution of clothing or a household item with minimal monetary value, such as used socks or undergarments. IRS says the price a buyer actually pays for a used item in a store such as a thrift shop is an indication of value, but dismissed as inaccurate "standard value listings" supplied by organizations like the Salvation Army. It also says valuation under a fixed formula or method (e.g., percentage of replacement cost), doesn't work well for used clothing. (Code Sec. 170(f)(16))[16]

¶ 2104 Fundraising events, entertainment, etc., for charity.

Where amounts are paid in connection with admission to fundraising events for charity (e.g., shows, lotteries and athletic events), the receipt of tickets or other privileges raises a presumption that the payment isn't a gift. Taxpayer must show that a clearly identifiable part of the payment is a gift. Only the part made with the intention of making a gift *and* for which taxpayer receives no consideration qualifies as a contribution. [17] The charity must show (in its solicitation, tickets, receipts or other related documents) the value (or reasonable

---

7. ¶K-2915; ¶1704.27; TD ¶330,275
8. ¶K-2921; ¶1704.26; TD ¶330,276
9. ¶K-2925; ¶1704.28; TD ¶330,277
10. ¶K-2804; ¶1624.395; TD ¶330,204
11. ¶K-2871; ¶1704.30; TD ¶332,613
12. ¶K-2953; ¶1704.20; TD ¶330,203

13. ¶K-3110, K-3111; ¶1704.38; TD ¶330,242
14. ¶K-3047; ¶1704.38; TD ¶330,231
15. ¶H-1013; TD ¶130,507
16. ¶K-3177.6; ¶1704.41.
17. ¶K-3089; ¶1704.38; TD ¶330,245

estimate) of the event, and how much of the contribution is deductible. [18] For an organization's fundraising disclosure requirements, see ¶4119.

However, the donor may deduct a contribution in full if the benefit is inconsequential or insubstantial. This applies if the charity informs patrons how much is deductible *and* any of these tests is met: (1) the fair market value (FMV) of all benefits received in connection with the payment is not more than 2% of the payment, or the following dollar figures: $89 for 2007 ($91 for 2008), if less; or (2) the payment is at least $44.50 for 2007 ($45.50 for 2008) and in connection with it the donor receives only token benefits (bookmarks, calendars, mugs, posters, tee shirts, etc.) generally costing less than $8.90 for 2007 ($9.10 for 2008), or (3) the charity mails or otherwise distributes free, unordered items to patrons. [19]

A taxpayer may rely on either a contemporaneous written acknowledgment (for contributions of $250 or more, see ¶2137) or a written disclosure statement (for quid pro quo contributions of more than $75, see ¶4119) for the FMV of any goods or services he receives from the charity. The taxpayer can't treat an estimate as the FMV where he knows, or has reason to know, it's unreasonable. (Reg § 1.170A-1(h)(4))[20] Payment to a college or university where the donor receives a *right to buy* seating at an athletic event (even in a skybox) is 80% deductible as a contribution. No amount paid for the tickets themselves is deductible. (Code Sec. 170(l))[21] Taxpayer's failure to use the ticket, etc., doesn't increase the amount of the deduction. [22]

Amounts paid for raffle tickets, to play bingo, etc., aren't contributions [23] (for deduction as a gambling loss, see ¶1786).

¶ 2105 Charitable contribution v. business expense.

Transfers to a charity that are directly related to a taxpayer's business and are made with a "reasonable expectation of financial return commensurate with" the amount transferred may be deductible as business expenses, and not as charitable contributions. But no business expense deduction is allowed for the transfer if *any* part of it is deductible as a charitable contribution. (Reg § 1.162-15(a)(2))[24]

observation: Business expense treatment may be preferable where the "contribution" exceeds the charitable deduction ceiling, ¶2124 *et seq.*

¶ 2106 Gift of property.

A gift of property to a qualified charitable donee (¶2102) is a charitable contribution to the extent of the property's fair market value (FMV) at the time of the gift, whether or not it has appreciated (Reg § 1.170A-1(c)), except for gifts of ordinary income-type property (¶2107), and certain gifts of tangible personal property or capital gain property (¶2110).[25] For substantiation requirements, see ¶2136.

The property's FMV is reduced for restrictions placed by the donor on marketability or use (e.g., 3-year bar on transfer or license of donated patent). [26]

No gain is realized on a charitable contribution of appreciated property (except for certain bargain sales, see ¶2112).[27]

observation: This means the taxpayer can deduct his basis in the property plus his paper profit, which he isn't taxable on.

---

18. ¶K-3105; ¶1704.38; TD ¶330,257
19. ¶K-3106; ¶1704.38; TD ¶330,262
20. ¶K-3087.2; ¶1704.38; TD ¶334,016
21. ¶K-3100; ¶1704.38; TD ¶330,256
22. ¶K-3094; TD ¶330,250

23. ¶K-3090; ¶1704.38; TD ¶330,246
24. ¶K-3068 *et seq.*; ¶1624.363; TD ¶334,700 *et seq.*
25. ¶K-3150 *et seq.*; ¶1704.40 *et seq.*; TD ¶331,601
26. ¶K-3151; TD ¶331,601
27. ¶K-3208 *et seq.*, ¶K-3179 *et seq.*; ¶1704.43; TD ¶331,679

Taxpayer's charitable deduction for the gift can't exceed the property's FMV (at contribution), even if it's less than his basis. [28] Nor is taxpayer allowed a loss deduction on the difference between the property's basis and FMV. [29]

Special rules apply to gifts of patents [30] and taxidermy property. [31]

¶ 2107 Gift of ordinary income-type appreciated property—deduction reduced.

For charitable gifts of ordinary income-type property (below), the amount contributed (property's fair market value (FMV), ¶2106) must be reduced by the amount which would have been recognized as gain other than long-term capital gain if the property had been sold by the donor for its then FMV. (Code Sec. 170(e)(1))[32] For exceptions, see ¶2108 *et seq.*

Ordinary income-type property is property which, if sold by taxpayer (donor) at its FMV on the date it was contributed, would have resulted in *some* amount of gain other than long-term capital gain. (Code Sec. 170(e)(1)) This includes: inventory or other property held for sale to customers; Code Sec. 306 stock (¶3535 *et seq.*); capital assets held for less than the long-term holding period as of the date contributed; property subject to depreciation, etc., recapture; property used in taxpayer's trade or business; and art works, letters, memoranda and similar property created by or for taxpayer. (Reg § 1.170A-4(b))[33]

For contributions before Jan. 1, 2008, taxpayers that aren't C corporations and donate "apparently wholesome food" inventory to eligible charities are entitled to the same enhanced deduction available to C corporations (see ¶2108), except that the deduction can't exceed 10% of net income as specially calculated. (Code Sec. 170(e)(3)(C)(i)(I))[34]

⚡*caution:* Check http://ria.thomson.com/federaltaxhandbook to see if this provision has been extended.

¶ 2108 Enhanced deductions for C corporation gifts of property for specific purposes.

A C corporation may claim an enhanced deduction equal to the lesser of (a) basis plus half of the property's appreciation, or (b) twice the property's basis, for:

(1) Contributions of inventory, property held primarily for sale to customers in the ordinary course of its trade or business, or depreciable or real property used in its trade or business, if the contribution is to an exempt Code Sec. 501(c)(3) organization (other than certain private foundations) that uses the property solely for the care of the ill, the needy or infants, and that meets other specified requirements. (Code Sec. 170(e)(3)(A))[35]

(2) Contributions before Jan. 1, 2008, of (a) food inventory (it must be apparently wholesome food, i.e., meant for human consumption and meet certain quality and labeling standards); and (b) qualified contributions of book inventory to certain public schools if donee certification requirements are met. (Code Sec. 170(e)(3)(C), Code Sec. 170(e)(3)(D))[36]

(3) Certain contributions of scientific equipment or apparatus constructed by the taxpayer to a higher education institution or a tax-exempt organization (but not a private foundation) organized and operated primarily to conduct scientific research. (Code Sec. 170(e)(4))[37]

(4) For tax years beginning before 2008, certain contributions of computer technology or equipment (software, computer or peripheral equipment, and fiber optic cable) to schools or libraries for use in the U.S. for educational purposes that is related to the donee's purpose

---

28. ¶K-3151; ¶1704.41; TD ¶331,601
29. ¶M-1015; TD ¶331,679
30. ¶K-3177.1; ¶1704.42; TD ¶331,616.2
31. ¶K-3171.1
32. ¶K-3158 *et seq.*; ¶1704.42; TD ¶331,609

33. ¶K-3161; ¶1704.42; TD ¶331,610
34. ¶K-3201.1; ¶1704.42; TD ¶331,702
35. ¶K-3201 *et seq.*; ¶1704.42; TD ¶331,701 *et seq.*
36. ¶K-3201 *et seq.*; ¶1704.42; TD ¶331,701 *et seq.*
37. ¶K-3221 *et seq.*; ¶1704.42; TD ¶331,721 *et seq.*

or function. (Code Sec. 170(e)(6))[38]

⊘*caution:* Check http://ria.thomson.com/federaltaxhandbook to see if provisions (2) and (4), above have been extended.

¶ 2109 Property contribution where taxpayer realizes income on gift.

If a taxpayer realizes income (ordinary income or capital gain) on his gift of property, his charitable deduction isn't subject to the reduction described at ¶2107. Thus, he may deduct the full fair market value of donated installment obligations, obligations issued at a discount, or other receivables. (Reg § 1.170A-4(a))[39]

¶ 2110 Limits on contributions of tangible personal property; gifts to certain private foundations.

For certain gifts, the amount treated as contributed and deductible (subject to deduction ceilings, see ¶2124 *et seq.*) is the property's fair market value (FMV) *reduced* by the total amount of the gain that would have been long-term capital gain (determined without regard to Code Sec. 1221(b)(3), see ¶2622) if the property were sold for its then FMV. (Code Sec. 170(e)(1)(B))[40] The donor's charitable deduction is thus limited to his basis for these contributions:

. . . tangible personal property that's unrelated to the donee's exempt function (e.g., art to a church that then sells it) (Code Sec. 170(e)(1)(B)(i)); and

. . . any capital gain property except for publicly traded stock (limited to aggregate contributions of not more than 10% of the value of a corporation's outstanding stock by a donor and his family) given to a private foundation that isn't an operating foundation or community foundation and that doesn't make timely qualifying distributions. (Code Sec. 170(e)(1)(B)(ii), Code Sec. 170(e)(5)).[41]

Contributions of tangible personal property for which a FMV deduction is claimed, but which is not used for exempt purposes, if the donee sells or disposes of tangible personal property with a claimed value of at least $5,000: (1) in the year of contribution, the deduction is limited to the taxpayer's basis; or (2) after the year of contribution but within the 3 year period beginning on the contribution date, the donor includes in income the amount of the claimed deduction in excess of his basis in the property. These rules do not apply if the organization makes a proper certification to IRS. A $10,000 penalty applies for fraudulent identifications of property (i.e., stating it is exempt use property while knowing it was not intended for such use). (Code Sec. 170(e)(1)(B)(i)(II), Code Sec. 170(e)(7), Code Sec. 6720B)[42]

¶ 2111 Liabilities transferred as part of contribution.

The donor's charitable contribution must be reduced by any liability that's assumed (e.g., by the donee) in connection with the gift. (Reg § 1.170A-3(d)) Where the donor transfers property subject to a liability, the amount of that debt is treated as an amount realized for purposes of the bargain sale rules, see ¶2112 (but not for the rule at ¶2109).[43]

A reduction also must be made for the amount of any interest on the liability attributable to any period after the contribution was made. (Code Sec. 170(f)(5))[44]

---

38. ¶K-3241 *et seq.*; ¶1704.42; TD ¶331,741 *et seq.*
39. ¶K-3178 *et seq.*; TD ¶331,618
40. ¶K-3167 *et seq.*; ¶1704.42; TD ¶331,615
41. ¶K-3167 *et seq.*; ¶1704.42; TD ¶331,615

42. ¶K-3167; ¶V-2704.1; ¶1704.42.
43. ¶K-3155, K-3198; ¶1704.44; TD ¶331,605
44. ¶K-3157; ¶1704.44; TD ¶331,607

¶ 2112 Bargain sale to charity.

A taxpayer who sells property to (or exchanges it with) a charity and receives less than its fair market value (FMV) may treat the "bargain" element as a charitable contribution. (Code Sec. 1011(b); Reg § 1.170A-4(c)(2)) In computing the deduction, the amount considered contributed (excess of FMV over selling price) must be reduced by the amount of any required adjustment for ordinary income-type appreciated property (¶2107) for the contribution portion. (Reg § 1.170A-4(c), Reg § 1.1011-2(a))[45]

But the donor generally also realizes taxable gain on the sale. His basis for measuring gain is only the portion of his total cost or other basis for the property that the bargain selling price (amount realized) bears to its FMV. (Code Sec. 1011(b); Reg § 1.1011-2) This is basis times the selling price, divided by FMV. (Reg § 1.170A-4(c)(2)(i))[46]

Illustration: J owns long-term stock that cost $12,000 and is worth $20,000 when he sells it to charity for $12,000. A contribution deduction of $8,000 ($20,000 – $12,000) is allowable. J's basis for the stock is reduced to $7,200 ($12,000 cost × $12,000 selling price ÷ $20,000 FMV) against his $12,000 selling price, giving J a $4,800 taxable gain. [47]

¶ 2113 Gift of stock to charity followed by redemption ("charitable bail-out").

Owners of closely held corporations may in effect withdraw earnings from their firms tax-free by making a charitable contribution of their corporate stock, which the corporation then redeems. As long as the charity has no legal obligation to sell back the stock, the donor is allowed a charitable deduction even if the redemption was preplanned. [48] However, a contribution of stock which is then redeemed from a private foundation may be subject to self-dealing penalty excise taxes (¶4127).

¶ 2114 Contributions of partial interests in property.

For transfers in trust, a contribution of a partial interest in property (e.g., where the donor transfers only his right to use the property, ¶2120, or his income interest in it) qualifies for a charitable deduction if the interest is:

- a remainder interest transferred to a charitable remainder trust (CRT, ¶2116), or a pooled income fund (¶2117), (Code Sec. 170(f)(2)(A)); or
- an income interest in a charitable lead trust (¶2119). (Code Sec. 170(f)(2)(B))[49]

For transfers not in trust, no charitable deduction is allowed for a contribution of less than the donor's entire interest in the donated property except to the extent the deduction would have been allowed had the transfer been in trust. (Code Sec. 170(f)(3)(A))[50] However, this bar doesn't apply to contributions of:

- A remainder interest in a personal residence or a farm. (Code Sec. 170(f)(3)(B)(i));[1]
- An undivided portion of taxpayer's entire interest (even if partial) in property (Code Sec. 170(f)(3)(B)(ii)), such as a remainder or income interest. [2] No deduction is allowed for a contribution of an undivided portion of a taxpayer's entire interest in tangible personal property unless, immediately before the contribution, all interests in the property are held by the taxpayer or the taxpayer and the donee. Additionally, the FMV of any additional contribution of a fractional interest in property is the lesser of: (1) its FMV at the time of the initial fractional contribution, or (2) its FMV at the time of the additional contribution.

45. ¶K-3190; ¶1704.43; TD ¶331,690
46. ¶K-3194; ¶1704.43; TD ¶331,690
47. ¶K-3194; ¶1704.43; TD ¶331,690
48. ¶K-3186; TD ¶331,686

49. ¶K-3250 *et seq.*; ¶1704.46; TD ¶331,619 *et seq.*
50. ¶K-3250 *et seq.*; ¶1704.45; TD ¶331,619 *et seq.*
1. ¶K-3440 *et seq.*; ¶1704.45; TD ¶331,619
2. ¶K-3451 *et seq.*; ¶1704.45; TD ¶331,621

(Code Sec. 170(o)(1)(A), Code Sec. 170(o)(2)) The deduction is recaptured under certain circumstances. (Code Sec. 170(o)(3)(A), Code Sec. 2522(e)(3)(A)) Similar rules apply for transfer-tax purposes.[3]

• A partial interest in property where *all* of taxpayer's interests in the property are given to one or more charities (e.g., income interest to one charity and remainder interest to another charity). (Reg § 1.170A-6(a));[4]

• A partial interest in real property (including remainders and perpetual restrictions) exclusively for "conservation purposes," including qualifying facade easements. (Code Sec. 170(f)(3)(B)(iii), Code Sec. 170(h))[5] A facade easement must, among other things: preserve the building's entire exterior and prohibit any change inconsistent with its historical character; donee and donor must enter into a written agreement certifying that donee is able and committed to manage and enforce the restriction; and (for contributions made in a tax year beginning after Aug. 17, 2006) a donor must include with the tax return an appraisal, pictures of the property, description of the restriction, and (for contributions made after Feb. 13, 2007) pay a $500 fee for deductions exceeding $10,000. The deduction is reduced to reflect any rehabilitation credits claimed for the property during the preceding five years. (Code Sec. 170(f)(13), Code Sec. 170(h))[6]

¶ 2115   No charitable deduction for "personal benefit contract" (charitable split-dollar insurance) transactions.

No charitable deduction is allowed for a transfer to or for the use of a charity if the charity directly or indirectly pays or paid any premium on any personal benefit contract (e.g., split-dollar life insurance, see ¶1267) for the transferor. Also, no deduction is allowed if there is an understanding or expectation that any person will directly or indirectly pay any premium on any such contract for the transferor. A charity must pay an excise tax (use Form 8870) if it or any such person pays such premiums. (Code Sec. 170(f)(10))[7]

¶ 2116   Charitable remainder trusts (CRTs)—CRATs and CRUTs.

A charitable remainder trust (CRT) is a trust formed to make current distributions to one or more noncharitable income beneficiaries and to pay the entire remainder to charity or use it for a charitable purpose, that is *either* a "charitable remainder annuity trust" (CRAT) or a "charitable remainder unitrust" (CRUT). (Code Sec. 664(d); Reg § 1.664-1)[8]

¶ 2117   Pooled income funds.

A pooled income fund is a trust formed to pay income to one or more noncharitable beneficiaries and the remainder to charity. It must be maintained by the donee charity (no donor or income beneficiary may be a trustee) and meet certain other requirements. (Code Sec. 642(c)(5); Reg § 1.642(c)-5)[9]

¶ 2118   Contributions to donor advised funds.

Donor advised funds (DAFs) are charitable accounts set up and sponsored by an organization to which donors contribute and provide advice on the account's distributions and investments, although the sponsoring organization must have final say on the actual distributions and investments. Post-Feb. 13, 2007 contributions to DAFs are deductible only if: (1) the sponsoring organization is not one listed in Code Sec. 170(f)(18)(A) (e.g., a war veteran's

3. ¶K-3472.2; ¶1704.45
4. ¶K-3473; ¶1704.45; TD ¶331,621
5. ¶K-3473 *et seq.*; ¶1704.45; TD ¶331,625
6. ¶K-3473 *et seq.*; ¶1704.45; TD ¶331,625

7. ¶K-3661, K-3667; ¶1704.305; TD ¶331,622
8. ¶K-3261 *et seq.*, ¶K-3291 *et seq.*; TD ¶331,629
9. ¶K-3363 *et seq.*; ¶s 1704.46, 6424.03; TD ¶331,632

organization or domestic fraternal lodge); and (2) the donor obtains contemporaneous written acknowledgment from the sponsoring organization certifying it has legal control over the contribution. (Code Sec. 170(f)(18)(A))[10]

¶ 2119 Contribution of income interest in trust—charitable lead trusts.

A charitable deduction is allowed for a contribution of an income interest in trust (remainder to a noncharity) *only* if: (1) the donor is taxable on the trust income, and (2) the donated income interest is either a "guaranteed annuity" or a "unitrust interest." (Code Sec. 170(f)(2)(B); Reg § 1.170A-6) This type of trust is a "charitable lead trust." [11]

¶ 2120 Contributing use of property.

A taxpayer who gives a charity the *right to use* property (e.g., rent-free use of office space), while retaining the property itself, can't take a charitable deduction for the rental or other value of this right (under the partial-interest gift rules, ¶2114). (Code Sec. 170(f)(3)(A))[12]

¶ 2121 Performing services for charity and related deductible transportation expenses.

No charitable deduction is allowed for the value of services a taxpayer renders to charity. (Reg § 1.170A-1(g))[13]

However, the taxpayer is allowed a charitable deduction for his unreimbursed out-of-pocket expenses (for travel expenses, see ¶2122) necessarily incurred in performing services (other than lobbying) free for a charity. (Code Sec. 170(f)(6); Reg § 1.170A-1(g))[14]

A taxpayer who uses his car in performing these services may deduct 14¢ per mile as a contribution (Code Sec. 170(i)) or his actual (unreimbursed) expenses for gas and oil. Parking fees and tolls are deductible in either case, as are deductions otherwise allowable for interest or taxes connected with the car, but not depreciation, insurance and repairs. [15]

¶ 2122 Charitable travel expenses.

No charitable deduction is allowed for taxpayer's travel expenses (including meals and lodging), whether or not reimbursed, while away from home unless there's no significant element of personal pleasure, recreation or vacation in the travel. (Code Sec. 170(j)) Even then, deduction is limited to amounts necessarily incurred for meals and lodging while away from home overnight in rendering these services. [16]

¶ 2123 Maintaining student in taxpayer's home.

A charitable deduction is allowed to a taxpayer who, under a written agreement with a charity and without compensation, maintains an elementary or high school student (who isn't his dependent or relative) in his home. (Code Sec. 170(g); Reg § 1.170A-2)[17] The charitable contribution in any year is the amount so contributed, but not more than $50 times the number of full calendar months (15 days or more is a "month") during the year for which the individual was a member of taxpayer's household and a full-time student. (Code Sec. 170(g); Reg § 1.170A-2(b))[18]

---

10. ¶K-3987; ¶1704.285
11. ¶K-3345 *et seq.*; ¶1704.46; TD ¶331,633
12. ¶K-3440.2; ¶1704.45; TD ¶331,626
13. ¶K-3551; ¶1704.36; TD ¶332,301
14. ¶K-3601 *et seq.*; ¶1704.37; TD ¶332,301 *et seq.*

15. ¶K-3614 *et seq.*; ¶1704.37; TD ¶332,614 *et seq.*
16. ¶K-3620 *et seq.*; ¶s 1704.37, 2744.01; TD ¶332,620 *et seq.*
17. ¶K-3650 *et seq.*; ¶1704.33; TD ¶332,650 *et seq.*
18. ¶K-3651; ¶1704.33; TD ¶332,651

¶ 2124   Charitable deduction ceilings for individuals.

There's a ceiling on the amount an individual may deduct each year as a charitable contribution, based both on the type of property contributed and the type of charity to which the contribution is made. The ceilings (below) for any tax year are a percentage of taxpayer's "contribution base" (below) for the year, subject to an overall 50% ceiling for all charitable gifts. (Code Sec. 170(b)(1))[19] For carryover of excess contributions, see ¶2130.

If the contributions are all to "50% charities" (listed at ¶2125), the year's ceiling is 50% of taxpayer's contribution base for the year, except for contributions of appreciated capital gain property (¶2127). (Code Sec. 170(b)(1)(A))[20]

If the contributions are all to "30% charities" (¶2126), or are "for the use" of *any* charities, the ceiling is 30% of taxpayer's contribution base (except for contributions of appreciated capital gain property, see ¶2127) or, if less, 50% of his contribution base minus his contributions to 50% charities. (Code Sec. 170(b)(1)(B); Reg § 1.170A-8(c))[21]

An individual's "contribution base" for a year is his adjusted gross income (AGI, see ¶3102) for the year, but without deducting any NOL carryback to that year. (Code Sec. 170(b)(1)(F))[22]

For spouses filing joint returns, these ceilings apply to the couple's combined contributions and their combined contribution base. (Reg § 1.170A-2(a)(1), Reg § 1.170A-8(a)(1))[23]

For qualified conservation contributions (i.e., contribution of a qualified real property interest to a qualified organization exclusively for conservation) made in tax years beginning in 2006 and 2007, the 30% limit is 50% of the contribution base less all other charitable contributions, and the carryforward period (¶2130) is 15 years. For qualified farmers and ranchers (more than 50% of gross income from farming as defined at Code Sec. 2032A(e)), the limit is 100% of the contribution base less all other charitable contributions. For property in agriculture or livestock production to be eligible for the 100% limit, the qualified real property interest must include a restriction that the property remain generally available for such production. (Code Sec. 170(b)(1)(E), Code Sec. 170(b)(2)) In a tax year in which an individual has made a qualified conservation contribution and one or more contributions subject to the limitations in Code Sec. 170(b)(1), the qualified conservation contribution may be taken into account only after taking into account contributions subject to the limitations in Code Sec. 170(b)(1).[24]

⓪*caution:* Check http://ria.thomson.com/federaltaxhandbook to see if this provision has been extended.

¶ 2125   50% charities.

For purposes of the deduction ceilings for individuals (¶2124), "50% charities" are:

(1) churches (or church conventions or associations);

(2) tax-exempt educational organizations;

(3) tax-exempt hospitals and certain medical research organizations;

(4) certain organizations holding property for state and local colleges and universities;

(5) a U.S. state or possession, or any political subdivision of any of these, or the U.S. or the District of Columbia, if the contribution is for exclusively public purposes;

(6) organizations organized and operated exclusively for charitable, religious, educational, scientific or literary purposes, or for the prevention of cruelty to children or animals, or to

---

19. ¶K-3670; ¶1704.05; TD ¶333,001
20. ¶K-3671; ¶1704.05; TD ¶333,004
21. ¶s K-3671, K-3674, K-3684 *et seq.*; ¶s 1704.05, 1704.10 *et seq.*;
    TD ¶333,009

22. ¶K-3672; ¶1704.05; TD ¶333,002
23. ¶K-3673; ¶1704.06; TD ¶333,003
24. ¶K-3694.1 *et seq.*; ¶1704.11 *et seq.*

foster national or international amateur sports competition if they normally get a substantial part of their support from the government or general public;

(7) certain private foundations;

(8) certain membership organizations more than one-third of whose support comes from the public. (Code Sec. 170(b)(1)(A))[25]

¶ 2126   30% charities.

For purposes of the ceilings on an individual's charitable deduction (¶2124), "30% charities" are qualifying charitable organizations (¶2102), that aren't 50% charities (¶2125), e.g., war veterans' organizations, fraternal orders, cemetery companies, and certain private non-operating foundations. (Code Sec. 170(b)(1)(B); Reg § 1.170A-8(c))[26]

¶ 2127   Gifts of appreciated capital gain property to 50% charities—30% ceiling.

An individual's deduction ceiling in the tax year for gifts of certain appreciated capital gain property (below) to 50% charities is 30% of his contribution base (¶2124), unless he makes an election to reduce the amount of his contribution (in which case the 50% ceiling applies, see ¶2128). (Code Sec. 170(b)(1)(C))[27] For ceiling on gifts to 30% charities, see ¶2129.

This rule applies to any capital asset which, if sold for fair market value at contribution, would have given rise to long-term capital gain, *other than* property subject to the reduction at ¶2110. (Code Sec. 170(b)(1)(C))[28]

¶ 2128   Individual's election of 50% ceiling for appreciated property contributions.

An individual donor whose gift of capital gain property to a 50% charity is otherwise subject to the 30% ceiling (¶2127) may elect the 50% ceiling for the gift *but only* if he reduces the amount of his contribution (as described at ¶2107)—i.e., his contribution is limited to his basis in the property. (Code Sec. 170(b)(1)(C)(iii))[29]

🅡 recommendation: Elect where the appreciation is small (value of increased current deduction is greater than loss of eventual deduction of appreciation) or where the 30% limit will prevent deduction of the appreciation even over the carryover period (¶2130).

Once made, the election applies to all gifts of capital gain property (¶2127) to 50% charities made by the donor in the tax year. In computing carryovers to this year, contributions of this property in an earlier year for which the election was *not* made are reduced as if they were subject to the reduction when made. (Code Sec. 170(b)(1)(C)(iii); Reg § 1.170A-8(d)(2))[30]

Elect by attaching a statement specified in the regs, to the original income tax return for the election year. (Reg § 1.170A-8(d)(2)(iii))[31]

¶ 2129   Gifts of appreciated capital gain property to 30% charities—20% ceiling.

An individual's deduction ceiling for gifts of appreciated long-term capital gain property to 30% charities is 20% of his contribution base (¶2124) (and there's no election like the one for gifts to 50% charities, see ¶2128). (Code Sec. 170(b)(1)(D))[32]

---

25. ¶K-3720 *et seq.*; ¶1704.08; TD ¶333,005
26. ¶K-3684 *et seq.*; ¶1704.10 *et seq.*; TD ¶333,010
27. ¶K-3686, K-3687; ¶1704.11; TD ¶333,013, 333,014
28. ¶K-3687; ¶1704.05; TD ¶333,014

29. ¶K-3689; ¶1704.11; TD ¶333,018
30. ¶K-3689 *et seq.*; ¶1704.11; TD ¶333,018
31. ¶K-3690; TD ¶333,019
32. ¶K-3694; ¶1704.11; TD ¶333,017

¶ 2130   Carryover of excess charitable contributions by individuals.

If an individual's charitable gifts for a tax year exceed the percentage ceilings for the year (¶2124), the excess may generally be carried forward and deducted for up to five years (subject to the later year's ceiling). (Code Sec. 170(d)(1)) A statement must be filed with the return for the year the carryover is deducted. The carryforward is available even if the individual didn't itemize his deductions in the contribution year. (Reg §   1.170A-10(a)(2))[33]

For a 15-year carryforward period for qualified conservation contributions in 2006 and 2007, see ¶2124.

Contributions are deductible in the following order, up to 50% of the contribution base:

(1) Contributions qualifying for the 50% charity limit (¶2125).

(2) Contributions qualifying for the 30% charity limit (¶2126) up to the lesser of:

. . . 30% of the contribution base, or

. . . (a) 50% of the contribution base minus (b) contributions to 50% limit organizations. For this purpose, (b) includes contributions of capital gain property subject to the 30% limit (¶2127).

(3) Contributions of capital gain property subject to the 30% limit (up to the lesser of 30% of the contribution base or 50% of the contribution base minus other contributions to 50% organizations).

(4) Contributions qualifying for the 20% limit (¶2129) up to the lesser of:

. . . 20% of the contribution base,

. . . 30% of the contribution base minus contributions subject to the 30% limit,

. . . 30% of the contribution base minus contributions of capital gain property subject to the special 30% limit, or

. . . 50% of the contribution base minus the total of contributions to 50% and 30% limit organizations. (Code Sec. 170(b)(1))[34]

Where charitable contributions in more than one limitation category are carried over, the ordering rules are applied to determine the deduction limits for each category of contribution. Starting with the first (50% limitation) category, the allowable deduction limit is determined. Current contributions in that category are deducted first. Next, within that category, amounts carried over are deducted, up to the limitation amount for the category. Then, the same process is applied to the next limitation category according to the ordering rules. (Reg § 1.170A-10(b), Reg § 1.170A-10(c)) If there are carryovers from two or more years in any category, the carryover from the earlier year is considered first. [35]

¶ 2131   Excess charitable contributions on decedent's final return.

If an individual dies, any charitable contribution that can't be used on the decedent's final return (under the normal ceilings, see ¶2124) is lost. (Reg § 1.170A-10(d)(4)(iii))[36]

¶ 2132   Corporation's 10% charitable deduction ceiling and five-year carryover.

A corporation's charitable deduction for a tax year can't exceed 10% of its taxable income for the year. Taxable income for this purpose is computed without deductions for charitable contributions or dividends received, or net operating loss or capital loss carrybacks to the

---

33. ¶K-3701 *et seq.*, ¶K-3711; ¶1704.13; TD ¶333,301, 333,310
34. ¶K-3701 *et seq.*; ¶s 1704.05, 1704.13; TD ¶333,302

35. ¶K-3701 *et seq.*; ¶1704.05; TD ¶333,307
36. ¶K-3710; ¶1704.13; TD ¶333,306

year. (Code Sec. 170(b)(2); Reg § 1.170A-11(a))[37] To the extent contributions in any year exceed this limit, the excess can be carried forward and deducted for five years. (Code Sec. 170(d)(2))[38]

For certain farm-related qualified conservation contributions made in tax years beginning in 2006 or 2007 by nonpublicly traded corporations that are qualified farmers, the limit is 100% of taxable income less all other charitable contributions; see ¶2124. (Code Sec. 170(b)(2)(B)(i)(II))

caution: Check http://ria.thomson.com/federaltaxhandbook to see if this provision has been extended.

¶ 2133 When to deduct charitable contributions.

A charitable contribution is deductible in the tax year it's paid (subject to percentage ceilings, see ¶2124, ¶2132) (Code Sec. 170(a)), regardless of the donor's accounting method (except for accrual method corporations, see ¶2134) or when the gift was pledged. (Reg § 1.170A-1(a))[39]

A contribution is "paid" when it's unconditionally delivered to the donee. A contribution by check that's delivered unconditionally is paid when delivered, if it clears in due course. If the check is mailed unconditionally and clears in due course, the contribution is paid when mailed. (Reg § 1.170A-1(b))[40]

A contribution charged on a credit card is deductible by a cash basis donor in the year the charge is made, *not* in any later year when the credit card company is paid. [41]

¶ 2134 Accrual method corporation's election to deduct contribution paid 2-1/2 months after year-end.

An accrual method corporation whose board of directors has authorized a charitable contribution during the tax year may elect to deduct all or part of the contribution in that (authorization) year, if the contribution is paid by the 15th day of the third month following the close of the year. (Code Sec. 170(a)(2))[42]

Elect by reporting the contribution in the return and attaching a declaration signed by a principal officer together with a copy of the directors' resolution authorizing the contribution. (Code Sec. 170(a)(2); Reg § 1.170A-11(b))[43]

¶ 2135 Specialized Rules for Claiming Charitable Contributions—$250, $500 and $5,000 Rules.

Taxpayers (donors) must substantiate their charitable deductions, and supply appraisals and other information for certain property contributions. No charitable deduction is allowed for a contribution of $250 or more unless taxpayer substantiates it by a contemporaneous written acknowledgement from the donee. Special rules apply for contributions of cars, boats, and planes.

¶ 2136 Charitable contributions must be substantiated; donor's receipt.

A charitable deduction isn't allowed unless the taxpayer can prove his right to it. (Code Sec. 170(a)(1))[44] For *donee's* information return requirement, see ¶4750.

For cash contributions, the taxpayer must keep either a cancelled check, receipt or other

37. ¶K-3830 *et seq.*; ¶1704.14; TD ¶333,022
38. ¶K-3830 *et seq.*; ¶1704.14; TD ¶333,315
39. ¶K-3851; ¶s 1704.02, 1704.03; TD ¶333,701
40. ¶K-3858 *et seq.*; ¶1704.02; TD ¶333,706
41. ¶K-3861; ¶1704.02; TD ¶333,707
42. ¶K-3882 *et seq.*; ¶1704.03; TD ¶333,718
43. ¶K-3883; ¶1704.03; TD ¶333,718
44. ¶K-3901 *et seq.*; ¶1704.50, TD ¶334,001

reliable evidence. (Reg § 1.170A-13(a)(1))[45] For contributions made in tax years beginning after Aug. 17, 2006, a taxpayer can't deduct *any* contribution of a cash, check, or other monetary gift unless he maintains as a record of the contribution a bank record or a written communication from the donee organization showing its name, plus the date and amount of the contribution. (Code Sec. 170(f)(17)) For contributions of property (other than cash), the taxpayer must have a receipt from the donee and keep records showing the donee's name and describing the gift. (Reg § 1.170A-13(b)(1))[46]

For contributions made via payroll deductions, the taxpayer must retain a pay stub, Form W-2, or other employer document showing the amount withheld for the purpose of payment to the donee plus a pledge card or similar donee document showing the donee's name. [47]

Additional substantiation is required for: contributions of $250 or more (¶2137); noncash contributions exceeding $500 (¶2138); and contributions of cars, boats and planes (¶2139).

¶ 2137   Substantiation requirement for contributions of $250 or more.

No charitable deduction is allowed for any (cash or property) contribution of $250 or more unless taxpayer substantiates it by a contemporaneous written acknowledgement (not just a cancelled check) from the donee (or its agent). (Code Sec. 170(f)(8)(A); Reg § 1.170A-13(f)(1))[48]

In general, the written acknowledgment must state: (1) the amount of cash and a description (but not the value) of any property other than cash contributed; (2) whether the donee provided any goods or services in consideration for the contribution; (3) a description and good-faith estimate of the value of those goods or services; and (4) if the goods or services consist entirely of intangible religious benefits (e.g., admission to a religious ceremony, but not religious school tuition or fees), a statement to that effect. (Code Sec. 170(f)(8)(B)(i); Reg § 1.170A-13(f)(2)) Special requirements apply for gifts to a pooled income fund (¶2117). (Reg § 1.170A-13(f)(13))[49]

The written acknowledgement requirement doesn't apply:

. . . if the donee files a substantiating return (under regs to be issued),   (Code Sec. 170(f)(8)(D));[50] or

. . . to transfers to a charitable lead trust (¶2119), charitable remainder annuity trust or charitable remainder unitrust (¶2116). (Reg § 1.170A-13(f)(13))[1]

Goods or services that have insubstantial value (¶2104), and certain annual membership benefits the charity provides to the taxpayer, the taxpayer's employees, or the partners of a partnership donor, in exchange for the contribution are disregarded in determining the $250 threshold. (Reg § 1.170A-13(f)(8)(i), Reg § 1.170A-13(f)(9)(i))[2]

Separate payments are generally treated as separate contributions and aren't aggregated (Reg § 1.170A-13(f)(1)).[3]

An employer's payment to a charity of $250 or more withheld from taxpayer's paycheck (the amount withheld from each single paycheck treated as a separate contribution), may be substantiated by a combination of (1) a pay stub, Form W-2, or other employer provided document showing the amount withheld for this purpose, and (2) a pledge card or other donee document which states it doesn't provide any consideration for the payroll contributions. (Reg § 1.170A-13(f)(11))[4]

---

45. ¶K-3919; ¶1704.50; TD ¶334,007
46. ¶s K-3926, K-3927; ¶1704.50; TD ¶334,011
47. ¶K-3939
48. ¶K-3933; ¶1704.50; TD ¶334,015
49. ¶K-3933 *et seq.*; ¶1704.50; TD ¶334,015 *et seq.*

50. ¶K-3938
1. ¶K-3940.3; ¶1704.50
2. ¶K-3934; ¶1704.38; TD ¶334,016
3. ¶K-3934; ¶1704.50; TD ¶334,017
4. ¶K-3940; ¶1704.50; TD ¶334,020

¶ 2138   Proving noncash contributions exceeding $500.

For noncash contributions that are:

(1) more than $500 but not more than $5,000, the donor must attach to its return a description of the contributed property. This requirement doesn't apply to a C corporation. (Code Sec. 170(f)(11)(B))

(2) more than $5,000 but not more than $500,000, the donor must obtain a "qualified appraisal" (one meeting specified IRS requirements) and attach to its return information about the property and appraisal (i.e., appraisal summary) as required by IRS. (Code Sec. 170(f)(11)(C))

(3) more than $500,000, the donor must attached a qualified appraisal to its return. (Code Sec. 170(f)(11)(D))

The above requirements in (2) and (3) don't apply to: patents, copyrights, etc. as described in Code Sec. 170(e)(1)(B)(iii) (¶2106); property described in Code Sec. 1221(a)(1) (e.g., stock in trade, inventory); publicly traded securities; and "qualified vehicle donations" (¶2139). (Code Sec. 170(f)(11)(A)(ii)(I))

IRS will disallow a deduction for property contributed if the above reporting requirements aren't met unless the failure was due to reasonable cause. (Code Sec. 170(f)(11)(A))[5]

¶ 2139   Charitable contributions of cars, boats and planes.

Special rules apply for charitable contributions of motor vehicles, boats and airplanes that aren't in taxpayer's inventory or held for sale in the ordinary course of his business ("qualified vehicle donations"), if the donation's claimed value exceeds $500. (Code Sec. 170(f)(12)) The donor's charitable deduction can't exceed the gross proceeds from the charity's sale proceeds unless:

(1) there's a "significant intervening use" of the vehicle by the charity (actual, significant use to substantially further the charity's regularly conducted activities) prior to its sale;

(2) the charity materially improves the vehicle (significantly increases its value) prior to its sale (minor repairs or routine maintenance aren't enough); or

(3) the charity sells it at a price significantly below FMV (or gives it away) to a needy individual, in direct furtherance of its charitable purpose of relieving the poor and distressed or the underprivileged who need vehicles.

If (1), (2), or (3) apply, the donor may claim a deduction for the vehicle's FMV, using the "blue book" value for a similar vehicle (until regs are issued, private party sale amount may be used).

A deduction for donated vehicles whose claimed value exceeds $500 isn't allowed unless the taxpayer substantiates the contribution by a contemporaneous written acknowledgement from the donee (on Form 1098-C). (Code Sec. 170(f)(12)(A)) It must:

. . . contain the donor's name and taxpayer identification number (TIN), the vehicle identification number (or similar number), and if exceptions (1), (2), or (3) in the list above apply, supporting details;

. . . indicate whether the donee provided goods or services in consideration of the vehicle (and, if so, describe them and estimate their value, or, if they consist solely of intangible religious benefits, a statement to that effect);

---

5. ¶K-3942; ¶1704.50; TD ¶334,024

. . . generally be made within 30 days after the vehicle's sale (within 30 days of the contri-bution if exceptions (1), (2) or (3) apply); and

. . . if the charity sells the vehicle and none of the three above exceptions apply, state that the vehicle was sold in an arm's length transaction between unrelated parties, show the gross proceeds, and declare that the deductible amount can't exceed the gross proceeds. [6]

¶ 2140 IRS "Statement of Value" for gifts of art appraised at $50,000 or more.

At the taxpayer's request, IRS will issue a Statement of Value that taxpayer may rely on to substantiate the value of an item of art (paintings, sculpture, antique furniture, carpets, rare manuscripts, historical memorabilia and similar objects) that has been appraised at $50,000 or more and transferred as a charitable gift. The taxpayer must request the statement before filing the return that first reports the gift, and must attach a copy of the statement (or of the request, if the statement hasn't been received yet) to that return. [7]

¶ 2141 Medical Expenses.

An individual who itemizes can deduct the amount by which certain unreimbursed medical and dental expenses paid during the year for himself, his spouse and his dependents exceed 7.5% of his adjusted gross income.

¶ 2142 How much is deductible—7.5%-of-adjusted-gross-income floor.

The amount of medical expenses (¶2145) an individual may deduct (on Schedule A, Form 1040) in a tax year is the amount by which his unreimbursed payments for those expenses exceed 7.5% of his adjusted gross income (AGI, ¶3102), for the year. (There's no ceiling on the deduction.) (Code Sec. 213(a))[8] But any expense allowed as a Code Sec. 21 dependent care credit (¶2351), Code Sec. 35 credit for health insurance costs (¶2347), or Code Sec. 162(l) self-employed medical insurance deduction (¶1533) can't be treated as a medical expense. (Code Sec. 213(e), Code Sec. 35(g)(2), Code Sec. 162(l)(3))[9]

⚫*observation:* The deduction is lost to the extent the medical expenses don't exceed 7.5% of AGI. There's no carryover.

⚫*caution:* For the percentage floor on deductible medical expenses for purposes of the alternative minimum tax, see ¶3208.

¶ 2143 Whose medical expenses may taxpayer deduct?

A taxpayer may deduct his own medical expenses, and those of his spouse and dependents if the status as spouse, etc., exists either when the medical care was rendered or when the expenses were paid. (Code Sec. 213(a); Reg § 1.213-1(e)(3)) For this purpose, "dependent" is defined in Code Sec. 152 (see ¶3119), determined without the gross income test for qualifying relatives, the rule that a joint return filer can't be a dependent, and the rule that a dependent is ineligible to have dependents (Code Sec. 213(a); Reg § 1.213-1(a)(3)(i)) A child of divorced parents is considered a dependent of both if Code Sec. 152(e) applies (see ¶3125), so that each parent may deduct the medical expenses he or she pays for the child. (Code Sec. 213(d)(5))[10] An organ donor's medical expenses are deductible by the payor, whether donor or recipient. [11]

---

6. ¶K-3948.1; ¶1704.41; TD ¶334,028.1
7. ¶T-10080 *et seq.*; ¶1704.50; TD ¶526,012
8. ¶K-2000 *et seq.*; ¶2134 *et seq.*; TD ¶346,001

9. ¶K-2003; ¶s 2134, 2134.04; TD ¶346,002
10. ¶K-2300 *et seq.*; ¶s 2134.01, 2134.02; TD ¶346,011
11. ¶K-2159; TD ¶346,008

¶ 2144 Decedent's medical expenses.

Expenses for a decedent's medical care that are paid out of his estate are treated as paid by him (and may be deducted) in the year incurred if: (1) they're paid within one year after his death, (2) they aren't deducted for federal estate tax purposes, and (3) a statement is filed with the income tax return (or amended return) showing that the expenses weren't allowed for estate tax purposes and that the estate tax deduction is waived. (Code Sec. 213(c))[12]

⚫️observation: The choice of an income tax or estate tax deduction depends primarily on the extent to which the expense is deductible for income tax purposes, the decedent's top income tax rate, and the top effective estate tax rate.

¶ 2145 What kinds of medical expenses are deductible?

Deductible medical expenses are amounts paid for the diagnosis, mitigation, treatment, prevention of disease or for the purpose of affecting the body's structure or function (Code Sec. 213(d)(1))[13] and the costs of nursing services (Reg § 1.213-1(e)(1)(ii))[14] (and related insurance payments, ¶2146, and transportation, ¶2149).

The cost of the following is deductible as medical expenses:

... Eyeglasses, artificial teeth or limbs (Reg § 1.213-1(e)(1)(ii)), hearing aids, and similar items.[15]

... Discretionary medical procedures affecting the body's structure or function, including legal abortions and procedures to prevent or facilitate pregnancy (e.g., egg donor fees). [16]

... Eye surgery to correct defective vision, including laser procedures (e.g., LASIK). [17]

... Smoking cessation programs [18] and prescribed drugs designed to alleviate nicotine withdrawal, but not non-prescription nicotine gum and nicotine patches. [19]

... Attending a medical conference on a chronic disease suffered by an individual, his spouse, or dependent (but not meal and lodging costs, ¶2150).[20]

... Legally procured prescription drugs (e.g., not aspirin) and insulin. (Code Sec. 213(b), Code Sec. 213(d)(3)) A controlled substance (such as marijuana) obtained for medical purposes, in violation of the federal Controlled Substances Act, isn't legally procured and is nondeductible even if state law permits its doctor-prescribed use. [21]

... Weight-loss program for treatment of a specific disease (e.g., obesity, hypertension), but not the cost of diet food.[22]

... Diagnostic tests aiding in the detection of heart attack, diabetes, cancer, and other diseases (but not the collection and storage of DNA, absent a showing of how the DNA will be used for medical diagnosis). [23]

Expenses that aren't deductible as medical care include:

... Expenses merely beneficial to the individual's general health. (Reg § 1.213-1(e)(1)(ii))[24]

... Costs of cosmetic surgery or similar procedure (e.g., teeth whitening), unless necessary to ameliorate a deformity arising from, or directly related to, a congenital abnormality, a personal injury resulting from an accident or trauma or a disfiguring disease (Code Sec. 213(d)(9))—e.g., breast reconstruction surgery after cancer mastectomy. [25]

---

12. ¶K-2405, C-9556; ¶2134.03; TD ¶346,020
13. ¶K-2100 *et seq.*; ¶s 2134.04, 2134.08; TD ¶346,003
14. ¶K-2111; ¶2134.04; TD ¶346,506
15. ¶K-2162; ¶2134.04; TD ¶348,012
16. ¶K-2110; ¶2134.04; TD ¶346,505
17. ¶K-2162
18. ¶K-2117; ¶2134.04; TD ¶346,508

19. ¶K-2137; ¶2134.04; TD ¶346,505
20. ¶K-2161; ¶2134.04; TD ¶346,010
21. ¶K-2137 *et seq.*; ¶2134.04, 2134.06; TD ¶347,003
22. ¶K-2116
23. ¶K-2105.1; TD ¶346,502.5
24. ¶K-2103; ¶2134.04; TD ¶347,003
25. ¶K-2109; ¶2134.04; TD ¶346,505

. . . Payments for illegal operations or treatments. (Reg § 1.213-1(e)(1)(ii))[26]

Qualified long-term care services are treated as medical care (Code Sec. 213(d)(1)(C)) (unless provided by a relative who isn't a licensed professional, or by a related corporation or partnership. (Code Sec. 213(d)(11))) These services include necessary diagnostic, preventive, therapeutic, curing, treating, mitigating, and rehabilitative services, and maintenance or personal care services, which are required by a chronically ill individual and provided under a plan of care prescribed by a licensed health care practitioner. (Code Sec. 7702B(c)(1))[27]

¶ 2146 Accident and health insurance; Medicare.

The cost of insurance that's deductible as a medical expense is limited to amounts paid for insurance that covers *medical care* as defined at ¶2145. (Code Sec. 213(d)(1)(D))[28]

Amounts paid as *voluntary* premiums under Part B of Medicare (supplementary medical insurance benefits for the aged and disabled) are deductible as medical care, as are voluntary premiums under Medicare Part A (basic Medicare) (Code Sec. 213(d)(1)(D)), but not the *mandatory* employment or self-employment taxes paid for basic coverage under Medicare A. (Reg § 1.213-1(e)(4)(i)(a))[29]

When an insurance contract covers both medical care and other items (e.g., loss of income), no amount is treated as for medical care *unless:* the charge for medical insurance is separately stated, the amount treated as paid for medical insurance doesn't exceed the separately-stated charge, *and* the charge isn't unreasonably large in relation to the total premium for the contract. (Code Sec. 213(d)(6))[30]

Medical expenses include premiums paid for a qualified long-term care insurance contract, up to annual limits. For an individual whose attained age before the close of the tax year is:

. . . 40 or less, the limit is $290 for 2007 ($310 for 2008);

. . . more than 40, but not more than 50, the limit is $550 for 2007 ($580 for 2008);

. . . more than 50, but not more than 60, the limit is $1,110 for 2007 ($1,150 for 2008);

. . . more than 60, but not more than 70, the limit is $2,950 for 2007 ($3,080 for 2008);

. . . more than 70, the limit is $3,680 for 2007 ($3,850 for 2008). (Code Sec. 213(d)(10))[31]

Qualified long-term care insurance contracts must provide only coverage of qualified long-term care services, must not pay or reimburse expenses to the extent the expenses are reimbursable under Medicare (or would be but for a deductible or coinsurance amount), must be guaranteed renewable, and must meet other detailed requirements. (Code Sec. 7702B(b)) [32]

¶ 2147 Deductible costs of care at hospitals and other institutions.

The cost of in-patient care (including meals and lodging, see ¶2150) furnished by a hospital is a deductible medical expense. (Reg § 1.213-1(e)(1)(v))[33]

The cost of in-patient care (including meals and lodging) at a medical-care institution that is *not* a hospital qualifies if the individual is there primarily for the availability of medical care (as defined at ¶2145), and the meals and lodging are a necessary incident to that care. If this test isn't met, only that part of the cost attributable to medical care qualifies. Medical care status depends on the patient's condition and the nature of the services he receives —not on the nature of the institution, which may be federal, state, local or private. Where this test is met, a medical deduction is allowed for:

26. ¶K-2106; ¶2134.04; TD ¶346,503
27. ¶s K-2100, K-2122.1; ¶2134.03; TD ¶346,005
28. ¶K-2140 *et seq.*; ¶2134.08; TD ¶346,301
29. ¶K-2140; ¶2134.08; TD ¶346,301

30. ¶K-2141; ¶2134.08; TD ¶346,302
31. ¶K-2141.1; ¶2134.075; TD ¶346,303
32. ¶K-2141.1 *et seq.*; ¶77,02B4; TD ¶346,304
33. ¶K-2142; ¶2134.04; TD ¶347,501

... costs (including tuition, meals and lodging) of a mentally or physically handicapped person at a special school (Reg § 1.213-1(e)(1)(v)), e.g., a school for children with learning disabilities like dyslexia. Costs allocable to medical care at a regular school qualify if the school supplies a cost breakdown; [34]

... costs of a nursing home or home for the aged. But if the person isn't there principally for medical reasons, only the cost of medical care qualifies. (Reg § 1.213-1(e)(1)(v))[35]

¶ 2148   "Medical" capital expenses for equipment or improvements.

Amounts incurred for elevators, swimming pools and other permanent improvements to taxpayer's property (including capital expenditures to accommodate a residence to a physically handicapped individual) may be deductible medical expenses (¶2145) if the primary purpose is for the medical care of taxpayer, his spouse or dependents. But the medical deduction is limited to that portion of the expenses that exceeds the amount by which the improvement increases the value of taxpayer's property. (Reg § 1.213-1(e)(1)(iii))[36]

illustration: On his doctor's advice, J installs an elevator in his two-story, single family home to avoid climbing stairs and to alleviate his heart condition. The cost of installing it is $5,000 and it decreases the value of J's home by $3,000 (because buyers don't want a single family home with an elevator). The full $5,000 is a medical expense.

Some expenses incurred by or for a physically handicapped individual to remove structural barriers in his residence to accommodate his physical condition (e.g., constructing access ramps, widening doorways, installing support bars) are presumed not to increase the value of the residence and may be deductible in full. (Reg § 1.213-1(e)(1)(iii))[37]

Capital expenditures that are related only to the sick person and are detachable from the property aren't permanent improvements, so their full cost can be a medical expense, e.g., detachable inclinators and air conditioners. (Reg § 1.213-1(e)(1)(iii))[38]

All the costs of operating or maintaining a medical capital asset are deductible, even if none or only a portion of the cost of the asset itself qualifies. (Reg § 1.213-1(e)(1)(iii))[39]

¶ 2149   Transportation expenses for medical care.

The costs of transportation primarily for and essential to medical care (¶2145) qualify as medical expenses. (Code Sec. 213(d)(1)(B)) This includes food and lodging expense (¶2150) while en route to the place of medical treatment (Reg § 1.213-1(e)(1)(iv)), as well as taxi, train, plane and bus fares and the cost of ambulance services. [40]

Deductible medical expenses also include certain out-of-pocket car expenses, e.g., for gas, oil, parking fees and tolls, but not depreciation, repair, insurance or maintenance. Instead of claiming the actual costs of gas and oil, taxpayer may for 2007 deduct a flat 20¢ for each mile he uses the car for qualified medical transportation. [41]

However, no medical expense deduction is permitted for the cost of commuting to and from work even if taxpayer's illness or disability requires a special method of transportation. [42]

¶ 2150   "Away from home" expenses (meals and lodging)—$50 per night rule.

Expenses for meals and lodging away from home aren't medical expenses unless they're part of the cost of care in a hospital or other institution (¶2147) or medical travel (¶2149).[43]

---

34. ¶K-2143 *et seq.*; ¶s 2134.10, 2134.11; TD ¶347,502
35. ¶K-2147; ¶2134.11; TD ¶347,504
36. ¶K-2180 *et seq.*; ¶2134.13; TD ¶348,009
37. ¶K-2181; ¶2134.13; TD ¶348,010
38. ¶K-2192; ¶s 2134.04, 2134.12; TD ¶348,012

39. ¶K-2182; ¶2134.13; TD ¶348,011
40. ¶K-2200 *et seq.*; ¶s 2134.04, 2134.09; TD ¶348,500
41. ¶K-2214 *et seq.*; ¶s 2134.04, 2134.09; TD ¶348,514 *et seq.*
42. ¶K-2202; ¶2134.09; TD ¶348,502
43. ¶K-2217; TD ¶348,517

Taxpayer may deduct as a medical expense amounts paid for lodging (not food) while away from home, that is primarily for and essential to medical care in a hospital or equivalent, up to $50 per night for each individual. (Code Sec. 213(d)(2))[44]

No deduction is allowed for lavish or extravagant lodging or where the travel has any significant element of personal pleasure, recreation or vacation. (Code Sec. 213(d)(2)(B))[45]

¶ 2151   When to deduct medical expenses; prepaid insurance.

Only medical expenses actually paid during the tax year are deductible. (Code Sec. 213(a)) Deduction is thus allowed for payments in the year even though the expenses were incurred in an earlier year. (Reg § 1.213-1(a)(1)) If the payment is made by credit card, the amount is deductible in the year the charge is made regardless of when the credit card bill is paid. [46]

Advance payment of anticipated medical expenses doesn't qualify for a current deduction unless there is a contractual obligation to pay in the current year. [47]

Certain insurance premiums paid by a taxpayer who is under 65 during the payment year, for medical care for himself, his spouse and dependents for the period *after* he reaches 65 are deductible in the year paid. (Reg § 1.213-1(e)(4)(i)(b))[48]

¶ 2152   Medical expenses compensated for by insurance or otherwise.

Medical expenses aren't deductible if they have been compensated for by insurance or otherwise. (Code Sec. 213(a)) Taxpayer must reduce his medical expenses by amounts so compensated before applying the 7.5%-of-AGI floor (¶2142). But no reduction is required for amounts received as compensation for loss of earnings or as damages for personal injuries. [49]

If reimbursements in a tax year exceed medical expenses in that year, no medical deduction is allowed.[50] Any part of the excess that's attributable to an employer's contribution is taxable; the rest is tax-free. [1] For reimbursement in later year, see ¶2153.

¶ 2153   Reimbursement in year after medical expenses are paid.

If a taxpayer is reimbursed for medical expenses in a year after he paid (and deducted) them, he must report the reimbursement as income to the extent attributable to the earlier deduction (Reg § 1.213-1(g))—i.e., to the extent he got a "tax benefit," see ¶1205.[2]

¶ 2154   Alimony or Separate Maintenance. ████████████

Payments of alimony or separate maintenance made under a divorce or separation instrument are deductible by the payor spouse and taxable to the payee spouse. Alimony must be paid in cash and must not continue beyond the death of the payee spouse. A payment that's fixed as child support isn't alimony.

¶ 2155   Tax treatment of alimony or separate maintenance payments.

Alimony or separate maintenance (¶2156) payments are taxable to the payee spouse, in the year received. (Code Sec. 71(a); Reg § 1.71-1(b)(5))[3]

The payments are deductible by the payor spouse in the year paid, as a deduction from gross income. (Code Sec. 62(a)(10), Code Sec. 215(a)) The payor doesn't have to itemize to be allowed the deduction. [4]

---

44. ¶K-2218; ¶s 2134.04, 2134.09; TD ¶348,518
45. ¶K-2218; ¶s 2134.04, 2134.09; TD ¶348,518
46. ¶K-2401; ¶2134.03; TD ¶346,016
47. ¶K-2403; ¶2134.03; TD ¶346,018
48. ¶K-2404; ¶2134.03; TD ¶346,019
49. ¶K-2601 *et seq.*; ¶s 2134.14, 2134.15; TD ¶346,021

50. ¶K-2605; TD ¶346,025
1. ¶H-1114; ¶2134.15; TD ¶133,012
2. ¶K-2604; ¶2134.15; TD ¶346,024
3. ¶J-1413, K-6001; ¶714 *et seq.*, ¶2154; TD ¶198,502, 341,001
4. ¶A-2621, K-6002; ¶714.10, 2154 *et seq.*; TD ¶341,502, 560,720

These rules don't apply if the spouses file a joint return with each other. (Code Sec. 71(e))[5] For requirement that the spouses live apart, see ¶2158.

¶ 2156 Alimony requirements.

To qualify as alimony, a payment must be made in cash, under a divorce or separation instrument (¶2157). (Code Sec. 71(b)(1)) A transfer of property other than cash can't be alimony[6] (for "nonalimony" designation of a cash transfer, see ¶2162).

There must be no requirement that payments continue beyond the death of the payee spouse (e.g., to the estate) or that any substitute payment (in cash or property) be made after the death of the payee spouse —i.e., the payments must end at the payee spouse's death. (Code Sec. 71(b)(1)(D)) If this rule isn't satisfied, *none* of the payments (even those made during the payee spouse's life) is alimony. (Reg § 1.71-1T(b), Q&A-10) If it isn't clear from the divorce or separation agreement whether payments cease at the payee spouse's death, local law controls.[7]

🖊️*recommendation:* To make sure of alimony treatment, the divorce or separation instrument should specify that otherwise qualifying payments will cease at the death of the recipient. Where alimony treatment isn't desired, the instrument should specify that payments aren't to be treated as alimony (see ¶2162).

¶ 2157 Payments must be under a divorce or separation instrument.

To be alimony, a payment must be made under a divorce or separation instrument. (Code Sec. 71(b)(1)(A)).[8] This means a:

(1) decree of divorce or separate maintenance or a written instrument issued incident to the decree,

(2) written separation agreement, or

(3) decree not described in (1) e.g., a temporary support order. (Code Sec. 71(b)(2))[9]

If made under a decree of divorce or separate maintenance (or a written instrument incident to the decree), the payment must be made after the decree. (Reg § 1.71-1(b)(1)(i))[10] If made under a separation agreement, the payment must be made after the execution of that agreement. (Reg § 1.71-1(b)(2))[11]

¶ 2158 Separate household requirement for alimony.

Spouses who are legally separated (but not divorced) under a divorce or separate maintenance decree must not live in the same household when the payment is made, or it won't be alimony (¶2156). (Code Sec. 71(b)(1)(C)) But if the spouses aren't legally separated, a payment under a written separation agreement or temporary support order may be alimony even if they are members of the same household. (Reg § 1.71-1T(b), Q&A 9)[12]

The spouses aren't treated as members of the same household if one spouse is preparing to leave it, and does leave within one month after the payment. [13]

---

5. ¶K-6001; ¶714.03; TD ¶341,501
6. ¶K-6005; ¶714.01; TD ¶341,505
7. ¶K-6036 *et seq.*; ¶714.01; TD ¶341,536 *et seq.*
8. ¶K-6013; ¶714; TD ¶341,513
9. ¶K-6013; ¶714.01; TD ¶341,513

10. ¶K-6018; ¶714.06; TD ¶341,518
11. ¶K-6018; ¶714.06; TD ¶341,518
12. ¶K-6035; ¶s 714.01, 714.06; TD ¶341,535
13. ¶K-6035; ¶714.01; TD ¶341,535

¶ 2159 "Alimony" payments to a third party.

Payments made in cash by the payor spouse to a third party on behalf of the payee spouse under the terms of the divorce or separation instrument can be alimony (¶2156). (Code Sec. 71(b)(1)(A)) Payments are on behalf of the payee spouse if they satisfy an obligation to that spouse. Thus, cash payments of the payee spouse's rent, mortgage, tax or tuition liabilities that the payor spouse makes as required by the instrument can qualify as alimony, as can payments made to a third party (e.g., a charity) at the payee spouse's written request if the spouses intend them to be alimony. [14]

But payments made to maintain property *owned by the payor spouse* but used by the payee spouse (including mortgage payments, realty taxes, and insurance premiums) are *not* payments on behalf of the payee spouse (i.e., not alimony) even if made under the terms of the divorce or separation instrument. (Reg § 1.71-1T(b))[15]

A payor spouse who is required by the divorce or separation instrument to pay the mortgage on a home he owns jointly with the payee spouse may deduct one-half of those payments as alimony, if they otherwise qualify (the rest may be deductible as qualified residence interest if paid on a qualified home, see ¶1730 *et seq.*).[16]

¶ 2160 Life insurance contracts as alimony.

Premiums that one spouse pays for insurance on his life as required by the divorce or separation instrument are alimony if the other (payee) spouse owns the policy. [17]

¶ 2161 Support payments for the payor's children aren't alimony.

A payment under a divorce or separation instrument that's "fixed" (or treated as fixed) as support for a child of the payor spouse *isn't* alimony. (Code Sec. 71(c)(1))[18] This applies if the instrument designates a specified amount of money or a part of a payment to be child support. The actual amount may fluctuate. (Reg § 1.71-1T(c))[19]

A portion of a payment may be *treated* as fixed if the payment is to be reduced on the happening of a specified contingency relating to the child (Code Sec. 71(c)(2)), e.g., on the child's 18th birthday, or when he dies, marries or leaves school. [20] A payment may also be treated as fixed if it ends or is reduced at a time that can clearly be associated with the contingency. (Reg § 1.71-1T(c))[21]

If a divorce or separation instrument provides a specified amount for alimony and a specified amount for child support, and the payor spouse pays the payee spouse less than the amount designated for child support, then the *entire* payment is treated as child support and no part is treated as alimony. (Code Sec. 71(c)(3))[22]

¶ 2162 Designating that payments aren't to be treated as alimony.

If a divorce or separation instrument designates a payment that would otherwise qualify as alimony as *not* to be treated as alimony (e.g., as a property settlement), the payment won't qualify as alimony. (Code Sec. 71(b)(1)(B); Reg § 1.71-1T, Q&A 8)[23]

---

14. ¶K-6006; ¶714.01; TD ¶341,506
15. ¶K-6007; TD ¶341,507
16. ¶K-6008; TD ¶341,508
17. ¶K-6010; ¶714.01; TD ¶341,510
18. ¶K-6046; ¶714.02; TD ¶342,001

19. ¶K-6047; TD ¶342,002
20. ¶K-6049; ¶714.02; TD ¶342,004
21. ¶K-6049; ¶714.02; TD ¶342,002
22. ¶K-6048; ¶714.02; TD ¶342,003
23. ¶K-6033; ¶714.01; TD ¶341,533

¶ 2163   Alimony trusts.

A payor spouse can't deduct payments the payee spouse receives from an alimony trust which aren't includable in the payor's income under the Code Sec. 682 trust rules. (Code Sec. 215(d))[24] Under those rules, a wife who's divorced or legally separated, or separated under a written separation agreement, includes in her gross income her share of trust income that (without this rule) would be includible in her husband's income. This shifts the liability for tax on the income from the husband to the wife. But amounts payable for support of the husband's minor children are taxable to the husband. (Code Sec. 682(a))[25]

¶ 2164   Recapture rules—excess front-loading of alimony.

If there are "excess" alimony payments ("front-loading"), the payor spouse must "recapture" the "excess" by including it in his gross income for the third post-separation year (below) (Code Sec. 71(f)(1)(A)) (on Form 1040, line 11, cross out "received" and write "recapture").[26] The same amount is deducted by the payee spouse in computing adjusted gross income for *the payee's* third post-separation year (on Form 1040, line 31a; cross out "paid" and write "recapture"). (Code Sec. 71(f)(1)(B))[27]

The "recapture" amount is the sum of:

(1) the excess of (a) the alimony or separate maintenance payments in the second post-separation year, over (b) the sum of the payments in the third year plus $15,000 (Code Sec. 71(f)(2)(B)); *plus*

(2) the excess of (a) the payments in the first post-separation year, over (b) the sum of the average of the payments in the second year (minus any excess payment in (1), above) and third year, plus $15,000. (Code Sec. 71(f)(2)(A))[28]

✪ illustration: H makes alimony payments of $50,000 in the first post-separation year, $20,000 in the second year, and nothing in the third year. H must recapture $32,500: $5,000 from the second year ($20,000 – ($0 + $15,000)) and $27,500 from the first year ($50,000 – ($7,500 + $15,000)), where the $7,500 equals $15,000 ($20,000 – $5,000) ÷ 2, i.e., the average of the second and third year payments after reduction of the second year payments by the $5,000 recaptured from the second year.[29]

✪ observation: The payor spouse is in effect allowed to pay up to $15,000 of excess alimony in each of the first two post-separation years without recapturing the excess.

The first post-separation year is the first calendar year in which the payor spouse paid alimony, etc., to the payee spouse. The second and third post-separation years are the succeeding calendar years. (Code Sec. 71(f)(6))[30]

There's no recapture if payments cease because either spouse dies or the payee spouse remarries before the close of the third post-separation year. Nor does recapture apply to temporary support payments or payments that fluctuate because of a continuing liability to pay, for at least three years, a fixed portion of income from business, property or services (including self-employment). (Code Sec. 71(f)(5))[31]

---

24. ¶K-6009; ¶2154.02; TD ¶341,509
25. ¶K-5432 *et seq.*; ¶6824; TD ¶657,039
26. ¶K-6043, K-6044; ¶714.03; TD ¶341,543, 341,544
27. ¶K-6044; ¶714.03; TD ¶341,544

28. ¶K-6044; ¶714.03; TD ¶341,544
29. ¶K-6044; ¶714.03; TD ¶341,545
30. ¶K-6045; ¶714.03; TD ¶341,546
31. ¶K-6043; ¶714.03; TD ¶341,547

¶ 2165   Pre-'85 instruments—alimony rules.

The alimony rules discussed at ¶2154 *et seq.*, don't apply to a pre-'85 instrument unless it is: (1) modified after '84 to expressly provide that those (post-'84) rules are to apply, or (2) incorporated into a post-'84 divorce decree that changes the terms of the payments. [32]

To be alimony under a pre-'85 instrument, payments must be "periodic;" see Reg § 1.71-1(d).[33]

Any part of a periodic payment that the decree, instrument or agreement *specifically fixed* as for support of the payor's minor children isn't alimony. (Reg § 1.71-1(c))[34]

¶ 2166   "Nonbusiness" Expenses. ■■■■■■■■■■■■■

Individuals may deduct most ordinary and necessary expenses that, though not connected with their trade or business, are paid or incurred for the collection or production of income; the management, conservation or maintenance of property held for the production of income; or the determination, collection or refund of any tax.

But a *personal expense* or a *capital expenditure* for which deductions are barred can't be deducted as a nonbusiness expense. (Code Sec. 262(a), Code Sec. 263; Reg § 1.212-1(e))[35]

For 2%-of-adjusted gross income (AGI) floor on nonbusiness deductions, see ¶3110. For reduction in itemized deductions if AGI exceeds specified amounts, see ¶3114.

caution: For nonbusiness expenses under the alternative minimum tax, see ¶3208.

¶ 2167   "Nonbusiness" (investment) expenses.

Taxpayer may deduct a wide variety of expenses related to his investments (not amounting to a business) if they are ordinary and necessary for the production or collection of income, or for the management, conservation or maintenance of property held for the production of income. (Code Sec. 212(1), Code Sec. 212(2))[36]

Home office expenses allocable to "nonbusiness" investment activities aren't deductible (but this doesn't affect deductions for interest, taxes or casualty losses). (Code Sec. 280A)[37]

Expenses of a convention, seminar, or similar meeting aren't deductible as nonbusiness (investment) expenses. (Code Sec. 274(h)(7))[38]

¶ 2168   Tax determination costs.

Individuals may deduct all the ordinary and necessary expenses incurred in connection with the determination, collection, or refund of any tax (for legal fees, see ¶2169). (Code Sec. 212(3)) This applies to income, estate, gift, property and any other tax imposed by federal, state, municipal or foreign authorities. Included are the costs of: preparing tax returns, determining the extent of liability, contesting tax liability (including transferee liability[39]), getting tax counsel, protesting assessments, prosecuting refunds, compromising liability (Reg § 1.212-1(e)), a tax text used by an individual to prepare his own tax return, [40] tax advice[41] (including divorce and estate planning [42]), property appraisal to substantiate a claimed deduction, [43] and contesting civil penalties, whether taxpayer is successful or not. [44]

32. ¶K-6100 *et seq.*; ¶714; TD ¶343,007
33. ¶K-6138 *et seq.*; ¶714.13; TD ¶343,005
34. ¶K-6192 *et seq.*; ¶714.16
35. ¶s L-1400, L-1415, L-5601; ¶s 2124 *et seq.*, 2624, 2634; TD ¶255,507, 256,201
36. ¶L-1401 *et seq.*; ¶2124 *et seq.*; TD ¶336,001
37. ¶L-1305; ¶280A4; TD ¶258,002

38. ¶L-1724; ¶s 2124.01, 2744.07; TD ¶291,021
39. ¶L-3015; TD ¶307,205
40. ¶L-3001 *et seq.*; ¶2124.14; TD ¶307,206
41. ¶L-3007; ¶2124.14; TD ¶307,210
42. ¶L-3010, L-3009; ¶2124.14; TD ¶307,208, 307,209
43. ¶L-3005; TD ¶307,206
44. ¶L-3006; ¶2124.14; TD ¶307,206

¶ 2169   "Nonbusiness" legal expenses.

An individual may deduct nonbusiness legal fees, e.g., attorney's fees, court costs, etc., if incurred to produce income, preserve income-producing property, etc. (Reg § 1.212-1(k))[45], as a miscellaneous itemized deduction (see ¶3110).[46]

Nonbusiness legal expenses incurred to acquire, perfect, or defend title to property are *not* deductible, but any of those costs that are allocable to collecting accrued rents on the property may be deducted. (Reg § 1.212-1(k))[47]

Legal expenses in connection with divorce, separation or a support decree are personal expenses which cannot be deducted by either spouse (Reg § 1.262-1(b)(7))[48] *except that*:

. . . the part of legal fees attributable to the production or collection of taxable alimony is deductible by the payee spouse (Reg § 1.262-1)[49] and

. . . taxpayer can deduct fees paid to his attorney for tax research and advice relating to a divorce and property settlement if the fee for the tax work is segregated, *but not* legal fees he pays to his spouse's attorney for tax advice given to the spouse. [50]

¶ 2170   Tax-exempt income expenses.

A taxpayer may not deduct costs incurred in the production of tax-exempt income (Code Sec. 265(a)(1))[1] (such as interest on indebtedness incurred or continued to buy or carry tax-exempt securities, see ¶1723). If expenses are attributable to both taxable and tax-exempt income, and can't be specifically identified, they must be prorated. (Reg § 1.265-1(c))[2]

¶ 2171   Premature withdrawal penalties.

An individual may deduct any interest or principal he forfeits to a bank or other financial institution as a penalty for premature withdrawal from a time savings account, certificate of deposit or similar deposit. The penalty is deductible from gross income in computing adjusted gross income (AGI, ¶3102), (Code Sec. 62(a)(9)) and[3] not as an interest expense (so it can't be netted against interest income, and taxpayer doesn't have to itemize). [4]

¶ 2172   Bond Premium Amortization. ▬▬▬▬▬▬▬▬▬▬▬▬▬▬▬▬▬▬▬▬

Any premium on tax-exempt bonds must be amortized. A premium on taxable bonds may be amortized at the holder's election. The amortized amount reduces basis and, for taxable bonds, is treated as an offset to the interest received.

Premium on tax-exempt bonds *must* be amortized. (Code Sec. 171(a)(2); Reg § 1.171-1(c)(1)) Premium on taxable bonds *may* be amortized at the holder's option (see ¶2173). (Code Sec. 171(a)(1), Code Sec. 171(c); Reg § 1.171-1(c)(2))[5] For securities dealers, see ¶2176.

"Bonds" include a bond, debenture, note, or certificate or other evidence of indebtedness. (Code Sec. 171(d); Reg § 1.171-1(d)(1)) But the bond premium amortization rules don't apply to certain specified debt obligations. (Reg § 1.171-1(b)(2))[6]

Bond premium generally arises when the stated interest rate on the bond is higher than the market yield for the bond at the time of purchase. The amount of premium on a bond is the excess of the holder's basis in the bond immediately after its acquisition over the sum of

45. ¶L-2902 *et seq.*; ¶2124.12; TD ¶305,005
46. ¶L-2903; ¶674; TD ¶305,002
47. ¶L-2908 *et seq.*; ¶2124.12; TD ¶305,018
48. ¶L-2962; ¶s 2124.13, 2624; TD ¶305,064
49. ¶L-2965; ¶s 2124.13, 2624; TD ¶305,067
50. ¶L-3010; ¶2124.13; TD ¶307,208

1. ¶K-9000 *et seq.*; ¶2654; TD ¶653,017
2. ¶K-9002; ¶2654; TD ¶653,017
3. ¶K-5880; ¶624; TD ¶560,719
4. TD ¶560,719
5. ¶K-5611; ¶s 1714.01, 10,164; TD ¶318,201
6. ¶K-5614; ¶1714.01; TD ¶318,204

all amounts payable on the bond after the acquisition date (other than payments of qualified stated interest, ¶1315). (Reg § 1.171-1(d)(1))[7] Basis for this purpose is the holder's basis for determining loss on sale. (Code Sec. 171(b)(1)(A); Reg § 1.171-1(e)(1)(i))[8]

If a convertible bond is purchased at a premium, any amount attributable to the conversion feature of the bond is excluded from amortizable bond premium. (Code Sec. 171(b)(1))[9] Regs provide special rules for variable rate debt instruments, inflation-indexed debt instruments, and bonds subject to contingencies. (Reg § 1.171-3)[10] For amortization of callable bonds, see ¶2174.

The regs discussed above don't apply for bonds acquired before Mar. 2, '98, unless an election is made. (Reg § 1.171-5(a)(1))[11]

¶ 2173   Amortization deduction, basis reduction.

For *tax-exempt* bonds, no deduction is allowed for the amortizable bond premium for a tax year. (Code Sec. 171(a)(2))[12] The basis of the bond is reduced by the amortizable bond premium barred as a deduction. (Code Sec. 1016(a)(5)); Reg § 1.1016-5(b)(3))[13]

For *taxable* bonds, a deduction *is* allowed for the amortizable bond premium (Code Sec. 171(a)(1)) if the election at ¶2175 is made. The bond premium (computed under a constant-yield method based on yield to maturity (Code Sec. 171(b)(3)(A); Reg § 1.171-1(a)(1)) allocable to an accrual period is deducted as an offset to the qualified stated interest (¶1315) allocable to the period. (Code Sec. 171(e); Reg § 1.171-2(a)(1))[14] The holder's basis in the bond is reduced by the offset amount. (Code Sec. 1016(a)(5))[15]

observation: If the holder of a taxable bond doesn't elect to amortize bond premium, the premium will be recovered when the bond is redeemed or sold.

¶ 2174   Amortization of callable bonds.

The holder of a taxable bond generally amortizes bond premium by reference to the bond's stated maturity date (see ¶2173) even if the bond is likely to be called. (Code Sec. 171(b)(1)(B)(ii); Reg § 1.171-3(c)(4)(ii)(A), Reg § 1.171-3(e), Ex. 2)[16]

If the issuer calls the bond, the holder can deduct the unamortized bond premium (excess of the bond's adjusted basis as of the start of the year over the greater of (a) the amount received on early redemption or (b) the amount due on maturity). (Code Sec. 171(b)(2); Reg § 1.171-3(c)(5)(ii), Reg § 1.171-3(e), Ex. 2)[17]

¶ 2175   Making the election to amortize bond premium.

The election to amortize bond premium on taxable bonds (¶2172) is made by (a) offsetting interest income with bond premium in the holder's timely filed return for the first tax year to which the election applies and (b) attaching an election statement to the return. (Code Sec. 171(c)(2); Reg § 1.171-4(a)(1)) IRS consent to make the election isn't needed. (Reg § 1.171-5(c)(1))[18]

A holder who has elected to treat all interest on the bond as original issue discount (OID, ¶1314) is treated as having elected to amortize bond premium. (Reg § 1.171-4(a)(2))[19]

Once made, the election (unless revoked with IRS consent) is binding for the year made and

---

7. ¶K-5616; ¶1714; TD ¶318,206
8. ¶K-5611; ¶1714.02; TD ¶318,201
9. ¶K-5622; ¶1714.035; TD ¶318,212
10. ¶K-5624 *et seq.*; ¶1714.036 *et seq.*; TD ¶318,214 *et seq.*
11. ¶K-5633; ¶1714.01; TD ¶318,223
12. ¶K-5611; ¶1714; TD ¶318,201
13. ¶P-5043; ¶10,164; TD ¶216,026

14. ¶K-5611; ¶1714.03; TD ¶318,201
15. ¶P-5043; ¶10,164; TD ¶216,026
16. ¶K-5627; ¶1714.03; TD ¶318,217
17. ¶K-5628; ¶1714.03; TD ¶318,218
18. ¶K-5633; ¶1714.04; TD ¶318,223
19. ¶K-5633; ¶1714.04; TD ¶318,223

later years. It applies to all taxable bonds held by the taxpayer at the beginning of the first tax year to which the election applies, and also to all taxable bonds thereafter acquired by the taxpayer. (Code Sec. 171(c)(2), Reg § 1.171-4(b))[20]

recommendation: Generally, the election should be made because it provides a current interest income offset which is preferable to a future capital loss deduction.

¶ 2176 Dealers in securities—bond premium amortization.

Taxable bonds that are the holder's stock in trade, or held primarily for sale to customers in the ordinary course of the holder's trade or business, or of a kind that would be included in inventory if on hand at the end of the tax year, aren't subject to the bond amortization rules. (Code Sec. 171(d); Reg § 1.171-1(b)(2)(iv)) Thus, dealers can't amortize the bond premium. [21]

Tax-exempt bonds held primarily for sale to customers in the ordinary course of the holder's trade or business must be adjusted for amortizable bond premium. (Code Sec. 75(a))[22]

---

20. ¶K-5633; ¶1714.04; TD ¶318,223
21. ¶K-5651; ¶1714.01; TD ¶318,213

22. ¶K-5651; ¶754; TD ¶318,251

Chapter 7 Education—Tax Credits, Exclusions, Deductions

¶ 2200   **Education—Tax Credits, Exclusions, Deductions.** ▬▬▬▬▬▬▬▬

There are a number of tax breaks designed specifically to help defray the costs of saving and paying for higher education, and one (the Coverdell education savings account) that helps with pre-college costs as well.

There are three main categories of tax breaks for education:

(1) Tax credits, see ¶2201 *et seq.*,

(2) Exclusions, see ¶2205 *et seq.*, and

(3) Deductions, see ¶2222 *et seq.*

Other tax breaks. Pre-age-59-1/2 distributions from traditional IRAs and Roth IRAs are excepted from the 10% premature distribution penalty tax to the extent they don't exceed qualified higher education expenses for the distribution year; see ¶4344 and ¶4357. Additionally, there's an unlimited gift-tax exclusion for gifts made on behalf of another individual directly to a qualifying educational organization; see ¶5040.

¶ 2201   **Tax Credits for Higher Education** ▬▬▬▬▬▬▬▬▬▬▬▬▬▬

An individual taxpayer may claim an income tax credit for the Hope scholarship credit (¶2202) and the Lifetime Learning credit (¶2203) for higher education expenses at accredited post-secondary educational institutions paid for themselves, their spouses, and their dependents. The Hope credit is available only for qualified expenses of the first two years of undergraduate education; the Lifetime Learning credit is available for qualified expenses of any post-high school education at "eligible educational institutions." Both credits can't be claimed in the same tax year for expenses of any one student (see ¶2203), and phase out for higher-income taxpayers (see ¶2202).

¶ 2202   **Hope scholarship credit—Form 8863.**

Individuals may elect (on Form 8863, attached to an original or amended return filed by the limitations period for filing a claim for credit or refund for the year the credit is claimed) a personal nonrefundable tax credit equal to 100% of up to $1,100 for 2007 ($1,200 for 2008) of qualified higher-education tuition and related expenses (¶2204) plus 50% of the next $1,100 of expenses ($1,200 for 2008) paid for education furnished to an eligible student in an academic period. Thus, for 2007, the maximum credit is $1,650 a year for *each* eligible student ($1,800 for 2008). (Code Sec. 25A(a)(1); Code Sec. 25A(b)(1))

For 2007, availability of the Hope credit phases out ratably for taxpayers with modified AGI (AGI increased by foreign, possessions, and Puerto Rico income exclusions) of $47,000 to $57,000 ($94,000 to $114,000 for joint filers). (Code Sec. 25A(d)) For 2008, the phaseout ranges are $48,000 to $58,000 ($96,000 to $116,000 for joint filers). Married taxpayers must file jointly to claim the credit. (Code Sec. 25A(g)(6)) The student's name and TIN must be included on the return of the taxpayer claiming the credit. (Code Sec. 25A(g)(1)) The Hope (or Lifetime Learning credit, ¶2203) and tax-free Coverdell education savings account (ESA) distributions (¶2205) are allowed for the same student for the same year, as long as a credit isn't claimed for education expenses used to generate the tax-free Coverdell ESA distribution. (Code Sec. 530(d)(2)(C)(i))

The Hope credit may be elected for a student's expenses only for two tax years, and only for students who have not completed the first two years of post-secondary education as of the beginning of the tax year. (Code Sec. 25A(b)(2); Reg § 1.25A-3(d)(1)(iii)) Additionally, for at

---

References beginning with a single letter are to paragraphs in RIA's Federal Tax Coordinator 2d and RIA's Analysis of Federal Taxes: Income. Those beginning with numbers are to paragraphs in RIA's United States Tax Reporter. Those beginning with TD are to paragraphs in RIA's Tax Desk.

least one academic period during the year, the student must be enrolled for at least half of the normal full-time workload for his course of study. (Code Sec. 25A(b)(3)(B), Reg § 1.25A-3(d)(1)(ii))

If a dependency deduction for an individual is allowed to another taxpayer, the dependent can't claim the Hope credit, and qualified tuition and expenses paid by the dependent during the tax year are treated as paid by the taxpayer who is allowed the dependency deduction. (Code Sec. 25A(g)(3)) If a third party (not the taxpayer, spouse, or dependent) pays a student's qualified expenses directly to an educational institution, the student is treated as receiving the payment from the third party and, in turn, paying the expenses. If the student in such a case is claimed as a dependent on another's return, the expenses deemed to be paid by the student would be treated as expenses of the taxpayer claiming the student as a dependent. (Reg § 1.25A-5(a), Reg § 1.25A-5(b)) If a taxpayer is eligible to but does not claim a student as a dependent, only the student can claim the education credit for the student's qualified tuition and related expenses. (Reg § 1.25A-1(f))

observation: It may pay for a parent not to claim the student as a dependent if (1) the parent can't claim education credits because of high modified AGI, and (2) the student pays or is deemed to pay the expense and has sufficient tax liability to claim the credit.

If qualified tuition and expenses are paid during one tax year for an academic period that begins during the first 3 months of the next tax year, the academic period is treated for Hope credit purposes as beginning in the earlier year. (Code Sec. 25A(g)(4)) Thus, the credit is allowed only in the tax year in which the expenses are paid. (Reg § 1.25A-3(e)) Special rules apply for tuition refunds and excludable tuition assistance received after the tax year in which qualified tuition and related expenses are paid. (Reg § 1.25A-5(c), Reg § 1.25A-5(f)) A Hope credit isn't allowed for a student convicted (as of the end of the tax year for which the credit is claimed) of a felony offense for possessing or distributing a controlled substance. (Code Sec. 25A(b)(2)(D))[1]

¶ 2203   Lifetime Learning credit—Form 8863.

Taxpayers may elect (use Form 8863) a Lifetime Learning credit equal to 20% of up to $10,000 of qualified tuition and related expenses paid (defined at ¶2204) during the tax year. The maximum credit is $2,000. (Code Sec. 25A(a)(2); Code Sec. 25A(c)(1))

Unlike the Hope credit (¶2202), which is available for the qualifying expenses of each qualifying student, the Lifetime Learning credit is available only per taxpayer. So, for example, a joint filing couple with two children could claim no more than a $2,000 Lifetime Learning credit, even if each family member is a qualifying student with qualifying expenses.

The same phaseout rules, treatment of expenses paid by dependent, adjustment for tax-free scholarships, etc., treatment of certain prepayments, denial of double benefit, denial of credit to marrieds not filing jointly, and nonresident alien bar that apply for Hope credit purposes (¶2202) also apply to the Lifetime Learning credit. (Code Sec. 25A(d); Code Sec. 25A(e); Code Sec. 25A(f); Code Sec. 25A(g); Code Sec. 25A(h))

Expenses for a student for whom a Hope scholarship credit (¶2202) is allowed for the tax year don't qualify for the Lifetime Learning credit. (Code Sec. 25A(c)(2))[2]

¶ 2204   Qualified tuition and related expenses for education credit purposes

Qualified tuition and related expenses for Hope credit (¶2202) and Lifetime Learning credit ((¶2203) purposes means tuition and fees required for the enrollment or attendance of the taxpayer, his spouse, or tax dependent, at a post-secondary educational institution eligible to

---

1. ¶A-4500 *et seq.*; ¶25A4; TD ¶568,923   2. ¶A-4500 *et seq.*; ¶25A4; TD ¶568,933

participate in the federal student loan program. [3]

Student activity fees and fees for course-related books, supplies, and equipment qualify for the Hope or Lifetime Learning credit only if they must be paid directly to the educational institution for the enrollment or attendance of the student. (Reg § 1.25A-2(d)(2)) Room and board, insurance, transportation, or other similar personal, living, or family expenses, don't qualify for the Hope or Lifetime Learning credit, whether or not paid to an educational institution. (Code Sec. 25A(f); Reg § 1.25A-2(d)(2), Reg § 1.25A-2(d)(3))

The cost of any course of instruction at an eligible institution taken to acquire or improve job skills qualifies for the Lifetime Learning credit, but not the Hope credit, even if it involves sports, games, hobbies, or is a noncredit course. (Code Sec. 25A(c)(2)(B), Reg § 1.25A-2(d)(5))

Qualified tuition and related expenses must be reduced by scholarship amounts excludable from income under Code Sec. 117 (¶2216), educational assistance under chapter 30 through 35 of title 38 U.S. Code or under chapter 1606 of title 10 U.S. Code, and other tax-free payments. However, qualified amounts are not reduced by amounts paid by gift, bequest, devise, or inheritance. (Code Sec. 25A(g)(2)) No credit is allowed for any expense for which an income tax deduction is allowed. (Code Sec. 25A(g)(5)) Special rules apply for tuition refunds and excludable tuition assistance received after the tax year in which qualified tuition and related expenses are paid. (Reg § 1.25A-2(d)(2))

¶ 2205　Coverdell Education Savings Accounts (ESAs)

Taxpayers can contribute up to $2,000 per year to Coverdell Education Savings Accounts (ESAs), formerly called education IRAs, for beneficiaries under age 18 (and special needs beneficiaries of any age). The account is exempt from income tax, and distributions are tax-free if used for qualified education expenses.

¶ 2206　Coverdell Education Savings Accounts (ESAs)—Form 5305-E and 5305-EA.

A Coverdell Education Savings Account (ESA) is a trust (Form 5305-E) or custodial account (Form 5305-EA) created exclusively for the purpose of paying an individual beneficiary's qualified education expenses. (Code Sec. 530(b)(1), Code Sec. 530(g)) These accounts are exempt from tax except for the unrelated business income tax. (Code Sec. 530(a)) Allowable annual contributions to Coverdell ESAs (no more than $2,000 per beneficiary to all accounts) aren't deductible, but distributions from Coverdell ESAs for qualified education expenses are tax-free (¶2208).

Coverdell ESAs can't invest in life insurance contracts, and, except for common trust or investment funds, trust assets can't be commingled. The account balance must be distributed to the beneficiary within 30 days after he turns age 30 (unless he has special needs), or, if sooner, to the beneficiary's estate within 30 days after the beneficiary's death (Code Sec. 530(b)(1), Code Sec. 530(d)(8)),[4] unless transferred to a family member's Coverdell ESA. see ¶2208.

¶ 2207　Contributions to Coverdell ESAs.

Annual contributions to Coverdell Education Savings Accounts (ESAs) for any beneficiary can't exceed $2,000, must be made in cash, and can't be made after the beneficiary turns age 18 (unless the beneficiary has special needs). (Code Sec. 530(b)(1)(A)) Coverdell ESA contributions for a year may be made as late as the unextended tax return due date for that year. (Code Sec. 530(b)(4))[5]

If the contributor is an individual, the $2,000 limit phases out ratably between $95,000 and

3. ¶A-4474 *et seq.*; ¶25A4.07; TD ¶568,937
4. ¶A-4615; ¶5304; TD ¶147,215
5. ¶A-4606; ¶5304

$110,000 ($190,000 and $220,000 for joint filers) of modified AGI (AGI plus income excluded under Code Sec. 911, Code Sec. 931, and Code Sec. 933) (Code Sec. 530(c))[6]

☛*observation:* Thus, a corporation may contribute to a Coverdell ESA that has an employee's child as beneficiary. The contribution would, however, be taxed to the employee.

Excess contributions are subject to a 6% excise tax in the contribution year and each year that an excess amount is in the account (report on Form 5329, Part V). However, the excise tax doesn't apply to rollover contributions, or contributions (with net earnings attributable to the excess contributions) returned before June 1 of the year following the contribution year. (Code Sec. 4973(e))[7]

For the gift tax treatment of Coverdell ESAs, see ¶5040.

¶ 2208 Distributions from Coverdell ESAs.

A distribution from a Coverdell ESA is included in the gross income of the distributee generally as provided under the annuity rules of Code Sec. 72. (Code Sec. 530(d)(1)) Thus, distributions consist of a pro-rata share of principal (recovered tax-free) and accumulated earnings (which *may* be excludable under the Coverdell ESA rules). Distributions from a Coverdell ESA are entirely excluded if qualified education expenses of the beneficiary equal or exceed total Coverdell ESA distributions for the year. (Code Sec. 530(d)(2)(A))

Qualified education expenses are:

. . . Higher education tuition, fees, books, and supplies, and, for half-time or greater students, certain room and board charges. (Code Sec. 530(b)(2)(A))

. . . Elementary and secondary (K through 12) public, private or religious school tuition and expenses, including tutoring, room and board, transportation, uniforms, and extended day programs. (Code Sec. 530(b)(4))

. . . Special needs services for special needs beneficiaries enrolled in any of the above types of schools. (Code Sec. 530(b)(2)(A), Code Sec. 530(b)(3)(B))

. . . The purchase of any computer technology or equipment or expenses for Internet access and related services for use by the beneficiary and his family during any of the years that the beneficiary is in school, but not expenses for computer software designed for sports, games or hobbies unless it is predominantly educational in nature. (Code Sec. 530(b)(4))

. . . Contributions to a qualified tuition program (QTP, see ¶2209) on behalf of a designated beneficiary, (Code Sec. 530(b)(2)(B))[8] but in applying the Code Sec. 72 annuity rules to a Coverdell ESA distribution that's contributed to a qualified tuition program (¶2210) for a designated beneficiary, any part of the contribution which is not includible in gross income (because it doesn't exceed the beneficiary's qualified education expenses) won't result in an increase in the investment in the contract. (Code Sec. 530(b)(2)(B))

Qualified education expenses are reduced by the same tax-free scholarships and similar payments that reduce qualified tuition and related expenses for education credit purposes (¶2204) (Code Sec. 530(d)(2)(C)(i)(I)), and by the expenses taken into account in determining the education credit (¶2201).[9]

Distributions aren't taxed if rolled over within 60 days (but not more than once in a 12-month period) into a Coverdell ESA for the same beneficiary or a member of the beneficiary's family (as defined at ¶2212) who is under age 30. (Code Sec. 530(d)(5), Code Sec. 530(d)(6))[10] A Coverdell ESA transfer to a beneficiary's family member under a divorce decree or after the beneficiary's death also isn't taxable. (Code Sec. 530(d)(7))

---

6. ¶A-4604; ¶5304; TD ¶147,204
7. ¶A-4607; ¶49,734; TD ¶147,205
8. ¶A-4610; ¶5304; TD ¶147,210

9. ¶A-4612; ¶5304; TD ¶147,212
10. ¶A-4619; ¶5304; TD ¶147,219

If Coverdell ESA distributions exceed qualified tuition expenses in a year, part of the earnings portion of the distributions is excludable and the balance of the earnings portion is taxable. The excludable part of the distributions is the earnings portion of the distributions times a fraction having as its numerator the year's qualified education expenses and as its denominator the year's total distributions. (Code Sec. 530(d)(2)(B))[11] Any savings bond redemption proceeds transferred to a Coverdell ESA in a tax-free transfer under Code Sec. 135 (see ¶2221) do *not* increase the investment in the contract in applying the Code Sec. 72 rules to the taxation of Coverdell ESA distributions. (Code Sec. 135(c)(2)(C))

Any taxable amount also is subject to a 10% additional tax, but not (1) if made on or after the beneficiary's death or disability, (2) to the extent the taxable amount doesn't exceed (a) the amount of a tax-free scholarship received by the beneficiary, or (b) the "advanced education costs" received by the beneficiary at a U.S. service academy (e.g., U.S. Military Academy), (3) if the distribution is taxable solely because of the rule (explained above) reducing the total amount of qualified education expenses by the expenses taken into account in determining the education credit for the year, or (4) if the tax is attributable to income on a contribution withdrawn (along with associated income) before June 1 of the year following the contribution year. (Code Sec. 530(d)(4))

If aggregate distributions from Coverdell ESAs and qualified tuition programs (¶2209) in a year exceed an individual's qualified education expenses, the expenses must be allocated among the distributions. (Code Sec. 530(d)(2)(D)) No deduction, credit, or exclusion is allowed under any other Code provision for an education expense taken into account in determining the Coverdell ESA exclusion. (Code Sec. 530(d)(2)(D))[12]

¶ 2209 Qualified Tuition Programs (QTPs) — "Sec. 529 Plans." ▮▮▮▮▮▮▮

Distributions from a qualified tuition program (QTP, also known as a "Sec. 529 plan") are excludable to the extent used to pay for qualified higher education expenses.

¶ 2210 Qualified tuition programs (QTPs).

Distributions from a QTP (or "Sec. 529 plan") are excludable to the extent used to pay for qualified higher education expenses. A QTP is a tax-exempt program established and maintained by a state (including a state agency or instrumentality), or one or more eligible educational institutions (including private ones) under which a taxpayer may:

(1) buy tuition credits or certificates on behalf of a designated beneficiary (¶2212) which entitle the beneficiary to a waiver or payment of qualified higher education expenses (¶2211) — i.e., a prepaid educational services account, or

(2) make contributions to an account set up to meet the designated beneficiary's qualified higher education expenses — i.e., an educational savings account. This option is available only for state (or state agency or instrumentality) programs. (Code Sec. 529(b)(1)(A); Prop Reg. § 1.529-2(c) ["Taxpayer may rely,"])[13]

🅡*observation:* Prepaid educational services accounts allow credits or certificates to be purchased at the current tuition rate, even though they won't be used for some time.

A QTP must require all purchases or contributions to be made in cash (there is no dollar limit on contributions), provide separate accounting for each designated beneficiary, prohibit the contributor and designated beneficiary from directing, indirectly or directly, the investment of contributions (or earnings), prohibit pledging an interest in the program as security, and provide adequate safeguards to prevent contributions in excess of amounts necessary for

---

11. ¶A-4609; ¶5304; TD ¶147,209   13. ¶A-4727; ¶5294; TD ¶672,302
12. ¶A-4609 *et seq.*; ¶5304 *et seq.*; TD ¶147,214

the beneficiary's qualified higher education expenses. (Code Sec. 529(b))[14] A QTP maintained by a private educational institution generally must get a ruling that it meets applicable requirements. (Code Sec. 529(b)(1))[15]

For the gift-tax treatment of contributions to a QTP, see ¶5040.

¶ 2211 Tax treatment of distributions from qualified tuition programs.

Distributions from a qualified tuition program (QTP) are includible in the distributee's income under the Code Sec. 72 annuity rules, to the extent not excluded under any other Code provision. (Code Sec. 529(c)(3)(A))[16]

In-kind distributions (e.g., tuition credits or waivers, payment vouchers) from state-sponsored QTPs aren't includible in gross income if the benefit, if paid for by the distributee, would have been a payment of a qualified higher education expense. (Code Sec. 529(c)(3)(B); Prop Reg. § 1.529-1(c), ["Taxpayer may rely,"])[17]

Cash distributions are fully excludable if they don't exceed qualified higher education expenses, reduced by expenses for which in-kind distributions were received. If cash distributions exceed qualified expenses, the amount otherwise includible under the Code Sec. 72 annuity rules is reduced by the ratio of qualified expenses to distributions. (Code Sec. 529(c)(3)(B)(ii))[18]

Qualified higher education expenses for QTP purposes are: (1) tuition, fees, books, supplies, equipment required for the enrollment or attendance of a designated beneficiary (¶2212) at an eligible educational institution, and expenses for special needs services; and (2) room and board costs (subject to a limit) for students who are at least half-time. (Code Sec. 529(e)(3))[19]

For QTP exclusion purposes, total annual qualified higher education expenses are reduced by excludable scholarships or educational assistance received, and by any qualified higher education expenses taken into account in determining the HOPE and Lifetime Learning credits (¶2201 *et seq.*) allowed to the taxpayer or any other person. (Code Sec. 529(c)(3)(B)(v))[20]

Distributions from a QTP aren't taxed if transferred (rolled over) within 60 days (but not more than once in 12 months) to another QTP for the same designated beneficiary or to a QTP for a member of the designated beneficiary's family (¶2212). (Code Sec. 529(c)(3)(C)(iii))[21] A change in the designated beneficiary isn't a distribution if the new beneficiary is a member of the old beneficiary's family; see ¶2212. (Code Sec. 529(c)(3)(C)(ii))[22]

A 10% additional tax applies to QTP distributions includible in gross income, in the same way, and with the same exceptions, as for Coverdell ESA distributions (see ¶2217). (Code Sec. 529(c)(6))[23]

If total distributions from a QTP and from a Coverdell ESA (see ¶2205 *et seq.*) exceed qualified higher education expenses otherwise taken into account under the QTP rules (after the above reductions), the taxpayer must allocate the expenses among the distributions for purposes of determining the QTP exclusion. (Code Sec. 529(c)(3)(B)(vi))[24]

¶ 2212 Designated beneficiary of a qualified tuition program.

The designated beneficiary of a qualified tuition program (QTP, see ¶2210) is:

(1) the individual so designated at the start of participation in the QTP; (Code

14. ¶A-4727; ¶5294; TD ¶672,302
15. ¶A-4729; ¶5294; TD ¶672,302
16. ¶A-4709 *et seq.*; ¶5294.02; TD ¶147,101 *et seq.*
17. ¶A-4709; ¶5294.02; TD ¶147,101
18. ¶A-4709; ¶5294.02; TD ¶147,101
19. ¶A-4711; ¶5294; TD ¶672,310

20. ¶A-4709; ¶5294.02; TD ¶147,101
21. ¶A-4721; ¶5294.02; TD ¶147,105
22. ¶A-4722; ¶5294.02; TD ¶147,107
23. ¶A-4720; ¶5294.02; TD ¶147,109
24. ¶A-4716; ¶5294.02; TD ¶147,101

Sec. 529(e)(1)(A))

(2) where beneficiaries are changed and the new one is a member of the same family (spouses, individuals meeting the relationship tests at ¶3119, spouses of these individuals, and first cousins of the beneficiary), the individual who is the new beneficiary; (Code Sec. 529(e)(1)(B); Code Sec. 529(e)(2))

(3) in the case of an interest in a QTP purchased by a state or eligible educational institution as part of a scholarship program it operates, the individual receiving the interest as a scholarship. (Code Sec. 529(e)(1)(C))[25]

¶ 2213 Employer-Provided Educational Benefits; Scholarships and Fellowships. ▆▆▆▆

An employee may exclude the value of educational benefits provided by an employer if the benefit qualifies as a working condition fringe or is provided under an educational assistance program. Qualified tuition reductions for employees of educational institutions and qualifying scholarships and fellowships also are excludable.

¶ 2214 When education benefits are excluded as working condition fringes.

Employer-provided educational expenses are excludable from an employee's income as a working condition fringe benefit to the extent that if the employee paid for the benefit, the amount paid could have qualified as a deductible employee business expense. For the criteria that apply in determining if education is a deductible employee business expense, see ¶2229. (Reg § 1.132-1(f); Reg § 1.132-5(a)(2))[26]

No business expense deduction is allowed for expenses incurred to meet minimum job qualifications, or qualify for a new trade or business.

¶ 2215 Exclusion for employer-provided educational assistance under a qualified program.

An employee may exclude educational assistance provided under an employer's qualified educational assistance program, up to an annual maximum of $5,250. (Code Sec. 127(a)(1)) The education received need not be job-related. (Code Sec. 127(a)(2))

Expenses paid by an employer for education or training provided to the employee that aren't excludable under this provision can only be excluded from income if they qualify as a working condition fringe benefit (¶2214). (Code Sec. 132(j)(8))

"Educational assistance" means the employer's payment for or provision of tuition, fees, books, supplies and equipment under an educational assistance program, including amounts for graduate-level courses. It doesn't include meals, lodging, transportation, or tools or supplies (other than textbooks) that may be retained after the course ends. (Code Sec. 127(c)(1); Reg § 1.127-2(c)(3))[27]

Eligibility requirements can't discriminate in favor of "highly compensated employees" (see ¶4325). (Code Sec. 127(b)(2); Reg § 1.127-2(e)(1))[28] No deduction or credit can be taken by the employee for any amount excluded from income. (Code Sec. 127(c)(7))[29]

¶ 2216 Exclusion for qualifying scholarships and fellowships.

A scholarship or fellowship isn't taxable, to the extent it's a "qualified scholarship" granted to a degree candidate at an educational organization and isn't a stipend (¶2218). (Code Sec. 117(a), Code Sec. 117(c))[30] A "qualified scholarship" is any amount received as a

---

25. ¶A-4701; ¶5294; TD ¶672,309

26. ¶H-2052; ¶1324.05; TD ¶136,516

27. ¶H-2065; ¶1274.01; TD ¶136,525

28. ¶H-2069; ¶1274.01; TD ¶136,526

29. ¶H-2064; ¶1274.01; TD ¶136,525

30. ¶J-1230; ¶1174.01; TD ¶193,501

scholarship and used for tuition and fees required for enrollment at an educational organization, and for required fees, books, supplies and equipment. (Code Sec. 117(b)(2))[31] An "educational organization" is one that normally maintains a regular faculty, curriculum and regularly enrolled student body in attendance. (Code Sec. 117(b)(2)(A))[32]

¶ 2217   Exclusion for qualified tuition reductions for school employees.

Qualified tuition reductions for employees of educational institutions are excluded from the recipient's gross income. (Code Sec. 117(d)) A "qualified tuition reduction" is the amount of tuition reduction provided to an employee of an educational organization for below-graduate-level education (not services, see ¶2218) at that or a similar institution, for the employee (whether active, retired, or disabled), or the employee's spouse or dependent children. (Code Sec. 117(d)(2)) But a tuition reduction for a graduate student engaged in teaching or research can be tax-free. (Code Sec. 117(d)(5))[33]

A qualified tuition reduction provided with respect to a highly compensated employee (¶4325) is excludable only if it's available to all employees on a nondiscriminatory basis. (Code Sec. 117(d)(3))[34]

¶ 2218   Payments for teaching or research.

The exclusions for qualified scholarships (¶2216) and qualified tuition reductions (¶2217) don't apply to any amount received that represents payment for teaching, research or other services performed by the student as a condition for receiving the qualified benefit. (Code Sec. 117(c)(1))[35] This no-payment-for-services rule doesn't apply to amounts received under certain health professions scholarship programs. (Code Sec. 117(c)(2)).[36]

¶ 2219   Higher Education Exclusion for Savings Bond Income. ▪▪▪▪▪▪▪▪

Qualified U.S. savings bond income is excluded if redemption proceeds don't exceed qualified higher education expenses. The exclusion phases out at higher levels of modified adjusted gross income.

¶ 2220   Exclusion of savings bond income—Form 8815.

An individual who pays qualified higher education expenses (¶2221) during a tax year excludes from that year's gross income any amount of income from the redemption, that year, of any "qualified U.S. savings bond" (Series EE bond issued after '89, or Series I bond). (Code Sec. 135(a), Code Sec. 135(c)(1))[37] Use Form 8815 to compute the exclusion. Form 8818 (one per bond) may be used to keep a record of the redemptions. [38]

If taxpayer's aggregate redemption proceeds (principal plus interest) for a tax year exceed the qualified higher education expenses paid that year, the excluded interest is limited to the otherwise excludable amount times this fraction: the qualified expenses paid that year, divided by the year's aggregate redemption proceeds. (Code Sec. 135(b)(1))[39]

Illustration: Taxpayer redeems $8,000 of qualified U.S. savings bonds ($4,000 interest, $4000 principal) and pays qualified higher education expenses of $6,000. The exclusion ratio is 75% ($6,000 ÷ $8,000), so $3,000 of the interest (75% × $4,000) (and the $4,000 principal) is excludable. [40]

---

31. ¶J-1232; ¶1174.01; TD ¶193,502
32. ¶J-1244; ¶1174.01; TD ¶193,507
33. ¶J-1252 *et seq.*; ¶1174.02; TD ¶193,512
34. ¶J-1255; ¶1174.02; TD ¶193,514
35. ¶J-1258; ¶1174.01; TD ¶193,517

36. ¶J-1258.1; ¶1174.05; TD ¶193,517
37. ¶J-3051; ¶1354 *et seq.*; TD ¶157,001
38. ¶J-3051; ¶1354.02; TD ¶157,001
39. ¶J-3052; ¶1354.02; TD ¶157,002
40. ¶J-3052; ¶1354.02; TD ¶157,002

A married individual must file a joint return to get the exclusion. (Code Sec. 135(d)(2))[41]

The individual must have bought the bond(s) after having reached age 24 (Code Sec. 135(c)(1)(B)) and must be the sole owner (or joint owner with his spouse). The exclusion isn't available to the owner of a bond that was bought by another individual (other than a spouse). Nor is it available to a parent who buys the bonds and puts them in the name of a child or other dependent. But the owner may designate an individual (including a child) as the beneficiary for amounts payable at death without losing the exclusion. [42]

For 2007, the exclusion phases out for a taxpayer whose modified adjusted gross income (modified AGI, see below) for the year exceeds $65,600 ($98,400 on a joint return). For 2008, the phaseout amount is $67,100 ($100,650 on a joint return). The amount of the reduction in the exclusion (but not below zero) equals the amount otherwise excludable (*but for* this phaseout) times this fraction: the excess of modified AGI over the appropriate phaseout amount, divided by $15,000 ($30,000 for a joint return). (Code Sec. 135(b)(2)) Thus, the exclusion is not available in 2007 when modified AGI reaches $80,600, or $128,400 for a joint return ($82,100, or $130,650 for a joint return, for 2008). [43]

The exclusion generally applies only if the owner redeems the bonds, i.e., not if he transfers them to the educational institution (see ¶2221 for exceptions).[44]

Modified AGI is AGI determined without the Code Sec. 221 deduction for interest on a qualified education loan (¶2225), the Code Sec. 222 deduction for higher education expenses (¶2223), the Code Sec. 199 U.S. production activities deduction (¶1614), the savings bond interest exclusion, itself, or the Code Sec. 911, Code Sec. 931, and Code Sec. 933 exclusions for income earned abroad or the Code Sec. 137 exclusion for employer-provided adoption assistance (¶1255). (Code Sec. 135(c)(4))[45]

¶ 2221   Qualified higher education expenses for savings bonds exclusion.

For purposes of the savings bond exclusion (¶2220), qualified higher education expenses are tuition and fees required for the enrollment or attendance of taxpayer, taxpayer's spouse or any dependent for whom taxpayer is allowed a dependency exemption (¶3119), at an eligible educational institution, (Code Sec. 135(c)(2)(A)) e.g., most colleges, junior colleges, nursing schools and vocational schools. (Code Sec. 135(c)(3)) Expenses with respect to any course or other education involving sports, games or hobbies, other than as part of a degree program, don't count. (Code Sec. 135(c)(2)(B))[46] The transfer of redemption proceeds to a qualified tuition program (¶2209) or to a Coverdell education savings account (see ¶2214) for the taxpayer (or his spouse or dependent) also is a qualified higher education expense. (Code Sec. 135(c)(2)(C))[47]

Expenses otherwise taken into account must be reduced by amounts received for excludable qualified scholarships (¶2216), certain educational assistance allowances and other tax-exempt payments (other than gifts, bequests, devises or inheritances), and a payment, waiver, or reimbursement of qualified higher education expenses under a qualified tuition program. (Code Sec. 135(d)(1))[48] The amount of qualified higher education expenses also must be reduced by the amount of such expenses taken into account in figuring the exclusions for distributions from Coverdell education savings accounts (¶2214) and qualified tuition programs (¶2209), and by expenses taken into account in determining the Hope and Lifetime Learning credit (¶2201) allowed to the taxpayer or any other person with respect to those expenses. This reduction is made before applying the rules reducing the excluded amount where redemption proceeds exceed higher education expenses and where taxpayer's modified

41. ¶J-3051; ¶1354; TD ¶157,001
42. ¶s J-3055, J-3056; ¶1354.01; TD ¶s 157,005, 157,006
43. ¶J-3053; ¶1354.03; TD ¶157,003
44. ¶J-3051; ¶1354.02; TD ¶157,001

45. ¶J-3054; ¶1354.03; TD ¶157,004
46. ¶s J-3057, J-3061; ¶1354.02; TD ¶s 157,007, 157,011
47. ¶J-3059; ¶1354; TD ¶157,009
48. ¶J-3060; ¶1354.02; TD ¶157,010

AGI exceeds specified dollar amounts) (see ¶2220). (Code Sec. 135(d)(2))[49]

¶ 2222   Above-the-Line Deduction for Higher-Education Expenses (before 2008) ▬▬▬

For payments before 2008, eligible individuals can claim an above-the-line deduction for higher education expenses.

¶ 2223   Above-the-line deduction for higher-education expenses before 2008 — Form 8917.

For payments made before 2008, eligible individuals may deduct (on Form 8917) higher education expenses (¶2224)—i.e., "qualified tuition and related expenses" of the taxpayer, his spouse, or dependents —as an adjustment to gross income to arrive at adjusted gross income. (Code Sec. 222(a)) The higher education deduction can't exceed:

. . . $4,000 for taxpayers whose modified AGI for the tax year doesn't exceed $65,000 ($130,000 for a joint return);

. . . $2,000 for taxpayers whose modified AGI exceeds $65,000 ($130,000 for a joint return), but doesn't exceed $80,000 ($160,000 for a joint return); and

. . . zero for other taxpayers. (Code Sec. 222(b)(2)(B))

caution: Check www.riahome.com/federaltaxhandbook to see if this provision has been extended.

Modified AGI is AGI determined without regard to the higher-education expense, the U.S. production activities deduction (¶1614) or the exclusions for foreign, possessions, and Puerto Rico income. (Code Sec. 222(b)(2))

The deduction for higher-education expenses is allowed for any tax year only to the extent the qualified tuition and related expenses are for enrollment at a higher education institution during that year, except that the deduction is allowed for expenses paid during a tax year if the expenses are in connection with an academic term beginning during that year or during the first 3 months of the next year. (Code Sec. 222(d)(3))

The higher-education expense deduction isn't allowed:

. . . unless the taxpayer includes on his tax return for the relevant year the name and TIN of the individual for whom the higher education expenses were paid, (Code Sec. 222(d)(2))

. . . for any expense for which a deduction is allowed to the taxpayer under any other provision of Chapter 1 of the Code, (Code Sec. 222(c)(1))

. . . for a tax year with respect to an individual's qualified tuition and related expenses if he or any other person elects to claim a Hope credit or Lifetime Learning credit (see ¶2201 *et seq.*) with respect to that individual for that year. (Code Sec. 222(c)(2)(A))

Higher-education expense deductions may not be claimed by a taxpayer who: files separately for the tax year (Code Sec. 222(d)(4)); may be claimed as a dependent (¶3119) on another's return (Code Sec. 222(c)(3)); or is a nonresident alien for any part of the tax year, unless so treated under a Code Sec. 6013(g) or Code Sec. 6013(h) election (to treat a spouse as a resident alien) by a U.S. citizen or resident with a nonresident alien spouse. (Code Sec. 222(d)(5))[50]

¶ 2224   Higher-education expenses for the pre-2008 above-the-line deduction.

For purposes of the above-the line deduction for higher-education expenses (¶2223), higher education expenses consist of qualified tuition and related expenses, defined the same way as

---

49. ¶J-3060; ¶1354; TD ¶157,010   50. ¶A-4471; ¶2224; TD ¶352,001

for Hope and Lifetime Learning Credit purposes (¶2201), but reduced by the amount of the expenses that are taken into account in determining amounts excluded under: Code Sec. 135 (interest on bonds used to pay for higher education expenses, ¶2219), Code Sec. 529(c)(1) (distributions from qualified tuition plans, but limited to the excludible earnings from such plans, ¶2209) and Code Sec. 530(d)(1) (full amount of distributions from Coverdell education savings accounts, ¶2205). Qualified tuition and related expenses also are reduced by certain excludible scholarships and other payments. (Code Sec. 222(c)(2)(B), Code Sec. 222(d)(1))[1]

¶ 2225   Deduction for Interest Paid on Qualified Education Loans.

Qualifying individuals may claim an above-the-line deduction for up to $2,500 of interest paid on a qualified higher education loan.

¶ 2226   Up to $2,500 of qualified education loan interest deductible above-the-line.

Student loan interest generally is treated as personal interest and thus isn't deductible. However, individuals may deduct a maximum of $2,500 annually for interest paid on qualified higher education loans. (Code Sec. 221)[2] The deduction is claimed as an adjustment to gross income to arrive at adjusted gross income. (Code Sec. 62(a)(17))[3] There's no deduction for any amount for which a deduction is allowable under any other Code provision (e.g., home equity loan; see ¶1734). (Code Sec. 221(e)(1))[4]

For 2007, the deduction phases out ratably for taxpayers with modified AGI between $55,000 and $70,000 ($110,000 and $140,000 for joint returns). For 2008, the phaseout range is between $55,000 and $70,000 ($115,000 and $145,000 for joint returns). (Code Sec. 221(b)(2)(B)) Modified AGI is AGI figured without regard to the deduction for qualified education loan interest, the deduction for qualified higher education expenses (¶2222), the Code Sec. 199 U.S. production activities deduction (¶1614), and without regard to the exclusions for foreign, possession, and Puerto Rico income. (Code Sec. 221(b)(2)(C)(i))[5]

A person who is claimed as a dependent on another's return can't claim the education interest deduction. (Code Sec. 221(c))[6] The deduction may be claimed only by a person legally obligated to make the interest payments. (Reg § 1.221-1(b))[7] Married couples must file joint returns to take the deduction. (Code Sec. 221(e)(3))[8]

For information reporting requirements for interest payments received on qualified education loans, see ¶4750.

¶ 2227   Qualified education loan defined.

A qualified higher education loan is any debt incurred by the taxpayer solely to pay qualified higher education expenses that are: (1) incurred on behalf of the taxpayer, the taxpayer's spouse, or any dependent of the taxpayer as of the time the debt was incurred; (2) paid or incurred within a reasonable period of time before or after the debt is incurred; and (3) attributable to education furnished during a period when the recipient was an eligible student (as defined for Hope credit purposes, i.e., at least a half-time student, see ¶2202). (Code Sec. 221(d)(1))

Revolving lines of credit generally aren't qualified education loans unless the borrower agreed to use the line of credit to pay only qualifying higher education expenses. A qualified education loan includes debt used to refinance debt that qualifies as a qualified education loan, but doesn't include certain debt owed to a related person or a loan under a qualified

---

1. ¶A-4474; ¶2224
2. ¶K-5500 *et seq.*; ¶2214; TD ¶314,100 *et seq.*
3. ¶K-5501; ¶2214
4. ¶K-5503.2; ¶2214.02; TD ¶314,109

5. ¶K-5502; ¶2214.01; TD ¶314,106
6. ¶K-5503
7. ¶K-5501.1
8. ¶K-5501

employer plan. (Code Sec. 221(e)(1))[9]

Qualified higher education expenses include tuition, fees, room and board, and related expenses, but must be reduced by the amount excluded by reason of such expenses under the rules for: employer-provided educational assistance benefits (¶2215), income from U.S. Savings Bonds used to pay higher education expenses (¶2219), Coverdell education savings accounts (¶2205), qualified tuition plans (¶2209), and scholarship or fellowship grants (¶2216). (Code Sec. 221(d)(2)) They also must be reduced by veterans' and armed forces' educational assistance allowances and any other educational assistance excludable from the student's gross income (other than as a gift, bequest, devise or inheritance). (Reg §   1.221-1(f)(2))[10]

¶ 2228   Education Expenses Related to Business or Employment. ▬▬▬▬▬▬▬▬

A taxpayer can deduct costs incurred to maintain or improve skills required in his business or employment, but not costs incurred to meet minimum requirements for a trade or profession or to qualify for a new trade or profession.

¶ 2229   When business- or employment-related expenses are deductible.

Education expenses are deductible if made by a taxpayer either to maintain or improve skills required in his business or employment or to meet the express requirements of his employer, or the requirements of law or regs, imposed as a condition to retaining his salary, status or employment. (Reg §   1.162-5)[11]

A lawyer who has actually practiced law may generally deduct the expenses of any further legal education on the grounds that it maintains or improves required skills even though the education qualifies him to practice as a specialist. [12] A non-lawyer employed in allied fields where a legal education is helpful or customary can't deduct legal education costs. (Reg §   1.162-5(b)(3))[13]

Deductions aren't allowed if the education:

. . . is needed to meet the minimum requirements for taxpayer's present or intended employment, trade, business or profession (Reg §   1.162-5(b)(2))[14] or

. . . is undertaken to fulfill general education aspirations or for other personal reasons, [15] or

. . . is part of a program of study that will lead to qualifying the individual in a new trade or business. (Reg §   1.162-5(b)(3)(i))[16]

Expenses that are otherwise deductible won't be disallowed because the course of studies leads to a degree. (Reg §   1.162-5(a))[17]

Self-employed taxpayers claim education deductions on Schedule C, C-EZ, or F of Form 1040; employees claim unreimbursed education expenses as miscellaneous itemized deductions on Schedule A, Form 1040.

¶ 2230   Travel and transportation expenses of education.

The expenses of travel as a form of education aren't deductible. (Code Sec. 274(m)(2))[18] However, travel expenses that are a necessary adjunct to other deductible education expenses may be deductible. [19]

Local transportation expenses for deductible education are deductible. These are expenses incurred in going directly from work to school, and, if the taxpayer is regularly employed and

---

9. ¶K-5504; ¶2214.02; TD ¶314,110
10. ¶K-5504.3
11. ¶L-3701; ¶1624.185; TD ¶302,001
12. ¶s L-3724, L-3722; ¶1624.185; TD ¶302,020
13. ¶L-3720 *et seq.*; TD ¶302,020 *et seq.*
14. ¶L-3713; ¶1624.185; TD ¶302,020

15. ¶L-3704; ¶1624.193; TD ¶302,001
16. ¶L-3715; ¶1624.185; TD ¶302,015
17. ¶L-3701; ¶1624.185; TD ¶302,001
18. ¶L-3734; ¶1624.185; TD ¶302,034
19. ¶L-3734; ¶1624.185; TD ¶302,034

goes to school on a strictly temporary basis, the costs of returning from school to home. A regularly employed taxpayer who goes from home to school on a temporary basis also may deduct the round-trip costs of transportation in going from home to school to home. In general, attendance at school is temporary if it is realistically expected to last (and does in fact last) for one year or less. [20]

Costs of seminar cruises or tours are disallowed if taken primarily for personal purposes even though part of the time is devoted to qualifying professional education. [21] Even if not for personal purposes, the deduction is limited under the rules at ¶1550 and ¶1551.

¶ 2231 Teachers' education expenses.

If the minimum teaching requirements have *already* been met, a teacher may deduct the expense of any education required to retain his or her position, salary or status, even if the education will qualify the teacher to teach a new or different subject. (Reg § 1.162-5) Costs of courses to renew a provisional teaching certificate, or that lead to a *permanent* certificate are deductible if necessary to continue teaching. [22] The cost of education to maintain or improve skills is deductible even if it leads to an advanced degree (Reg § 1.162-5(c)) or qualifies the teacher for a change of duties. (Reg § 1.162-5(b))[23] Education to meet minimum requirements isn't deductible. (Reg § 1.162-5(b)(2))[24]

¶ 2232 Limited above-the-line deduction for educator expenses—before 2008.

For tax years beginning before 2008, an eligible educator —a grade K through 12 teacher, instructor, counselor, principal, or aide in a school for at least 900 hours during a school year (Code Sec. 62(d)(1))—may claim an "above the line deduction" (i.e., an adjustment to gross income to arrive at adjusted gross income) for up to $250 of trade or business expenses paid or incurred for books, supplies (other than nonathletic supplies for courses of instruction in health or physical education), computer equipment (including related software and services) and other equipment, and supplementary materials used in the classroom. (Code Sec. 62(a)(2)(D))

Ⓡ*caution:* Check www.ria.thomson.com/federaltaxhandbook to see if this provision has been extended.

---

20. ¶L-3730; ¶1624.185; TD ¶302,030
21. ¶L-3733; ¶2744.04; TD ¶302,033
22. ¶L-3703; ¶1624.185; TD ¶302,003

23. ¶L-3705; ¶1624.185; TD ¶302,025
24. ¶L-3714; ¶1624.185; TD ¶302,005

Chapter 8   Tax Credits

¶ 2300   Tax Credits.

Tax credits are either business credits intended to provide special incentives for the achievement of certain economic objectives, or personal credits, which provide tax benefits to certain taxpayers (e.g., the elderly or disabled, etc.). The foreign tax credit, however, may apply to both business and nonbusiness taxpayers.

The three main categories of tax credits are:

(1) The business incentive credits, see ¶2301 *et seq.*

(2) The personal (refundable and nonrefundable) credits, see ¶2340 *et seq.*

(3) The foreign tax credit, see ¶2369 *et seq.*

For credit for alternative minimum tax, see ¶2367.

For tax credits attributable to certain "passive" activities, see ¶1810 *et seq.*

¶ 2301   Business Incentive Credits.

Certain business incentive credits are combined into one "general business credit" for purposes of determining each credit's allowance limitation for the tax year.

¶ 2302   General business credit—Form 3800.

The general business credit is made up of:

... the investment credit (Code Sec. 38(b)(1)), see ¶2307 *et seq.*) (which includes the rehabilitation credit (¶2308), the energy credit (¶2311), and the qualifying advanced coal and gasification project credits (¶2312);

... the work opportunity credit (Code Sec. 38(b)(2)), see ¶2314 *et seq.*;

... the alcohol fuel credit (Code Sec. 38(b)(3)), see ¶2317;

... the incremental research credit (Code Sec. 38(b)(4)), see ¶2318;

... the low-income housing credit (Code Sec. 38(b)(5)), see ¶2319 *et seq.*;

... the enhanced oil recovery credit (Code Sec. 38(b)(6)), see ¶2321;

... the disabled access credit (Code Sec. 38(b)(7)), see ¶2322;

... the credit for producing electricity from renewable resources (Code Sec. 38(b)(8)), see ¶2323;

... the empowerment zone employment credit (Code Sec. 38(b)(9)), see ¶2324;

... the Indian employment credit (Code Sec. 38(b)(10)), see ¶2327;

... the employer social security credit (Code Sec. 38(b)(11)), ¶2328;

... the orphan drug credit (Code Sec. 38(b)(12)), see ¶2329;

... the new markets credit (Code Sec. 38(b)(13)), see ¶2331;

... the employer-provided child care credit (Code Sec. 38(b)(15)), see ¶2332;

... the small employer pension plan startup credit (Code Sec. 38(b)(14)), see ¶2333;

... the railroad track maintenance credit (Code Sec. 38(b)(16), Code Sec. 45G);

... the biodiesel fuel credit (Code Sec. 38(b)(17)), see ¶2334;

... the low sulfur diesel fuel production credit (Code Sec. 38(b)(18)), see ¶2335;

... the marginal oil and gas well production credit (Code Sec. 38(b)(19)), see ¶2336;

... the distilled spirits credit (Code Sec. 38(b)(20); Code Sec. 5011(a));

... the advanced nuclear power facility production credit (Code Sec. 38(b)(21); Code

References beginning with a single letter are to paragraphs in RIA's Federal Tax Coordinator 2d and RIA's Analysis of Federal Taxes: Income. Those beginning with numbers are to paragraphs in RIA's United States Tax Reporter. Those beginning with TD are to paragraphs in RIA's Tax Desk.

329

Sec. 45J(a));

. . . the nonconventional source production credit (Code Sec. 38(b)(22)), see ¶2339;

. . . the new energy efficient home credit (Code Sec. 38(b)(23)), see ¶2337;

. . . the energy efficient appliance credit (Code Sec. 38(b)(24)), see ¶2338;

. . . the applicable portion (that attributable to depreciable property) of the alternative motor vehicle credit (Code Sec. 38(b)(25)), see ¶2362;

. . . the applicable portion (that attributable to depreciable property) of the alternative fuel vehicle refueling property credit (Code Sec. 38(b)(26)), see ¶2363; and

. . . the mine rescue training credit for tax years beginning before 2009. (Code Sec. 38(b)(31), Code Sec. 45N)

The credit for excise tax payments to the Trans-Alaska Pipeline Liability Fund (Code Sec. 4612(e)(1)), the renewal community employment credit (Code Sec. 1400H(a)), see ¶2325), and the community development corporation credit (¶2330) aren't included in the above Code Sec. 38(b) list, but are also part of the current year business credit.

¶ 2303　Limitation on general business credits based on tax liability.

A credit is allowed against income tax for a particular tax year equal to the sum of: (1) the business credit carry *forwards* carried to the tax year, (2) the *current year* business credit, and (3) the business credit carry *backs* carried to the tax year. (Code Sec. 38(a))[1]

The credit allowed for any tax year (except for the empowerment zone employment credit, the New York Liberty Zone business employee credit, and "specified credits," see below) is limited to the excess of taxpayer's "net income tax" over the greater of: (1) the tentative minimum tax for the tax year, or (2) 25% of the amount of the taxpayer's "net regular tax" that exceeds $25,000. (Code Sec. 38(c)(1))[2] Husbands and wives who file separate returns are each limited to $12,500 instead of $25,000, but if either spouse has no carryforward, carryback or current year general business credit in the tax year that ends within or with the other spouse's tax year, the other spouse gets the full amount of $25,000. (Code Sec. 38(c)(5)(A))[3]

For estates and trusts, the $25,000 amount is reduced to an amount equal to $25,000 multiplied by a fraction (numerator is the total income of the estate or trust not allocated to beneficiaries, denominator is the total income of the estate or trust). (Code Sec. 38(c)(5)(D))[4]

Net income tax is the sum of the regular tax liability and the alternative minimum tax (AMT), ¶3200), reduced by the credits listed below. Net regular tax is the regular tax liability reduced by the sum of the following credits (Code Sec. 38(c)(1)): (1) household and dependent care credit (Code Sec. 21); (2) credit for the elderly and the permanently and totally disabled (Code Sec. 22); (3) adoption credit (Code Sec. 23); (4) child tax credit (Code Sec. 24); (5) mortgage credit (Code Sec. 25); (6) Hope scholarship and Lifetime learning credits (Code Sec. 25A); (7) credit for making elective deferrals and IRA contributions (Code Sec. 25B); (8) nonbusiness energy property credit (Code Sec. 25C); (9) residential energy efficient property (Code Sec. 25D); (10) possessions tax credits (for American Samoa) (Code Sec. 27 and Code Sec. 936); (11) alternative fuel production credit (Code Sec. 45K); (12) alternative motor vehicle credit (Code Sec. 30B); (13) qualified alternative fuel vehicle refueling property credit (Code Sec. 30C); and (14) first-time homebuyer credit for District of Columbia (Code Sec. 1400C(g)).[5]

The empowerment zone employment credit is limited to the excess of the taxpayer's net income tax over the greater of: (1) 75% of his tentative minimum tax, or (2) 25% of so much of

---

1. ¶L-15200; ¶384.01 - ¶384.03; TD ¶380,500
2. ¶L-15202; ¶384.02; TD ¶380,502
3. ¶L-15204; ¶384.02; TD ¶380,505
4. ¶L-15207; ¶384.02; TD ¶380,507
5. ¶L-15202; ¶384.02, 384.03; TD ¶380,502

his net regular tax liability as exceeds $25,000. This limitation is reduced by the general credits (not including the empowerment zone employment credit, New York Liberty Zone business employee credit, and other specified credits, see below) allowed for the tax year. (Code Sec. 38(c)(2)) The effect is that the empowerment zone employment credit may be used to offset up to 25% of a taxpayer's AMT.[6]

"Specified credits" may offset 100% of a taxpayer's AMT. (Code Sec. 38(c)(4)) They include: (1) credits determined under Code Sec. 45 (¶2323) to the extent attributable to electricity or refined coal produced at a facility which is originally placed in service after Oct. 22, 2004 and during the four-year period beginning on the date the facility was originally placed in service; (2) the alcohol fuel credit; (¶2317) (Code Sec. 38(c)(4)(B)); (3) the Indian coal production credit during the 4-year period it's first placed in service; (Code Sec. 45(e)) and (4) in tax years beginning after 2006, the FICA tip credit (¶2328) and the work opportunity tax credit (¶2314).

¶ 2304 Carryback and carryforward of general business credits.

There's a one-year carryback (five-year carryback for the marginal well production credit, see ¶2336) and 20-year carryforward (on Form 3800). (Code Sec. 39(a)) No part of any unused current business credit attributable to a component credit may be carried back to tax years before the first tax year that the component credit was allowable. (Code Sec. 39(d))[7]

¶ 2305 Deduction for unused general business credits after the carryover period.

If any portion of a qualified business credit (investment credit, work opportunity credit, alcohol fuels credit, incremental research credit, enhanced oil recovery credit, empowerment zone employment credit, employer social security credit, new markets tax credit, small employer pension plan startup credit, Indian employment credit, biodiesel fuels credit, low sulfur diesel fuel production credit, and new energy efficient home credit —but not including the nonconventional fuel production credit (Code Sec. 196(c))—hasn't been allowed after the carryover period expires, the taxpayer is allowed to deduct the unused portion in the first tax year after the last tax year of the carryover period (or in the tax year of the taxpayer's death or cessation if earlier). (Code Sec. 196(a), Code Sec. 196(b)) But, for the research credit for a tax year beginning before '90 and for the investment tax credit (other than the rehabilitation credit), the deduction is 50% of the unused amount. (Code Sec. 196(d))[8]

¶ 2306 Ordering rules for the general business credits.

The order in which the component credits of the general business credit are used in a tax year or as a carryback or carryforward is determined on the basis of the order they are listed in Code Sec. 38(b) (¶2302) as of the close of the tax year in which the credit is used. (Code Sec. 38(d)(1)) The order in which the component credits of the business investment credit are used is determined on the basis of the order they are listed in Code Sec. 46 as of the close of the tax year in which the credit is used. (Code Sec. 38(d)(2))

Carryovers of pre-'87 ESOP credits are used as if they were added to the end of the list in Code Sec. 38(b). (Code Sec. 38(d)(3)(A)) Carryovers of pre-'91 regular investment credits are used before the rehabilitation credit. (Code Sec. 38(d)(3)(B)(ii))[9]

¶ 2307 The investment tax credits—Form 3468.

The Code Sec. 46 investment tax credit (claimed on Form 3468) consists of: (1) the rehabilitation investment credit (Code Sec. 47), see ¶2308 *et seq.*; (2) the energy credit (Code

6. ¶L-15202.1; ¶384.02; TD ¶380,503
7. ¶L-15209; ¶384.01, ¶384.03; TD ¶380,509

8. ¶L-15212; ¶1964.01; TD ¶380,510
9. ¶L-15208; ¶384.01; TD ¶380,508

Sec. 48(a)), see ¶2311;[10] (3) the qualifying advanced coal project credit (Code Sec. 48A), see ¶2312;[11] and (4) the qualifying gasification project credit. (Code Sec. 48B(e)), see ¶2312.[12]

Property qualifying for the rehabilitation credit (depreciable or amortizable property) is treated as investment credit property. (Code Sec. 50(a)(5)) But certain otherwise qualified property is denied the applicable credit if it is:

. . . Property used "predominantly" outside the U.S., except for property listed in Code Sec. 168(g)(4)—dealing with rolling stock, spacecraft, satellites, etc. (Code Sec. 50(b)(1))

. . . Property used predominantly to furnish, or in connection with the furnishing of, permanent lodging, except for certain nonlodging commercial facilities, lodging facilities used by transients, certified historic structures, and energy property. (Code Sec. 50(b)(2))

. . . Property used by certain tax-exempt organizations. (Code Sec. 50(b)(3)) If property is leased to a partnership or other pass-through entity, a proportionate share of the property is treated as leased to each tax-exempt entity partner (under the rules of Code Sec. 168(h)(5) and (6)) in determining whether any portion of the property is tax-exempt use property. (Code Sec. 50(b)(4))

. . . Property used by the U.S. or other governmental units, except for short-lease property. (Code Sec. 50(b)(4))[13]

Pass-through to lessee. A lessee of new investment credit property may be entitled to take the investment credit on the property if the lessor elects to pass it to him. (Code Sec. 50(d); Reg § 1.48-4) The election statement is described in the regs. (Reg § 1.48-4(f), Reg § 1.48-4(g)) The effect is to treat the lessee as having acquired the property for its fair market value, but the lessor's basis is used instead when lessor and lessee are members of the same controlled group. The lessee uses the same investment credit life for the property as the lessor.[14]

But a lessor's election to pass the investment credit from property with an over 14-year ADR depreciation "class life" to his lessee results in only a partial transfer of the credit if the lease is for a period that is less than 80% of the property's "class life" and isn't a "net lease." (Reg § 1.48-4(a)(2))[15]

At-risk rules impact. If there is a net decrease in the amount of nonqualified nonrecourse financing (under the at-risk rules, ¶1803, *et seq.*) as of the close of a tax year following that in which property was placed in service, the net decrease is treated as an increase in the credit base for the property. Thus, an increase in the amount that the taxpayer has at risk for a particular investment credit property is additional qualified investment. (Code Sec. 49(a)(2))[16]

¶ 2308   Rehabilitation investment credits.

The rehabilitation credit for a building is 10% (20% for a certified historic structure) of the qualified rehabilitation expenditure. (Code Sec. 47(a)) A rehabilitated building (other than a certified historic structure) is eligible for the credit only if the building was first placed in service before '36. (Code Sec. 47(c)(1)(B))[17]

The credit is 13% (26% for a certified historic structure) of the qualified rehabilitation expenditures for eligible buildings located in the Gulf Opportunity (GO) Zone paid or incurred before Jan. 1, 2009. (Code Sec. 1400N(h))[18] The GO Zone is the area entitled to individual assistance or individual and public assistance from FEMA (Federal Emergency Management Agency) as a result of the President's declaration of a major disaster on account of Hurricane

10. ¶L-16500; ¶s 474, 484; TD ¶381,400
11. ¶L-16450; ¶s 48A4; TD ¶396,100
12. ¶L-16470; ¶s 48B4; TD ¶396,200
13. ¶L-16501; ¶504.01; TD ¶381,401
14. ¶s L-16506, L-17010 *et seq.*; ¶484.10; TD ¶381,403

15. ¶L-17015; ¶484.10
16. ¶L-16505; ¶494; TD ¶381,402
17. ¶L-16103; ¶484.13; TD ¶381,503
18. ¶L-16120; ¶14,00N4.04; TD ¶381,518.1

Katrina (this area is also referred to as the "Hurricane Katrina core disaster area"). (Code Sec. 1400M)

A qualified rehabilitation expenditure is any amount charged to capital account and incurred in connection with the rehabilitation (including reconstruction, or an addition or improvement) of a qualified rehabilitated building (¶2309) that's depreciable under Code Sec. 168, and is nonresidential real property, residential rental property, or real property with a class life of more than 12.5 years. Expenditures for which straight-line depreciation isn't used are not qualified expenditures. (Code Sec. 47(c)(2)[19] If bonus first-year depreciation (¶1935) is claimed for the building, the credit may be claimed only if the taxpayer depreciates the remaining adjusted depreciable basis of rehabilitation expenses using the straight line method. (Reg § 1.168(k)-1(f)(10)), Reg § 1.1400L(b)-1(f)(9))[20]

Also excluded are expenditures in connection with the rehabilitation of a building that are allocable to that portion of the building that is (or that may reasonably be expected to be) tax-exempt-use property. (Code Sec. 47(c)(2)(B)(v))[21]

In addition to owner-taxpayers of qualified property, the rehabilitation credits are available to lessees for qualified expenditures incurred by them, but only if, on the rehabilitation's completion date, the remaining term of the lease (without regard to renewal) is at least the recovery period under Code Sec. 168(c). (Code Sec. 47(c)(2)(B)(vi))[22]

¶ 2309 Which buildings qualify for the rehabilitation credit?

The term "qualified rehabilitated building" means any building (and its structural components) that satisfies all of the following requirements:

(1) Except for a certified historic structure, the building was first placed in service before '36, see ¶2308.

(2) The building has been substantially rehabilitated (see below).

(3) The building was placed in service before the beginning of the rehabilitation.

(4) For any building other than a certified historic structure, the building retains in place (a) at least 75% of the external walls (including at least 50% as external walls), and (b) at least 75% of its internal structural framework.

(5) The building must be depreciable or amortizable. (Code Sec. 47(c)(1)(A))[23]

A substantial rehabilitation ((2), above) is one in which the qualified rehabilitation expenditures during the 24-month period selected by the taxpayer (as prescribed in regs) and ending with or within the year exceed the greater of: (1) $5,000; or (2) the adjusted basis of the building and its structural components as of the first day of the 24-month period, or of the holding period (without regard to reconstruction), whichever is later. (Code Sec. 47(c)(1)(C)(i)) Rehabilitation includes reconstruction. (Code Sec. 47(c)(1)(D))[24]

In the case of any rehabilitation that may reasonably be expected to be completed in phases set forth in architectural plans and specifications completed before the rehabilitation begins, a 60-month (instead of 24-month) period applies. For certain buildings located in the GO Zone (¶2308), Rita Gulf Opportunity (GO) Zone, or Wilma GO Zone on which rehabilitation had begun, this 24-month or 60-month is tolled for 12 months. (Code Sec. 47(c)(1)(C)(ii))[25] The Rita GO Zone is the part of the Hurricane Rita disaster area determined by the President to warrant individual or individual and public assistance because of Hurricane Rita; and the Wilma GO Zone is the portion of the Hurricane Wilma disaster area determined by the President to warrant individual or individual and public assistance because of Hurricane

19. ¶L-16102; ¶474; TD ¶381,502
20. ¶L-16102.1; ¶1684.025, ¶14,00L4.05; TD ¶381,502
21. ¶L-16115; ¶474; TD ¶381,516
22. ¶L-16102; ¶474; TD ¶381,501

23. ¶L-16101, L-16103; ¶474; TD ¶381,503
24. ¶L-16106; ¶474; TD ¶381,506
25. ¶L-16113; ¶474; TD ¶381,514

Wilma. (Code Sec. 1400M)

¶ 2310   Progress expenditure rehabilitation credit—Form 3468.

If any building being rehabilitated by or for the taxpayer has a "normal rehabilitation period" of two years or more, and it's reasonable to expect the building to be a qualified rehabilitated building (¶2309) in the hands of the taxpayer when placed in service (Code Sec. 47(d)(2)), the taxpayer may irrevocably elect (on Form 3468) to account for qualified rehabilitation expenditures made with respect to that property as follows: (Code Sec. 47(d)(1); Reg § 1.46-5(g)(1))

(1) where it's reasonable to believe that more than half these expenditures will be made *directly* by the taxpayer, any qualified rehabilitation expenditure is taken into account for the tax year it's properly chargeable to capital account (i.e., includible in computing the property's basis), and

(2) where it's reasonable to believe that no more than half the qualified expenditure will be made directly by the taxpayer, any qualified rehabilitation expenditure is taken into account in the tax year it's paid. [26]

¶ 2311   Energy credit—Form 3468.

A taxpayer may be eligible to claim (on Form 3468) the following energy credits (in each case, the percentage is applied to the basis of eligible energy property placed in service during the year):

(1) 30% for qualified fuel cell property, (Code Sec. 48(a)(2)(A)(i)(I)) i.e., a fuel cell power plant with a nameplate capacity of at least 0.5 kilowatt of electricity using an electrochemical process, and an electricity only generation efficiency of greater than 30%. The credit can't exceed an amount equal to $500 for each 0.5 kilowatt of capacity. The credit isn't available after 2008. (Code Sec. 48(c))

(2) 30% for solar energy property, (Code Sec. 48(a)(2)(A)(i)(II)) i.e., equipment that uses solar energy to generate electricity, to heat or cool (or provide hot water for) a structure, or to provide solar process heat (but not for heating a swimming pool). (Code Sec. 48(a)(3)(A)(i)) The 30% credit is available only for periods ending before 2009. (Code Sec. 48(a)(2)(A)(i)(II)) After 2008, the credit will be 10%. (Code Sec. 48(a)(2)(ii))

(3) 30% for solar energy to illuminate the inside of a structure using fiber optic distributed sunlight, but only for periods ending before 2009. (Code Sec. 48(a)(2)(A)(i)(III), Code Sec. 48(a)(3)(A)(ii))

(4) 10% for equipment used to produce, distribute, or use energy derived from a geothermal deposit. (Code Sec. 48(a)(2)(A)(ii), Code Sec. 48(a)(3)(A)(iii))

(5) 10% for qualified microturbine property, (Code Sec. 48(a)(2)(A)(ii), Code Sec. 48(a)(3)(A)(iv)) i.e., a stationary microturbine powerplant with a nameplate capacity of less than 2,000 kilowatts, and has an electricity only generation efficiency of not less than 26% at International Standard Organization conditions. A credit for qualified microturbine property can't exceed $200 for each kilowatt of the property's capacity. The credit is not available after 2008. (Code Sec. 48(c)(2))

No credit is allowed for property unless it is depreciable or amortizable; its construction, reconstruction or erection is completed by the taxpayer or, if acquired by the taxpayer, its original use begins with the taxpayer; and it meets the official quality and performance standards in effect at the time of acquisition. (Code Sec. 48(a)(3))

---

26. ¶L-16200; ¶474; TD ¶381,519

No credit is allowed for public utility property (Code Sec. 48(a)(3)) (except for certain qualified microturbine property used predominantly in a telephone or telegraph service business (Code Sec. 48(c)(2)(D)), or for property that also qualifies for the rehabilitation credit. (Code Sec. 48(a)(2))[27] If property is financed in whole or in part by subsidized financing or tax-exempt private activity bonds, the amount taken into account as qualified investment is proportionately reduced. (Code Sec. 48(a)(4))[28]

¶ 2312   Credits for qualifying advanced coal projects and gasification projects.

A credit can be claimed for investments in qualifying advanced coal projects. The credit is 20% of the qualified investment for the tax year in integrated gasification combined cycle projects, and 15% of the qualified investment for the tax year in projects that use other advanced coal-based generation technologies. (Code Sec. 48A(a))[29] A separate investment credit can also be claimed for qualified investment in qualifying gasification projects. The credit is 20% of the qualified investment for the tax year. (Code Sec. 48B(a)) This credit is not allowed for any qualified investment for which the above Code Sec. 48A credit is allowed. (Code Sec. 48B(e))[30]

¶ 2313   Recapture of investment credits—Form 4255.

If investment credit property is disposed of or ceases to be investment credit property for the taxpayer before the end of the recapture period, the credit taken for all earlier years is recaptured on Form 4255 (i.e., added to the tax liability for the recapture year). (Code Sec. 50(a)(1)) The recapture percentage is 100% during the first full year after the property is placed in service. This percentage decreases by 20 percentage points every succeeding full year. There's no recapture after the fifth full year. (Code Sec. 50(a)(1)) Recapture applies only to credit used to reduce tax liability. If any part of it isn't used, carrybacks and carryovers of the credit must be appropriately adjusted. (Code Sec. 50(a)(3))

No recapture applies to a transfer by reason of death (Code Sec. 50(a)(4)(A)), a mere change in form of doing business (Code Sec. 50(a)(4)(B)), or a transfer between spouses or incident to divorce (under the rules of Code Sec. 1041(a)). (Code Sec. 50(a)(5)(B))[31]

Different recapture computation methods apply to progress expenditures credit (¶2310) depending on whether the recapture year occurs before or after the progress expenditure property is placed in service. (Code Sec. 50(a)(2))[32]

If the amount of nonqualified nonrecourse financing (¶1809) for at-risk property increases as of the close of the tax year, then the tax for the tax year is increased by the total decrease in credits allowed in earlier tax years that would result if the credit base for the earlier credits had been reduced by the amount of the increase in the nonqualified nonrecourse financing. For purposes of computing recapture, the increase in nonqualified nonrecourse financing is treated as reducing the credit base and correspondingly reducing the qualified investment in the year the property was placed in service. (Code Sec. 49(b)(1)) The transfer of (or an agreement to transfer) any evidence of indebtedness won't be treated as an increase in nonqualified nonrecourse financing, if the transfer occurs (or the agreement is entered into) more than one year after the indebtedness was incurred. (Code Sec. 49(b)(2))[33]

If the taxpayer fails to pay the principal on a level payment nonqualified nonrecourse loan (¶1809) used for qualified energy property, the taxpayer is treated as increasing the amount of nonqualified nonrecourse financing to the extent of the credit recapture. (Code Sec. 49(b)(3))[34]

27. ¶L-16502; ¶484; TD ¶381,601
28. ¶L-16504; ¶484; TD ¶381,603
29. ¶L-16450; ¶s 48A4; TD ¶396,100
30. ¶L-16470; ¶s 48B4; TD ¶396,200

31. ¶L-17301; ¶504.02; TD ¶381,405
32. ¶L-17314; ¶504.02; TD ¶381,407
33. ¶L-17307; ¶494; TD ¶381,408
34. ¶L-16419; ¶494; TD ¶381,607

¶ 2314 Work opportunity tax credit before September 2011—Form 5884.

The work opportunity tax credit (WOTC) allows employers who hire members of certain targeted groups (¶2315) before September 2011 to get a credit against income tax (use Form 5884) of a percentage of first-year wages up to $6,000 per employee ($12,000 for qualified veterans who begin work after May 25, 2007; and $3,000 for qualified summer youth employees). Where the employee is a long-term family assistance (LTFA) recipient (¶2315), the credit is a percentage of first *and* second year wages, up to $10,000 per employee. (Code Sec. 51)

✐*observation:* Before 2007, the employer's credit for hiring LTFA recipients was a separate welfare-to-work credit under former Code Sec. 51A.

Generally, the percentage of qualifying wages is 40% of first-year wages, for a maximum credit of $2,400 (.4 × $6,000) (Code Sec. 51(a)); it's 25% for employees who have completed at least 120 hours, but less than 400 hours of service for the employer. (Code Sec. 51(i)) However, for LTFA recipients, it includes an additional 50% of qualified-second year wages for a maximum credit of $9,000 [(.4 × $10,000) + (.5 × $10,000)]. (Code Sec. 51(e))[35]

The credit reduces the employer's wage deduction dollar-for-dollar. (Code Sec. 280C(a); Reg § 1.280C-1)[36] But the taxpayer can elect not to take the credit. (Code Sec. 51(j))[37]

Wages paid (1) for federally funded on-the-job training, (Code Sec. 51(c)(2)(A))[38] and (2) to an individual who performs the same or substantially similar services as those of employees participating in or affected by a strike or lockout at the employer's plant don't qualify for the credit. (Code Sec. 51(c)(3))[39] Creditable wages are reduced by the amount of supplementation payments made to the employer for an employee under section 482(e) of the Social Security Act. (Code Sec. 51(c)(2)(B))[40]

¶ 2315 Targeted groups for work opportunity credit—Form 8850.

The targeted groups are: Qualified IV-A recipients (qualified recipients of aid to families with dependent children or successor program), qualified veterans, qualified ex-felons, designated community residents who begin work after May 25, 2007 (i.e., the former "high-risk youths" targeted group but with the maximum age requirement raised and the residency requirement expanded to include rural renewal residents), vocational rehabilitation referrals, qualified summer youth employees, qualified food stamp recipients, qualified SSI recipients, and long-term family assistance recipients, i.e., members of a family that receives or received assistance under a IV-A program for a minimum period of time. (Code Sec. 51(d))[41]

To be eligible for the credit, a new employee must be certified as a member of a targeted group by a State Employment Security Agency (SESA). The employer can either get the certification by the day the prospective employee begins work or complete a pre-screening notice (use Form 8850) for the employee by the day he is offered employment, and submit it to the SESA (not to IRS) as part of a request for certification within 28 days (21 days for employees who begin work before 2007) after the employee begins work. (Code Sec. 51(d)(13))[42] No credit is allowed for employees who are related to the employer or to certain owners of the employer. (Code Sec. 51(i))[43]

35. ¶L-17775 *et seq.*; ¶514; TD ¶380,700
36. ¶L-17780; ¶514; TD ¶380,703
37. ¶L-17781; ¶514; TD ¶380,704
38. ¶L-17784.2; ¶514; TD ¶380,707
39. ¶L-17783.3; ¶514; TD ¶380,707

40. ¶L-17783; ¶514
41. ¶L-17776 *et seq.*; ¶514; TD ¶380,701
42. ¶L-17784.1; ¶514; TD ¶380,708
43. ¶L-17784.2; ¶514; TD ¶380,709

¶ 2316 Work opportunity tax credit for Hurricane Katrina employees.

A Hurricane Katrina employee is treated as a member of a targeted group (¶2315) for purposes of the work opportunity tax credit (WOTC, ¶2315). (KETRA § 201(a); KETRA § 201(d))) A Hurricane Katrina employee is an individual who on Aug. 28, 2005, had a principal place of abode in the Hurricane Katrina core disaster area (i.e., the GO Zone, see ¶2308), and who is hired during the 2-year period beginning on Aug. 28, 2005 for a position the principal place of employment of which is located in the core disaster area. (KETRA § 201(b)) An individual that provides the employer with reasonable evidence that he is a Hurricane Katrina employee meets the WOTC certification requirements. (KETRA § 201(c)) The rule that denies the credit for employees who had been previously employed by the employer doesn't apply to the first hire of a Hurricane Katrina employee, unless he was an employee on Aug. 28, 2005. (KETRA § 201(d))

¶ 2317 Alcohol fuels credit before 2011—Form 6478; refundable fuel excise tax credits

Alcohol fuels credit. A credit (computed on Form 6478) is allowed for alcohol (other than that produced from petroleum, natural gas, coal or peat, or with a proof less than 150) (Code Sec. 40(d)(1)) used as a fuel. The credit equals the sum of: (1) the alcohol mixture credit, (2) the alcohol credit, and (3) the small ethanol producer credit. (Code Sec. 40(a))

The credit applies to sales or uses before 2011, except for periods during which the removal-at-terminal excise tax on gasoline, diesel fuel and kerosene drops to 4.3¢ a gallon (Code Sec. 40(e)(1)) (which is scheduled to occur after Sept. 30, 2011. [44] (Code Sec. 4081(d)(1)) The credit cannot be carried over to any tax year beginning after the three-tax year period beginning with the tax year in which the credit ceases to apply. (Code Sec. 40(e)(2)) The fuel credit will be reduced to take into account excise tax exemptions. (Code Sec. 40(c))

The alcohol mixture credit is 60¢ for each 190-or-greater-proof gallon of alcohol used by the taxpayer in the production of a qualified mixture. A "qualified mixture" is a mixture of alcohol and gasoline or of alcohol and a special fuel that is either sold by the taxpayer producing the mixture to any person for use as a fuel or used as a fuel by the taxpayer producing the mixture. (Code Sec. 40(b)(1), Code Sec. 40(h)(1))

The alcohol credit is 60¢ per gallon of 190-or-greater proof alcohol that during the tax year is either: (1) used by the taxpayer as a fuel in a trade or business, or (2) sold by the taxpayer at retail to a person and placed in the fuel tank of that person's vehicle. (Code Sec. 40(b)(2)(A), Code Sec. 40(h)(1)(A))

A taxpayer gets no credit as a user (under (1) above) for any alcohol that was sold in a retail sale described in (2), above. (Code Sec. 40(b)(2)(B))

If the alcohol has a proof of at least 150 but less than 190, the alcohol mixture credit and the alcohol credit is 45¢ per gallon. (Code Sec. 40(b)(3), Code Sec. 40(h)(1)(B))

A tax of 60¢ per gallon (reported on Form 720) applies if a credit was taken and the mixture or alcohol is used other than as a fuel, the mixture is separated, or the alcohol is mixed. For alcohol with a proof less than 190 the tax is 45¢ per gallon. (Code Sec. 40(d)(3), Code Sec. 40(h)(1)(C))

A "small" ethanol producer is eligible for a credit of 10¢ per gallon of qualified ethanol fuel production. The credit is limited to 15 million gallons of production. (Code Sec. 40(b)(4)) A small producer is one whose productive capacity for alcohol does not exceed 60 million gallons at any time during the tax year. For this purpose, "alcohol" is defined as methanol or ethanol,

44. ¶L-17518; TD ¶382,210

without regard to proof or source restrictions. (Code Sec. 40(g)) A recapture tax of 10¢ per gallon is imposed on alcohol not used as fuel and reported on Form 720. [45] (Code Sec. 40(d)(3)(C)) A cooperative can elect to pass through the small ethanol producer credit to its patrons. (Code Sec. 40(g)(6))

A taxpayer can elect not to take the alcohol fuel credit (Code Sec. 40(f)(1)) simply by not taking the credit. (Reg § 301.9100-6T(f))[46]

¶ 2318   Incremental research expenses credit before 2008—Form 6765.

The research expense credit (claimed on Form 6765) equals the sum of:

(1) 20% of the excess (if any) of the qualified research expenses for the tax year over a base amount, (unless the taxpayer elects either the alternative incremental credit or the alternative simplified research credit, which would then replace this item (1)).

(2) The "university basic research credit," i.e., 20% of the basic research payments determined under Code Sec. 41(e)(1)(A).

(3) 20% of the taxpayer's expenditures on qualified energy research undertaken by an energy research consortium. (Code Sec. 41(a))[47]

The credit terminates for amounts paid or incurred after 2007. (Code Sec. 41(h)(1))

caution: Check http://ria.thomson.com/federaltaxhandbook to see if this provision has been extended.

The base amount is a fixed-base percentage of taxpayer's average annual gross receipts from a U.S. trade or business (and includes its foreign sub's gross receipts), net of returns and allowances, for the four tax years before the credit year, and can't be less than 50% of the year's qualified research expenses. The fixed base percentage for a non-startup company that isn't using the alternative incremental credit is the percentage (not exceeding 16%) that taxpayer's total qualified research expenses is of total gross receipts for tax years beginning after '83 and before '89.

Except when a taxpayer elects the alternative incremental credit or the alternative simplified research credit described below, the Code assigns a fixed-base percentage of 3% in making the base amount computation for each of its first five tax years in which a "startup company" has qualified research expenses. (Code Sec. 41(c)(3)(B)(ii)(I)) For the second five tax years, the fixed-base percentage is not pre-set at 3%. Instead, it is a specified amount of the ratio or percentage —increased annually during this second five year period —determined by dividing qualified research expenses by gross receipts. [48]

To qualify for the Code Sec. 41 research credit, research must be conducted within the U.S. (including Puerto Rico and U.S. possessions). (Code Sec. 41(d), Code Sec. 41(f)) An expense must:

(a) qualify as a research and experimental expenditure under Code Sec. 174;

(b) relate to research undertaken for the purpose of discovering information that is technological in nature and the application of which is intended to be useful in developing a new or improved business component of the taxpayer; and

(c) be for research in which substantially all of the activities constitute elements of a process of experimentation that relates to a new or improved function, performance, reliability or quality. (Code Sec. 41(d)(1); Reg § 1.41-4(a)(5))

Additional tests apply to research costs of software developed for the taxpayer's internal use. (Code Sec. 41(d)(4)(E)) Certain activities (e.g., marketing, surveys, duplication of existing

---

45. ¶L-17507; TD ¶382,207
46. ¶L-17504; ¶404.04; TD ¶382,208

47. ¶L-15300 et seq.; ¶414 et seq.; TD ¶384,002
48. ¶L-15309 et seq.; ¶414 et seq.; TD ¶384,015

business components, post-commercial-production activities) aren't qualified expenses. (Code Sec. 41(d)(4)) To pass the second test, research must be intended to eliminate uncertainty about the development or improvement of a business component, and the process of experimentation must fundamentally rely on principles of the physical or biological sciences, engineering, or computer science. A taxpayer may use existing technologies and may rely on existing principles of these sciences. Courts generally have applied these tests strictly. [49] The issuance of certain patents is conclusive evidence that a taxpayer has discovered technological-in-nature information that is intended to eliminate uncertainty about the development or improvement of a business component. (Reg § 1.41-4(a)(3)(iii))

"Qualified research expenses" are amounts the taxpayer pays or incurs during the tax year "in carrying on any trade or business" (including certain "start-up" costs) of the taxpayer for: "in-house" research expenses, which consist of certain wages and supplies, and "contract" research expenses, i.e., 65% of amounts paid to certain nonemployees, and 100% of the taxpayer's expenditures to eligible small businesses, universities, and federal laboratories for qualified energy research. (Code Sec. 41(b); Reg § 1.41-2)[50]

Any expense taken into account in computing the clinical testing expense credit (¶2329) for a tax year cannot be taken into account in computing the credit for incremental research expenses. (Code Sec. 45C(c)(1)) But, any qualified clinical testing expenses for any tax year which are qualified research expenses are to be taken into account in determining "base period research expenses" in later tax years. (Code Sec. 45C(c)(2))[1]

No deduction is allowed for that portion of the otherwise deductible qualified research expenses or basic research expenses that equals the research credit for the tax year. (Code Sec. 280C(c)(1)) If a taxpayer capitalizes rather than deducts expenses, the amount of such expenses capitalized during the year must be reduced by the excess of the credit over the amount allowable (without regard to the above disallowance) as a deduction for the tax year. (Code Sec. 280C(c)(2))[2] But a taxpayer may avoid this reduction for any tax year by claiming a reduced credit for the year. The election limits the taxpayer to a credit in the amount of the research credit before any reduction less the product of that credit amount times the maximum corporate tax rate. (Code Sec. 280C(c)(3))[3]

Alternative incremental research credit. Taxpayers electing this credit are assigned a three-tiered fixed base percentage under which a credit rate of:

... 3% applies to the extent that a taxpayer's current-year research expenses exceed a base amount computed by using a fixed-base percentage of 1% but do not exceed a base amount computed by using a fixed base percentage of 1.5%;

... 4% applies to the extent that a taxpayer's current-year research expenses exceed a base amount computed by using a fixed-base percentage of 1.5% but don't exceed a base amount computed by using a fixed base percentage of 2%; and

... 5% applies to the extent that a taxpayer's current-year research expenses exceed a base amount computed by using a fixed-base percentage of 2%. (Code Sec. 41(c)(4)(A))

The rates are prorated for a tax year that straddles Dec. 31, 2007. (TRHCA § 104(b)(3))

The election, made on Form 6765, applies to the election year and all later years unless revoked with IRS's consent. (Code Sec. 41(c)(4)(B))[4]

Alternative simplified research credit. For tax years ending after 2006, a taxpayer can elect this credit equal to 12% of the excess of the qualified research expenses for the tax year over 50% of the average qualified research expenses for the three tax years preceding the tax year for which the credit is being determined. (Code Sec. 41(c)(5)(A)) If a taxpayer has no qualified

49. ¶L-15412
50. ¶L-15401 *et seq.*; ¶414.01; TD ¶384,008
1. ¶L-15606; ¶414.04

2. ¶L-3131; ¶s 280C4, 414.04; TD ¶306,508
3. ¶L-15308; ¶s 280C4, 414.04; TD ¶384,019
4. ¶L-15302.1; ¶414.01;TD ¶384,003

research expenses in any one of the three preceding tax years, the alternative simplified research credit is 6% of the qualified research expenses for the tax year for which the credit is being determined. (Code Sec. 41(c)(5)(B)) The election applies to the tax year for which it is made and all following tax years unless revoked with IRS's consent. The election cannot be made for any tax year to which an election of the alternative incremental credit applies. (Code Sec. 41(c)(5)(C)) An election of the alternative incremental credit that applies to a tax year that includes Jan. 1, 2007, will be treated as revoked with IRS's consent (for that and later years) if the taxpayer elects the alternative simplified credit for the year. (TRHCA § 104(c)(2)) However, the alternative incremental credit and the alternative simplified credit can apply to a tax year that straddles Dec. 31, 2007. (TRHCA § 104(c)(4)) The alternative simplified credit is prorated for a tax year that straddles Dec. 31, 2007. (TRHCA § 104(c)(4))

University basic research credit. The 20% university basic research credit component applies to 100% of cash expenditures by corporations (except S corporations, personal holding companies, or service organizations) for basic research over the sum of: (1) the minimum basic research amount, plus (2) the maintenance-of-effort amount. (Code Sec. 41(e); Reg § 1.41-7)[5]

The "minimum basic research amount" (Code Sec. 41(e)(4); Reg § 1.41-7) is the greatest of: (1) 1% of the average amount paid for in-house and contract research expenses during the base period (the three tax years before the first tax year beginning after '83); (Code Sec. 41(e)(7)(B)) (2) the contract research expense for the base period; or (3) 50% of the basic research payments if taxpayer wasn't in existence for a full year in the base period. [6]

The maintenance-of-effort amount is: (1) the average charitable contribution to all educational institutions during the base period (see above) multiplied by the cost-of-living adjustment, *minus* (2) the charitable contributions to educational institutions for the year. (Code Sec. 41(e)(5)(A))[7]

¶ 2319 Low-income housing credit for qualified buildings—Form 8609; Form 8586.

The low-income housing credit is allowed annually over a ten-year "credit period" beginning with the tax year the qualified building is placed in service, or, under an irrevocable election (on Form 8609), the next tax year. (Code Sec. 42(f)(1)) The credit period for an existing building can't begin before the first tax year of the tax period for rehabilitation expenses for the building. (Code Sec. 42(f)(5)(A))[8]

The credit equals the qualified basis of the qualified building times the applicable percentage (see below) (Code Sec. 42(a)) prescribed by IRS for the month placed in service or elected in agreement with the housing credit agency. (Code Sec. 42(b)(2)(A)) The building owner can't claim a credit amount in excess of the allocation received from the state or housing credit agency for that year. (Reg § 1.42-1T(e)(1))[9]

IRS prescribes percentages that will yield, over a ten-year period, credit amounts that will have a present value equal to 70% of the qualified basis of new buildings (not federally subsidized) and 30% of the qualified basis of existing buildings and federally subsidized new buildings as follow: (Code Sec. 42(b)(2)):[10]

Month	Year	70% present value credit	30% present value credit
Nov.	2007	8.08%	3.46%
Oct.	2007	8.07%	3.46%
Sept.	2007	8.15%	3.49%
Aug.	2007	8.21%	3.52%

---

5. ¶L-15501 *et seq.*; ¶s 414.01, 414.02; TD ¶384,018
6. ¶s L-15508, L-15507; ¶414.02
7. ¶L-15509; ¶414.02

8. ¶L-15700 *et seq.*; ¶424.10, 424.55; TD ¶383,001
9. ¶L-15702; ¶424.10; TD ¶383,001
10. ¶L-15718; ¶424.10; TD ¶383,001

July	2007	8.18%	3.50%
June	2007	8.11%	3.48%
May	2007	8.11%	3.47%
Apr.	2007	8.10%	3.47%
Mar.	2007	8.15%	3.49%
Feb.	2007	8.11%	3.48%
Jan.	2007	8.08%	3.46%
Dec.	2006	8.12%	3.48%

A credit for rehabilitation expenditures (treated as a separate building (Code Sec. 42(e)(1))) is allowed only if during any 24-month period they are the greater of: 10% of the building's adjusted basis or $3,000 per low-income unit. (Code Sec. 42(e)(3)(A))

To claim the credit, taxpayers must file Form 8586 for each tax year in the ten-year credit period. (Code Sec. 42(g)(4))[11] Form 8609 must be filed once with the taxpayer's income tax return.[12]

A qualified low-income building is a building that at all times during the "compliance period" of 15 tax years beginning with the first tax year of the credit period, is part of a qualified low-income housing project. (Code Sec. 42(c)(2), Code Sec. 42(i)(1), Code Sec. 42(g)) In addition, no credit is allowed unless an extended low income housing commitment (for an additional 15-year period) between the taxpayer and the housing credit agency is in effect at the end of the tax year. (Code Sec. 42(h)(6))[13]

¶ 2320 Recapture of low-income housing credit—Form 8611; Form 8693.

If, at the close of any year in the compliance period, the qualified basis of a building is less than it was at the close of the earlier tax year, the taxpayer's tax for the year is increased (Code Sec. 42(j)(1), Code Sec. 42(j)(4)(B)) by the sum of:

(1) the total decrease in taxpayer's general business tax credits for all earlier tax years that would have resulted if the accelerated portion of the credit (see below) allowable for the earlier tax years weren't allowed for all earlier tax years for the decrease in qualified basis, plus

(2) an amount of nondeductible interest on (1), above, computed at the rate charged for overpayment of tax, see ¶4853. (Code Sec. 42(j)(2))

The accelerated portion of the credit for the earlier tax years is the excess of the total credit allowed for the earlier tax years over the total credit that would have been allowable for those years if the total credit that would have been allowable for the entire compliance period were allowable ratably over 15 years. (Code Sec. 42(j)(3))[14]

Recapture (on Form 8611) results from a disposition of a building or interest in one unless: (1) the taxpayer furnishes a bond (using Form 8693) of a term and in an amount satisfactory to IRS, and (2) it's reasonably expected that the building will continue to be operated as a qualified low-income building for its remaining compliance period. (Code Sec. 42(j)(6))[15]

¶ 2321 Enhanced oil recovery credit—Form 8830.

The enhanced oil recovery (EOR) credit (claimed on Form 8830) for any tax year is 15% of the taxpayer's qualified enhanced oil recovery costs for the tax year. (Code Sec. 43(a)) These are amounts paid or incurred for: (1) qualifying tangible property that's depreciable or amortizable; (2) qualifying tertiary injectant acquisition and use costs that qualify for a deduction

---

11. ¶S-3456; ¶424.50; TD ¶383,002
12. ¶S-3451; ¶424.50; TD ¶383,002
13. ¶L-15719 *et seq.*; ¶424.60; TD ¶383,004

14. ¶L-16050 *et seq.*; ¶424.85; TD ¶383,014
15. ¶L-16050 *et seq.*; ¶424.85; TD ¶383,014

under Code Sec. 193; (3) qualifying intangible drilling and development costs (IDCs) that are eligible for the Code Sec. 263(c) expensing election; and (4) for tax years beginning after 2004, Alaska gas treatment plant construction costs. (Code Sec. 43(c)(1)) The credit is phased out as the average per barrel wellhead price of domestic crude oil ("reference price," see ¶2339) for the last calendar year that ended before the tax year in question exceeds $28 (adjusted for inflation). (Code Sec. 43(b))[16] The credit is completely phased out for 2007. [17]

¶ 2322   Disabled access credit—Form 8826.

An "eligible small business" may elect (on Form 8826) to apply a credit against income tax of 50% of the amount of "eligible access expenditures" for the tax year that's over $250 and not more than $10,250. (Code Sec. 44(a))

observation: Thus, the maximum amount of the credit for any tax year is $5,000, 50% of ($10,250 – $250).

For partnerships and S corporations this limitation applies at both the entity and the individual partner or shareholder levels. (Code Sec. 44(d)(3))

An "eligible small business" for any tax year is any person who either: (1) has gross receipts that don't exceed $1 million for the tax year *before* that in which the credit is elected, net of returns and allowances, or (2) employed no more than 30 full-time employees in the tax year *before* the tax year in which the credit is elected; an employee who is employed at least 30 hours a week for 20 or more calendar weeks in the tax year is considered to be full-time. (Code Sec. 44(b), Code Sec. 44(d)(5))

Eligible access expenditures are amounts paid or incurred to enable the business to comply with the Americans With Disabilities Act of '90 (as in effect on Nov. 5, '90). (Code Sec. 44(c)(1)) These expenses include *only* expenses that are necessary to comply with the Disabilities Act, that are paid or incurred: (1) for the purpose of removing architectural, communication, physical or transportation barriers in connection with any facility first placed in service before Nov. 6, '90, which prevent a business from being accessible to, or usable by, individuals with disabilities; (2) to provide qualified interpreters or other effective methods of making aurally delivered materials available to individuals with hearing impairments; (3) to provide qualified readers, taped texts and other effective methods of making visually delivered materials available to individuals with visual impairments; (4) to acquire or modify equipment or devices for individuals with disabilities; or (5) to provide other similar services, modifications, materials or equipment. (Code Sec. 44(c))[18] Software expenses to improve access to a business website are ineligible for the disabled access credit. [19]

¶ 2323   Credit for producing electricity from renewable resources—Form 8835.

A renewable electricity production credit (claimed on Form 8835) is allowed for electricity produced by taxpayers from: (1) wind, (2) "closed-loop biomass" (generally, organic plants, except timber, grown for the sole purpose of being used to generate electricity), (3) "open-loop biomass" (e.g., agricultural livestock waste nutrients such as poultry waste, solid wood waste materials), (4) geothermal energy, (5) small irrigation power, (6) municipal solid waste, (7) qualified hydropower production, and (8) solar energy. Qualified facilities for (1) through (7) must be originally placed in service before 2009 (for (8), before 2006). (Code Sec. 45(a), Code Sec. 45(c))[20] The electricity production credit is generally available for a 10-year period beginning on the placed-in-service date of the qualifying facility for electricity produced during that period for property placed in service after Aug. 8, 2005. (Code Sec. 45(a)(2)(A)) The 10-year

16. ¶L-17615; ¶434.01; TD ¶384,050

17. ¶L-17600 *et seq.*; ¶434 *et seq.*; TD ¶384,046

18. ¶L-17900 *et seq.*; ¶444; TD ¶382,500 *et seq.*

19. ¶L-17902; TD ¶382,502

20. ¶L-17751 *et seq.*; ¶454; TD ¶384,054

credit period for a qualified hydropower facility begins on the date that the qualifying efficiency improvements or additions to capacity are placed in service. (Code Sec. 45(d)(9)(C)) For open-loop biomass, geothermal and solar energy, small irrigation power, and municipal solid waste facilities placed in service before Aug. 8, 2005, a five-year credit period applies. For open-loop biomass facilities not using agricultural livestock waste nutrients placed in service before Oct. 22, 2004, a five-year credit period beginning on Jan. 1, 2005 applies. (Code Sec. 45(b)(4)(B))

For 2007, the credit is 2.0¢ per kilowatt hour. (Code Sec. 45(a)) But, for electricity produced and sold at any qualifying facility using open-loop biomass, small irrigation power, landfill gas, trash combustion, or hydropower the amount of the credit (before it's indexed for inflation for the calendar year), is reduced by one-half (.95¢ per kilowatt hour). (Code Sec. 45(b)(4)) The credit is allowed for qualified electricity sold to an unrelated person (Code Sec. 45(a)(2)(B))[21] and produced from domestic or U.S. possession facilities originally placed in service by the taxpayer (a) after '92 (for closed-loop biomass facility), after '93 (for a wind energy facility), after Aug. 8, 2005 for a hydropower facility, after Oct. 22, 2004 (for facilities using agricultural livestock waste nutrients open-loop biomass, geothermal energy, solar energy, small irrigation power, or municipal solid waste), and (b) before 2008. (Code Sec. 45(d))[22] Taxpayers are entitled to the credit in proportion to their ownership interest in the qualifying facility. (Code Sec. 45(e)(3))[23]

The credit is proportionately phased out when the national average price of electricity produced from the applicable renewable resource exceeds a specified, inflation-adjusted threshold price per kilowatt hour. (Code Sec. 45(b)(1)) There is no phaseout for 2007.[24]

For refined coal produced and sold to an unrelated person in tax years ending after Oct. 22, 2004, a credit applies for the domestic production of refined coal from a qualified facility placed in service after Oct. 22, 2004 and before 2009. (Code Sec. 45(c)(7); Code Sec. 45(d)(8)) The credit is allowed during a ten-year period beginning on the date the facility is originally placed in service. The credit is equal to $5.877 for 2007 (as indexed for inflation) per ton of qualified refined coal and phases out as the market price of refined coal exceeds certain threshold levels. (Code Sec. 45(e)(8)) No phaseout applies for 2007.[25]

For Indian coal sold before Jan. 1, 2013, from a qualified facility placed in service before 2009, an Indian coal production credit is allowed. (Code Sec. 45(e)(10))[26]

¶ 2324 Empowerment zone employment credit before 2008—Form 8844.

Employers are entitled to an empowerment zone employment credit (claimed on Form 8844) for any tax year equal to 20% of the qualified zone wages paid or incurred during the calendar year that ends with or within that tax year. (Code Sec. 1396(a); Code Sec. 1400(d)) The amount of qualified zone wages taken into account for each employee can't exceed $15,000 for a calendar year. (Code Sec. 1396(c)(2)) Thus, the maximum credit per qualified employee is $3,000 per year.[27]

Qualified zone wages don't include wages taken into account for the work opportunity credit (¶2314), and the $15,000 maximum amount above is reduced by the amount of wages taken into account for the work opportunity credit. (Code Sec. 1396(c)(3))[28]

The employer's deduction for wages paid must be reduced by the empowerment zone employment credit for the year. (Code Sec. 280C(a))[29]

⚫*caution:* Check http://ria.thomson.com/federaltaxhandbook to see if this provision has

21. ¶L-17754; ¶454; TD ¶384,054
22. ¶L-17771.1; ¶454; TD ¶384,054
23. ¶L-17755; ¶454; TD ¶384,055
24. ¶L-17760 *et seq.*; ¶454; TD ¶384,056
25. ¶L-17771.7; ¶454.16; TD ¶384,054.1

26. ¶L-17771.8; ¶454.17; TD ¶384,054.1
27. ¶L-15630 *et seq.*; ¶13,964; TD ¶384,021
28. ¶L-15632; ¶13,964; TD ¶384,024
29. ¶L-15639.2; ¶13,964; TD ¶384,030

been extended.

¶ 2325   Renewal community employment credit.

For wages paid or incurred before 2010, a "renewal community" (as designated under Code Sec. 1400E) is treated, subject to modifications, as an "empowerment zone" for purposes of Code Sec. 1396 (which provides an employment credit for certain wages paid by employers in empowerment zones, see ¶2324). (Code Sec. 1400H(a))

In applying Code Sec. 1396 to renewal communities, (1) the credit is 15% of qualified wages, and (2) the maximum amount of qualified wages that can be used to figure the credit is $10,000 per employee per year. (Code Sec. 1400H(b))

Qualified wages for purposes of the renewal community employment credit don't include amounts taken into account in figuring the work opportunity credit, and the $10,000 of maximum wages per qualified employee is reduced by the amount of wages used to figure either credit.[30]

¶ 2326   Credit for qualified zone academy bonds before 2008—Form 8860.

Banks, insurance companies, and other corporations actively engaged in the lending business that hold qualified zone academy bonds are entitled to a nonrefundable tax credit (Code Sec. 1397E(a)) (use Form 8860) equal to a credit rate published daily by Bureau of Public Debt on its Internet site multiplied by the face amount of the bonds held on each credit allowance date (Code Sec. 1397E(b)) (the day before each annual anniversary of the bonds' issuance). (Code Sec. 1397E(f)(1)) A holder that cannot use all or a portion of the credit to reduce its tax liability is allowed a deduction for the unused portion of the credit for the tax year that includes the credit allowance date. (Reg § 1.1397E-1(f)(2)) Qualified zone academy bonds are certain state or local government bonds issued in '98 through 2007, subject to an overall $400 million national annual limitation, whose proceeds are used for certain purposes by public schools located in an empowerment zone or enterprise community, or that have a certain percentage of low-income students, to which private sources contribute certain amounts of goods or services. (Code Sec. 1397E(d))

caution: Check http://ria.thomson.com/federaltaxhandbook to see if this provision has been extended.

The credit is includible in gross income (without regard to the tax liability limitation on the credit). (Code Sec. 1397E(g); Reg § 1.1397E-1(f)(1)) Where qualified zone academy bonds pay stated interest or are issued at a discount, the interest or discount also is taxable. (Reg § 1.1397E-1(f)(1))[31]

¶ 2327   Indian employment credit before 2008—Form 8845.

For tax years beginning before 2008 (Code Sec. 45A(f)),[32] the Indian employment credit (claimed on Form 8845) is 20% of the excess, if any, of the sum of qualified wages and qualified employee health insurance costs (not in excess of $20,000 per employee) paid or incurred (other than paid under salary reduction arrangements) to qualified employees (enrolled Indian tribe members and their spouses who meet certain requirements) during the tax year (Code Sec. 45A(a)(1); Code Sec. 45A(b)(2)) over the sum of these same costs paid or incurred in calendar year '93 —determined as if the Indian employment credit had been in

---

30. ¶L-15661; ¶14,00H4; TD ¶384,601   32. ¶L-15670 *et seq.*; ¶45A4; TD ¶384,039
31. ¶L-15645 *et seq.*; ¶1397E4

effect in '93. (Code Sec. 45A(a)(2); Code Sec. 45A(c)) Tax credits claimed for certain terminated employees are recaptured. (Code Sec. 45A(d)) Deductions for wages and health insurance costs are reduced by the credit. (Code Sec. 280C(a))

caution: Check http://ria.thomson.com/federaltaxhandbook to see if this provision has been extended.

¶ 2328 Elective employer social security credit for employee cash tips—Form 8846.

A food and beverage establishment is allowed a credit (on Form 8846) for the amount of the employer's FICA tax obligation (7.65%) attributable to employee tips received for providing, delivering, or serving food or beverages (whether or not the tips are reported as required by Code Sec. 6053). However, no credit is given for tips used to meet the federal minimum wage rate. (Code Sec. 45B) For tips received for services performed after 2006, employers determine their Code Sec. 45B credit using the minimum wage in effect on Jan. 1, 2007, even if the minimum wage increases (Code Sec. 45B(b)(1)) Thus, in 2007, when the federal minimum wage increases to $5.85 from $5.15 per hour, employers may still use the $5.15 rate to compute their allowable credit. [33]

No deduction is allowed for any amount taken into account in determining the employer social security credit. (Code Sec. 45B(c)) A taxpayer can elect to have the credit not apply for any tax year. (Code Sec. 45B(d)) [34]

¶ 2329 Qualified clinical testing expense ("orphan drug") credit—Form 8820.

A taxpayer that incurs qualified clinical testing expenses for drugs for rare diseases may claim (on Form 8820) a credit equal to 50% of those expenses for the tax year. (Code Sec. 45C) [35] Qualified clinical testing expenses are amounts which, with certain modifications, would qualify as "qualified research expenses" for the incremental research expenses credit (¶2318). (Code Sec. 45C(b)(1))

¶ 2330 Credit for pre-July '99 contributions to community development corporations—Form 8847.

A taxpayer can claim a credit (on Form 8847) for qualified contributions made before July '99 (including certain long-term loans and investments) to selected community development corporations (CDCs, listed in the instructions to Form 8847). The credit is 5% of the qualified contribution for each tax year during the credit period, i.e., the 10-year period beginning with the tax year in which the contribution is made. Thus, the taxpayer may claim a total of 50% of the contribution during the 10-year credit period. [36]

¶ 2331 New markets tax credit—Form 8874.

A "new markets tax credit" applies for qualified equity investments to acquire stock in a community development entity (CDE). A CDE is any domestic corporation or partnership (1) whose primary mission is serving or providing investment capital for low-income communities or low-income persons, (2) that maintains accountability to residents of low-income communities through representation on governing or advisory boards of the CDE, and (3) is certified by the Treasury Dept. as an eligible CDE. A qualified equity investment means stock or a similar equity interest acquired directly from a CDE for cash. Substantially all (at least 85%, reduced to 75% for the final year of the 7-year credit period) of the cash must be used by

33. ¶L-17860 *et seq.*; ¶45B4; TD ¶382,000 *et seq.*
34. ¶L-17860 *et seq.*; ¶45B4; TD ¶382,005
35. ¶L-15600 *et seq.*; ¶45C4
36. ¶L-15650 *et seq.*; ¶384.01; TD ¶384,031

the CDE to make investments in, or loans to, qualified active businesses located in low-income communities or certain financial services to businesses and residents in low-income communities. (Code Sec. 45D; Reg § 1.45D-1(c)(5))[37]

The new markets tax credit (claim on Form 8874) is: (a) 5% for the year in which the equity interest is purchased from the CDE and for the first two anniversary dates after the purchase (for a total credit of 15%), *plus* (b) 6% on each anniversary date thereafter for the following four years (for a total of 24%).[38]

The credit is recaptured if the entity fails to continue to be a CDE or the interest is redeemed within seven years, unless it is permitted to correct its failure, and does so. (Code Sec. 45D(g); Reg § 1.45D-1(e))[39] Nationally, the maximum annual amount of qualifying equity investments is capped at specified amounts through 2008 (Code Sec. 45D) (for 2007, increased limits apply for investments in the GO Zone (¶2308)). (Code Sec. 1400N(m)(2))

caution: Check http://ria.thomson.com/federaltaxhandbook to see if this provision has been extended.

¶ 2332   Credit for employer-provided child care—Form 8882.

A tax credit for "employer-provided child care" (Code Sec. 45F(a)) is equal to the sum of the following expenses for the tax year:

(1) 25% of qualified child care expenses, which are expenses to buy, build, rehabilitate, or expand property to be used as part of a qualified child care facility of the taxpayer (i.e., the employer), for which a deduction for depreciation (or amortization) is allowable, and which isn't part of the principal residence of the taxpayer or any of its employees. Qualifying child care expenses also include operating costs of a qualified child care facility of the taxpayer (including costs related to employee training, scholarship programs, and to providing increased compensation to employees with higher levels of child care training), and amounts paid under a contract with a qualified child care facility to provide child care services to the taxpayer's employees. (Code Sec. 45F(c)(1)(A)) Qualified child care expenses don't include expenses in excess of the FMV of the care. (Code Sec. 45F(c)(1)(B))

(2) 10% of qualified child care resource and referral expenses, which are amounts paid or incurred under a contract to provide child care resource and referral services to an employee of the taxpayer.[40]

The amount of the credit can't exceed $150,000 for any tax year. (Code Sec. 45F(b))[41]

Generally, for purposes of (1), above, a qualified child care facility is one principally used to provide child care assistance, and which meets the requirements of the State or local government in which it is located, including its licensing as a child care facility. (Code Sec. 45F(c)(2)(A)) The facility must be open to the taxpayer's employees during the tax year, and, if it is the taxpayer's principal trade or business, at least 30% of its enrollees must be dependents of the taxpayer's employees. [42]

The provision of child care resource and referral services or facilities can't discriminate in favor of highly compensated employees (within the meaning of Code Sec. 414(q)) (see ¶4325). (Code Sec. 45F(c)(2)(B); Code Sec. 45F(c)(3))[43]

A taxpayer claiming a Code Sec. 45F credit for acquiring, constructing, rehabilitating, or expanding a qualified child care facility must reduce its basis in the facility by the amount of the credits. (Code Sec. 45F(f)(1)(A))[44] No deduction or credit is allowed under any other income tax provision for the amount of the credit determined under Code Sec. 45F. (Code

---

37. ¶L-17920 *et seq.*; ¶45D4 *et seq.*; TD ¶384,700 *et seq.*
38. ¶L-17922; ¶45D4; TD ¶384,702
39. ¶L-17928; ¶45D4.10; TD ¶384,713
40. ¶L-17870 *et seq.*; ¶45F4; TD ¶382,100 *et seq.*

41. ¶L-17872; ¶45F4; TD ¶382,102
42. ¶L-17874; ¶45F4; TD ¶382,104
43. ¶L-17875; ¶45F4; TD ¶382,105
44. ¶L-17876; ¶45F4; TD ¶382,106

Sec. 45F(f)(2))[45]

Credit-recapture rules apply for the first ten years after a qualified child care facility is placed in service. (Code Sec. 45F(d))[46]

For purposes of the Code Sec. 45F credit all persons treated as a single employer under Code Sec. 52(a) or Code Sec. 52(b) are treated as one taxpayer. Regs are to address credit allocations between an estate or trust and its beneficiaries, and among partners of a partnership. (Code Sec. 45F(e))[47][48]

¶ 2333   Small employer pension plan startup credit—Form 8881.

Eligible small employers that adopt a new qualified defined benefit or defined contribution plan (including a Code Sec. 401(k) plan, SIMPLE plan, or simplified employee pension) may claim a nonrefundable credit. The credit is equal to 50% of administrative and retirement-related education expenses for the plan for each of the first three plan years, with a maximum credit of $500 for each year. The first credit year is the tax year that includes the date the plan becomes effective, or, electively, the preceding tax year. (Code Sec. 45E(a), Code Sec. 45E(b), Code Sec. 45E(d)(3))[49]

The pension plan startup credit is available only to businesses that did not employ, in the preceding year, more than 100 employees with compensation of at least $5,000. But, an employer isn't an eligible employer if, during the three-tax year period immediately preceding the first tax year for which the credit is otherwise allowable, it or any member of any controlled group including the employer (or any predecessor of either) established or maintained a qualified employer plan to which contributions were made, or benefits were accrued, for substantially the same employees that are in the qualified employer plan. (Code Sec. 45E(c)(2))[50] For purposes of Code Sec. 45E, all persons treated as a single employer under Code Sec. 52(a) or Code Sec. 52(b) or Code Sec. 414(m) or Code Sec. 414(o) are treated as one taxpayer. (Code Sec. 45E(e)(1))[1] To be eligible for the credit, the plan must cover at least one nonhighly compensated employee. If the credit is for the cost of a payroll-deduction IRA plan, it must be made available to all employees who have worked with the employer for at least three months. (Code Sec. 45E(d)(1))[2]

No deduction is allowed for that portion of the qualified startup costs paid or incurred for the tax year which is equal to the credit. (Code Sec. 45E(e)(2))[3] An eligible employer may elect not to have the credit apply for any tax year. (Code Sec. 45E(e)(3))[4]

¶ 2334   Biodiesel fuel credit—Form 8864.

For fuels produced and sold or used before 2009 (Code Sec. 40A(g)), a taxpayer can claim a credit (on Form 8864) for biodiesel fuels equal to the sum of: (1) a biodiesel mixture credit of 50¢ per gallon of biodiesel used in the production of a qualified biodiesel mixture; (2) a biodiesel credit of 50¢ per gallon of biodiesel, not in a mixture, that's used as a fuel in the taxpayer's trade or business, or sold at retail and placed in a vehicle fuel tank; and (3) for an eligible small agri-biodiesel producer, a small agri-biodiesel producer credit of 10¢ per gallon of agri-biodiesel (up to a 15 million gallon maximum) that is: (a) used by the producer, or sold by the producer for use, in the production of a qualified biodiesel mixture in a trade or business or as fuel in a trade or business, or (b) sold at retail and placed in a vehicle fuel tank by the producer or a person buying from the producer. (Code Sec. 40A(a); Code Sec. 40A(b)) For purposes of (1) and (2), where the biodiesel is agri-biodiesel, the credits are computed

45. ¶L-17877; ¶45F4; TD ¶382,107
46. ¶L-17878; ¶45F4.01; TD ¶382,108
47. ¶L-17879; TD ¶382,109
48. ¶L-17870; ¶45F4; TD ¶382,100
49. ¶L-15690 *et seq.*; ¶45E4; TD ¶384,060 *et seq.*

50. ¶L-15692; ¶45E4; TD ¶384,202
1. ¶L-15699.1; TD ¶384,202
2. ¶L-15694; TD ¶384,202
3. ¶L-15698; ¶45E4; TD ¶384,208
4. ¶L-15699; ¶45E4; TD ¶384,209

using $1.00 for each gallon of agri-biodiesel. (Code Sec. 40A(b)(3))[5]

"Renewable diesel" is treated in the same manner as biodiesel, but for (1) and (2), the credits are computed using $1.00 for each gallon. (Code Sec. 40A(f))[6]

¶ 2335   Low sulfur diesel fuel production credit—Form 8896.

Small business refiners can claim (on Form 8896) a credit of 5¢ per gallon of low sulfur diesel fuel (diesel fuel with sulfur content of 15 parts per million (ppm) or less (Code Sec. 45H(c)(5)), to a maximum of 25% of the refiner's qualified capital costs, reduced by the aggregate low sulfur diesel fuel credits for all earlier tax years for the facility. (Code Sec. 45H(a); Code Sec. 45H(b)(1)) For a small business refiner with average daily domestic refinery runs for the 1-year period ending on Dec. 31, 2002 of more than 155,000 barrels, the 25% must be reduced (not below zero) by the product of the above percentage (before application of this rule) and the ratio of the excess over 155,000 barrels to 50,000 barrels. (Code Sec. 45H(b)(2))[7]

¶ 2336   Marginal well production credit.

A credit is allowed for domestic crude oil or natural gas produced from a "qualified marginal well." The credit amount is $3 per barrel of qualified crude oil production and 50¢ per 1,000 cubic feet of qualified natural gas production. (Code Sec. 45I(a); Code Sec. 45I(b)) The credit is phased out if (1) the average barrel wellhead price of domestic crude oil not subject to U.S. regulation for the last calendar year that ended before the tax year in question exceeds $18 (adjusted for inflation) or (2) the average wellhead price per 1,000 cubic feet for domestic natural gas for the last calendar year that ended before the tax year in question exceeds $2.00 (adjusted for inflation). (Code Sec. 45I(b)(2)) Generally, there is a 1,095 barrel (or barrel-of-oil equivalent) limit on the amount of production that qualifies for the credit. (Code Sec. 45I(c))[8]

¶ 2337   New energy efficient home credit.

For homes acquired before 2009, eligible contractors (including manufacturers of manufactured homes) that construct new energy-efficient homes can qualify for a $2,000 or $1,000 credit per qualifying home. (Code Sec. 45L(a); Code Sec. 45L(g))[9] A structure qualifies for the credit if it meets specific energy saving requirements, and its construction, which includes substantial reconstruction and rehabilitation, is substantially completed after Aug. 8, 2005. It must be located in the U.S. (Code Sec. 45L(a); Code Sec. 45L(b)(2))[10] A property's basis is reduced by the amount of credit claimed. (Code Sec. 45L(e))[11]

A home (including a manufactured one) qualifies for the $2,000 credit if it is certified to have a projected 50% reduction in the level of annual heating and cooling energy consumption, compared to comparable dwellings, and at least one-fifth of the 50% reduction is from its building envelope component improvements —insulation materials or systems specifically and primarily designed to reduce heat loss or gain, exterior windows (including skylights), doors, and any duct sealing and infiltration reduction measures. (Code Sec. 45L(a)(2); Code Sec. 45L(c))[12]

A manufactured home qualifies for a $1,000 credit if it is either (1) certified to have a projected 30% reduction in the level of annual heating and cooling energy consumption, compared to comparable dwellings, and its building envelope component improvements account for at least one-third of the 30% reduction, or (2) it meets the requirements under the

---

5. ¶L-17570; ¶40A4; TD ¶382,400
6. ¶L-17585; ¶40A4.05; TD ¶382,409
7. ¶L-17550; ¶45H4; TD ¶382,300
8. ¶L-17720; ¶45I4; TD ¶384,059

9. ¶L-17940; ¶45L4; TD ¶569,570
10. ¶L-17944; ¶45L4; TD ¶569,574
11. ¶L-17949.3; ¶45L4; TD ¶569,579.1
12. ¶L-17947; ¶45L4; TD ¶569,575

Energy Star Labeled Homes program. (Code Sec. 45L(a)(2); Code Sec. 45L(c)(3))[13]

¶ 2338 Energy efficient appliance credit.

For appliances produced before 2008, manufacturers can qualify for a credit for producing energy efficient dishwashers, clothes washers, and refrigerators. The credit depends on the type of appliance and how much energy it saves. The maximum tax credit is $100 per dishwasher or clothes washer, and $175 per refrigerator. (Code Sec. 45M(b)) Appliances eligible for the credit include only those produced by the taxpayer during the calendar year in the U.S. that exceed the average amount of production by the taxpayer in the U.S. during the three prior calendar years (for refrigerators, 110% of average production). (Code Sec. 45M(c)) A taxpayer can't claim credits in excess of $75 million for all tax years, and can't claim credits in excess of $20 million for the manufacture of certain refrigerators. The credit allowed in a tax year for all eligible appliances can't exceed 2% of the average annual gross receipts of the taxpayer for the 3 tax years preceding the tax year in which the credit is determined. (Code Sec. 45M(e))[14]

caution: Check http://ria.thomson.com/federaltaxhandbook to see if this provision has been extended.

¶ 2339 Alternate (nonconventional source) fuel production credit

A $3 per barrel of oil-equivalent (measured on a btu basis) tax credit (claimed by attaching a self-made schedule to the return) is allowed for the production of qualified fuels sold to an unrelated party. (Code Sec. 45K(a))[15] The $3 amount, except in the case of gas from a tight formation, is adjusted for inflation ($4.72 for calendar year 2006; the 2007 figure won't be released until 2008). (Code Sec. 45K(b)(2))[16] The credit phases out as the annual average wellhead price per barrel for all domestic crude oil not subject to U.S. regulation rises from $23.50 to $29.50 per barrel (as adjusted for inflation). Thus, the credit per barrel equivalent of qualified fuel sold in calendar year 2006 is reduced by $2.31. (Code Sec. 45K(b)(1))[17]

The credit is allowed for gas produced from biomass; and liquid, gaseous or solid synthetic fuels produced from coal (Code Sec. 45K(c))[18] that is sold before 2008. (Code Sec. 45K(f))[19] Special placed in service rules apply to a facility that produces gas from biomass or produces liquid, gaseous or solid synthetic fuels from coal (including lignite). (Code Sec. 45K(f))[20]

There is a production credit of $3 per barrel-of-oil equivalent (indexed for inflation) for qualified facilities, placed in service before Jan. 1, '93, or after June 30, '98 and before Jan. 1, 2010, that produce coke or coke gas (other than from petroleum based products). The amount of credit-eligible coke produced cannot exceed an average barrel-of-oil equivalent of 4,000 barrels a day. No phaseout applies. (Code Sec. 45K(g))[21]

¶ 2340 Personal (Refundable and Nonrefundable) Credits. ▬▬▬▬▬

Taxpayers, whether or not in business, may qualify for one or more personal credits. Some of these credits are refundable, i.e., the excess of the credit over taxpayer's tax liability is refunded to the taxpayer; others are not.

The *refundable* credits are the credits:

. . . for earned income by certain taxpayers, see ¶2341 *et seq.*;

. . . for additional child credit for families with three or more children, see ¶2358;

---

13. ¶L-17949; ¶45L4; TD ¶569,577
14. ¶L-17950; ¶45M4; TD ¶569,580
15. ¶L-17700 *et seq.*; ¶45K4; TD ¶396,001
16. ¶L-17704; ¶45K4.02
17. ¶L-17710; ¶45K4.02; TD ¶396,001

18. ¶L-17702; ¶45K4.01; TD ¶396,001
19. ¶L-17700; ¶45K4.04; TD ¶396,001
20. ¶L-17705.1; ¶45K4.01; TD ¶396,001
21. ¶L-17706.1; ¶45K4; TD ¶396,001

... for health insurance costs of displaced workers and PBGC pension recipients, see ¶2347;

... for income tax withheld, see ¶2348;

... for excess social security tax withheld, see ¶2349;

... for child credit (only for certain taxpayers), see ¶2358;

... for capital gain tax paid by a RIC and allocated to the shareholder, (¶4201) and

... for excise tax for certain nontaxable uses of fuels. (Code Sec. 6420, Code Sec. 6421, Code Sec. 6427(l))

The *non*refundable credits are:

... the credit for the elderly and the permanently and totally disabled, see ¶2350;

... the credit for household and dependent care expenses, see ¶2351 *et seq.*;

... the credit for adoption expenses, see ¶2356;

... the regular child tax credit for certain taxpayers, see ¶2357;

... the mortgage credit, see ¶2359;

... the Hope scholarship and Lifetime Learning credits, see ¶2201 *et seq.*;

... the pre-2008 nonbusiness energy property credit, see ¶2360;

... the residential energy efficient property credit, see ¶2361;

... the "saver's" credit for elective deferrals and IRA contributions, see ¶2365;

... the alternative motor vehicle credit for vehicles, see ¶2362;

... the alternative fuel vehicle refueling property, see ¶2363;

... the pre-2008 first-time DC homebuyer credit, see ¶2364;

... the alternative minimum tax credit, see ¶2367; and

... the credit for holders of clean renewable energy bonds, see ¶2368

For the limit on the combined amount of certain personal nonrefundable credits, see ¶2366.

¶ 2341   Earned income credit—overview—Schedule EIC.

An eligible individual (¶2343) is allowed a credit equal to the credit percentage times the amount of the individual's earned income for the tax year that doesn't exceed the statutory earned income amount. (Code Sec. 32(a)(1)) The EIC for a tax year can't be more than the excess (if any) of (1) the credit percentage of the earned income amount, over (2) the phaseout percentage of so much of adjusted gross income (or if greater, earned income) of the individual for the tax year as exceeds the phaseout amount. (Code Sec. 32(a)(2)) These amounts are determined as follows (phaseout amount in table is for other than joint filers). [22]

Qualifying Children:	The Credit % is:	The Earned Income Amount is:	The Phaseout % is:	The Phaseout Amount is:
FOR 2007				
No qualifying children	7.65%	$ 5,590	7.65%	$ 7,000
1 qualifying child	34%	$ 8,390	15.98%	$15,390
2 or more qualifying children	40%	$11,790	21.06%	$15,390

The 2007 phaseout amount for joint filers is $9,000 for no qualifying children, and $17,390 for one, two, or more qualifying children.

The maximum credit for 2007 is $428 (no qualifying children), $2,853 (one qualifying child), or $4,716 (two or more qualifying children). [23] The EIC for 2007 is completely phased out at

---

22. ¶A-4201 *et seq.*; ¶324 *et seq.*; TD ¶569,001   23. ¶A-4201; ¶324 *et seq.*; TD ¶569,001

the following amounts of earned income (or AGI, whichever is greater): [24]

 . . . no qualifying children, $12,590 ($14,590 for joint filers),

 . . . one qualifying child, $33,241 ($35,241 for joint filers), and

 . . . two or more qualifying children, $37,783 ($39,783 for joint filers).

No credit is allowed if the taxpayer has excess disqualified income, see ¶2344.

No credit is allowed for 10 years after a year in which the EIC was claimed fraudulently (2 years for erroneously claimed credit due to reckless or intentional disregard of the rules). If the EIC is denied under deficiency procedures, including administrative procedures (but not mathematical or clerical errors), no credit is allowed for any later tax year unless the taxpayer provides information IRS requires to demonstrate eligibility (Code Sec. 32(k); Reg § 1.32-3(b)) (use Form 8862). (Reg § 1.32-3(c))[25]

A taxpayer with a qualifying child claims the credit on Form 1040 or Form 1040A and attaches Form 1040A or 1040, Schedule EIC. An individual who has no qualified children can claim the credit on Form 1040, Form 1040A, or Form 1040EZ. [26]

For advance payment of the earned income credit, see ¶2346. For due diligence requirements for return preparers, see ¶4887.

¶ 2342   Earned income defined for EIC purposes.

Earned income for EIC purposes includes wages, salaries, tips, other employee compensation and an individual's net earnings from self-employment less one-half of the self-employment tax under Code Sec. 164(f) (¶1755). Compensation that is earned income includes wages, salaries, tips, and other employee compensation only if such amounts are includible in gross income. (Code Sec. 32(c)(2)(A)) For tax years ending before 2008, taxpayers may elect to treat combat pay as earned income for purposes of the earned income credit. (Code Sec. 32(c)(2)(B)(vi))

✐caution: Check http://ria.thomson.com/federaltaxhandbook to see if this provision has been extended.

Earned income is reduced by any net loss in earnings from self-employment (Reg § 1.32-2(c)(2)) and *doesn't* include any amount received as a pension or an annuity, any amount subject to the 30% withholding tax on U.S. income (not connected with U.S. business) of nonresident alien individuals (Code Sec. 32(c)(2)(B)), unemployment compensation, worker's compensation (Reg § 1.32-2(c)(2)), amounts earned while an inmate in a penal institution, or amounts received for "workfare" services to the extent subsidized by a state program. (Code Sec. 32(c)(2)(B)(iv)) Earned income is determined without regard to any community property laws. (Code Sec. 32(c)(2))[27]

¶ 2343   Eligible individual defined for EIC purposes.

Any individual who has a "qualifying child" (¶2345) for the tax year is an eligible individual. (Code Sec. 32(c)(1)(A)(i)) An individual who doesn't have a qualifying child for the tax year is also an eligible individual *if:*

 . . . the individual's principal place of abode is in the U.S. for more than half the tax year (U.S. Armed Forces personnel are considered to have their personal abode in the U.S. for the time they are stationed outside the U.S. on extended active duty),

 . . . either the individual or the individual's spouse (if any) is older than 24 but younger than 65 before the end of the tax year,

---

24. ¶A-4202   26. ¶A-4201; TD ¶569,002
25. ¶A-4205 *et seq.*; ¶324.02; TD ¶569,007   27. ¶A-4222; ¶324.05; TD ¶569,023

. . . the individual can't be claimed as the dependent of another taxpayer for any tax year beginning in the same calendar year as the individual's tax year (Code Sec. 32(c)(1)(A)(ii)), and

. . . the individual isn't a nonresident alien for any part of the tax year, or has elected under Code Sec. 6013(g) or Code Sec. 6013(h) to be treated as a U.S. resident. (Code Sec. 32(c)(1)(D))[28]

A person can't be an eligible individual unless he includes his (and his spouse's) taxpayer identification number (TIN, social security number, not an individual taxpayer identification number (ITIN) or adoption taxpayer identification number (ATIN)) and the name, age, and TIN (not ITIN or ATIN) of any qualifying child on the return for the tax year. (Code Sec. 32(m); Code Sec. 32(c)(1)(F); Code Sec. 32(c)(3)(D))[29]

Someone who is a qualifying child (¶2345) cannot be treated as an eligible individual in the same year. (Code Sec. 32(c)(1)(B)) Nor can any individual who elects to exclude foreign earned income for the tax year be an eligible individual for that tax year. (Code Sec. 32(c)(1)(C))[30]

Married individuals are eligible for only one credit on their combined earned income and must file a joint return to claim the credit. (Code Sec. 32(d))[31]

Except where a short-period return is filed due to an individual's death, only individuals filing a return for a full 12-month year can claim the credit. (Code Sec. 32(e))

¶ 2344   No child credit where disqualified income is more than $2,900 in 2007.

A taxpayer with "disqualified income" over $2,900 in 2007 ($2,950 in 2008) cannot claim the earned income credit. (Code Sec. 32(i)(1))[32] Disqualified income means:

(1) interest or dividends to the extent includible in gross income for the tax year (Code Sec. 32(i)(2)(A));

(2) tax exempt interest received or accrued during the tax year. (Code Sec. 32(i)(2)(B)) Tax exempt interest is defined by reference to the rules requiring disclosure of the amount of tax exempt interest on the return;

(3) the excess (if any) of gross income from nonbusiness rents or royalties (Code Sec. 32(i)(2)(C)(i)) over the sum of (a) the noninterest deductions that are clearly and directly allocable to that gross income (Code Sec. 32(i)(2)(C)(ii)(I)) and (b) the interest deductions properly allocable to the gross income; (Code Sec. 32(i)(2)(C)(ii)(II))[33]

(4) the taxpayer's capital gain net income for the year (Code Sec. 32(i)(2)(D)) (but gain that is treated as long-term capital gain under Code Sec. 1231(a)(1) (¶2684 *et seq.*) is not disqualified income);[34] and

(5) the excess, if any, of the aggregate income from all passive activities for the year (determined without regard to any amount otherwise included in earned income, or the other disqualified income described above) over the aggregate losses from all passive activities for the tax year (as so determined). (Code Sec. 32(i)(2)(E))[35]

¶ 2345   Qualifying child defined.

A "qualifying child" for purposes of the earned income credit (EIC), means a qualifying child of the taxpayer, as defined for purposes of the dependency exemption in Code Sec. 152(c) (see ¶3120) but without the requirement that the child not have provided more than half of his or her own support, and without regard to a release of the dependency exemption by a

28. ¶A-4209, A-4217; ¶324.02; TD ¶569,009, 569,017
29. ¶A-4219; TD ¶569,020
30. ¶A-4209; ¶324.02; TD ¶569,009
31. ¶A-4221; ¶324.02; TD ¶569,022
32. ¶A-4205; ¶324.02; TD ¶569,004
33. ¶A-4205; ¶324.02; TD ¶569,005
34. ¶A-4205; ¶324.02; TD ¶569,005
35. ¶A-4204; ¶324.02; TD ¶569,005

custodial parent (¶3125). (Code Sec. 32(c)(3)(A))[36]

¶ 2346 Advance payment of earned income credit—Form W-5.

An eligible individual may elect to receive advance payment of the earned income credit by providing his or her employer with a Form W-5. (Code Sec. 3507(b))[37] The amount advanced depends on the employee's earnings in the pay period, and is determined from IRS tables. (Code Sec. 3507(c)(1))[38] The employer adds the advance payment to the employee's paycheck. The advance payment is reflected in the employee's Form W-2 as a separate item. (Code Sec. 6051(a)(7)) Everyone who has received advanced payments of earned income during the year must file an income tax return. (Code Sec. 6012(a)(8)) Advance payments in excess of the employee's earned income credit are recaptured. (Code Sec. 32(g))[39]

¶ 2347 Refundable credit for health insurance costs of trade-displaced workers and PBGC pension recipients—Form 8885.

An "eligible individual" may claim (file Form 8885 with Form 1040) a refundable health coverage tax credit (HCTC) equal to 65% of his qualifying health insurance costs. (Code Sec. 35)[40] An "eligible individual" is someone who is an (1) "eligible TAA recipient" as defined in Code Sec. 35(c)(1)(A),[41] (2) "eligible alternative TAA recipient" as defined in Code Sec. 35(c)(1)(B),[42] or (3) "eligible PBGC pension recipient," namely any individual who, for any month, has attained age 55 as of the first day of that month, and is for that month receiving a benefit any portion of which is paid by the Pension Benefit Guaranty Corporation (PBGC) under title IV of the Employee Retirement Income Security Act of 1974 (ERISA), dealing with plan terminations. (Code Sec. 35(c)(4)(B))[43]

Eligibility for the credit is determined on a monthly basis. A month is an eligible coverage month if as of the first day of that month the taxpayer is an "eligible individual" (defined above), is covered by qualified health insurance, doesn't have other specified coverage as defined at Code Sec. 35(f) (in general, some form of subsidized coverage), and isn't imprisoned under federal, state, or local authority. (Code Sec. 35(b)) The credit for health insurance costs can't be claimed by an individual who may be claimed as a dependent on another person's tax return. (Code Sec. 35(g)(4)) IRS must pay the refundable health insurance costs credit in advance. (Code Sec. 7527)[44]

¶ 2348 Credit for income tax withheld.

The amount of income tax withheld from wages, pensions, annuities, gambling winnings, etc., in a calendar year is a credit for the last tax year beginning in that calendar year. (Code Sec. 31(a))[45] The credit for amounts withheld under the backup withholding rules (¶3043 *et seq.*) is allowed for the tax year of the recipient of the income in which the income is received. (Code Sec. 31(c))[46]

If a husband and wife file separate returns, each must claim credit for the actual amount of tax withheld from his or her salary or wages. In a community property state, each spouse may claim a credit for half of the tax withheld on community wages. (Code Sec. 31(a); Reg § 1.31-1(a))[47]

---

36. ¶A-4210 *et seq.*; ¶324.02; TD ¶569,010 *et seq.*
37. ¶H-4855; ¶324.03; TD ¶569,028
38. ¶H-4858; ¶324.03; TD ¶569,028
39. ¶H-4855 *et seq.*; ¶324.03; TD ¶569,028
40. ¶A-4231; ¶354; TD ¶569,401
41. ¶A-4232; ¶354; TD ¶569,402

42. ¶A-4233; ¶354; TD ¶569,402
43. ¶A-4233; ¶354; TD ¶569,402
44. ¶H-4871; ¶75,274; TD ¶569,406
45. ¶A-4005 *et seq.*; ¶314.01; TD ¶568,502
46. ¶J-9009; ¶s 314.01, 34,064; TD ¶568,504
47. ¶A-4006; ¶314.01; TD ¶568,503

¶ 2349   Credit for excess social security tax withheld.

Where more than the maximum social security tax (see ¶1107) is withheld from an employee's wages because he worked for two or more employers, the excess may be claimed as a credit against his income tax on his return. (Code Sec. 31(b)(1), Code Sec. 6413(c)(1); Reg § 1.31-2(a)(2), Reg § 31.6413(c)-1) If a husband and wife both work, the ceiling is applied separately to each. If more than the maximum was withheld by one employer, the employee can't claim the excess against his income tax. His employer should repay him the over-collection.[48]

¶ 2350   Credit for the elderly and the permanently and totally disabled.

The credit is available to an individual who: (1) reaches 65 before the end of the tax year, or (2) is under 65 at the end of the tax year, is retired with a permanent and total disability, and receives disability income from a public or private employer. (Code Sec. 22(b))[49]

Permanently and totally disabled means that the individual is unable to engage in any substantial gainful activity because of a medically determinable physical or mental impairment that can be expected to result in death, or that has lasted or can be expected to last for a continuous period of at least 12 months. (Code Sec. 22(e)(3))[50]

Married individuals must file a joint return to claim the credit unless they qualify as married living apart, see ¶3132. (Code Sec. 22(e)(1)) A nonresident alien isn't eligible for the credit (Code Sec. 22(f)), unless he's married to a U.S. spouse with whom he files jointly, and both elect to be taxed on worldwide income. (Reg § 1.37-1(d))[1]

The credit is 15% of the specified initial amount (Step 1 below), reduced by both an amount that is based on the taxpayer's adjusted gross income (Step 2) and the sum of the taxpayer's incomes from tax-free pensions and annuities (Step 3) (use Form 1040, Schedule R, or Form 1040A, Schedule 3):

Step (1): The initial amount for which the credit may be computed is:

. . . $5,000 for a single person, 65 or over;

. . . $5,000 for a married couple filing jointly if only one spouse is a qualified individual, 65 or over;

. . . $7,500 for a married couple filing jointly and both spouses are qualified individuals and 65 or over;

. . . $3,750 for a married individual, 65 or over, filing a separate return. (Code Sec. 22(c)(2)(A)) For individuals under age 65, see below.

Step (2): Where a taxpayer's adjusted gross income (AGI) exceeds certain amounts, the applicable initial amount determined in Step (1) (above) must be reduced by one-half of the excess. The reduction is one-half of AGI in excess of $7,500 for a single person and $10,000 for a married person filing jointly ($5,000 if filing separately). (Code Sec. 22(d)) The reduction applies regardless of the taxpayer's age.

🅡observation: Step (2) (above) eliminates the credit for joint filers with AGI of at least $25,000 (if both are 65 or over) or of at least $20,000 (if one is), and for a single person with AGI of at least $17,500.

Step (3): The initial amount as adjusted under Step (2) (above) must be further reduced by the sum of the amounts received by the individual (or, in the case of a joint return, by either spouse) as a pension or annuity or as a disability benefit that's: (a) excluded from gross

---

48. ¶A-4002; ¶314.02; TD ¶568,506   50. ¶A-4102; ¶224.02; TD ¶568,705
49. ¶A-4101; ¶224; TD ¶568,702   1. ¶A-4101; TD ¶568,702

income and payable under title II of the Social Security Act, the Railroad Retirement Act of '74, or a law administered by the VA; or (b) excluded from gross income under any provision of law not in the Internal Revenue Code. (Code Sec. 22(c)(3)(A))

IRS requires a physician's statement (part of Schedule R or Schedule 3). For joint returns where both spouses retired on permanent and total disability, each spouse must file a physician's statement. [2]

For purposes of the above rules, a social security benefit, as defined under the Code Sec. 86 rules (¶1279), or workmen's compensation that reduces such a benefit, is treated as an amount received as a pension or annuity. (Code Sec. 86(f)(1)) [3]

Taxpayers under age 65 compute the credit in the same way as above, except that the "initial amount" is limited to the lower of the initial amount shown in Step (1), above, or

. . . for other than joint returns, the taxpayer's disability income for the year;

. . . for a married couple filing jointly, neither of whom has reached age 65, the sum of the spouses' disability income;

. . . for a married couple filing jointly, only one of whom has reached age 65, the sum of $5,000 plus the disability income of the spouse who hasn't reached age 65. (Code Sec. 22(c)(2)(B)) [4]

¶ 2351 Credit for household and dependent care ("child-care") expenses.

The credit is 35% of employment-related expenses (¶2353) incurred by taxpayers with adjusted gross income (AGI) of $15,000 or less. The percentage decreases by 1% for each $2,000 (or fraction of that amount) of AGI over $15,000, but not below 20%. (Code Sec. 21(a)(1), Code Sec. 21(a)(2), Reg § 1.21-1(a)) [5]

The maximum amount of employment-related expenses that may be used to compute the credit is $3,000 for expenses incurred for one qualifying individual, or $6,000, if incurred for two or more qualifying individuals, at any time during the tax year. (Code Sec. 21(c); Reg § 1.21-2(a)(1)) But, these maximum dollar amounts must be reduced, dollar-for-dollar, by the aggregate amount excludable from gross income under the Code Sec. 129 (¶1271) dependent care assistance exclusion. (Code Sec. 21(c), Reg § 1.21-2(a)) [6]

A taxpayer must incur employment-related expenses (¶2353) that enable the taxpayer to be gainfully employed. If the other requirements are satisfied, an otherwise eligible taxpayer may claim the credit for a child who lives with the taxpayer for more than half the year, even if the taxpayer doesn't provide more than half the cost of maintaining the household. A taxpayer may claim the credit if he has one or more "qualifying individuals" (¶2352). (Code Sec. 21(a), Reg § 1.21-1(b)) [7]

¶ 2352 Qualifying individual defined.

A qualifying individual means someone who:

. . . is under the age of 13 and for whom the taxpayer is entitled to a dependency exemption as defined in Code Sec. 152(a)(1) (Code Sec. 21(b)(1)(A), Reg § 1.21-1(b)(1));

. . . is a taxpayer's dependent who is physically or mentally incapable of caring for himself or herself and who has the same principal place of abode as the taxpayer for more than half of the tax year. For this purpose, "dependent" is defined in Code Sec. 152 (see ¶3119), determined without the gross income test for qualifying relatives, the rule that a joint return filer can't be a dependent, and the rule that a dependent is ineligible to have

---

2. ¶A-4102; TD ¶568,706
3. ¶s A-4105, A-4107; ¶224.02; TD ¶568,709
4. ¶A-4106; ¶224.02; TD ¶568,704

5. ¶A-4301; ¶214; TD ¶569,301
6. ¶A-4303; ¶214.04; TD ¶569,303
7. ¶s A-4301, A-4316 *et seq.*; ¶214.03; TD ¶569,301

dependents (Code Sec. 21(b)(1)(B), Reg § 1.21-1(b)(1)); or

. . . the taxpayer's spouse, if the spouse is physically or mentally incapable of caring for himself or herself and has the same principal place of abode as the taxpayer for more than half of the tax year. (Code Sec. 21(b)(1)(C), Reg § 1.21-1(b)(1))[8]

¶ 2353 Employment-related expenses.

Employment-related expenses qualifying for the household and dependent care credit include expenses for household services and for the care of qualifying individuals. Thus, costs of a housekeeper, maid, babysitter, or cook ordinarily qualify. Payments for services provided outside the taxpayer's household are taken into account only if incurred for the care of: a dependent who is under 13 years old, or any other qualifying individual (¶2352) who regularly spends at least eight hours each day in the taxpayer's household. (Code Sec. 21(b)(2)(B), Reg § 1.21-1(e)(1))[9]

But, the expenses incurred for services that are performed by a *dependent care center* qualify for the credit only if the center complies with all applicable laws and regulations of a state or unit of local government, and the dependent in whose behalf the expenses are incurred spends at least eight hours each day in the taxpayer's household. (Code Sec. 21(b)(2)(B), Code Sec. 21(b)(2)(C), Reg § 1.21-1(e))[10]

(RIA) observation: Thus the credit isn't available for expenses of full institutional care.

Payments to relatives of a taxpayer or to members of his household for services are counted in computing the credit only if the person to whom the payments are made isn't a dependent of the taxpayer or his spouse or a child of the taxpayer who is under age 19 at the close of the tax year. (Code Sec. 21(e)(6), Reg § 1.21-4(a))[11]

¶ 2354 Earned income limit on employment-related expenses.

The amount of employment-related expenses that may be taken into account can't exceed, in the case of an individual who isn't married at the close of the tax year, that individual's earned income, or, in the case of an individual who is married at the close of the tax year, the lesser of the individual's earned income or the earned income of the spouse for the year (even if only married for part of the year). (Code Sec. 21(d)(1), Reg § 1.21-2(b))[12]

The income considered to be earned by a spouse who is a full-time student or who is incapable of self-care is $250 per month if there's one qualifying individual in the household, and $500 a month if there are two or more qualifying individuals. But, this income is deemed to be earned only by one spouse for any given month. (Code Sec. 21(d)(2), Reg § 1.21-2(b)(4))[13]

¶ 2355 Claiming the child-care credit—Form 2441, or Form 1040A Schedule 2.

The credit (claimed on Form 2441 if Form 1040 is filed, or Form 1040A, Schedule 2) is available to married couples only if they file a joint return. (Code Sec. 21(e)(2), Reg § 1.21-3(a))[14]

A married individual living apart from his spouse may claim the credit on a separate return if he maintains a household and furnishes over one-half the cost of that household for the tax year, which is the principal place of abode of a qualifying individual for more than half of the tax year, and from which the other spouse is absent for the last six months of the tax year. (Code Sec. 21(e)(4), Reg § 1.21-3(b))[15]

---

8. ¶A-4312; ¶214.02; TD ¶569,312
9. ¶A-4320; ¶214.03; TD ¶569,318
10. ¶A-4320 *et seq.*; ¶214.03; TD ¶569,322
11. ¶A-4324; ¶214.01; TD ¶569,325

12. ¶A-4305; ¶214.05; TD ¶569,305
13. ¶A-4307; ¶214.06; TD ¶569,306
14. ¶s A-4300, A-4310; ¶214.07; TD ¶569,310
15. ¶A-4311; ¶214.07; TD ¶569,311

Divorced or legally separated parents who seek to claim the credit for an under-13-year-old child must meet the custody test. That is, where the child receives more than half of his support during the year from his parents, and is in the custody of one or both of the parents for more than half of the calendar year, he's a qualifying individual for the parent who has the longer custody, i.e., that parent may claim him for purposes of the credit. That parent need *not* be able to claim the child as a dependent and may even have released the dependency exemption, ¶3125, to the other parent. (Code Sec. 21(e)(5), Reg § 1.21-1(b)(5))[16]

No credit can be claimed unless the taxpayer reports on his or her Form 2441 (or Form 1040A, Schedule 2) the correct name, address and taxpayer identification number of the dependent care provider. A tax-exempt provider doesn't have to supply a TIN. (Code Sec. 21(e)(9)) The dependent care provider should provide this information and certify the TIN on Form W-10. If the care provider doesn't comply with a request, the taxpayer should furnish whatever information is available, and include a statement that the other required information was requested but wasn't given. [17]

No credit is permitted for any qualifying individual unless his taxpayer identification number (TIN) is included on the return claiming the credit. (Code Sec. 21(e)(10))[18]

¶ 2356 Adoption expense credit—Form 8839.

An individual may claim an income tax credit (use Form 8839 with Form 1040 or Form 1040A) for qualified adoption expenses. (Code Sec. 23(a)(1)), which are reasonable and necessary adoption fees, court costs, attorney fees, and other expenses that are directly related to and the principal purpose of which is the taxpayer's legal adoption of an eligible child. (Code Sec. 23(d)(1)(A))[19] The total amount that may be taken as a credit for all tax years for the adoption of a child is $11,390 for 2007 ($11,650 for 2008). The credit for the adoption of a special-needs child is $11,390 for 2007 ($11,650 for 2008) regardless of whether the taxpayer has qualified adoption expenses, reduced by aggregate adoption expenses for the tax year the adoption becomes final and all earlier tax years. (Code Sec. 23(a)(2), Code Sec. 23(a)(3))

The credit begins to phase out if the taxpayer's adjusted gross income (as modified in a special way) exceeds $170,820 for 2007 ($174,730 for 2008), and is fully eliminated when it reaches $210,820 for 2007 ($214,730 for 2008) of modified AGI. (Code Sec. 23(b)(2))

For tax years for which Code Sec. 26(a)(2) would limit personal nonrefundable credits (see ¶2366), the credit is limited to the excess of the sum of the regular tax liability, plus the alternative minimum tax (AMT), over the sum of the nonrefundable personal credits, other than the adoption credit, allowable under Code Sec. 21 through Code Sec. 26, plus the foreign tax credit for the tax year. (Code Sec. 23(b)(4)) Excess credits can be carried forward, but not to any tax year following the fifth tax year after that in which the credit arose. (Code Sec. 23(c)(3))

observation: Thus, the adoption credit is allowed against AMT.

To get the credit, married individuals must file jointly and the taxpayer must include (if known) the name, age and taxpayer identification number (TIN) of the child on the return. (Code Sec. 23(f))

The credit for an expense paid or incurred before the tax year in which the adoption becomes final is allowed for the tax year following the tax year during which it is paid or incurred. For an expense paid or incurred during or after the tax year in which the adoption becomes final the credit is allowed for the tax year in which it's paid or incurred. The credit for a foreign adoption isn't available unless the adoption becomes final. Expenses paid or incurred in the year the foreign adoption is finalized or in an earlier year are allowed in the

---

16. ¶A-4314; ¶214.07; TD ¶569,314
17. ¶A-4327; ¶214.08 *et seq.*; TD ¶569,328
18. ¶A-4326; TD ¶569,327
19. ¶A-4400 *et seq.*; ¶234; TD ¶569,501 *et seq.*

year the adoption is final; and expenses after the year the foreign adoption becomes final are taken into account when paid or incurred. (Code Sec. 23(e)) In some cases, taxpayers may treat adoptions as final where the competent authority enters a decree of adoption or a home state enters a decree of re-adoption. [20] A taxpayer can't claim a credit for any employer-reimbursed adoption expense (¶1255).

¶ 2357   Child tax credit.

Before 2010, individuals may claim a maximum child tax credit of $1,000 for each qualifying child (¶3120) under age 17 at the close of the calendar year in which the tax year begins.

The amount of the credit allowable is reduced (not below zero) by $50 for each $1,000 (or fraction thereof) of modified AGI (AGI increased by excluded foreign, possessions, and Puerto Rico income) above $110,000 for joint filers, $75,000 for unmarried individuals, and $55,000 for marrieds filing separately. (Code Sec. 24(b))

For tax years for which Code Sec. 26(a)(2) would limit personal nonrefundable credits (see ¶2366), the child tax credit allowed for any tax year may not exceed the excess of: (1) the sum of: the regular tax liability, plus alternative minimum tax (AMT) liability, over (2) the sum of the credits under Code Sec. 21 through Code Sec. 26 (other than the child tax credit, the adoption expense credit, and the "saver's" credit for elective deferrals and IRA contributions), plus the foreign tax credit. (Code Sec. 24(b)(3))

observation: Thus, the child credit is allowed against AMT.

No child credit is allowed for a child for a tax year unless the taxpayer includes the child's name and TIN on the return for the year. (Code Sec. 24(e)) Except for a short year on account of the taxpayer's death, no credit is allowed for a short tax year. (Code Sec. 24(f))[21]

¶ 2358   When child tax credit is refundable.

The child tax credit is refundable, but only to the extent of the *greater of*: (1) 15% of earned income above $11,750 for 2007 ($12,050 for 2008), or (2) for a taxpayer with three or more qualifying children, the excess of his social security taxes for the tax year over his earned income credit for the year. (Code Sec. 24(d))[22]

Any amount excluded from gross income under Code Sec. 112 (combat-zone pay, see ¶1224) is treated as earned income for purposes of computing the refundable portion of the child tax credit. (Code Sec. 24(d)(1))

observation: While a certain level of earned income is needed for the child credit to be refundable, earned income isn't required for the credit to be claimed against income tax liability.

¶ 2359   Credit for interest on mortgage under QMCC program—Form 8396.

Under a qualified mortgage credit certificate program established by a state or local government, a taxpayer can take a credit (on Form 8396). (Code Sec. 25(a)) The credit is equal to the mortgage credit certificate rate multiplied by the interest paid by the taxpayer on a mortgage. (Code Sec. 25(a))[23] If the credit rate exceeds 20%, the maximum amount of the credit is $2,000. (Code Sec. 25(a)(2)(A))[24] The credit is subject to recapture on Form 8828 if the taxpayer sells or otherwise disposes of his residence within nine years after the mortgage loan was provided. (Code Sec. 143(m))[25]

20. ¶A-4402; ¶234; TD ¶569,502
21. ¶A-4050 *et seq.*; ¶244; TD ¶569,101
22. ¶A-4055; ¶244; TD ¶569,105
23. ¶A-4008; ¶254.01; TD ¶568,507
24. ¶A-4009; ¶254.01; TD ¶568,508
25. ¶I-4901; ¶1434.02

¶ 2360 Nonbusiness energy property credit—Form 5695.

For property placed in service before 2008 (Code Sec. 25C(g), a taxpayer can claim (on Form 5695) a lifetime nonrefundable credit of up to $500 for making qualifying energy saving improvements to his home, but only $200 of this credit amount may be for qualifying window expenditures. (Code Sec. 25C(a); Code Sec. 25C(b)) The expenses must be made on or in connection with a dwelling unit located in the U.S., owned and used by the taxpayer as his principal residence (as defined in Code Sec. 121), and originally placed in service by the taxpayer. (Code Sec. 25C(c); Code Sec. 25C(d))[26]

The credit per improvement is:

(1) 10% of the cost of energy efficient building envelope components which meet criteria established by the 2000 International Energy Conservation Code. These consist of: insulation materials or systems that reduce heat loss/gain; exterior windows (including skylights); exterior doors; and certain metal roofs with special coatings (which meet the Energy Star requirements) designed to reduce heat gain. (Code Sec. 25C(c)(2)) The components must be expected to last for at least five years. (Code Sec. 25C(c)) A manufacturer's certification that a component meets energy requirements can be relied on by taxpayers until IRS withdraws it. The 5-year requirement is met if the manufacturer offers a 2-year warranty to repair or replace at no extra charge.

(2) Residential energy property expenses (including labor costs for onsite preparation, assembly, or original installation (Code Sec. 25C(d))) which meet specific standards set forth in Code Sec. 25C(d)(2)(B) and Code Sec. 25C(d)(2)(C), in an amount up to:

... $300 for the cost of energy-efficient building property (electric heat pump water heater, electric heat pump; geothermal heat pump, central air conditioner, and natural gas, propane, or oil water heater meeting specific energy efficiency standards).

... $150 for a natural gas, propane, or oil furnace or hot water boiler.

... $50 for an advanced main air circulating fan. (Code Sec. 25C(a)(1); Code Sec. 25C(b)(3); Code Sec. 25C(d)(2))[27]

Any expense that otherwise qualifies for the credit won't fail to qualify merely because it was made for two or more dwelling units. In those cases, the amount of the credit is computed separately for the amount of the expenditure made for each dwelling unit. (Code Sec. 25C(e)(2)(B))[28] If a credit is allowed for an expense for a property, the increase in the basis of that property that would otherwise result is reduced by the credit allowed. (Code Sec. 25C(f); Code Sec. 1016(a)(34))[29]

caution: Check http://ria.thomson.com/federaltaxhandbook to see if this provision has been extended.

¶ 2361 Residential energy efficient property credit—Form 5695.

For property placed in service before 2009 (Code Sec. 25D(g)), an individual is allowed an annual credit (on Form 5695) for the purchase of residential energy efficient property equal to the sum of:

(1) 30% of the amount paid for qualified solar energy property (i.e., property that uses solar power to generate electricity in a home), up to a maximum credit of $2,000;

(2) 30% of the amount paid for qualified solar water heating property, up to a maximum credit of $2,000; and

---

26. ¶A-4750; ¶25C4; TD ¶569,550
27. ¶A-4751; ¶25C4; TD ¶569,551

28. ¶A-4755; ¶25C4; TD ¶569,555
29. ¶A-4757; ¶25C4; TD ¶569,557

(3) 30% of the amount paid for qualified fuel cell property, up to a maximum credit of $500 for each 0.5 kilowatt of capacity. (Code Sec. 25D(a); Code Sec. 25D(b))[30]

The equipment in (1) and (2) can be installed in a taxpayer's residence (including a vacation home). The equipment in (3) must be installed in a taxpayer's principal residence (as defined in Code Sec. 121), which may include a co-op or condo. (Code Sec. 25D(d); Code Sec. 25D(e)) Cost includes installation as well as hardware costs. (Code Sec. 25D(e)(1)) All three types of equipment must be installed in a home located in the U.S. (Code Sec. 25D(d)), and can't be used to heat a swimming pool or hot tub. (Code Sec. 25D(e)(3)) The above $2,000 and $500 amounts are determined without regard to carryovers of unused credits from previous years. (Code Sec. 25D(b)(1))[31]

An expenditure will be treated as made when the original installation is completed, except that an expenditure in connection with the construction or reconstruction of a structure will be treated as made when the taxpayer's original use of the constructed or reconstructed structure begins. (Code Sec. 25D(e)(8))[32]

¶ 2362 Alternative motor vehicle credit vehicles—Form 8910.

Taxpayers can claim (on Form 8910) an alternative motor vehicle credit for qualifying vehicles. The portion of this credit attributable to a vehicle that is depreciable is treated as part of the general business credit (¶2302). The remainder credit is a personal credit that may offset the excess of the regular tax liability (reduced by the sum of the credits allowed under Code Sec. 21 through Code Sec. 26 (nonrefundable personal credits), Code Sec. 27 (foreign tax credit), and Code Sec. 30 (qualified electric vehicles credit), over the tentative minimum tax for the tax year. (Code Sec. 30B(g))[33] As a result, even a person who is not subject to the AMT may not be able to claim the maximum allowable credit, or any credit, for a qualified vehicle. If a taxpayer's regular tax liability is zero, the amount of the credit taken as a personal credit is zero; the credit can't be carried forward or back to another tax year. [34]

The credit is allowed to the vehicle owner (or lessor of a vehicle subject to a lease) for the year the vehicle is placed in service. (Code Sec. 30B(b)) A vehicle must be used predominantly in the U.S.to qualify for the credit. Any deduction otherwise allowable under Code Sec. 179A is reduced by the amount of the credit allowable. No credit is allowable for the portion of the cost of any property taken into account under Code Sec. 179 expensing. (Code Sec. 30B(h)(7))

The credit is the sum of the following four credits: (Code Sec. 30B)

New qualified fuel cell motor vehicle credit for the purchase of a fuel cell vehicle (before 2015 (Code Sec. 30B(j))) is determined by a base credit amount that depends upon the weight class of the vehicle, and, in the case of automobiles or light trucks, an additional credit amount that depends upon the rated fuel economy of the vehicle compared to a base fuel economy. A qualifying fuel cell vehicle is a one that is propelled by power derived from one or more cells which convert chemical energy directly into electricity by combining oxygen with hydrogen fuel which is stored on board the vehicle. (Code Sec. 30B(b))[35] The 2005 and 2006 Honda FCX is certified for a $12,000 credit.

New advance lean-burn technology motor vehicle credit for the purchase (before 2011 (Code Sec. 30B(j))) of an advanced lean burn technology motor vehicle is the sum of two components: a fuel economy credit amount that varies with the rated fuel economy of the vehicle compared to a 2002 model year standard and a conservation credit based on the estimated lifetime fuel savings of a qualifying vehicle compared to a comparable 2002 model year vehicle. A qualifying advanced lean-burn technology motor vehicle is a passenger auto or light truck with an

---

30. ¶A-4781; ¶25D4; TD ¶569,561
31. ¶A-4782; ¶25D4; TD ¶569,562
32. ¶A-4783; ¶25D4; TD ¶569,563

33. ¶L-18021; ¶30B4; TD ¶397,101
34. ¶L-18026; TD ¶397,106
35. ¶L-18024; ¶30B4.01; TD ¶397,104

internal combustion engine that's designed to operate primarily using more air than is necessary for complete combustion of the fuel, incorporates direct injection, and achieves at least 125% of the 2002 model year city fuel economy. (Code Sec. 30B(c))[36]

New qualified alternative fuel motor vehicle credit is equal to 50% of a vehicle's incremental cost, plus an additional 30% if the vehicle meets certain emissions standards, but not more than between $4,000 and $32,000 depending upon the weight of the vehicle (for property purchased before 2011). (Code Sec. 30B(j)) A new qualified alternative fuel motor vehicle is a motor vehicle that's only capable of operating on an alternative fuel, compressed natural gas, liquefied natural gas, liquefied petroleum gas, hydrogen, and any liquid fuel that is at least 85% methanol. (Code Sec. 30B(e))[37] The 2005, 2006, 2007 and 2008 Honda Civic GX is certified for a $4,000 credit.

New qualified hybrid motor vehicle credit for a purchase (before 2011 for a passenger car or light truck, before 2010 for other vehicles (Code Sec. 30B(j)) of an auto or light truck (vehicles weighing 8,500 pounds or less). The credit amount varies with the vehicle's rated fuel economy compared to the 2002 model year. A new qualified hybrid motor vehicle is a motor vehicle that draws propulsion energy from onboard sources of stored energy which include both an internal combustion engine or heat engine using combustible fuel and a rechargeable energy storage system (e.g., batteries). (Code Sec. 30B(d))[38] Vehicles certified for the credit (and applicable *full* credit amount) as of the date this publication went to press are: **Toyota (see phaseout, below)** *2007* Camry Hybrid ($2,600) and Lexus GS 450h ($1,550), *2007 and 2006* Lexus 2WD and 4WD RX400h ($2,200), Highlander 2WD and 4WD Hybrid ($2,600), and *2007, 2006 and 2005* Prius ($3,150); **Honda** *2008* Civic CVT ($2,100), *2007 and 2006* Accord Hybrid ($1,300, but $650 without updated calibration), and Civic Hybrid ($2,100), *2006* Insight ($1,450), and *2005* Accord Hybrid ($650), Insight ($1,450), and Civic Hybrid ($1,700); **Ford** *2008* Escape Hybrid ($3,000 for 2WD; $2,200 for 4WD), Mercury Mariner Hybrid ($3,000 for 2WD; $2,200 for 4WD), *2007, 2006 and 2005* Escape ($2,600 for 2WD; $1,950 for 4WD), *2007 and 2006* 4WD Mercury Mariner ($1,950), Saturn 2007 Vue GreenLine ($650); **GMC** *2008* Chevrolet Malibu Hybrid ($1,300), *2008 and 2007* Saturn Aura Hybrid ($1,300), *2007 and 2006* Silverado Hybrid, and Sierra Hybrid ($250 for 2WD; $650 for 4WD); **Nissan** *2007* Altima Hybrid ($2,350); and **Mazda** *2008* Tribute Hybrid ($3,000 for 2WD; $2,200 for 4WD).

Phaseout. The credit (as listed above) for advanced lean burn technology and hybrid motor vehicles phases out beginning in the second calendar quarter following that in which a manufacturer sells its 60,000th qualified vehicle for use in the U.S. (50% credit reduction in second and third quarter; 75% in fourth and fifth quarter; 0 credit allowed thereafter) (Code Sec. 30B(f)) Except for cars manufactured by Toyota (reduced credit beginning Oct. 1, 2006; no credit after Sept. 30, 2007), no phaseout applies for 2007. [39]

¶ 2363 Alternative fuel vehicle refueling property.

For property placed in service before 2010 (2015 for property relating to hydrogen) (Code Sec. 30C(g)), a taxpayer can elect to claim a tax credit equal to 30% of the cost of any qualified alternative fuel vehicle refueling property (QAFVR property) placed in service by the taxpayer during the tax year. (Code Sec. 30C(a); Code Sec. 30C(e)(4)) The credit can't exceed $30,000 for depreciable property. (Code Sec. 30C(b)(1)) and $1,000 for any other QAFVR property. (Code Sec. 30C(b)(2))[40] QAFVR property is defined in Code Sec. 179A(d) but with certain modifications. (Code Sec. 30C(c)(1)) Property installed on property that is used as the taxpayer's principal residence under Code Sec. 121 doesn't need to be depreciable. (Code Sec. 30C(c)(2))[41]

---

36. ¶L-18025; ¶30B4.02; TD ¶397,105
37. ¶L-18029.1; ¶30B4.06; TD ¶397,110
38. ¶L-18026; ¶30B4.03; TD ¶397,106

39. ¶L-18028; ¶30B4.04; TD ¶397,108
40. ¶L-18041; ¶30C4; TD ¶397,201
41. ¶L-18043; ¶30C4.02; TD ¶397,203

The portion of the credit that is attributable to depreciable property is treated as a part of the general business credit. (Code Sec. 30C(d)(1)) The remaining part of the credit can't exceed the excess of: the regular tax liability for the tax year reduced by the sum of the credits allowable under Code Sec. 21 through Code Sec. 26 (nonrefundable personal credits), Code Sec. 27 (foreign tax credit), Code Sec. 30 (electric vehicle credit), and Code Sec. 30B (the alternative motor vehicle credit) over the tentative minimum tax for the tax year. (Code Sec. 30C(d)(2))

¶ 2364   First-time homebuyer credit for District of Columbia before 2008.

An individual who hasn't had an ownership interest in a principal residence in the District of Columbia (and, if married, whose spouse hasn't had such an interest) in the one-year period before acquiring a principal residence in the District of Columbia is permitted a one-time only nonrefundable personal tax credit (use Form 8859) of up to $5,000 of the acquired residence's purchase price (Code Sec. 1400C(a); Code Sec. 1400C(c); Code Sec. 1400C(g)), for purchases before 2008. (Code Sec. 1400C(i)) The credit phases out ratably between modified AGI (AGI increased by the foreign earned income, possessions, and Puerto Rico exclusions) of $70,000 and $90,000 ($110,000 and $130,000 for joint filers). (Code Sec. 1400C(b)) The maximum credit for a married individual filing separately is $2,500. The basis of the residence is reduced by the amount of the credit claimed. (Code Sec. 1400C(h))[42]

⊘caution: Check http://ria.thomson.com/federaltaxhandbook to see if this provision has been extended.

¶ 2365   "Saver's" credit for elective deferrals and IRA contributions

An eligible lower-income taxpayer can claim a nonrefundable tax credit for the applicable percentage (below) of up to $2,000 of his qualified retirement savings contributions — "the saver's credit." (Code Sec. 25B(a)) The applicable percentage (50%, 20%, or 10%) depends on filing status and AGI. For tax years beginning in 2007, adjusted for inflation, the amounts are:

. . . Joint filers: $0 to $31,000, 50%; $31,000 to $34,000, 20%; and $34,000 to $52,000, 10% (no credit if AGI is above $52,000).

. . . Heads of households: $0 to $23,250, 50%; $23,250 to $25,500, 20%; and $25,500 to $39,000, 10% (no credit if AGI is above $39,000).

. . . All other filers: $0 to $15,500, 50%; $15,500 to $17,000, 20%; and $17,000 to $26,000, 10% (no credit if AGI is above $26,000).

For tax years beginning in 2008, the amounts are:

. . . Joint filers: $0 to $32,000, 50%; $32,000 to $34,500, 20%; and $34,500 to $53,000, 10% (no credit if AGI is above $53,000).

. . . Heads of households: $0 to $24,000, 50%; $24,000 to $25,875, 20%; and $25,875 to $39,750, 10% (no credit if AGI is above $39,750).

. . . All other filers: $0 to $16,000, 50%; $16,000 to $17,250, 20%; and $17,250 to $26,500, 10% (no credit if AGI is above $26,000).

The taxpayer's AGI is determined without regard to the Code Sec. 911, Code Sec. 931, and Code Sec. 933 foreign income exclusions. (Code Sec. 25B(e))

The credit is in addition to any deduction or exclusion that would otherwise apply for a contribution. Only an individual who is 18 or over (other than a full-time student, or an individual allowed as a dependent on another taxpayer's return for a tax year beginning in

---

42. ¶A-4250 *et seq.*; ¶1400C4; TD ¶568,800 *et seq.*

the calendar year in which the individual's tax year begins) is eligible for the credit. (Code Sec. 25B(c))

For tax years for which Code Sec. 26(a)(2) would limit personal nonrefundable tax credits (see ¶2366), the credit is limited to the excess of: (1) the sum of: the regular tax liability, plus alternative minimum tax liability, over (2) the sum of the credits under Code Sec. 21 through Code Sec. 26 (other than the adoption expense credit and the saver's credit), plus the foreign tax credit. (Code Sec. 25B(g))

The credit is available for elective contributions to Code Sec. 401(k) plans, Code Sec. 403(b) annuities, Code Sec. 457 plans, SIMPLE or SEP plans, traditional or Roth IRAs, and voluntary after-tax employee contributions to a qualified retirement plan. (Code Sec. 25B(d)(1))

The amount of any credit-eligible contribution is reduced (but not below zero) by the following distributions during a testing period: taxable distributions received by the taxpayer and spouse from any of the above savings arrangements; or distributions from a Roth IRA or Roth account (whether or not taxable) that are not qualified rollover contributions to a Roth IRA or rollovers to a Roth account. The testing period is (1) the tax year for which the credit is claimed, (2) the preceding two tax years, and (3) the period after the end of the tax year and before the due date for filing the taxpayer's return for the year. (Code Sec. 25B(d)(2)) Certain distributions enumerated in Code Sec. 25B(d)(2)(C), such qualified plan loans not treated as distributions, won't reduce a credit-eligible contribution. [43]

¶ 2366　Limit on combined amount of certain personal nonrefundable credits.

For 2006, the combined total of the child and dependent care credit (¶2351 *et seq.*), credit for the elderly and permanently and totally disabled (¶2350), mortgage credit (¶2359), child tax credit (¶2357), Hope and Lifetime Learning credits (¶2201 *et seq.*), adoption credit (¶2356), lower income saver's credit (¶2365), the DC homebuyer credit (¶2364), the nonbusiness energy property credit (¶2360), and the residential energy efficient property credit (¶2361) was limited to the sum of: (1) regular tax liability reduced by the foreign tax credit allowable under Code Sec. 27(a) (¶2369), and (2) the alternative minimum tax (AMT). (Code Sec. 26(a)(2))

ⓇⒾⒶ*observation:* Thus these personal credits could offset the alternative minimum tax.

At press time, Code Sec. 26(a)(2) provided that for tax years beginning after 2006, these credits (other than the adoption credit, the child tax credit, and the low-income saver's credit) are allowed only to the extent that their aggregate amount doesn't exceed the excess of: (a) the taxpayer's regular tax liability, over (b) his tentative minimum tax, determined without regard to the alternative minimum tax foreign tax credit.

ⓇⒾⒶ*caution:* In an Oct. 30, 2007 letter to IRS's Acting Commissioner, the Chairmen and Ranking Members of the House Ways and Means Committee and the Senate Finance Committee pledged to pass legislation that for 2007 would allow nonrefundable personal credits to offset regular taxes and the AMT. In other words, for the limitation on the combined total of personal nonrefundable credits that may be claimed, they pledged to apply the same rules for 2007 as applied for 2006. Check http://ria.thomson.com/federaltaxhandbook for the latest news on this change and other legislative changes affecting 2007 returns and 2008 tax years.

Regular tax liability doesn't include the following types of tax: (Code Sec. 26(b)(2))

(1) The alternative minimum tax. (Code Sec. 55)

(2) Penalty taxes on certain premature distributions. (Code Sec. 72(m)(5)(B), Code Sec. 72(q), Code Sec. 72(v))

---

43. ¶A-4451; ¶25B4; TD ¶569,200

(3) Tax on nonqualified withdrawals from capital construction funds. (Code Sec. 7518(g)(6))

(4) Accumulated earnings tax. (Code Sec. 531)

(5) Personal holding company tax. (Code Sec. 541)

(6) Certain recoveries of foreign expropriation losses. (Code Sec. 1351(d)(1))

(7) Tax on certain built-in gains of S corporations. (Code Sec. 1374)

(8) Tax imposed when passive investment income of an S corporation having Subchapter C earnings and profits exceeds 25% of gross receipts. (Code Sec. 1375)

(9) Tax on transfers of high-yield interest to disqualified holders of FASITs. (Former Code Sec. 860K)

(10) The 30% tax on U.S. source income earned by nonresident aliens and foreign corporations. (Code Sec. 871(a), Code Sec. 881)

(11) The interest paid as additional income on tax deferred by installment sales of timeshares and residential lots. (Code Sec. 453(l)(3), Code Sec. 453A(c))

(12) Recapture of federal subsidy from use of mortgage bonds and mortgage credit certificates. (Code Sec. 143(m))

(13) Tax on transfers of residual interests in a REMIC to a disqualified organization. (Former Code Sec. 860E(e))

(14) The branch profits tax. (Code Sec. 884)

(15) Additional tax on Archer MSA distributions and health savings account (HSA) distributions not used for medical expenses. (Code Sec. 220(f)(4), Code Sec. 223(f)(4))

(16) Additional tax on distributions from Coverdell education savings accounts not used for higher education expenses. (Code Sec. 530(d)(4))

(17) Penalty tax for certain distributions from Medicare Advantage MSA not used for qualified medical expenses. (Code Sec. 138(c)(2))[44]

(18) For amounts deferred after Dec. 31, 2004, any interest and penalties for violations of the nonqualified deferred compensation rules. (Code Sec. 409A)[45]

¶ 2367   Credit for alternative minimum tax—Form 8801; Form 8827.

This is a credit (computed on Form 8801, Form 8827 for corporations) equal to the adjusted net minimum tax that a taxpayer paid in all previous years for "deferral preferences" (and for a corporation also "exclusion preferences"), less any minimum tax credits taken in those years. (Code Sec. 53(a), Code Sec. 53(b)) The credit is limited to the excess of: (1) taxpayer's regular tax liability (¶2366), for the year to which the credit is being carried, *over* (2) the sum of the following for the year to which the credit is being carried: all nonrefundable tax credits, and the tentative minimum tax (¶3201). (Code Sec. 53(c))

For small corporations exempt from AMT (¶3203), the limitation on the use of the AMT credit for any exempt year is applied by reducing the amount of regular tax liability (after reduction by credits under Code Sec. 53(c)(1)) by 25% of the amount in excess of $25,000. (Code Sec. 55(e)(5))

A taxpayer's adjusted net minimum tax ("ANMT") is:

(1) the total alternative minimum tax for the year,

(2) less the amount of alternative minimum tax liability that would have arisen if the only applicable preferences and alternative minimum tax adjustments were "exclusion preferences," plus

(3) the amount of electric vehicle credit not allowed solely by reason of the limitation on that credit that's a function of the taxpayer's tentative minimum tax. (Code

---

44. ¶L-18100 *et seq.*; ¶264, 264.01; TD ¶569,601   45. ¶L-18103; ¶264.01; TD ¶398,001

Sec. 53(d)(1)(B))

A corporation's ANMT, is the sum of items (1) and (3).[46]

Deferral preferences are all of the alternative minimum tax preferences and adjustments except those for: (1) percentage depletion, (2) tax-exempt interest, (3) exclusion of a portion of the gain on qualified small business stock, (4) alternative tax itemized deductions of noncorporate taxpayers, (5) the standard deduction, (6) personal exemptions, and (7) the exclusion of gain from qualified small business stock.

The preferences/alternative minimum tax adjustments that aren't deferral preferences are "exclusion preferences."[47]

Refundable part of minimum tax credit. For tax years beginning after Dec. 20, 2006, if an individual has a long-term unused minimum tax credit for any tax year beginning before Jan. 1, 2013, the Code Sec. 53(c) limit (see above) can't be less than the AMT refundable credit for the tax year. The credit is subject to a phaseout and is refundable. (Code Sec. 53(e)) The long-term unused minimum tax credit for any tax year is the portion of the minimum tax credit determined under Code Sec. 53(b) (i.e., the excess of ANMT for all earlier tax years over the minimum tax credit for those years) attributable to the ANMT for tax years before the third tax year immediately preceding the tax year. (Code Sec. 53(e)(3)(A)) For this purpose, credits are treated as allowed under Code Sec. 53(a) on a first-in, first-out (FIFO) basis. (Code Sec. 53(e)(3)(B))

The AMT refundable credit amount is reduced by the applicable percentage under Code Sec. 151(d)(3)(B) (i.e., the percentage reduction in the personal exemption amount) for an individual whose adjusted gross income for a tax year exceeds the threshold amount in Code Sec. 151(d)(3)(C) (i.e., the AGI threshold at which the deduction for personal exemptions phases out). For this purpose, AGI is determined without regard to Code Sec. 911 (foreign earned income exclusion), Code Sec. 931 (exclusion for bona fide residents of American Samoa), and Code Sec. 933 (exclusion for Puerto Rico residents). (Code Sec. 53(e)(2)(B))

¶ 2368   Clean renewable energy bond credit.

For bonds issued before 2009, taxpayers who hold "clean renewable energy bonds" (CREBs) on specified dates during the year are entitled to a nonrefundable credit equal to a portion of the bond's outstanding face amount. (Code Sec. 54(a)) The credit is includable in income, and is treated as interest income (Code Sec. 54(g)), but may be claimed against regular income tax and alternative minimum tax liability. (Code Sec. 54(c)(1))[48]

¶ 2369   Foreign Tax Credit. ▄▄▄▄▄▄▄▄▄▄▄▄▄▄▄▄▄▄▄▄▄▄▄▄▄▄▄▄▄

Most U.S. taxpayers who pay income taxes to foreign governments may deduct those taxes for U.S. tax purposes or may credit them dollar-for-dollar against their U.S. income tax liability on world-wide income.

The foreign tax credit is elective and is allowed against U.S. income tax for income tax paid to a foreign country (or province, state, city, etc., thereof) or U.S. possession. (Code Sec. 901; Reg § 1.901-1(a)) Taxpayers may choose each year between taking a credit or a deduction for foreign income taxes. (Code Sec. 27, Code Sec. 164) If credit is claimed for any foreign income taxes, no deductions may be claimed for other foreign income taxes, but other foreign taxes otherwise deductible (e.g., foreign real property taxes) may be deducted. (Reg § 1.901-1(c)) IRS will issue regs to disallow foreign tax credits for abusive tax-motivated transactions that yield little economic benefit relative to expected U.S. tax benefits.[49] Under the partnership rules, IRS has targeted certain transactions in which U.S. partners (or U.S. shareholders of

46. ¶A-8802; ¶534; TD ¶691,501
47. ¶A-8804; ¶534; TD ¶691,504

48. ¶L-16480; ¶544; TD ¶384,800
49. ¶O-4365; ¶9044.05; TD ¶391,001

partners that are controlled foreign corporations) attempt, through special partnership allocations, to claim foreign tax credits that are not matched by income subject to U.S. tax.
(Reg § 1.704-1)

Except for the "deemed" foreign tax paid (¶2377), the credit is allowed only to the person
on whom the tax was imposed, but a U.S. citizen or resident alien, who is a member of a
partnership or a beneficiary of an estate or trust, or stockholder of a regulated investment
company that made the necessary election, may claim (as a credit) his share of the foreign tax
paid or accrued by the partnership, estate, trust or mutual fund. On a joint return, the credit
is for the taxes of both spouses. (Code Sec. 853, Code Sec. 901)[50]

For tax years beginning after 2006, for purpose of the rule limiting the foreign tax credit to
the taxpayer's U.S. tax liability, an individual's U.S. tax is reduced by the sum of nonrefundable personal credits (other than the adoption credit, the child tax credit and the credit for
elective deferrals and IRA contributions) allowable for the year. (Code Sec. 904(h))

Credit is allowed to:

• *U.S. citizens* (except to the extent they are entitled to U.S. tax exemption for earned
income from U.S. possessions and foreign countries); (Code Sec. 901(b)(1), Code Sec. 911(a),
Code Sec. 931(a), Code Sec. 932; Reg § 1.901-1(g), Reg § 1.911-6(a))

• *domestic corporations* (Code Sec. 901(b)(1)) or electing possessions corporations (Code
Sec. 901(g));

• *aliens* residing in the U.S., or residing during the entire tax year in Puerto Rico (Code
Sec. 901(b)(3));

• *partners or beneficiaries* of an estate or trust who are U.S. citizens, residents of the U.S.
or Puerto Rico, alien residents of the U.S. or Puerto Rico, domestic corporations, foreign
corporations or nonresident aliens described below (Code Sec. 901(b)(5));

• *settlors or other persons* who would be treated as owners of a foreign trust but for Code
Sec. 672(f) (Code Sec. 901(b)(5));

• *domestic or resident estates and trusts* (to the extent allocable to the estate or trust
rather than the beneficiaries) (Code Sec. 642(a));

• *stockholders of a DISC or former DISC* (Code Sec. 901(d));

• *FSCs* to a limited extent. (Code Sec. 906(b)(5); Reg § 1.921-3T(d)(2)(i))

Nonresident aliens and foreign corporations can claim the credit *only* for foreign or possessions tax on certain income effectively connected with their U.S. business. (Code Sec. 906)[1]

Although the Code Sec. 936 possessions tax credit, in lieu of the foreign tax credit, has
generally been phased out, it still applies for American Samoa for the first two tax years of
certain corporations beginning after 2005 and before 2008. [2]

For the limit on the credit for alternative minimum tax purposes, see ¶3213.

¶ 2370   When and how to claim foreign tax credit—Form 1116; Form 1118.

The credit is claimed on Form 1116 by an individual, trust or estate, and on Form 1118 by
a corporation. (Reg § 1.905-2(a)(1))[3]

Accrual basis taxpayers take the tax as a credit in the tax year it accrues, cash basis
taxpayers in the tax year it's paid. But, cash basis taxpayers can make a binding election to
take credit, for *all* qualified foreign taxes, in the year they accrue rather than are paid. (Code
Sec. 905(a); Reg § 1.905-1(a))[4]

---

50. ¶O-4410 *et seq.*; ¶9014 *et seq.*; TD ¶392,004   3. ¶O-5501; ¶9054.02; TD ¶391,013
1. ¶O-4108; ¶9014.01; TD ¶392,001   4. ¶O-5504; ¶9054.01; TD ¶391,014
2. ¶O-1500.1; ¶9314.06; TD ¶394,500.1

¶ 2371   What taxes qualify for foreign tax credit?

A foreign levy (i.e., a payment required from a person by a foreign country) qualifies as a creditable foreign tax only if: (1) it is a tax, and (2) its predominant character is that of an income tax in the U.S. sense. (Reg § 1.901-2(a)(1))

Income taxes, war profits taxes and excess profits taxes paid or accrued during the tax year to a foreign country or a U.S. possession qualify for the foreign tax credit. (Code Sec. 901(b)(1)) A tax "in lieu of" such a tax also qualifies. (Code Sec. 903)

Foreign taxes on wages, dividends, interest and royalties normally qualify for the credit. (Reg § 1.901-2(a))[5]

No credit is allowed for taxes paid or accrued for income attributable to a period beginning six months after a country becomes a country that the U.S. doesn't recognize, that the U.S. has severed relations (or doesn't conduct relations) with, or that the Secretary of State has designated as a country that repeatedly provides support for acts of international terrorism. (Code Sec. 901(j)(1), Code Sec. 901(j)(2))[6] The denial of the foreign tax credit won't apply if the President determines that a waiver of the foreign tax credit denial will be in the U.S. national interest and will expand trade and investment opportunities for U.S. companies in that country, and the other conditions at Code Sec. 901(j)(5) are met. For denial of the credit to participants in an international boycott, see ¶4639.

¶ 2372   Limitations on the foreign tax credit.

The foreign tax credit is computed separately for different categories of income. The credit for each category is the lesser of: (1) the amount of foreign taxes paid or accrued with respect to that category, or (2) the U.S. tax on the foreign income in that category. (Code Sec. 901(b), Code Sec. 904(a), Code Sec. 904(d)) The following formula determines the credit: (Total taxable income within the separate category from all foreign sources ÷ Total taxable income) × U.S. income tax = Maximum credit for that category. [7]

The taxpayer adds up its net income and net losses within each category from all sources outside the U.S. and calculates that category's separate foreign tax credit limitation. There are two categories: passive category income and general category income. For tax years beginning before 2007, there were nine categories: passive income, high withholding tax interest, financial services income, certain dividends from a DISC, shipping income, taxable foreign trade income, certain distributions from foreign sales corporations (FSC) or former FSCs, and income not described in the above categories (general overall category). Dividends from 10% to 50% U.S.-owned foreign corporations are treated as income described in one of the separate limitation categories in proportion to the ratio of: the portion of the earnings and profits (E&P) attributable to income described in that category, to total E&P. (Code Sec. 904(d); Reg § 1.904-5T)[8]

The limitation doesn't apply to individuals with no more than $300 ($600 for joint filers) of creditable foreign taxes and no foreign source income other than qualified passive income who elect to be exempt from it. No carryover of excess foreign taxes is permitted to or from a tax year for which the election applies. (Code Sec. 904(j)) If the election is made, Form 1116 doesn't have to be filed.

Under the foreign tax credit limitation calculation rules, special rules may apply to the treatment of short-term capital gains and "qualifying dividends" (¶1288) and some lower-level-income non-corporate taxpayers can elect out of certain complex adjustments. [9]

---

5. ¶O-4200 *et seq.*; ¶9014.02; TD ¶391,005
6. ¶O-4007 *et seq.*; ¶9014.07; TD ¶391,012
7. ¶O-4401; ¶9044 *et seq.*; TD ¶393,001

8. ¶O-4300 *et seq.*; ¶9044.01; TD ¶393,006
9. ¶O-4404.1 *et seq.*

(Reg § 1.904(b)-1(b)(3), Reg § 1.904(b)-1(a)(1), Reg § 1.904(b)-1(f)(4))

Additional restrictions apply on foreign tax credits for foreign mineral income (Reg § 1.901-3(a))[10] and foreign oil and gas extraction income. (Reg § 1.907(a)-1, Reg § 1.907(b)-1, Reg § 1.907(c)-1, Reg § 1.907(d)-1, Reg § 1.907(f)-1)[11]

Special holding period requirements apply for claiming a foreign tax credit for withheld tax on dividends, and, effective for amounts paid or accrued after Nov. 21, 2004 on other items of income or gain, such as interest. (Code Sec. 901(l))

¶ 2373 Determining foreign taxable income.

The foreign tax credit can't exceed the foreign tax paid or accrued. If the taxpayer has no foreign source income that's taxable in the U.S., no credit is allowed. [12] For treatment of certain foreign source income as domestic income, see ¶2374. (Code Sec. 904(a), Code Sec. 904(b), Code Sec. 904(f))

Taxable income from foreign sources for purposes of the tax credit includes capital gain only up to the lesser of foreign capital gain or the excess of *all* capital gains over capital losses. Where there's a capital gain rate differential a special rule applies which limits the amount of the net foreign source capital gain or loss that's counted as foreign income in the numerator of the fraction at ¶2372. (Code Sec. 904(b)(1), Code Sec. 904(b)(2); Reg § 1.904(b)-1(b)(1), Reg § 1.904(b)-1(b)(2))[13]

¶ 2374 Source rules for foreign tax credit purposes; recapture of foreign losses.

In applying the credit limitation (¶2372), certain amounts derived from a U.S.-owned foreign corporation that are included in gross income as Subpart F income (¶4630), interest, dividends, or income from a qualifying electing fund (QEF) (¶4636), are treated as U.S.-source income (¶4654) (Code Sec. 904(g)(1))[14] notwithstanding any contrary treaty obligation unless the treaty expressly shows an attempt to override the rule. [15]

A taxpayer's "overall foreign losses" in a separate limitation category are recharacterized as U.S.-source ("recaptured") if foreign operations in later years produce a profit in that category, or if foreign business property in that category is disposed of. One-half (more if the taxpayer so elects) of foreign taxable income in any year is recharacterized as U.S.-source income (but limited to the amount of income in the separate limitation category that offsets the U.S. income), until the amount recharacterized equals the amount of those offsetting losses. Where a foreign loss in one separate limitation category offsets income in a second limitation category, income in a later year in the first category will be recharacterized as income in the second category up to the amount of the original offset. (Code Sec. 904(f)) Form 1118, Schedule J is used by corporations to keep track of these amounts. [16]

Special overall foreign loss recapture rules apply generally to controlled foreign corporation (CFC) (¶4629) stock dispositions after Oct. 22, 2004. (Code Sec. 904(f)(3)(D))

For tax years beginning after 2006, taxpayers sustaining an overall domestic loss can recharacterize it as foreign source for succeeding tax years in an amount equal to the lesser of: the full amount of the loss not carried back to prior tax years, or 50% of the taxpayer's U.S. source taxable income for the succeeding tax year. (Code Sec. 904(g))[17]

---

10. ¶O-5100 *et seq.*; ¶9014.02
11. ¶O-5200 *et seq.*
12. ¶O-4401 *et seq.*; ¶9044.01; TD ¶393,001
13. ¶O-4404; ¶9044.01; TD ¶393,005

14. ¶O-4501 *et seq.*; ¶9044.01
15. ¶O-4511; ¶9044.01
16. ¶O-4700 *et seq.*; ¶9044.01; TD ¶393,020 *et seq.*
17. ¶O-4720.1; ¶9044.01; TD ¶393,024

¶ 2375   Carryover and carryback of excess foreign tax.

If foreign income taxes paid or accrued exceed the amount that may be credited for the tax year, the excess is carried back one year (two years for credits arising in a tax year beginning before Oct, 23, 2004) and forward ten years (five years for credits that can be carried forward to any tax year ending before Oct. 23, 2004) (Code Sec. 904(c), Code Sec. 907(f))[18]

¶ 2376   Determining amount of foreign tax payments.

Payments of foreign income taxes must be translated into dollars using the exchange rates in effect at the time of the payments. (Reg § 1.905-3T(b)) Accrual taxpayers generally translate foreign taxes at the average exchange rate for the tax year to which the taxes relate unless (1) the taxes are paid more than two years after the close of the tax year to which they relate; (2) the taxes are paid before the year to which they relate; (3) the taxes are denominated in an inflationary currency; or (4) for tax years beginning after 2004, a taxpayer elects not to use the average exchange rate for foreign taxes paid in any currency other than the taxpayer's functional currency. (Code Sec. 986(a)(1)) Foreign taxes to which this rule doesn't apply are translated into U.S. dollars using the exchange rates in effect when the taxes are paid. (Code Sec. 986(a)(2))[19]

¶ 2377   Domestic corporation's credit for foreign tax on foreign affiliate.

A domestic corporation is deemed to have paid, and may claim credit for, a portion of the foreign taxes paid or accrued by a foreign corporation in which it holds at least 10% of the voting stock (first tier corporation). A domestic corporation is also deemed to have paid a portion of the taxes paid or accrued by a foreign second through sixth tier corporation in certain cases. (Code Sec. 902; Reg § 1.902-1)[20]

The domestic corporation claims the credit against dividend income from the foreign affiliate, and has to treat a portion of the foreign tax paid by that affiliate as additional taxable dividend income (called "gross up"). (Code Sec. 78, Code Sec. 902; Reg § 1.78-1(a))

To claim a foreign tax credit for taxes imposed on dividends, or for taxes deemed paid for stock, the taxpayer (except for registered or licensed securities dealers or brokers for stock held in the active conduct of a foreign securities dealer business) must hold the stock for a minimum holding period. If a credit is disallowed under these rules neither the deduction disallowance (¶1755) nor the gross-up applies. (Code Sec. 901(k))

---

18. ¶O-4601 *et seq.*; ¶9044.02; TD ¶394,001   20. ¶O-4800 *et seq.*; ¶9024.01
19. ¶O-5300; ¶9864.01

Chapter 9 Sales and Exchanges—Tax Free Exchanges—Basis

¶ 2400 Gain or Loss on Sales or Exchanges. ■■■■■■■■■■

When a taxpayer sells or exchanges property at a price higher than his cost or tax basis, he realizes a gain. If he sells at less than his basis, he realizes a loss. He doesn't realize gain or loss when property merely goes up or down in value.

¶ 2401 Computing gain or loss on a sale or exchange.

Taxpayers have gain to the extent the amount realized from a sale or exchange exceeds their adjusted basis (usually cost, increased for improvements and decreased for depreciation or amortization). If the adjusted basis of the property disposed of exceeds the amount realized, the difference is a loss. (Code Sec. 1001(a))[1]

illustration: In Year 1, S bought a machine for $10,000 and placed it in service. S used it solely in business. For Years 1 and 2, S claims total depreciation deductions of $6,300. S sells the machine for $2,700 in Year 3. S's loss is $1,000: $3,700 adjusted basis ($10,000 – $6,300) less $2,700 received on the sale.

observation: Whether gain or loss is recognized in the year of sale depends on whether it was realized in a taxable or tax-deferred transaction.

¶ 2402 Amount realized.

The amount realized on a sale or other disposition of property is the amount of money plus the fair market value (FMV) of any property received by the seller. (Code Sec. 1001(b))[2] Where the buyer of property assumes a debt of the seller, or pays one (e.g., pays seller's taxes or legal fees), the amount of the debt is added to the amount realized by the seller. (Reg § 1.1001-2(a))[3] FMV is the price at which the property would change hands between a willing buyer and a willing seller, neither being under any compulsion to buy or sell and both having reasonable knowledge of relevant facts. (Reg § 1.170A-1(c)(2); Reg § 1.412(c)(2)-1(c)(1); Reg § 1.1445-1(g)(7))[4]

If a taxpayer sells a capital asset, his selling expenses (such as brokers' commissions) ordinarily reduce the amount realized, thus reducing the gain or increasing the loss realized on the sale.[5]

For the effect of unstated interest on a deferred payment sale or installment sale of property, see ¶1307.

¶ 2403 Amount realized on sale of property subject to a debt.

If property is sold subject to a mortgage or other debt, the amount of the mortgage is included in the sales price whether or not the seller is personally liable on the mortgage debt. This is so whether or not the buyer assumes the mortgage. [6]

In determining the gain or loss on property, its fair market value is treated as being not less than the amount of the nonrecourse debt to which it's subject. (Code Sec. 7701(g))[7]

---

1. ¶I-2501; ¶10,014; TD ¶222,001
2. ¶I-2502; ¶10,014; TD ¶222,002
3. ¶I-2517; ¶10,014.03; TD ¶222,011
4. ¶P-6002; ¶10,114.25; TD ¶481,001

5. ¶I-2531 *et seq.*; ¶10,014; TD ¶222,023
6. ¶I-2517; ¶10,014.03; TD ¶222,011
7. ¶I-2522; TD ¶222,019

References beginning with a single letter are to paragraphs in RIA's Federal Tax Coordinator 2d and RIA's Analysis of Federal Taxes: Income. Those beginning with numbers are to paragraphs in RIA's United States Tax Reporter. Those beginning with TD are to paragraphs in RIA's Tax Desk.

¶ 2404 Open sales.

When a seller receives payment in the form of a property right or obligation whose value depends on future events, if the seller can prove that the right or obligation has no ascertainable value, he reports gain only when the proceeds from the obligation exceed his basis, and loss is fixed only when further payments can't reasonably be expected. [8] For contingent payment sales and open sales under the installment sale rules, see ¶ 2455.

¶ 2405 Repossession of mortgaged real estate.

When real property is sold and the sale gives rise to a debt to the seller secured by the real property (a purchase-money mortgage or similar lien), and the seller later repossesses the property (through voluntary transfer or foreclosure) because of actual or imminent default by the buyer, then (1) no loss results to the seller from the repossession or reacquisition, nor does the mortgage debt become worthless; and (2) the seller's gain on repossession is limited to the money and the value of other property (except the repossessed property) received by the seller with respect to the original sale to the extent these amounts haven't already been reported as income. The resulting gain can't exceed the gain on the original sale. (Code Sec. 1038)[9]

If a homeseller's gain isn't recognized under the exclusion rules explained at ¶ 2442 and he repossesses the home and then resells it within one year after the date of the repossession, the above rules don't apply; the resale of the home is treated as part of the transaction constituting the original sale of the property. (Code Sec. 1038(e))[10]

⌖ *observation:* If the resale isn't made within one year, the regular repossession rules above apply.

¶ 2406 Personal property repossessed.

Gain or loss to the seller on repossession of personal property sold in a deferred payment transaction not on the installment method is the difference between the fair market value of the property when repossessed and the basis of the defaulted obligation (decreased by amounts paid on the note and increased for costs incurred in connection with the repossession). Gain or loss is reported in the year of repossession. [11]

¶ 2407 When cash basis taxpayers report gain or loss.

A cash basis seller reports gain on a sale or exchange in the year the sales proceeds are received, actually or constructively. A loss is reported in the year the transaction is completed by a fixed, identifiable event. [12]

¶ 2408 When accrual basis taxpayers report gain or loss.

An accrual basis seller reports gain or loss in the year the sale is completed and an unqualified right to the purchase price arises —usually when title passes to the buyer. [13] For securities sales, see ¶2410.

¶ 2409 Delivery of deed or title in escrow.

Where both the deed (or other evidence of title) and the purchase price are placed in escrow pending examination and approval of the title by the buyer, a sale isn't completed (and gain

---

8. ¶G-6567 *et seq.*; ¶4534.49; TD ¶467,015
9. ¶G-6851 *et seq.*; ¶10,384; TD ¶471,001
10. ¶G-6877 *et seq.*; ¶10384; TD ¶471,013

11. ¶G-6801; TD ¶471,020
12. ¶I-2601; ¶4514.001; TD ¶222,401
13. ¶I-2602; ¶4464.07; TD ¶222,402

or loss isn't realized) until the buyer signifies approval. Until then, the seller doesn't have an unqualified right to payment. Once the buyer approves title, the seller can't postpone reporting gain by directing the escrow agent to hold the payment. [14]

But if the deed is delivered in escrow as security for the performance of an unconditional obligation of the buyer (usually payment of the purchase price), the sale is completed when the deed is delivered and the buyer enters into possession of the property. [15]

¶ 2410 Sales and exchanges of securities.

Gain or loss on the sale of securities arises when the seller has sold or committed himself to sell specific shares. [16] Gain or loss on the exchange of securities arises when the taxpayer acquires a right to specific securities. [17]

In stock exchange transactions, cash and accrual basis taxpayers realize gain or loss on the trade date, and not on the later settlement date. [18] For short sales, see ¶ 2639.

¶ 2411 Sales of load mutual funds with reinvestment right.

A load charge incurred in buying mutual fund shares is disregarded (in whole or in part) in computing gain or loss on the disposition of those shares within 90 days, if the buyer was given a reinvestment right under which shares in the same (or another) mutual fund could be bought at less than the usual load charge. The load charge is disregarded to the extent of the reduction in the load charge on the later purchase. (Code Sec. 852(f))[19]

¶ 2412 Significant modification of debt instrument treated as exchange.

A significant modification of a debt instrument results in an exchange of the original debt instrument for a modified instrument that differs materially either in kind or in extent. (Reg § 1.1001-3(b))[20]

observation: The like-kind exchange rules (¶2418 *et seq.*) don't apply to exchanges of bonds, notes or other evidences of indebtedness. Exchanges of corporate bonds, but not of government bonds, may be tax-free under the reorganization provisions of the Code, but only to the extent the principal amount isn't increased. Thus, in most cases, an exchange (or modification which is considered an exchange for tax purposes) results in the holder's recognizing gain or loss. For example, if a modification of a debt instrument results in a reduction of the debtor's debt, the debtor will have cancellation of debt income. (¶1388)

Examples of significant modifications in the terms of a debt instrument include:

. . . A change in the yield of a debt instrument, if the yield varies from the annual yield on the unmodified instrument (determined as of the date of the modification) by more than the greater of: 1/4 of 1% (25 basis points), or 5% of the annual yield of the unmodified instrument (.05 × annual yield). (Reg § 1.1001-3(e)(2)(ii))

. . . A modification that changes the timing of payments (including any resulting change in the amount of payments), if it results in the material deferral of scheduled payments. (Reg § 1.1001-3(e)(3)(i))

Qualifying taxpayers may elect to treat a substitution of certain publicly traded debt instruments for new ones as a realization event even if the substitution doesn't result in a significant modification of the terms of the old debt instrument, and therefore is not an exchange for tax purposes. Electing taxpayers do not recognize any realized gain or loss on

---

14. ¶I-1112; ¶4514.087; TD ¶220,608
15. ¶I-1124; ¶s 4514.101; TD ¶222,030
16. ¶I-2615; ¶12,234.07; TD ¶222,601
17. ¶I-2616; ¶s 12,234.07, 4514.112; TD ¶222,603

18. ¶I-2615.1; ¶4514.112; TD ¶222,602
19. ¶P-5038 *et seq.*; ¶8524.02; TD ¶216,021
20. ¶I-1050 *et seq.*; ¶10,014.83; TD ¶220,400 *et seq.*

the date of the substitution. Instead, gain or loss generally is taken into account as income or deductions over the term of the new debt instruments. [21]

¶ 2413   Nontaxable Exchanges.

A taxpayer doesn't recognize gain or loss on exchanges of common or preferred stock for other common or preferred stock of the same corporation. A corporation doesn't recognize gain or loss when it sells or exchanges its own stock for property or services. Certain U.S. obligations can be exchanged tax-free. Additionally, Code Sec. 1043 allows deferral of gain for conflict of interest sales by certain federal employees and related persons..

¶ 2414   Stock for stock of same corporation.

No gain or loss is recognized on the exchange of common stock for other common, or preferred stock for other preferred, of the same corporation. (Code Sec. 1036(a)) It's tax-free whether between a shareholder and the corporation or between two shareholders. [22]

Nonqualified preferred stock (¶3514) is treated as property other than stock for purposes of the rule allowing tax-deferred exchanges of preferred stock in the same corporation. (Code Sec. 1036(b))[23]

An exchange between individual shareholders, of common for preferred stock in the same corporation, isn't tax-free. (Reg § 1.1036-1(a))[24] However, reorganization exchanges of stock for stock or stock and securities of the same or different corporations may be tax-free, see ¶3541 *et seq.*

¶ 2415   Corporation's sale or exchange of its own stock for property or services.

A corporation doesn't recognize gain or loss on the sale or exchange of its stock (including treasury stock) for money, other property or services. (Code Sec. 1032(a); Reg § 1.1032-1)[25] And it doesn't recognize gain or loss on the lapse of an option (warrant) to buy or sell its stock (including treasury stock). (Code Sec. 1032(a); Reg § 1.1032-3(d))[26]

¶ 2416   Tax-free exchanges of U.S. obligations.

IRS regs may provide for the tax-free exchange of one U.S. obligation (bond, note, etc.) for another. (Code Sec. 1037(a)) The Treasury designates the specific obligations it will exchange for the previously issued obligations without recognition of gain or loss. [27]

¶ 2417   Tax-free exchanges of insurance policies and annuities.

No gain or loss is recognized upon the exchange of a life insurance contract for another or for an endowment or annuity contract, an endowment contract for an annuity or endowment contract providing for regular payments beginning at a date not later than the beginning date under the old contract, or an annuity contract for another. To qualify for tax-free exchange treatment, the insured or annuitant must remain the same. (Code Sec. 1035) The direct transfer of a portion of funds from one annuity contract to another annuity contract qualifies as a nontaxable exchange under Code Sec. 1035. Thus, the direct exchange of part of the cash surrender value of an annuity contract for a new annuity contract issued by a second insurance company is tax-free even though the original annuity contract continued to exist. [28]

To the extent provided in regs, the rules allowing a tax-free exchange of insurance policies

---

21. ¶I-1081.8; ¶10,014.83; TD ¶220,411
22. ¶I-3301; ¶10,364; TD ¶225,501
23. ¶I-3301.1; ¶10,364; TD ¶225,501
24. ¶I-3301; TD ¶225,501

25. ¶I-3201; ¶I-3208; ¶10,324; TD ¶233,401
26. ¶I-6517; ¶10,324; TD ¶252,010
27. ¶I-3400 *et seq.*; ¶10,374; TD ¶227,301
28. ¶J-5301 *et seq.*; ¶10,354; TD ¶146,616

and annuities don't apply to any exchange having the effect of transferring property to a non-U.S. person. (Code Sec. 1035(b)(3))[29]

For exchanges occurring after 2009, no gain or loss will be recognized on the exchange of a life insurance contract or an annuity contract for a qualified long-term care contract. (Code Sec. 1035(a))[30]

¶ 2418   "Like-Kind" (Code Sec. 1031) Exchanges. ▮▮▮▮▮▮▮▮▮▮▮▮▮▮▮▮▮▮

No gain or loss is recognized where business or investment property is exchanged solely for like-kind property. Multi-party exchanges may qualify. However, gain, but not loss, is recognized if boot is also received.

This nonrecognition provision doesn't apply to: stock in trade (inventory) and other property held primarily for sale; stocks, bonds, and notes; choses in action; interests in a partnership; certificates of trust or beneficial interest; or other securities or evidences of indebtedness or interest. (Code Sec. 1031(a))[31]

Nonrecognition under Code Sec. 1031 is mandatory if the conditions are met. [32]

Report on Form 8824, in addition to Form 1040, Schedule D, Form 4797, or Form 6252 (whichever applies). [33]

¶ 2419   Like-kind defined.

"Like-kind" refers to the nature, character, or class of the property, not to its grade or quality. Thus, an exchange of real estate for real estate is an exchange of "like-kind" property. It doesn't matter where the real estate is located (but foreign and U.S. real property can't be like-kind) or whether it's improved or not. (Code Sec. 1031(h); Reg § 1.1031(a)-1(b))[34]

Personal property used predominantly in the U.S. and personal property used predominantly outside the U.S. aren't like kind. (Code Sec. 1031(h)(2)(A)) In general, predominant use of relinquished property is determined based on the 2-year period that ends when the property is relinquished, and predominant use of the replacement property is determined based on the 2-year period beginning on the acquisition date. (Code Sec. 1031(h)(2)(B))[35]

Depreciable tangible personal property is exchanged for property of a "like kind" if it is exchanged for property of a like kind or like class. It is of a like class to other depreciable tangible personal property if the exchanged properties are either within the same General Asset Class or within the same Product Class. (Reg § 1.1031(a)-2(b)(1)) General asset classes are set forth by Revenue Procedure (Reg § 1.1031(a)-2(b)(2)); product classes are in Sectors 31, 32, and 33 (pertaining to manufacturing industries) of the North American Industry Classification System (NAICS) Manual. (Reg § 1.1031(a)-2(b)(3))[36]

No like classes are provided for nondepreciable or intangible personal property (e.g., a patent or copyright); an exchange of such property qualifies for nonrecognition only if the exchanged properties are of a like kind. (Reg § 1.1031(a)-2(c)(1)) The goodwill or going concern value of a business can't be like-kind property. (Reg § 1.1031(a)-2(c)(2))[37]

An exchange of real property for a 30-year leasehold on real property is a like-kind exchange. (Reg § 1.1031(a)-1(c))[38] An exchange of real property for an interest in a Delaware statutory trust (DST) that owned real property was like-kind since the DST was a grantor trust (¶3956) and the taxpayers (who received DST interests as replacement property) were treated as owning undivided fractional shares of the real property held by the DST. [39] Also, an

---

29. ¶J-5306.1; ¶10,354; TD ¶146,623
30. ¶J-5301; ¶10,354; TD ¶146,616
31. ¶I-3050 *et seq.*; ¶10,314 *et seq.*; TD ¶223,601 *et seq.*
32. ¶I-3052; TD ¶223,603
33. ¶I-3051; TD ¶223,602
34. ¶I-3059; ¶10,314.02; TD ¶223,701

35. ¶I-3064.1; ¶10,314.04; TD ¶223,706
36. ¶I-3060 *et seq.*; ¶10,314.02; TD ¶223,703 *et seq.*
37. ¶I-3065; ¶10,314.02; TD ¶223,707
38. ¶I-3076; ¶10,314.03; TD ¶223,716
39. ¶I-3074

undivided fractional interest in real property may qualify as like-kind replacement property for other real property.[40]

Trade-ins are a common type of nontaxable exchange. Whether the taxpayer pays money or not, the trade-in is still a nontaxable exchange. (Reg § 1.1031(a)-1(c))[41]

¶ 2420 Multi-party (including deferred) nontaxable exchanges.

If a taxpayer wants to (or will only) exchange his property for like-kind property, but the party who wants taxpayer's property doesn't own the like-kind property, the taxpayer can still set up a nontaxable exchange if the other party acquires the like-kind property and taxpayer then exchanges his property for that like-kind property.

V *illustration:* A holds Whiteacre for investment. He doesn't want to sell it if that would result in tax, but he would exchange it for Blackacre. B wants Whiteacre. C owns Blackacre and is willing to sell, but doesn't want Whiteacre. B buys Blackacre from C for cash. A transfers Whiteacre to B for Blackacre. The exchange is nontaxable to A.

The exchange is nontaxable (if the time limits at ¶2423 are met) even where the taxpayer transfers property in exchange for a written promise by the transferee to deliver like-kind property to the taxpayer in the future, i.e., a deferred or nonsimultaneous exchange.

A multiparty nontaxable exchange can be set up by using a qualified intermediary (someone other than the taxpayer or a "disqualified person," e.g., taxpayer's agent) to facilitate the transaction. (Reg § 1.1031(k)-1(g)(4)) Reverse exchanges (replacement property is acquired before the relinquished property is transferred) may be implemented using qualified exchange accommodation arrangements under IRS-approved safe-harbor rules. However, the safe harbor rules do not apply to replacement property owned by the taxpayer within the 180-day period ending on the date of transfer of ownership of the property to an exchange accommodation titleholder. IRS recognizes, however, that under case law, some reverse exchanges may still qualify even if they do not meet the safe harbor requirements. [42]

¶ 2421 Taxing "boot" in otherwise nontaxable exchange.

If a taxpayer receives boot —money or any other property that doesn't qualify for nonrecognition of gain—in an otherwise nontaxable exchange of stock (¶2414), insurance policies (¶2417), like-kind property (¶2418), or U.S. obligations (¶2416), then gain to the taxpayer is recognized (is taxable) in an amount not exceeding the value of the boot received (Code Sec. 1031(b)), but loss to the taxpayer isn't recognized (isn't deductible) to any extent. (Code Sec. 1031(c))[43]

V *illustration:* Taxpayer exchanges business real estate worth $50,000 and having an adjusted basis of $30,000 for business real estate worth $40,000 plus $10,000 cash. His total gain is $20,000 ($40,000 + $10,000 – $30,000 basis), but the amount recognized is limited to the boot—$10,000. The tax on the remaining $10,000 gain is deferred because the transaction qualifies as a like-kind exchange.

Where the taxpayer gives money in the nontaxable exchange, no gain is recognized. But if the boot given is property other than money, gain or loss may be recognized. Thus, where stock that has depreciated in value is given in connection with a nontaxable exchange of real estate, loss on the stock is recognized to the extent the stock's adjusted basis exceeds its fair market value. (Reg § 1.1031(d)-1(e))[44]

---

40. ¶I-3092.1; TD ¶224,003.1
41. ¶I-3057; ¶10,314.15; TD ¶223,708
42. ¶I-3095 *et seq.*; ¶10,314.10; TD ¶224,800 *et seq.*

43. ¶I-3160; ¶10,314.11; TD ¶225,001
44. ¶I-3163; ¶10,314.11; TD ¶225,001

¶ 2422   Assumption of liabilities.

Liabilities assumed are treated as a cash equivalent (boot). Whether a liability is "assumed" for this purpose is determined under Code Sec. 357(d) (see ¶3516). (Code Sec. 1031(d)) The taxpayer who assumes the liability is the one giving the boot, while the taxpayer whose liability is assumed *receives* the boot.[45] If each party assumes a liability of the other, only the net liability is boot given or received. (Reg § 1.1031(b)-1(c))

⊘*illustration:* Taxpayer's investment realty has an adjusted basis of $40,000, a value of $115,000, and has a mortgage of $60,000. He exchanges his property for investment real estate which is worth $100,000 and has a $50,000 mortgage, and he also gets $5,000 cash. Each party to the exchange assumes the liability of the other. Taxpayer's realized gain is $75,000, since he receives consideration of $115,000: (1) property worth $50,000 ($100,000 value − $50,000 mortgage), (2) $60,000 mortgage on the property *he* transfers, and (3) $5,000 cash, while his adjusted basis was $40,000. But the gain *recognized* is limited to the boot of $15,000, computed as follows:

Mortgage on property given up by taxpayer	$60,000
Mortgage on property received by taxpayer	50,000
Net reduction of taxpayer's indebtedness	$10,000
Cash paid to taxpayer	5,000
Maximum gain to be recognized	$15,000

In determining the basis of the property received in a nontaxable exchange, liabilities assumed by the other party are treated as money (boot) received by the taxpayer. (Reg § 1.1031(d)-2)

¶ 2423   Time limits on like-kind exchanges.

Like-kind treatment is barred if the property to be received is not identified (e.g., by being specified in the contract) on or before 45 days after the transfer, or isn't received within 180 days after the transfer or by the due date (with extensions) of the return for the year of transfer if earlier. (Code Sec. 1031(a)(3))[46] There's no good faith exception to these deadlines,[47] but the deadlines may be extended for like-kind exchanges affected by disasters. [48]

¶ 2424   Related-party exchanges.

Where a taxpayer exchanges like-kind property with a related (under Code Sec. 267(b), see ¶2448, or Code Sec. 707(b)(1), see ¶3731) taxpayer and, within two years of the date of the last transfer that was part of the exchange, either party disposes of the property received in the exchange, then gain or loss not recognized in the exchange is recognized on the date the later disposition occurs. A disposition includes indirect transfers. Exceptions are made for death, certain involuntary conversions, and non-tax-avoidance transactions. (Code Sec. 1031(f))[49] Form 8824 must be filed for the year of the exchange *and also* for the two years following the exchange. [50]

A qualified intermediary (¶2420) cannot be used to circumvent the limitations that would have applied to a direct exchange between the related parties. [1]

---

45. ¶I-3165; ¶10,314.12; TD ¶225,005
46. ¶I-3099; ¶10,314.08; TD ¶224,209
47. ¶I-3101; TD ¶224,209
48. ¶S-8012; TD ¶904,003

49. ¶I-3132 *et seq.*; ¶10,314.07; TD ¶224,701
50. ¶I-3132; TD ¶224,701
1. ¶I-3137

¶ 2425   Exchanges of multiple properties.

These are exchanges in which more than one "exchange group" (see below) is created, or exchanges in which only one exchange group is created but there is more than one property being transferred or received within that exchange group. To compute gain, (1) separate the properties transferred into "exchange groups," (2) offset all liabilities assumed by the taxpayer as part of the exchange by all liabilities of which the taxpayer is relieved as part of the exchange, with the excess liabilities assumed or relieved allocated among the exchange groups, and (3) apply the rules of Code Sec. 1031 and the regs separately to each exchange group to determine the amount of gain recognized in the exchange and the basis of the properties received in the exchange. (Reg § 1.1031(j)-1(a)(2)(i))

Each "exchange group" consists of the properties transferred and received in the exchange, all of which are of a like kind or like class. (Reg § 1.1031(j)-1(b)(2)(i))[2]

¶ 2426   Rollover of Gain From Certain Sales ▮▮▮▮▮▮▮▮▮▮▮▮▮▮▮▮▮▮▮▮▮▮▮▮▮▮▮▮

Eligible taxpayers may elect to roll over gain from (1) the sale of publicly traded securities tax-free into an investment in a Specialized Small Business Investment Company (SSBIC) (¶2427), (2) the sale of qualified empowerment zone assets (¶2428), and (3) the sale of qualified small business stock (¶2429), if certain holding period and reinvestment requirements are met.

¶ 2427   Rollover of securities sale gain into SSBICs.

An individual and a C corporation may elect to limit the amount of capital gain they recognize on the sale of "publicly traded securities" (securities traded on an open market) to the excess of the amount realized on the sale, over (1) the cost of any common stock or partnership interest in a specialized small business investment company (SSBIC) bought during the 60-day period beginning on the sale date, reduced by (2) any part of that cost previously taken into account under this rule. (Code Sec. 1044(a); Code Sec. 1044(c)(1))[3]

An SSBIC is any partnership or corporation licensed by the Small Business Administration under Sec. 301(d) of the Small Business Investment Act of '58 as in effect on May 13, '93. (Code Sec. 1044(c)(3))[4]

The gain an individual may roll over under the SSBIC rules for any tax year may not exceed the lesser of: $50,000, or $500,000 reduced by any gain excluded (rolled over) under this rule in all preceding years. (Code Sec. 1044(b)(1)) For married persons filing separately, the limits are $25,000 and $250,000, respectively. (Code Sec. 1044(b)(3))[5]

A C corporation's rollover for any tax year may not exceed the lesser of $250,000 or $1,000,000 reduced by any gain excluded under this rule in all preceding years. (Code Sec. 1044(b)(2)) This includes exclusions by members of the corporation's controlled group, or by its predecessor. (Code Sec. 1044(b)(4))[6]

Elect by reporting the entire gain from the sale of the publicly traded securities on Schedule D of the return on or before the due date (including extensions) for the year the publicly traded securities are sold and by attaching a statement to Schedule D showing (1) how the nonrecognized gain was calculated; (2) the SSBIC in which common stock or a partnership interest was purchased and the date the stock or interest was purchased; and (3) the basis of the SSBIC stock or interest. (Reg § 1.1044(a)-1(b))[7]

For the effect of gain not recognized under the SSBIC rules upon taxpayer's basis in an

---

2. ¶I-3138 *et seq.*; ¶10,314.10; TD ¶225,408   5. ¶I-3792; ¶10,444; TD ¶225,504
3. ¶I-3791; ¶10,444; TD ¶225,503   6. ¶I-3793; ¶10,444; TD ¶225,504
4. ¶I-3794; ¶10,444; TD ¶225,503   7. ¶I-3795; ¶10,444; TD ¶225,505

SSBIC investment, see ¶2505.

¶ 2428 Election to roll over gain from qualified empowerment zone assets.

A taxpayer can elect to defer recognition of capital gain on the sale of a qualified empowerment zone asset acquired after Dec. 21, 2000 and before 2010, and held for more than one year where replacement empowerment zone assets are purchased within 60 days. (Code Sec. 1397B(a)) DC Enterprise Zone assets aren't eligible for the tax-free rollover treatment. (Code Sec. 1397B(b)(1)(B))

The rollover rules do not apply to any gain treated as ordinary income or any gain attributable to real property, or an intangible asset, which is not an integral part of an enterprise zone business. (Code Sec. 1397B(b)(2))

If the rollover is elected, capital gain from the sale of a qualified empowerment zone asset is recognized only to the extent that the amount realized from the sale exceeds the cost of any qualified empowerment zone asset (with respect to the same zone as the asset sold) purchased during the 60-day period beginning on the sale date, reduced by any part of the cost previously taken into account under this rollover rule.

The basis of the replacement zone asset is reduced by gain not recognized on the rollover, but this rule doesn't apply for purposes of Code Sec. 1202 (exclusion for gain on the sale of small business stock; see ¶2648). (Code Sec. 1397B(b)(4))

The holding period of the replacement zone asset includes the holding period of the original zone asset, except that the replacement asset must actually be held for more than one year to qualify for another tax-free rollover. (Code Sec. 1223(15); Code Sec. 1397B(b)(5)(A))[8]

¶ 2429 Election to roll over capital gain from sale of qualified small business stock.

Taxpayers other than corporations may elect to roll over capital gain from the sale of qualified small business stock (defined at ¶2649) held for more than six months, so that gain is recognized only to the extent that the amount realized exceeds (1) the cost of qualified small business stock bought during the 60-day period beginning on the sale date, reduced by (2) any part of the cost previously taken into account under the rule. (Code Sec. 1045(a))

Rules similar to the rules that, under Code Sec. 1202(g) (¶2648), determine which holders of interests in pass-through entities are eligible for the 50% exclusion of gain from the sale of QSBS, apply to the rollover of gain from the sale of QSBS by a pass-through entity. (Code Sec. 1045(b)(5))[9]

The holding period of the replacement stock includes the holding period of the stock sold, but not for purposes of determining whether the 6-month holding period required for rollovers is met. To qualify as small business stock, the issuing corporation must meet an active business test during substantially all of the taxpayer's holding period for the stock. For purposes of the rollover provision, the replacement stock must meet this active business requirement for the six-month period following the purchase. (Code Sec. 1045(b)(4))[10]

For adjustments to basis of the replacement qualified small business stock, see ¶2506.

¶ 2430 Involuntary Conversions.

No gain is recognized when property is compulsorily or involuntarily converted into property similar or related in service or use. Where property is involuntarily converted into money or into property that isn't similar or related in service or use, a

---

8. ¶I-3430 *et seq.*; ¶13,97B4; TD ¶227,350 *et seq.*   10. ¶I-9204; ¶10,454; TD ¶247,204
9. ¶I-9201; ¶10,454; TD ¶247,201

taxpayer can avoid tax on any gain, if he so elects and he buys property that's similar or related in service or use or if he acquires control of a corporation that owns such property (or acquires the property within a specified time). The cost of the replacement property must be equal to or more than the net proceeds from the converted property. And the replacement must generally be made within two years after the close of the first tax year in which any part of the gain is realized. (Code Sec. 1033)

A loss on an involuntary conversion is recognized or not recognized without regard to the involuntary conversion rules. (Reg § 1.1033(a)-1(a))[11]

Individuals use Form 1040 Schedule D, to report gain or loss from an involuntary conversion. Form 4797 is used to report an involuntary conversion of assets used in a trade or business.[12]

¶ 2431 Nonrecognition of gain on involuntary conversions.

Where property is involuntarily converted into other property similar or related in service or use to the converted property, no gain is recognized. (Code Sec. 1033(a)(1)) However, where the taxpayer receives dissimilar property or cash when his property is involuntarily converted, he must, within a specified time, buy "replacement" property, see ¶2438,[13] or must buy 80% control of a corporation owning or, within the specified time, acquiring replacement property.[14] Gain is recognized only to the extent the amount realized on the conversion exceeds the cost of the replacement property. (Code Sec. 1033(a)(2)(A))[15]

illustration: X's insured property having a basis of $10,000 is destroyed by fire. The insurance is $15,000, so X has a $5,000 gain. If X timely buys replacement property for $13,000, $2,000 of the gain is taxable ($15,000 – $13,000). If the new property costs $15,000, none of the gain is taxed.

If a principal residence is involuntarily converted and gain is excluded under Code Sec. 121 (¶2442), then the amount realized for purposes of the involuntary conversion provisions is the amount realized less the excluded gain. (Code Sec. 121(d)(5)(B))

illustration: A taxpayer had a $300,000 gain upon the involuntary conversion of his principal residence (amount realized is $350,000), and $250,000 of the gain was excluded under Code Sec. 121. The taxpayer can avoid a current tax on the remaining $50,000 of realized gain through the timely purchase (¶2441) of a residence costing at least $100,000.

A business that realized gain from a state disaster relief grant to reimburse it for disaster-related damage to real and personal property may elect to defer the gain to the extent that an amount equal to the grant proceeds is used to timely purchase property similar or related in service or use to the destroyed or damaged property. [16]

¶ 2432 Involuntary conversion defined.

An involuntary conversion is the compulsory or involuntary conversion of taxpayer's property into similar property, dissimilar property or money as a result of the property's destruction, theft, seizure, requisition or condemnation (actual or threatened). (Code Sec. 1033(a))

Involuntary conversion includes certain sales —sales in actual or threatened condemnation (¶2435), certain sales (or the destruction) of livestock due to disease (Code Sec. 1033(d)), and the sale or exchange of livestock (in excess of the number taxpayer would sell if he followed his usual business practices) solely on account of drought, flood, or other weather-related

11. ¶I-3701; ¶10,334; TD ¶229,701
12. ¶I-3773; TD ¶229,702
13. ¶I-3700 *et seq.*; ¶10,334 *et seq.*; TD ¶229,701

14. ¶I-3743; ¶10,334.23; TD ¶229,736
15. ¶I-3701; ¶10,334.31; TD ¶229,743
16. ¶I-3702; TD ¶229,713

conditions. (Code Sec. 1033(e)(1))[17]

If property is sold or otherwise transferred to the federal government, a state or local government, or an Indian tribal government to implement hazard mitigation under the Robert T. Stafford Disaster Relief and Emergency Assistance Act (as in effect on Apr. 15, 2005) or the National Flood Insurance Act (as in effect on that date), the sale or transfer is treated as an involuntary conversion. (Code Sec. 1033(k))[18]

¶ 2433 Principal residence or contents converted as result of presidentially declared disaster.

If the taxpayer's principal residence, or any of its contents, is compulsorily or involuntarily converted because of a "Presidentially declared disaster", any gain resulting from the receipt of insurance proceeds for personal property that was part of the contents of the residence and wasn't "scheduled property" for insurance purposes, isn't recognized, regardless of the use to which the taxpayer puts those proceeds. (Code Sec. 1033(h)(1)) [19] Insurance proceeds received for the home or its "separately scheduled" contents are treated as received for a single item of property, and any property which is similar or related in service or use to the residence so converted (or its contents) is treated for purposes of the involuntary conversion rules as property similar or related in service or use to that single item of property. [20] For the extended replacement period that applies, see ¶2441.

¶ 2434 Insurance that compensates for the loss of the right to use property.

Insurance proceeds that compensate for the loss of the right to use the property due to loss or destruction may qualify for nonrecognition as involuntary conversion proceeds, but the proceeds of a use and occupancy insurance contract that expressly insures against actual lost profits don't qualify and are treated as taxable income. (Reg § 1.1033(a)-2(c)(8))[21]

¶ 2435 Condemnations—actual or threatened.

A disposition under the threat or imminence of condemnation is treated as an involuntary conversion. (Code Sec. 1033(a)(2)(E)(ii))

Threat or imminence of condemnation exists (1) when taxpayer is informed, orally or in writing, by a representative of a governmental body or authorized public official, that the body or official has decided to acquire the property, and taxpayer has reasonable grounds to believe that condemnation proceedings will be initiated if he doesn't voluntarily sell, and (2) where the taxpayer gets information as to a decision to acquire the property for public use through a report in the news media, if a representative of the governmental body or public official involved confirms the published report and taxpayer has reasonable grounds to believe that the necessary steps to condemn will be taken if he doesn't sell. [22]

Sales to third parties (as distinguished from the condemning agency) also qualify as involuntary conversions if made under the threat or imminence of condemnation. [23]

¶ 2436 Amount of condemnation awards.

Condemnation proceeds cannot be greater than the amount specifically awarded for the requisitioned property. It may, however, be less if there are any legal or other expenses or special assessment which must be deducted. But sums withheld from the award to pay liens on the property don't reduce the amount realized. [24]

---

17. ¶N-1216 *et seq.*; ¶10,334.01; TD ¶229,713.1
18. ¶I-3716.1; ¶10,334.01; TD ¶193,606
19. ¶I-3772.1 *et seq.*; ¶10,334.40; TD ¶229,750
20. ¶I-3772.2; ¶10,334.40; TD ¶229,750

21. ¶I-3724; ¶10,334.12; TD ¶229,749
22. ¶I-3703; ¶10,334.02; TD ¶229,713
23. ¶I-3706; TD ¶229,714
24. ¶I-3764; ¶10,334.31; TD ¶229,745

¶ 2437   Severance damages.

Where only part of the property is condemned, the owner may be paid severance damages as compensation for a loss of value in the part of the property retained. Severance damages may be paid, for example, because of impairment of access to the property retained. [25]

Payments are considered severance damages only if specifically agreed to in the condemnation proceeding; otherwise, the entire award is considered made for the condemned property. [26]

Where severance damage proceeds are used to acquire replacement property, the taxpayer may elect nonrecognition under the involuntary conversion rules with respect to any gain from receipt of the severance damages. [27]

¶ 2438   Replacement property.

The replacement property must be similar or related in service or use to the property replaced. (Code Sec. 1033(a)(1)) "Similar or related in service or use" means the use of the replacement property must be substantially similar to the use of the replaced property. [28]

This test as applied to an owner-lessor of property looks to the use of the replacement property from the lessor's viewpoint, not the lessee's. If the replacement property involves similar business risks, management and landlord services, etc., it will qualify even though the lessee's use of the new property differs from the lessee's use of the old. [29]

Tangible property acquired and held for productive use in a trade or business is treated as similar or related in service or use to property that (a) was held for investment or for productive use on a trade or business, and (b) was involuntarily converted as a result of a disaster for which a presidential determination was made. (Code Sec. 1033(h)(2))

illustration: If a business loses its delivery truck in a presidentially declared disaster, it can avoid current tax on the gain realized by timely (¶2441) reinvesting the insurance proceeds in a production machine.

If, because of drought, flood, or other weather-related conditions or soil contamination or other environmental contamination, it is not feasible for the taxpayer to reinvest the proceeds from compulsorily or involuntarily converted livestock (see ¶2432) in property similar or related in use to the old livestock, he may reinvest the proceeds in other property used for farming purposes. In the case of soil contamination or other environmental contamination, other property used for farming purposes includes real property. (Code Sec. 1033(f)) [30]

¶ 2439   Related-person exception to nonrecognition rule.

Nonrecognition treatment for gain in an involuntary conversion isn't permitted if a taxpayer described below acquires replacement property or stock from a related party (under Code Sec. 267(b), see ¶2448, or Code Sec. 707(b)(1), see ¶3731):

. . . C corporations.

. . . A partnership if one or more C corporations own, directly or indirectly under Code Sec. 707(b)(3) (¶3733), more than 50% of the capital interest or the profits interest of the partnership at the time of the involuntary conversion.

. . . Any other taxpayer (including an individual) if, with respect to property which is involuntarily converted during the tax year, the aggregate realized gain on property on which there is realized gain exceeds $100,000. (Code Sec. 1033(i)(2))[31]

---

25. ¶I-3768; ¶10,334.14; TD ¶229,747
26. ¶I-3770; ¶10,334.14; TD ¶229,747
27. ¶I-3768; ¶10,334.14; TD ¶229,747
28. ¶I-3725; ¶10,334.22; TD ¶229,727

29. ¶I-3730; TD ¶229,730
30. ¶N-1220; ¶10,334.08; TD ¶118,003
31. ¶s I-3733.1; I-3733.2, I-3734; ¶10,334.221; TD ¶229,722

However, nonrecognition does apply to the extent the related party acquired the replacement property or stock from an unrelated party, within the period allowed for the acquisition of replacement property or stock. (Code Sec. 1033(i)(1))[32]

In the case of a partnership (or S corporation), this denial of nonrecognition rule applies to a partnership (or S corporation) and to each partner (or S shareholder). Thus, the annual $100,000 limit applies to both the entity and each partner (or S corporation shareholder).' [33]

¶ 2440   Replacement of condemned real estate.

A replacement of condemned real estate held for productive business use or for rental or investment qualifies for nonrecognition treatment if the replacement property is property of a like-kind. (Code Sec. 1033(g)(1)) Determination of whether replacement property is of like-kind is made under the rules at ¶2418, rather than the "similar use" rule. For example, improved realty isn't similar in use to unimproved realty (Reg § 1.1033(a)-2(c)(9)(i)), but the two properties are of like-kind. [34]

The like-kind rule doesn't apply to real estate held primarily for sale (Code Sec. 1033(g)(1)) or where control of a corporation owning replacement property is acquired. (Code Sec. 1033(g)(2))[35]

¶ 2441   Replacement period.

Converted property must be replaced within a period:

(1) beginning with (a) the date the property was destroyed, stolen, condemned, etc., or (b) the date condemnation or requisition was first threatened or became imminent, whichever is earlier (Code Sec. 1033(a)(2)(B)), and

(2) ending (a) two years after the close of the first tax year in which any part of the gain is realized (three years in the case of condemnation or threat of condemnation of real property described at ¶2440; four years for principal residences converted due to presidentially declared disasters, see ¶2433), or (b) at a later date allowed by IRS upon application by the taxpayer. (Code Sec. 1033(a)(2)(B), Code Sec. 1033(g)(4)) The replacement period is extended to five years for property involuntarily converted in the Hurricane Katrina disaster area and compulsorily or involuntarily converted after Aug. 24, 2005, by reason of Hurricane Katrina, if substantially all of the use of the replacement property is within the Hurricane Katrina disaster area. [36]

If a taxpayer sells livestock on account of drought, flood, or other weather-related conditions (see ¶2438) which result in the area being designated as eligible for assistance by the federal government, the replacement period is extended to four years. This four-year period may be extended further by IRS on a regional basis if the weather-related conditions continue for more than three years. (Code Sec. 1033(e)(2)) And for tax years ending after Sept. 25, 2006, IRS has done so until the end of taxpayers' first tax year ending after the first drought-free year (as specially defined) for applicable regions. [37]

¶ 2442   Exclusion of Gain on Principal Residence. ▬▬▬▬▬▬▬▬

A taxpayer can exclude from income up to $250,000 of gain ($500,000 for joint filers meeting certain conditions) from the sale of a home owned and used by the taxpayer as a principal residence for at least 2 of the 5 years before the sale.

The full exclusion doesn't apply if, within the 2-year period ending on the sale date, the exclusion applied to another home sale by the taxpayer. (Code Sec. 121(a), Code

---

32. ¶I-3733.1; ¶10,334.221; TD ¶229,722   35. ¶I-3727; ¶10,334.22, 10,334.23; TD ¶229,728
33. ¶I-3733.2; ¶10,334.221; TD ¶229,723   36. ¶I-3772.8; TD ¶229,754.2
34. ¶I-3727; ¶10,334.22 *et seq.*; TD ¶229,728   37. ¶N-1216.1; ¶10,334.08; TD ¶229,713.2

Sec. 121(b)(3))[38]

Married taxpayers filing jointly for the year of sale may exclude up to $500,000 of home-sale gain if (1) either spouse owned the home for at least 2 of the 5 years before the sale, (2) both spouses used the home as a principal residence for at least 2 of the 5 years before the sale, and (3) neither spouse is ineligible for the full exclusion because of the once-every-2-year limit. (Code Sec. 121(b)(2)(A))[39]

For the excludible amount where married taxpayers aren't eligible for the full $500,000 exclusion, see ¶2444.

The exchange or involuntary conversion (destruction (but only if the residence is totally destroyed) as well as condemnation) of a principal residence is treated as a sale for purposes of the homesale exclusion. (Code Sec. 121(a); Code Sec. 121(d)(5)(A))[40] A taxpayer may elect not to apply the exclusion to the sale or exchange of a principal residence. (Code Sec. 121(f))[41]

The exclusion doesn't apply to gain attributable to post-May 6, '97 depreciation claimed for rental or business use of a principal residence. (Code Sec. 121(d)(6))[42]

If property is used for both residential and business (or investment) purposes, no allocation of gain is required if both the residential and non-residential portions of the property are within the same dwelling unit, but gain isn't excludible to the extent of any post-May 6, '97, depreciation. However, gain is allocated if the part of the home for which the use requirement isn't met is separate from the dwelling unit. (Reg § 1.121-1(e)(1))[43]

The exclusion isn't available to individuals subject to the expatriate tax rules (see ¶4658) (Code Sec. 121(e))[44]

For a taxpayer who acquired a home in a like-kind exchange (¶2418 *et seq.*) in which any gain wasn't recognized, or a donee of such a taxpayer, the exclusion doesn't apply for the 5-year period beginning with the date of the acquisition. (Code Sec. 121(d)(10))[45]

If home-sale gain is entirely excluded under Code Sec. 121, the transaction is not reported on the return at all. However, Schedule D entries are necessary if there is taxable gain on the home sale (e.g., realized gain exceeds the excludible amount).

A member of the uniformed services or the Foreign Service or, for sales or exchanges after Dec. 20, 2006, and before 2011, an employee of the intelligence community, may elect to suspend the 5-year period for measuring ownership and use during any period that he or his spouse is serving on extended duty at a duty station which is at least 50 miles from the residence or while residing under Government orders in Government quarters. However, in the case of an employee of the intelligence community, that extended duty must be at a duty station located outside the U.S. (Code Sec. 121(d)(9)(C)) The 5-year period can't be extended by more than 10 years. (Code Sec. 121(d)(9)(B))

¶ 2443   Reduced exclusion for partially qualifying principal residence sales.

A reduced maximum exclusion may apply to taxpayers who sell their principal residence but (1) fail to qualify for the 2-out-of-5-year ownership and use rule, or (2) previously sold another home within the two year period ending on the sale date of the current home in a transaction to which the exclusion applied (¶2442). If the taxpayer's failure to meet either rule occurs because he must sell the home due to a change of place of employment, health, or to the extent provided by regs, other unforeseen circumstances, then he may be entitled to a reduced maximum exclusion. Under these circumstances, the maximum gain that can be excluded is equal to the full $250,000 or $500,000 exclusion times a fraction having as its

---

38. ¶I-4520 *et seq.*; ¶1214.; TD ¶225,700 *et seq.*
39. ¶I-4536; ¶1214.02; TD ¶225,716
40. ¶I-4565; ¶1214.14; TD ¶225,745
41. ¶I-4570; ¶1214.20; TD ¶225,753

42. ¶I-4568; ¶1214.06; TD ¶225,748
43. ¶I-4532 *et seq.*; ¶1214.06; TD ¶225,712 *et seq.*
44. ¶I-4569; ¶1214.18; TD ¶225,749
45. ¶I-4561.1; ¶1214.14; TD ¶225,741.1

numerator the shorter of (a) aggregate periods of ownership and use of the home by the taxpayer as a principal residence during the 5 years ending on the sale date, or (b) the period of time after the last sale to which the exclusion applied, and before the date of the current sale, and having 2 years (or its equivalent in months) as its denominator. (Code Sec. 121(c)(2))[46]

illustration: S, a single taxpayer, sells her principal residence because she has a new job in another city. On the sale date, she has owned the home and used it as her principal residence for the last 18 months. She has never excluded gain from another home sale. Since S fails to meet the use and ownership requirements for the exclusion because of a change in place of employment, the amount of gain excluded by her can't exceed $187,500 ($250,000 times 1.5 years of ownership and use divided by 2 years). Thus, if S realized a gain of $50,000 on her home sale, all of it would be excludible.

The up-to-ten-year suspension for qualifying military services or Foreign Service members or intelligence community employees explained at ¶2442 may be elected to determine the amount of the reduced exclusion. (Code Sec. 121(d)(9)(A))

To claim a reduced maximum exclusion, the sale or exchange must be made because of a change of place of employment, health, or unforeseen circumstances. If a safe harbor in the regs applies, a sale is deemed to be made by reason of a change in place of employment, health, or unforeseen circumstances. If a safe harbor does not apply, a sale or exchange is by reason of a change in place of employment, health, or unforeseen circumstances only if the primary reason for the sale or exchange is one of those reasons. (Reg § 1.121-3(b))

A sale or exchange is because of a change in place of employment, if, in the case of a qualified individual (taxpayer, spouse, co-owner of the residence, or a person whose principal place of abode is in the same household as the taxpayer), the primary reason for the sale or exchange is a change in the location of the individual's employment (including self-employment). Under a safe harbor, this condition is treated as met if (1) the new place of employment is at least 50 miles farther from the residence sold or exchanged than was the former place of employment (for the unemployed, 50 miles between the new place of employment and the residence sold or exchanged), and (2) the change in place of employment occurs during the taxpayer's ownership and use of the home as his principal residence. (Reg § 1.121-3(c))[47]

The health condition is met if the primary reason for the sale is (1) to obtain, provide, or facilitate the diagnosis, cure, mitigation, or treatment of disease, illness, or injury of a qualified individual, or (2) to obtain or provide medical or personal care for a qualified individual suffering from a disease, illness, or injury. A qualified individual includes those listed above under change of employment, plus (a) the taxpayer's family members listed in Code Sec. 152(a) (other than paragraph (9)), even if they aren't his dependents; and (b) descendants of the taxpayer's grandparent (e.g., first cousins). A sale or exchange doesn't qualify for the health condition if it is merely beneficial to the general health or well-being of the individual. Under a safe harbor, the health condition is treated as met if a doctor recommends a change of residence for the health reasons listed above in (1) and (2). (Reg § 1.121-3(d))[48]

A sale or exchange is caused by unforeseen circumstances if the primary reason for the sale or exchange is an event that the taxpayer could not reasonably have anticipated before purchasing and occupying the residence. A sale or exchange by reason of unforeseen circumstances (other than a circumstance covered by one of the safe harbors listed in regs, such as an involuntary conversion, or death of a qualified individual, or designated by IRS as an unforeseen circumstance in published guidance or in a ruling issued to a specific taxpayer) does not qualify for the reduced maximum exclusion if the primary reason for the sale or

---

46. ¶I-4557; ¶1214.08; TD ¶225,737   48. ¶I-4545 *et seq.*; ¶1214.08; TD ¶225,725 *et seq.*
47. ¶I-4542 *et seq.*; ¶1214.08; TD ¶225,722 *et seq.*

exchange is a preference for a different residence or an improvement in financial circumstances. (Reg § 1.121-3(e))[49]

¶ 2444   Amount excludible if married taxpayers ineligible for full exclusion.

If married taxpayers filing a joint return aren't eligible for the $500,000 maximum exclusion under the rules explained at ¶2442, the amount of the exclusion that they may claim is the sum of each spouse's maximum exclusion determined on a separate basis as if they had not been married. However, for purposes of this rule, each spouse is treated as owning the property during the period that either spouse owned the property. (Code Sec. 121(b)(2)(B))[50]

⬥illustration: When Al and Betty were married, Betty moved into the house Al had been using as his principal residence for over 20 years. Neither of them had previously sold a principal residence. They both used the house as their principal residence for six months after their marriage, and then Al sold the house because of a change of place of employment. Al had a gain of $600,000 on the sale. Both Al and Betty are treated as owning the house for at least two years but Betty used it as her principal residence for only six months. Al can exclude $250,000 of the gain on the sale since he meets both the two-year ownership and the two-year use requirements, but Betty can exclude only $62,500 of the gain (¼ of $250,000). The total amount excludable is $312,500, i.e., $250,000 plus $62,500.

¶ 2445   Ownership and use test to qualify for homesale exclusion

In general, the full homesale exclusion applies only if the taxpayer owned the home and used it as a principal residence for at least 2 of the 5 years ending on the date that it is sold. (Code Sec. 121(a))

A taxpayer is treated as the owner and seller of the residence held by a trust during the period that he is treated as the owner of the trust or the portion of the trust that includes the residence under the rules of Code Sec. 671 through Code Sec. 679 (grantors and others treated as substantial owners), see ¶3956 *et seq.* Similar treatment applies to certain single-owner entities. (Reg § 1.121-1(c)(3))[1]

Each unmarried taxpayer who jointly owns a principal residence may be eligible to exclude from gross income up to $250,000 of gain that is attributable to that taxpayer's interest in the property. (Reg § 1.121-2(a)(2))[2]

Gain from the sale or exchange of partial interests (other than interests remaining after the sale or exchange of a remainder interest) in the taxpayer's principal residence is excludible if the interest sold or exchanged includes an interest in the dwelling unit. Only one maximum limitation amount of $250,000 ($500,000 for certain joint returns) applies to the combined sales or exchanges of partial interests. (Reg § 1.121-4(e))[3]

The bankruptcy estate of an individual in a chapter 7 or 11 bankruptcy case under title 11 of the United States Code succeeds to and takes into account his homesale exclusion if the individual otherwise satisfies the requirements. (Reg § 1.1398-3)[4]

Under the following circumstances, a taxpayer may "tack on" someone else's ownership and/or use period to his or her own ownership and/or use period.

. . . An unmarried individual whose spouse was deceased on the homesale date may tack on the decedent's ownership and use period to his or her own ownership and use period. (Code Sec. 121(d)(2))[5]

49. ¶I-4547 *et seq.*; ¶1214.08; TD ¶225,727 *et seq.*
50. ¶I-4537; ¶1214.02; TD ¶225,717
1. ¶I-4529 *et seq.*; ¶1214.12; TD ¶225,709 *et seq.*
2. ¶I-4535; ¶1214.02; TD ¶225,715

3. ¶I-4567; ¶1214.16; TD ¶225,747
4. ¶C-9718.01; ¶13,984.01; TD ¶225,742
5. ¶I-4559; ¶1214.10; TD ¶225,739

. . . An individual who receives a home in a Code Sec. 1041(a) transaction (¶2447), such as a tax-free transfer from one spouse to another, may tack on the transferor's ownership period to his or her own ownership period. (Code Sec. 121(d)(3)(A))[6]

. . . An individual is treated as using a home as his or her principal residence during any period of ownership that the individual's spouse or former spouse is granted use of the property under a divorce or separation instrument. (Code Sec. 121(d)(3)(B))[7]

A relief provision applies to a taxpayer who becomes physically or mentally incapable of self-care and, during the 5-year period ending on the home's sale date, owns and uses the home as a principal residence for periods aggregating at least 1 year. Here, the taxpayer is treated as having used the home as a principal residence during any time in the 5-year period in which he owns the home and lives in a facility (including a nursing home) licensed by a state or political subdivision to care for someone in the taxpayer's condition. (Code Sec. 121(d)(7))[8] The up-to-ten-year suspension for qualifying military services, Foreign Services members, or employees of an intelligence community (¶2442) also may be elected for this relief provision. (Code Sec. 121(d)(9)(A))

Effective for individuals dying after 2009, the home-sale exclusion will be extended to decedents' estates, heirs and trusts that were qualified revocable trusts immediately before such an individual's death so that they will be allowed to take into account the decedent's ownership and use of the home while alive. (Code Sec. 121(d)(9))[9]

¶ 2446   Sales and Exchanges Between Related Taxpayers. ▰▰▰▰▰

No gain or loss is recognized on a transfer of property between spouses (or former spouses incident to divorce). No deduction is allowed for any loss from the sale or exchange of property between specified related taxpayers. A loss from a transfer between members of the same controlled group is generally deferred until the property is transferred outside the group.

¶ 2447   Gain or loss on transfer to spouse.

No gain or loss is recognized on a transfer of property to (or in trust for the benefit of) the transferor's spouse, or to a former spouse incident to a divorce. (Code Sec. 1041(a))[10] Certain transfers to third parties on behalf of (i.e., in satisfaction of an obligation or liability of) the spouse or former spouse qualify for nonrecognition. (Reg § 1.1041-1T(c))[11] However, the no-gain-or-loss rule doesn't apply to transfers in trust where liability exceeds basis (Code Sec. 1041(e)),[12] to transfers in trust of installment obligations (Code Sec. 453B(g)),[13] or where the transferee spouse is a nonresident alien. (Code Sec. 1041(d))[14]

A transfer of property is incident to divorce if it occurs within one year after the date the marriage ceases (Code Sec. 1041(c)(1)) or the transfer is related to the cessation of the marriage. (Code Sec. 1041(c)(2)) A transfer is related to the cessation if the transfer is under a divorce or separation instrument and the transfer occurs not more than six years after the date the marriage ceases. For later transfers, there's a presumption that the transfer isn't related to the cessation. (Reg § 1.1041-1T(b), Q&A-7)[15]

¶ 2448   Losses from sales and exchanges between related taxpayers.

No deduction is allowed for losses from sales or exchanges between certain related taxpayers. (Code Sec. 267(a)) The following are related taxpayers:

6. ¶I-4558; ¶1214.10; TD ¶225,738
7. ¶I-4558; ¶1214.10; TD ¶225,738
8. ¶I-4563; ¶1214.14; TD ¶225,743
9. ¶I-4560; ¶1214.14; TD ¶225,740
10. ¶s I-3609, I-3601; ¶10,414; TD ¶228,201

11. ¶I-3604; ¶10,414; TD ¶228,205
12. ¶I-3605; ¶10,414; TD ¶228,206
13. ¶I-3606; ¶10,414; TD ¶228,207
14. ¶I-3608; ¶10,414
15. ¶I-3610; ¶10,414; TD ¶228,302

Members of the seller's family, but only brothers and sisters (whole or half blood), spouse, ancestors and lineal descendants. (Code Sec. 267(a), Code Sec. 267(b)(1), Code Sec. 267(c)(4))[16] In-laws aren't members of the seller's family. [17]

Controlled corporations. A taxpayer and his controlled corporation, and a fiduciary and a corporation controlled by the trust or grantor. Control is direct or indirect ownership of more than 50% in value of the outstanding stock. (Code Sec. 267(b)(2), Code Sec. 267(b)(8))

Control group member. Corporations that are members of the same controlled group of corporations. (Code Sec. 267(b)(3))[18] Loss from a sale or exchange between members of a controlled group is deferred, as explained at ¶2450.

A corporation and a partnership if the same persons own more than 50% in value of the outstanding stock of the corporation, and more than 50% of the capital interest, or the profits interest, in the partnership. (Code Sec. 267(b)(10))[19]

An S corporation and another S corporation if the same persons own more than 50% in value of the outstanding stock of each corporation. (Code Sec. 267(b)(11))

An S corporation and a C corporation if the same persons own more than 50% in value of the outstanding stock of each corporation. (Code Sec. 267(b)(12))[20]

An estate and a beneficiary of that estate, except in the case of a sale or exchange in satisfaction of a pecuniary bequest. (Code Sec. 267(b)(13))

Trustees, grantors, and beneficiaries, that is, the grantor and the fiduciary of a trust; the fiduciary and the beneficiary of a trust; the fiduciaries of two different trusts with the same grantor; a fiduciary of one trust and the beneficiary of another trust with the same grantor; and a trust fiduciary and a corporation more than 50% in value of the outstanding stock of which is owned directly or indirectly by or for the trust or its grantor. (Code Sec. 267(b)(4), Code Sec. 267(b)(5), Code Sec. 267(b)(6), Code Sec. 267(b)(7), Code Sec. 267(b)(8))[21]

Exempt organizations. A person and an exempt organization controlled, directly or indirectly, by that person or the members of his family. (Code Sec. 267(b)(9))[22]

In applying the related taxpayer rules, ownership of stock is attributed to the taxpayer as follows:

(1) A stockholder is considered to own a proportionate share of the stock owned by the corporation.

(2) A partner is considered to own a proportionate share of the stock owned by the partnership.

(3) If an individual owns some stock in a corporation, he's considered the owner of stock owned by his partner.

(4) A beneficiary is considered to own a proportionate share of the stock owned by the trust or estate.

(5) An individual is considered to own stock owned by members of his family, as defined above, whether or not he's the actual owner of stock in the same corporation. (Code Sec. 267(c); Reg § 1.267(c)-1)[23]

¶ 2449   Later sale by related buyer.

A related buyer is allowed to reduce his gain on property he resells at a gain by the loss disallowed to his seller if these conditions are met: (1) a loss deduction was barred under the

---

16. ¶I-3512; ¶s 2674.03, 26,74.04; TD ¶227,905
17. ¶I-3515; ¶2674.03; TD ¶227,907
18. ¶I-3522; ¶2674.05; TD ¶227,910
19. ¶I-3532; ¶s 2674.03, 2674.04; TD ¶227,921

20. ¶I-3531; ¶2674.05; TD ¶227,920
21. ¶I-3527; ¶2674.03; TD ¶227,917
22. ¶I-3530; ¶2674.03; TD ¶227,904
23. ¶I-3516; ¶2674.04; TD ¶227,913

rules on related taxpayers (¶2448), (2) the resale or exchange is at a gain, and the property is either the property on which the loss was disallowed or property the basis of which is determined by reference to the basis of that property, and (3) the loss deduction on the original sale to the taxpayer wasn't barred under the wash sale rules (¶2461). (Code Sec. 267(d); Reg § 1.267(d)-1)[24]

Illustration: H sells to his wife, B, for $5,500, farmland, with an adjusted basis for determining loss to him of $8,000. The loss of $2,500 is not allowable to H. B exchanges the farmland, held for investment purposes, with an unrelated individual, for two city lots, also held for investment purposes. The basis of the city lots in the hands of B ($5,500) is a substituted basis determined by reference to the basis of the farmland. Later, B sells the city lots for $10,000. Although her realized gain is $4,500 ($10,000 minus $5,500), her recognized gain is only $2,000, the excess of the realized gain of $4,500 over the loss of $2,500 not allowable to H. (Reg § 1.267(d)-1(a)(4), Ex (4))

¶ 2450   Loss between members of controlled group.

With some exceptions, a loss from a transfer between members of the same controlled group is deferred (rather than denied). The loss is recognized when the property is transferred outside the group if the loss would be recognized under consolidated return principles. (Code Sec. 267(f)(2))[25]

For purposes of any Code section other than Code Sec. 267 which refers to a relationship which would result in a disallowance of losses under Code Sec. 267, deferral under Code Sec. 267(f)(2) is treated as a disallowance. (Code Sec. 267(f)(4))[26]

¶ 2451   Gain on sale of employer stock to ESOP or EWOC.

A taxpayer (but not a C corporation) or executor who sells qualified securities (certain common stock) to an employee stock ownership plan (ESOP) or eligible worker-owned cooperative (EWOC) that holds specified percentages of the securities, may elect nonrecognition of gain if the seller buys "qualified replacement property" (securities of another corporation that doesn't exceed certain passive income limits) within a specified period of time. The seller's gain is recognized only to the extent the proceeds of sale exceed his cost for the replacement property. Nonrecognition treatment applies only if the gain on the sale of the stock would otherwise have been long-term capital gain. (Code Sec. 1042)[27]

The deferral of gain under Code Sec. 1042 also applies to the sale of stock of a qualified refiner or processor to an eligible farmer's cooperative. (Code Sec. 1042(g)(1))

¶ 2452   Installment Sales and Other Deferred Payment Sales. ▬▬▬▬▬▬▬

Under the installment method, a nondealer (unless he elects out) reports gain on a sale as payments are received, instead of reporting all the gain in the year of sale.

For unstated interest on installment (and other deferred payment) sales, see ¶1307 *et seq.*

¶ 2453   Reporting gain under the installment sale rules—Form 6252.

The installment sale rules must be used to report gain on the disposition of non-dealer property where at least one payment is to be received after the close of the tax year in which the disposition occurs (Code Sec. 453(b)(1)) unless the taxpayer elects not to use the installment method (see ¶2456) or the transaction is one for which the installment method can't be used (see ¶2454).[28] The amount of a payment that's income to the taxpayer is that portion of

---

24. ¶I-3541; ¶2674; TD ¶227,927
25. ¶s E-8250, I-3524 *et seq.*; ¶2674.05; TD ¶227,912
26. ¶I-3524 *et seq.*; TD ¶227,912

27. ¶H-12103 *et seq.*; ¶10,424
28. ¶G-6000 *et seq.*; ¶4534.01; TD ¶461,000 *et seq.*

the installment payments received in the year that the gross profit realized or to be realized bears to the total contract price (the "gross profit ratio"). (Code Sec. 453(c); Reg § 15A.453-1(b)(2)(i))[29]

◈illustration: Taxpayer sells personal-use property for a gross profit of $2,000 at a contract price of $8,000. The gross profit ratio is 25% ($2,000 ÷ $8,000). Therefore, 25% of each payment collected on the sale (including the down payment) is gain and is included in gross income for the tax year it's collected. The ratio remains constant for all installment payments received on the sale.

Payments include:

(a) amounts actually received by the seller (e.g, cash, other property, foreign currency, marketable securities, or evidences of indebtedness of persons other than the buyer. (Reg § 15A.453-1(b)(3)(i))[30] Evidences of indebtedness of the buyer are treated as payment if they are payable on demand or readily tradable. (Code Sec. 453(f)(4)) [31]

(b) the buyer's payments of the seller's selling expenses, [32] and

(c) the amount by which qualifying debt assumed or taken subject to by the buyer exceeds the seller's basis. (Reg § 15A.453-1(b)(3)(i))[33]

Gross profit is the selling price less the property's adjusted basis (as increased by selling expenses). (Reg § 15A.453-1(b)(2)(v))[34] The selling price is the gross selling price without reduction to reflect any existing mortgage or other encumbrance on the property (whether assumed or taken subject to by the buyer) and without reduction to reflect any selling expenses. Neither interest (whether stated or unstated) nor original issue discount is part of the selling price. (Reg § 15A.453-1(b)(2)(ii))

Gain recaptured under Code Sec. 1245 (¶2695) or Code Sec. 1250 (¶2696), including gain attributable to the Code Sec. 179 expense election, (¶1944 *et seq.*), or so much of the unrealized receivables under Code Sec. 751 (¶3755) as relates to Code Sec. 1245 or Code Sec. 1250, is fully taxed as ordinary income in the year of sale. Only gain that isn't recapture income is taken into account under the installment method. (Code Sec. 453(i))[35] The recaptured amount is added to the adjusted basis of the property for purposes of determining basis recovered and gain recognized from each installment. [36]

While gain on the sale of a partnership interest qualifies for installment reporting, gain attributable to inventories and unrealized receivables held by the partnership does not. [37]

The total contract price is the selling price, reduced by debt on the property that the buyer assumes (or takes subject to) but only to the extent of the seller's basis in the property. (Reg § 15A.453-1(b)(2)(iii))[38]

¶ 2454 Where installment method can't be used.

The installment method cannot be used by dealers in property, real or personal (Code Sec. 453(b)(2)).[39] However, the installment method may be used for:

• dispositions by farmers (not merchants) of any property used or produced in the trade or business of farming (Code Sec. 453(l)(2)(A)); and

• dispositions to an individual in the ordinary course of a taxpayer's trade or business of the following but only if interest is paid on the tax deferred when the installment method is used: (Code Sec. 453(l)(2)(B))

---

29. ¶G-6052 *et seq.*; ¶4534.21; TD ¶462,003
30. ¶G-6151; ¶4534.22 *et seq.*; TD ¶462,501 *et seq.*
31. ¶G-6163; ¶4534.23; TD ¶462,509
32. TD ¶462,503
33. ¶G-6155; ¶4534.27; TD ¶462,504
34. ¶G-6053; ¶4534.21; TD ¶462,004

35. ¶G-6097 *et seq.*; ¶4534.05; TD ¶462,018
36. ¶G-6097; ¶4534.05; TD ¶462,018
37. ¶G-6010; ¶4534.05; TD ¶461,005
38. ¶G-6060; ¶4534.21; TD ¶462,013
39. ¶G-6601; ¶G-6014.1; ¶4534.01; ¶4534.03; TD ¶466,001; TD ¶461,008

... a timeshare right to use, or a timeshare right to an ownership interest in, residential real property for not more than six weeks per year, or a right to use specified campgrounds for recreational purposes (timeshare rights or ownership interests held by the spouse, children, grandchildren or parents of an individual are treated as held by the individual), or

: ... any residential lots, but only if the taxpayer (or any related person) isn't to make any improvements with respect to the lots. [40]

The installment method can't be used for:

... Sales of stock or securities traded on an established securities market (Code Sec. 453(k)(2)(A)), but it can be used for unregistered restricted stock sold in a private placement. [41]

... Sales at a loss. [42]

... Sales of depreciable property between persons related within the Code Sec. 1239(b) rules (¶2691), and the Code Sec. 707(b)(1)(B) rules, ¶3731 *et seq.*)[43] unless it's established to IRS's satisfaction that the sale didn't have as one of its principal purposes the avoidance of federal tax. (Code Sec. 453(g))[44]

¶ 2455   Contingent payment sales.

The installment method is used to report contingent payment sales (sales or other dispositions of property in a tax year in which the total selling price can't be determined at the close of that.tax year), unless the taxpayer elects not to use the installment method. (Reg § 15A.453-1(c)(1)) In general, basis is allocated to payments received and to be received by treating the stated maximum selling price as the selling price. (Reg § 15A.453-1(c)(2)(i)) However:

... If the maximum selling price can't be determined, but the maximum period over which payments may be received is fixed, the seller's basis is allocated to the tax years in which payments may be received in equal annual increments. (Reg § 15A.453-1(c)(3)(i))

... If the agreement neither specifies a maximum selling price nor limits payments to a fixed period, the transaction may be a sale or payments under the agreement may be rent or royalty income. If the transaction is a sale, basis (including selling expenses) generally is recovered in equal annual increments over a period of 15 years starting with the date of sale. (Reg § 15A.453-1(c)(4))

A seller may (if IRS grants permission) use an alternative basis recovery method if it's able to demonstrate that applying the normal basis recovery rule would substantially and inappropriately defer recovery of basis. (Reg § 15A.453-1(c)(7))[45]

¶ 2456   Electing out of the installment method.

An election not to have the installment method apply to a sale is made by reporting an amount realized equal to the selling price (including the full face amount of any installment obligation) on the tax return filed for the year the sale occurs. (Reg § 15A.453-1(d)(3)(i))[46]

The election out must be made on or before the due date (including extensions) for filing the return for the year of sale. (Code Sec. 453(d)(2))[47] A late election is allowed only if IRS concludes taxpayer had good cause for the failure to timely elect. (Reg § 15A.453-1(d)(3)(ii))[48]

40. ¶G-6600 *et seq.*; ¶4534.01; TD ¶466,003 *et seq.*
41. ¶G-6016 *et seq.*; ¶4534.01; TD ¶461,012
42. ¶G-6015; ¶4534.01; TD ¶461,011
43. ¶G-6208; ¶4534.17; TD ¶463,503
44. ¶G-6201; ¶4534.17; TD ¶463,501

45. ¶G-6280; ¶4534.30; TD ¶463,020
46. ¶G-6360; ¶4534.08; TD ¶461,503
47. ¶G-6352; ¶4534.08; TD ¶461,502
48. ¶G-6353; ¶4534.08; TD ¶461,502

An election out may be revoked only with IRS consent. (Code Sec. 453(d)(3))[49]

⚫️observation: Consider electing out of the installment method if the seller will be in a much higher tax bracket in post-sale years than in the sale year, or if he is selling a property with large suspended passive activity losses (if installment method is used, these losses only become available to offset nonpassive income as payments are made; see ¶1840).

A taxpayer who elects not to report a deferred-payment sale on the installment method recognizes gain on the sale according to his method of accounting. The receipt of an installment obligation is treated as a receipt of property equal to the fair market value (FMV) of the obligation. (Reg § 15A.453-1(d)(2)(i))[50]

¶ 2457 Character of installment gain where depreciable realty is sold.

When depreciable real property is sold by a noncorporate taxpayer, the gain may be partially 25%-rate gain (unrecaptured section 1250 gain subject to a maximum tax of 25%, see ¶2605), and partially adjusted net capital gain (taxed at a maximum rate of 15%, see ¶2604). If there are both types of gain, the 25%-rate gain is taken into account as payments are received before any adjusted net capital gain is included. (Reg § 1.453-12(a)) If the taxpayer is otherwise in a tax bracket below 25%, the 25%-rate gain is taxed at a 15% or 10% rate, and the adjusted net capital gain is taxed at a 5% rate.

⚫️illustration: T sells depreciable real property for a total price of $150,000. He has a total gain of $30,000, $20,000 of which is 25%-rate gain, and $10,000 of which is adjusted net capital gain. The sales price is payable in five equal annual installments of $30,000, with the first installment due in the year of sale. T takes $6,000 of gain into account as each installment is paid. The entire gain of $6,000 on the receipt of the first three installments, and $2,000 of the gain on the receipt of the fourth installment, is taxed as 25%-rate gain. The remaining $4,000 of gain on the fourth installment and the entire $6,000 of gain on the fifth installment is taxed at a maximum rate of 15%.

Net section 1231 gain that would otherwise be taxed as long-term capital gain, is taxed as ordinary income to the extent of non-recaptured net section 1231 losses for the preceding five years (¶2685). If net section 1231 gain for a tax year consists of both 25%-rate gain and adjusted net capital gain, the 25%-rate gain is recharacterized as ordinary income first. This rule also applies to installment payments. (Reg § 1.453-12(d), Ex. 3)[1]

¶ 2458 Sale, exchange, or satisfaction of installment obligations.

For installment obligations satisfied at face value, gain or loss is computed under the general rules (¶2453) for computing income on the installment method. [2]

If an installment obligation is satisfied at other than face or is sold or exchanged, gain or loss is the difference between the basis of the obligation and the amount realized. If it's distributed, transmitted, or disposed of other than by sale or exchange, gain or loss is the difference between its basis and its fair market value, (Code Sec. 453B(a)) [3] except that if it's distributed in a complete liquidation of a subsidiary to which Code Sec. 337(a) applies (¶3575), no gain is recognized. (Code Sec. 453B(d)) [4] If there's a repossession by the seller of the personal property sold following the buyer's default (i.e., a disposition of the installment obligation by the seller), [5] the seller's gain or loss is: (1) the fair market value of the property, plus anything received from the buyer in addition to the repossessed property; minus (2) the

49. ¶G-6362; ¶4534.08; TD ¶461,509
50. ¶G-6351, G-6550 *et seq.*; ¶4534.45 *et seq.*; TD ¶467,001
1. ¶G-6000 *et seq.* ¶4534; TD ¶461,000 *et seq.*
2. ¶G-6052; ¶4534.22; TD ¶465,002

3. ¶G-6454 *et seq.*; ¶453B4.05; TD ¶465,004
4. ¶G-6489; ¶453B4.11; TD ¶465,037
5. ¶G-6476; ¶453B4.07; TD ¶465,044

seller's basis in the installment obligation, plus any expense in connection with the repossession.[6] Transmission of an installment obligation at death doesn't result in gain or loss to the decedent. (Code Sec. 453B(c); Reg § 1.451-1(b)(2))[7]

The basis of an obligation is the excess of its face value over the amount equal to the income that would be returnable if the obligation were fully satisfied. (Code Sec. 453B(b))[8]

☑ *observation:* Since this excess always equals the unrecovered cost, the "basis" is the unrecovered cost.

¶ 2459   Sale to related person who then resells.

If a person disposes of property in an installment sale (first disposition) to a related person (see below) who then disposes of the property (second disposition) within two years of the first disposition, and before all payments are made on the first disposition, the amount the related person (the buyer in the first disposition) realizes as a result of the second disposition is treated as being received by the original seller at the time of the second disposition. (Code Sec. 453(e)(1), Code Sec. 453(e)(2))

The amount treated as received by the person making the first disposition because of the second disposition can't be more than:

. . . the lesser of the total amount realized on any second disposition of the property occurring in the tax year, or the total contract price for the first disposition; minus

. . . the sum of the aggregate amount of payments received with respect to the first disposition before the close of the tax year in which the second disposition occurs, and the aggregate amount treated as received with respect to the first disposition because of earlier dispositions of installment obligations by related persons. (Code Sec. 453(e)(3))[9]

For purposes of these rules, if the second disposition isn't a sale or exchange, the property's FMV is treated as the amount realized. (Code Sec. 453(e)(4))

A "related person" is someone whose stock would be attributed to the initial seller under Code Sec. 318(a) (¶3534), other than under the option attribution rules, or a person who bears a relationship to the initial seller under Code Sec. 267(b) (¶2448) for purposes of the rules disallowing the deduction of losses on sales between related persons. (Code Sec. 453(f)(1))[10]

Exceptions exist for involuntary conversions, deaths, corporations' reacquisition of their own stock, and where IRS rules out tax avoidance. (Code Sec. 453(e)(6), Code Sec. 453(e)(7))[11]

The two-year period stops running when puts, options, or short sales, etc., are involved. (Code Sec. 453(e)(2)(B))[12] For marketable securities, there's no two-year limit. (Code Sec. 453(e)(2)(A))[13]

¶ 2460   Sales of certain property for more than $150,000—"pledge and interest" rule.

The following rules apply to an installment sale of "any" property (except personal use or farm property, and dealer sales of timeshares or residential lots) where the selling price is over $150,000: (Code Sec. 453A)[14]

(1) If an installment obligation from the sale plus all other installment obligations that arose from dispositions during the tax year and are still outstanding at the close of the tax

6. ¶G-6481; ¶453B4.07; TD ¶465,048
7. ¶G-6507; ¶453B4.13; TD ¶465,019
8. ¶G-6456; ¶453B4.07; TD ¶465,006
9. ¶G-6401; ¶4534.18; TD ¶464,500 *et seq.*
10. ¶G-6416; ¶4534.18; TD ¶464,503

11. ¶G-6411; ¶4534.18; TD ¶464,512
12. ¶G-6409; ¶4534.18; TD ¶464,510
13. ¶G-6408; ¶4534.18; TD ¶464,510
14. ¶G-6300 *et seq.*; ¶453A4; TD ¶464,001

year total over $5,000,000, the seller must pay, as additional tax, interest at the underpayment rate (¶4865) on the deferred tax attributable to those installment obligations.

(2) If an installment obligation from the sale becomes security for any indebtedness, the net proceeds of the indebtedness is treated as a payment of the obligation as of the later of the time the indebtedness becomes secured or the proceeds of the indebtedness are received by the seller. Payment of indebtedness is treated as secured by an interest in an installment obligation to the extent that an arrangement allows the taxpayer to satisfy all or part of the debt with the installment obligation (i.e., gives him the *right* to repay the loan by transferring the installment note to his creditor). (Code Sec. 453A(d)(4))

¶ 2461   Wash Sales.

No loss deduction is allowed for any loss from any sale or other disposition of stock or securities (including contracts or options to acquire or sell stock or securities) if within a period beginning 30 days before and ending 30 days after the sale the taxpayer acquires, or has entered into a contract or option to acquire, substantially identical stock or securities.

¶ 2462   Wash sale loss disallowance rule.

Losses on the sale of (or on a contract or option to sell) stock or securities are not deductible if, within a period beginning 30 days before the date of the sale and ending 30 days after the date of the sale, the taxpayer acquires or has entered into a contract or option to acquire stock or securities that are substantially identical. (Code Sec. 1091(a); Reg § 1.1091-1(a))[15]

⬥*illustration:* June 1: T buys 100 shares of Corp A stock for $15 per share. Dec. 1: T buys 100 shares of Corp A stock for $10 per share. Dec. 31: T sells the 100 shares of Corp A stock bought on June 1 for $10 per share realizing a $500 loss. No loss deduction is allowed because substantially identical stock was purchased within 30 days before the sale. The same result would occur if the second purchase had been made on the following Jan. 30.

⬥*caution:* This rule can ensnare investors (including investors in mutual funds) who participate in automatic dividend reinvestment plans. Where an investor sells, at a loss, only some of the shares the investor owns in an entity and, within the prohibited time, a dividend is paid on the remaining shares, the automatic reinvestment of that dividend is a purchase of substantially identical securities.

"Substantially identical securities" requires something less than precise correspondence. Stock or securities of different issuers or obligors are not substantially identical. Stock or securities of the same issuer are substantially identical if they are substantially the same in all important particulars. [16]

⬥*observation:* It is often possible to recognize losses by selling a particular security and investing the proceeds in a similar but not substantially identical security (e.g., sell common stock in one drug company and buy stock in another drug company, or sell stock in one exchange-traded fund and buy stock in another exchange-traded fund that invests in the same types of securities).

The wash sale rule also disallows a loss on the closing of a short sale of stock or securities, or the sale, exchange, or termination of a securities futures contract to sell, if, within the period beginning 30 days before the date the short sale is closed and ending 30 days after that date: (1) substantially identical stock or securities are sold, or (2) another short sale of (or securities futures contracts to sell) substantially identical stock or securities is entered into. (Code Sec. 1091(e))[17]

---

15. ¶I-3901; ¶10,914; TD ¶227,001   17. ¶I-3905; ¶10,914; TD ¶227,006
16. ¶I-3914 *et seq.*; ¶10,914; TD ¶227,019

Special wash sale rules apply to residual interests in REMICs, (Code Sec. 860F(d))[18] and to tax straddles. (Reg § 1.1092(b)-1T, Reg § 1.1092(b)-5T)[19]

The wash sale rule doesn't apply to a dealer in stocks or securities if the loss is sustained in a transaction made in the ordinary course of that business. (Code Sec. 1091(a))[20]

For the basis of the acquired stock, see ¶2499. For the holding period, see ¶2667 *et seq.*

¶ 2463   Basis of Property. ▬▬▬▬▬▬▬▬▬▬▬▬▬▬▬▬▬▬▬

Basis is the amount of investment in property for tax purposes. It is the point of departure for determining gain or loss on the disposition of the property, for computing annual deductions for depreciation, amortization, depletion, casualty losses, bad debts, and losses from "at-risk" activities, and for many other tax computations. A taxpayer's basis for property acquired in a taxable exchange is usually its cost, subject to certain adjustments.

In general, basis for computing loss and gain is the same, whatever the transaction may be. But the basis for computing loss differs from the basis for computing gain for (1) property converted from personal use to business or income-producing use (¶2473), and (2) property acquired by gift (¶2508).

For determining basis in corporate transactions and in nontaxable exchanges, see ¶2482 *et seq.*

For basis of property acquired by gift, from a decedent or a spouse, see ¶2507 *et seq.*

¶ 2464   Cost as basis.

The original basis for property is its cost to the taxpayer, except where otherwise specifically provided (Code Sec. 1012) or where the transaction is not made at arm's length (see below). Cost is the amount paid in cash, liabilities incurred (¶2465), or other property. (Reg § 1.1012-1(a))[21] Payments made in connection with the acquisition of property, e.g., commissions and legal fees, are included in basis as part of the property's cost. [22]

IRS and most courts say that the cost basis of property received in an arm's length taxable exchange is the fair market value of the property *received* in the exchange, at the time of the exchange unless the fair market value of the property received cannot be determined with a fair degree of certainty. Then the fair market value of the property given up will be used as a way of valuing the property received. However, a substantial minority of courts say the cost basis of property received in an arm's length taxable exchange is the fair market value of the property given up, not the property received. [23]

When property isn't bought in an arms-length deal, its basis is its fair market value. This can occur in sham transactions, or where the buyer, for personal reasons, pays more than what the property is worth (e.g., to help out a friend). [24]

¶ 2465   Mortgages and other liabilities as part of basis.

Taxpayer's cost of property includes the amount of a mortgage or other liability that he assumes in connection with the purchase, plus the amount of any liabilities that the purchased property is subject to (whether or not the taxpayer assumes the liabilities). [25] Redeemable ground rents are treated as mortgages. (Code Sec. 1055)[26]

🅡 *illustration:* J buys a building by paying $20,000 cash and giving an $80,000 mortgage.

---

18. ¶s I-3902, I-3903; ¶860A4; TD ¶227,011 *et seq.*
19. ¶I-7528; ¶10,924; TD ¶228,418
20. ¶I-3917; ¶10,914; TD ¶227,020
21. ¶P-1119; ¶10,124 *et seq.*; TD ¶211,100
22. ¶P-1102; ¶10,124.03; TD ¶213,505

23. ¶P-1114; ¶10,124.46; TD ¶211,106
24. ¶P-1108; ¶10,124.22; TD ¶211,104
25. ¶P-1104 *et seq.*; ¶10,124.04; TD ¶211,118
26. ¶P-1175; ¶10,554; TD ¶211,138

J's basis is $100,000. It would also be $100,000 if instead J assumed an existing $80,000 mortgage. And it would be $100,000 if, in addition to paying $20,000 cash, J acquired the building subject to the mortgage without assuming it, or if J agreed to pay $80,000 but no mortgage was involved, or if J agreed to pay his seller's debt of $80,000.

Mortgages or other liabilities aren't part of the cost if they are contingent *and* there's a clear indication they might never have to be paid or that taxpayer doesn't intend to pay. [27]

¶ 2466 Effect of OID and unstated interest on basis.

If the OID rules (¶1751 *et seq.*) or the unstated interest rules (¶1707), apply so that a part of a debt included in the buyer's cost for the property is treated as OID or unstated interest, the buyer's basis doesn't include the OID or interest portion. [28] However, to the extent that OID or unstated interest is capitalized rather than deducted it's included in basis. (Reg § 1.483-2(a)(1)(i))[29]

For adjustments to the basis of OID instruments, see ¶2470.

¶ 2467 Basis of repossessed mortgaged real estate.

A seller's basis in repossessed property is equal to the adjusted basis of the mortgage debt (determined under Code Sec. 453 and Code Sec. 1011) to the seller (as of the date of repossession), *plus* the sum of: (1) the repossession gain, and (2) the amount of money and the fair market value of other property (other than the buyer's obligations) which the seller transfers in connection with the repossession. [30]

If the mortgage debt isn't discharged on repossession, the seller's basis in the mortgage debt is zero. (Code Sec. 1038(c))

¶ 2468 Satisfaction of debt or claim with property.

The cost basis of property received in whole or partial satisfaction of a debt or claim is the amount of the debt or claim satisfied but not more than the property's fair market value. [31]

¶ 2469 Property acquired through exercise of options.

The basis of property acquired by exercising of an option or warrant other than an option granted for services is (a) the basis of the option plus (b) the option price. [32]

¶ 2470 Holder's basis in certain debt instruments acquired at a discount.

The holder's basis in a debt instrument issued with original issue discount (OID) is increased by the OID currently included in gross income under the rules discussed at ¶1313 *et seq.* (Code Sec. 1272(d)(2))[33] This rule applies for inflation-indexed debt instruments (¶1333), whose basis also must be reduced for deflation adjustments.

Short-term debt instruments. If the holder includes the daily portions of acquisition discount (or OID) in gross income, that holder increases his basis in the debt instrument by the amount so included. (Code Sec. 1283(d)(1))[34]

Tax-exempt obligations issued with OID. A holder's basis is increased by the amount of OID that the holder would have had to include in gross income currently if the obligation had not been tax-exempt. (Code Sec. 1288(a)(2), Code Sec. 1288(b)(3))[35]

---

27. ¶P-1134; ¶10,124.04; TD ¶211,104
28. ¶s P-1138, P-1139; TD ¶211,120, TD ¶211,121
29. ¶P-1815; TD ¶211,120
30. ¶G-6872; ¶10,384; TD ¶471,009
31. ¶P-1116; ¶10,384; TD ¶211,107

32. ¶P-1165 *et seq.*; ¶10,124.13; TD ¶211,133
33. ¶P-5044; ¶12,714.01; TD ¶216,028
34. ¶P-5047; ¶12,814.01; TD ¶216,028
35. ¶P-5048; ¶12884; TD ¶216,028

Market-discount bonds. Under regs to be issued, adjustments are made to bonds to reflect gain recognized under the market-discount bond rules discussed at ¶1326 *et seq.* (Code Sec. 1276(d))[36] Where the election is made to include accrued market discount in income currently, the basis of the bond is increased by the amount of income so included. (Code Sec. 1278(b)(4))[37]

For determining cost of, and original basis in, property received in exchange for an OID debt instrument, see ¶2466.

¶ 2471   Cost of intangible assets.

The basis of goodwill, a patent, a copyright, or a covenant not to compete is the amount taxpayer paid for it. [38]

Where a patent is obtained from the government, the basis is the cost of development, such as research and experimental expenditures (but not if deducted currently), drawings, attorneys' and governmental fees, etc. The value of any time spent on an invention isn't part of an inventor's basis. The basis of a copyright acquired from the government is the cost of securing the copyright from the government, including the cost of producing the work covered by the copyright, but not including the value of the author's time. [39]

Accounts receivable in the hands of a cash basis taxpayer have a zero basis. [40]

¶ 2472   Basis allocation, including "applicable asset acquisitions."

If a single transaction involves a number of separate properties, the total cost is allocated to establish the cost of the individual properties. The total basis is allocated to each item in proportion to the fair market value of each item at the time of acquisition. [41]

However, for an applicable asset acquisition (defined below), the residual method must be used to allocate the purchase price. Under the residual method, the purchase price is reduced first by the amount of cash, demand deposits, and similar accounts. The amount remaining is allocated among the following assets in proportion to (but not in excess of) their fair market value on the purchase date in the following order: (1) certificates of deposit, U.S. Government securities, readily marketable stock or securities, foreign currency, and other items designated by IRS; (2) all assets other than those in the other categories; (3) all section 197 intangibles (¶1979) except those in the nature of goodwill and going concern value; and (4) section 197 intangibles in the nature of goodwill and going concern value.

The parties to an applicable asset acquisition may agree in writing to an allocation of consideration for, or a determination of the fair market value of, any asset (including covenants not to compete) in the acquisition. The parties are bound by the allocation or valuation unless IRS determines that it's not appropriate. (Code Sec. 1060(a); Reg § 1.1060-1(c)(4), Reg § 1.1060-1(e))[42]

An applicable asset acquisition is any direct or indirect transfer of a group of assets that is a trade or business in the hands of either the seller or buyer if (except for certain like-kind exchanges) the buyer's basis in the transferred assets is determined wholly by reference to the buyer's consideration. (Code Sec. 1060(c); Reg § 1.1060-1(b)(1))[43]

The buyer and seller have to provide IRS with specified information about the assets (use Form 8594). (Code Sec. 1060(b); Reg § 1.1060-1(e)(1))[44]

---

36. ¶J-4573; ¶12,764.01
37. ¶J-4573 *et seq.*; ¶12,764.02; TD ¶154,005
38. ¶P-1178, P-1179, P-1180; ¶10,124.38; TD ¶212,511, 212,514
39. ¶P-1178; ¶10,124.38; TD ¶211,111
40. ¶P-1121; TD ¶211,108

41. ¶P-1300 *et seq.*; ¶10,124.55; TD ¶212,500
42. ¶P-1400 *et seq.*; ¶10,604; TD ¶212,001 *et seq.*
43. ¶P-1402 *et seq.*; ¶10,604; TD ¶212,002
44. ¶S-4301; ¶10,604; TD ¶212,012

¶ 2473   Personal use property converted to business use.

When a residence or other nonbusiness property is converted from personal use to business or income-producing use, for purposes of calculating losses or depreciation (but not for purposes of calculating gain) the basis for the property on the date of its conversion is the lower of its adjusted basis or fair market value on that date. This basis must thereafter be adjusted for depreciation, etc., after conversion. (Reg § 1.167(g)-1)[45]

¶ 2474   Adjusted basis.

Basis must be increased or decreased to reflect certain events, such as capital improvements or depreciation, whether the original basis was cost or something else. [46]

The basis of property is adjusted (increased) to include the amount of the capital expenditures with respect to the property. (Code Sec. 1016(a)(1))[47] A lessee's basis for his leasehold is increased by his capital expenditures. [48] However, a lessee's capital improvements don't increase or diminish the lessor's basis of the leased property. (Code Sec. 1019)[49]

Basis can't be increased for items that are deductible as expenses, except for items the taxpayer has capitalized, such as carrying charges, see ¶1666.

For the effect on basis of capitalizing taxes, carrying charges, etc., see ¶1656.

For adjusted basis for alternative minimum tax purposes, see ¶3212.

¶ 2475   Contributions and returns of capital.

A stockholder's contribution of property to his corporation will increase his basis for his corporate stock.[50] A partner's contribution of cash to his partnership increases his basis in his partnership interest. See ¶3738 *et seq.*

Basis must be reduced for receipts representing a return of capital (Code Sec. 1016(a)(1); Reg § 1.1016-2(a)) such as damages taxpayer received for injury to property. [1]

illustration: In Year 1, P, on the calendar-year basis, bought for $80,000 real property to be used as a factory. P also paid commissions of $2,000 and title search and legal fees of $600. The total cost of $82,600 was allocated $10,325 to the land and $72,275 to the building. P immediately spent $20,000 in remodeling the building. P was allowed depreciation deductions of $27,600 for Years 1 through 4. In Year 4 the building suffered an uninsured deductible $5,000 casualty loss from fire. This loss was deducted. The adjusted basis of the property as of Jan. 1, Year 5, is:

		Land	Building
Original cost, including fees and commissions		$10,325	$72,275
Adjustment to basis:			
Add: Improvement			20,000
			$92,275
Subtract:			
Depreciation	$27,600		
Casualty loss	5,000		32,600
Adjusted basis Jan. 1, Year 5		$10,325	$59,675

45. ¶P-1908; ¶1674.037; TD ¶213,017
46. ¶P-1700 *et seq.*; ¶s 10,114, 10,164.01; TD ¶213,000 *et seq.*
47. ¶P-1801; ¶10,164.01; TD ¶213,501
48. ¶L-6510; ¶10,164

49. ¶P-1809; ¶10,194; TD ¶213,504
50. ¶F-1916; ¶10,164.02
1. ¶P-1821; ¶10,164.03; TD ¶213,515

¶ 2476   Depreciation, amortization, and other deductions.

Basis must be reduced for depreciation, cost recovery, amounts expensed under Code Sec. 179, amounts claimed under the Code Sec. 1400I commercial revitalization deduction, or amortization deductions with respect to the property. The amount of the reduction is the larger of (1) the amount of the depreciation, cost recovery, amortization, or depletion deductions *allowable* under the law, or (2) the amount that was actually *allowed* and resulted in a reduction of tax. (Code Sec. 1016(a)(2)

Basis must also be reduced for the Code Sec. 179D energy efficient commercial building property deduction for property placed in service after 2005 and before 2008. (Code Sec. 1016(a)(32))

Allowable depreciation (or cost recovery) is the amount the taxpayer was entitled to deduct under the law, whether or not he actually took more or less and whether or not a tax benefit results. Where a taxpayer didn't adopt a depreciation method under Code Sec. 167, the amount allowable is figured under the straight-line method. (Code Sec. 1016(a))[2]

The depreciation (or cost recovery) *allowed* is the amount claimed on a tax return and allowed by IRS.[3]

In the case of business autos for which the optional business standard mileage rate, see ¶1561, is used, depreciation is considered to have been allowed at the rate of 16¢ for 2004, 17¢ for 2005 and 2006, and 19¢ for 2007.[4]

¶ 2477   Partial losses due to casualty or theft.

If property is partly lost or destroyed through casualty or theft, the basis is reduced by (1) the amount of insurance or other reimbursement received, and (2) the amount of deductible loss. No reduction is required for the amount of a loss which is not deductible under the rule (discussed at ¶1793 *et seq.*) barring deduction for the first $100 of casualty or theft loss or for the amount of loss below the 10%-of-AGI floor.

Expenditures with respect to such property, e.g., to remove debris and to restore the property to pre-casualty condition, increase the basis, unless they are deducted as repairs.   [5]

¶ 2478   Basis of credit property reduced by certain credits earned.

The basis of investment credit property (¶2307), for purposes of computing depreciation or cost recovery deductions and gain or loss, must be reduced by 100% of the amount of the credit for which the property qualifies. (Code Sec. 50(c)(1))[6] The basis of energy credit property (¶2311) must be reduced by 50% of the allowed credit. (Code Sec. 50(c)(3)(A))[7] Special rules apply for assets placed in service before '86 and for qualified progress expenditures.   [8]

If a pre-2007 credit is taken for the cost of a qualified electric vehicle, the basis of the property is reduced by the amount of the credit. (Code Sec. 30(d)(1))[9]

The basis of property also must be reduced for certain other credits such as: the Code Sec. 25C nonbusiness energy property credit for property placed in service before 2008 (Code Sec. 1016(a)(34)); the Code Sec. 25D residential energy efficient property credit for property placed in service before 2009 (Code Sec. 1016(a)(35)); the Code Sec. 30B alternative motor vehicle credit (Code Sec. 1016(a)(36)); the Code Sec. 45F credit for employer-provided child care (Code Sec. 1016(a)(28)); and the Code Sec. 45L new energy efficient homes credit for homes acquired

---

2. ¶P-1902; ¶1674.085; TD ¶214,002
3. ¶P-1903; ¶s 1674, 1684; TD ¶214,003
4. ¶P-1909; ¶1624.157; TD ¶214,007
5. ¶P-1811; ¶1654.304; TD ¶213,503

6. ¶P-2004; ¶504.03; TD ¶213,006
7. ¶P-2005, ¶P-2006; ¶504.03; TD ¶213,006
8. ¶s P-2002, P-2003
9. ¶L-18015; ¶304; TD ¶397,007

before 2009. (Code Sec. 1016(a)(33))

¶ 2479 Recaptured tax credits.

Where certain tax credits are recaptured, a percentage of the recapture amount is added back to basis immediately before the event causing the recapture. The term "recapture amount" means any increase in tax (or adjustment in carrybacks or carryovers) due to the credit recapture provision. (Code Sec. 50(c)(2), Code Sec. 50(c)(3))[10]

¶ 2480 Special lessor-lessee rule doesn't require basis-reduction adjustment.

A lessor of certain credit property who elects to pass the credit for the leased property to the lessee is not required to make the basis-reduction adjustment (¶2478). (Code Sec. 50(d)(5))[11]

¶ 2481 Basis in partnership or S corporation.

The basis of a partner's interest in a partnership or of a shareholder's stock in an S corporation is adjusted to reflect a partner's or shareholder's share of the required adjustments to the basis of partnership or S corporation property when credits are either allowed or recaptured. (Code Sec. 50(c)(5))[12]

¶ 2482 Property Acquired in Nontaxable Exchanges. ▆▆▆▆▆▆▆▆

The basis of property received in a nontaxable exchange, depending on the type of transaction, generally will be the same as its basis in the hands of the transferor or will be the same as the basis of the property transferred by the recipient in the exchange. If gain is recognized in part on the transaction, the basis of the property received may have to be adjusted.

¶ 2483 Basis of property received by corporation in tax-free transfer.

The basis of property received by a controlled corporation in a tax-free transfer, whether upon the incorporation of the corporation or otherwise, see ¶3510 *et seq.*, is equal to the basis of the property in the transferor's hands increased by any gain recognized by the transferor on the transfer. (Code Sec. 362(a)(1))[13]

The basis to a corporation of property acquired from a shareholder as a contribution to capital equals the basis of that property in the hands of the shareholder increased by the gain (if any) recognized by the shareholder on the transfer. (Code Sec. 362(a)(2))[14]

For limitations on an increase in basis due to the assumption of a liability and/or a built-in loss, see ¶2485.

¶ 2484 Acquirer's basis in property received in reorganization.

The basis of property received by the acquiring corporation in a tax-free reorganization (¶3541), is the transferor's (target's) basis increased by any gain recognized to the target. However, if the property consists of stock or securities of the target, this rule applies only if the property was acquired in exchange for stock or securities of the acquirer or the acquirer's parent corporation. (Code Sec. 362(b))[15]

For when an acquirer must reduce basis in assets received in a tax-free reorganization if the transferor has cancellation of debt income in connection with the transfer, see ¶1392.

---

10. ¶P-2007; ¶504.03; TD ¶213,006
11. ¶P-2008; TD ¶213,007
12. ¶P-2009; TD ¶213,008

13. ¶F-1851; ¶3624.01; TD ¶232,001
14. ¶F-1851; ¶3624.03; TD ¶232,309
15. ¶F-4305; ¶3624.02; TD ¶233,501

For limitations on basis increase due to the assumption of a liability, see ¶2485.

¶ 2485 Limits on basis increase due to assumption of liability and/or built-in loss.

For purposes of the basis increase in the case of a tax-free transfer to a controlled corporation (¶2483) or in a reorganization exchange (see ¶2484), the property's basis can't be increased above its fair market value (FMV) on account of gain recognized by the transferor as a result of a liability assumed by the transferee. For this purpose, FMV is determined without regard to Code Sec. 7701(g) (which generally provides that a property's FMV is not less than the amount of nonrecourse debt to which it is subject). (Code Sec. 362(d)(1))[16]

Also, if property transferred was not taxable in the hands of the transferor but is taxable in the hands of the transferee corporation, and the total basis for the property in the hands of the transferee would otherwise (if not for this basis limitation rule) exceed its fair market value, then the basis for each property in the hands of the transferee is its fair market value. (Code Sec. 362(e)(1)) If this rule doesn't apply, a second carryover basis limitation rule (not limited to property as to which the transferor would not have recognized gain or loss) limits the total basis for property transferred by any transferor to its fair market value. (Code Sec. 362(e)(2)) However, the transferor and transferee can jointly elect to reduce the basis of the stock received by the transferor instead of the basis of the assets transferred in the hands of the transferee. (Code Sec. 362(e)(2)(C)) IRS has prescribed how to make the election. [17]

¶ 2486 Target's basis in property received in reorganization.

The basis of property (other than stock and securities of another corporation that is a party to the reorganization, see ¶3553 *et seq.*) received under a plan of reorganization by the target equals the fair market value of the property. (Code Sec. 358(a)(2), Code Sec. 358(f))[18]

¶ 2487 Taxable acquisition of property by corporation for its stocks or bonds.

In cases other than tax-free contributions or reorganizations, the basis of property a corporation acquires in exchange for its stock is the fair market value of the stock at the time of the exchange.[19] The cost to a corporation of property it acquires in exchange for its bonds is the face amount of the bonds.[20] For bonds with OID or unstated interest, see ¶2466.

¶ 2488 Basis of property to distributee shareholders or security holders.

For purposes of determining basis, property received by a distributee in connection with a transfer to a controlled corporation, a reorganization, or a corporate division (¶3510 *et seq.*), is classified as either nonrecognition property or other property. "Nonrecognition property" is property received without recognition of gain or loss to the recipient (stock in the transferee corporation in the case of a transfer to a controlled corporation, and stock or securities in the distributing corporation in tax-free reorganizations and corporate divisions). (Code Sec. 358(a)(1)) "Other property" is anything except "nonrecognition property" and money.

The basis of "nonrecognition property" is the same as the basis of the property given up in the exchange except that this amount is (1) decreased by any money received, by the fair market value of any "other property" received, and by the loss, if any, recognized by the distributee on the exchange; and (2) increased by any part of the distribution that is treated as a dividend, and by any other gain recognized by the distributee on the exchange. (Code Sec. 358(a)(1))[21] The basis must be allocated among the nonrecognition property received in

---

16. ¶F-1852; ¶3624.01; TD ¶232,002

17. ¶F-1871 *et seq.*; ¶3624.02; ¶3624.03; TD ¶232,001

18. ¶F-4304; ¶3584.02; TD ¶233,301

19. ¶P-1158; ¶10,124.47; TD ¶211,130

20. ¶P-1160; TD ¶211,130

21. ¶F-4034; ¶3584.02; TD ¶232,541 *et seq.*

the transaction without recognition of gain or loss. (Reg § 1.358-2(a)(2))[22]

Where, as part of the consideration for the transfer of the distributee corporation's property to the acquirer, another party to the deal assumes a liability of the distributee, the assumption of that liability is treated as though it were money received by the distributee on the reorganization exchange (for basis purposes only). (Code Sec. 358(d)(1))[23]

⊘ *observation:* Thus, the basis of the nonrecognition property received by the distributee on the exchange is reduced by an amount equal to the liabilities assumed.

IRS may provide adjustments for divisive reorganization transactions (¶3557) among affiliated group members. (Code Sec. 358(g))

IRS has issued regs for determining the basis of stock or securities received in connection with a corporate reorganization or a corporate division. (Reg § 1.358-1; Reg § 1.358-2).[24]

¶ 2489 Basis of other property received in tax-free transfer or reorganization.

The basis of property, other than stock or securities, received by a shareholder upon a tax-free transfer to a controlled corporation, a reorganization, or a corporate division (¶3510 *et seq.*) is its fair market value. (Code Sec. 358(a)(2))[25]

¶ 2490 Basis of property received in complete liquidation of corporation.

If property is received in a complete liquidation and any gain or loss is recognized on the receipt of the property, its basis in the hands of the shareholder-distributee is its fair market value at the time of the distribution. (Code Sec. 334(a))[26]

¶ 2491 Basis after partnership incorporates.

If a partnership incorporates, the basis of the corporation in the partnership's property and the basis of the former partners in their stock in the corporation depends on the method used to incorporate.

If the partnership transfers all of its assets subject to its liabilities to a newly formed corporation in return for all its stock, then distributes the stock to the partners, the corporation's basis in the partnership's assets is equal to the partnership's basis in the assets before the transaction and each partner's basis in the stock of the corporation is equal to the adjusted basis of that partner's interest in the partnership.

If the partnership distributes all of its assets subject to liabilities to the partners, who in turn transfer them to the new corporation for its stock, the corporation's basis in its assets is the same as the partners' basis in the assets prior to their contribution to the corporation and the partners' basis in the stock of the corporation is the same as their basis in the assets distributed in liquidation reduced by liabilities assumed by the corporation.

If the partners transfer their interests in the partnership to the new corporation in exchange for its stock and the corporation then liquidates the partnership, the corporation's basis in its assets is equal to the partners' basis in their partnership interests before the transaction and the partners' basis in their stock is equal to their basis in their partnership interests reduced by the liabilities assumed by the corporation. [27]

---

22. ¶F-4036; ¶3584.03; TD ¶232,544
23. ¶F-4035; ¶3584.02; TD ¶232,543
24. ¶F-1802 *et seq.*; ¶F-4036 *et seq.*; ¶3584 *et seq.*
25. ¶s F-1804, F-4034, F-4304, F-5014; ¶3584.02 ; TD ¶231,912,

TD ¶232,542, TD ¶233,304
26. ¶F-13119; ¶3344.01; TD ¶245,427
27. ¶s F-1011, F-1805; TD ¶231,015

¶ 2492   Property received as a dividend.

The basis for property received as a dividend, including stock or stock rights received as a taxable stock dividend, is its fair market value on the date of distribution. (Code Sec. 301(d))[28]

¶ 2493   Basis allocation for nontaxable stock dividend.

If a shareholder gets a nontaxable dividend of stock or stock rights, the (adjusted) basis of the old stock (that is, of the stock on which the dividend was distributed) is allocated between the old and new stock (or rights) in proportion to the fair market value of each on the date of distribution. (Code Sec. 307(a)) Where only part of the stock dividend is nontaxable, the basis of the old stock is allocated between the old stock and that part of the new stock (or rights) which isn't taxable, in proportion to the fair market value of each on the date of distribution. The date of distribution is, in both cases, the date on which the new stock (or the stock rights) was distributed, not the record date. [29]

illustration: S bought one share of voting common for $45. The corporation distributed two new shares of voting common for each share held. This gave S three shares of voting common with a basis of $15 each. If he had owned two shares before the distribution, one purchased for $30 and the other for $45, he would have six shares: three with a basis of $10 each, and three with a basis of $15 each.

If the fair market value of stock rights at the time of distribution is less than 15% of the fair market value of the stock on which they were distributed, the basis for the rights received is zero unless the taxpayer elects to allocate basis to the rights. (Code Sec. 307(b)(1))[30]

¶ 2494   Basis of stock acquired through dividend reinvestment plans.

If a corporation allows shareholders to receive dividends in either cash or stock, then, depending on the situation, the receipt of stock is treated either as the receipt of a taxable stock dividend because the shareholder has the choice of receiving either cash or stock or as the receipt of a cash dividend which the shareholder used to buy stock (in some cases, at a discount). If the transaction is treated as a stock dividend, the shareholder's basis is equal to the value of the shares received at the time of the receipt. On the other hand, if the transaction is treated as a cash dividend, the shareholder's basis in the shares is equal to the amount of the cash he could have received. [31]

¶ 2495   Effect of extraordinary dividends on corporate shareholders' basis.

Corporate shareholders may have to reduce their basis in stock (at the beginning of the ex-dividend date) by the nontaxed part of an extraordinary dividend. When the nontaxed part of an extraordinary dividend exceeds the basis of the stock, gain is recognized to the extent of the excess in the year the extraordinary dividend is received. (Code Sec. 1059)[32]

¶ 2496   Identifying shares transferred.

Where taxpayer can adequately identify which shares of stock, or which bonds, are transferred, the basis used is the basis of that stock or those bonds. Shares of stock or bonds are adequately identified where it can be shown that the shares or bonds that were delivered to the transferee are from a lot acquired on a certain date or for a certain price. (Reg § 1.1012-1(c)(1))[33]

---

28. ¶P-5400 *et seq.*; ¶3014.03; TD ¶217,501 *et seq.*
29. ¶P-5301; ¶3074.01 *et seq.*; TD ¶217,001
30. ¶P-5303; ¶3074.03; TD ¶217,002

31. ¶P-5402; TD ¶174,008
32. ¶P-5100 *et seq.*; ¶10,594; TD ¶216,022
33. ¶P-5202; ¶10,124.78; TD ¶218,002 *et seq.*

If a number of lots were acquired and the ones sold can't be adequately identified, a first-in, first-out (FIFO) rule applies. (Reg § 1.1012-1(c)(1)) But it applies only to the particular account from which the stock or bonds were transferred, so that stock or bonds in another account, even though acquired earlier, are disregarded. [34]

¶ 2497 Adequate identification v. wrong delivery.

In certain situations, if a taxpayer specifically identifies certain shares of stock or bonds as the ones to be transferred, and certain other conditions are met, these will be treated as the ones transferred even though some other lot is actually delivered. This rule applies (1) for sales of stock or bonds held by a broker or agent (Reg § 1.1012-1(c)(3)(i)), (2) where a single certificate represents different lots of stock (Reg § 1.1012-1(c)(3)(ii)), and (3) for certain transfers by a trustee, executor or administrator. (Reg § 1.1012-1(c)(4))[35]

¶ 2498 Methods for determining basis of mutual fund shares.

A taxpayer who sells mutual fund shares held by a custodian or agent may elect to determine the basis of the shares sold by determining the average basis of the shares on either a "single-category method" or a "double-category method." [36] Generally, the single-category method groups in one category all shares regardless of holding period; the double-category method divides all shares by their holding period. The basis is then averaged over all the shares in their respective category. (Reg § 1.1012-1(e)) A shareholder who doesn't elect either of the above methods uses the normal first-in, first-out (FIFO) method for determining which shares were sold, see ¶2496.

¶ 2499 Basis of stock acquired in wash sale.

Where a loss is disallowed under the wash sale rule (¶2461), the basis of the acquired stock takes account of the unrecognized loss in the following manner: (Code Sec. 1091(d))

(1) If the sales price is less than the repurchase price, the basis of the new stock is the basis of the stock sold plus the difference between the repurchase and the sales prices.

Illustration: T owns 100 shares of X company common which cost $100 per share. On May 1, T sells the 100 shares at $80 per share. On May 20, T buys 100 shares of X common at $90 per share. No loss is allowed on the May 1 sale. The basis of each share acquired May 20 is $110, i.e., the basis of the shares sold ($100) plus the $10 difference between the repurchase and sale prices ($90 – $80). (Reg § 1.1091-2(a))

(2) If the sales price is more than the repurchase price, the basis of the new stock is the basis of the stock sold minus the difference between the sale and the repurchase prices. [37]

Illustration: If, in the above illustration, the May 1 sale price had been $90 per share and the May 20 repurchase price was $80 per share, the basis of each share acquired May 20 would be $90, i.e., the basis of shares sold ($100) minus the difference between the sale and repurchase prices ($90 – $80). (Reg § 1.1091-2(a))

¶ 2500 Basis of properties after nontaxable exchange.

The basis of property received in a like-kind exchange or certain other nontaxable exchanges where no part of the gain is recognized is the adjusted basis of the property traded away. (Code Sec. 1031(d))

If money is received as part of the exchange and some gain is recognized, basis in the

34. ¶P-5212 *et seq.*; ¶10,124.83; TD ¶218,011
35. ¶P-5200 *et seq.* ¶10,124.78; TD ¶218,002 *et seq.*

36. ¶P-5214; ¶10,124.7801; TD ¶218,013
37. ¶P-5019; ¶10,914; TD ¶216,007

property received is decreased by the money received and increased by the gain recognized. Reg § 1.1031(d)-1(b)) If money is paid, basis is increased by the amount paid. (Reg § 1.1031(d)-1(a))

If other property (boot) is received and some gain is recognized, basis must be allocated (according to fair market value) to all the properties received. (Reg § 1.1031(d)-1(c))

If boot is given as part of the exchange, and gain or loss is recognized on transfer of the boot, the basis of the nonrecognition property received is the total basis of all the properties given, increased by any recognized gain on the boot, or decreased by any recognized loss on the boot. (Reg § 1.1031(d)-1(e))[38]

¶ 2501   Basis after exchange of multiple properties.

In an exchange of multiple properties qualifying for nonrecognition of gain or loss (see ¶2425), the aggregate basis of properties received in each of the "exchange groups" is determined under regs. (Reg § 1.1031(j)-1(c))[39]

¶ 2502   Basis of replacement property after involuntary conversion.

If property is involuntarily converted directly into similar property and gain on the conversion isn't recognized under Code Sec. 1033(a)(1) (see ¶2431), the basis of the property received is the basis of the converted property (1) decreased by the amount of any money received that wasn't spent in acquiring similar property, and (2) increased by the amount of gain recognized, or decreased by the amount of loss recognized. (Code Sec. 1033(b)(1))

Where the taxpayer's property is involuntarily converted into money or other property that isn't similar or related in use to the converted property (¶2431) and, within the prescribed period (¶2441), the taxpayer purchases other property that is similar or related in service or use to the converted property, and elects not to recognize any part of the gain, the basis of the replacement property is its cost, reduced by the amount of gain that isn't recognized. If more than one piece of property is bought as replacement, the basis (cost less nonrecognized gain) is allocated to each piece in proportion to its respective cost. (Code Sec. 1033(b)(2))[40]

Where a taxpayer satisfies the replacement property requirement by buying a controlling stock interest in a corporation (¶2431), the corporation reduces its basis in its assets by the amount by which the taxpayer reduces its basis in the stock. (Code Sec. 1033(b)(3))[41]

¶ 2503   Basis of new residence where gain was rolled over from old residence (pre-May 7, '97 sales).

Under the home sale rollover rules that applied to pre-May 7, '97, sales as well as to transactions covered by certain elective transition rules, when a taxpayer bought a new principal residence and thereby avoided recognition of all or part of the gain on the sale of the old principal residence, the taxpayer's basis in the new residence is the cost of the new residence minus the gain not recognized on sale of the old residence. [42]

¶ 2504   Basis of replacement for stock sold to ESOP or EWOC.

If the seller of qualified securities to an ESOP or EWOC reinvests in qualified replacement property and elects nonrecognition of gain (¶2451), the basis in the qualified replacement property is reduced by the gain not recognized. If more than one item of replacement property is bought, the basis reduction is allocated among each item of replacement property (as the

38. ¶I-3176 *et seq.*; ¶10,314.13; TD ¶225,203
39. ¶I-3193; ¶10,314.14; TD ¶225,409
40. ¶P-1154; ¶10,334.33; TD ¶211,128

41. ¶P-1154.1; ¶10,334.231; TD ¶211,129
42. ¶I-4649; ¶10,344.05; TD ¶225,839

cost of that item bears to the cost of all the items). (Code Sec. 1042(d))[43]

¶ 2505 Basis for SSBIC rollovers.

Any gain not recognized under the SSBIC rollover rules (¶2427), reduces taxpayer's basis in any SSBIC investment made during the 60-day rollover period. If taxpayer makes more than one SSBIC investment during this period, the bases of those other investments are reduced in the order they were acquired. (Code Sec. 1044(d))[44]

¶ 2506 Basis for Qualified Small Business Stock rollovers.

Gain from the sale of qualified small business stock that isn't recognized because of the Code Sec. 1045(a) rollover election (see ¶2429) reduces (in the order acquired) the basis for determining gain or loss of any qualified small business stock that's purchased by the taxpayer within the 60-day rollover period beginning on the sale date. (Code Sec. 1045(b)(3))[45]

¶ 2507 Property Acquired by Gift, from a Decedent, or from a Spouse. ▬▬▬▬

Special rules apply to determine the basis of property acquired by gift, from a decedent, or from a spouse.

For the basis of property acquired by a gift or transfer in trust during the life of the transferor, see ¶2508 *et seq.*

For the basis of property acquired from a decedent, see ¶2512 *et seq.*

For basis of property acquired from a decedent dying after 2009, see ¶2523.

For the basis of property acquired from a spouse (or former spouse), see ¶2524.

¶ 2508 Basis of property acquired by gift and transfer in trust.

A donee's original or unadjusted basis (that is, the basis before adjustments made while the donee owned it) for property the donee acquires by gift is the same as the property's adjusted basis in the hands of the donor, or in the hands of the last preceding owner who didn't acquire the property by gift. (Code Sec. 1015(a))[46] But if the property's fair market value at the date of the gift is lower than that adjusted basis, then the property's basis for determining *loss* is its fair market value on that date. (Code Sec. 1015(a))[47]

Since two different methods determine basis of property acquired as a gift, it's possible that neither gain nor loss determined in reference to basis will be realized when the donee sells or exchanges the property. (Reg § 1.1015-1(a)(2))[48]

⦿ *illustration:* Taxpayer acquires by gift income-producing property with an adjusted basis of $100,000 at the date of gift. The fair market value on the date of gift is $90,000. Taxpayer later sells the property for $95,000. Taxpayer has neither gain nor loss, since the basis for determining gain is $100,000 and the basis for determining loss is $90,000.

If a transfer in trust is made for consideration (whether full and adequate, or less) the basis is the same as it would be in the hands of the grantor, increased by the amount of gain or decreased by the amount of loss recognized to the grantor upon the transfer under the law applicable to the year in which the transfer was made. (Code Sec. 1015(b)) [49]

For part sales and part gifts, see ¶2509.

---

43. ¶H-12110; ¶10,424
44. ¶I-3791; ¶10,444; TD ¶225,503
45. ¶I-9206; ¶10,454; TD ¶247,208
46. ¶P-3103; ¶10,154.01; TD ¶215,002

47. ¶P-3104; ¶10,154.01; TD ¶215,002
48. ¶P-3105; TD ¶215,002
49. ¶P-3112; ¶10,154.16; TD ¶215,018

¶ 2509　Basis after transfer that is part purchase, part gift.

Where a transfer of property is in part a purchase and in part a gift, the transferee's basis is the greater of cost or the transferor's adjusted basis for the property at the time of the transfer.[50] However, for determining loss, the basis can't exceed the property's fair market value at the time of transfer. (Reg § 1.1015-4) In either event, basis is increased to the extent of any gift tax paid (¶2511).

¶ 2510　Basis rules for donees of partial interests.

If two or more donees receive partial interests in the same property, the basis to each is his or her proportionate part of the donor's basis. To determine the part of total basis allowable to life tenants and remaindermen, apply the rules at ¶2522. (Reg § 1.1015-1(b))[1]

¶ 2511　Increase in basis for gift tax paid.

If the property's fair market value at the date of the gift is greater than the donor's adjusted basis, the donee's basis (donor's adjusted basis) is increased by the part of the gift tax paid that is attributable to the net appreciation in value of the gift. This portion is determined by multiplying the gift tax paid by a fraction whose numerator is the net appreciation in value of the gift and whose denominator is the amount of the gift. (Code Sec. 1015(d)(6))

If a gift consists of more than one item of property, the gift tax paid with respect to each item is computed by allocating to each item a proportionate part of the gift tax paid with respect to the gift. If more than one gift was made during the calendar year (or preceding calendar period), the total tax paid must be apportioned to each gift to determine the amount paid on each gift. (Code Sec. 1015(d)(2))

The gift tax paid on a husband-wife split gift is the sum of the taxes, computed separately, paid with respect to each half of the gift. (Code Sec. 1015(d)(3); Reg § 1.1015-5(b)(3))[2]

¶ 2512　Property acquired from a decedent.

The basis of property acquired from a decedent by inheritance, bequest, devise, etc. (see ¶2515), that hasn't been sold, exchanged, or otherwise disposed of before the decedent's death, is generally equal to its fair market value at the date of the decedent's death. (Code Sec. 1014(a)(1)) However, if:

(1) the fiduciary elects for estate tax purposes to value the decedent's gross estate at the alternate valuation date (¶5027), the basis of the property is its fair market value at that alternate date (Code Sec. 1014(a)(2));

(2) the fiduciary elects for estate tax purposes the special use valuation method of valuing farm or other closely held business real property included in the decedent's gross estate (¶5028), the basis of the real property is its value determined for purposes of the special use valuation election (rather than its fair market value). (Code Sec. 1014(a)(3))[3]

(3) land acquired at death is subject to a qualified conservation easement, it is excluded from the decedent's gross estate under the rules explained at ¶5027, and its basis (to the extent that it's subject to the easement) is the basis in the hands of the decedent. (Code Sec. 1014(a)(4))[4]

Fair market value on the date of the decedent's death (or the alternate valuation date, if

---

50. ¶P-1113; ¶10,154; TD ¶215,006
1. ¶P-3131; ¶10,154.06; TD ¶215,016
2. ¶P-3108; ¶10,154.01; TD ¶215,004 *et seq.*

3. ¶P-4001; ¶s 10,144, 10,144.05; TD ¶215,501
4. ¶P-4021.1; ¶10,144; TD ¶215,517

applicable) doesn't apply to determine the basis of property:

... that's appreciated property reacquired by the donor within one year of transfer to decedent, see ¶2514;

... included in the decedent's estate but disposed of by the taxpayer before the decedent's death, see ¶2516;

... that's stock in a DISC or former DISC (Code Sec. 1014(d)), or of certain foreign entities; or

... that is a right to receive income in respect of a decedent (Code Sec. 1014(c)), see ¶3967.[5]

For the basis of property acquired from a decedent dying after 2009, see ¶2523.

¶ 2513 When estate tax value is also income tax basis.

The fair market value of property at the decedent's death or at the alternate valuation date as appraised for federal estate tax purposes (or, if no federal estate tax return is required to be filed, the fair market value of the property appraised as of the date of death for purpose of state inheritance taxes) is considered to be also the fair market value for purposes of determining the income tax basis of property acquired from a decedent. (Reg § 1.1014-3(a))[6] But the value for estate tax purposes is only presumptively correct for basis purposes. Except where facts have been misrepresented, neither taxpayer nor IRS is barred from using a value for basis purposes that differs from the value accepted for estate tax purposes. However, where a discount is allowed in valuing property (e.g., artwork) for estate tax purposes, full value generally will not be allowed in valuing the same property for estate tax purposes. [7]

¶ 2514 Appreciated property reacquired by donor.

If: (1) appreciated property was acquired by the decedent by gift during the one-year period ending at death, and (2) that property is acquired from the decedent by (or passes from the decedent to) the donor of the property (or the donor's spouse), the basis of the property in the hands of the donor (or spouse) is the adjusted basis of the property in the decedent's hands immediately before his death. (Code Sec. 1014(e)(1))[8]

¶ 2515 When is property considered acquired from a decedent?

Property is acquired from a decedent if it is acquired by bequest, devise, or inheritance, or if it is acquired by the decedent's estate from the decedent. (Code Sec. 1014(b)(1))[9] Property acquired from a decedent also includes certain pre-death transfers and other classes of property, as explained at ¶2519 *et seq.*

Qualified terminable interest property (QTIP) that is includible in a surviving spouse's estate (¶5009), is treated as passing from that surviving spouse for purposes of determining the remaindermen's basis. (Code Sec. 1014(b)(10))[10]

Property acquired from a decedent doesn't include:

... Property the fiduciary acquires after the decedent's death, the basis of which to the fiduciary (or a distributee, if it's distributed) is its cost or other basis with appropriate adjustments. (Reg § 1.1014-3(c))[11]

... Property bought from a decedent's estate. Its basis to the buyer is its cost or other basis with appropriate adjustments. [12]

... Income in respect of a decedent (IRD, see ¶3967). (Code Sec. 1014(c)) Its basis is equal to

5. ¶P-4001; ¶10,144.02; TD ¶215,518 *et seq.*
6. ¶P-4022; ¶10,144.03; TD ¶215,506
7. ¶s P-4023, P-4024; TD ¶215,506
8. ¶P-4002; ¶10,144.02; TD ¶215,522

9. ¶P-4102; ¶10,144.01; TD ¶215,507
10. ¶P-4104; ¶10,144.01; TD ¶215,507
11. ¶P-4054; ¶10,144.02; TD ¶215,511
12. ¶P-4118; TD ¶215,511

the decedent's basis (if any). [13]

. . . Property transferred by the executor, administrator or trustee to a beneficiary in discharge of a specific pecuniary bequest. The beneficiary's basis is the fair market value of the property on the date of the transfer. (Reg § 1.1014-4(a)(3))[14]

¶ 2516 Property acquired from decedent and included in decedent's gross estate.

Property is considered to have been acquired from a decedent if it was acquired from a decedent by reason of: death, form of ownership, or other conditions and the property is required to be included in determining the value of the decedent's gross estate whether or not an estate tax return is required or an estate tax is payable. Acquisitions covered by this rule include acquisitions as surviving joint tenant or tenant by the entireties (see ¶2517), acquisitions through exercise or failure to exercise a power of appointment (¶2520), and gifts within three years of death (if includible in gross estate for estate tax purposes, see ¶5003). (Reg § 1.1014-2(b))[15]

If property received as a gift (including a gift in trust) is disposed of by the donee before the donor's death, the property isn't treated as acquired from a decedent and the donee's basis is determined under the rules for gifts, see ¶2508. But property received in exchange for such gift property, or property acquired through reinvesting proceeds of sale of such gift property (or property acquired in further exchange or reinvestments), is treated as acquired from a decedent if it is includible in the decedent's gross estate. (Reg § 1.1014-3(d))[16]

¶ 2517 Tenants by the entirety and joint tenants.

Property that a person acquires as the surviving tenant by the entireties or as a surviving joint tenant is property acquired from a decedent to the extent the property is includible in the decedent's gross estate. The part of the property that's treated as acquired from the decedent gets a stepped-up basis. [17]

The reduction in basis for depreciation and similar deductions is required only for depreciation, etc., allowed to the surviving joint owner, whose new basis is at issue. (Code Sec. 1014(b)(9)) Special rules apply to determine how depreciation is allocated to a husband and wife who file joint returns. (Reg § 1.1014-6(a)(2))[18]

¶ 2518 Community property.

Where a spouse dies owning community property and at least one-half of the entire community interest is includible in the deceased spouse's gross estate (whether or not an estate tax return is required or an estate tax is payable), the surviving spouse's interest is treated as property acquired from a decedent. (Code Sec. 1014(b)(6))[19]

🅡*observation:* Under the above rule, the surviving spouse's share of the community property plus the decedent's share (included in the decedent's estate) is treated as property acquired from the decedent. Thus, both shares get a stepped-up basis.

¶ 2519 Inter vivos trust with power to revoke, alter, etc.

Property acquired from a decedent includes property that the decedent during his lifetime transferred in trust to pay the trust income to, or on the order of, the decedent, where the decedent also reserved to himself at all times before his death the right to (1) revoke the trust

---

13. ¶P-4003; ¶10,144.02; TD ¶215,523
14. ¶P-4055; TD ¶215,511
15. ¶P-4103; ¶10,144.01; TD ¶215,011
16. ¶P-3124; TD ¶215,012

17. ¶P-4115; ¶10,144.01; TD ¶215,502
18. ¶P-4028 *et seq.*; ¶10,144.01; TD ¶215,502
19. ¶P-4112; ¶10,144.01; TD ¶215,510

(Code Sec. 1014(b)(2)), or (2) make any change in the enjoyment of the trust through the exercise of a power to alter, amend, or terminate the trust (whether alone or with the consent of another not having an interest adverse to his). (Code Sec. 1014(b)(3))[20]

¶ 2520 Power to appoint property.

Property acquired from a decedent includes property passing without full and adequate consideration under a general power of appointment exercised by the decedent in his will. (Code Sec. 1014(b)(4))[21]

¶ 2521 Basis of postponed or contingent remainder interests.

Taxpayer's basis for property acquired from a decedent is determined on the date of the decedent's death under the rules at ¶2512 *et seq.*, whether or not, at the decedent's death, the taxpayer's interest was conditional or contingent, and whether or not the taxpayer can immediately possess and enjoy the property. (Reg § 1.1014-4(a)(2))[22]

¶ 2522 Multiple interests in one property.

Where more than one person has an interest in property acquired from a decedent, the basis in the property is determined and adjusted without regard to the multiple interests. Therefore, a life tenant makes basis adjustments for depreciation as if he were the absolute owner. His basis adjustments are an adjustment in the hands of every person who receives an interest by reason of the decedent's death. (Reg § 1.1014-4(b))[23]

¶ 2523 Basis of property acquired from a decedent dying after 2009.

Effective for individuals dying after 2009, when estate and GST taxes will be completely repealed (see ¶5000), the basis of property acquired from a decedent, in the hands of the person acquiring or receiving it, generally will be the lower of the fair market value on the date of the decedent's death or the adjusted basis of the property immediately before the death of the decedent. (Code Sec. 1022(a)) However, each estate will receive $1.3 million of basis to be added to the carryover basis of any one or more of the assets held at death. (Code Sec. 1022(b)(2)(B)) Also, an estate generally will receive additional basis equal to the sum of (a) the decedent's unused capital loss carryforwards, (b) the decedent's unused net operating loss carryforwards, and (c) the amount of losses that would have been allowable under Code Sec. 165 if the property acquired from the decedent had been sold at fair market value immediately before death. (Code Sec. 1022(b)(2)(C)) Also, estates will be allowed an additional $3 million of basis, to be allocated among the assets passing to a surviving spouse. (Code Sec. 1022(c)) However, no addition to basis may increase the new basis of any asset above its fair market value on the date of death. (Code Sec. 1022(d)(2))[24]

For post-2010 sunset provisions, see ¶1114.

¶ 2524 Basis of property transferred between spouses or incident to a divorce.

The transferee is treated as acquiring the property by gift and the transferee's basis in the property received is the adjusted basis that the transferor had in the property. (Code Sec. 1041(b)) This rule applies even where the transaction is a sale between the spouses or where the transferee-spouse pays a sum of money to the transferor-spouse (as required under the divorce settlement) for the transfer of title to the property to the transferee-spouse. (Reg § 1.1041-1T(a), Q&A – 2) This carryover basis rule applies whether the adjusted basis of

20. ¶P-4109; ¶10,154.17; TD ¶215,508
21. ¶P-4110; ¶10,144.01; TD ¶215,509
22. ¶P-4018; TD ¶215,503

23. ¶P-4014 *et seq.*; ¶10,144.06; TD ¶215,505
24. ¶P-4060; ¶10,224.02

the transferred property is less than, equal to, or greater than its fair market value at the time of transfer and applies for purposes of determining loss as well as gain, upon later sale by the transferee. (Reg § 1.1041-1T(d), Q&A–11)[25] Exceptions apply to certain transfers in trust (where liabilities assumed by the trust exceed the transferor's adjusted basis) (Code Sec. 1041(e)) and to transfers of installment obligations into a trust (Code Sec. 453B(g)). [26]

The transferor must, at the time of the transfer, give the transferee records sufficient to determine the adjusted basis and holding period of the property at the date of transfer. (Reg § 1.1041-1T(e), Q&A–14)[27]

---

25. ¶P-1146; ¶10,414; TD ¶211,124   27. ¶P-1153; ¶10,414; TD ¶211,127
26. ¶P-1147; ¶10,414; TD ¶211,125

Chapter 10 Capital Gains and Losses—Section 1231— Depreciation Recapture

¶ 2600 Capital Gains and Losses.

The tax treatment of capital gains and losses depends on whether the gains and losses are long-term or short-term and on whether the taxpayer is a corporation or not. For noncorporate taxpayers, the maximum tax rate on net long-term capital gains is lower than the top rate on ordinary income. The maximum tax rate on long-term capital gains depends on the type of capital asset sold, and the taxpayer's marginal tax rate (the top rate of tax on the person's ordinary income). The long-term capital gains of corporations, and the short-term gains of corporations and of noncorporate taxpayers, are taxable at the same rates as their ordinary income. The deduction for capital losses is limited, but unused capital losses of noncorporate taxpayers may be carried over indefinitely (¶2612) and unused capital losses of corporate taxpayers can generally be carried back for three years and carried over for five years, see ¶2615.

The main features of the income tax treatment of capital gains and losses are:

. . . Short-term capital gains and losses are netted, long-term capital gains and losses are netted, and then long- and short-term are netted with each other (¶2602 et seq.). Further netting may be required if a noncorporate taxpayer has capital losses as well as long-term capital gain subject to differing maximum rates of tax. (¶2609)

. . . A net capital gain (excess of net long-term capital gain over net short-term capital loss) of a noncorporate taxpayer is generally taxed more favorably than ordinary income. The maximum tax rate depends on whether the net capital gain is adjusted net capital gain, generally taxed no higher than 5% (0% in tax years beginning after 2007) or 15% depending on the taxpayer's marginal tax bracket (¶2603), collectibles gain (¶2607) or section 1202 gain (¶2608), taxed no higher than 28% (¶2606), or unrecaptured section 1250 gain, which is taxed no higher than 25% (¶2605).

. . . Section 1231 nets gains and losses to arrive at a net of long-term capital gain or ordinary loss (¶2610 and ¶2684 et seq.).

. . . Recapture provisions restrict the possibility of converting ordinary income into capital gains via cost recovery or depreciation (¶2692 et seq.).

Capital gains and losses are the gains and losses from sales or exchanges (¶2676) of capital assets (¶2617). But capital gain treatment also applies to gains in certain transactions involving assets that aren't capital assets (such as depreciable property used in business, ¶2686).[1]

⊘observation: Not all losses (capital or ordinary) are deductible. An individual can only deduct losses incurred in business or transactions for profit, or resulting from a casualty or theft. Thus, a loss on a sale of a personal residence is a nondeductible capital loss.

Report capital gains and losses on Schedule D of the applicable return (e.g., for individuals, Form 1040). Taxpayers may report the total of their capital gains and losses transactions on Schedule D and provide details on attachments such as brokers' statements. Individuals whose only capital gains are capital gains distributions (other than unreported section 1250 gain or collectibles gain) reported on Form 1099-DIV do not have to file a Schedule D. They enter capital gains on Form 1040 or 1040A and complete a capital gain tax worksheet in the instructions.

---

1. ¶I-5100 et seq.; ¶12,214 et seq.; TD ¶223,300 et seq.

References beginning with a single letter are to paragraphs in RIA's Federal Tax Coordinator 2d and RIA's Analysis of Federal Taxes: Income. Those beginning with numbers are to paragraphs in RIA's United States Tax Reporter. Those beginning with TD are to paragraphs in RIA's Tax Desk.

For the deduction when stock or securities become worthless, see ¶1781.

For tax years beginning after 2010, a "sunset" provision provides that amendments made by Sec. 301 of the Jobs and Growth Tax Relief Reconciliation Act of 2003 (PL 108-27, 5/28/2003) won't apply. Instead, the rules in effect for capital gains taken into account before May 6, 2003 will apply. Under those rules, after 2010, long-term capital gains of noncorporate taxpayers now taxed at a rate of 5% will be taxed at a rate of 10% (8% for assets held over five years), and long-term capital gains now taxed at a rate of 15% will be taxed at a rate of 20% (18% for assets held over five years). [2]

¶ 2601   Tax effect of capital asset sales and exchanges.

If a capital asset is held for not more than the short-term holding period (¶2667), the gain or loss from its sale or exchange is short-term. If held for more than the short-term holding period, gain or loss is long-term. (Code Sec. 1222)[3]

Short-term capital gains and losses are netted to get net short-term capital gain or net short-term capital loss. (Code Sec. 1222(5), Code Sec. 1222(6))

Long-term capital gains and losses are netted to get net long-term capital gain or net long-term capital loss. (Code Sec. 1222(7), Code Sec. 1222(8))

There's a further netting if one group shows a loss and the other a gain:

If there's a net short-term gain, it's taxable (both for noncorporate and corporate taxpayers) at the same rate as ordinary income. [4]

If capital losses exceed capital gains , see ¶2611 *et seq.* (noncorporate) or ¶2615 (corporate).

If net long-term capital gains exceed net short-term capital losses , the excess is net capital gain, taxed under the rules at ¶2603 to ¶2611 (individuals and other noncorporate taxpayers) or ¶2613 *et seq.* (corporate taxpayers). (Code Sec. 1222(11))

¶ 2602   Capital gain net income defined.

A taxpayer who has an excess of capital gains over capital losses (whether long-term or short-term) for the tax year, has "capital gain net income" (Code Sec. 1222(9)), which is included in gross income. [5]

¶ 2603   Noncorporate taxpayers' tax on net capital gain.

A noncorporate taxpayer's net capital gain is taxed as follows:

. . . Net capital gain that is adjusted net capital gain (¶2604) is taxed at a maximum rate of 15%. If the adjusted net capital gain would otherwise be taxed at a rate below 25% if it were ordinary income, it is taxed at a 5% rate (at a zero percent rate for tax years beginning after 2007). (Code Sec. 1(h)(1)(B), Code Sec. 1(h)(1)(C))

. . . That part of net capital gain attributable to unrecaptured section 1250 gain (¶2605) is taxed at a maximum rate of 25%. (Code Sec. 1(h)(1)(D))

. . . Net capital gain attributable to collectibles gain (¶2607), and section 1202 gain (¶2608) is taxed at a maximum rate of 28%. (Code Sec. 1(h)(1)(E), Code Sec. 1(h)(4))[6]

IRS is authorized to issue regs applying the applicable rates for long-term capital gain to sales by passthrough entities and sales of interests in those entities. (Code Sec. 1(h)(9))[7]

Sellers of interests in S corporations, partnerships, and trusts held for more than one year

---

2. ¶T-11062; ¶79,006.87; TD ¶880,014
3. ¶s I-5103, I-5102; ¶s 12,224.01, 12,224.02; TD ¶223,501
4. ¶s I-5111, I-5116; ¶12,224.01; TD ¶223,326

5. ¶I-5111; ¶12,224.03; TD ¶223,306
6. ¶I-5110; ¶14.08; TD ¶223,309
7. ¶I-5110.14; ¶14.08; TD ¶223,324

recognize collectibles gain if the entity owns such appreciated assets at the time of sale. (Code Sec. 1(h)(5)(B)) Regs explain how to figure the seller's deemed collectibles gain and his residual long-term gain or loss and use the same approach for sales of interests in various entities. (Reg § 1.1(h)-1) See ¶3765 for the regs' approach in the context of sales of partnership interests, which also may cause a partner to recognize unrecaptured section 1250 gain. However, sales of interests in S corporations and trusts don't trigger unrecaptured section 1250 gain — only collectibles gain and residual long-term capital gain or loss. [8]

For netting rules where the noncorporate taxpayer has capital losses, see ¶2609.

¶ 2604 Adjusted net capital gain defined.

Adjusted net capital gain is net capital gain (¶2601) determined without taking qualified dividend income (see ¶1288) into account less the amount that the taxpayer takes into account as investment income under Code Sec. 163(d)(4)(B)(iii) (see ¶1729), reduced (but not below zero) by the sum of:

. . . unrecaptured section 1250 gain (¶2605), and

. . . 28% rate gain (as defined at ¶2606), and increased by

the amount of qualified dividend income. (Code Sec. 1(h)(3))[9]

observation: Effectively, adjusted net capital gain is the sum of that part of a taxpayer's net capital gain that is eligible to be taxed at a maximum rate of 15% or 5% (0% in tax years beginning after 2007) (see ¶2603), plus the amount of qualified dividend income.

¶ 2605 Noncorporate taxpayer's unrecaptured section 1250 gain taxed at a maximum rate of 25%.

Unrecaptured section 1250 gain, taxed at a maximum rate of 25%, is the excess (if any) of:

(1) the amount of long-term capital gain (¶2601) which is not otherwise treated as ordinary income, and which would be treated as ordinary income if Code Sec. 1250(b)(1) recapture applied to all depreciation (rather than only to depreciation in excess of straight line), and the applicable percentage under Code Sec. 1250(a) (¶2696) were 100%, over

(2) the excess (if any) of the amount of losses taken into account in computing 28% rate gain (¶2606) over the amount of gains taken into account in computing 28% rate gain. (Code Sec. 1(h)(6))[10]

The amount in (1), above, from sales exchanges and conversions described in Code Sec. 1231(a)(3)(A) (i.e., section 1231 gain, see ¶2684) for any tax year can't exceed the net section 1231 gain (see ¶2685) for that tax year. (Code Sec. 1(h)(6)(B))

observation: Under MACRS, real property must be depreciated using the straight-line method (¶1925). Thus, any gain on the sale or exchange of such property that's attributable to depreciation will be unrecaptured section 1250 gain if held for more than one year.

illustration: Y, an individual, sells nonresidential real property on Aug. 15 for $200,000, realizing a gain of $50,000. This is Y's only transaction involving a capital asset for the year. Y has held the property for more than one year. He depreciated the property using MACRS, and claimed $25,000 of depreciation during his ownership. There is no depreciation recapture under Code Sec. 1250(b)(1) because Y didn't claim accelerated depreciation. However, $25,000 of Y's gain, representing depreciation deductions claimed by Y, is unrecaptured section 1250 gain.

---

8. ¶I-5110.12; ¶14.08; TD ¶223,322
9. ¶I-5110.10; ¶14.08; TD ¶223,320

10. ¶I-5110.8; ¶14.08; TD ¶223,317

For how to handle unrecaptured section 1250 gain where a sale of real property is reported on the installment method, see ¶2457.

For how unrecaptured section 1250 gain can arise on sale of a partnership interest, see ¶3765.

¶ 2606   Noncorporate taxpayer's 28% rate gain.

The term 28% rate gain means the sum of collectibles (¶2607) gain and losses and section 1202 gain, less the sum of collectibles loss, the net short-term capital loss for the tax year, and the long-term capital loss carryover to the tax year. (Code Sec. 1(h)(5))[11]

⊘observation: As a result of the way 28% rate gain is defined, a long-term capital loss carryover from an earlier tax year will always be used first to offset 28% rate gain. The netting process is explained in more detail at ¶2609.

¶ 2607   Noncorporate taxpayer's collectibles gain or loss.

Collectibles gain or loss is gain or loss from the sale or exchange of a collectible which is a capital asset held for more than one year, but only to the extent such gain or loss is taken into account in computing gross income. (Code Sec. 1(h)(5)) Any work of art, rug or antique, metal or gem, stamp or coin, alcoholic beverage, or any other tangible personal property specified by IRS for this purpose is a collectible. [12]

For how collectibles gain can arise on the sale of interests in a partnership, S corporation, or trust, see ¶2603.

¶ 2608   Noncorporate taxpayers' section 1202 gain.

Section 1202 gain is the excess of (1) the gain that would be excluded on the sale of certain small business stock under Code Sec. 1202, if the percentage limitations of Code Sec. 1202(a) (50% or 60% exclusion of gain on the disposition of qualifying small business stock held over five years, see ¶2648) didn't apply, less (2) the gain actually excluded under Code Sec. 1202. (Code Sec. 1(h)(7))[13]

⊘observation: If 50% of the gain on the disposition of qualifying small business stock is excluded from gross income, the 50% includible in gross income is taxed at a maximum rate of 28% (since it's excluded from adjusted net capital gain). This makes the maximum effective rate on the gain from the sale of qualified small business stock 14%.

See ¶3208 for AMT treatment of section 1202 gain.

¶ 2609   Netting rules where taxpayer has capital losses.

The following netting and ordering rules apply where the taxpayer has capital losses:

(1) Short-term capital losses are applied first to reduce short-term capital gains, if any, otherwise taxable at ordinary income rates. If there's a net short-term capital loss, it reduces any net long-term gain from the 28% group, then gain from the 25% group, and finally reduces adjusted net capital gain (15% or lower group).

(2) Long-term capital losses are handled as follows:

. . . A net loss from the 28% group (including long-term capital loss carryovers from prior years) is used first to reduce gain from the 25% group, then to reduce adjusted net capital gain (15 or lower group).

---

11. ¶I-5110.11; ¶14.08; TD ¶223,321   13. ¶I-5110.13; ¶14.08; TD ¶223,323
12. ¶I-5110.12; ¶14.08; TD ¶223,322

... A net loss from the 15% or lower group is used first to reduce net gain from the 28% group, then to reduce gain from the 25% group. [14]

illustration: T, in the 33% bracket, has a 28%-group loss of $40,000 from the sale of collectibles. T has unrecaptured section 1250 gain of $25,000 (in the 25% group), and adjusted net capital gain of $25,000. T's net capital gain is $10,000 (total gain of $50,000 less $40,000 loss). T's 28% group loss completely offsets the unrecaptured section 1250 gain of $25,000, and $15,000 of adjusted net capital gain, leaving him with adjusted net capital gain of $10,000.

¶ 2610 Noncorporate taxpayer's non-recaptured net section 1231 losses.

If any amount is treated as ordinary income under Code Sec. 1231(c) (relating to capital gain/ordinary loss treatment of gains and losses from the sale or exchange, or involuntary conversion, of property used in the trade or business and certain property held for the production of income, see ¶2685), that amount must be allocated among the separate categories of net section 1231 gain in the manner to be prescribed by forms or regulations. (Code Sec. 1(h)(8)) The amount to be treated as ordinary income is allocated first to any net section 1231 gain in the 28% group, then to any section 1231 gain in the 25% group, and then to any net section 1231 gain in the 5% or lower group. [15]

¶ 2611 Capital losses of noncorporate taxpayers.

A noncorporate taxpayer may deduct capital losses only to the extent of capital gains plus (if the losses exceed the gains) the lower of:

(1) $3,000 ($1,500 for married individuals filing separate returns), or

(2) the excess of the losses over the gains. (Code Sec. 1211(b))[16]

illustration: B has a short-term capital loss of $100 and a long-term capital loss of $3,600 for his tax year. His total capital loss for the tax year is $3,700. This capital loss is deductible from ordinary income up to a maximum of $3,000. See ¶2612 for carrying over the excess capital loss.

A noncorporate taxpayer's capital losses for a tax year consist of the capital losses sustained during the year plus the total of all capital losses sustained in other years that are carried to that tax year (¶2612). (Code Sec. 1212(b); Reg § 1.1211-1(b)(1))[17]

¶ 2612 Noncorporate capital loss carryovers.

If an individual, trust or estate sustains a net capital loss that exceeds the maximum deductible in the current year (¶2611), the excess is carried forward to later years indefinitely until it's absorbed. (Code Sec. 1212(b)) Carry*backs* aren't allowed.[18] A decedent's unused capital loss is lost; it can't be carried over. [19] For the use in tax years beginning after 2009 of a decedent's unused capital losses to increase his estate's basis in his capital assets, see ¶2523.

The capital loss keeps its original character as long- or short-term when carried over. (Code Sec. 1212(b)(1))[20]

For purposes of determining the amount of excess long-term or short-term capital loss that is carried over, that excess is reduced by assuming the existence of a short-term capital gain equal in amount to the lesser of: (1) $3,000 ($1,500 for marrieds filing separately), (2) the

---

14. ¶I-5107; TD ¶223,307
15. ¶I-9003.1
16. ¶I-5112; ¶12,114; TD ¶223,327
17. ¶I-5113; ¶12,124 *et seq.*; TD ¶223,305

18. ¶I-5122; ¶12,124.01; TD ¶223,336
19. ¶I-5133; TD ¶223,344
20. ¶I-5123; ¶12,124.01; TD ¶223,337

excess of allowed losses over gains (¶2611), or (3) "adjusted taxable income." Adjusted taxable income is taxable income (a) increased by the lesser of the amounts computed in (1) and (2), above, (which is the amount described in ¶2611) (b) increased by the personal exemption. For this purpose, any excess of deductions allowed over gross income is taken into account as negative taxable income. (Code Sec. 1212(b)(2))[21]

¶ 2613 Capital gains of corporate taxpayers.

Corporate taxpayers must include capital gains in full in gross income but only to the extent that they exceed capital losses. [22]

¶ 2614 Corporation's alternative tax on capital gains.

A corporation with an excess of net long-term capital gain over net short-term capital loss ("net capital gain") (Code Sec. 1222(11)) pays an alternative tax instead of the regular corporate tax if the alternative tax is smaller. The alternative tax applies a tax rate of 35% to the corporation's net capital gain, but only if the top regular corporate tax rate for the year (see ¶1112) is higher than 35% (determined without regard to the additional tax on (1) the corporation's taxable income over $100,000, and (2) the corporation's taxable income over $15,000,000). (Code Sec. 1201(a))[23]

observation: Thus, the alternative tax doesn't apply for 2007, since the top corporate rate is 35%.

¶ 2615 Corporation's capital losses.

Corporations may deduct capital losses only to the extent of their capital gains. Excess capital losses can't be deducted from a corporation's ordinary income. (Code Sec. 1211(a))[24]

A corporation's capital losses in excess of its capital gains for the current year are carried back three years, but only to the extent the loss isn't attributable to a foreign expropriation capital loss and to the extent that the carryback doesn't increase or produce a net operating loss for the tax year to which it's carried back. (Code Sec. 1212(a)(1)(A)) A net capital loss can't be carried back to a tax year in which the corporation is either a foreign personal holding company, a regulated investment company, a real estate investment trust or a foreign investment company electing to distribute income currently. (Code Sec. 1212(a)(3))

The carryforward period is five years (eight years for regulated investment companies; ten years for foreign expropriation capital losses). (Code Sec. 1212(a)(1)(B), Code Sec. 1212(a)(1)(C))[25]

A capital loss carryback or carryover is treated as a short-term capital loss whether or not it was short-term when sustained. (Code Sec. 1212(a)(1)) A carryover from one year can't be included in computing a new net capital loss for another year. (Code Sec. 1222(10))[26]

¶ 2616 Assets to Which Capital Gain and Loss Rules Apply. ▆▆▆▆▆▆

The capital gain or loss rules apply to assets that are capital in nature. An asset's character depends upon what it is and what use it has in taxpayer's hands.

¶ 2617 Capital assets defined.

Capital assets include all assets held by the taxpayer except:

(1) Stock in trade of the taxpayer or other property of a kind that would properly be

---

21. ¶I-5123; ¶12,124.01; TD ¶223,337
22. ¶I-5116; ¶12,224.03; TD ¶223,331
23. ¶I-5117; ¶12,014; TD ¶223,332

24. ¶I-5121; ¶12,114; TD ¶223,335
25. ¶I-5125; ¶12,124.04; TD ¶223,339
26. ¶I-5125; ¶12,124.04; TD ¶223,341

included in the inventory of the taxpayer if on hand at the close of the tax year.

(2) Property held by the taxpayer primarily for sale to customers in the ordinary course of his trade or business.

(3) Accounts or notes receivable acquired in the ordinary course of a trade or business for services rendered or from the sale of any properties described in (1) or (2), above.

(4) Depreciable property (and amortizable Code Sec. 197 intangibles) used in the taxpayer's trade or business.

(5) Real property used in the taxpayer's trade or business.

(6) Certain copyrights, and literary, artistic, or musical works (unless, for musical works or copyrights in them, the election discussed at ¶2622 is made).

(7) Certain letters, memoranda or similar property, see ¶2622.

(8) U.S. government publications (e.g., Congressional Record) received from the government without charge or below the price sold to the public, in the hands of the recipient and carryover-basis transferees.

(9) Commodities derivative financial instruments held by a commodities derivatives dealer (except for certain instruments not connected to the dealing activity).

(10) Any hedging transaction (e.g., to manage risk of price changes or currency fluctuations) clearly identified as such before the close of the day on which it was acquired, originated, or entered.

(11) Supplies of a type regularly used or consumed by the taxpayer in the ordinary course of the taxpayer's trade or business. (Code Sec. 1221(a))[27]

Property held for personal use is a capital asset, as is property used for the production of income (even if depreciable). But inventory, and real estate and depreciable property used in taxpayer's trade or business, aren't capital assets. (Reg § 1.1221-1(b)) Examples of capital assets include stock and securities held for investment, [28] including tax-exempt bonds [29] (discussed at ¶2636). The right to receive future lottery payments is not a capital asset (a payment received in exchange for that right is ordinary income, not capital gain). [30]

¶ 2618 Hedging transactions.

The term capital asset doesn't include property that's part of a hedging transaction. (Reg § 1.1221-2(a)) A hedging transaction is a transaction that a taxpayer enters into in the normal course of the taxpayer's trade or business, primarily to reduce the risk of price changes or currency fluctuations with respect to ordinary property, or to reduce the risk of interest rate or price changes or currency fluctuations with respect to borrowings or ordinary obligations. (Reg § 1.1221-2(b)(1)) Property is ordinary property if its sale or exchange by the taxpayer couldn't produce capital gain or loss regardless of the holding period. An obligation is an ordinary obligation if performance or termination of the obligation by the taxpayer could not produce capital gain or loss. (Reg § 1.1221-2(b)) Thus, hedging in corn futures (to stabilize the cost of corn inventory) as an integral part of a taxpayer's inventory-purchase system produces ordinary income and loss. [31]

A taxpayer must identify a transaction (including recycling an existing hedge) as a hedging transaction before the close of the day he enters it. (Reg § 1.1221-2(f)(1))[32]

The accounting method used for a hedging transaction must clearly reflect income and reasonably match the timing of the transaction with the timing of the item(s) being hedged. Special rules detail the accounting methods for various transactions. (Reg § 1.446-4)[33]

27. ¶I-6001; ¶12,214; TD ¶249,001
28. ¶I-6003; ¶12,214.21; TD ¶250,000
29. ¶I-7801
30. ¶I-6824.1

31. ¶I-6231 *et seq.*; ¶12,214.80; TD ¶250,006
32. ¶I-6250; ¶12,214.80; TD ¶250,007
33. ¶G-2519 *et seq.*; ¶4464.01; TD ¶447,501 *et seq.*

¶ 2619   Options to buy or sell.

Gain or loss from the sale or exchange of a noncompensatory option to buy or sell property is considered a gain or loss from the sale or exchange of a capital asset if the optioned property is (or would be if acquired) a capital asset in the taxpayer's hands. (Code Sec. 1234(a)(1); Reg § 1.1234-1(a))[34] If the holder of an option incurs a loss because he fails to exercise the option, the option is considered to have been sold or exchanged on the date it expires. (Code Sec. 1234(a)(2); Reg § 1.1234-1(b))[35]

A dealer in options is considered a dealer in the property subject to the option, and any gain or loss received from sale or exchange of the option is ordinary. (Reg § 1.1234-1(d))[36]

¶ 2620   "Put" and "call" options; straddles.

There are no tax consequences to the buyer or writer of an option until the option is exercised, otherwise closed out or lapses. The holder treats the premium paid as a nondeductible capital expenditure at the time of payment. The premium isn't included in income of the writer at the time of receipt.[37] The premium received by the writer for granting a "put" or "call" option that's not exercised ("lapses"), so that the writer simply keeps the money, is generally treated as ordinary income, and gain or loss to the writer on repurchase of an option ("closing transaction") is also generally ordinary. (Reg § 1.1234-1(b)) However, gain or loss to a nondealer from a lapse or closing transaction involving options in stocks, securities, commodities or commodity futures is treated as short-term capital gain or loss. (Code Sec. 1234(b); Reg § 1.1234-3)[38]

Where a put is exercised, the premium received by the writer for granting the option is deducted from the option price for the property in determining the net basis to the writer of the property purchased. The holder deducts the premium from the amount received from the writer, in computing the gain or loss realized on the sale. Where a call is exercised, the premium received by the writer (i.e., seller) for granting the option is added to the sale proceeds received. This is included in the holder's (buyer's) basis for the property.[39]

illustration: A bought a 180-day put from B for $5,000 that gave A the right to sell 1,000 shares of stock to B for $50,000. The stock originally cost A $25,000. The put was timely exercised. A has a gain of $20,000 on the sale ($50,000, less $30,000 ($5,000 paid for put and $25,000 original cost of stock). B's basis in the stock is $45,000 ($50,000 paid to A on the exercise of the put, less $5,000 received by B from A for the put).

When the put or call is bought from the original holder (or his assignee), the buyer is treated as a holder, and the amount paid by him to the original holder is likewise treated as a premium. However, the original holder is not treated as a writer, and must include that premium in his amount realized upon disposition of the option, see ¶2619.[40]

observation: Thus, if a holder (other than a dealer) of a put or call option on publicly traded stock closes out a position by selling the option on an exchange, the gain or loss is a capital gain or loss.

A "straddle" option combines a put and a call. (Reg § 1.1234-3(e))[41]

IRS may issue regs to carry out the purposes of the constructive sale rules (¶2637 *et seq.*). (Code Sec. 1259(f)) IRS may treat as constructive sales certain transactions that have substantially the same effect as those specified at ¶2637 (i.e., short sales, offsetting notional

34. ¶I-6504; ¶12,344; TD ¶252,002
35. ¶I-6510; ¶12,344; TD ¶252,003
36. ¶I-6509; ¶12,344.03
37. ¶s I-6521, I-6522; ¶12,344 *et seq.* TD ¶252,001, 252,005
38. ¶I-6515; ¶12,344 *et seq.*; TD ¶252,006

39. ¶s I-6530, I-6531; ¶s 12,344.03, 12,344.04; TD ¶252,008, 252,009
40. ¶I-6523; ¶s 12,344.03, 12,344.04; TD ¶252,002
41. ¶I-6528; ¶12,344.06

principal contracts and futures or forward contracts to deliver the same or substantially similar property), namely those that have the effect of eliminating substantially all of the taxpayer's risk of loss and opportunity for income or gain. [42]

¶ 2621   Patents.

If an individual inventor or his financial backer transfers (other than by gift, inheritance or devise) all substantial rights to a patent, or an undivided interest (e.g., a half, a third) in those rights, the transfer is considered a sale or exchange of a long-term capital asset even though the transferor hasn't held the patent property for the period required for long-term treatment (see ¶2667), and even though the payments to the seller are: (1) made periodically during the buyer's use of the property, or (2) contingent on the productivity, use or disposition of the buyer's rights in the property (i.e., are like royalties). (Code Sec. 1235(a))[43]

It's not necessary that the patent or patent application be in existence at the time of that transfer for long-term capital gain treatment to apply. (Reg § 1.1235-2(a))[44]

This treatment doesn't apply to a transfer by the inventor's employer. (Code Sec. 1235(b)(2)(A))[45] Nor does it apply to transfers made (directly or indirectly) to or by certain persons related to the inventor. (Code Sec. 1235(b)(2)(B); Reg § 1.1235-2(f))[46]

Transferors that don't qualify for this special long-term capital gain treatment nevertheless qualify for capital gain or loss treatment if they can establish that the patent is a capital asset or a Section 1231 asset. (Reg § 1.1235-1(b))[47]

The long-term capital gain rule doesn't apply unless all substantial rights (or an undivided interest in those rights) are transferred. (Reg § 1.1235-2(b))[48]

¶ 2622   Copyrights, literary, musical, artistic composition, etc.

Copyrights, literary, artistic, and (except as noted below) musical compositions, etc., aren't capital assets or Section 1231 assets if the taxpayer is either (1) the author or creator of property through his own personal efforts, or (2) the donee of the author or creator, or one who otherwise has a basis for the property determined in whole or in part by reference to the basis in the hands of that donor.

A letter, memorandum or similar property prepared or produced for a taxpayer isn't a capital asset to him (or his donee or other carryover-basis transferee). (Code Sec. 1221(a)(3))[49]

For sales or exchanges in tax years beginning after May 17, 2006, a taxpayer may elect to treat a sale or exchange of musical compositions or copyrights in musical works created by the taxpayer's personal efforts (or having a basis determined by reference to the basis in the hands of a taxpayer whose personal efforts created them) as the sale or exchange of a capital asset. (Code Sec. 1221(b)(3))[50]

Where a taxpayer inherits creative property (such as a copyright, composition or similar property) from a decedent dying after 2009, and the taxpayer's basis for figuring gain from a sale or exchange is determined in whole or in part by reference to the basis of certain earlier holders of the property under the modified-carryover-basis-at-death rules of Code Sec. 1022 (¶2523), the property is a capital asset. (Code Sec. 1221(a)(3)(C))[1]

42. ¶I-7747 *et seq.*; ¶12,594
43. ¶I-8301; ¶12,354; TD ¶229,101
44. ¶I-8307
45. ¶I-8322; ¶12,354.04; TD ¶229,102
46. ¶s I-8301, I-8325; ¶12,354.06; TD ¶229,112

47. ¶I-6700; TD ¶229,101
48. ¶I-8301; ¶12,354.09; TD ¶229,106
49. ¶I-6601 *et seq.*; ¶12,214; TD ¶252,501
50. ¶I-6601; ¶12,214.45; TD ¶252,501
1. ¶I-6601.2; ¶12,214.45

¶ 2623   Real property.

Real property held primarily for sale in the ordinary course of the taxpayer's trade or business doesn't qualify as a capital asset. Whether particular real estate sold is a capital asset is decided on a case by case basis taking into consideration many factors including number and taxpayer's frequency of sales, subdividing and promotional activities. [2]

¶ 2624   Five-year land subdivision rule for noncorporate taxpayers.

A taxpayer other than a C corporation (e.g., an individual, trust, estate or S corporation) won't be treated as holding land primarily for sale to customers merely because the taxpayer subdivided a tract of land into lots or parcels and engaged in advertising, promotion, selling activities or the use of sales agents in selling lots in the subdivision, if the taxpayer:

. . . hasn't previously held any part of the same land primarily for sale to customers in the ordinary course of business, and, in the year of sale doesn't hold any other real estate for sale to customers;

. . . doesn't (while he holds the land or as part of a contract of sale with the buyer) make "substantial improvements" on the land that substantially increase the value of the lot sold (except, if elected, improvements needed to make marketable land that has been held for ten years or more); and

. . . either has owned the land for five years or more, or acquired it by inheritance or devise. (Code Sec. 1237(a); Reg § 1.1237-1(a)(2), Reg § 1.1237-1(a)(5), Reg § 1.1237-1(b)(1))[3]

However, if more than five lots or parcels in the same tract are sold or exchanged, gain from any sale or exchange (which occurs in or after the tax year in which the sixth lot or parcel is sold or exchanged) of any lot or parcel covered by the above 5-year rule will be treated as ordinary income to the extent of 5% of the selling price. (Code Sec. 1237(b)(1), Reg § 1.1237-1(e)(2))

The sale or exchange of qualifying subdivided land that's business property can result in an ordinary loss, see ¶2684. (Reg § 1.1237-1(f))[4]

¶ 2625   Sale of a sole proprietorship.

When a sole proprietorship is sold, there isn't a sale of just one asset (the business). Rather, there's a sale of the individual assets that comprise the business. Thus, gain or loss on some assets will be ordinary while on others it will be capital. [5]

¶ 2626   Allocation of selling price on sale of business.

If assets of a going business are sold, the selling price must be allocated among the assets (including goodwill) for purposes of determining gain or loss (and the type of gain or loss, e.g., capital gain or ordinary income) separately for each. Allocation is made under the rules for determining the buyer's basis in each of them, see ¶2472.[6]

¶ 2627   Goodwill and covenants not to compete.

Goodwill is a capital asset, unless it is treated as an amortizable section 197 intangible under the rules explained at ¶1977 *et seq.* To the extent that the Code Sec. 197 rules don't apply, proceeds from the sale of a business that are allocable (¶2626) to goodwill are taxed

---

2. ¶I-6300 *et seq.*; ¶12,214; TD ¶250,502
3. ¶I-6400 *et seq.* ¶12,374.01; TD ¶251,501
4. ¶I-6424; TD ¶251,512

5. ¶I-8501; ¶12,214.53; TD ¶229,401
6. ¶I-8506 *et seq.*; ¶12,214.51; TD ¶212,000

under the capital gain and loss rules, [7] and payments for a covenant not to compete that is severable from the sale of goodwill results in ordinary income. [8]

¶ 2628   Investments by dealer in securities.

A securities dealer who buys securities for resale to customers may also hold securities purchased as investments for the dealer's own account. But gain from the sale or exchange of those securities won't be capital gain unless (1) the security is clearly identified in the dealer's records as a security held for investment on the day it is acquired, and (2) the security is not held by the dealer primarily for sale to customers in the ordinary course of a trade or business at any time after the acquisition date. (Code Sec. 1236(a))[9]

A loss is a capital loss if the security has ever been clearly identified in the dealer's records as held for investment, even though held primarily for sale at the time of its disposition. (Code Sec. 1236(b); Reg § 1.1236-1(b))[10]

¶ 2629   Franchise, trademark or trade name transfers.

The transfer of a franchise, trademark or trade name isn't a sale or exchange of a capital asset if the transferor retains any significant power, right or continuing interest (such as the right to terminate at will, prescribe standards of quality or require the transferee to sell only the transferor's products). (Code Sec. 1253(a), Code Sec. 1253(b)(2))[11] In any case, ordinary income treatment applies to payments received by a transferor that are contingent on production, use, or disposition of a franchise, trademark or trade name. (Code Sec. 1253(c))[12]

For deduction of these payments, see ¶1620; for amortization of payments made for the transfer of a franchise, trademark, or trade name, see ¶1979.

¶ 2630   Life estates, etc.

A life tenant, a tenant for a term of years, or an income beneficiary of a trust is generally entitled to capital gain on the sale of that interest. [13] However, where the interest was acquired by gift, from a decedent, by a transfer in trust or by a transfer from a spouse (or a former spouse incident to divorce), that part of the basis that's determined under the Code rules for those types of acquisitions (e.g., fair market value basis where acquired from a decedent dying before 2010, see ¶2516) isn't taken into account in computing gain or loss on the sale or exchange of the interest, unless the entire interest in the underlying property is transferred in the same transaction. (Code Sec. 1001(e); Reg § 1.1001-1(f))[14]

¶ 2631   Small business investment company (SBIC) stock.

Losses from the sale, exchange or worthlessness of SBIC stock are deductible by a shareholder as an ordinary loss attributable to the shareholder's business. (Code Sec. 1242; Reg § 1.1242-1) Gains on the sale or exchange of SBIC stock are capital gains. [15]

¶ 2632   Regulated investment company stock.

A loss realized on the sale or exchange of stock in a regulated investment company is a long-term capital loss to the extent of any long-term capital gain realized via a distribution made with respect to the stock, if the taxpayer held the stock for six months or less. Rules for periodic liquidations differ. (Code Sec. 852(b)(4))[16]

---

7. ¶I-8601; ¶12,214.55; TD ¶229,501
8. ¶I-8603; ¶12,214.56; TD ¶229,502
9. ¶I-6209; ¶12,364.01; TD ¶250,004
10. ¶I-6215; ¶12,364.01; TD ¶250,004
11. ¶s I-8401; ¶12,534 *et seq.*; TD ¶229,301

12. ¶I-8412; ¶12,534.01; TD ¶229,306
13. ¶I-7014; ¶12,214.66
14. ¶P-3129; ¶10,144.07; TD ¶215,015
15. ¶I-9543; ¶12,424 *et seq.*
16. ¶E-6162; ¶8524.02

¶ 2633   Sale or exchange of debt instruments issued with original issue discount.

If a debt instrument is issued with original issue discount (OID) as defined at ¶1314, and if at the time of original issue there was an intention to call the debt instrument before maturity, any gain realized on the sale or exchange of the instrument is treated as ordinary income to the extent the gain doesn't exceed the OID reduced by the part of the OID previously included in the income of any holder. For purposes of this rule, any part of the OID that would have been included in the income of the holder had there been no acquisition premium is treated as if it had been included. (Code Sec. 1271(a)(2)(A))

The above rule doesn't apply to tax-exempt obligations or to the sale or exchange by a holder who purchased the debt instrument at a premium. (Code Sec. 1271(a)(2)(B)) [17]

¶ 2634   Sale or exchange of short-term government obligations.

On the sale or exchange of any short-term government obligation, any gain realized that doesn't exceed an amount equal to the ratable share of the acquisition discount is treated as ordinary income (Code Sec. 1271(a)(3)(A)) unless the seller was required to include the acquisition discount in gross income currently under the rules at ¶1328. (Code Sec. 1283(d)(3)) [18]

¶ 2635   Sale or exchange of short-term nongovernment obligations.

On the sale or exchange of any short-term nongovernment obligation, any gain realized that doesn't exceed an amount equal to the ratable share of OID is treated as ordinary income (Code Sec. 1271(a)(4)(A) unless the seller was required to include the acquisition discount in gross income currently under the rules at ¶1328. (Code Sec. 1283(d)(3)) [19]

¶ 2636   Sale or exchange of tax-free bonds.

The sale or exchange of tax-exempt obligations is a taxable event even if the interest on the bonds is exempt. The seller has gain to the extent that the amount realized exceeds his adjusted basis (see ¶2474) in the bonds. The seller's basis for this purpose means the price he paid, whether or not he bought the bonds at a discount. However, the holder of a tax-exempt bond issued with original issue discount (OID) can increase his adjusted basis of the bond by the amount of OID accrued during the period the bond is held. [20]

¶ 2637   Constructive Sales of Appreciated Financial Positions. ▮▮▮▮▮▮▮▮▮▮▮▮▮▮▮▮

The constructive sale rules restrict a taxpayer's ability to defer recognition of gain on appreciated property he owns even though he locks in his gain and limits risk of loss through the use of short-sales-against-the-box and similar transactions. In general, the taxpayer is treated as constructively selling property he owns if he borrows and sells the same or substantially identical property.

A taxpayer must recognize gain (but not loss) upon entering into a constructive sale of any appreciated financial position in stock, a partnership interest, or certain debt instruments. (Code Sec. 1259) In general, an appreciated financial position is any position with respect to any stock, debt instrument, or partnership interest if there would be gain if the position were sold, assigned, or otherwise terminated at its fair market value. (Code Sec. 1259(b)(1)) Except as provided at ¶2638, a constructive sale of an appreciated position occurs when the taxpayer (or a related person):

(1) enters into a short sale of the same or substantially identical property,

---

17. ¶I-8001; ¶s 12,714, 12,714.01, 12,714.02; TD ¶227,601
18. ¶I-8004; ¶12,714.05; TD ¶227,602

19. ¶I-8005; ¶12,714.05; ¶12,814; TD ¶227,603
20. ¶I-4001 *et seq.*; TD ¶227,401 *et seq.*

(2)   enters into an offsetting notional principal contract with respect to the same or substantially identical property,

(3)   enters into a futures or forward contract to deliver the same or substantially identical property,

(4)   in the case of an appreciated financial position that's a short sale or a contract described in (2) or (3) above with respect to any property, the taxpayer acquires the same or substantially identical property, or

(5)   to the extent prescribed in regs, enters into one or more other transactions (or acquires one or more positions) that have substantially the same effect as a transaction described in (1), (2), (3), or (4) above. (Code Sec. 1259(c)(1))[21]

Persons are "related" with respect to a transaction if their relationship is described in Code Sec. 267(b) (¶2448) or Code Sec. 707(b) (¶3731), and the transaction is entered into with a view toward avoiding the purposes of the constructive sale rules. (Code Sec. 1259(c)(4))[22]

The constructive sale rules don't apply to a short sale of stock that the seller borrows if he doesn't hold substantially identical property at the time of the sale. However, if he acquires the same stock that he borrowed and sold, and has a gain, the constructive sale rules apply on the acquisition date even if the acquired stock isn't delivered to the lender. [23]

As a result of a constructive sale,

. . . the taxpayer recognizes gain as if the position were sold, assigned, or otherwise terminated at its FMV value on the constructive sale date (Code Sec. 1259(a)(2)), and

. . . for purposes of applying the Code for periods after the constructive sale, (1) an appropriate adjustment is made in the amount of gain or loss later realized on the position for the gain taken into account because of the constructive sale rule, and (2) a new holding period for the position begins as if the taxpayer had acquired the position on the date of the constructive sale. (Code Sec. 1259(a)(2))[24]

☝*illustration:* On May 1, Year 1, S bought 100 shares of ABC stock for $10,000. On Sept. 3, Year 1, S sold short 100 shares of ABC stock for $16,000. He made no other transactions involving ABC stock for the rest of Year 1 and the first 30 days of Year 2. S's short sale is treated as a constructive sale of an appreciated financial position because a sale of the ABC stock on the date of the short sale would have resulted in a gain. S recognizes a $6,000 short-term capital gain from the constructive sale and he has a new holding period in his ABC stock that begins on Sept. 3, Year 1.

The term "appreciated financial position" does *not* include (1) certain positions with respect to nonconvertible debt if certain specified conditions with respect to principal and interest are met (Code Sec. 1259(b)(2)(A)); (2) any hedge with respect to a position described in (1), above (Code Sec. 1259(b)(2)(B)); and (3) any position which is marked to market under any Code section or the regs under those Code sections. (Code Sec. 1259(b)(2)(C))[25]

¶ 2638   Exceptions to constructive sale rules.

A taxpayer is not treated as having made a constructive sale solely because the taxpayer enters a contract for the sale of any stock, debt instrument, or partnership interest which isn't a marketable security if the contract settles within one year after the date the contract is entered. (Code Sec. 1259(c)(2))[26] In addition, any transaction which would otherwise cause a constructive sale during the tax year is disregarded if:

(1)   it's closed on or before the 30th day after the close of the tax year it was entered,

---

21. ¶I-7732; ¶12,594; TD ¶228,602
22. ¶I-7733; ¶12,594; TD ¶228,603
23. ¶I-7732.1; TD ¶228,602.1

24. ¶I-7731; ¶12,594; TD ¶228,601
25. ¶I-7739; ¶12,594; TD ¶228,609
26. ¶I-7736; ¶12,594; TD ¶228,606

(2)   the taxpayer holds the appreciated financial position to which the transaction relates (e.g., the stock where the transaction is a short sale) throughout the 60-day period beginning on the date the transaction is closed, and

(3)   at no time during that 60-day period is the taxpayer's risk of loss reduced with respect to the position (applying the principles of Code Sec. 246(c)(4), relating to suspension of the holding period where the risk of loss is diminished for purposes of the dividends received deduction, see ¶3312). (Code Sec. 1259(c)(3)(A))[27]

⌾ *observation:* If a taxpayer meets the above requirements, a "short sale against the box" is not a constructive sale as long as he remains at risk with respect to the appreciated financial position for sixty days after the closing.

If a transaction which would otherwise cause a constructive sale of an appreciated financial position, is closed during the tax year or during the 30 days after the close of the tax year, the third requirement above isn't violated if the taxpayer enters another transaction during that 60-day period if that transaction:

... also would otherwise be treated as a constructive sale of that appreciated financial position,

... is closed on or before the 30th day after the close of the tax year in which the transaction (described in (1) above) occurs,

... the appreciated financial position is held throughout the 60-day period beginning on the date the transaction is closed, and

... at no time during that 60-day period is the taxpayer's risk of loss with respect to the position reduced by reason of a circumstance which would be described in Code Sec. 246(c)(4). (Code Sec. 1259(c)(3)(B))[28]

¶ 2639   Short Sales. ▰▰▰▰▰▰▰▰▰▰▰▰▰▰▰▰▰▰▰▰▰▰▰▰▰▰▰

In a short sale, an investor sells a security for delivery in the future. The short seller may meet his obligation to deliver by buying the security on the delivery ("closing") date. If the security has declined in value by the time he closes or covers the sale, he has a gain equal to the price at which he sold minus his cost; if the value has increased, his purchase price is higher than the sale price, and the short seller has a loss. The nature of the gain or loss on a short sale depends upon the nature of the property used to close the short transaction.

If the property used to close the short sale is a capital asset in the hands of the short seller, the gain or loss on the transaction is capital gain or loss. (Code Sec. 1233(a); Reg § 1.1233-1(a)(2))[29] Where the property used to close the short sale is a capital asset, the period the taxpayer held the property determines whether the gain or loss is long or short term, unless the limits at ¶2640 *et seq.* apply. (Reg § 1.1233-1(a)(3))[30]

⌾ *caution:* Entering into certain short sales may result in a taxpayer recognizing gain under the constructive sale rules (¶2637 *et seq.*).

Entering into a securities futures contract (¶2661) to sell is treated as a short sale and the settlement of the contract is treated as the closing of the short sale for determining whether gain or loss is long- or short-term and for the holding period rules at ¶2670. (Code Sec. 1233(e)(2)(E))[31]

For the effect of the wash sale rules on short sales, see ¶2462.

---

27. ¶I-7737; ¶12,594; TD ¶228,607
28. ¶I-7738; ¶12,594; TD ¶228,608
29. ¶I-7704; ¶12,334.01; TD ¶228,901

30. ¶I-7708; ¶12,334.01; TD ¶228,905
31. ¶I-7712.2; ¶12,334.09; TD ¶228,911.1

¶ 2640   Capital gain limits on short sales.

The capital gain realized by the seller in a short sale is short-term, regardless of the actual holding period, where the seller either: (1) as of the date of the short sale, has owned for not more than one year (determined without regard to the effect of the short sale on the holding period, see ¶2670) property that's "substantially identical" (¶2462) to that which he used to close the sale, or (2) after the short sale and on or before its closing, he acquires substantially identical property. (Code Sec. 1233(b); Reg § 1.1233-1(c)(2)) This doesn't apply to any capital gain on property in excess of the amount of substantially identical property. This keeps the taxpayer from turning what would normally be a short-term capital gain into a long-term capital gain. [32]

The above rule applies only to stocks, securities and commodity futures. (Code Sec. 1233(e)(2)(A))[33]

¶ 2641   Capital loss limits on short sales.

If property "substantially identical" (¶2462) to that sold short was held by the taxpayer for more than one year as of the sale date, any loss on closing of the short sale is long-term capital loss, regardless of how long he held the property used to close the sale. (Code Sec. 1233(d)) This doesn't apply to any capital loss on property used to close the short sale in excess of the amount of substantially identical property. (Code Sec. 1233(e)(1))[34] This rule applies only to stocks, securities and commodity futures. (Code Sec. 1233(e)(2)(A))[35]

¶ 2642   Commodity futures and hedging transactions.

Commodity transactions are generally subject to the same rules for short sales as stocks and securities. (Reg § 1.1233-1(b)) A commodity future is a contract to buy some fixed amount of a commodity at a future date at a fixed price. Gain or loss from the short sale of a commodity future is capital gain or loss if the future used to close the short sale is a capital asset to the taxpayer. However, the short sale rules don't apply where the sale of the commodity future is a bona fide hedging transaction, see ¶2660. (Code Sec. 1233(g); Reg § 1.1233-1(b))[36] A transaction is a bona fide hedging transaction if the commodity future purchased is directly related to the taxpayer's business, e.g., flour millers buying and selling wheat futures.[37]

¶ 2643   Gain recognition required when property sold short becomes worthless.

If a taxpayer enters into a short sale of property, and that property becomes substantially worthless, the taxpayer recognizes gain in the same manner as if the short sale were closed when the property becomes substantially worthless. (Code Sec. 1233(h)(1))[38] To the extent provided in regs, this rule will also apply for any option with respect to property, any offsetting notional principal contract with respect to property, any futures or forward contract to deliver any property, and any other similar transaction. (Code Sec. 1233(h)(1))[39]

Where property becomes substantially worthless during a tax year and any short sale of the property remains open at that time, then the statutory period for the assessment of any deficiency attributable to any part of the gain on the transaction doesn't expire before the earlier of: (1) the date which is three years after the date IRS is notified by the taxpayer (in a manner that IRS may prescribe by regs) of the substantial worthlessness of the property, or

---

32. ¶I-7710; ¶s 12,334.03, 12,334.06; TD ¶228,907
33. ¶I-7709; ¶12,334.09; TD ¶228,905
34. ¶I-7714; TD ¶228,907
35. ¶I-7709; ¶12,334.03; TD ¶228,905

36. ¶I-7724; ¶12,334.01; TD ¶228,901
37. ¶I-7724; ¶s 12,214.80, 12,334.12
38. ¶I-7707.1; ¶12,334.02; TD ¶228,917
39. ; ¶12,334.02; TD ¶228,615

(2) the date which is six years after the date the return for the tax year during which the position became substantially worthless is filed. In addition, the deficiency may be assessed before the expiration of the assessment period described above in spite of any other law or rule of law which would otherwise prevent the assessment. (Code Sec. 1233(h)(2))[40]

¶ 2644   Section 1244 ("Small Business Corporation") Stock. ▂▂▂▂▂▂

Loss on the sale, exchange or worthlessness of Section 1244 stock is deductible, within limits, as an ordinary loss, even though gain on the stock is capital gain. This ordinary deduction is available only to individuals, and only if the individual (or a partnership) was the original purchaser. Transferees of these original purchasers don't qualify. (Code Sec. 1244(a))[41]

The aggregate amount of the ordinary loss is limited to $50,000 on separate returns and $100,000 on joint returns each year. Spouses may deduct the $100,000 maximum in a joint return even if only one spouse owned the stock. (Code Sec. 1244(b))[42]

A loss on qualifying Section 1244 stock is deductible as an ordinary loss attributable to the shareholder's business. As such, the loss is deductible in full from gross income and may give rise to a net operating loss. Losses exceeding the limits must be treated as regular capital losses. (Reg § 1.1244(b)-1(a))[43]

¶ 2645   Qualifying for Section 1244 ordinary loss treatment.

To qualify as Section 1244 stock, all of the following tests must be met: (Code Sec. 1244(c))[44]

. . . The stock must be stock of a domestic corporation. It may be common or preferred, voting or nonvoting). (Reg § 1.1244(c)-1(b))[45]

. . . The stock must have been issued for money or property (other than stock and securities). But stock issued for the cancellation of corporate debt (not evidenced by a security or issued for services) does qualify. Stock issued for services rendered or to be rendered to, or for the benefit of, the issuing corporation, does not qualify. (Reg § 1.1244(c)-1(d)(1))[46]

. . . The issuing corporation must have met a test in which it shows that over 50% of its receipts were from business operations. [47]

. . . The stock had to be issued by a domestic "small business" corporation, see ¶2647.[48]

¶ 2646   How to claim the Section 1244 ordinary loss—Form 4797.

Claim the ordinary loss on Form 4797 (attached to Form 1040). No information statement is required to be filed with the return but records must be maintained to establish a loss and whether the stock qualifies as Section 1244 stock. (Reg § 1.1244(e)-1(b))[49]

¶ 2647   Small business corporation (SBC) defined.

A corporation is an SBC if at the time the stock is issued its capital receipts don't exceed $1,000,000. (Special designation rules must be met for stock issued in a year capital receipts do exceed $1,000,000.)[50] Capital receipts means the aggregate amount of money and other property received by the corporation for stock, as a contribution to capital, and as paid-in surplus. This includes amounts received for the Section 1244 stock and for all stock issued

---

40. ¶T-4221.2; ¶12,334.02; TD ¶228,917
41. ¶I-9503; ¶12,444.02; TD ¶247,301
42. ¶I-9505; ¶12,444.01; TD ¶247,359
43. ¶I-9502; ¶12,444; TD ¶247,362
44. ¶I-9508 *et seq.*; ¶12,444.03; TD ¶247,336
45. ¶I-9509; ¶12,444.03; TD ¶247,302 *et seq.*

46. ¶I-9511, I-9512; ¶12,444.03; TD ¶247,309 *et seq.*
47. ¶I-9524 *et seq.*; ¶12,444.03; TD ¶247,302
48. ¶I-9517; ¶12444.03; TD ¶247,325 *et seq.*
49. ¶I-9537, I-9538; ¶12,444.05; TD ¶247,363, 247,365
50. ¶I-9518 *et seq.*; ¶12,444.04; TD ¶247,326

previously. (Code Sec. 1244(c)(3)(A))[1]

¶ 2648 Partial exclusion of Gain from Qualified Small Business Stock (QSBS). ▬▬▬▬

Noncorporate taxpayers may exclude 50% of the gain (60% on certain Empowerment Zone stock) on the disposition of QSBS.

A taxpayer other than a corporation may exclude 50% of the gain on the disposition of QSBS.issued after Aug. 10, '93 and held over five years. (Code Sec. 1202(a)(1))[2] However, a taxpayer (or a related party) who takes an off-setting short position before the required five-year holding period is completed cannot exclude gain from the disposition of QSBS. (Code Sec. 1202(j))[3]

The exclusion is 60% for gain on the sale of empowerment zone stock (but not District of Columbia Enterprise Zone stock) acquired after Dec. 21, 2000, held for more than five years, and not attributable to periods after 2014. The empowerment zone stock must be in a corporation that qualifies as an enterprise zone business under Code Sec. 1397C(b) during substantially all of the taxpayer's holding period. (Code Sec. 1202(a)(2)) [4]

For each corporation in which the taxpayer invests, the total amount of gain eligible for the partial exclusion for a tax year may not exceed the greater of:

... $10,000,000 ($5,000,000 for marrieds filing separately) (Code Sec. 1202(b)(1)(A), Code Sec. 1202(b)(3)(A)) reduced by taxpayer's total gain on dispositions of the corporation's stock that he took into account in earlier years. (Code Sec. 1202(b)(1)(A)) The amount of eligible gain is allocated equally between spouses who file jointly, to apply this limit to later years (Code Sec. 1202(b)(3)(B)); or

... ten times the aggregate adjusted bases of any of the corporation's QSBS that taxpayer disposed of during the year. (Code Sec. 1202(b)(1)(B)) For this purpose, the adjusted basis of any stock doesn't include any additions to basis after the date it was originally issued (Code Sec. 1202(b)(1)), or any reductions for SSBIC rollovers (¶2505). (Code Sec. 1044(d))[5]

The exclusion is denied where the corporation redeems stock from the taxpayer or a related person during certain periods, or buys its own stock in excess of certain amounts during specified periods. (Code Sec. 1202(c)(3))[6]

Additional rules apply where pass-through entities hold the stock. (Code Sec. 1202(g))[7]

For the rollover of gain from QSBS to other QSBS, see ¶2429.

For alternative minimum tax treatment of the exclusion, see ¶3208.

¶ 2649 Qualified small business stock (QSBS) defined.

Qualified small business stock (QSBS) is any stock in a C corporation which is originally issued after Aug. 10, '93 if:

... as of the date of issuance, the corporation is a qualified small business. (Code Sec. 1202(c)(1)(A)) This means a domestic C corporation whose total gross assets (treating all members of the same parent-subsidiary controlled group as one corporation) at all times after Aug. 10, '93 and before the issuance, and immediately after the issuance (taking into account amounts received in the issuance), don't exceed $50,000,000, and that meets certain reporting requirements (Code Sec. 1202(d));

... the taxpayer claiming the exclusion acquired the stock at its original issuance for money or other property (not stock) or as compensation for services provided to the corporation

1. ¶I-9518; ¶12,444.04; TD ¶247,327
2. ¶I-9100.1; ¶12,024; TD ¶246,601
3. ¶I-9115; ¶12,024.03; TD ¶246,610
4. ¶I-9100.1A; ¶12,024; TD ¶246,602

5. ¶I-9112 *et seq.*; ¶12,024.01; TD ¶246,603 *et seq.*
6. ¶I-9102; ¶12,024; TD ¶246,637
7. ¶I-9116; ¶s 12,024, 12,024.03; TD ¶246,612

(other than services performed as an underwriter) (Code Sec. 1202(c)(1)(B)); *and*

. . . during substantially all of taxpayer's holding period for the stock, the corporation is a C corporation (other than certain excluded corporations) *and* meets an active business test. (Code Sec. 1202(c)(2)(A), Code Sec. 1202(e)) An SSBIC (¶2427) meets the active business test.[8]

¶ 2650   Tax- Free Capital Gains for Investment in Renewal Communities and DC Zone Assets. ▬▬▬▬▬▬

Taxpayers will be able to exclude all capital gains realized from the sale of certain qualifying community renewal or DC Zone assets held for more than 5 years.

¶ 2651   Tax-free capital gains from sale of qualifying community renewal assets held for more than 5 years

Taxpayers will be able to exclude 100% of their "qualified capital gain" recognized on the sale or exchange of a "qualified community asset" if the asset is (1) acquired after 2001 and before 2010 and (2) held for more than 5 years. (Code Sec. 1400F(a); Code Sec. 1400F(b)(2)(A)(i); Code Sec. 1400F(b)(3)(A); Code Sec. 1400F(b)(4)(A)(i))

"Qualified capital gain" is gain recognized on the sale or exchange of a capital asset, or property used in a trade or business, as defined in Code Sec. 1231(b), see ¶2686. (Code Sec. 1400F(c)(1)) It doesn't include (1) any gain attributable to periods before 2002 or after 2014 (Code Sec. 1400F(c)(2)), (2) gain recaptured under Code Sec. 1245 (¶2695) or under Code Sec. 1250 (¶2696) (including gain that would be recaptured if Code Sec. 1250 applied to all depreciation rather than just to additional depreciation) (Code Sec. 1400F(c)(3); Code Sec. 1400B(e)(3)), (3) gain attributable to real property, or an intangible asset, that isn't integral to a "renewal community business" (as defined in Code Sec. 1400G) (Code Sec. 1400F(c)(3); Code Sec. 1400B(e)(4)), and (4) gain attributable in whole or in part to certain related-party transactions. (Code Sec. 1400F(c)(3); Code Sec. 1400B(e)(5)).

A "qualified community asset" is qualifying stock in a U.S. corporation (defined in Code Sec. 1400F(b)(2)), a qualifying capital or a profits interest in a U.S. partnership (defined in Code Sec. 1400F(b)(3)), or qualifying community business property (defined in Code Sec. 1400F(b)(4)).

Special rules apply for subsequent holders of qualifying property (Code Sec. 1400F(d)), and where qualifying community assets cease to qualify as a renewal community business (or property ceases to be used in such a business) after the 5-year period beginning after the date the taxpayer acquired the assets. (Code Sec. 1400F(d))[9]

¶ 2652   Tax-free gain from the sale or exchange of qualifying D.C. Zone assets.

Gross income doesn't include qualified capital gain from the sale or exchange of any DC Zone asset held for more than five years. Qualified capital gain is any gain recognized on the sale or exchange of: a capital asset, or property used in the trade or business. (Code Sec. 1400B(a), Code Sec. 1400B(e)(1)(B))

Qualified capital gain does *not* include any gain (1) attributable to periods before '98 or after 2012 (Code Sec. 1400B(e)(2)), (2) which would be treated as ordinary income under the recapture rules of Code Sec. 1245 (¶2695) or Code Sec. 1250 (¶2696) if Code Sec. 1250 applied to all depreciation rather than the additional depreciation (Code Sec. 1400B(e)(3)), (3) which is attributable to real property, or an intangible asset, that is not an integral part of a DC Zone business (Code Sec. 1400B(e)(4)), or (4) is attributable, directly or indirectly, in whole or in part, to a transaction with a related person (under Code Sec. 267(b) or Code Sec. 707(b)(1)).

---

8.   ¶I-9102 *et seq.*; ¶12,024.02; TD ¶246,639 *et seq.*   9.   ¶I-8801 *et seq.*; ¶14,00F4; TD ¶229,952 *et seq.*

(Code Sec. 1400B(e)(5))

In general, a DC Zone asset is qualifying DC Zone business stock, DC Zone partnership interests, and DC Zone business property, acquired before 2008. (Code Sec. 1400B(b)(1) [10]

¶ 2653 Tax Straddles and Section 1256 Contracts

Losses on certain unregulated straddles are deferred, to the extent taxpayer has an offsetting unrecognized gain. Related interest and carrying charges must be capitalized. Regulated futures contracts are subject to the "mark-to-market" rule which treats the unrealized capital gain (or loss) from the contract for the year as 60% long-term and 40% short-term. Hedging transactions are excepted from these rules.

There are a number of rules provided to restrict tax avoidance opportunities in commodity futures straddles and to curb certain tax shelters involving tax straddles. [11]

Under the constructive sale rules (¶2637), a taxpayer must recognize gain (but not loss) upon entering into a constructive sale of any appreciated financial position in stock, a partnership interest, or certain debt instruments. (Code Sec. 1259). The constructive sale rules generally are intended to apply to transactions that are identified as hedging or straddle transactions under other Code provisions such as Code Sec. 1092(a)(2) (dealing with a special rule for straddles that are identified as straddles at the close of a tax year), Code Sec. 1092(b)(2) (dealing with regs with respect to identified mixed straddles, ¶2658), Code Sec. 1092(e) (dealing with an exception for hedging transactions), and Code Sec. 1256(e) (dealing with the nonapplication of the mark-to-market rules to hedging transactions, ¶2660).[12]

¶ 2654 Straddle defined.

A straddle is "offsetting positions" with respect to personal property. (Code Sec. 1092(c)(1)) A "position" is an interest, including a futures or forward contract or option, in personal property. (Code Sec. 1092(d)(2)) In general, personal property does not include stock (but it does include stock options and contracts to buy stock). (Code Sec. 1092(d)(3)(A)) However, stock is included in the definition of personal property for straddle purposes if (1) the stock is part of a straddle in which at least one of the offsetting positions is either an option to buy or sell the stock or substantially identical stock or securities, or a position on substantially similar or related property (other than stock); or (2) the stock is in a corporation formed or availed of to take positions in personal property that offset positions taken by any shareholder. (Code Sec. 1092(d)(3)(B))

A taxpayer holds "offsetting positions" if he has reduced his risk of loss from holding the property by holding one (or more) other positions, whether or not the items of personal property involved in the different positions are the same kind. (Code Sec. 1092(c)(2)(A))[13]

¶ 2655 Recognition of losses postponed on certain nonregulated futures straddles (loss deferral rule).

Loss deductions on nonregulated straddles, that is, those straddle positions not on the "mark-to-market" system (see ¶2656), are limited to the amount by which the losses exceed "unrecognized gains" on any offsetting straddle positions. Losses in excess of the limitation (deferred losses) are carried forward to the next year and are subject to the deferral rules in that year. (Code Sec. 1092(a)(1))[14]

---

10. ¶I-8750 *et seq.*; ¶14,00B4; TD ¶246,550 *et seq.*
11. ¶I-7500 *et seq.*; ¶10,924; TD ¶228,401
12. ¶I-7746

13. ¶I-7504; ¶10,924; TD ¶228,406
14. ¶I-7523; ¶10,924; TD ¶228,403

¶ 2656   Regulated futures contracts, etc. (Section 1256 contracts), under "mark-to-market" system.

Taxpayers must report (on Form 6781) gains and losses from regulated futures contracts and other "Section 1256 contracts" (¶2657) on an annual basis under the "mark-to-market" rule. All Section 1256 contracts must be marked to market at year end. Each Section 1256 contract held by a taxpayer is treated as if it were sold for fair market value on the last business day of the year. (Code Sec. 1256(a)(1)) If a taxpayer holds Section 1256 contracts at the beginning of a tax year, any gain or loss later realized on the contracts must be adjusted to reflect any gain or loss taken into account with respect to the contracts in an earlier year. (Code Sec. 1256(a)(2))

Any capital gain or loss on a Section 1256 futures contract that is marked-to-market is treated as if 40% of the gain or loss is short-term capital gain or loss, and as if 60% of the gain or loss is long-term capital gain or loss. (Code Sec. 1256(a)(3))[15]

The wash sale rules (¶2462) don't apply to losses taken into account when a Section 1256 contract is marked to market. (Code Sec. 1256(f)(5))[16]

¶ 2657   Section 1256 contracts defined.

Section 1256 contracts include: regulated futures contracts, foreign currency contracts, nonequity options, dealer equity options, and dealer securities futures contracts (¶2663) (Code Sec. 1256(b))[17] For a partnership that's a qualified fund, Section 1256 contracts include bank forward contracts, foreign currency futures contracts, and similar instruments prescribed by IRS regs. (Code Sec. 988(c)(1)(E)(iv)(I))[18]

¶ 2658   Election for mixed straddles.

If straddles are composed of at least one position in a Section 1256 contract (¶2657) and one or more positions in interests in property that aren't Section 1256 contracts, a taxpayer may elect on Form 6781 to exclude all positions in the mixed straddle, including Section 1256 contracts, from the mark-to-market rules in which case they will be subject to the loss deferral, wash sale, and short sale rules, and the straddle won't be a mixed straddle. (Code Sec. 1256(d))[19] If that election isn't made, so that the straddle is a mixed straddle, a taxpayer may elect to offset gains and losses in the mixed straddle by either separately identifying the positions of the mixed straddle, or establishing a mixed straddle account. (Reg § 1.1092(b)-4T(f))[20]

¶ 2659   Carryback election for losses from Section 1256 contracts—Form 6781.

Noncorporate taxpayers can elect (on Form 6781) to have net commodity futures capital losses carried back three years and applied against net commodities futures capital gains during that period. (Code Sec. 1212(c)) The carryback applies only if, after netting Section 1256 contracts with capital gains and losses from other sources, there's a net capital loss for the tax year that, but for the election, would be a capital loss carryforward under the normal rules (¶2612). The lesser of the net capital loss or the net loss resulting from the application of the mark-to-market rule is a "net Section 1256 contracts loss" which may be carried back. (Code Sec. 1212(c)(4)) Capital losses carried back must be treated as if 40% of the losses are short-term capital losses and 60% are long-term capital losses. (Code Sec. 1212(c)(1)) The

15. ¶I-7602, ¶I-7603.3; ¶12,564 *et seq.*; TD ¶228,700 *et seq.*
16. ¶I-7602; ¶12,564.02; TD ¶228,701
17. ¶I-7604; ¶12,564.01; TD ¶228,704

18. ¶I-7607; ¶9884.01
19. ¶I-7616; ¶12,564.03; TD ¶228,714
20. ¶I-7543 *et seq.*; ¶10,924

losses must be absorbed in the earliest year to which they may be carried back. Any remainder is then carried forward to the next year. The losses may be applied in the carryback year against the lesser of "net Section 1256 contracts gain" or capital gain net income for that year. (Code Sec. 1212(c)(5))

Capital losses that are carried forward, to the extent they were determined under the mark-to-market rule, continue to be treated as losses from Section 1256 contracts in the year to which they are carried. (Code Sec. 1212(c)(6))[21]

¶ 2660   Hedging transactions not covered by the mark-to-market rules.

The "mark-to-market" rules don't apply to "hedging transactions" as defined in Code Sec. 1256(e)(2). (Code Sec. 1256(e)(1))[22]

¶ 2661   Securities Futures Contracts

Gain or loss from a securities futures contract generally has the same character as gain or loss from transactions in the underlying security. A dealer securities futures contract is treated as a section 1256 contract.

¶ 2662   Gain or loss from nondealer securities futures contracts.

Gain or loss on the sale, exchange, or termination of a securities futures contract (as defined in Code Sec. 1234B(c)) generally has the same character as gain or loss from transactions in the underlying security. (Code Sec. 1234B(a)(1)) For example, if the underlying asset would be a capital asset in the hands of the taxpayer, gain or loss from the sale of the contract is capital gain or loss. This rule does not apply to securities futures contracts that are not capital assets because they are Code Sec. 1221(a)(1) inventory assets, are identified as Code Sec. 1221(a)(7) hedging transactions, or any income derived in connection with a contract which would otherwise not be capital gain. (Code Sec. 1234B(a)(2))[23]

Except as provided in regs to Code Sec. 1092(b) or Code Sec. 1234B, or in Code Sec. 1233, capital gain or loss from the sale, exchange, or termination of a securities futures contract to sell property is treated as short-term capital gain or loss. (Code Sec. 1234B(b))

If the security to which a securities futures contract (that is not a Code Sec. 1256 contract (see ¶2663)) is acquired in satisfaction of that contract, the taxpayer's holding period for the security includes the period for which the taxpayer held the contract if the contract was a capital asset in the taxpayer's hands. (Code Sec. 1223(14))

¶ 2663   Dealer securities futures contracts are section 1256 contracts.

Dealer securities futures contracts are treated as Code Sec. 1256 contracts (see ¶2656). (Code Sec. 1256(b)(5)) A dealer securities futures contract is any securities futures contract (see ¶2662) and any option to enter into such a contract that (1) is entered into by the dealer (or, in the case of an option, is purchased or granted by the dealer) in the normal course of his activity of dealing in such contracts or options, as the case may be (Code Sec. 1256(g)(9)(A)(i)), and (2) is traded on a qualified board or exchange. (Code Sec. 1256(g)(9)(A)(ii))[24]

¶ 2664   Conversion and Constructive Ownership Transactions

Capital gain on the disposition of property that was part of a conversion transaction (i.e., functionally equivalent to a loan) is treated as ordinary income. Certain gains from derivative contracts (constructive ownership transactions) with respect to financial assets are recharacterized as ordinary income.

---

21. ¶I-7606; ¶12,124.02; TD ¶228,706
22. ¶I-7620; ¶12,564.05; TD ¶250,006

23. ¶I-6280 *et seq.*; ¶12,34A4; TD ¶250,200 *et seq.*
24. ¶I-7615.1; ¶12,564.01; TD ¶228,712

¶ 2665   Gain recharacterized on conversion transactions similar to loans.

Gain recognized on the disposition or other termination of any position held as part of a conversion transaction (defined below), that would otherwise be treated as capital gain, is treated as ordinary income, to the extent it doesn't exceed the applicable imputed income amount. (Code Sec. 1258(a))[25] The applicable imputed income amount equals the excess of (1) taxpayer's net investment in the transaction multiplied by 120% of (a) the applicable federal rate (¶1116), compounded semiannually, for the period covered by the transaction, if the transaction has a definite term, or of (b) the federal short-term rates (compounded daily) in effect under Code Sec. 6621(b) for the period of the conversion transaction, if the term of the transaction is indefinite, over (2) the amount already so treated with respect to the same transaction. (Code Sec. 1258(b), Code Sec. 1258(d)(2))[26]

When a taxpayer disposes or terminates all positions of an identified (as part of the same transaction, on taxpayer's books and records) netting transaction within a 14-day period in a single tax year, all gains and losses on those positions realized within that period are netted to determine the amount of gain treated as ordinary income. (Reg § 1.1258-1(b))[27]

A conversion transaction is any transaction where substantially all of taxpayer's expected net return is attributable to the time value of his net investment, and which is:

... the holding of any property (whether or not actively traded) and substantially contemporaneous making of a contract to sell that or substantially identical property at a price determined in accordance with the contract (Code Sec. 1258(c)(2)(A));

... a straddle (¶2654) of actively traded personal property (Code Sec. 1258(c)(2)(B));

... any other transaction that is marketed or sold as producing capital gains, and substantially all of the expected return from that transaction is attributable to the time value of the taxpayer's net investment in the transaction (Code Sec. 1258(c)(2)(C)); or

... a conversion transaction as specified in regs to be issued. (Code Sec. 1258(c)(2)(D))[28]

Conversion transactions don't include transactions of options dealers and commodities traders in the normal course of their trade or business. (Code Sec. 1258(d)(5)(A))[29]

¶ 2666   Certain long-term capital gains from constructive ownership transactions are recharacterized as ordinary income

The amount of long-term capital gain a taxpayer can recognize from certain derivative contracts (constructive ownership transactions (defined in Code Sec. 1260(d))) with respect to certain financial assets is limited, and an interest charge is imposed on the tax underpayment for each year that the constructive ownership transaction was open. (Code Sec. 1260) If a taxpayer has gain from a constructive ownership transaction with respect to any financial asset and that gain would otherwise be treated as a long-term capital gain, then (1) the gain is treated as ordinary income to the extent it exceeds the net underlying long-term capital gain, and (2) to the extent gain is treated as long-term capital gain, the determination of the capital gain rate (or rates) applicable to the gain under Code Sec. 1(h) (i.e., the individual capital gains rates) is determined on the basis of the respective rate (or rates) that would have applied to the net underlying long-term capital gain. (Code Sec. 1260(a))[30]

¶ 2667   Holding Period. ▰▰▰▰▰▰▰▰▰▰▰▰▰▰▰▰▰

The length of time that a capital asset is held before its sale or exchange determines whether the proceeds from the sale or exchange are taxable as long-term capital gain

---

25. ¶I-8200 *et seq.*; ¶12,584; TD ¶227,801

26. ¶I-8208; ¶12,584; TD ¶227,806

27. ¶I-8209.1 *et seq.*; ¶12,584; TD ¶227,802

28. ¶I-8205; ¶12,584; TD ¶227,805

29. ¶I-8210 *et seq.*; ¶12,584

30. ¶I-8251; ¶12,604

or loss or as short-term capital gain or loss.

The length of time an asset is held is also crucial in qualifying for Section 1231 (capital gain/ordinary loss) treatment, see ¶2686.

Holding a capital asset for the short-term holding period (one year or less) results in short-term capital gain or loss on the sale or exchange of that asset. (Code Sec. 1222(1), Code Sec. 1222(2)) Holding a capital asset for the long-term holding period (more than one year) results in long-term capital gain or loss on the sale or exchange of that asset. (Code Sec. 1222(3), Code Sec. 1222(4))[31]

The holding period is more than six months for futures transactions in any commodity subject to the rules of a board of trade or commodity exchange. (Code Sec. 1222)[32]

¶ 2668   How to measure the holding period.

The holding period is computed in terms of calendar months, not days. [33] It begins on the day after the day of acquisition and ends on the day of sale, exchange or other disposition. Thus, the taxpayer excludes the day of acquisition but includes the date of disposition. [34]

illustration: A capital asset is acquired on Feb. 15. To meet the long-term holding period, it must be held until Feb. 16 of the following year. To meet the more-than-six-month long-term holding period for a commodity future (¶2667), it must be held until Aug. 16. If the asset were acquired on Jan. 31, it would have to be held until Feb. 1 of the following year to meet the more-than-one-year holding period, or until Aug. 1 to meet the more-than-six-month period.

¶ 2669   Holding period of partnership interest.

A partner doesn't have a divided holding period in his partnership interest unless he acquired portions of it at different times or in exchange for property transferred at the same time but resulting in different holding periods. (Reg § 1.1223-3(a)) The holding period of a portion of a partnership interest is determined based on a fraction equal to the fair market value (FMV) of the portion of the partnership interest received in the transaction to which the holding period relates over the FMV of the entire partnership interest (determined immediately after the transaction). (Reg § 1.1223-3(b))[35]

illustration: A contributes $5,000 and a nondepreciable capital asset that he's held for two years to a partnership for a 50% interest in it. His basis in the capital asset is $5,000, and its FMV is $10,000. After the exchange, A's basis in his interest in the partnership is $10,000, and the FMV of the interest is $15,000. Because he received one-third of the interest in the partnership for $5,000 in cash, his holding period in one-third of the interest received begins on the day after the contribution. A received two-thirds of the interest in the partnership in exchange for the capital asset ($10,000/$15,000). Under Code Sec. 1223(1), he has a two-year holding period in two-thirds of the interest received in the partnership.

¶ 2670   Holding period for stocks and securities.

The holding period for stocks and securities acquired by purchase, whether on a registered securities exchange or in the "over-the-counter" market, is determined by reference to the "trade date" on which the stock or security is acquired and the "trade date" on which it is sold. The "settlement dates" aren't considered. [36]

---

31. ¶I-8901; ¶12,234; TD ¶223,501
32. ¶I-8971; ¶12,234.27; TD ¶223,550
33. ¶I-8904; ¶12,234.01; TD ¶223,504

34. ¶s I-8904, I-8906; ¶12,234.01; TD ¶223,502
35. ¶I-8934.1; ¶12,234.29; TD ¶223,556
36. ¶I-8914 *et seq.*; ¶12,234.07; TD ¶223,513

The holding period for stock or securities acquired from a corporation by the exercise of rights begins on and includes the day the rights are exercised. (Code Sec. 1223(5); Reg § 1.1223-1(f))[37]

The holding period for property "substantially identical" to that sold short in a transaction to which the rule at ¶2640 applies is considered to begin on the day the short sale is closed or, if earlier, on the date the property is sold, given away or otherwise disposed of. (Code Sec. 1233(b)(2); Reg § 1.1233-1(c)(2))[38]

The holding period for stock, stock rights or other property received as a taxable dividend begins on the date the distribution is actually or constructively received. [39] If the distribution is tax-free, the holding period for the stock, etc., includes the period that the underlying stock was held. (Code Sec. 1223(4); Reg § 1.1223-1(e))[40]

The holding period for restricted stock (or property) begins after it is substantially vested, unless an election (¶1219) is made to include the property in income in the year of transfer, in which case it begins just after the transfer. (Code Sec. 83(f); Reg § 1.83-4(a))[41]

Where the loss on a sale of stock or securities is disallowed under the "wash sale" rules (¶2461), the holding period for the new similar stock includes the holding period for the old stock that was sold. (Code Sec. 1223(3))[42]

The holding period for U.S. Treasury bonds and notes is measured from the acquisition date; for those sold at auction, this is the date the Treasury gives notice of acceptance to bidders; for those sold in a subscription offering at a specified interest rate, it's the date the buyer submits an offer. [43]

If an individual elects to roll over gain from qualified small business stock (QSBS) by way of the timely acquisition of other QSBS stock (¶2428) the holding period for the acquired QSBS stock includes the holding period for the sold QSBS stock. (Code Sec. 1223(13))[44]

¶ 2671   Property acquired through options.

The holding period for property acquired through the exercise of an option begins the day after the option is exercised. [45]

¶ 2672   Holding period for property inherited from a decedent.

The holding period of property acquired from a decedent starts with the date of death. [46] However, property acquired from a decedent which is sold within the short-term capital gain holding period after the decedent's death is considered to be held for the *long*-term capital gain holding period if the person selling the property has a basis that is determined under Code Sec. 1014 (by reference to the property's fair market value on date of death or alternate valuation date). (Code Sec. 1223(9))[47]

The long-term holding period is also met where special use valuation property (¶5028) is acquired by a "qualified heir" from the decedent's estate, and is sold within the short-term holding period to another "qualified heir." (Code Sec. 1223(10))[48]

The holding period of the surviving spouse's share of community property that vested at the time of the acquisition by the community (as opposed to the share inherited from the deceased spouse) starts from the date of acquisition. [49]

---

37. ¶I-8924; ¶12,234.25; TD ¶223,520
38. ¶I-7720; ¶12,334.03; TD ¶228,919
39. ¶I-8918; TD ¶223,517
40. ¶I-8921; ¶12,234.25; TD ¶223,518
41. ¶I-8916; ¶834 *et seq.*; TD ¶223,515
42. ¶I-8929; ¶12,234.25; TD ¶223,525
43. ¶I-8915; TD ¶223,514

44. ¶I-9207; ¶12,234.24
45. ¶I-8949; ¶12,234.10; TD ¶223,541
46. ¶I-8944; ¶12,234.21; TD ¶223,537
47. ¶I-8942; ¶12,234.21; TD ¶223,535
48. ¶I-8943; ¶12,234.21; TD ¶223,536
49. ¶I-8945; ¶12,234.21; TD ¶223,538

¶ 2673　Holding period for gifts.

The holding period for property acquired by gift includes the donor's holding period if the property has the same basis for gain or loss (see ¶2463 *et seq.*) in whole or in part in the hands of the donee as it would have in the donor's hands. (Code Sec. 1223(2); Reg § 1.1223-1(b)) But if the property is sold by the donee at a loss based on its market value on the date of the gift (and not the donor's basis), the holding period starts from the date of the gift. [50]

¶ 2674　Tax-free exchange property.

The holding period for property received in a partially or wholly tax-free exchange (¶2413), includes the holding period for the property surrendered. This "tacking on" applies where the new property has the same basis, in whole or in part, as the old property (Code Sec. 1223(1)), e.g., like-kind exchanges, tax-free stock distributions (¶2670), involuntary conversions (¶2675), or incorporations and tax-free corporate reorganizations (¶3510 *et seq.*).[1]

¶ 2675　Replacements for property lost or damaged in an involuntary conversion.

The holding period of the original property is tacked on to that of property acquired to replace property lost or damaged in an involuntary conversion (¶2430 *et seq.*), where gain isn't recognized.[2]

¶ 2676　Sales and Exchanges. ■■■■■■■■■■■■■■■■■■■■■■■■■■■■■

Unless a transaction involving a capital asset is treated as a sale or exchange, any resulting gain or loss doesn't qualify as capital gain or loss.

A sale is a transfer of property for an amount of money or a money equivalent that is fixed or determinable. An exchange is a transfer of property for property other than money or a cash equivalent. (Reg § 1.1002-1(d))[3]

To qualify as a sale or exchange, the transaction must be complete, and bona fide in all respects. If it's real in substance as well as form, it qualifies as a sale or exchange even though it was designed to reduce taxes. [4] Where shareholders deal with their corporation, or family members sell or exchange property among themselves, IRS scrutinizes the deal closely. If a sale or exchange is a sham, IRS can disallow any of the sought-after tax consequences. [5]

¶ 2677　Gain or loss from certain terminations treated as capital gain or loss.

Gain or loss attributable to the cancellation, lapse, expiration, or other termination of the following is treated as gain or loss from the sale of a capital asset:

(1) a right or obligation (other than a securities futures contract under Code Sec. 1234B) with respect to property which is (or on acquisition would be) a capital asset in the hands of the taxpayer (Code Sec. 1234A(1)), or

(2) a section 1256 contract (¶2657) not described in (1) above which is a capital asset in the hands of the taxpayer. (Code Sec. 1234A(2)).

These rules don't apply to the retirement of any debt instrument (whether or not through a trust or other participation arrangement). (Code Sec. 1234A)[6]

🔖 *observation:* It's not clear whether the rule discussed in (1), above, would change the

50. ¶I-8966; ¶12,234.22; TD ¶223,511
1. ¶I-8960 *et seq.*; ¶12,234.18; TD ¶223,507
2. ¶I-8963; ¶12,234.18; TD ¶223,507
3. ¶I-1002, I-1104; ¶12,224.07; TD ¶220,201

4. ¶I-1212 *et seq.*; ¶12,224.07; TD ¶220,600 *et seq.*
5. ¶I-1201 *et seq.*; TD ¶220,801
6. ¶I-7619; ¶12,34A4; TD ¶221,208

rule discussed at ¶1340 that amounts received by a lessor for the cancellation of a lease are rent taxable as ordinary income.

¶ 2678   Retirement of debt instruments.

In general, amounts received by a holder on retirement of a debt instrument are treated as received in exchange for the debt instrument. (Code Sec. 1271(a)(1))

¶ 2679   Payment with property as a sale.

A debtor realizes gain or loss when he transfers property to his creditor in complete or partial satisfaction of his debt. The transfer is treated as a sale or exchange of the property by the debtor. Gain or loss is the difference between the amount of debt satisfied and the basis of the transferred property. [7]

¶ 2680   Cancellation of lease or distribution agreement as sale or exchange.

Amounts received by a lessee or tenant for the cancellation of a lease, or by a distributor of goods for the cancellation of a distributorship agreement, are considered amounts received *in exchange* for the lease or agreement. (Code Sec. 1241)[8] Thus, Section 1231 treatment (see ¶2684) is available for gain or loss from the cancellation of a business lease or distributorship held long-term. If the lease was for the tenant's home, a gain would be taxed as a capital gain, but any loss wouldn't be deductible. [9]

¶ 2681   Convertible bonds.

No gain or loss is realized upon the conversion of bonds into stock of the *same* corporation under a conversion privilege set forth in the terms of the bond. [10]

¶ 2682   Sale with leaseback, reservations or restrictions.

The fact that a sale of property is accompanied by a leaseback doesn't bar recognizing the sale as closed for tax purposes. [11] But a leaseback of realty (including renewal options) extending for 30 years or more may be considered an exchange of like-kind property in which gain or loss isn't recognized. [12] A sale restricting the buyer's use of the property may be recognized as a completed sale, as where stock is sold subject to security-device restrictions, [13] but if the rights retained are significant enough, the seller may be considered as selling only a partial interest or as granting a license to use. [14]

¶ 2683   Part gift, part sale; conditional gifts.

If an owner combines a gift with a sale (e.g., to a family member) gain is realized to the extent the price received exceeds the owner's adjusted basis. (Reg § 1.1001-1(e))[15]

If a donor gives appreciated property to a donee on condition the donee pay the donor's gift tax, there's a sale by the donor for the amount of the gift tax. To the extent the gift tax paid by the donee exceeds the donor's basis, the donor has income. [16]

¶ 2684   Capital Gain-Ordinary Loss Rule. ■■■■■■■■■■■■■■■■■

Under Section 1231, if there's a net gain for the tax year from sales, exchanges, and

7. ¶I-1501 *et seq.*; ¶10,014.17; TD ¶221,401
8. ¶I-1400 *et seq.*; ¶12,414 *et seq.*; TD ¶221,201
9. ¶M-1500; ¶12,414
10. ¶I-1909; ¶10,014.42; TD ¶221,600
11. ¶I-1122; TD ¶220,620
12. ¶I-3077; TD ¶223,717
13. ¶I-1125
14. ¶I-1602 *et seq.*
15. ¶I-1006; ¶10,014.06; TD ¶220,205
16. ¶I-1007; TD ¶222,411

involuntary or compulsory conversions of certain assets, it's treated as long-term capital gain. A net loss is treated as an ordinary loss.

¶ 2685 Applying the Section 1231 rules—Form 4797.

If the recognized gains are greater than the recognized losses on sales, exchanges and involuntary conversions of Section 1231 assets, the net amount is treated as a long-term capital gain, except as discussed below. But, if those losses are greater than those gains, the net amount is treated as an ordinary loss. (Code Sec. 1231(a); Reg § 1.1231-1(b))[17] Section 1231 gains and losses are reported and netted on Form 4797.

A net Section 1231 gain is treated as ordinary income to the extent of nonrecaptured net Section 1231 losses. (Code Sec. 1231(c)(1))

A nonrecaptured net Section 1231 loss is the net Section 1231 loss for the five most recent preceding tax years that hasn't been offset by a net Section 1231 gain in an intervening tax year. (Code Sec. 1231(c)(2)) Net Section 1231 gain means the excess of the Section 1231 gains over the Section 1231 losses. Net Section 1231 loss means the excess of the Section 1231 losses over the Section 1231 gains. (Code Sec. 1231(c)(3), Code Sec. 1231(c)(4))[18]

illustration: X Corp, a calendar year taxpayer, had a net Section 1231 loss of $1,000,000 in 2003 that was offset against ordinary income. X Corp had no net Section 1231 gain in 2004, 2005, or 2006, but has a net Section 1231 gain of $1,400,000 (consisting of a $2,000,000 gain on condemnation of land, and a $600,000 loss on the sale of machinery) in 2007. $1,000,000 of the net Section 1231 gain for 2007 is treated as ordinary income, and the remaining $400,000 is treated as long-term capital gain.

If the recognized losses from involuntary conversions arising from fire, storm, shipwreck or other casualty, or from theft, exceed the recognized gain, they aren't included in the Section 1231 computations. (Code Sec. 1231(a)(4), Code Sec. 1231(c)(5))[19]

Capital gain treatment under Section 1231 is also barred to the extent that the depreciation recapture rules apply, see ¶2692 *et seq.*

¶ 2686 Section 1231 assets defined.

Section 1231 assets are certain assets used in taxpayer's trade or business that were held for more than one year at the time of disposition. Except as explained below, these assets include depreciable tangible and intangible personal property, and real property, whether or not depreciable. They include timber, certain livestock (other than poultry), and unharvested crops that are transferred with land. (Code Sec. 1231(b))

They don't include: (1) inventory, (2) property held primarily for sale to customers in the ordinary course of the taxpayer's business, (3) copyrights, artistic, literary, or musical compositions (unless, for musical compositions or copyrights in them, the election discussed at ¶2622 is made), letters or memoranda, or similar property, in the hands of the creator or other taxpayer described in Code Sec. 1221(a)(3), and (4) U.S. government publications obtained without charge or below the price sold to the general public. (Code Sec. 1231(b); Reg § 1.1231-1(c))[20]

Property held for rent usually is treated as property used in business, but IRS (with the support of some, but not all, courts) denies this status where rental activity is slight. [21]

---

17. ¶I-9001; ¶12,314; TD ¶223,201
18. ¶I-9003; ¶12,314.15; TD ¶223,205
19. ¶I-9004; ¶s 12,314.09, 12,314.15; TD ¶223,206

20. ¶I-9007 *et seq.*; ¶12,314 *et seq.*; TD ¶223,208
21. ¶I-9013; ¶12,314.02 *et seq.*; TD ¶223,213

¶ 2687 Timber cutting treated as sale or exchange—Form T.

A taxpayer may elect to treat the cutting of timber as a sale or exchange qualifying for Section 1231 capital gain-ordinary loss treatment. (Code Sec. 631(a), Code Sec. 1231(b)(2))[22] Taxpayers who elect must file Form T with their returns. [23]

The taxpayer must have owned the timber, or held a contract right to cut it, for more than one year before the timber is cut. (Code Sec. 631(a); Reg § 1.631-1(b)(1)) The timber must be cut for sale or for use in the taxpayer's business. (Reg § 1.631-1)[24]

Once made, the election can be revoked only with IRS's consent (Code Sec. 631(a)) unless it was made for a tax year ending before Oct. 23, 2004 in which case it can be revoked for any later tax year without IRS's consent. [25]

¶ 2688 Timber, coal or U.S. iron ore sold with a retained economic interest.

A disposition of timber, coal or U.S. iron ore held more than 1-year qualifies for Section 1231 treatment if disposed of under a contract in which the taxpayer retains an economic interest. (Code Sec. 631(b), Code Sec. 631(c), Code Sec. 1231(b)(2); Reg § 1.631-2(a)(1), Reg § 1.631-3(a)(1))[26] For sales of timber after 2004, Section 1231 treatment also applies if the owner makes an outright sale of the timber even if no economic interest is retained. (Code Sec. 631(b))[27]

When the disposition qualifies for Section 1231 treatment, no cost depletion deduction (¶1982) is allowed. (Reg § 1.611-1(b)(2)) And, for dispositions of coal and iron ore, no percentage depletion deduction is allowed if the maximum tax rate for the year on net capital gain is less than the maximum rate for ordinary income. (Code Sec. 631(c); Reg § 1.611-1(b)(2))[28]

¶ 2689 Advance payments for timber, coal or domestic iron ore.

Advance or minimum royalty payments or other amounts received or accrued before cutting of timber or before the mining of coal or iron ore (disposed of with a retained economic interest) are treated as realized from a sale subject to Section 1231 if the contract of disposal provides that they are to be applied as payment for timber cut later or coal or iron ore mined later. (Reg § 1.631-2(d)(1), Reg § 1.631-3(c)(1)) But if the right to cut or to mine ends or is abandoned before the timber, coal or iron ore that has been paid for is cut or mined, the advance payments for them are ordinary income. (Reg § 1.631-2(d)(2), Reg § 1.631-3(c)(2))

If the taxpayer elects to treat the date of payment as the date of disposal of timber (Code Sec. 631(b); Reg § 1.631-2(b)(1)), Section 1231 applies only if the timber is held for the required period at the time of the advance payment. (Reg § 1.631-2(c)(2)) If the election isn't made, the required holding period is measured as of the time it's cut. (Reg § 1.631-2(d)(1))[29] This election is made by attaching a specified statement to the return (filed not later than the due date, including extensions) for the year payment is received. (Reg § 1.631-2(c))[30]

¶ 2690 Sale of Depreciable Property to Related Parties. ▰▰▰▰▰▰

Any recognized gain on the sale or exchange of depreciable property is ordinary income if it's made directly or indirectly between related persons.

---

22. ¶N-6201; ¶12,314; TD ¶271,603
23. ¶N-6213
24. ¶N-6208; ¶6314.01 *et seq.*; TD ¶271,603
25. ¶N-6212.1; ¶6314.02; TD ¶271,604
26. ¶N-7001 *et seq.*; ¶6314; TD ¶223,208

27. ¶N-7001.1; ¶6314
28. ¶N-7021; ¶6114.013
29. ¶N-7025 *et seq.*; ¶6314 *et seq.*
30. ¶N-7026

¶ 2691　Capital gain bar on sales or exchanges of depreciable property.

In a direct or indirect sale or exchange of property between related persons, any gain recognized is treated as ordinary income if that property is, in the hands of the transferee, subject to the Code Sec. 167 allowance for depreciation, or an amortizable Code Sec. 197 intangible asset. (Code Sec. 197(f)(7), Code Sec. 1239(a)) It also applies to property that would be subject to depreciation except that the buyer has elected amortization instead of depreciation (Reg § 1.1239-1(a)), and to patent applications. (Code Sec. 1239(e))[31]

Related persons are:

(1) a person and all entities that are controlled entities with respect to that person (see below) (Code Sec. 1239(b)(1));

(2) a taxpayer and any trust in which the taxpayer or his spouse is a beneficiary (unless the interest is a remote contingent interest) (Code Sec. 1239(b)(2));

(3) an employer and any person related to the employer (within the meaning of (1) and (2) above) (Code Sec. 1239(d)(1));

(4) a welfare benefit fund controlled directly or indirectly by anyone in (3), above (Code Sec. 1239(d)(2)); and

(5) an executor of an estate and a beneficiary of the estate (except in the case of a sale or exchange in satisfaction of a pecuniary bequest). (Code Sec. 1239(b)(3))[32]

A controlled entity ((l), above) means, with respect to any person:

. . . a corporation more than 50% of the value of the stock of which is owned (directly or indirectly) by or for the person (Code Sec. 1239(c)(1)(A)),

. . . a partnership more than 50% of the capital interest or profits interest in which is owned (directly or indirectly) by or for the person (Code Sec. 1239(c)(1)(B)), or

. . . any entity that is a related person to the person under Code Sec. 267(b)(3) (controlled group of corporations), Code Sec. 267(b)(10) (certain related corporations and partnerships), Code Sec. 267(b)(11) (S corporations controlled by the same person) or Code Sec. 267(b)(12) (S corporations and C corporations controlled by the same person). (Code Sec. 1239(c)(1)(C))

And, under Code Sec. 267(c), there is attribution for stock owned by children, grandchildren, ancestors and siblings, as well as by the spouse. (Code Sec. 1239(c)(2))[33]

¶ 2692　Depreciation Recapture. ▆▆▆▆▆▆▆▆▆▆▆▆▆▆

Two provisions restrict the possibility of converting ordinary income into capital gains by use of depreciation or amortization deductions.

One applies to personal property that is Section 1245 property; the other, to real property that is Section 1250 property. (Code Sec. 1245(a)(3), Code Sec. 1250(c)) Recapture applies only to the extent of gain on a sale or other "disposition" (¶2699) of property. (Code Sec. 1245(a)(1), Code Sec. 1250(a)) Compute recapture on Form 4797.

> ⚫*recommendation:* To avoid realizing recapture income, consider trading in the property for replacement property in a tax-free exchange, and using depreciable property to exhaustion, instead of selling it, if practical.

---

31. ¶I-8702; ¶12,394; TD ¶229,601
32. ¶I-8703 *et seq.*; ¶12,394; TD ¶229,602

33. ¶I-8708; ¶12,394; TD ¶229,605

¶ 2693   What is Section 1245 property?

Section 1245 property includes:

(1) all MACRS property other than residential real property (27.5-year class) and nonresidential real property (39-year class; 31.5-year class if placed in service before May 13, '93);

(2) all ACRS property other than 19-year, 18-year or 15-year real property: (a) that is residential rental property, (b) that is foreign-held realty, (c) with respect to which an optional (straight-line) cost recovery period was elected, or (d) that includes any one of certain categories of subsidized low-income rental housing;

(3) other property subject to the depreciation rules of Code Sec. 167 or the amortization rules of Code Sec. 197 (¶1979) that's personal property, certain real property (not including buildings) and real property to the extent of certain amortization (or Code Sec. 179) deductions taken.[34]

Section 1245 property includes property, other than a building or its structural components, used as an integral part of manufacturing, production or extraction, or for furnishing transportation, communication or other public utility services, and research or storage facilities used in connection with any of these activities. It also includes single purpose agricultural or horticultural structures, and storage facilities (except buildings and their structural components) used in distributing petroleum or any primary product of petroleum. (Code Sec. 1245(a)(3); Reg § 1.1245-3)[35]

¶ 2694   What is Section 1250 property?

All real property subject to depreciation that isn't Section 1245 property is Section 1250 property. (Code Sec. 1250(c)) Thus, Section 1250 property includes:

(1) MACRS residential real property (in the 27.5-year class) and nonresidential real property (in the 39-year class; 31.5-year class if placed in service before May 13, '93).

(2) The types of ACRS real property that aren't Section 1245 property, see ¶2693.

(3) The following real property placed in service before '81: (a) depreciable intangible real property, such as a leasehold interest in land, (b) all depreciable buildings and their structural components, and (c) other depreciable real property excluded from the definition of Section 1245 property (¶2693). (Reg § 1.1250-1(e)(3))[36]

¶ 2695   Recapture rules for Section 1245 property.

A gain on the disposition (¶2699) of Section 1245 property is treated as ordinary income to the extent of depreciation or amortization allowed or allowable on the property. (Code Sec. 1245(a))[37] The following deductions are treated as amortization for purposes of the Section 1245 recapture rules: the expense deduction under Code Sec. 179 (¶1944 *et seq.*); the deduction for clean fuel vehicles placed in service before 2006 under Code Sec. 179A; the deductions for refining costs under Code Sec. 179B and Code Sec. 179C (¶1970); the deduction for the cost of energy efficient commercial buildings under ¶179D (¶1971); the deduction for the costs incurred before 2009 of qualified film and TV productions under Code Sec. 181 (¶1969); qualified architectural and transportation barrier removal expenses under Code Sec. 190 (¶1667); and reforestation expenses under Code Sec. 194 (¶1974). (Code Sec. 1245(a)(2)(C))[38]

---

34. ¶I-10101 *et seq.*; ¶12,454.01; TD ¶223,105
35. ¶I-10101; ¶12,454.01; TD ¶223,105
36. ¶I-10112 *et seq.*; ¶12,504.01; TD ¶223,109

37. ¶I-10200 *et seq.*; ¶12,454; TD ¶223,102
38. ¶I-10204; ¶12,454.05; TD ¶223,103

The environmental remediation expensing deduction (¶1669) (Code Sec. 198(e)),[39] the commercial revitalization deduction (¶1976) (Code Sec. 1400I(f)(2)),[40] and the amortization of a Section 197 intangible (¶1979) (Code Sec. 197(f)(7)) also are subject to recapture under Code Sec. 1245.[41]

The amount of gain treated as ordinary income on the disposition is limited to the lower of:

(1) the recomputed basis of the property minus the adjusted basis of the property. (Code Sec. 1245(a)(1)(A)) Recomputed basis is the adjusted basis of the property increased by the recapturable depreciation and amortization deductions reflected in the adjusted basis (Code Sec. 1245(a)(2)); or

(2) in the case of a sale, exchange or involuntary conversion, the amount realized minus the adjusted basis of the property; or in the case of any other disposition, the fair market value of the property minus the adjusted basis of the property. (Code Sec. 1245(a)(1)(B))[42]

If a taxpayer disposes of more than one amortizable Code Sec. 197 intangible (¶1979) after Aug. 8, 2005 in a transaction or a series of related transactions, all of the amortizable intangibles are treated as one Code Sec. 1245 property for purposes of the recapture rules. However, this rule does not apply to such an intangible if its adjusted basis exceeds its fair market value. (Code Sec. 1245(b)(8))

¶ 2696   Recapture rules for Section 1250 property.

Part or all of the gain on the sale or other disposition (¶2699) of Section 1250 property may be treated as ordinary income. (Code Sec. 1250(a))[43] But where property was held more than one year, there's no depreciation recapture if it was depreciated via straight line. (Code Sec. 1250(b)) Thus, Section 1250 recapture doesn't apply to residential rental or nonresidential real property depreciated under MACRS. For Section 1250 property held more than one year, the amount of gain treated as ordinary income is the lower of (1) the "applicable percentage" of the portion of the "additional depreciation" (see below) attributable to periods after '75, or (2) in the case of a sale, exchange or involuntary conversion, the excess of the amount realized over the adjusted basis, or in the case of any other disposition, the fair market value of the property over its adjusted basis. (Code Sec. 1250(a)(1))[44]

Special rules apply to determine the amount to be recaptured as ordinary income for (a) additional depreciation attributable to periods after '69 and before '76 to determine the amount to be recaptured as ordinary income (Code Sec. 1250(a)(2)),[45] and (b) additional depreciation attributable to periods before '70. (Code Sec. 1250(a)(3))[46]

Additional depreciation is the excess of actual post-'63 depreciation deductions over the amount that would have resulted during the same period had the straight-line method been used for the entire period the property was held. (Code Sec. 1250(b)(1); Code Sec. 1250(b)(3))[47] For additional amounts for corporations, see ¶2697.

The applicable percentage differs depending upon various factors, including whether the property is nonresidential real property, residential real property or low income housing. [48]

For the tax treatment of a noncorporate taxpayer's unrecaptured Code Sec. 1250 gain, see ¶2605.

---

39. ¶L-6150.3; ¶1984
40. ¶L-12709; ¶14,00I4; TD ¶269,308
41. ¶L-7981.2; ¶1974; TD ¶223,103
42. ¶I-10200; ¶12,454.05; TD ¶223,102
43. ¶I-10400 *et seq.*; ¶12,504; TD ¶223,107

44. ¶I-10400 *et seq.*; ¶12,504.06; TD ¶223,110
45. ¶I-10402; ¶12,504.06; TD ¶223,110
46. ¶I-10402; ¶12,504.06; TD ¶223,110
47. ¶I-10403; ¶12,504.06; TD ¶223,110
48. ¶I-10417 *et seq.*; ¶s 12,394, 12,504.06; TD ¶223,111

¶ 2697   Additional 20% recapture on disposition of realty by corporations.

For sales or other dispositions (of both residential and nonresidential property), 20% of the amount by which the gain recapturable if Section 1245 rules applied exceeds the gain recaptured under Section 1250 is treated as ordinary income (to the extent of gain) to a corporation. (Code Sec. 291(a))[49] This rule applies to an S corporation only if it was formerly a C corporation for any of the three immediately preceding tax years. (Code Sec. 1363(b)(4))[50]

¶ 2698   Treatment of basis reduction for investment credit.

In determining the recapturable amount, the reduction of basis for the investment credit is treated as a deduction allowed for depreciation. (Code Sec. 50(c)(4)(A))[1] However, this basis reduction is disregarded in computing straight-line depreciation for purposes of determining "additional depreciation" subject to recapture for Section 1250 property. (Code Sec. 50(c)(4)(B))[2]

¶ 2699   Transactions and events that trigger or escape depreciation recapture.

The following is a list of transactions and events that either trigger or escape depreciation recapture:

* A sale in a sale and leaseback transaction, a sale under a conditional sales contract, and a transfer of title back to the seller, creditor, or new purchaser upon foreclosure of a security interest, triggers recapture, but not a transfer of legal title to a creditor upon creation of a security interest, or a transfer of legal title to a debtor upon termination of a security interest. (Reg § 1.1245-1(a)(3), Reg § 1.1250-1(a)(2)(i))

* Trade-ins, exchanges and involuntary conversions. Section 1245 depreciation not recaptured unless gain is recognized or non-Section 1245 property is acquired. (Code Sec. 1245(b)(4); Reg § 1.1245-4(b)) Section 1250 depreciation not recaptured except where gain is recognized, stock is bought to acquire control of a corporation owning replacement property, or non-Section 1250 property is acquired. (Code Sec. 1250(d)(4); Reg § 1.1250-3(d))

* Conversion to personal use doesn't trigger recapture, but a later sale will.

* Lease termination or disposition where depreciation was taken by lessee (or sublessee). Generally recaptured. (Reg § 1.1245-2(a)(3)(i))

* Incorporation of a business. Not recaptured except to the extent that gain is otherwise recognized. (Code Sec. 1245(b)(3), Code Sec. 1250(d)(3); Reg § 1.1245-4(c), Reg § 1.1250-3(c))

* Corporate distributions in kind including liquidating distributions. Generally recaptured except in tax-free complete liquidation of a subsidiary with carryover basis (recaptured on disposition by parent-transferee). (Code Sec. 1245(b)(3), Code Sec. 1250(d)(3); Reg § 1.1245-4(c), Reg § 1.1250-3(c))

* Corporate split-ups and reorganizations. Generally not recaptured except to extent that gain is otherwise recognized on transfer of the property. (Code Sec. 1245(b)(3), Code Sec. 1250(d)(3); Reg § 1.1245-4(c), Reg § 1.1250-3(c))

* S corporations. Not recaptured on election or termination of status.

* Partnerships. Recaptured on sale of partnership interest. Not recaptured on contribution to a partnership but may be if property is subject to a liability. (Code Sec. 1245(a), Code Sec. 1245(b)(6), Code Sec. 1250(a), Code Sec. 1250(d)(6); Reg § 1.1245-1(e), Reg § 1.1250-

49. ¶I-10422 *et seq.*; ¶2914; TD ¶223,108
50. ¶I-10422; ¶2914, 13634.01; TD ¶614,503,

1. ¶I-10204; ¶12,454 *et seq.*; TD ¶223,103
2. ¶I-10507

3(f))

• Gifts. Not recaptured, but recapturable depreciation carried over to donee. (Code Sec. 1245(b)(1), Code Sec. 1250(d)(1); Reg § 1.1245-2(a)(4), Reg § 1.1250-3(a))

• Death of owner. Neither recaptured nor carried over (except as provided under the Code Sec. 691 rules (income in respect of a decedent). (Code Sec. 1245(b)(2), Code Sec. 1250(d)(2); Reg § 1.1245-4(b), Reg § 1.1250-3(b))[3]

• Gain realized by an estate or trust from distribution of depreciable property in satisfaction of a fixed dollar bequest or from a distribution in kind where gain or loss is realized by election is recapturable. (Reg § 1.1245-4(b), Reg § 1.1250-3(b))[4]

For the effect of depreciation recapture on installment sales, see ¶2453.

¶ 2700 Special recapture rules for listed property.

A reduction of business use of listed property (¶1950 *et seq.*) from more-than-50% to 50% or less triggers recapture of excess depreciation previously taken. (Code Sec. 280F(b)(2)(A)) "Excess depreciation" means depreciation allowable for years before the first year in which the property wasn't predominantly used in a qualified business use, over the amount of depreciation which would have been allowable for those years if the property hadn't been predominantly used in a qualified business use for the year it was acquired and there had been no Section 179 expense election for the property. (Code Sec. 280F(b)(2)(B))[5]

---

3. ¶I-10002, I-10301 *et seq.*; ¶s 12,454.03, 12,504.01; TD ¶223,114   5. ¶L-10032; ¶280F4; TD ¶267,625
4. ¶C-7154; ¶s 12,454.03, 12,504.01; TD ¶223,114

Chapter 11 Tax Accounting—Inventories

¶ 2800 Accounting Periods. ▐███████████████████████████

Each taxpayer must compute taxable income and file a return on the basis of an accounting period called a tax year. An S corporation generally has to use a calendar year as its tax year unless it specially elects to use a fiscal year. So does a personal service corporation. A partnership generally has to use a "majority interest tax year" unless it makes the fiscal year election.

¶ 2801 Tax year.

Taxpayers must compute their taxable income on the basis of their tax year. (Code Sec. 441(a); Reg § 1.441-1(a)) "Tax year" is the taxpayer's annual accounting period (the annual period on the basis of which the taxpayer regularly computes his income in keeping his books) (Code Sec. 441(c)), but only if that's the calendar year or a fiscal year. (Code Sec. 441(b)(1))[1]

The calendar year is the 12-month period ending on Dec. 31. (Code Sec. 441(d)) A taxpayer must use the calendar year, if the taxpayer keeps no books (unless it gets IRS consent to use a fiscal year (Reg § 1.441-1(c)(2))), or has no annual accounting period, or has an annual accounting period that doesn't qualify as a fiscal year (Code Sec. 441(b)(2), Code Sec. 441(g)), or if the taxpayer hasn't established a fiscal year. (Reg § 1.441-1(b)(1)(iv))[2]

A fiscal year is any 12-month period ending on the last day of a month other than December, or the 52-53 week tax year described at ¶2802. (Code Sec. 441(e))[3]

If a return is properly made for a period of less than 12 months (see ¶2804), the tax year is the short tax year for which the return is made. (Code Sec. 441(b)(3))[4]

Certain taxpayers must use a required tax year. (Code Sec. 441(f)(3), Code Sec. 441(f)(4), Reg § 1.441-1(b)(2))

¶ 2802 Tax year of 52-53 weeks.

A 52-53 week tax year varies from 52 to 53 weeks and always ends on the same day of the week. The day chosen must be either the day of the week that last occurs in a calendar month or the day that falls nearest to the end of the calendar month (in which case the last day of the tax year may fall in the next month). (Code Sec. 441(f)(1); Reg § 1.441-2(a)(1)) A taxpayer may elect a 52-53 week tax year if it otherwise satisfies Code Sec. 441 and its regs. (Reg § 1.441-2(a)(3))[5]

Wherever the applicability of any provision of the Code, or filing date, is expressed in terms of tax years beginning, including, or ending with reference to a specified date that's the first or last day of the month, the actual opening and closing dates of 52-53 week years are disregarded. The year is considered to begin on the first day of the calendar month beginning nearest to the first day of that tax year, and to end on the last day of the calendar month ending nearest to the last day of that tax year. (Code Sec. 441(f)(2)(A))[6]

If a pass-through entity or an pass-through owner, or both, use a 52-53-week tax year and the tax years of both end with reference to the same calendar month, then, for purposes of determining the tax year in which pass-through items are taken into account by its owner, the owner's tax is deemed to end on the last day of the pass-through's tax year. (Reg § 1.441-

---

1. ¶G-1000 *et seq.*; ¶4414; TD ¶431,001
2. ¶s G-1001, G-1003; ¶4414; TD ¶431,001
3. ¶G-1004; ¶4414; TD ¶431,006
4. ¶s G-1001; ¶4414; TD ¶431,001
5. ¶G-1101; ¶4414; TD ¶432,501
6. ¶G-1103; ¶4414; TD ¶432,503

References beginning with a single letter are to paragraphs in RIA's Federal Tax Coordinator 2d and RIA's Analysis of Federal Taxes: Income. Those beginning with numbers are to paragraphs in RIA's United States Tax Reporter. Those beginning with TD are to paragraphs in RIA's Tax Desk.

2(e)(1)) Similarly, if the tax year of a personal service corporation (PSC) and an employee-owner end with reference to the same calendar month, then for purposes of determining the tax year in which an employee-owner takes into account items that are deductible by the PSC and includible in the income of the employee-owner, the employee-owner's tax year is deemed to end on the last day of the PSC's tax year. (Reg § 1.441-2(e)(2))

¶ 2803 Establishing a tax year.

A new taxpayer generally may adopt any tax year that satisfies Code Sec. 441 and its regs, without IRS approval, by filing its first federal income tax return using that tax year. (Reg § 1.441-1(c)(1)) However, a newly formed partnership, S corporation, or personal service corporation that wants to adopt a tax year other than its required tax year, a tax year elected under Code Sec. 444 (¶2813), or a 52-53 week tax year (¶2802) that ends with reference to its required tax year or one elected under Code Sec. 444 must establish a business purpose and get IRS approval. (Reg § 1.441-1(c)(2)) Use Form 1128 following IRS procedures. [7]

If taxpayer's "annual accounting period" (¶2801), as established by the basis on which taxpayer keeps his books, is the calendar year or a fiscal year, his tax year is that annual accounting period. (Code Sec. 441(b)(1), Code Sec. 441(c)) Otherwise, the taxpayer must use the calendar year as his tax year. (Code Sec. 441(b)(2), Code Sec. 441(g))[8]

A new taxpayer using a 52-53 week tax year (¶2802) must file a statement (specified in the regs) with the return for its first 52-53 week tax year. (Reg § 1.441-2(b)(1)(ii))[9]

¶ 2804 Short tax years.

A taxpayer must use a tax "year" of less than 12 months if: (1) the taxpayer isn't in existence for what would otherwise be his full tax year (Code Sec. 443(a)(2));[10] or (2) the taxpayer properly changes his annual accounting period (¶2814). (Code Sec. 443(a)(1))[11] But if the short year arises because of the taxpayer's death, his last return may be filed and the tax paid as if he had lived to the end of his last tax year. (Reg § 1.443-1(a)(2))[12]

For filing requirements for short years, see ¶ 4717 and ¶ 4725.

¶ 2805 Computing tax for a short year.

If the short year results from a change of the taxpayer's annual accounting period, the short period's taxable income must be annualized. (Code Sec. 443(b))

Under the general method of annualization, gross income for the short period (less allowable deductions for the short period and, for individuals, the ratable amount of personal exemptions) is multiplied by 12 (months) and divided by the number of months in the short period. The result is the annualized taxable income on which the tentative tax is computed. The tax due is arrived at by multiplying the tentative tax by the number of months in the short period and dividing by 12. (Code Sec. 443(b)(1); Reg § 1.443-1(b)(1)(i))[13] Special annualization rules apply to the alternative minimum tax. (Code Sec. 443(d))[14]

There are exceptions to the annualization requirements for self-employment tax, accumulated earnings tax, personal holding company tax, undistributed foreign personal holding company income and income of regulated investment companies. [15]

The net operating loss (NOL) deduction can reduce actual income for the short period before computing short period income on an annual basis. Therefore, if the NOL deduction

---

7. ¶4414; TD ¶432,001
8. ¶G-1051; ¶4414; TD ¶432,001
9. ¶s G-1054, G-1753; ¶4414; TD ¶432,004
10. ¶G-1153; ¶4434; TD ¶431,011
11. ¶G-1155; ¶4434; TD ¶431,011

12. ¶G-1154; ¶4434; TD ¶431,011
13. ¶G-1166; ¶4434; TD ¶431,012
14. ¶A-8119; ¶4434; TD ¶691,018
15. ¶G-1163; ¶4434

wipes out short period actual income there would be nothing to annualize and therefore no short period taxable income. [16]

The income is *not* annualized if the short year is caused by the taxpayer not being in existence for a full tax year. (Code Sec. 443(b)) In this case, tax is computed as if the short period were a full year, and individuals need not prorate their personal exemptions. (Reg § 1.443-1(a)(2))[17]

If a taxpayer changes to or from a 52-53 week year, income for the short period must be annualized, with this exception: if the short period is 359 days or more, it is treated as a full tax year, while if it is six days or less it is added to the following tax year. (Reg § 1.443-1(b)(1)(ii))[18]

¶ 2806   Optional look-back method of computing tax for the short period.

The annualizing method at ¶2805 may create a tax hardship for taxpayers who have a disproportionately large amount of taxable income in the short period. To avoid this, taxpayers may use an optional method that computes the tax for the full 12 months starting at the beginning of the short year and prorates the tax according to the amount of income earned in the short period. (Code Sec. 443(b)(2))

The optional method is available only on a claim for credit or refund, filed no later than the due date (including extensions) of taxpayer's return for the first tax year that ends on or after the day that is 12 months after the first day of the short period. (Reg § 1.443-1(b)(2)(v)(a))[19]

¶ 2807   Tax year of sole proprietorship.

A sole proprietorship must use the same tax year as the proprietor. Thus, a calendar year employee who later operates as a sole proprietorship must use the calendar year for the proprietorship unless he gets IRS consent to use a fiscal year. [20]

¶ 2808   Tax years of trusts and estates.

Trusts must use the calendar year, except for trusts exempt from tax under Code Sec. 501(a), wholly charitable trusts described in Code Sec. 4947(a)(1) (Code Sec. 644)[21] and grantor trusts.[22] Estates may adopt either a calendar year or a fiscal year. [23]

¶ 2809   Tax years of foreign sales corporations and DISCs.

Foreign Sales Corporations (FSCs) and Domestic International Sales Corporations (DISCs) must use the tax year of the shareholder (or group of shareholders with the same 12-month tax year) with the highest percentage of voting power. (Code Sec. 441(h)(1))[24]

¶ 2810   Tax year of S corporation.

An S corporation (unless it makes the election at ¶2813, or elects a 52-53 week tax year (¶2802) ending with reference to its required year) must have a "required year," i.e., a calendar year or any other accounting year for which it shows a business purpose satisfactory to IRS; use Form 2553. (Code Sec. 1378; Reg § 1.441-1(b)(2)(i)(L); Reg § 1.441-1(b)(2)(ii)(B); Reg § 1.1378-1(a))[25]

---

16. ¶G-1166; ¶4434; TD ¶431,012
17. ¶G-1162; ¶4434; TD ¶431,012
18. ¶G-1108; ¶4434
19. ¶G-1170 *et seq.*; ¶4434; TD ¶431,013
20. ¶G-1062; ¶4414; TD ¶432,006

21. ¶G-1400; ¶6454; TD ¶651,009
22. ¶G-1401; ¶6454; TD ¶651,009
23. ¶C-7008; ¶4414; TD ¶661,008
24. ¶O-1726; ¶4414
25. ¶G-1250; ¶13,784; TD ¶433,201

¶ 2811   Tax year of personal service corporation.

The tax year of a personal service corporation (PSC) must be a calendar year unless the corporation makes the election at ¶2813, elects a 52-53 week tax year ending with reference to the calendar year or the year elected under the rules at ¶2813, or can satisfy IRS that there's a business purpose for a different tax year. (Code Sec. 441(i)(1); Reg § 1.441-1(b)(2)(i)(B); Reg § 1.441-3(a))[26]

A PSC is, as defined under the rules permitting IRS to reallocate PSC income and deductions (¶2859), any corporation whose principal activity is the performance of personal services that are substantially performed by employee-owners. But for this purpose PSC doesn't include S corporations, and the term "owner-employee" includes all employees with *any* stock ownership in the corporation. In determining ownership, attribution from a corporation (under Code Sec. 318(a)(2)(C)) is applied if *any* stock is owned by the shareholder in that corporation. (Code Sec. 441(i)(2))[27] Certain independent contractors who own stock in the corporation and perform personal services for or on behalf of it are treated as employees. (Reg § 1.441-3(g)(2))[28]

The performance of personal services is considered the corporation's principal activity if the corporation's compensation cost for a testing period for activities that are considered the performance of personal services exceeds 50% of its total compensation cost for the period. (Reg § 1.441-3(e)(1)) The testing period is the preceding tax year (or, for a corporation's first tax year, the period beginning the first day of the first tax year and ending the last day of that tax year or, if earlier, the last day of the calendar year in which that tax year began). (Reg § 1.441-3(c)(2)) Personal services are substantially performed by employee-owners if during the testing period more than 20% of the corporation's compensation cost (excluding qualified plan or SEP contributions) attributable to the performance of personal services is attributable to personal services performed by employee-owners. (Reg § 1.441-3(f)); Reg § 1.441-3(e)(2)(ii))[29]

¶ 2812   Tax year of partnership—"majority interest tax year."

Unless the partnership makes the election at ¶2813, or can satisfy IRS that there's a business purpose for a different tax year (Code Sec. 706(b)(1)(C))[30] a partnership must adopt:

(1) the "majority interest tax year" (Code Sec. 706(b)(1)(B)(i))—the tax year of one or more of the partners having an aggregate interest in partnership profits and capital of more than 50% on each testing day (the first day of the partnership's tax year as otherwise determined, or days prescribed by IRS) (Code Sec. 706(b)(4)(A));

(2) the tax year of all its principal (5%-or-more) partners, if there's no majority interest tax year (Code Sec. 706(b)(1)(B)(ii));

(3) the "least-aggregate-deferral" year, if there's no majority interest tax year and the principal partners don't have the same tax year. (Code Sec. 706(b)(1)(B)(iii); Reg § 1.706-1(b)(2)(i)(C))[31]

A partnership may have a tax year other than its required year if it makes an election under Code Sec. 444 (¶2813), elects to use a 52-53-week tax year (¶2802) that ends with reference to its required year or a tax year elected under Code Sec. 444, or establishes a business purpose for it and gets IRS approval. (Reg § 1.706-1(b)(2)(ii))

A partnership that's required to change to a majority-interest tax year isn't required to change to another tax year for either of the two tax years following the year of change. (Code

---

26. ¶G-1300; ¶4414; TD ¶433,401
27. ¶G-1302; ¶4414; TD ¶433,403
28. ¶G-1306; ¶4414

29. ¶G-1303; ¶4414
30. ¶G-1200 *et seq.*; ¶7064.01; TD ¶433,002
31. ¶G-1200 *et seq.*; ¶7064.01; TD ¶433,001

Sec. 706(b)(4)(B))[32]

A partnership tax year ends as dictated by the accounting period selected or required, except that it closes earlier: (1) for a partner who sells his entire interest or whose interest is completely liquidated (Code Sec. 706(c); (Reg § 1.706-1(c)(2)(i)), and (2) with respect to all its partners on the date the partnership terminates for tax purposes. (Reg § 1.706-1(c)(1))[33]

¶ 2813   Section 444 election of tax year other than required tax year—Form 8716; Form 8752; Form 1120, Schedule H.

An S corporation, personal service corporation (PSC), or partnership may elect (on Form 8716) to have a tax year other than the required tax year (Code Sec. 444(a)), but only if the deferral period (number of months between beginning of elected fiscal tax year and following Dec. 31) for the tax year elected isn't longer than three months. (Code Sec. 444(b)(1); Reg § 1.444-1T(b))[34]

A partnership or S corporation that elects has to make a "required payment" (report on Form 8752) that approximates the tax the partners or S corporation shareholders would have paid on short-period income if the election hadn't been made. (Code Sec. 7519; Reg § 1.444-3T)[35]

A PSC that elects a fiscal tax year but doesn't make required minimum distributions to its employee-owners before the end of the calendar year must postpone part or all of its corresponding deduction to its next fiscal tax year. (Code Sec. 280H) To figure the required minimum distribution and maximum deductible amount, use Form 1120, Schedule H. [36]

¶ 2814   How to change accounting periods—Form 1128.

A taxpayer must get prior IRS approval to change accounting periods unless the change is authorized by the Code or one of those listed at ¶2815. (Reg § 1.441-1(e); Reg § 1.442-1(a))[37]

IRS will approve a request for a change in tax years only if the taxpayer establishes a substantial business purpose for the change, [38] and agrees to any terms, conditions or adjustments required to effect the change, including any that IRS feels are necessary to avoid a substantial distortion of the taxpayer's income as a result of the change. (Reg § 1.442-1(b)(1))[39]

To request IRS approval, file Form 1128 within the time and in the manner as provided in IRS administrative procedures. (Reg § 1.442-1(b)(1), (3))[40] Fiscal year individuals must follow an exclusive procedure to change to a calendar year. [41]

If a taxpayer changed its annual accounting period within 48 months before the last month of the requested tax year, a copy of the application for the previous change, the ruling letter, and any other related correspondence from IRS, must be attached to the application. [42]

Limitations apply to the carryback of certain NOLs and capital losses generated in the short period necessary to effect a change of tax year. [43]

¶ 2815   "No prior approval needed" changes of accounting period.

A taxpayer that has adopted a tax year generally must continue to use it unless it obtains IRS approval to change or is otherwise authorized to change without the IRS approval under

---

32. ¶G-1201; ¶7064.01
33. ¶G-1224, G-1225; ¶7064.02; TD ¶433,024
34. ¶G-1500 *et seq.*; ¶4444; TD ¶434,003
35. ¶s G-1500, G-1550; ¶75,194; TD ¶434,012
36. ¶G-1600; ¶280H4; TD ¶434,014
37. ¶G-1800; ¶4424; TD ¶435,000

38. ¶G-1803 *et seq.*; ¶4424; TD ¶435,015
39. ¶G-1812 *et seq.*; ¶4424
40. ¶G-1701.1; ¶4424; TD ¶435,002
41. ¶G-1726; ¶4424; TD ¶436,001
42. ¶G-1882
43. ¶G-1827 *et seq.*; ¶4424; TD ¶439,027

the Code (e.g., Code Sec. 444, ¶2813) or regs. (Reg § 1.442-1(a))[44] A taxpayer may change his annual accounting period without IRS approval, or with "automatic" IRS approval, where the taxpayer:

. . . changes to a 52-53 week tax year that ends with reference to the same calendar month as the month ending his previous tax year (Reg § 1.441-2(b)(2));[45]

. . . is an individual who marries a person with a different tax year (Reg § 1.442-1(d)(1));[46]

. . . is an individual with a fiscal year tax year who changes to a calendar year tax year; [47]

. . . is a partnership changing its tax year to meet the tests described at ¶2812;[48]

. . . is a C corporation that meets certain tests; [49]

. . . is an S corporation changing its tax year to meet the tests described at ¶2810;[50]

. . . is a personal service corporation changing to a calendar year or a 52-53 week tax year ending with reference to a calendar year; (Reg § 1.441-3(b)(2))[1]

. . . is a subsidiary corporation required to change its tax year to that of members of its affiliated group that file a consolidated return. (Reg § 1.442-1(c))

¶ 2816 Accounting Methods. ▬▬▬▬▬▬▬▬

Methods of tax accounting are the methods and systems by which taxpayers determine the amount of their income, gains, losses, deductions and credits, as well as the time when those items must be realized and recognized. Various methods of tax accounting are permissible, but each must be used consistently, and each must clearly reflect income.

¶ 2817 Establishing a method of accounting.

Because a taxpayer's book accounting method determines his accounting method, a taxpayer establishes a tax accounting method by setting up books, keeping accounts, and preparing income tax returns under any of the permissible methods. The method first used in accounting for business income and deductions in connection with each trade or business, as evidenced in the taxpayer's income tax return in which the income or deductions are first reported, must be followed consistently after that. (Reg § 1.446-1(d)(1))[2] The requirement to maintain books and records can be met by using certain electronic storage systems. [3]

A taxpayer may use one method of accounting to keep personal books and another to keep the books for his trade or business. But the two must be strictly separated. (Reg § 1.446-1(c)(1)(iv)(b))

A taxpayer whose only income is wages doesn't have to keep formal books in order to establish an accounting method, but may establish a method of accounting by means of tax returns (or copies) or other records. (Reg § 1.446-1(b)(2))[4]

A new taxpayer may adopt a method of accounting in connection with filing the first income tax return. An existing taxpayer entering into a business that's separate and distinct from any trade or business that the taxpayer previously carried on may adopt a method of accounting for the separate and distinct business in connection with filing the first tax return reporting income from the business. (Reg § 1.446-1(e)(1))[5]

Use of different accounting methods isn't permitted if there's a creation or shifting of profits or losses between the taxpayer's various trades or businesses (e.g., by using inventory

---

44. ¶G-1701; ¶s 4424, 7064.01; TD ¶435,001
45. ¶G-1101; ¶4414; TD ¶432,501
46. ¶G-1708; ¶4424; TD ¶435,013
47. ¶G-1725; ¶4424; TD ¶436,001
48. ¶G-1222; ¶4424; TD ¶433,020
49. ¶G-1800 *et seq.*; ¶4424; TD ¶435,008

50. ¶G-1250.1; ¶13,784; TD ¶433,201
1. ¶G-1301; ¶4424; TD ¶433,402
2. ¶G-2051; ¶4464.01; TD ¶440,518
3. ¶G-2019; ¶60,014; TD ¶440,509 *et seq.*
4. ¶G-2051; TD ¶440,518
5. ¶G-2051; ¶4464.01; TD ¶440,518

adjustments, sales, purchases or expenses, and this results in a distortion of the taxpayer's income). (Reg § 1.446-1(d)(3))[6]

Taxpayers may use any combination of the cash, accrual, and specifically permitted special methods of accounting if the combination clearly reflects income and is consistently used. (Reg § 1.446-1(c)(1)(iv))[7]

¶ 2818   Limits on choice of accounting methods.

The accrual method is mandatory for purchases and sales (unless IRS consents to a change) where inventories must be used. (Reg § 1.446-1(c)(2)(i)) Inventories must be used where the production, purchase or sale of merchandise is an income-producing factor. (Reg § 1.446-1(a)(4)(i))[8] However, exceptions apply for certain small businesses:

- *$1 million or less average gross receipts.* Taxpayers (other than tax shelters) with 3-year average annual gross receipts of $1 million or less do not have to account for inventories or use an accrual method of accounting. Instead they may treat merchandise inventory in the same way that cash method taxpayers must treat material or supplies that are not inciden- tal (under Reg § 1.162-3). Generally, a taxpayer has average annual gross receipts of $1 million or less if for each earlier tax year, its (or its predecessor's) average annual gross receipts for the 3-tax-year period ending with the applicable prior tax year does not exceed $1 million (using the method of accounting actually used for federal tax purposes). [9]

- *More than $1 million but not more than $10 million average gross receipts.* Qualifying small businesses with 3-year average annual gross receipts of more than $1,000,000 but not more than $10,000,000 that are not prohibited from using the cash method under Code Sec. 448 (see below) and otherwise would have to keep inventories and use accrual account- ing may, instead, use the cash method for an eligible trade or business. Generally, a taxpayer has average annual gross receipts of $10 million or less if, for each prior tax year ending after Dec. 30, 2000, its average annual gross receipts for the 3-tax-year period ending with the applicable prior tax year does not exceed $10 million. Qualifying small businesses that may use the cash method for all of their trades and businesses are: (1) businesses whose principal business activity for the immediately preceding tax year is other than mining, manufacturing, wholesale trade, retail trade, or information industries; (2) service providers, including those providing property incident to those services; and (3) fabricators or modifiers of tangible personal property on demand in accordance with cus- tomer design or specifications. [10]

C corporations (other than qualified personal service corporations), and partnerships with a C corporation (other than a qualified personal service corporation) as a partner, with average annual gross receipts of more than $5 million for any prior 3-tax-year period (or the period of its existence, if less) can't use the cash method. Tax shelters can't use the cash method in any event. (Code Sec. 448(a))[11] The limitation on the cash method doesn't apply to farming busi- nesses (except tax shelters) (Code Sec. 448(b)(1)), but for special farm accounting rules, see ¶4504 *et seq.* [12] For purposes of these restrictions, an accounting method that records some but not all items on the cash method (i.e., a hybrid method) is treated as the cash method of accounting. (Reg § 1.448-1T(a)(4))[13] Tax-exempt trusts are treated as C corporations with respect to unrelated trade or business income. (Code Sec. 448(d)(6))[14]

---

6. ¶G-2052; ¶4464.01; TD ¶440,803
7. ¶G-2003; ¶4464.09; TD ¶440,802
8. ¶G-5000; ¶4464.07; TD ¶440,827
9. ¶G-5005A, ¶G-5005.3; ¶4714.10; TD ¶450,508
10. ¶G-5005.4; ¶4714.15

11. ¶G-2054; ¶4484; TD ¶440,806
12. ¶G-2057; ¶s 614.053, 4474; TD ¶440,814
13. ¶G-2054; ¶4484; TD ¶440,806
14. ¶G-2055; ¶4484; TD ¶440,806

¶ 2819   The Cash Method of Accounting.

Under the cash method, gross income includes cash or property actually or constructively received during the tax year. Deductions are usually taken in the year cash or property is actually paid or transferred. It doesn't matter when the income was earned, or when the expense was incurred.

¶ 2820   Cash basis accounting.

Under the cash basis method of accounting, income is reported when cash or property is actually or constructively received (¶2822), and deductions are taken in the year cash or property is paid or transferred. [15]

For income a taxpayer receives under a claim of right, see ¶1204. For restrictions on use of the cash method by certain taxpayers, see ¶2818; for exceptions to those restrictions for small businesses, see ¶2818.

¶ 2821   When is a check income?

A check issued by a solvent payor is income when received by a cash basis payee, unless there's a restriction on the payee's right to cash the check. [16] Receipt of a check by an agent is considered receipt by the principal. [17]

¶ 2822   Constructive receipt of income.

Income not actually received is constructively received and reportable if it's within the taxpayer's control. Cash basis taxpayers must report money unconditionally subject to their demand as income, even if they haven't received it. [18] There's no constructive receipt if the amount is available only on surrender of a valuable right, [19] or if there are substantial limits on the right to receive it. (Reg § 1.451-2(a))[20]

¶ 2823   Timing of deductions under the cash method.

Cash method taxpayers generally take deductions (if otherwise allowable) in the year the items are paid. (Reg § 1.461-1(a)(1))[21] There's no constructive payment doctrine. [22]

Where an expense (e.g., rent or an insurance premium) relates to a period covering more than 12 months, IRS and most courts agree that the deduction must be spread over the period to which the expense applies. [23] For an exception for points paid on a home mortgage, see ¶1746. For deduction of prepaid taxes, see ¶1766.

A check is payment when delivered, not when cashed, if it's honored when it's first presented for payment. [24]

¶ 2824   The Accrual Method of Accounting.

Under the accrual method, income is reported in the tax year in which the right to the income becomes fixed and the amount of the income can be determined with reasonable accuracy. Deductions are claimed in the period in which all events have occurred that determine the fact of the liability and the amount of the liability can be determined with reasonable accuracy.

---

15. ¶G-2410 *et seq.*; ¶s 4464.05, 4514.003; TD ¶441,001
16. ¶G-2415; ¶s 4514.003, 4514.004; TD ¶441,003
17. ¶G-2419; TD ¶441,002
18. ¶G-2424; ¶4514.036 *et seq.*; TD ¶441,005
19. ¶G-2426; ¶4514.036; TD ¶441,007

20. ¶G-2425; ¶4514.036; TD ¶441,006
21. ¶G-2436 *et seq.*; ¶4614.01; TD ¶441,401
22. ¶G-2443; TD ¶441,409
23. ¶s L-3526 *et seq.*, L-6616 *et seq.*; ¶1624.081; TD ¶441,410
24. ¶G-2438; ¶4614.02; TD ¶441,404

¶ 2825   Accrual basis accounting.

Income accrues and must be reported in the year all events have occurred that determine taxpayer's right to receive it (¶2832), and the amount can be determined with reasonable accuracy (Reg § 1.451-1(a)), even if it's received in a later year. That is, the right to receive the income must not be contingent on a future event; the amount must be reasonably susceptible of accurate estimate; and there must be a reasonable expectation that it will be received in due course.[25]

Accrual basis taxpayers do not need to accrue income from the performance of services that, based on their experience, will not be collected if, among other things, interest isn't charged on the debt and there is no penalty for late payment. This "nonaccrual experience method" is available only for: (1) amounts owing for services in the fields of health, law, engineering, architecture, accounting, actuarial science, performing arts, or consulting, or (2) other services, if the taxpayer's three-year average annual gross receipts doesn't exceed $5 million. Uncollectible amounts may be determined using specified safe-harbor methods. (Code Sec. 448(d)(5)) A taxpayer's nonaccrual experience method must be tested against actual experience unless he has adopted one of the five safe harbor methods in the regs. (Reg § 1.448-2(d))[26]

¶ 2826   Contingent rights to income.

Where the right to income is contingent on a future event, an accrual basis taxpayer doesn't have to recognize the income until that event occurs. [27]

Advance payments to a retailer under which it agreed to purchase specified amounts from its supplier were held by a court to be income on receipt. But another court found similar cash advances by a wholesaler to a retailer in exchange for a volume purchase commitment not includible on receipt; they were contingent on the purchases being made. Generally adopting the latter approach, IRS allows taxpayers to adopt an Advance Trade Discount Method of accounting in which advance trade discount aren't recognized as income on receipt by accrual method taxpayer with inventories but instead are taken into account in the amount and manner that the retailer accounts for the discount in its financial statements. [28]

Where litigation is involved and liability to the taxpayer is admitted, the income must be recognized if the taxpayer can accurately estimate the amount of recovery. [29] But if liability isn't admitted, the income accrues when the litigation is concluded or settlement reached, whichever is earlier. [30] An offer in compromise is income when the dispute is settled or the offer is unconditionally accepted. [31]

¶ 2827   Income accrual for disputed liability for goods.

If an accrual method taxpayer overbills a customer due to clerical error and the customer discovers the error and, in the following year, disputes its liability, gross income accrues in the year of sale for the correct amount. An accrual method taxpayer does not accrue income in the year of sale if, during that year, the customer disputes its liability because incorrect goods were shipped. However, income does accrue in the year of sale if excess quantities of goods are shipped and the customer agrees to pay for them. [32]

---

25. ¶G-2471; ¶4514.012; TD ¶441,701
26. ¶G-2501 *et seq.*; ¶4514.023 *et seq.*; TD ¶441,707
27. ¶s G-2484, G-2485; ¶s 4514.011, 4514.012; TD ¶441,703
28. ¶G-2483

29. ¶G-2506; ¶s 4514.021, 4514.055; TD ¶441,704
30. ¶G-2506; ¶4514.055; TD ¶441,704
31. ¶s G-2506, G-2507; ¶4514.058
32. ¶G-2511.1

¶ 2828 Dealers' reserves.

Dealers commonly discount customers' notes with a finance company that keeps a portion of the amount due the dealer as security against possible default by the customer. A dealer that uses the accrual method must include the full amount of the discount price, undiminished by the portion retained by the finance company —the "dealer reserve," in income as soon as the notes are sold to the finance company. This is so even if the dealer assigned the notes to the finance company "without recourse."[33]

¶ 2829 Deferral method for certain advance payments.

Under the deferral method of accounting for advance payments, accrual basis taxpayers can defer to the next succeeding tax year the inclusion in gross income of specified advance payments to the extent the advance payments are not recognized in revenues (or, in certain cases, are not earned) in the tax year of receipt. Except for certain short tax years of less than 93 days, deferral to a tax year later than the next succeeding tax year isn't allowed. Alternately, taxpayer, under the full inclusion method of accounting for advance payments, can include the full amount of advance payments in gross income in the tax year of receipt, whether or not the taxpayer earns the full amount of advance payments in that tax year. [34]

An advance payment is eligible for the deferral method if :

(A) including the payment in income for the tax year of receipt generally is a permitted method of accounting for tax purposes (without regard to the revenue procedure authorizing the deferral method));

(B) taxpayer recognizes the payment (partially or completely) in revenues in its applicable financial statement for a later tax year (or, if doesn't have one, it earns the payment, partially or completely, in a later tax year); and

(C) the payment is for: services; sale of goods (other than goods for which the taxpayer uses the deferral method of Reg § 1.451-5(b)(1)(ii)); use (including by license or lease) of intellectual property; occupancy or use of property ancillary to the provision of services; sale, lease, or license of computer software; guaranty or warranty contracts ancillary to the preceding items; subscriptions (other than those for which an election under Code Sec. 455 is in effect), whether or not provided in a tangible or intangible format; organization membership (other than those for which an election under Code Sec. 456 is in effect); or any combination of the preceding items.

> **illustration:** Accrual method, calendar year C Corp sells and repairs TVs. On July 1, 2007, C receives an advance payment for a 2-year contract under which it will repair or replace broken parts in a customer's TV. In its applicable financial statement, C recognizes ¼ of the payment in revenues for 2007, ½ in revenues for 2008, and ¼ in revenues for 2009. Under the deferral method, C includes ¼ of the payment in gross income for 2007 and the remaining ¾ of the payment in gross income for 2008.

> **observation:** Given the deferral possibilities outlined above, cash-basis service providers who bill in advance should consider switching to the accrual method. The benefits of deferring reporting a portion of cash receipts for one year (on an ongoing basis, if applicable), should be compared with the costs and effort of making the accounting method change.

Payments ineligible for the deferral method include rent (unless it's for the use of intellectual property, occupancy or use of property ancillary to the provision of services, or software) and payments for financial instruments (e.g., debt instruments, letters of credit). [35]

---

33. ¶G-2513; ¶4514.017; TD ¶441,702
34. ¶G-2548; ¶4514.191; TD ¶441,712

35. ¶G-2548; ¶4514.191; TD ¶441,712

¶ 2830   Advance payments received for merchandise or construction.

Advance merchandise payments and advance payments under long-term construction contracts are reported by accrual method taxpayers when the income is properly accruable under their method of accounting.[36] But that method must be used for all tax reporting and for credit purposes. (Reg § 1.451-5(b))[37]

An accrual basis taxpayer or a taxpayer using one of the long-term contract methods (¶2848 *et seq.*) can defer reporting an advance payment received under an agreement for the sale or other disposition in a future tax year of goods held primarily for sale to customers, or for the building, installing, constructing or manufacturing of items, where the work isn't completed in the year the advance payment is received. (Reg § 1.451-5(a)(1)) Deferral also applies to advance payments for services to be performed under the agreement as an integral part of the above activities, and for gift certificates. (Reg § 1.451-5(a)(2))[38] Amounts due and payable under the contract are treated as advance payments received. (Reg § 1.451-5(a))[39]

There's a limited deferral for certain inventoriable goods. Where a payment for goods is received several years before they are delivered, taxpayer can postpone reporting the advance payments for one year past the year total advance payments first equal or exceed the anticipated cost of the goods. Thereafter, all prepayments received are reported and actual or expected costs deducted. (Reg § 1.451-5(c))[40] A taxpayer who defers reporting advance payments for merchandise must attach an annual information schedule to its tax return for each year. (Reg § 1.451-5(d))[41]

Use Form 3115 (¶2840) to get IRS consent to switch to deferral. (Reg § 1.451-5(e))[42]

¶ 2831   Advance payments or security deposits.

Amounts received as security aren't taxable until used. A deposit that guarantees the customer's payment of amounts owed to the creditor isn't a deposit but an advance payment includible in income (unless deferred, see ¶2820 and ¶2831), while a deposit securing someone's property is a true security deposit and not an advance payment. [43]

¶ 2832   Timing of expense deductions—all-events test.

Expenses are deductible under the accrual method in the period in which: (1) all events have occurred that determine the fact of the liability; (2) the amount of the liability can be determined with reasonable accuracy; and (3) economic performance (¶2833) has occurred. (Code Sec. 461(h)(4), Reg § 1.461-1(a)(2)) The fact of a liability—generally, the earlier of the event fixing the liability (e.g., the required performance) or when payment is due —isn't established by executing a contract for services to be provided in the future. A reasonable estimate of the liability must be accrued for the tax year in which it was incurred. If there is a difference between the estimate and the amount finally determined, the difference must be added to or deducted from income when the final determination is made. [44] But an automobile company couldn't deduct its anticipated warranty costs under the accrual method based on estimates; until a claim had been filed under the warranty, liability for it remained contingent.[45]

Where the accrual doesn't involve a current expense, but results in the creation of an asset having a useful life extending substantially beyond the end of the tax year, the deduction

---

36. ¶G-2592 *et seq.*; ¶s 4514.121 *et seq.*, 4514.191; TD ¶441,715
37. ¶G-2595; TD ¶441,715
38. ¶s G-2592, G-2594; TD ¶441,715
39. ¶G-2599; ¶4514.121 *et seq.*; TD ¶441,715
40. ¶G-2596; ¶4514.166; TD ¶441,717
41. ¶G-2597; TD ¶441,718
42. ¶G-2598; TD ¶441,719
43. ¶J-1435 *et seq.*; ¶s 4514.193, 4514.194; TD ¶441,711
44. ¶G-2620 *et seq.*; ¶4614.15; TD ¶442,000
45. ¶G-2620 *et seq.*; ¶4614.15; TD ¶442,000

must be taken as depreciation, amortization or similar deduction. (Reg § 1.461-1(a)(2))[46]

An accrual basis taxpayer may deduct a properly accrued expense, regardless of whether he has actually paid that expense. [47]

¶ 2833 Economic performance.

Accrual basis taxpayers won't be considered to have met the all-events test (¶2832), until economic performance has occurred. (Code Sec. 461(h))[48] Economic performance occurs when the property or service to which the accrual relates is actually provided or used. (Code Sec. 461(h)(2)(A))[49] A taxpayer is allowed to treat property or services as provided when he pays for them, but only if he can reasonably expect the property or services to be provided by the other person within 3½ months after the payment is made. (Reg § 1.461-4(d)(6)(ii))[50]

Certain "recurring" expenditures may be treated as incurred in the year the all events test is otherwise met, even though economic performance doesn't occur until the following year. This applies if:

(1) economic performance occurs on or before the date taxpayer files a timely (including extensions) return for the tax year the expense is accrued or, if shorter, 8 ½ months after the close of that year; and

(2) the item is recurring and taxpayer consistently treats items of that kind as incurred in the tax year the all-events test (not including the economic performance test) is met; and

(3) the item is either not a material item or its accrual in the year before economic performance results in a more proper match against income than would be achieved by accruing it in the year of economic performance. (Code Sec. 461(h)(3)(A); Reg § 1.461-5(b))[1]

A taxpayer can adopt the recurring item exception as part of its method of accounting for any type of income for the first tax year that type of item is incurred. (Reg § 1.461-5(d)(1)) Tax shelters can't use the recurring item exception. (Code Sec. 461(i)(1); Reg § 1.461-5(c))[2]

The above 3½ month rule and 8½ month recurring item exception apply only to property or services completely provided within that period; a prorated deduction isn't allowed where all services to be performed aren't provided within that period.

¶ 2834 Accruing contested liability.

An otherwise deductible expense isn't allowable, as long as the taxpayer denies and contests the liability, until the contest is resolved by agreement or final court decision. [3] However, a deduction is allowed in the year of transfer (payment) where:

(1) the taxpayer contests an asserted liability;

(2) the taxpayer transfers money or other property to satisfy the liability;

(3) the contest with respect to the asserted liability exists after the transfer; and

(4) but for the contest, a deduction would be allowed for the tax year of the transfer (or an earlier year). (Code Sec. 461(f)) The contest need not involve court proceedings. [4]

Except as provided under Code Sec. 468B (¶2835), economic performance does not occur when a taxpayer transfers money or property to a trust, escrow account, or court to provide for the satisfaction of a contested workers compensation, tort, or a liability that arises out of a breach of contract or violation of law and requires a payment or a series of payments to another person unless the trust, escrow account, or court is the claimant, or the taxpayer's

---

46. ¶G-2620; ¶4614.15; TD ¶442,001
47. ¶G-2620; ¶4614.15; TD ¶442,000
48. ¶G-2653; ¶4614.15; TD ¶442,012
49. ¶G-2656; ¶4614.15; TD ¶442,013
50. ¶G-2656; ¶4614.15; TD ¶442,014

1. ¶G-2686; ¶4614.15; TD ¶442,035
2. ¶G-2458; ¶4614.15; TD ¶442,035
3. ¶G-2643; ¶s 4614.56, 4614.59; TD ¶442,006
4. ¶G-2645; ¶s 4614.56, 4614.59; TD ¶442,007

payment discharges the taxpayer's liability to the claimant. (Reg § 1.461-2(e)(2)(ii))[5]

¶ 2835 Accrual basis taxpayer's payments for tort liabilities.

If the liability of a taxpayer requires a payment to another person that arises out of a tort, "economic performance" (¶2833) occurs as the payments are made. (Code Sec. 461(h)(2)(C))[6] A qualified payment to a court-ordered or designated settlement fund that extinguishes a taxpayer's tort liability is economic performance for the liability as the payment is made. The present or future claims against the taxpayer must arise out of personal injury, death or property damage. (Code Sec. 468B)[7]

¶ 2836 Accrual basis taxpayer's payables to related cash basis taxpayer.

An accrual basis taxpayer can deduct expenses and interest owed to a related cash basis person only when payment is made and the amount involved is includible in the gross income of the cash basis payee. (Code Sec. 267(a)(2)) That is, an accrual basis taxpayer is treated as on the cash method for purposes of deducting amounts owed to a related cash basis person. [8]

The rule applies in general to all deductible expenses if the timing of the deduction depends on the taxpayer's method of accounting or on electing to expense the item. But it doesn't apply to defer the deduction of otherwise deductible original issue discount or below-market loan interest. (Reg § 1.267(a)-2T(b), Q&A-2) Nor does it apply to defer the deduction of otherwise deductible depreciation, or amortization, except as to amounts owed to a related person for interest, rent or for the performance or nonperformance of services (which amount the payor capitalized or treated as a deferred expense). (Reg § 1.267(a)-2T(b), Q&A-4)[9]

The above rule barring an accrual method corporation from deducting unpaid accrued interest on a loan made to the company from its cash-basis owner, continues to apply after the loan is sold by the owner to an unrelated third-party. Interest that accrued in years before the sale cannot be deducted by the corporation until the unrelated party includes it in income. However, interest that accrues in the year of the sale can be deducted before it is paid. [10]

¶ 2837 Changes of Accounting Methods. ████████████████████

Usually, taxpayers may change their methods of accounting only with IRS consent, and only on IRS-imposed terms. However, automatic consent is available in certain circumstances where IRS-prescribed procedures are followed.

¶ 2838 IRS permission to change method of accounting.

Generally, once a taxpayer has adopted an accounting method, he must continue to use it until: IRS requires him to change the method, or he requests, and gets, IRS permission to change. (Code Sec. 446(e); Reg § 1.446-1(e)(2)) This is so even if the taxpayer has been using an incorrect method, or a method that doesn't clearly reflect income. [11] Taxpayers can't, without IRS consent, retroactively change from an erroneous to a permissible accounting method by filing amended returns, even if the time for amending the return for the first year in which the erroneous method was used hasn't expired. [12]

Taxpayers under examination [13] or before an appeals office [14] or federal court [15] may request prospective accounting method changes in certain circumstances.

For automatic consent procedures for certain accounting method changes, see ¶2845.

---

5. ¶G-2645; ¶4614.56; TD ¶442,007
6. ¶G-2736; ¶4614.15; TD ¶442,019
7. ¶G-2788 *et seq.*; ¶468B4; TD ¶442,025
8. ¶G-2700 *et seq.*; ¶2674; TD ¶442,027
9. ¶G-2701 *et seq.*; ¶2674; TD ¶442,028
10. ¶G-2701

11. ¶G-2201; ¶4464; TD ¶442,601
12. ¶G-2201; ¶s 4464.21, 4464.22; TD ¶442,601
13. ¶G-2237; ¶4464.22; TD ¶442,605
14. ¶G-2256.1; ¶4464.22; TD ¶442,605
15. ¶G-2257.1; ¶4464.22; TD ¶442,605

For changes to inventory methods, see ¶2881.

¶ 2839 What is a change in accounting method?

A change in accounting method is a change of the taxpayer's overall method of accounting or a change in the treatment of a material item of income or expense. Changes in overall methods of accounting include changes:

... from the cash to accrual basis, or vice-versa;

... from the long-term contract method to the cash or accrual method, or vice-versa;

... from one basis of inventory valuation to another;

... to or from a specialized basis, e.g., the crop basis. (Reg § 1.446-1(e)(2)(ii))[16]

A material item is any item that involves the proper time for the inclusion of the item in income or the taking of a deduction. It doesn't include corrections of mathematical or posting errors, or errors in computing tax liability. (Reg § 1.446-1(e)(2)(ii))[17]

Depreciation changes that aren't accounting method changes include: adjustments in the useful life of a depreciable or amortizable asset for which depreciation is determined under Code Sec. 167 (other than under current (or former) Code Sec. 168, Code Sec. 1400I, and Code Sec. 1400L); changes in computing depreciation or amortization allowances in the tax year in which the use of an asset changes in the hands of the same taxpayer; changes in depreciation caused by certain revocations of elections and late elections; and changes in the placed-in service date. (Reg § 1.446-1(e)(2)(ii), Reg § 1.167(e)-1(2))

However, most changes in computing depreciation (or amortization) are treated as accounting method changes. Changes that are accounting method changes include changes: in depreciation or amortization methods, recovery periods or conventions, e.g., half-year to midquarter (but a switch from 200% or 150% declining balance to straight line is allowable without IRS's consent in the first tax year in which it produces a higher allowance); from regular MACRS to the alternative depreciation system; in claiming bonus first-year depreciation without electing; from treating property as nondepreciable or nonamortizable to depreciable or amortizable (or vice versa); and from depreciating or amortizing an item to deducting it as an expense (or vice versa). (Reg § 1.167(e)-1(a)(1), Reg § 1.446-1(e)(2)(ii))[18]

¶ 2840 Applying for a change in accounting method—Form 3115.

An application for change generally must be filed with IRS on the latest version of Form 3115 by the end of the tax year of the change. (Reg § 1.446-1(e)(3)(i))[19] However, automatic consent accounting method change requests (¶2845), may be made on Form 3115:

(1) with a timely filed (including extensions) original income tax return for the change year (file a copy with the IRS National Office), or

(2) within six months of the original tax return due date (excluding extensions) for the change year, if the taxpayer (a) timely filed (including extensions) its return for the change year; (b) files an amended return within the six-month extension period; (c) attaches the original Form 3115 to the amended return; (d) files a copy with the national office at the same time or sooner; and (e) writes "FILED PURSUANT TO Reg § 301.9100-2" at the top of the application.[20]

Extensions won't be granted except in unusual and compelling circumstances. The taxpayer must include all information required by the form, and state that he agrees to the conditions set by IRS and will take into account any required adjustments (¶2841).[21]

---

16. ¶G-2103; ¶4464.21; ¶4464.24; TD ¶442,403
17. ¶G-2104; ¶4464.24; TD ¶442,404
18. ¶G-2106.1; ¶4464.25; TD ¶442,407

19. ¶G-2225; ¶4464.22; TD ¶442,601
20. ¶G-2203.9; ¶4464.225
21. ¶G-2220 *et seq.*; ¶4464.22

¶ 2841   Adjustments required on change—Code Sec. 481(a) adjustments.

In any year in which taxpayer uses a different tax accounting method from the method used in the preceding year, Code Sec. 481(a) adjustments must be made to prevent items of income or expense from being duplicated or entirely omitted. (Reg § 1.446-1(e)(3)(i))[22] The adjustments must take into account inventories, accounts receivable, accounts payable, and any other necessary items. (Reg § 1.481-1(b))[23] The adjustments can be positive (increasing taxable income), or negative (decreasing taxable income). (Reg § 1.481-1(c))[24]

¶ 2842   When Code Sec. 481(a) adjustments are taken into account.

Except as noted below or where the Code or another federal statute provides otherwise, the Code Sec. 481(a) adjustment required as a result of an accounting method change (¶2841), must be taken into account in the year of change —i.e., the first tax year in which the taxpayer's method of accounting is different from that used in the previous tax year. (Code Sec. 481(a); Reg § 1.481-1(a)(1)) This applies to both positive and negative adjustments. (Reg § 1.481-1(c))[25]

Instead of taking the Code Sec. 481(a) adjustment into account in the year of change, taxpayer may take it into account over an appropriate period agreed to (in writing) by IRS. (Code Sec. 481(c); Reg § 1.481-4(a), Reg § 1.481-4(b)) The adjustment must be taken into account ratably over the years included in the adjustment inclusion period (¶2843).[26]

¶ 2843   Adjustment inclusion periods prescribed by IRS—four-year/one-year rules.

The Code Sec. 481(a) adjustment period for voluntary accounting method changes, including automatic consent changes (¶2845) is one tax year for negative adjustments and four tax years for positive adjustments beginning with the year of change. [27] However, taxpayers may elect to account for a positive adjustment in the year of change if it's less than $25,000. Cooperatives generally must take the adjustment into account for the year of change. Taxpayers that terminate their existence or cease to engage in a trade or business must take any remaining balance into account in the year of the cessation or termination. Except for LIFO discontinuance, acceleration of a Code Sec. 481(a) adjustment isn't required on conversion from C to S corporation status, or vice versa. [28]

If an accounting method issue (an issue regarding whether the taxpayer's accounting treatment of an item is proper, but only if changing the taxpayer's treatment of that item could constitute a change in accounting method) results from an examination, any resulting positive Code Sec. 481(a) adjustment is made in the earliest tax year under examination, with a one-year Code Sec. 481(a) adjustment period. [29]

Situations with a different "adjustment inclusion period" are explained at the place in this Handbook where the item subject to the accounting rule is discussed.

¶ 2844   Relief for high-impact adjustments.

Where Code Sec. 481(a) adjustments increase taxable income of the change-over year by more than $3,000, the taxpayer can compute his tax for that year using whichever of these two methods produces the lower tax:

(1) *Three-year allocation* —The tax that would have resulted if one-third of the increase had been included in taxable income in each of the two preceding years and in the change-

---

22. ¶G-2215; ¶4464.21; TD ¶443,301
23. ¶G-2290 *et seq.*; ¶4814; TD ¶443,301
24. ¶G-2304; ¶4814; TD ¶443,302
25. ¶G-2360; ¶4814; TD ¶440,817

26. ¶G-2309; ¶4814; TD ¶443,304
27. ¶G-2311; ¶4814; TD ¶443,303
28. ¶G-2308; ¶4814; TD ¶443,303
29. ¶G-2308; ¶4464.21; TD ¶442,555

over year. (Code Sec. 481(b)(1); Reg § 1.481-2(a))

(2) *Allocation of specific years under new method of accounting* —Where the taxpayer establishes his taxable income under the new method of accounting for one or more tax years consecutively preceding the year of change (in which the old method was actually used), the tax is reduced to the amount that would have been paid if:

(a) the tax for the preceding years was figured under the new method, and

(b) the then remaining adjustments were allocated to the change-over year. (Code Sec. 481(b)(2); Reg § 1.481-2(b))[30]

In making the above computations, the entire Code Sec. 481(a) adjustment required as a result of the accounting method change is taken into account. (Reg § 1.481-1(d))[31]

¶ 2845 Automatic consent procedures for certain accounting method changes

IRS provides automatic procedures for obtaining IRS consent to make some accounting method changes. Many of these are contained in *Rev Proc 2002-9*, 2002-1 CB 327, which for changes within its scope is the exclusive means of obtaining an accounting method change. [32] Some of the more commonly applicable "automatic consent" items are those involving: permissible to permissible accounting method for depreciation; uniform capitalization methods of small resellers; cash or hybrid method to accrual method; series E or EE U.S. savings bonds; timing of incurring liabilities for employee compensation, workers' compensation, and payroll taxes; change from LIFO; retail safe harbor method (and certain other methods) for estimating inventory shrinkage; and capitalizing costs incurred in acquiring or creating intangible assets. There is generally no user fees for automatic-consent accounting method change requests. [33] For applying for an automatic consent accounting method change, see ¶2840.

¶ 2846 Reserves for Expenses.

Taxpayers often maintain accounting reserves for various future liabilities. Generally, no deduction is allowed for additions to these reserves.

¶ 2847 Reserves for estimated expenses and contingent liabilities.

Deduction or exclusion from income isn't allowed for additions to reserves for estimated expenses or contingent liabilities, even if reserves are required by state law or by contract, unless the reserve is expressly authorized by the Code (e.g., depreciation) [34] or is a reserve for trading stamps or coupons (Reg § 1.451-4(a))[35] or for container deposits. However, the use of this method for container deposits applies only where the containers are leased or loaned (*not* sold). Thus, no reserve is permitted for refundable deposits on empty beverage containers under states' environmental and conservation laws. The deposits are includible in income when received and refunds are deductible when paid. [36]

¶ 2848 Long-Term Contracts.

Long-term contracts generally must be accounted for by the percentage-of-completion method. For how to account for long-term contracts for alternative minimum tax purposes, see ¶3207.

---

30. ¶G-2401; ¶4814; TD ¶443,304
31. ¶G-2401; ¶4814; TD ¶443,304
32. ¶G-2203 *et seq.*; ¶4464; TD ¶442,606 *et seq.*
33. ¶G-2203.13

34. ¶s G-2733, G-2737; ¶4514.017; TD ¶442,036
35. ¶G-2742; ¶s 4514.161, 4514.163; TD ¶442,037
36. ¶G-2740; TD ¶442,039

¶ 2849   Accounting for long-term contracts.

Taxpayers must account for long-term contracts (except for certain home and other real property construction contracts, see ¶2850) under the percentage-of-completion method (¶2852), subject to an election to use a modified percentage-of-completion method ("10% method," see ¶2853). (Code Sec. 460)[37]

A long-term contract is any contract for the manufacture, building, installation, or construction of property, if not completed in the tax year in which entered into. (Code Sec. 460(f)(1); Reg § 1.460-1(b)(1)) Whether the taxpayer reasonably expected that the contract would be completed within the tax year is not relevant. [38] But a manufacturing contract isn't long-term unless it involves manufacture of a unique item (of a type not normally included in inventory), or an item that normally requires more than 12 months to complete. [39] (Code Sec. 460(f)(2))

¶ 2850   Exception for small construction contracts.

Home construction contracts (specially defined) aren't limited to the percentage-of-completion method. Nor are any other real property construction contracts if originally estimated to be completed within two years of the contract start date, and if the taxpayer's average annual gross receipts for the three previous tax years don't exceed $10 million (including receipts of certain related businesses). (Code Sec. 460(e); Reg § 1.460-3(b)) Regs provide reporting methods for exempt contracts. (Reg § 1.460-4(c))[40]

¶ 2851   Allocation of costs to long-term contracts.

All costs that directly benefit, or are incurred by reason of, a long-term contract (including research and experimental costs) must be allocated to the contract in the same manner as costs were allocated to extended-period long-term contracts entered into before Mar. 1, '86, under Code Sec. 451 and former Reg. § 1.451-3(d) except that past service pension costs must be allocated to the contract. Also, in the case of a cost-plus contract or a federal long-term contract or subcontract, any other costs (e.g., general and administrative expenses) must be allocated to the contract if identified by the taxpayer (or a related person) as being attributable to it under the contract, or under federal, state, or local law or regulation. (Code Sec. 460(c)(1), Code Sec. 460(c)(2))[41] Interest costs are allocated to long-term contracts in a way that's similar to the way interest costs are allocated under the uniform capitalization rules (Code Sec. 263A(f)) (¶1660) that apply to property produced by a taxpayer. (Code Sec. 460(c)(3); Reg § 1.460-5(b)(2)(v))[42]

The allocation rules don't apply to any expenses for unsuccessful bids and proposals; marketing, selling, and advertising expenses; or independent research and development expenses (IR&D). IR&D expenses don't include expenses directly attributable to a long-term contract in existence when the expenses are incurred, or expenses under an agreement to perform research and development. (Code Sec. 460(c)(4), Code Sec. 460(c)(5))[43]

Alternatively, a taxpayer may elect to use the simplified cost-to-cost allocation method, under which a contract's completion factor is determined based upon only direct material costs; direct labor costs; and depreciation, amortization, and cost recovery allowances on equipment and facilities directly used to manufacture or construct the subject matter of the contract. Material or labor costs associated with a subcontractor's activities must be allocated to the contract. A taxpayer electing this method must use it to apply the look-back method

---

37. ¶s G-3100, G-3229; ¶4514.125; TD ¶445,001
38. ¶G-3103; ¶4604; TD ¶445,027
39. ¶s G-3102, G-3106; ¶4604; TD ¶445,029
40. ¶G-3209; ¶4604; TD ¶445,033

41. ¶G-3143 *et seq.*; ¶s 4514.132, 4604; TD ¶445,016
42. ¶G-3150; ¶s 4514.132, 4604; TD ¶445,019
43. ¶G-3154 *et seq.*; ¶4604; TD ¶445,021

(¶2854) and to determine alternative minimum taxable income. Elect the simplified cost-to-cost method for all long-term contracts entered into during the tax year by using it on the original federal income tax return for the election year. The election isn't available if the percentage-of-completion method (¶2852) is not used for all long-term contracts or if the 10% method (¶2853) is used. (Code Sec. 460(b)(3)(A); Reg § 1.460-5(c))[44]

Home construction contracts and real property construction contracts not subject to long-term contract accounting restrictions (¶2849) are exempt from the above cost allocation rules other than the interest allocation rules. (Code Sec. 460(e))[45]

¶ 2852 Percentage-of-completion method.

Under this method, a long-term contract's percentage of completion must be determined by comparing costs allocated to the contract and incurred before the close of the tax year, with estimated total contract costs. (Code Sec. 460(b)(1)(A)) Events that occur after the end of the tax year that are reasonably subject to estimate as of the last day of the tax year are taken into account.[46]

Gross income recognized in a particular year under the percentage-of-completion method equals total revenue expected from the contract times the cumulative percentage of the contract completed as of the end of the tax year, less the total cumulative amount of contract revenue required to be included in gross income in all preceding tax years. (This can result in a deductible loss for a year if total estimated contract costs increase.) (Reg § 1.460-4(b)(2))[47]

If the total contract price has not been included in gross income by the completion year, the taxpayer must include the remaining portion of the total contract price in gross income for the following tax year. (Reg § 1.460-4(b)(3))

When the contract is completed (or, for amounts received or accrued after completion, when those amounts are received or accrued), the taxpayer must either pay or is entitled to receive interest computed under the look-back method discussed at ¶2854. (Code Sec. 460(b)(1)(B))[48]

Although an aircraft manufacturer's long-term contract was completed for income tax purposes when the Navy cancelled the contract, gain or loss couldn't be determined while millions (if not billions) of dollars remained in dispute in pending litigation. [49]

¶ 2853 Modified percentage-of-completion method—"the 10% method."

For purposes of the percentage-of-completion method (¶2852), a taxpayer may elect not to recognize income under the contract and not to take into account any costs allocable to the long-term contract for any tax year if, as of the end of the tax year, less than 10% of the estimated total contract costs have been incurred. (Code Sec. 460(b)(5)) Elect by using the 10% method for all long-term contracts entered into during the tax year on the original federal income tax return for the election year. If elected, the method is used to apply the look-back method (¶2854) and to determine alternative minimum taxable income. It can't be used if the simplified cost-to-cost method (¶2851) is used. (Reg § 1.460-4(b)(6)(ii))[50]

¶ 2854 Look-back method for interest on tax—Form 8697.

In the tax year a long-term contract (with exceptions, below) is completed, the taxpayer must compare the amount of taxes paid in previous years under the percentage method with the tax that would have been owed if actual, rather than anticipated, costs and contract price

---

44. ¶G-3138; ¶4604; TD ¶445,023
45. ¶G-3209 *et seq.*; ¶4604; TD ¶445,033
46. ¶s G-3123; ¶4604; TD ¶445,002
47. ¶G-3126 *et seq.*; ¶4604; TD ¶445,002

48. ¶G-3156; ¶4604; TD ¶445,044
49. ¶G-3124.1; ¶4604.
50. ¶G-3229 *et seq.*; ¶4604; TD ¶445,088

had been used to compute gross income. Interest at the "adjusted overpayment rate" (overpayment rate (¶4853) for the calendar quarter in which the "interest accrual period" begins) for any "interest accrual period" (period beginning the day after the return due date, without extensions, and ending on the return due date of the following tax year) is owed by or payable to the taxpayer (use Form 8697) if there is, respectively, an underpayment or overpayment for any tax year. (Code Sec. 460(b)(2), Code Sec. 460(b)(7))[1] For pass-through entities, see ¶2855.

Taxpayers may elect (for all contracts completed in the election year and all future years, revocable only with IRS consent) not to apply the look-back method if at the close of each contract year before the tax year in which the look-back method would otherwise have to be applied, the cumulative taxable income (or loss) under the contract (using estimated contract price and costs) is within 10% of the cumulative look-back income or loss under the contract. (Code Sec. 460(b)(6)) Elect by attaching a statement to a timely filed (including extensions) original return for the election year. (Reg § 1.460-6(j))[2]

The look-back method doesn't apply to any contract whose gross price (at completion) doesn't exceed the lesser of $1,000,000 or 1% of taxpayer's average annual gross receipts for the three tax years preceding the tax year the contract was completed if the contract is completed within two years of its start date. (Code Sec. 460(b)(3)(B))[3] Nor does it apply to home construction contracts or others described at ¶2850. (Reg § 1.460-6(b)(2))[4]

¶ 2855 Simplified look-back marginal-impact method for pass-through entities.

For partnerships, S corporations and trusts (that aren't 50% or more held directly or indirectly by five or fewer persons), a simplified look-back marginal-impact method is applied at the entity level if substantially all the income from the contract is U.S.-source. The amount of taxes treated as overpaid or underpaid under a contract in any year is found by multiplying the amount of contract income over- or under-reported for the year by the top marginal tax rate applicable for the year. (Code Sec. 460(b)(4); Reg § 1.460-6(d)(1))[5] Individuals, C corporations and owners of closely-held pass-through entities may elect to use this method. Also, widely-held pass-through entities may use it for foreign contracts. (Reg § 1.460-6(d)(4))[6]

¶ 2856 Long-term contract following mid-contract change.

The tax treatment following a mid-contract change in taxpayer of a long-term contract depends on whether the change is a "constructive completion transaction" or a "step-in-the-shoes transaction." In a constructive completion transaction, the old taxpayer is treated as completing the contract and the new taxpayer as entering into a new contract on the transaction date. This approach applies to any transaction not subject to the step-in-the-shoes approach. (Reg § 1.460-4(k)(2)) In general, with a step-in-the-shoes transaction, the old taxpayer's obligation to account for the contract terminates on the transaction date and is assumed by the new taxpayer. The new taxpayer assumes the old taxpayer's methods of accounting for the contract, with both the contract price and allocable contract costs based on amounts taken into account by both parties. Special rules apply to the treatment of certain partnership transactions. (Reg § 1.460-4(k); Reg § 1.460-6(g))[7]

¶ 2857 Reconstruction of Income by IRS. ■■■■■■■■■■■■■■■■

Where taxpayer's records are inadequate, IRS can reconstruct taxpayer's income by whatever method will in its opinion most clearly reflect income.

1. ¶G-3161 *et seq.*; ¶4604; TD ¶445,054
2. ¶G-3203.1; ¶4604; TD ¶445,049
3. ¶G-3158; ¶4604; TD ¶445,050 *et seq.*
4. ¶G-3159; TD ¶445,051

5. ¶G-3195 *et seq.*; ¶4604; TD ¶445,074
6. ¶G-3201; ¶4604; TD ¶445,074
7. ¶G-3246; ¶4604.04

The methods most often used are:

The net worth method. Here, IRS attempts to establish an opening net worth or total value of the taxpayer's assets at the beginning of a given year. It then proves increases in the taxpayer's net worth for each later year during the period under examination and calculates the difference between the adjusted net values of the taxpayer's assets at the beginning and end of each of the years involved. The taxpayer's nondeductible expenditures, including living expenses, are added to these increases. If the resulting figure for any year is substantially greater than the taxable income reported by the taxpayer for that year, IRS treats the excess as unreported taxable income. [8]

Bank deposit method. The bank deposit method assumes that all deposits represent income unless the taxpayer can show otherwise. [9]

Percentage markup method. IRS determines taxpayer's net income by applying certain percentages, e.g., gross profit to sales, or net income to gross income, or net income to sales, derived from other taxpayers in the same kind of business. [10]

¶ 2858 Reallocations of Income by IRS. ▬▬▬▬▬▬▬▬▬

IRS is authorized (under Code Sec. 482) to distribute, apportion, or allocate gross income, deductions, credits or allowances among two or more organizations, trades, or businesses owned or controlled by the same interests in order to prevent tax evasion or to reflect the true taxable income of any of those entities. A similar rule also allows IRS to reallocate tax items (under Code Sec. 269A) for a personal service corporation.

IRS can reallocate income under Code Sec. 482 regardless of the entities' *motives* for shifting it, and can reallocate even if the shift was unintentional. (Reg § 1.482-1(c))[11]

If an allocation is made for a transaction between controlled taxpayers, IRS will also take into account the effect of any other non-arm's length transaction between the same controlled taxpayers in the same tax year which will result in a setoff against the original allocation. (Reg § 1.482-1(g)(4)(i)) Procedures have been issued for notifying IRS of a proposed setoff.[12]

For tax years beginning after 2007, regs on the tax treatment of services transactions ensure that valuable intangibles cannot be transferred outside the U.S. for less than arm's length consideration, and update guidance on the transfer pricing methods to determine the arm's-length price in services transactions. (Reg § 1.482-9T)[13]

Under advance pricing agreements (APAs) with IRS, taxpayers can prospectively determine and apply transfer pricing methodologies to international transactions by related foreign or domestic taxpayers. [14] APAs and related background information can't be released to the public. (Code Sec. 6103(b); Code Sec. 6110(b))

¶ 2859 Reallocation of personal service corporation income.

To prevent tax avoidance or evasion or to clearly reflect income, IRS may allocate all income, deductions, credits, exclusions and other allowances between a personal service corporation (PSC) and its employee-owner who owns more than 10% of the PSC stock (on any day in the tax year) if:substantially all of its services are performed by or for one other corporation, partnership, or entity (including related parties) and are availed of principally to avoid federal income tax by securing for any employee-owner significant tax benefits that he

---

8. ¶G-2912; ¶s 4464.41, 4464.42; TD ¶444,010
9. ¶G-2941; ¶s 4464.41, 4464.67; TD ¶444,027
10. ¶G-2948; ¶s 4464.41, 4464.76; TD ¶444,031
11. ¶G-4018; ¶4824

12. ¶G-4108; ¶4824.08
13. ¶G-4200; ¶G-4500; ¶4824.04; ¶4824.06
14. ¶G-4700 *et seq.*; ¶4824.07

wouldn't otherwise have. (Code Sec. 269A(a))[15] A PSC is one whose principal activity is the performance of personal services, substantially all of which are performed by employee-owners for one other corporation, partnership, or entity (including related parties). The Code Sec. 318 attribution rules apply for purposes of the 10% test, except that for purposes of applying the Code Sec. 318(a)(2)(C) rules, attribution is triggered by 5% rather than 50% stock ownership. (Code Sec. 269A(b)(2))[16]

¶ 2860   Previously Reported Income Repayments.

Taxpayers who must repay amounts they previously reported as income may deduct the repayments in the year the repayments are made. If the amount repaid exceeds $3,000, the taxpayer may recover the tax paid on that amount in the year he reported it, if that gives him the greater tax benefit.

¶ 2861   Deducting the repayment of previously reported income.

A taxpayer who must repay previously-reported income is entitled to deduct the amount repaid.[17] For relief where the repayment exceeds $3,000, see ¶2862.

For a cash basis taxpayer, the year of the deduction, and accordingly the year that the special computation might be available, is the year the income previously reported was repaid. If the taxpayer reported the income as constructively received, the year of deduction is the year he had to relinquish his claim to the income. (Reg § 1.1341-1(e))[18]

For an accrual basis taxpayer, the year of deduction is the year liability for repayment becomes fixed. Where the taxpayer received the income reported, the year of deduction is the year it's finally established the taxpayer had no unrestricted right to it. (Reg § 1.1341-1(e))[19]

¶ 2862   Repayments that exceed $3,000.

If the amount of the deduction allowed for a tax year (¶2861) with respect to an item reported as income in an earlier tax year is more than $3,000, and:

. . . that item was included in gross income in the earlier year because it appeared that the taxpayer had an unrestricted right to it then; and

. . . the deduction is allowed because it was shown after the close of the earlier year that taxpayer did *not* have an unrestricted right to all or part of that item, then the tax for the year in which the deduction is allowed is the lesser of:

(1) the tax for that year computed with the deduction,

(2) the tax for that year computed *without the deduction,* minus the decrease in tax for the earlier year that would result solely from excluding the deductible repayment. (Code Sec. 1341(a))

This relief for repayments exceeding $3,000 doesn't apply:

. . . where repayment is required because of a liability that arose later, as distinguished from absence of an unrestricted right to the income previously reported; [20]

. . . where an item was originally included in gross income by reason of the sale or other disposition of stock-in-trade, or other property includible in inventory if on hand at close of the earlier tax year, or property held primarily for sale to customers in the ordinary course of business—i.e., it doesn't apply to sales returns and allowances and similar items (Code Sec. 1341(b)(2); Reg § 1.1341-1(f));

---

15. ¶G-4751; ¶269A4
16. ¶G-4756; ¶269A4
17. ¶G-3001; ¶13,414; TD ¶203,015

18. ¶G-3027; ¶13,414.01; TD ¶444,520
19. ¶G-3028; ¶13,414.01; TD ¶444,520
20. ¶G-2308; ¶13,414; TD ¶444,511

... to deductions attributable to bad debts or to legal fees and other expenses incurred in contesting the repayment of income previously included. (Reg § 1.1341-1(g), Reg § 1.1341-1(h))[21]

¶ 2863 Inventories.

Where producing, buying or selling merchandise is an income-producing factor, inventories are needed to determine the correct cost of goods sold.

Inventories serve to allocate the expense of buying merchandise to the year in which that merchandise is sold. [22]

Inventories must be used whenever IRS finds their use is needed to clearly determine a taxpayer's income. (Code Sec. 471) Generally, this is the case where the "production, purchase or sale of merchandise" is an income-producing factor. (Reg § 1.471-1)[23] A taxpayer that must use inventories also must use the accrual method of accounting for its purchases and sales. (Reg § 1.446-1)[24] However, IRS has excepted non-tax-shelters with average annual gross receipts of $1 million or less from having to account for inventories and certain taxpayers with not more than $10 million average annual gross receipts, see ¶2818. Also, pending the release of further guidance IRS will not assert that construction contractors must maintain inventory accounts for the supplies used in their businesses. [25]

⊘caution: Under the uniform inventory inclusion and capitalization rules (¶1660 *et seq.*), certain direct and indirect costs are either included in inventory or capitalized.

¶ 2864 What goods are included in inventory?

Inventories include all merchandise that is held for sale in the ordinary course of business or that is to become a physical part of merchandise intended for sale. Inventories generally cover finished or partly finished goods as well as raw materials and supplies acquired for sale or that will physically become a part of merchandise intended for sale. For items to be included in inventory, taxpayer must have title. (Reg § 1.471-1)[26] Prescription drugs and similar items administered by healthcare providers are not merchandise. [27]

Merchandise shipped on approval or sold on sample is kept in the seller's inventory until its acceptance. Consigned goods or goods in the hands of others for processing (e.g., dyeing) and returnable in kind are kept in the consignor's inventory. A seller's inventory includes goods he has contracted to sell but not yet segregated and applied to the contract, while a buyer's inventory includes merchandise in transit to him or that for other reasons hasn't been reduced to possession but to which he has title. But a buyer does *not* include in inventory goods ordered for future delivery. [28]

Containers that are to be *sold* with the merchandise they contain should be included in the seller's inventory, regardless of whether they are returnable. If the containers are merely leased or loaned with a deposit received to guarantee the return, they aren't included in inventory since they aren't part of the merchandise held for sale. In that case they can be inventoried at cost the same as supplies, considered as fixed assets and depreciated, or, if they have a useful life of less than a year, currently deducted. [29]

Under an IRS accounting method safe harbor, rotable spare parts (parts that can be reserviced or repaired and used repeatedly) can be capitalized and depreciated, rather than included in inventory. [30]

21. ¶s G-3032, G-3034, G-3035; ¶13,414.01; TD ¶444,523
22. ¶G-5000 *et seq.*; ¶4714; TD ¶450,500
23. ¶G-5001; ¶4714; TD ¶450,501
24. ¶G-2089; ¶4464.07; TD ¶450,506
25. ¶G-5001

26. ¶G-5006 *et seq.*; ¶4714; TD ¶450,509 *et seq.*
27. ¶G-5001
28. ¶G-5009; ¶4714; TD ¶450,517
29. ¶G-5010; ¶4714; TD ¶450,513
30. ¶G-5006.1; TD ¶265,444

¶ 2865   Valuing inventory.

The two most commonly recognized bases of valuing inventories are: (1) cost, and (2) cost or market, whichever is lower. (Reg § 1.471-2(c))[31] Farmers may use other valuation methods, see ¶4512 *et seq.* For inventories of dealers in securities, see ¶2879.

Consistency from year to year in whatever inventory procedure is adopted is of first importance. (Reg § 1.471-2(b))[32]

¶ 2866   Valuation of unsalable, slow-moving and traded-in goods.

Any goods in inventory that are unsalable at normal prices or in the normal way because of damage, imperfections, style changes, etc., can at the taxpayer's option be written down — that is, valued at selling prices less direct costs of disposition, whether the cost or the lower of cost or market method is used. If the goods consist of raw materials or partly finished goods held for use or consumption, they must be valued upon a reasonable basis, considering the usability and condition of the goods, but in no case at less than scrap value. (Reg § 1.471-2(c))[33] Selling price means the actual price at which goods are offered for sale during a period ending not later than 30 days after the date of inventory. (Reg § 1.472-2(c))[34]

Normal but slow-moving inventory (i.e., goods in excess of current demand) can't be written down based on arbitrary cut-off time periods. [35]

¶ 2867   Prohibited valuation methods and practices.

The following aren't permitted:

(1) Deducting from inventory a reserve for price changes or an estimated depreciation in the value of inventory (but for permissible estimates of inventory shrinkage, see ¶2868).

(2) Valuing work in process, or other parts of the inventory, at a nominal price or at less than its proper value.

(3) Omitting portions of the stock on hand.

(4) Using a constant price or nominal value for so-called normal quantity of material or goods in stock.

(5) Segregating indirect production costs into fixed and variable classifications and allocating only the variable costs to the cost of goods produced while treating fixed costs as currently deductible (the "direct cost" method).

(6) Treating all or substantially all indirect production costs (whether classified as fixed or variable) as currently deductible (the "prime cost" method). (Reg § 1.471-2(f))[36]

¶ 2868   Estimates of inventory shrinkage.

A method of determining inventories doesn't fail to clearly reflect income solely because it uses estimates of inventory shrinkage that are confirmed by a physical count only after the last day of the tax year if the taxpayer: (1) normally does a physical count at each location on a regular and consistent basis, and (2) makes proper adjustments to inventories and to its estimating methods if estimates are greater or less than actual shrinkage. (Code Sec. 471(b)) Use the automatic consent procedure (¶2845), with some modifications, to change to the retail safe harbor method of estimating inventory shrinkage (using a historical ratio of shrinkage-to-sales to estimate shrinkage occurring between the last physical inventory and the end of

---

31. ¶G-5101; ¶s 4714.21, 4714.41, 4714.51; TD ¶451,001
32. ¶G-5002; ¶4714.21; TD ¶450,502
33. ¶G-5159; ¶4714.35; TD ¶451,510

34. ¶G-5161; ¶4714.35; TD ¶451,511
35. ¶G-5164; TD ¶451,514
36. ¶G-5124; ¶4714.21; TD ¶451,020

the tax year), or to a method that clearly reflects income other than the retail safe harbor method if the method being changed from didn't estimate inventory shrinkage. [37]

¶ 2869 What is cost?

The cost of goods on hand at the start of an accounting period is the amount at which they were valued in the closing inventory of the period before. (Reg § 1.471-3(a))[38]

The cost of the goods purchased ordinarily is the invoice price reduced by trade or other discounts. Strictly cash discounts approximating a fair interest rate may be deducted at the option of the taxpayer if the method is consistently followed. (Reg § 1.471-3(b))[39] To this net invoice price should be added transportation or other necessary charges incurred in acquiring possession of the goods. (Reg § 1.471-3(b))[40]

The costs of goods produced by the taxpayer include, in addition to the opening inventory, cost of raw materials and supplies entering into or consumed in manufacture, regular and overtime direct labor costs, and the indirect costs required to be included under the "full absorption" method. (Reg § 1.471-3(c))[41]

For the uniform capitalization rules for including costs in inventory, see ¶1660 *et seq.*

¶ 2870 Valuing inventory using the lower of cost or market method.

Under this method, market value on the inventory date is compared with the cost of each item. The lower of the two is the inventory value of the item. Total inventory is the aggregate of the inventory values so computed for each item in the inventory. It is *not* the lower of the total cost or total market value of all items. (Reg § 1.471-4(c))[42]

¶ 2871 Market value defined.

Market value normally means the current bid price prevailing at the inventory date for the particular merchandise in the volume usually purchased by the taxpayer. Market price is applied to: (1) goods purchased and on hand, and (2) the basic elements of cost (materials, labor and overhead) of goods in process of manufacture and of finished goods on hand. (Reg § 1.471-4(a))[43]

Market price may not be applied to goods on hand or in process if the merchandise is covered by a firm sales contract at fixed prices (i.e., not legally subject to cancellation by either buyer or seller). If, under the contract, the taxpayer is protected against actual loss, the goods must be inventoried at cost with no deduction for inventory decline. (Reg § 1.471-4(a)) Moreover, goods covered by firm sales contracts at the end of the year must be valued at cost even though the contracts are cancelled after the close of the year at the customer's request. [44] If the contract gives the seller an almost certain loss, IRS says the seller isn't allowed to write the inventory down but must value it at cost, thus taking the loss when actually realized (Reg § 1.471-4(a)), but some courts disagree. [45]

A taxpayer may write down inventory below market if in the regular course of business he has offered the merchandise for sale at below-market prices. (Reg § 1.471-4(b))

If no market exists, or if quotations are nominal because of an inactive market, the taxpayer must use whatever evidence of a fair market price at the date or dates nearest his inventory date as may be available, e.g., specific purchases and sales made by the taxpayer or others in reasonable volume and in good faith, or compensation paid for cancellation of

37. ¶G-5120.1; ¶4714.38; TD ¶451,014
38. ¶G-5102; ¶4714.41; TD ¶451,002
39. ¶G-5107, G-5108; ¶4714.41; TD ¶451,003
40. ¶G-5103, G-5110; ¶4714.41; TD ¶451,006
41. ¶s G-5102 *et seq.*, G-5402; ¶4714.41

42. ¶G-5150; ¶4714.51; TD ¶451,501
43. ¶G-5151; ¶4714.51; TD ¶451,502
44. ¶G-5154 *et seq.*; ¶4714.51; TD ¶451,505
45. ¶G-5154 *et seq.*; ¶4714.51; TD ¶451,503

contracts for purchase commitments. (Reg § 1.471-4(b))[46]

¶ 2872   Inventory cost identification methods.

Under the specific identification method, goods are matched with their invoices (less appropriate discounts) to find the cost of each item. [47]

Where it isn't possible or practicable to identify each item of inventory with its cost, an assumption must be made to determine which items were sold and which remain in inventory. Although only two methods of costing intermingled merchandise are specifically approved (the "first-in, first-out" (FIFO) and the "last-in, first-out" (LIFO) methods, ¶2873), any method that comes within the best accounting practice of the particular business and clearly reflects income is acceptable. Two permissible cost identification methods are averaging the cost of each type or grade of goods in the inventory (¶2875), and mainly relying on the taxpayer's accounting records to arrive at the correct inventory value (¶2877). The base stock method (the assumption that a certain portion of inventory will be maintained from year to year and therefore need not be revalued) isn't permitted. [48]

The inventory price index computation (IPIC) method, under which inventory price indexes are computed with reference to consumer or producer price indexes published by the U.S. Bureau of Labor Statistics (BLS) (Code Sec. 472(f); Reg § 1.472-8(e)(3)) is intended to simplify the use of the dollar-value LIFO method (¶2875).[49]

¶ 2873   FIFO (first-in, first-out) and LIFO (last-in, first-out).

Under the FIFO method, the cost of goods that are so intermingled they cannot be identified with specific invoices is considered to be the cost of goods most recently purchased or produced. (Reg § 1.471-2(d))[50]

Under the "last-in, first-out" method of inventory valuation, the most recently purchased merchandise is treated as the first sold. (Code Sec. 472(b)(1))[1] LIFO may generally be used only where inventory is valued at cost. (Reg § 1.472-2(b))[2] If a taxpayer had written down inventory to a lower market value, the difference between that value and cost must be restored to income ratably over a three-year period (beginning with the year of the election to LIFO). (Code Sec. 472(d))[3]

In order to use LIFO for tax purposes, the enterprise must also use LIFO in its reports to partners, stockholders, etc., and for credit purposes. (Code Sec. 472(c))[4]

Qualifying heavy equipment dealers using LIFO or FIFO may, like auto dealers, use replacement cost to determine the cost of their heavy parts inventory under safe harbor rules. [5]

¶ 2874   Electing LIFO—Form 970.

File Form 970 (or other acceptable statement) with the return for the tax year as of the close of which LIFO is first to be used (Reg § 1.472-3)[6] or re-elected in the fifth or later tax year after changing from LIFO (otherwise IRS permission is needed for the change, see ¶2838 *et seq.*) Once made, the election applies to all later years unless IRS grants permission to change. (Reg § 1.472-5)[7] Automatic consent procedures (¶2845) apply to adoption of certain specialized LIFO methods and to changes from LIFO.

---

46. ¶G-5157; ¶4714.51; TD ¶451,508
47. ¶s G-5121, G-5265; ¶4714.41; TD ¶452,020
48. ¶G-5125 *et seq.*; ¶4714.41
49. ¶G-5253; ¶4724; TD ¶452,055
50. ¶G-5121; ¶4714.41; TD ¶451,017
1. ¶G-5200; ¶4724; TD ¶452,001

2. ¶G-5212; ¶4724; TD ¶452,001
3. ¶G-5208; ¶4724; TD ¶452,009
4. ¶G-5307; ¶4724; TD ¶452,076
5. ¶G-5248.4.
6. ¶G-5202; ¶4724; TD ¶452,003
7. ¶G-5201; ¶4724; TD ¶452,002

¶ 2875   Dollar value LIFO and simplified dollar value LIFO.

Under this method a taxpayer who deals in a large variety of products may value inventory by the use of the dollar value rather than natural units. The assumption is that items in the inventory are homogeneous. The taxpayer is therefore required to break up the inventory into a series of "pools"—the natural business unit pool or multiple pools. (Reg § 1.472-8)[8] Any taxpayer electing to use the dollar-value LIFO method can elect to compute an inventory price index in accordance with the Inventory Price Index Computation method (Reg § 1.472-8(e)(3)(ii), see ¶2872.

An eligible small business may elect to use a simplified dollar-value method of pricing inventories for purposes of the LIFO method. Under this method, the cost of each grade of goods is averaged. (Code Sec. 474(a)) An eligible small business is a taxpayer whose average annual gross receipts don't exceed $5,000,000 for the three-tax-year period ending immediately before the tax year. (Code Sec. 474(c))[9]

¶ 2876   Retailers' inventory.

Retailers can value each item of merchandise in stock at the end of the year at its retail selling price but adjusted to approximate cost by eliminating the average percent of markup. (Reg § 1.471-8(a))[10] This retail inventory method may be used in conjunction with FIFO and specific identification methods, as well as LIFO, if the taxpayer adjusts his selling price for both markups and markdowns. (Reg § 1.471-8(g))[11] Price change adjustments are determined by reference generally to U.S. Bureau of Labor Statistics price indexes. (Reg § 1.472-1(k))[12]

¶ 2877   Book (perpetual) inventory method.

Under this method inventory accounts are charged with the actual cost of goods purchased or produced, and credited with the cost of goods used, transferred or sold. The net amount is considered to be the cost of the goods on hand, if the balances shown on the books are adjusted at reasonable intervals to conform to physical inventories. (Reg § 1.471-2(d))[13]

¶ 2878   Miners' and manufacturers' inventory.

Miners and manufacturers who use a single process or uniform series of processes, and derive a product of two or more kinds, sizes or grades with a unit cost substantially alike, may allocate a share of total cost to each kind, size or grade as a basis for pricing inventories. (Reg § 1.471-7)[14]

¶ 2879   Securities and commodities dealers' inventories—mark-to-market rules.

Any security that's inventory in the hands of a securities dealer must be included in inventory at its fair market value. (Code Sec. 475(a)(1)) In the case of a non-inventory security that's held at the close of a tax year, the dealer must recognize gain or loss as if the security were sold for its fair market value on the last business day of that year, and any gain or loss must be taken into account for that tax year, generally as ordinary income or loss. (Code Sec. 475(a)(2); Code Sec. 475(d)(3))[15] A "security" doesn't include any security held for investment, certain other securities, and hedges of those securities (but only if the hedge is clearly identified as a hedge in the dealer's records before the close of the business day on

8. ¶G-5245 *et seq.*; ¶4724; TD ¶452,046
9. ¶G-5302 *et seq.*; ¶4744; TD ¶452,070
10. ¶G-5351; ¶4724.06; TD ¶453,001
11. ¶G-5357; ¶4724.06; TD ¶453,006
12. ¶G-5362; ¶4724.06; TD ¶453,011
13. ¶G-5119; ¶4714.21; TD ¶451,013
14. ¶G-5020; ¶4714.85; TD ¶450,520
15. ¶I-7652; ¶4754

which it was acquired, originated or entered into). (Code Sec. 475(b)) [16] A security also doesn't include nonfinancial customer paper arising from the sale of nonfinancial goods or services by sellers or providers of those goods or services which are held by them (or related parties) at all times since issue. (Code Sec. 475(c)(4))[17] Commodities dealers may elect (under interim procedures[18]) to apply the mark-to-market rules to commodities held by them in the same way that the rules apply to securities held by securities dealers. (Code Sec. 475(e)(1)) Once made, the election may be revoked only with IRS consent. (Code Sec. 475(e)(3))[19] Where the Code Sec. 475 rules don't apply, a securities dealer inventories securities at: (1) cost, (2) lower of cost or market, or (3) market value. (Reg § 1.471-5)[20]

A dealer is one who regularly buys and sells securities to customers (or enters into or terminates positions in securities with customers) in the ordinary course of business. (Code Sec. 475(c)(1))[21] If one's sole business is trading in securities he's not a dealer [22] (but for the mark-to-market election by traders, see ¶2880).

¶ 2880   Mark-to-market election for securities and commodities traders.

A person engaged in the trade or business of securities trader or commodities trader may elect (under interim procedures[23]) to have the following mark-to-market rules apply to the trade or business: (1) gain or loss is recognized on any security (or commodity) held in connection with the trade or business at the close of any tax year as if the security (or commodity) were sold for its fair market value on the last business day of the tax year, and (2) gain or loss is taken into account for the tax year (Code Sec. 475(f)(1)(A), Code Sec. 475(f)(2)) as ordinary income or loss. Once made, the election may be revoked only with IRS consent. (Code Sec. 475(f)(3)) These elective mark-to-market rules don't apply to securities or commodities that have no connection to the electing person's trading activities if they are clearly identified as such before the close of the day acquired. (Code Sec. 475(f)(1)(B)) Securities and commodities subject to this election aren't subject to the constructive sale rules of Code Sec. 1259 (¶2637). (Code Sec. 475(f)(1)(C))[24]

¶ 2881   Changing inventory method—Form 3115.

A change in the method of valuing inventory, with the exception of a change to LIFO (¶2874) and to certain specialized LIFO methods (¶2845), requires IRS approval. This includes adoption of either: (1) cost, or (2) cost or market, whichever is lower, where the taxpayer has been on a different basis, and changes to and from the various methods of determining inventory costs. Use Form 3115, under the rules at ¶2840. (Reg § 1.446-1(e))[25] An automatic consent procedure also applies for certain taxpayers changing *from* LIFO (¶2845).[26]

---

16. ¶I-7657 *et seq.*; ¶4754
17. ¶I-7657.1; ¶4754
18. ¶I-7669; ¶4754.02
19. ¶I-7667 *et seq.*; ¶4754.01
20. ¶G-5021; ¶s 4754, 4714.67
21. ¶G-5023; ¶4754

22. ¶I-7656.1; ¶4754
23. ¶I-7675; ¶4754.02
24. ¶I-7670 *et seq.*; ¶4754.01
25. ¶s G-2101 *et seq.*, G-5201 *et seq.*; ¶4464.21; TD ¶451,022
26. ¶G-5217 *et seq.*; ¶s 263A4.10, 4464.21, 4724; TD ¶452,018

Chapter 12   Withholding Tax on Wages and Other Income Payments

¶ 3000   Withholding on Wages. ▬▬▬▬▬▬▬▬▬▬▬▬▬▬▬▬▬▬

Employers must withhold income tax from wages paid to employees, but not from amounts paid to independent contractors. "Wages" includes most forms of taxable compensation. Employees are entitled to minimum, and sometimes additional, withholding exemptions or allowances. Withheld tax must be paid through tax deposits or electronic funds transfers.

For withholding on certain federal payments (e.g., social security payments), see ¶3009. For other nonpayroll withholding (backup withholding, withholding for pension, annuities, and gambling winnings, etc.), see ¶3030. For withholding from U.S. source amounts paid to nonresident aliens and foreign corporations, see ¶4666.

¶ 3001   Withholding by employers.

Employers must withhold. (Code Sec. 3402(a)(1); Reg § 31.3402(a)-1(b))[1] An employer is any person or organization for whom an individual performs any service as an employee. (Code Sec. 3401(d)) An employer includes any person paying wages to a former employee, (Reg § 31.3401(d)-1(b)) and includes tax-exempt organizations. (Reg § 31.3401(d)-1(d))[2] Employers who outsource some or all of their payroll responsibilities remain liable for all taxes, penalties and interest due. [3]

If the actual employer doesn't have control over the payment of wages, the person who does have control must withhold. (Code Sec. 3401(d)(1)) A lender, surety or other person is personally liable for the employee income tax required to be withheld if he: (1) directly pays wages to another's employees (Code Sec. 3505(a)), or (2) supplies funds specifically for the payment of the wages of another's employees knowing the employer can't or doesn't intend to pay payroll taxes. In the case of (2), liability is limited to 25% of the amount supplied (inclusive of interest). (Code Sec. 3505(b); Reg § 31.3505-1(b))

Where a one-person unincorporated business entity (e.g., an LLC) does not elect treatment as a corporation under the "check-the-box" rules, the sole owner is personally liable for withholding, since the entity is disregarded. [4] For wages paid before 2009, IRS will accept reporting and payment of employment taxes for the employees of a disregarded entity (¶3701): either (1) as though the employees of the disregarded entity are employed directly by its owner, under the owner's name and taxpayer identification number; or (2) separately calculated, reported, and paid by each state law entity for its own employees, under its own name and taxpayer identification number. In either event, the owner of the disregarded entity retains ultimate responsibility for the employment tax obligations. For post-2008 wages, a disregarded single-owner entity will be treated as a separate entity (i.e., as a corporation) for purposes of employment taxes and related reporting requirements. (Reg § 1.1361-4(a)(7) , Reg § 301.7701-2(c)(2)) An owner of a disregarded entity treated as a sole proprietorship is subject to self-employment taxes. (Reg § 301.7701-2(c)(2))[5]

If a person pays wages on behalf of a nonresident employer not engaged in trade or business in the U.S., that person must withhold. (Code Sec. 3401(d)(2))[6]

---

1. ¶H-4222; ¶34,024; TD ¶531,001
2. ¶H-4226; ¶34,014.60; TD ¶534,001
3. ¶V-1664
4. ¶D-1151; ¶77014.14; TD ¶580,521
5. ¶H-4223; TD ¶534,002
6. ¶s H-4229, H-4236, H-4374; ¶34,014.60; TD ¶532,038

References beginning with a single letter are to paragraphs in RIA's Federal Tax Coordinator 2d and RIA's Analysis of Federal Taxes: Income. Those beginning with numbers are to paragraphs in RIA's United States Tax Reporter. Those beginning with TD are to paragraphs in RIA's Tax Desk.

¶ 3002   Employees defined.

Every individual who performs services subject to the will and control of an employer both as to what is to be done and how it's to be done, is an employee for withholding purposes. It doesn't matter that the employee has considerable discretion and freedom of action, so long as the employer has the *legal right* to control both the method and the result of the services. (Reg § 31.3401(c)-1(b)) For how IRS determines whether a worker is an employee or independent contractor, see ¶3003.

It doesn't matter that the employee is designated a partner, agent or independent contractor, or how payments are measured or paid or what they're called. (Reg § 31.3401(c)-1(e))[7]

No distinction is made between classes of employees. Managers and other supervisory personnel are employees. An officer of a corporation is an employee (Code Sec. 3401(c)), but a director in his capacity as director isn't an employee. (Reg § 31.3401(c)-1(f))[8]

Persons in business for themselves aren't employees. For example, self-employed physicians, lawyers, dentists, veterinarians, construction contractors and others who offer their services to the public aren't employees. (Reg § 31.3401(c)-1(c))[9]

Qualified real estate agents and direct sellers are treated as independent contractors, not employees. (Code Sec. 3508(a))[10]

Statutory employees, such as certain drivers, life insurance salespersons, home workers, and other salespersons, who are treated as employees for FICA purposes (Code Sec. 3121(d)(3)) but aren't common law employees (¶3002), aren't employees for income tax purposes.[11]

Crew leaders who pay agricultural laborers that they provide to another person are employers unless a written contract designates them as employees of that person. (Code Sec. 3401(g))[12]

observation: A person not treated as an employee for income tax purposes can't be covered under employee plans, e.g., medical reimbursement and group-term life insurance plans.

If payment is made for services rendered and the payor isn't sure whether the payee is an employee or independent contractor, the payor may get an IRS ruling by filing Form SS-8. (Reg § 31.3401(d)-1(d))[13] Adverse rulings can be reviewed by the Tax Court (Code Sec. 7436) after IRS sends an adverse notice of determination.[14]

¶ 3003   How IRS determines employee or independent contractor status.

To determine whether a worker is an independent contractor or an employee, IRS examines the relationship between the worker and the business, and considers all evidence of control and independence. The facts that provide this evidence fall into the following three categories:

(1) *Behavioral control* covers facts that show whether the business has a right to direct and control how the work is done through instructions, training, or other means. Employees are generally given instructions on when and where to work, what tools to use, where to purchase supplies, what order to follow, etc.

(2) *Financial control* covers facts that show whether the business has a right to control the

---

7. ¶H-4251; ¶34,014.37; TD ¶535,001
8. ¶H-4252; ¶s 34,014.39, 34,014.40; TD ¶535,003
9. ¶H-4258; ¶34,014.47, 34,014.48, 34,014.50, 34,014.61; TD ¶535,001
10. ¶H-4283; ¶34,014.37; TD ¶535,032

11. ¶H-4300; ¶624.03; TD ¶542,007
12. ¶H-4227; ¶34,014.18
13. ¶H-4282; ¶34,014.37; TD ¶535,008
14. ¶U-2143; ¶74,364; TD ¶806,067

financial and business aspects of the worker's job. This includes the extent to which the worker has unreimbursed business expenses; the extent of his investment in the facilities being used; the extent to which he makes his services available to the relevant market; how he is paid; and the extent to which he can realize a profit or incur a loss.

(3) *Type of relationship* includes written contracts describing the relationship the parties intended to create; the extent to which the worker is available to perform services for other, similar businesses; whether the business provides the worker with employee-type benefits, such as insurance, a pension plan, vacation pay, or sick pay; the permanency of the relationship; and the extent to which services performed by the worker are a key aspect of the company's regular business.

IRS's three-category approach essentially distills the 20-factor test IRS had used to determine whether a worker was an employee or an independent contractor. [15]

In certain cases in which a taxpayer has a reasonable basis for treating an individual as a nonemployee (e.g., judicial precedent, IRS ruling, past audit allowance), a special statutory rule (section 530 of the '78 Revenue Act) may allow nonemployee treatment regardless of the above factors.[16]

¶ 3004 Wages subject to withholding.

"Wages" cover all types of employee compensation, including salaries, fees, bonuses, commissions and fringe benefits. It's immaterial whether payments are based on the hour, day, week, month, year or on a piecework or percentage plan, or whether they're called wages, salaries, fees, etc. (Code Sec. 3401(a); Reg § 31.3401(a)-1(a)(2), Reg § 31.3401(a)-1(a)(3))[17] Bonuses received for signing employment contracts are wages, as are payments received for canceling employment contracts.[18] Wages also include amounts includible in an employee's gross income for failure to comply with the Code Sec. 409A deferred compensation rules (¶1276). (Code Sec. 3401(a)) For withholding purposes they are treated as paid in the year they are includable in gross income.[19]

Noncash wages are the fair market value of the goods, lodging, meals or other consideration given for services. (Reg § 31.3401(a)-1(a)(4))[20]

Vacation allowances[21] and back pay, including retroactive wage increases, are wages. (Reg § 31.3401(a)-1(b)(3))[22] Supplemental unemployment compensation benefits are treated as wages for income tax purposes (Code Sec. 3402(o)(1)(A), Code Sec. 3402(o)(2)),[23] but some disagreement exists about whether they are subject to FICA.[24]

Withholding is computed on gross wages before any deductions by the employer for social security tax, pensions, union dues, insurance, etc. (Reg § 31.3401(a)-1(b)(5))[25]

¶ 3005 Tips.

Wages includes tips. (Code Sec. 3401(f)) However, withholding isn't required on cash tips of less than $20 a month received by an employee, or for tips paid in any medium other than cash (such as passes, tickets or other goods or commodities). (Code Sec. 3401(a)(16); Reg § 31.3401(a)(16)-1) But if cash tips amount to $20 or more in a month, none of the cash tips are exempt. The $20 test is applied separately with respect to cash tips received by the employee for his services to each employer. (Reg § 31.3401(a)(16)-1[26] (For the business tax credit for employer FICA tax paid on tips for food and beverage service, see ¶2328.)

---

15. ¶H-4259; TD ¶535,009
16. ¶H-4303 *et seq.*; ¶34,014.375; TD ¶537,003
17. ¶H-4326; ¶s 34,014.02, 34,014.09; TD ¶532,001
18. ¶H-4360.2, ¶H-4361.1
19. ¶H-4326; ¶H-4333.1;¶34,014.025; TD ¶532,046
20. ¶H-4327; ¶34,014.09; TD ¶532,001

21. ¶H-4364; ¶34,014.04; TD ¶532,029
22. ¶H-4355; ¶34,014.09; TD ¶532,024
23. ¶H-4351
24. ¶H-4664
25. ¶H-4331; TD ¶532,001
26. ¶H-4341; ¶34,014.31; TD ¶532,011

¶ 3006   Exempt "wages"—fringes, reimbursed expenses, domestic service, etc.

The following aren't wages subject to income tax withholding:

. . . Fringe benefits if it's reasonable to believe that the employee will be able to exclude them from income as a qualified scholarship, a no-additional-cost service, a qualified employee discount, a working condition fringe, a de minimis fringe, a qualified transportation fringe, a qualified moving expense reimbursement, an on-premises athletic facility, or an employee achievement award. (Code Sec. 3401(a)(19))[27] (For the employer's election not to withhold on a vehicle fringe benefit, see ¶3007.)

. . . Amounts specifically advanced or reimbursed to employees for traveling or other ordinary and necessary expenses incurred or reasonably expected to be incurred in the employer's business. But they must be either paid separately, or specifically identified if combined with wages in a single payment. (Reg § 31.3401(a)-4(a)) If a reimbursement or other expense allowance arrangement meets the requirements of Code Sec. 62(c) (¶3104, i.e., an "accountable plan"), payments that don't exceed the substantiated expenses aren't wages and aren't subject to withholding. Payments that aren't substantiated within a reasonable period of time or are in excess of substantiated expenses are wages and subject to withholding. Per diem or mileage allowances at a rate in excess of the deemed substantiated amount are subject to withholding. If the arrangement doesn't meet the Code Sec. 62(c) requirements (i.e., a "nonaccountable plan"), all amounts paid are wages and subject to withholding. (Reg § 31.3401(a)-4(a), Reg § 31.3401(a)-4(b), Reg § 1.62-2(h)(1), Reg § 1.62-2(h)(2))[28]

. . . Moving expense reimbursements, if a corresponding deduction is allowable under the normal Code Sec. 217 rules, see ¶1645, (determined without regard to the Code Sec. 274(n) percentage limit on meal expenses). (Code Sec. 3401(a)(15))[29]

. . . Tips, under the circumstances at ¶3005.

. . . Benefits paid by a labor union to workers unemployed because of a strike or lockout. [30]

. . . Payments for agricultural labor except if during the year: (1) cash payments to an employee are $150 or more, or (2) the employer pays all such employees $2,500 or more (unless the employee is a hand harvest laborer who is paid on a customary basis, commutes daily to the farm from his permanent residence and was employed in agriculture less than 13 weeks during the prior year). (Code Sec. 3401(a)(2); Code Sec. 3121(a)(8))[31]

. . . Payments for domestic service in a private home, local college club or fraternity or sorority chapter. (Code Sec. 3401(a)(3))[32]

. . . Certain payments for services by a U.S. citizen for an employer outside the U.S. (Code Sec. 3401(a)(8)(A)(i))[33]

. . . Premiums paid by an employer for group term insurance on an employee's life. (Code Sec. 3401(a)(14))[34]

. . . Payments to or on behalf of an employee or his beneficiary to or from a qualified plan (except payments for services rendered by an employee of the plan) (Code Sec. 3401(a)(12)(A)); to or under a qualified annuity plan (Code Sec. 3401(a)(12)(B)); under a SIMPLE retirement account (Code Sec. 3401(a)(12)(D)); to or under a governmental section 457 plan (Code Sec. 3401(a)(12)(E)); or, if it's reasonable to believe the employee will be entitled to exclude the payment, for contributions to a simplified employee pension for an employee. (Code Sec. 3401(a)(12)(C))[35]

27. ¶H-4400 *et seq.*; ¶s 34,014.09, 34,024; TD ¶533,001
28. ¶H-4340; ¶34,014.03; TD ¶532,004
29. ¶H-4418; ¶34,014.30; TD ¶533,014
30. ¶H-4354; ¶34,014.10; TD ¶532,023
31. ¶H-4426; ¶34,014.18; TD ¶536,023

32. ¶H-4450 *et seq.*; ¶34,014.19; TD ¶536,006
33. ¶s H-4442, H-4443; ¶34,014.23; TD ¶536,013
34. ¶H-1518 *et seq.*, ¶H-4400 *et seq.*; ¶34,014.29
35. ¶H-10500 *et seq.*; ¶34,014.27; TD ¶553,237

... Payments made under educational assistance or dependent care programs if it's reasonable to believe that the employee can exclude them. (Code Sec. 3401(a)(18))[36]

... Payment of deceased employee's accrued wages to his estate or beneficiaries. [37]

... Combat zone compensation excludible under Code Sec. 112. (Code Sec. 3401(a)(1)) [38]

... Employer contributions to medical savings accounts. (Code Sec. 3401(a)(21), Code Sec. 3401(a)(22))[39]

... Qualified adoption expenses paid under an employer's adoption assistance program. [40]

... Disqualifying dispositions of stock acquired through the exercise of an incentive stock option (ISO) or an option under an employee stock purchase plan (ESPP) (Code Sec. 421(b)) or with respect to any amount treated as compensation as a result of the ESPP discount option rule which treats a part of the gain on a disposition of stock acquired through the exercise of an option under an ESPP as compensation income if the option price at which the stock was acquired was between 85% and 100% of its fair market value at the time the option was granted. (Code Sec. 423(c))[41]

¶ 3007 Employer's election not to withhold on vehicle fringe benefit.

Employers may elect not to withhold on an employee's use of an employer-provided vehicle where that use is wages to the employee. The employer must notify the employee of the election and include the amount of the benefit on a timely furnished Form W-2. (Code Sec. 3402(s))[42]

¶ 3008 Withholding on sick pay—Form W-4S.

If the recipient of sick pay that isn't wages requests the payor (on Form W-4S) to withhold a specified amount of at least $20 from each payment, the payor must withhold that amount. (Code Sec. 3402(o)(1)(C); Reg § 31.3402(o)-3(b)) An employee doesn't have to request withholding if his employer makes the sick payments since employers are required to withhold income tax from sick pay. [43]

¶ 3009 Voluntary withholding agreements—Form W-4 and Form W-4V.

Household, and other employees who aren't subject to income tax withholding may elect to have tax withheld, if their employers agree. (Code Sec. 3402(p)) Other employees can also have their withholding increased voluntarily. (Code Sec. 3402(i))

The rules generally applicable to mandatory withholding, including withholding rates and tables, apply to the voluntary withholding. An employee requests voluntary withholding by filing a Form W-4 with his employer —unless he wants the voluntary withholding to apply for a *limited period of time.* In that case, he must also give the employer a statement that includes the date the voluntary withholding is to terminate.

A voluntary withholding agreement may be terminated by employer or employee by giving advance notice to the other in accordance with the regs. (Reg § 31.3402(p)-1)[44]

A taxpayer can request voluntary withholding at a rate of 7%, 10%, 15%, or 25% on certain federal payments, including Social Security benefits, crop disaster payments, and Commodity Credit Corporation loans (Code Sec. 3402(p)(1)), and at a 10% rate on unemployment compensation payments (¶1281). (Code Sec. 3402(p)(2)) Use Form W-4V.[45]

---

36. ¶H-4401; ¶34,014.05; TD ¶533,001
37. ¶H-4350; ¶34,014.07; TD ¶532,019
38. ¶H-4447; ¶34,014.17; TD ¶536,004
39. ¶H-4326; ¶34,014.67; TD ¶533,001
40. ¶H-4401; TD ¶533,001

41. ¶H-4448.2; TD ¶532,035.1
42. ¶s H-4411, H-4412; ¶34,024.27; TD ¶533,010
43. ¶H-4337; ¶H-4481 *et seq.*; ¶34,024.25; TD ¶532,015
44. ¶H-4477 *et seq.*; ¶34,024.19; TD ¶538,049 *et seq.*
45. ¶H-4483 *et seq.*; ¶34,024.25; TD ¶538,053 *et seq.*

¶ 3010   Fringe benefits.

Fringe benefits must be treated as paid at least annually. Except for transfers of either personal property of a kind normally held for investment or real property (which must be reported when they are actually paid), an employer may elect to treat fringe benefits as paid quarterly, semiannually, annually, or on another basis. An employer may also treat a fringe benefit as paid in installments, even if the entire benefit is paid at one time. Benefits provided in a calendar year must be treated as paid by Dec. 31 of that year. [46]

Employers may treat fringe benefits as part of regular wages for the payroll period and compute withholding on the total, or instead withhold 25% of the value of the benefit from regular wages. (Reg § 31.3501(a)-1T, Q&A-10) Any noncash fringe benefit provided in a calendar quarter may be treated as provided on the last day of that quarter. (Reg § 31.3501(a)-1T, Q&A-1)[47]

For when withholding isn't required on a presumptively tax-free fringe benefit, see ¶3006. For the election to not withhold on the value of a vehicle fringe benefit provided to the employee, see ¶3007.

¶ 3011   Supplemental wage payments.

Withholding on bonuses, commissions, overtime pay or other supplemental wages paid:

. . . *with regular wages*, should be determined as if the total supplemental and regular wages were a single payment for the regular payroll period; (Reg § 31.3402(g)-1(a))

. . . *at a different time*, can be determined by adding the supplemental wages either to the regular wages for the current payroll period or to the last preceding payroll period within the same calendar year; (Reg § 31.3402(g)-1(a))

. . . *where tax has been withheld on regular wages*, generally can be determined by using a flat rate of not less than 25% without allowance for exemptions and without reference to any regular wage payment. (Reg § 31.3402(g)-1(a)) Where tax has been withheld on regular wages (during the calendar year of the payment or the preceding one), withholding generally can be determined (at the employer's option) by using a flat rate of 25% without allowance for exemptions and without reference to any regular wage payment, if the supplemental wages are either paid at a different time than the regular wages or are separately stated on the employer's payroll records. (Reg § 31.3402(g)-1(a))[48]

However, for supplemental wage payments totalling more than $1 million for a calendar year, the withholding rate is increased to the maximum tax rate under Code Sec. 1 (35% for 2007).[49] The employer has the option of treating either the entire supplemental payment or just that which brings the total payment over $1 million as subject to this mandatory withholding. (Reg § 31.3402(g)-1(a)(4)(iv))[50]

Where tax isn't withheld from regular wages for employees who receive both regular wages and supplemental wages (e.g., tips), the flat supplemental withholding rate can't be used; the tips are added to the current or preceding regular wage payment and withholding is computed at the regular graduated rates. [1] A payment qualifies as supplemental wages even if no regular wages have been paid to the employee.

Extra pay for working during a vacation period is treated as a supplemental wage payment. (Reg § 31.3402(g)-1(c))[2] Employers have the option to treat tips and overtime pay as either regular or supplemental wages. (Reg § 31.3402(g)-1(a))[3]

---

46. ¶H-4403; ¶34,024; TD ¶533,002 *et seq.*
47. ¶H-4404 *et seq.*; ¶s 34,024, 34,024.27; TD ¶533,003
48. ¶s H-4509, H-4510, H-4511; ¶34,024.13; TD ¶538,018
49. ¶H-4542; ¶34,024.13; TD ¶538,019.1

50. ¶H-4505 *et seq.*; ¶34,024.13; TD ¶538,017
1. ¶H-4507; TD ¶538,017
2. ¶H-4508; ¶34,024.13; TD ¶538,017
3. ¶H-4505 *et seq.*; ¶34,024.13; TD ¶538,017

¶ 3012 Computing the amount withheld—percentage and wage bracket methods.

There are two principal systems of withholding: (1) the percentage or exact method, and (2) the wage bracket method. Whichever method is used, the employer applies the withholding allowances and marital status indicated by the employee, see ¶3014 *et seq.* For variations of these two methods, see ¶3013.

Under the percentage method, the income tax to be withheld is computed as follows:

(1) Multiply the amount of *one* withholding exemption (from a table provided by IRS) by the number of withholding exemptions claimed.

(2) Subtract the amount claimed in (1) (above) from the employee's wages.

(3) Compute the tax by referring to the appropriate percentage table. There are tables for both single persons (including heads of household) and married persons. For each category, there is a weekly, biweekly, semimonthly, monthly, quarterly, semiannual, annual and a daily (or miscellaneous period) table. (Code Sec. 3402(b))[4]

Wage bracket table method. These tables show the amount to be withheld from various amounts paid to employees with different numbers of withholding exemptions. The tables may be used for weekly, biweekly, semi-monthly, monthly, and daily or miscellaneous payroll periods. (Code Sec. 3402(c))[5]

¶ 3013 Alternative withholding methods.

IRS also authorizes withholding on the basis of: (1) annualized wages, (2) cumulative wages, (3) part-year employment, (4) average estimated wages, and (5) any other method that results in substantially the same amount of withholding as the percentage method. (Methods (2) and (3) are at the employee's request.) (Code Sec. 3402(h))[6]

¶ 3014 Employee's withholding allowance certificate—Form W-4.

An employer should ask each new employee to fill out a Form W-4 withholding allowance certificate before employment begins. (Code Sec. 3402(f)(2)(A)) Employers must take into account the marital status and exemptions and allowances of each employee on the basis of that Form W-4. A certificate filed by a new employee is effective on the first payment of wages. (Code Sec. 3402(f)(3)) If an employee fails to furnish a certificate, the employer must withhold tax as if the employee were a single person with no withholding exemptions or allowances. (Code Sec. 3401(e); Reg § 31.3402(f)(2)-1(e))[7]

An employer can establish a system for its employees to file Form W-4 electronically. (Reg § 31.3402(f)(5)-1(c))[8]

¶ 3015 Withholding exemptions.

An employee is allowed: (1) a regular exemption for himself, unless he's claimed as another's dependent; (2) a regular exemption for his spouse, unless the spouse is employed and claims a regular exemption; (3) an exemption for each dependent he may claim on his tax return; (Code Sec. 3402(f)(1); Reg § 31.3402(f)(1)-1)[9] and (4) additional withholding allowances, ¶3016.

A taxpayer working for more than one employer must allocate his allowances on separate

---

4. ¶H-4493; ¶s 34,024.02, 34,024.04; TD ¶538,004
5. ¶H-4494; ¶s 34,024.02, 34,024.18; TD ¶538,005
6. ¶H-4492; ¶34,024.18; TD ¶538,006 *et seq.*

7. ¶H-4523 *et seq.*; ¶34,024.09 *et seq.*; TD ¶538,031
8. ¶H-4523.1 *et seq.*; ¶34,024.11; TD ¶538,039
9. ¶H-4512; ¶34,024.10; TD ¶538,020

Form W-4S filed with each employer. (Code Sec. 3402(f)(7); Reg § 31.3402(m)-1(f)(2))[10]

The withholding exemption allowance is the same amount as allowed for a personal exemption, ¶3115. (Code Sec. 3402(a)(2))[11]

¶ 3016   Additional withholding allowances.

Employees may claim (on Form W-4) additional withholding allowances for: estimated tax credits like those shown on Form 1040, except for any earned income credit if the employee is receiving advance payment of it (¶2346); and estimated itemized deductions and other deductions including the additional standard deduction for the aged and blind, but only if his spouse doesn't have in effect a Form W-4 claiming the same allowances. (Code Sec. 3402(m); Reg § 31.3402(m)-1)[12]

✪/caution: A taxpayer who has too little tax withheld because he has claimed too many withholding allowances may have to pay a penalty for underpayment of estimated tax, see ¶3156.

An additional withholding allowance (called a "standard deduction allowance") can be claimed by an employee who is single and has only one job; is married and has only one job, if his spouse does not work; or if his wages from a second job or his spouse's wages (or the total of both) are $1,000 or less. (Code Sec. 3402(f)(1)(E); Reg § 31.3402(f)(1)-1(e))[13]

¶ 3017   Employees with no tax liability.

Employees with no tax liability can be exempt from income tax withholding. To qualify, the employee certifies on Form W-4 to his employer that he expects to have no federal income tax liability for the current year, *and* he had no federal income tax liability in the preceding year. (Code Sec. 3402(n); Reg § 31.3402(n)-1)[14]

An employee who can be claimed as a dependent on someone else's tax return (whether or not actually claimed) cannot claim exemption from withholding if his income exceeds $850 and includes more than $300 of unearned income for 2007, such as interest and dividends. Special calculations have to be made by an employee who is 65 or older and/or blind. [15]

¶ 3018   Amending withholding certificate.

The employee *must* amend his Form W-4, reducing the number of allowances, within ten days: (Code Sec. 3402(f)(2)(B); Reg § 31.3402(f)(2)-1(b))

. . . when the spouse he has been claiming is divorced or legally separated from him, or claims her own allowance on a separate W-4;

. . . when he loses the right to exemption for a claimed dependent;

. . . when he loses the right to the number of withholding allowances he has claimed. [16] The employer must give effect to an amended W-4 no later than the beginning of the first payroll period ending (or the first payment of wages made without regard to a payroll period) on or after the 30th day after the day the amended W-4 is furnished. (Code Sec. 3402(f)(3)(B)(i))[17]

An amended Form W-4 must be filed by Dec. 1 if the number of allowances is expected to *decrease* for next year. If the change resulting in the decrease occurs in December, the amended Form must be furnished within ten days of the date of the change. The number of allowances drops if a spouse or dependent died during the year or an individual will no longer

10. ¶H-4516; ¶34,024.10; TD ¶538,024   14. ¶H-4526; ¶34,024.24; TD ¶538,034
11. ¶H-4512; ¶34,024.10; TD ¶538,020   15. ¶H-4526; ¶34,024.24; TD ¶538,034
12. ¶H-4518 *et seq.*; ¶s 34,024.10, 34,024.23; TD ¶538,026   16. ¶H-4531; ¶34,024.11; TD ¶538,040
13. ¶H-4513; ¶34,024.10; TD ¶538,021   17. ¶H-4534; ¶34,024.11; TD ¶538,041.1

qualify as a dependent. [18]

If the number of allowances is expected to increase next year, the employee can amend his W-4 by Dec. 1. If the change arises in December, the amended W-4 may be filed on or after the date of the change. (Code Sec. 3402(f)(2)(C); Reg § 31.3402(f)(2)-1(c)) This W-4 doesn't take effect and isn't to be made effective with respect to any payment of wages in the calendar year it's furnished. (Code Sec. 3402(f)(3)(B)(iii))[19]

¶ 3019 Employer withholding tax return—Form 941.

Every employer (except household employers, see ¶3028) must file with IRS a quarterly return reporting withheld income taxes on Form 941. (Reg § 31.6011(a)-1, Reg § 31.6011(a)-4) Employers must submit copies of W-4S to IRS only when directed to do so by written notice or as directed in published guidance. (Reg § 31.3402(f)(2)-1(g)(1)) Where a serious underwithholding problem is found to exist for a particular employee, IRS will notify the employer to withhold income tax from that employee at a more appropriate rate (i.e., issue a "lock-in letter"). (Reg § 31.3402(f)(2)-1(g)(2))[20]

In certain cases (e.g., for taxpayers who must separately account, see ¶3024) IRS can require monthly wage withholding returns. (Reg § 31.6011(a)-5(a)(1))[21]

Form 941 must be filed by Apr. 30, July 31, Oct. 31 and Jan. 31 for the calendar quarters ending Mar. 31, June 30, Sept. 30 and Dec. 31, respectively, unless monthly filing is required. But the returns may be filed ten days later if timely deposits in full payment of the tax are made. (Reg § 31.6071(a)-1(a))[22]

Form 941, Schedule D, can be used to explain reporting discrepancies after (1) statutory mergers and consolidations, and (2) acquisitions satisfying the requirements for predecessor-successor status (here, discrepancies may arise between amounts reported to the Social Security Administration on Form W-2 and amounts reported to IRS on Form 941). [23]

Employers with annual employment tax liabilities of $1,000 or less who have received written notification from IRS that they qualify for the program can file Form 944 annually, instead of Form 941. (Reg § 31.6011(a)-4T(a)(4))[24]

For nonpayroll withholding (backup withholding, withholding for pension, annuities, and gambling winnings, etc.), see ¶3030.

¶ 3020 Errors in withholding and payment of tax.

Where underwithholding of FICA and income tax is ascertained before the return is filed, the employer must report and pay the correct amount of tax by the due date of the return. (Reg § 31.6151-1, Reg § 31.6205-1(b)(1), Reg § 31.6205-1(c)(1); Prop Reg. § 31.6205-1(b)(1), Prop Reg. § 31.6205-1(c)(1)["Taxpayer may rely," Preamble to Prop Reg 12/10/92]) [25]

Where underpayment of FICA and income tax is ascertained after the return is filed, the additional amount due should be reported on a return filed by the due date for the return period in which the error is ascertained (in order to qualify for an interest-free adjustment). (Reg § 31.6205-1(b)(2); Prop Reg. § 31.6205-1(b)(3)["Taxpayer may rely," Preamble to Prop Reg 12/10/92]) An underpayment or underwithholding may not be corrected interest-free after receipt of notice and demand. (Reg § 31.6205-1(a)(6)) Corrections are interest-free only if made before the *earlier* of receipt of (1) notice and demand, or (2) notice of determination concerning worker classification. (Reg § 31.6205-1(a)(6))[26]

18. ¶H-4532; ¶34,024.11; TD ¶538,041
19. ¶H-4532; ¶34,024.11; TD ¶538,041
20. ¶S-2603; ¶s 34,024, 35,014.02; TD ¶557,001
21. ¶S-2604; ¶60,114.11; TD ¶557,004
22. ¶S-4918; ¶60,114.11; TD ¶557,002

23. ¶S-3195.1
24. ¶S-4918
25. ¶S-5525; ¶35,014.05; TD ¶559,516
26. ¶S-5526; ¶35,014.05; TD ¶559,517

If *more* than the correct FICA and income tax is collected from an employee and paid to IRS, the employer should:

(1) repay the overcollection to the employee in any later return period in the same calendar year and get a dated written receipt from the employee, or

(2) reimburse the employee by reducing the tax to be withheld for the balance of the same calendar year. (Reg § 31.6413(a)-1(b)(1))[27]

An employer shouldn't report or pay to IRS an overage of tax if the employer: (1) repays the overwithholding to the employee before the return for the period is filed and before the end of the calendar year in which the overcollection was made and (2) gets and keeps the written receipt of the employee showing the date and amount of the repayment. (Reg § 31.6413(a)-1(a)(1), Reg § 31.6413(a)-1(a)(2))[28]

¶ 3021   Wage and tax statement—Form W-2.

An employer in business must give each employee copies of Form W-2, on or before Jan. 31 of the year after the calendar year for which the wages were paid. If an employee leaves the job before the end of the calendar year and isn't expected to return within the calendar year, Form W-2 must be given to him not later than 30 days after the employer receives a written request for it from the employee, if that 30-day period ends before Jan. 31. (Code Sec. 6051; Reg § 31.6051-1(d))[29]

¶ 3022   Nonreceipt of Form W-2 by employee—Form 4852.

If an employee doesn't receive a Form W-2, he should ask his employer for it. If the employer doesn't provide the form, the taxpayer should telephone IRS toll-free at the number listed in the income tax return instructions; IRS will ask the employer to send a copy or duplicate form. If the employee hasn't received a Form W-2 in time to file his tax return, he should file a return estimating wages and the income tax withheld on Form 4852. [30]

¶ 3023   Earned income credit notice to employees with no tax withheld—Notice 797.

An employer must notify any employee who has not had any tax withheld from his wages (other than an employee who certifies, see ¶3017, that he has no tax liability) that the employee may be eligible for a refund because of the earned income credit (¶2341 *et seq.*). IRS Notice 797 or a written statement containing an exact reproduction of the wording in Notice 797 must be used and must be furnished within one week (before or after) the date the employee should receive a timely Form W-2 or, if none is required, before Feb. 8th of the following calendar year. (Reg § 31.6051-1(h))[31]

¶ 3024   Separate accounting for employment tax.

IRS can require an employer who fails to collect, account for, deposit, etc., income or related employment taxes or make timely deposits or file returns to make deposits in a special trust account. (Code Sec. 7512; Reg § 301.7512-1(b))[32]

---

27. ¶S-5529; ¶35,014.05; TD ¶559,520

28. ¶S-5530; TD ¶559,521

29. ¶S-4930; ¶60,514

30. ¶S-3193; TD ¶812,025

31. ¶H-4851 *et seq.*; ¶s 324.04, 60,514; TD ¶569,027

32. ¶S-5541 *et seq.*; ¶75,124; TD ¶531,002

¶ 3025   Deposit of employment taxes.

An employer is either a monthly or semi-weekly depositor. (Reg § 31.6302-1(a))

An employer is a monthly depositor for the entire calendar year if the aggregate amount of employment taxes reported for the lookback period (i.e., the 12-month period ended the preceding June 30) is $50,000 or less. (Reg § 31.6302-1(b)(2)(i), Reg § 31.6302-1(b)(4)) These employers must deposit taxes on or before the 15th day of the following month. (Reg § 31.6302-1(c)(1))[33]

An employer is a semi-weekly depositor for the entire calendar year if the aggregate amount of employment taxes reported for the lookback period (i.e., the 12-month period ended the preceding June 30) exceeds $50,000. (Reg § 31.6302-1(b)(3), Reg § 31.6302-1(b)(4)) The employer must deposit taxes on or before the following dates. (Reg § 31.6302-1(c)(2))[34]

If the wage payment date is:

... Wednesday, Thursday, and/or Friday, the deposit date is on or before the following Wednesday.

... Saturday, Sunday, Monday, and/or Tuesday, the deposit date is on or before the following Friday.

If a return period (quarterly or annual) ends during a semi-weekly period, the employer must designate on his deposit coupon the proper return period for which the deposits relates (the period in which the payment is made). If the return period ends during a semi-weekly period during which the employer has two or more payment dates, two deposit obligations may exist. (Reg § 31.6302-1(c)(2)(ii))[35]

Notwithstanding the above rules, under the "one-day rule," if on any day an employer has $100,000 or more of employment taxes accumulated, these taxes must be deposited by the close of the next banking day. (Reg § 31.6302-1(c)(3)) The day after a monthly depositor becomes subject to the one-day rule it becomes a semi-weekly depositor for the remainder of that calendar year and for the following calendar year. (Reg § 31.6302-1(b)(2)(ii))[36]

If a tax deposit day isn't a banking day, deposits are timely if made on the next day that is a banking day. (Reg § 31.6302-1(c)(4)) In addition, if one of the three weekdays following the close of a semi-weekly period is a bank holiday, the employer has an extra banking day to deposit taxes. (Reg § 31.6302-1(c)(2)(iii))[37]

Deposits are considered timely if mailed (postmarked, or date marked by a designated delivery service, see ¶4759) at least two days before the due date if the deposit is actually received by the bank. (Code Sec. 7502(e)) But a deposit of $20,000 or more by a person who is required to make a deposit more than once a month must be actually received by the due date. (Code Sec. 7502(e)(3))[38]

Some taxpayers must deposit taxes by electronic funds transfer (¶3027).

¶ 3026   Deposit safe harbor and de minimis rules.

Under the single deposit safe harbor, an employer will be considered to have satisfied his deposit obligations if:

(1) the amount of any shortfall (the excess of the amount required to be deposited over the amount deposited for the applicable period —monthly, semi-weekly or daily) doesn't exceed the greater of $100 or 2% of the amount of employment taxes required to be deposited

---

33. ¶S-5503; ¶63,014; TD ¶559,503
34. ¶S-5506; ¶63,014; TD ¶559,504
35. ¶S-5507; ¶63,014; TD ¶559,505

36. ¶S-5510; ¶63,014; TD ¶559,507
37. ¶S-5512; ¶63,014; TD ¶559,508
38. ¶T-10777 *et seq.*; ¶63,014, 75,024

(Reg § 31.6302-1(f)(1)(i), Reg § 31.6302-1(f)(2)), and

(2) the employer deposits the shortfall on or before the shortfall make-up date. (Reg § 31.6302-1(f)(1)(ii)) For a monthly depositor this is no later than the due date for the quarterly return. For a semi-weekly or a one-day depositor this is on or before the first Wednesday or Friday (whichever is earlier) falling on or after the 15th day of the month following the month the deposit was required to be made. (Reg § 31.6302-1(f)(3))[39]

Under a de minimis rule, an employer with accumulated employment taxes of less than $2,500 for a return period (quarterly or annual) doesn't have to make deposits and can instead remit his full liability with a timely filed return for the period. (Reg § 31.6302-1(f)(4))[40]

¶ 3027   Tax deposits by electronic funds transfer.

Unless exempted, taxpayers whose aggregate annual deposits of certain taxes exceeded $200,000 in a tax year must deposit taxes by electronic funds transfer. (Code Sec. 6302(h); Reg § 31.6302-1(h)(2)(i)(A)) Once taxpayers exceed the $200,000 threshold, they have a one-year grace period before being required to use EFT. They must then use EFT in all later years even if their deposits fall below the threshold. (Reg § 31.6302-1(h)(2)(ii)) The EFT rules apply to return periods beginning after Dec. 31 of the year following the year in which the threshold is exceeded. (Reg § 31.6302-1(h)(2)(i))[41]

A taxpayer required to deposit by EFT must use the Electronic Federal Tax Payment System (EFTPS) to make federal tax deposits. [42] Taxpayers must enroll in EFTPS before they can make EFT deposits. Enroll on-line at www.eftps.com. [43] EFTPS deposits may be initiated directly via EFTPS-Online, EFTPS-PC Software supplied by IRS, or EFTPS-Phone, or through a financial institution using an Automated Clearing House (ACH) credit transaction. Under this system, payments can be made weekly, monthly, or quarterly, and businesses can schedule payments up to 120 days in advance of the due date. Scheduled payments can be changed or cancelled up to two business days in advance of the scheduled date. Tax practitioners and payroll companies can use EFTPS to make payments on behalf of their clients without having to register for EFTPS (although their clients must do so). [44]

Federal income taxes (including estimated taxes) (Reg § 1.6302-4), estate (Reg § 20.6302-1) and gift taxes (Reg § 25.6302-1), employment taxes (Reg § 31.6302-1(h)(2)(iii)), and various excise taxes (Reg § 40.6302(a)-1) may be made voluntarily by EFT. [45]

A taxpayer required to deposit taxes by EFT that (without reasonable cause) deposits by other means is subject to the Code Sec. 6656 failure to deposit penalty. [46]

To induce employers who are not required to use the EFT system to use it, IRS is offering a refund of a previously paid federal tax deposit penalty with interest. To qualify, the employer must use EFT for one year (four consecutive quarters), make all Form 941 payments on time, and have previously fully paid the penalty. IRS automatically determines which employers have achieved the four quarters of EFT compliance and reverses the most recent full-paid FTD penalty minus any outstanding taxes. [47]

¶ 3028   Payment of Domestic Service Employment Tax ("Nanny tax") ▬▬▬▬

Domestic service employment taxes (income tax, FICA, and FUTA) can be paid in a lump sum when the employer's income tax return is filed.

39. ¶S-5513 *et seq.*; ¶63,014; TD ¶559,509
40. ¶S-5516; ¶63,014; TD ¶559,510
41. ¶S-5620 *et seq.*; ¶63,014; TD ¶559,850 *et seq.*
42. ¶S-5621; TD ¶559,857
43. ¶S-5630; TD ¶559,857
44. ¶S-5631 *et seq.*; TD ¶559,851 *et seq.*
45. ¶S-5629; TD ¶559,863 *et seq.*
46. ¶V-1658; TD ¶559,853
47. ¶S-5629

¶ 3029 "Nanny tax"—Form 1040, Schedule H.

Employers of domestic service employees must file annual returns of domestic service employment taxes on a calendar-year basis (Code Sec. 3510(a)(1)) on or before the 15th day of the fourth month following the close of the employer's tax year. (Code Sec. 3510(a)(2)) Household employers report withheld income and FICA tax for their household employees on their individual income tax return (Form 1040, Schedule H) and need employer identification numbers (EINs, apply on Form SS-4). [48]

Annual Form 940 (FUTA) doesn't have to be filed for domestic employees. There is no requirement to make deposits of domestic service employment taxes, or to pay installments of these taxes under Code Sec. 6157 (Code Sec. 3510(a)(3)), dealing with quarterly payment of FUTA tax.

"Domestic service employment taxes" are: (1) any FICA and FUTA taxes on remuneration paid for domestic service in a private home of the employer (for dollar threshold see below), and (2) and any income tax on these payments that is withheld under the Code Sec. 3402(p) voluntary withholding agreement rules (¶3009) (for the otherwise applicable exemption from income tax withholding on domestic service employment, see ¶3006). (Code Sec. 3510(c))[49]

Domestic service is service of a household nature performed in and about the private home of the person for whom the services are performed. (Reg § 31.3121(a)(7)-1(a); Reg § 31.3401(a)(3)-1(a))[50]

Noncash payments for domestic services in an employer's private home are excluded from FICA wages. Cash remuneration paid by an employer for domestic service in the employer's private home isn't FICA wages if the cash remuneration paid during the year is less than the "applicable dollar threshold"—$1,500 in 2007 ($1,600 in 2008). (Code Sec. 3121(a)(7); Code Sec. 3121(x))[1]

🛈*observation:* The dollar threshold applies separately to each domestic employee. Thus, if an employer pays $1,450 each to a babysitter and a housekeeper in 2007, no FICA tax is due for either.

Domestic service performed in the private home of the employer in any year by an individual under the age of 18 during any portion of the year is excepted from employment for FICA if the service isn't the principal occupation of the employee. (Code Sec. 3121(b)(21))[2]

Form W-2. An employer must furnish Form W-2 to household employees whose wages are subject to Social Security taxes even if they aren't subject to income tax withholding. (Reg § 31.6051-1(b)(1)) Use a Form W-3 transmittal to file even one Form W-2. [3]

¶ 3030 Nonpayroll Withheld Taxes. ▆▆▆▆▆▆▆▆▆

Income tax on gambling winnings, payments subject to backup withholding, retirement plan payments, IRAs, annuities and certain other deferred compensation are withheld under "nonpayroll withheld taxes" rules.

The employment tax deposit rules of ¶3025 *et seq.* apply to determine the time and manner of making deposits of nonpayroll withheld taxes. (Reg § 31.6302-4(a))[4] Whether a taxpayer is a monthly or a semi-weekly depositor for a calendar year is based on an annual determination and generally depends on the aggregate amount of nonpayroll withheld taxes reported by the taxpayer for the "lookback period"—i.e., the second calendar year preceding the current calendar year. Thus, the lookback period for calendar year 2007 is calendar year 2005. A new

48. ¶S-2608; ¶35,104; TD ¶557,007
49. ¶S-2608.3; ¶35,104
50. ¶H-4654; TD ¶536,006
1. ¶H-4653 *et seq.*; ¶35,104; TD ¶544,009

2. ¶H-4611.1
3. ¶S-3159; TD ¶812,004
4. ¶S-5584 *et seq.*; ¶63,014

taxpayer is treated as having nonpayroll withheld taxes of zero for any calendar year in which the taxpayer didn't exist. (Reg § 31.6302-4(c)(2)(iv))[5]

A taxpayer is a monthly depositor of nonpayroll withheld taxes for a calendar year if the amount of nonpayroll withheld taxes accumulated in the lookback period is $50,000 or less. A taxpayer ceases to be a monthly depositor of nonpayroll withheld taxes on the first day after the taxpayer is subject to the "one-day rule" (¶3025) with respect to nonpayroll withheld taxes. At that time, the taxpayer immediately becomes a semi-weekly depositor of nonpayroll withheld taxes for the remainder of the calendar year and the succeeding calendar year. (Reg § 31.6302-4(c)(2)(ii))

A taxpayer is a semi-weekly depositor of nonpayroll withheld taxes for a calendar year if the amount of nonpayroll withheld taxes accumulated in the lookback period exceeds $50,000. (Reg § 31.6302-4(c)(2)(iii))

Nonpayroll withheld taxes are income taxes withheld from: gambling winnings (¶3032) (Reg § 31.6302-4(b)(1)); retirement pay for services in the Armed Forces under Code Sec. 3402 (Reg § 31.6302-4(b)(2); retirement plan payments, IRAs, annuities and certain other deferred compensation (¶3033) (Reg § 31.6302-4(b)(3)); certain payments by governmental entities made after 2010 (Code Sec. 3402(t)); and under the backup withholding rules (¶3043). (Reg § 31.6302-4(b)(5))[6]

For the requirement that some taxpayers deposit nonpayroll withheld taxes by electronic funds transfer (EFT), see ¶3027.

¶ 3031   Annual nonpayroll tax return—Form 945.

Taxpayers who withhold income tax from nonpayroll payments must report the withholding annually on Form 945. The return must be filed on or before Jan. 31 following the calendar year. However, if timely deposits of tax have been made, the return may be filed by Feb. 10. (Reg § 31.6071(a)-1(a)(1))[7]

¶ 3032   Withholding on gambling winnings—Form W-2G and Form 5754.

Payors must withhold 25% on proceeds of more than $5,000 (Code Sec. 3402(q)(1)) from:

(1) a wagering transaction in a parimutuel pool with respect to horse races, dog races or jai alai if the amount of the proceeds is at least 300 times as large as the amount wagered; (Code Sec. 3402(q)(3)(C)(ii))

(2) a wager placed in a state-conducted lottery; (Code Sec. 3402(q)(3)(B))

(3) a sweepstakes, wagering pool or lottery (other than a state-conducted lottery); or (Code Sec. 3402(q)(3)(C)(i))

(4) all other wagering transactions if the amount of the proceeds is at least 300 times as large as the amount wagered. (Code Sec. 3402(q)(3)(A))[8]

"Proceeds" means amount received from the wager reduced by the amount of the wager. (Code Sec. 3402(q)(4)(A))[9] Amounts paid with respect to identical wagers are treated as paid with respect to a single wager. (Reg § 31.3402(q)-1(c)(1)(ii))[10]

A person who receives gambling winnings subject to withholding must provide certain information on Form W-2G or Form 5754 and give it to the payor. (Code Sec. 3402(q)(6); Reg § 31.3402(q)-1(e))[11]

The above withholding rules don't apply to slot machines, keno and bingo winnings. (Code

---

5. ¶S-5585; ¶63,014; TD ¶559,005

6. ¶S-5581; ¶63,014

7. ¶S-2609.1 *et seq.*, S-4918; TD ¶559,000 *et seq.*

8. ¶J-8603; ¶34,024.26; TD ¶554,001 *et seq.*

9. ¶J-8606 *et seq.*; ¶34,024.26; TD ¶554,002

10. ¶J-8610; ¶34,024.26; TD ¶554,006

11. ¶J-8614; ¶34,024.26; TD ¶554,010

Sec. 3402(q)(5)) However, backup withholding (¶3043) may apply.[12] And a payor must file Form a W-2G for every person the payor pays $1,200 or more in winnings from slot machines or bingo, or $1,500 or more from Keno (after deducting the cost of the winning Keno game). (Reg § 7.6041-1)[13]

Withholding on Indian casino profits. Withholding equal to a payment's proportionate share of annualized tax is required under tables provided by IRS (Reg § 31.3402(r)-1(a)(2)) on payments to Indian tribal members from the net revenue of most gambling activities of the tribe (i.e., class II and III gaming activities). (Code Sec. 3402(r))[14]

¶ 3033 Pension, Annuity and Other Withholding. ▬▬▬▬▬

Withholding of 20% is required on any designated distribution that's an eligible rollover distribution, unless there's a direct trustee-to-trustee transfer. Withholding is required on periodic and lump-sum payments from certain employee plans and certain annuities. However, certain recipients may elect not to have tax withheld.

¶ 3034 Mandatory 20% withholding on eligible rollover distributions.

Unless a distributee elects to have the distribution paid directly to an eligible retirement plan under the Code Sec. 401(a)(31)(A) trustee-to-trustee rules (¶4319), a payor must withhold 20% of any designated distribution that's an "eligible rollover distribution" as defined by Code Sec. 402(f)(2)(A). The Code Sec. 3405(a) and Code Sec. 3405(b) elective withholding rules (¶3035 *et seq.*) don't apply to an eligible rollover distribution. (Code Sec. 3405(c); Reg § 31.3405(c)-1, Q&A-1)[15]

An eligible rollover distribution (reported by the payor on Form 1099-R) (Reg § 31.3405(c)-1, Q&A-16) is any distribution to an employee from a qualified trust (not from an IRA, SEP, or SIMPLE plan) *other than:*

. . . a required distribution under Code Sec. 401(a)(9);

. . . any distribution that is one of a series of substantially equal periodic payments made (a) not less frequently than annually for the life (or life expectancy) of the employee (or joint lives or expectancies of the employee and his designated beneficiary), or (b) for a specified period of ten years or more; or

. . . a hardship distribution from a 401(k) or 403(b) plan. (Code Sec. 3405(c)(3), Code Sec. 402(c)(4), Code Sec. 402(f)(2)(A), Code Sec. 403(b)(8)(B); Reg § 1.402(c)-2, Q&A-3[16]

No withholding is required: (1) if the total distribution paid to the distributee under the plan within one tax year is expected to be less than $200; or (Reg § 31.3405(c)-1, Q&A-14[17] (2) for qualified hurricane distributions, see ¶4344. (Code Sec. 1400Q(a))[18]

¶ 3035 Required withholding for designated distributions.

Withholding is required for designated distributions (Code Sec. 3405(d)(1)),[19] but the recipient generally may elect out, see ¶3037, unless the distribution is an eligible rollover distribution, see ¶3034. Designated distributions are periodic as well as nonperiodic (including lump-sum) payments from pension, profit sharing, stock bonus or other employer deferred compensation plans, as well as from IRAs (other than Roth IRAs) and commercial annuities, whether or not the contract was purchased under an employer's plan for employees. (Code Sec. 3405(e)) Annuity payments and other distributions under a state or local government deferred compensation plan, other than a Code Sec. 457 plan, including the Civil Service

---

12. ¶J-8604; ¶34,024.26; TD ¶554,002
13. ¶S-3697; ¶60,414; TD ¶816,025
14. ¶J-8616.1; ¶34,024.261; TD ¶554,013
15. ¶J-8577 *et seq.*; ¶34,054; TD ¶553,244 *et seq.*

16. ¶J-8586; ¶4024.04; TD ¶553,246
17. ¶s J-8584; ¶4014.22; TD ¶553,247
18. ¶H-11006.1; ¶14,00Q4; TD ¶553,244
19. ¶J-8501 *et seq.*; ¶34,054; TD ¶553,204

Retirement System are subject to income tax withholding as well. (Reg § 35.3405-1T, Q&A A-22, -23)[20]

The payor of a designated distribution must withhold and is liable for the payment of the tax (unless the payee elects out). But in the case of a qualified pension, profit sharing, stock bonus, annuity, or 457 governmental plan, the plan administrator has the responsibility, unless he directs the payor to withhold and provides the payor with the information set out in the regs. In that case, the responsibility reverts to the payor. (Code Sec. 3405(d); Reg § 35.3405-1T, Q&A E-3)[21]

¶ 3036   Withholding from periodic payments.

Tax must be withheld in accordance with a recipient's withholding certificate or, if none, by treating the payee as a married individual claiming three withholding exemptions (Code Sec. 3405(a)(4))[22] even if the payor is aware the payee is single. (Reg § 35.3405-1T, Q&A B-4) The amount to be withheld is calculated separately from any amounts that actually are wages to the payee for the same period. (Reg § 35.3405-1T, Q&A B-1)

¶ 3037   Election out of withholding on periodic payments—Form W-4P.

A recipient of periodic payments (except for certain U.S. citizens and expatriates living abroad, see ¶3041) may elect not to have any tax withheld. The election remains in effect until revoked. (Code Sec. 3405(a)(2))[23] Elect (or revoke) on Form W-4P.[24]

If the recipient doesn't furnish his taxpayer identification number (TIN) to the payor or if IRS has notified the payor that the TIN furnished is incorrect, an election out of withholding isn't effective. (Code Sec. 3405(e)(12))[25]

For periodic payments that are "eligible rollover distributions," see ¶3034.

¶ 3038   Withholding from nonperiodic distributions.

The payor of any nonperiodic distribution that is not an eligible rollover distribution subject to 20% mandatory withholding (¶3034) must withhold an amount equal to 10% of that distribution (Code Sec. 3405(b)(1)),[26] unless the recipient elects out of withholding (¶3039).

¶ 3039   Electing out of withholding on nonperiodic distributions—Form W-4P.

A payee (except for recipients of eligible rollover distributions (¶3034), and certain U.S. citizens and expatriates living abroad (¶3041)) may elect exemption from withholding for any nonperiodic distribution. The election is made on Form W-4P on a distribution-by-distribution basis. (Code Sec. 3405(b)(2)(A), Code Sec. 3405(b)(2)(B))[27]

If the recipient doesn't furnish his taxpayer identification number (TIN) to the payor or if IRS has notified the payor that the TIN furnished is incorrect, an election out of withholding isn't effective. (Code Sec. 3405(e)(12))[28]

¶ 3040   Payor must notify payee of right to elect to have no tax withheld.

For periodic payments, the notice to make, renew, or revoke the election out of withholding is required no earlier than six months before and no later than the date of the first payment. For nonperiodic payments the notice should be given not earlier than six months before the

---

20. ¶J-8504 *et seq.*; ¶34,054; TD ¶553,203
21. ¶J-8518 *et seq.*; ¶34,054; TD ¶553,205
22. ¶J-8525; ¶34,054; TD ¶553,220
23. ¶J-8526; ¶34,054; TD ¶553,221
24. ¶J-8528; ¶34,054; TD ¶553,221

25. ¶J-8513; TD ¶553,212
26. ¶J-8533; ¶34,054; TD ¶553,227
27. ¶J-8539; ¶34,054; TD ¶553,230
28. ¶J-8513; ¶34,054; TD ¶553,212

distribution and not later than the time that will give the payee reasonable time to elect out. (Code Sec. 3405(e)(10)(B); Reg § 35.3405-1T, Q&A D-4, Reg § 35.3405-1T, Q&A D-9)[29] The notice must state that withholding will apply unless the payee elects otherwise, and if he elects no withholding, estimated tax may apply. A sample statement is in the regs.(Reg § 35.3405-1T, Q&A D-21, Reg § 35.3405-1T, Q&A D-25)[30]

¶ 3041 Electing out of withholding where payment is delivered outside the U.S.

An election out of withholding can't be made for any periodic or nonperiodic payment that is to be delivered outside the U.S. and its possessions (Code Sec. 3405(e)(13)(A)) *unless* the recipient certifies to the payor that the recipient is neither a U.S. citizen, a resident alien, nor a nonresident alien who in the last ten years has lost his U.S. citizenship in order to avoid U.S. taxes and is therefore subject to Code Sec. 877. (Code Sec. 3405(e)(13)(B))[31]

¶ 3042 Backup Withholding. ▄▄▄▄▄▄▄▄▄▄▄▄▄▄▄▄▄

A payor of any reportable payment must withhold a specified percentage of the payment.

¶ 3043 When backup withholding is required.

A payor of any reportable payment (¶3044) must withhold 28% of the payment if:

(1) The payee has failed to furnish his taxpayer identification number (TIN) to the payor (Code Sec. 3406(a)(1)(A)) or furnishes an "obviously incorrect number," (Code Sec. 3406(h)(1)) i.e., one without nine digits or which includes letters of the alphabet. (Reg § 31.3406(h)-1(b))

(2) IRS or a broker has notified (the "B-notice") the payor that the TIN furnished by the payee is incorrect. (Code Sec. 3406(a)(1), Code Sec. 3406(d)(2))

(3) There has been a notified payee underreporting with respect to interest and dividends. (Code Sec. 3406(a)(1)(C))

(4) The payee has failed to make the exemption certification (on Form W-9) with respect to interest and dividends. (Code Sec. 3406(a)(1)(D))[32]

Backup withholding doesn't apply to any payment made to an organization exempt from tax under Code Sec. 501(a) (with certain exceptions); the U.S., a state, the District of Columbia, a U.S. possession, or their political subdivisions; a foreign government or its political subdivisions; an international organization; any wholly-owned agency or instrumentality of any of the above political entities; or any other person specified in regs. (Code Sec. 3406(g)(1)) Payments to a fiduciary or nominee account, or to an exempt recipient (Reg § 31.3406(d)-5(b)) aren't subject to backup withholding. [33]

¶ 3044 Reportable payments.

Reportable payments include most payments for which information returns are required, such as an interest or dividend payment. (Code Sec. 3406(b)(1))[34] Original issue discount (OID) is treated as a payment of interest for backup withholding purposes, but the amount withheld is limited to the cash paid. (Reg § 31.3406(b)(2)-2(a))[35]

Reportable payments are treated as if they were wages. Amounts deducted and withheld are treated as if they were deducted and withheld from wages. (Code Sec. 3406(h)(10))[36]

---

29. ¶J-8528 *et seq.*, ¶J-8539 *et seq.*; ¶34,054; TD ¶553,223
30. ¶J-8541, J-8543; ¶34,054; TD ¶553,223
31. ¶J-8554; ¶34,054
32. ¶J-9001; ¶34,064; TD ¶554,501

33. ¶J-9109; ¶34,064; TD ¶554,502
34. ¶J-9101; ¶34,064; TD ¶554,503
35. ¶J-9111; ¶34,064
36. ¶J-9009; TD ¶554,501

¶ 3045   How to stop backup withholding.

A payee can stop backup withholding once it has started, by showing that there was no underreporting, correcting any underreporting, showing that backup withholding will cause undue hardship and that it's unlikely he will underreport again, or showing that a bona fide dispute exists as to whether there has been any underreporting. (Reg § 35a.3406-2(g)(1); Reg § 31.3406(c)-1(g)) If IRS determines that backup withholding should stop, it will give the payee a written certification to that effect and notify payors and brokers to stop withholding. (Reg § 35a.3406-2(h)(1), Reg § 35a.3406-2(d)(1), Reg § 31.3406(c)-1(g)(1))

Withholding must stop as of the close of the day before the "stop date" (generally 30 days after receipt of the stop notice from IRS or a copy of the certification IRS gave the payee, whichever is earlier). (Code Sec. 3406(e)(3)(C)) The payor may elect to shorten or eliminate the 30-day period. (Code Sec. 3406(e)(5)(C); Reg § 35a.3406-2(e)(2)(iii), Reg § 31.3406(c)-1(e)(2)(i)(B))[37]

---

37. ¶J-9607; ¶34,064; TD ¶554,513

Chapter 13 Individual's Tax Computation—Kiddie Tax—Self-Employment Tax—Estimated Tax

¶ 3100 How Income Tax on Individuals is Computed. ▬▬▬▬▬▬▬

The annual income tax liability of an individual on taxable income is computed by using either the tax rate schedules or (when taxable income is less than $100,000) the tax tables, see ¶1101 *et seq.* The tax liability so determined is increased for some individuals by other taxes, e.g., the self-employment tax and the alternative minimum tax, and is reduced by certain credits.

For taxation of unearned income of children subject to the kiddie tax, see ¶3134 *et seq.*

For the threshold amounts of gross income that must be reached before a tax return must be filed, see ¶4701.

¶ 3101 Steps in computing taxable income.

An individual taxpayer first computes gross income —generally all income from all sources (Code Sec. 61), see ¶1200 *et seq.*

From gross income, taxpayer subtracts the deductions specified at ¶3102 to reach adjusted gross income (AGI). (Code Sec. 62)

Finally, taxpayers who itemize reduce AGI by allowable deductions and personal exemptions (¶3115) (Code Sec. 63(a)), see ¶3109 *et seq.* Nonitemizers reduce AGI by the standard deduction (¶3112) and personal exemptions. (Code Sec. 63(b))[1]

¶ 3102 Deductions in arriving at adjusted gross income (AGI).

Subtract the following deductions from gross income to arrive at AGI: (Code Sec. 62)[2]

... Trade or business expenses (¶1508) (other than unreimbursed employee business expenses, see ¶3104). For business-related deductions of "statutory employees," see ¶3103.

... Self-employed medical insurance premiums, ¶1533.

... Moving expenses, ¶1645 *et seq.*

... 50% of self-employment tax, ¶1755.

... Amortization of reforestation expenditures, ¶1974.

... Amounts forfeited to a bank or savings institution for premature withdrawal of funds from a deposit account, ¶2171.

... Alimony and separate maintenance payments, ¶2154 *et seq.*

... Employee expenses that are reimbursed by the employer or a third party, ¶3104.

... Employee business expenses of certain performing artists (¶3105) and of state and local government employees compensated on a fee basis, ¶3106.

... Jury duty pay remitted to an employer, ¶3107.

... Contributions to tax-favored retirement plans for the self-employed, ¶4310.

... Contributions to individual retirement accounts (IRAs), ¶4351.

... The "total taxable amount" of a lump-sum distribution from a retirement plan to a participant who reached age 50 before '86, ¶4339.

... Deductions in connection with property held for the production of rents or royalties.

... Depreciation and depletion deductions of a life tenant or an income beneficiary of a

---

1. ¶A-2500 *et seq.*; ¶634; TD ¶560,500 *et seq.*   2. ¶A-2601; ¶624; TD ¶560,702

References beginning with a single letter are to paragraphs in RIA's Federal Tax Coordinator 2d and RIA's Analysis of Federal Taxes: Income. Those beginning with numbers are to paragraphs in RIA's United States Tax Reporter. Those beginning with TD are to paragraphs in RIA's Tax Desk.

trust, or of an heir, legatee or devisee of an estate,   ¶3927.

. . . Losses from the sale or exchange of property,   ¶2400.

. . . Repayment of supplemental unemployment compensation benefits.

. . . Certain foreign housing costs by individuals having income earned abroad,   ¶4615.

. . . Contributions to an Archer medical savings account (Archer MSA, see   ¶1528).

. . . Contributions to a health savings account (HSA, see   ¶1529)

. . . Deduction for interest on qualified education loans,   ¶2225 *et seq.*

. . . Payments for deductible higher education expenses,   ¶2222 *et seq.*

. . . Up to $250 of qualifying expenses of educators,   ¶2232.

. . . Certain unreimbursed travel expenses of National Guard and Reserve members,   ¶1554.

. . . Attorney fees and court costs of civil rights suits,   ¶3108.

¶ 3103   Business-related expenses of "statutory employees."

For purposes of computing adjusted gross income, the allowable deductions attributable to the services rendered by a statutory employee (drivers, life insurance salespersons, home workers and other salespersons meeting certain conditions) are treated as trade or business expenses (deductible on Schedule C, rather than as itemized deductions). [3]

¶ 3104   Reimbursed and unreimbursed employee expenses.

An employee can deduct from gross income in computing adjusted gross income employee expenses for which the employee is reimbursed by the employer, its agent, or third party (for whom the employee performs a benefit as an employee of the employer) under an express agreement for reimbursement or other expense allowance under an accountable plan. (There's no normal "deduction," however, since the reimbursement is excluded from the employee's gross income. That is, there's no deduction to the extent there's no inclusion of the reimbursement.) (Code Sec. 62(a)(2)(A); Reg § 1.62-2(c)(4))[4] The expense must be otherwise allowable as a deduction (i.e., not a personal expense). [5]

If the reimbursement is for less than the total expenses paid or incurred by the employee, the unreimbursed expenses are deductible from *adjusted* gross income (not gross income), as an itemized deduction, subject to, for example, the 2%-of-AGI floor (¶3110), and the percentage limit on meal and entertainment expenses (¶1570). (Reg § 1.62-1T(e)(3))[6]

A reimbursement or other expense allowance arrangement under an accountable plan is one that meets tests for (1) business connection, (2) substantiation, and (3) return of amounts in excess of expenses. (Reg § 1.62-2(c)(2)) See ¶1574 *et seq.* for details.

A payor can have more than one arrangement with respect to one employee. (Reg § 1.62-2(c)(1))[7]

¶ 3105   Expenses of certain performing artists.

Expenses of certain performing artists are deductible (use Form 2106 or Form 2106-EZ) in arriving at adjusted gross income despite the general disallowance of unreimbursed employee business expenses as above-the-line deductions. (Code Sec. 62(a)(2)(B)) To qualify, the taxpayer must have earned at least $200 as a performing artist from each of at least two employers during the tax year. (Code Sec. 62(b)(1)(A), Code Sec. 62(b)(2)) In addition, the allowable expenses must exceed 10% of gross income from the services, and AGI for the year

---

3. ¶A-2603; ¶624.03; TD ¶560,704   6. ¶A-2605; ¶624.02; TD ¶561,003
4. ¶A-2604; ¶624.02; TD ¶561,001   7. ¶L-4703.2; TD ¶561,006
5. ¶A-2602; ¶624.02; TD ¶561,001

(before deducting these expenses) cannot exceed $16,000. (Code Sec. 62(b)(1)(B), Code Sec. 62(b)(1)(C)) A married performing artist who lives with his spouse at any time during the year must file a joint return to deduct these expenses in arriving at AGI. (Code Sec. 62(b)(3)(A)) The two-employer requirement and 10%-of-gross-income test are applied separately to each spouse, but the $16,000 test is applied to their combined income. (Code Sec. 62(b)(3)(B))[8]

¶ 3106 Business expenses of state and local government officials compensated on a fee basis.

Employee business expenses relating to service as an official of a state or local government (or a political subdivision thereof) are deductible in computing AGI, if the official is compensated on a fee basis. (Code Sec. 62(a)(2)(C))[9]

¶ 3107 Jury duty pay remitted to an employer.

An individual may deduct jury pay from gross income if the employer requires the individual to remit the pay in exchange for a payment by the employer of compensation for the period the individual was performing jury duty. (Code Sec. 62(a)(13))[10]

¶ 3108 Attorney fees and court costs of civil rights suits.

Deductible attorney fees and court costs paid for judgments and settlements, by, or on behalf of, the taxpayer in connection with an action involving a claim (1) of unlawful discrimination, (2) of a violation of subchapter III of chapter 37 of title 31, United States Code ("Claims Against the U.S. Government") or (3) made under section 1862(b)(3)(A) of the Social Security Act (42 U.S.C. 1395y(b)(3)(A)) (private cause of action under the Medicare Secondary Payer statute) are deductible from gross income. (Code Sec. 62(a)(20))[11]

¶ 3109 Itemized deductions.

Itemized deductions are all allowable deductions except those subtracted from gross income in arriving at adjusted gross income (¶3102), and except the deductions for personal exemptions. (Code Sec. 63(d))[12]

⟨RIA⟩/caution: For treatment of itemized deductions for alternative minimum tax purposes, see ¶3208.

¶ 3110 Miscellaneous itemized deductions—2%-of-AGI floor.

Miscellaneous itemized deductions are allowed only to the extent that they, in the aggregate, exceed 2% of adjusted gross income. (Code Sec. 67(a))[13] To the extent any other limit or restriction is placed on a miscellaneous itemized deduction, that other limit applies before the 2% floor. For example, the 2% floor is applied after the percentage limit for business meals and entertainment (¶1570). (Reg § 1.67-1T(a)(2))[14]

⟨RIA⟩/observation: Miscellaneous itemized deductions that don't exceed 2% of AGI are lost. There's no carryover.

Miscellaneous itemized deductions are itemized deductions *other than* deductions for medical expenses; taxes; interest; charitable contributions; casualty and theft losses; gambling

---

8. ¶A-2611; ¶624.02; TD ¶560,705
9. ¶A-2611.1; ¶624.02; TD ¶560,706
10. ¶A-2623; ¶624.04; TD ¶560,723
11. ¶A-2628; ¶624.04; TD ¶560,715.2

12. ¶A-2700 *et seq.*; ¶634; TD ¶561,201
13. ¶A-2711 *et seq.*; ¶674; TD ¶561,601
14. ¶A-2711; ¶674; TD ¶561,601

losses (of non-professional gamblers); impairment-related work expenses; estate tax on income in respect of a decedent; personal property used in a short sale; restored amounts held under a claim of right; annuity payments that cease before investment is recovered; amortizable bond premium; payments by tenant-stockholders in connection with co-op housing corporations. (Code Sec. 67(b))

Miscellaneous itemized deductions *include* unreimbursed employee business expenses, including union and professional dues and home office expenses; expenses related to investment income or property, such as investment counsel or advisory fees; any allowable losses from traditional IRAs (¶4357) or Roth IRAs (¶4373); tax return preparation costs and related expenses (for deduction of tax determination costs as business expenses, see ¶1513); appraisal fees paid to determine the amount of a casualty loss or a charitable contribution of property; and hobby expenses to the extent of hobby income. (Reg § 1.67-1T(a)(1))[15]

If an expense relates to both a trade or business activity (not subject to the 2% floor) and a production of income or tax preparation activity (subject to the 2% floor) the taxpayer must allocate it between the activities on a reasonable basis. (Reg § 1.67-1T(c))[16]

¶ 3111   Application of 2% floor to partners, S corporation shareholders and other interests in pass-through entities.

A partner or S corporation shareholder must take into account separately his or her distributive or pro rata share of the partnership's or S corporation's miscellaneous itemized deductions. Similarly, the 2% floor applies to the grantor (or other person treated as the owner) of a grantor trust with respect to items treated as miscellaneous itemized deductions of the grantor (or other owner). (Reg § 1.67-2T(b)(1))[17] Similar rules apply to affected investors in common trust funds (Reg § 1.67-2T(d)(1)(ii)),[18] nonpublicly offered regulated investment companies (RICs) (Reg § 1.67-2T(e)(1)(ii))[19] and REMICs. (Reg § 1.67-3T(b)(1))[20]

The above rules don't apply to publicly offered RICs (Code Sec. 67(c)(2)), cooperatives, and REITs. (Code Sec. 67(c)(3))[21] For estates and trusts, see ¶3921.

¶ 3112   Standard deduction.

The standard deduction is the sum of the basic standard deduction and the additional standard deduction, (Code Sec. 63(c)(1))[22] as adjusted each year for inflation. (Code Sec. 63(c)(4))[23] The basic standard deduction amounts are: [24]

Basic Standard Deduction

Filing Status	2007	2008
Joint filers and surviving spouses	$10,700	$10,900
Heads of household	7,850	8,000
Singles	5,350	5,450
Marrieds filing separately	5,350	5,450

The basic standard deduction of individuals who can be claimed as dependents by another taxpayer can't exceed the greater of (a) $850 (for 2007, $900 for 2008) or (b) $300 (for 2007 and 2008) plus the individual's earned income. But the basic standard deduction can't be more than the regular basic standard deduction amount shown above ($5,350 in 2007 and

---

15. ¶A-2722 *et seq.*; ¶674; TD ¶561,603
16. ¶A-2722 *et seq.*; ¶674; TD ¶561,603
17. ¶A-2715; ¶674; TD ¶561,610
18. ¶A-2716; ¶674; TD ¶561,611
19. ¶A-2717; ¶674; TD ¶561,612

20. ¶A-2714; ¶674; TD ¶561,608
21. ¶A-2714; ¶674; TD ¶561,601
22. ¶A-2801; ¶634; TD ¶562,001
23. ¶A-2801; ¶634; TD ¶562,001
24. ¶A-2803; ¶634; TD ¶562,003

$5,450 in 2008). (Code Sec. 63(c)(5))[25]

The standard deduction is zero for:

. . . a married individual filing separately whose spouse itemizes deductions;

. . . a nonresident alien individual;

. . . an individual filing a short-year return due to a change of accounting period. (Code Sec. 63(c)(6))[26]

On a decedent's final return, the fiduciary may claim the full amount of the appropriate standard deduction regardless of the date of death. [27]

Elderly and blind taxpayers get an additional standard deduction. (Code Sec. 63(c)(3)) A taxpayer who is 65 before the close of his tax year is entitled to the additional standard deduction for the elderly. (Code Sec. 63(f)(1))[28] The additional standard deduction amounts are: (Code Sec. 63(f)(1), Code Sec. 63(f)(2), Code Sec. 63(f)(3); Code Sec. 63(c)(4))[29]

Additional Standard Deduction

Filing Status	2007	2008
Marrieds and surviving spouses	$1,050	$1,050
Heads of household	1,300	1,350
Singles	1,300	1,350

One who is both elderly and blind is entitled to each additional standard deduction. (Code Sec. 63(c)(3))[30]

A married individual who files a separate return can claim a spouse's additional standard deduction if the spouse has no gross income and isn't the dependent of another taxpayer. (Code Sec. 63(f)(1)(B), Code Sec. 63(f)(2)(B), Code Sec. 151(b))[31]

A taxpayer who is blind must attach a statement saying so to the return; one who is partially blind must attach certification from an eye doctor. Where a physician certifies the blindness is irreversible, certification is necessary only once. [32]

🅡ⁱᵃ*caution:* For treatment of the standard deduction for alternative minimum tax purposes, see ¶3208.

¶ 3113 Election to itemize deductions in computing taxable income.

No itemized deductions are allowed unless an election to itemize is made on the return. (Code Sec. 63(e)(1), Code Sec. 63(e)(2)) A taxpayer who elects to itemize and wants to switch to the standard deduction, or vice versa, can do so. But the change cannot be made unless a separately filing spouse makes a consistent change (Code Sec. 63(e)(3)(A)), and both spouses consent in writing to the assessment of any deficiency resulting from the change. (Code Sec. 63(e)(3)(B))[33]

¶ 3114 Reduction in itemized deductions—3%/80% rule for pre-2010 tax years.

If an individual's adjusted gross income exceeds the "applicable amount" (see below), certain otherwise allowable itemized deductions are reduced by the lesser of:

(1) 3% of the excess of adjusted gross income over the applicable amount, or

---

25. ¶A-2806; ¶634; TD ¶562,003
26. ¶A-2802; ¶634; TD ¶562,002
27. ¶C-9603; ¶60,124.04; TD ¶579,507
28. ¶A-2806; ¶634; TD ¶562,005
29. ¶A-2806; ¶634; TD ¶562,004

30. ¶A-2804; ¶634; TD ¶562,004
31. ¶A-2804; TD ¶562,004
32. ¶A-2808; TD ¶562,006
33. ¶A-2702; ¶634; TD ¶561,202

(2) 80% of the itemized deductions otherwise allowable for the tax year. (Code Sec. 68(a))[34]

The reduction is determined after the application of any other limits on an itemized deduction (Code Sec. 68(d))[35] and doesn't apply to the deductions for medical expenses, investment interest, nonbusiness casualty and theft losses, and gambling losses. (Code Sec. 68(c))[36]

For 2007, the applicable amount is $156,400 ($78,200 for married filing separately). For 2008, it's $159,950 ($79,975 for married filing separately). (Code Sec. 68(b)(1)) A taxpayer loses only ⅔ for 2007 (⅓ for 2008 and 2009) of the amount he would otherwise lose under the regular reduction computation. (Code Sec. 68(f)) The reduction rule itself ends after 2009. (Code Sec. 68(g))[37]

🅁illustration: In 2007, a joint filing married couple has AGI of $456,400, which is $300,000 over the limit. Their itemized deductions that are subject to the limit equal $100,000. They start out losing 3% of $300,000 or $9,000. But they get to keep $3,000 of that so they only lose $6,000 of their deductions. Now assume the same couple has AGI that is $3 million over the limit. They could theoretically lose $90,000 (.03 times $3 million) of their affected $100,000 of deductions. But, after applying the 80% limit, they could not lose more than $80,000. But for 2007, they lose only ⅔ of that amount or $53,333.

¶ 3115 Deduction for personal exemptions.

Each taxpayer may be entitled to an exemption for himself and spouse (¶3118), and may qualify for an additional exemption for each dependent (¶3119 *et seq.*).

The exemption amount is $3,400 for 2007, and $3,500 for 2008. (Code Sec. 151(d))[38]

However, an individual (e.g., a child) who can be claimed as a dependent by another (e.g., the child's parent) can't claim a personal exemption for himself. (Code Sec. 151(d)(2))[39]

The personal exemption phase-out rules (¶3117) don't apply in determining whether a deduction for a personal exemption is available to another taxpayer. (Code Sec. 151(d)(3)(D))[40]

🅁caution: The child can't claim a personal exemption even if the parent doesn't take the dependency exemption.

A resident alien can claim personal and dependency exemptions under the same rules as U.S. citizens. But no joint return can be made if either the husband or wife is a nonresident at any time during the year, unless the nonresident alien spouse elects to file a joint return and be treated as a resident for tax purposes. (Code Sec. 6013(g); Reg § 1.6013-1(b))[41]

🅁caution: For treatment of personal exemptions for alternative minimum tax purposes, see ¶3208.

No exemption is allowed for any individual unless the individual's TIN is included on the return claiming the exemption. (Code Sec. 151(e))[42]

¶ 3116 Effect of death on personal exemptions.

The deduction for personal exemptions on a decedent's final return isn't reduced or prorated because the return is for a short year. (Reg § 1.443-1(a)(2)) However, if the decedent could be claimed as a dependent by another taxpayer (e.g., a parent), the decedent's personal exemption isn't allowed on the final return. [43]

If one spouse dies during the year, the survivor can claim the deceased spouse's exemption

---

34. ¶A-2731; ¶684; TD ¶561,801
35. ¶A-2731; ¶684; TD ¶561,803
36. ¶A-2731; ¶684; TD ¶561,802
37. ¶A-2731; ¶684; TD ¶561,801
38. ¶A-3500; ¶1514; TD ¶562,201

39. ¶A-3500 *et seq.*; ¶1514; TD ¶562,203
40. ¶A-3500 *et seq.*; ¶1514;TD ¶564,401
41. ¶A-3507, A-1800; ¶60,134; TD ¶570,601, TD ¶567,500
42. ¶A-3501.1, A-3603; ¶s 1514, 61,094; TD ¶562,400
43. ¶C-9602; TD ¶579,508

on a joint return, unless the survivor remarries during the same year. [44] A surviving spouse who has no gross income for the year his spouse died can be claimed as an exemption on the final separate return of the decedent. [45]

¶ 3117   Phase-out of personal exemptions for pre-2010 tax years.

The personal exemption amount of a taxpayer whose adjusted gross income (AGI) exceeds a specified threshold amount, described below, is reduced by an "applicable percentage." (Code Sec. 151(d)(3)(A)) This applicable percentage is 2% for each $2,500 (or fraction thereof) by which the AGI of a taxpayer (other than a married taxpayer filing separately) exceeds the threshold amount for that taxpayer. For married persons filing separately, the applicable percentage is 2% for each $1,250 (or fraction of that amount) by which the taxpayer's AGI exceeds the threshold amount. The applicable percentage can't exceed 100%. For 2007, the threshold amounts are $234,600 (joint return or surviving spouse), $195,500 (head of household), $156,400 (single) and $117,300 (married filing separately). For 2008, these figures are $239,950, $199,950, $159,950 and $119,975, respectively. (Code Sec. 151(d)(3)(B))

Before 2007, the phaseout rule could have eliminated exemptions completely. However, for 2007, a taxpayer only loses ⅔ (⅓ for 2008 and 2009) of the amount he would otherwise lose. For those with more than $122,500 ($61,250 for married filing separately) over the limit, this works out so that for 2007 each exemption equals ⅓ of its regular amount. The phaseout rule ends after 2009. (Code Sec. 151(d)(3)(E))[46]

⊘ *illustration:* On their jointly filed 2007 return, a married couple with AGI of $380,000 claims 4 exemptions which normally would total $13,600 ($3,400 × 4). Their AGI is more than $122,500 over the 2007 limit of $234,600. Thus, they get four exemptions of $1133.33 each for a total of $4,533, which is ⅓ of $13,600. The phaseout is more complex where AGI is not more than $122,500 ($61,250 for married filing separately) over the limit. For example, assume a married couple with four exemptions has 2007 AGI of $264,600, which is $30,000 over the $234,600 limit. The four exemptions normally would be $13,600 ($3,400 × 4). However, they lose 2% of their exemptions for every $2,500 they are over the limit. Dividing $2,500 into $30,000 yields 12, which when multiplied by .02 equals .24. Thus, they lose .24 of the $13,600 or $3,264. But for 2007, they only lose ⅔ of the amount they would otherwise lose or in this case $2,176. Therefore, their 2007 exemptions total $11,424 ($13,600 − $2,176).

¶ 3118   Exemptions for spouse.

If a married couple files a joint return, each spouse is allowed one personal exemption, whether or not a spouse has gross income or is a dependent of another taxpayer (though the *other* taxpayer will be denied an exemption, see ¶3119). (Reg § 1.151-1(b))[47]

⊘ *illustration:* Son and his wife file a joint return, but son's mother supports him for the entire tax year while he's in college. Son can claim a personal exemption for himself, but even if all other dependency tests are met, the mother can't claim a dependency exemption for her son.

On a separate return, the taxpayer may claim an exemption for a spouse only if, for the calendar year in which the taxpayer's tax year begins, the spouse has *no gross income, and* isn't the dependent of another. (Code Sec. 151(b))[48]

⊘ *observation:* If the son's wife (above) filed a separate return, she couldn't claim an exemption for her husband, since he's a dependent of his mother.

44. ¶A-3504; ¶1514.01; TD ¶562,204
45. ¶A-3504; ¶1514.01; TD ¶562,204
46. ¶A-3502; ¶1514; TD ¶564,401

47. ¶A-3501; ¶1514.01; TD ¶562,203
48. ¶A-3501; ¶1514.01; TD ¶562,203

¶ 3119   Exemption for dependents.

A taxpayer is entitled to a deduction equal to the exemption amount (¶3115) for each person who qualifies as his "dependent." (Code Sec. 151(c))

A person qualifies as the taxpayer's dependent if the person is the taxpayer's qualifying child (¶3120) or qualifying relative (¶3121) (Code Sec. 152(a)) However, if an individual is a dependent of a taxpayer for any tax year of that taxpayer that begins in a calendar year, the individual is treated as having no dependents for any tax year of the individual beginning in that calendar year. (Code Sec. 152(b)(1)) Also, an individual won't be treated as a dependent of a taxpayer if the individual has made a joint return with the individual's spouse for the tax year that begins in the calendar year in which the tax year of the taxpayer begins. (Code Sec. 152(b)(2)) Furthermore, an individual who isn't a U.S. citizen or national can't be a dependent unless he or she is a resident of the U.S., Canada or Mexico. However, a nonresident alien child can qualify as a dependent if he is legally adopted by the taxpayer or is lawfully placed with him for legal adoption by the taxpayer, provided that he has the same principal place of abode as the taxpayer and is a member of the taxpayer's household, and the taxpayer is a U.S. citizen or national. (Code Sec. 152(b)(3))[49]

¶ 3120   Qualifying child.

A "qualifying child" (¶3119) is an individual who: (1) bears a relationship to the taxpayer specified below; (2) has the same principal place of abode as the taxpayer for more than one-half of that tax year; (3) hasn't attained a specified age (see below) ; and (4) hasn't provided over one-half of his or her own support for the calendar year in which the taxpayer's tax year begins. (Code Sec. 152(c)(1), Code Sec. 152(c)(2))

The following relationships of an individual to the taxpayer meet requirement (1), above:

. . . a child (defined below) of the taxpayer or a descendant of such a child (Code Sec. 152(c)(2)(A)) , or

. . . a brother, sister, stepbrother, or stepsister of the taxpayer or a descendant of these relatives. (Code Sec. 152(c)(2)(B)) The terms "brother" and "sister" include a brother or sister by the half blood. (Code Sec. 152(f)(4))

For purposes of the definition of a dependent, the term "child" means an individual who is:

. . . a son, daughter, stepson, or stepdaughter of the taxpayer (Code Sec. 152(f)(1)(A)(i)) , or

. . . an eligible foster child of the taxpayer (Code Sec. 152(f)(1)(A)(i)) , i.e., an individual who is placed with the taxpayer by an authorized placement agency or by judgment, decree, or other order of any court of competent jurisdiction. (Code Sec. 152(f)(1)(C))

In determining whether an individual is a son, daughter, stepson, stepdaughter, brother, or sister of the taxpayer, a legally adopted individual of the taxpayer, or an individual who is lawfully placed with the taxpayer for legal adoption by the taxpayer, is treated as a child of that individual by blood. (Code Sec. 152(f)(1)(B))

An individual meets the age requirement in (3), above, if he:

. . . hasn't attained the age of 19 as of the close of the calendar year in which the tax year of the taxpayer begins;

. . . is a student who hasn't attained the age of 24 as of the close of that calendar year; or

. . . is permanently and totally disabled, as defined in Code Sec. 22(e)(3), at any time during the calendar year. (Code Sec. 152(c)(3))

---

49. ¶A-3601; ¶1524; TD ¶562,401

observation: If a child of the taxpayer doesn't meet the definition of a "qualifying child," for example, because he doesn't meet the age test, he may still qualify as a dependent under the "qualifying relative" test, ¶3121.

If an individual may be and is claimed as a qualifying child by two or more taxpayers for a tax year beginning in the same calendar year, the following tie-breaking rules apply (generally uniformly to all provisions relying on the same definition, according to IRS):

- If only one of the taxpayers claiming the individual as a qualifying child is the individual's parent, the individual is treated as the qualifying child of his or her parent.

- If more than one parent claims the child as a qualifying child and the parents don't file a joint return together, the child is treated as the qualifying child of:

... the parent with whom the child resided for the longest period of time during the tax year, or

... if the child resides with both parents for the same amount of time during the tax year, the parent with the highest adjusted gross income.

- If an individual isn't claimed by either parent, the individual is treated as the qualifying child of the taxpayer with the highest adjusted gross income for the tax year. (Code Sec. 152(c)(4))[50]

¶ 3121   Qualifying relative.

A "qualifying relative" (¶3119) is an individual:

(1)   who bears a specified relationship to the taxpayer;

(2)   whose gross income for the calendar year in which that tax year begins is less than the exemption amount;

(3)   with respect to whom the taxpayer provides over one-half of his or her support for the calendar year in which that tax year begins; and

(4)   who isn't a qualifying child (¶3120) of that taxpayer or of any other taxpayer for any tax year that begins in the calendar year in which that tax year begins. (Code Sec. 152(d)(1))

The following relationships of an individual to the taxpayer meet the relationship test (item (1), above): a child or a descendant of a child including foster and adopted children who qualify under the rules in ¶3120; a brother, sister, stepbrother, or stepsister; the father or mother, or an ancestor of either; stepfather or stepmother; a nephew or niece; an uncle or aunt; a son-in-law, daughter-in-law, father-in-law, mother-in-law, brother-in-law, or sister-in-law; and an individual (other than an individual who, at any time during the tax year, was the spouse, determined without regard to Code Sec. 7703, of the taxpayer) who, for the tax year of the taxpayer, has as such individual's principal place of abode the home of the taxpayer and is a member of the taxpayer's household. (Code Sec. 152(d)(2))[1]

¶ 3122   Multiple support agreement—Form 2120.

For purposes of the support test for qualifying relatives (¶3121), over one-half of the support of an individual for a calendar year is treated as received from the taxpayer if:

... no one person contributed over one-half of that support;

... over one-half of that support was received from two or more persons each of whom, but for the fact that any such person alone didn't contribute over one-half of that support, would have been entitled to claim the individual as a dependent for a tax year that begins

---

50. ¶A-3605.2; ¶1524; TD ¶562,408   1. ¶A-3605.6; ¶1524; TD ¶562,412

in that calendar year;

. . . the taxpayer contributed over 10% of that support; and

. . . each other person who contributed over 10% of that support agrees not to claim that person as a dependent by giving the taxpayer a signed statement to that effect. The statements needn't be filed with IRS but a Form 2120 showing the names, addresses and social security numbers of the other eligible persons must be attached to Form 1040 or Form 1040A. (Code Sec. 152(d)(3); Reg § 1.152-3(c))[2]

¶ 3123   "Support" defined.

Support includes:[3]

. . . food, school lunches, toilet articles and haircuts;

. . . clothing;

. . . recreation, including toys, summer camp, horseback riding, entertainment and vacation expenses;

. . . medical and dental care, including premiums on accident and health insurance;

. . . child care expenses, even though a credit is also allowed for these expenses;

. . . allowances, gifts;

. . . son's or daughter's wedding costs;

. . . lodging—when furnished in kind, it's measured by its fair market value rather than actual cost (Reg § 1.152-1(a)(2));[4]

. . . education—these costs include board, uniforms at military schools, and tuition, even where free schooling is available. Scholarship payments received by a dependent are treated as support furnished by someone other than the taxpayer. However, scholarships aren't counted in determining whether the taxpayer furnished more than half the dependent's support if these tests are met:

(1) the dependent is a child (including stepchild, foster child, or child adopted or placed for adoption) of taxpayer, and

(2) is a full-time student at an educational institution (Reg § 1.152-1(c));[5]

. . . social security benefits received by a child and used for his support are considered provided by the child (Reg § 1.152-1(a)(2)(ii));[6]

. . . Armed Forces dependency allotments —the amount contributed by the government *and* the amount withheld from the pay of the member of the Armed Forces are treated as contributed by the member.[7]

¶ 3124   Allocating support of several contributors to several dependents.

Where more than one member of a household contributes towards expenses that are equally applicable to all members of the household, the contributors are presumed (absent contrary evidence) to have pooled their contributions towards the support of all members. The total contributed is divided equally among the members as amounts paid for their support, unless there is proof of how much was actually spent for particular members. [8]

---

2. ¶A-3605.6; ¶1524; TD ¶562,412
3. ¶A-3711 *et seq.*; ¶1524.06; TD ¶563,302
4. ¶A-3714 *et seq.*; ¶1524.09; TD ¶563,309
5. ¶A-3721; ¶1524.07; TD ¶563,316

6. ¶A-3712; TD ¶563,306
7. ¶A-3711; ¶1524.09; TD ¶563,305
8. ¶A-3708; TD ¶563,325

¶ 3125   Release of dependency exemption by custodial parent

A child is treated as being the "qualifying child" (¶3120) or "qualifying relative" (¶3121) of the noncustodial parent for a calendar year if:

(1) the child receives over one-half of his support during the calendar year from his parents;

(2) the child's parents satisfy one of the following requirements:

(a) they are divorced or legally separated under a decree of divorce or separate maintenance;

(b) they are separated under a written separation agreement; or

(c) they live apart at all times during the last six months of the calendar year;

(3) the child is in the custody of one or both of his parents for more than one-half of the calendar year;

(4) the custodial parent signs a written declaration (in the manner and form that IRS prescribes) stating that he won't claim that child as a dependent for the tax year beginning in that calendar year, and

(5) the noncustodial parent attaches that written declaration to the noncustodial parent's return for the tax year beginning during that calendar year. (Code Sec. 152(e)(1), Code Sec. 152(e)(2))

A child is also treated as the qualifying child or qualifying relative of the noncustodial parent for any calendar year if a "qualified pre-'85 instrument" has been executed between the custodial and noncustodial parents. (Code Sec. 152(e)(3)(A))

The custodial parent is the parent having custody for the greater portion of the calendar year. (Code Sec. 152(e)(4)(A))

The above rules apply notwithstanding: (i) the requirement of Code Sec. 152(c)(1)(B) that a qualifying child have the same principal place of abode as the taxpayer for more than half the year, see ¶3120; (ii) the tie-breaking rules of Code Sec. 152(c)(4), see ¶3120; or (iii) the support test for qualifying relatives in Code Sec. 152(d)(1)(C), see ¶3121. (Code Sec. 152(e)(1))

The rules on release of the dependency exemption don't apply where, under the rules for multiple support agreements in Code Sec. 152(d)(3) (¶3122), more than half of the child's support is treated as having been received from a taxpayer. (Code Sec. 152(e)(5))

For purposes of these rules, if a parent remarries, support of a child received from this remarried parent's spouse is treated as received from the parent. (Code Sec. 152(e)(6))[9]

¶ 3126   Dependents of married couples.

On a joint return, the married couple can claim exemptions for all persons who are dependents of either or both spouses. On a separate return, however, a spouse can claim exemptions only for his or her own dependents. [10]

If a husband and wife in a community property state file separate returns, they can divide the total of their exemptions for dependents between them, but they can't divide between them an exemption for any one dependent. [11]

---

9. ¶A-3851; ¶1524.10; TD ¶564,051   11. ¶A-3605.1; TD ¶562,407
10. ¶A-3607; ¶1524.03

¶ 3127   Effect of death on exemption for dependent.

If a dependent died during the year, and the dependency tests were met for the part of the year he lived, the taxpayer can claim a full exemption for him. [12]

In determining relationships that qualify the taxpayer for an exemption (¶3120, ¶3121) death or divorce doesn't terminate relationships established by marriage. For example, the relationship of son-in-law and father-in-law survives the spouse's death. (Reg § 1.152-2(d))[13]

¶ 3128   Exemption and other tax breaks for kidnapped children.

Solely for the purposes listed below, a taxpayer's child who is presumed by law enforcement authorities to have been kidnapped by a non-family member, and who had, for the tax year in which the kidnapping occurred, the same principal place of abode as the taxpayer for more than one-half of the portion of that year before the kidnapping date, is treated as meeting the requirement that a qualifying child (¶3120) have the same principal place of abode as the taxpayer for more than half the tax year for all tax years ending during the period that the individual is kidnapped. (Code Sec. 152(f)(6)(A)) This rule applies for purposes of the dependency deduction; the child tax credit; surviving spouse or a head of a household status ; and the earned income credit. (Code Sec. 152(f)(6)(B)) Comparable treatment applies to certain qualifying relatives (¶3120). (Code Sec. 152(f)(6)(C))[14]

¶ 3129   Tax rate schedules for individuals.

There's a tax rate schedule for:

(1) Single persons (not married at year's end), including certain marrieds living apart (¶3132), see ¶1102. These rates are more favorable than those for marrieds filing separate returns, but less favorable than head of household and (generally) joint return rates.

(2) Married couples filing joint returns, and certain widows and widowers who qualify as "surviving spouses" (¶3131), see ¶1103. These are often the most favorable rates.

(3) Heads of household, see ¶1105. These rates are more favorable than those for single persons.

(4) Married persons filing separate returns, see ¶1104—the least favorable rates. (Code Sec. 1)[15]

There are six tax brackets with rates of 10%, 15%, 25%, 28%, 33% and 35%. (Code Sec. 1)[16]

¶ 3130   Tax tables.

IRS has drawn up tax tables, based on the tax rates. (Code Sec. 3(a)(1))[17] The 2007 table for Form 1040, Form 1040A or Form 1040EZ filers with taxable income less than $100,000 is reproduced at ¶1110. However, the tables aren't used by those who file a short period return because they changed their accounting period. (Code Sec. 3(b)(1))[18]

¶ 3131   When surviving spouse (qualifying widow(er)) gets benefit of joint return rates.

A surviving spouse (qualifying widow(er)) whose spouse died during either of the surviving spouse's two tax years immediately preceding the tax year (Code Sec. 2(a)(1)) is taxed at joint

---

12. ¶A-3602; ¶1524.03; TD ¶562,403
13. ¶A-3607; ¶1524.03; TD ¶562,414
14. ¶A-3601.1; ¶1514.02; TD ¶562,402
15. ¶A-1003 *et seq.*; ¶14.08; TD ¶560,504

16. ¶A-1100; ¶14.08; TD ¶568,201
17. ¶A-1100; ¶34 *et seq.*; TD ¶568,251
18. ¶A-1100; ¶34.02; TD ¶568,251

return rates (Code Sec. 1(a)(2)) if the surviving spouse:

. . . hasn't remarried at any time before the close of the tax year (Code Sec. 2(a)(2)(A)),

. . . "maintains" (pays more than 50% of the costs of) a household as his or her home which is the "principal place of abode" of a son or daughter (including adopted and foster children) or a stepson or stepdaughter,

. . . is entitled to a dependency deduction for at least one child (Code Sec. 2(a)(1)), and

. . . was entitled to file a joint return with the deceased spouse for the year of death. (Code Sec. 2(a)(2)(B))[19]

observation: These surviving spouse rules *don't* apply for the year the spouse died, but for when a joint return can be filed (and thus joint return rates used) in a year a spouse dies, see ¶4707.

Spouses of individuals in "missing status" as a result of "combat zone" or "qualified hazardous duty area" service can use different rules. When an MIA or POW is officially determined to be dead, and is removed from the missing status rolls, surviving spouse status doesn't depend on the actual date of death. The relevant date is the date of the official determination, or, if earlier, two years after the date of official termination of combat activities in that zone. If a later actual death is established, that date will control. (Code Sec. 2(a)(3)) [20]

¶ 3132 Certain married individuals living apart treated as unmarried.

A married taxpayer is considered single for tax purposes if he or she meets all of the following tests:

(1) Files a separate return.

(2) Maintains as his or her home a household that for more than half the tax year is the principal place of abode of "a child within the meaning of Code Sec. 152(f)(1)," see ¶3120, for whom taxpayer is entitled to a dependency deduction even if the custodial parent allows the other parent to claim the exemption for the child. (Code Sec. 7703(b)(1))

(3) Furnishes more than half the cost of maintaining the household. (Code Sec. 7703(b)(2))

(4) Doesn't have the other spouse living with him or her during the last six months of the tax year. (Code Sec. 7703(b)(3))[21]

These individuals, if they otherwise qualify, can use head of household rates.

Both spouses, or either spouse, can qualify as an unmarried taxpayer by meeting the tests. If one spouse qualifies and the other doesn't, the spouse who doesn't must use married-filing-separately rates. [22]

¶ 3133 Head of household status.

An unmarried taxpayer may qualify as a head of household by maintaining as his home a household that is the principal place of abode for more than half the year of:

. . . a qualifying child of the taxpayer (as defined in Code Sec. 152(c), see ¶3120, but determined without reference to Code Sec. 152(e), see ¶3125), or

. . . a person who would be the taxpayer's qualifying child if the taxpayer hadn't released the dependency deduction to the noncustodial parent (¶3125). (Code Sec. 2(b)(1)(A)(i))

However, the taxpayer won't qualify as a head of household if the qualifying child is

19. ¶A-1700 *et seq.*; ¶24.02; TD ¶567,002
20. ¶A-1703; ¶24.02; TD ¶567,003

21. ¶A-1610 *et seq.*; ¶77,034.01; TD ¶566,511
22. ¶A-1403; ¶77,034.01; TD ¶566,511

married at the close of the taxpayer's tax year (Code Sec. 2(b)(1)(A)(i)(I)), and isn't a dependent of the taxpayer because he filed a joint return (Code Sec. 152(b)(2)) or because he isn't a U.S. citizen or resident (Code Sec. 152(b)(3)), or both. (Code Sec. 2(b)(1)(A)(i)(II))

Also, an unmarried taxpayer may claim head-of-household status if he or she (1) pays more than half of the cost of maintaining as his or her home a household that is the principal place of abode for more than half the year of an individual for whom the taxpayer may claim a dependency exemption (Code Sec. 2(b)(1)(A)(i)), or (2) maintains a household (not necessarily his own) that for the tax year is the principal place of abode for either of his parents, if taxpayer is entitled to a dependency deduction for either parent. (Code Sec. 2(b)(1)(B))[23]

¶ 3134 Tax on Unearned Income of Children—Kiddie Tax ▬▬▬▬▬▬▬▬▬▬▬

A child subject to the kiddie tax (see ¶3135) pays tax at his or her parents' highest marginal rate on the child's unearned income over $1,700 (for 2007, $1,800 for 2008) if that tax is higher than what the child would otherwise pay on it and the child does not file a joint return for the tax year. The parents can instead elect to include on their own return the child's gross income in excess of $1,700 (for 2007, $1,800 for 2008). Distributions from certain qualified disability trusts are excepted from the kiddie tax. (Code Sec. 1(g)(4))

The child pays a tax (computed on Form 8615) equal to the *greater* of:

(1) the sum of (a) the tax that would be imposed if the taxable income of the child for the tax year were reduced by the net unearned income (¶3136) of the child, plus (b) the child's share of the allocable parental tax (below) (Code Sec. 1(g)(1)(B)), or

(2) the tax imposed on the child without regard to (1), above (Code Sec. 1(g)(1)(A)), that is, the tax imposed on the child as a single person. [24]

The "child's share" of the allocable parental tax ((1), above) equals the amount that bears the same ratio to the total allocable parental tax (below) as the child's net unearned income bears to the aggregate net unearned income of all children of the parent to whom this tax applies. (Code Sec. 1(g)(3)(B))[25]

The "allocable parental tax" is the excess of: (1) the tax that would be imposed by these rules on the parent's taxable income if that income included the net unearned income of all children of the parent to whom these rules apply, over (2) the tax imposed on the parent without regard to these rules. (Code Sec. 1(g)(3)(A))[26]

⟳/caution: For the child's alternative minimum tax, see ¶3204.

¶ 3135 Child subject to kiddie tax.

A child is subject to the kiddie tax if either parent is alive at the end of the tax year; the child does not file a joint return for the tax year and (1) the child hasn't reached age 18 before the close of the tax year or, (2) for tax years beginning after May 25, 2007, the child's earned income doesn't exceed one-half of his support and the child is age 18 or is a full time student age 19-23. (Code Sec. 1(g)(2))[27]

¶ 3136 Net unearned income.

"Net unearned income" is adjusted gross unearned income reduced by the sum of the amounts determined under (1), (2) and (3), below. (Code Sec. 1(g)(4)(A); Reg § 1.1(i)-1T, Q&A6) These are:

---

23. ¶A-1400; ¶24.03; TD ¶565,500
24. ¶A-1300 *et seq.*; ¶14.09; TD ¶568,301
25. ¶A-1310; ¶14.09; TD ¶568,310

26. ¶A-1311; ¶14.09; TD ¶568,311
27. ¶A-1301; ¶14.09; TD ¶568,301

(1) the amount in effect for the tax year under Code Sec. 63(c)(5)(A) (Code Sec. 1(g)(4)(A)(ii)(I); Reg § 1.1(i)-1T, Q&A6) (relating to one of the components of the standard deduction which is allowable to a child who can be claimed as a dependent on another person's return, specifically, $850 for 2007;

(2) the greater of (a) the amount in (1), above, or (b) the amount of the itemized deductions which are directly connected with the production of the unearned income if the child itemizes deductions (Code Sec. 1(g)(4)(A)(ii)(II); Reg § 1.1(i)-1T, Q&A6);

(3) adjustments to income attributable to the unearned (investment) income, such as the penalty on early withdrawal of savings. [28]

However, net unearned income for any tax year can't exceed the child's taxable income for the year. (Code Sec. 1(g)(4)(B))

As a result of the above rules, for 2007, the child's first $850 ($900 in 2008) of unearned income isn't taxed at all, the next $850 ($900 in 2008) of unearned income is taxed at the child's tax rate, and the excess of the child's unearned income is taxed at the parent's marginal rate. [29]

Earned income means earned income as defined in Code Sec. 911(d)(2), i.e., income attributable to wages, salaries, or other amounts received as compensation for personal services. (Code Sec. 1(g)(4)(A)(i); Reg § 1.1(i)-1T, Q&A6) Thus, any social security or pension benefits paid to the child would be unearned, not earned, income. (Reg § 1.1(i)-1T, Q&A9)[30]

¶ 3137 Parents' election to claim child's unearned income on parent's return— Form 8814.

A parent can elect (on Form 8814) to include in the parent's gross income for the tax year the child's gross income in excess of $1,700 for 2007 ($1,800 for 2008). (Code Sec. 1(g)(7)(B)(i)) The child is then treated as having no gross income for the year and isn't required to file a return. (Code Sec. 1(g)(7)(A))

For 2007, this election only applies if the child's gross income is only from interest and dividends, is more than $850 and less than $8,500, and the child made no estimated tax payments and backup withholding didn't apply. For 2008, these figures are $900 and $9,000, respectively. (Code Sec. 1(g)(7)(A))[31]

For 2007, the electing parent's tax equals the sum of the tax determined with the child's gross income in excess of $1,700, plus 10% of the lesser of (a) $850 or (b) the excess of the child's income over $850. For 2008, these figures are $1,800 and $900. (Code Sec. 1(g)(7)(B)(ii)) Any interest income that is a tax preference item of the child is treated as that of the parent. (Code Sec. 1(g)(7)(B)(iii))[32]

⟨RIA⟩*illustration:* S, age 6, received $2,300 in interest income in 2007. He has no other income, no itemized deductions, and isn't subject to backup withholding. No estimated tax payments were made with his name or social security number. His parents elect to include S's income on their tax return instead of filing a return for him. They include $600 of S's gross income on their tax return ($2,300 minus $1,700). They also must pay an additional tax of $85 (10% of $850). If the parents are in the 28% bracket, the total tax cost to them of the election is $253 ($85 plus $168 (28% of $600)).

⟨RIA⟩*caution:* The election could increase total family taxes, because the income picked up from the child could lower various tax breaks of the parent that are geared to AGI.

---

28. ¶A-1305; ¶14.09; TD ¶568,305
29. ¶A-1304 *et seq.*; ¶14.09; TD ¶568,305
30. ¶A-1307; ¶14.09; TD ¶568,307

31. ¶A-1326; ¶14.11; TD ¶568,400
32. ¶A-1327; ¶14.11; TD ¶568,401

¶ 3138   Self-Employment Tax

Self-employed persons pay social security and Medicare taxes for themselves as part of their income tax. This self-employment tax is based on net earnings from self-employment, not on taxable income.

Combined social security (OASDI) and Medicare (hospital insurance) taxes are imposed on self-employment income.[33] For contribution bases and rates for these taxes, see ¶1108.

Compute the tax on Form 1040, Schedule SE.

¶ 3139   Self-employment income subject to self-employment tax.

Self-employment income consists of net earnings from self-employment (¶3140). However, in computing the self-employment tax, the maximum amount of self-employment income subject to OASDI is the excess of the applicable contribution base (¶3138) in effect for the calendar year in which the tax year begins *minus* any wages subject to OASDI received by the individual in the same tax year. But if net earnings from self-employment are *less* than $400, no self-employment tax is imposed. (Code Sec. 1402(b))[34]

observation: Since a 7.65% deduction, ¶3140, is allowed from net profits from a trade or business (i.e., net earnings from self-employment before the 7.65% deduction), the actual net profits from a trade or business that an individual is allowed before becoming subject to the self-employment tax is $433.13 (92.35% of $433.13 equals $400).

¶ 3140   Net earnings from self-employment.

This is gross income, under the individual's income tax accounting method, from a trade or business carried on by him, less allowable deductions attributable to that business, plus the distributive share of partnership taxable income or loss from a partnership of which he is a member. (Reg § 1.1402(a)-1)[35] Among the deductions allowed is an amount equal to 7.65% times the taxpayer's net earnings from self-employment for the tax year (determined without regard to this deduction). (Code Sec. 1402(a)(12))[36]

Statutory employees (¶3103) aren't subject to the self-employment tax (they are subject to FICA instead) even though they are treated as self-employed for income tax purposes. (Code Sec. 1402(d), Code Sec. 3121(d)(3))[37]

If a person has a part-time business and a regular job as an employee, the income from the part-time business is included in determining net earnings from self-employment. [38]

In computing the gross income and deductions of a trade or business or the distributive share of partnership ordinary income or loss, the following items are excluded:

. . . operating loss carrybacks and carryovers;

. . . nonbusiness deductions;[39]

. . . the deduction for a self-employed person's health insurance costs (Code Sec. 162(l)(4));[40]

. . . deduction for personal exemptions;

. . . standard deduction;

. . . foreign expropriation loss deduction. (Code Sec. 1402(a))[41]

Net earnings from self-employment don't include:

33. ¶A-6036; ¶14,024.02; TD ¶575,500
34. ¶A-6031; ¶14,024.02; TD ¶576,001
35. ¶A-6100 *et seq.*; ¶14,024.07; TD ¶576,012
36. ¶A-6114; ¶14,024; TD ¶576,025
37. ¶A-6081; ¶14,024.09; TD ¶542,007

38. ¶A-6083; ¶14,024; TD ¶576,036
39. ¶s A-6105, A-6113; ¶14,024; TD ¶576,023
40. ¶A-6105; ¶1624.403; TD ¶576,018
41. ¶s A-6105, A-6113; ¶14,024; TD ¶576,211

... certain income received by a retired partner under a written plan of the partnership; [42]

... dividends or interest on investments (Code Sec. 1402(a)(2)); [43]

... gains (or deduction for losses) from property that's not inventory or held for sale to customers (Code Sec. 1402(a)(3)); [44] but gains and losses derived by option and commodity dealers in the normal course of trading in options and regulated futures subject to mark-to-market rules are included in net earnings from self-employment (Code Sec. 1402(i)); [45]

... gain or loss of a securities or commodities trader that is treated as ordinary solely by reason of the election of mark-to-market treatment (Code Sec. 475(f)(1)(D)); [46]

... qualified disaster relief payments or qualified disaster mitigation payments (Code Sec. 139(d)); [47]

... rents from real estate held for income or value growth, (Code Sec. 1402(a)(1)) but rent is self-employment earnings if received by real estate dealers who get rent on property held for sale to customers in the normal course of business (Reg § 1.1402(a)-4(a)) [48] or if the rent is for living quarters where *services* (e.g., maid service) are also rendered primarily for the occupant's convenience (Reg § 1.1402(a)-4(c)(2)) such as in hotels, boarding houses, tourist camps or homes, parking lots, warehouses and storage garages; [49]

... rents paid in crop shares unless the landowner is a real estate dealer, materially participates in the production of the crop or controls and directs the farming operation and pays the farmer at a fixed rate as his employee (Reg § 1.1402(a)-4(b)); [50]

... certain termination payments received by former insurance salesmen (Code Sec. 1402(k)); [1]

... a shareholder's share of the income of an S corporation, whether distributed or not. [2]

A passive activity loss that's disallowed for income tax purposes isn't taken into account in computing net earnings from self-employment. (Reg § 1.469-1T(d)(3)) [3]

¶ 3141 Partner's self-employment tax.

A partner's net earnings from self-employment are, generally, his distributive share of the partnership's income arising out of the trade or business of the partnership plus his guaranteed payments. (Reg § 1.1402(a)-1(a)(2)) [4] Losses from one business offset the income of another. (Reg § 1.1402(a)-2(c)) [5]

The distributive share of any item of income or loss of a limited partner is excluded. But this exclusion doesn't apply to guaranteed payments to that partner for services actually rendered to or on behalf of the partnership, to the extent the payments are shown to be remuneration for those services. (Code Sec. 1402(a)(13)) [6]

¶ 3142 Husbands and wives.

Tax on self-employment income is computed on the separate self-employment income of each spouse, whether or not they file joint returns. But the spouses are jointly and severally liable for self-employment tax due on a joint return. (Reg § 1.6017-1(b)) [7]

---

42. ¶A-6166; ¶14,024.16; TD ¶576,018
43. ¶A-6108; ¶14,024.05; TD ¶576,021
44. ¶A-6109; ¶14,024.06; TD ¶576,022
45. ¶A-6112; ¶14,024.06; TD ¶576,017
46. ¶A-6112.1; ¶4754.01; TD ¶576,017
47. ¶A-6105; ¶1394; TD ¶576,018
48. ¶A-6106; ¶14,024.04; TD ¶576,018
49. ¶A-6107; ¶14,024.04; TD ¶576,020

50. ¶A-6202 *et seq.*; ¶14,024.04; TD ¶576,018
1. ¶A-6032.1; ¶14,024.155; TD ¶576,009
2. ¶A-6084; TD ¶576,037
3. ¶M-4603; ¶4694.47; TD ¶411,002
4. ¶A-6150 *et seq.*; ¶14,024.16; TD ¶575,502
5. ¶A-6103; TD ¶576,011
6. ¶A-6158; ¶14,024.16; TD ¶576,207
7. ¶S-1812; ¶60,174; TD ¶570,607

¶ 3143   Optional determination of nonfarm self-employment earnings.

An optional method of computing nonfarm self-employment earnings by individuals who are regularly self-employed may be used. It permits individuals to compute their nonfarm self-employment earnings as the smaller of (1) 66 ⅔% of gross self-employment income, or (2) $1,600. (Code Sec. 1402(a))

This method may be used for a tax year only if all these conditions are met:

(1) The individual's net nonfarm profits are less than $1,733.

(2) The individual's net nonfarm profits are less than 72.189% of gross nonfarm income.

(3) The individual's actual net earnings from self-employment were $400 or more in at least two of the three immediately preceding tax years.

(4) The individual has not previously used this method for more than four tax years.

observation: The $1,733 limit above is the maximum amount that, when reduced by the deduction for one-half of the 15.30% self-employment tax, yields the Code limit of $1,600.

observation: The 72.189% limit is the percentage that, when multiplied by 92.35%, yields the Code limit of 66.67% (i.e., 72.189% × 92.35%).

The election is made on the return by computing self-employment earnings under the optional method. The election may be made or revoked after the return is filed, by filing an amended return. (Code Sec. 1402(a))[8]

¶ 3144   Who is subject to tax?

The self-employment tax is a tax on self-employed persons. Income earned as an employee isn't subject to self-employment tax, [9] with these exceptions:

. . . Members of the clergy, see ¶3145.

. . . Persons 18 or older employed to sell magazines and newspapers to the public at a fixed price and whose compensation is the excess of the fixed price over their cost. (Code Sec. 1402(c)(2)(A))[10]

. . . U.S. citizens employed by a foreign government, or its wholly owned instrumentality, or an international organization (e.g., the U.N.). (Code Sec. 1402(c)(2)(C))[11]

. . . Fishing boat crewmen who work on a boat that normally has fewer than 10 crew members and who get no fixed remuneration other than a share of the catch and certain small cash payments. (Code Sec. 1402(c)(2)(F))[12]

. . . Sharecroppers whose earnings depend on production. [13]

. . . State or local government official whose pay is *solely* fees, unless the services are covered by social security under a federal-state agreement. (Code Sec. 1402(c)(1))[14]

Members of religious sects in existence since Dec. 31, '50 who are conscientiously opposed to social security benefits may apply (on Form 4029) for exemption. (Code Sec. 1402(g))[15]

¶ 3145   Members of the clergy.

Members of the clergy, members of religious orders who haven't taken a vow of poverty, and Christian Science practitioners are subject to self-employment tax on services performed

---

8. ¶A-6117; ¶14,024.20; TD ¶576,028
9. ¶A-6092; ¶14,024.09; TD ¶576,049
10. ¶A-6092; ¶14,024.09; TD ¶576,049
11. ¶A-6097; ¶14,024.09; TD ¶576,053

12. ¶A-6090; ¶14,024.14; TD ¶576,047
13. ¶A-6202; ¶14,024.04; TD ¶576,066
14. ¶A-6095; ¶14,024.13; TD ¶576,051
15. ¶A-6327; ¶14,024.15; TD ¶576,092

in the exercise of their ministry *unless* they irrevocably elect (on Form 4361) *not* to be covered. (Code Sec. 1402(e))[16]

¶ 3146   Farmers.

Self-employed persons must pay the self-employment tax on the income from their farming operations and on conservation reserve rental payments. (Code Sec. 1402(a)) Since a farmer has an optional method of computing the self-employment tax on his farm income (¶3147), it may be necessary to distinguish farm income from other self-employment income. Farm income comes from an operation on a farm in which more than half the time is devoted to farming activities. (Reg § 1.1402(a)-13(a)(1))[17]

¶ 3147   Farmer's optional computation method.

If gross income from farming is $2,400 or less, then the farmer may use two-thirds of his gross income as his net self-employment earnings. The method can be used to either raise or lower tax. If gross income from farming is more than $2,400 and net farm profits are less than $1,733, the farmer may report $1,600 as his net self-employment earnings. [18]

¶ 3148   Using both optional farm method and optional nonfarm method.

If a self-employed individual has both nonfarm and farm income, he may only use the nonfarm option (¶3143) if his actual net earnings from nonfarm self-employment are less than $1,600. In all combined cases, net nonfarm earnings must be less than two-thirds of gross nonfarm profits to use the nonfarm option. If a self-employed individual qualifies to use both options, he may report less than actual total net earnings but not less than actual net earnings from nonfarm self-employment alone.

If both options are used in figuring net earnings from self-employment, the maximum combined total of net earnings from self-employment for any tax year can't be more than $1,600. (Code Sec. 1402(a); Reg § 1.1402(a)-15)[19]

¶ 3149   Individual Estimated Tax

An individual must pay 25% of a "required annual payment" by Apr. 15, June 15, Sept. 15 and Jan. 15, to avoid an underpayment penalty. The required annual payment for most taxpayers is the lower of 90% of the tax shown on the current year's return or 100% of the tax shown on the prior year's return even if filed late. (For making 2007 estimates, however, taxpayers whose adjusted gross income on their 2006 return is over $150,000 (over $75,000 if married filing separately) must pay the lower of 90% of their 2007 tax or 110% of their 2006 tax.) There's no underpayment penalty if the tax shown on the return (after withholding) is less than $1,000. There's also no penalty if other specified exceptions or waivers apply.

To avoid the underpayment penalty, an individual must either: (1) pay each "required installment" (¶3150) by the due date of that installment (¶3153), (2) meet one of more of the exceptions to the penalty (¶3157), or (3) get a waiver of the penalty (¶3158).[20]

Make estimated tax payments on payment-voucher Form 1040-ES (Form 1040-ES(NR) for nonresident aliens), by phone or online using a MasterCard, VISA, American Express, or Discover Card and calling 1-888-PAY-1040 (1-888-729-1040) or 1-800-2PAY-TAX (1-800-272-9829) or pointing your browser to www.pay1040.com or www.officialpayments.com, or by EFTPS using the Internet or phone.[21]

---

16. ¶A-6321; ¶14,024.10; TD ¶576,075
17. ¶A-6201; ¶614.051; TD ¶576,064
18. ¶A-6120; ¶14,024,20; TD ¶576,030

19. ¶A-6118; ¶14,024.20; TD ¶576,032
20. ¶S-5200; ¶66,544 *et seq.*; TD ¶571,300
21. ¶S-5253; ¶63,114; TD ¶571,341

¶ 3150   Amount of required installment.

Unless the annualized income method at ¶3151 is used, the amount of each required installment is 25% of the "required annual payment." The required annual payment is the lower of: (1) 90% of the tax shown on the current year's return (or, if no return is filed, 90% of the current year tax), or (2) 100% of the tax shown on the individual's previous year's return, if that tax year was a tax year of 12 months and the taxpayer filed a return for that year, even a late one. (Code Sec. 6654(d)(1))[22]

Different rules apply to those with adjusted gross income on the preceding year's return exceeding $150,000 (exceeding $75,000 for marrieds filing separately). For 2007 estimated tax, the required annual payment for individuals with adjusted gross income on their 2006 return exceeding $150,000 (exceeding $75,000 for marrieds filing separately) is the lower of (1), above, or 110% of the tax shown on the 2006 return. (Code Sec. 6654(d)(1)(C))[23]

¶ 3151   Annualized income method.

For any installment for which the taxpayer establishes that the "annualized income installment" (below) is less than the required installment determined under the rules at ¶3150, the annualized income installment becomes the required installment. (Code Sec. 6654(d)(2)(A)(i)) The annualized income installment is the excess (if any) of:

(1) an amount equal to the "applicable percentage" (below) of the tax computed by placing on an annualized basis the taxable income, alternative minimum taxable income, and adjusted self-employment income as defined below, for the months in the tax year ending before the due date for the installment, over

(2) the sum of any earlier required installments for the tax year. (Code Sec. 6654(d)(2)(B))

The applicable percentages are 22.5%, 45%, 67.5% and 90%, respectively, for the first, second, third and fourth required installments. (Code Sec. 6654(d)(2)(C)(ii))

Adjusted self-employment income means self-employment income except that wages for the calendar months preceding the installment due date must be annualized in a manner consistent with the method for annualizing taxable income, alternative minimum taxable income and adjusted self-employment income. (Code Sec. 6654(d)(2)(C)(iii))

If for any installment, the required installment is the annualized income installment, then the amount by which the installment determined under the rules at ¶3150 exceeds the annualized income installment must be added to the next required installment that isn't an annualized income installment. (Code Sec. 6654(d)(2)(A)(ii))[24]

¶ 3152   Withholding as payment of estimated tax.

Any withholding is treated as a payment of estimated tax. An equal part of the withheld tax is considered paid on each installment date unless the individual establishes the dates the amounts were actually withheld. (Code Sec. 6654(g)(1))[25]

✦recommendation: This means a taxpayer who may otherwise be subject to an underpayment penalty for earlier periods in the year can avoid or reduce the penalty by increasing withholding in later months.

---

22. ¶S-5204; ¶66,544.03; TD ¶571,304   24. ¶S-5219; ¶66,544.04; TD ¶571,312 *et seq.*
23. ¶S-5204.1; ¶66,544.03; TD ¶571,305   25. ¶S-5248; ¶66,544; TD ¶571,342

¶ 3153 Time for paying installments.

Calendar year taxpayers other than farmers and fishermen (see ¶3154) and nonresident aliens (¶3155) must pay estimated taxes in four installments, due by Apr. 15, June 15, Sept. 15 of the current year, and Jan. 15 of the following tax year. (Code Sec. 6654(c))[26] The last installment, ordinarily due on Jan. 15, needn't be paid if taxpayer files his return and pays the tax shown to be due on it by Jan. 31. (Code Sec. 6654(h))[27]

¶ 3154 Farmers and fishermen.

A person for whom at least 66 ⅔% of gross income for the current or preceding tax year comes from farming or fishing[28] doesn't have to pay estimated tax if he files his return and pays the tax on or before Mar. 1 of the following year. If he doesn't file and pay on or before Mar. 1 he need only make one estimated tax payment for the year, which is due on or before Jan. 15 of the next tax year.[29] Also, he substitutes 66 ⅔% for 90% in the required installment calculation in ¶3150. (Code Sec. 6654(i))[30]

¶ 3155 Nonresident aliens.

Nonresident aliens have three required installments: June 15, Sept. 15, and Jan. 15 of the following year. (Code Sec. 6654(j)(2))[31] The required installments are 50%, 25% and 25%, respectively, of the required annual payment (¶3150). (Code Sec. 6654(j)(3)(A)) For purposes of the annualized income method (¶3151), the applicable percentages are 45%, 67.5% and 90%, respectively. (Code Sec. 6654(j)(3)(B))[32]

¶ 3156 Penalty for underpayment of estimated tax.

The penalty for underpayment equals the product of the interest rate (using simple interest) (Code Sec. 6622(b)) on deficiencies (¶4865), times the amount of the underpayment (below) for the period of the underpayment (below). (Code Sec. 6654(a))[33]

The *amount of the underpayment* is the excess of the "required installment" (¶3150) over any amount paid on or before the due date of the installment. (Code Sec. 6654(b)(1))

The *period of underpayment* runs from that due date to the earlier of: (1) Apr. 15 following the close of the tax year, or (2) the date the underpayment is paid. (Code Sec. 6654(b)(2)) For purposes of (2), above, a payment is credited against unpaid installments in the order the installments are required to be paid. (Code Sec. 6654(b)(3))[34]

Form 2210 (Form 2210F for farmers and fishermen) may be used to compute the penalty,[35] or IRS will figure the penalty and send a bill.[36]

¶ 3157 Exceptions to underpayment penalty.

The underpayment penalty doesn't apply:

(1) if the tax shown on the return (or the tax due if no return is filed) is less than $1,000 after reduction for withholding tax paid, (Code Sec. 6654(e)(1))[37] or

(2) if the individual was a U.S. citizen or resident for the entire preceding tax year, that tax year was 12 months, and the individual had no tax liability for that year, (Code

---

26. ¶S-5241; ¶s 66,544, 66,544.02; TD ¶571,335
27. ¶S-5268; ¶s 66,544, 66,544.02; TD ¶571,362
28. ¶S-5238; ¶66,544.06; TD ¶571,332
29. ¶S-5247; ¶66,544.06; TD ¶571,340
30. ¶S-5237; ¶66,544.06; TD ¶571,332
31. ¶S-5246; ¶66,544.07

32. ¶S-5236; ¶66,544.07
33. ¶S-5260; ¶66,544.02; TD ¶571,353
34. ¶S-5261 *et seq.*; ¶66,544.02; TD ¶571,356
35. ¶S-5265; TD ¶571,359
36. ¶S-5260; ¶66,544.05
37. ¶S-5266; TD ¶571,360

Sec. 6654(e)(2))[38] or

(3) for the fourth installment, if the individual (who isn't a farmer or fisherman, ¶3154) files his return by the end of the first month after the tax year (Jan. 31 for calendar year taxpayers), and pays in full the tax computed on the return, (Code Sec. 6654(h))[39] or

(4) under certain circumstances with respect to a period during which a Title 11 bankruptcy case is pending. (Code Sec. 6658(a))[40]

¶ 3158   Waiver of penalty.

The underpayment penalty may be waived by IRS:

(1) if failure to pay was due to casualty, disaster, or other unusual circumstances where it would be inequitable or against good conscience to impose the penalty, or

(2) for reasonable cause during the first two years after the taxpayer retires (after reaching age 62) or becomes disabled. (Code Sec. 6654(e)(3))[41]

38. ¶S-5267; ¶66,544.05; TD ¶571,361
39. ¶S-5268; ¶66,544.02; TD ¶571,362
40. ¶V-7378; ¶66,584; TD ¶571,363
41. ¶S-5270; ¶66,544.05; TD ¶571,365

Chapter 14   Alternative Minimum Tax

¶ 3200   Alternative Minimum Tax. ▬▬▬▬▬▬▬▬▬▬▬▬▬▬▬▬▬▬▬▬▬

The alternative minimum tax equals the excess (if any) of the tentative minimum tax over the regular tax.

The AMT was designed to prevent a taxpayer from avoiding all tax liability by using exclusions, deductions, and credits. It's paid only if and to the extent it exceeds the taxpayer's regular tax. (Code Sec. 55(a)) Taxpayers who are subject to the regular tax generally are subject to the AMT. (Code Sec. 55(a), Code Sec. 55(b)) Thus, partnerships (Code Sec. 701) and S corporations (Code Sec. 1363(a)) aren't subject to AMT but their shareholders and partners are. Foreign corporations are subject only as to taxable income effectively connected with conduct of a trade or business in the U.S. (Code Sec. 882(a)(1)) Certain small corporations are exempt from AMT, see ¶3203.[1]

For the AMT credit available in tax years that follow years in which a taxpayer was liable for the AMT, see ¶2367.

¶ 3201   Computing the AMT—Form 6251; Form 4626.

The alternative minimum tax (AMT) equals the excess (if any) of the tentative minimum tax for the tax year, over the regular tax for the tax year. (Code Sec. 55(a)) AMT is computed on Form 6251 for individuals, Schedule I (Form 1041) for fiduciaries (estates and trusts), or Form 4626 for C corporations.[2]

For a noncorporate taxpayer (other than a married person filing separately), the tentative minimum tax for the tax year is equal to 26% of the "taxable excess" (defined below) that doesn't exceed $175,000, plus 28% of the taxable excess above $175,000, reduced by the AMT foreign tax credit for the tax year. (Code Sec. 55(b)(1)(A)(i)) For marrieds filing separately, $87,500 replaces $175,000 above. (Code Sec. 55(b)(1)(A)(iii)) However tentative minimum tax attributable to capital asset sales and exchanges and qualified dividend income is determined using the rates that apply to long-term gains for regular tax purposes, see   ¶2603. "Taxable excess" means the excess of alternative minimum taxable income (AMTI) for the tax year over the "exemption amount" (¶3202). (Code Sec. 55(b)(1)(A)(ii))[3]

For a corporation, the tentative minimum tax (Code Sec. 55(b)(1)) for the tax year is 20% of AMTI for the tax year in excess of the exemption amount, reduced by the AMT foreign tax credit for the tax year (¶3213). (Code Sec. 55(b)(1)(B)) (But for the tentative minimum tax for small corporations, see ¶3203.)

All Code provisions that apply in determining regular taxable income also apply in determining AMTI. (Reg § 1.55-1(a)) For example, the limitations on the use of capital losses by noncorporate taxpayers (¶2611, ¶2612), and by corporate taxpayers (¶2615) also apply for AMTI purposes. Thus, an individual who exercised incentive stock options (ISOs) in Year 1 to buy company stock couldn't use the AMT capital losses he realized in Year 2 when the company went bankrupt and his stock became worthless, to reduce his Year 1 AMTI since the capital losses of noncorporate taxpayers can only be carried forward and not carried back. [4]

AMTI is taxable income, plus or minus various "adjustments," plus tax preferences, see ¶3205 et seq. (Code Sec. 55(b)(2))[5] No adjustment is permitted to the taxable income starting point for a regular tax deduction that was reduced due to use of a tax credit that isn't allowed for AMT purposes.[6] The AMT can apply if a taxpayer has only adjustments even if he has no

---

1. ¶A-8130 et seq.; ¶554; TD ¶691,000

2. ¶A-8101; ¶554.01; TD ¶691,001

3. ¶A-8101; ¶554.01; TD ¶691,002

4. ¶A-8108; ¶554.01; TD ¶691,007

5. ¶A-8101; ¶554.01; TD ¶691,001

6. ¶A-8108

References beginning with a single letter are to paragraphs in RIA's Federal Tax Coordinator 2d and RIA's Analysis of Federal Taxes: Income. Those beginning with numbers are to paragraphs in RIA's United States Tax Reporter. Those beginning with TD are to paragraphs in RIA's Tax Desk.

tax preferences. Preferences are just one component of the AMT calculation; a taxpayer without preferences must still compute AMT with the adjustments. [7]

In taking the Code Sec. 199 production activity deduction (¶1614) into account for purposes of determining AMTI: (1) qualified production activities income (¶1616) is determined without regard to any adjustments under Code Sec. 56 through Code Sec. 59; and (2) for a corporation, the Code Sec. 199(a)(1)(B) taxable income limit (¶1615) on the deduction is applied by substituting "AMTI" for "taxable income." (Code Sec.199(d)(6); Reg § 1.199-8(d))[8]

If a taxpayer's regular tax is determined by reference to an amount other than taxable income (e.g., unrelated business taxable income of an exempt organization), that amount is treated as taxable income in determining AMTI. (Code Sec. 55(b)(2))

There are rules for the apportionment of items that are treated differently for AMT purposes among holders of interests in regulated investment companies, real estate investment trusts, and common trust funds. (Code Sec. 59(d))[9]

The regular tax is the regular tax liability used for determining the limitation on various nonrefundable credits (¶2366), reduced by the regular (as opposed to the AMT) foreign tax credit (¶2369), and without the inclusion of any investment credit recapture (¶2313), low-income housing credit recapture, or any increase under Code Sec. 45(e)(11)(C) in the income tax of a cooperative passing through credits for electricity produced from renewable resources to its patrons. (Code Sec. 55(c)(1))[10]

In computing regular tax liability for AMT purposes, income averaging for farmers and fishermen is not taken into account. (Code Sec. 55(c)(1)) [11]

observation: This means that income averaging does not cause the AMT of farmers and fishermen who use three-year income averaging to increase since the regular tax for AMT purposes is computed as though income averaging had not been used.

¶ 3202   AMT exemption amount.

At press time, Code Sec. 55(d)(3) provided that for tax years beginning after 2006, the exempt portion of an individual's alternative minimum taxable income (AMTI) is:

. . . *Married individuals filing jointly and surviving spouses,* $45,000, less 25% of AMTI exceeding $150,000 (zero exemption when AMTI is $330,000);

. . . *Unmarried individuals,* $33,750, less 25% of AMTI exceeding $112,500 (zero exemption when AMTI is $247,500); and

. . . *Married individuals filing separately,* $22,500 less 25% of AMTI exceeding $75,000 (zero exemption when AMTI is $165,000). (Code Sec. 55(d)(1)) But AMTI of married individuals filing separately is increased by the lesser of $22,500 or 25% of the excess of AMTI (without regard to the exemption reduction) over $165,000.

caution: In an Oct. 30, 2007 letter to IRS's Acting Commissioner, the Chairmen and Ranking members of the House Ways and Means Committee and the Senate Finance Committee pledged to pass legislation that would set the AMT exemption amount for 2007 (before phaseout) at $44,350 for individuals and $66,250 for married taxpayers filing jointly. (As a corollary, the AMT exemption for marrieds filing separately would increase to $33,125, half the joint filer amount.) Check http://ria.thomson.com/federaltaxhandbook for the latest news on this change and other legislative changes affecting the 2007 return and the 2008 tax year.

---

7. ¶A-8109
8. ¶A-8103.1; ¶1994.130; TD ¶691,003.1
9. ¶A-8111; ¶594; TD ¶691,010

10. ¶A-8105; ¶554.01; TD ¶691,005
11. ¶A-8105; ¶554.01; TD ¶691,005

For estates and trusts, the AMT exemption amount is $22,500, less 25% of AMTI exceeding $75,000 (zero exemption when AMTI is $165,000).

For corporations, the AMT exemption amount is $40,000, less 25% of AMTI exceeding $150,000 (thus, zero exemption when AMTI is $310,000 or more).

In no case can the exemption amount be less than zero. (Code Sec. 55(d))[12]

¶ 3203 AMT exemption for "small corporations."

The tentative minimum tax (¶3201) of a corporation is zero (making the corporation exempt from AMT) for a tax year if its average annual gross receipts (determined by applying Code Sec. 448(c)(2) and Code Sec. 448(c)(3) (¶2818)) (Code Sec. 55(e)(1)(D)) for all three-tax-year periods beginning after '93 and ending before the tax year don't exceed $7,500,000. (Code Sec. 55(e)(1)(A)) However, the gross receipts test is applied by substituting $5,000,000 for $7,500,000 for the first three-tax-year period (or portion thereof) of the corporation that's taken into account under the test. (Code Sec. 55(e)(1)(B))

Notwithstanding the above tests, a corporation is exempt from AMT for its first tax year (Code Sec. 55(e)(1)(C)) unless it fails the gross receipts test because its gross receipts are aggregated with an existing corporation (under Code Sec. 448(c)(2)) or it's treated as having a predecessor corporation (under Code Sec. 448(c)(3)(D)).

A corporation that has been exempt from AMT that ceases to meet the gross receipts test becomes subject to AMT prospectively from the first day of the first tax year for which the gross receipts test isn't met, except that the Code Sec. 56(g)(4)(A) ACE depreciation adjustment (¶3210) doesn't apply. (Code Sec. 55(e)(2)) However, prospective-only application doesn't apply to certain items carried over in Code Sec. 381 transactions (¶3562) or to other property with a basis carried over from a transferor. (Code Sec. 55(e)(3))[13] For a limitation on the AMT credit for corporations exempt from AMT, see ¶2367.

¶ 3204 AMT of a child subject to the kiddie tax.

The child's AMT exemption amount can't exceed the child's earned income for the tax year plus $6,300 for 2007 ($6,400 for 2008). (Code Sec. 59(j)) But the exemption computed under this limit can't be more than the child's regular AMT exemption, i.e., for an unmarried individual, before a phaseout (¶3202).[14]

✒️*caution:* For proposed legislation affecting a child's regular AMT exemption, see ¶3202. Check http://ria.thomson.com/federaltaxhandbook for the latest news on this and other legislative changes affecting the 2007 return and 2008 tax year.

¶ 3205 Adjustments and tax preferences.

AMT adjustments differ from preferences. Adjustments involve a *substitution* of AMT treatment of an item for the regular tax treatment. A preference involves the *addition* of the difference between the AMT treatment and the regular tax treatment. Some (but not all) adjustments can be negative amounts, i.e., they may result in alternative minimum taxable income that's less than taxable income. Tax preferences can't be negative amounts. [15]

¶ 3206 Depreciation adjustment.

Except as provided below, the following rules apply to all taxpayers subject to the AMT, for depreciable property placed in service after Dec. 31, '86 (and after July 31, '86 and before Jan. 1, '87, for which the taxpayer elected to have the MACRS rules (¶1906 *et seq.*) apply):

---

12. ¶A-8160 *et seq.*; ¶554.01; TD ¶691,300
13. ¶A-8140 *et seq.*; ¶554; TD ¶691,301 *et seq.*

14. ¶A-8163; ¶594; TD ¶691,303
15. ¶A-8190; ¶s 564, 574; TD ¶695,501

(1)   For property placed in service before '99: Code Sec. 1250 property and property depreciated under the straight-line method for regular tax purposes is depreciated for AMT purposes using the Alternative Depreciation System (ADS) (¶1931). For property for which accelerated depreciation is used for regular tax purposes, AMT depreciation is computed using ADS recovery periods and 150% declining balance method (switching to straight-line in the year necessary to maximize the allowance).

(2)   For property placed in service after '98, AMT depreciation is computed using the 150% declining balance method (switching to straight-line in the year necessary to maximize the allowance), except that straight line is used for Code Sec. 1250 property (¶2694) and other property for which straight line depreciation is used for regular tax purposes. The recovery period is the same for AMT and regular tax purposes. (Code Sec. 56(a)(1)(A), Code Sec. 56(a)(1)(C)(ii))

The AMT adjustment (i.e., the amount that must be added or subtracted in the calculation of alternative minimum taxable income) that's generated by the above calculations is determined by subtracting the amount of AMT depreciation for all property covered by the above rule from the MACRS depreciation for that property.

The above rules don't apply to: (1) certain property to which the MACRS rules don't apply, and natural gas gathering lines placed in service after Apr. 11, 2005 (Code Sec. 56(a)(1)(B), Code Sec. 56(a)(1)(C));[16] (2) qualified property under Code Sec. 168(k) (bonus first-year depreciation, ¶1935), under Code Sec. 1400L(b) (bonus first-year depreciation for qualified Liberty Zone property, ¶1942), or under Code Sec. 1400N(d) (bonus first-year depreciation allowance for GO Zone property, ¶1941); (Code Sec. 168(k)(2)(G), Code Sec. 1400L(b)(2)(E), Code Sec. 1400N(d)(4))[17] and (3) qualified Indian reservation property placed in service after '93. (Code Sec. 168(j)(3))[18]

¶ 3207   Other tax preferences and adjustments applicable to all taxpayers.

(1) Tax exempt interest earned on certain private activity bonds is a preference item. (Code Sec. 57(a)(5))[19]

(2) Except for independent oil and gas producers and royalty owners, the excess of the percentage depletion over the adjusted basis (before considering the current year's depletion) of the property at the end of the year is a preference item. (Code Sec. 57(a)(1))[20]

(3) Excess intangible drilling costs are a preference. This is the excess of the allowable expense deduction for the tax year for intangible drilling and development costs for oil, gas and geothermal wells, over the amount that would have been allowable had the costs been capitalized and straight-line recovery of intangibles used with respect to them. For integrated oil companies the preference equals this excess reduced by 65% of the net income received from all oil and gas properties. For taxpayers other than integrated oil companies, the preference applies only to the extent that, had it applied fully, it would have increased alternative minimum taxable income (AMTI)) by an amount that exceeds 40% of the AMTI for the tax year determined without the intangible drilling cost preference and without the alternative tax NOL deduction. (Code Sec. 57(a)(2))[21]

(4) The deduction for amortization of pollution control facilities is an adjustment. For facilities placed in service after '86 and before '99, the AMT deduction is the amount allowable under the Alternative Depreciation System (ADS). The Code Sec. 291(a)(5) 20% cutback (¶1972), which applies for purposes of computing a corporation's pollution control facility amortization deduction for regular tax purposes, doesn't apply for the AMT. For facilities placed in service after '98, the deduction is determined under Code Sec. 168 using straight-

---

16. ¶A-8221 *et seq.*; ¶564.01; TD ¶695,500 *et seq.*

17. ¶A-8221; ¶1684.029; ¶1400L4.07

18. ¶L-8806; ¶1684.01

19. ¶A-8201; ¶574; TD ¶696,501

20. ¶A-8233; ¶574; TD ¶696,518

21. ¶A-8239; ¶574; TD ¶696,533

line. (Code Sec. 56(a)(5))[22]

(5) Mining exploration and development costs are adjusted. A deduction is allowed for the amount that results from capitalizing mine exploration and development expenditures (¶1623 *et seq.*) (without regard to the Code Sec. 291(b)(1) 30% cutback) and amortizing them on a straight-line basis over ten years. (Code Sec. 56(a)(2)(A))[23]

(6) For long-term contracts (adjustment), AMTI is computed using the percentage-of-completion method of accounting for long-term contracts. (Code Sec. 56(a)(3))[24] For small construction contracts (under Code Sec. 460(e)(1), ¶2850) percentage of contract completed is found by using the simplified method for allocating costs in Code Sec. 460(b)(4) (¶2855).[25]

(7) Alcohol fuel credit amount (adjustment): amount includible in gross income (¶1206) isn't included in AMTI. (Code Sec. 56(a)(7))[26]

¶ 3208   AMT preferences and adjustments for noncorporate taxpayers only.

(1) *Itemized deductions adjustment.* Itemized deductions for AMT purposes are computed the same as for regular tax purposes, except:

. . . Medical expenses are deductible only to the extent they exceed 10% of the taxpayer's adjusted gross income. (Code Sec. 56(b)(1)(B))

. . . Property, income, and state and local general sales, taxes aren't deductible unless they are deductible in computing adjusted gross income. (Code Sec. 56(b)(1)(A)(ii))

. . . Qualified "housing interest," rather than qualified "residence" interest, is deductible (Code Sec. 56(b)(1)(C); Code Sec. 56(e)) (so that home equity indebtedness isn't allowed for AMT purposes, unless used to buy, build, or substantially improve the taxpayer's principal residence or one other qualified residence).

. . . Net investment income (the limit on the deduction for investment interest) for AMT purposes, equals the sum of interest on tax exempt bonds that's includible in alternative minimum taxable income (AMTI, ¶3207), net of expenses associated with that interest, plus net investment income for regular tax purposes. (Code Sec. 56(b)(1)(C))

. . . No deduction is allowed for miscellaneous itemized deductions. (Code Sec. 56(b)(1)(A)(i))

Itemized deductions otherwise allowed in computing AMTI income are *not* reduced by the regular-tax Code Sec. 68 overall limit on itemized deductions (¶3114). (Code Sec. 56(b)(1)(F))[27]

(2) *Standard deduction and personal exemptions adjustments.* The standard deduction and the deduction for personal exemptions (including the personal exemptions for trusts and estates) *aren't* allowed. (Code Sec. 56(b)(1)(E))[28]

(3) *State, etc., tax recoveries adjustment.* If an itemized deduction for state, etc., taxes paid is permitted for regular tax purposes but is denied for AMT purposes (above), and any portion of that tax is refunded, the refund isn't included in AMTI. (Code Sec. 56(b)(1)(D))[29]

(4) *Research and experimental expenditures adjustment.* The deduction allowed is the amount that results from capitalizing Code Sec. 174(a) research and experimental expenditures (¶1601) and amortizing them on a straight-line basis over ten years. (Code Sec. 56(b)(2)(A)(ii)) This rule doesn't apply to expenses incurred after '90 in an activity in which the taxpayer materially participates under Code Sec. 469(h) (¶1828 *et seq.*). (Code Sec. 56(b)(2)(D))[30]

---

22. ¶A-8237; TD ¶696,531
23. ¶A-8235; ¶564.01; TD ¶696,529
24. ¶A-8202; ¶574; TD ¶696,502
25. ¶A-8204; ¶564.01; TD ¶696,504
26. ¶A-8247; ¶564.01; TD ¶696,540

27. ¶A-8306; ¶564.02; TD ¶697,006 *et seq.*
28. ¶A-8305; ¶A-8315; ¶564.02; TD ¶697,005; TD ¶697,015
29. ¶A-8309; ¶564.02; TD ¶697,009
30. ¶A-8316; ¶564.02; TD ¶697,016

(5) *Incentive stock options (ISOs) adjustment.* The Code Sec. 83 restricted property rules (which may require earlier recognition of income, ¶1218), rather than the Code Sec. 421 stock option rules (¶1222), apply, unless the stock is acquired and disposed of in the same tax year. (Code Sec. 56(b)(3))[31] Thus, a taxpayer who makes a Code Sec. 83(b) election (¶1219) on the exercise of an ISOs will not recognize income for regular tax purposes (because Code Sec. 421 applies), but will recognize income for AMT purposes.) [32]

(6) *Qualified small business stock exclusion preference.* For tax years beginning before 2011, 7% of the amount excluded from gross income at the disposition of "qualified small business stock" (¶2648 *et seq.*) is an AMT preference. (So if 50% of gain is excluded, the preference is 7% of 50%, or 3.5% of the total gain.) (Code Sec. 57(a)(7)) [33]

¶ 3209 Preferences and adjustments applicable to all noncorporate taxpayers and to certain corporations.

(1) *Farm losses.* No loss is permitted from any "tax shelter farm activity" of any noncorporate taxpayer or personal service corporation, except to the extent the taxpayer is insolvent at the close of the tax year. A tax shelter farm activity is either (a) a farming syndicate, or (b) any other activity consisting of farming that's a passive activity, unless the taxpayer materially participates in the activity. (Code Sec. 58(a))[34]

(2) *Passive losses.* The rules limiting the deduction for regular tax purposes of losses from passive activities (¶1810 *et seq.*) apply for AMT purposes except that:

. . . the amount of losses that otherwise would be disallowed under the regular tax limitation is reduced by the amount, if any, by which the taxpayer is insolvent; and

. . . in computing income and losses from passive activities, other AMT adjustments and preferences are taken into consideration. (Code Sec. 58(b))[35]

(3) *Circulation expenditures.* Noncorporate taxpayers and personal holding companies may deduct the amount that results from capitalizing circulation expenditures and amortizing them over three years (¶1619). (Code Sec. 56(b)(2))[36]

¶ 3210 Earnings and profits adjustments only applicable to corporations

Alternative minimum taxable income (AMTI) of a corporation is *increased* by 75% of the amount by which adjusted current earnings (ACE), as defined below, exceeds AMTI determined without regard to this adjustment or the AMT net operating loss deduction (ATNOLD). (Code Sec. 56(c)(1), Code Sec. 56(g)(1)) This rule doesn't apply to S corporations, regulated investment companies, real estate investment trusts, and real estate mortgage investment conduits, and financial asset securitization investment trusts. (Code Sec. 56(g)(6)) If AMTI (before this adjustment and the ATNOLD) exceeds the amount of ACE, AMTI is *reduced* by 75% of the difference. This reduction, however, is limited to the aggregate amount of increases in AMTI under this provision in earlier years. (Code Sec. 56(g)(2))[37]

Adjusted current earnings (ACE) is AMTI, plus those items that are included in earnings and profits (E&P) as computed for purposes of Subchapter C but that never enter into the calculation of regular or alternative minimum taxable income (e.g., interest on certain tax-exempt bonds). In addition, there are numerous adjustments: including adjustments requiring a special method for depreciation for property placed in service before '94, [38] including the

31. ¶A-8302; ¶A-8303; ¶564.02; TD ¶697,002
32. ¶H-2508.2; TD ¶696,507
33. ¶A-8304; ¶574; TD ¶697,004
34. ¶A-8242; ¶584; TD ¶699,001

35. ¶A-8244; ¶584; TD ¶699,003
36. ¶A-8245; ¶564.02; TD ¶699,004
37. ¶A-8401; ¶564.03; TD ¶698,001
38. ¶A-8406; ¶s 564.01, 564.03; TD ¶698,002

"inside buildup" on life insurance contracts in ACE, disallowing the dividends received deduction and the use of the installment method, and providing for certain of the statutory adjustments required in calculating earnings and profits. [39] The Code Sec. 199 deduction (¶1614) is allowed for purposes of computing ACE. (Code Sec. 56(g)(3), Code Sec. 56(g)(4))[40]

✔️observation: The Code Sec. 199 deduction is deductible in computing a corporation's ACE, even though it's not deductible in computing its E&P for regular tax purposes.

Special adjustments apply for Blue Cross, Blue Shield and similar organizations (Code Sec. 56(c)(3))[41] and for certain merchant marine capital construction funds (Code Sec. 56(c)(2)).[42]

¶ 3211 Alternative tax net operating loss deduction.

There is an adjustment for AMT purposes under which the regular net operating loss deduction (RNOLD, see ¶1841 *et seq.*) isn't allowed and instead, an alternative tax net operating deduction (ATNOLD) is allowed. [43]

In general, the ATNOLD is the same as the RNOLD except that: (1) the amount of the ATNOLD is limited to 90% of the alternative minimum taxable income determined without regard to the ATNOLD and the Code Sec. 199 production activity deduction (¶1615),[44] and (2) for any loss year beginning after '86, the ATNOLD is determined with each of the AMT adjustments and reduced by each of the items of tax preference (but only to the extent the tax preference item increased the NOL for the year). (Code Sec. 56(d))[45] However, the above 90%-of-AMTI limitation doesn't apply to carrybacks and carryovers of 2001 and 2002 NOLs, or to carrybacks and carryovers of qualified GO Zone losses (¶1844). Carrybacks and carryovers of these NOLs can offset 100% of AMTI. (Code Sec. 56(d)(1)(A)), Code Sec. 1400N(k)(1)(B))

For corporations, regular NOL carryforwards from tax years beginning before Jan. 1, '87, may be carried forward as alternative tax NOLs to the first tax year for which the AMT applies (Code Sec. 56(d)(2)(B)) and to later years until used up. (Code Sec. 56(d))[46]

An election to forgo the regular NOL carryback period (¶1845) also applies for ATNOLD purposes. (The election must be made for regular tax purposes to get it for AMT purposes.) [47] The difference between the regular tax basis and AMT basis (¶3212) on the exercise of an incentive stock option isn't an adjustment and doesn't result in an ATNOL.

¶ 3212 Different adjusted basis for some property.

For AMT purposes, the adjusted bases of the following types of property are computed by taking into consideration the AMT preference or adjustment listed below with the property:

(1) Depreciable property subject to the AMT depreciation adjustment, described at ¶3206.

(2) Property with respect to which circulation or research and experimental expenditures (described at ¶3208 and ¶3209) were paid or incurred after Dec. 31, '86.

(3) Property with respect to which mine exploration or development expenditures (described at ¶3207) were paid or incurred after Dec. 31, '86.

(4) Pollution control facilities (described at ¶3207) placed in service after Dec. 31, '86. (Code Sec. 56(a)(6))

(5) Stock acquired under an incentive stock option (ISO). Generally, the basis of the stock is determined under the Code Sec. 83 rules rather than the Code Sec. 421 rules (¶3208). (Code Sec. 56(b)(3))[48]

---

39. ¶A-8431 *et seq.*; ¶564.03; TD ¶698,027
40. ¶A-8411 *et seq.*; ¶564.03; TD ¶698,010
41. ¶A-8197; ¶564.03
42. ¶A-8198; ¶564.03
43. ¶A-8210 *et seq.*; ¶564.01; TD ¶696,000 *et seq.*

44. ¶A-8212; ¶564.01; TD ¶696,001
45. ¶A-8214; ¶564.01; TD ¶696,005
46. ¶A-8214; ¶564.01; TD ¶696,004
47. ¶A-8216; ¶564.01; TD ¶696,006
48. ¶A-8193; ¶564.01 *et seq.*; TD ¶695,502

¶ 3213   Foreign tax credit.

Since the alternative minimum tax foreign tax credit is calculated differently than the regular foreign tax credit (¶2369), taxpayers must separately apply, for AMT purposes, the Code Sec. 904 limitation on the amount of the credit, to reflect the differences between regular taxable income and alternative minimum taxable income (AMTI). (Code Sec. 59(a)(1))

If a taxpayer so elects for the first tax year for which he claims an AMT foreign tax credit, the foreign tax credit limitation can be figured in a simplified way, based on the proportion that regular taxable income from sources outside the U.S. (but not in excess of the taxpayer's entire alternative minimum taxable income) bears to the entire AMTI for the tax year. (Code Sec. 59(a)(3)(A); Code Sec. 59(a)(3)(B)(i)) Once made, this election applies to all tax years and can be revoked only with IRS consent. (Code Sec. 59(a)(3)(B)(ii)) This election permits taxpayers to use foreign source regular taxable income in computing their AMT foreign tax credit limitation, eliminating the need to reallocate and reapportion every deduction. [49]

---

49. ¶A-8183; ¶594; TD ¶691,403

Chapter 15 Corporations—Accumulated Earnings Tax—Personal Holding Companies—Consolidated Returns—Estimated Tax—S Corporations

¶ 3300 Taxation of Corporations.

A corporation is an entity distinct from its shareholders. How a corporation is taxed depends on whether it is a C corporation or an S corporation.

¶ 3301 What is a corporation for tax purposes?

Under regs that set forth a "check-the-box" system of classifying entities for federal tax purposes, the following business entities are mandatorily classified as corporations:

. . . A business entity organized under a federal or state statute, or under a statute of a federally recognized Indian tribe, if the statute describes or refers to the entity as incorporated or as a corporation, body corporate, or body politic.

. . . An association as determined under Reg § 301.7701-3.

. . . A business entity organized under a state statute, if the statute describes or refers to the entity as a joint-stock company or joint-stock association.

. . . An insurance company.

. . . A state-chartered business entity conducting banking activities, if any of its deposits are insured under the Federal Deposit Insurance Act.

. . . A business entity wholly owned by a state or any of its political subdivisions.

. . . A business entity that's taxable as a corporation under a provision of the Code other than Code Sec. 7701(a)(3), such as a publicly traded partnership.

. . . Certain foreign business entities ("per se" corporations) (Reg § 301.7701-2(b)(8)), and the business entities formed under the laws of U.S. territories and possessions. (Reg § 301.7701-2(b))[1]

Under the "check-the-box" regs, if a joint undertaking is an entity separate from its owners for federal tax purposes, the entity is a business entity and not a trust, and the business entity is an "eligible entity" (i.e., not mandatorily classified as a corporation), it may elect its classification for federal tax purposes. An eligible entity with at least two members may elect to be classified as a partnership or as an association (and thus as a corporation). An eligible entity with a single owner may elect to be classified as an association or to be disregarded as an entity separate from its owner. [2] An eligible entity that wishes to elect a classification other than its default classification, or any eligible entity that wishes to change its classification does so by filing Form 8832 with the IRS Center designated on the form. [3]

An entity organized in more than one jurisdiction is treated as a corporation for federal tax purposes if it is so treated in any of those jurisdictions. (Reg § 301.7701-2(b)(9))[4]

¶ 3302 Publicly traded partnerships (PTPs) as corporations.

A publicly traded partnership (PTP) is taxable as a corporation. (Code Sec. 7704(a))[5] A partnership is a PTP if interests in the partnership either: (1) are traded on an established securities market (including, besides a national exchange, a regional or local exchange, certain foreign exchanges, and an interdealer quotation system), or (2) are readily tradable on a

---

1. ¶D-1102; ¶77,014.14; TD ¶580,501
2. ¶D-1151; ¶77,014.15; TD ¶580,501
3. ¶D-1166; ¶77,014.15; TD ¶580,511

4. ¶D-1101.1; ¶77,014.14; TD ¶600,202
5. ¶D-1321; ¶77,044; TD ¶600,202

References beginning with a single letter are to paragraphs in RIA's Federal Tax Coordinator 2d and RIA's Analysis of Federal Taxes: Income. Those beginning with numbers are to paragraphs in RIA's United States Tax Reporter. Those beginning with TD are to paragraphs in RIA's Tax Desk.

secondary market or its substantial equivalent. (Code Sec. 7704(b); Reg § 1.7704-1)[6]

However, a PTP won't be treated as a corporation if, for each tax year beginning after '87, at least 90% of its gross income is specified passive-type income, and certain other requirements are met. (Code Sec. 7704(c))[7] The corporate estimated tax rules of Code Sec. 6655 (¶3346 *et seq.*) apply to this tax. (Code Sec. 7704(g)(3)(C))[8]

For how C corporations are taxed, see ¶3303 *et seq.*

For how S corporations are taxed, see ¶3353 *et seq.*

¶ 3303   How C Corporations Are Taxed.

C corporations generally are subject to tax at graduated rates on their taxable income. The benefits of the graduated rates phase out after taxable income reaches a specified amount.

For the rates at which a C corporation's income is taxed, and for the amount at which the graduated rates are phased out, see ¶1112. For limits on the use of graduated rates and other tax benefits by members of a controlled group of corporations, see ¶3342.

C corporations that are qualified personal service corporations (PSCs, see ¶3334) are taxed at a flat 35% rate. (Code Sec. 11(b)(2))[9]

Some C corporations are also subject to an alternative minimum tax (¶3200 *et seq.*).

For penalty taxes imposed on corporations with unreasonable earnings accumulations, see ¶3316 *et seq.*

For personal holding company tax, see ¶3323 *et seq.*

For taxation of corporations making certain outbound transfers, see ¶3586.

For corporate income tax returns generally, see ¶4725.

¶ 3304   C corporation's taxable income.

A C corporation's taxable income equals its gross income less the deductions allowed by the Code. (Code Sec. 63)[10] A C corporation's gross income doesn't include contributions to its capital. (Code Sec. 118)[11] For a C corporation's gain or loss from distributing property to its shareholders, see ¶3521 *et seq.*

¶ 3305   Computing a C corporation's tax.

A C corporation's tax is computed by applying the Code Sec. 11 rates in effect for its tax year (¶1112) to its taxable income (¶3304) for that year, and then subtracting any available tax credits (¶2300 *et seq.*).[12]

Special rules apply for computing the tax for years that straddle a rate change (Code Sec. 15(a))[13] and for short tax years, see ¶2805.

For reporting and paying the tax, see ¶4725 *et seq.*

¶ 3306   Dividends-Received Deduction.

Corporate shareholders are allowed a deduction for dividends received.

---

6. ¶D-1343; ¶77,044.03
7. ¶D-1363 *et seq.*; ¶77,044
8. ¶D-1322; ¶77,044.03
9. ¶D-1006; ¶s 114.01, 114.02; TD ¶600,901

10. ¶D-1001; ¶634; TD ¶600,501
11. ¶F-1901; ¶1184; TD ¶600,501
12. ¶D-1001 *et seq.*; ¶114.01; TD ¶600,501
13. ¶D-1009 *et seq.*; ¶154.01; TD ¶600,506

¶ 3307　Deduction for dividends from domestic corporations—70%, 80%, and 100% deductions.

Subject to specific disallowances, reductions, and limitations (¶3311 *et seq.*), a C corporation may deduct 70% of the dividends received or accrued from domestic corporations. (Code Sec. 243(a)(1))[14] The deduction is 80% for dividends received or accrued from a corporation at least 20% of the stock of which (not counting preferred stock described in Code Sec. 1504(a)(4)) is owned, by vote and value, by the corporate shareholder. (Code Sec. 243(c))[15]

Members of an affiliated group (as specially defined) that file separate returns may deduct 100% of the dividends received from other group members if certain requirements are met. (Code Sec. 243(a)(3), Code Sec. 243(b))[16]

For a small business investment company's dividends-received deduction, see ¶4205.

The deduction applies to taxable dividends (¶1285 *et seq.*), (Code Sec. 243(a)), "boot" dividends (¶3554), consent dividends (¶3339)[17] and the "dividend equivalent" portion of high yield OID obligations (¶1753). (Code Sec. 163(e)(5)(B))[18] For dividends that aren't deductible, see ¶3315.

¶ 3308　Dividends from regulated investment companies (RICs)—mutual fund dividends.

A dividend (other than capital gain or exempt-interest dividends) from a RIC (e.g., a mutual fund) is eligible for the dividends-received deduction to the extent of the amounts the RIC received from domestic corporations that it would have been allowed to treat as dividends in computing its own dividends-received deduction if it had been a regular corporation. (Code Sec. 243(d)(2), Code Sec. 854(b)(4))[19]

¶ 3309　Dividends on certain public utility preferred stock.

Dividends received from a public utility are eligible for the dividends-received deduction, but the deduction is reduced if the utility was entitled to a dividends- *paid* deduction (¶3335) on those dividends. (Code Sec. 244(a))[20]

¶ 3310　Dividends from foreign corporations and possession corporations.

A U.S. corporation that owns at least 10% (by vote or value) of the stock of a foreign corporation (other than a foreign passive investment company) may deduct the applicable percentage (70% or 80%, see ¶3307) of the U.S.-source portion of the dividends from that corporation. (Code Sec. 245(a)(1), Code Sec. 245(a)(2))[21]

The U.S.-source portion of any dividend is the amount that bears the same ratio to the dividend that the payor's post-'86 undistributed U.S. earnings bears to its total post-'86 undistributed earnings. (Code Sec. 245(a)(3), Code Sec. 245(a)(4), Code Sec. 245(a)(5))[22] Special rules apply for dividends paid out of pre-'87 earnings. [23]

A 100% dividends-received deduction is allowed (instead of the above percentage deductions) if all the foreign corporation's gross income is effectively connected with its U.S. business in the year the dividends are earned, and all its outstanding stock is owned by the U.S. payee both in that year and in the payee's tax year in which the dividends are received. (Code

---

14. ¶D-2201; ¶2434.01; TD ¶600,509
15. ¶D-2205 *et seq.*; ¶2434.01; TD ¶600,509
16. ¶D-2223 *et seq.*; ¶2434.01; TD ¶600,509
17. ¶D-2209 *et seq.*; ¶2434.01; TD ¶602,019
18. ¶D-2221; ¶1634.051; TD ¶600,512

19. ¶D-2216, ¶E-6163; ¶8524.02; TD ¶600,512
20. ¶D-2222; ¶2434.02; TD ¶600,512
21. ¶D-2244; ¶2434.03; TD ¶600,509
22. ¶s D-2244, D-2246; ¶2434.03
23. ¶D-2246; ¶2434.03

Sec. 245(b))[24]

For DISC dividends, see ¶3315.

¶ 3311   Taxable income limit on dividends-received deduction.

A corporation's percentage dividends-received deduction (but not the 100% deduction) for any tax year can't exceed the applicable percentage (below) of its taxable income. (Code Sec. 246(b)(1)) But this limit doesn't apply for any tax year for which the shareholder has a net operating loss (NOL). (Code Sec. 246(b)(2))[25]

A corporation's dividends-received deduction is generally limited to 70% of its taxable income. But if the dividends are received *only* from 20%-owned corporations the deduction is limited to 80% of taxable income. If a corporation receives dividends from both 20%-owned *and* non-20%-owned corporations, the taxable income limit is applied first to the "20%-owned" dividends so that their deduction can't exceed 80% of taxable income. (Code Sec. 246(b)(3)(A)) If this 80% limit isn't exceeded, a separate limit is then applied to the "non-20%-owned" dividends so that their deduction doesn't exceed 70% of taxable income (as reduced by the total amount of the "20%-owned" dividends). (Code Sec. 246(b)(3)(B))[26]

For this purpose, taxable income is computed without regard to the deductions for capital loss carrybacks, NOLs, dividends received, and the deduction for income attributable to domestic production activities (¶1616), and without regard to any basis reduction for extraordinary dividends (¶2495). (Code Sec. 246(b)(1))[27]

¶ 3312   Holding period requirements.

No dividends-received deduction is allowed for any dividend on any share of stock that's held by the taxpayer for 45 days or less during the 91-day period beginning on the date that is 45 days before the date on which the stock becomes ex-dividend with respect to the dividend (90 days or less out of the relevant 181-day period for any preferred stock with respect to which the taxpayer gets dividends that are attributable to a period or periods aggregating in excess of 366 days). (Code Sec. 246(c)) In other words, a dividends received deduction is allowed only if the taxpayer's holding period for the dividend paying stock is satisfied over a period immediately before or immediately after the taxpayer becomes entitled to receive the dividend.[28]

In determining how long the shareholder has held the stock, the day of disposition but not the day of acquisition is taken into account. (Code Sec. 246(c)(3)(A))[29]

The shareholder's holding period for the stock is suspended (reduced) for any period during which, while holding the stock, the shareholder:

(1) has an option to sell, is under a contractual obligation to sell, has made (and not closed) a short sale of, or is the grantor of an option to buy, substantially identical stock or securities (as defined under the "wash sale" rules, see ¶2461). (Code Sec. 246(c)(4)(A), Code Sec. 246(c)(4)(B); Reg § 1.246-3(c)(2))[30]

(2) has diminished its risk of loss by holding one or more other positions with respect to substantially similar or related property (i.e., the fair market values (FMV) of the stock and the property primarily reflect a single firm or enterprise and changes in the stock's FMV are reasonably expected to approximate (directly or indirectly) changes in the property's FMV), where changes in the FMVs of the stock and the positions are reasonably expected to vary inversely. (Code Sec. 246(c)(4)(C); Reg § 1.246-5)[31]

---

24. ¶D-2247; ¶2434.03; TD ¶600,509
25. ¶s D-2251, D-2252; ¶2434.04; TD ¶600,518
26. ¶D-2253; ¶2434.04; TD ¶600,518
27. ¶D-2251; ¶2434.04; TD ¶600,518

28. ¶D-2263; ¶2434.04; TD ¶600,516
29. ¶D-2263; ¶2434.04
30. ¶s D-2264, D-2266; ¶2434.04; TD ¶600,517
31. ¶D-2268 *et seq.*; ¶2434.04; TD ¶600,517

¶ 3313 No dividends-received deduction where shareholder is obligated to make certain payments.

A corporate shareholder gets no dividends-received deduction for any dividends received on any stock acquired after July 18, '84 to the extent the shareholder is under an obligation (by a short sale or otherwise) to make related payments with respect to positions in substantially similar or related property (as defined at ¶3312). (Code Sec. 246(c)(1)(B))[32]

¶ 3314 Deduction reduced for dividends on debt-financed portfolio stock.

The 70% and 80% dividends-received deduction (but not the 100% deduction) is reduced for dividends on debt-financed portfolio stock with a holding period that began after July 18, '84. As reduced, the applicable percentage for deducting these dividends equals: (1) 70% (80% for dividends from 20%-owned corporations), multiplied by (2) 100% minus the "average indebtedness percentage." (Code Sec. 246A(a), Code Sec. 246A(b)) The reduction for any dividend may not exceed the interest deduction (including short sale expense) allocable to that dividend. (Code Sec. 246A(e))[33]

¶ 3315 Dividends from certain corporations aren't deductible.

No dividends-received deduction is allowed for dividends from:

. . . a corporation that's exempt from tax as a charitable organization under Code Sec. 501 or as a farmer's cooperative under Code Sec. 521. (Code Sec. 246(a)(1))[34]

. . . a DISC (¶4627) or former DISC to the extent paid out of accumulated DISC income or previously taxed income, or amounts considered distributed in the year of qualification as a DISC. (Code Sec. 246(d))[35]

. . . a REIT. (Code Sec. 243(d)(3))[36]

. . . a mutual savings bank, savings and loan associations and other banks allowed a deduction under Code Sec. 591. (Code Sec. 243(d)(1))[37] However, certain dividends from federal home loan banks qualify to the extent set out in a specific formula. (Code Sec. 246(a)(2))[38]

¶ 3316 Accumulated Earnings Tax. ▬▬▬▬▬▬▬

Every corporation, unless specifically exempt, that accumulates earnings and profits (rather than distributes them) in order to avoid the imposition of income tax on its shareholders is subject to an annual accumulated earnings (penalty) tax, equal to 15% (for tax years beginning after 2002 and before 2009) of its "accumulated taxable income" for the year. The tax is in addition to the regular corporate tax.

¶ 3317 Purpose to avoid tax versus "reasonable needs" of the business.

The accumulated earnings penalty tax is only imposed on a corporation whose earnings and profits (E&P) were accumulated with the purpose of avoiding income tax on its shareholders. (Code Sec. 532(a))[39] A corporation that accumulates E&P beyond the reasonable needs of its business is considered to have done so to avoid tax on its shareholders *unless* it proves the contrary by the preponderance of the evidence. (Code Sec. 533(a))[40]

An accumulation is in excess of the reasonable needs of a business if it exceeds the amount that a prudent business person would consider appropriate for the present purposes of the

32. ¶D-2261; ¶2434.04; TD ¶600,515
33. ¶D-2255; ¶2434.05; TD ¶600,520
34. ¶D-2213; ¶2434.04; TD ¶600,513
35. ¶D-2212; ¶2434.04; TD ¶600,513
36. ¶D-2215; ¶2434.01; TD ¶600,513

37. ¶D-2211; ¶2434.01; TD ¶600,513
38. ¶s D-2214, D-2219; ¶2434.04; TD ¶600,512
39. ¶D-2601; ¶5324.01; TD ¶601,001
40. ¶D-2704; ¶s 5324.01, 5374; TD ¶601,014

business and for its reasonably anticipated future needs. (Code Sec. 537; Reg § 1.537-1(a); Reg § 1.537-1(b)(1))[41] The reasonable needs of a corporation's business include the Code Sec. 303 redemption needs of the business (Code Sec. 537(a)(2)[42] and the excess business holdings redemption needs of the business. (Code Sec. 537(a)(3))[43]

Corporations facing an accumulated earnings tax may use a formula to compute the amount reasonably needed for working capital, to test their liability for the penalty. The Tax Court in Bardahl Manufacturing Corp held that necessary working capital should be determined by: (1) calculating a corporation's operating cycle percentage (the period of time, expressed as a percent of a year, needed to convert cash to inventory, inventory to sales and accounts receivable, and accounts receivable to cash), and then (2) multiplying that percentage times the corporation's total operating expenses for the year (cost of goods sold and other expenses). The result of this two-step Bardahl formula is the amount of liquid assets necessary to meet the ordinary operating expenses for one complete operating cycle. [44]

A corporation with a history of paying dividends isn't likely to be hit with the penalty. [45]

¶ 3318 Application of the accumulated earnings tax.

The tax applies to every corporation (unless specifically exempt, see ¶3319), regardless of the number of shareholders (Code Sec. 532(a), Code Sec. 532(c))—i.e., even if it's widely held.[46]

The tax applies to foreign corporations on their U.S.-source income if *any* of their shareholders is subject to U.S. income tax on distributions. (Reg § 1.532-1(c))[47]

The accumulated earnings tax is in addition to other income taxes imposed on the corporation, and is assessed and paid with those taxes. (Code Sec. 531; Reg § 1.531-1)[48]

For permissible accumulations, see ¶3322.

¶ 3319 Corporations exempt from the accumulated earnings tax.

The accumulated earnings tax *doesn't apply* to:

... personal holding companies (subject to their own penalty tax, see ¶3323); (Code Sec. 532(b)(1))

... tax-exempt corporations; (Code Sec. 532(b)(2))

... passive foreign investment companies (¶4634); (Code Sec. 532(b)(3))

... S corporations (¶3353 *et seq.*). (Code Sec. 1363(a))[49]

¶ 3320 Accumulated earnings tax rate.

For tax years beginning after 2002 and before 2009, the accumulated earnings tax is 15% of accumulated taxable income (¶3321). (Code Sec. 531)[50]

¶ 3321 Accumulated taxable income.

A corporation's accumulated taxable income is its taxable income, adjusted as described below, *minus:* (1) the dividends-paid deduction (¶3335), and (2) the accumulated earnings credit (¶3322). (Code Sec. 535(a))[1]

---

41. ¶s D-2779, D-2792; ¶s 5314, 5374; TD ¶601,019;)¶D-2783; ¶5374; TD ¶601,019
42. ¶D-2828;¶5374; TD ¶601,030
43. ¶D-2830; ¶5374; TD ¶601,030
44. ¶D-2848; ¶5374; TD ¶601,032
45. ¶D-2715; ¶5374; TD ¶601,016

46. ¶s D-2602, D-2603; ¶5324; TD ¶601,002
47. ¶D-2607; ¶5324; TD ¶601,003
48. ¶D-2601, V-2053; ¶5314; TD ¶601,001
49. ¶D-2602; ¶5324; TD ¶601,002
50. ¶D-2601; ¶s 5324.01, 5354; TD ¶601,001
1. ¶D-2901; ¶5354.01; TD ¶601,009

The corporation's taxable income is *reduced* by:

... federal income and excess profits taxes accrued during the tax year (not the accumulated earnings tax or the personal holding company tax) (Code Sec. 535(b)(1));

... taxes of foreign countries and U.S. possessions accrued or deemed paid by a domestic corporation and included in the foreign tax credit (¶2369 *et seq.*) (Code Sec. 535(b)(1));[2]

... charitable contributions in excess of the deduction ceiling (¶2132) (Code Sec. 535(b)(2));[3]

... net capital gains (less attributable taxes). (Code Sec. 535(b)(6)(A)) A mere holding or investment company deducts net *short*-term capital gain (less attributable taxes) to the extent it doesn't exceed capital loss carryover to the year (Code Sec. 535(b)(8)(B)); other corporations must reduce their net capital gain deduction by net capital losses from any earlier year (Code Sec. 535(b)(7)(A), Code Sec. 535(b)(8)(B));[4]

... net capital losses. (Code Sec. 535(b)(5)(A)) A mere holding or investment company gets no net capital loss deduction (Code Sec. 535(b)(8)(A)); any other corporation must reduce its net capital loss deduction by the lesser of: (1) its nonrecaptured capital gain deduction, or (2) its accumulated E&P as of the close of the preceding tax year. (Code Sec. 535(b)(5))[5]

Taxable income is *increased* by:

... special corporate deductions (e.g., for dividends received (¶3306 *et seq.*), but not for organizational expenditures) (Code Sec. 535(b)(3));

... net operating loss deduction (¶1841 *et seq.*) (Code Sec. 535(b)(4));

... capital loss carryback or carryover (¶2615). (Code Sec. 535(b)(7)(B))[6]

¶ 3322 Accumulated earnings credit.

For corporations other than a mere holding or investment company, the accumulated earnings credit equals the *greater* of:

(1) $250,000 ($150,000 for certain service corporations) *plus* dividends paid during the first 2 ½ months of the tax year *minus* accumulated earnings and profits (E&P) at the end of the preceding tax year (Code Sec. 535(c)(2), Code Sec. 535(c)(4)); or

(2) an amount equal to that part of the E&P for the tax year that are retained for the reasonable needs of the business *minus* the net capital gain deduction, if any, allowed in adjusting the corporation's taxable income (¶3321). (Code Sec. 535(c)(1)) The E&P "retained" for a tax year is the amount in excess of dividends-paid deduction (¶3336). (Code Sec. 535(c)(4))[7]

A mere holding or investment company's accumulated earnings credit is the amount, if any, by which $250,000 plus dividends paid in the first 2 ½ months of the tax year exceeds accumulated E&P at the close of the preceding year. (Code Sec. 535(c)(3), Code Sec. 535(c)(4))[8]

🅡🅘🅐 *observation:* A mere holding or investment company gets no credit for reasonable needs.

¶ 3323 Personal Holding Company Tax. ▰▰▰▰▰▰▰▰▰▰▰▰

A closely held corporation whose income is largely of investment character may be a personal holding company (PHC), in which case a penalty tax of 15% (for tax years beginning after 2002 and before 2009) is imposed on the "personal holding company income" it doesn't distribute, in addition to regular income taxes.

2. ¶D-2913; ¶5354.01; TD ¶601,009
3. ¶D-2906; ¶5354.01; TD ¶601,009
4. ¶D-2908; ¶5354.01; TD ¶601,009
5. ¶D-2911; ¶5354.01; TD ¶601,009

6. ¶D-2907; ¶5354.01; TD ¶601,009
7. ¶D-2915; ¶5354.01; TD ¶601,012
8. ¶D-2915; ¶5354.01; TD ¶601,013

¶ 3324   Tax on personal holding companies (PHCs).

For any year in which a corporation is a personal holding company (PHC, see ¶3326), it is liable for a 15% (for tax years beginning after 2002 and before 2009) penalty tax on its undistributed PHC income, in addition to "regular" income tax. (Code Sec. 541)[9] The tax is reported on Form 1120, Schedule PH. (Reg § 1.6012-2(b))[10]

The foreign tax credit isn't allowed against the PHC tax. (Reg § 1.545-2(a)(3))[11]

¶ 3325   Undistributed PHC income subject to the PHC penalty tax.

A corporation's undistributed PHC income that is subject to the PHC tax is its taxable income (Code Sec. 545(a))[12] adjusted as described below.

. . . The following amounts are *subtracted* from taxable income:

. . . Federal income tax accrued during the year, and U.S. possession and foreign income taxes not deductible in computing taxable income. (Code Sec. 545(b)(1))[13]

. . . Excess charitable contributions, i.e., amounts over the *corporate* ceiling up to the amount allowed under the *individual* ceiling, ¶2124 *et seq.* (Code Sec. 545(b)(2))[14]

. . . Net capital gain (i.e., excess of net long-term capital gain over net short-term capital loss), minus income taxes attributable to that excess. (Code Sec. 545(b)(5))[15]

. . . One-year net operating loss (NOL) carryforward, i.e., NOL from the preceding tax year. (Code Sec. 545(b)(4))[16]

. . . Dividends-paid deduction (¶3335 *et seq.*). (Code Sec. 545(a))[17]

. . . The following amounts are *added* to taxable income:

. . . Special corporate deductions, e.g., for dividends received (¶3306 *et seq.*). (Code Sec. 545(b)(3))[18]

. . . NOL deduction. (Code Sec. 545(b)(4))[19]

. . . Expenses and depreciation exceeding income from property (unless income was highest obtainable). (Code Sec. 545(b)(6))[20]

¶ 3326   What is a personal holding company (PHC)?

Any corporation (unless specifically exempted, see ¶3327) is a personal holding company (PHC) if, for the tax year:

. . . at any time during the last half of the year more than 50% in value of its outstanding stock is owned, directly or indirectly, by or for not more than five individuals ("stock ownership test," see ¶3328); *and*

. . . at least 60% of its adjusted ordinary gross income is PHC income ("adjusted ordinary gross income test," see ¶3329). (Code Sec. 542(a))[21]

---

9. ¶D-3202; ¶5414; TD ¶601,501
10. ¶D-3601; ¶5454.02; TD ¶609,805
11. ¶D-3619; ¶9014
12. ¶D-3603; ¶5454; TD ¶601,516
13. ¶D-3606; ¶5454; TD ¶601,516
14. ¶D-3609; ¶5454; TD ¶601,516
15. ¶D-3610; ¶5454; TD ¶601,516

16. ¶D-3614; ¶5454; TD ¶601,516
17. ¶D-3800; ¶5454; TD ¶601,516
18. ¶D-3613; ¶5454; TD ¶601,516
19. ¶D-3614; ¶5454; TD ¶601,516
20. ¶D-3615; ¶5454; TD ¶601,516
21. ¶D-3203; ¶5424; TD ¶601,502

¶ 3327   Corporations exempt from PHC classification.

The following cannot be PHCs:

... S corporations (¶3353 *et seq.*) (Code Sec. 1363(a));

... tax-exempt corporations (Code Sec. 542(c)(1));

... banks or domestic building and loan associations (Code Sec. 542(c)(2));

... life insurance companies (Code Sec. 542(c)(3));

... surety companies (Code Sec. 542(c)(4));

... certain active lending or finance companies (Code Sec. 542(c)(6), Code Sec. 542(d));

... small business investment companies (¶2631), if no shareholders own, directly or indirectly, a 5%-or-more interest in a small business concern to which the investment company provides funds (Code Sec. 542(c)(7));

... corporations subject to the jurisdiction of a court in a bankruptcy case or in a receivership, foreclosure or similar proceeding in a federal or state court if the proceedings aren't primarily to avoid the PHC tax (Code Sec. 542(c)(8)); and

... foreign corporations. (Code Sec. 542(c)(5))

¶ 3328   Determining stock ownership.

For purposes of the PHC tests (¶3326), an individual is the owner of any stock he owns directly or indirectly (Code Sec. 542(a)(2)), or constructively under these rules:

(1) Stock owned by or for a corporation, partnership, estate or trust is considered owned proportionately by its shareholders, partners or beneficiaries. (Code Sec. 544(a)(1))[22]

(2) Stock owned by or for an individual's family or partner is considered owned by the individual. An individual's family includes only his brothers and sisters (whether by the whole or half blood), spouse, ancestors and lineal descendants. (Code Sec. 544(a)(2))[23]

(3) If any person has an option to acquire stock, the stock subject to the option is considered owned by that person. An option to acquire the option, and each one of a series of these options, is considered an option to acquire the stock. (Code Sec. 544(a)(3))[24]

Stock that may be considered owned by an individual under either rule (2) or rule (3) is considered owned by him under rule (3). (Code Sec. 544(a)(6))[25]

Rules (2) and (3) apply only if the result is to make the corporation a PHC or to make income PHC income (¶3330). (Code Sec. 544(a)(4))[26]

Stock *constructively* owned by a person under rule (1) or rule (3) is considered *actually* owned by that person for purposes of again applying rule (1), or applying rule (2), to make *another* person the *constructive* owner of the same stock. (Code Sec. 544(a)(5))[27]

Only outstanding stock (i.e., not Treasury stock) is counted. (Reg § 1.542-3(b))[28] Outstanding securities convertible into stock are considered outstanding stock *but only if* converting them would make the corporation a PHC or the income PHC income (except where there are differing conversion dates). (Code Sec. 544(b))[29]

---

22. ¶D-3406; ¶5444.01; TD ¶601,512
23. ¶D-3408; ¶5444.01; TD ¶601,512
24. ¶D-3410; ¶5444.01; TD ¶601,512
25. ¶D-3411; ¶5444.01 *et seq.*; TD ¶601,512

26. ¶s D-3408, D-3410; ¶5444.01; TD ¶601,512
27. ¶D-3411; ¶5444.01; TD ¶601,512
28. ¶D-3402; ¶5424.04; TD ¶601,510
29. ¶D-3412; ¶5444.01 *et seq.*; TD ¶601,513

¶ 3329   Adjusted ordinary gross income used in PHC test.

For purposes of the PHC tests (¶3326), *adjusted ordinary gross income* is ordinary gross income (below) minus certain interest income, with these adjustments: for each of the separate categories of rents, mineral, oil and gas royalties, working interests in an oil or gas well and property produced by the taxpayer, gross income from the category is reduced (but not below zero) by certain expenses allocated to each category. (Code Sec. 543(b)(2))[30]

Ordinary gross income is gross income minus all gains from the sale or other disposition of capital assets (including unstated interest) and of Code Sec. 1231(b) assets. (Code Sec. 543(b)(1))[31]

¶ 3330   Personal holding company (PHC) income used in PHC test.

For purposes of the PHC tests (¶3326), PHC income is the portion of adjusted ordinary gross income (¶3329), that consists of: dividends; interest; annuities; rents (¶3331); mineral, oil and gas royalties; copyright, patent, etc., royalties (but not certain "active business computer software royalties"); produced film rents; compensation for more-than-25% shareholder's use of corporate property (¶3332); amounts received under personal service contracts (¶3333); and amounts received from estates and trusts. (Code Sec. 543(a))[32]

¶ 3331   Rents.

The adjusted income from rents is PHC income (¶3330), unless *both* these tests are met:

(1) adjusted income from rents is 50% or more of adjusted ordinary gross income (¶3329); *and*

(2) certain other *undistributed* "PHC income" (as specially defined) is 10% or less of ordinary gross income (¶3329). This "PHC income" *includes* copyright royalties and adjusted income from mineral, oil and gas royalties but *excludes* rents and compensation for a 25%-or-more shareholder's use of corporate property. The 10% test is met if the total of (a) dividends paid during the tax year, plus (b) late-paid dividends (¶3337), plus (c) consent dividends (¶3339), equals or exceeds the amount, if any, by which "PHC income" exceeds 10% of ordinary gross income. (Code Sec. 543(a)(2))[33]

Rents are compensation (however designated) for the use of, or the right to use, property (Code Sec. 543(a)(1)(A), Code Sec. 543(b)(3)), *except* for: compensation for a shareholder's use of corporate property that is PHC income (¶3332), copyright royalties, produced film rents, or compensation for the right to use any tangible personal property manufactured or produced by the corporation, if during the tax year it's engaged in substantial manufacturing or production of property of the same type. (Code Sec. 543(b)(3))[34]

¶ 3332   Compensation for use of corporate property by a 25%-or-more shareholder.

Amounts received by the corporation from a shareholder as compensation for the use of, or right to use, tangible property of the corporation is included in the corporation's PHC income (¶3330), if, during the tax year, 25% or more in value of the corporation's outstanding stock is owned by or for an individual entitled to use that property (directly or through a sublease). (Code Sec. 543(a)(6)(A)) But this doesn't apply if the corporation's PHC income doesn't exceed 10% of its ordinary gross income (¶3329). This specially defined PHC income is computed by *excluding* adjusted income from rents and compensation for a 25%-or-more shareholder's use

---

30. ¶D-3506; ¶5424.03; TD ¶601,504
31. ¶D-3505; ¶5424.03; TD ¶601,504
32. ¶D-3507; ¶5434 *et seq.*; TD ¶601,505

33. ¶D-3522; ¶5434.07; TD ¶601,506
34. ¶D-3524; ¶s 5434.06, 5434.07, 5434.09

of tangible corporate property, and by *including* copyright royalties and adjusted income from mineral, oil and gas royalties. (Code Sec. 543(a)(6))[35]

¶ 3333 Receipts under personal service contract.

PHC income (¶3330) includes amounts received under a contract under which the corporation furnishes personal services, and amounts received from the sale or other disposition of the contract, if:

(1) some person other than the corporation has the right to designate (by name or description) the individual who performs the services, or if the individual who is to perform the services is so designated in the contract, *and*

(2) at some time during the tax year 25% or more in value of the corporation's outstanding stock is owned, directly or indirectly, by or for that individual. (Code Sec. 543(a)(7); Reg § 1.543-1(b)(8)(i))[36]

¶ 3334 Qualified Personal Service Corporations

Qualified personal service corporations (PSCs) are subject to special rules, including the rate that they are taxed at (a flat 35%) and the accounting method that they may use (cash). A corporation is a PSC if it meets two tests:

(1) Substantially all of its activities involve the performance of services in the fields of health, law, engineering, architecture, accounting, actuarial science, performing arts, or consulting. "Substantially all" means that 95% or more of the time spent by the corporation's employees, serving in their capacity as employees, is devoted to performing such services. Brokerage services, including commission-based financial services, are excepted from consulting services.

(2) Substantially all (95% or more) of the stock by value (not including treasury shares) is held directly or indirectly by: employees performing the services or retired employees who had performed such services; or the estates of such employees, or any other person who, during the two-year period starting with the date that such an employee died, acquired that individual's stock because his death. (Code Sec. 448(d)(2); Reg § 1.448-1T(e)(4))[37]

For the tax rate applicable to qualified PSCs see ¶3303. For the rules on allowable accounting methods, see ¶2818. For the tax year of personal service corporations, see ¶2811.

¶ 3335 Dividend Distributions to Cut Special Taxes on Corporations.

A deduction for dividends paid is allowed in computing the accumulated earnings and personal holding company penalty taxes, and in determining a corporation's qualification as a regulated investment company (e.g., mutual fund) or real estate investment trust (REIT). A deduction is also allowed in some cases for undistributed amounts shareholders consent to report as dividends.

Depending on the entity involved, the dividends-paid deduction may consist of:

(1) dividends paid during the tax year (¶3336),

(2) "late paid" dividends (¶3337),

(3) liquidating dividends (¶3338),

(4) consent dividends (¶3339),

(5) dividend carryover — only for personal holding companies (PHCs) (¶3340), and

(6) deficiency dividends (¶3341) — only for PHCs. (Code Sec. 561; Reg § 1.561-1)[38]

---

35. ¶D-3527; ¶5434.06; TD ¶601,514
36. ¶D-3531; ¶5434.05; TD ¶601,515

37. ¶G-2058; ¶4484; TD ¶440,809
38. ¶D-3800; ¶5614; TD ¶602,000 *et seq.*

¶ 3336   Dividends paid during the tax year.

The dividends-paid deduction includes dividends paid during the tax year. (Code Sec. 561(a)(1)) But the dividend must actually be paid, [39] and must actually be received by the shareholder in the year for which the deduction is claimed. (Reg § 1.561-2(a)(1))[40]

No deduction is allowed if the dividend is preferential, i.e., it must be pro rata. (Code Sec. 562(c); Reg § 1.562-2(a))[41]

The amount of "dividends" paid is the amount by which the distribution reduces the corporation's earnings and profits (E&P). (Code Sec. 316(a), Code Sec. 562(a))[42]

A PHC's (¶3323 *et seq.*) dividends-paid deduction may equal its undistributed PHC income even if this exceeds its E&P. (Code Sec. 316(b)(2), Code Sec. 562(a))[43]

¶ 3337   Deduction for "late paid" dividends.

A corporation may treat dividends paid after the close of the tax year but within the first 2 ½ months of the next year ("late paid dividends") as paid on the last day of the earlier year, for purposes of the accumulated earnings (¶3316 *et seq.*), and, if elected (on the earlier year return), PHC (¶3323 *et seq.*) penalty taxes. (Code Sec. 563(a), Code Sec. 563(b))[44]

¶ 3338   Liquidating distributions.

Corporations (including mutual funds and REITs) other than PHCs may include liquidating distributions in their dividends-paid deduction, to the extent the distribution is properly chargeable to E&P. (Code Sec. 562(b)(1)(A))[45] Where there's a deficit in E&P at the start of the tax year of distribution, no dividends-paid deduction is allowed if current E&P for that year doesn't exceed the deficit. (Reg § 1.562-1(b)(1))[46] A liquidation for this purpose includes a redemption of stock to which Code Sec. 302 applies (¶3526 *et seq.*), other than a redemption by a mere investment or holding company. (Code Sec. 562(b)(1))[47]

If a *complete* liquidation of a corporation other than a PHC occurs within 24 months after the plan of liquidation is adopted, any distribution under the plan within the 24-month period is treated as a dividend for this purpose, to the extent of the corporation's E&P for the tax year of the distribution, computed without regard to capital losses. (Code Sec. 562(b)(1)(B)) Thus, the dividends-paid deduction is allowed for the amount of the distribution up to the amount of current E&P even if there's an E&P deficit at the start of the year. (Reg § 1.562-1(b)(1))[48]

For PHCs, only distributions made within 24 months after the plan of liquidation is adopted qualify for the dividends-paid deduction. [49] Distributions (in this period) to *corporate* shareholders qualify to the extent the undistributed PHC income for the tax year of the distribution is allocable to corporate shareholders. (Code Sec. 562(b)(2))[50] Distributions to *noncorporate* shareholders qualify if the corporation designates the amount distributed as a dividend and notifies the shareholders that it must be reported as a dividend. (Code Sec. 316(b)(2)(B), Code Sec. 562(b)(2))[1]

---

39. ¶D-3806; ¶5614.01; TD ¶602,003
40. ¶D-3810; ¶5614.01
41. ¶D-3819 *et seq.*; ¶5624.06; TD ¶602,003
42. ¶D-3807; ¶s 3164 *et seq.*, 5614, 5624; TD ¶602,004
43. ¶D-3807; ¶s 3164.03, 5614; TD ¶602,005
44. ¶D-3825 *et seq.*; ¶5634; TD ¶602,007
45. ¶D-3828; ¶5624.02; TD ¶602,010

46. ¶D-3835; ¶5624.02; TD ¶602,013
47. ¶D-3829; ¶s 5624.02, 5624.05; TD ¶602,010
48. ¶D-3836; ¶5624.02; TD ¶602,014
49. ¶D-3837; ¶s 3164.03, 5624.02; TD ¶602,015
50. ¶D-3844 *et seq.*; ¶5624.02; TD ¶602,018
1. ¶D-3838 *et seq.*; ¶s 3164.03, 5624.02; TD ¶602,016

¶ 3339 Consent dividends—Form 972 and Form 973.

A corporation may claim a dividends-paid deduction for amounts with respect to "consent" stock (below) it doesn't actually pay out as dividends, if those who are shareholders on the last day of its tax year consent (on Form 972) to report these hypothetical amounts as dividend income on their tax returns. (Code Sec. 565(a); Reg § 1.565-1(a), Reg § 1.565-1(b))[2]

This amount is treated for all tax purposes as if it had been distributed in money to the consenting shareholder on the last day of the corporation's tax year, and contributed to the corporation's capital by the shareholder on the same day. (Code Sec. 565(c))[3]

Consent stock includes common stock, and preferred stock with unlimited participation rights. (Code Sec. 565(c); Reg § 1.565-6(a)(1))[4]

The corporation must file the Form 972 duly executed by each consenting shareholder, and a return on Form 973, with its income tax return not later than the due date (with extensions) of the return. (Reg § 1.565-1(b)(3))

¶ 3340 Dividend carryover for PHC.

A PHC may increase its dividends-paid deduction for the tax year by the excess of: (1) dividends paid in the two preceding tax years, over (2) its undistributed PHC income for those years. (Code Sec. 564; Reg § 1.564-1)[5]

¶ 3341 PHC deficiency dividend deduction—Form 976.

If a corporation is "determined" to be liable for a deficiency in PHC tax (¶3323 *et seq.*) for any tax year, it may reduce or eliminate the deficiency (or get a refund of part or all of any deficiency paid) by making a "deficiency dividend" distribution and then claiming a deduction (on Form 976) for it. This deduction is allowed only for purposes of determining the *PHC tax* for that year (but not any interest, additional amounts or assessable penalties computed with respect to the PHC tax). (Code Sec. 547(a))[6]

The deduction isn't allowed if the determination finds that any part of the deficiency is due to fraud or willful failure to file a timely income tax return. (Code Sec. 547(g))[7]

A "determination" is a final court decision, a closing agreement, or a signed agreement with IRS relating to PHC tax liability. (Code Sec. 547(c))[8]

¶ 3342 Limit on Multiple Tax Benefits For "Controlled Groups." ▮▮▮▮▮▮

For a controlled group of corporations filing separate returns, the corporate tax brackets are applied to the group's total taxable income, and the group is allowed only one accumulated earnings tax credit, and one alternative minimum tax exemption amount. (Code Sec. 1561).

A *parent-subsidiary controlled group* consists of one or more chains of corporations connected through stock ownership with a common parent where:

. . . the common parent owns stock having at least 80% of the total combined voting power of all classes of stock entitled to vote or at least 80% of the total value of shares of all classes of stock, of at least one other corporation in the chain; *and*

. . . at least 80% of the stock (combined voting power or value) of each corporation in the chain (other than the parent) is owned by one or more of the other corporations in the

---

2. ¶s D-3851, D-3854, D-3861; ¶5654; TD ¶602,019

3. ¶D-3853; ¶5654; TD ¶602,021

4. ¶s D-3859, D-3861; ¶5654; TD ¶602,024

5. ¶D-3869; ¶5644; TD ¶602,030

6. ¶s D-3703, D-3716; ¶5474; TD ¶601,519

7. ¶D-3719; ¶5474; TD ¶601,517

8. ¶D-3705; ¶5474; TD ¶601,517

chain. (Code Sec. 1563(a)(1))[9]

For purposes of the rules governing corporate tax brackets (¶1112), the accumulated earnings credit (¶3322), and the minimum tax exemption (¶3202), a *brother-sister controlled group* consists of two or more corporations if (a) more than 50% of the total combined voting power of all classes of stock, or (b) more than 50% of the value of all shares of stock, of each corporation is owned by five or fewer persons who are individuals, estates, or trusts, taking into account the stock ownership of each person only to the extent the stock ownership is identical for each corporation. (Code Sec. 1563(a)(2), Code Sec. 1563(f)(5); Reg § 1.1563-1T(a)(3)(ii)(C))[10]

Specific constructive ownership rules apply in determining whether these stock ownership tests are met. (Code Sec. 1563(d))[11]

¶ 3343   Consolidated Returns by Affiliated Groups. ▬▬▬▬▬▬▬▬▬▬▬

An affiliated group can elect to file a single consolidated return instead of each group member filing a separate return.

Any affiliated group of one or more chains of "includible" corporations (¶3344) connected through the requisite stock ownership with a common parent may file a consolidated return in place of separate returns by each member (Code Sec. 1501, Code Sec. 1502, Code Sec. 1503, Code Sec. 1504, Code Sec. 1505)[12] Generally, once this election to file a consolidated return is made, the group must continue to file a consolidated return. (Reg § 1.1502-75(a)(2))[13]

Tax saving considerations usually determine whether to file a consolidated return. Advantages of consolidated returns include:

. . . operating losses of one group member offset operating profits of other members. [14]

. . . capital losses of one group member offset capital gains of other members. [15]

. . . deferral of income on intercompany distributions. [16]

. . . group's ability to use of foreign taxes paid by a member in excess of its limitation on foreign tax credits. [17]

. . . the 70% or 80% dividends-received deduction for dividends received from unrelated corporations, that may not be fully usable on a separate return basis because of the income limitation rule, may be fully used in a consolidated return. (¶3307)[18]

Regs prescribe detailed rules for treating items of income, gain, deduction, and loss of members from intercompany transactions. The rules are designed to clearly reflect the group's taxable income as a whole by preventing intercompany transactions from crediting, accelerating, avoiding, or deferring consolidated taxable income or consolidated tax liability. (Reg § 1.1502-13)[19]

Except as discussed below, no deduction is allowed for any loss recognized by a member of a consolidated group on the disposition of stock of a subsidiary. Likewise, if the basis of a member of a consolidated group exceeds its value immediately before deconsolidation (i.e., before it becomes held outside the group), the basis of the stock is reduced at that time to its value. However, to the extent the taxpayer establishes that the loss or basis is not attributable to the recognition of built-in gain (net of directly related expenses, including, in certain cases, federal income tax related to the gain recognition), on the disposition of an asset (including stock and securities), losses on subsidiary dispositions are not disallowed and basis

9. ¶E-10601; ¶15,634; TD ¶607,501
10. ¶E-10613, ¶15,634; TD ¶607,509
11. ¶E-10700 *et seq.*; ¶15,634; TD ¶607,702 *et seq.*
12. ¶E-7500 *et seq.*; ¶15,014 *et seq.*; TD ¶603,601
13. ¶E-10000; ¶15,024.16; TD ¶606,801
14. ¶E-7503; ¶15,024; TD ¶603,203

15. ¶E-7503; ¶15,024; TD ¶603,203
16. ¶E-9050 *et seq.*; ¶15,024; TD ¶603,203
17. ¶E-9050 *et seq.*; ¶15,024; TD ¶603,203
18. ¶E-8903; ¶2434.01; TD ¶603,203
19. ¶E-8250 *et seq.*; ¶15,024; TD ¶604,500 *et seq.*

is not reduced. The loss disallowance rule does not apply to loss from the disposition of stock of a member of a consolidated group to the extent that, as a result of same plan or arrangement, gain is taken into account by members of the same group on the stock of the same member having the same material terms. Similarly, basis is not reduced on deconsolidation of a member of a consolidated group to the extent that gain is taken into account by members of the group on the stock of the same member as a consequence of the same plan or arrangement. (Reg § 1.337(d)-2)[20]

Special anti-avoidance rules bar the circumvention of the basis redetermination and loss suspension rules,[21] including rules aimed at preventing groups from avoiding the loss suspension rule by "reimporting" losses to the group. (Reg § 1.1502-35T(g)(3))[22]

A corporation that is subject to tax on its worldwide income in the U.S. and a foreign jurisdiction (e.g. a company incorporated in the U.S. but managed and controlled in another country) is referred to as a "dual resident corporation" (DRC). If a DRC is a resident of a foreign country that permits its losses to offset the income of other commonly controlled foreign corporate residents, then the DRC could use a single loss to offset both foreign and U.S. taxable income.[23] The use of a dual consolidate loss to offset the income of a domestic affiliate is permitted only if the loss does not offset the income of a foreign corporation under foreign law. (Reg § 1.1503(d)-8)[24]

¶ 3344 "Affiliated group" defined.

In order to qualify as an affiliated group:

(1) the common parent must directly own at least 80% of the total voting power and 80% of the total value of the stock in at least one other "includible" corporation; *and*

(2) one or more of the other includible corporations must directly own at least 80% of the stock (by vote or value) in each of the remaining includible corporations (i.e., not the parent). (Code Sec. 1504(a))[25]

All corporations connected through these stock ownership requirements are "includible" corporations *except*:

. . . tax-exempt organizations;

. . . life insurance companies, except (under certain conditions) where two or more insurance companies are themselves an affiliated group;

. . . RICs (mutual funds) and REITs (¶4201 *et seq.*);

. . . foreign corporations, except for certain Mexican or Canadian subs of a U.S. parent;

. . . corporations that have a Code Sec. 936 election (possessions tax credit) in effect for the tax year;

. . . DISCs (¶4627);

. . . S corporations. (Code Sec. 1504(b), Code Sec. 1504(c))[26]

¶ 3345 Forms for consolidated reporting—Form 851, Form 1120, and Form 1122.

A consolidated return is made by the common parent on Form 1120 with an attached Form 851 (affiliation schedule), and a Form 1122 (consent) signed by each sub unless a consolidated return was filed (or required) for the preceding tax year. (Reg § 1.1502-75(b), Reg § 1.1502-75(h))[27]

---

20. ¶E-8640 *et seq.*; ¶3374.025; TD ¶605,251
21. ¶E-8566; ¶3374.025
22. ¶E-8569; ¶3374.025
23. ¶E-9200 *et seq.*; ¶15,024.005; TD ¶606,008

24. ¶E-9139.1 *et seq.*; ¶15,024.005
25. ¶E-7601; ¶s 15,024.16, 15,024.17; TD ¶603,300
26. ¶E-7646; ¶s 15,024, 15,024.17; TD ¶603,301
27. ¶E-7754 *et seq.*; ¶15,024.16; TD ¶603,603

¶ 3346   Corporate Estimated Tax. ▰▰▰▰▰▰▰▰▰▰▰▰▰

Corporations (including S corporations) owing $500 or more in income tax for the tax year must make estimated tax payments, or be subject to penalty.

For quick refund where a corporation pays *too much* in estimated tax, see ¶4851.

¶ 3347   The required annual payment.

A corporation must make installment payments (¶3349) of its "required annual payment," which equals the *lesser* of:

(1) 100% of the tax shown on its return for the year (or if no return is filed, 100% of its tax for that year); or

(2) 100% of the tax shown on its return for the preceding tax year (except as noted below). (Code Sec. 6655(d)(1)(B))[28]

A corporation's required annual payment can't be based on the preceding year's tax if:

. . . it didn't file a return for the preceding tax year showing a liability for tax (Code Sec. 6655(d)(1)) (a return showing zero tax, e.g., because of a net operating loss (NOL), isn't a return showing a liability for tax);

. . . the preceding tax year was less than 12 months (Code Sec. 6655(d)(1)); or

. . . it's a "large corporation" (below). (Code Sec. 6655(d)(2)(A)) However, a large corporation may use its last year's tax to determine the amount of its first required installment for any tax year, but it must recapture any resulting reduction in that first installment, by increasing its next required installment by the amount of the reduction. (Code Sec. 6655(d)(2)(B))[29]

A corporation is "large" in any tax year if it (or any predecessor corporation) had taxable income of $1,000,000 or more for any of the three immediately preceding tax years. For this purpose, taxable income doesn't include carryback or carryover of NOLs or capital losses. Special rules apply to controlled groups. (Code Sec. 6655(g)(2))[30]

¶ 3348   What is "tax" for estimated tax purposes?

A corporation's "tax" for estimated tax purposes is the excess of: (1) the sum of its regular corporate (income) tax, the alternative minimum tax, and (for foreign corporations) the tax on gross transportation income (¶4652), over (2) the sum of its tax credits. (Code Sec. 6655(g)(1))[31]

For S corporations, regular corporate taxes also include: built-in gains tax (¶3365) or tax on net capital gains for certain S corporations (¶3364), tax on excess passive income (¶3368), and tax on recapture of pre-S election investment credit (Code Sec. 6655(g)(4)(A)), but not the LIFO recapture tax (¶3367).[32]

Special rules apply for foreign corporations, insurance companies and tax-exempt organizations (for unrelated business income tax). (Code Sec. 6655(g)(1), Code Sec. 6655(g)(3))[33]

¶ 3349   "Required installments" of corporate estimated tax.

A corporation pays its estimated tax (electronically, if required, see ¶3027, otherwise on Form 8109) — except for certain large corporations — in four equal installments ("required installments") of its "required annual payment" (¶3347). (Code Sec. 6655(c)(1), Code

---

28. ¶s S-5327, S-5328; ¶66,554; TD ¶609,211 *et seq.*
29. ¶S-5328 *et seq.*; ¶66,554; TD ¶609,218
30. ¶S-5331 *et seq.*; ¶66,554; TD ¶609,221

31. ¶S-5322; ¶66,554; TD ¶609,205
32. ¶S-5401; ¶66,554; TD ¶628,501
33. ¶S-5321 *et seq.*, S-5421; ¶66,554

Sec. 6655(d)(1)(A)) For a calendar year corporation, the installments are due as follows: first, Apr. 15; second, June 15; third, Sept. 15; fourth, Dec. 15. (Code Sec. 6655(c)(2)) For a fiscal year corporation, they are due on the 15th day of the corresponding months of the tax year (Code Sec. 6655(i)(1)) (i.e., the fourth, sixth, ninth and 12th months). [34]

However, estimated tax payments for corporations with assets of $1 billion or more (determined as of the end of the preceding tax year) are made under the following schedule:

... the amount of any required installment of corporate estimated tax that is otherwise due in July, Aug., or Sept. of 2012 is 115% of that amount,

... the amount of any required installment of corporate estimated tax that is otherwise due in July, Aug., or Sept. of 2013 is 100.75% of that amount, and

... the amount of the next required installment after the installments described directly above is appropriately reduced to reflect the amount of the increase in the earlier installment. (TIPRA § 401)[35]

illustration: X Corporation, a corporation with assets of $1 billion or more, has a required installment of estimated tax due on Sept. 15, 2012, that is otherwise calculated to be $400,000. X must make an estimated tax payment of $460,000 (115% of $400,000) by Sept. 15, 2012. X reduce its next required installment by $60,000 ($460,000 minus $400,000).

Notwithstanding the above rules, 20.5% of the amount of any required installment of estimated tax of *any* corporation that is otherwise due on Sept. 15, 2010 is not due until Oct. 1, 2010, and 27.5% of the amount of any required installment of corporate estimated tax that is otherwise due on Sept. 15, 2011 is not due until Oct. 1, 2011. (TIPRA § 401)

For lower installments in certain situations, see ¶3350 and ¶3351.

¶ 3350 Lower "annualized income installment" as required installment—Form 8842.

A corporation may use an "annualized income installment" as its estimated tax installment, if that's less than the "required installment" (¶3349). (Code Sec. 6655(e)(1)(A))[36]

The annualized income installment is the excess (if any) of:

(1) the applicable percentage (25%, 50%, 75%, and 100% for the first, second, third and fourth installments, respectively) of the full year's tax, computed by placing on an annualized basis (under regs to be issued) the taxable income (taking into account Code Sec. 936(h) and Code Sec. 951(a) inclusions (Code Sec. 6655(e)(4))), alternative minimum taxable income, and modified alternative minimum taxable income for the months to which the installment applies (i.e., the first three months (first and second installments), first six months (third), and first nine months (fourth)), *over*

(2) the sum of any earlier required installments for the tax year. (Code Sec. 6655(e)(2)(A), Code Sec. 6655(e)(2)(B))[37]

Alternatively, a corporation may elect (on Form 8842, by the due date of the first installment (Reg § 1.6655(e)-1(b))) to determine its annualized income based on its income for *either:* (1) the first two months (first installment), first four months (second), first seven months (third) and first ten months (fourth); *or* (2) the first three months (first), first five months (second), first eight months (third), and first 11 months (fourth). (Code Sec. 6655(e)(2)(C))[38]

Any reduction in an installment resulting from using the annualization method must be

---

34. ¶S-5353; ¶66,554; TD ¶609,201
35. ¶S-5353; ¶66,554; TD ¶609,201
36. ¶S-5326; ¶66,554; TD ¶609,216

37. ¶S-5338 *et seq.*; ¶66,554; TD ¶609,223
38. ¶S-5340.1; ¶66,554; TD ¶609,226

made up (recaptured). This is done by increasing the amount of the next required installment that *isn't* determined under the annualization method, by the amount of the reduction. (Code Sec. 6655(e)(1)(B))[39]

¶ 3351   Use of lower "adjusted seasonal installment" as required installment.

A corporation may use an "adjusted seasonal installment" as its estimated tax installment if it's less than the required installment (¶3349) or the annualized income installment (Code Sec. 6655(e)(1)(A)), but only if the corporation's "base period percentage" (below) for any six consecutive months of the tax year is at least 70%. (Code Sec. 6655(e)(3)(B))[40]

A corporation computes its adjusted seasonal installment by: (1) ·computing the taxable income for all months during the tax year before the filing month (i.e., the month the installment is required to be paid), (2) dividing this amount by the base period percentage for those preceding months, (3) determining the tax on the result, (4) multiplying that tax by the base period percentage for the filing month and all preceding months in the tax year (Code Sec. 6655(e)(3)(C), Code Sec. 6655(e)(3)(D)(ii)), and Code Sec. 6655(e)(5) subtracting the aggregate of all earlier required installments. (Code Sec. 6655(e)(3)(A))[41]

The "base period percentage" for any specific period of months is the average percent that the corporation's taxable income for the corresponding months in each of the three preceding tax years bears to its taxable income for those three years. (Code Sec. 6655(e)(3)(D)(i))[42]

Any reduction in an installment resulting from the adjusted seasonal method must be made up (recaptured), by increasing the amount of the next required installment that *isn't* determined under the adjusted seasonal method, by the amount of the reduction. (Code Sec. 6655(e)(1)(B))[43]

¶ 3352   Penalty for failure to pay estimated tax—Form 2220.

A corporation that underpays its estimated tax must add to its income tax an amount equal to the underpayment interest rate (¶4865) times the amount of the underpayment, for the period of the underpayment. (Code Sec. 6655(a)) Compute on Form 2220.[44]

The amount of the underpayment is the excess of the required installment (¶3349) over the amount (if any) of the installment paid on or before the due date for the installment. (Code Sec. 6655(b)(1))[45]

The period of the underpayment runs from the due date for the installment to the earlier of: (1) the 15th day of the third month after the close of the tax year, or (2) with respect to any portion of the underpayment, the date the portion is paid. (Code Sec. 6655(b)(2)) For this purpose, a payment of estimated tax is credited against unpaid required installments in the order those installments were due. (Code Sec. 6655(b)(3))[46]

No estimated tax penalty is imposed for any tax year if the tax shown on the return for that year (or if no return is filed, the tax liability) is less than $500. (Code Sec. 6655(f))[47] Nor is the penalty imposed for a period in which the failure to pay the required installment(s) results from a pending Title 11 bankruptcy case. (Code Sec. 6658(a))[48]

¶ 3353   S Corporations. ■■■■■■■■■■■■■■■■■■■■■■■■■■■■■■■

An eligible corporation may elect to be taxed as an S corporation which, with limited

---

39. ¶S-5347; ¶66,554; TD ¶609,232
40. ¶S-5344; ¶66,554; TD ¶609,233
41. ¶S-5345 *et seq.*; ¶66,554; TD ¶609,234
42. ¶S-5346; ¶66,554; TD ¶609,235
43. ¶S-5348; ¶66,554; TD ¶609,236

44. ¶S-5358; ¶66,554; TD ¶609,208
45. ¶S-5359; ¶66,554; TD ¶609,209
46. ¶S-5360; ¶66,554; TD ¶609,210
47. ¶S-5363; ¶66,554; TD ¶609,213
48. ¶V-7378; TD ¶571,363

exceptions, isn't taxed at the corporate level. Instead, its items of income, loss, deduction and credit are passed through to, and taken into account by, its shareholders in computing their individual tax liabilities.

¶ 3354 S election eligibility.

An S corporation is a corporation for which an election to be taxed under Subchapter S of the Code is in effect. (Code Sec. 1361(a)(1))[49] Only a small business corporation may elect to be an S corporation. (Code Sec. 1362(a)(1))[50] A corporation (or an unincorporated entity that's taxable as a corporation) qualifies as a small business corporation if it meets all of the following requirements:[1]

(1) It must be a domestic corporation (created under the law of the U.S. or of any state). (Code Sec. 1361(b)(1))[2]

(2) It must not be *ineligible*. (Code Sec. 1361(b)(1), Reg § 1.1361-1(d))

A corporation is ineligible if it:

. . . is a financial institution that uses a reserve method of accounting for bad debts,

. . . is taxable as an insurance company (with certain exceptions),

. . . is a DISC or former DISC (¶4627) (Code Sec. 1361(b)(2)), or

. . . is a taxable mortgage pool. (Reg § 301.7701(i)-4(c)(1))[3]

(3) It can't have more than 100 shareholders, see ¶3356. (Code Sec. 1361(b)(1)(A), Reg § 1.1361-1(e))[4]

(4) All shareholders must be individuals, decedents' estates, bankruptcy estates, trusts described at ¶3357, or tax-exempt Code Sec. 501(c)(3) charitable organizations (Code Sec. 1361(b)(1)(B), Reg § 1.1361-1(f)), except that an otherwise eligible S corporation can be wholly owned by another S corporation, see ¶3355. A partnership can hold S corporation stock as a nominee for an eligible shareholder. (Reg § 1.1361-1(e)(1))[5]

(5) No shareholder may be a nonresident alien (Code Sec. 1361(b)(1)(C)), or be married to a nonresident alien who has a current ownership interest in his stock under local law (unless the spouses elect under Code Sec. 6013(g) to be taxed as U.S. residents (¶3115)). (Reg § 1.1361-1(g)(1))[6]

(6) It must have only one class of stock, see ¶3358. (Code Sec. 1361(b)(1)(D), Reg § 1.1361-1(b)(1))[7]

For additional tests that must be met after the S election is made, see ¶3379.

¶ 3355 S corporation subsidiaries.

S corporations may have 80%-or-more owned C ("regular") corporation subsidiaries and wholly-owned S corporation subsidiaries. (Code Sec. 1361(b))

A C corporation subsidiary is treated as a separate taxpayer. If it operates profitably, it pays tax on its income. If it operates at a loss, it cannot pass the loss through to the S corporation. A C corporation subsidiary may file a consolidated return with other C corporations with which it is affiliated. The S corporation cannot be included in this return, however (see ¶3344).

An S corporation cannot have a corporate shareholder. (Code Sec. 1361(b)(1)(B),

---

49. ¶D-1421; ¶13,614 *et seq.*; TD ¶611,001
50. ¶D-1431; ¶13,614; TD ¶611,001
1. ¶D-1431; ¶13,614; TD ¶611,001
2. ¶D-1432; ¶13,614.01; TD ¶611,001
3. ¶D-1434 *et seq.*; ¶13,614.01, 77,014.53; TD ¶611,002

4. ¶D-1441; ¶13,614.02; TD ¶611,003
5. ¶D-1445; ¶13,614.03; TD ¶611,005
6. ¶D-1457; ¶13,614.03; TD ¶611,001
7. ¶D-1496; ¶13,614.04; TD ¶611,043

Reg § 1.1361-1(f)) This rule ordinarily prevents a subsidiary from being an S corporation. However, an S corporation can have an S corporation subsidiary if it owns 100% of the subsidiary's stock, the sub is not an ineligible corporation, and the S corporation parent elects (on Form 8869)[8]) to treat the subsidiary as a qualified subchapter S subsidiary (QSub). (Code Sec. 1361(b)(3)(B), Reg § 1.1361-2, Reg § 1.1361-3)[9]

A QSub isn't treated as a separate corporation for federal tax purposes; rather, its assets, liabilities, and items of income, deduction, and credit are treated as those of the parent S corporation. (Code Sec. 1361(b)(3)(A), Reg § 1.1361-4)[10] However, except to the extent otherwise provided by IRS, QSubs are treated as separate entities for purposes of making information returns. (Code Sec. 1361(b)(3)(E))[11]

If a QSub loses its qualification, (1) for tax years beginning before 2007, the sub is treated as a new corporation that, immediately before it lost qualification, acquired all of its assets and assumed all of its liabilities from the S corporation in exchange for its stock, and (2) for tax years beginning after 2006, the sub is treated as if it sold an undivided interest in its assets (based on a percentage of the stock sold) and transferred the remaining assets to itself in a tax-free incorporation. Thus, in a post-2006 tax year, an S corporation sells 21% of the stock of its QSub to an unrelated party, it will recognize 21% of the gain on the QSub's assets and will not recognize the remaining gain. (Code Sec. 1361(b)(3)(C), Reg § 1.1361-5)[12] If QSub status terminates, the corporation or its successor may not elect QSub status or S corporation status before its fifth year beginning after the first tax year for which the termination was effective, without IRS consent. (Code Sec. 1361(b)(3)(D), Reg § 1.1361-5(c))[13] For elections and terminations after 2004, IRS may waive inadvertent or invalid QSub elections and terminations of elections. (Code Sec. 1362(f))[14]

A QSub uses the parent S corporation's EIN. If the election terminates, the sub must get an EIN; but if the entity either had an EIN before becoming a QSub or got an EIN while it was a QSub, it must use that EIN. (Reg § 301.6109-1(i))[15]

¶ 3356 Number of shareholders.

In applying the 100-shareholder limit (¶3354), everyone who owns stock is counted separately, even if the stock is owned jointly with someone else (e.g., joint tenant, tenant in common), except as follows:

(1) A husband and wife (and their estates) are treated as one shareholder, no matter how the stock is held (separately, jointly, etc.). (Code Sec. 1361(c)(1)(A)(i); Reg § 1.1361-1(e)(2))[16]

(2) Where stock is owned by a grantor trust and also by the grantor directly, they are treated as one shareholder. [17]

(3) All members of a family and their estates are treated as one shareholder. Family members include the common ancestor, lineal descendants of the common ancestor, and the spouses (or former spouses) of the lineal descendants or common ancestor. But, an individual isn't considered a common ancestor if, on the applicable date, the individual was more than six generations removed from the youngest generation of shareholders who would (but for this limitation) be family members. For this purpose, a spouse (or former spouse) is treated as being of the same generation as the individual to which such spouse is (or was) married. Adopted children are treated as children if they are (i) legally adopted children, (ii) children who are lawfully placed with an individual for legal adoption and (iii) eligible foster children (defined under Code Sec. 152(f)(1)(C), ¶3120) (Code Sec. 1361(c)(1)) The applicable date is the latest of: the date the S election was made; the earliest date that a

---

8. ¶D-1539; ¶13,614.05; TD ¶611,006
9. ¶D-1540; ¶13,614.05; TD ¶611,006
10. ¶D-1531; ¶13,614.05; TD ¶611,006
11. ¶D-1532; ¶13,614.05; TD ¶611,007
12. ¶D-1536; ¶13,614.05; TD ¶611,006

13. ¶D-1538; ¶13,614.05; TD ¶611,006
14. ¶D-1564.1; ¶13,624.03; TD ¶623,018
15. ¶D-1532; ¶13,614.05; TD ¶611,007
16. ¶D-1447; ¶s 13,614.02, 13,614.03; TD ¶611,003
17. ¶D-1461; ¶s 13,614.02, 13,614.03; TD ¶611,003

family member holds stock in the S corporation; or Oct. 22, 2004. (Code Sec. 1361(c)(1)(B)(ii))[18]

Each potential current beneficiary (i.e., one who may receive a discretionary distribution of income or principal during the relevant period) of an electing small business trust is treated as a shareholder in applying the limit. The trust is treated as the shareholder for periods when there's no potential current beneficiary. (Code Sec. 1361(c)(2)(B)(v); Reg § 1.1361-1(m)(4)) However, unexercised powers of appointment are not taken into account in determining potential current beneficiaries. In addition, a person who first becomes a potential current beneficiary during the one-year period ending with the date of the trust's disposition of all of its stock in an S corporation, isn't a potential current beneficiary of that corporation. (Code Sec. 1361(e)(2))[19]

¶ 3357   Trusts as shareholders.

Only the following trusts may be S corporation shareholders:

(1) Grantor trusts—domestic trusts that are treated as being owned by an individual ("grantor") who is a U.S. citizen or resident, during the period the trust holds the S corporation stock. The grantor, not the trust, is treated as the shareholder. (Code Sec. 1361(c)(2)(A)(i), Code Sec. 1361(c)(2)(B)(i); Reg § 1.1361-1(h)(1)(i), Reg § 1.1361-1(h)(3)(i)(A)) But after the grantor dies, the trust may continue as the shareholder for two years. (Code Sec. 1361(c)(2)(A)(ii))[20]

(2) Code Sec. 678 trusts —where a person other than the grantor is treated as the substantial owner of the trust, during the period the trust holds the S corporation stock. The deemed owner, who must be a U.S. citizen or resident, is treated as the shareholder. (Code Sec. 1361(c)(2)(A)(i), Code Sec. 1361(c)(2)(B)(i); Reg § 1.1361-1(h)(1)(i), Reg § 1.1361-1(h)(3)(i)(A))[21]

(3) Voting trusts, but each beneficiary is counted as a separate shareholder. (Code Sec. 1361(c)(2)(A)(iv), Code Sec. 1361(c)(2)(B)(iv); Reg § 1.1361-1(h)(1)(v), Reg § 1.1361-1(h)(3)(i)(E))[22]

(4) Testamentary trusts, for 2-years beginning with the day when stock was transferred to the trust under the testator's will. (Code Sec. 1361(c)(2)(A)(iii); Reg § 1.1361-1(h)(1)(iv))[23]

(5) "Qualified Subchapter S trusts" (QSSTs), if the beneficiary elects (on Form 2553, in certain circumstances) to be treated as the owner of the trust so that it is eligible to hold the S stock (as in (1), above), and is treated as the shareholder. (Code Sec. 1361(d); Reg § 1.1361-1(j)) For purposes of applying the passive activity loss rules (¶1810 *et seq.*) and the at-risk rules (¶1803 *et seq.*) to a beneficiary of a QSST, a disposition of S corporation stock by a QSST is treated as a disposition by that beneficiary. (Code Sec. 1361(d)(1)(C))[24]

A QSST can be converted to an electing small business trust if certain conditions are met.[25]

(6) "Electing small business trusts (ESBTs)." (Code Sec. 1361(c)(2)(A)(v), Code Sec. 1361(e), Reg § 1.1361-1(m)) These trusts are subject to fewer restrictions than QSSTs but carry a heavy tax cost, see ¶3910. To elect, the trustee must sign and file a specified statement with the service center with which the corporation files its income tax return. In the case of a newly electing S corporation, the trustee can attach the ESBT's consent to the Form 2553.[26] An ESBT can be converted to a QSST if certain conditions are met. [27]

---

18. ¶D-1447.1; ¶13,614.02; TD ¶611,003.1
19. ¶D-1484 *et seq.*; ¶13,614.03; TD ¶611,037
20. ¶s D-1460, D-1461; ¶13,614.03; TD ¶611,018
21. ¶D-1461; ¶13,614.03; TD ¶611,018
22. ¶D-1492; ¶13,614.03; TD ¶611,017

23. ¶D-1491; ¶13,614.03; TD ¶611,017
24. ¶D-1465 *et seq.*; ¶13,614.03; TD ¶611,020 *et seq.*
25. ¶D-1489; ¶13,614.03; TD ¶611,041
26. ¶D-1482; ¶13,614.03; TD ¶611,034
27. ¶D-1490; ¶13,614.03; TD ¶611,042

(7)   Tax exempt Code Sec. 401(a) qualified plan trusts. (Code Sec. 1361(c)(6))[28]

¶ 3358   One class of stock.

A corporation is treated as having only one class of stock (¶3354), if:

. . . all outstanding shares of its stock confer identical rights to distribution and liquidation proceeds, based on certain governing provisions (i.e., corporate charter, by-laws, state law, etc.) (Reg § 1.1361-1(l)(1), Reg § 1.1361-1(l)(2)(i)); and

. . . it hasn't issued any instrument or obligation or entered into any arrangement that's treated as a second class of stock. (Reg § 1.1361-1(l)(4))[29]

The one-class-of-stock rule isn't violated *solely* because of differences in voting rights. Thus, voting and nonvoting common can be issued. (Code Sec. 1361(c)(4))[30]

Buy-sell agreements among shareholders, redemption agreements and agreements restricting the transferability of stock generally won't violate the one-class-of-stock rule *unless:* (1) a principal purpose of the agreement is to circumvent the rule, and (2) it establishes a purchase price for the stock that's significantly above or below its fair market value (FMV). (Reg § 1.1361-1(l)(2)(iii))[31]

A call option, warrant or similar instrument is, with certain exceptions, treated as a second class of stock if it's substantially certain to be exercised and has a strike price substantially below the stock's FMV on the date it's issued, transferred to an ineligible shareholder, or materially modified. (Reg § 1.1361-1(l)(4)(iii)(A))[32]

Straight debt isn't treated as a second class of stock if specified safe harbor rules are met. (Code Sec. 1361(c)(5)(A), Code Sec. 1361(c)(5)(B))[33] However, any instrument, obligation or arrangement is, with certain exceptions, treated as a second class of stock if: (1) it constitutes equity or otherwise results in the holder being treated as the owner of stock under general tax law, and (2) its principal purpose is to circumvent these rules. (Reg § 1.1361-1(l)(4))[34] Restricted bank director stock is not taken into account for the one class of stock requirement. (Code Sec. 1361(f)(1))[35]

¶ 3359   How to elect S corporation status—Form 2553.

The S election is made by the corporation (Code Sec. 1362(a)(1)) by filing a Form 2553 signed by its authorized officer, with the required shareholder consents (¶3360) (and IRS user fee), at the IRS Service Center designated on the form. (Reg § 1.1362-6(a)(2))[36]

An S election for a tax year may be made during the preceding tax year, or by the 15th day of the third month of the tax year for which it's to be effective. (Code Sec. 1362(b)(1)) If this first tax year is less than two months and 15 days, the election must be made no later than two months and 15 days after the first day of that year. (Code Sec. 1362(b)(4))[37]

An S election will be effective retroactively to the first day of a tax year *only if:*

. . . on all days in the tax year before the day the election is made, the corporation would have been eligible to elect (Code Sec. 1362(b)(2)(B)(i)), *and*

. . . all persons who were shareholders at any time during the tax year before the day of the election, but who aren't shareholders on that date, consent (along with persons who *are* shareholders, see ¶3360). (Code Sec. 1362(b)(2)(B)(ii))[38]

---

28. ¶D-1493; ¶13,614.03
29. ¶D-1496 *et seq.*; ¶13,614.04; TD ¶611,043
30. ¶D-1499; ¶13,614.04; TD ¶611,043
31. ¶D-1507 *et seq.*; ¶13,614.04; TD ¶611,045
32. ¶D-1523; ¶13,614.04; TD ¶611,046
33. ¶D-1517; ¶13,614.04; TD ¶611,046

34. ¶D-1512 *et seq.*; ¶13,614.04; TD ¶611,046
35. ¶D-1444.1; ¶13,614.02
36. ¶D-1552, ¶T-10004; ¶s 13,624, 13,624.01; TD ¶612,001
37. ¶s D-1565, D-1568; ¶13,624.01; TD ¶612,011
38. ¶D-1566; ¶13,624.01; TD ¶612,009

If either of the above conditions isn't met, the election is treated as made for the next tax year. (Code Sec. 1362(b)(2))[39]

IRS may waive invalid elections (e.g., because of an inadvertent failure to get all the necessary consents, ¶3360, or to qualify to elect S status). (Code Sec. 1362(f))[40] For IRS's authority to treat late elections or nonexistent elections as timely, see ¶3361.

¶ 3360 Shareholder consents.

All shareholders owning stock in the corporation on the day it elects S status must consent to the election. (Code Sec. 1362(a)(2); Reg § 1.1362-6(b)(2)(i))[41]

The consents may be given on Form 2553 (¶3359), or on separate statements attached to the Form 2553. (Reg § 1.1362-6(b))[42]

A shareholder's failure to file a timely consent won't invalidate an otherwise valid timely filed election if consents are filed within an extended period of time as granted by IRS, and IRS is satisfied that: (1) there was reasonable cause for the failure; (2) the extension was requested within a reasonable time; and (3) its interests won't be jeopardized by treating the election as valid. (Reg § 1.1362-6(b)(3)(iii)(A))[43]

¶ 3361 Relief for late or nonexistent S elections

If an S election is made after the date (specified at ¶3359) for making it, or if no election is made, and IRS determines there was reasonable cause for the failure to timely elect, IRS can treat the election as timely made. (Code Sec. 1362(b)(5)) Generally the relief is obtained through the issuance of a private letter ruling. [44]

IRS has provided procedures for requesting relief for a failure to make a timely valid S corporation election without asking for a private letter ruling (e.g., automatic relief) where the entity fails to qualify for its intended status as an S corporation, electing small business trust (ESBT), qualified Subchapter S trust (QSST), or qualified Subchapter S subsidiary (QSub) on the intended effective status date solely because of the failure to file the appropriate election in a timely fashion. [45]

Special rules apply for requests for automatic relief when a community property spouse fails to timely consent to an S corporation election. [46]

¶ 3362 "Taxable income" of an S corporation.

An S corporation's taxable income is computed in the same manner as an individual's taxable income *except that*: (Code Sec. 1363(b))[47]

(1) Items of income (including tax-exempt interest), loss, deduction or credit must be separately stated if their separate treatment by a shareholder could affect his tax liability. (Code Sec. 1363(b)(1))

(2) The corporation can't take the following deductions allowed to individuals: personal exemptions; foreign taxes; charitable contributions; net operating loss (NOL) deduction; additional itemized deductions; and oil and gas depletion. (Code Sec. 1363(b)(2))

(3) A deduction is allowed for the amortization of the corporation's organization expenditures under Code Sec. 248 (¶3520). (Code Sec. 1363(b)(3))[48]

39. ¶D-1566; ¶13,624.01; TD ¶612,009
40. ¶D-1564.1; ¶13,614.03; TD ¶612,006
41. ¶D-1554; ¶13,624.01; TD ¶612,002
42. ¶D-1555; ¶13,624.01; TD ¶612,001
43. ¶D-1564.2; ¶13,624.03; TD ¶612,004

44. ¶D-1572.1; ¶13,624.01; TD ¶612,014
45. ¶D-1572.2; *et seq.*;¶13,624.03; TD ¶612,014 *et seq.*
46. ¶D-1572.3; ¶13,624.03; TD ¶612,016; TD ¶612,006.5
47. ¶D-1591; ¶13,634.01; TD ¶614,501
48. ¶D-1594; ¶13,634.01; TD ¶614,501

(4) The Code Sec. 291 rules that reduce certain corporate tax benefits apply to an S corporation (or any predecessor) that was a C corporation for any of the 3 immediately preceding tax years. (Code Sec. 1363(b)(4))[49]

Except as otherwise provided in the Code, or to the extent inconsistent with the Subchapter S rules, the Subchapter C rules (transfers to related corporations, redemptions, reorganizations, liquidations, etc., see ¶3510 *et seq.*) apply to an S corporation and its shareholders. (Code Sec. 1371(a))[50] But there are these modifications:

. . . With respect to liquidating distributions, no gain or loss is recognized on distributions of installment obligations where the shareholders' receipt of them (as part of a 12-month complete liquidation) isn't treated as payment for their stock by reason of Code Sec. 453(h)(1). (Code Sec. 453B(h)(1))[1]

. . . Except for the organization expenditures deduction (above), Code provisions governing the computation of taxable income which apply only to corporations (e.g., dividends-received deduction, ¶3306) don't apply to S corporations. (Code Sec. 1363(b))[2]

. . . Limitations on the amount allowed for: (1) expensing certain depreciable assets (Code Sec. 179(d)(8)), and (2) writing off reforestation expenses (Code Sec. 194(b)(2)(B)) are determined at both the corporate and shareholder level. [3]

. . . An item (e.g., an NOL) cannot be carried over from a year the corporation was a C corporation (C year) to an S year (except in computing the built-in gains tax, see ¶3365). (Code Sec. 1371(b)(1)) However, the Tenth Circuit has held that S corporations may carry disallowed passive losses from C to S years. [4]

¶ 3363   Deductions for fringe benefits.

In applying the Code's fringe benefit rules, an S corporation is treated as a partnership and its more-than-2% shareholders are treated as partners. (Code Sec. 1372) Fringe benefits furnished by an S corporation to its more-than-2% shareholder-employees are treated like partnership guaranteed payments. [5]

observation: An S corporation is entitled to deduct the cost of fringe benefits for its more-than-2% shareholder-employees, who are required to include the value of those benefits in income.

¶ 3364   Taxation of S corporations.

An S corporation is generally exempt from federal income taxes. (Code Sec. 1363(a))[6] Instead, the corporation's income is passed through, and taxed, to its shareholders (¶3370). But some S corporations may be subject to one or more of these corporate-level taxes: the tax on recognized built-in gains (¶3365); the tax on excess net passive income (¶3368); the tax on LIFO recapture (¶3367); the tax on capital gains attributable to certain substituted basis property, if S election was made before '87; [7] the tax on recapture of investment credit. [8] For an S corporation's liability to make estimated tax payments, see ¶3346 *et seq.*

¶ 3365   Built-in gains tax.

An S corporation is subject to a corporate-level built-in gains tax in any tax year beginning in the recognition period (below) in which it has a "net recognized built-in gain" (¶3366).

49. ¶D-1595; ¶13,634.01; TD ¶614,503
50. ¶D-1602; ¶13,714; TD ¶614,511
1. ¶s D-1600, D-1601; ¶453B4.11; TD ¶614,509
2. ¶D-1595; ¶13,634.01; TD ¶614,503
3. ¶D-1596; ¶1794.01; TD ¶614,504

4. ¶D-1603; ¶13,714.01; TD ¶614,510
5. ¶D-1621; ¶13,724; TD ¶614,505
6. ¶D-1641; ¶13,634; TD ¶615,001
7. ¶D-1674 *et seq.*; ¶13,744.02; TD ¶615,002
8. ¶s D-1640, D-1685; ¶13,714.03; TD ¶615,029

(Code Sec. 1374(a)) But the tax is imposed only on S corporations that were formerly C corporations. (Code Sec. 1374(c)(1))[9]

The built-in gains tax may be imposed where property is transferred to an S corporation and basis for the property is determined by its basis to a C corporation (treated as the S corporation's predecessor). (Code Sec. 1374(d)(8)(A); Reg § 1.1374-1(e))[10]

The built-in gains tax (computed on Form 1120, Schedule D) equals the highest corporate rate (¶1112) times the net recognized built-in gain. (Code Sec. 1374(b)(1))[11]

In this computation, net recognized built-in gains are taken into account only to the extent of the excess of the net *unrealized* built-in gain over net recognized built-in gains for earlier tax years in the recognition period. (Code Sec. 1374(c)(2); Reg § 1.1374-2(a))[12] Net unrealized built-in gain means the excess (if any) of: (1) the fair market value of the S corporation's assets (including inventory) over (2) the aggregate adjusted basis of the assets, at the start of its first tax year as an S corporation ("S tax year"). (Code Sec. 1374(d)(1))[13]

The recognition period is the ten-year period beginning on the first day of the corporation's first S tax year. (Code Sec. 1374(d)(7))[14]

The built-in gains tax applies to transactions occurring after Dec. 26, '94, regardless of the date of the S corporation's election. (Reg § 1.1374-8(a))[15]

Regs prevent gain or loss from being counted twice for the built-in gains tax when a C corp converting to S status owns stock in a subsidiary that's later liquidated. (Reg § 1.1374-3)[16]

¶ 3366 Net recognized built-in gain defined.

The *net recognized built-in gain* for any tax year in the recognition period (¶3365) is the *lesser of:* (1) the amount that would be the S corporation's taxable income for that year if only recognized built-in gains (below) and recognized built-in losses are taken into account, or (2) the taxable income for that year determined without taking into account NOL carryovers or special corporate deductions, e.g., for dividends received. (Code Sec. 1374(d)(2)(A))[17] However, if (1) is more than (2), the excess is treated as recognized built-in gain in the next tax year, but only if the S election was made after Mar. 31, '88. (Code Sec. 1374(d)(2)(B); Reg § 1.1374-2(c))[18]

Recognized built-in gain means any gain recognized (and certain related amounts taken into account) during the recognition period on the disposition of any asset held on the first day of the corporation's first S tax year (¶3365), but only to the extent the gain doesn't exceed the excess (if any) of the asset's fair market value over its adjusted basis, on that first day. (Code Sec. 1374(d)(3); Reg § 1.1374-4)[19]

Special rules apply to determine an S corporation's recognized built-in gain on the disposition of transferred-basis and exchanged-basis property acquired after it became an S corporation. (Code Sec. 1374(d)(8); Reg § 1.1374-8)[20]

¶ 3367 LIFO recapture.

A C corporation that maintained its inventory using the last-in first-out (LIFO) method for its last tax year before the S corporation election is effective must include a "LIFO recapture amount" in its income for that last C corporation year. (Code Sec. 1363(d)(1))[21] In addition, a

9. ¶D-1643; ¶13,744.01; TD ¶615,002
10. ¶D-1650; ¶13,744.01; TD ¶615,002
11. ¶D-1657; ¶13,744.01; TD ¶615,004
12. ¶D-1657; ¶13,744.01; TD ¶615,003
13. ¶D-1658; ¶13,744.01; TD ¶615,015
14. ¶D-1655; ¶13,744.01; TD ¶615,014
15. ¶D-1666; ¶13,744.03; TD ¶615,020

16. ¶D-1650.1; ¶13,744.01
17. ¶D-1644; ¶13,744.01; TD ¶615,003
18. ¶D-1645; ¶13,744.01; TD ¶615,005
19. ¶D-1646 *et seq.*; ¶13,744.01; TD ¶615,007
20. ¶D-1650 *et seq.*; ¶13,744.01; TD ¶615,012
21. ¶D-1581; ¶13,634.02; TD ¶613,001

C corp that transfers LIFO inventory to an S corp must include a LIFO recapture amount in income the year of the transfer. (Reg § 1.1363-2(a))[22]

The "LIFO recapture amount" is the excess (if any) of the inventory amount under FIFO over the inventory amount under LIFO, at the close of the last C corporation tax year. (Code Sec. 1363(d)(3))[23]

Any resulting increase in tax is payable in four equal installments over four tax years. The first installment must be paid on or before the due date (without regard to extensions) for the tax return for the last year for which the corporation was a C corporation. The other three installments must be paid on or before the due date for the corporation's return for the three succeeding tax years. (Code Sec. 1363(d)(2))[24]

A C corporation holding LIFO inventory indirectly through a partnership must recognize a lookthrough LIFO recapture amount if it either elects to be an S corporation or transfers its partnership interest to an S corporation in a nonrecognition transaction. (Reg § 1.1363-2(b))[25]

¶ 3368   Tax on excess net passive income.

A corporate-level tax is imposed on an S corporation's "excess net passive income" (below) for any tax year in which it has: (1) accumulated earnings and profits (i.e., E&P from a year it was taxed as a C corporation) at the close of the tax year, and (2) passive investment income (¶3369) that exceeds 25% of gross receipts (¶3369). This tax is imposed at the highest regular corporate rate. (Code Sec. 1375(a))[26]

IRS can waive the tax if the S corporation shows that its determination of no year-end Subchapter C E&P was made in good faith, and that within a reasonable time after it was determined otherwise, those E&P were distributed. (Code Sec. 1375(d))[27]

Net passive income is passive investment income reduced by deductions directly connected with the production of that income. (Code Sec. 1375(b)(2)) A deduction item that is attributable partly to passive investment income and partly to other income is allocated on a reasonable basis. (Reg § 1.1375-1(b)(3)(ii))[28] But passive investment income may not be reduced by the NOL deduction or any of the special corporate deductions (e.g., for dividends received). (Code Sec. 1375(b)(2))[29]

Excess net passive income means that amount that bears the same ratio to the total net passive income for the year as: (1) the amount by which the passive investment income for the tax year exceeds 25% of gross receipts for the year ("excess passive investment income"), bears to (2) the total passive investment income for the tax year. However, an S corporation's excess net passive income for the year can't exceed its taxable income for the year computed as though it were a C corporation but without any NOL deduction or any of the special corporate deductions described above. (Code Sec. 1375(b)(1))[30]

¶ 3369   "Passive investment income" and "gross receipts" defined.

For purposes of the tax on excess net passive income (¶3368), and involuntary terminations (¶3379), passive investment income means gross receipts derived from royalties, rents, dividends, interest, annuities, and, for tax years beginning before May 26, 2007, (to the extent of gains) sales or exchanges of stock or securities. (Code Sec. 1362(d)(3)(C), Code Sec. 1375(b)(3))[31]

However, in the case of a bank, a bank holding company, a financial holding company, or a

---

22. ¶D-1583; ¶13,634.02; TD ¶613,003
23. ¶D-1582; ¶13,634.02; TD ¶613,002
24. ¶D-1585; ¶13,634.02; TD ¶613,007
25. ¶D-1582.1; ¶13,634.02
26. ¶D-1690 *et seq.*; ¶13,754; TD ¶615,021

27. ¶D-1696; ¶13,754.01; TD ¶615,026
28. ¶D-1693 *et seq.*; TD ¶615,023
29. ¶D-1693; ¶13,754; TD ¶615,023
30. ¶D-1692; ¶13,754; TD ¶615,025
31. ¶D-1713 *et seq.*; ¶s 13,624.02, 13,754; TD ¶615,022

depository institution holding company, passive investment income does not include (1) interest income earned by the bank or company or (2) dividends on assets that must be held by the bank or company. (Code Sec. 1362(d)(3)(C)(v)(I))[32]

Gross receipts are the total amount received or accrued under the S corporation's accounting method before reduction for returns, allowances, cost, or deductions. But gross receipts don't include amounts received in nontaxable sales or exchanges except to the extent gain is recognized by the corporation. (Code Sec. 1362(d)(3), Code Sec. 1375(b)(3))[33]

Special rules apply to determine gross receipts from the sale of capital assets. [34]

¶ 3370 Taxation of S corporation's shareholders.

An S corporation's income is taxed directly to its shareholders by allocating the corporation's items of income, loss, deduction and credit for each day in its tax year pro rata among the persons who were shareholders on that day. (Code Sec. 1366(a)(1), Reg § 1.1366-1(a), Code Sec. 1377(a)(1))[35]

Items of income, loss, deduction and credit are separately allocated to each shareholder whenever separate treatment could affect the tax liability of a shareholder. (Code Sec. 1366(a)(1)(A), Reg § 1.1366-1(a)) Under regs, the following S corporation items must be taken into account separately:

. . . The combined net amount of gains and losses from sales or exchanges of capital assets grouped by applicable holding periods, Code Sec. 1(h) tax rates, and by any other classification that may be relevant in determining the shareholder's tax liability.

. . . The combined net amount of gains and losses from sales or exchanges of Code Sec. 1231 property grouped by applicable holding periods, Code Sec. 1(h) tax rates, and by any other classification that may be relevant in determining the shareholder's tax liability.

. . . The charitable contributions, grouped by the Code Sec. 170(b) percentage limitations (see ¶2124 *et seq.*), paid by the corporation within its tax year.

. . . The foreign taxes paid (or accrued) by the corporation.

. . . Each of separate items involved in determining credits, except credits for certain uses of gasoline and special fuels.

. . . Each of these separate items: Code Sec. 165(d) gains and losses from wagering transactions; Code Sec. 175 soil and water conservation expenditures, Code Sec. 179 expense election deductions; Code Sec. 213 medical, dental, etc., additional itemized deductions for individuals under Code Sec. 212 *et seq.*; and any other deductions subject to the Code Sec. 67 or Code Sec. 68 limitations on itemized deductions.

. . . Any of the corporation's items of portfolio income or loss, and related expenses, as defined in the regulations under Code Sec. 469.

. . . The corporation's tax-exempt income, i.e., income that is permanently excludible from gross income.

. . . The corporation's alternative minimum tax adjustments described in Code Sec. 56, and Code Sec. 58 and tax preference items described in Code Sec. 57; and

. . . Any item identified in IRS guidance (including forms and instructions) as an item required to be separately stated. (Reg § 1.1366-1(a)(2))[36]

The character of any item in the shareholder's hands is determined as if the item had been realized directly from the source from which the corporation realized it, or as if it had been incurred in the same manner as incurred by the corporation. (Code Sec. 1366(b),

---

32. ¶D-1737.1; ¶13,624.02
33. ¶s D-1702, D-1703; ¶13,624.02; TD ¶615,022
34. ¶D-1701 *et seq.*; ¶13,624; TD ¶615,503

35. ¶D-1761 *et seq.*; ¶13,664; TD ¶614,701
36. ¶D-1765; ¶13,664; TD ¶614,701

Reg § 1.1366-1(b))[37]

A shareholder's share of an S corporation's items is taken into account in his tax year that includes the last day of the corporation's tax year (¶2810). (Code Sec. 1366(a)(1), Reg § 1.1366-1(a)(1))[38]

If a shareholder sells all of his S corporation stock during the corporation's tax year and if all affected shareholders (all terminating shareholders and their transferees) consent (by attaching a specified statement to Form 1120S for the tax year during which the shareholder's entire interest is terminated), the corporation's tax year can be split into two tax years, the first of which ends on the date the seller's interest in the S corporation is terminated. Items will be allocated between those tax years according to the books. (Code Sec. 1377(a)(2); Reg § 1.1377-1(b))[39] This also applies where the S corporation elects to terminate its tax year because of a "qualifying disposition." (Reg § 1.1368-1(g))[40]

✔️observation: This election makes it possible to see that items of income, etc., are allocated to shareholders based on when they actually held their respective interests in the corporation. Otherwise, the terminating and acquiring shareholders can be taxed on the corporation's operations for a part of the year when they didn't own the stock.

✔️recommendation: In negotiating the sales price of the stock, take account of whether the election is to be made, and the resulting tax consequences to the terminating seller and acquiring buyer. Since the seller and buyer may have adverse interests as to the election, specify in the sales contract whether the election is or isn't to be made.

If a shareholder dies (or a trust terminates) before the end of an S corporation tax year, his (or its) pro rata part of the corporation's items is reported on his (its) final return. (Code Sec. 1366(a)(1))[41]

¶ 3371 Amount passed through to shareholders reduced for corporate-level taxes.

The amount of any corporate-level built-in gains tax (¶3365) that's imposed on an S corporation is treated as a loss sustained by the corporation during the tax year. The character of the loss is determined by allocating it proportionately among the recognized built-in gains giving rise to the tax. (Code Sec. 1366(f)(2), Reg § 1.1366-4(b)) If a corporate-level tax is imposed on an S corporation's excess net passive income (¶3368), each item of passive investment income that's passed through to a shareholder is reduced by a pro rata part of that tax. (Code Sec. 1366(f)(3), Reg § 1.1366-4(c))[42]

¶ 3372 Shareholders' deductions and losses limited to basis.

All deductions and losses of an S corporation (e.g., capital losses and NOLs) are passed through to and (except as otherwise limited by the Code) deductible by shareholders. However, a shareholder may deduct his pro rata share of these passed-through items only to the extent of his adjusted basis (¶3374) in his S corporation stock, determined by taking into account the increases in basis for his share of the S corporation income during the year, and the decreases in basis for nondividend distributions for the year, plus any debt owed to him by the corporation. A shareholder gets no basis increase for debts of the corporation that he guaranties. (Code Sec. 1366(d)(1), Reg § 1.1366-2)[43]

Any deduction or loss that can't be deducted (for lack of basis) is suspended and may be carried over to be used whenever the shareholder has basis to apply against all or part of the amount the shareholder carried over. The loss is personal to the shareholder to whom it is

---

37. ¶D-1762; ¶13,664; TD ¶614,703
38. ¶D-1764; ¶13,774; TD ¶614,702
39. ¶D-1769; ¶13,774; TD ¶614,707
40. ¶D-1771; ¶13,684.09; TD ¶614,711

41. ¶D-1774; ¶13,664; TD ¶614,715
42. ¶D-1767; ¶13,664.02; TD ¶614,705
43. ¶D-1775; ¶13,664; TD ¶614,716

disallowed and suspended, and cannot be transferred in any manner. However, where there is a post-2004 tax-free transfer of S corporation stock to a spouse or to a former spouse incident to divorce (¶2447), any disallowed losses or deductions are carried over to the spouse or former spouse. (Code Sec. 1366(d)(2), Reg § 1.1366-2(a)(2))[44] Special rules apply where the S corporation is in bankruptcy or is insolvent. (Code Sec. 108(d)(7)(B))[45]

If an S corporation's stock, or the debt it owes to a shareholder, becomes worthless in any tax year of the corporation or shareholder, the corporate items for that year will be taken into account by the shareholders and the adjustments to basis of stock or debt will be made, before the worthlessness is taken into account. (Code Sec. 1367(b)(3))[46]

¶ 3373 Consistent treatment on shareholder's return and S corporation's return— Form 8082.

A shareholder must on his own return treat a Subchapter S item in a manner that is consistent with the treatment of that item on the corporation's return (Form 1120S). A shareholder that treats a Subchapter S item differently must notify IRS of the inconsistency (Code Sec. 6037) on Form 8082.[47]

¶ 3374 Shareholder's basis in S corporation's stock or debt.

A shareholder's basis in the stock of an S corporation is *increased* by his share of the corporation's income items that are passed through to him —i.e., its separately and non-separately computed income items (including tax-exempt income) and the excess of the deduction for depletion over the basis of depletable property. (Code Sec. 1367(a)(1); Reg § 1.1367-1(b)) Debt discharge income of an S corporation that is excluded from its income is not income to a shareholder, and, thus, does not increase shareholder basis in the S corporation's stock. [48] Basis in stock is *decreased* (but not below zero) by: the shareholder's share of the corporation's items of deduction, loss and nondeductible expenses (except those chargeable to capital account); the shareholder's depletion deduction for oil and gas property; and distributions to the shareholder that aren't taxable as dividends. (Code Sec. 1367(a)(2); Reg § 1.1367-1(c))[49]

In any tax year of an S corporation when the total of the amount of items (other than distributions) that reduce a shareholder's basis in stock exceeds the amount that would reduce that basis to zero, the balance is applied to reduce the basis (but not below zero) of any shareholder debt in the S corporation. (Code Sec. 1367(b)(2)(A); Reg § 1.1367-2(b))[50]

If the shareholder's basis in S corporation debt in any tax year is reduced below his original basis in it, that basis must be increased to (but not above) its original amount, before the shareholder's basis in *stock* is increased. (Code Sec. 1367(b)(2)(B); Reg § 1.1367-2(b)) Thus, to the extent that, in any later year, the total amount of items that increase basis exceed the total amount of items that decrease basis, the net increase is applied first to increase the basis of debt to its original level before it is applied to increase the basis of stock. [1]

¶ 3375 Tax treatment of S corporation distributions.

The amount of a distribution from an S corporation to a shareholder equals the amount of cash distributed plus the fair market value (at distribution) of any other property distributed. (Code Sec. 301(c), Code Sec. 1368(a))[2]

If an S corporation has no accumulated earnings and profits (E&P), the amount distributed

---

44. ¶D-1785; ¶13,664; TD ¶614,718
45. ¶D-1786; ¶1084.03; TD ¶614,718
46. ¶D-1789; ¶13,674; TD ¶614,722
47. ¶D-1801; ¶60,374; TD ¶614,724
48. ¶D-1863; ¶13,674; TD ¶617,001

49. ¶D-1865; ¶13,674; TD ¶617,001
50. ¶D-1877; ¶13,674; TD ¶617,007
1. ¶D-1881; ¶13,674; TD ¶617,009
2. ¶D-1813; ¶13,684; TD ¶616,501

reduces the shareholder's basis in his stock (¶3374). If the amount exceeds basis, the excess is treated as payment in exchange for stock, (Code Sec. 1368(b)(2)) i.e., as capital gain. [3]

If an S corporation has accumulated E&P, its distributions are treated as follows: (Code Sec. 1368(c))[4]

(1) The portion of the distribution that doesn't exceed the accumulated adjustments account (AAA, see ¶3377) is taxed the same as a distribution from an S corporation with no accumulated E&P (above). If more than one distribution is made in a tax year, and the total amount distributed exceeds the amount in the AAA at the end of that year, the balance in that account is allocated among the distributions in proportion to the size of each distribution. (Code Sec. 1368(c)(1))[5]

(2) The portion of the distribution that remains after applying (1) is treated as a dividend to the extent it doesn't exceed the S corporation's accumulated E&P. (Code Sec. 1368(c)(2))

(3) Any portion of the distribution remaining after applying (2) is treated the same as a distribution by an S corporation with no accumulated E&P. (Code Sec. 1368(c)(3))[6]

The tax effects of an S corporation's distributions to shareholders with respect to stock are determined only after taking into account:

(1) adjustments that increase the basis of the shareholder's stock and

(2) adjustments to the accumulated adjustments account (AAA), other than for distributions to shareholders and without regard to any net negative adjustments, for the S corporation's tax year. (Code Sec. 1368(d), Reg § 1.1368-1(e)(2))[7]

🅡🅘🅐 *observation:* The effect of taking the basis increases, but not the decreases, into account is that the shareholder may receive more nontaxable distributions, at the cost of a decrease in the amount of loss that he may deduct.

An S corporation may elect, with the consent of all affected shareholders (i.e., to whom distributions are made), to treat distributions as made out of accumulated E&P *before* being made out of the AAA. (Code Sec. 1368(e)(3); Reg § 1.1368-1(f)(2))[8]

¶ 3376   S corporation's earnings and profits.

An S corporation has no current E&P for any tax year beginning after '82, for which the S election is in effect.[9] No adjustments are made in the amount of a corporation's E&P for the period it is an S corporation during tax years beginning after '82, except as follows: (Code Sec. 1371(c)(1))

. . . E&P are reduced to reflect distributions that are taxable to the shareholders as dividends. (Code Sec. 1371(c)(3))

. . . E&P are adjusted (up or down) to reflect the effect of redemptions, liquidations, tax-free reorganizations and corporate divisions. (Code Sec. 1371(c)(2))

. . . E&P are reduced to reflect any tax paid by an S corporation because of the recapture of a pre-S election investment credit. (Code Sec. 1371(d)(3))[10]

. . . E&P are adjusted for LIFO recapture tax. (¶3367) (Code Sec. 1363(d)(5)[11]

Also, a corporation that was an S corporation for any tax year beginning before Jan. 1, '83 and was not an S corporation for its first tax year beginning after Dec. 31, '96 reduces its accumulated E&P (for the first tax year beginning after May 25, 2007) by an amount equal to

---

3. ¶D-1815; ¶s 13,684, 13,684.07; TD ¶616,502
4. ¶s D-1817, D-1816; ¶13,684.01; TD ¶616,502
5. ¶D-1816, D-1819; ¶13,684.01; TD ¶616,502
6. ¶s D-1817, D-1816; ¶13,684.01; TD ¶616,502
7. ¶D-1818

8. ¶D-1835; ¶13,684.03; TD ¶616,509
9. ¶D-1631; ¶13,684.01 *et seq.*; TD ¶616,507
10. ¶D-1633; ¶13,714.03; TD ¶616,507
11. ¶D-1581; TD ¶616,507

the portion (if any) of the accumulated E&P that was accumulated in any pre-'83 S corporation years. (Small Business and Work Opportunity Tax Act of 2007 § 8235) [12]

¶ 3377 Accumulated adjustments account (AAA)

The accumulated adjustment account (AAA) is a corporate account consisting of the corporation's income that was previously taxed to its shareholders and not distributed. An S corporation's AAA[13] is increased each tax year by:

(1) Separately computed items of income (other than tax-exempt interest).

(2) Nonseparately computed income.

(3) The excess of deductions for depletion over the basis of property subject to depletion. (Code Sec. 1368(e)(1); Reg § 1.1368-2(a)(2))[14]

The AAA is decreased each tax year by:

(a) Items of separately computed loss and deduction.

(b) Nonseparately computed loss.

(c) Nondeductible expenses (other than expenses chargeable to capital account) unless related to tax-exempt income.

(d) The amount of the shareholder's deduction for depletion under Code Sec. 611 with respect to oil and gas wells.

(e) Distributions from an S corporation that has no E&P and distributions that are made out of the AAA.

(f) The amount that was treated as paid out of the AAA on redemptions that were treated as payments in exchange for stock under Code Sec. 302(a) or Code Sec. 303(a). That amount is the same percentage of the amount in the account before the redemption, that the number of redeemed shares was of the total number of outstanding shares before the redemption. (Code Sec. 1368(e)(1); Reg § 1.1368-2(a)(3))[15]

Special ordering rules apply with regard to the above mentioned increases and decreases. (Reg § 1.1368-2(a)(5))[16]

Where there is a net negative adjustment for the tax year, any net loss for the year is disregarded in adjusting the AAA for purposes of distributions made during the tax year. (Code Sec. 1368(e)(1)(C))[17]

The balance in an S corporation's AAA at the end of a tax year may be reduced below zero if the items that reduce the AAA exceed the sum of the AAA plus the items that increase the AAA (items (1) – (3), above). (Code Sec. 1368(e)(1)(A)) Income in a later year will cause the AAA to become positive only after the negative balance has been restored as illustrated in regs. (Reg § 1.1368-3)[18]

The AAA isn't to be adjusted (i.e., reduced) for federal taxes attributable to any tax year when the S corporation was a C corporation. (Code Sec. 1368(e)(1))[19]

If distributions made during the year exceed the AAA at the close of the tax year, then the AAA is allocated pro rata among each of the distributions (Code Sec. 1368(c); Reg § 1.1368-2(b)(1))[20]

Special rules apply to distributions after the S election is terminated. (Code Sec. 1371(e))[21]

---

12. ¶D-1632; ¶13,684.07
13. ¶D-1823; ¶13,684.02; TD ¶616,506
14. ¶D-1824; ¶13,684.02; TD ¶616,506
15. ¶D-1825, D-1827; ¶13,684.02; TD ¶616,506
16. ¶D-1829; ¶13,684.02; TD ¶616,506

17. ¶D-1826.1; TD ¶616,506
18. ¶D-1830; ¶13,684.02; TD ¶616,506
19. ¶D-1823; ¶13,684.02; TD ¶616,506
20. ¶D-1819; ¶13,684.02; TD ¶616,505
21. ¶D-1846 *et seq.*; ¶13,714.04; TD ¶616,516

¶ 3378   Voluntary revocation of the S election; rescission.

A corporation's S election may be revoked with the consent of holders of a majority of the corporation's issued and outstanding stock (including non-voting stock). (Code Sec. 1362(d)(1); Reg § 1.1362-2(a)(1))[22]

If no effective date is specified, a revocation is effective for the tax year in which made, if made by the 15th day of the third month of that year. Otherwise, it will be effective as of the first day of the next tax year. (Code Sec. 1362(d)(1)(C))[23] However, if the revocation specifies that it is to be effective on a date that is on or after the date it's made, it will be effective on that date even if it causes the corporation's tax year to be split. (Code Sec. 1362(d)(1)(D))[24]

A corporation may *rescind* the revocation at any time before it becomes effective. A rescission may be made only with the consent of each person who consented to the revocation and of each person who became a shareholder during the period from the day after the date the revocation was made through the date the rescission is made. (Reg § 1.1362-2(a)(4))[25]

¶ 3379   Involuntary termination of S election.

A corporation's S election is terminated if:

(1) The corporation ceases to meet any of the S corporation eligibility requirements discussed at ¶3354. (Code Sec. 1362(d)(2)(A)) The termination is effective as of the day the eligibility requirement is no longer met. (Code Sec. 1362(d)(2)(B))[26]

(2) The S corporation's passive investment income (¶3369) exceeds 25% of its gross receipts for three consecutive tax years *if* at the end of each of those years, the corporation had accumulated E&P (¶3368). The termination is effective as of the first day of the first tax year beginning after the third of these years. (Code Sec. 1362(d)(3)(A))[27]

IRS can waive inadvertent terminations if certain conditions are met. (Code Sec. 1362(f)) Regs explain how to request relief. (Reg § 1.1362-4(c))[28] IRS has waived termination where, for example, the S corporation temporarily had an ineligible shareholder such as a nonresident alien, an ineligible trust or another corporation, and where the S corporation had an ineligible subsidiary. [29]

A corporation's filing a voluntary bankruptcy petition does not terminate its S corporation election.[30]

¶ 3380   When new S election can be made after termination or revocation.

After a revocation or termination of its S election, a corporation must wait five years before making a new S election unless IRS consents to an earlier election. (Code Sec. 1362(g))[31]

---

22. ¶D-1901; ¶13,624.02; TD ¶623,001
23. ¶D-1903; ¶13,624.02; TD ¶623,003
24. ¶D-1905; ¶13,624.02; TD ¶623,003
25. ¶D-1907 *et seq.*; ¶13,624.02; TD ¶623,005
26. ¶D-1911; ¶13,624.02; TD ¶623,006

27. ¶D-1914; ¶13,624.02; TD ¶623,008
28. ¶D-1928; ¶13,624.03; TD ¶623,018
29. ¶D-1937 *et seq.*; TD ¶623,025
30. ¶D-1911
31. ¶s D-1951, D-1953; ¶13,624.02; TD ¶623,023

Chapter 16 Corporate Transactions—Organization—
Distributions—Reorganization—Acquisitions—
Liquidation

¶ 3510 Incorporations and Transfers to Controlled Corporations—Code Sec. 351 Transfers.

Incorporating a business or transferring property to a controlled corporation can be partly or wholly tax-free if technical rules are satisfied. But purposely failing to satisfy those rules may not make a transfer taxable in all cases. [1]

No gain or loss is recognized if property (¶3511) is transferred to a corporation solely in exchange for stock (¶3512) of that corporation, if immediately after the transfer, the transferor or transferors are in control (¶3513) of the corporation. (Code Sec. 351(a))[2] For exceptions, see ¶3517 and ¶3518.

For transfers to foreign corporations, see ¶3586.

For basis of property received in the transfer, see ¶2483.

¶ 3511 Property defined.

Property that may be transferred tax-free in a Code Sec. 351 transfer includes cash, tangible property and intangible personal property (e.g., stock, partnership interests, patent rights and working interests in oil and gas properties). [3]

Property doesn't include:

... services by a transferor to the transferee corporation (Code Sec. 351(d)(1));[4]

... indebtedness of the transferee corporation not evidenced by a security (Code Sec. 351(d)(2));[5] or

... interest on indebtedness of the transferee that accrued on or after the start of the transferor's holding period for the debt. (Code Sec. 351(d)(3))[6]

¶ 3512 Exchange for "stock."

For purposes of the "solely in exchange for stock" test, "stock" doesn't include (1) stock rights, options or warrants (Reg § 1.351-1(a)), or (2) nonqualified preferred stock. (Code Sec. 351(g)) (¶3554)[7]

Shares in an association, joint stock company or insurance company are treated as stock. (Code Sec. 7701(a)(7))[8] Stock can be owned even if no stock certificate is issued. [9]

¶ 3513 Control defined.

For purposes of the "control" requirement, control is as defined in Code Sec. 368(c) —i.e., ownership of at least 80% of the transferee's voting stock and at least 80% of all its other classes of stock (¶3551). (Code Sec. 351(a))[10] This requires transferors as a group to hold at least 80% of the voting power immediately after the transfer, but not every transferor has to hold voting stock. Some of the transferors can receive voting stock and others can receive

1. ¶F-1014; TD ¶231,014
2. ¶F-1001; ¶3514.01; TD ¶231,001
3. ¶F-1101 et seq.; ¶3514.03; TD ¶231,004
4. ¶F-1104; ¶3514.03; TD ¶231,004
5. ¶F-1102; TD ¶231,004
6. ¶F-1103; TD ¶231,004
7. ¶F-1004; ¶3514.04; TD ¶231,005
8. ¶F-1004; ¶3514.04; TD ¶231,005
9. ¶F-1004 et seq.; ¶3514.05; TD ¶231,005
10. ¶s F-1200 et seq., F-5501 et seq.; ¶3514.05; TD ¶231,701

References beginning with a single letter are to paragraphs in RIA's Federal Tax Coordinator 2d and RIA's Analysis of Federal Taxes: Income. Those beginning with numbers are to paragraphs in RIA's United States Tax Reporter. Those beginning with TD are to paragraphs in RIA's Tax Desk.

nonvoting preferred as long as the combined stock ownership meets the control test. A corporate transferor's transfer of stock it receives to shareholders doesn't affect the determination of control for this purpose. (Code Sec. 351(c))[11]

¶ 3514   Tax where transferors get cash or property ("boot").

If "boot" (defined at ¶3554) is received by the transferors in addition to "stock," and the exchange otherwise qualifies as a tax-free Code Sec. 351 transfer

. . . loss isn't recognized to a transferor, but

. . . gain is recognized to the transferor up to the amount of "boot" received (e.g., cash, the fair market value of other property). (Code Sec. 351(b))[12]

¶ 3515   Assumption of liabilities.

When the corporation assumes (see ¶3516) liabilities in connection with an otherwise tax-free transfer to a controlled corporation, the transfer is still tax-free, *except:* (Code Sec. 357(a))[13]

. . . If the transferor's principal purpose for having the controlled corporation assume the liabilities is tax avoidance or isn't a bona fide business purpose, *the full amount* of all assumed liabilities, even those assumed for nontax avoidance or valid business purposes, is treated as boot and is taxed under the rule at ¶3514. (Code Sec. 357(b)(1))[14]

. . . If the total liabilities assumed exceed the transferor's adjusted basis in the transferred property, gain is recognized to the extent of the excess. (Code Sec. 357(c)(1))[15]

Where both the tax avoidance rule and excess liability rule apply, tax avoidance takes precedence—i.e., all liabilities are treated as boot. (Code Sec. 357(c)(2)(A))[16]

The assumption of a liability whose payment by the transferor would have resulted in a deduction generally is excluded from the excess liability rule. (Code Sec. 357(c)(3)(A)) However, if the basis of stock received by a transferor as part of a tax-free exchange with a controlled corporation exceeds the stock's fair market value (FMV), the basis of stock received in the tax-free transfer is reduced (but not below the stock's FMV) by the amount of any liability that (1) is assumed by another person as part of the exchange, and (2) did not otherwise reduce the transferor's basis in the stock because of the assumption. Except as provided by IRS, this rule doesn't apply if as part of the exchange the trade or business (or substantially all of the assets) with which the liability is associated is transferred to a corporation. (Code Sec. 358(h))[17]

The assumption of excess liability rule does not apply if (1) an acquiring corporation in a Type A, C, D or G reorganization satisfies Code Sec. 354(b)(1) (i.e., the acquiring corporation acquires substantially all of the transferor's assets, and the stock or other property received by the transferor is distributed as part of the reorganization plan), (2) assumes liabilities of the acquired corporation exceeding the basis of the assets transferred, and (3) the transaction also qualifies as a transfer to a controlled corporation under Code Sec. 351. [18]

¶ 3516   When a liability is treated as "assumed."

For purposes of the rules discussed at ¶3515, except as provided in regs,

. . . *a recourse liability* is treated as having been "assumed" if, based on all the facts and

---

11. ¶F-1202; TD ¶231,702
12. ¶F-1501; ¶3514.10; TD ¶231,302
13. ¶F-1509; ¶3574.01; TD ¶231,501
14. ¶F-1511 *et seq.*; ¶3574.02; TD ¶231,504

15. ¶F-1515 *et seq.*; ¶3574.03; TD ¶231,507
16. ¶F-1519; ¶3574.02; TD ¶231,510
17. ¶F-1803.1; TD ¶231,905
18. ¶F-4204; ; TD ¶235,008

circumstances, the transferee has agreed to, and is expected to, satisfy it (whether or not the transferor has been relieved of the liability); (Code Sec. 357(d)(1)(A)) and

. . . *a nonrecourse liability* is treated as having been assumed by the transferee of any asset subject to the liability, except that the amount of the liability treated as assumed must be reduced to reflect the value of any other assets subject to the same nonrecourse liability that haven't been transferred to the transferee. The reduction is the lesser of:

(1) the amount of the nonrecourse liability the owner of the other assets has agreed with the transferee to satisfy, and is expected to satisfy, or

(2) the fair market value of the other, untransferred assets, determined without regard to Code Sec. 7701(g) (which generally provides that property subject to a nonrecourse debt is worth at least the amount of the debt). (Code Sec. 357(d)(2))[19]

🅥*observation:* If the owner of untransferred assets securing a nonrecourse debt doesn't agree to pay any of it, the amount of the liability treated as assumed by the transferee isn't reduced at all, which could cause liabilities to exceed basis and result in gain recognition.

For the limitation on the transferee's basis increase, see ¶2485.

¶ 3517   Swap funds—transfers to investment companies.

If property is transferred to an "investment company" in exchange for its stock, gain or loss is recognized. (Code Sec. 351(e)(1))[20] A transfer is to an investment company where it results in diversification of the transferor's interests and the transferee is a regulated investment company (mutual fund), a real estate investment trust (REIT), or a corporation more than 80% of the value of whose assets (excluding cash and nonconvertible debt obligations) are held for investment and are readily marketable securities or interests in other mutual funds or REITs. (Reg § 1.351-1(c)(1))[21] Specified types of property, including money, are treated as stock or securities in determining whether a corporation is an investment company. (Code Sec. 351(e)(1))[22] Diversification results if a significant portion of the assets transferred by two or more transferors are nonidentical (Reg § 1.351-1(c)(5))[23] but not if each transferor transfers a portfolio of already diversified assets. (Reg § 1.351-1(c)(6))[24]

¶ 3518   Transfer of debtor's property in a bankruptcy or similar proceeding.

The Code Sec. 351 rules don't apply to transfers in a bankruptcy, receivership, foreclosure or similar proceeding (including agency receivership proceedings involving banks). Any gain or loss is recognized to the extent the stock received by the debtor in exchange for his assets is used to satisfy his indebtedness. (Code Sec. 351(e)(2))[25]

¶ 3519   Gain or loss to corporation on issuance of stock.

A corporation recognizes no gain or loss when it exchanges its stock for property or money. This is true whether the issue or subscription price is above or below par or stated value, and whether the stock is original issue or treasury stock. (Code Sec. 1032(a))[26] Similarly, no gain or loss is recognized in otherwise taxable transactions where a corporation or partnership acquires stock directly or indirectly from the issuing corporation in what otherwise would be a transferred basis transaction, and immediately transfers it to acquire money or other property (including services), and no party receiving the issuing corporation stock receives a substituted basis in the stock of the issuing corporation. (Reg § 1.1032-3(b), Reg § 1.1032-

19. ¶F-1509.2; ¶3574.01; TD ¶231,502
20. ¶F-1301; ¶3514.06; TD ¶232,102
21. ¶F-1302; ¶3514.06; TD ¶232,102
22. ¶F-1303; ¶3514.06; TD ¶232,101

23. ¶F-1307; ¶3514.06; TD ¶232,103
24. ¶F-1307.1; ¶3514.06; TD ¶232,103
25. ¶F-1308; ¶3514.07; TD ¶231,018
26. ¶I-3201; ¶10,324; TD ¶233,401

3(c))[27] (For stock issued to a creditor in satisfaction of the corporation's debt, see ¶1398.)

¶ 3520   Deductibility of the costs of organizing a corporation.

A corporation can elect to deduct in the tax year it begins business up to $5,000 of its organization expenditures. The $5,000 amount is reduced (but not below zero) by the amount, if any, by which the total of the organization expenditures exceeds $50,000. Organizational expenditures in excess of the amount deductible in the year the corporation begins business are deductible ratably over the 180-month period beginning with the month in which it begins business. (Code Sec. 248(a))

Qualifying expenses include outlays for legal services, incorporation fees and temporary directors' fees and organizational meeting costs. (Code Sec. 248(b); Reg § 1.248-1) However, costs of issuing stock can't be deducted. [28]

¶ 3521   Corporate Distributions; Earnings and Profits (E&P). ▬▬▬▬▬▬▬▬

A distribution of property (i.e., money, securities, and any other property except stock of the distributing corporation)[29] by a corporation to its shareholders is taxable to the shareholders as a dividend, to the extent it's made out of current or accumulated earnings and profits (E&P) (¶1285 *et seq.*). The amount of a distribution is reduced by an associated liability only if it is assumed by the shareholder within the meaning of Code Sec. 357(d). (Reg § 1.301-1(g)) (¶3516)

¶ 3522   Earnings and profits (E&P).

As discussed at ¶1285 *et seq.*, a distribution of money or other property by a corporation to its shareholders is treated as a dividend, taxable as ordinary income to the extent it is made out of current and accumulated earnings and profits (E&P). The portion of the distribution in excess of E&P is treated as a return of capital to the extent of the shareholder's basis in his stock in the distributing corporation (his cost or net capital investment). (Code Sec. 301(c)) The remainder of the distribution, if any, is generally taxed as capital gain. [30] For tax treatment of the distributing corporation, see ¶3538 *et seq.*

E&P as computed under the tax laws isn't the same as "earned surplus" or "retained earnings" under financial accounting concepts (nor is it the same as taxable income). Adjustments for specified transactions may have to be made to determine the increase or decrease in E&P for a particular tax year (¶3525). Some adjustments are designed to conform E&P to economic income. (Code Sec. 312(n))[31]

✐caution: For increases in E&P for alternative minimum tax purposes, see ¶3210.

¶ 3523   How distributions affect E&P.

With some exceptions (below), distributions of property reduce E&P by the sum of:

(1) The amount of money distributed. (Code Sec. 312(a)(1))[32]

(2) The principal (face) amount of the corporation's obligations (i.e., its own notes, bonds, etc.) distributed without original issue discount (OID) (as determined under the rules discussed at ¶1313 *et seq.*). (Code Sec. 312(a)(2))[33]

(3) The aggregate issue price of the corporation's obligations distributed *with* OID. (Code Sec. 312(a)(2))[34]

---

27. ¶I-3213
28. ¶s L-5206, L-5207; ¶2484; TD ¶301,028
29. ¶J-2351; ¶3014.01
30. ¶J-2352 *et seq.*; ¶3014; TD ¶172,001

31. ¶F-10007; ¶s 3124.01, 3124.07; TD ¶171,021
32. ¶F-10502; ¶3124.02; TD ¶171,008
33. ¶F-10503; ¶3124.02; TD ¶171,008
34. ¶F-10504; ¶3124.02; TD ¶171,008

(4) The adjusted basis of other distributed property (for appreciated property, see below) (Code Sec. 312(a)(3), Code Sec. 312(b))[35] determined for purposes of computing E&P. (Code Sec. 312(b)(1))[36] This may not be the same as the property's basis for regular income tax purposes, since depreciation allowances may differ for E&P and taxable income purposes (see ¶3524).[37]

Distributions of appreciated property increase E&P to the extent of the gain (FMV over the adjusted basis) realized by the distributing corporation on the distribution of appreciated property (other than the corporation's own obligations) to its shareholders. (Code Sec. 312(b)(1))[38]

Liabilities assumed by the distributee and any liabilities to which the distributed property is subject reduce the E&P. (Code Sec. 312(c))[39]

Distributions in redemption that are treated as payment for stock (¶3526) reduce E&P by an amount not in excess of the ratable share of the distributing corporation's E&P attributable to the redeemed stock. (Code Sec. 312(n)(7))[40]

Reorganization and other tax-free distributions don't reduce E&P, if no gain is recognized to the distributee. (Code Sec. 312(d); Reg § 1.312-11(b), Reg § 1.312-11(c))[41]

Tax-free distributions of stock or rights in the distributing corporation don't reduce E&P. (Code Sec. 312(d); Reg § 1.312-1(d)) But if the distribution is *taxable* to shareholders (see ¶1296), E&P is reduced by the FMV of the taxable portion of the stock or rights. (Reg § 1.312-1(d))[42]

Distributions to 20% corporate shareholders may require adjustments to E&P solely for purposes of determining the distributee's income and basis. (Code Sec. 301(e))[43]

¶ 3524 Effect of depreciation on E&P.

Deductions allowed for depreciation in computing E&P are often less than those allowed in computing taxable income (¶1900 *et seq.*), as follows:

... For *MACRS* property (other than expensed property, see below), the deduction must be computed under the alternative depreciation system (ADS) even if a different system is used in computing taxable income. (Code Sec. 312(k)(3)(A))[44]

🅡🅘🅐/*observation:* This applies even for property for which the "bonus" first year depreciation under Code Sec. 168(k) (¶1935 *et seq.*) is taken.

... For *ACRS* property placed in service before '87, the deduction is computed by using the straight-line method over the regular or alternative ACRS recovery periods, which may be longer than those used in computing taxable income. [45]

... For *depreciable property* placed in service before '81, the deduction is computed by using the straight-line or a similar method (e.g., units of production) even if an accelerated depreciation method is used in computing taxable income. [46]

... For *expensed* property (Code Sec. 179 and Code Sec. 179A property), the cost is deducted ratably over five tax years. (Code Sec. 312(k)(3)(B))[47]

35. ¶F-10505; ¶3124.02; TD ¶171,008
36. ¶F-10505; ¶s 3124.02, 3124.04; TD ¶171,008
37. ¶F-10300 *et seq.*; ¶3124.01 *et seq.*; TD ¶171,008
38. ¶F-10506; ¶3124.02; TD ¶171,011
39. ¶F-10508; ¶3124.02; TD ¶171,011
40. ¶F-10701; ¶3124.07; TD ¶171,034
41. ¶F-10801; ¶3124.02; TD ¶171,034

42. ¶F-10509 *et seq.*; ¶3124.02; TD ¶171,015
43. ¶F-10601 *et seq.*; ¶3014; TD ¶171,008
44. ¶F-10303; ¶3124.04; TD ¶171,022
45. ¶F-10307; ¶3124.04; TD ¶171,022
46. ¶F-10309; ¶3124.04; TD ¶171,022
47. ¶F-10304; ¶3124.04; TD ¶171,023

¶ 3525   Other adjustments to E&P.

Here are how other key items are treated in computing E&P:

Circulation expenses must be capitalized and treated as part of the basis of the asset to which they relate even if they are deducted currently in computing taxable income. (Code Sec. 312(n)(3))[48]

Completed contract method of accounting can't be used for E&P purposes. The percentage of completion method must be used instead. (Code Sec. 312(n)(6))[49]

Construction period carrying charges (interest, property taxes, etc.) must be capitalized as part of the assets to which they are allocable. (Code Sec. 312(n)(1)(A)) The capitalized amounts must be written off for E&P purposes, as is the asset itself. [50]

Depletion is taken into account on a *cost,* not percentage, basis. (Reg § 1.312-6(c)(1))[1]

Estimated tax payments by a cash method taxpayer reduce E&P in the year paid. [2]

Exempt income (e.g., state or local bond interest) increases E&P. (Reg § 1.312-6(b))[3]

Installment sale principal amounts must be treated as received in the year of sale, i.e., as if the corporation didn't use the installment method. (Code Sec. 312(n)(5))[4]

Intangible drilling and development costs that are deductible when paid or incurred for taxable income purposes (other than costs incurred in connection with a nonproductive well) must be capitalized and deducted ratably over a 60-month period for E&P purposes. (Code Sec. 312(n)(2)(A))[5]

Income tax liabilities reduce E&P as of the close of the tax year, for an accrual basis corporation, and according to some courts, a cash basis corporation. (IRS and other courts say a cash basis corporation reduces E&P only when the tax is *paid.*)[6]

Life insurance proceeds increase E&P if the corporation is the beneficiary even if not includible in taxable income. [7]

LIFO recapture amount increases or decreases at the close of each tax year increase or decrease E&P by the same amount. (Code Sec. 312(n)(4))[8]

Losses may be recognized though not allowed as a deduction. The mere fact that the losses aren't allowed doesn't prevent a decrease in E&P by the disallowed amount. [9]

Mineral exploration and development costs that are deductible for taxable income purposes must be capitalized and deducted ratably over a 120-month period for E&P purposes. (Code Sec. 312(n)(2)(B))[10]

Loss carryovers and carrybacks don't reduce E&P of the year to which they are carried. Nor does a reduction of a loss carryover increase E&P in a later carryover year. [11]

Organization expenses must be capitalized and treated as part of the basis of the asset to which they relate even if they are amortized in computing taxable income. (Code Sec. 312(n)(3))[12]

Premiums paid for insuring lives of corporate officers reduce E&P even if not deductible in computing taxable income. [13]

48. ¶F-10206; ¶3124.07; TD ¶171,019
49. ¶F-10008; ¶3124.07; TD ¶171,021
50. ¶F-10208; ¶3124.07; TD ¶171,025
1. ¶F-10314; ¶3124.04; TD ¶171,024
2. ¶F-10224; ¶3124.03; TD ¶171,009
3. ¶F-10101; ¶s 3124.01, 3124.07; TD ¶171,012
4. ¶F-10405; ¶3124.07; TD ¶171,021
5. ¶F-10221; ¶3124.07; TD ¶171,026

6. ¶F-10223, F-10225; ¶3124.03; TD ¶171,009
7. ¶F-10102; ¶3124.07; TD ¶171,012
8. ¶F-10212; ¶3124.07; TD ¶171,021
9. ¶F-10403; ¶3124.05
10. ¶F-10220; ¶3124.07; TD ¶171,026
11. ¶F-10012; ¶3124.03; TD ¶171,032
12. ¶F-10204; ¶3124.07; TD ¶171,028
13. ¶F-10234; TD ¶175,042

¶ 3526   Stock Redemptions. ▬▬▬▬▬▬▬▬▬▬▬▬▬▬▬▬▬▬▬▬▬▬▬

The acquisition by a corporation of its own stock from a shareholder in exchange for cash or property is treated as a distribution to the shareholder (taxable under the rules described at ¶¶1285 *et seq.*) unless it qualifies as a redemption, in which case the distribution is treated as payment for the stock (i.e., as a sale or exchange, for which capital gain treatment is allowed if the stock is a capital asset).

Stock is treated as redeemed if the corporation acquires its stock from a shareholder in exchange for cash or property, whether or not the stock acquired is cancelled, retired or held as treasury stock. (Code Sec. 317(b))[14]

If a redemption fits within any of the following categories, the distribution of cash or property to the redeeming shareholder is treated as a payment in exchange for stock: (Code Sec. 302(a))[15]

(1) A redemption that's "substantially disproportionate" with respect to the redeeming shareholder, see ¶3527.

(2) A complete redemption of all of a shareholder's stock in the corporation, see ¶3528.

(3) A redemption that is "not essentially equivalent to a dividend," see ¶3530.

(4) A redemption of stock held by a noncorporate shareholder, in partial liquidation of the distributing corporation, see ¶3531.

(5) A redemption of a decedent's stock to pay death taxes, see ¶3532.

¶ 3527   Substantially disproportionate redemptions.

A redemption is "substantially disproportionate" if *both* of these tests are satisfied:

(1) *80% test.* Immediately after the redemption, the ratio of the shareholder's voting stock to the corporation's total outstanding voting stock is less than 80% of that ratio immediately before the redemption. The same 80% test must also be met with regard to the corporation's *common stock,* voting and nonvoting. Where there's more than one class of common stock, the 80% test is based on the fair market value of the aggregate shares of the different classes. (Code Sec. 302(b)(2)(C))

(2) *50% test.* Immediately after the redemption, the shareholder owns less than 50%, by vote, of the corporation's total voting stock. (Code Sec. 302(b)(2)(B))[16]

For constructive ownership rules that apply to the above tests, see ¶3534.

A redemption solely of nonvoting stock doesn't qualify as substantially disproportionate. But if voting stock is also redeemed at the same time and in a redemption that qualifies as substantially disproportionate, the redemption of nonvoting stock (other than Section 306 stock) will also qualify as substantially disproportionate. (Reg § 1.302-3(a))[17]

¶ 3528   Complete redemptions—termination of a shareholder's interest in the corporation.

To qualify as a complete redemption, all stock owned (or treated as owned under the constructive ownership rules, see ¶3534 (unless waived, see ¶3529) by the shareholder in the corporation must be redeemed. (Code Sec. 302(b)(3)) Thus, if a shareholder owns both common and preferred stock, the redemption of all the shares of only one of the classes doesn't qualify as a complete redemption. [18]

---

14. ¶F-11001; ¶3174.01; TD ¶241,002
15. ¶F-11101 *et seq.*; ¶3024.02 *et seq.*; TD ¶241,001
16. ¶F-11203 *et seq.*; ¶3024.04; TD ¶242,000 *et seq.*

17. ¶F-11212; ¶3024.04; TD ¶242,014
18. ¶F-11301 *et seq.*; ¶3024.05; TD ¶241,201

A redemption on the installment basis can qualify as a complete redemption if the corporation and the shareholder are bound by a purchase agreement to complete the redemption by a certain date and for a maximum price. [19]

¶ 3529 Family attribution rules waived on complete redemptions.

In applying the complete redemption tests (¶3528), the Code Sec. 318(a)(1) family attribution rules (¶3534) won't apply (but the other constructive ownership rules, described at ¶3534, will still apply) to any shareholder whose actually-owned stock is completely redeemed if:

(1) immediately after the redemption he has no personal financial interest in the corporation ("prohibited interest"), other than as a creditor;

(2) he no longer serves as director, officer or employee;

(3) he doesn't acquire any prohibited interest (except by inheritance) or position within ten years after the date of the redemption;

(4) he didn't acquire any of the redeemed stock from close family members, and didn't transfer any stock to them, within ten years before the redemption, except for an acquisition or transfer not principally motivated by tax avoidance; *and*

(5) he attaches a separate statement (in duplicate) to his income tax return for the year of redemption, in which he states that he hasn't acquired any new prohibited interest in the company (except by inheritance) and that he will notify the district director within 30 days after acquiring any new interest. (Code Sec. 302(c)(2); Reg § 1.302-4)[20]

If a distribution qualifies both as a partial liquidation (i.e., substantially disproportionate redemption (¶3527) or a redemption not essentially equivalent to a dividend (¶3530)) and as a complete termination of the shareholder's interest, and if the shareholder relies on Code Sec. 302(c)(2) for a waiver of the family attribution rules, the shareholder is not subject to the ten-year prohibition on the acquisition of an interest in the corporation. (Code Sec. 302(b)(5))[21]

Entity waiver rule. A partnership, estate, trust or corporation (entity) can waive the family attribution rule as applied to the stock that the entity's partner, beneficiary or shareholder owns constructively by attribution from that person's family, if the entity and each related person (e.g., individual partner) meet the above tests and agree to be jointly and severally liable for any tax deficiency resulting from any acquisition of an interest within the ten-year period. (Code Sec. 302(c)(2)(C)) This prevents reattribution to the partnership, etc., of stock that would otherwise be attributed first to its individual partner (because his family actually owned the stock).[22]

¶ 3530 Redemptions not essentially equivalent to a dividend.

A redemption isn't essentially equivalent to a dividend if it results in a meaningful reduction in the redeemed shareholder's proportionate interest in the distributing corporation, without regard to how it affects the distributing corporation. (Reg § 1.302-2(b))[23]

A redemption from a sole shareholder and a redemption that's pro rata can't result in any reduction in the redeemed shareholder's proportionate interest in the distributing corporation.[24]

A redemption from a shareholder with over 50% of the voting power usually results in a meaningful reduction if that shareholder's voting power is reduced to 50% or less. [25]

19. ¶F-11307; ¶3024.05; TD ¶241,211
20. ¶F-11313 *et seq.*; ¶3024.05; TD ¶241,401 *et seq.*
21. ¶F-11311 *et seq.*; ¶3024.05; TD ¶241,405
22. ¶F-11314; ¶3024.05; TD ¶241,403

23. ¶F-11402; ¶3024.03; TD ¶242,201
24. ¶F-11407; ¶3024.03; TD ¶242,208
25. ¶F-11418; ¶3024.03; TD ¶242,225

A redemption of voting stock from a substantial minority shareholder results in a meaningful reduction if, after the redemption, the number of shareholders the redeemed shareholder must act in concert with to control the corporation is increased. [26]

Any redemption of voting stock from a low percentage minority shareholder usually is treated as a meaningful reduction. [27]

Redemptions of nonvoting preferred stock from shareholders who own no common stock and no voting stock of any class always result in a meaningful reduction. [28]

The constructive ownership rules (¶3534) apply in determining the redeemed shareholder's ownership of stock in the distributing corporation before and after the redemption (Code Sec. 302(c)(1)) even if no stock is actually owned after the redemption. For these purposes, stock held in a voting trust is treated as owned by the beneficial owner and not the trustee. [29]

¶ 3531   Redemptions in partial liquidation of a noncorporate shareholder.

A redemption distribution is treated as made in partial liquidation if it is (1) made with respect to a noncorporate shareholder, (2) not essentially equivalent to a dividend (based on the effect to the distributing corporation), and (3) made under a plan within the tax year in which the plan is adopted or the next tax year. (Code Sec. 302(b)(4); Code Sec. 302(e)(1))[30] Partial liquidations are meant to include cases involving the genuine contraction of a corporate business. (Reg § 1.346-1(a))[31]

If a corporation is engaged in two or more active trades or businesses for five years or more, a distribution in partial liquidation won't be essentially equivalent to a dividend if the corporation terminates one of the businesses, distributes all of the assets of the discontinued business (or its sales proceeds), and continues to operate the second business. (Code Sec. 302(e)(2), Code Sec. 302(e)(3))[32]

¶ 3532   Redemption of decedent's stock to pay death taxes.

Distributions in redemption of stock included in a decedent's gross estate for federal estate tax purposes are treated as payment for stock up to the sum of: (1) all death taxes (federal and state), including interest, and (2) funeral and administration expenses allowable as federal estate tax deductions (Code Sec. 303(a))[33] *but only if* these three tests are met:

(1) The value of the redeeming corporation's stock included in the estate must exceed 35% of the decedent's adjusted gross estate. (Code Sec. 303(b)(2)(A)) Stock in two or more corporations is treated as stock of a single corporation if 20% or more in value of the outstanding stock of each corporation is included in the estate. A surviving spouse's interest in stock held with the decedent as community property, joint tenants, tenants by the entirety or tenants in common is treated as included in the decedent's gross estate for these purposes (Code Sec. 303(b)(2)(B))[34] as are shares of stock transferred by gift within three years of a decedent's death. [35]

(2) The redemption distribution must take place after the decedent's death and within three years and 90 days after the estate tax return is filed (or due, if filed early), or, in some cases, by later specified dates. (Code Sec. 303(b)(1))[36]

(3) The redeemed shareholder must bear the burden of the taxes or expenses —i.e., his interest must be reduced (directly or through a binding obligation to contribute) by any payment of death taxes or funeral and administration expenses. (Code Sec. 303(b)(3))[37]

26. ¶F-11424; ¶3024.03
27. ¶F-11425; ¶3024.03; TD ¶242,213
28. ¶F-11429 *et seq.*; ¶3024.03; TD ¶242,218
29. ¶F-11410 *et seq.*; ¶3024.03; TD ¶242,009
30. ¶F-11500 *et seq.*; ¶3024.06; TD ¶242,604
31. ¶F-11509; ¶3024.06; TD ¶242,614

32. ¶F-11516 *et seq.*; ¶3024.06; TD ¶242,608
33. ¶F-11600 *et seq.*; ¶3034.01; TD ¶243,001
34. ¶F-11605 *et seq.*; ¶3034.01; TD ¶243,013 *et seq.*
35. ¶F-11604; ¶3034.01; TD ¶243,012
36. ¶F-11613; ¶3034.01; TD ¶243,018
37. ¶F-11617; ¶3034.01; TD ¶243,009

¶ 3533   Sales between related corporations as redemptions.

If shareholders who control (defined below) two corporations that are related to one another, sell stock they own in one of the controlled corporations (issuer) to the related controlled corporation (acquirer) in return for cash or other property, the sale is treated: (1) as a redemption by the *acquirer* if the acquirer is a brother corporation to the issuer (Code Sec. 304(a)(1)), or (2) as a redemption by the *issuer* if the issuer is a parent of the acquirer. (Code Sec. 304(a)(2))[38]

Whether a redemption is treated as payment in exchange for stock or as an ordinary income dividend is determined by applying the tests at ¶3526 *et seq.* to the redeemed shareholder's interest in the issuer after the redemption. (Code Sec. 304(a))[39] If the transaction is treated as a dividend, the E&P of both corporations are taken into account to determine the amount of the dividend. Under an ordering rule, the E&P is treated as first coming out of the acquirer's E&P (to the extent of its E&P) and then coming out of the issuer's E&P (to the extent of its E&P). (Code Sec. 304(b)(2))[40] These rules apply even absent a motive to convert ordinary income to capital gain. [41] If the purchaser in a related-party stock sale is a foreign corporation, special rules apply to determine E&P. (Code Sec. 304(b)(5))[42]

If a deemed distribution from a stock sale between brother-sister corporations is treated as a dividend (as opposed to a sale or exchange), (1) the stock that was sold is deemed to have been transferred by the selling corporation to the buying corporation for stock of the buyer in a tax-free transfer to a controlled corporation, and (2) the buyer is deemed to have redeemed the stock that is treated as having been issued to the seller in the constructive transfer. (Code Sec. 304(a)(1)) This prevents the seller from using the dividends-received deduction to shelter any part of the deemed distribution. [43]

A corporation is a parent if it controls another corporation. (Code Sec. 304(a)(2)) A brother-sister relationship exists where the same person or persons controls each of two corporations. (Code Sec. 304(a)(1)) For these purposes, "control" means ownership of stock possessing at least 50% of the total combined voting power of all classes of the voting stock, or at least 50% of the total value of all classes of stock. (Code Sec. 304(c)(1))[44] Constructive ownership rules similar to those at ¶3534, but with certain modifications, apply in determining whether control exists. (Code Sec. 304(c)(3)(A))[45]

The parent-sub redemption rules apply even if, as a result of the constructive ownership rules, a brother-sister relationship also exists. [46]

¶ 3534   Constructive ownership.

For purposes of the stock redemption rules, a person is treated as owning not only his own direct holdings, but also those of certain closely related taxpayers: (Code Sec. 302(c))

...*Family attribution.*   An individual is considered as owning stock owned, directly or indirectly, by his spouse (unless divorced or legally separated), children (including adopted children), grandchildren and parents. (Code Sec. 318(a)(1))[47]

...*Attribution to and from S corporations, partnerships and estates.*   Stock owned by or for an S corporation, partnership or estate is considered as owned proportionately by its shareholders, partners, or beneficiaries. (Code Sec. 318(a)(2)(A), Code Sec. 318(a)(5)(E)) Stock owned by or for an S corporation shareholder, partner or estate beneficiary is attributed in full to the S corporation, partnership or estate. (Code Sec. 318(a)(3)(A), Code

---

38. ¶F-11704 *et seq.*; ¶3044 *et seq.*; TD ¶243,302 *et seq.*
39. ¶F-11704; ¶s 3044.02, 3044.03; TD ¶243,301
40. ¶F-11706; ¶3044.02; TD ¶243,303
41. ¶F-11710
42. ¶F-11719.2

43. ¶F-11716; ¶3044.03; TD ¶243,311
44. ¶F-11711; ¶3044.01; TD ¶243,307
45. ¶F-11720 *et seq.*; ¶3044.01; TD ¶243,323
46. ¶F-11723; ¶3044.04; TD ¶243,321
47. ¶F-11803 *et seq.*; ¶3184.02; TD ¶243,627

Sec. 318(a)(5)(E))[48]

. . . Attribution to and from trusts (except an exempt employee's trust). Stock owned by or for a trust is considered owned by its beneficiaries in proportion to their actuarial interest in the trust. (Code Sec. 318(a)(2)(B)(i)) Stock owned by or for a trust beneficiary is attributed in full to the trust unless the beneficiary's interest in the trust is a remote contingent interest. (Code Sec. 318(a)(3)(B)(i))[49]

. . . Attribution to and from C corporations. A 50%-or-more shareholder in a C corporation is considered as owning his proportionate share of stock in other corporations owned by the C corporation. (Code Sec. 318(a)(2)(C)) A C corporation is considered as owning all the stock (except its own) owned by its 50%-or-more shareholder. (Code Sec. 318(a)(3)(C))[50]

. . . Option attribution. The holder of an option to buy stock is treated as the owner of the stock covered by the option. (Code Sec. 318(a)(4)) This includes an option that isn't exercisable until after the lapse of a fixed time. [1]

Stock constructively owned by a person is considered as actually owned by him for purposes of further attribution, (Code Sec. 318(a)(5)(A))[2] *except* in the following situations where "double" or "sidewise" attribution is prohibited:

. . . Stock constructively owned by a person under the family attribution rules won't be attributed further to make another family member the constructive owner of that stock. (Code Sec. 318(a)(5)(B))[3]

illustration: If father and son each actually own 50 shares in a corporation, each is treated as owning all 100 shares. But the father's *constructive* ownership of the 50 shares actually owned by his son can't be attributed from him to his daughter. She is considered owner of only her father's *actual* 50 shares.

. . . Stock constructively owned by a partnership, estate, trust or corporation can't be further attributed from the partnership, etc., to make another (partner, heir, beneficiary or shareholder) the constructive owner of that stock. (Code Sec. 318(a)(5)(C))[4]

¶ 3535 Section 306 Preferred Stock Bail-Outs.

Certain stock issued as a stock dividend or in a corporate reorganization is treated as Section 306 stock. Generally, a shareholder will have ordinary income if Section 306 stock is redeemed or sold.

¶ 3536 Dispositions of Section 306 stock.

If Section 306 stock (¶3537) is redeemed by the corporation, the amount paid to the redeeming shareholders is treated as any current distribution of property subject to the normal dividend rules, see ¶¶1285 *et seq.* (Code Sec. 306(a)(2))[5]

If the Section 306 stock is sold (or otherwise disposed of) to an outsider (i.e., not a redemption), the entire amount realized is treated as ordinary *nondividend* income, up to the amount that would have been a dividend to the disposing shareholder if at the time the stock was distributed the corporation had made a cash distribution of the stock's then fair market value. (Code Sec. 306(a)(1)(A))[6] No loss is recognized. (Code Sec. 306(a)(1)(B))[7]

These dispositions of Section 306 stock aren't subject to the ordinary income "taint":

. . . a complete redemption of all the shareholder's stock (Code Sec. 306(b)(1)(B));

48. ¶F-11812 *et seq.*; ¶3184.03; TD ¶243,615 *et seq.*
49. ¶F-11827 *et seq.*; ¶3184.04; TD ¶243,618
50. ¶F-11808 *et seq.*; ¶3184.05; TD ¶243,614
1. ¶F-11834 *et seq.*; ¶3184.06; TD ¶243,632
2. ¶F-11805
3. ¶F-11804; ¶3184.07; TD ¶243,629

4. ¶s F-11811, F-11814, F-11824, F-11832; ¶3184.07; TD ¶243,623 *et seq.*
5. ¶F-12106; ¶3064.02; TD ¶244,406
6. ¶s F-12103, F-12101; ¶3064.02; TD ¶244,401
7. ¶F-12103; ¶3064.02; TD ¶244,403

. . . a complete termination of a shareholder's stock interest by any other disposition that leaves him without any stock actually or constructively owned (Code Sec. 306(b)(1)(A));

. . . a partial liquidation redemption from a noncorporate shareholder (Code Sec. 306(b)(1)(B));

. . . a redemption in a complete liquidation of the corporation (Code Sec. 306(b)(2));

. . . any nontaxable disposition, e.g., an exchange of stock in a reorganization or a gift of the tainted stock (but the stock remains tainted in the transferee's hands) (Code Sec. 306(b)(3));

. . . any disposition (including a redemption) of Section 306 stock if IRS is satisfied that federal income tax avoidance wasn't a principal purpose: (1) for the distribution and disposition of the tainted stock, or (2) if the underlying stock is disposed of before or simultaneously with the tainted stock, for the disposition of the tainted stock. (Code Sec. 306(b)(4)) Showing that the corporation that issued the Section 306 stock is widely held isn't enough to make the exception apply. [8]

¶ 3537   Stock treated as Section 306 stock.

"Section 306 stock" includes:

(1) Stock received as a stock dividend, *other than common issued with respect to common,* any part of which was nontaxable on receipt. (Code Sec. 306(c)(1)(A)) Usually this is preferred distributed on common. [9]

(2) Stock *(other than common)* received in a corporate reorganization, spin-off, split-up or split-off, to the extent that (a) the transaction was substantially the same as the receipt of a stock dividend, or (b) the stock was received in exchange for Section 306 stock. (Code Sec. 306(c)(1)(B)) [10]

(3) Stock (except stock described in (2), above) whose basis is determined by reference to the basis of Section 306 stock. (Code Sec. 306(c)(1)(C)) [11]

✔ observation: This means that once stock has the Section 306 "taint" it remains tainted in the hand of any transferee (e.g., a donee) who takes the same basis as his transferor.

(4) Preferred stock received in a Code Sec. 351 transfer (except for certain bank transfers), provided that if, cash had been distributed instead of the preferred stock, part of the cash would have been a dividend (applying the related corporation redemption rules, see ¶3531). (Code Sec. 306(c)(3)(A)) [12]

✔ observation: If gain is recognized on the receipt of nonqualified preferred stock (¶3554) it won't be section 306 stock.

Excluded from Section 306 classification is any stock, whatever its class, that at the time of its distribution wouldn't *in any part* have been a dividend if cash had been distributed instead of stock because the corporation had no current or accumulated earnings and profits. (Code Sec. 306(c)(2)) [13]

¶ 3538   Nonliquidating Property Distributions. ▬▬▬▬▬▬▬▬

A corporation recognizes taxable gain when it makes a nonliquidating distribution (e.g., redemption, dividend) of appreciated property (other than its own obligations) to its shareholders, as if the property had been sold, at the time of the distribution, to the distributee for its then fair market value. (Code Sec. 311(b)(1)) [14]

---

8. ¶F-12108 *et seq.*; ¶3064.02; TD ¶244,413
9. ¶F-12122; ¶3064.01; TD ¶244,408
10. ¶F-12124 *et seq.*; ¶3064.01; TD ¶244,408
11. ¶F-12128; ¶3064.01; TD ¶244,408

12. ¶F-12123; ¶3064.01; TD ¶244,408
13. ¶F-12132; ¶3064.01; TD ¶244,411
14. ¶F-14004 *et seq.*; ¶3114.01; TD ¶244,203

A corporation recognizes no loss on a nonliquidating distribution of property. (Code Sec. 311(a)(2))[15] IRS must issue regs to prevent taxpayers from circumventing gain recognition on appreciated property distributions through use of other Code or reg provisions. (Code Sec. 346(b))

Neither gain nor loss is recognized by a corporation on distributions of its own stock or stock rights. (Code Sec. 305(a))

For distributed property is subject to a liability, see ¶3539.

For how nonliquidating distributions affect earnings and profits, see ¶3523.

¶ 3539 Distribution of property subject to a liability.

If a corporation's nonliquidating distribution consists of property subject to a liability in excess of basis, or if a shareholder assumes a liability of the distributor corporation in connection with the distribution, then in computing the corporation's gain on the distribution (¶3538), the property's fair market value (FMV) is treated as not less than the amount of those liabilities. (Code Sec. 311(b)(2))[16] If the liability is unsecured, it's allocated among all the distributed assets (including any asset that secures another liability) according to their relative FMVs. [17]

¶ 3540 Distributions of stock or stock rights.

Except for distributions of appreciated property, a corporation doesn't recognize gain or loss on distributions (not in complete liquidation) of its own stock or of rights to acquire its own stock. (Code Sec. 311(a)(1))[18]

¶ 3541 Corporate Reorganizations.

If one corporation transfers property to another corporation solely in exchange for stock or securities of the other corporation and the exchange is made pursuant to a plan of reorganization, neither corporation will recognize gain or loss on the exchange, provided the transaction complies with strict statutory and regulatory requirements.

¶ 3542 Conditions common to all reorganizations.

These definitions and requirements apply to all reorganization types (except as noted below). Failure to meet any requirement may disqualify a reorganization and can result in recognized gain and/or dividend treatment. [19]

Plan of reorganization. There must be a "plan" of reorganization. (Code Sec. 354(a)(1)) The plan should be in writing (though not required by the Code), since the regs require a copy of it to be filed with the returns of all corporate parties (below). (Reg § 1.368-3)[20]

A party to a reorganization. The stock or securities exchanged must be those of a "party to the reorganization." (Code Sec. 354(a)(1))[21] A "party" includes any corporation resulting from the reorganization, such as the survivor in a merger, the consolidated company, etc., as well as the corporations merged, consolidated, etc. (Code Sec. 368(b)) A "party" also can include a parent corporation, in some cases. [22]

Continuity of interest. The continuity of proprietary interest doctrine, set out in regs, incorporates the judicial requirement that the former target shareholders retain a significant

15. ¶F-14002; ¶3114.01; TD ¶244,209
16. ¶s F-14005, F-14402; ¶3114.01; TD ¶244,204
17. ¶F-14006; ¶3114.01; TD ¶244,206
18. ¶F-14002; ¶3114; TD ¶244,209

19. ¶F-3500 *et seq.*; ¶3684; TD ¶232,508
20. ¶s F-4009; ¶3684.09; TD ¶232,509
21. ¶F-4013 *et seq.*; ¶3684.08; TD ¶232,501
22. ¶F-4013; ¶3684.08; TD ¶232,517

equity participation in the target corporation following the reorganization.

A proprietary interest is preserved if: (1) it is exchanged for a proprietary interest in the issuing corporation, (2) it is exchanged by the acquiring corporation for a direct interest in the target corporation enterprise, or (3) it otherwise continues as a proprietary interest in the target corporation. (Reg § 1.368-1(e))[23]

Continuity of business enterprise. An acquiring corporation must either: (1) continue the target's "historic business" (in general, its most recent business unless the most recent business was entered under the plan of reorganization), or (2) use a significant portion of the target's "historic business assets" in a business. (Reg § 1.368-1(d)(1); Reg § 1.368-1(d)(2)) To satisfy the continuity of business enterprise requirement, a business and assets do not have to be conducted or held directly by the acquirer, but may be conducted or held through one or more of the members of the acquirer's "qualified group" (one or more chains of corporations connected through stock ownership, if the acquirer has 80% control of at least one of them and each of the other corporations is controlled by one of the other corporations). (Reg § 1.368-1(d)(4)(ii))[24]

Business purpose. Where there's no business purpose, the transaction isn't treated as a reorganization.[25]

The continuity of interest and continuity of business enterprise requirements, above, do not apply to recapitalizations involving a single corporation (Type E reorganizations, see ¶3548),[26] or to change-in-identity reorganizations (Type F, see ¶3549) (Reg § 1.368-1(b))[27]

¶ 3543   Reorganizations involving investment companies.

Tax-free reorganization treatment is denied to an exchange of assets or stock of two or more investment companies[28] if the result of the exchange is to achieve significantly more diversity of investment for the shareholders of any one of the companies than existed before the exchange. The rule only affects treatment of the exchange with respect to the undiversified investment company, and its shareholders and security holders. An investment company is considered undiversified unless it's a regulated investment company (e.g., a mutual fund),[29] a real estate investment trust,[30] or a corporation that meets the diversified investment company requirements of Code Sec. 368(a)(2)(F)(ii). (Code Sec. 368(a)(2)(F))[31]

¶ 3544   Type A: Merger or consolidation.

A Type A reorganization is a merger or consolidation effected under the statute or statutes necessary to effect the merger or consolidation. (Code Sec. 368(a)(1)(A); Reg § 1.368-2(b)(1)(ii))[32]

Where the acquirer uses its parent's stock to acquire "substantially all" (¶3546) of the target's properties, the transaction is a forward triangular merger. (Code Sec. 368(a)(2)(D))[33] The acquirer's stock may be transferred to another subsidiary of parent following a forward triangular merger.[34] If the sub (using its parent's voting stock) merges into the target, the transaction is a reverse triangular merger. (Code Sec. 368(a)(2)(E))[35] A reverse triangular merger is a tax-free reorganization despite a later sale of half of the target's operating assets.[36] A sub's merger into the target followed by an upstream merger into the parent is a statutory merger.[37] The merger of a target corporation into the acquiring corporation's wholly

---

23. ¶s F-3501, F-3600 *et seq.*; ¶3684.10; TD ¶236,202
24. ¶F-3701 *et seq.*; ¶3684.11; TD ¶236,401
25. ¶F-3800 *et seq.*; ¶3684.12, ¶79,006.07; TD ¶236,500 *et seq.*
26. ¶F-3626; ¶3684.05; TD ¶236,221
27. ¶F-3107; ¶3684.06; TD ¶236,408
28. ¶F-2103
29. ¶E-6001; ¶8514
30. ¶E-6500; ¶8564

31. ¶F-2101 *et seq.*; ¶3684.14
32. ¶F-2201; ¶3684.01; TD ¶234,100
33. ¶F-2301 *et seq.*; ¶3684.01; TD ¶234,200
34. ¶F-2308.1
35. ¶F-2401 *et seq.*; ¶3684.01; TD ¶234,400
36. ¶F-2413
37. ¶F-2407

owned limited liability company (LLC) qualified as a statutory merger. [38]

The merger of a disregarded entity into a corporation doesn't qualify as a tax-free statutory merger or consolidation, although the merger of a corporation into a disregarded entity may qualify. (Reg § 1.368-2)[39]

For triangular reorgs where at least one of the parties is foreign, see ¶3545.

¶ 3545 Type B: Stock for stock.

A Type B reorganization is the acquisition by one corporation of stock in a second (target) corporation in exchange *solely* for the acquiring corporation's *voting stock* (or voting stock of its parent—a triangular B reorganization), if the acquiring corporation has "control" (¶3551) of the target immediately after the exchange. (Code Sec. 368(a)(1)(B)) An acquiring corporation that transfers property other than voting stock in connection with a Type B reorganization plan (e.g., to nonshareholders) doesn't violate the solely-for-voting-stock requirement as long as the target's *stock* is acquired solely for voting stock. [40]

IRS will issue regs under Code Sec. 367(b), effective for transactions occurring after May 30, 2007, which will treat a subsidiary (S) as having made a Code Sec. 301(c) distribution to its parent (P) where P or S (or both) are foreign, and, as part of a reorganization S acquires P stock from either P or P's shareholders in exchange for property and S uses the P stock to acquire a target in a triangular reorganization (i.e., a so called "Killer B" transaction). [41]

¶ 3546 Type C: Acquiring "substantially all" of target's assets for stock.

A Type C reorganization is the acquisition by one corporation of "substantially all" of the properties of a second (target) corporation in exchange for voting stock of the acquiring corporation (or its parent—a triangular C reorganization). Except as noted below, liabilities assumed by the acquiring corporation are disregarded. (Code Sec. 368(a)(1)(C))[42]

There's no rule of thumb as to what is "substantially all" of the target's properties, and how much can be safely retained by the transferor (target), although cases have held that certain percentages met (92%) or failed (61%, 68%) the requirement. [43] For purposes of a favorable advance ruling from IRS, the target must transfer at least 90% of the fair market value of the net assets and at least 70% of the fair market value of the gross assets that it held immediately before the transfer. [44]

Also, the transaction won't qualify as a C reorganization unless, under the reorganization plan, the target distributes to its shareholders (i.e., liquidates) all the stock, securities and other property received under the plan, as well as its other properties. But IRS may waive this distribution requirement under certain conditions. (Code Sec. 368(a)(2)(G))[45]

For a corporation to meet the requirement that it acquire substantially all of the property of another corporation in exchange for voting stock, at least 80% of the fair market value of all the property must be acquired solely for voting stock. The remainder of the property may be acquired for cash or other property without disqualifying the transaction as a C type reorganization. If any cash or other property is transferred, liabilities assumed with respect to acquired properties are treated as cash. (Code Sec. 368(a)(2)(B))[46] Preexisting ownership by an acquiring corporation of a portion of the target's stock does not, in and of itself, prevent the solely-for-voting-stock requirement from being satisfied. (Reg § 1.368-2(d)(4))[47]

For triangular reorganizations where at least one of the parties is foreign, see ¶3545.

---

38. ¶F-2201.2
39. ¶F-2201.2 *et seq.*; ¶3684.01
40. ¶F-2500 *et seq.*; ¶3684.02; TD ¶234,601 *et seq.*
41. ¶F-6649.2; ¶3674.04.
42. ¶F-2600 *et seq.*; ¶3684.03; TD ¶235,001

43. ¶F-2618; ¶3684.03; TD ¶235,018
44. ¶F-2618, F-2620; ¶3684.03; TD ¶235,020
45. ¶F-2629; ¶3684.03; TD ¶235,025
46. ¶F-2613; ¶3684.03; TD ¶235,014
47. ¶F-2617; ¶3684.03; TD ¶235,017

¶ 3547   Type D: Transfer of assets to subsidiary.

A Type D reorganization is the transfer by one corporation of all or part of its assets to a second corporation, if immediately after the transfer, the transferor and/or its shareholders are in "control" (¶3551) of the transferee corporation *and* the transferor either:

. . . under the plan of reorganization, distributes all of its assets (including stock and securities) of the transferee to its shareholders as a part of the transferor's liquidation ("acquisitive" or "nondivisive" D); or

. . . distributes the stock and securities of the transferee in a tax-free spin-off, split-off or split-up (corporate separation, or "divisive" D, see ¶3557 *et seq.*). (Code Sec. 368(a)(1)(D))[48]

This distribution requirement will be treated as satisfied, even if there is no actual distribution of stock or securities of the transferee corporation, if the same person or persons own, directly or indirectly, all of the stock of the transferor and transferee corporations in identical proportions. (Reg § 1.368-2T(l)(2))[49]

A Type D transaction may also qualify as a Type C, in which case it will be treated only as a Type D. (Code Sec. 368(a)(2)(A))[50]

An acquiring corporation's transfer of the target corporation's assets to a controlled subsidiary as part of a plan of reorganization won't prevent a transaction otherwise qualifying as a D reorganization from so qualifying. [1]

D reorganization treatment applies where, under an integrated plan, a parent corporation sells the stock of a wholly owned subsidiary for cash to another wholly owned subsidiary and the acquired subsidiary liquidates into the purchasing subsidiary. [2]

¶ 3548   Type E: Recapitalization.

A Type E reorganization is a "recapitalization" or change in the capital structure of a single corporation. (Code Sec. 368(a)(1)(E)) Recapitalizations include:

. . . issuance of preferred stock in discharge of outstanding bonds;

. . . exchanging one class of common for another class of common, or preferred for common (but new preferred may be Section 306 stock, see ¶3534), or vice-versa; (Reg § 1.368-2(e))

. . . exchanging old bonds for new bonds with a different face value, interest rate or the like;

. . . changes in stock or securities effected by a change in the corporate charter. [3]

¶ 3549   Type F: Change in Identity.

A Type F reorganization is limited to a change in identity, form or place of organization *of one corporation,* (Code Sec. 368(a)(1)(F)) but may include a reincorporation as part of a plan that includes a public stock offering, a merger, or a C reorganization. [4]

¶ 3550   Type G: Bankruptcy.

A Type G reorganization is the transfer by a corporation of all or part of its assets to another corporation (including a "bridge bank") under a court-approved reorganization plan in a Title 11 or similar case (e.g., bankruptcy, receivership, or foreclosure) but only if stock or

---

48. ¶s F-2004, F-2700 *et seq.*; ¶3684.04; TD ¶237,000
49. ¶F-2708
50. ¶s F-2004, F-2700 *et seq.*; ¶3684.04; TD ¶237,000
1. ¶F-2702.1

2. ¶F-2701.1
3. ¶F-3000 *et seq.*; ¶3684.05; TD ¶235,601
4. ¶F-3100 *et seq.*; ¶3684.06; TD ¶235,801

securities of the corporation to which the assets are transferred are distributed in a transaction that qualifies under Code Secs. 354, 355 or 356. (Code Sec. 368(a)(1)(G), Code Sec. 368(a)(3)(A))[5] The acquirer can use its parent's stock to acquire the debtor corporation, in a triangular Type G reorganization. (Code Sec. 368(a)(2)(D))[6]

¶ 3551 Control defined.

For purposes of the rules for reorganizations (other than nondivisive Type Ds, see below), "control" is the ownership of:

. . . stock possessing at least 80% of the total combined voting power of all voting stock, *and*

. . . at least 80% of the total number of shares of each class of nonvoting stock. (Code Sec. 368(c))[7]

If the Code Sec. 355 requirements for a tax-free corporate division are satisfied (¶3558), control for purposes of determining the tax treatment of transfers to the controlled corporation isn't affected by later transfers by shareholders of the distributed controlled corporation stock or by the fact that the corporation whose stock was distributed issues additional stock. (Code Sec. 368(a)(2)(H)(ii))[8]

For nondivisive Type Ds, "control" is defined under the related corporation redemption rules (i.e., 50%, rather than 80%, ownership, see ¶3533) (Code Sec. 368(a)(2)(H)(i))[9]

¶ 3552 How reorganization exchanges are taxed to shareholders.

If under a plan of reorganization, the holder of stock or securities receives in the exchange only stock in a corporation that's a party to the reorganization, the recipient recognizes no gain or loss. Nonrecognition also applies when securities of a corporate party to the reorganization are received in exchange for other securities, if the principal (face) amount of the securities received isn't more than the face amount given up. (Code Sec. 354(a)(1))[10] Nonqualified preferred stock (¶3554) received for stock that isn't nonqualified preferred stock isn't stock or securities for this purpose unless it's received in a recapitalization (¶3548) of a family-owned corporation. (Code Sec. 354(a)(2)(C))[11] (For nonqualified preferred stock and excess securities as "boot," see ¶3554.)

Stock rights (except rights to acquire nonqualified preferred stock (defined at ¶3554) (Reg § 1.356-6(a)(2)) not received as part of a family corporation recapitalization (¶3548) (Reg § 1.356-6(b)(1))) are treated as securities with no principal amount. (Reg § 1.354-1(e), Reg § 1.355-1(c))[12]

The nonrecognition rules don't apply to D or G reorganizations unless the transferee corporation receives substantially all of the transferor's assets, and the stock, securities and other property received by the transferor, as well as its remaining assets, are distributed by the transferor under the reorganization plan. (Code Sec. 354(b))[13]

If the nonrecognition rules would apply to an exchange but for the fact that property other than stock or securities is also received in the exchange (boot, see ¶3554), gain is recognized only up to the sum of the money and the fair market value of the other property received. (Code Sec. 356(a)(1))[14]

Gain recognized by a shareholder in a reorganization (i.e., where boot is received) is treated as a dividend if the exchange has the effect of a distribution. The gain is treated as ordinary income to the extent of the taxpayer's ratable share of the accumulated earnings and profits

5. ¶F-3200 *et seq.*; ¶3684.07; TD ¶236,001
6. ¶F-3207; ¶3684.07; TD ¶236,007
7. ¶F-4502, ¶F-5500 *et seq.*; ¶3684.13; TD ¶236,701
8. ¶F-4502; ¶3684.13; TD ¶237,003
9. ¶F-2702; ¶3684.13; TD ¶235,404

10. ¶F-4001, F-4022; ¶s 3544.01, 3544.03; TD ¶232,501
11. ¶F-4001, F-4001.1; ¶s 3544.01, 3544.03; TD ¶232,501
12. ¶F-4012; ¶3544.06; TD ¶232,514
13. ¶s F-2701, F-3205; ¶3544.02; TD ¶235,401
14. ¶F-4017; ¶3564.02; TD ¶232,529

of the distributing corporation. The balance is treated as gain from the sale or exchange of property. (Code Sec. 356(a)(2))[15] In determining if dividend treatment applies, the redemption tests, (¶3526 *et seq.*) are applied to the transaction as though the consideration paid in the reorganization were entirely in the form of acquirer stock, and as though, after the reorganization, the boot had been distributed in redemption of a portion of that stock. [16]

For basis of property received in the exchange, see ¶2488.

¶ 3553   How reorganization exchanges are taxed to corporate parties.

No gain or loss is recognized by a corporation that is a party to a reorganization (¶3542) that exchanges property solely for stock or securities of another corporation that is also a party to that reorganization. (Code Sec. 361(a))[17] If the corporation receives other property or money (boot, see ¶3554) in addition to stock or securities, then:

. . . if the recipient distributes all of the boot, it doesn't recognize gain on the exchange (but may recognize gain on the distribution of appreciated property, see below).

. . . if any part of the boot isn't distributed, gain is recognized on the exchange but only to the extent of the undistributed boot. (Code Sec. 361(b))[18]

Gain or loss isn't recognized on the distribution of "qualified property" received under the plan of reorganization. "Qualified property" is stock (or the right to acquire stock) in the distributing corporation, and stock or obligations of another party to the reorganization that are received in the reorganization exchange. Gain (but not loss) is recognized on the distribution of property that isn't qualified property. (Code Sec. 361(c))[19]

For acquirer's basis in property received in the exchange, see ¶2484. For target's basis, see ¶2486.

¶ 3554   Boot.

Boot is money or the fair market value (FMV) of property other than stock or securities of a party to the reorganization (¶3542) that's received by the target in exchange for its property, or by target shareholders in exchange for their stock, under the plan of reorganization. [20] Nonqualified preferred stock received for stock other than nonqualified preferred stock is boot unless received in a recapitalization of a family-owned corporation. (Code Sec. 356(e))[21] "Nonqualified preferred stock" is generally preferred stock that the issuer is required to redeem, or is more likely than not to redeem, or preferred stock with a dividend rate that varies with changes in interest rates or other similar indices.(Code Sec. 351(g)(2)).[22] For effect of liabilities, see ¶3555.

Securities in corporations not parties to the reorganization are always "boot" so that any gain on the exchange is taxable to the extent of the securities' FMV. For securities in corporations that are parties to the reorganization, only the excess face amount of securities received over the face amount of securities surrendered is boot. If no securities are surrendered, the FMV of any securities received is boot. (Code Sec. 354(a)(2), Code Sec. 356(d)) A stock right treated as a security having no principal amount (¶3552) isn't boot whether or not securities are surrendered in the exchange. (Reg § 1.356-3(b))[23]

---

15. ¶F-4017; ¶3564.02; TD ¶232,533
16. ¶F-4026; ¶3564.02; TD ¶244,000 *et seq.*
17. ¶F-4100 *et seq.*; ¶3614.01; TD ¶233,001
18. ¶F-4106 *et seq.*; ¶3614.01; TD ¶233,003
19. ¶F-4108 *et seq.*; ¶3614.03; TD ¶233,007

20. ¶F-4017; ¶3564.01; TD ¶231,305
21. ¶F-4001.1; ¶3564.01; TD ¶231,305
22. ¶F-1530; ¶3514.13; TD ¶231,306
23. ¶F-4021 *et seq.*; ¶3564.01; TD ¶238,006

¶ 3555   Assumption or transfer of liabilities.

Where a person that's a party to a reorganization (¶3542) exchanges property for stock or securities in a corporation, and the corporation also assumes the person's liabilities, the assumed liabilities aren't considered boot (¶3554) for the purpose of *recognizing* gain. (Code Sec. 357(a))[24]

But if the principal purpose for the assumption of the liabilities is tax avoidance, or is something other than a bona fide business purpose, *all* the liabilities assumed are treated as cash (i.e., boot) for purposes of both computing *and* recognizing gain. (Code Sec. 357(b))[25]

For a Type D reorganization (¶3547) where stock or securities of the transferee corporation are distributed in a transaction that qualifies as a tax-free separation under Code Sec. 355 (¶3557), if the sum of the liabilities assumed exceeds the total adjusted basis of the property transferred, the excess is taxed as a gain from the sale or exchange of property (capital gain or ordinary, depending on the character of the property in the hands of the transferor). (Code Sec. 357(c))[26]

For what constitutes assumption of a liability for these purposes, see ¶3516.

¶ 3556   Deductibility of reorganization costs.

Attorneys' fees and other expenses incurred in connection with a corporate reorganization aren't deductible business expenses but are capital expenditures (see ¶1654 *et seq.*) because they give a benefit to the corporation that extends beyond the year incurred. [27]

If a proposed reorganization is abandoned, the costs are deductible in the year of abandonment. [28]

¶ 3557   Spin-Offs, Split-Offs and Split-Ups. ▅▅▅▅▅▅▅▅▅▅▅▅▅▅▅▅

A corporate division may be accomplished on a tax-free basis in the form of a (1) *spin-off*, i.e., a pro rata distribution of a controlled corporation's stock to the distributing corporation's shareholders without requiring the shareholders to surrender any of their distributing corporation stock; (2) *split-off*, i.e., a pro rata or non pro rata distribution of a controlled corporation's stock to one or more of the distributing corporation's shareholders in exchange for stock held in the distributing corporation; or (3) *split-up*, i.e., a transfer of all the businesses of a distributing corporation to controlled corporations followed by a distribution of the stock of the controlled corporations to the distributing corporation's shareholders and the liquidation of the distributing corporation. The distribution of the stock of the controlled corporations to the distributing corporation's shareholders can be pro rata or non pro rata. [29]

¶ 3558   Requirements for a tax-free spin-off, split-off or split-up.

The requirements for a tax-free spin-off, split-off or split-up are as follows:

(1) The distributing corporation (P) must distribute to its shareholders with respect to their stock, or to its security holders in exchange for their securities, solely stock or securities in a corporation (S) that it "controls" (¶3551) immediately before the distribution. (Code Sec. 355(a)(1)) Nonqualified preferred stock (¶3514) received in exchange for other than nonqualified preferred stock is not stock or securities for this purpose. (Code Sec. 355(a)(3)(D))[30]

---

24. ¶F-4201; ¶3574.01; TD ¶231,501
25. ¶F-4202; ¶3574.02; TD ¶231,504
26. ¶F-4203; ¶3574.03; TD ¶233,203
27. ¶L-5401; ¶2484; TD ¶301,037

28. ¶L-5416; ¶2484; TD ¶301,047
29. ¶F-4600 *et seq.*; ¶3554.01; TD ¶237,001
30. ¶F-4608; ¶3544.01; TD ¶237,002

(2) The transaction must not be used principally as a device for distributing earnings and profits (E&P) of either P or S. (Code Sec. 355(a)(1)(B)) The regs specify "devise factors" (the presence of which are evidence of a device) and nondevice factors, and certain distributions that ordinarily aren't considered to have been used principally as a device even though device factors are present. (Reg § 1.355-2(d))[31]

(3) There must be a "continuity of interest" (¶3542). The pre-distribution shareholders of P must end up with an amount of stock which establishes a continuity of interest in both P and S, though not necessarily proportionately (see (6), below). (Reg § 1.355-2(c)(1))[32]

(4) Both P and S (or each controlled subsidiary) must be engaged immediately after the distribution in the active conduct of a trade or business (Code Sec. 355(b)(1)(A)) A corporation satisfies the active conduct of a trade or business test if, and only if, it is engaged in the active conduct of a trade or business, (Code Sec. 355(b)(3)(A)) with all members of the corporation's separate affiliated group being treated as one corporation. (Code Sec. 355(b)(3)(B))[33] These trades or businesses must have been actively conducted throughout the five-year period ending on the date the sub's stock is distributed. (Code Sec. 355(b)(2)(B))[34]

(5) The active trade or business in (4), above, must not have been acquired during the above five-year period in a transaction in which gain or loss was recognized. (Code Sec. 355(b)(2)(C))[35] IRS found that a distributing corporation failed this requirement despite the fact that it acquired an interest in an LLC's business in a tax-free Code Sec. 721(a) transaction (¶3710).[36]

(6) A distribution doesn't qualify as a tax-free Code Sec. 355 corporate division if immediately after the transaction (including any series of related transactions): (1) either the distributing or controlled corporation is a disqualified investment corporation, [37] and (2) any person that did not hold 50% or more of either the voting power or value of stock in the disqualified investment corporation immediately before the transaction holds a 50% or greater interest (voting or value). (Code Sec. Sec. 355(g))[38]

(7) P must distribute either all its stock or securities in S, or at least an amount of S stock that's treated as "control" (¶3551). The distributions don't have to be pro rata, or under a plan of reorganization. But if P retains *any* stock or securities in S, tax avoidance must not be a principal purpose for the retention. (Code Sec. 355(a)(1)(D), Code Sec. 355(a)(2))[39]

Even if all the above requirements are met, there must be one or more corporate business purposes for the transaction for it to be tax-free. (Reg § 1.355-2(b))[40] IRS has established guidelines for whether a corporate business purpose exists. [41]

¶ 3559   Boot in a Sec. 355 transaction—tax on shareholders.

The receipt of boot in an otherwise tax-free spin-off, split-off or split-up (¶3558) may trigger a tax on the shareholders. Boot includes cash and the fair market value of:

... *any property* (including stock warrants, short-term notes, etc.) *except* (subject to the limitations below) stock or securities (other than nonqualified preferred stock (¶3554) (Code Sec. 356(e)) in the spun-off corporation (S) (Code Sec. 356(a));

... *any excess in the face amount of securities* of S received over the face amount of securities in distributing corporation (P) which are surrendered. (Code Sec. 355(a)(3)(A), Code Sec. 356(d)(2)(C)) Stock rights are treated as securities having no principal amounts. (Reg § 1.355-1(c))

31. ¶F-4701 *et seq.*; ¶3554.01; TD ¶237,201
32. ¶F-4613; ¶3554.03; TD ¶237,014
33. ¶F-4802 *et seq.*; ¶3554.02; TD ¶237,426.1
34. ¶F-4819; ¶3554.02; TD ¶237,403
35. ¶F-4826 *et seq.*; ¶3554.02; TD ¶237,409
36. ¶F-4826

37. ¶F-5403; ¶3544.035
38. ¶F-5401; ¶3554.035;TD ¶237,004.1
39. ¶F-4602 *et seq.*; ¶3544.01; TD ¶237,007
40. ¶F-4900 *et seq.*; ¶3554.03; TD ¶237,701
41. ¶F-4902 *et seq.*; ¶3554.03; TD ¶237,702

...*stock in S* that P acquired in a partially or wholly taxable transaction during the five-year period preceding the distribution. (Code Sec. 355(a)(3)(B))[42]

Boot received in a spin-off (where no stock or securities of P are surrendered) is treated like a Code Sec. 301 dividend (¶1286). (Code Sec. 356(b))[43]

Boot received in a split-off or split-up (where stock or securities of P are surrendered) is taxable to the recipient to the extent gain is recognized, but not in excess of the value of the boot received. (Code Sec. 356(a)(1)) If, however, the exchange "has the effect of the distribution of a dividend," it is treated as a dividend to the extent of the taxpayer's ratable share of accumulated earnings and profits. The remainder, if any, of the recognized gain is generally treated as capital gain. (Code Sec. 356(a)(2))[44] In determining whether boot has the effect of a dividend, the transaction is treated as though the shareholder had retained the P stock which he actually surrendered in exchange for S stock, and had received the boot in exchange for an amount of P stock with a value equal to the amount of the boot; the redemption rules (¶3526 *et seq.*) are then applied to determine whether the boot is treated as a dividend. [45]

No loss is recognized, whether or not boot is received. (Code Sec. 355(a), Code Sec. 356(c))[46]

For shareholders' basis in property received, see ¶2488.

¶ 3560 How distributing corporation is taxed.

No gain or loss is recognized by a distributing corporation (P) on its distribution of stock or securities of a corporation it controls (S) in a tax-free corporate separation (Code Sec. 355(c)(1); Code Sec. 361) unless (1) the distribution is "disqualified" (below), in which case P recognizes gain (but not loss) as if the property were sold for its fair market value (FMV). If the property distributed is subject to a liability and the distributee assumes the liability, the FMV of the property will be treated as no less than the assumed liability. (Code Sec. 355(c)(2), Code Sec. 355(d)(1) *et seq.*)[47] or (2) pursuant to a "plan or series of related transactions" there is an acquisition (direct or indirect) of a 50% or greater interest in either the controlled or distributing corporation following the distribution, in which case the distributing corporation generally must recognize gain as if it had sold the stock or securities of the controlled corporation to the distributee for FMV immediately before the distribution. (Code Sec. 355(e)) Regs defining "a plan or a series of related transactions" for these purposes contain a number of safe-harbors that can be relied on to avoid triggering gain recognition under the above rules. (Reg § 1.355-7)[48] A tax-free division isn't available for distributions from one affiliated group member to another except as provided in regs, if the distribution is part of a plan under which anyone acquires (directly or indirectly) a 50% or greater interest in either the distributing or a controlled corporation, determined after application of Code Sec. 355(e). (Code Sec. 355(f))[49]

A distribution is "disqualified" (unless it doesn't violate the purpose of Code Sec. 355(d) (Reg § 1.355-6(c)(4)(i))) if: (1) immediately after the distribution any shareholder (or any two or more shareholders acting under a plan (Reg § 1.355-6(b)(3))) hold (actually or constructively) at least 50% of the stock of P or S, and (2) that stock was purchased (or acquired) within the immediately preceding five-year period, or was received as a distribution on P stock that was purchased (or acquired) within that period. (Code Sec. 355(c), Code Sec. 355(d))[50]

---

42. ¶F-5003 *et seq.*; ¶s 3554.01, 3564.02; TD ¶238,004 *et seq.*
43. ¶F-5000 *et seq.*; ¶3564.02; TD ¶238,004
44. ¶F-5000 *et seq.*; ¶3564.02; TD ¶238,003
45. ¶F-4026; ¶3564.02; TD ¶232,534
46. ¶F-5000 *et seq.*; ¶3564.02; TD ¶238,204

47. ¶F-5201 *et seq.*; ¶s 3554.01, 3554.04; TD ¶238,205
48. ¶F-5301; ¶s 3554 *et seq.*
49. ¶F-4630 *et seq.*; TD ¶237,004
50. ¶F-5202 *et seq.*; ¶3554.04; TD ¶238,404

¶ 3561   Carryovers of Tax Items.

A corporation that acquires the assets of another corporation in certain tax-free reorganizations or liquidations also carries over numerous tax items of the transferor (predecessor) corporation.

The predecessor's tax items are carried over to the successor corporation only in a:

. . . *Type A, C or F reorganization;*

. . . *Type D or G reorganization,* but only if the transferor transfers substantially all its assets to the acquiring corporation and then (in effect) completely liquidates; or

. . . *complete liquidation of an 80% subsidiary.* (Code Sec. 381(a))[1]

¶ 3562   Tax items that are carried over.

In transactions that come within the Code's carryover provisions, the acquiring corporation succeeds to and takes into account the following tax items of the transferor: (Code Sec. 381(c))[2] accounting method; amortization of bond discount or premium; capital loss carryovers; charitable contributions carryover; depreciation allowance and method; earnings and profits (E&P); employee benefit plan contributions; general business credit; installment method; inventory method; involuntary conversions; minimum tax credit; mining development and exploration expenses; net operating loss carryovers; percentage depletion on extraction of ores or minerals from waste or residue of earlier mining; personal holding company (PHC) deficiency dividend; PHC dividend carryover; real estate investment trust (REIT) or regulated investment company (mutual fund) deficiency dividend; tax benefit items; items under Subchapter U (dealing with enterprise zones), as prescribed by regs. [3]

Tax attributes to which an acquiring corporation succeeds, including the basis of property acquired, must reflect reductions for cancellation of debt. (Reg § 1.108-7(c))[4]

¶ 3563   Tax Avoidance Acquisition Bar to Tax Benefits.

Under Code Sec. 269, any deduction, credit or other allowance may be disallowed where, for the principal purpose of tax avoidance:

. . . any person or persons acquire, directly or indirectly, stock having at least 50% of the total combined voting power of all classes of a corporation's voting stock, or at least 50% of the total value of all classes of its stock; or

. . . any corporation acquires, directly or indirectly, property of another corporation not controlled, directly or indirectly, by the acquirer (or its shareholders) immediately before the acquisition, if the acquirer takes a carryover basis in the property. (Code Sec. 269(a))[5]

IRS may also apply these disallowances where a target that a corporation acquired in a qualified stock purchase *without* making a Code Sec. 338 election (¶3579) is liquidated primarily for tax avoidance or evasion, under a plan of liquidation adopted within two years after the acquisition date. (Code Sec. 269(b))[6]

¶ 3564   Limits On Use of Built-in Gains of One Corporation to Offset Losses of Another Corporation.

If one corporation is acquired by another corporation, limits are placed on the extent to which built-in gains of one of the corporations (gain corporation) can be used to offset the other corporation's pre-acquisition losses.

---

1. ¶F-7000 *et seq.*; ¶3814.01; TD ¶240,100
2. ¶F-7012; ¶3814.02; TD ¶240,101
3. ¶F-7012, F-7098, F-7099; ¶3814.02; TD ¶240,101
4. ¶J-7404.2; ¶1084.02; TD ¶188,016.1
5. ¶F-7900 *et seq.*; ¶2694; TD ¶240,702
6. ¶F-7923 *et seq.*; ¶2694; TD ¶240,703

If a corporation acquires directly (or through one or more other corporations) control of another corporation, or acquires the assets of another corporation in a Type A, C or D reorganization, and either corporation is a gain corporation, then any income of either corporation attributable to recognized built-in gain within a five year period beginning on the date of the ownership change (¶3569) can't be offset by any pre-acquisition loss of the other corporation. (Code Sec. 384(a))[7] Control means stock ownership that satisfies the requirements at ¶3343. (Code Sec. 384(c)(5))[8]

Similar rules limit the use of any excess credit or net capital loss. (Code Sec. 384(d))[9]

The offset prohibition rules don't apply to any pre-acquisition loss of any corporation if that corporation and the gain corporation were members of the same controlled group at all times during the five-year period ending on the acquisition date (or shorter period of either corporation's existence). (Code Sec. 384(b))[10]

¶ 3565   Trafficking in NOLs and Other Carryovers—Section 382 Limitation. ▰▰▰▰

If an ownership change occurs with respect to a loss corporation, that corporation's taxable income for any post-change year can be offset by pre-change losses only to the extent of a certain percent of the value of the corporation at the time of the change. Similar rules limit the use of capital loss carryovers and carryovers of certain credits.

¶ 3566   "Section 382 limitation" on use of loss carryforwards after ownership change.

The taxable income of a loss corporation for any tax year ending after an ownership change (¶3569) may be offset by pre-change loss carryforwards only to the extent of the Section 382 limitation for that year. (Code Sec. 382(a))[11] For limits on credit carryforwards, see ¶3570.

A loss corporation is a corporation entitled to use a net operating loss (NOL) carryover or having an NOL for the tax year in which the ownership change occurs. (Code Sec. 382(k)(1))[12]

The Section 382 limitation for any post-change year is equal to the value of the loss corporation immediately before the ownership change multiplied by the long-term tax-exempt rate (¶3567). (Code Sec. 382(b)(1))[13] Special rules apply to determine the value of the loss corporation. (Code Sec. 382(e)(1), Code Sec. 382(e)(2), Code Sec. 382(l)(1)(A), Code Sec. 382(l)(4))[14]

The Section 382 limitation for any year is (within limits) *increased* by any recognized built-in gain for the year if the loss corporation had net unrealized built-in gain, and by Code Sec. 338 gains recognized in that year. Recognized built-in gain is gain recognized on the disposition of an asset within a "recognition period" (the five-year period starting on the date of the ownership change), but only if the asset was held immediately before the change date and only to the extent of the excess of the asset's fair market value over its adjusted basis, on that date. (Code Sec. 382(h)(1))[15]

IRS has issued guidance on how to apply Code Sec. 382(h), consisting of two approaches taxpayers may use and rely on as safe harbors until final or temporary regs are issued. "The 1374 approach" generally incorporates the rules of Code Sec. 1374(d) under which built-in gain and loss are computed for the S corp tax on net unrecognized built-in gain (see ¶3365). Alternatively, "the 338 approach" generally identifies items of recognized built-in gain and loss by comparing the loss corporation's actual items of income, gain, deduction, and loss with those that would have resulted if a Code Sec. 338 election had been made with respect to a

---

7. ¶s F-7851, F-7852; ¶3844 *et seq.*; TD ¶240,801
8. ¶F-7853; ¶3844.01; TD ¶240,813
9. ¶F-7875 *et seq.*; ¶3844.04; TD ¶240,806
10. ¶F-7860 *et seq.*; ¶3844.01; TD ¶240,804
11. ¶F-7201; ¶3824.01; TD ¶240,302

12. ¶F-7203; ¶3824.01
13. ¶F-7251; ¶3824.12; TD ¶240,314
14. ¶F-7301 *et seq.*; ¶3824.12; TD ¶240,315
15. ¶F-7340 *et seq.*; ¶3824.25; TD ¶240,319

hypothetical purchase of all the outstanding stock of the loss corporation on the change date (see ¶3579).[16]

Special rules apply to determine the amount (and applicability) of the Section 382 limitation for the tax year in which the ownership change occurs. (Code Sec. 382(b)(3))[17]

The Section 382 limitation doesn't apply if the old loss corporation is under the jurisdiction of a court in a bankruptcy, receivership, foreclosure, or similar proceeding (unless it elects not to have this exception apply). (Code Sec. 382(l)(5); Reg § 1.382-9(i))[18]

Special rules apply for consolidated (Reg § 1.1502-90 to Reg § 1.1502-96, and Reg § 1.1502-98 to Reg § 1.1502-99) and controlled groups (Reg § 1.382-8), and for successive ownership changes. (Reg § 1.382-5(d))

¶ 3567 Long-term tax-exempt rate.

Long-term tax-exempt rate means the highest of the adjusted federal long-term rates in effect for any month in the three-calendar month period ending with the calendar month in which the ownership change occurs. (Code Sec. 382(f))[19] The long-term tax-exempt rate for ownership changes in:[20]

Nov. 2007 is 4.49%	July 2007 is 4.32%	Mar. 2007 is 4.18%
Oct. 2007 is 4.50%	June 2007 is 4.15%	Feb. 2007 is 4.14%
Sep. 2007 is 4.50%	May 2007 is 4.18%	Jan. 2007 is 4.15%
Aug. 2007 is 4.50%	Apr. 2007 is 4.18%	Dec. 2006 is 4.22%

¶ 3568 Pre-change losses and credits subject to Section 382 limitation.

The losses and credits that are subject to the Section 382 limitation (¶3566) are: (1) any net operating losses (NOLs) of the old loss corporation that are carried forward to the tax year ending with the ownership change or in which the change date occurs; (2) any NOL of the old loss corporation for the tax year in which the ownership change occurs to the extent the loss is allocable to the period in that year on or before the change date; (3) any recognized built-in loss for any tax year if a part of that tax year is in the recognition period. (¶3566); (4) any pre-change capital loss (below); and (5) any pre-change credits (below). (Code Sec. 382(d)(1); Reg § 1.382-2(a)(2))[21]

Pre-change capital losses are losses described in (1) –(3), above, but with respect to capital losses. (Reg § 1.383-1(c)(2))[22]

Pre-change credits are excess foreign taxes under Code Sec. 904(c), unused Code Sec. 38 business credits, and the available Code Sec. 53 minimum tax credit, to the extent attributable to periods ending on or before the change date. (Reg § 1.383-1(c)(3))[23]

¶ 3569 Ownership change defined.

There is an ownership change if, immediately after any owner shift involving a "5% shareholder" or an equity structure shift:

. . . the percentage of the stock of the loss corporation owned by one or more 5% shareholders has increased by more than 50 percentage points, over

. . . the lowest percentage of stock of the loss corporation owned by those shareholders at any time during a three-year testing period. (Code Sec. 382(g)(1))[24]

16. ¶F-7341 *et seq.*; ¶3824.25; TD ¶240,321
17. ¶F-7255 *et seq.*; ¶3824.12; TD ¶240,323
18. ¶F-7700 *et seq.*; ¶3824.26; TD ¶240,325
19. ¶F-7336; ¶3824.12; TD ¶240,316
20. ¶F-7336; ¶3824.12; TD ¶240,316

21. ¶F-7363; ¶s 3824, 3824.01, 3824.25
22. ¶F-7386; ¶3834.01; TD ¶240,329
23. ¶F-7408; ¶3834.01; TD ¶240,330
24. ¶F-7441; ¶3824.02; TD ¶240,303

A 5% shareholder is any person holding 5% or more (by value) of the stock of the corporation at any time during the testing period. (Code Sec. 382(h)(7)) Special aggregation rules treat groups of shareholders as though they were a single shareholder, for this purpose. (Reg § 1.382-2T)[25]

The percentage of stock owned is determined on the basis of value. Nonvoting preferred stock is generally not taken into account. (Code Sec. 382(k)(6))[26] But certain nonstock interests may be treated as stock. (Reg § 1.382-2T(f)(18)(iii))[27]

¶ 3570 Limitations on credit and capital loss carryforwards—Section 383 limitation.

Code Sec. 383 provides limitations on the use of unused general business credits, unused minimum tax credits, excess foreign taxes and net capital losses similar to the limits on net operating loss carryovers. If an ownership change occurs to a loss corporation, the Section 382 limitation (¶3566) for a post-change year applies to limit the amount of taxable income and regular tax liability that may be offset, respectively, by pre-change capital losses and pre-change credits (¶3568) of the new loss corporation. (Code Sec. 383; Reg § 1.383-1(b))[28]

¶ 3571 Order of absorption of Section 382 limitation.

A loss corporation must absorb its Section 382 limitation in the following order for each post-change year: (1) pre-change losses that are built-in capital losses recognized during that year, (2) pre-change losses that are capital loss carryovers, (3) pre-change losses that are built-in ordinary losses recognized during that year, (4) pre-change losses that are net operating loss carryovers, (5) pre-change credits for excess foreign taxes carried forward under Code Sec. 904(c), (6) pre-change credits that are unused general business credits carried over under Code Sec. 39, and (7) pre-change credits that are unused minimum tax credits under Code Sec. 53. (Reg § 1.383-1(d)(2))[29]

The losses absorb the Section 382 limitation on a dollar-for-dollar basis, but the credits must be converted to a "deduction equivalent" for this purpose. (Reg § 1.383-1(e)(2))[30]

¶ 3572 Corporate Liquidations. ▬▬▬▬▬▬▬▬▬▬▬▬

If a corporation distributes its assets to its shareholders in complete liquidation, the shareholders generally recognize capital gain or loss on the receipt of the distributions. A corporation generally recognizes taxable gain or loss on the distribution or sale of property in liquidation.

¶ 3573 Shareholder's tax on liquidating distributions.

Amounts received by a shareholder in a distribution in complete liquidation of a corporation are treated as payment in exchange for the stock. (Code Sec. 331(a))[31]

observation: This means that a distribution in complete liquidation usually results in capital gain or loss to the shareholder.

Gain or loss is the total amount distributed less the shareholder's basis for his stock. (Reg § 1.331-1(b)) The amount of the distribution is the sum of the cash plus the fair market value of any other property (reduced by any liability assumed) received by the shareholder in exchange for his stock. (Code Sec. 1001(b))[32]

---

25. ¶F-7500 *et seq.*; ¶3824.15
26. ¶F-7505 *et seq.*; ¶s 3824.01, 3824.10; TD ¶240,303
27. ¶F-7603; ¶3824.10; TD ¶240,312
28. ¶F-7400 *et seq.*; ¶E-8953.1; ¶3834.01; TD ¶240,328

29. ¶F-7360, F-7405; ¶3834.01; TD ¶240,331
30. ¶F-7361, F-7404; ¶3834.01; TD ¶240,331
31. ¶F-13101; ¶3314.01; TD ¶245,401
32. ¶F-13108; ¶3314.01; TD ¶245,402

A shareholder who receives a series of distributions in complete liquidation of the corporation reports his gain only after he first recovers the cost or other basis of all his stock. [33]

For basis of property received in the distribution, see ¶2490.

¶ 3574   How corporations are taxed on liquidation.

A liquidating corporation recognizes taxable gain or loss on distributions of property as if the property had been sold to the distributee for its fair market value (FMV). (Code Sec. 336(a)) If the distributed property is subject to a liability, or if any shareholder assumes a liability of the liquidating corporation in connection with the distribution, the property's FMV is treated as not less than the amount of the liability. (Code Sec. 336(b))[34]

There are exceptions to recognition of gain or loss for certain liquidating distributions:

. . . by 80%-owned subsidiaries to the parent corporation, see ¶3575; or

. . . in connection with tax-free reorganizations, see ¶3551, ¶3558. (Code Sec. 336(c))[35]

¶ 3575   Liquidation of 80% subs.

When a parent corporation completely liquidates its 80%-owned sub, the *parent* (as shareholder) doesn't recognize gain or loss on the liquidating distributions (Code Sec. 332(a)), whether the distributions are of *cash* or other property,[36] if the following requirements are met:

(1) The parent must own at least 80% of the sub's total voting stock and at least 80% of the total value of all the sub's stock, on the date the plan of liquidation is adopted and until the final liquidating distribution is received. (Code Sec. 332(b)(1))[37]

(2) The distributions must be made under a plan of *complete* liquidation, and in complete redemption of all of the sub's stock. (Code Sec. 332(b)(2), Code Sec. 332(b)(3))[38]

(3) If the sub distributes all its assets in complete liquidation *in one tax year,* its liquidation plan or resolution needn't specify a completion time. But if complete distribution doesn't occur within one tax year, the plan must specifically provide for all liquidating distributions to be made within three years from the close of the tax year in which the first distribution is made. (Code Sec. 332(b); Reg § 1.332-4(a))[39]

If the above requirements are met, the parent will *carry over* the sub's basis in the assets distributed. (Code Sec. 334(b)(1))[40] Special rules apply to debt owed to the parent by its sub. (Reg § 1.332-7)[41]

Where a distribution from a regulated investment company (RIC) or a real estate investment trust (REIT) qualifies as a distribution in complete liquidation of the RIC or REIT under Code Sec. 332(b),[42] the corporation receiving the distribution is required to include in income as a dividend from the RIC or REIT an amount equal to the dividends-paid deduction allowable to the RIC or REIT by reason of the distribution. [43] (Code Sec. 332(c))

Minority shareholders don't qualify for nonrecognition. They must recognize gain or loss under the regular liquidation rules (¶3573). (Reg § 1.332-5)[44]

---

33. ¶F-13112; ¶3314.01; TD ¶245,406
34. ¶F-14401 *et seq.*; ¶3364.01; TD ¶245,201 *et seq.*
35. ¶F-14401 *et seq.*; ¶3364.01; TD ¶233,011
36. ¶F-13200 *et seq.*; ¶3324; TD ¶245,701
37. ¶F-13202 *et seq.*; ¶3324.01; TD ¶245,703
38. ¶F-13207 *et seq.*; ¶3324.01; TD ¶245,714

39. ¶F-13209; ¶3324.01; TD ¶245,712
40. ¶F-13227 *et seq.*; ¶3344.01; TD ¶245,733
41. ¶F-13216; ¶3324.01; TD ¶245,737
42. ¶F-13201; ¶3324.02; TD ¶245,701
43. ¶D-3800 *et seq.*; ¶D-3828
44. ¶F-13223; ¶3324.01; TD ¶245,738

¶ 3576   How 80% subsidiary is taxed on liquidating distributions.

A liquidating sub doesn't recognize any gain or loss on liquidating distributions to its 80% distributee-parent, but it recognizes gain (but not loss) on distributions to minority shareholders. (Code Sec. 336(d)(3), Code Sec. 337(a))[45] However, a C corporation generally recognizes gain on property converted to RIC or REIT property unless the RIC or REIT elects to be subject to Code Sec. 1374 (¶3365) built-in gain treatment. (Reg § 1.337(d)-7(c)(1))

¶ 3577   Taxation of asset transfer to exempt entity or change to exempt entity status.

A corporation must recognize gain or loss on either the transfer of its assets to a tax-exempt entity or on a change in the corporation's status from taxable to tax-exempt, subject to a number of exceptions. (Reg § 1.337(d)-4).[46]

¶ 3578   Deductibility of costs of corporate dissolution and liquidation.

Filing fees, attorney's and accountant's fees and other expenditures, including payments for tax advice, incurred in connection with the complete liquidation and dissolution of a corporation are generally deductible in full by the dissolved corporation. [47]

¶ 3579   Code Sec. 338 Election to Treat a Stock Purchase as an Asset Purchase. ▰▰▰▰

A corporate acquirer that makes a qualified stock purchase of the stock of another corporation (target) may be able to get a stepped-up basis for the target's assets by making a Code Sec. 338 election to treat the stock purchase as an asset purchase.

⚡observation: The Code Sec. 338 election can best be used where the target has losses to offset gains, owns predominantly depreciated property, or will benefit from stepped-up basis through deductions for depreciation or amortization.

⚡caution: If a Code Sec. 338 election is made, the target may have to recognize gain from the "sale" of its assets (see ¶3580). In addition, if the seller's basis in the target stock is less than the stock's fair market value, the seller must recognize gain on the sale of the stock.

For "qualified stock purchase" requirement, see ¶3581.

For consistency requirement, see ¶3582.

For an election where a target is a member of a consolidated return group, see ¶3584.

For how and when to make the Code Sec. 338 election, see ¶3583.

¶ 3580   Effect of Code Sec. 338 election.

If the Code Sec. 338 election is made, the target is treated (for tax purposes only) as two corporations: an "old target," and a "new target." The old target is treated as though it had sold its assets as of the close of the acquisition date for their fair market value (FMV) (i.e., the "aggregate deemed sale price") in a single transaction. (Code Sec. 338(a)(1); Reg § 1.338-4(a))[48]

⚡observation: Gain or loss is recognized by old target on the deemed sale to the extent of the difference between the FMV of the old target's assets and its basis in those assets.

---

45. ¶F-14500 *et seq.*; ¶3374.01; TD ¶246,201
46. ¶F-14609 *et seq.*; ¶3374.03
47. ¶L-5500 *et seq.*; ¶2484; TD ¶301,048
48. ¶s F-8301, F-8302; ¶3384.05; TD ¶239,018

The new target is treated as though it had purchased all of the assets of the old target as of the beginning of the day after the acquisition date (Code Sec. 338(a)(2)), for an amount equal to the sum of: the grossed-up basis of the acquirer's recently purchased stock, the basis of the acquirer's nonrecently purchased stock, the target's liabilities, and other relevant items. This sum (as adjusted) is the target's "adjusted grossed-up basis" for the assets. (Code Sec. 338(b)(1), Code Sec. 338(b)(2); Reg § 1.338-5(b)(1))[49]

The acquirer may step-up its basis in the target's assets by making a "gain recognition election" (on Form 8023, see ¶3583). (Code Sec. 338(b)(3); Reg § 1.338-5(d)(3))[50] Regs specify how basis is allocated among the target's assets. (Code Sec. 338(b)(5); Reg § 1.338-6)[1]

¶ 3581   "Qualified stock purchase" requirement.

The Code Sec. 338 election may be made only if the acquirer makes a qualified stock purchase of the target. (Code Sec. 338(a))[2]

A qualified stock purchase means one corporation's (acquirer's) purchase, in one or more transactions during a 12-month acquisition period, of another (target) corporation's stock, if the shares so purchased have at least 80% of the target's total combined voting power and at least 80% of the value of all the target's stock. (Code Sec. 338(d)(3))[3]

¶ 3582   Consistency as to purchases from target or target affiliate.

The Code provides that purchases by a purchasing corporation with respect to a target or a target affiliate must be treated consistently (all as stock purchases or all as asset purchases) if made within a consistency period (below). (Code Sec. 338(e), Code Sec. 338(f)) But under the regs, the consistency rules apply only where gain on the sale of an asset (or stock in a Code Sec. 338(h)(10) election, see ¶3584) results in a step-up in the seller's basis in the target's stock under the consolidated return regs. And the rules (instead of resulting in a deemed election) require the acquirer to take a carryover basis in the acquired stock. (Reg § 1.338-5(a))[4]

observation: A corporation recognizes gain on a sale in liquidation of the corporation. The consistency rules are limited to specific situations where the gain on the appreciated assets of the corporation isn't fully taxed.

Consistency period means the period consisting of: (1) the one-year period before the beginning of the 12-month acquisition period, (2) that part of the acquisition period up to and including the acquisition date (i.e., the date on which the last purchase of stock needed to complete a qualified stock purchase is made) and (3) the one-year period beginning on the day after the acquisition date. (Code Sec. 338(h)(4)(A))[5]

¶ 3583   Making the Code Sec. 338 election—Form 8023.

The acquirer makes the Code Sec. 338 election on Form 8023 on or before the 15th day of the ninth month beginning after the month in which the acquisition date occurs. (Code Sec. 338(g)(1), Code Sec. 338(g)(2); Reg § 1.338-2(d))[6] Once made, the election is irrevocable. (Code Sec. 338(g)(3))[7]

49. ¶F-8601 *et seq.*; ¶3384.09; TD ¶239,021
50. ¶F-8511; ¶3384.09; TD ¶239,023
1. ¶F-8601; ¶3384.10; TD ¶212,004.1
2. ¶F-8101; ¶3384; TD ¶239,013
3. ¶F-8101; ¶3384.02; TD ¶239,002

4. ¶F-8201 *et seq.*; ¶3384.11; TD ¶239,015
5. ¶F-8917; ¶3384.11; TD ¶239,017
6. ¶F-8831 *et seq.*; ¶3384.01TD ¶239,027
7. ¶F-8833; ¶3384.01; TD ¶239,027

¶ 3584 Election by selling consolidated group to recognize gain or loss on deemed sale of target's assets—Code Sec. 338(h)(10) election.

If a qualified stock purchase (¶3581) of the stock of a member of a selling consolidated return group (selling group) is made, the acquirer and the selling group can jointly elect (on Form 8023, see ¶3583) to have the selling group recognize (and report) gain or loss as though the target sold all of its assets in a single taxable transaction while still a member of the selling group. (Code Sec. 338(h)(10); Reg § 1.338(h)(10)-1(c))[8]

In addition, making the Code Sec. 338(h)(10) election will have these tax effects:

. . . No gain or loss will be recognized by the selling group on the actual sale of target stock in a qualified stock purchase.

. . . The target is treated as if, at the close of the acquisition date but after the deemed sale, it had distributed all of its assets in a complete liquidation under Code Sec. 331 (¶3574), or under the 80% sub liquidation rules (¶3575).

. . . If the acquirer owns nonrecently purchased target stock, it is deemed to have made a "gain recognition election" with respect to that stock.

. . . The acquirer's adjusted gross-up basis in the target is determined under the rules described at ¶3580, with adjustments. (Reg § 1.338(h)(10)-1(d))[9]

¶ 3585 Collapsible Corporation Rules Repealed. ▬▬▬▬▬

The Jobs and Growth Tax Relief Reconciliation Act of 2003 (P.L. #108-27, 5/28/03) repealed the collapsible corporation rules, effective for tax years beginning after 2002 and before 2009. Before the enactment of P.L. 108-27, these rules denied capital gain treatment for shareholders' gains from the liquidation (or sale of stock) of their corporation where the profit was attributable to ordinary income assets of the corporation.

¶ 3586 Transfers to Foreign Corporations—Code Sec. 367 Transfers. ▬▬▬▬

The transfer of property to a foreign corporation by a U.S. person generally won't qualify as a tax-free reorganization because the foreign corporation won't be treated as a corporation for U.S. tax purposes. (Code Sec. 367(a)(1))

This general rule applies to transfers and exchanges under Code Sec. 332 (complete liquidations of a subsidiary); Code Sec. 351 (transfers to a controlled corporation); Code Sec. 354 (tax-free reorganizations, including Type A reorgs); Code Sec. 356 (reorganizations and spin-offs, etc., with boot); Code Sec. 361 (reorganizations); and Code Sec. 355 (spin-offs, split-offs and split-ups), where corporate status is essential for the operation of the nonrecognition rules. (Code Sec. 367(a)(1), Code Sec. 367(c))[10]

This gain recognition rule does not apply, however, to transfers of

. . . stock or securities of a foreign corporation to a foreign corporation that is party to an exchange or reorganization provided certain requirements are met; (Code Sec. 367(a)(2); Reg § 1.367(a)-3(b))[11]

. . . stock or securities of a domestic corporation to a foreign corporation provided certain requirements are met; (Reg § 1.367(a)-3(c))[12]

. . . property used in the active conduct of a trade or business outside the U.S., if reporting requirements are met. (Code Sec. 367(a)(3); Reg § 1.367(a)-2T)) Subject to basis adjustments and any other conditions, the active business exception applies in the case of an

---

8. ¶F-8820 *et seq.*; ¶3384.075; TD ¶239,031
9. ¶F-8800 *et seq.*; ¶s 3384.075, 3384.09; TD ¶239,031
10. ¶F-6000 *et seq.*; ¶3674.01

11. ¶F-6201 *et seq.*; ¶3674.02
12. ¶F-6209; ¶3674.02

exchange described in Code Sec. 361(a) or (b), if the transferor corporation is controlled by five or fewer domestic corporations. (Code Sec. 367(a)(5))[13] Inventory and certain other types of property can't be transferred free of tax, even if they are used in the active conduct of a trade or business. (Code Sec. 367(a)(3)(B)(i))[14]

. . . certain property designated in regs in order to carry out the purposes of these rules. (Code Sec. 367(a)(6))

In addition, if, in a Code Sec. 354 or Code Sec. 356 exchange, a U.S. person exchanges stock or securities of a foreign corporation in a Type E reorganization, or U.S. person exchanges stock or securities of a domestic or foreign corporation for stock of a foreign corporation in an asset reorganization that is not treated as an indirect stock transfer, [15] the exchange is not a transfer to a foreign corporation subject to Code Sec. 367(a). (Reg § 1.367(a)-3(a))[16]

Special rules apply where the assets of a U.S. person's foreign branch are transferred to a foreign corporation. (Code Sec. 367(a)(3)(C))[17]

Special rules apply to Code Sec. 355 spin-offs, etc. (Code Sec. 367(e)(1))[18]

Special rules apply to liquidations into a foreign parent. (Code Sec. 367(e)(2)) (Reg § 1.367(e)-2)

Some of the above exceptions to the Code Sec. 367(a) gain recognition rule require the filing of a gain recognition agreement (GRA) under which the U.S. transferor agrees to include in income the gain realized but not recognized on the initial transfer if certain events (triggering events) occur before the close of the fifth full tax year following the year of the transfer. (Reg § 1.367(a)-3)[19]

Temporary regs provide that certain nonrecognition transactions (including asset reorganizations and nontaxable liquidations) occurring after Mar. 6, 2007, are not triggering events, if certain requirements are satisfied. (Reg § 1.367(a)-8T)[20]

To the extent provided in regs, if a U.S. person transfers property to a foreign corporation as paid-in surplus or a contribution to capital in a transaction not otherwise described in Code Sec. 367, the transfer is treated as a sale or exchange for the fair market value of the property, and the transferor must recognize as gain the excess of the property's fair market value over the adjusted basis. (Code Sec. 367(f))

Special rules apply for carrying over of tax attributes (¶3561 and ¶3562) to the acquiring corporation in reorganizations and liquidations involving foreign corporations. (Reg § 1.367(b)-2, Reg § 1.367(b)-3, Reg § 1.367(b)-6, Reg § 1.367(b)-7 and Reg § 1.367(b)-9)[21]

When a U.S. person transfers intangibles to a foreign corporation in a Code Sec. 351 or Code Sec. 361 transaction, the transferor is treated as having sold the property for contingent payments, and recognizes ordinary income reflecting those payments over the life of the property. (Code Sec. 367(d))[22]

---

13. ¶F-6128; ¶3674.02
14. ¶F-6101 *et seq.*; ¶3674.02
15. ¶F-6227; ¶3674.02
16. ¶F-6201; ¶3674.02
17. ¶F-6129 *et seq.*; ¶3674.02

18. ¶F-6801; ¶3674.01
19. ¶F-6300; ¶3674.01 *et seq.*; TD ¶644,714
20. ¶F-6311 *et seq.*; ¶3674.02
21. ¶F-6912
22. ¶F-6501 *et seq.*; ¶3674.03

Chapter 17   Partnerships

¶ 3700   Partnerships. ▆▆▆▆▆▆▆▆▆▆

For tax purposes, a partnership is a business entity that has elected, or defaulted to, partnership classification under "check-the-box" entity classification regulations.

¶ 3701   Partnership defined.

A "partnership" includes a syndicate, group, pool, joint venture or other unincorporated organization through, or by means of which, any business, financial operation or venture is carried on if it isn't, within the meaning of the Code, a corporation, trust or estate. (Code Sec. 761(a))[1] Under the "check-the-box" entity classification regs, a partnership is a business entity, with two or more members, that isn't mandatorily classified as a corporation, and that has elected, or defaulted to, partnership tax status. (Reg § 301.7701-2(c))[2] Under default provisions, unless a domestic eligible entity elects otherwise, it's a partnership if it has two or more members. (Reg § 301.7701-3(b)(1)(i))[3] In general, an eligible entity that wishes to elect a classification other than its default classification, or that wishes to change its classification, does so by filing Form 8832. (Reg § 301.7701-3(c)(1)(i))[4] A partnership that changes to an association is deemed to contribute all of its assets and liabilities to the association in exchange for stock in it. Then, the partnership is deemed to liquidate by distributing the stock to its partners. (Reg § 301.7701-3(g)(1)(i))[5] An eligible entity classified as a partnership becomes disregarded as an entity separate from its owner when the entity's membership is reduced to one member. (Reg § 301.7701-3(f)(2).[6] A qualified joint venture conducted by a husband and wife who file a joint return for the tax year is not treated as a partnership for tax purposes if the spouses so elect. (Code Sec. 761(f)(1))[7]

For tax years of a partnership, see ¶2812.

For partnership tax returns (including Schedule K-1 (Form 1065)), see ¶4733.

¶ 3702   Electing large partnerships.

Simplified flow-through reporting (Form 1065-B) applies for an electing large partnership, i.e., a partnership with at least 100 partners in the prior tax year that elects simplified reporting under Code Sec. 771 through Code Sec. 777. (Code Sec. 775(a)(1))[8] These rules differ from the regular rules for tax partners (¶3715 *et seq.*), in that, for example, fewer partnership items pass through to partners (Code Sec. 772)[9] and limitations on deductions and credits generally are applied at the partnership level. (Code Sec. 773)[10]

¶ 3703   Limited liability companies (LLCs).

Limited liability companies (LLCs) are a creation of state law. LLCs are owned (in some cases managed) by members, who aren't personally liable for the LLC's debts or obligations. [11]

Under the "check-the-box" entity classification rules (¶3701), if an LLC isn't mandatorily classified as a corporation, it's an "eligible entity" that may elect (on Form 8832) to be classified for tax purposes either as a partnership or as a corporation (Reg § 301.7701-2(c)), except that a single member LLC that doesn't elect to be a corporation is treated as not

---

1. ¶B-1000 *et seq.*; ¶7614.01, 7614.03; TD ¶580,101
2. ¶D-1151; ¶77,014.15; TD ¶580,501
3. ¶D-1152; ¶77,014.15; TD ¶580,521
4. ¶D-1158; ¶77,014.15; TD ¶580,511
5. ¶D-1170; ¶77,014.155; TD ¶580,517
6. ¶D-1171; ¶77,014.165; TD ¶580,505

7. ¶B-1222; ¶7614.02
8. ¶B-4401 *et seq.*; ¶7754; TD ¶594,101
9. ¶B-4402 *et seq.*; ¶7724; TD ¶594,112
10. ¶B-4410 *et seq.*; ¶7734; TD ¶594,109
11. ¶D-1150 *et seq.*; TD ¶582,500 *et seq.*

References beginning with a single letter are to paragraphs in RIA's Federal Tax Coordinator 2d and RIA's Analysis of Federal Taxes: Income. Those beginning with numbers are to paragraphs in RIA's United States Tax Reporter. Those beginning with TD are to paragraphs in RIA's Tax Desk.

having any entity status, i.e., it can't be treated as a partnership. (Reg § 301.7701-2(a), Reg § 301.7701-2(c)(2)(i))[12]

⊙ observation: If an LLC is characterized as a partnership for federal tax purposes, the limited liability company form will offer the flow-through of tax attributes, as well as limited liability. Pass-through of tax attributes and limited liability are also available to S corporations. S corporations are, however, subject to many restrictions, including restrictions on the number and kind of shareholders, which don't apply to limited liability companies.

¶ 3704 Family partnerships.

If capital isn't a material income-producing factor, a family member is recognized as a partner only if he contributes substantial services. [13]

If capital is a material income-producing factor in the enterprise, a valid family partnership may be created by gift of a capital interest. (Code Sec. 704(e)(1))[14]

The donee-partner's distributive share of partnership income is included in his gross income subject to two limitations:

... It must be determined after allowance of reasonable compensation for services rendered to the partnership by the donor.

... The donee's share attributable to donated capital must not be proportionately greater than the donor's share attributable to his capital. (Code Sec. 704(e)(2))[15]

A capital interest purchased from a partner by the partner's spouse, ancestor, lineal descendant or any trust for the primary benefit of such persons, is considered to be a gift of the partnership interest by the seller to the buyer. (Code Sec. 704(e)(3))[16]

A donee or purchaser of a capital interest in a family partnership isn't recognized as a partner unless the transfer to him is bona fide. (Reg § 1.704-1(e)(1)(iii))[17]

A minor child generally won't be recognized as a partner unless either: (1) the child is shown to be competent (despite legal disability under state law) to manage his or her own property, or (2) control of the child's interest is exercised by a fiduciary for the child's sole benefit, subject to any required judicial supervision. (Reg § 1.704-1(e)(2)(viii))[18]

¶ 3705 Election to be excluded from partnership rules.

Certain unincorporated organizations can elect to be excluded from the partnership rules, i.e., exempt from Subchapter K of the Code (or only some of those provisions under a partial exclusion election). The election is available only if the income of each separate member of the partnership can be adequately determined without computation of partnership taxable income. (Code Sec. 761(a); Reg § 1.761-2(a)(1))[19] The election is available for:

... "Investing partnerships" whose members own property as co-owners, reserve the right separately to dispose of their share of property, and aren't engaged in the active conduct of a business. (Reg § 1.761-2(a)(2))[20]

... "Operating agreement groups" under which a number of co-owners engage in the joint production, extraction or use of property, but not for the purpose of selling services or property produced or extracted. (Reg § 1.761-2(a)(3))[21]

... Syndications formed for a short period by dealers in securities to underwrite, sell or

12. ¶D-1167; ¶77,014.15
13. ¶B-3422; ¶7044.17; TD ¶588,713
14. ¶B-3402; ¶7044.14; TD ¶588,702
15. ¶B-3423; ¶7044.12; TD ¶588,714
16. ¶B-3426; ¶7044.11; TD ¶588,702

17. ¶B-3408; ¶7044.15; TD ¶588,706
18. ¶B-3416; ¶7044.15; TD ¶588,708
19. ¶B-1200 *et seq.*; ¶7614.02; TD ¶581,006
20. ¶B-1207; ¶7614.02; TD ¶581,012
21. ¶B-1208; ¶7614.02; TD ¶581,013

distribute an issue of securities. (Code Sec. 761(a)(3))[22]

¶ 3706 Partnerships v. other forms of doing business.

Partnerships are "pass-through entities" —that is, their income is subject to tax only once, at the partner level. They share this characteristic with S corporations, but not C corporations (whose income is taxed twice, at the corporate and again at the shareholder level). Partnerships also offer these advantages over S corporations:

. . . There are no limitations on who may be a partner, or on how many persons may be partners, unlike an S corporation, which is subject to limitations on who may be a shareholder and on how many shareholders the corporation may have, see ¶3354.

. . . There is far greater flexibility in allocating the enterprise's profits, losses and credits (by means of special allocations, see ¶3724 *et seq.*) among partners of a partnership than among shareholders of an S corporation, see ¶3370.

. . . A partner's basis in his partnership interest, unlike a shareholder's basis in S corporation shares, includes the partner's share of partnership liabilities, see ¶3759 *et seq.*

¶ 3707 Organization and syndication fees.

No deduction is allowed to a partnership or to any partner for any amounts paid or incurred to organize a partnership or to promote the sale of, or to sell, an interest in that partnership, except as described below. (Code Sec. 709(a))[23]

A partnership may elect to deduct in the tax year it begins business up to $5,000 of its organization expenses. The $5,000 amount is reduced (but not below zero) by the amount, if any, by which the total of the organization expenses exceeds $50,000. Organization expenses in excess of the amount deductible in the year the partnership begins business are deductible ratably over the 180-month period beginning with the month in which it begins business. If a partnership is liquidated before the end of the 180-month period, any organization expenses not yet deducted may be deducted as a loss. (Code Sec. 709(b)(1))

For amounts paid or incurred before Oct. 23, 2004, the organization expenses could, at the partnership's election (use Form 4562, together with election statement as specified in the regs), be amortized over not less than 60 months, starting the month the partnership began business. Any unamortized expenses could be deducted as a loss if the partnership is liquidated before the end of the 60-month period. [24]

Syndication expenses aren't amortizable and must be capitalized. They are expenses connected with the marketing of interests in the partnership. (Reg § 1.709-2(b)) Syndication expenses can't be deducted as a loss when the partnership is liquidated (Reg § 1.709-1(b)(2)) or the syndication effort is abandoned. [25]

For an election to deduct start-up costs, see ¶1501.

¶ 3708 Partnership anti-abuse rules.

If a partnership is formed or used in connection with a transaction with a principal purpose of substantially reducing the present value of the partners' total tax liability in a manner that is inconsistent with the intent of subchapter K, IRS may recast the transaction as appropriate to achieve a tax result that is consistent with the intent of subchapter K. [26] These anti-abuse rules apply only with respect to federal income taxes. (Reg § 1.701-2(h))[27]

22. ¶B-1215; ¶7614.02
23. ¶B-1301; ¶7094; TD ¶581,201
24. ¶B-1302; ¶7094.01; TD ¶581,202

25. ¶B-1308; ¶7094.04; TD ¶581,207
26. ¶B-1251; ¶7014; TD ¶580,107
27. ¶B-1250 *et seq.*; ¶7014; TD ¶580,107

IRS also may treat a partnership as an aggregate of its partners, in whole or in part, (except as described below) as appropriate in order to carry out the purpose of any provision of the Code or regs. (Reg § 1.701-2(e)(1)) But IRS may not treat a partnership as an aggregate to the extent that:

(1) a Code or reg provision prescribes the treatment of a partnership (in whole or in part) as an entity and

(2) that treatment and the ultimate tax results, taking into account all the relevant facts and circumstances, are clearly contemplated by that provision. (Reg § 1.701-2(e)(2))[28]

¶ 3709   Treatment of Contributions to a Partnership. ▬▬▬▬▬▬▬

Contributions from a partner to a partnership are generally tax-free.

¶ 3710   Contributions to a partnership.

Whether contributions to a partnership's capital are made on formation of the partnership or later no gain or loss is ordinarily recognized to the partners or the partnership. (Code Sec. 721; Reg § 1.721-1) However, this rule doesn't apply where a partner acts in his individual capacity (not in his capacity as a partner) in a transaction with the partnership (¶3729); a partner contributes property to a partnership and the partnership assumes a liability of the partner, with the resulting decrease in the partner's liabilities being treated as a distribution of money to the contributing partner (¶3744); or in the situations listed at ¶3711 *et seq.*[29] Also, IRS has regulatory authority (1) to provide for gain recognition in cases where the gain would otherwise be transferred to foreign partners (Code Sec. 721(c)) and (2) to treat intangibles transferred to a foreign partnership as sold. (Code Sec. 721(d)) Depreciation recapture isn't triggered (Code Sec. 1245(b)(3), Code Sec. 1245(b)(6), Code Sec. 1250(d)(3))[30] and investment credit isn't recaptured as long as the transfer is a mere change in the form of conducting the business of the contributing partner. (Reg § 1.47-3(f)(6), Ex (5))[31]

For gain or loss on the distribution of contributed built-in gain or loss property, see ¶3752.

¶ 3711   Exchange fund partnerships.

Gain is recognized where a transfer of appreciated stocks, securities or other property is made to a partnership that would be treated as an investment company under Code Sec. 351 were the partnership a corporation. (Code Sec. 721(b)) The partnership is treated as an investment company if, after the exchange, over 80% of the value of its assets (excluding cash and nonconvertible debt) are held for investment and are readily marketable stocks or securities (or interests in REITs or in regulated investment companies). Specified categories of assets are treated as "stock and securities" and are taken into account, whether or not marketable, in determining investment company status. [32]

¶ 3712   Contribution of services.

Where a taxpayer receives a capital interest in a partnership in exchange for services, that interest is taxable compensation income to him. When the income must be recognized depends on the facts and circumstances, including whether there are any restrictions on the taxpayer's right to withdraw from the partnership or otherwise dispose of the partnership interest. (Reg § 1.721-1(b)(1))[33]

---

28. ¶B-1255; ¶7014; TD ¶580,109
29. ¶B-1401; ¶7214; TD ¶581,401
30. ¶s I-10311, I-10503; ¶7214.01; TD ¶223,114

31. ¶L-17418; ¶474.03; TD ¶381,409
32. ¶B-1410; ¶7214.02; TD ¶581,409
33. ¶B-1407 *et seq.*; ¶7214.01; TD ¶581,406

Where a taxpayer receives a profits interest in a partnership (even if substantially unvested) in exchange for services, IRS won't treat the transaction as giving rise to compensation income, unless: (1) the profits interest relates to a substantially certain and predictable stream of income from partnership assets; (2) the partner disposes of the profits interest within two years; or (3) the profits interest is a limited partnership interest in a publicly traded partnership. Cases hold that no income is includible where the profit interest has only speculative value. [34]

¶ 3713 Partnership's basis in property contributed to it.

Property received by a partnership from a contributing partner takes the same basis in the partnership's hands as it had in the contributing partner's hands at the time of the contribution (increased by any gain recognized if the partnership is an "investment company partnership," see ¶3711). (Code Sec. 723; Reg § 1.723-1)[35]

¶ 3714 Partnership's holding period for contributed property.

A partnership's holding period for property contributed to it includes the contributing partner's holding period. (Code Sec. 1223(2); Reg § 1.723-1)[36]

¶ 3715 Partnership Income and Deductions.

A partnership is essentially a conduit which passes through to each partner his share of income and deductions generated by the partnership.

¶ 3716 Partners taxed on partnership income.

The partners, not the partnership, are taxed on the partnership's income. (Code Sec. 701) The partnership only files an information return (Form 1065, see ¶4733) showing each partner's distributive share of the partnership income, gains, losses, etc. Each partner includes his share of these items on his own return. (Code Sec. 702)[37]

¶ 3717 Partnership taxable income.

Partnership taxable income is computed the same as an individual's except the following deductions aren't allowed:

. . . standard deduction (Code Sec. 63(c)(6)(D));

. . . personal exemptions;

. . . charitable contributions;

. . . nonbusiness expenses, medical expenses, alimony, retirement savings under Code Sec. 219 and taxes and interest paid to cooperative housing corporations;

. . . capital loss carryovers;

. . . net operating loss deduction;

. . . taxes paid to a foreign country or U.S. possession that can be taken as a credit or as a deduction (income and similar taxes);

. . . oil and gas well depletion. (Code Sec. 703(a)(2); Reg § 1.703-1(a)(2))[38]

---

34. ¶B-1408; ¶7214.01; TD ¶581,407
35. ¶B-1418; ¶7234.01; TD ¶581,411
36. ¶B-1419; ¶7234.01; TD ¶581,412

37. ¶B-1900 *et seq.*; ¶7014; TD ¶584,000 *et seq.*
38. ¶B-1901; ¶7034.01; TD ¶584,001

¶ 3718   "Separately stated" items of income and deductions.

Partnerships are required to "state separately" —that is, to compute as separate items — certain classes of income and deductions. These are then directly "passed through" to the partnership's partners, who take them into account for tax purposes by including their distributive share of each of the classes as separate items on their tax returns. (Code Sec. 702(a))

Key items that must be separately stated are:

. . . charitable contributions;

. . . dividends for which a dividends-received deduction is allowed or qualified dividend income eligible for capital gains treatment ;

. . . foreign and U.S. possessions taxes eligible for foreign tax credit;

. . . income, gains and losses from the sale or exchange of unrealized receivables and substantially appreciated inventory;

. . . income, gain, loss, deduction or credit items that are specially allocated under the partnership agreement;

. . . intangible drilling and development expenses;

. . . long-term capital gains and losses;

. . . 28% rate gains and losses;

. . . mining explorations expenditures;

. . . nonbusiness production of income expenses;

. . . recoveries of tax benefit items;

. . . Code Sec. 1231 gains and losses;

. . . short-term capital gains and losses;

. . . soil and water conservation expenses.

Partnerships must also separately state —and partners must separately take into account their distributive share of —any partnership item, if separately stating that item would result in a tax liability for any partner different from that partner's tax liability if the item weren't separately stated. (Reg § 1.702-1(a)(8)(ii))[39]

¶ 3719   Items not required to be separately stated.

After determining which of its items of income, gains, losses, deductions and credits must be separately stated, a partnership computes its taxable income or loss based on items that don't have to be separately stated. The partnership's partners, in computing their income tax liabilities, take into account their distributive shares of the partnership's nonseparately stated income or loss, as well as their distributive shares of each separately stated item. (Code Sec. 702(a)(8); Reg § 1.702-1(a)(9))[40]

¶ 3720   Character of partnership income.

Each item passed through to the partners and separately stated on their returns has the same character as if realized or incurred directly by the partnership. (Code Sec. 702(b); Reg § 1.702-1(b))[41]

---

39. ¶B-1903; ¶7024.01; TD ¶584,003
40. ¶B-1904; ¶7024.01; TD ¶584,004

41. ¶B-1905; ¶7024.02; TD ¶584,005

¶ 3721 Consistent treatment on partner's and partnership's return— Form 8082.

A partner must, on his own return, treat a partnership item in a manner that's consistent with the treatment of that item on the partnership's return. (Code Sec. 6222(a)) A partner that treats a partnership item differently must notify IRS of the inconsistency on Form 8082. (Code Sec. 6222(b))[42]

The above consistency rule doesn't apply to certain small partnerships that aren't covered by the unified audit and review procedures for partnerships (¶4841). (Code Sec. 6231(a)(1)(B))[43]

¶ 3722 When partnership income is reported by the partners.

Each partner reports his distributive share of the partnership income, deductions and other items (including guaranteed salary and interest payments) for a partnership tax year on his individual return for his tax year within or with which the partnership tax year (discussed at ¶2812) ends. (Code Sec. 706(a); Reg § 1.706-1(a))[44]

If two partnership tax years end within a partner's individual tax year, he must report in that year his share of the partnership income for both partnership years. [45]

¶ 3723 Elections.

Elections affecting partnership taxable income must be made by the partnership except for certain elections involving discharge of indebtedness, foreign tax credits, mining exploration costs, and the election by nonresident alien individuals and foreign corporations regarding income from U.S. real property, which must be made by each partner for himself. [46]

¶ 3724 Partnership Allocations.

A partner's distributive share of income, gain, loss, deduction or credit is controlled by the partnership agreement, unless there is no partnership agreement or the allocation in the agreement has no substantial economic effect; then the allocation is made in accordance with the partner's interest in the partnership.

¶ 3725 Allocation rules.

A partnership's allocations (the partners' distributive shares) of partnership income, gains, losses, deductions and credits are normally determined by the partnership agreement. (Code Sec. 704(a)) If, however, the partnership agreement fails to make such allocations, they must be determined in accord with the partners' interests in the partnership. (Code Sec. 704(b)(1)) If the partnership agreement does make allocations of partnership items, these will be respected for tax purposes if:

. . . they have substantial economic effect, see ¶3726; or

. . . they are in accord with the partners' interests in the partnership; or

. . . they are treated as being in accord with the partners' interests in the partnership. (Code Sec. 704(b); Reg § 1.704-1(b)(1))[47]

Special allocation rules apply to: built-in gain and loss property (¶3752); tax preferences associated with pre-'87 cost recovery property; [48] income, gains, losses, etc., with respect to property whose book value differs from its adjusted basis; [49] tax credits and credit recapture

---

42. ¶B-1801; ¶62,214; TD ¶584,010
43. ¶B-1800; ¶62,214.10
44. ¶B-1701; ¶7064; TD ¶584,008
45. ¶B-1701; TD ¶584,008

46. ¶B-1907; ¶7034.02; TD ¶584,007
47. ¶B-2401; ¶7044 *et seq.*; TD ¶586,101
48. ¶B-2901
49. ¶B-2902; ¶7044.07; TD ¶586,101

amounts;[50] creditable foreign taxes;[1] "excess percentage depletion;"[2] the basis of partnership oil and gas properties;[3] recapture income under Code Sec. 1245 and Code Sec. 1250;[4] and allocations attributable to the partnership's nonrecourse debt.[5]

Retroactive allocations — that is, allocations that give particular partners shares of partnership items of income, expense, etc., that were paid or accrued before these partners joined the partnership — aren't permitted. (Code Sec. 706(d)(1))[6]

Except to the extent provided in regs to be issued, if there is a change in any partner's interest during any partnership tax year, each partner's share of any "allocable cash basis item" is determined by assigning the appropriate portion of the item to each day in the period to which the item is attributable. (Code Sec. 706(d)(2))

If a portion of any allocable cash basis item is attributable to a period preceding the partnership tax year, it will be assigned to the first day of the tax year. (Code Sec. 706(d)(2)(C)) Any amount which would be allocated under that procedure to a person who is not a partner on the first day of the partnership's tax year is capitalized by the partnership and added to the basis of the partnership assets in accordance with the basis allocation rules of Code Sec. 755. (Code Sec. 706(d)(2)(D)) Similarly, a portion of an item attributable to a period following the tax year is to be assigned to the last day of the tax year. (Code Sec. 706(d)(2)(C))

¶ 3726   Determining whether an allocation has substantial economic effect.

An allocation of partnership income, gain, loss, deduction or credit among partners has substantial economic effect if it passes a two-part test applied as of the end of the partnership year to which the allocation relates.

First, the allocation must have economic effect. (Reg § 1.704-1(b)(2)(i)) This means that it must be consistent with the underlying economic arrangement of the partners. An allocation will be treated as having economic effect only if throughout the full term of the partnership, the partnership agreement states:

(1) the partners' capital accounts are to be determined and maintained according to rules set forth in the regs (see ¶3727);

(2) when the partnership liquidates, or a partner's interest is liquidated, liquidating distributions are to be made according to the partners' positive capital account balances; and

(3) a partner with a deficit balance in his capital account after the liquidation of his partnership interest is unconditionally obligated to restore the amount of the deficit to the partnership. (Reg § 1.704-1(b)(2)(ii))[7]

Second, the economic effect of the allocation must be substantial. (Reg § 1.704-1(b)(2)(i)) The economic effect of an allocation is substantial if there's a reasonable possibility that it will affect substantially the dollar amounts to be received by the partners from the partnership, independent of the tax consequences. (Reg § 1.704-1(b)(2)(iii))[8]

observation: Generally speaking, the economic effect test is designed to ensure that partnership allocations of income and gain ultimately correspond to real distributions of money and property, and that allocations of deductions, losses and credits ultimately correspond to the partners' actual liabilities for partnership expenses and losses. The substantiality test is designed to ensure that the economic effects of an allocation don't arise principally from the tax character of the allocated item — for example, from the fact that an

---

50. ¶B-2903; ¶7044.07; TD ¶586,101
1. ¶B-2903.1; ¶7044.07
2. ¶B-2904; ¶7044.07; TD ¶586,101
3. ¶B-2905; ¶7044.07; TD ¶586,101
4. ¶B-2906 *et seq.*; ¶7044.07; TD ¶587,405

5. ¶B-3001 *et seq.*; ¶7044.08; TD ¶587,600
6. ¶B-3201; ¶7064.02; TD ¶588,501
7. ¶B-2503 *et seq.*; ¶7044.03; TD ¶586,503
8. ¶B-2700 *et seq.*; ¶7044.02; TD ¶586,519

income item is tax-exempt or foreign-sourced, or that a loss is from the sale of partnership property used in its trade or business.

¶ 3727 Partner capital account rules.

For partner capital accounts to be determined and maintained properly for purposes of the economic effect rules (see ¶3726), each partner's account must be increased by cash contributed by the partner (including cash treated as contributed when the partner assumes partnership liabilities), and by the fair market value of property contributed by the partner (net of liabilities secured by the property). The account must also be increased by the partner's allocable share of partnership income and gain, including tax-exempt income, book income (not tax income) for property whose book value differs from basis, and unrealized income with respect to accounts receivable and certain other accrued but unpaid items.

Each account must be decreased by cash distributed to the partner (including cash treated as distributed when the partnership assumes partner liabilities), and by the fair market value of property distributed to the partner (net of liabilities secured by the property). The account must also be decreased by the partner's allocable share of partnership expenditures that are neither deductible nor capitalizable, and partnership loss and deduction, including book (not tax) loss for property whose book value differs from basis, and unrealized deductions for accounts payable and certain other accrued but unpaid items.

Capital account adjustments may also be required when partnership property is revalued or distributed, and on the transfer of a partnership interest. For example, partnership property may be revalued (and capital accounts adjusted) if property is contributed by, or distributed to, a partner in exchange for a partnership interest. Revaluation is also allowed where a partnership interest is granted as payment for services.

An adjustment may also be required if an optional basis adjustment election is in effect (see ¶3775) and property is distributed or an interest is transferred. (Reg § 1.704-1(b)(2)(iv))[9]

¶ 3728 Partner's Dealings with Partnership. ▬▬▬▬▬▬▬▬▬▬

Partners may deal with their partnerships in other than their capacity as partners. "Guaranteed payments" to partners are generally treated as made to nonpartners. Certain sales between partners and their partnerships establish the character of any gain, and require the deferral of loss.

¶ 3729 "Separate entity" transactions between partner and partnership.

If a partner provides services for or transfers property to his partnership, he may be treated as dealing with the partnership either as a member or as an outsider. If there's a related allocation and distribution of partnership income (direct or indirect), and the transaction on the whole is properly characterized as a sale or exchange between a partnership and an outsider, it will be treated in that way. (Code Sec. 707(a)(2)(A), Code Sec. 707(a)(2)(B))[10]

¶ 3730 Guaranteed payments.

Guaranteed payments are payments to a partner for services or capital *without regard to partnership income.* [11] Guaranteed payments for a partner's services or capital are treated like salary payments to employees or interest payments to creditors, not like partnership distributions. (Code Sec. 707(c); Reg § 1.707-1(c))[12]

For a guaranteed payment to be deductible as a business expense by the partnership, it

---

9. ¶B-2600 *et seq.*; ¶7044.04; TD ¶587,000
10. ¶B-2000 *et seq.*; ¶7074.01; TD ¶584,501

11. ¶B-2005; ¶7074.04; TD ¶584,505
12. ¶B-2006 *et seq.*; ¶7074.04; TD ¶584,505

must meet the business expense tests as if the payment had been made to a person who wasn't a member of the partnership. (Code Sec. 707(c))[13] In determining whether a partnership can deduct or must capitalize a guaranteed payment, the regular capital expenditure rules apply. (Code Sec. 707(c))[14]

When a partnership makes a guaranteed payment using property other than cash, it is treated as a sale or exchange of that property by the partnership on which gain is recognized, and not a partnership distribution treated as discussed at ¶3743.[15]

¶ 3731 Losses on sales and exchanges with controlled partnership.

No deduction is allowed for losses from sales or exchanges between:

. . . a partnership and a person owning, directly or indirectly, over 50% of the capital interest, or profits interest, in the partnership; or

. . . two partnerships in which the same persons own over 50% of the capital or profits interests.

For constructive ownership rules, see ¶3733.

If property on which a loss was disallowed under the above rule is later sold by the transferee at a gain, the gain is taxable only to the extent it exceeds the loss previously disallowed. (Code Sec. 707(b)(1); Reg § 1.707-1(b)(1))[16]

¶ 3732 Gain on sale or exchange with controlled partnership.

The character of the property in the hands of the transferee, immediately after the transfer, determines the character of a *gain to the transferor* on a direct or indirect sale or exchange of property between:

. . . a partnership and a person owning, directly or indirectly, over 50% of the capital interest, or profits interest, in the partnership; or

. . . two partnerships in which the same persons own, directly or indirectly, more than 50% of the capital interest or profits interest in each. (Code Sec. 707(b)(2); Reg § 1.707-1(b)(2))[17]

For constructive ownership rules, see ¶3733.

¶ 3733 Constructive ownership of partnership interests.

In determining the percentage of ownership of partnership interests for purposes of ¶3731 and ¶3732, the constructive ownership rules for stock under Code Sec. 267(c) (¶2448) apply (substituting "capital or profits interest" for "stock"), except that a partner isn't considered as owning the interest of his partners (unless they are relatives, etc.). (Code Sec. 707(b)(3))[18]

¶ 3734 Limitations on a Partner's Deductible Loss. ▪▪▪▪▪▪

A partner's deduction for partnership losses may not exceed the basis of his interest in the partnership. However, partners (although not partnerships) are allowed loss carrybacks and carryovers.

¶ 3735 Limitation on partner's share of partnership loss.

A partner can deduct his distributive share of partnership *losses* only up to the amount of the adjusted basis of his interest in the partnership (¶3738 *et seq.*) at the end of the partnership's loss year. (Code Sec. 704(d))

---

13. ¶B-2001; ¶7074.04; TD ¶584,505
14. ¶B-2009; ¶7074.04; TD ¶584,507
15. ¶B-2009.1

16. ¶B-2016; ¶7074.03; TD ¶584,514
17. ¶B-2017; ¶7074.03; TD ¶584,515
18. ¶B-2018; ¶7074.03; TD ¶584,516

Where a partnership has more than one class of losses (e.g., capital losses, Code Sec. 1231 losses, and operating losses) in the same year and a partner's total share of those losses exceeds the adjusted basis of his partnership interest, the limitation is allocated proportionately to each type of loss. (Reg § 1.704-1(d))

Excess losses disallowed to a partner in any year are carried over, and are deductible by him at the end of the partnership year in which the adjusted basis of the partner's interest at the end of the year exceeds zero (before reduction by that year's loss). (Reg § 1.704-1(d)(4))[19]

For limits on a partner's loss under the at-risk rules, see ¶1804 *et seq.*, and under the passive activity rules, see ¶1813 *et seq.*, ¶1819, and ¶1831.

¶ 3736 Basis adjustments made before applying loss limitations.

In determining whether a partner's deductible share of partnership loss exceeds (and is thus limited by) his basis in his partnership interest (¶3735), the basis adjustments described at ¶3740 are made first. (Reg § 1.704-1(d)(2))[20]

¶ 3737 Loss carrybacks and carryovers.

A carryover or carryback of net operating losses isn't allowed to a partnership but a partner may carry back or carry over his share of the partnership's net business loss for any year to the extent it can't be used by that partner in the year it's passed through to him. (Code Sec. 702)[21]

¶ 3738 Basis of Partnership Interest.

A partner's basis for his interest in a partnership ("outside basis") depends on how he acquired it: It may be the amount of cash he contributed to the partnership, the adjusted basis of the property he contributed or the amount he paid to purchase it.

¶ 3739 Initial basis of partnership interest.

A partner's interest acquired by a tax-free contribution of money or property to the partnership has a basis equal to the amount of money plus the partner's adjusted basis for the property when contributed. (Code Sec. 722)[22] If the contributed property is subject to indebtedness or if liabilities of the partner are assumed by the partnership, the basis of the contributing partner's interest is reduced by the portion of the indebtedness assumed by the other partners. (Reg § 1.722-1)[23]

A partner's capital interest acquired for services has a basis equal to the value of the capital interest acquired. (Reg § 1.722-1)[24]

A partner's interest acquired by purchase or inheritance has a basis determined under the general basis rules (¶2463 *et seq.*). (Code Sec. 742; Reg § 1.742-1)[25]

A partner may have a divided holding period in his partnership interest, see ¶2669. (Reg § 1.1223-3)[26]

¶ 3740 Adjustments to basis of partner's interest.

The basis of a partner's interest is increased:

. . . by further contributions (but not by his own personal note given to the partnership); [27]

19. ¶B-3500 *et seq.*; ¶7044.10; TD ¶589,001 *et seq.*
20. ¶B-3501 *et seq.*; ¶7044.10; TD ¶589,001
21. ¶B-3508; ¶7024.01; TD ¶589,007
22. ¶B-1502; ¶7224.01; TD ¶581,418
23. ¶B-1506; ¶7224.01; TD ¶581,422

24. ¶B-1502; ¶7224.02; TD ¶581,418
25. ¶B-1501; ¶7424.01; TD ¶581,415
26. ¶I-8934.1; ¶12,234.29; TD ¶223,556
27. ¶B-1504; ¶7054.01; TD ¶581,418

... by the cost of additional interests purchased or inherited, see ¶3739; (Code Sec. 742)

... by any increase in his share of partnership liabilities since the increase is treated as a contribution of money to the partnership, see ¶3760;[28]

... by his distributive share of partnership income, including tax-exempt income and any excess of net long-term capital gains over losses; (Code Sec. 705(a)(1))

... by his distributive share of the excess of percentage depletion deductions over the basis of the depletable property. (Code Sec. 705(a)(1))[29]

The basis of a partner's interest is reduced (but not below zero) by:

... the adjusted basis allocable to any part of his interest sold or otherwise transferred; [30]

... the amount of money and the adjusted basis of partnership property distributed to him in nonliquidating distributions; (Code Sec. 705(a)(2), Code Sec. 733)[31]

... by any decrease in his share of partnership liabilities since the decrease is treated as a distribution of money by the partnership, see ¶3760;

... his distributive share of partnership losses (including capital losses) *and* nondeductible expenditures not chargeable to the capital account (Code Sec. 705(a); Reg § 1.705-1(a)) (for the partner's distributive share of losses in excess of his adjusted basis, see ¶3735);

... his percentage depletion deduction for partnership oil and gas property to the extent the deduction doesn't exceed his allocated proportionate share of the property's basis. (Code Sec. 705(a)(3))[32]

Regs have been issued to prevent the acceleration or duplication of losses through a partnership's assumption of obligations that are not treated as resulting in a deemed cash contribution or distribution by or to the partner under the rules discussed at ¶3759. These obligations are called "Reg § 1.752-7 liabilities." Where such a liability is assumed by a partnership from a partner in a property contribution by a partner to a partnership in exchange for a partnership interest (a Code Sec. 721(a) contribution), the liability is treated as having a built-in loss (see ¶3752) equal to the amount of the liability as of the date of the partnership's assumption of the liability. (Reg § 1.752-7)[33]

Regs prevent inappropriate increases or decreases in the basis of a corporate partner's interest in a partnership resulting from the partnership's disposition of the corporate partner's stock, for gain or loss allocated on stock sales after Dec. 6, '99. (Reg § 1.705-2)[34]

¶ 3741 Alternative adjusted basis computation.

The adjusted basis of a partner's interest may be determined under a "short-cut" method by reference to what would be his proportionate share of the adjusted basis of the partnership property upon a termination of the partnership (Code Sec. 705(b)) where: (1) it isn't practicable to use the regular rule, or (2) IRS is satisfied the result under the alternative method won't vary substantially from that under the regular rule. (Reg § 1.705-1(b))[35]

¶ 3742 Distributions to a Partner.

A partnership generally doesn't recognize gain or loss on a distribution to a partner, but the partner often will recognize gain or loss.

---

28. ¶B-1506; ¶7524; TD ¶581,422
29. ¶B-1507; ¶7054.01; TD ¶581,423
30. ¶B-3805
31. ¶B-1505; ¶7334.01; TD ¶581,423

32. ¶B-1507; ¶7054.02; TD ¶581,423
33. ¶B-1506.1; ¶7524.04; TD ¶581,422.2
34. ¶B-1504.1; ¶7054.03
35. ¶B-1514; ¶7054.04; TD ¶581,428

¶ 3743   Partnership's gain or loss on distribution.

No gain or loss is recognized to a partnership on a distribution to a partner of money or other property, except where a disproportionate distribution is treated as a sale by the partnership, see ¶3754. (Code Sec. 731(b)) This rule applies generally to both current and liquidating distributions. [36]

¶ 3744   Partner's gain or loss on receipt of distribution.

Gain or loss isn't recognized to a partner on receipt of a current or liquidating distribution from a partnership, except as follows:

... Gain is recognized to the extent that *money* (defined to include marketable securities, see ¶3745) distributed exceeds the adjusted basis of the partner's interest in the partnership immediately before the distribution. (Code Sec. 731(a))[37] This is treated as a gain from sale or exchange of the partner's interest. (Reg § 1.731-1(a)(3))[38] A reduction in a partner's liabilities (due either to the partnership's assumption of them or a reduction in the partner's share of partnership liabilities) is treated as a money distribution. (Code Sec. 752(b))[39]

... Loss is recognized to the extent the adjusted basis of the partner's interest exceeds the sum of any money, and the basis to the distributee of any unrealized receivables and inventories received if the distribution is in liquidation of the partner's interest in the partnership *and* no other property is distributed. This is treated as a loss from sale or exchange of the partner's interest in the partnership. (Code Sec. 731(a))[40]

If gain or loss is recognized under one of the above rules, the partnership may elect to, or may have to, adjust the basis of its assets, as explained at ¶3775 *et seq.*

The above rules on recognition of a partner's gains and losses don't apply to (Code Sec. 731(c); Reg § 1.731-1(c)):[41]

... disproportionate distributions treated as sales or exchanges of property, see ¶3754;

... liquidation payments made to a retiring partner or to a deceased partner's successor in interest treated as a share of income or as guaranteed payments, see ¶3769;

... recognition of precontribution gain under Code Sec. 737, see ¶3752.

Where a partnership took cash it would have distributed to a partner in liquidation of his interest and used it buy a house he wanted and then distributed the house to him, the partner was treated as receiving the cash as part of distribution and not the house. Thus, the attempt to reduce the partner's gain on the distribution was unsuccessful. [42]

¶ 3745   Distribution of marketable securities treated as cash.

Subject to exceptions, a distribution of marketable securities (stock and other equity instruments, evidences of indebtedness, precious metals commodities, options, forward or futures contracts, notional principal contracts and derivatives) is treated as a distribution of money. They are taken into account at their fair market value as of the date of the distribution. (Code Sec. 731(c); Reg § 1.731-2)

Gain is recognized by a distributee partner to the extent that the cash and the fair market value of the marketable securities exceeds the basis of the partner's interest in the partnership. But where a partner realizes a loss on a distribution of marketable securities, the loss

---

36. ¶B-3601; ¶7314.01; TD ¶589,501
37. ¶B-3602; ¶7314.01; TD ¶589,502
38. ¶B-3602; ¶7314.01; TD ¶589,502
39. ¶B-3608; ¶7524.01; TD ¶582,002

40. ¶B-3603; ¶7314.01; TD ¶589,508
41. ¶B-3605; ¶7314.01; TD ¶589,510
42. ¶B-3612

isn't recognized. These rules are applied after the application of the rules that treat a shift in the partners' interests in accounts receivables and substantially appreciated inventory as a sale. (Code Sec. 731(a))[43]

The amount of marketable securities taken into account under the above rule is reduced (but not below zero) by the excess (if any) of:

(1) the partner's distributive share of the net gain that would be recognized if all marketable securities of the same class and issuer as the distributed securities held by the partnership were sold (immediately before the transaction to which the distribution relates) by the partnership for fair market value, over

(2) the partner's distributive share of the net gain that's attributable to the marketable securities of the same class and issuer as the distributed securities held by the partnership immediately after the transaction, determined using the fair market value described in (1) above. (Code Sec. 731(c)(3)(B))

All marketable securities held by the partnership are treated as marketable securities of the same class and issuer as the distributed securities. (Reg § 1.731-2(b))[44]

¶ 3746   Partner's holding period.

A partner's holding period for property distributed to him in kind includes the period the partnership held the property. (Code Sec. 735(b)) If contributed to the partnership by a partner, the recipient partner's holding period also includes the period that the property was held by the contributing partner before contribution. (Reg § 1.735-1(b))[45]

¶ 3747   Character of certain contributed property.

When a partner contributes what was an unrealized receivable in his hands to a partnership, the partnership's gain or loss on disposition of the item will still be ordinary income or loss. (Code Sec. 724(a)) The same rule applies to contributed inventory, but in this case, ordinary income or loss will result only if the assets are disposed of by the partnership within five years of the contribution. (Code Sec. 724(b))[46]

If a partner contributes a capital asset with a basis higher than its fair market value, and the partnership disposes of it within five years of the contribution, the partnership's loss will be a capital loss to the extent of the basis/value variance upon contribution. (Code Sec. 724(c))[47]

If any of the above property is disposed of by the partnership in a nontaxable disposition, the above rules apply to the substituted basis property that results. (Code Sec. 724(d)(3))[48]

¶ 3748   Partner's basis for property received in nonliquidating distributions.

The basis to a partner of property distributed to him, in kind, other than in liquidation of his partnership interest, is the same as the property's adjusted basis to the partnership immediately before the distribution. But the basis of the property to the partner may not exceed the adjusted basis of his interest in the partnership reduced by any money distributed to him in the same transaction. (Code Sec. 732(a); Reg § 1.732-1(a))[49]

---

43. ¶B-3602.1 *et seq.*; ¶7314.01; TD ¶588,035
44. ¶B-3602.2; ¶7314.01
45. ¶B-3706; ¶7354.02; TD ¶589,523
46. ¶B-1420; ¶7244; TD ¶581,413
47. ¶B-1421; ¶7244; TD ¶581,414
48. ¶B-1422; ¶7244.01; TD ¶581,415
49. ¶B-3701; ¶7324.01; TD ¶589,518

¶ 3749 Partner's basis for property distributed in liquidation.

A partner's basis for property distributed in liquidation of his partnership interest is the same as the adjusted basis for his partnership interest reduced by any money distributed to him in the same transaction. However, the partner's basis in inventory and unrealized receivables cannot exceed the basis the partnership had in such items. (Code Sec. 732(b); Code Sec. 732(c); Reg § 1.732-1(b))[50]

¶ 3750 Basis adjustments to assets of corporation whose stock is distributed to corporate partner.

A corporate partner that receives a distribution of stock in another corporation ("distributed corporation") must, subject to limitations and exceptions, reduce the basis of the distributed corporation's assets if:

. . . the corporate partner "controls" (by 80% vote and value) the distributed corporation immediately after the distribution or at any time thereafter, and

. . . the partnership's adjusted basis in the stock of the distributed corporation immediately before the distribution exceeded the corporate partner's adjusted basis in such stock immediately after the distribution. (Code Sec. 732(f)(1))[1]

The basis reduction equals the excess described above and is applied to the property held by the distributed corporation following the distribution, if the corporate partner then has control of the distributed corporation. (Code Sec. 732(f)(1))[2]

The basis reduction cannot exceed the lesser of:

(A) the amount by which (i) the sum of the aggregate adjusted bases of the property and the amount of money of the distributed corporation exceeds (ii) the corporate partner's adjusted basis in the stock of the distributed corporation, or

(B) the adjusted basis of any property of the distributed corporation (determined before the reduction). (Code Sec. 732(f)(3))[3]

If, in applying the basis-reduction rule, the amount by which basis is to be reduced exceeds the aggregate adjusted bases of the property of the distributed corporation, then the excess is recognized by the corporate partner as long-term capital gain and increases its basis in the stock of the distributed corporation. (Code Sec. 732(f)(4))[4]

¶ 3751 Allocation of basis to distributed property when limited by basis of partner's interest.

In a current distribution in which the partner's basis in his partnership interest is less than the partnership's basis in the property distributed and in a liquidating distribution, the partner's basis in his partnership interest (reduced by any money received) must be allocated among the distributed property in the following manner:

(1) First, to any unrealized receivables and inventory items in an amount equal to the adjusted basis of each such property to the partnership. (Code Sec. 732(c)(1)(A)(i)) If the basis to be allocated is less than the sum of the adjusted bases of these properties in the hands of the partnership, a basis decrease is applied as described below. (Code Sec. 732(c)(1)(A)(ii), Reg § 1.732-1(c)(1)(i))

(2) To the extent any basis isn't allocated under (1), basis is allocated to other distributed

50. ¶B-3702; ¶7324.01; TD ¶589,519   3. ¶B-3704.1; ¶7324.03
1. ¶B-3704; ¶7324.03   4. ¶B-3704.2; ¶7324.03
2. ¶B-3704; ¶7324.03

properties. This allocation is made by assigning to each property its adjusted basis in the hands of the partnership (Code Sec. 732(c)(1)(B)(i), Reg § 1.732-1(c)(1)(ii)) and then increasing or decreasing the basis to the extent any increase or decrease in basis is required in order for the adjusted bases of the other distributed properties to equal the remaining basis under the rules described below. (Code Sec. 732(c)(1)(B)(ii), Reg § 1.732-1(c)(1)(ii))

Any basis *increase* is allocated (i) first to properties with unrealized appreciation in proportion to their respective amounts of unrealized appreciation before such increase (but only to the extent of each property's unrealized appreciation) (Code Sec. 732(c)(2)(A), Reg § 1.732-1(c)(2)(ii)) and (ii) to the extent the required increase isn't allocated under (i), in proportion to the respective fair market values of the properties. (Code Sec. 732(c)(2)(B), Reg § 1.732-1(c)(2)(ii))

Any basis *decrease* is allocated (a) first to properties with unrealized depreciation in proportion to their respective amounts of unrealized appreciation before such decrease (but only to the extent of each property's unrealized depreciation) (Code Sec. 732(c)(3)(A), Reg § 1.732-1(c)(2)(i)) and (b) to the extent the required decrease isn't allocated under (a), in proportion to the respective bases of the properties (as adjusted under (a)). (Code Sec. 732(c)(3)(B), Reg § 1.732-1(c)(2)(i))[5]

¶ 3752   Built-in gain or loss property—seven-year rule.

If the basis of property contributed to a partnership by a partner is different from the property's fair market value at the time of contribution (i.e., there is built-in gain or loss), then the following rules apply:

If the partnership distributes property contributed to it either directly or indirectly to a partner or partners *other than the contributing partner* within seven years of the contribution, then the distributed property is treated as sold by the partnership for its fair market value at the time of the distribution, and the contributing partner must recognize any gain or loss from this constructive sale in an amount equal to the amount of gain or loss that would have been allocated to him if the property had actually been sold. (Code Sec. 704(c)(1)(B), Reg § 1.704-4(a)(5), Ex (1))[6]

Where property is distributed to the partner *who contributed the property,* the partner will recognize as gain the lesser of (a) the excess of the fair market value of the property over the adjusted basis of the partner's interest in the partnership immediately before the distribution (reduced, but not below zero, by any money also received, where money is defined to include marketable securities, see ¶3745), or (b) the partner's net precontribution gain, i.e., the gain that would have been recognized by the distributee partner under the rules discussed, above, if all property held by the partnership immediately before the distribution that had been contributed to it by the distributee partner within seven years of the distribution, was distributed to another partner. (Code Sec. 737(a), Code Sec. 737(b))[7] Distributions of property previously contributed by the distributee partner aren't taken into account for purposes of determining (a) and (b), above. (Code Sec. 737(d)(1))[8]

Special rules apply if the partnership distributes to the contributing partner property that's of "like kind" to the contributed property (within the meaning of Code Sec. 1031, see ¶2418) to limit recognition of gain by the contributing partner. (Code Sec. 704(c)(2))[9]

The rules requiring gain recognition on distributions described above do not apply when a partnership transfers all of its assets and liabilities to a partnership in exchange for an

5. ¶B-3703; ¶7324.01; TD ¶589,521   8. ¶B-3135; ¶7374.03; TD ¶588,037
6. ¶B-3125; ¶7044.09; TD ¶588,019   9. ¶B-3127 *et seq.*; ¶7044.09; TD ¶588,025
7. ¶B-3133 *et seq.*; ¶7374; TD ¶588,031

interest in the transferee partnership, and distributes the interest to its partners in liquidation as part of the same plan (a merger). With respect to a later distribution of "built-in gain" property that was transferred, the seven-year period begins when the property was originally contributed to the transferor partnership, and not from the date of the transfer to the transferee partnership. However, for post-Jan. 19, 2005 distributions, the merger is considered a contribution of assets, so a new seven-year period begins but only with respect to the appreciation in value that occurred while the property was held by the transferor partnership. [10]

Income, gain, loss and deductions with respect to property which was contributed to the partnership after Mar. 31, '84 is to be shared among the partners so as to take into account the difference between the property's fair market value and its basis at the time of the contribution. (Code Sec. 704(c)(1)(A)) Built-in gain or loss must be allocated using a reasonable method, i.e., the traditional method following the ceiling rule or with curative allocations, the remedial allocation method or another method appropriate to the circumstances. (Reg § 1.704-3(a)(1)) With respect to property contributed before Apr. 1, '84, a similar special allocation applies only if the partnership agreement so provides. [11]

If any property contributed to a partnership after Oct. 22, 2004 has a built-in loss, then:

. . . the built-in loss is taken into account only in determining the amount of items allocated to the contributing partner, and

. . . except as provided in regs, in determining the amount of items allocated to other partners, the basis of the contributed property in the hands of the partnership is treated as being equal to its fair market value at the time of the contribution. (Code Sec. 704(c)(1)(C))

If a partnership makes an installment sale of built-in gain or loss property, the installment obligation it receives (after Nov. 23, 2003), is treated as built-in gain or loss property. (Reg § 1.704-3(a)(8)(ii))[12]

¶ 3753   Disproportionate Distributions. ▬

Disproportionate distributions of partnership property that includes "unrealized receivables" and "substantially appreciated inventory" (so-called "hot assets") may trigger ordinary income, gain or loss to both the partnership and its partners.

¶ 3754   Disproportionate distributions defined.

A disproportionate distribution of partnership assets to a partner is treated as a sale or exchange that may result in recognition of gain or loss to the partner and the partnership. The rule applies to all distributions, both liquidating and nonliquidating except for: (1) a distribution of contributed property to the same partner who contributed it; and (2) liquidation payments to a retiring or deceased partner that are treated as ordinary income under the rules at ¶3769. (Code Sec. 751(b))[13]

A distribution is "disproportionate" if a partner receives more than his proportionate share of partnership property in the first of the following categories and less than his proportionate share of property in the second category, or vice versa:

. . . "hot assets"—unrealized receivables (including recapturable deductions, certain transfers of franchises, trademarks or trade names, see ¶3755) and substantially appreciated inventory items, see ¶3756;

. . . other property (including money). [14]

In such a case, a partner, in effect, sells or exchanges part or all of his share in property of

---

10. ¶B-3130.2; ¶7044.097; TD ¶588,024
11. ¶B-3103 *et seq.*; ¶7044.09; TD ¶588,001
12. ¶B-3100; ¶7044.09; TD ¶588,014

13. ¶B-3905 *et seq.*; ¶7514.01; TD ¶591,003
14. ¶B-3905; ¶7514.01; TD ¶591,003

one category for property of the other category, see ¶3757. The general rules on partnership distributions apply to the balance of the distribution not treated as a sale or exchange. (Reg § 1.751-1(b))[15]

The partners may agree as to which particular assets in one category shall be considered to have been sold or exchanged for particular assets in the other category. Absent such an agreement, a proportionate part of each asset relinquished in one category will be considered to have been sold or exchanged for excess assets received in the other category. (Reg § 1.751-1(g))[16]

¶ 3755 "Unrealized receivables."

Unrealized receivables include any contractual or other rights to payment for:

. . . goods delivered, or to be delivered, to the extent the proceeds would be treated as amounts received from sale or exchange of noncapital assets;

. . . services rendered, or to be rendered.

Such receivables are included only to the extent not previously includible in income under the method of accounting used by the partnership. (Code Sec. 751(c))[17]

Unrealized receivables also include (other than for payments to retiring partners or deceased partners under Code Sec. 736, see ¶3769): (Code Sec. 751(c))

. . . depreciation recapturable under Code Sec. 1245 and Code Sec. 1250;

. . . mine exploration deductions recapturable under Code Sec. 617;

. . . soil and water conservation deductions recapturable under Code Sec. 1252;

. . . recapturable deductions for oil, gas or certain geothermal well intangible costs under Code Sec. 1254;

. . . understated rental income under a Code Sec. 467 rental agrement; [18]

. . . DISC stock;

. . . stock in certain foreign corporations as described in Code Sec. 1248 (¶4631);[19]

. . . market discount bonds, to the extent they would give rise to ordinary income if sold by the partnership (¶1326);

. . . short term obligations as defined in Code Sec. 1283 (¶1328);[20]

. . . franchises, trademarks or trade names whose transfer is treated as a sale of a noncapital asset under Code Sec. 1253. [21]

¶ 3756 "Inventory items" and "substantially appreciated" inventory items.

Inventory items include property properly includible in inventory and property held primarily for sale to customers in the ordinary course of business (Code Sec. 751(d)(1)), as well as:

. . . any other property that would produce ordinary income on sale or exchange by the partnership (Code Sec. 751(d)(2)), including accounts receivable for goods or services and unrealized receivables as described at ¶3755; (Reg § 1.751-1(d)(2)(ii))

. . . any other property held by the partnership that would be inventory items, as defined above, if held by the selling or distributee-partner. (Code Sec. 751(d)(3)) However, this rule doesn't apply to property actually distributed to a partner. (Reg § 1.751-1(d)(2)(iii))[22]

Inventory items are "substantially appreciated" in value if the fair market value of *all* such

---

15. ¶B-3910 *et seq.*; ¶7514.01; TD ¶591,006
16. ¶B-3902 *et seq.*; ¶7514.01; TD ¶591,006
17. ¶B-3914; ¶7514.02; TD ¶591,010
18. ¶B-3916; ¶7514.02; TD ¶591,012

19. ¶B-3918; ¶7514.02; TD ¶591,011
20. ¶B-3920; ¶7514.02; TD ¶591,013
21. ¶B-3919; ¶7514.02; TD ¶591,014
22. ¶B-3921; ¶7514.02; TD ¶591,015

items (including unrealized receivables) exceeds 120% of their adjusted basis to the partnership. (Code Sec. 751(b)(3)(A)) The 120% limit is computed by excluding any item acquired principally to avoid meeting it. (Code Sec. 751(b)(3)(B))

If the test is met on the basis of all inventory items, a distribution of any inventory item is a distribution of a substantially appreciated one even though the particular item may not have appreciated at all. If the test isn't met on the basis of all items, no distribution of an inventory item is a distribution of a substantially appreciated item. (Reg § 1.751-1(d)(1))[23]

¶ 3757   Gain or loss on disproportionate distribution.

If a distributee-partner receives *more* than his share of unrealized receivables and substantially appreciated inventory items and *less* than his share of other property (including money), he is considered to have sold or exchanged the portion of his share of the other property that he relinquished for the excess unrealized receivables and substantially appreciated inventory items he received. (Reg § 1.751-1(b)(2)(i), Reg § 1.751-1(b)(2)(iii))

The partnership (as constituted after the distribution) is considered to have sold or exchanged the excess other property distributed to the partner for the unrealized receivables and substantially appreciated inventory items he relinquished. (Reg § 1.751-1(b)(2)(i), Reg § 1.751-1(b)(2)(ii))[24]

Rules analogous to those described above apply where the distributee partner receives a disproportionate distribution of *less* than his share of unrealized receivables and substantially appreciated inventory items and *more* than his share of other property (including money). (Reg § 1.751-1(b)(3))[25]

¶ 3758   Character of unrealized receivables and inventory to a distributee-partner.

Gain or loss on disposition of unrealized receivables and inventory by a distributee-partner is:

... in the case of *unrealized receivables* , ordinary gain or loss; (Code Sec. 735(a)(1))

... in the case of *inventory items* (whether or not substantially appreciated) sold or exchanged within five years from the date of the distribution, ordinary gain or loss. (Code Sec. 735(a)(2)) If disposed of after five years from the date of distribution, the character of the gain or loss depends upon the character of the item in the partner's hands on the date of disposition. (Reg § 1.735-1(a)(2))[26]

¶ 3759   Liabilities of Partnerships and Partners. ▬▬▬▬▬▬▬▬

Changes in partners' shares of partnership liabilities are treated as cash contributions to, or distributions by, the partnership. Partners' shares of partnership liabilities depend on whether the liability is recourse or nonrecourse.

¶ 3760   Partnership liabilities.

If a partner's share of the partnership liabilities increases, or if he assumes any partnership liabilities, it's treated as a contribution of money from the partner to the partnership. (Code Sec. 752(a); Reg § 1.752-1(b))[27]

If a partner's share of the partnership liabilities decreases, or if the partnership assumes any of his liabilities, it's treated as a distribution of money to the partner. (Code Sec. 752(b); Reg § 1.752-1(c))[28]

---

23. ¶B-3922; ¶7514.02; TD ¶591,016
24. ¶B-3910 *et seq.*; ¶7514.01; TD ¶591,003
25. ¶B-3911; ¶7514.01; TD ¶591,008

26. ¶B-3705; ¶7354.01; TD ¶589,522
27. ¶B-1601; ¶7524.01; TD ¶582,004
28. ¶B-1602; ¶7524.01; TD ¶582,004

An unassumed liability to which property is subject is considered a liability of the owner of the property (e.g., the partnership) to the extent of its fair market value. (Code Sec. 752(c))[29]

For these purposes and for determining "Reg § 1.752-7 liabilities" (see ¶3740), a liability is any fixed or contingent obligation to make payment without regard to whether the obligation is otherwise taken into account for tax purposes. Obligations include, but are not limited to, debt obligations, environmental obligations, tort obligations, contract obligations, pension obligations, obligations under a short sale, and obligations under derivative financial instruments such as options, forward contracts, and futures contracts. (Reg § 1.752-1(a)(4)(ii))[30]

¶ 3761   Share of recourse liabilities.

A partnership debt is a recourse liability to the extent that any partner bears the economic risk of loss for the liability.[31] A partner's share of a recourse liability is the part of the economic risk of loss for the liability the partner bears. (Reg § 1.752-1(a)(1))[32]

Generally, a partner bears the economic risk of loss for a partnership liability to the extent that he (or a related person) would be obligated to pay the creditor or contribute to the partnership (and wouldn't be entitled to reimbursement) in case of a constructive liquidation. (Reg § 1.752-2(b)(1))[33]

¶ 3762   Share of nonrecourse liabilities.

If no partner bears the economic risk of loss for a partnership liability (e.g., unassumed mortgages), the liability is nonrecourse. (Reg § 1.752-1(a)(2)) Nonrecourse liabilities of a partnership are first allocated among all the partners to reflect their shares of:

... "partnership minimum gain" (gain on the disposition of property subject to a nonrecourse liability that exceeds its adjusted basis); and

... the gain that would be allocated to the partners under Code Sec. 704(c), or under similar principles in connection with a revaluation of partnership property, if, in a taxable transaction, the partnership disposed of all property subject to a nonrecourse liability in satisfaction of those liabilities and for no other consideration.

Any excess is allocated among the partners in proportion to their interests in partnership profits. The partnership agreement may specify the partners' profit interests as long as those interests are reasonably consistent with allocations (which have substantial economic effect) of some significant item of partnership income or gain among the partners. Alternatively, the excess may be allocated in accordance with the manner in which it's expected that the deductions attributable to the nonrecourse debt will be allocated. In addition, for liabilities incurred or assumed by a partnership after Oct. 30, 2000 (or before Oct. 31, 2000 in tax years ending after Oct. 30, 2000, if the taxpayer chooses) the excess may be allocated based on the excess gain attributable to the property securing the liability. (Reg § 1.752-3(a))[34]

¶ 3763   Transfer and Liquidation of Partnership Interest. ▬▬▬▬▬▬▬

The transfer or liquidation of a partnership interest, while generally resulting in capital gain or loss, is subject to special rules that may turn part of the gain or loss from capital to ordinary.

---

29. ¶B-1608; ¶7524.01; TD ¶582,007
30. ¶B-1607; ¶7524.01.
31. ¶B-1651; ¶7524.03; TD ¶582,012

32. ¶B-1653 *et seq.*; ¶7524.03; TD ¶582,011
33. ¶B-1654 *et seq.*; ¶7524.03; TD ¶582,013
34. ¶B-1670; ¶7524.03; TD ¶582,017

¶ 3764   Liquidation v. sale of partner's interest.

Withdrawal of a partner from a partnership ordinarily may be accomplished either by a retiring partner's sale or liquidation of his interest in the partnership.

Where a partner's interest is liquidated, payments are taxable to that partner as guaranteed payments or income distributions to the extent they exceed the value of his interest in the partnership property (¶3768 *et seq.*).[35]

Where a partner *sells* his interest, payments to him that exceed his basis for his interest are capital gain except to the extent of payments for unrealized receivables and inventory items (¶3765 *et seq.*). (Code Sec. 741; Reg § 1.741-1)[36]

¶ 3765   Sale or exchange of partnership interest.

If a partner sells or exchanges all or a part of his interest in the partnership after holding it for more than one-year, he may recognize ordinary income, collectibles gain (¶2607), section 1250 gain, and residual long-term capital gain or loss. (Reg § 1.1(h)-1(a)) He recognizes ordinary income to the extent, see ¶3766, his gain is attributable to unrealized receivables (¶3755) and inventory (¶3756). (Code Sec. 741, Code Sec. 751(a), Code Sec. 751(c))[37]

The capital gain or loss is the difference between:

. . . the amount realized *reduced* by the portion attributable to unrealized receivables and inventory; *and*

. . . the transferor-partner's adjusted basis for the partnership interest transferred *reduced* by the portion attributable to unrealized receivables and inventory. (Reg § 1.741-1(a))[38]

The seller's collectibles gain is the amount that would be allocated to him if the partnership had sold all of its collectibles for fair market value in a fully taxable transaction immediately before the sale of the interest in the entity. (Reg § 1.1(h)-1(b)(2)(ii)) The seller must take into account under Code Sec. 1(h)(6)(A)(i) in determining his unrecaptured section 1250 gain (¶2605), the amount of "section 1250 capital gain" that would be allocated to him if the partnership had sold all of its section 1250 property in a fully taxable transaction immediately before the transfer of the partnership interest. (Reg § 1.1(h)-1(b)(3)(ii)) The amount of residual long-term capital gain or loss recognized by a selling partner is the amount of long-term capital gain or loss that the partner would recognize under Code Sec. 741 (as explained above) minus (1) the collectibles gain allocable to the sold interest, and (2) the section 1250 gain allocable to the sold interest. (Reg § 1.1(h)-1(c))

¶ 3766   Ordinary gain or loss.

To the extent that money or property received by a partner in exchange for all or part of his partnership interest is attributable to his share of partnership unrealized receivables or inventory items—collectively Code Sec. 751 property —the gain or loss is ordinary income or loss. (Code Sec. 751(a))

The income or loss realized by a partner upon the sale or exchange of its interest in Code Sec. 751 property is the amount of income or loss from Code Sec. 751 property (including any remedial allocations) that would have been allocated to the partner (to the extent attributable to the partnership interest sold or exchanged) if the partnership had sold all of its property in a fully taxable transaction for cash in an amount equal to the fair market value of such property (taking into account the Code Sec. 7701(g) rule that the fair market value must be

35. ¶B-3811, B-4102; ¶7364.01; TD ¶590,507
36. ¶B-3801 *et seq.*; ¶7414.01; TD ¶590,502
37. ¶B-3802 *et seq.*; ¶7514.01; TD ¶590,502
38. ¶s B-3802, B-3901; ¶7414.01; TD ¶590,501

not less than the amount of the nonrecourse debt to which the property is subject) immediately before the partner's transfer of the interest in the partnership. Gain or loss attributable to Code Sec. 751 property is ordinary gain or loss. The difference between the amount of capital gain or loss that the partner would realize in the absence of Code Sec. 751 and the amount of ordinary income or loss is capital gain or loss on the sale of its partnership interest. (Reg § 1.751-1(a)(2))[39]

The basis for unrealized receivables includes all attributable costs or expenses paid or accrued but not previously taken into account under the partnership's method of accounting. (Reg § 1.751-1(c)(2)) The basis of any potential gain from the following property (treated as unrealized receivables) is zero: (1) mining exploration expenditures recapture under Code Sec. 617; (2) gain from stock of a DISC or a former DISC under Code Sec. 995(c); (3) depreciation recapture under Code Sec. 1245 and Code Sec. 1250; (4) gain from stock of a controlled foreign corporation under Code Sec. 1248(a); (5) gain from disposition of farm land under Code Sec. 1252(a)(1); (6) gain from transfers of franchises, trademarks, or trade names under Code Sec. 1253(a); or (7) oil, gas, or geothermal wells intangible drilling and development cost recapture under Code Sec. 1254. (Reg § 1.751-1(c)(5))[40]

¶ 3767   Sale of partnership business vs. sale of partnership assets.

Where *all* of the old partners sell out, whether the transaction is a sale of the partnership interests or a sale of the partnership assets generally depends on whether what was actually transferred was a going business or simply assets. [41]

¶ 3768   Payments After Partner's Death or Retirement.

When a partner either retires or dies and payments are made in liquidation of his partnership interest, the payments are broken down into several categories, which are treated as ordinary income or capital gains.

¶ 3769   Liquidation payments to retiring or deceased partners.

These payments may be for the partner's interest in the fair market value of the partnership assets, his interest in unrealized receivables or payments under an agreement akin to mutual insurance. These amounts have to be separately considered. [42]

Liquidation payments received by a retiring partner, a partner expelled from a partnership or by a deceased partner's successor in interest are treated as distributions taxable under the rules for regular distributions discussed at ¶3744 if they are for the partner's interest in partnership property, see ¶3770. (Code Sec. 736(b)(1))[43] Payments for *substantially appreciated* inventory (¶3756) may result in ordinary income under the rules governing disproportionate distributions (see ¶3757). (Reg § 1.736-1(b)(1))

Liquidation payments that aren't in exchange for partnership property are treated either as distributive shares of partnership income (if the amount is determined with regard to partnership income), or as guaranteed payments (if the amount is determined without regard to partnership income). (Code Sec. 736(a); Reg § 1.736-1(a)(3))[44]

¶ 3770   Payment for interest in partnership property.

Payments for partnership property don't include payments to a retiring or deceased general partner in a partnership in which capital isn't a material income-producing factor for (i) unrealized receivables (which for this purpose includes only accounts receivable and unbilled

39. ¶B-3901; ¶7514.01; TD ¶591,001   42. ¶B-4102 *et seq.*; ¶7364.01; TD ¶592,000 *et seq.*
40. ¶B-3903; TD ¶591,002   43. ¶B-4103; ¶7364.02; TD ¶592,001
41. ¶B-3809; TD ¶590,508   44. ¶B-4106; ¶7364.03; TD ¶592,005

amounts) or (ii) goodwill (unless the partnership agreement provides for payment with respect to goodwill). (Code Sec. 736(b)(2), Code Sec. 736(b)(3))[45]

¶ 3771 Allocation of payments between income and property.

The allocation problem comes up where payments are made over two or more years. Retirement or death payments must be allocated between the portion received in exchange for partnership property and the balance, received in the form of guaranteed payments or as a distributive share of partnership income. This allocation may be made in any manner in which the remaining partners and the withdrawing partner (or a deceased partner's successor in interest) agree. However, the *total* allocated to property must not exceed the fair market value of the property at the date of death or retirement. (Reg § 1.736-1(b)(5)(iii))

In the absence of an allocation agreement, payments will be apportioned between income and property, as follows:

. . . Payments that aren't fixed in amount are first treated as made in exchange for the partner's interest in partnership property to the extent of the value of that interest. Additional amounts are ordinary income. (Reg § 1.736-1(b)(5)(ii))

. . . Payments fixed in amount and to be received over a fixed number of years are apportioned year by year in accordance with the overall ratio of property payments to total payments. (Reg § 1.736-1(b)(5)(i))[46]

A payment for goodwill is treated as a payment made in exchange for partnership property where payment for goodwill is provided by the partnership agreement. (Reg § 1.736-1(b)(3))[47]

¶ 3772 Withdrawing partner's share of final year's income.

A retiring partner must pick up his distributive share of the partnership income for the partnership year in which he retires. His share of the partnership income for the year is allocable to him only for the portion of the year he was a member of the partnership. (Reg § 1.736-1(a)(4))[48]

¶ 3773 Income of deceased partner.

The tax year of a partnership closes with respect to a deceased partner on the date of his death. Thus, partnership items for the short partnership tax year that closes on the partner's death are included in his final return. (Code Sec. 706(c)(2))[49]

¶ 3774 Continuation of retiring or deceased partner's partner status.

A retiring partner or a deceased partner's successor in interest who receives retirement or death payments is regarded as a partner until his entire interest in the partnership is liquidated. Thus, even a two-person partnership isn't terminated until the retiring or deceased partner's interest is liquidated. (Reg § 1.708-1(b)(1)(i), Reg § 1.736-1(a)(6))[50]

¶ 3775 Special Basis Adjustments to Partnership Property. ▬▬▬▬▬

A partnership's basis in its assets ("inside basis") is unaffected by partnership distributions and transfers of partnership interests unless the partnership makes a special basis election. Under certain circumstances, the transferee of a partnership interest may elect to adjust the basis of property distributed to him as if the partnership had made the special basis election.

---

45. ¶B-4104; ¶7364.02; TD ¶592,004
46. ¶s B-4109, B-4110; ¶7364.01; TD ¶592,007
47. ¶B-4105; ¶7364.02; TD ¶592,004

48. ¶B-4102; ¶7064.02; TD ¶592,006
49. ¶B-4202; ¶7064.02; TD ¶592,502
50. ¶B-4112; ¶7084.03; TD ¶592,010

¶ 3776   Post-transfer adjustments to basis.

A transfer of a partnership interest by reason of a sale or exchange or the death of a partner causes a basis adjustment of the partnership's property if a basis adjustment election under Code Sec. 754 is in effect, or if the partnership has a substantial built-in loss immediately after the transfer. (Code Sec. 743(a)) A partnership is treated as having a substantial built-in loss if the partnership's adjusted basis in the partnership property is more than $250,000 more than the fair market value of that property. (Code Sec. 743(d)(1)) IRS has issued procedures for complying with the basis adjustments required in the case of substantial built-in losses. *For transfers before Oct. 23, 2004,* the rule that a basis adjustment results from a transfer if there is a substantial built-in loss was not in effect. [1]

However, a contribution of cash or property to the partnership does not cause a basis adjustment to the partnership's property, regardless of whether a basis adjustment election is in effect. (Reg § 1.743-1(a))[2] If the election is in effect, the partnership's basis in its property with respect to the transferee partner is increased by any excess of the partner's basis in his interest over his share of the basis of partnership property (or decreased if his basis in his interest is lower). (Reg § 1.743-1(b))[3] Regs provide rules for allocating the basis adjustment among the partnership's assets. (Reg § 1.755-1)[4]

¶ 3777   Post-distribution adjustments to basis of undistributed property.

The basis of partnership property is not adjusted when the partnership makes a distribution to a partner unless a basis adjustment election under Code Sec. 754 is in effect or (for distributions after Oct. 22, 2004), the partnership has a "substantial basis reduction" with respect to the distribution. (Code Sec. 734(a)) A substantial basis reduction exists where the sum of (i) the amount of the partner's loss on the distribution, and (ii) the basis increase to the distributed properties is over $250,000. (Code Sec. 734(d))[5] If an adjustment is made on a partnership distribution, the partnership's basis in its retained property (1) is increased by the amount of gain recognized by the distributee partner on the distribution, and the amount by which the basis of the distributed property in the hands of the partnership before the distribution exceeds the basis of the property in the hands of the distributee partner (Code Sec. 734(b)(1)), and (2) is decreased by the amount of loss recognized by the distributee partner on the distribution and the amount by which the basis of the distributed property in the hands of the distributee partner exceeds the basis the partnership had in the property before the distribution. (Code Sec. 734(b)(2)(B))[6] Regs provide rules for allocating the basis adjustment among the partnership's assets. (Reg § 1.755-1)[7]

However, effective for distributions after Oct. 22, 2004, in allocating any basis reduction in partnership property under Code Sec. 734(b) as a result of a distribution, no allocation may be made to stock in a corporation that is a partner in the partnership, or to the stock of any person related to the corporation, and any amount not allocable to stock is allocated to other partnership property. Where the reduction that must be allocated to other partnership property exceeds the aggregate adjusted basis of the other partnership property immediately before the required allocation, gain is recognized by the partnership to the extent of the excess. (Code Sec. 755(c))[8]

Where the basis of a partnership's recovery property is increased as a result of a distribution of property by the partnership, the increased portion of the basis is taken into account for depreciation purposes as if it were newly purchased recovery property that is placed in

---

1. ¶B-4008; ¶7434; TD ¶591,511
2. ¶B-4007 *et seq.*; ¶7434; TD ¶591,500 *et seq.*
3. ¶B-4007 *et seq.*; ¶7434; TD ¶591,500 *et seq.*
4. ¶B-4021 *et seq.*; ¶7554; TD ¶591,532

5. ¶B-4002.1; ¶7344; TD ¶591,504
6. ¶B-4002; ¶7344.01; TD ¶591,504
7. ¶B-4021 *et seq.*; ¶7554; TD ¶591,532
8. ¶B-4054.1; ¶7554

service when the distribution or transfer occurs. Any applicable recovery period and method may be used to determine the recovery (depreciation) deduction for the increased portion of the basis. However, no change in determining the recovery (depreciation) deduction for the portion of the basis of recovery property for which there is no increase is allowed. (Reg § 1.734-1(e)(1))[9]

Where the basis adjustment requires a decrease in the basis of partnership recovery property, the basis decrease must be accounted for over the remaining recovery period of the property beginning with the recovery period in which the basis is decreased. (Reg § 1.734-1(e)(2))[10]

¶ 3778 Partner's basis adjustments.

Where a partnership interest is transferred and the partnership later distributes property, but hasn't made the election described at ¶3776, the transferee-partner may elect to have the basis of the property distributed to him adjusted as if the partnership had made the election. The election to make the adjustment applies only for purposes of determining the basis of distributed property (other than money) in the partner's hands. It doesn't enable the partner to amend prior income tax returns to recompute income based on an adjusted basis. (Code Sec. 732(d)) Accordingly, in computing the adjustment, no deduction is made for any depletion or depreciation of that portion of the basis of partnership property which arises from the basis adjustment, since no depletion or depreciation on the basis adjustment for the period before the distribution is allowed or allowable unless the partnership had an election in effect. (Reg § 1.732-1(d)(1)(iv))[11]

The transferee-partner may make this election only with respect to property (other than money) distributed to him within two years after he acquired his interest by transfer. (Code Sec. 732(d))[12]

The adjustment is *required* (without regard to the two-year limit) if at the time the transferee-partner acquired the transferred partnership interest all three of the following conditions existed:

(1) The fair market value of all partnership property (other than money) exceeded 110% of its adjusted basis to the partnership.

(2) Allocation of basis under Code Sec. 732(c) (general rule for allocation of basis of distributed properties) upon a liquidation of his interest immediately after the transfer of the interest would have resulted in a shift of basis from property not subject to depreciation, depletion or amortization to property that is so subject.

(3) The post-transfer adjustment would change the basis to the transferee-partner of the property actually distributed. (Code Sec. 732(d); Reg § 1.732-1(d)(4))[13]

¶ 3779 Basis of unrealized receivables and inventory items distributed to a partner.

If unrealized receivables or inventory items are distributed to a *transferee partner* who has a special basis adjustment for those assets under either the post-transfer adjustment rule (¶3776) or the distributed property adjustment rule (¶3777), the partnership's adjusted basis, immediately before distribution, of any unrealized receivables or inventory items distributed to such a partner takes into account the following portions of the post-transfer or distributed property basis adjustments that the distributee partner has for those assets:

---

9. ¶B-4007; ¶7344.01; TD ¶591,509
10. ¶B-4007; ¶7344.01; TD ¶591,509
11. ¶B-4029; ¶7324.01; TD ¶591,537

12. ¶B-4029; ¶7324.01; TD ¶591,537
13. ¶B-4033; ¶7324.01; TD ¶591,540

. . . The entire amount of the post-transfer or distributed property basis adjustments *if* the distributee-partner receives his entire share of the fair market value of the unrealized receivables or inventory items of the partnership.

. . . The same proportion of the post-transfer or distributed property basis adjustments as the value of the unrealized receivables or inventory items distributed to him bears to his entire share of the total value of all those items of the partnership, *if* the distributee-partner gets less than his entire share of those items. (Reg § 1.732-2(c))[14]

¶ 3780   Electing basis adjustments.

The election to adjust the basis of the partnership assets on a distribution or a sale or transfer of a partnership interest (¶3776, ¶3777) is made by the partnership filing a statement of election with the partnership return for the tax year during which the transfer of interest or the distribution of property occurs. (Code Sec. 754; Reg § 1.754-1(b))

Once made, the election applies to all current and future distributions and transfers until revoked. (Code Sec. 754; Reg § 1.754-1(a))[15]

A transferee-partner who wishes to make the distributed property adjustment (¶3778), must elect as follows:

. . . If the distribution includes any depreciable, depletable, or amortizable property, elect with the return for the distribution year.

. . . If it doesn't include any such property, elect not later than the first tax year in which the basis of any of the distributed property is pertinent in determining the transferee-partner's tax. (Reg § 1.732-1(d)(2), Reg § 1.732-1(d)(3))[16]

¶ 3781   Terminations.

A partnership ordinarily terminates only on discontinuance of operations as a partnership, or on sale or exchange of 50% or more of the total interests in the partnership.

¶ 3782   Termination of partnership.

A partnership terminates for tax purposes (whether or not it has terminated under applicable local law) when:

. . . it stops doing business as a partnership, or

. . . 50% or more of the total interest in partnership capital and profits changes hands by sale or exchange (or by distribution, unless excepted by regs) within 12 consecutive months. (Code Sec. 708, Code Sec. 761(e); Reg § 1.708-1(b)(1))[17] There has been such a change if a corporation transfers its 50% or more interest in a partnership to a new or different corporation in connection with a tax-free corporate reorganization. [18]

As a result of this sale or exchange, the partnership is deemed to transfer all of its assets and liabilities to a new partnership in exchange for an interest in the new partnership, and immediately after that, the terminated partnership is deemed to distribute interests in the new partnership to the purchasing partner and the remaining partners in liquidation of the terminated partnership, either for the continuation of the business of the new partnership or for its dissolution and winding up. (Reg § 1.708-1(b)(4))[19]

The sale may be made to an existing partner or an outsider. It may be made by one or more persons. A gift, bequest, or inheritance or liquidation of a partnership interest doesn't count;

---

14. ¶B-4018; TD ¶591,520
15. ¶B-4023; ¶7544.01; TD ¶591,501
16. ¶B-4031; ¶7324.01; TD ¶591,538

17. ¶B-4301; ¶7084; TD ¶594,001
18. ¶B-4303; ¶7084.05; TD ¶594,004
19. ¶B-4305; ¶7084; TD ¶594,006

nor does a contribution of property to a partnership in exchange for a partnership interest, even if this produces a 50% or more change. (Reg § 1.708-1(b)(2))[20]

¶ 3783 Split-up of partnership.

If a partnership splits up into two or more partnerships, each resulting partnership is considered a continuation of the old partnership as long as the members of the resulting partnership had more than a 50% interest in the capital and profits of the old partnership. A resulting partnership whose members had an interest of only 50% or less in the old partnership is treated as a new partnership.

If the members of none of the resulting partnerships had more than a 50% interest in the old partnership, the old partnership is considered terminated as of the date of the division, and all the resulting partnerships are treated as new partnerships. (Code Sec. 708(b)(2)(B); Reg § 1.708-1(d)(2))[21]

Any members of the original partnership who do not become members of a resulting partnership that is treated as a continuation of the original partnership are considered to have had their partnership interests liquidated as of the date of the division. (Reg § 1.708-1(d)(1))

For divisions, the resulting partnership that is treated as the divided partnership must file a return for the tax year of the partnership that has been divided and must retain the employer identification number (EIN) of the prior partnership. All other resulting partnerships that are regarded as continuing and new partnerships must file separate returns for the tax year beginning on the day after the date of the division with new EINs for each partnership. (Reg § 1.708-1(d)(2))

---

20. ¶B-4303; ¶7084.02; TD ¶594,004   21. ¶B-4307; ¶7084.06; TD ¶594,008

Chapter 18   Trusts—Estates—Decedents

¶ 3900   Trust and Estate Income Tax Rules

Trusts and estates are generally treated as separate taxpayers and, with some important qualifications, are taxed in the same way as individuals.

¶ 3901   Taxation of trusts and estates—Form 1041.

Trust and estate income is normally taxed to the fiduciary (that is, to the trust or estate itself), if retained by the trust, or to the beneficiary, if distributed. Thus, if the fiduciary passes on income to the beneficiary, the trust or estate deducts the distributed income which then becomes taxable to the beneficiary. A special yardstick called "distributable net income" (DNI) (see ¶3935 and ¶3937), is used to limit both the amount deducted by the trust or estate as a distribution and the amount taxed to the beneficiary. (Code Sec. 643, Code Sec. 651, Code Sec. 652, Code Sec. 661, Code Sec. 662)[1]

The income that's passed on to the beneficiary has the same tax attributes in the beneficiary's hands as when received by the fiduciary, see ¶3946.

Trusts and estates compute their tax under a separate, unfavorable tax rate schedule (¶1106) that has five brackets and that quickly reaches the top marginal rate. (Code Sec. 1(e))[2] Trusts and estates can't use the tax tables to figure their tax. (Code Sec. 3(b)(2))

⚠ *caution:* For treatment of trusts and estates for purposes of the alternative minimum tax, see ¶3200 *et seq.*

A foreign trust or estate is taxed as if it were a nonresident alien individual who isn't present in the U.S. at any time, see ¶4644 *et seq.*, subject to special rules for trusts. (Code Sec. 641(b))[3]

For income tax returns of trusts and estates (Form 1041, Schedule K-1), see ¶4735 *et seq.* Beneficiaries must report items consistently with the entity's return or notify IRS (on Form 8082) of the inconsistency. (Code Sec. 6034A(c)).[4]

For the tax years of trusts and estates, see ¶2808.

¶ 3902   Election to treat revocable trust as part of estate—Form 8855.

An election can be made to have an individual's revocable trust treated as part of his estate for income tax purposes. (Code Sec. 645) If there is an executor, the trustee and the executor make the election by filing Form 8855. If there is no executor, the trustee makes the election by filing Form 8855. (Reg § 1.645-1(c))[5]

¶ 3903   Estimated tax payments by trusts and estates—Form 1041-ES.

All trusts and certain estates must make estimated income tax payments (using Form 1041-ES and vouchers) under rules similar to those that apply to individuals, with certain adjustments. (Code Sec. 6654(l)(1))[6] Trusts and estates generally have 45 days to compute their estimated tax payments under the annualization rules. (Code Sec. 6654(l)(4))[7]

Estates and grantor trusts that receive the residue of a probate estate are exempt from making estimated tax payments for their first two tax years after the date of decedent's

---

1. ¶C-2600 *et seq.*, ¶C-7000 *et seq.*; ¶6414; TD ¶s 651,001, 661,001
2. ¶s C-1003 *et seq.*, C-7002 *et seq.*; ¶6414; TD ¶s 651,003, 661,003
3. ¶C-1014 *et seq.*, ¶O-10118; ¶6414; TD ¶665,501
4. ¶s C-3081, C-9081; ¶60,34A4; TD ¶665,029, TD ¶655,500

5. ¶C-1021 *et seq.*; ¶6454; TD ¶661,002
6. ¶s-5300 *et seq.*; ¶66,544.08; TD ¶658,501
7. ¶S-5304; ¶6434.08; TD ¶658,506

References beginning with a single letter are to paragraphs in RIA's Federal Tax Coordinator 2d and RIA's Analysis of Federal Taxes: Income. Those beginning with numbers are to paragraphs in RIA's United States Tax Reporter. Those beginning with TD are to paragraphs in RIA's Tax Desk.

death. (Code Sec. 6654(l)(2))[8] Charitable trusts subject to tax under Code Sec. 511 are subject to corporate, not individual estimated taxes. (Code Sec. 6654(l)(3), Code Sec. 6655(g)(3))[9]

A mechanism exists for crediting estimated taxes paid by an ESBT, ¶3910, to its owner. [10]

¶ 3904 Estimated tax payments for trusts and estates with short year.

A trust or estate with a short tax year must pay estimated tax installments on or before the 15th day of the 4th, 6th and 9th month of such tax year, and the 15th day of the first month of the following year. For a short tax year in which the trust or estate terminates, installments due before the last day of the short year must be paid, and a final installment must be paid by the 15th day of the first month following the month the short year ends. [11]

¶ 3905 Election to treat estimated tax payments as paid by beneficiary—Form 1041-T.

A trustee may elect (on Form 1041-T) to treat any part of the trust's estimated tax payments as paid by a beneficiary. Any amount so treated is considered paid or credited to the beneficiary on the last day of the trust's tax year and is considered an estimated tax payment made by the beneficiary on Jan. 15, following the trust's tax year. (Code Sec. 643(g)(1))[12]

This election is available to an estate if a tax year is reasonably expected to be its last tax year. (Code Sec. 643(g)(3))

Elect on or before the *65th day* after the tax year. (Code Sec. 643(g)(2)) Attach Form 1041-T to Form 1041 only if the election is made with Form 1041. Otherwise, file Form 1041-T separately. The election is irrevocable. (Reg § 301.9100-8(a)(4))[13]

🅡 *observation:* The income tax return of a trust or estate is normally due 3 ½ months after the close of its tax year, see ¶2808. Thus the election must be made before the due date of this return.

¶ 3906 Trust's termination.

When a trust terminates, it ends as a separate tax entity and no longer reports gross income or claims the deductions, credits, etc. (Reg § 1.641(b)-3(d))

Though the duration of a trust may depend on the occurrence of a particular event under the trust instrument, e.g., the life beneficiary reaching a specified age, for tax purposes the trust will nevertheless continue for a reasonable period beyond this time to allow for the orderly completion of administration. (Reg § 1.641(b)-3(b))[14]

For unused deductions allowed to a beneficiary on a trust's termination, see ¶3951.

¶ 3907 Estate's termination.

An estate's status as a separate taxpayer exists only during the period of administration and settlement of the estate. (Code Sec. 641(a)(3)) This period starts with the individual's death and generally extends for the entire time actually required to perform the ordinary duties of administration, such as collecting assets and paying legacies and debts. [15] If estate administration is unduly prolonged, IRS considers the estate terminated for tax purposes after expiration of a reasonable period (considering the estate's assets) for performance by the

8. ¶s S-5302, S-5203; ¶66,544.08; TD ¶s 658,502, 666,002
9. ¶s S-5301, S-5420; ¶66,554; TD ¶658,500
10. ¶S-5310.1
11. ¶S-5311; ¶6434.08; TD ¶658,503

12. ¶S-5309; ¶66,544.08; TD ¶654,022
13. ¶S-5310; ¶6434.08; TD ¶658,510
14. ¶C-1012; ¶6414.07; TD ¶651,011
15. ¶C-7010; ¶6414.03; TD ¶661,010

executor of all the duties of administration. (Reg § 1.641(b)-3(a))[16]

For unused deductions allowed to a beneficiary on an estate's termination, see ¶3951.

¶ 3908   Trusts taxed as business entity.

The fact that any organization is technically cast in the trust form, by conveying title to property to trustees for the benefit of persons designated as beneficiaries, won't change the real character of the organization if the organization is more properly classified as a business entity under Reg § 301.7701-2. (Reg § 301.7701-4(b))[17]

¶ 3909   Liquidating Trusts.

Liquidating trusts are ordinary trusts if their primary purpose is to liquidate the assets transferred to them. They are corporations if liquidation is only an incidental or ultimate intention and the primary objective is to continue normal business operations for an indefinite time. (Reg § 301.7701-4(d))[18]

¶ 3910   Electing Small Business Trusts for holding S Stock.

Electing small business trusts (ESBTs) may hold stock of an S corporation. For the portion of an ESBT consisting of S stock, the normal pass-through rules don't apply; instead, the trust is taxed at a flat rate of 35% on its taxable ordinary income as specially computed and its capital gains are taxed at the preferential rates that apply for individuals. And, for tax years beginning after 2006, interest paid or accrued on debt incurred to acquire S stock is taken into account in determining the income of the S portion of an ESBT. (Code Sec. 641(c)) A grantor trust may elect to be an ESBT and if it does, the trust consists of a grantor portion, an S portion, and a non-S portion. The items of income, deduction, and credit attributable to the grantor portion are taxed to the deemed owner of that portion. The S portion is taxed under the special rules of Code Sec. 641(c), while the non-S portion is subject to the normal trust rules. (Reg § 1.641(c)-1)[19]

¶ 3911   Environmental Remediation Trusts.

An environmental remediation trust is treated as a grantor trust. Each contributor is taxed on the portion of the trust relating to his contributions. (Reg § 301.7701-4(e))[20]

¶ 3912   Funeral trusts—Form 1041-QFT.

A pre-need funeral trust allows an individual to buy funeral services or merchandise from a funeral home or cemetery in advance of death. A trustee of a qualified funeral trust may elect simplified tax treatment for the trust on Form 1041-QFT, if it would otherwise be treated as a grantor trust. (Code Sec. 685)[21]

¶ 3913   Multiple trusts.

If a grantor creates several or "multiple" trusts, each trust is treated as a separate taxpayer. Several separate trusts may be created even though there is only one trust instrument and only one trustee. [22]

Two or more trusts are treated as one if: (1) the trusts have substantially the same grantor

---

16. ¶C-7011 *et seq.*; ¶6414.03; TD ¶661,010
17. ¶C-5003; ¶77,014.13; TD ¶651,025
18. ¶C-5015; ¶77,014.17; TD ¶651,027
19. ¶C-5700 *et seq.*; ¶6414.08; TD ¶657,500 *et seq.*

20. ¶C-5035.1; ¶77,014.12; TD ¶657,005
21. ¶C-1013.1; ¶6854; TD ¶657,018
22. ¶C-5150 *et seq.*; ¶6434.07; TD ¶651,034

or grantors and substantially the same primary beneficiary or beneficiaries, and (2) a principal purpose of the trusts is avoidance of federal income tax. (Code Sec. 643(f)) However, if a trust was irrevocable on Mar. 1, '84, this consolidation rule applies only to that portion of the trust attributable to contributions to corpus after Mar. 1, '84. [23]

¶ 3914 Charitable remainder annuity trust and charitable remainder unitrust.

These types of trusts (¶2116) are not subject to income tax. However, if they have unrelated business taxable income (UBTI) for a post-2006 tax year, they must pay an excise tax equal to 100% of the UBTI. (Code Sec. 664(c); Reg § 1.664-1(a)(1))[24]

¶ 3915 Pooled income fund.

A pooled income fund (PIF) formed to pay income to noncharitable beneficiaries and the remainder to charity (¶2117) generally is taxed under the trust rules [25] even if it isn't a trust under local law. (Reg § 1.642(c)-5(a)(2))[26] However, a PIF is allowed a charitable deduction for any and all long-term capital gain that is, under the terms of its governing instrument, permanently set aside for charitable purposes during the tax year. (Code Sec. 642(c)(3); Reg § 1.642(c)-2(c)) No amount of net long-term capital gain will be considered "permanently set aside for charitable purposes" if, under the terms of the PIF's governing instrument and applicable local law, the trustee has the power, whether or not exercised, to satisfy the income beneficiaries' right to income by the payment of either:

. . . an amount equal to a fixed percentage of the fair market value of the PIF's assets, whether determined annually or averaged on a multiple year basis; or

. . . any amount that takes into account unrealized appreciation in the value of the PIF's assets. (Reg § 1.642(c)-2(c))[27]

¶ 3916 Gross income of trusts and estates.

What would be gross income in the hands of an individual is gross income when received by a trust or estate —dividends, interest, rents, royalties, capital gains, ordinary gains, etc. (Reg § 1.641(a)-2)[28]

Gross income includes income accumulated or held for future distribution under the terms of a will or trust, income that's currently distributable, income received by a deceased's estate during administration or settlement, and income that, in the fiduciary's discretion, may be either accumulated or distributed. (Code Sec. 641(a))[29]

¶ 3917 Income from real estate passing directly to heirs.

Where under local law, real property is subject to an estate's administration, the income from it is that of the estate for the period that the estate is under administration. [30]

Where state law vests legal title to decedent's real estate upon his death directly in his heirs, devisees, or other beneficiaries, income from it is taxed to the beneficiaries and not the estate. (Reg § 1.661(a)-2(e)) But where because of insufficiency of funds to pay the deceased's debts, property is sold at the direction of the court, the gain realized upon the sale is, for tax purposes, divided between the heirs and the estate in proportion to the amount of the proceeds received by each. [31]

---

23. ¶C-5154; ¶6434.07; TD ¶651,034
24. ¶C-5039; ¶6644; TD ¶651,030
25. ¶s C-2312, C-2316; TD ¶651,031
26. ¶C-5040; TD ¶651,031
27. ¶C-2316; ¶6424.03

28. ¶s C-2100 *et seq.*, C-7100 *et seq.*; ¶6414; TD ¶s 652,001, 662,001
29. ¶s C-2101, C-7101; ¶6414 *et seq.*; TD ¶s 652,001, 662,001
30. ¶C-7105; TD ¶662,009
31. ¶C-7109; TD ¶662,009

¶ 3918   Gain or loss on distribution of property in kind.

Gain or loss is realized by a trust or estate (or the other beneficiaries) by reason of a distribution of property in kind if the distribution is in satisfaction of a right to receive a specific dollar amount, specific property other than that distributed, or income, if income is required to be distributed currently. In addition, gain or loss is realized if the trustee or executor makes the Code Sec. 643(e) election to recognize gain or loss. (Reg §   1.661(a)-2(f))[32]

Trusts and estates may not deduct a loss on property to which a Code Sec. 643(e)(3) election applies because of the rule barring loss deductions on sales between related parties. See ¶2448.

Different rules are slated to apply for estates of individuals dying in 2010.

¶ 3919   Estate income from community property.

If a married decedent dies leaving community property, the income from one-half of the property is taxable to the estate and the income from the other half is taxable to the surviving spouse.[33]

¶ 3920   Deductions and credits of trusts and estates.

Deductions and credits of trusts and estates are basically those allowed to individuals except for the special deduction rules discussed in the following paragraphs. (Code Sec. 641(b); Reg § 1.641(b)-1)[34]

¶ 3921   Two percent floor on miscellaneous itemized deductions.

For purposes of this floor (see ¶3110), the adjusted gross income of a trust or estate is computed the same as for an individual, except the deductions for: (1) costs paid or incurred in connection with the administration of the trust or estate (¶3922) that wouldn't have been incurred if the property weren't held in the trust or estate (the Sixth Circuit has held this includes investment counseling fees paid by the trust to aid the trustees in discharging their fiduciary duty to the trust beneficiaries —but several other courts disagree and the Supreme Court has agreed to resolve the issue); (2) the trust's or estate's personal exemptions (¶3928); and (3) distribution deductions (¶3934 and ¶3936), are allowed as deductions in arriving at adjusted gross income. (Code Sec. 67(e)) Thus, these expenses aren't subject to the floor.

Amounts that wouldn't be allowable as miscellaneous itemized deductions if paid directly by an individual can't be indirectly deducted through grantor trusts. (Code Sec. 67(c); Reg § 1.67-2T(g)(1), Reg § 1.67-2T(g)(2))

¶ 3922   Administration expenses.

Reasonable amounts paid or incurred by the fiduciary of an estate or trust on account of administration expenses, including fiduciaries' fees and litigation expenses, that are ordinary and necessary in the performance of duties of administration are deductible. (Reg §   1.212-1(i)) Deductible items include commissions and legal fees, whether allocable to corpus or income.[35] For the election to deduct these expenses against income or estate tax, see   ¶3925.

---

32. ¶s C-2151, C-7151; ¶6614.01; TD ¶s 652,006, 662,018

33. ¶C-7108; ¶6414.06; TD ¶662,008

34. ¶s C-2200 *et seq.*, C-7200 *et seq.*; ¶6414; TD ¶s 651,001,

661,001

35. ¶s C-2217, C-7215; ¶s 2124.09, 6424; TD ¶s 653,016, 663,014

¶ 3923 Interest deductions.

An estate or trust may deduct interest to the same extent as an individual, see ¶1700 *et seq*. Thus, an estate or trust is subject to the bar on the deduction of "personal" interest. But otherwise deductible interest on estate tax deferred because of a closely held business interest or a reversionary interest (see ¶5035) isn't subject to this limit (Code Sec. 163(h)), except that for estates of individuals dying after '97 and, if elected, of individuals dying before '98, interest on estate tax deferred because of a closely held business interest isn't deductible. (Code Sec. 163(k))[36]

¶ 3924 Expenses of exempt income.

No deduction may be taken for *any* expenses allocable to tax-exempt income. (Code Sec. 265; Reg § 1.212-1(i))[37]

¶ 3925 Election to take either income tax or estate tax deduction.

Administration expenses, including commissions and other selling expenses, and casualty and theft losses during administration may be taken either: (1) as a deduction (or as an offset against the sales price of property in determining gain or loss) in computing the estate's taxable income for *income tax* purposes, or (2) as a deduction in computing the decedent's taxable estate for *estate tax* purposes, but not both. (Code Sec. 642(g)) To take the income tax deduction, the executor should file in duplicate (a) a statement that the amount involved hasn't already been taken as a deduction for federal estate tax purposes, and (b) a waiver of the right to take it as an estate tax deduction. (Reg § 1.642(g)-1)[38]

Some items or portion of an item can be deducted for income tax purposes if the statement and waiver are filed, while a similar item or different portion of the same item can be taken for estate tax purposes. (Reg § 1.642(g)-2)[39]

Similar rules apply for purposes of the generation-skipping transfer tax. (Code Sec. 642(g))[40]

¶ 3926 Deductions that can be claimed for both income and estate tax purposes.

The rule barring deductions for *both* income tax and estate tax purposes (¶3925) doesn't apply to obligations of the decedent for interest, taxes and expenses that are allowable as deductions in respect of a decedent as explained at ¶3970 (Reg § 1.642(g)-2), or items that qualify for deduction on the estate tax return as claims against the estate, such as divorce settlement payments. [41]

¶ 3927 Depreciation and depletion.

Depreciation and depletion deductions of trust or estate property must be apportioned as follows:

For a *trust*, these deductions are generally apportioned between the beneficiaries and the trustee on the basis of the trust income allocable to each. (Code Sec. 167(d), Code Sec. 611(b)(3), Code Sec. 642(e))[42] But if the trustee is required or permitted by the trust instrument or local law to maintain a reserve for the deduction, the deduction belongs to the trust to the extent that income is actually set aside for the reserve. Apart from this, the regs

---

36. ¶K-5513; ¶s 1634.013, 1634.054; TD ¶663,010
37. ¶s C-2217, C-2219, C-7217; ¶2654; TD ¶s 653,016, 663,014
38. ¶C-7226 *et seq.*; ¶6424.07; TD ¶s 663,025, 776,082
39. ¶C-7232; ¶6424.07; TD ¶s 663,025, 77,6,082
40. ¶C-7227; ¶6424.07; TD ¶663,026
41. ¶s C-7234, C-7235; ¶6914.04; TD ¶663,033, TD ¶776,082
42. ¶C-2222 *et seq.*; ¶6424.06; TD ¶s 653,019, 663,019

bar any deduction by the trust or a beneficiary that exceeds the trust's or beneficiary's allocable share of trust income. (Reg § 1.167(h)-1(b), Reg § 1.611-1(c)(4))[43]

For an *estate*, the deductions are apportioned between the estate and the heirs, legatees and devisees on the basis of the estate income allocable to each, regardless of the terms of the will. (Code Sec. 167(d), Code Sec. 611(b)(4))[44]

¶ 3928 Personal exemption.

An estate is entitled to a deduction for a personal exemption of $600. (Code Sec. 642(b))[45]

A trust that's required to distribute all of its income currently has a $300 exemption (even for a year in which it makes a corpus distribution or a charitable contribution). All other trusts deduct $100. (Code Sec. 642(b); Reg § 1.642(b)-1)[46]

¶ 3929 Standard deduction.

The standard deduction of a trust or estate is zero. (Code Sec. 63(c)(6)(D))[47]

¶ 3930 Net operating loss.

Trusts and estates are entitled to the net operating loss (NOL) deduction. (Code Sec. 642(d)) In computing the NOL, the charitable deduction and the deduction for distributions are disregarded. (Reg § 1.642(d)-1)[48]

¶ 3931 Charitable contributions—Form 1041-A.

An estate or trust may deduct any amount of gross income, without limitation, that, under the terms of the governing instrument is *paid* during the tax year for a charitable purpose. (Code Sec. 642(c)(1); Reg § 1.642(c)-1(a))[49] These deductions aren't subject to the 2% floor on miscellaneous itemized deductions, see ¶3110. (Code Sec. 67(b)(4)) File Form 1041-A for a trust that claims a charitable deduction under Code Sec. 642(c). Use Form 8868 for an extension, see ¶4124.

Estates are allowed to deduct any amount of gross income, without limit, which under the terms of the governing instrument is, during the tax year, permanently *set aside* for a charitable purpose. (Code Sec. 642(c)(2); Reg § 1.642(c)-2(a), Reg § 1.642(c)-2(b))[50] *Trusts* are denied the set-aside deduction, except for pooled income funds. (Code Sec. 642(c)(2), Code Sec. 642(c)(3); Reg § 1.642(c)-2(b), Reg § 1.642(c)-2(c))[1]

Contributions made out of tax-exempt income, such as state or municipal bond interest, aren't deductible. (Reg § 1.642(c)-3(b), Reg § 1.643(a)-5(b))[2]

¶ 3932 Election to accelerate charitable deduction.

A fiduciary of a trust or estate can elect to treat a contribution actually paid in one tax year as paid in the preceding tax year. (Code Sec. 642(c)(1))[3]

The election to accelerate the deduction must be made not later than the time, including extensions, prescribed for filing the income tax return for the tax year *following the tax year* to which the deductions are pushed back. Elect by attaching a statement to the return or

---

43. ¶C-2214, C-2224; ¶6424.06; TD ¶653,019
44. ¶C-7220; ¶s 1674.119, 6424.06; TD ¶663,019
45. ¶C-7207; ¶6424.01; TD ¶663,006
46. ¶C-2206; ¶6424.01; TD ¶653,004
47. ¶s C-2204, C-7205; ¶634; TD ¶s 653,003, 663,004
48. ¶s C-2226, C-7222; ¶6424.05; TD ¶s 653,022, 663,021

49. ¶s C-2301 *et seq.*, C-7301 *et seq.*; ¶6424.02; TD ¶s 653,023, 663,036
50. ¶C-7311; ¶6424.02; TD ¶663,036
1. ¶C-2312 *et seq.*; ¶6424.03; TD ¶653,031
2. ¶s C-2308, C-7308; ¶6424.02; TD ¶s 653,029, 663,042
3. ¶s C-2303, C-7304; ¶6424.02; TD ¶s 653,026, 663,039

amended return for the year to which the deductions are pushed back. (Reg § 1.642(c)-1(b))[4]

¶ 3933 Deduction for distributions to beneficiaries of trusts and estates.

A deduction is allowed for distributions to beneficiaries up to the "distributable net income" (DNI) of the trust or estate for the tax year. (Code Sec. 651(b), Code Sec. 661(a))[5] The distribution deduction of a trust depends upon whether the trust is a simple trust (¶3934) or a complex trust (¶3936).

A "simple" trust is one that makes no distribution other than of current income and the terms of which require all of its income to be distributed currently and do not provide for charitable or similar contributions. A "complex" trust permits accumulation of income or charitable contributions or distributes principal.

A trust may shift its character from simple to complex and vice versa. (Reg § 1.651(a)-1, Reg § 1.661(a)-1)[6]

¶ 3934 Distributions deduction of a simple trust.

This deduction for a simple trust is the amount of its income for the tax year that's required to be distributed currently, up to the ceiling of its DNI for the year (¶3935). (Code Sec. 651(b)) Tax-exempt income is excluded both from accounting income and DNI in figuring the deduction. (Reg § 1.651(b)-1)[7]

¶ 3935 Distributable net income of a simple trust.

The starting point is *taxable* income, i.e., gross income minus deductions. These adjustments are then made to taxable income:

(1) Add back the deduction for personal exemption and any deduction for distributions. (Code Sec. 643(a)(1), Code Sec. 643(a)(2); Reg § 1.643(a)-1, Reg § 1.643(a)-2)

(2) Subtract any extraordinary dividends (in cash or property) and taxable stock dividends that the trustee doesn't pay or credit because he determines they are allocable to principal. (Code Sec. 643(a)(4); Reg § 1.643(a)-4)

(3) Subtract any capital gains that are allocated to principal and aren't paid, credited or required to be distributed during the tax year. Also add back any capital losses, except to the extent they are taken into account in computing capital gains that are paid, credited or required to be distributed during the tax year. And add back any gain excluded under Code Sec. 1202 on the sale of stock in a qualified small business corporation. (Code Sec. 643(a)(3); Reg § 1.643(a)-3(b))[8]

Gains from the sale or exchange of capital assets are included in DNI to the extent they are allocated to: (i) income; (ii) corpus, but treated consistently by the fiduciary on the trust's books, records, and tax returns as part of a distribution to a beneficiary; or (iii) corpus, but actually distributed to the beneficiary or used by the fiduciary in determining the amount that is distributed or required to be distributed to a beneficiary. (Reg § 1.643(a)-3(b)) If income under the state statute is defined as, or consists of, a unitrust amount, a discretionary power to allocate gains to income must also be exercised consistently and the amount so allocated may not be greater than the excess of the unitrust amount over the amount of DNI determined without regard to the forgoing rule. (Reg § 1.643(a)-3(b)(1))[9]

---

4. ¶s C-2305, C-7305; ¶6424.02; TD ¶s 653,027, 663,039
5. ¶s C-2501, C-8001; ¶6514; TD ¶s 654,001, 664,001
6. ¶C-2501; ¶6514.01; TD ¶654,030

7. ¶C-2603 *et seq.*; ¶6514.01; TD ¶654,013
8. ¶C-2606 *et seq.*; ¶6434.01; TD ¶654,032
9. ¶C-2608; ¶6434.01; TD ¶654,034

¶ 3936   Distributions deduction of a complex trust or estate.

A complex trust or estate deducts, up to its DNI ceiling for the year (¶3937), the sum of:

(1) any income for the tax year required to be distributed currently (¶3938); and

(2) any other amounts, whether income or principal, properly paid or credited or required to be distributed for that tax year (¶3939). (Code Sec. 661(a); Reg § 1.661(a)-2(a))[10]

No distributions deduction may be taken for any portion of DNI that represents an item, such as tax-exempt interest, that isn't included in the gross income of the trust or estate. (Code Sec. 661(c); Reg § 1.661(c)-1) Unless the instrument or local law requires another allocation, the distribution is considered to contain the same proportion of tax-exempt items entering into DNI as the total tax-exempt income bears to total DNI. (Code Sec. 661(b); Reg § 1.661(b)-1)[11]

¶ 3937   Distributable net income for a complex trust or estate.

The DNI of a complex trust or an estate is its taxable income with these adjustments:

(1) No deduction for distributions or personal exemption is allowed. (Code Sec. 643(a)(1))

(2) Capital gains are excluded unless: allocated to income; allocated to corpus, but treated consistently by the fiduciary on its books, records, and tax returns as part of a distribution to a beneficiary; allocated to corpus but actually distributed to the beneficiary or used by the fiduciary in determining the amount that is distributed or required to be distributed to a beneficiary; or allowed as a charitable deduction. Capital losses are excluded except to the extent they enter into a determination of any capital gains paid, credited or required to be distributed to a beneficiary during the tax year. Add back any gain excluded under Code Sec. 1202 on the sale of stock in a qualified small business corporation. (Code Sec. 643(a)(3); Reg § 1.643(a)-3(b))

(3) Tax-exempt interest, reduced by allocable, nondeductible expenses, is *included* except to the extent allocable to the charitable deduction. (Code Sec. 643(a)(5); Reg § 1.643(a)-5)[12]

¶ 3938   "Income required to be distributed currently."

Income required to be distributed currently means accounting income of the trust or estate determined under the trust instrument or will and applicable local law. It doesn't include items of gross income that the fiduciary allocates to corpus. (Code Sec. 643(b))

The definition of accounting income in the regs reflects changed state law definitions. Thus, an allocation of amounts between income and principal pursuant to applicable local law will be respected if local law provides for a reasonable apportionment between the income and remainder beneficiaries of the total return of the trust for the year, including ordinary and tax-exempt income, capital gains, and appreciation. (Reg § 1.643(b)-1)

A distribution required to be made out of income or corpus, such as an annuity, is considered to be out of currently distributable income to the extent it's paid out of income for the tax year. (Code Sec. 661(a)(1); Reg § 1.661(a)-2(b))

Currently distributable income is deductible for the tax year of the trust or estate in which it is received even though, as a matter of practical necessity, it isn't distributed until after the end of that year. (Reg § 1.651(a)-2(a), Reg § 1.651(a)-2(b))[13]

---

10. ¶s C-2701, C-8101; ¶6614.01; TD ¶s 654,037, 664,001

11. ¶s C-2707, C-8107; TD ¶s 654,043, 664,036.

12. ¶s C-2702 *et seq.*, C-8102 *et seq.*; ¶6434.01; TD ¶s 654,038,

664,030

13. ¶s C-2504 *et seq.*, C-8003 *et seq.*; ¶s 6434.03, 6514.01, 6624.01; TD ¶s 654,003, 664,003

¶ 3939 "Other amounts properly paid or credited or required to be distributed."

Other amounts properly paid or credited or required to be distributed must be actually distributed or at least made available on demand by the beneficiary. Even though designated by the fiduciary as a payment of *principal* of the trust or estate, a distribution actually paid or made available is deductible by the fiduciary as a distribution of "other amounts." It isn't necessary that the distribution actually be made out of income. (Code Sec. 661(a); Reg § 1.661(a)-2(c))[14] An amount that a trust has elected to treat as an estimated tax payment by a beneficiary (¶3905) is a deductible distribution. (Code Sec. 643(g))[15]

¶ 3940 Deduction for distribution of property in kind.

Distributions of property in kind qualify for deduction as other amounts paid. (Reg § 1.661(a)-2(c)) If the trust or estate elects to recognize gain or loss (¶3918), the property distributed is taken into account at its fair market value for purposes of the distribution deduction. If the election isn't made, the property is taken into account only to the extent of the lesser of the basis of the property in the hands of the beneficiary (¶3949) or the fair market value of the property. (Code Sec. 643(e)(2), Code Sec. 643(e)(3))[16]

¶ 3941 Family support allowances—"widow's allowance."

Family support allowances (for a decedent's widow or dependent) paid by an estate under a court order or decree, or under local law, are treated as estate distributions deductible by the estate, subject to the regular DNI deduction ceiling. (Reg § 1.661(a)-2(e), Reg § 1.662(a)-2(c))[17]

¶ 3942 Nonqualifying distributions.

No *distributions* deduction is allowed for:

... distributions to charity (Reg § 1.663(a)-2);[18]

... the value of any interest in real estate, title to which passes directly from decedent to his heirs and devisees (Reg § 1.661(a)-2(e));[19]

... a gift or bequest of specific property or of a specific sum of money that is paid or credited all at once or in not more than three installments —an amount that can be paid only from income isn't considered a gift or bequest of a specific sum of money and is therefore includible in the distributions deduction (Code Sec. 663(a)(1));[20]

... any amount reported as a distribution in an earlier year's return because it was credited or required to be distributed in the earlier year (Code Sec. 663(a)(3); Reg § 1.663(a)-3);[21]

... any amount paid or credited within the first 65 days of the current year which the fiduciary elected to treat as paid or credited in the preceding year, see ¶3943.

¶ 3943 Trust's and estate's election to deduct "late paid" distributions—the "65-day rule."

The fiduciary of a complex trust and the executor of an estate can elect, by checking a box on Form 1041, to treat an amount properly paid or credited within the first 65 days of any tax

14. ¶s C-2524 *et seq.*, C-8014 *et seq.*; ¶s 6614.01, 6624.01; TD ¶s 654,018, 664,013
15. ¶C-2530; ¶6434.08; TD ¶654,022
16. ¶s C-2525, C-8015; ¶6434.05; TD ¶s 654,019, 664,014
17. ¶C-8011; ¶6614.01; TD ¶664,011

18. ¶s C-2533, C-8026; ¶6614.01; TD ¶s 65,4,027, 664,025
19. ¶C-8027; TD ¶664,026
20. ¶s C-2531 *et seq.*, C-8022 *et seq.*; ¶6614.01; TD ¶s 65,4,024, 664,021
21. ¶s C-2534, C-8028; ¶6614.01; TD ¶s 654,028, 664,027

year of the trust as paid or credited on the last day of the preceding tax year. (Code Sec. 663(b))[22] This gives the trustee or executor time to determine income earned by the trust for the year, and the opportunity to deduct distributions of that income on the return for the year earned.

The amount to which the election applies can't exceed the greater of: (1) the entity's accounting income for the year for which the election is made, or (2) its DNI for that year, in each case reduced by any amounts paid, credited, or required to be distributed in that year other than amounts considered paid or credited in a preceding tax year by reason of the "65-day" rule. (Reg § 1.663(b)-1(a))[23]

¶ 3944   Amount taxed to beneficiary of a simple trust.

The beneficiary of a simple trust is in general taxed on the *lower* of these two items:

(1) the amount of trust income for the tax year of the trust required to be distributed to the beneficiary currently whether distributed or not; or

(2) the beneficiary's proportionate share of the trust's DNI. (Code Sec. 652(a); Reg § 1.652(a)-1)

DNI is computed as explained at ¶3935, except that for this purpose it includes tax-exempt interest minus allocable deductions. (Code Sec. 643(a)(5)) Tax-exempt income items, however, aren't taxable to the beneficiary because of the character rule explained at ¶3946. Income from outside U.S. sources is included for foreign trusts. (Code Sec. 643(a)(6))[24]

¶ 3945   Amount taxed to beneficiary of a complex trust or estate.

The beneficiary of a complex trust or of an estate includes in gross income the sum of the following amounts, subject to the DNI ceiling (see below) and the elimination of tax-exempt items under the character rule (¶3946):

(1) income required to be distributed to him currently (though not actually distributed), which includes an annuity or other amount required to be paid out of income or corpus, to the extent it is paid out of income for the tax year; and

(2) all other amounts (whether from income or principal) properly paid, credited or required to be distributed to him for the tax year (Code Sec. 662(a))[25] including income from property distributed in-kind, see ¶3949. (Reg § 1.662(a)-3(b))

DNI ceiling. A beneficiary of a complex trust or an estate need not report as income more than his share of DNI, so that the total amount of income reported by all beneficiaries cannot exceed the total DNI of the trust or estate for the tax year. For this purpose, the beneficiaries are divided into two groups or "tiers:"

(1) The first tier is composed of beneficiaries entitled to income distributions currently, that is "income required to be distributed currently."

(2) The second tier is composed of beneficiaries receiving or entitled to receive other "noncurrent" distributions. (Code Sec. 662(a); Reg § 1.662(a)-3(c))[26]

First-tier beneficiaries report, in the aggregate, the amount of their current distributions, up to the amount of DNI for the tax year of the trust or estate, computed as explained at ¶3937 without any charitable deduction. Thus, if the total of first-tier distributions is equal to or less than DNI (without charitable deduction), each first-tier beneficiary reports his full

---

22. ¶C-2713, ¶C-8113; ¶6634.03; TD ¶654,052, TD ¶664,047
23. ¶C-2713, ¶C-8113; ¶6634.03; TD ¶654,052
24. ¶C-3001; ¶s 6524, 6524.02, 6434.01; TD ¶655,001

25. ¶s C-3006 *et seq.*, C-9001 *et seq.*; ¶6624; TD ¶s 655,006, 665,001
26. ¶s C-3010, C-9006; ¶6624; TD ¶s 655,009, 665,005

share of the distributions. (Code Sec. 662(a)(1))[27]

But if the total of first-tier distributions exceeds DNI (without charitable deduction) each beneficiary reports an amount equal to his pro rata share of DNI (without charitable deduction). (Code Sec. 662(a)(1); Reg § 1.662(a)-2(b))[28]

Second-tier beneficiaries report, in the aggregate, the amount of their second-tier distributions up to the DNI of the trust or estate as reduced for first-tier distributions of current income. For this purpose, DNI is computed *with* allowance of any charitable deduction.

If the total of second-tier distributions equals or is less than the ceiling (DNI as reduced for first-tier distributions), each second-tier beneficiary reports his or her full share of the second-tier distributions. But, if the total of second-tier distributions exceeds the ceiling, each second-tier beneficiary reports only his pro rata share of the ceiling amount. (Code Sec. 662(a)(2); Reg § 1.662(a)-3(c))[29]

¶ 3946   Character of trust's and estate's income in beneficiary's hands.

For simple trusts, complex trusts and estates, the amounts taxable to the beneficiaries have the same character (e.g., as tax-exempt income) in the hands of the beneficiaries as the amounts had when received by the trust or estate. (Code Sec. 652(b), Code Sec. 662(b); Reg § 1.652(b)-1, Reg § 1.662(b)-1)[30]

Unless the instrument specifically allocates different classes of income to different beneficiaries, amounts distributed are treated as consisting of the same proportion of each class of items entering into the computation of DNI as the total of each class bears to the total DNI of the trust or estate. (Code Sec. 652(b), Code Sec. 662(b); Reg § 1.652(b)-1, Reg § 1.662(b)-1)[31]

Allocation of deductions. Deductions that enter into the computation of DNI are allocated among the various classes as follows:

. . . Deductions *directly* attributable to a particular class of income (interest, rents, dividends, capital gains, etc.) are allocated to that class.

. . . If deductions *directly* attributable to a class of income exceed that class, the excess may be allocated to any other class (including capital gains) included in DNI in the manner shown below for deductions not directly attributable, except that excess deductions directly attributable to tax-exempt income cannot be used to reduce any other class of income.

. . . Deductions not directly attributable to a specific class of income can be allocated to any item of income (including capital gains) included in DNI, but a part must be allocated proportionately to tax-exempt income. Examples of these "neutral" deductions are trustees' commissions (both income and corpus), and state income and personal property taxes. (Reg § 1.652(b)-3)[32]

A *charitable deduction* by an estate or complex trust is allocated just before the other deductions. Allocation follows the terms of the instrument or local law, but if these are silent, the charitable deduction is allocated to each class of income items in the proportion the total that each class bears to the total of all classes. (Reg § 1.643(a)-5(b), Reg § 1.662(b)-2)[33]

---

27. ¶s C-3011 *et seq.*, C-9007 *et seq.*; ¶6624; TD ¶s 655,010, 665,006
28. ¶s C-3011, C-9008; ¶6624; TD ¶s 655,011, 665,007
29. ¶s C-3013, C-9009; ¶6624; TD ¶s 655,012, 665,008
30. ¶s C-3002, C-3016, C-9012; ¶s 6524.03, 6624.03; TD ¶s 655,002, 655,015, 665,011

31. ¶s C-3003, C-3016, C-9012; ¶s 6524.02, 6624.02; TD ¶s 655,005, 655,015, 665,011
32. ¶s C-3004, C-3017, C-9013; ¶s 6524, 6524.02, 6624.02; TD ¶s 655,005, 655,016, 665,012
33. ¶s C-3018, C-9015; ¶6624; TD ¶655,017, 665,014

¶ 3947   Beneficiaries' separate shares treated separately.

If a complex trust accumulates income for one beneficiary and distributes principal to another beneficiary, the normal tax rules would impose a tax burden on the recipient of principal since he in effect must pay tax on income accumulated for the other beneficiary. To prevent this, the "separate share rule" treats substantially separate and independent shares of different beneficiaries of a single trust as though each share represented a separate trust. This applies *only* in computing DNI as a ceiling on the amount deductible by the trust and taxable to the beneficiaries (Code Sec. 663(c); Reg § 1.663(c)-1(b)), only to complex trusts, and is mandatory. (Reg § 1.663(c)-1(d))[34] A similar separate share rule applies to beneficiaries of estates of decedents dying after Aug. 5, '97. (Code Sec. 663(c), Reg § 1.663(c)-1(a))[35] A surviving spouse's elective share is a separate share, [36] as is a pecuniary formula bequest unless it's not entitled to income or to share in appreciation or depreciation and it can paid or credited in more than three installments. (Reg § 1.663(c)-4(b))[37]

¶ 3948   When a beneficiary is taxed.

Current distributions (amounts required to be distributed currently) are taxed to the beneficiary when they are required to be distributed even though not actually distributed. Other distributions are taxed to a beneficiary when they are made or credited, or required to be made. (Code Sec. 652(a), Code Sec. 662(a); Reg § 1.662(a)-3(a))[38]

If a beneficiary's tax year is different from that of the estate or trust, the beneficiary includes his share of the trust or estate income in his return for the tax year in which the tax year of the trust or estate ends. (Code Sec. 652(c), Code Sec. 662(c))[39]

Upon termination of an estate, a beneficiary must include in his calendar year return income received from the estate during both the estate's fiscal year and final short year where both years end within his calendar year. [40]

Where the 65-day rule is elected (¶3943), the beneficiary is considered as receiving the distribution in his tax year that includes the close of the trust's or estate's tax year in which the distribution is considered made. (Reg § 1.663(b)-1(a)(2)(ii))[41]

¶ 3949   Distributions in kind includible in a beneficiary's income.

For property distributed in kind, the amount taken into account under Code Sec. 662(a)(2) (¶3945) for purposes of determining the amount includible in the beneficiary's income and for purposes of determining his basis in the property depends on whether the estate or trust elected to recognize gain or loss on the distribution (see ¶3918).

If the estate or trust elects , the property is taken into account at its fair market value. (Code Sec. 643(e)(3))

If the estate or trust doesn't elect , the property is taken into account only to the extent of the lesser of: (1) the fair market value of the property, or (2) its basis in the hands of the beneficiary. (Code Sec. 643(e)(2))[42]

The beneficiary's basis for property distributed in kind is the adjusted basis of the property in the hands of the estate or trust immediately before the distribution, adjusted for any gain or loss recognized by the estate or trust on the distribution. (Code Sec. 643(e)(1))[43]

---

34. ¶C-2711 *et seq.*; ¶6634.01; TD ¶654,047
35. ¶C-8111; ¶6634.01; TD ¶664,040
36. ¶C-8112.1; ¶6634.01; TD ¶664,042
37. ¶C-8112.2; ¶6634.01; TD ¶664,043
38. ¶s C-3025, C-9017; ¶s 6524.01, 6624.01; TD ¶s 655,020, 665,016
39. ¶s C-3026, C-9018; ¶s 6524.04, 6624.04; TD ¶s 655,021, 665,017
40. ¶C-9018; TD ¶665,017
41. ¶C-3028, ¶C-9019; ¶6634.03; TD ¶655,020
42. ¶s C-3009, C-9004; ¶6434.05; TD ¶s 655,008, 665,003
43. ¶s C-3009, C-9004; ¶6614.01; TD ¶s 655,008, 665,003

¶ 3950 Nontaxable gifts and bequests.

A beneficiary isn't taxable on any amount paid or credited as a gift or bequest of specific property or of a specific sum of money, and that is paid or credited all at once or in not more than three installments. But an amount that can be paid only from *income* isn't excludable. (Code Sec. 663(a)(1); Reg § 1.102-1(c))[44]

¶ 3951 Beneficiaries' deductions on estate or trust termination.

Beneficiaries who succeed to property of a trust or estate on its termination can deduct as a miscellaneous itemized deduction the unused deductions in excess of gross income for the last tax year of the trust or estate, other than the personal exemption and charitable contributions. The deduction by the beneficiary is allowed only for his tax year in which the trust or estate terminates. It is taken into account in computing the beneficiary's items of tax preference. (Code Sec. 642(h); Reg § 1.642(h)-2(a))[45]

¶ 3952 Taxation of beneficiaries of charitable remainder trusts—CRTs.

Amounts paid to an income beneficiary of a CRT retain the character they had in the hands of the trust, with this qualification: each payment is treated as consisting of: (1) ordinary income, to the extent of the trust's ordinary income for that year and undistributed ordinary income for earlier years, (2) capital gain, to the extent of capital gain for that year and undistributed capital gain (determined on a cumulative net basis) for earlier years, (3) other income (e.g., tax-exempt interest), to the extent of that income for that year and undistributed amounts for earlier years, and (4) trust corpus. (Code Sec. 664(a), Code Sec. 664(b); Reg § 1.664-1(d)(1)) Within categories (1) and (2), items are assigned to different classes to reflect rate differences (e.g., qualified dividends and different capital gain classes). (Reg § 1.664-1(d)(1)(i)(b)) Regs prevent individuals from using charitable remainder trusts to cash in appreciated property without being taxed currently. (Reg § 1.643(a)-8)[46]

¶ 3953 Distribution of accumulated trust income—"throwback" rules.

The "throwback rules" tax beneficiaries on distributions of income accumulated by the trust before the year of distribution, as though the income had been distributed currently to the beneficiaries in the years received by the trust. (Reg § 1.665(a)-0A(a)(1))[47]

The throwback rules apply to foreign trusts, domestic trusts previously treated as foreign trusts (except as provided in regs), and domestic trusts created before Mar. 1, '84, that would be treated as multiple trusts under Code Sec. 643(f). (Code Sec. 665(c))

The throwback rules generally apply only to complex trusts. Estates aren't subject to the throwback rules. (Code Sec. 666; Reg § 1.665(a)-0A(d))[48]

The fiduciary of a trust subject to the throwback rules must complete Schedule J (Form 1041) and attach it to the trust's return. [49]

¶ 3954 Distributions exempt from the throwback rules.

These distributions are exempt from the throwback rules:

• Distributions of income accumulated before birth of beneficiary or before beneficiary reaches age 21. But this exclusion doesn't apply to distributions from a foreign trust or to

---

44. ¶s C-2531, C-8022; ¶6634.02; TD ¶s 654,024, 664,021
45. ¶s C-3033 *et seq.*, C-9053 *et seq.*; ¶6434.04; TD ¶s 655,025, 665,022
46. ¶C-3051; ¶6644.01; TD ¶655,030
47. ¶C-4001; ¶6664; TD ¶656,001
48. ¶C-4002; ¶6664; TD ¶656,002
49. ¶C-4001; ¶6664; TD ¶656,001

certain distributions from multiple trusts. (Code Sec. 665(b))[50]

• Distributions not exceeding accounting income. (Code Sec. 665(b))[1]

¶ 3955 Beneficiary's tax under throwback rules—Form 4970.

The beneficiary includes in his income for the current year:

... the amount of the accumulation distribution considered distributed; and

... the trust's income tax considered distributed. (Code Sec. 667(a), Code Sec. 666(b))[2]

The beneficiary's total tax liability for the current year is:

(1) a partial tax on the beneficiary's taxable income *reduced* by the total amounts considered distributed to the beneficiary under the throwback rules; *plus*

(2) a partial tax on the amounts considered distributed under the throwback rules (Code Sec. 667(a)); *plus*

(3) in the case of a foreign trust, a special nondeductible interest charge. (Code Sec. 667(b))[3]

The beneficiary's partial tax under (2) is computed (on Form 4970) under a special "short-cut" method and is then reduced by any estate tax or generation-skipping transfer tax attributable to the partial tax. (Code Sec. 667(b)(6))[4]

¶ 3956 Grantor or others taxed as owner of trust—Grantor trust rules.

A trust grantor or another person with power over the trust or its property may (instead of the fiduciary) be taxed on its income as the "owner" of the trust. These grantor trust rules are discussed at ¶3957 *et seq.*[5] These rules don't apply to charitable remainder trusts or pooled income funds. (Reg § 1.671-1(d)[6] These rules generally apply only to the extent they result in amounts being currently taken into account in computing the income of a U.S. citizen, resident or domestic corporation. (Code Sec. 672(f); Reg § 1.672(f)-1, Reg § 1.672(f)-2, Reg § 1.672(f)-3)

RIA *observation:* Thus, the grantor trust rules generally don't apply where they would treat a foreign person as owner of the trust. This ensures that either the U.S. or the foreign jurisdiction taxes the trust income.

For purposes of these rules, a grantor includes any person who creates a trust, or directly or indirectly makes a gratuitous transfer of property, including cash, to a trust. (Reg § 1.671-2(e))[7]

These rules may be applicable to the entire trust or, where appropriate, to only a specific portion of a trust. (Reg § 1.671-3(a))[8] If a grantor or other person is considered to be the owner of the *entire* trust, he computes his own personal income tax by taking into account all trust income, deductions and credits, as though the trust didn't exist. (Reg § 1.671-3(a)(1)) But, where a grantor is treated as owner solely because of his interest in trust *income*, he takes into account only his share of trust items that would be reported by a current income beneficiary. (Reg § 1.671-3(c))[9]

For purposes of taxing the grantor as the owner of a trust, the grantor is treated as holding any power or interest held by any individual who was the spouse of the grantor at the time of the creation of the power or the interest, or who became the spouse of the grantor after the creation, but only for periods after the individual became the spouse. (Code Sec. 672(e)(1))

---

50. ¶C-4007; ¶6664; TD ¶656,005
1. ¶C-4008; ¶6664; TD ¶656,005
2. ¶C-4101; ¶6664; TD ¶656,008
3. ¶C-4101; ¶6664; TD ¶656,009
4. ¶C-4100 *et seq.*; ¶6664; TD ¶656,009

5. ¶C-5200 *et seq.*; ¶6714; TD ¶657,000
6. ¶C-5216; ¶6714; TD ¶655,030
7. ¶C-5201; ¶6714; TD ¶657,001
8. ¶C-5207 *et seq.*; ¶6714; TD ¶657,013
9. ¶C-5209 *et seq.*; ¶6714; TD ¶657,012

This rule applies only to transfers in trust made after Mar. 1, '86. [10]

A "defective grantor trust" is a trust intentionally structured so that the grantor, rather than the trust or its beneficiaries, will be taxed on the trust's income without the trust being included in the grantor's estate. A defective grantor trust can lower income taxes where the grantor is in a lower bracket than the beneficiary or some income would be accumulated in the trust and taxed at the highly compressed trust tax brackets. The grantor's payment of income tax on trust income taxed to him is not a gift to the beneficiaries. If a defective grantor trust or applicable state law requires the trustee to reimburse the grantor for the income tax on trust income, the full value of the trust property will be included in the grantor's gross estate for trusts created after Oct. 3, 2004. [11]

¶ 3957 Power to revoke.

If the grantor of a trust reserves the power to take back title to the trust funds for himself, he is considered the owner of the trust, whether or not he actually exercises that power. (Code Sec. 671, Code Sec. 676) The power to get back the trust funds may be a power to revoke, terminate, alter or amend, or to appoint. (Reg § 1.676(a)-1)

The grantor is taxed if he can exercise the power alone, if it can be exercised only by another who is regarded as a *nonadverse* party, or if it can be exercised by both the grantor and a nonadverse party together. (Code Sec. 676(a))[12] The grantor is not taxed if the power can be exercised only by or with consent of an adverse party. (Code Sec. 672(a), Code Sec. 676(a); Reg § 1.676(a)-1)[13]

An "adverse party" is any person with a substantial beneficial interest in the trust (including a general power of appointment over trust property) which would be adversely affected by the exercise or non-exercise of his power with regards to the trust. (Code Sec. 672(a)) A beneficiary is ordinarily an adverse party. (Reg § 1.672(a)-1(b)) A "nonadverse party" has either no beneficial interest, or one that is not substantial, or one which would not be adversely affected by the exercise of his power with regard to the trust. (Code Sec. 672(b); Reg § 1.672(b)-1)[14]

¶ 3958 Income for grantor, spouse or dependent.

The grantor of a trust is treated as its owner and taxed on its income, if the trust income is:

. . . distributed actually or constructively to the grantor or his spouse;

. . . held or accumulated for future distribution to the grantor or his spouse; or

. . . applied to pay premiums on life insurance policies taken out on the life of the grantor or his spouse (and not irrevocably payable to charities). (Code Sec. 677(a))

The income isn't taxable to the grantor if the application of the income to any of these purposes requires the approval of an adverse party (¶3957). (Reg § 1.677(a)-1(b))[15]

If trust income is *actually* used to support a beneficiary (other than the grantor's spouse) whom the grantor is legally obligated to support, such as his minor children, the grantor is taxable on that income. But the mere fact that trust income *may* be so used doesn't make him taxable, unless the use is discretionary with the grantor as an *individual* (not trustee). (Reg § 1.677(b)-1(d), Reg § 1.677(b)-1(e), Reg § 1.677(b)-1(f))[16]

---

10. ¶C-5204 *et seq.*; ¶6724.02; TD ¶657,009
11. ¶C-5200; ¶6714
12. ¶C-5301; ¶6764; TD ¶657,025
13. ¶C-5303; ¶6764; TD ¶657,025

14. ¶C-5312 *et seq.*; ¶6724.01; TD ¶657,027
15. ¶C-5401; ¶6774.01; TD ¶657,029
16. ¶C-5423; ¶6774.04; TD ¶657,033

¶ 3959   Reversionary interests.

For transfers in trust made after Mar. 1, '86, the grantor of a trust is generally taxable as the owner on its income if he has a reversionary interest in the corpus or income and, as of the inception of the trust, the value of that interest is more than 5% of the value of the trust. (Code Sec. 673(a)) The value of the reversionary interest must be determined by assuming the maximum exercise of discretion in favor of the grantor. (Code Sec. 673(c)) But the possibility that an interest may return to the grantor solely by intestacy is disregarded in determining whether there's a more than 5% interest.

Any postponement of the date specified for the reacquisition of possession or enjoyment of the reversionary interest is treated as a new transfer in trust starting with the date the postponement is effective and terminating with the date prescribed by the postponement. However, income for any period isn't included in income of the grantor by reason of this rule if it wouldn't be includible in the absence of the postponement. (Code Sec. 673(d))

The grantor isn't treated as the owner where the reversionary interest takes effect on the death before age 21 of a beneficiary who: (1) is a lineal descendant of the grantor, and (2) holds all present interests in the trust. (Code Sec. 673(b))[17]

¶ 3960   Power to control beneficial enjoyment (including "sprinkling" and "spray" powers).

Trust income is generally taxable to the grantor as the owner of the trust property if the beneficial enjoyment of trust corpus or income is subject to a power of disposition that may be exercised by him personally, or by a nonadverse party (¶3957), or both, and requires no consent or approval of an adverse party (¶3957). (Code Sec. 674)[18]

Similarly, the grantor will be taxed if he retains certain administrative powers, such as borrowing powers and dealing with the trust for less than full consideration. (Code Sec. 675)[19]

But certain relatively broad powers to shift benefits may be given to "independent" trustees without causing the grantor to be taxed on the income as owner. These so called "sprinkling" and "spray" powers permit the trustee to distribute, apportion or accumulate income, or to pay out corpus to or among beneficiaries (Code Sec. 674(c)), but not to add beneficiaries except to include after-born or after-adopted children. These powers vested solely in trustees won't cause the grantor to be taxed as the owner of the trust if the grantor isn't eligible as a trustee or co-trustee and no more than half the trustees vested with the power are related or subordinate parties subservient to the wishes of the grantor. (Code Sec. 674(c), Code Sec. 674(d); Reg § 1.674(d)-2(b))

Also, a power to distribute, apportion or accumulate income won't subject the grantor to tax if he and his spouse (living with him) are ineligible to exercise the power as trustee or co-trustee and the power is limited by a reasonably definite external standard set forth in the trust instrument, such as needs for education, sickness, support in an accustomed manner, etc. (Code Sec. 674(d); Reg § 1.674(d)-1)[20]

¶ 3961   Person other than the grantor as owner (including "Crummey" powers).

A trustee, beneficiary, or some other person may be taxable on the income as the owner, if that person:

. . . has a power exercisable solely by himself to vest the corpus, or income from it, in himself; or

---

17. ¶C-5450 *et seq.*; ¶6734.01; TD ¶657,041
18. ¶C-5531; ¶6744; TD ¶657,000

19. ¶C-5551 *et seq.*; ¶6754; TD ¶657,057
20. ¶C-5542 *et seq.*; ¶6744; TD ¶657,055

. . . has previously modified or released such a power and afterward retains sufficient control which would make the grantor taxable under the rules discussed at ¶3956 *et seq.* (Code Sec. 678)[21]

IRS says a beneficiary of a "Crummey" power (noncumulative right to withdraw a specified amount of property transferred to a trust within a specified period) will be treated as owner under the above rule. [22]

¶ 3962 Foreign trust grantors or other transferors—Form 3520, Form 3520-A.

If a U.S. person (e.g., a grantor) makes a transfer to a foreign trust with a U.S. beneficiary, the income of the trust (including foreign source income) will be taxed currently to the transferor as the owner of the trust. (Code Sec. 679(a)(1); Reg § 1.679-1) This rule doesn't apply where the transfer is: (1) by reason of death, (2) for fair market value, or (3) to a foreign employee benefit or charitable trust. (Code Sec. 679(a); Reg § 1.679-4) Regs spell out when a foreign trust that has received property from a U.S. transferor is treated as having a U.S. beneficiary. (Reg § 1.679-2)[23]

The U.S. person must report (use Form 3520) gratuitous transfers to a foreign trust. (Code Sec. 6048(a)(3))[24]

The above rules also apply to (1) certain foreign persons who transfer property to a foreign trust and later become a U.S. person (Code Sec. 679(a)(4); Reg § 1.679-5(a)) and (2) to a U.S. person who transferred property to a domestic trust that becomes a foreign trust during the transferor's life. (Code Sec. 679(a)(5); Reg § 1.679-6(b))[25]

A foreign trust with a U.S. owner must file Form 3520-A to satisfy information reporting requirements. (Code Sec. 6048(b)(1))[26]

¶ 3963 Beneficiary treated as grantor of trust to the extent of gifts to foreign grantor.

Where a foreign person would ordinarily be treated as the owner of any portion of a trust, *and* the trust has a beneficiary who is a U.S. person, the beneficiary generally is treated as the grantor of that portion to the extent the beneficiary has after Nov. 5, '90, made transfers by gift (directly or indirectly) to the foreign grantor. Gifts which are excluded from the calculation of gift tax under Code Sec. 2503(b) (generally, gifts of present interests of up to $12,000 per calendar year, see ¶5046) aren't included. (Code Sec. 672(f)(5); Reg § 1.672(f)-5) This rule applies even if the beneficiary wasn't a U.S. person at the time of the transfer. [27]

¶ 3964 Decedent's Income and Deductions. ████████████████████

A decedent's last tax year ends on his death. A cash basis decedent's final return includes only the income he actually or constructively received before he died. An accrual basis decedent's return includes income and deductions properly accruable at death (but not solely by reason of death). After-death income and deductions "in respect of a decedent" must be reported by decedent's estate or others who acquire his rights or obligations.

21. ¶C-5571; ¶6784; TD ¶657,058
22. ¶C-5574; ¶6784
23. ¶C-5600 *et seq.*; ¶6794; TD ¶657,060
24. ¶S-3644 *et seq.*; ¶60,484; TD ¶659,025
25. ¶s C-5603.1, C-5603.2; ¶6794; TD ¶657,062
26. ¶S-3645; ¶60,484; TD ¶659,024
27. ¶C-5218.31; ¶6724.03; TD ¶657,059

¶ 3965 Income includible and deductions taken on decedent's last return.

The last tax year of a decedent ends with the day of his death. (Reg § 1.451-1(b))[28]

For a *cash basis* decedent, include only the income received, actually or constructively, up to the end of the day of death (Code Sec. 691(a); Reg § 1.451-1(b)(1), Reg § 1.691(a)-1(b)), and deduct expenses only to the extent paid before death (except for the special deduction for the unrecovered investment in an annuity contract, see ¶3966, and certain medical expenses paid within one year after death, see ¶2144).[29]

For an *accrual basis* decedent, include income and deductions computed on the accrual method (including the deduction for the unrecovered investment in an annuity contract, ¶3966). But an amount of income or deduction accrued *solely* by reason of death isn't includible on the final return. (Code Sec. 451(b), Code Sec. 461(b))[30]

¶ 3966 Deduction for unrecovered investment in annuity contract.

A decedent's unrecovered investment in an annuity contract is an itemized deduction (*not* subject to the 2%-of-AGI floor) (Code Sec. 67(b)(10)) for the decedent's last tax year, if the annuity payments cease by reason of his death. (Code Sec. 72(b)(3)(A))[31]

¶ 3967 Income in respect of a decedent (IRD, after-death income).

Income in respect of a decedent (IRD) covers income (including capital gain) which a decedent had a right to receive but that: (1) wasn't actually or constructively received by a cash basis decedent, or (2) wasn't accrued by an accrual basis decedent. IRD includes insurance renewal commissions, a monthly pension paid to deceased employee's widow, taxable distributions from a qualified employee plan or IRA, a death benefit under a deferred annuity contract, partnership income of a deceased partner (Reg § 1.742-1) and S corporation income of a deceased shareholder. (Code Sec. 1374(b)(4))[32]

¶ 3968 Installment obligations, including self-cancelling installment notes (SCINs).

Uncollected installment obligations held by the decedent and disposed of at his death are income in respect of a decedent (Code Sec. 453B(c); Reg § 1.691(a)-5(a)) and not reported on the decedent's final return. (Code Sec. 691(a)(4)) The amount of the income in respect of a decedent is the excess of the face amount of the obligation over its basis in the hands of the decedent. (Code Sec. 453B(b); Code Sec. 691(a)(4)) On collecting the face amount, the executor, beneficiary or other recipient includes in gross income the same proportion of the payment that would have been reported by the decedent if he had lived and received the payment. (Reg § 1.691(a)-5(a))

If the executor or beneficiary transfers the installment obligation, the amount included in gross income for the tax year of the transfer is the fair market value of the obligation at the time of the transfer plus any excess of sales proceeds over fair market value (if it's sold) minus an amount equal to the basis of the obligation in the hands of the decedent (adjusted to reflect the receipt of any installment payments since the decedent's death). (Code Sec. 691(a)(4); Reg § 1.691(a)-5(b))

If the installment obligation is transferred to the obligor or is cancelled by the executor, any previously unreported gain from the installment sale will be recognized by the seller's estate. (Code Sec. 691(a)(5)) The result is the same where payments due on an installment note are

28. ¶C-9601; ¶6914; TD ¶579,501
29. ¶s C-9556, C-9605; ¶6914; TD ¶579,503
30. ¶s C-9606, C-9608; ¶6914.03; TD ¶579,504

31. ¶C-9608; ¶674; TD ¶579,506
32. ¶C-9505 *et seq.*; ¶s 6914, 6914.03; TD ¶578,505

extinguished at the holder's death under a provision contained in the sales agreement and installment note, i.e., a "death-terminating" installment note or self-cancelling installment note (SCIN).[33]

¶ 3969 Who is taxed on income in respect of a decedent?

A decedent's income in respect of a decedent not includible on his last return must be reported, for the tax year when received, by:

. . . the decedent's estate, if it acquired the right to receive the item of income from the decedent;

. . . the person who, by reason of the decedent's death, acquires the right to the income whenever this right isn't acquired by the decedent's estate from the decedent; or

. . . the person who acquires the right from the decedent by bequest, devise or inheritance, if the amount is received after distribution by the decedent's estate of the right to the income. (Code Sec. 691(a)(1))[34]

The character of income in respect of a decedent is the same as it would have been in the hands of the decedent, if he had lived and received the income. (Code Sec. 691(a)(3); Reg § 1.691(a)-3(a))[35]

¶ 3970 Decedent's deductions and credits available to estate or beneficiaries.

Deductions for a decedent's Code Sec. 162 business expenses, Code Sec. 212 expenses for the production of income, interest, taxes, depletion and the credit for foreign taxes are available to the decedent's estate if the estate is liable for the obligation giving rise to the deduction or credit and it isn't allowable in the decedent's final (or any previous) return. If not available to the estate, the deduction or credit may be taken by the person who acquires an interest in the decedent's property from the decedent by reason of the decedent's death, or by bequest, devise or inheritance, subject to the obligation to which the deduction or credit relates. (Code Sec. 691(b))[36]

¶ 3971 Deduction for estate tax attributable to income in respect of a decedent.

The decedent's right to income in respect of a decedent (IRD) is frequently included in his gross estate for federal estate and generation-skipping tax purposes although it's taxed as income to the recipient. As a relief, the recipient of the IRD can deduct the estate and generation-skipping tax attributable to inclusion of the right to income in the gross estate. (Code Sec. 691(c)(1); Reg § 1.691(c)-1(a)) This relief is available to an individual only if he itemizes his deductions but the deduction isn't subject to the 2%-of-AGI floor. (Code Sec. 67(b)(8))[37]

If the IRD includes capital gains or qualified dividends, the Code in effect treats the deduction as an offset against the capital gains or qualified dividends. For purposes of computing (1) the limitation on capital losses under Code Sec. 1211, (2) the maximum tax on a noncorporate taxpayer's capital gains or qualified dividends under Code Sec. 1(h), (3) the alternative tax on a corporation's capital gains, and (4) the partial exclusion of gain realized on the disposition of qualified small business stock, the amount of any gain taken into account that is treated as income in respect of a decedent must be reduced (but not below zero) by the amount of the allowable deduction for estate tax attributable to that gain. (Code Sec. 691(c)(4))[38]

---

33. ¶C-9528; ¶6914; TD ¶578,528
34. ¶C-9501; ¶6914; TD ¶578,501
35. ¶C-9506; ¶6914.05; TD ¶578,506

36. ¶C-9551; ¶6914.04; TD ¶579,001
37. ¶C-9557 *et seq.*; ¶674; TD ¶579,007
38. ¶C-9563; ¶6914.07; TD ¶579,012

Annuity payments received by the surviving annuitant of a joint and survivor annuity are income in respect of a decedent of the deceased annuitant to the extent that the payments are includible in gross income of the survivor. The portion of the estate tax attributable to the survivor's annuity is allowable as a deduction to the survivor over his life expectancy (determined under IRS tables). (Code Sec. 691(d); Reg § 1.691(d)-1(c))[39]

¶ 3972   Bankruptcy Estate for Bankrupt Individual. ▅▅▅▅▅▅▅▅▅▅▅▅▅▅▅

The bankruptcy estate of an individual is treated as a separate taxable entity for income tax purposes, subject to special rules.

¶ 3973   Bankruptcy estate as separate taxable entity.

The separate entity rules apply if a bankruptcy case involving an *individual* debtor (not a corporation or partnership) is brought under Chapter 7 (relating to liquidations) or Chapter 11 (reorganizations) of Title 11 of the U.S. Code. (Code Sec. 1398(a))[40]

For income tax returns of bankruptcy estates (Form 1040 and Form 1041), see ¶4739.

¶ 3974   Debtor's election to close tax year.

An individual debtor can elect to close his tax year as of the day before the date the bankruptcy case commences. (Code Sec. 1398(d)(2)(A), Code Sec. 1398(d)(3)) If the election is made, the debtor's tax year that otherwise would include the commencement date is divided into two "short" tax years. The first year ends on the day before the commencement date; the second begins on the commencement date. (Code Sec. 1398(d)(2)(A))[41]

¶ 3975   Taxation of bankruptcy estate.

The gross income of the bankruptcy estate of an individual consists of: (1) any gross income of the individual debtor (other than any amount received or accrued as income by the debtor before the commencement of the case), that under the substantive law of bankruptcy (Title 11 of the U.S. Code), is property of the bankruptcy estate, and (2) the gross income of the estate beginning on and after the date the case commenced. (Code Sec. 1398(e)(1))[42]

Except as otherwise provided, the taxable income of the bankruptcy estate is computed the same as in the case of an individual. (Code Sec. 1398(c)(1))[43] The estate is allowed a personal exemption deduction equal to that of an individual (two exemptions for married debtors jointly filing for bankruptcy)[44] and the same standard deduction as married individuals filing separately. (Code Sec. 1398(c)(3)) The tax rate schedule applicable to the estate is the same as for married individuals filing separate returns. (Code Sec. 1398(c)(2))[45]

The estate succeeds to various income tax attributes of the debtor (including certain carryovers and unused passive activity and at-risk losses). (Code Sec. 1398(g); Reg § 1.1398-1, Reg § 1.1398-2)[46]

¶ 3976   Deduction of business and administrative expenses.

An amount paid or incurred by the bankruptcy estate is deductible or creditable by the estate to the same extent that the item would be by the debtor had the debtor remained in the same trades, businesses or activities after the case commenced as before and had the debtor paid or incurred the amount. (Code Sec. 1398(e)(3))[47]

---

39. ¶C-9569; ¶6914.07; TD ¶579,018
40. ¶C-9701; ¶13,984; TD ¶578,001
41. ¶C-9802 *et seq.*; ¶13,984.05; TD ¶577,504
42. ¶C-9711; ¶13,984.01; TD ¶578,004
43. ¶C-9708; ¶13,984.01; TD ¶578,009

44. ¶C-9709; ¶13,984.01; TD ¶578,011
45. ¶C-9707; ¶13,984.01; TD ¶578,012
46. ¶C-9718; ¶13,984.02; TD ¶578,015
47. ¶C-9714; ¶13,984.01; TD ¶578,005

The estate can deduct: (1) any administrative expense allowed under 11 U.S. Sec. 503 (11 USCS 503), and (2) any court fees and costs assessed against the estate under Chapter 123 of Title 28 of the U.S. Code. (Code Sec. 1398(h)(1))[48]

¶ 3977 Carrybacks and carryovers.

Any deduction for administrative and related expenses not used in the current year can be carried back by the estate three years and carried forward seven years (Code Sec. 1398(h)(2)), but only to a tax year of the *estate,* not of the debtor. (Code Sec. 1398(h)(2)(D))

The administrative expense carrybacks and carryovers that may be carried to a particular tax year are "stacked" after the net operating loss deductions (allowed by Code Sec. 172) are computed for the particular year. (Code Sec. 1398(h)(2)(C))[49]

If the bankruptcy estate itself incurs a net operating loss (apart from losses passing to the estate from the individual debtor), the bankruptcy estate can carry back its net operating losses not only to earlier tax years of the estate, but also to tax years of the debtor before the year in which the case commenced. (Code Sec. 1398(j)(2)(A))[50]

¶ 3978 Tax attributes on termination of estate.

On termination of the bankruptcy estate, the debtor succeeds to various tax attributes of the estate (including certain carryovers). (Code Sec. 1398(i))[1]

---

48. ¶C-9715; ¶13,984.01; TD ¶578,006
49. ¶C-9720; ¶s 1724.05, 13,984.01; TD ¶578,007

50. ¶C-9721; ¶s 1724.05, 13,984.01; TD ¶578,013
1. ¶C-9812; ¶13,984.02; TD ¶577,512

Chapter 19   Exempt Organizations

¶ 4100   Tax-Exempt Organizations. ▬▬▬▬▬▬▬▬▬▬▬▬

Certain nonprofit organizations are exempt from federal income taxation, but they may be taxable on income from unrelated businesses they conduct.

Exempt organizations include:

... U.S. corporate instrumentalities organized under an Act of Congress (Code Sec. 501(c)(1));[1]

... corporations exclusively holding title to property, and collecting and remitting the income from it (less expenses) to an exempt organization (Code Sec. 501(c)(2));[2]

... religious, charitable, scientific, literary and educational organizations, organizations testing for public safety, organizations that foster national or international amateur sports competition, those organized and operated for preventing cruelty to children or animals, see ¶4102 (Code Sec. 501(c)(3)), qualified charitable risk pools, (Code Sec. 501(n)) cooperative hospital (Code Sec. 501(e)) and educational organization (Code Sec. 501(f)) service organizations;[3]

... religious and apostolic organizations, ¶4105;

... nonprofit civic organizations operated exclusively for social welfare, and local employees' associations whose net earnings are used solely for charitable, educational or recreational purposes (Code Sec. 501(c)(4));[4]

... labor, agricultural or horticultural organizations (Code Sec. 501(c)(5), Code Sec. 501(g));[5]

... chambers of commerce, business leagues, real estate boards, boards of trade or professional football leagues not organized for profit or private benefit (Code Sec. 501(c)(6));[6]

... social clubs organized for pleasure, recreation and other nonprofitable purposes (¶4107) (Code Sec. 501(c)(7)) and fraternal beneficiary societies, orders or associations operating under the lodge system and providing life, sick, accident or other benefits to members and their dependents (Code Sec. 501(c)(8));[7]

... domestic fraternal societies operating under the lodge system that don't provide payment of benefits, if their net earnings are devoted exclusively to religious, charitable, etc., and fraternal purposes (Code Sec. 501(c)(10));[8]

... voluntary employees' beneficiary associations providing benefit payments to members and their dependents (Code Sec. 501(c)(9));[9]

... local teachers' retirement fund associations (Code Sec. 501(c)(11));[10]

... certain local benevolent life insurance associations, mutual ditch or irrigation companies, mutual or cooperative telephone companies or like organizations, (Code Sec. 501(c)(12));[11]

... nonprofit cemetery companies and burial corporations (Code Sec. 501(c)(13));[12]

... credit unions and certain entities organized before Sept. 1, '57 to provide reserve funds and insure shares or deposits in building and loan associations, cooperative banks or mutual savings banks (Code Sec. 501(c)(14));[13]

... certain nonlife insurance companies (Code Sec. 501(c)(15));[14]

---

1. ¶D-6301; ¶5014.03
2. ¶D-5801; ¶5014.04; TD ¶672,542
3. ¶D-5950 *et seq.*; ¶5014.04;TD ¶670,500 *et seq.*
4. ¶D-5100 *et seq.*; ¶5014.13; TD ¶672,501
5. ¶D-4600 *et seq.*; ¶5014.14; TD ¶672,508
6. ¶D-4800 *et seq.*; ¶5014.15; TD ¶671,501
7. ¶D-4300 *et seq.*; ¶5014.17; TD ¶671,007

8. ¶D-4304; ¶5014.19; TD ¶671,010
9. ¶D-4400 *et seq.*; ¶5014.18; TD ¶672,001
10. ¶D-5500 *et seq.*; ¶5014.20
11. ¶D-6100 *et seq.*; ¶5014.21
12. ¶D-6000 *et seq.*; ¶5014.22
13. ¶D-4900 *et seq.*; ¶5014.23
14. ¶D-5900 *et seq.*; ¶5014.24

References beginning with a single letter are to paragraphs in RIA's Federal Tax Coordinator 2d and RIA's Analysis of Federal Taxes: Income. Those beginning with numbers are to paragraphs in RIA's United States Tax Reporter. Those beginning with TD are to paragraphs in RIA's Tax Desk.

... farmers' cooperatives that are crop financing corporations (Code Sec. 501(c)(16));[15]

... supplemental unemployment benefit plans (SUBs) (Code Sec. 501(c)(17));[16]

... certain domestic veterans' organizations (Code Sec. 501(c)(19));[17]

... qualified employee benefit trusts (¶4319);

... trusts established by the Pension Benefit Guaranty Corporation (PBGC) in connection with a terminated plan (Code Sec. 501(c)(24));[18]

... pooled real estate investment funds of exempt organizations (Code Sec. 501(c)(25));[19]

... certain trusts created before June 25, '59, to pay benefits under a pension plan funded only by employee contributions (Code Sec. 501(c)(18));[20] black lung benefit trusts (Code Sec. 501(c)(21)); and[21] state sponsored workmen's compensation reinsurance organizations established before June 1, '96 (Code Sec. 501(c)(27)(A));[22]

... organizations (including mutual insurance companies) providing worker's compensation (Code Sec. 501(c)(27)(B));

... state sponsored high-risk health coverage organizations (Code Sec. 501(c)(26));[23] and

... qualified tuition programs. (Code Sec. 529)[24]

IRS may suspend the tax-exempt status of an organization designated or identified as a terrorist organization. (Code Sec. 501(p))[25]

For private foundations, see ¶4125 *et seq.*

¶ 4101   Feeder organizations.

An organization operated for the primary purpose of carrying on a business for profit (not just holding title to property) is taxable on all its income, even if all its profits are payable to exempt organizations. (Code Sec. 502(a); Reg § 1.502-1(a))[26]

But this type of "feeder" organization is exempt if it's controlled by and furnishes its services *solely* to: a single exempt organization, an exempt parent organization and its exempt subs, or exempt subs having a common parent. (Reg § 1.502-1(b))[27]

¶ 4102   Religious, charitable, educational and similar organizations.

A corporation, community chest, fund, foundation, or other organization is exempt if:

... it's both organized *and* operated exclusively for: religious, charitable, scientific, literary or educational (including certain child care) purposes; public safety testing; prevention of cruelty to children or animals; or fostering national or international amateur sports competition (even if it has local or regional membership); (Code Sec. 501(c)(3); Reg § 1.501(c)(3)-1(a))

... no part of its net earnings inures to benefit any private shareholder or individual; *and*

... no substantial part of its activities consists of carrying on propaganda or otherwise attempting to influence legislation, i.e., lobbying (subject to an election, see ¶4103), or intervening in any political campaign for or against any candidate (Code Sec. 501(c)(3)[28] — i.e., it can't be an "action" organization. (Reg § 1.501(c)(3)-1(c)(3)) IRS guidance shows examples of prohibited and permissible political activities of tax-exempts. [29] (For excise tax on these expenditures, see ¶4104.)

---

15. ¶E-1041 *et seq.*; ¶5014.25
16. ¶D-4500; ¶5014.26
17. ¶D-5200 *et seq.*; ¶5014.28; TD ¶672,022
18. ¶D-5303
19. ¶D-5850 *et seq.*; ¶5014.32; TD ¶672,546
20. ¶D-5400 *et seq.*; ¶5014.27
21. ¶D-6200 *et seq.*; ¶5014.30
22. ¶D-6340; ¶5014.40

23. ¶D-6320; ¶5014.39
24. ¶A-4701; ¶5294
25. ¶D-4001A; ¶5014.44
26. ¶D-7101; ¶5024
27. ¶D-7103; ¶5024.01
28. ¶D-4101; ¶5014.05; TD ¶670,601
29. ¶D-6401; TD ¶677,001

IRS guidance explains when organizations providing down payment assistance to home buyers qualify for exemption. [30]

For "private foundation" presumption, see ¶4125.

¶ 4103 Lobbying expenditures election for Code Sec. 501(c)(3) organizations— Form 5768.

Certain Code Sec. 501(c)(3) organizations (other than church-related ones or private foundations) may elect (on Form 5768) to make limited lobbying expenditures without losing their exempt status. (Code Sec. 501(h)) [31] The election is effective for all tax years that end after it's made, and that begin before it's revoked. (Code Sec. 501(h)(6)) [32]

An electing charity's permissible lobbying expenditures for any tax year can't exceed ("general limit") the *lesser of:* (1) $1,000,000, or (2) the sum of 20% of the first $500,000 it paid or incurred for exempt purposes (including related administrative costs) for the year, plus 15% of the second $500,000, plus 10% of the third $500,000, plus 5% of any additional such expenditures. (Code Sec. 4911(c)(2); Reg § 56.4911-1(c)(1)) Also, only 25% of this lobbying amount may go to influencing legislation ("grass roots expenditures"). (Code Sec. 4911(c)(4); Reg § 56.4911-1(c)(2)) [33] Charities must keep records of these expenditures (and show them on their annual returns, see ¶4124). (Reg § 56.4911-6) [34]

In any tax year an electing charity's lobbying expenditures exceed either the general or the grass roots limit, a 25% excise tax is imposed on that excess. If both limits are exceeded, the tax is imposed on the greater excess. (Code Sec. 4911(a), Code Sec. 4911(b)) [35] Pay the tax on Form 4720. Use Form 8868 for an extension, see ¶4124. [36]

Also, an electing charity can lose its tax exemption if its lobbying expenditures over a four-year period exceed 150% of either limit. (Code Sec. 501(h)(1), Code Sec. 501(h)(2)) [37] For the excise tax that applies if that happens, see ¶4104.

¶ 4104 Excise tax on Code Sec. 501(c)(3) organizations' political and lobbying expenditures—Form 4720.

A Code Sec. 501(c)(3) organization is subject to a two-tier excise tax on its *political expenditures.* An initial tax of 10% of the expenditure is imposed on the organization, and an initial 2 ½% tax (up to $5,000 per expenditure) is imposed on any organization manager who willfully and without reasonable cause agreed to the expenditure. (Code Sec. 4955(a), Code Sec. 4955(c)(2); Reg § 53.4955-1(b)) [38] Form 4720 is used to report these taxes. Use Form 8868 for an extension, see ¶4124. [39] Additional taxes are imposed on both the organization (100%) and management (50%, up to $10,000 per expenditure) if the expenditure isn't corrected within a reasonable time. (Code Sec. 4955(b), Code Sec. 4955(c)(2)) [40]

A Code Sec. 501(c)(3) organization (other than charities making the lobbying expense election (¶4103), private foundations and church-related organizations) whose *lobbying expenditures* for a tax year cause it to lose its tax exemption is subject to a 5% tax on those disqualifying amounts. The 5% tax also is imposed on any organization manager who agreed to the expenditure knowing that disqualification could result. (Code Sec. 4912) [41] Use Form 4720. Use Form 8868 for an extension, see ¶4124. [42]

IRS may also seek to enjoin a Code Sec. 501(c)(3) organization from engaging in flagrant

---

30. ¶D-4101
31. ¶D-6500 *et seq.*, ¶D-6571; ¶5014.12, ¶60,334; TD ¶677,020 *et seq.*
32. ¶D-6501; ¶5014.12; TD ¶677,023
33. ¶D-6507 *et seq.*; ¶49,114; TD ¶677,027
34. ¶D-6571; TD ¶677,028
35. ¶D-6532 *et seq.*; ¶5014.12, 49,114; TD ¶677,047

36. ¶S-2512; TD ¶688,030
37. ¶D-6572 *et seq.*; ¶5014.12; TD ¶677,042
38. ¶D-6421 *et seq.*; ¶49,554; TD ¶677,005
39. ¶S-2512; TD ¶688,029
40. ¶D-6421 *et seq.*; ¶49,554; TD ¶677,005
41. ¶D-6417 *et seq.*; ¶49,124; TD ¶677,017
42. ¶S-2512; TD ¶688,030

political activities. (Code Sec. 7409(a); Reg § 301.7409-1(a))[43]

¶ 4105 Religious or apostolic associations.

Even if an organization carries on business activities so that it can't be exempt under Code Sec. 501(c)(3) (as *exclusively* for exempt purposes), it still can be exempt as a *religious or apostolic association.* The organization may thus be exempt if it has a common or community treasury, and if its income (whether or not distributed) is taxed pro rata to its members, as a dividend received, for the organization's tax year ending with or within the member's tax year. (Code Sec. 501(d); Reg § 1.501(d)-1)[44]

❤️observation: Exemption under Code Sec. 501(c)(3) is preferable because it means that contributions to the organization also may be deductible, see ¶2102.

¶ 4106 Civic leagues for social welfare.

A civic league is exempt if it isn't organized or operated for profit; is operated exclusively for the promotion of social welfare; no part of its net earnings inures to the benefit of any private shareholder or individual; (Code Sec. 501(c)(4)) and no substantial part of its activities consists of providing commercial-type insurance. (Code Sec. 501(m)(1))[45]

¶ 4107 Social clubs.

For a social club to be exempt, it must be organized and operated substantially for pleasure, recreation or other nonprofit purposes, its governing instruments or written policies can't provide for discrimination based on color, race or religion, and no part of its earnings may benefit any private shareholder. (Code Sec. 501(c)(7))[46]

Up to 35% of a social club's gross receipts (including investment income) may be from sources outside of its membership. Within this 35%, not more than 15% of gross receipts may be from the general public's (i.e., not members or their guests) use of the club's facilities or services.[47]

If the club fails the 35% or 15% tests (and a facts and circumstances test) in any tax year, all of its income, even amounts (reduced by allocable costs) received from members, is subject to tax in that year. (Code Sec. 277)[48]

¶ 4108 Nondiscrimination requirements for VEBAs and SUBs.

A VEBA or SUB won't be exempt unless it satisfies nondiscrimination rules similar to those applicable to qualified employee benefit plans (¶4324). (Code Sec. 501(c)(17)(A), Code Sec. 505(a)(1), Code Sec. 505(b)(1))[49]

¶ 4109 Political organizations—Form 1120-POL; Form 990; Form 990-EZ; Form 8871; Form 8872; Form 8453-X.

A political organization is a party, committee, association, fund (including certain newsletter funds) or other organization (whether or not incorporated) that's organized and operated primarily to accept contributions and/or make expenditures for an "exempt function," e.g., influencing or attempting to influence the selection, nomination, election or appointment of any individual to public office. (Code Sec. 527(e)(1), Code Sec. 527(e)(2), Code Sec. 527(g))[50] Subject to exceptions, political organizations must (1) give notice of status electronically (use

43. ¶V-2712; ¶74,094
44. ¶D-5601; ¶5014.33
45. ¶D-5100 *et seq.*; ¶5014.13; TD ¶672,501
46. ¶D-4201; ¶5014.16; TD ¶671,001

47. ¶D-4206; ¶5014.16; TD ¶671,004
48. ¶D-4206; ¶5014.16; TD ¶671,001
49. ¶s D-4418, D-4501, D-6351; ¶5054; TD ¶672,011
50. ¶s D-5002, D-5021; ¶5274; TD ¶672,513

Form 8871 and Form 8453-X), (2) provide periodic reports of contributions and expenditures, electronically in some cases (use Form 8872) and (3) file annual returns. Although generally tax-exempt (Code Sec. 527(a)), a political organization is taxed, at the *highest* corporate rate, on income (minus connected expenses) that isn't from its exempt function. (Code Sec. 527(b)(1), Code Sec. 527(c))[1] A political organization, whether or not tax-exempt, that has more than $100 of taxable income must file an annual income tax return on Form 1120-POL. (Code Sec. 6012(a)(6)) Only tax-exempt political organizations may have to file annual information returns. Subject to exceptions, a tax-exempt political organization (other than a qualified state or local political organization) with $25,000 or more of annual gross receipts must file Form 990. Qualified state or local political organizations must file Form 990 if they have annual gross receipts of $100,000 or more. (Code Sec. 6033(g)(1)) Tax-exempt organizations with gross receipts of less than $100,000 and assets less than $250,000 may file Form 990-EZ. Tax-exempt organizations with gross receipts of less than $25,000 need not file Form 990 or Form 990-EZ. IRS has provided a safe harbor for establishing that a political organization's failure to report certain contributor information on Form 8872 was due to reasonable cause and not due to willful neglect. [2]

IRS has a website for political organizations to electronically file documents and allow public access and searches for contributions and expenditures.

¶ 4110   Homeowners' associations—Form 1120-H.

Associations for the management of residential real estate and condominiums and timeshare associations (but not cooperative housing corporations) that meet an organization and operation test and an income test may elect (by filing Form 1120-H) to be treated as exempt organizations. (Code Sec. 528(a), Code Sec. 528(c))[3] Electing associations are taxed at a 30% (32% for timeshare associations) rate on income other than amounts received as dues, fees or assessments from members. (Code Sec. 528(b))[4] This taxable income must be reported on Form 1120-H.[5]

¶ 4111   Loss of exemption for exempt employee trusts engaging in prohibited transactions.

Some employee trusts (including church and governmental plans) will lose or be denied their exemption from income tax (and are subject to an excise tax, see ¶4347) if they engage in "prohibited transactions." (Code Sec. 503(a)(1))[6]

A prohibited transaction occurs if a trust engages in an activity with its creator, a substantial contributor or person related to either, in which it:

(1) lends any part of its income or corpus without receiving adequate security and a reasonable rate of interest;

(2) pays any compensation in excess of a reasonable allowance for personal services actually rendered;

(3) makes any part of its services available on a preferential basis;

(4) makes any substantial purchase of securities or any other property for more than adequate consideration;

(5) sells any substantial part of its securities or any other property for less than adequate consideration; or

(6) engages in any other transaction that results in a substantial diversion of its income or

---

1. ¶D-5008; ¶5274; TD ¶672,518
2. ¶S-1921; ¶5274; TD ¶672,518
3. ¶D-5701 *et seq.*; ¶5284; TD ¶672,531 *et seq.*
4. ¶D-5712; ¶5284; TD ¶672,539
5. ¶S-1922; ¶5284; TD ¶609,812
6. ¶D-6700 *et seq.*; ¶5034.01

corpus. (Code Sec. 503(b))[7]

¶ 4112 Excise tax on excess benefit transactions by disqualified persons and organization managers—Form 4720.

Penalty excise taxes are imposed on disqualified persons and organization managers who benefit from an excess benefit transaction with a Code Sec. 501(c)(3) or Code Sec. 501(c)(4) organization (other than a private foundation), or that was such an organization at any time within five years before the transaction. (Code Sec. 4958(a); Reg § 53.4958-1) An excess benefit transaction is one in which the exempt organization provides a benefit directly or indirectly to or for the use of a disqualified person (any person in a position to exercise substantial influence over the organization at any time during the five years before the transaction (Code Sec. 4958(f); Reg § 53.4958-4), or certain related parties, that exceeds the value of the consideration, including services, received in exchange. (Code Sec. 4958(c)) [8]

The disqualified person is liable for a tax of 25% of the excess benefit (200% if the transaction is not corrected by the time a deficiency notice is mailed or the tax is assessed). (Code Sec. 4958(a)(1), Code Sec. 4958(b); Reg § 53.4958-1)[9] An organization manager (officer, director, trustee, etc.) who knowingly participates in an excess benefit transaction is liable for a tax of the lesser of 10% or $10,000 ($20,000 for tax years beginning after Aug. 17, 2006). (Code Sec. 4958(a)(2), Code Sec. 4958(d)(2))[10] Certain post-Aug. 17, 2006 distributions from a donor advised fund to a donor, donor advisor, or related person are automatically treated as excess benefit transactions. (Code Sec. 4958(c)(2)) Excess benefit transactions of Code Sec. 509(a)(3) supporting organizations are determined under special rules for transactions occurring after Aug. 17, 2006. (Code Sec. 4958(c)(3))[11] IRS may abate the first-tier taxes for reasonable cause. (Code Sec. 4962(b))[12] Persons liable for excess benefit transaction excise taxes report them on Form 4720. (Reg § 53.6071-1(f)) Use Form 8868 for an extension, see ¶4124.

¶ 4113 Excise tax on entities that are parties to prohibited tax shelter transactions, and on entity managers who knowingly approve prohibited tax shelter transactions.

Generally effective for tax years ending after May 17, 2006, with respect to transactions entered into before, on, or after that date, excise taxes are imposed on (1) certain tax-exempt entities that are parties to "prohibited tax shelter transactions" (Code Sec. 4965(a)(1)) and (2) "entity managers" of tax-exempt entities who approve the entity as a party (or otherwise cause the entity to be a party) to a prohibited tax shelter transaction and know or have reason to know that the transaction is a prohibited tax shelter transaction. (Code Sec. 4965(a)(2)) IRS has issued proposed reliance regs under Code Sec. 4965 that would define "party" and address other aspects of the above taxes. (Prop Reg. § 53.4965-1 through Prop Reg. § 53.4965-9 ["Taxpayers may rely"])[13]

¶ 4114 Tax-exempt entities must disclose participation in prohibited tax shelter transactions to IRS or face penalties—Form 8886-T.

Every tax-exempt entity described in Code Sec. 4965(c) that is a party to a prohibited tax shelter transaction (¶4113) must disclose to IRS (on Form 8886-T): (a) that the entity is a party to the prohibited tax shelter transaction; and (b) the identity of any other party to the transaction which is known to such tax-exempt entity (Code Sec. 6033(a)(2))[14] The penalty for

7. ¶D-6702 *et seq.*; ¶5034.02
8. ¶D-6650 *et seq.*; ¶49,584; TD ¶676,500
9. ¶D-6652; ¶49,584
10. ¶D-6653; ¶49,584

11. ¶D-6654; ¶49,584
12. ¶D-6652; ¶49,624
13. ¶D-8301; ¶49,654
14. ¶S-2895; ¶60,334

failing to comply is $100 for each day during which such failure continues, not to exceed $50,000 with respect to any one disclosure. IRS may make a written demand on any entity or manager subject to the penalty for nondisclosure, specifying a reasonable future date by which the required disclosure must be filed. Failure to comply with the demand is subject to an additional penalty of $100 for each day after the expiration of the time specified in the demand during which such failure continues, not to exceed $10,000 with respect to any one disclosure. (Code Sec. 6652(c)(3)(B)(ii))[15] For non-plan entities, these penalties are imposed on the tax-exempt entity. For plan entities, they are imposed on the entity manager of the tax-exempt entity.

Any taxable party to a prohibited tax shelter transaction must disclose by statement to any tax-exempt entity that is a party to the transaction that it's a prohibited tax shelter transaction. (Code Sec. 6011(g))[16]

¶ 4115 Donee organization must acknowledge and report qualified vehicle donations—Form 1098-C.

An organization that receives a post-2004 charitable contribution of a "qualified vehicle" (¶2139) must provide the donor with a contemporaneous written acknowledgement of the contribution if the claimed value is more than $500, and report the information to IRS (use Form 1098-C) or face a penalty, which also applies for furnishing a false or fraudulent acknowledgement. It also must indicate whether the donee provided any goods or services in consideration for the vehicle, and, if so, a description and good faith estimate of their value, or, if they consist solely of intangible religious benefits, a statement to that effect. (Code Sec. 170(f)(12)(B))[17]

¶ 4116 Application for exemption—advance rulings—Form 1023; Form 1024.

An organization must apply in writing (on Form 1023 for Code Sec. 501(c)(3) organizations, Form 1024 for most others, and with the appropriate user fee with for an IRS ruling or determination that it's exempt from federal income tax. (Reg § 1.501(a)-1(a)(2)) A parent organization's exemption doesn't cover its subsidiary. [18] But organizations under the general control of a central organization may apply on a group basis. [19] When applying for tax-exempt status, sponsoring organizations must notify IRS of any donor advised fund they maintain or intend to maintain. (Code Sec. 508(f))

¶ 4117 Modification or revocation of exemption.

IRS may modify or revoke rulings and determination letters that granted exempt status to an organization (e.g., for failure to comply with exemption requirements, or prohibited transactions, see ¶4111). (Reg § 601.201(n)(6)) The revocation may be retroactive, in which case deficiencies and penalties may be imposed for open years. [20]

¶ 4118 Disclosure of nondeductibility of contributions.

Certain exempt organizations that aren't eligible to receive deductible contributions must expressly state that fact (in a conspicuous and easily recognizable format) in every fundraising solicitation. (Code Sec. 6113)[21]

---

15. ¶V-2538; ¶66,524.01
16. ¶S-4440; ¶60,114.023
17. ¶K-3948.2; ¶67,204; TD ¶861,084
18. ¶T-10450 *et seq.*; ¶5014.01; TD ¶670,502

19. ¶T-10481; ¶5014.01
20. ¶s T-10485, T-10486
21. ¶D-4004 *et seq.*; ¶61,134; TD ¶673,001

¶ 4119 Disclosure requirement for quid pro quo contributions.

Certain charities that are eligible to receive deductible contributions must, in connection with soliciting or receiving a quid pro quo contribution in excess of $75, inform the donor in writing that his charitable deduction is limited to the excess of his contribution over the value of the goods or services provided by the charity (with a good faith estimate, made by using any reasonable method in good faith, of the value of those goods and services). (Code Sec. 6115; Reg § 1.6115-1)[22]

¶ 4120 Disclosure of annual return and exemption application—Form 990; Form 990-PF; Form 990-T; Form 4720.

A Code Sec. 501(c) or Code Sec. 501(d) organization must make a copy of its annual returns (Form 990) for the last three years and its exempt status application and supporting documents available for inspection during business hours but religious or apostolic organizations don't have to make K-1s available. (Code Sec. 6104(a), Code Sec. 6104(b), Code Sec. 6104(d); Reg § 301.6104(d)-3)[23] The organization must provide a copy of the application without charge, except reasonable reproduction and mailing costs, to any individual who requests it. Copies must be provided within 30 days, for written requests, or immediately for in-person requests. (Code Sec. 6104(d)(1); Reg § 301.6104(d)-3) Requests don't have to be honored if the information has been made widely available or if the request is determined by IRS to be part of a harassment campaign. (Code Sec. 6104(d)(4); Reg § 301.6104(d)-2, Reg § 301.6104(d)-3)[24] These requirements apply to annual information returns (Form 990-PF and Form 4720) of private foundations, which also must disclose names and addresses of contributors. (Reg § 301.6104(d)-1(b)(4)(ii))[25] Returns of certain political organizations (¶4109) also are subject to disclosure requirements. (Code Sec. 6104(a), Code Sec. 6104(b), Code Sec. 6104(d))[26] Code Sec. 501(c)(3) organizations (¶4102) must make available for public inspection copies of their annual unrelated business income tax (UBIT) returns (Form 990-T) filed after Aug. 17, 2006. (Code Sec. 6104(d)(1)(A)(ii)) IRS has issued interim guidance on meeting this requirement pending the issuance of regs. [27]

¶ 4121 Unrelated business income tax—Form 990-T.

Exempt organizations (other than U.S. corporate instrumentalities and certain other exempt organizations) are subject to a tax on income (¶4122) from any unrelated business (defined below). (Code Sec. 511(a), Code Sec. 512(a), Code Sec. 512(b)(12); Reg § 1.511-2(a)(1))[28] Form 990-T is used to report and pay the tax. (Reg § 1.6012-2(e), Reg § 1.6012-3(a)(5))[29] Imposition of this tax doesn't affect the organization's exempt status. (Code Sec. 501(b), Code Sec. 511)[30]

An unrelated business is a trade or business (i.e., carried on for the production of income, whether or not profit results) regularly carried on (including seasonally) by the organization, that isn't substantially related (aside from providing funds) to the exercise or performance of its exempt purpose or function. (Code Sec. 513(a), Code Sec. 513(c); Reg § 1.513-1)[31] An unrelated trade or business doesn't include the activity of soliciting and receiving qualified sponsorship payments (payments from a person engaged in a trade or business with respect to which the person won't get any substantial return benefit other than the use or acknowledgement of the donor's name or logo as part of a sponsored event or certain goods or services

22. ¶s K-3101, K-3102; ¶61,154; TD ¶s 330,257, 330,259
23. ¶S-6601 *et seq.*; ¶61,044
24. ¶S-6609.1; ¶61,044
25. ¶S-6603; ¶61,044
26. ¶S-6642 *et seq.*; ¶61,044

27. ¶S-6603; ¶61,044
28. ¶D-6800 *et seq.*; ¶5114 *et seq.*; TD ¶681,000 *et seq.*
29. ¶S-2101; ¶5114; TD ¶688,501
30. ¶D-6801; ¶5114
31. ¶D-6804 *et seq.*; ¶5134.01; TD ¶681,019

that have an insubstantial value). (Code Sec. 513(i), Reg § 1.513-4)[32] Regs provide guidance on whether a tour activity is an unrelated business. (Reg § 1.513-7)[33] For tax years beginning after Aug. 17, 2006 (one year later for existing organizations), debt management plan services are an unrelated trade or business, if the organization is not a tax-exempt credit counseling organization. (Code Sec. 513(j))[34]

For exempt SUBs, qualified employee pension, etc., trusts, and nonexempt trusts, *any* business it regularly carries on is "unrelated." (Code Sec. 513(b))[35]

But an unrelated business doesn't include an activity where substantially all the work is performed for the organization without compensation, e.g., by volunteers. (Code Sec. 513(a)(1))[36]

The rules on assessment, collection, and penalties applicable to income tax, including estimated tax and foreign tax credit, apply. (Code Sec. 515, Code Sec. 6655(g)(3)(A); Reg § 1.511-3(a)) The corporate tax rates and filing dates apply if the organization is a corporation, and those for trusts if it's a charitable trust. (Code Sec. 511(a), Code Sec. 511(b))[37]

Tax-exempt organizations must make estimated tax payments on their unrelated business taxable income. (Code Sec. 6655(g)(3)) [38]

¶ 4122   Unrelated business taxable income (UBTI) defined.

Unrelated business taxable income (UBTI) is the gross income derived from any unrelated trade or business (¶4121), less directly connected allowable deductions, but with certain exceptions (below), additions and limitations (Code Sec. 512(a), Code Sec. 512(b)), including a specific deduction of $1,000. (Code Sec. 512(b)(12))[39]

UBTI does not include gain or loss from the qualified sale, exchange, or other disposition by an eligible taxpayer of any qualifying brownfield property acquired after 2004 and before 2010. (Code Sec. 512(b)(18)(A) [sic Code Sec. 512(b)(19)(A)])[40]

Social clubs, VEBAs, SUBs and veterans organizations are allowed special exclusions. (Code Sec. 512(a)(3))[41] A charitable organization's income or gain from ownership of S corporation stock is UBTI. (Code Sec. 512(e)) [42]

Dividends (except certain insurance income received from a controlled foreign corporation (Code Sec. 512(b)(17))), interest, rents, royalties, annuities, payments with respect to securities loans, loan commitment fees, and gains or losses from property dispositions are excluded from UBTI, as are gains or losses from the lapse or termination of options to buy or sell securities or real property, or from the forfeiture of good-faith deposits to buy, sell, or lease real property in connection with the organization's investment activities, (Code Sec. 512(b))[43] and annual dues of up to $139 for 2008, ($136 for 2007) per member received by agricultural or horticultural organizations. (Code Sec. 512(d)) [44]

But to the extent the dividends, etc., are attributable to property acquired through debt financing ("debt-financed property," see ¶4123), they *are* included in UBTI. The includible portion (computed separately for each property) equals a percentage (not over 100%) of the dividends, etc., derived from the property during the tax year, based on the ratio of: (1) the average acquisition indebtedness, to (2) the average adjusted basis of debt-financed property, for the year. (Code Sec. 514(a)(1))[45] This same percentage also is used to compute the allowable deductions for that property (other than capital loss carryovers or depreciation). (Code

---

32. ¶D-6819 *et seq.*; ¶5134.02; TD ¶681,026
33. ¶D-6829.1; ¶5134.03
34. ¶D-6848; ¶5134
35. ¶D-6807; ¶5134; TD ¶681,034
36. ¶D-6836; ¶5134; TD ¶681,028
37. ¶D-6928 *et seq.*; TD ¶681,002
38. ¶S-5421; ¶66,554; TD ¶689,001

39. ¶D-6900 *et seq.*; ¶5124; TD ¶681,004
40. ¶D-6911.3; ¶5124.01
41. ¶D-6929 *et seq.*; ¶5124; TD ¶681,034
42. ¶D-6916.1; TD ¶681,012
43. ¶D-6901 *et seq.*; ¶5124; TD ¶681,006
44. ¶D-6847; ¶5124; TD ¶681,033
45. ¶D-6901 *et seq.*; ¶5144; TD ¶682,001 *et seq.*

Sec. 514(a)(2), Code Sec. 514(a)(3))[46]

Payments of interest, rents, royalties and annuities ("specified payments") made by a controlled entity to its tax-exempt parent in 2006 or 2007 are included in UBTI to the extent they exceed fair market value. (Code Sec. 512(b)(13)(E))[47]

¶ 4123   Property acquired through debt financing—"debt-financed property."

Debt-financed property, with certain exceptions, is any property held to produce income (including gains from its disposition, as well as rents, dividends and other recurring income) (Code Sec. 514(b); Reg § 1.514(b)-1(a)), with respect to which there's an acquisition indebtedness at any time during the tax year. [48]

"Acquisition indebtedness" for any property generally means: (1) the unpaid amount of indebtedness incurred by the organization in acquiring or improving the property; and (2) indebtedness incurred at other times which *but for* the acquisition or improvement wouldn't have been incurred (if incurred after the acquisition, etc., the debt must have been reasonably foreseeable at that time). (Code Sec. 514(c))[49]

Any mortgage or other lien on the acquired property is considered incurred in that acquisition, whether or not it's thus assumed by the organization. (Code Sec. 514(c)(2)(A))[50]

¶ 4124   Exempt organization returns—Form 990; Form 8868.

In general, every organization that's exempt from tax, or whose exemption application is pending, must file an annual information return (Form 990 series) and keep the records and make sworn statements as required by IRS. (Code Sec. 6033; Reg § 1.6033-2)[1] For returns filed for tax years ending after Aug. 17, 2006, Code Sec. 509(a)(3) supporting organizations must file annual information returns (Code Sec. 6033(a)(3)(B)) containing specific information (Code Sec. 6033(l))[2] Certain exempt organizations that acquire interests in life insurance contracts within two years after Aug. 17, 2006 must file an information return or face a penalty. (Code Sec. 6050V, Code Sec. 6724(d)(1)(B)(xiv), Code Sec. 6721(e)(2)(D))[3] For private foundations, see ¶4131.

The return must show the organization's total lobbying and political expenditures for the year (Code Sec. 6033(b)(8)), (except political expenditures of nonpolitical organizations taxed under Code Sec. 527(f) (Code Sec. 6033(e)(1)(B)(iii)))[4] and the total amount of dues and similar receipts to which the expenditures are allocable. There are exceptions for Code Sec. 501(c)(3) organizations' in-house expenditures not exceeding $2,000 (Code Sec. 6033(e)(1))[5] and certain nondeductible dues. [6]

As a result of IRS discretion, the filing requirement does not apply to an organization, other than a private foundation, whose gross receipts in each tax year are normally not more than $25,000[7] but organizations exempted under this rule must file annual notices with IRS effective for notices and returns for annual periods beginning after 2006. Use Form 990-N, "Electronic Notice (e-Postcard) for Tax-Exempt Organizations Not Required to File Form 990 or 990-EZ." (Code Sec. 6033(i))[8] There's no monetary penalty for failure to file the notice. (Code Sec. 6652(c)(1)(E))[9]

For returns due after Aug. 17, 2006, information returns of parent tax-exempt organizations must include information about transactions with controlled entities. (Code

46. ¶s D-7007, D-7010; ¶5144; TD ¶682,001
47. ¶D-6913.2; ¶5124
48. ¶D-7012 *et seq.*; ¶5144; TD ¶682,005
49. ¶D-7040 *et seq.*; ¶5144; TD ¶682,005
50. ¶D-7043; ¶5144; TD ¶682,007
1. ¶S-2801 *et seq.*; ¶60,334; TD ¶688,001
2. ¶S-2823.1

3. ¶S-2896; ¶60,50V4
4. ¶S-2853; ¶60,334; TD ¶688,016
5. ¶s S-2858.1, S-2858.2; ¶60,334
6. ¶S-2858.3; ¶60,334
7. ¶S-2827
8. ¶S-2801.1; ¶60,334
9. ¶V-1907; ¶6,524

Sec. 6033(h))[10]

For returns filed for tax years ending after Aug. 17, 2006, sponsoring organizations must disclose information about donor advised funds on information returns. (Code Sec. 6033(k))

The return must be for the organization's annual accounting period or if it has none, the calendar year. (Reg § 1.6033-2(b)) It must be filed by the fifteenth day of the fifth full month after this annual period (May 15 for a calendar year organization). (Reg § 1.6033-2(e))[11]

An exempt organization required to file a return on Form 990 (except for Form 990-C), Form 1041-A, Form 4720, Form 5227, or Form 8870 may obtain an automatic three-month filing extension by filing on or before the return due date a Form 8868 showing the full amount properly estimated as tax, and remitting the full amount of properly estimated unpaid tax. (Reg § 1.6081-9(a))

For returns and notices for annual periods beginning after 2006, an exempt organization's failure to file the required information return or notice for three consecutive years will result in the revocation of its exempt status. IRS will publish and maintain a list of organizations whose status has been so revoked (Code Sec. 6033(j))[12]

Most exempt organizations must file an information return (with Form 990) on liquidation, dissolution, termination or contraction if it was exempt for any of its last five years. (Code Sec. 6043(b))[13]

For tax years ending on or after Dec. 31, 2006, tax-exempt organizations must electronically file their Forms 990, if they have $10 million or more in total assets and file 250 or more returns a year. In addition, private foundations and charitable trusts must e-file Forms 990-PF, regardless of their asset size, if they file at least 250 returns. (Reg § 301.6033-4T)[14] For other information return requirements, see ¶4750.

¶ 4125   Private foundations and Donor Advised Funds. ■■■■■■■■■■■■

Private foundations are generally exempt from income tax, but are subject to excise taxes, notification requirements and other restrictions.

A private foundation is any domestic or foreign religious, scientific, charitable, etc., organization described in Code Sec. 501(c)(3) (¶4102) *other than* organizations that:

(1) are "50% charities" (¶2125), except operating foundations and membership organizations (Code Sec. 509(a)(1));[15]

(2) meet detailed public support tests (Code Sec. 509(a)(2), Code Sec. 509(d));[16]

(3) operate exclusively for the benefit of one or more of the above organizations (as Type I, Type II, or Type III supporting organizations) and aren't controlled by disqualified persons (¶4127, other than foundation managers) (Code Sec. 509(a)(3));[17]

(4) are organized and operated exclusively for testing for public safety. (Code Sec. 509(a)(4))[18]

Strict accountability requirements apply to qualify as a Type III supporting organization (Code Sec. 509(f)(1));[19] and Type I and Type II supporting organizations lose their status as non-private foundations if they accept gifts from prohibited persons. (Code Sec. 509(f)(2)(A))[20]

A Code Sec. 501(c)(3) organization (other than a church or an organization whose annual gross receipts don't exceed $5,000) is presumed to be a private foundation unless it notifies IRS to the contrary (Code Sec. 508(b), Code Sec. 508(c))[21] on Form 1023 within 15 months

---

10. ¶S-2862.2
11. ¶S-4928; ¶60,334; TD ¶688,003
12. ¶S-2802; ¶60,334
13. ¶S-2883; ¶60,334; TD ¶815,008
14. ¶S-2822.2; ¶60,334; TD ¶688,001
15. ¶D-7203; ¶5074; TD ¶683,506

16. ¶s D-7204, D-7207, D-7209; ¶5074; TD ¶683,507
17. ¶D-7212 *et seq.*; ¶5074; TD ¶683,508
18. ¶D-7202; ¶5074; TD ¶670,632
19. ¶D-7211; ¶5074
20. ¶D-7211; ¶5074
21. ¶s D-7216, D-7217; ¶5074; TD ¶683,503

from the end of the month it was organized. (Reg § 1.508-1(b)(2))[22]

Because of recent law changes made by the Pension Protection Act of 2006 (PPA), IRS recognizes that organizations classified as supporting organizations under Code Sec. 509(a)(3) may wish to seek reclassification under Code Sec. 509(a)(1) or Code Sec. 509(a)(2) and has established a procedure for doing so.[23] IRS has also issued detailed guidance on the PPA changes affecting exempt organizations.

¶ 4126 Taxable trusts and foreign organizations subject to private foundation rules—Form 1041-A; Form 5227.

Certain charitable trusts and split interest trusts, and foreign organizations meeting the private foundation definition (¶4125), may be subject to the private foundation excise taxes (¶4127) and rules on prohibited acts, but not the notification requirements. (Code Sec. 4947, Code Sec. 4948) File Form 1041-A for a split interest trust. Use Form 8868 for an extension, see ¶4124. Use Form 5227 to report the financial activities of a split-interest trust and to determine if it is treated as a private foundation and is subject to excise tax. Use Form 8868 for an extension, see ¶4124.[24]

¶ 4127 Excise taxes on private foundations—Form 990-PF; Form 4720.

Private foundations may be subject to the following excise taxes.

Net investment income. An *exempt* private foundation is liable for an excise tax of 2% on its net investment income for the tax year. (Code Sec. 4940(a); Reg § 53.4940-1)[25] The tax is reduced to 1% if the foundation makes certain charitable distributions (Code Sec. 4940(e))[26] and is eliminated altogether for certain operating foundations. (Code Sec. 4940(d))[27] For a *taxable* foundation, the excise tax equals the amount (if any) by which: (1) the sum of 2% of its net investment income (computed as if it were exempt) plus the unrelated business income tax (¶4122) that would have been imposed on it had it been exempt, *exceeds* (2) the income tax actually imposed on it for the tax year. (Code Sec. 4940(b))[28] Report the tax on Form 990-PF. (Reg § 53.6011-1(d))[29]

Self-dealing. An excise tax is imposed when a disqualified person (substantial contributors, foundation managers, and specified owners, family members and related entities of these, as well as government officials) (Code Sec. 4946(a)(1)) engages in any of certain acts of self-dealing with a private foundation.[30]

For *each* act of self-dealing (Code Sec. 4941(a), Code Sec. 4941(b));[31] the disqualified person (except foundation managers) is subject to an initial tax of 5% (10% for tax years beginning after Aug. 17, 2006) on the amount (not exceeding the amount he actually benefits) involved (Code Sec. 4941(a)(1); Reg § 53.4941(a)-1(a))[32] and a 200% additional tax if the self-dealing isn't timely corrected. (Code Sec. 4941(b)(1))[33] Any foundation manager who knowingly participates in the act is subject to an initial 2 ½% tax (5% for tax years beginning after Aug. 17, 2006) (Code Sec. 4941(a)(2))[34] and, if he refuses to agree with all or part of the correction, an additional 50% tax. (Code Sec. 4941(b)(2))[35] Managers may be jointly and severally liable, but their maximum liability for any one act is $10,000 in initial tax and $10,000 in additional tax ($20,000 in each case for tax years beginning after Aug. 17, 2006). (Code Sec. 4941(c))[36] Report the initial taxes on Form 4720. (Reg § 53.6011-1(b)) Use Form 8868 for an extension,

22. ¶T-10464; ¶5074; TD ¶683,503
23. ¶T-10492
24. ¶s D-7300 *et seq.*, D-7400 *et seq.*; ¶s 49,474, 49,484; TD ¶688,009
25. ¶D-7501; ¶49,404; TD ¶684,001
26. ¶D-7503; ¶49,404; TD ¶684,006
27. ¶D-7504; ¶49,404; TD ¶684,009
28. ¶D-7506; ¶49,404.

29. ¶S-2511; ¶60,334; TD ¶684,001
30. ¶D-7600 *et seq.*; ¶s 49,414; 49,464; TD ¶684,500
31. ¶s D-7606, D-7608; ¶49,414.02; TD ¶684,500
32. ¶D-7601; ¶49,414.02; TD ¶684,501
33. ¶D-7602; ¶49,414.02; TD ¶684,503
34. ¶D-7602; ¶49,414.02; TD ¶684,504
35. ¶D-7602; ¶49,414.02; TD ¶684,505
36. ¶s D-7603, D-7604; ¶49,414.02; TD ¶684,506

see ¶4124.[37]

Failure to distribute income. A foundation (other than an operating foundation) that fails to distribute its income for a tax year by the end of the *next* year is subject to an initial tax equal to 15% (30% for tax years beginning after Aug. 17, 2006) of the income (based on a minimum investment return) (Code Sec. 4942(a); Reg § 53.4942(a)-1(a)), which IRS may abate for reasonable cause (Code Sec. 4962(a))[38] and a 100% additional tax if the foundation fails to distribute the income by the date the initial tax is assessed or IRS issues a 90-day letter for it. (Code Sec. 4942(b))[39] Distributions after Aug. 17, 2006 by nonoperating private foundations to certain supporting organizations are not qualifying distributions. (Code Sec. 4942(g)(4))[40] Report the initial taxes on Form 4720. (Reg § 53.6011-1(b)) Use Form 8868 for an extension, see ¶4124.[41]

Excess business holdings. A foundation that has any excess business holdings is subject to an initial tax (which IRS may abate for reasonable cause) equal to 5% (10% for tax years beginning after Aug. 17, 2006) of those excess holdings, based on their value on the day during the tax year when those holdings were the greatest. (Code Sec. 4943(a), Code Sec. 4962)[42] If the foundation fails to timely correct its holdings, an additional 200% tax is imposed. (Code Sec. 4943(b))[43] For tax years beginning after Aug. 17, 2006, subject to transition rules, the excess business holding tax applies to donor advised funds (Code Sec. 4943(e))[44] and the excess business holdings rules apply to certain supporting organizations. (Code Sec. 4943(f))[45] Report the initial taxes on Form 4720. (Reg § 53.6011-1(b)) Use Form 8868 for an extension, see ¶4124.[46]

Investments that jeopardize a foundation's charitable purpose. An excise tax is imposed if a foundation makes investments that jeopardize its charitable purpose. An initial tax of 5% (10% for tax years beginning after Aug. 17, 2006) of the amount invested is imposed on the foundation *and* on any foundation manager who knowingly participated in the investment. (Code Sec. 4944(a))[47] Additional taxes are imposed on the foundation (25%) if the investment is not timely removed from jeopardy (Code Sec. 4944(b)(1))[48] and on any manager (5%) who refuses to agree to removing the investment from jeopardy. (Code Sec. 4944(b)(2))[49] Foundation managers may be jointly and severally liable for these taxes, but the initial tax on management with respect to any one investment is limited to $5,000, and the additional tax to $10,000 (these figures are doubled for tax years beginning after Aug. 17, 2006). (Code Sec. 4944(d))[50] Report the initial taxes on Form 4720. (Reg § 53.6011-1(b)) Use Form 8868 for an extension, see ¶4124.[1]

Propaganda, legislative activities and other taxable expenditures. An excise tax is imposed for engaging in propaganda or legislative activities or for making other taxable expenditures. An initial tax equal to 10% (20% for tax years beginning after Aug. 17, 2006) of the amount of the taxable expenditure is imposed on the foundation, and a 2 ½% (5% for tax years beginning after Aug. 17, 2006) initial tax is imposed on any foundation manager who willfully agreed to the expenditure. (Code Sec. 4945(a))[2] An additional tax is imposed on the foundation (100%) if the expenditure isn't timely corrected, and on any foundation manager (50%) who refuses to agree to part or all of the correction. (Code Sec. 4945(b))[3] Foundation managers may be jointly and severally liable, but the maximum tax that may be imposed on them for any one taxable expenditure is $5,000 of initial tax and $10,000 ($20,000 for tax years beginning after Aug. 17, 2006) of additional tax. (Code Sec. 4945(c)) These taxes don't apply if the political

37. ¶S-2511; TD ¶684,504
38. ¶s D-7701, D-8201; ¶s 49,424, 49,614; TD ¶685,001
39. ¶s D-7701, D-7706; ¶49,424.01; TD ¶685,002
40. ¶D-7711; ¶49,424.03
41. ¶S-2511; TD ¶685,001
42. ¶s D-7800 *et seq.*, D-8201; ¶s 49,434, 49,614; TD ¶685,509
43. ¶D-7801; ¶49,434; TD ¶685,509
44. ¶D-7801; ¶49,434
45. ¶D-7800 *et seq.*; ¶49,434

46. ¶S-2511; TD ¶685,509
47. ¶s D-7901, D-7903; ¶s 49,444, 49,614; TD ¶685,503
48. ¶D-7905; ¶49,444; TD ¶685,505
49. ¶D-7906; ¶49,444; TD ¶685,507
50. ¶D-7907; ¶49,444; TD ¶685,508
1. ¶S-2511; TD ¶685,501
2. ¶D-8001; ¶s 49,454 *et seq.*, 49,614 *et seq.*; TD ¶685,018
3. ¶D-8001; ¶49,454.02; TD ¶685,019

expenditures tax (¶4104) applies. (Code Sec. 4955(e))[4] Report the initial taxes on Form 4720. (Reg § 53.6011-1(b)) Use Form 8868 for an extension, see ¶4124.[5]

¶ 4128 Termination of private foundation status; termination tax—Form 990-PF.

Except as otherwise provided below, an organization's status as a private foundation may terminate only if either: (1) the organization notifies IRS of its intent to terminate, or (2) the organization is guilty of willful repeated acts or omissions or of a willful and flagrant act or omission resulting in liability for any of the excise taxes on private foundations (see ¶4127), and IRS notifies the organization that it's liable for tax on termination of its status as a private foundation. (Code Sec. 507(a))[6]

The organization must pay a tax (use Form 990-PF, see ¶4131) on termination of its private foundation status. Unless abated by IRS, the tax equals the lesser of: (1) the aggregate tax benefit (as adequately substantiated by the foundation) resulting from its Code Sec. 501(c)(3) status, or (2) the value of its net assets. (Code Sec. 507(c), Code Sec. 507(g))[7]

Where there's no willful repeated acts or omissions or willful and flagrant acts or omissions resulting in private foundation excise tax liability, a private foundation's status may be terminated without imposition of the tax on termination, if: (a) it distributes all its net assets to one or more public charities that have been in existence as such for at least 60 calendar months before the distribution (IRS guidance illustrates termination under this rule); or (b) it notifies IRS of its intent to terminate, and the organization becomes a public charity for a continuous 60- month period. (Code Sec. 507(b))[8]

¶ 4129 Excise tax on taxable distributions from donor advised funds

For tax years beginning after Aug. 17, 2006, if a taxable distribution is made from a donor advised fund (see below):

(1) a tax equal to 20% of the amount distributed is imposed and must be paid by the donor advised fund's sponsoring organization (Code Sec. 4966(a)(1)); and

(2) a tax equal to 5% of the amount distributed is imposed if any fund manager agreed to the making of a distribution knowing that it was a taxable distribution. The tax must be paid by any fund manager who agreed to the making of the distribution. (Code Sec. 4966(a)(2))[9]

The maximum amount of tax imposed by item (2) as to any one taxable distribution is $10,000. (Code Sec. 4966(b)(2))

Subject to exceptions, a *donor advised fund* is a fund or account which is:

(1) separately identified by reference to contributions of a donor or donors,

(2) owned and controlled by a sponsoring organization, and

(3) as to which a donor (or any person appointed or designated by the donor) has, or reasonably expects to have, advisory privileges as to the distribution or investment of amounts held in the fund or account by reason of the donor's status as a donor. (Code Sec. 4966(d)(2))

¶ 4130 Excise taxes imposed on prohibited benefits received by a donor, donor advisor or related person from a donor advised fund.

For tax years beginning after Aug. 17, 2006, if a distribution from a donor advised fund

---

4. ¶D-8003; ¶49,554; TD ¶684,500
5. ¶S-2511; ¶s 60,114.04, 60,334; TD ¶685,017
6. ¶s D-7220, D-7222; ¶5074; TD ¶683,509

7. ¶D-7228; ¶5074
8. ¶D-7223; ¶5074
9. ¶D-8152 *et seq.*; ¶49,664

(¶4129) results in a donor, donor advisor, or a related person (Subsection (d) person as set forth in Code Sec. 4967(d)) receiving directly or indirectly a more than incidental benefit as a result of the distribution:

(1) A tax equal to 125% of the amount of the benefit is imposed on the advice of any Subsection (d) person to have a sponsoring organization make the distribution. The tax must be paid by the Subsection (d) person who advises that a distribution be made or who receives a benefit as a result of the distribution. (Code Sec. 4967(a)(1))

(2) A tax equal to 10% of the amount of the benefit is imposed on the agreement of any fund manager to the making of the distribution knowing that the distribution would confer a benefit described at item (1) (above). This tax must be paid by the fund manager who agreed to the making of the distribution. (Code Sec. 4967(a)(2)) However, the maximum amount of tax imposed on a fund manager as to any distribution is $10,000. (Code Sec. 4967(c)(2))[10]

Tax is not imposed as to any distribution as to which tax has been imposed under the Code Sec. 4958 excess benefit transaction rules, ¶4112. (Code Sec. 4967(b))

¶ 4131   Annual return of private foundations—Form 990-PF.

A private foundation must file an annual information return on Form 990-PF (Reg § 1.6033-2(a)(2)(i)) on or before the fifteenth day of the fifth month following the close of the tax year. (Reg § 1.6033-2(e))[11] For return disclosure requirements, see ¶4120. Certain private foundations must file returns electronically. (Reg § 301.6033-4T)

---

10. ¶D-8160 *et seq.*; ¶49,674   11. ¶s S-2801, S-4928; ¶60,334; TD ¶688,021

Chapter 20 RICs (Mutual Funds), REITs, REMICs, Banks and Other Special Corporations

¶ 4200 Special Corporations and Other Entities. ▌▌▌▌▌▌▌▌▌▌▌▌▌▌▌▌▌▌▌

Regulated investment companies (mutual funds), real estate investment trusts, real estate mortgage investment conduits, and certain other entities get special tax treatment.

¶ 4201 Regulated investment companies (RICs)—mutual funds.

If it makes certain distributions, a RIC (mutual fund) is taxed only on: (1) the undistributed portion of its ordinary net income, at the regular corporate rates; and (2) the undistributed portion of its net long-term capital gains, at the corporate capital gains rate. (Code Sec. 852(b))[1] The RIC isn't taxed on the amounts it distributes to shareholders, thus allowing it to pass through ordinary income, net capital gains, qualified dividend income eligible for capital gain treatment, dividend income eligible for the corporate dividends-received deduction, and certain other items to them (see ¶1298) without any tax at the RIC level (if requirements are met). (Code Sec. 852(b))[2] For "late-paid" and year-end dividends, see ¶4203.

The RIC's *undistributed* capital gains may also be designated (on Form 2439) and passed through to the shareholders (but the RIC pays tax (on Form 2438) on the retained gains). The effects of designation are that the shareholders: (1) include their shares of the undistributed capital gains in income, (2) get a credit or refund for their shares of the tax the RIC paid on these amounts (so that only one tax is paid), and (3) get a basis step-up in their shares equal to the difference between the amount of the includible capital gains from the dividend and the tax the shareholder is deemed to have paid with respect to those shares. (Code Sec. 852(b)(3)(D))[3]

A RIC is a domestic corporation that at all times in the tax year is registered with the SEC as a management company or unit investment trust, has an election in effect to be treated as a business development company under the '40 Investment Company Act, or is a mutual or common trust fund other than an "investment company" under that Act. (Code Sec. 851(a))[4] It must also meet gross income, (Code Sec. 851(b)(2))[5] diversification, (Code Sec. 851(b)(3))[6] and E&P tests, (Code Sec. 852(a)(2))[7] make certain distributions (Code Sec. 852(a)(1))[8] *and* elect on its return (Form 1120-RIC) to be taxed as a RIC. (Code Sec. 851(b)(1))[9]

¶ 4202 Real estate investment trusts (REITs).

REITs are generally taxed only on amounts not distributed to their shareholders or beneficiaries, as follows: (1) at *regular* corporate rates on undistributed earnings and profits and net capital gains, and (2) at the *highest* corporate rate on net income from foreclosure property. (Code Sec. 857(b))[10] A REIT may pass through the character of its capital gains and qualified dividend income taxed as capital gains to its shareholders, see ¶1299. In addition, a REIT's *undistributed* capital gains may be passed through to the shareholders (on Form 2439). The REIT pays tax on the retained gains (on Form 2438) and the shareholders: (1) include their shares of the undistributed capital gains in income, (2) get a credit or refund for their shares of the tax the REIT paid on these amounts (so that only one tax is paid), and (3)

---

1. ¶E-6100 *et seq.*; ¶8524.10
2. ¶E-6150; ¶8524.02
3. ¶E-6155; ¶8524.02; TD ¶173,001
4. ¶E-6001 *et seq.*; ¶8514
5. ¶E-6004; ¶8514.02

6. ¶s E-6012, E-6015; ¶8514.04
7. ¶E-6020; ¶8524.01
8. ¶E-6101; ¶8524.01
9. ¶E-6002; ¶8514.01
10. ¶E-6600 *et seq.*; ¶8574.01

References beginning with a single letter are to paragraphs in RIA's Federal Tax Coordinator 2d and RIA's Analysis of Federal Taxes: Income. Those beginning with numbers are to paragraphs in RIA's United States Tax Reporter. Those beginning with TD are to paragraphs in RIA's Tax Desk.

get a basis step-up in their shares equal to the difference between the amount of the includible capital gains from the dividend and the tax the shareholder is deemed to have paid with respect to those shares. (Code Sec. 857(b)(3)(D))[11] For "late-paid" and year-end dividends, see ¶4203.

The REIT must be a calendar-year (Code Sec. 859) corporation, trust or association that meets certain requirements as to the source of income, earnings and profits, type of its investments, nature of its activities, and its relationships with financially interested parties (Code Sec. 856(a)), and certain recordkeeping and distribution requirements. (Code Sec. 857(a)) And it must elect on its return (Form 1120-REIT) to be a REIT. (Code Sec. 856(c)(1); Reg § 1.856-2(b))[12]

✪ observation: REITs are designed to do for real estate investors what mutual funds (RICs, see ¶4201) do for investors in securities —i.e., pool resources and get a return on capital without paying a corporate tax on the gain.

¶ 4203   RIC (mutual fund) and REIT dividends paid after close of tax year; year-end dividends.

A RIC (¶4201) or REIT (¶4202) may elect to treat all or part of any dividend paid after the end of a tax year ("late-paid dividends") as paid during the year, if the dividend is: (1) declared before the due date of the return (REITs must state a dollar amount), and (2) paid not later than the first regular dividend date after declaration, but in no case later than 12 months after the end of the tax year. (Code Sec. 855(a), Code Sec. 858(a))[13]

A dividend declared by a RIC or REIT in October, November or December of any calendar year, that's payable to shareholders of record on a specified date in one of those months, is considered to have been paid on Dec. 31 if the dividend is actually paid during January of the following calendar year. (Code Sec. 852(b)(7), Code Sec. 857(b)(9))[14]

For shareholders' tax on these dividends, see ¶1298 (RICs) and ¶1299 (REITs).

¶ 4204   Real estate mortgage investment conduits (REMICs).

REMICs are fixed mortgage pools with multiple classes ("regular" and "residual" (Code Sec. 860G(a)(1), Code Sec. 860G(a)(2); Reg § 1.860G-1)) of investment interests, that have elected REMIC status (on Form 1066). (Code Sec. 860D; Reg § 1.860D-1)[15] REMICs, which are treated as partnerships for procedural purposes (Code Sec. 860F(e))[16] generally aren't taxable. (Code Sec. 860A(a))[17] The REMIC's income is allocated to, and taken into account by, the holders of its interests. (Code Sec. 860A(b)) REMICs report on Form 1066.[18]

Although not subject to federal income tax, a REMIC is subject to penalty taxes on: income from foreclosure property (Code Sec. 860G(c)), contributions after the start-up date (Code Sec. 860G(d)), and prohibited transactions (Code Sec. 860F(a)), and an excise tax (reported on Form 8831) on certain transfers of residual interests. (Code Sec. 860E(e))[19]

¶ 4205   Small business investment companies (SBICs).

SBICs are licensed and operated under the Small Business Investment Act of '58.[20] They are subject to these special tax rules:

---

11. ¶E-6617.1; ¶8574.02
12. ¶s E-6501, E-6623; ¶8564.02
13. ¶s E-6201, E-6701;¶s 8554, 8584
14. ¶s E-6202, E-6704;¶s 8554.01, 8574.02; TD ¶172,005
15. ¶s E-6901, E-6903; ¶860A4
16. ¶E-6927; ¶860A4

17. ¶E-6917; ¶860A4
18. ¶E-7000 et seq.; ¶s 860A4.01, 860A4.02
19. ¶E-6920 et seq.; ¶E-7106; ¶s 860A4.05, 860A4.06, 860A4.07; TD ¶162,010
20. ¶I-9541; ¶12,424.01

... Loss on stock received through the conversion of convertible debentures originally acquired for long-term equity capital supplied to small business concerns is a fully deductible ordinary loss. (Code Sec. 1243)[21]

... An SBIC's gain or loss on sale of bonds, debentures, etc., (regardless of issuer) is ordinary gain or loss. (Code Sec. 582(c); Reg § 1.582-1(d))[22]

... Dividends the SBIC receives from taxable domestic corporations are 100% deductible. (Code Sec. 243(a)(2))[23]

... An SBIC is exempt from personal holding company tax (¶3323 *et seq.*), unless at any time in the tax year any shareholder of the SBIC owns, directly or indirectly, a 5%-or-more interest in the companies financed by the SBIC. (Code Sec. 542(c)(8))[24]

¶ 4206 Cooperatives (co-ops).

A cooperative is an entity in which the same persons are both owners and customers. Although some co-ops are *classified* as "exempt," most co-ops are taxed like any ordinary business corporation, and at the regular corporate rates, but with a specific deduction for patronage dividends, see ¶4207. (Code Sec. 1382(b)) "Exempt" farmers' co-ops also may deduct certain nonpatronage distributions. (Code Sec. 1382(c))[25]

¶ 4207 Patronage dividends and per-unit retain allocations.

Both "exempt" farmers' co-ops and nonexempt co-ops exclude (deduct) from their income amounts paid as patronage dividends or per-unit retain allocations. (Code Sec. 1381(a), Code Sec. 1382(b))[26] For deduction of nonpatronage dividends, see ¶4208. For how the patrons or shareholders treat these amounts, see ¶1300.

A patronage dividend represents distributions of net earnings among the cooperators and other patrons on the basis of each person's patronage. (Code Sec. 1388(a))[27] It may be paid in money, a certificate of indebtedness, or other property, including a qualified written notice of allocation.[28]

A per-unit retain allocation is an allocation by a co-op to a patron with respect to products marketed for him. (Code Sec. 1388(f))[29]

A written notice of allocation must disclose the dollar amount allocated to the patron and the portion that is a patronage dividend. (Code Sec. 1388(b); Reg § 1.1388-1(b))[30]

¶ 4208 Nonpatronage distributions deductible by exempt co-ops.

In addition to patronage distributions (¶4207), an "exempt" farmers' co-op may also deduct: dividends paid during the tax year on its capital stock and on any other evidence of proprietary interest in the co-op (Code Sec. 1382(c)(1); Reg § 1.1382-3(b)) distributions to patrons on a patronage basis out of earnings from nonpatronage sources (Code Sec. 1382(c)(2)(A); Reg § 1.1382-3(c), Reg § 1.1382-3(c)(3)) payments in redemption of non-qualified written notices of allocation issued to patrons on a patronage basis with respect to earnings from nonpatronage sources. (Code Sec. 1382(c)(2)(B); Reg § 1.1382-3(d))[31]

21. ¶I-9542; ¶12,424.02; TD ¶372,006
22. ¶I-9544
23. ¶D-2243; ¶12,424.02
24. ¶D-3311; ¶5424.02; TD ¶601,503
25. ¶E-1100 *et seq.*; ¶13,814.01
26. ¶E-1100 *et seq.*; ¶13,814.01

27. ¶E-1104; ¶13,814.05
28. ¶E-1120; ¶13,814.01
29. ¶E-1126; ¶13,814.14
30. ¶E-1123; ¶13,814.02
31. ¶s E-1140, E-1141, E-1142; ¶13,814.01

¶ 4209   Taxation of banks and other financial institutions.

Banks are generally taxed like regular corporations (Reg § 1.581-1), except that: [32]

Gains and losses from sales or exchanges of bonds, debentures, notes or certificates or other evidences of indebtedness (including any regular or residual interest in a REMIC, see ¶4204) are treated as ordinary gains and losses. (Code Sec. 582(c)(1)) Sales of stock and securities are subject to the regular wash sale provisions, see ¶2461. [33]

Interest paid or credited on deposits or CDs is deductible (special rules apply to frozen deposits). [34] But no deduction is allowed for any portion of interest expense that's allocable (comparing the bank's adjusted bases in taxable and exempt investments) to investment in tax-exempts. (Code Sec. 265(b)(1), Code Sec. 265(b)(2)) [35] However, interest allocable to tax-exempts acquired (or treated as acquired) before Aug. 8, '86, is 80% deductible (100% deductible if acquired before '83). (Code Sec. 291(a)(3), Code Sec. 291(e)(1)(B)) [36]

Bad debts. Banks generally must treat bad debts (e.g., losses on loans) by taking a specific deduction ("charge-off") for the debt but non-large banks can choose to deduct additions to bad debt reserves. (Code Sec. 585(a)) [37] Banks using reserves must use the experience method to compute the additions. Under this method, the additions can't bring the reserve above the bank's loans outstanding at year-end, times a six-year moving average percentage (ratio of total bad debts to total outstanding loans). (Code Sec. 585(b)) [38]

Losses a bank incurs on account of its deposits in other banks must be specifically deducted, whether or not it uses the reserve method for other bad debts. [39]

Worthless securities. A bad debt deduction is allowed to banks for total or partial worthlessness (¶1781) of debts evidenced by securities. (Code Sec. 582(a)) Under the charge-off method, a bank's debt is conclusively presumed to be worthless where the charge-off is made under specific orders or in conformance with established policies, of federal or state supervisory authorities, or is in accordance with a properly made "conformity" election. (Reg § 1.166-2(d)) [40]

Mutual savings banks or stock associations, savings and loan associations, building and loan associations, and cooperative banks are subject to special tax rules. [41]

¶ 4210   Common trust funds.

A common trust fund isn't subject to tax (Code Sec. 584(b)) but must file a return (on Form 1065) and pass through its income or loss and other items attributable to each participant. (Reg § 1.6032-1) [42] A common trust fund is a fund maintained by a bank or trust company exclusively to collectively invest and reinvest moneys that it, in its capacity as a trustee, executor, administrator, guardian or custodian, contributes to the fund. (Code Sec. 584(a)) [43]

¶ 4211   Taxation of insurance companies.

Life insurance companies are taxed, at the regular corporate rates, on their "life insurance company taxable income" (LICTI). (Code Sec. 801(a)(1)) [44] LICTI is life insurance company gross income minus general deductions and, if applicable, the small life insurance company

---

32. ¶E-3000 *et seq.*, ¶E-3300 *et seq.*; ¶5814
33. ¶E-3022 *et seq.*; ¶5824
34. ¶E-3105; ¶5914
35. ¶E-3108; ¶2654
36. ¶s E-3111, E-3124; ¶2914
37. ¶E-3201, ¶E-3224
38. ¶E-3227; ¶5854
39. ¶E-3139
40. ¶E-3201 *et seq.*; ¶5824
41. ¶E-3300 *et seq.*; ¶5814
42. ¶s E-3600 *et seq.*, S-4105; ¶s 5844, 60,324
43. ¶E-3600 *et seq.*; ¶5844
44. ¶E-4801; ¶8014

deduction. (Code Sec. 803(a), Code Sec. 804)[45] Gain from the redemption at maturity of certain market discount bonds is taxed under a special rule. [46]

A corporation (whether stock, mutual, or mutual benefit) is taxed as a life insurance company if: (1) it's an insurance company, (2) it's engaged in the business of issuing life insurance and annuity contracts, and (3) it meets a reserve test. (Code Sec. 816(a))[47]

Nonlife insurance companies (stock and mutual) are taxed like corporations generally (¶3303 *et seq.*), with certain deductions peculiar to insurance. Gross income is investment and underwriting income, and gain or loss from property dispositions. (Code Sec. 831, Code Sec. 832)[48] Certain small nonlife insurance companies may elect to be taxed only on investment income, (Code Sec. 831(b))[49] and others may be exempt. (Code Sec. 501(c)(15))[50]

---

45. ¶E-4801 *et seq.*; ¶s 8034, 8044
46. ¶E-4819
47. ¶E-5401; ¶8164

48. ¶E-5500 *et seq.*; ¶8324.01
49. ¶E-5503; ¶8314
50. ¶D-5901

Chapter 21 Pension and Profit-Sharing Plans—401(k) Plans—Roth 401(k) Plans—IRAs—Roth IRAs— SEPs—SIMPLE Plans

¶ 4310 Employee Benefit Plans.

Qualified pension, profit-sharing and stock bonus plans offer substantial tax benefits to sponsor-employers and their employees.

The principal tax advantages are:

. . . the employer gets an immediate deduction for contributions under the plan (Code Sec. 404);[1]

. . . the income earned by funds while held under the plan is tax-exempt (Code Sec. 501(a));[2]

. . . the employee isn't taxed on his share of the fund until amounts are distributed to him (usually after retirement), ¶4337 et seq., (Code Sec. 402; Reg § 1.402(a)-1);[3]

. . . qualifying "lump-sum" distributions for those born before '36 can get favorable tax treatment, ¶4338, (Code Sec. 402(d));[4]

. . . amounts transferred in a direct trustee-to-trustee transfer are excluded from income (¶4359) (Code Sec. 402(e)(6)) and eligible rollover distributions can be rolled over tax-free to eligible retirement plans (¶4359) (Code Sec. 402(c)(1));[5]

. . . tax is deferred on qualifying distributions of appreciated employer stock until the stock is sold, see ¶4340. (Code Sec. 402(e)(4))[6]

For the small-employer retirement plan start-up tax credit, see ¶2333.

¶ 4311 Pension plans.

A qualified pension plan provides systematically for the payment of definitely determinable benefits to employees (and their beneficiaries) after retirement over a period of years, usually for life.[7] Retirement benefits are generally measured by such factors as years of the employee's service and compensation received. (Reg § 1.401-1(b)(1)(i))[8] Benefits under a defined benefit plan are "definitely determinable" if they are determined actuarially, on a basis that precludes employer discretion. (Code Sec. 401(a)(25))[9] A money-purchase plan —contributions geared to a fixed formula (e.g., 10% of compensation), rather than to profits —is a pension plan if the plan "designates" its intent to be a money purchase pension plan. (Code Sec. 401(a)(27)(B); Reg § 1.401-1(b)(1)(i))[10]

¶ 4312 Profit-sharing and stock-bonus plans.

A qualified profit-sharing plan must have a definite, predetermined formula for allocating contributions made under the plan among the participants, and for distributing the funds accumulated under the plan only after a fixed number of years, the attainment of a stated age or upon the occurrence of some event (such as disability, retirement, death or severance of employment). (Reg § 1.401-1(b)(1)(ii))[11]

Contributions can be made to a qualified profit-sharing plan whether or not the employer

---

1. ¶H-10000 et seq.; ¶4014; TD ¶280,101
2. ¶H-10500 et seq.; ¶4014; TD ¶280,101
3. ¶H-11006 et seq.; ¶4014; TD ¶280,101
4. ¶H-11200 et seq.; ¶4014; TD ¶280,101
5. ¶H-8250 et seq.; ¶s 4014.27, 4024.04; TD ¶280,101
6. ¶H-11500 et seq.; ¶s 4014, 4024.02; TD ¶280,101
7. ¶H-5328; ¶4014.02; TD ¶280,105
8. ¶H-5328; ¶4014.02; TD ¶280,102
9. ¶H-5328; ¶4014.10; TD ¶280,102
10. ¶s H-5205, H-5337; ¶4014.02; TD ¶280,107
11. ¶H-5337 et seq.; ¶4014.03; TD ¶280,109

References beginning with a single letter are to paragraphs in RIA's Federal Tax Coordinator 2d and RIA's Analysis of Federal Taxes: Income. Those beginning with numbers are to paragraphs in RIA's United States Tax Reporter. Those beginning with TD are to paragraphs in RIA's Tax Desk.

has current or accumulated profits, and whether or not the employer is a tax-exempt organization. (Code Sec. 401(a)(27)(A))[12]

A qualified stock bonus plan provides benefits in the form of the employer-corporation's own stock. Stock bonus plans must generally satisfy the qualification requirements that apply to profit sharing plans, plus some additional requirements. [13]

¶ 4313 Cash balance and other hybrid pension plans.

Cash balance plans are defined benefit plans that resemble defined contribution plans in that they determine an employee's benefit by reference to the employee's "cash balance" or other hypothetical account. Each employee's hypothetical account is the sum of the hypothetical pay credit allocations for earlier plan years, plus subsequent interest adjustments through normal retirement age. Under another type of hybrid plan called a pension equity plan (PEP), benefits typically are described as a percentage of the participant's final average pay, with the percentage determined on the basis of points received for each year of service. .

For periods beginning on or after June 29, 2005, for "applicable defined benefit plans" (i.e., cash balance, pension equity, and other hybrid plans), if a participant's accrued plan benefit, determined as of any date under the plan's terms, would be equal to or greater than that of any similarly situated, younger individual who is (or could be) a participant, the plan won't be treated as violating the age discrimination rules. (Code Sec. 411(b)(5))

An applicable defined benefit plan fails to meet the age discrimination rules unless it provides that the interest credit rate (or an equivalent amount) for any plan year does not exceed a "market rate of return." A plan is not treated as failing to meet the "market rate of return" requirement merely because it provides for a reasonable minimum guaranteed rate of return, or a rate of return equal to the greater of a fixed or variable rate of return. (Code Sec. 411(b)(5))[14]

¶ 4314 Employee stock ownership plans (ESOPs).

An ESOP is a qualified defined contribution plan that is either a stock bonus plan, or a combination stock bonus and money purchase plan, that invests primarily in employer securities (Code Sec. 4975(e)(7)), and is formally designated as an ESOP. [15]

To ensure that S corporation ESOPs benefit a broad range of employees, restrictions apply under Code Sec. 409(p) that generally prohibit the accrual or allocation of S corp. stock to certain disqualified persons in an ESOP where 10% owners hold 50% or more of the interests in the S corp. (Code Sec. 409(p), Reg § 1.409(p)-1)[16]

¶ 4315 Annuity plans.

The tax advantages of a qualified plan can be obtained without a trust by using contributions to buy retirement annuities directly from an insurance company. (Code Sec. 403(a)(1), Code Sec. 404(a)(2))[17] For Code Sec. 403(b) "tax-sheltered annuities" for employees of tax-exempt organizations and public schools, see ¶4388 *et seq.*

¶ 4316 "Thrift" and "savings" plans.

A thrift plan is in the nature of a profit-sharing plan and provides for the contribution by the participants of a specified percentage (the same for all participants) of their salaries. This employee contribution is then matched by the employer, either dollar for dollar or in some

---

12. ¶H-5337; ¶4014.03; TD ¶280,109
13. ¶H-5209; ¶4014.04; TD ¶280,111
14. ¶H-6272.2 *et seq.*; ¶4114.33; TD ¶286,020

15. ¶H-9300 *et seq.*; ¶49,754; TD ¶280,112
16. ¶H-5337; ¶4014.03; TD ¶280,109
17. ¶H-5212 *et seq.*; ¶4034; TD ¶280,113

other specified manner, out of profits. [18]

A savings plan permits employees to make voluntary employee contributions which aren't limited to any specific percentage of compensation. [19]

These plans may allow withdrawal of the voluntary employee contributions (plus earnings) before retirement or termination. [20]

¶ 4317   401(k) plans—$15,500 elective deferral for 2007 and 2008.

Cash or deferred arrangements (CODAs), popularly known as "401(k)" plans (from Code Sec. 401(k)) allow an employee to choose whether the employer should pay a certain amount directly to the employee in cash, or should instead pay that amount on the employee's behalf to a qualified trust under a profit-sharing plan, a stock bonus plan, a pre-ERISA money purchase plan or a rural cooperative defined contribution pension plan. (Code Sec. 401(k))[21] For salary-reduction arrangements similar to 401(k) plans under SIMPLE retirement plans, SEPs established before '97, and tax-sheltered annuities, see ¶4382, ¶4381, and ¶4388.

An employee may elect to defer a maximum of $15,500 on a pre-tax basis under a 401(k) plan, SEP, or Code Sec. 403(b) tax-sheltered annuity (¶4388) for 2007 (and 2008), as adjusted for inflation. (Code Sec. 402(g)(1), Code Sec. 402(g)(5))[22] Individuals who attain age 50 by the end of the plan year may make (if their plan permits (Reg § 1.414(v)-1(a)) additional pre-tax "catch-up" contributions of up to $5,000 for 2007 (and 2008), as adjusted for inflation. (Code Sec. 414(v)(2)(B)(i), Code Sec. 414(v)(2)(C)) The maximum catch-up amounts apply to all qualified plans, tax sheltered annuity plans, SEPs and SIMPLE plans of an employer on an aggregated basis, as if all plans were a single plan. (Code Sec. 414(v)(2)(D))[23]

Excess deferrals must be either corrected (i.e., distributed) by Apr. 15 of the following tax year (Reg § 1.402(g)-1(e)(2)(ii)), or included in the employee's gross income. (Reg § 1.402(g)-1(a))[24]

A 401(k) plan must meet all the normal tax qualification rules (¶4319), including the nondiscrimination rules (¶4324), and, in addition, all of the following requirements:

(1) amounts must not be distributable except by reason of (a) retirement, death, disability or other separation from employment, including certain transfers in connection with the sale of a business, (b) hardship (see below) or attainment of age 59 ½ (for profit-sharing or stock bonus plans), (c) in a lump sum on termination of the plan, or (d) in a lump sum, on the employer's disposition of (i) substantially all of its trade or business assets, or (ii) a subsidiary (Code Sec. 401(k)(2)(B))[25] (for loans from 401(k) plans, see ¶4343);

(2) employer contributions made under the employee's election must be nonforfeitable at all times (Code Sec. 401(k)(2)(C));[26] and

(3) a covered employee must be able to elect to have the employer make plan contributions on the employee's behalf or make the payment directly to the employee in cash (Code Sec. 401(k)(2)(A))[27] ("negative elections" may be permitted for employees who don't affirmatively elect to receive cash); [28]

(4) elective deferrals under the plan (as aggregated with all other plans, etc., of the employer) must be prohibited from exceeding the above indexed dollar limits; [29] and

(5) special nondiscrimination rules that require the plan to satisfy one of two "actual

---

18. ¶H-5214; TD ¶280,114
19. ¶H-5215; TD ¶280,114
20. ¶H-5313; TD ¶280,114
21. ¶H-8950 *et seq.*; ¶4014.17; TD ¶280,116
22. ¶H-9151; ¶4024; TD ¶284,025
23. ¶H-9246; ¶4144.26; TD ¶284,116

24. ¶H-9151 *et seq.*; ¶s 4014.17, 4154.015; TD ¶284,024 *et seq.*
25. ¶H-9201 *et seq.*; ¶4014.17
26. ¶H-9001; ¶4014.17; TD ¶284,003
27. ¶H-8954; ¶4014.17; TD ¶284,003
28. ¶H-8962.1; TD ¶284,007
29. ¶s H-9150, H-9159; ¶4014.17; TD ¶284,003

deferral percentage tests," so highly compensated employees can't elect to defer a disproportionately higher amount of their salary, must be met. (Code Sec. 401(k)(3)(A))[30] A 401(k) plan is treated as meeting these requirements if it's a "SIMPLE" plan (¶4382), that meets specified matching or nonelective contribution tests and other requirements. (Code Sec. 401(k)(11))[31] An alternative nondiscrimination safe-harbor based on employer matching or nonelective contributions also is available. (Code Sec. 401(k)(12))[32]

Similar rules apply to employer and matching contributions under Code Sec. 401(m). (Code Sec. 401(m)(3))[33]

For plan years beginning after 2007, a nondiscrimination safe harbor applies for automatic enrollment 401(k) programs meeting certain contribution, vesting, and withdrawal requirements. (Code Sec. 401(k)(13)(A))

Similar rules apply for 403(b) plans, see ¶4388.

A Code Sec. 401(k) plan can include a qualified Roth contribution program; see ¶4375.

An in-service distribution on account of hardship may only be made if the employee has "an immediate heavy financial need" and the distribution is "necessary to meet such need." But a distribution may be considered for hardship only to the extent that, as shown by the employee, the need can't be relieved by certain alternate sources, e.g., loans, insurance. (Reg § 1.401(k)-1(d)(2))[34]

Beginning Aug, 17, 2006 and thereafter, 401(k) plans may permit hardship distributions for the medical, tuition, funeral etc. expenses of a named plan beneficiary, or of a person who has an unconditional right to all or a part of the participant's account balance on the participant's death.[35]

Hardship distributions are not rollover-eligible, see ¶4359.

For the special rules that apply to qualified hurricane distributions from, and rollovers to, 401(k) (and other qualified) plans, see ¶4344.

For the small-employer retirement plan start-up tax credit, see ¶2333. For the saver's credit for lower-income taxpayers' elective contributions to 401(k) plans, see ¶2365.

¶ 4318 Defined contribution and defined benefit plans.

Certain rules governing employee benefit plans specifically apply either to "defined contribution plans" or to "defined benefit plans."

A "defined contribution plan" provides for individual accounts for participants and for benefits based on those accounts. (Code Sec. 414(i)) Included are money purchase pension plans, profit-sharing plans and stock bonus plans.

A "defined benefit plan" is a pension plan other than a defined contribution plan. (Code Sec. 414(j)) It provides for the payments of definitely determinable benefits to the employee over a period of years, usually for life, after retirement. (Reg § 1.401-1(b)(1)(i))[36]

For plan years beginning after 2009, employers with 500 or fewer employees may establish a combined defined benefit – 401(k) plan. In general, the defined benefit rules apply to the defined benefit portion of the plan and the defined contribution rules apply to the defined contribution portions of the plan. The 401(k) component must have automatic enrollment and must meet minimum matching contribution requirements. (Code Sec. 414(x))

30. ¶H-9051 *et seq.*; ¶4014.17; TD ¶284,003
31. ¶H-9087; ¶4014.1735; TD ¶284,022
32. ¶H-6513.1; ¶4014.21; TD ¶284,003
33. ¶H-9051 *et seq.*; ¶4014.176; *et seq.* TD ¶284,042

34. ¶H-9211 *et seq.*; ¶4014.17
35. ¶H-9211 *et seq.*; ¶4014.17
36. ¶H-5200 *et seq.*; ¶s 4014.02, 4014.03; TD ¶280,100

¶ 4319   Qualification requirements for a qualified employee plan.

The chief requirements for tax qualification of an employee benefit plan and tax-exempt trust are:

(1) The plan must be a definite written program [37] that's communicated to the employees. (Reg § 1.401-1(a)(2)) [38]

(2) The plan must be established by the employer for the *exclusive* benefit of the employees or their beneficiaries. (Code Sec. 401(a)(1)) [39]

(3) The plan must generally provide that benefits can't be assigned, except for transfers under a qualified domestic relations order (QDRO) and judgments or settlements for certain ERISA crimes and violations. (Code Sec. 401(a)(13); Reg § 1.401(a)-13(g)(2)) [40]

(4) The plan must meet special tests based on coverage and eligibility of employees to participate (¶4322).

(5) The plan must not discriminate in favor of highly compensated employees with respect to contributions or benefits (¶4324).

(6) The plan must be properly funded (¶4329), and must meet certain vesting requirements (¶4321).

(7) Under a defined benefit plan, forfeitures must not be applied to increase the benefits of the employees. (Code Sec. 401(a)(8)) [41]

(8) A pension plan (and certain other plans) must in general pay a married participant's benefits in the form of a qualified joint and survivor annuity, unless the participant elects otherwise (with written spousal consent). The monthly survivor benefit must be at least 50% of the joint benefit. (Code Sec. 417(b)) [42] For plan years beginning after 2007, plans that offer a qualified joint and survivor annuity must offer, as an option, a joint and survivor benefit that provides at least a 75% survivor benefit. (Code Sec. 417(a)(1)(A), Code Sec. 417(g))

(9) In the event of a merger or consolidation with, or transfer of assets or liabilities to, any other plan, each participant must be entitled to a termination benefit after the merger, etc., at least equal to his pre-merger termination benefit. (Code Sec. 401(a)(12)) [43]

(10) The plan may not provide for contributions or benefits that exceed specified overall limitations (Code Sec. 401(a)(16)) [44] (¶4327).

(11) The plan must provide that benefit payments begin (unless otherwise elected) no later than the 60th day after the plan year in which occurs the latest of: (a) the date the participant reaches age 65 (or earlier retirement age), (b) the 10th anniversary of the employee's participation in the plan, or (c) the date the participant terminates service. (Code Sec. 401(a)(14); Reg § 1.401(a)-14(a)) [45]

Qualified pension plans may allow employees age 62 or older to receive in-service distributions (i.e. receive plan benefits before retirement). (Code Sec. 401(a)(36); Reg § 1.401(a)-1(b)(1)(i)) [46]

(12) The plan must provide certain required minimum distribution rules (Code Sec. 401(a)(9) (¶4345).

(13) A pension plan can't allow withdrawal of employer contributions before termination of employment, or of the plan. [47] But employer contributions accumulated in a profit-sharing plan may be distributed after a fixed number of years (not less than two years).

---

37. ¶H-5301; ¶4014.05; TD ¶286,001
38. ¶H-5303; ¶4014.05
39. ¶H-5304; ¶4014.09; TD ¶286,001
40. ¶H-8200 *et seq.*; ¶4014.14
41. ¶H-7502; ¶4014.11; TD ¶286,032
42. ¶H-8611; ¶4174.02

43. ¶H-8800 *et seq.*; ¶4014.07
44. ¶H-5901 *et seq.*; ¶4154; TD ¶282,001
45. ¶H-8301; ¶4014.15; TD ¶286,034
46. ¶H-8273.2; ¶4014.141
47. ¶H-5310; TD ¶286,003

(Reg § 1.401-1(b)(1)(ii))[48] A profit-sharing plan may also permit withdrawal of employer contributions for hardship[49] or by participants with at least 60 months of participation. [50]

(14) Every plan must provide that a distributee of an eligible rollover distribution may elect to have the distribution transferred directly to an eligible retirement plan (¶4359). (Code Sec. 401(a)(31)(A); Reg § 1.401(a)(31)-1)[1] Plans also must adhere to certain involuntary cash-out rollover rules (see ¶4359). (Code Sec. 401(a)(31)(B))

(15) The plan can't reduce plan benefits (including death or disability) to account for post-separation social security benefit increases. (Code Sec. 401(a)(15))[2]

(16) A plan may take into account only the first $225,000 for 2007 ($230,000 for 2008, as indexed for inflation) of each employee's annual compensation. (Code Sec. 401(a)(17))[3]

(17) Defined benefit plans other than government plans must meet minimum participation requirements (¶4323) (Code Sec. 401(a)(26)) in addition to the coverage and eligibility requirements (¶4322).[4]

(18) If a plan member elects to have an eligible rollover distribution paid directly to a specified eligible retirement plan, the plan must make the distribution in the form of direct trustee-to-trustee transfer. (Code Sec. 401(a)(31))[5]

¶ 4320 Incidental benefits.

Life or accident and health insurance features that are incidental to the primary benefit of a qualified plan, may be included to a limited extent. (Reg § 1.401-1(b)(1)(i), Reg § 1.401-1(b)(1)(ii))[6]

¶ 4321 Vesting of benefits.

Plans must provide that a participant's right to his accrued benefit (defined below) vests at certain rates during the years of his employment. Benefits derived from employee contributions must be 100% vested at all times. (Code Sec. 411(a); Reg § 1.411(a)-1(a)(2)) Benefits derived from employer contributions must become nonforfeitable when the employee reaches normal retirement age (defined below). (Code Sec. 411(a)) The plan also must meet one of two alternative minimum vesting standards for vesting in benefits derived from employer contributions before normal retirement age: (1) a five-year cliff schedule requiring full vesting after five years of service, or (2) a three-to-seven year graded schedule requiring 20% vesting after three years of service and 20% additional vesting in each of the following years. (Code Sec. 411(a)(2); Reg § 1.411(a)-3T) Slightly faster vesting (three-year cliff or two-to-six year graded) applies to all employer contributions (non-elective employer contributions as well as matching contributions). (Code Sec. 411(a)(12), Code Sec. 411(a)(2)(B))[7]

For plan years beginning after 2006, the accelerated three-year cliff or two-to-six year phased vesting applies to *all* employer contributions in a defined contribution plan (non-elective employer contributions as well as matching contributions). (Code Sec. 411(a)(2)(B))[8] A plan may have one vesting schedule for employer nonelective contributions for plan years beginning after Dec. 31, 2006, and another vesting schedule for contributions for employer nonelective contributions for plan years beginning before Jan. 1, 2007, if certain requirements are met.[9]

Accrued benefit means the participant's annual benefit (or its actuarial equivalent) starting at normal retirement age (defined benefit plans) or the balance in the participant's account

---

48. ¶H-5346; TD ¶280,109
49. ¶H-5348
50. ¶H-5346
1. ¶H-8250 *et seq.*; TD ¶144,037
2. ¶H-5311; ¶4014.22; TD ¶286,022
3. ¶H-5919; ¶4014.18; TD ¶280,505

4. ¶H-5700 *et seq.*; ¶4014.25; TD ¶286,007
5. ¶H-8251; ¶4014.27
6. ¶H-8104 *et seq.*; ¶4014.13; TD ¶280,105
7. ¶H-7400 *et seq.*; ¶s 4114, 4114.01; TD ¶286,028
8. ¶H-7410 ; ¶4114.01
9. ¶H-74102.4.

(defined contribution plans). (Code Sec. 411(a)(7)(A))[10]

Normal retirement age is the earlier of the time a participant attains normal retirement age under the plan or the later of: (1) the time the participant reaches age 65, or (2) the 5th anniversary of the individual's participation in the plan. (Code Sec. 411(a)(8))[11]

Beginning May 22, 2007, IRS regs allow plans to set normal retirement age lower than age 65, so long as this age isn't earlier than the earliest age that is reasonably representative of the typical age for the industry in which the covered workforce is employed. The regs establish age 62 (coinciding with the rule allowing in-service distributions to employees age 62 or older, see ¶4319) as a safe harbor for this requirement. (Reg § 1.401(a)-1(b)(2)) IRS has provided temporary relief for plans with normal retirement ages earlier than 62 to comply with these requirements. [12]

¶ 4322   Coverage and eligibility requirements.

A qualified plan other than a government plan must meet special tests designed to ensure adequate coverage of rank and file employees and avoid discrimination.

The plan must, on at least one day in each quarter of its tax year, either: (1) benefit 70% of the employees who aren't "highly compensated" (¶4325), (2) benefit a percentage of nonhighly compensated employees that is at least 70% of the highly compensated benefiting, or (3) meet a test under which the average benefit for the nonhighly compensated is at least 70% of the average benefit for the highly compensated. (Code Sec. 410(b)(1)) This "average benefits test" also requires that the plan benefit employees under a nondiscriminatory classification. (Code Sec. 410(b)(2))[13] However, a plan maintained by an employer that has no employees other than highly compensated employees for a year is treated as meeting the coverage requirement for the year. (Code Sec. 410(b)(6)(F))[14]

A qualified plan can't require as a condition of participation that any employee complete a period of service extending beyond the later of the date he: (1) reaches age 21, or (2) completes one year of service (or two years, if the plan provides full and immediate vesting for all participants). (Code Sec. 410(a)(1)(A), Code Sec. 410(a)(1)(B)(i))[15]

¶ 4323   Minimum participation requirement—the 50-employee/40% test.

A defined benefit plan other than a governmental plan isn't qualified unless, on each day of the plan year, the plan benefits at least the lesser of (a) 50 employees of the employer, or (b) the greater of 40% of employees, or 2 employees (or 1 employee if there is only 1 employee). (Code Sec. 401(a)(26)(A))[16] Instead of meeting the test on each day of the plan year, compliance on a single representative "snapshot" day during the year is sufficient. (Reg § 1.401(a)(26)-7(b))[17]

¶ 4324   Contributions or benefits must be nondiscriminatory.

Contributions or benefits under a plan other than a governmental plan must not discriminate in favor of "highly compensated employees", see ¶4325. (Code Sec. 401(a)(4))[18] To comply, a plan must satisfy three requirements: (1) either the contributions or benefits under the plan must be nondiscriminatory in amount, (2) the plan's optional forms of benefit, ancillary benefits (e.g., disability benefits), and other rights and features (e.g., plan loans and investment alternatives) must be made available to employees in a nondiscriminatory manner, and (3) the effect of the plan under certain plan amendments, grants of past service credit, and

---

10. ¶H-7200 *et seq.*; ¶4114.06; TD ¶286,020
11. ¶H-7404; ¶4114.08; TD ¶286,027
12. ¶H-7404; ¶4114.08; TD ¶286,027
13. ¶H-5410 *et seq.*; ¶s 4104.11, 4104.12; TD ¶286,006
14. ¶H-5410; ¶4104.12

15. ¶s H-5804, H-5807 *et seq.*; ¶4104.02; TD ¶286,008
16. ¶H-5701 *et seq.*; ¶4014.25; TD ¶286,007
17. ¶H-5704; ¶4014.25
18. ¶H-6100 *et seq.*; ¶4014.19; TD ¶286,010

plan terminations must be nondiscriminatory. (Reg § 1.401(a)(4)-1(b))[19] Defined benefit plans can be cross-tested for discrimination on the basis of equivalent employer contributions to profit-sharing plans, and vice versa. (Reg § 1.401(a)(4)-8) "Catch-up" elective deferrals by older employees (¶4317) are not subject to nondiscrimination requirements, above, but all eligible employees must have the opportunity to make these "catch-up" contributions (the "universal availability" requirement). (Code Sec. 414(v)(3)(B))[20]

¶ 4325 Who is a highly compensated employee.

A highly compensated employee is an employee who (1) was a 5% owner at any time during the determination year or the preceding year, or (2) for the preceding year, received more than $100,000 for 2007 ($105,000 for 2008) in compensation from the employer and, if the employer elects, also was in the "top-paid group" (top 20%) of employees for that year. (Code Sec. 414(q))[21]

¶ 4326 Plans covering self-employed persons (Keogh plans).

A person who is a "self-employed individual," i.e., derives "earned income" from a business or profession that he owns or conducts, or who has earned income from a partnership in which he is a partner, or has other self-employment income (such as director's fees), can establish and be covered by a qualified retirement plan (sometimes called a Keogh plan). (Code Sec. 401(c)(1))[22] Earned income for this purpose consists essentially of earnings attributable to personal services, whether from a sole proprietorship, partnership or other unincorporated venture, derived from the trade or business with respect to which the plan is established. (Code Sec. 401(c)(2), Code Sec. 401(d))[23]

Elective deferrals (up to $15,500 for 2007 and 2008) made by self-employed individuals to 401(k) plans aren't subject to the deduction limit (¶4334) applicable to profit-sharing plans (and salary-reduction SEPs). Thus, a self-employed can make deferrals to a 401(k) plan without being penalized by having those deferrals reduce the otherwise available contributions that could be made to his profit-sharing plan. (Code Sec. 404(n))[24]

¶ 4327 Overall limitations on plan contributions and benefits.

A plan can't be qualified if it provides for contributions or benefits that exceed the overall limitations described below.

Benefits under a defined benefit plan will disqualify the plan if the "annual benefit" for each participant beginning at age 65 exceeds the lesser of: (1) $180,000 for 2007 ($185,000 for 2008), but actuarially reduced if benefit begins before age 62, and raised if it begins after age 65), or (2) 100% of the participant's average compensation for his three high consecutive years of active plan participation. (Code Sec. 415(b), Reg § 1.415(b)-1(a)(1))[25] The maximum dollar benefit is reduced if the employee has less than ten years of plan participation when retirement benefits begin. (Code Sec. 415(b)(5)) This reduction doesn't apply to pro rata benefit increases under a terminating plan if there is no discrimination in favor of highly compensated employees. (Code Sec. 4980(d)(4)(C))[26] Neither the dollar nor the percentage limitation applies if the annual benefit payable under a defined benefit plan doesn't exceed $10,000 and the employer has never had a defined contribution plan in which the employee participated. (Code Sec. 415(b)(4))[27]

Annual additions under a defined contribution plan may not exceed the lesser of: (1)

19. ¶H-6350 *et seq.*; ¶4014.19; TD ¶286,010
20. ¶H-9247.1; ¶4144.26; TD ¶284,119
21. ¶H-6702; ¶s 4144.21, 4154.015; TD ¶286,012
22. ¶s H-5218, H-9500 *et seq.*; ¶4014.24; TD ¶284,500 *et seq.*
23. ¶H-9512 *et seq.*; ¶4014.24; TD ¶284,522

24. ¶H-10120 *et seq.*; ¶4044.08
25. ¶H-5950; ¶4154.02; TD ¶287,002
26. ¶H-5962; ¶4154.02
27. ¶H-5965; ¶4154.02; TD ¶282,002

$45,000 for 2007 ($46,000 for 2008), or (2) 100% of the participant's compensation. (Code Sec. 415(c)(1)) Annual additions include employer contributions, employee contributions other than qualified cost-of-living contributions to a defined benefit plan (Code Sec. 415(k)(2)(A)), and employee forfeitures. (Code Sec. 415(c), Reg § 1.415(c)-1(a)(1))[28]

For plan limitation years beginning after June 30, 2007, new regs governing limits on contributions and benefits under qualified plans take effect that reflect changes made to these rules over the past 25 years. [29]

Special rules apply the limits to certain ESOPs. (Code Sec. 415(c)(6), Reg § 1.415(c)-1(f))[30]

Benefits provided to alternate payees under any qualified domestic relations order (QDRO) relating to a participant's benefits must be aggregated with benefits provided to the participant from all defined benefit and defined contribution plans in applying the Code Sec. 415 limitations. [31]

¶ 4328   Additional qualification requirements for "top-heavy" plans.

A "top-heavy" plan must meet specified additional requirements in the areas of minimum vesting and minimum benefits or contributions for non-key employees, in determining contributions or benefits. (Code Sec. 416(a))[32] SIMPLE retirement plans (¶4382) and Code Sec. 401(k) plans that meet safe-harbor nondiscrimination requirements, aren't subject to the top-heavy rules. (Code Sec. 416(g)(4)(G), Code Sec. 416(g)(4)(H))[33]

Vesting requirements.   For any plan year for which a plan is a top-heavy plan, an employee's rights to accrued benefits must be 100% vested after three years of service or, at the employer's option, 20% vested after two years' service and 20% in each of the following years (100% vested after six years of service). (Code Sec. 416(b))[34]

Minimum benefits or contributions. A top-heavy defined benefit plan must provide a minimum annual retirement benefit, not integrated with social security, for each non-key employee equal to the lesser of: (1) 2% of the participant's average compensation for years in the testing period multiplied by his years of service with the employer, or (2) 20% of his average compensation in the years in the testing period. (Code Sec. 416(c)(1))[35]

In a defined contribution plan, the employer must contribute for each non-key employee not less than 3% of that employee's compensation (including employer matching contributions). (Code Sec. 416(c)(2))[36]

¶ 4329   Minimum funding requirements.

Defined benefit and money purchase plans (including target benefit plans) must maintain a "minimum funding standard account," to which credits and charges (including interest) are made, and satisfy a "minimum funding standard" each plan year. (Code Sec. 412(a), Code Sec. 412(b))[37]

For plan years beginning after 2007, single-employer plans need no longer maintain a minimum funding standard account, and single-employer plan liabilities are determined using a 3-segment yield curve developed from a 24-month average of the yield on the top three grades of corporate bonds. Under the new funding rules, the liability for benefits earned under the plan in past years is the plan's target liability; the liability for benefit accruals in the current year is the plan's normal cost. A plan's minimum contribution requirement for a year is the normal cost plus amounts required to amortize any funding shortfall over seven

---

28. ¶H-6000 *et seq.*; ¶4154.06; TD ¶287,003
29. ¶H-5900 *et seq.*; ¶H-6000 *et seq.*¶4154.01 *et seq.*
30. ¶H-6016; ¶4154.09
31. ¶s H-5950, H-6000, H-8217 *et seq.*; ¶4154.02
32. ¶H-8000 *et seq.*; ¶4164; TD ¶286,002

33. ¶H-8001 *et seq.*; ¶4164.02; TD ¶286,002
34. ¶H-7423; ¶4164.04; TD ¶286,030
35. ¶H-8025; ¶4164.05; TD ¶286,025
36. ¶H-8032; ¶4164.06; TD ¶286,026
37. ¶H-7600 *et seq.*; ¶4124.01; TD ¶286,015

years. (Code Sec. 430(h))

Liabilities are increased for "at risk" plans (single-employer plans whose funding target attainment percentage is both less than 80% without regard to at-risk liabilities and less than 70% counting at-risk liabilities). (Code Sec. 430(d), Code Sec. 430(i))

For plan years beginning after 2007, new minimum funding rules also apply to multiemployer plans. (Code Sec. 431)[38]

¶ 4330   Returning veteran's pension rights.

An employee who returns to a civilian employer following qualified military service is entitled to restoration of certain qualified plan benefits that would have accrued but for the absence due to military service. Qualified military service of a reemployed person must not be treated as a break in service, and must be considered service with the employer for purposes of determining the nonforfeitability and the accrual of the individual's benefits. (Code Sec. 414(u)(8)(B))[39] "Make-up" contributions in excess of the usual contribution and deduction limits for the year made, and suspension of plan loan repayment during uniformed service do not cause loss of a plan's qualified status. (Code Sec. 414(u)(1); Code Sec. 414(u)(4))[40] Plans must permit returning employees to make additional elective deferrals and employee contributions, and must make matching contributions that would have been required had the deferral been made during the period of military service. (Code Sec. 414(u)(2)(A)) Report make-up contributions on Form W-2 or a separate statement identifying the type of plan, years involved, and amounts. [41]

¶ 4331   How to get IRS approval of plan—Form 5300; Form 5307.

Although advance IRS approval isn't required, it's desirable and customary to seek it by requesting a determination letter on special forms issued by IRS (e.g., Form 5300). [42]

Master and prototype plans.   Instead of establishing a plan on its own, an employer may adopt (use Form 5307) a qualified plan using an IRS-approved master or prototype plan prepared and sponsored by trade or professional associations, banks, insurance companies or regulated investment companies (mutual funds). [43] IRS has adopted a system of remedial amendment cycles for issuing determination letters for individually designed plans, and six-year amendment/approval cycles for pre-approved plans. [44]

For the small-employer retirement plan start-up tax credit, see   ¶2333.

¶ 4332   Employee contributions and employer matching contributions.

A plan may require an employee to contribute to the plan, as a condition to participation, or it may permit such contributions, or both, if no discrimination results. [45]

Employee contributions and employer matching contributions under defined contribution plans (and those under a defined benefit plan treated as made under a defined contribution plan) must meet a nondiscrimination test that restricts the extent to which the actual contribution percentage (ACP) of eligible highly compensated employees can exceed the ACP for all other eligible employees. (Code Sec. 401(m), Code Sec. 414(k)(2)) The current year ACP for highly compensated employees is compared to the previous year's, or, electively, the current year's ACP for other employees. (Code Sec. 401(m)(2)) The ACP test can be satisfied using a safe-harbor. (Code Sec. 401(m)(11))[46] "SIMPLE" plans (¶4382) are deemed to satisfy the ACP

---

38. ¶H-9738.0 *et seq.*; ¶4314 *et seq.*
39. ¶H-9951; TD ¶286,040
40. ¶H-9952 *et seq.*; TD ¶286,041 *et seq.*
41. ¶H-9956; TD ¶286,041
42. ¶T-10500 *et seq.*; ¶4014.01

43. ¶T-10631; ¶4014.01
44. ¶H-8760 *et seq.*
45. ¶H-6510 *et seq.*; ¶4014.21
46. ¶H-6565; ¶4014.21

test. (Code Sec. 401(m)(10))[47]

Defined contribution plans generally must allow participants to immediately diversify any employee contributions or elective deferrals invested in employer securities into at least 3 other investment options. For employer contributions, other than elective deferrals, invested in employer securities, the same diversification rights must be given to participants with at least 3 years of service, or each beneficiary of such participants or deceased participants. (Code Sec. 401(a)(35)) A plan is not treated as holding employer securities to which the diversification rules apply if the securities are held by either a registered investment company or a regulated pooled investment vehicle. The diversification requirements are phased in over a 3-year period (2007 through 2009 plan years). (Code Sec. 401(a)(35)(H)(i)(I))[48]

¶ 4333   Ceiling on deductions for contributions to pension and annuity plans.

Subject to applicable limits (see following) an employer can deduct its timely paid (¶4336) contributions to a qualified plan. (Code Sec. 404(a); Reg § 1.404(a)-1(b))[49] However, the plan to which the contribution is made must be in existence by the end of the employer's tax year.[50]

The employer may choose one of three alternative special ceilings on annual deductions for contributions to a pension or annuity plan, to get the largest deduction: [1]

(1) The "level cost" ceiling permits a deduction equal to an amount necessary to provide for all participating employees the remaining unfunded cost of their past and current service credits, distributed as a level amount (or level percentage of compensation) over the entire future remaining service of each employee. If the remaining unfunded cost with respect to any three individuals is more than 50% of the total remaining unfunded cost, the unfunded cost attributable to those three must be distributed over at least five tax years. (Code Sec. 404(a)(1)(A)(ii))

(2) The "normal cost" ceiling permits the employer to deduct contributions equal to (a) the "normal cost" (cost of credits for current services determined as though past service credits had been properly funded), plus (b) an amount necessary to amortize the cost of past service or supplementary or annuity credits provided by the plan in equal annual payments (until fully amortized) over ten years. (Code Sec. 404(a)(1)(A)(iii))

(3) If the minimum funding standard (¶4329) exceeds the "level cost" or "normal cost" ceiling applicable to the plan, the employer can deduct the amount necessary to satisfy the minimum funding standard. (Code Sec. 404(a)(1)(A)(i))

The maximum annual deduction under the above ceilings, however, cannot generally exceed the full funding limitation for the year (Code Sec. 404(a)(1)(A)) or be less than the plan's unfunded current liability. [2] Money purchase and target benefit plans also are subject to the 25%-of-compensation deduction limit that applies to profit-sharing plans (¶4334). (Code Sec. 404(a)(3)(A)(v))[3]

Contributions in excess of the amount deductible (except contributions to SIMPLE plans (¶4382) for household workers (Code Sec. 4972(c)(6))) are subject to a nondeductible 10% excise tax in certain cases (Code Sec. 4972), but may be carried over and deducted in later years, subject to the above limitations. (Code Sec. 404(a)(1)(E))[4]

For tax years beginning after 2007, for contributions to a single-employer defined benefit pension plan, the maximum deductible amount is equal to the greater of:

(1) the excess (if any) of (A) the sum of: the plan's funding target, the plan's target normal

---

47. ¶H-6513; ¶4014.21
48. ¶4014.12
49. ¶H-10001; ¶4044.01; TD ¶280,500
50. ¶H-10021; ¶4044.02; TD ¶280,518

1. ¶H-10102 *et seq.*; ¶4044.04; TD ¶281,006
2. ¶H-10105 *et seq.*; ¶4044.04; TD ¶281,006
3. ; ¶4044.07; TD ¶281,006
4. ¶H-10125 *et seq.*; ¶4044.04; TD ¶280,500

cost, and a cushion amount for a plan year, over (B) the value of plan assets (as determined under minimum funding rules); and

(2) the minimum required contribution for the plan year. (Code Sec. 404(o))[5]

¶ 4334 Ceiling on deductions for contributions to profit-sharing and stock bonus plans.

The special ceiling on deductions for contributions under a profit-sharing, stock-bonus, or "SIMPLE" plan is 25% of the aggregate compensation (exclusive of qualified plan contributions) paid or accrued during the tax year for all employees participating in the plan. (Code Sec. 404(a)(3)(A); Code Sec. 404(m)(1); Reg § 1.404(a)-9(c)) Contributions in excess of this limit may be carried over and deducted in a later year to the extent that contributions for that later year are below the applicable percentage limit for that year. (Code Sec. 404(a)(3)(A)(ii))[6]

The percentage of compensation limit on deductible contributions to a stock bonus or profit-sharing plan for a self-employed individual (Keogh plan) is 25% of "earned income," which is 25% of net earnings from self-employment less the self-employment tax deduction and deductible qualified plan contributions. (Code Sec. 404(a)(8)(B))[7]

Elective deferrals (¶4317) are not subject to the deduction limits for stock bonus and profit sharing plans, combination defined contribution and defined benefit plans, or ESOPs. (Code Sec. 404(n))[8] Compensation includes elective deferral amounts, amounts deferred to a cafeteria plan, and certain pre-disability compensation. (Code Sec. 404(a)(12))[9]

¶ 4335 Deduction ceiling for combinations of qualified plans.

If there is a mixture of one or more defined contribution plans and one or more defined benefit plans, or any combination of two or more pension trusts, annuity plans, and stock bonus or profit-sharing trusts, an overall limit on deductible contributions applies. Under this limitation, the total amount deductible for *all* plans is the greater of: (1) 25% of the compensation (exclusive of qualified plan contributions) paid or accrued during the tax year to the beneficiaries of the various trusts or plans, or (2) the total contributions to the trusts or plans to the extent those contributions don't exceed the amount necessary to satisfy the Code Sec. 412 minimum funding standards. For years after 2007, the amount necessary to satisfy the Code Sec. 412 minimum funding standard must not be less than the plan's funding shortfall under Code Sec. 430. (Code Sec. 404(a)(7)(A))

The 25% limit does not apply if the only amounts contributed to the defined compensation plan are elective deferrals. (Code Sec. 404(a)(7)(C)(ii))[10] Further, the combined plan limit applies only to employer contributions to one or more defined contribution plans to the extent the contributions exceed 6% of the compensation otherwise paid or accrued to plan beneficiaries during the tax year. [11]

For contributions for tax years beginning after 2007, in determining the limit on deductions where there is a combination of one or more defined benefit and one or more defined contribution plans, any defined benefit plan guaranteed by the PBGC is not taken into account. (Code Sec. 404(a)(7)(C)(iv))

---

5. ¶H-10102.1; ¶4044.02
6. ¶H-10202; ¶4044.06; TD ¶281,302
7. ¶H-10204; ¶4044.08; TD ¶281,305
8. ¶H-10202; ¶4044.08; TD ¶281,302

9. ¶H-10203; ¶4044.08; TD ¶281,303
10. ¶H-10120 *et seq.*; ¶4044.09; TD ¶281,014
11. ¶H-10120

¶ 4336   Timely payment requirement.

A contribution actually must be paid to the trust or under the plan to be deductible. (Code Sec. 404(a))[12] However, payments (including those made to "SIMPLE" plans (¶4382) (Code Sec. 404(m)(2)(B)), made after the end of a year are considered paid on the last day of the year if paid by the employer no later than the due date of its tax return (including extensions). (Code Sec. 404(a)(6))[13] This applies to both cash and accrual employers, even if other accrual requirements are not met. (Reg § 1.404(a)-1(c))[14]

¶ 4337   How employees are taxed.

Apart from certain "lump-sum" payments qualifying for the preferential tax treatment (¶4338 *et seq.*), and "rollovers" (¶4359), distributions from a qualified plan (reported to recipients on Form 1099-R) generally are taxed to the employee under the annuity rules (¶1355 *et seq.*) in the year distributed or otherwise made available to the employee. (Code Sec. 402(a); Reg § 1.402(a)-1(a)) Thus, the excess of the distribution (cash or fair market value of property) over the amount of any after-tax plan contributions made by the employee, is ordinary income. (Code Sec. 402; Reg § 1.402(a)-1(a)(1)(i))[15]

Certain early (¶4344) distributions are subject to penalty.

¶ 4338   Preferential treatment for certain lump-sum distributions.

Distributions from a qualified plan to an employee or his beneficiaries, that are lump-sum distributions, are taxable as ordinary income, subject to special elections for pre-'74 capital gain treatment and/or ten-year forward averaging (¶4339) for those born before '36.

A lump-sum distribution eligible for preferential tax treatment is a distribution or payment from an exempt trust or annuity within one tax year of the recipient of the balance to the credit of the participant (excluding amounts payable to an alternate payee under a qualified domestic relations order (QDRO), which separately can qualify for lump-sum treatment to the alternate payee): (1) on account of an employee's (other than a self-employed's) separation from service; or (2) after attaining age 59 ½ (regardless of his separation from service); or (3) on account of his death; or (4) on account of disability. (Code Sec. 402(e)(4)(D))[16]

¶ 4339   Lump-sum distribution elections for participants who reached age 50 before '86—Form 4972.

A participant who reached age 50 before '86 (or an individual, estate or trust that receives a distribution with respect to that employee) is permitted:

(1) to elect capital gains treatment at a flat 20% rate without regard to the phase-out of elective capital gains treatment of distributions for pre-'74 plan participation, and

(2) to elect ten-year averaging at '86 tax rates with respect to a lump-sum distribution. This election (use Form 4972) can only be made once with respect to an employee. [17]

¶ 4340   Lump-sum distributions of securities of employer corporation.

If a lump sum distribution consists in part of securities of the employer, the net unrealized appreciation in value of the securities while held by the trust is not taxed to the recipient at the time of distribution. But the same amount also is excluded from the recipient's basis in

---

12. ¶H-10010; ¶4044.01; TD ¶280,506
13. ¶H-10016; ¶4044.01; TD ¶280,513
14. ¶H-10017; ¶4044.01; TD ¶280,513

15. ¶H-11006 *et seq.*; ¶4024; TD ¶141,002
16. ¶H-11200 *et seq.*; ¶4024.03; TD ¶142,001
17. ¶H-11229; ¶4024.03; TD ¶142,028

the securities, so that it's taken into account for tax purposes if and when the securities are later disposed of in a taxable transaction. The distributee, however, has the right to elect, on the tax return on which a distribution is required to be included, to have this rule not apply, i.e., to include any net unrealized appreciation in income. (Code Sec. 402(e)(4)(B); Reg § 1.402(a)-1(b)(1))[18] Net unrealized appreciation that isn't included in income at the time of distribution is long-term capital gain when it's realized in a later taxable transaction. (Reg § 1.402(a)-1(b)(1)(i))[19]

¶ 4341   Tax on current payments for life insurance protection.

The cost of current life insurance protection under a life insurance contract purchased with employer contributions to a qualified plan (or earnings thereon) is income to the insured employee for the tax year of purchase, where the benefits are payable to him or his beneficiaries. (Code Sec. 72(m)(3); Reg § 1.72-16(b)) The taxable amount is generally determined under IRS's "Table 2001," reproduced at ¶1267.[20]

¶ 4342   Tax on failure to notify participants of benefit-accrual reduction.

Defined benefit plans and individual account plans subject to minimum funding standards are subject to an excise tax of $100 per day per participant, subject to an overall dollar limit, for failure to provide written notice to any participant, employee organization, or alternate payee under a qualified domestic relations order within a reasonable time when the plan is amended to provide for a significant reduction in the rate of future benefit accrual. (Code Sec. 4980F(a); Reg § 54.4980F-1)[21] Plans with fewer than 100 participants or that offer participants the option to choose between a new benefit formula and the old one may be able to use a simplified notice form or be exempted by IRS from the notice requirements. (Code Sec. 4980F(e)(2)(A))[22]

¶ 4343   Loans from qualified plans.

A loan from a qualified plan isn't treated as a taxable distribution to the plan participant only if it must be repaid within five years (except for certain home loans), and doesn't exceed the *lesser* of: (1) $50,000, or (2) the greater of (a) ½ of the present value of the employee's nonforfeitable accrued benefit under the plan, or (b) $10,000. If a plan loan (when added to the employee's outstanding balance of all other plan loans at the time the loan is made and the highest outstanding loan balance during the year before the loan was made) exceeds these limits, the excess is treated (and taxed) as a plan distribution (¶4337). The entire amount of a plan loan that isn't required to be repaid within five years (except for certain home loans) is treated as a plan distribution. (Code Sec. 72(p))[23] The outstanding balance of a plan loan is treated as distributed if the borrower fails to make a scheduled loan repayment installment before any allowable grace period expires. (Reg § 1.72(p)-1, Q&A 10(b))[24] Loan repayment following a deemed distribution increases the participant's investment in the contract (basis). (Reg § 1.72(p)-1, Q&A 21)[25]

A plan loan must be amortized in substantially level payments, at least quarterly, over its term. (Code Sec. 72(p)(2)(C))[26] The level amortization requirement doesn't apply while the employee is on leave without pay for up to one year. (Reg § 1.72(p)-1, Q&A 9)[27]

Special rules apply to plan loans that were made before Jan. 1, 2007 to individuals who were affected by hurricanes Katrina, Rita, or Wilma. (Code Sec. 1400Q(c)(1))[28]

---

18. ¶s H-11501, H-11503; ¶4024.02; TD ¶142,058
19. ¶H-11510; TD ¶142,063
20. ¶H-10507 *et seq.*; ¶724.24; TD ¶141,081
21. ¶H-7374
22. ¶H-7368
23. ¶H-11067 *et seq.*; ¶724.23; TD ¶141,049 *et seq.*

24. ¶H-11070; ¶724.23; TD ¶141,049
25. ¶724.23; TD ¶141,049
26. ¶H-11068; ¶724.23; TD ¶141,054
27. ¶H-11068.1; ¶724.23; TD ¶141,067
28. ¶H-11067.2; ¶14,00Q4; TD ¶141,053.1

For loans as prohibited transactions, see ¶4347.

¶ 4344   Penalty for premature distributions—Form 5329.

Early withdrawals from a qualified retirement plan, SIMPLE plan, or IRA result in an additional tax (reported on Form 5329) equal to 10% of the amounts withdrawn that are includible in gross income. (Code Sec. 72(t)(1)) The additional tax applies to all withdrawals unless specifically excepted. Exceptions include distributions (i) made on or after age 59 ½; (ii) made to a beneficiary or estate on or after death; (iii) attributable to disability; (iv) from a qualified plan after an employee's separation from service after age 55; (v) not in excess of the amount allowable as a medical expense deduction for the year, whether or not the distributee itemizes; (vi) that are part of a series of substantially equal periodic (annual or more frequent) payments (made after separation from service if from a qualified plan) for the life (or life expectancy) of the employee or the joint lives (or joint life expectancies) of the employee and his beneficiary; (vii) from an IRA not exceeding amounts paid for medical insurance by IRA owners who have received unemployment compensation for at least 12 weeks (or could have except for being self-employed); (viii) from an IRA for qualified higher education expenses; (ix) from an IRA for qualified "first-home" purchases, subject to $10,000 lifetime cap; (x) from a qualified plan to an alternate payee under a qualified domestic relations order; and (xi) made on account of an IRS tax levy. (Code Sec. 72(t)(2), Code Sec. 72(t)(3))[29]

Taxpayers who used the annuitization or amortization methods to compute substantially equal payments can make a one-time switch to the required minimum distribution method, which generally requires smaller annual distributions, without triggering the 10% penalty. [30]

The additional tax is 25%, rather than 10% on amounts received from a SIMPLE retirement account (¶4382) during the employee's first two years of participation. (Code Sec. 72(t)(6))[31]

The tax applies to certain involuntary cash-outs and deemed distributions. It doesn't apply to amounts distributed from unfunded deferred compensation plans of tax-exempt employers or state and local government employees, i.e., Code Sec. 457 plans.[32]

The 10% early withdrawal tax does not apply to post-Aug. 17, 2006 distributions from a governmental defined benefit pension plan to a qualified public safety employee (e.g., firefighter or policeman) who separates from service after age 50. (Code Sec. 72(t)(10))

Special rules applied to "qualified hurricane distributions" made from eligible retirement plans before Jan. 1, 2007. (Code Sec. 1400Q(a)(1), Code Sec. 1400Q(a)(5), Code Sec. 1400Q(a)(6))[33]

If repayment of a qualified hurricane distribution is made within the three-year period beginning on the day after the date of the distribution, rollover treatment results, and the taxpayer is treated as having transferred the repayment amount to the eligible retirement plan or IRA in a direct trustee-to-trustee transfer (see ¶4359) within 60 days of the distribution. (Code Sec. 1400Q(a)(3))[34]

The 10% additional tax also does not apply to any "qualified reservist distribution" made to individuals ordered or called to active duty for more than 179 days after Sept. 11, 2001, and before Dec. 31, 2007. (Code Sec. 72(t)(2)(G)(i))[35] Recipients of such distributions may, at any time during the two-year period beginning on the day after the end of the active duty period, make contributions to their IRAs in an aggregate amount not to exceed the amount of the distribution (i.e., they may make "pay back" contributions). The two-year period ends Aug. 17, 2008. The regular IRA dollar contribution limits don't apply to "pay back" contributions,

---

29. ¶H-11100 *et seq.*; ¶724.22; TD ¶145,501   33. ¶H-11006.2; ¶14,00Q4;TD ¶141,002.2
30. ¶H-11107   34. ¶H-11006.4; ¶14,00Q4;TD ¶144,008.6
31. ¶H-12377; TD ¶282,815   35. ¶H-11116; ¶724.22; TD ¶145,513.1
32. ¶H-11101; ¶724.22

but these contributions aren't deductible. (Code Sec. 72(t)(2)(G)(i))[36]

⚫*caution:* Check http://ria.thomson.com/federaltaxhandbook to see if this provision has been changed.

¶ 4345   Required minimum distributions.

A qualified plan must provide that the employee's entire interest will be distributed, starting Apr. 1 of the calendar year following the later of the year in which he: (a) reaches age 70 ½ or (b) retires (except for 5% owners), no later than over (i) his life, (ii) his life and the life of a designated beneficiary, (iii) a period of not more than his life expectancy, or (iv) a period of not more than his life expectancy and that of a designated beneficiary. (Code Sec. 401(a)(9)(A), Code Sec. 401(a)(9)(C)) (Similar rules apply to IRAs, see ¶4357.) A qualified plan may provide that the required beginning date for all employees (including non-5% owners) is Apr. 1 of the calendar year following the calendar year in which the employee attained age 70 ½.[37]

Where distributions to a participant have begun, but he dies before his entire interest has been distributed, his remaining interest must be distributed at least as rapidly as under the method of distribution in effect at the date of his death. (Code Sec. 401(a)(9)(B)(i)) Where he dies before receiving any required plan distributions, his entire interest must be distributed within five years after his death, except where the employee's interest: (1) is distributed over the life of a designated beneficiary (or over a period not extending beyond the life expectancy of the beneficiary) and the distributions begin no later than one year after the date of the employee's death (Code Sec. 401(a)(9)(B)(ii), Code Sec. 401(a)(9)(B)(iii)), or (2) is distributed over the life of the surviving spouse (or over a period not extending beyond his life expectancy), and the distributions begin no later than the date on which the employee would have reached age 70 ½. If the surviving spouse dies before payments must begin, then the 5-year rule applies as if the surviving spouse were the employee. (Code Sec. 401(a)(9)(B)(iv))

Failure to make the required distributions is subject to an excise tax (report on Form 5329) equal to 50% of the minimum amount that should have been distributed over the amount actually distributed. (Code Sec. 4974(a))[38]

Lifetime distributions. The required minimum distribution (RMD) for each year is found by dividing the account balance as of the end of the preceding year by the age-based factor from the table in Reg § 1.401(a)(9)-9, Q&A 2. Portions of this table are excerpted below (the full table goes to age 115).

Uniform Lifetime Table

Employee's Age	Distribution Period	Employee's Age	Distribution Period
70	27.4	82	17.1
71	26.5	83	16.3
72	25.6	84	15.5
73	24.7	85	14.8
74	23.8	86	14.1
75	22.9	87	13.4
76	22.0	88	12.7
77	21.2	89	12.0
78	20.3	90	11.4
79	19.5	91	10.8
80	18.7	92	10.2
81	17.9	93	9.6

36. ¶H-11116.1; TD ¶145,513.2   38. ¶H-8500 *et seq.*; ¶49,744; TD ¶145,515
37. ¶H-8400 *et seq.*; ¶4014.15; TD ¶145,000

Employee's Age	Distribution Period
94	9.1
95	8.6

This table is used for lifetime distributions of the account owner regardless of the identity of the beneficiary or age differential between account owner and designated beneficiary, unless the account owner's spouse is the sole beneficiary and is more than 10 years younger than the account owner, in which case the distribution period may be measured by the joint life and last survivor life expectancy of the employee and spouse, using the life expectancies in the joint and last survivor table of Reg § 1.401(a)(9)-9, Q&A 3.[39]

Determination of designated beneficiary. The account owner's designated beneficiary is determined based on the beneficiaries designated as of the account owner's date of death who remain beneficiaries on Sept. 30 of the year following the year of the account owner's death. Any beneficiary eliminated by distribution of the benefit or through disclaimer (or otherwise) during the period between the account owner's death and Sept. 30 of the year following the year of death is disregarded in determining the designated beneficiary for purposes of calculating RMDs. (Reg § 1.409(a)(9)-4, Q&A 4(a)) Except for certain trusts (see below), only an individual may be a designated beneficiary for purposes of the RMD rules. (Reg § 1.401(a)(9)-4, Q&A 3)[40]

Trusts as beneficiaries. An underlying beneficiary of a trust may be treated as the account owner's designated beneficiary for RMD purposes when the trust is named as the beneficiary of a retirement plan or IRA, if certain requirements are met (e.g., documentation of the underlying beneficiaries of the trust must be provided timely to the plan administrator, and beneficiaries of the trust can be identified). (Reg § 1.401(a)(9)-4, Q&A 6(b), Reg § 1.401(a)(9)-4, Q&A 5)[41]

Post-death distributions. For non-annuity-type payouts after the death of the account owner:

. . . If the account has a designated beneficiary, and the account owner died before his required beginning date (generally, April 1 following the year in which the account owner attains age 70 ½), the remaining account balance may be paid out over the remaining life expectancy of the beneficiary, using the life expectancy of the beneficiary in the Single Life Table of Reg § 1.401(a)(9)-9, Q&A 1.

. . . If the account has a designated beneficiary, and the account owner died after the date he was required to begin receiving distributions, the remaining account balance may be paid out over the longer of the remaining life expectancy of the beneficiary or the remaining life expectancy of the account owner. In either instance, the life expectancy for post-death RMDs is determined using the Single Life Table of Reg § 1.401(a)(9)-9, Q&A 1.

. . . If the account does not have a designated beneficiary: (1) If the account owner dies after his required beginning date (generally, April 1 following the year in which the IRA owner attains age 70-1/2), the remaining balance is paid out over the remaining life expectancy of the account owner, using the Single Life Table of Reg § 1.401(a)(9)-9, Q&A 1. (2) If the account owner dies before his required beginning date, the account balance must be paid out no later than 5 years after the year of the owner's death. (Reg § 1.401(a)(9)-3, Q&A 1; Reg § 1.401(a)(9)-5, Q&A 5)[42]

The 50% excise tax on failures to make RMDs is waived during the first five years after the year of the account owner's death before the required beginning date if the entire benefit is

---

39. ¶H-8279; ¶4014.153
40. ¶H-8278; ¶4014.153

41. ¶H-8278.4; ¶4014.153
42. ¶H-8279.8; ¶4014.153

distributed by the end of the fifth year following the year of death. (Reg § 54.4974-2, Q&A 4)

Annuity type distributions. Separate rules apply to annuity type required distributions, namely defined-benefit (i.e., pension) plan RMDs, as well as annuity contracts purchased from firms such as insurance companies to make RMDs from other qualified plans and IRAs. (Reg § 1.401(a)(9)-6) Under these rules, distributions of an employee's entire interest must be paid in the form of periodic annuity payments for the employee's or beneficiary's life (or the joint lives of the employee and beneficiary) or over a comparable period certain. The payments must be nonincreasing or only increase as provided in the regs. (Reg § 1.401(a)(9)-6, Q&A 1)[43]

¶ 4346 Excise tax on employer reversions—Form 5330.

An "employer reversion" from a qualified plan (except for certain exempt employers and government plans) is, in addition to being includible in the employer's gross income, also subject to a 50% excise tax (20% in certain cases). (Code Sec. 4980(a), Code Sec. 4980(b), Code Sec. 4980(c)(1), Code Sec. 4980(d)) Pay with Form 5330 filed no later than the last day of the month following the month in which the reversion occurred. [44]

¶ 4347 Excise tax on prohibited transactions—Form 5330.

An excise tax is imposed on a disqualified person who takes part in a prohibited transaction with a qualified plan, IRA, or medical savings account. The tax (report on Form 5330 each year for each transaction (Reg § 54.6011-1(b))) is 15% of the amount involved in the prohibited transaction for each tax year (or part of the year) in the taxable period. And if the prohibited transaction isn't timely corrected, the disqualified person must pay an additional tax of 100% of the amount involved. (Code Sec. 4975(a), Code Sec. 4975(b)) The Eighth Circuit has held that certain transactions are "self-correcting," automatically avoiding the second tier 100% tax, but IRS disagrees. [45] Neither level of tax is imposed on a fiduciary acting only as such. (Code Sec. 4975(a))[46]

Providing investment advice through an "eligible investment advice arrangement" to participants and beneficiaries of a defined contribution plan who direct the investment of their accounts under the plan and to beneficiaries of IRAs (as well as HSAs, Archer MSAs, and Coverdell education savings accounts) is exempt from the prohibited transaction rules. (Code Sec. 4975(d)(17)) The Department of Labor has issued guidance on how the investment advice exemption is to be applied. [47]

A number of other transactions occurring after Aug. 17, 2006 also are exempt from the prohibited transaction rules, such as certain transactions between plans and service providers, for adequate consideration (Code Sec. 4975(d)(20)), certain cross trades of securities between a plan and a party in interest (Code Sec. 4975(d)(22)), and certain otherwise prohibited transactions involving the sale or exchange of securities and commodities between the plan and a party in interest that are corrected within 14 days (Code Sec. 4975(d)(23)).

¶ 4348 Transfers to health benefits accounts before 2014.

Before Jan. 1, 2014, excess pension assets may be transferred to a retiree health benefit account without being treated as either a prohibited transaction or a reversion to the employer if certain conditions are met. (Code Sec. 420(a))[48]

After Aug. 17, 2006, single-employer plans can use excess pension assets to fund future retiree health benefits by making qualified future transfers to retiree health benefit accounts,

---

43. ¶H-8280; ¶4014.153
44. ¶H-8900 *et seq.*; ¶49,804; TD ¶286,004
45. ¶H-12510; TD ¶287,501
46. ¶H-12514 *et seq.*; ¶49,754; TD ¶287,501
47. ¶H-12558.1; ¶49,754.01
48. ¶H-8163; ¶4204

providing that certain minimum cost requirements are maintained. Similar rules apply to "collectively bargained transfers" to fund collectively bargained retiree health liabilities. A qualified future transfer or collectively bargained transfer must meet the requirements applicable to qualified transfers, with certain modifications to the requirements, one of which is the minimum cost requirement. (Code Sec. 420(f))

For qualified future transfers, the minimum cost requirement is satisfied if, during the transfer period and the four subsequent years, the annual average amount of employer costs is not less than applicable employer cost determined for the transfer. For collectively bargained transfers, the minimum cost requirement is satisfied if each collectively bargained group health plan provides that the collectively bargained employer cost for each tax year in the collectively bargained cost maintenance period is not less than the amount specified by the collective bargaining agreement.

Qualified transfers taking place on or after May 26, 2007 may satisfy the minimum cost requirement by satisfying the minimum cost requirement that applies to a collectively bargained transfer. (Code Sec. 420(c)(3)(A)).[49]

For transfers made in tax years beginning after 2006, multiemployer plans may transfer excess pension assets to retiree health accounts. (Code Sec. 420(a)) For plan years beginning after 2007, the new funding rules for defined benefit plans (see ¶4329) are integrated into the rules on the transfer of excess pension assets to retiree health accounts. (Code Sec. 420(e)(2), (Code Sec. 420(e)(4)) Further, any assets transferred in a qualified transfer to a retiree health account will not be treated as assets in the plan for purpose of the minimum contribution rules. (Code Sec. 430(l))

¶ 4349   Distributions from governmental retirement plans for health and long-term care insurance for public safety officers.

Public safety officers may exclude from income governmental retirement plan distributions that don't exceed accident, health or long-term care insurance premiums for themselves, their spouses, and dependents, if the distributions are paid directly to insurers. The exclusion is limited to $3,000 per year. (Code Sec. 402(l), Code Sec. 403(a), Code Sec. 403(b), Code Sec. 457(a))[50]

¶ 4350   Plans that fail to qualify or that lose qualified status.

The following rules apply to a plan that fails to qualify or loses its qualified status:

Contributions to the trust by an employer are included in the gross income of the employee. (Code Sec. 402(b)) The employee must report the value of his interest in the employer's contributions the first time his interest isn't subject to substantial risk of forfeiture, or is transferable free of such risk, whichever occurs first. (Reg § 1.402(b)-1)[1]

An employer's contributions are deductible in the tax year in which an amount attributable to the contribution is includible in the gross income of employees participating in the plan (Code Sec. 404(a)(5)), even if the employer is an accrual basis taxpayer. [2]

The amount actually distributed or made available to the employee or other distributee (beneficiary, etc.) is taxable in the year distributed or made available under the regular annuity rules (¶1355 *et seq.*), with a minor exception for distribution of trust income before the annuity is to begin. (Code Sec. 402(b)(2))[3]

Premiums paid by an employer for an annuity contract not purchased under a qualified

---

49. ¶H-8173; ¶4204.01
50. ¶H-11089; ¶4024.02; TD ¶141,090.1
1. ¶H-3200 *et seq.*; ¶4024.01; TD ¶135,506

2. ¶H-3677 *et seq.*; ¶4044.16; TD ¶277,506
3. ¶H-3246; ¶4024.01; TD ¶135,505

annuity plan (¶4315), are included in the employee's gross income. Amounts actually paid or made available to any employee-beneficiary under the nonqualified annuity contract are taxed under regular annuity rules. (Code Sec. 403(c))[4]

¶ 4351   Retirement Savings Plans for Individuals (IRAs). ━━━━━━━━━━

Employees and self-employed individuals who aren't active participants in an employer-maintained retirement plan can set aside and deduct up to $4,000 for 2007 ($5,000 for 2008), for contributions to an individual retirement account (IRA), or for the purchase of individual retirement annuities or endowment contracts. An individual who is an active participant in an employer plan (or whose spouse is) can't make deductible IRA contributions unless his adjusted gross income is below specified levels (¶4352).

An individual retirement account (IRA) is a trust (or custodial account) created or organized in the U.S. with a written governing instrument. [5] The assets of the account must be invested in a trusteed or custodial account with a bank, savings and loan association, credit union or other qualified person. (Code Sec. 408(a)(2))[6]

IRAs may be set up by employers for employees and by unions for members if these employer- and association-sponsored IRAs separately account for the interest of each participant (or his spouse). (Code Sec. 408(c); Reg § 1.408-2(c))[7] Qualified retirement plans, tax-sheltered annuities, and government retirement plans may allow employees to make voluntary contributions to separate IRA or Roth IRA accounts or annuities. (Code Sec. 408(q))[8]

Except for rollover contributions (¶4359) the maximum amount that may be contributed to IRAs for any individual for a tax year is $4,000 for 2007, and $5,000 for 2008 and later. (Code Sec. 408(a)(1), Code Sec. 408(b)(4), Code Sec. 219(b)(1)(A), Code Sec. 219(b)(5)(A)) The $5,000 amount will be inflation adjusted after 2008. (Code Sec. 219(b)(5)(D))[9]

Individuals who turn age 50 before the close of the tax year may increase the maximum permitted annual contribution by $1,000. (Code Sec. 219(b)(5)(B))[10]

IRA funds can't be used to buy life insurance. (Code Sec. 408(a)(3))[11] IRA contributions may not be invested in "collectibles" (except for certain coins and bullion), the acquisition of which is treated as an includible distribution (and possibly subject to premature distribution penalties). (Code Sec. 408(m))[12]

Individual retirement annuities are nontransferable flexible premium annuity or endowment contracts issued by an insurance company. (Code Sec. 408(b))[13]

No tax is paid on income earned on contributions until the retirement savings are distributed or retirement bonds are cashed, at which time the distributions or retirement bond proceeds are taxable (Code Sec. 408(d)(1))[14] though the tax-free "rollover" provisions (¶4359) may apply. Rules penalize excess contributions, premature (before age 59 ½) distributions (¶4344), and certain distributions deferred beyond age 70 ½ (¶4357).

For deductible contributions, see ¶4352; for nondeductible contributions to traditional IRAs, see ¶4354.

For Roth IRAs, see ¶4367 *et seq.* For the saver's credit for lower-income taxpayers' contributions to IRAs, see ¶2365.

---

4. ¶H-3249; ¶4034.05; TD ¶135,506
5. ¶H-12201; ¶4084.02; TD ¶283,041
6. ¶H-12202 *et seq.*; ¶4084.02
7. ¶s H-12212, H-12213; ¶4084.02; TD ¶283,045
8. ¶H-12280; ¶4084.07
9. ¶H-12215; ¶2194.01; TD ¶283,001

10. ¶H-12215; ¶2194.01; TD ¶283,001
11. ¶H-12201; ¶4084.02
12. ¶H-12259; ¶4084.03; TD ¶143,012
13. ¶H-12208 *et seq.*; ¶4084.02; TD ¶283,042
14. ¶H-12253; ¶4084.03; TD ¶143,003

¶ 4352   Deduction for IRA.

An individual who isn't an active participant in certain employer-sponsored retirement plans, and whose spouse isn't an active participant, can deduct, for a tax year, cash contributions to an IRA for that year, up to the lesser of: (1) $4,000 for 2007 ($5,000 for 2008), plus catch-up contribution, if eligible, see ¶4351, or (2) 100% of the compensation that's includible in his gross income for that year. (Code Sec. 219(b)(1))[15] For spousal IRAs, see ¶4355.

If the individual (or his spouse) is an active plan participant (for any part of a plan year in his tax year), and has adjusted gross income (AGI) that exceeds an "applicable dollar limit," the IRA deduction limit is reduced (but not below zero) by an amount (rounded to the next lowest multiple of $10) that bears the same ratio to the dollar limit on the deduction that his (and his spouse's if a joint return is filed) AGI (determined without regard to the IRA deduction and with certain other modifications), minus the applicable dollar limit, bears to $10,000 ($20,000 for joint return filers after 2006, except for non-active plan participants whose spouses are active plan participants). (Code Sec. 219(g)(1), Code Sec. 219(g)(2), Code Sec. 219(g)(3)(A), Code Sec. 219(g)(7)(B)) But the maximum IRA deduction can't be reduced below $200 unless the applicable dollar limit is reduced to zero. (Code Sec. 219(g)(2)(B))[16] The applicable dollar limit is higher than the usual limit for an individual who is not an active participant in an employer plan during any part of the year, but whose spouse is an active plan participant. The higher limit does not apply to the active-participant spouse. (Code Sec. 219(g)(7))[17] The income limits for deductible contributions for active participants in an employer sponsored plan and non-active participants whose spouses are active participants (but not for marrieds filing separately) are indexed for inflation. (Code Sec. 219(g)(8))

For 2007, for joint filers, the deduction phaseout begins at AGI of $83,000 and is fully phased-out at AGI of $103,000 ($85,000 to $105,000 for 2008). For single filers, or heads of households, the deduction phaseout begins at AGI of $52,000 and is fully phased-out at AGI of $62,000 ($53,000 to $63,000 for 2008)). For marrieds filing separately, the deduction phaseout begins at AGI of zero, and is fully phased-out at AGI of $10,000. Finally, for a non-active participant whose spouse is an active participant, the deduction phaseout begins at AGI of $156,000 and is fully phased-out at AGI of $166,000 ($159,000 to $169,000 for 2008).

Spouses who file separate returns and live apart at all times during the year aren't treated as married for purposes of the IRA deduction phase-out. (Code Sec. 219(g)(4))[18]

"Compensation" means wages, salaries, commissions, tips, bonuses, professional fees and other amounts received for personal services. It doesn't include earnings from property, such as interest, rents and dividends, or pension and annuity payments or other deferred compensation. Only compensation includible in gross income is used. (Code Sec. 219(f)(1))[19] Compensation includes taxable alimony paid under a decree of divorce or separate maintenance. (Code Sec. 219(f)(1))[20]

The amount shown on Form W-2 as "Wages, tips, other compensation," less any amount shown as distributions from nonqualified plans can be used as "safe harbor" compensation. [21]

The "compensation" of a self-employed individual includes net earnings from self-employment reduced by any allowable deduction for contributions on his behalf to a tax-qualified plan, e.g., a Keogh plan. (Code Sec. 219(f)(1))[22] A self-employed individual's net earnings from self-employment are also reduced by the deduction allowed for one-half of the self-employment tax (¶1755). (Code Sec. 219(f)(1), Code Sec. 401(c)(2)(A)(vi))[23]

---

15. ¶H-12215; ¶2194; TD ¶283,001
16. ¶H-12217; ¶2194.02; TD ¶283,002
17. ¶H-5300; ¶408A4; TD ¶283,002*et seq.*
18. ¶H-12217; ¶2194.02; TD ¶283,002
19. ¶H-12226; ¶2194.01; TD ¶283,012

20. ¶H-12232; ¶2194.01; TD ¶283,018
21. ¶H-12226; TD ¶283,012
22. ¶H-12226; TD ¶283,012
23. ¶s H-9514, H-12228; TD ¶284,523

Combat pay excluded under Code Sec. 112 (¶1224) is treated as if it were includible compensation for IRA purposes. (Code Sec. 219(f)(7)) In addition, military personnel who received tax–free combat pay in either 2004 or 2005 may make IRA contributions for those years until May 28, 2009. [24]

No deduction is allowed for contributions for the benefit of an individual for the tax year he attains age 70 ½ or any later year. (Code Sec. 219(d)(1))[25]

The IRA must be established no later than the due date (*not* including extensions) of the taxpayer's income tax return for the year the deduction is claimed. To be deductible for the preceding tax year, the contribution also must be made by that date. (Code Sec. 219(f)(3))[26]

No part of a premium (under an IRA endowment policy) that's used to buy life insurance is deductible. (Code Sec. 219(d)(3))[27]

No deduction is permitted for a rollover contribution (¶4359) (Code Sec. 219(d)(2))[28] or for any contribution to an "inherited" IRA — one acquired by other than the surviving spouse as a result of the death of the employee-participant. (Code Sec. 219(d)(4))[29]

For tax years beginning after 2006 and before 2010, participants in a 401(k) plan, whose contributions the employer matched at least 50% with employer stock, can elect to make additional IRA contributions, up to 3 times the catch-up amount (see ¶4351), where the employer (or controlling corporation) is a debtor in bankruptcy, and an indictment or conviction resulted from transactions related to the bankruptcy. Qualifying participants who make the election can't make regular catch-up contributions. (Code Sec. 219(b)(5)(C))[30]

¶ 4353 Active participant defined.

An individual who (or whose spouse) is an active participant in a qualified pension, profit-sharing, stock bonus or annuity plan, government plan, tax-sheltered annuity plan, SEP, SIMPLE retirement plan, or certain other trusts can't make deductible IRA contributions unless his adjusted gross income falls with the dollar limits at ¶4352. (Code Sec. 219(g))[31]

An individual is an active participant for any tax year in which he's eligible to participate in a defined benefit plan, or any year in which employer or employee contributions or forfeitures are added to his account in a defined contribution plan. [32]

¶ 4354 Nondeductible IRA contributions—Form 8606.

An active participant in a qualified plan who may not be eligible to make deductible contributions either in whole or in part to an IRA (see ¶4353), can make (use Form 8606) designated nondeductible contributions (DNCs) to an IRA for a tax year (Code Sec. 408(o)(2)(C)(i)) up to the due date (*without* extensions) for the taxpayer's income tax return for that year. (Code Sec. 408(o)(3))[33]

The amount of any DNCs made in any tax year on behalf of an individual is limited to the excess of: (1) the lesser of $4,000 in 2007 ($5,000 for 2008), plus an additional $1,000 for those 50 and over, see ¶4351, or 100% of compensation (including the higher-earning spouse's compensation (¶4355)), over (2) the amount allowable as a deduction for IRA contributions by active participants. (Code Sec. 408(o)(2)(B)(i))[34]

A taxpayer can elect to treat an otherwise deductible contribution as a DNC, thereby increasing, to that extent, his DNC limit for that year. (Code Sec. 408(o)(2)(B)(ii))[35]

24. ¶H-12215.1 *et seq.*; TD ¶283,018.1
25. ¶H-12234; ¶2194.01; TD ¶283,020
26. ¶H-12233; ¶2194.01; TD ¶283,019
27. ¶H-12236; ¶2194.01; TD ¶283,022
28. ¶H-12235; TD ¶283,021
29. ¶H-12237; ¶2194.01; TD ¶283,023

30. ¶2194.01; ¶H-12215; TD ¶614,704
31. ¶H-12217 *et seq.*; ¶2194.02; TD ¶283,006
32. ¶H-12220 *et seq.*; ¶2194.02; TD ¶283,007
33. ¶s H-12238, H-12240; ¶4084.01; TD ¶283,024
34. ¶H-12239; ¶4084.01; TD ¶283,025
35. ¶H-12240; ¶4084.01; TD ¶283,027

DNCs and deductible contributions may be made to the same IRA. [36]

¶ 4355   Special IRA deduction rules for married taxpayers.

Married taxpayers can each make deductible contributions to separate IRAs, subject to the deduction phase-out rules at ¶4352 that apply if either or both are active participants in an employer retirement plan for any part of the tax year. [37]

An individual who files a joint return and has less taxable compensation than his spouse may contribute to a spousal IRA and deduct the lesser of (1) $4,000 in 2007 ($5,000 for 2008), plus an additional $1,000 for those 50 and over, see ¶4351, or (2) the sum of (a) that individual's includible compensation for the tax year, plus (b) the includible compensation of the individual's spouse reduced by the sum of the spouse's allowable IRA deduction, designated nondeductible IRA contribution, and Roth IRA contribution for that tax year. (Code Sec. 219(c))[38]

¶ 4356   Penalties for excess contributions—Form 5329.

An individual who contributes more to an IRA than he is entitled to deduct must pay (use Form 5329) a 6% excise tax on the excess *every year*. The tax for any particular year, however, can't exceed 6% of the value of the IRA (as of the close of the tax year). (Code Sec. 4973(a))

An excess contribution to an IRA is the sum of: (1) the excess of the amount contributed for the tax year (*other than* a contribution to a Roth IRA or a rollover contribution), over the amount allowable as a deduction for the contribution, plus (2) any excess contribution for the preceding tax year, *reduced by* the sum of taxable distributions for the tax year, distributions for the tax year of excess contributions after the due date of the return, and the excess (if any) of the maximum amount allowable as a deduction for the tax year, over the amount contributed to the IRA for the tax year (without regard to any deduction for a preceding year's excess contribution), *including* the amount contributed to a Roth IRA. (Code Sec. 4973(b))[39]

There's no 6% penalty for the year of the contribution (or any other year) if the taxpayer is allowed no IRA deduction for the excess *and* withdraws the excess (together with any net income earned on it) by the due date for filing his income tax return for the year the excess contribution was made. (Code Sec. 4973(b))[40]

For tax on excess contributions to Roth IRAs, see ¶4369.

¶ 4357   Distributions from IRAs and individual retirement annuities.

Payouts from an IRA can be made without penalty once the participant attains age 59 ½ (or earlier in the case of death, disability, annuitized payments, certain medical-related distributions, higher education expenses, certain first-time homebuyer expenses, and IRS levies, see ¶4344). These distributions can be made in a lump-sum or in installments and are taxable as ordinary income under the annuity rules (see ¶1355 *et seq.*), when received, except that distributions are tax-free if reinvested (i.e., "rolled over," see ¶4359 *et seq.*) within 60 days into that or another IRA. (Code Sec. 408(d)(3)(A))[41] (If not reinvested, the distribution is taxable in the year received, not the year in which the 60-day rollover period ends.) [42] A distribution from a SIMPLE retirement plan (¶4382) can't be rolled over tax-free except to another SIMPLE plan during the employee's first two years of participation in the plan. (Code Sec. 408(d)(3)(G))

36. ¶H-12238; ¶4084.01; TD ¶283,024
37. ¶H-12217; ¶2194.02; TD ¶283,002
38. ¶s H-12230, H-12231; ¶2194.01; TD ¶s 283,016, 283,017
39. ¶H-12242 *et seq.*; ¶49,734; TD ¶283,030

40. ¶H-12247 *et seq.*; ¶49,734; TD ¶283,031 *et seq.*
41. ¶H-12265; ¶4084.03; TD ¶143,003
42. ¶s H-11460, H-12253; ¶4084.03; TD ¶144,034

☛ *caution:* Although an IRA account can be used as a source for an interest-free "loan" (of up to 60 days), this can be done only once in a one-year period, see ¶4360.

Amounts distributed from an IRA are included in gross income under the Code Sec. 72 annuity rules. (Code Sec. 408(d)(1)) In applying the annuity rules, all IRAs (other than Roth IRAs) are treated as one contract, all distributions made during any tax year are treated as one distribution, and the value of the contract, income on the contract, and investment in it are determined at the end of the calendar year in which the tax year begins. (Code Sec. 408(d)(2))[43] Part of an individual's withdrawal from an IRA is excludible if he previously made nondeductible IRA contributions. The excludible part is (the amount withdrawn × [aggregate nondeductible IRA contributions ÷ aggregate balance on the last day of the tax year of all IRAs of the individual]). The sum of all distributions from all of the individual's IRAs during the year, including rollovers to Roth IRAs, is added to the denominator of the fraction, as are "outstanding rollovers" (amounts distributed within 60 days of the end of the tax year, not rolled over to another traditional IRA by the end of the year, but rolled over in the following year before the 60 days end). Neither the aggregate nondeductible contributions, nor the aggregate balance of all IRAs, includes amounts previously withdrawn. For purposes of the calculation, IRAs include all of the taxpayer's traditional IRAs, SEPs and SIMPLE IRAs.[44]

Up to $100,000 of taxable IRA distributions in 2006 and 2007 from a traditional (or Roth IRA, see ¶4368) may be excluded annually if the distribution is made: (1) directly by the IRA trustee to a Code Sec. 170(b)(1)(A) charity (see ¶2125) other than a Code Sec. 509(a)(3) organization (see ¶4125) or a Code Sec. 4966(d)(2) donor advised fund, see ¶4129; and (2) on or after the date the IRA owner attains age 70- ½. (Code Sec. 408(d)(8)(A)).[45]

A loss in an individual's traditional IRA is recognized only when *all* amounts have been distributed from *all* of the individual's traditional IRAs, and the amounts distributed are less than the individual's unrecovered basis (total nondeductible contributions) in his traditional IRAs.[46] For how to claim the loss, see ¶3110. For losses from Roth IRAs, see ¶4373.

Distributions from an IRA are reported on Form 1099-R. Distribution recipients who at any time made nondeductible contributions to a IRA (¶4354), must file Form 8606.

The transfer of an interest in an IRA (but not the distribution of funds from an IRA) to a spouse under a divorce or separation instrument isn't taxable (the transferred IRA is treated as the spouse's). (Code Sec. 408(d)(6))[47] Roth IRAs (¶4367 *et seq.*) are treated separately. (Code Sec. 408A(d)(4))

For the tax on early distributions from an IRA, see ¶4344.

Distribution of a participant's entire interest in his IRA (other than a Roth IRA, see ¶4373) must be made under rules similar to the Code Sec. 401(a)(9) required distribution rules for qualified plans (¶4345), (Code Sec. 408(a)(6), Code Sec. 408(b)(3)) except that required distributions from an IRA can't be deferred beyond age 70- ½ due to the account owner's not being retired (Code Sec. 401(a)(9)(C)(ii)(II)), see ¶4319. While the required minimum distribution must be separately calculated for each IRA an individual has, the amounts may then be totalled, and the total distribution taken from any one or more of the individual's IRAs. Failure to make the required distributions results in a nondeductible excise tax payable (on Form 5329) by the recipient. The tax is 50% of the excess of the minimum amount that should have been distributed over the amount actually distributed. (Code Sec. 4974(a))[48] IRS can waive the 50% tax if the shortfall in the amount distributed is due to "reasonable error" and reasonable corrective steps are taken. (Code Sec. 4974(c))[49]

---

43. ¶H-12253; ¶4084.03; TD ¶143,003
44. ¶H-12253; ¶4084.03; TD ¶143,003
45. ¶H-12253.2; ¶4084.03; ¶408A4; TD ¶143,003.2
46. ¶H-12255; TD ¶143,005

47. ¶H-12261; ¶4084.03; TD ¶143,013
48. ¶H-8501; ¶49,744; TD ¶145,515
49. ¶H-8508; ¶49,744

¶ 4358   Exemption of IRA from tax.

Income earned by an IRA is tax-exempt until distribution. This tax exemption doesn't apply to the unrelated business income tax, see ¶4121. Engaging in a prohibited transaction causes loss of the exemption. (Code Sec. 408(e))[50] Certain nominal gifts, free banking services, and free group term life insurance offered by banks for opening and contributing to an IRA are exempted from the prohibited transaction rules. [1]

If the owner of an individual retirement annuity borrows any money under, or by use of, the annuity contract, the contract stops being an individual retirement annuity as of the first day of the tax year, and the owner must include in income for that year an amount equal to the fair market value of the contract on the first day of the year. (Code Sec. 408(e)(3)) If the individual for whom an IRA is established uses the account or any portion of it as security for a loan, that portion is treated as distributed to that individual. (Code Sec. 408(e)(4))

¶ 4359   Tax-free rollovers from qualified plans.

A tax-free rollover from a qualified plan is any portion of the balance of an employee's credit in a qualified trust paid to the employee in an "eligible rollover distribution," any portion of which the employee then transfers to an "eligible retirement plan." (Code Sec. 402(c)(1))[2] A distribution must be rolled over within 60 days after receipt to be tax-free, but IRS may waive the 60-day rollover period for equitable reasons, including cases of casualty, disaster, or other events beyond an individual's control (Code Sec. 402(c)(3); Code Sec. 408(d)(3); Reg § 301.7508A-1(c)(1)) such as bank error, if certain conditions are met. [3]

An "eligible rollover distribution" is any distribution to an employee of all or any portion of the balance to the credit of the employee in a qualified trust. (Code Sec. 402(c)(4)) An "eligible rollover distribution" does *not* include:

(1) any distribution that's one of a series of substantially equal periodic payments made (at least annually) for (a) the life (or life expectancy) of the employee, or the joint lives (or joint life expectancies) of the employee and the employee's designated beneficiary, or (b) a specified period of ten years or more (Code Sec. 402(c)(4)(A));

(2) any distribution to the extent it is a required distribution under Code Sec. 401(a)(9); (Code Sec. 402(c)(4)(B); Reg § 1.402(c)-2) and

(3) any hardship distribution. (Code Sec. 402(c)(4)(C), Code Sec. 403(b)(8)(B))[4]

✪/caution: An eligible rollover distribution from a qualified plan is subject to 20% withholding, unless there's a direct trustee-to-trustee transfer, see ¶3034.

Amounts transferred in a direct trustee-to-trustee transfer (¶4319) are excludable from income for the tax year of the transfer. (Code Sec. 402(e)(6))[5]

Certain payments can't be rolled over, e.g., corrective distributions of excess 401(k) contributions, loans treated as deemed distributions, and dividends paid on employer securities. (Reg § 1.402(c)-2, Q&A 4) However, where a plan loan offset amount is treated as a default, it is an eligible rollover distribution that may be rolled over tax –free to an IRA. (Reg § 1.402(c)-2, Q&A 9)[6]

An "eligible retirement plan" is: (1) an individual retirement account (not a Roth IRA), (2) an individual retirement annuity (other than an endowment contract), (3) a qualified trust, (4) an annuity plan, (5) a Code Sec. 403(b) annuity, and (6) a governmental section 457 plan.

---

50. ¶H-12214; ¶4084.03; TD ¶283,044
1. ¶H-12530
2. ¶H-11402; ¶4024.04; TD ¶144,001
3. ¶H-11452; ¶H-11452.2; ¶4024.04; TD ¶144,034

4. ¶H-11406; ¶4024.04; TD ¶144,006
5. ¶H-11403; ¶4024.04; TD ¶144,003
6. ¶H-11415; ¶4014.27; TD ¶144,016

(Code Sec. 402(c)(8)(B))[7]

For the special recontribution rules that apply to qualified hurricane distributions, and to withdrawals for home purchases that were not made due to a hurricane, see ¶4344.

If noncash property (e.g., securities) is distributed, the employee can sell the property and roll over the proceeds. There's no gain or loss recognized on the sale if the full proceeds are rolled over. (Code Sec. 402(c)(6)(A))[8] If cash is distributed, it must be recontributed as cash. [9]

Plan administrators must inform recipients of potential rollovers in writing ("a section 402(f) notice") of the applicable rollover rules, no less than 30 days, and no more than 90 days before making an eligible rollover distribution (but the 30-day time period may be waived by a participant in certain cases, and a summary notice procedure also is available). (Code Sec. 402(f); Reg § 1.402(c)-2, Q&A 2; Reg § 1.402(f)-1, Q&A 2(b)) IRS has provided a model safe harbor explanation of this notice. [10]

Where a participant with a small accrued benefit (a nonforfeitable accrued benefit whose present value is $5,000 or less) is terminating his employment with the company sponsoring the plan, the plan may provide for the distribution of the employee's benefit without his consent, or the consent of his spouse (a "mandatory distribution" or an "involuntary cash-out distribution"). Such mandatory distributions must follow the automatic rollover rules. Under these rules, plans with mandatory distribution provisions must transfer the amount of the distribution to an IRA of a designated trustee or issuer where:

. . . the distribution of a nonforfeitable accrued benefit is more than $1,000, but no more than $5,000; and

. . . the plan participant (or beneficiary) receiving the distribution does not elect to have the distribution paid directly to another qualified plan or IRA (a direct rollover), and does not elect to receive the distribution himself. (Code Sec. 401(a)(31)(B))[11]

The plan administrator must also notify the distributee in writing, either separately or as part of the section 402(f) notice (see above), that the distribution may be transferred without cost or penalty to another IRA. [12] IRS has provided a transition period under which certain failures to follow the automatic rollover rules before 2006 won't be considered operational plan failures. [13]

For rollovers of after-tax contributions, see ¶4362.

¶ 4360 Other types of rollovers.

Permissible types of tax-free 60-day rollovers, besides those covered at ¶4359, include:

. . . Rollovers from one type of IRA (individual retirement account or individual retirement annuity) to the same or another type. But these rollovers may be made no more than once in a one-year period. (Code Sec. 408(d)(3))[14] Qualified rollovers from an IRA to a Roth IRA are disregarded for purposes of the one-year rule. (Code Sec. 408A(e)) However, a distribution from a SIMPLE retirement plan (¶4382) can't be rolled over tax-free except to another SIMPLE plan during the employee's first two years of participation in the plan. (Code Sec. 408(d)(3)(G))

. . . From one type of IRA (individual retirement account or individual retirement annuity) to an eligible retirement plan (¶4359) (limited to amount which would otherwise be included in gross income). (Code Sec. 408(d)(3)(A)(ii))

. . . Eligible rollover distributions from a section 403(b) plan to an eligible retirement plan

---

7. ¶H-11440; ¶4024.04; TD ¶144,023
8. ¶H-11448; ¶4024.04; TD ¶144,028
9. ¶H-11402; TD ¶144,001
10. ¶H-11455; ¶4024.04; TD ¶144,053

11. ¶H-8251.3; ¶4014.27; TD ¶144,037.1
12. ¶H-8251.6; TD ¶144,053
13. ¶H-8251.7
14. ¶H-11460 *et seq.*; ¶4084.03; TD ¶144,055

(¶4359) and from an eligible retirement plan to a section 403(b) plan. (Code Sec. 402(c)(8)(B), Code Sec. 403(b)(8)(A)(ii))

. . . Eligible rollover distributions from a section 457 plan to an eligible retirement plan (¶4359) and from an eligible retirement plan to a section 457 plan. (Code Sec. 402(c)(8)(B), Code Sec. 457(e)(16))

For post-2007 taxable rollovers to Roth IRAs, see ¶4363.

¶ 4361 Partial rollovers.

When an employee elects to roll over less than his entire distribution:

(1) the portion not rolled over is taxed under the regular rules for taxing ordinary income. Ten-year forward averaging and/or capital gains treatment, where applicable, for lump-sum distributions (¶4339) don't apply if any part of the lump-sum distribution is rolled over; (Code Sec. 402(c)(10), Code Sec. 402(d)(4)(K), before amended by Sec. 1401(a), P.L. 104-188, 8/20/96)

(2) the basis recovery rules of Code Sec. 72(e) apply to a distribution that's rolled over under Code Sec. 402(c); and

(3) any net unrealized appreciation in employer securities attributable to nondeductible employee contributions is subject to tax immediately. [15]

¶ 4362 Rollovers of after-tax contributions.

Generally, only otherwise taxable amounts of an eligible rollover distribution may be rolled over. However, the "nontaxable" portion of a eligible rollover distribution (attributable to after-tax employee contributions) may be rolled over to the extent that the "taxable" portion is rolled over to (1) an IRA, or (2) to a defined contribution plan or tax-sheltered Code Sec. 403(b) annuity) that will account separately for the taxable and nontaxable portions. In such a case, the amount transferred is treated as consisting first of the portion of the distribution that would be includible in income were it not for the rollover. (Code Sec. 402(c)(2)[16]

¶ 4363 Qualified plan to Roth IRA rollovers—after 2007.

Post-2007 distributions from qualified retirement plans, tax-sheltered Code Sec. 403(b) annuities, and governmental Code Sec. 457 plans may be rolled over directly into a Roth IRA, generally subject to the usual rules that apply to rollovers from a traditional IRA into a Roth IRA (see ¶4371). For example, a rollover from a qualified retirement plan into a Roth IRA is includible in gross income (except to the extent it represents a return of after-tax contributions), and the 10% early distribution tax does not apply. (Code Sec. 408A(e)) A rollover from a qualified plan, etc., to a Roth IRA doesn't count for purposes of the one-per-year rule. [17]

¶ 4364 One-time IRA to HSA rollovers—after 2006.

Taxpayers may make a one-time-only tax-free rollover, via direct trustee-to-trustee-transfer, from an IRA to a Health Savings Account (HSA) (¶1529). (Code Sec. 408(d)(9)) The rollover amount is nondeductible and is limited to the otherwise maximum deductible HSA contribution amount, computed on the basis of the type of coverage under the taxpayer's high deductible health plan (HDHP) at the time of the contribution. The rollover reduces the otherwise allowable HSA contribution amount.

Generally, only one rollover may be made during a taxpayer's lifetime, but if one is made

---

15. ¶H-11405 *et seq.*; ¶4024.04; TD ¶144,005
16. ¶H-12290.17; ¶408A4

17. ¶H-11444; ¶4024.04; TD ¶144,005.5

during a month in which he has self-only coverage as of the first day of the month, an additional rollover may be made during a subsequent month within the tax year in which he has family coverage. (Code Sec. 408(d)(9)(C)(ii))

If a taxpayer does not remain an eligible individual (except because of death or disability) during the testing period (begins with the month of the contribution and ends on the last day of the 12th month following that month), the amount of the IRA distribution that would otherwise have been includible is taxed to him and is subject to a 10% penalty tax. The amount is includible in income for the tax year of the first day during the testing period that the taxpayer is not an eligible individual. (Code Sec. 408(d)(9)(D))[18]

¶ 4365   Surviving spouse's rollover of distribution from decedent.

A surviving-spouse beneficiary may elect to treat the entire beneficiary interest in the decedent's IRA as the spouse-beneficiary's own IRA if he or she is the sole beneficiary of the IRA and has an unlimited right to withdraw amounts from it. However, this requirement is not satisfied if a trust is named beneficiary of the IRA even if the spouse is sole beneficiary of the trust. (Reg § 1.408-8, Q&A 5(a)) The election is made by the surviving spouse redesignating the account as an account in her name as IRA owner rather than as beneficiary. Alternatively, a surviving spouse is deemed to have made the election if, at any time, either of the following occurs: (1) any amount required to be distributed to the surviving spouse as beneficiary is not timely distributed, or (2) any additional amount is contributed to the IRA. (Reg § 1.408-8, Q&A 5(b)) If the election is made, the surviving spouse is considered the IRA owner for all purposes under the Code. (Reg § 1.408-8, Q&A 5(c))[19]

A surviving spouse may also roll a distribution from a qualified plan, annuity, or IRA over to any other qualified plan, annuity, or IRA in which the surviving spouse participates that accepts rollover contributions. (Code Sec. 402(c)(9), Code Sec. 408(d)(3)(C))[20]

¶ 4366   Rollover by beneficiary other than surviving spouse.

Pre-2007 distributions from an IRA or qualified plan to a beneficiary other than a surviving spouse of a deceased IRA owner or plan participant can't be rolled over to an IRA. (Code Sec. 408(d)(3)(C))[21] However, post-2006 distributions from qualified plans, tax–sheltered annuities (¶4388 *et seq.*), and Code Sec. 457 government plans may (if the plan so allows) be rolled over (in a direct trustee–to–trustee transfer, see ¶4319) to a non-spouse beneficiary's IRA that's established for the purpose of receiving the distribution. This "recipient IRA" is treated as an inherited IRA, and so is subject to the required minimum distribution (RMD) rules that apply to inherited IRAs of nonspouse beneficiaries (¶4345). To the extent provided by IRS, the change applies to benefits payable to a trust maintained for a designated beneficiary to the same extent it applies to the beneficiary. (Code Sec. 402(c)(11), Code Sec. 403(a)(4)(B), Code Sec. 457(e)(16)(B))[22]

¶ 4367   Roth IRAs. ▬▬▬▬▬▬▬▬▬▬▬▬▬▬▬▬▬▬▬▬▬▬

Taxpayers can make nondeductible contributions to Roth IRAs. Qualified distributions from Roth IRAs are tax-free and penalty-free. Roth IRAs aren't subject to the post-age 70-½ required distribution rules. Traditional IRAs can be rolled over penalty-free (but not tax-free) into Roth IRAs.

---

18. ¶H-12253.1A; ¶4084.03; TD ¶143,003.1A
19. ¶H-12270; TD ¶143,024
20. ¶H-11467 *et seq.*; ¶4084.03; TD ¶144,065

21. ¶H-11469; ¶4084.03; TD ¶144,065
22. ¶H-11437; ¶H-11438; TD ¶144,020; TD ¶144,021

¶ 4368   Roth IRAs—overview.

A Roth IRA is an IRA that is designated as a Roth IRA when it's established (Code Sec. 408A(b)); it's treated as a traditional IRA (¶4351 *et seq.*) except to the extent that special rules apply to it. (Code Sec. 408A(a)) Contributions to a Roth IRA aren't deductible (Code Sec. 408A(c)(1)), and are limited based on modified adjusted gross income (¶4369). Qualified distributions from a Roth IRA aren't included in income (Code Sec. 408A(d)(1)) and other distributions are treated as a return of investment to the extent of contributions to Roth IRAs (¶4373). (Code Sec. 408A(d)(4)) Rollovers from traditional IRAs to Roth IRAs are taxable, but not subject to the 10% premature distribution penalty tax. (Code Sec. 408A(d)(3))[23] (Reg § 1.408A-3; Reg § 1.408A-4;Reg § 1.408A-5)

Prototype Roth IRAs can currently accept eligible rollover contributions from designated Roth accounts (Roth 401(k) or Roth 403(b) arrangements, see ¶4375) without being amended to allow for these rollovers. But, amendments allowing for these rollovers must be adopted no later than Dec. 31, 2007. [24]

Use Form 5305-R, Form 5305-RA, and Form 5305-RB to set up Roth trust, custodial, and annuity accounts, respectively, with financial institutions.

¶ 4369   Contributions to Roth IRAs.

An individual can make annual nondeductible contributions to a Roth IRA in amounts up to $4,000 for 2007 ($5,000 for 2008 and thereafter), plus an additional $1,000 for those 50 and older, or 100% of compensation, if less, reduced by the amount of contributions for the tax year made to all other IRAs (Code Sec. 408A(c)(1); Code Sec. 408A(c)(2)) but not reduced by contributions to a SEP (¶4377) or SIMPLE plan (¶4382) (Code Sec. 408A(f)(2); Reg § 1.408A-3, Q&A 3(c))[25] The allowable contribution phases out ratably (in $10 increments) over the following levels of AGI:

- For joint filers, $156,000 to $166,000 for 2007 ($159,000 to $169,000 for 2008);
- For married persons filing separately, $0 to $10,000 for 2007 (and 2008); and
- For single taxpayers and heads of household, $99,000 to $114,000 for 2007 ($101,000 to $116,000 for 2008).

However, a $200 contribution may be made if the phase-out lowers the contribution limit to under $200 but more than $0. (Code Sec. 408A(c)(3)(A), Code Sec. 408A(c)(3)(B); Reg § 1.408A-3, Q&A 3(b))

AGI for purposes of the Roth IRA contribution phaseout is defined as it is for traditional IRA purposes (¶4352), except that it does not include income resulting from the conversion from a traditional IRA to a Roth IRA (¶4371). (Code Sec. 408A(c)(3)(C)(i); Reg § 1.408A-3, Q&A 5; Reg § 1.408A-3, Q&A 6(b))[26]

Ⓡ*observation:* The AGI-based contribution limits for Roth IRAs apply whether or not the taxpayer is a participant in a qualified retirement plan.

Roth IRA contributions for a year must be made by the unextended tax return due date for the contribution year. (Code Sec. 408A(c)(7); Reg § 1.408A-3, Q&A 2(b))[27] Unlike traditional IRAs, contributions are permitted after age 70 ½. (Code Sec. 408A(c)(4))[28] For rollover contributions, see ¶4371.

A 6% excise tax is imposed each year on excess contributions to an IRA (¶4356). Similar

---

23. ¶H-12290 *et seq.*; ¶408A4; TD ¶283,300 *et seq.*
24. ¶T-10708C; TD ¶283,318.1
25. ¶H-12290.7; ¶408A4; TD ¶283,306 *et seq.*

26. ¶H-12290.9; ¶408A4; TD ¶283,310
27. ¶H-12290.14; ¶408A4; TD ¶283,315
28. ¶H-12290.13; ¶408A4; TD ¶283,314

rules apply to a Roth IRA. (Code Sec. 4973(f))[29]

Any contribution distributed from a Roth IRA before the due date of the individual's tax return is treated as an amount not contributed. (Code Sec. 4973(f))[30]

For the saver's credit for lower-income taxpayers' contributions to Roth IRAs, see ¶2365.

¶ 4370 Recharacterizing (changing the nature of) IRA contributions.

A taxpayer may elect to recharacterize an IRA contribution, that is, treat a contribution to one type of IRA (Roth IRA or traditional IRA) as made to a different type of IRA. (Code Sec. 408A(d)(6); Reg § 1.408A-5)

⟨RIA⟩ *observation:* The recharacterization election allows a contribution to a traditional IRA to be treated as made to a Roth IRA, or a contribution to a Roth IRA to be treated as made to a traditional IRA. It also allows a taxpayer to "reverse" a traditional-IRA-to-Roth IRA conversion (¶4371), in other words, treat the conversion as if it had never been made.

To make the recharacterization election:

. . . The taxpayer must notify the trustees of the first (distributing) and second (receiving) IRAs of his election to recharacterize a contribution (regular or conversion), i.e., that he is electing for tax purposes to treat the contribution as having been made to the second IRA, instead of the first IRA. The taxpayer must provide the trustees with specified information (including the type and amount of the contribution being recharacterized) sufficient to effect the recharacterization transfer.

. . . The contribution (regular or conversion) originally made to first IRA, plus net income (if any) allocable to the contribution (Reg § 1.408A-10; Reg § 1.408A-5, Q&A 2(c)), must be transferred from the first IRA to the second IRA via a trustee-to-trustee transfer.

. . . The trustee-to-trustee transfer must be made on a timely basis. (Reg § 1.408A-5, Q&A-6)[31]

An IRA contribution for a tax year may be recharacterized as late as six months after the unextended due date for filing the return for that year. (Reg § 301.9100-2(b))[32]

A recharacterization election cannot be revoked after the transfer. (Reg § 1.408A-5, Q&A 6(b))

The contribution that is being recharacterized is treated as having been originally contributed to the second IRA on the same date and (in the case of a regular contribution) for the same tax year that the contribution was made to the first IRA. (Reg § 1.408A-5, Q&A 3)

⟨RIA⟩ *caution:* For the limit on *reconversion* to a Roth IRA following a recharacterization from a Roth IRA to a traditional IRA, see ¶4372.

¶ 4371 Conversions of traditional IRAs to Roth IRAs—Form 8606.

Taxpayers (other than marrieds filing separately) with AGI of $100,000 or less for a tax year (Code Sec. 408A(c)(3)(B)) may convert amounts in a traditional IRA to amounts in a Roth IRA in one of three ways:

(1) Rollover to a Roth IRA of a distribution from a traditional IRA within 60 days of the distribution.

(2) Trustee-to-trustee transfer from the trustee of the traditional IRA to the trustee of the Roth IRA.

(3) Transfer of an amount in a traditional IRA to a Roth IRA maintained by the same

---

29. ¶H-12242.1; ¶49,734; TD ¶283,032
30. ¶H-12242.1; ¶49,734; TD ¶283,032
31. ¶H-12290.22; ¶408A4; TD ¶283,328
32. ¶H-12290.23A; TD ¶283,331

trustee. (Code Sec. 408A(c)(3)(B); Reg § 1.408A-4, Q&A 1(b))

Amounts from a SEP-IRA (¶4378) or a SIMPLE IRA (¶4357) also may be converted to a Roth IRA, but a conversion from a SIMPLE IRA may be made only after the 2-year period beginning on the date on which the taxpayer first participated in any SIMPLE IRA maintained by the taxpayer's employer. (Reg § 1.408A-4, Q&A 4)

For purposes of conversions to Roth IRAs, AGI is defined as it is for traditional IRA purposes (¶4352), except that it does not include income resulting from the conversion from a traditional IRA to a Roth IRA. (Code Sec. 408A(c)(3)(C)(i); Reg § 1.408A-3, Q&A 5) AGI — for purposes of determining conversion eligibility only — will not include any required minimum distribution from an IRA under Code Sec. 408(a)(6) and Code Sec. 408(b)(3) (see ¶4357). (Code Sec. 408A(c)(3)(C)(i)); Reg § 1.408A-3, Q&A 6(b))[33]

The conversion is subject to tax (report on Form 8606) as if it were distributed from the traditional IRA and not recontributed to another IRA (¶4357) (Code Sec. 408A(d)(3)(A)(i)), but isn't subject to the 10% premature distribution tax. (Code Sec. 408A(d)(3)(A)(ii); Reg § 1.408A-4, Q&A 7)[34]

For tax years beginning after 2009, (1) the $100,000 modified AGI limit on conversions of traditional IRAs to Roth IRAs is eliminated, and (2) married taxpayers filing a separate return may convert amounts in a traditional IRA into a Roth IRA. (Code Sec. 408A(c)(3))[35] However, a complex income inclusion rule applies for conversions occurring in 2010. Unless a taxpayer elects otherwise, none of the gross income from the conversion is included in income in 2010; half of the income resulting from the conversion is includible in gross income in 2011 and the other half in 2012. (Code Sec. 408A(d)(3)(A))[36]

¶ 4372   Reconversion to Roth IRA.

A person who has converted an amount from a traditional IRA to a Roth IRA (¶4371) may not only transfer the amount back to a traditional IRA in a recharacterization (¶4370), but may later reconvert that amount from a traditional IRA to a Roth IRA, and, under certain circumstances, have his resulting income fixed at the time of the reconversion.

An IRA owner who converts an amount from a traditional IRA to a Roth IRA and then transfers that amount back to a traditional IRA by way of a recharacterization can't reconvert that amount from the traditional IRA to another Roth IRA before the beginning of the tax year following the tax year in which the amount was converted to a Roth IRA or, if later, the end of the 30-day period beginning on the day on which the IRA owner transfers the amount from the Roth IRA back to a traditional IRA by way of a recharacterization. This timing rule applies regardless of whether the recharacterization occurs during the tax year in which the amount was converted to a Roth IRA or the following tax year. (Reg § 1.408A-5, Q&A 9(a)(1))

⚓*observation:* This restriction prevents a taxpayer from recharacterizing a Roth IRA as a traditional IRA if the market value of the IRA has been substantially reduced, e.g., because of a sharp decline in the market value of stocks held in the IRA, and then immediately reconverting to a Roth IRA to take advantage of the lower market value in determining the income to be reported from the conversion.

A reconversion made before the later of the beginning of the next tax year or the end of the 30-day period that begins on the day of the recharacterization is treated as a failed conversion, subject to correction through a recharacterization back to a traditional IRA.

---

33. ¶H-12290.15; ¶408A4; TD ¶283,317   35. ¶H-12290.16A
34. ¶H-12290.20; ¶408A4; TD ¶283,326 *et seq.*   36. ¶H-12290.20B

(Reg § 1.408A-5, Q&A 9(a)(1)) A failed conversion results in a distribution from the traditional IRA that's subject to tax (and possibly penalty tax) followed by a regular contribution to the Roth IRA. To the extent it exceeds the annual contribution limit, the amount treated as a regular contribution to the Roth IRA is treated as an excess contribution subject to the excise tax under Code Sec. 4973. (Reg § 1.408A-4, Q&A 3(b), Reg § 1.408A-4, Q&A 1(d), Reg § 1.408A-5, Q&A 9(a)(1)) For purposes of the reconversion timing rules, above, a failed conversion resulting from not having satisfied the statutory requirements (e.g., the $100,000 modified AGI limit) is treated as a conversion in determining when an IRA owner may make a reconversion. (Reg § 1.408A-5, Q&A 9(a)(2))

¶ 4373 Distributions from Roth IRAs—Form 8606.

Qualified distributions. Qualified distributions from Roth IRAs aren't included in income. (Code Sec. 408A(d)(1)) These are distributions made after the five-tax-year period beginning with the first tax year for which the taxpayer or the taxpayer's spouse made a contribution to a Roth IRA established for the taxpayer, including a qualified rollover contribution from an IRA other than a Roth IRA (Code Sec. 408A(d)(2)(B)), and that are made:

(1) on or after attaining age 59 ½,

(2) at or after death (to a beneficiary or estate),

(3) on account of disability, or

(4) for a first-time home purchase expense under Code Sec. 72(t)(2)(F). (Code Sec. 408A(d)(2)(A), Code Sec. 408A(d)(5); Reg § 1.408A-6, Q&A 1)[37]

The five-year period for qualified distributions isn't recalculated when a Roth IRA owner dies. The five-year period for a beneficiary's inherited Roth IRA is determined independently of the period for any other Roth IRA that the beneficiary may have, except that the 5-year period for a spousal beneficiary with both an inherited Roth IRA and his own Roth IRA ends with the earlier of the five-year periods. (Reg § 1.408A-5, Q&A 7)

Corrective distributions made by the return due date, plus extensions, for the tax year of the contribution aren't qualified distributions. (Code Sec. 408A(d)(2)(C); Reg § 1.408A-6, Q&A 2)[38]

Nonqualified distributions. Distributions that aren't qualified distributions are treated as made first from contributions to all of an individual's Roth IRAs and are nontaxable to that extent; distributions in excess of contributions are taxable. (Code Sec. 408A(d)(4))[39]

Order of distributions. Distributions are treated as made from contributions to the Roth IRA to the extent that the distribution, when added to all previous distributions from the Roth IRA, doesn't exceed the total amount of all contributions. (Code Sec. 408A(d)(4)(B)(i)) Contributions are treated as withdrawn in the following order: first, contributions other than qualified rollover contributions (i.e., qualified conversions, see ¶4371); second, qualified rollover contributions (on a FIFO basis); third, a distribution allocable to a qualified rollover contribution is allocated first to the part of the contribution required to be included in gross income. (Code Sec. 408A(d)(4)(B)(ii); Reg § 1.408A-6, Q&A 8)[40] All of a taxpayer's Roth IRAs are treated as a single Roth IRA. (Code Sec. 408A(d)(4)(A), Code Sec. 408(d)(2))

If the taxpayer withdraws all amounts from all of his Roth IRAs, a loss is recognized if the amounts distributed are less than his unrecovered basis (regular and conversion contributions).[41] For how to claim the loss, see ¶3110.

Report Roth IRA distributions on Form 8606, Part III.

37. ¶H-12290.28; ¶408A4; TD ¶283,337
38. ¶H-12290.30; ¶408A4; TD ¶283,338
39. ¶H-12290.34; ¶408A4; TD ¶283,342

40. ¶H-12290.35; ¶408A4; TD ¶283,343
41. ¶H-12255; TD ¶143,005

Roth IRAs aren't subject to the required minimum distribution rules of Code Sec. 401(a)(9)(A) or the incidental benefit requirements of Code Sec. 401(a) (¶4345). Instead, after the Roth IRA owner's death, the distribution rules in Reg § 1.408-8 apply as though the Roth IRA owner died before his required beginning date. Thus, the entire Roth IRA must generally be distributed within five years of the owner's death unless it is distributed over the life expectancy of a designated beneficiary, and distributions commence prior to the end of the calendar year following the year of the owner's death. Where the sole beneficiary of a Roth IRA is the Roth IRA owner's surviving spouse, the spouse may delay distributions until the Roth IRA owner would have reached age 70 ½, or may treat the Roth IRA as his or her own. (Reg § 1.408A-6, Q&A 14(b)) (Code Sec. 408A(c)(5))[42]

For the 10% early distribution penalty tax, see ¶4374. For distributions from designated Roth accounts, see ¶4375.

¶ 4374   10% premature distribution tax on Roth IRA distributions.

As with other IRAs (¶4344) the Code Sec. 72(t) 10% early withdrawal tax applies to the portion of an early withdrawal that is includible in income. In addition, however, a distribution from a Roth IRA is subject to the early withdrawal tax as if it *were* includible in income, if that distribution (or any portion of it): (1) is allocable (under rules at ¶4373) to a "qualified rollover contribution;" and (2) is made within the five-tax year period beginning with the tax year for which the contribution was made. However, the 10% tax applies only to the extent that the amount of the qualified rollover contribution was includible in income. (Code Sec. 408A(d)(3)(F))[43]

¶ 4375   Designated Roth (Roth 401(k)) accounts ████████████████████████

An employer's Code Sec. 401(k) plan (¶4317) or Code Sec. 403(b) annuity (¶4388) may include a qualified Roth contribution program (i.e, a "Roth 401(k)") that allows participants to elect to have all or part of their elective deferrals treated as Roth contributions—that is to make "designated Roth contributions." (Code Sec. 402A) Designated Roth contributions, which are currently includible in income, aren't subject to the AGI based phaseouts for regular Roth IRA contributions (¶4369). Qualified distributions are excludable from income. (Code Sec. 402A(d))[44]

Designated Roth contributions. These are elective contributions under a 401(k) plan that are:

(1) designated irrevocably by the employee when he makes the cash or deferred arrangement (CODA) election as designated Roth contributions;

(2) treated by the employer as includible in the employee's income when he would have received the contribution in cash had he not made the CODA election (e.g., by treating the contributions as wages subject to applicable withholding requirements); and

(3) maintained by the plan in a separate account. (Code Sec. 402A(b)(2), Reg § 1.401(k)-1(f)(1), Reg § 1.401(k)-1(f)(2))

A 401(k) plan can't provide for designated Roth contributions unless it also offers pre-tax elective contributions. (Reg § 1.401(k)-1(f)(1)(i))

A designated Roth contribution must satisfy the requirements that apply to elective contributions made under a qualified CODA (i.e., a 401(k) plan), such as the nonforfeitability and distribution restrictions for elective contributions, and the Code Sec. 401(k) ADP (actual deferral percentage) test; see ¶4317. (Reg § 1.401(k)-1(f)(3))

42. ¶H-12290.42; ¶408A4; TD ¶283,351   44. ¶H-12295.1 *et seq.*; ¶402A4; TD ¶283,400 *et seq.*
43. ¶H-12290.38; ¶408A4; TD ¶283,346

Rollovers. A direct rollover from a designated Roth account may only be made to another designated Roth account under a qualified retirement plan (or Code Sec. 403(b) annuity) or to a Roth IRA, and only to the extent the direct rollover is permitted under the Code Sec. 402(c) rules (¶4359). (Reg § 1.401(k)-1(f)(4)(ii)) A designated Roth distribution to an employee may be rolled over by him into a Roth IRA (or to a designated Roth account) within a 60-day period. (Reg § 1.402A-1, Q&A 5.)

Distributions from designated Roths. A qualified distribution from a designated Roth is excluded from income if it meets the requirements for qualified distributions from Roth IRAs (¶4373), with the following differences:

. . . A distribution for a first-time home purchase isn't excluded. (Code Sec. 402A(d)(2)(A)

. . . the five-year period necessary for a distribution to be excluded begins on the first day of the employee's tax year for which he first had designated Roth contributions made to the plan. If a direct rollover is made from a designated Roth account under another plan, the five-year period begins on the first day for which the employee first had designated Roth contributions made to the other plan, if earlier. (Reg § 1.402A-1, Q&A 4)

. . . Designated Roth accounts are subject to the lifetime required minimum distribution (RMD) rules of Code Sec. 401(a)(9)(A) and Code Sec. 401(a)(9)(B) (¶4345). (Reg § 1.401(k)-1(f)(4)(i)) By contrast, a regular Roth IRA is not subject to the Code Sec. 401(a)(9)(A) lifetime RMD rules (¶4373).

A distribution from a designated Roth account that is not a qualified distribution is taxable to the distributee under the Code Sec. 72 rules, *not* under the regular Roth IRA ordering rules (¶4373). (Reg § 1.402A-1, Q&A 3)

¶ 4376   Deemed IRAs. ▬▬▬▬▬▬▬▬▬▬▬▬▬▬▬▬▬▬▬▬▬▬▬▬▬▬▬▬▬▬▬▬

Qualified plans, Code Sec. 403(b) annuities (¶4388), and governmental Code Sec. 457 plans may include a deemed IRA, which is a separate account or annuity in a qualified employer plan to which plan participants may make voluntary IRA or Roth IRA contributions.

The qualified plan must elect to allow employees to make voluntary employee contributions (designated as such by the employees) to a separate account or annuity (meeting the requirements for a traditional IRA or Roth IRA) established under the plan. However, the general requirement that IRA assets not be commingled does not apply to deemed IRAs. (Code Sec. 408(q))[45]

SEPs (see ¶4377) and SIMPLE IRAs (¶4382) cannot be used as deemed IRAs. (Reg § 1.408(q)-1(b))[46]

Contributions to a deemed IRA are treated as contributions to an IRA, and not as contributions to the qualified employer plan. Thus, a deemed IRA contribution is in addition to the $15,500 (for 2007 and 2008) maximum amount that can be contributed to a 401(k) plan (excluding catch-up contributions). (Code Sec. 408(q)(1))

The ceilings on modified adjusted gross income that limit a taxpayer's ability to make Roth IRA contributions or deductible contributions to a regular IRA also apply to voluntary contributions to a deemed IRA. (Code Sec. 408(q)(1)(B); Reg § 1.408(q)-1(f)(4)[47]

A deemed IRA isn't subject to the rules that apply to the qualified employer plan, so contributions to a deemed IRA are not taken into account in applying those rules to any other contributions under the plan. Thus, deemed IRA contributions don't count against the 100% of income or dollar limit on annual additions to defined contribution plans. (Reg § 1.408(q)-1(c))

---

45. ¶H-12280; ¶4084.07; TD ¶283,080   47. ¶H-12284; TD ¶283,084
46. ¶H-12280; ¶4084.07; TD ¶283,080

¶ 4377 Simplified Employee Pensions (SEPs) ▆▆▆▆▆▆▆▆▆▆▆▆▆▆▆▆▆▆▆▆

An employer can make deductible contributions on behalf of its employees to a simplified employee pension (SEP). These deductible employer contributions are excluded from the gross income of the employee.

¶ 4378 Simplified employee pension (SEP) defined.

A SEP is an individual retirement account or individual retirement annuity (IRA, see ¶4351), established by an employer by filing Form 5305-SEP, in which:

(1) The employer contributions are made only under a definite written allocation formula that is executed within the time for making a deductible contribution (¶4379)[48] that specifies (a) the requirements that an employee must satisfy to share in an allocation, and (b) how the allocated amount is computed. (Code Sec. 408(k)(5))[49]

(2) Employer contributions for a year must be made to each SEP of each employee who has reached age 21, performed service for the employer during at least three of the immediately preceding five years and has received at least $500 in compensation for 2007 (and 2008). (Code Sec. 408(k)(2))[50]

(3) The employer contributions don't discriminate in favor of highly compensated employees. (Code Sec. 408(k)(3)(A))[1]

(4) The employer contributions aren't conditional on the retention in the plan of any portion of the amounts contributed. (Code Sec. 408(k)(4))[2]

(5) The employer doesn't restrict employee withdrawals. (Code Sec. 408(k)(4)(B))[3]

(6) Elective deferrals made by each highly compensated employee under a salary reduction arrangement may not exceed the average of the deferral percentage of all other eligible employees multiplied by 1.25. (Code Sec. 408(k)(6)(A)(iii))[4]

Employer contributions are discriminatory unless they bear a uniform relationship to the first $225,000 (for 2007; $230,000 for 2008) of the compensation (including self-employed income) of each employee maintaining the SEP. (Code Sec. 408(k)(3)(C))[5]

Employees covered by a collective bargaining agreement and nonresident aliens may be excluded from participation in the plan and from the discrimination test under certain conditions. (Code Sec. 408(k)(3)(B))[6]

Maximum allowable contributions made by an employer to a SEP on behalf of an employee for any year cannot exceed the lesser of: (1) 25% of compensation (limited by the annual compensation limit, see ¶4319) from the employer includible in the employee's gross income for the year (determined without regard to the employer's contributions to the SEP), or (2) the dollar limitation for defined contribution plans ($45,000 for 2007; $46,000 for 2008, see ¶4327). (Special calculations are needed for self-employeds, like those for Keogh plans, see ¶4334.) Employee elective deferrals to a SEP (¶4381) do not count towards the limit. Where the SEP is integrated with social security, the dollar limitation in (2) is reduced by the amount taken into account above the integration level, in the case of a highly compensated employee. (Code Sec. 402(h)(2))[7]

48. ¶H-12303; ¶4084.05; TD ¶282,306
49. ¶H-12310; ¶4084.05; TD ¶282,306
50. ¶H-12305; ¶4084.05; TD ¶282,302
1. ¶H-12306; ¶4084.05; TD ¶282,303
2. ¶H-12309; ¶4084.05; TD ¶282,305

3. ¶H-12309; ¶4084.05; TD ¶282,305
4. ¶H-12321; ¶4084.05; TD ¶282,315
5. ¶H-12307; ¶4084.05; TD ¶282,304
6. ¶H-12306; TD ¶282,303
7. ¶s H-12308, H-12311; ¶4084.05; TD ¶282,307

¶ 4379   Employer's deduction for contributions to a SEP.

A contribution by an employer to a SEP is deductible for a tax year if made on account of that year and not later than the time prescribed for filing the return for that year plus extensions.[8] The deduction can't exceed 25% of the compensation paid to the employees during the calendar year, up to the defined contribution plan limit (¶4327). Contributions that exceed this limit can be carried over to, and deducted in, succeeding tax years in order of time. (Code Sec. 404(h))[9]

An employer may elect to use either the calendar year or, subject to such terms and conditions as IRS may prescribe, its own tax year as the computation period for purposes of determining contributions to a SEP. (Code Sec. 408(k)(7)) If the calendar year is used, contributions made for a year are deductible for the employer's tax year with which or within which the calendar year ends. If the employer's "regular" tax year is used, contributions are deductible for that tax year. For purposes of deductibility, contributions are treated as if they were made for a tax year if the contributions are made on account of the tax year and are made not later than the time prescribed by law for filing the return for the tax year, plus extensions. (Code Sec. 404(h)(1)(A), Code Sec. 404(h)(1)(B))[10] Special rules apply where the employer also contributes to other plans. (Code Sec. 404(h)(2), Code Sec. 404(h)(3))[11]

¶ 4380   Employee's treatment of SEP contributions and withdrawals.

Contributions made to a SEP by an employer on behalf of an employee are excluded from the employee's gross income, up to the deduction limits at ¶4379. (Code Sec. 402(h)(1)) Contributions in excess of those limits are taxed to the employee in the year made. (Code Sec. 402(h)(2))[12] Payments made from the SEP are taxed to the recipient under the IRA rules (¶4357). (Code Sec. 402(h)(3))[13]

¶ 4381   Salary reduction SEPs (SARSEPs).

Employers can no longer establish salary reduction SEPs. However, a SEP that's maintained by an employer (except for tax-exempt or governmental employers) with no more than 25 employees at any time during the year before a particular tax year may include a salary reduction arrangement with the SEP for that year, if the plan as in effect on Dec. 31, '96 had a salary reduction arrangement. Not less than 50% of the participating employees must be able to elect to have the employer either make contributions to the SEP on his behalf or pay him cash. The amount of the elective deferrals for any year must satisfy the CODA deferral limits, including catch-up contributions for those age 50 and over (¶4317). Also, the SEP must provide for distribution of excess contributions. (Code Sec. 408(k)(6))[14]

For the saver's credit for lower-income taxpayers' elective contributions to SEPs, see ¶2365.

¶ 4382   "SIMPLE" Retirement Plans. ■■■■■■■■■■■■■■■■■■■■■■■■■■■■■■■

An employer with 100 or fewer employees that doesn't have a qualified plan can establish a "SIMPLE" (savings incentive match plan for employees) retirement plan, without having to meet most requirements for qualified plans.

---

8. ¶H-12312 *et seq.*; ¶4084.05; TD ¶282,311
9. ¶H-12315; ¶4044.08; TD ¶282,309
10. ¶H-12317; ¶4044.08; TD ¶282,311
11. ¶H-12318 *et seq.*; ¶4084.05; TD ¶282,312

12. ¶H-12311; ¶4084.05; TD ¶282,307
13. ¶H-12319.3; TD ¶143,001
14. ¶H-12321; ¶4084.05; TD ¶282,314

¶ 4383   Employers eligible to adopt SIMPLE retirement plans.

A "SIMPLE retirement plan" can be adopted (use Form 5305-SIMPLE, Form 5304-SIM-PLE if there's no designated financial institution, or Form 5305-SA for a SIMPLE individual retirement custodial account) by an employer with 100 or fewer employees who received at least $5,000 of compensation from the employer for the preceding year (Code Sec. 408(p)(2)(C)(i)(I)) that doesn't have another employer-sponsored retirement plan (including a SEP or annuity plan), except for a collectively bargained plan covering employees ineligible to participate in the SIMPLE plan, to which contributions were made or benefits accrued for the year. (Code Sec. 408(p)(2)(D))[15] "Employee" includes a self-employed individual. (Code Sec. 408(p)(6)(B)) A qualifying employer that maintains a SIMPLE plan but later fails to qualify may continue to maintain the plan for two years after its last year of eligibility, subject to certain restrictions for acquisitions, dispositions and similar transactions. (Code Sec. 408(p)(2)(C)(i)(II), Code Sec. 408(p)(10))[16]

¶ 4384   "Qualified salary reduction arrangements" under SIMPLE plans.

Employees designate contributions to be made to a SIMPLE plan under a "qualified salary reduction arrangement." This is a written arrangement under which an employee may elect to have the employer make elective employer contributions (expressed as a percentage of compensation, or, if the employer permits, a specific dollar amount) to a SIMPLE retirement account on behalf of the employee, or to the employee directly in cash. The amount that an employee may elect for any year can't exceed $10,500 for 2007 (and 2008), with inflation indexing in later years. (Code Sec. 408(p)(2)(A)(i), Code Sec. 408(p)(2)(A)(ii), Code Sec. 408(p)(2)(E))[17] SIMPLE 401(k) or SIMPLE IRA participants who are age 50 or over by the end of the plan year may make additional catch-up contributions of up to $2,500 for 2007 (and 2008). (Code Sec. 414(v)(2)(B)(ii), Code Sec. 414(v)(2)(C))[18]

For the saver's credit for lower-income taxpayers' elective contributions to SIMPLE plans, see ¶2365.

The employer must make either:

(1) a matching contribution equal to the amount the employee contributes, up to 3% (Code Sec. 408(p)(2)(C)(ii)(I)) of the employee's compensation for the year, or, electively, as little as 1% in no more than two out of the previous five years, if the employer timely notifies the employees of the lower percentage (Code Sec. 408(p)(2)(C)(ii)(II))[19]; or

(2) a nonelective contribution of 2% of compensation for each employee eligible to participate who has at least $5,000 of compensation from the employer for the year. (Code Sec. 408(p)(2)(B)(i))[20]

No other contributions may be made. (Code Sec. 408(p)(2)(A)(iv); Code Sec. 408(p)(8)) Elective employer contributions must be made no later than 30-days after the month for which the contributions are to be made. (Code Sec. 408(p)(5)(A)(i)) Matching contributions and nonelective contributions must be made by the deductible contribution due date for the year. (Code Sec. 408(p)(5)(A)(ii))[21]

"Compensation" is wages for income tax withholding purposes plus the amount of the employee's elective deferrals (Code Sec. 408(p)(6)(A)(i)) (for a self-employed person, net self-employment earnings (under Code Sec. 1402(a)) without regard to the SIMPLE retirement plan provisions. (Code Sec. 408(p)(6)(A)(ii)) For purposes of determining contributions to a SIMPLE plan, the definition of compensation includes wages paid to domestic workers, even

---

15. ¶H-12351; ¶4084.06; TD ¶282,801
16. ¶H-12352.1; ¶4084.06; TD ¶282,801
17. ¶H-12357; ¶4084.06; TD ¶282,803
18. ¶H-9244.1; ¶4144.26; TD ¶284,114

19. ¶H-12359; ¶4084.06
20. ¶H-12360; ¶4084.06
21. ¶H-12364; ¶4084.06; TD ¶282,809

though those amounts are not subject to income tax withholding. (Code Sec. 408(p)(6)(A)(i))

The compensation taken into account for purposes of determining the amount of the 2% nonelective contribution can't exceed the limit on compensation (under Code Sec. 401(a)(17), see ¶4319) that may be taken into account for the year. (Code Sec. 408(p)(2)(B)(ii))[22]

¶ 4385 SIMPLE retirement account defined.

A "SIMPLE retirement account" into which employer contributions under a SIMPLE retirement plan are made), is an individual retirement account or annuity (Code Sec. 408(p)(1)) for which the only contributions allowed are contributions under a "qualified salary reduction arrangement" and that meets certain vesting, participation and administrative requirements (Code Sec. 408(p)(1)(A)). Employees' rights to all SIMPLE account contributions must be nonforfeitable. (Code Sec. 408(p)(3)) All employees (except those who can be excluded from a qualified plan (Code Sec. 408(p)(4)(B)) who received at least $5,000 in compensation from the employer during any two preceding years (Code Sec. 408(p)(4)(A)(i)), and are reasonably expected to receive at least $5,000 in compensation during the current year (Code Sec. 408(p)(4)(A)(ii)) must be eligible either to elect to make a salary reduction contribution or receive nonelective contributions. (Code Sec. 408(p)(4)(A))[23]

¶ 4386 Contributions to SIMPLE retirement accounts.

Employer contributions to SIMPLE accounts are deductible in the employer's tax year with which (or within which) the calendar year for which the contributions were made ends. (Code Sec. 404(m)(1); Code Sec. 404(m)(2)(A)) Contributions are treated as made for the tax year if they are made (a) on account of that year, and (b) not later than the time for filing that year's tax return (including extensions). (Code Sec. 404(m)(2)(B))[24]

✓*observation:* "Employer contributions" include elective contributions, matching contributions, and nonelective contributions.

Contributions to simplified employee pensions are excluded from the employee's income similar to the rules for SEPs under Code Sec. 402(h)(1) (¶4380). Employees aren't entitled to a deduction for employer contributions made on their behalf to a SIMPLE retirement account. (Code Sec. 219(b)(4)) Any elective contributions under a SIMPLE retirement plan are included in the sum of elective deferrals, subject to an annual limit on the amount that can be excluded from income. (Code Sec. 402(g)(3)(D))[25] Matching contributions on behalf of self-employed persons aren't treated as employer elective contributions for this purpose. (Code Sec. 408(p)(9))[26]

✓*observation:* Thus, matching SIMPLE contributions for a self-employed person don't count toward the annual limit on elective deferrals (¶4317).

¶ 4387 SIMPLE retirement account distributions.

Rules similar to those for distributions from simplified employee pensions (SEPs), apply to SIMPLE retirement accounts. (Code Sec. 402(k)) Thus, they are taxed under the rules relating to IRAs in the year of distribution. (Code Sec. 402(h)(3))[27] For tax-free rollovers of SIMPLE retirement account distributions, see ¶4357.[28] For early withdrawal penalties for SIMPLE account distributions, see ¶4344.[29]

¶ 4388 Tax-Sheltered 403(b) Annuities. ▬▬▬▬▬▬▬▬▬▬▬

Employees of tax-exempt educational, charitable, religious, etc., organizations, or

---

22. ¶H-12358; ¶4084.06
23. ¶H-12361; ¶4084.06; TD ¶282,807
24. ¶H-12372; ¶4084.06; TD ¶282,811
25. ¶H-12373; TD ¶282,813

26. ¶H-12357; ¶4084.06
27. ¶H-12374; ¶4084.06; TD ¶282,814
28. ¶H-12375; TD ¶282,816
29. ¶H-12377; TD ¶282,815

public schools get special tax advantages from annuities bought for them by the exempt employers.

Tax-sheltered annuities offer benefits similar to those under a qualified employee plan. The tax isn't imposed when the annuity is bought, but is deferred until payments are received. (Code Sec. 403(b); Reg § 1.403(b)-1)[30] These annuities may be bought only for common law employees of certain exempt educational, charitable, religious, etc., employers, and by or for certain self-employed ministers. (Code Sec. 403(b)(1)(A))[31] The annuity must be nonforfeitable (except for failure to pay premiums) and nontransferable. (Code Sec. 403(b)(1)(C); Reg § 1.401-9(b)(3))[32] Certain elective deferral limits must be met if the annuity is part of a salary reduction arrangement (¶4390). (Code Sec. 403(b)(1)(E))[33] Also, except for annuities bought by church employers, certain nondiscrimination tests must be met. (Code Sec. 403(b)(1)(D), Code Sec. 403(b)(12))[34] Tax-sheltered annuities are treated as defined contribution plans for purposes of the contribution limits (¶4327).[35]

For tax years beginning after 2008, IRS regs will reduce the extent to which the 403(b) rules differ from the rules for arrangements such as 401(k) plans, and 457(b) plans. Included among these changes are the requirement that a 403(b) plan be operated in accordance with a written plan document, that the 403(b) plan meet nondiscrimination "universal availability" requirement. One key change under the IRS regs takes effect before 2009. So-called 90-24 transfers, which allow a 403(b) contract to be exchanged for an annuity contract outside the plan without income inclusion, are no longer allowed as of Sept. 24, 2007. (Reg § 1.403(b)-1 through Reg § 1.403(b)-11)

¶ 4389   How tax-sheltered annuity arrangements work.

Employees of a qualifying employer can get a prescribed amount of their compensation in the form of a tax-sheltered annuity. The employee pays no immediate tax on the amount the employer pays for the annuity, but is taxed under the regular annuity rules (¶1355 *et seq.*) when the annuity payments are made. (Code Sec. 403(b)(1))[36]

The tax deferral is denied for distributions attributable to contributions made under a salary reduction agreement (¶4390), unless the annuity provides that payments may be paid only: (1) when the employee attains age 59 ½, separates from employment, dies, or becomes disabled, or (2) in the case of hardship. (Code Sec. 403(b)(11)) (The premature distribution penalty applies, ¶4344). (Code Sec. 72(t)) The contract may not provide for the distribution of any income attributable to such contributions in the case of hardship. (Code Sec. 403(b)(11))[37] Tax-sheltered annuities are subject to the loan rules at ¶4343. (Code Sec. 72(p)(4)(A))[38]

IRS has relaxed its rules so that 403(b) plans can choose to make hardship distributions available to victims of Hurricane Katrina, Rita or Wilma, and members of their families. In addition, special rules apply to qualified hurricane distributions from, and rollovers to, 403(b) plans, see ¶4344.

For rollovers to and from Code Sec. 403(b) plans, see ¶4359 and ¶4360.

¶ 4390   Tax-sheltered annuity salary-reduction agreements.

An employee of a qualifying employer can agree to reduce his salary or forego an increase as a means of contributing to a 403(b) plan. The rules that apply to cash or deferred arrangements under Code Sec. 401(k) (¶4317) determine how often a salary reduction may be entered into, the compensation to which the agreement applies, and the ability to revoke the agreement.[39]

---

30. ¶H-12400 *et seq.*; ¶4034.04; TD ¶135,506
31. ¶s H-12402, H-12409; ¶4034.04
32. ¶H-12415; ¶4034.04
33. ¶H-12427 *et seq.*; ¶4034.04
34. ¶H-12420; ¶4034.04

35. ¶H-12454 *et seq.*; ¶4034.04; TD ¶284,029
36. ¶H-12431
37. ¶H-12430; ¶4034.04
38. ¶H-11066; ¶724.23
39. ¶H-12419.1; ¶4034.04

All of the employer's employees (except those covered by a CODA or an eligible Code Sec. 457 plan for tax-exempt and governmental employers) must get a chance to elect to have the employer contribute more than $200 under the salary reduction agreement, on a nondiscriminatory basis, if *any* employee may so elect. (Code Sec. 403(b)(12)(A))[40] The employee's elective deferrals for a year can't exceed the CODA limits, including catch-up contributions for those age 50 or over (¶4317). (Code Sec. 403(b)(1)(E), Reg § 1.403(b)-4(c))[41]

A 403(b) plan can include a qualified Roth contribution program (see ¶4375).

For tax years beginning after 2008, the 403(b) annuity must be maintained pursuant to a written defined contribution plan that sets out all of the material terms and conditions for eligibility, benefits, distributions, etc. (Reg § 1.403(b)-3(b)(3)(i))

For the saver's credit for lower-income taxpayers' contributions to 403(b) annuities, see ¶2365.

¶ 4391 Tax-sheltered annuity contribution limit.

If a qualifying employer buys a tax-sheltered annuity for an employee and employee's rights are nonforfeitable, the premium paid is not taxable to the employee at that time, up to the applicable limit for a defined contribution plan under Code Sec. 415 (¶4327). (Code Sec. 403(b)(1), Code Sec. 415(c)(1), Code Sec. 415(k)(4), Reg § 1.403(b)-3(b)(3))[42]

Special limits apply for contributions by church plans. (Code Sec. 415(c)(7))

¶ 4392 "Includible compensation" and "years of service."

"Includible compensation" means the amount of compensation received by the employee from the qualified employer that is includible in his gross income (without regard to the exclusion for certain foreign source earned income) for the most recent period ending not later than the close of the employee's tax year that can be counted as one "year of service" and which precedes the tax year by no more than five years. Amounts contributed by the employer for tax-sheltered annuities are not included. Elective deferrals and any amount contributed or deferred by the employer at the employee's election that is excluded from income under Code Sec. 125 or Code Sec. 457 are included. (Code Sec. 403(b)(3))[43]

"Includible compensation" doesn't include any compensation *earned* when the employer wasn't a qualified employer. But it's immaterial whether the employer was qualified when the compensation is actually *received* by the employee.[44]

Similar rules will apply to compensation received from "eligible employers" for tax years after 2008. (Reg § 1.403(b)-2(b)(11))

The employee's "years of service," which can't be less than one, includes one year for each full year he was a full-time employee of the organization buying the annuity for him, plus a fraction of each year, as prescribed by regs, for each full year he was a part-time employee, or for each part of a year he was a full- or part-time employee. (Code Sec. 403(b)(4))[45]

For tax years after 2008, an employee's years of service equals the aggregate of the annual work periods during which he is employed by the eligible employer. (Reg § 1.403(b)-4(e))

---

40. ¶H-12420; ¶4034.04
41. ¶H-12427; ¶4034.04
42. ¶H-12439; ¶4034.04

43. ¶H-12443; ¶4034.04
44. ¶H-12443; ¶4034.04
45. ¶H-12444 *et seq.*; ¶4034.04

Chapter 22   Farmers

¶ 4500   Farmers.

Farmers get tax breaks not generally available to others: three-year income averaging, a generally longer NOL carryback period, favorable accounting and inventory methods, income deferrals, capital gain-ordinary loss treatment and the deduction of items normally capitalized.

¶ 4501   Farmers' income and expenses—Schedule F (Form 1040).

A farmer's gross income includes cash and the fair market value of goods received ("barter income") from crops, produce, poultry and livestock. (Reg § 1.61-4(c)) The value of produce consumed by the farmer and his family isn't included, but expenses incurred in raising that produce can't be deducted.[1] Payments from the National Tobacco Settlement Trust must be reported as income.[2]

Farmers may deduct the ordinary and necessary expenses of operating a farm for profit — e.g., rent, labor, feed (¶4514), fertilizer (¶4515). (Reg § 1.162-12(a))[3] For required capitalization of certain expenses, see ¶4518. Where farming isn't engaged in for profit, see ¶1779.

¶ 4502   Three-year averaging for farming or fishing income—Schedule J.

An individual (including a partner in a partnership and a shareholder of an S corporation, but not including an estate or trust) engaged in a farming or fishing business may elect three-year averaging of "elected farm income" (below) for regular income tax (but not for employment tax) purposes. If the election is made, the tax for the year is equal to the sum of (1) the tax computed on taxable income reduced by elected farm or fishing income, and (2) the increase in tax that would result if taxable income for the three prior tax years were increased by an amount equal to one-third of the elected farm or fishing income. Any adjustment under this provision for any tax year is taken into account in applying this provision for any later tax year. (Code Sec. 1301(a); Code Sec. 1301(b)(3); Reg § 1.1301-1(b)) Taxable income for prior years can be less than zero, but in that case any amount that may provide a benefit in another tax year (such as an NOL) is added back in determining base year taxable income. (Reg § 1.1301-1(d)(2))[4]

Elect by filing Form 1040, Schedule J with a return for the election year (including a late or amended return if the time for filing for a credit or refund has not expired). An individual may change or revoke a previous election, if the period of limitation on filing a claim for credit or refund has not expired for the election year. (Reg § 1.1301-1(c))

"Elected farm income" means the amount of taxable income for the tax year attributable to any farming or fishing business that's specified in the election to average farm or fishing income (Code Sec. 1301(b)(1)(A)) including farm wages paid to an S shareholder (Reg § 1.1301-1(e)(1)) and certain crop-share income. (Reg § 1.1301-1(b)(2)) Gain from the sale or other disposition of property (other than land) regularly used by the taxpayer in a farming or fishing business for a substantial period is treated as attributable to that farming business. (Code Sec. 1301(b)(1)(B); Reg § 1.1301-1(e)(1)(ii)(A))[5] A landlord is engaged in a farming business for farm averaging purposes for rental income based on a share of production (not fixed rent) from a tenant's farming business determined under a written agreement

---

1. ¶N-1151; ¶1624.340; TD ¶116,001
2. ¶N-1174
3. ¶N-1301; ¶1624.340; TD ¶297,501

4. ¶N-1500 *et seq.*; ¶13,014; TD ¶119,001 *et seq.*
5. ¶N-1500 *et seq.*; ¶13,014; TD ¶s 119,003, 119,004

References beginning with a single letter are to paragraphs in RIA's Federal Tax Coordinator 2d and RIA's Analysis of Federal Taxes: Income. Those beginning with numbers are to paragraphs in RIA's United States Tax Reporter. Those beginning with TD are to paragraphs in RIA's Tax Desk.

entered into before the tenant begins significant activities on the land. Tobacco quota payments don't qualify for income averaging. [6]

Electing income averaging does not cause the taxpayer's AMT to increase because regular tax liability for determining the AMT is computed as though the election had not been made, see ¶3201.

¶ 4503 Three- or five-year NOL carryback.

Although net operating losses (NOLs) generally may be carried back only two years, a taxpayer engaged in the business of farming gets a three-year carryback for NOLs (other than those that qualify for the five-year carryback, below) attributable to Presidentially declared disasters (Code Sec. 172(b)(1)(F)(ii)(III))[7], see ¶1843. And "farming losses" (any NOL attributable to the income and deductions of a farming business, but not in excess of the taxpayer's NOL for the year) may be carried back five years (Code Sec. 172(b)(1)(G)) (and forward for the regular 20-year period). [8] Farmers may elect (by the due date, including extensions, for the loss year, or, if a timely return was filed, on an amended return within six months of the original return due date) not to have the five-year carryback apply, in which case the regular NOL rules apply (¶1843); once made, the election is irrevocable for that year. (Code Sec. 172(i)(3))[9]

NOLs incurred before Jan. 1, 2007, by certain small timber owners in areas affected by Hurricane Katrina, Wilma, or Rita are treated as farming losses and allowed a 5-year carryback. (Code Sec. 1400N(i)(2))[10]

¶ 4504 Farmers' accounting methods.

Farmers (unless listed at ¶4509) may use the cash method (¶4505), the accrual method (¶4508), the crop method (¶4511), or a "hybrid" method combining any of these methods if it clearly reflects income (¶2817). (Reg § 1.61-4, Reg § 1.446-1(c), Reg § 1.471-6(a))[11]

While most taxpayers who produce, buy or sell merchandise must use inventories (and therefore the accrual method, see ¶2863), farmers may choose not to, except to the extent they are subject to the uniform capitalization rules (¶4518). (Reg § 1.471-6(a))[12] But a farmer who does use inventories must use the accrual method at least for purchases and sales. [13] However, IRS has excepted the following from having to account for inventories or use an accrual method of accounting: (1) any business with average annual gross receipts of $1 million or less; and (2) taxpayers whose principal business activity is not mining, manufacturing, wholesale trade, retail trade, or information industries, for all of their trades or businesses, if average annual gross receipts are $10 million ($5 million for C corporations) or less, see ¶2818.

¶ 4505 Cash method farmers.

Cash method farmers include income in the year actually or constructively received, whichever is earlier (¶2819). Gross income includes receipts of: (1) proceeds from sales of *raised* livestock or produce; (2) profits from the sale of any *purchased* property, including livestock, (3) breeding fees, (4) fees from renting teams, machinery or land, (5) taxable subsidy and conservation payments, (6) crop insurance proceeds, and (7) all other gross income. (Reg § 1.61-4(a))[14] For deferral of insurance proceeds and forced livestock sales, see ¶4507.

Expenses are ordinarily deductible in the year paid (other than the cost of animals and

---

6. ¶N-1501 *et seq.*; ¶13,014; TD ¶s 119,003, 119,004

7. ¶M-4305.2; ¶1724.436; TD ¶356,011

8. ¶M-4305.3; ¶1724.437; TD ¶356,012

9. ¶M-4305.4; ¶1724.437; TD ¶356,013

10. ¶M-4305.4; ¶14,00N4.05; TD ¶356,012.1

11. ¶N-1010 *et seq.*; ¶s 614.053, 4464.09; TD ¶118,001

12. ¶N-1100 *et seq.*; ¶4714.73; TD ¶118,002

13. ¶N-1017; TD ¶118,009

14. ¶N-1013; ¶614.054; TD ¶118,002

plants bought for resale, see ¶4506). (Reg § 1.61-4(a))[15] For feed expenses, see ¶4514, and for pre-paid expenses, see ¶4516. An option to accelerate the receipt of any payment under a production flexibility contract that is payable under the FAIR Act of 1996 as in effect on Dec. 17, '99 won't accelerate the recognition of income unless the option is exercised. (Sec. 525 of P.L. 106-170) The constructive receipt rules also don't apply to options to receive payments under the Farm Security and Rural Investment Act of 2002. [16]

¶ 4506 Cash method farmer's deduction of costs of purchased animals and plants—election to deduct in year bought or year sold.

Cash method farmers generally deduct the costs of animals and plants bought for resale only in the year the animals or plants are disposed of. (Reg § 1.61-4(a)) But for these animals and plants, a farmer may elect to deduct the costs either for the year they are purchased or for the year they are sold, if the method chosen clearly reflects income:

. . . baby chicks and pullets bought for raising and resale;

. . . hens bought for commercial egg production;

. . . seeds and young plants (other than Christmas trees, orchards and timber) bought for further development and cultivation before sale. (Reg § 1.162-12)[17]

The farmer makes the election by deducting the cost for the first year in which he buys the items. Once the farmer elects this option —which is a method of accounting—he must use it consistently until IRS consents to a change (¶2838).[18]

¶ 4507 One-year deferral elections for cash method farmers—"disaster" receipts.

A cash method farmer can elect to defer reporting certain insurance proceeds and federal disaster payments (including payments under Title II (but not Title I) of the '88 Disaster Assistance Act) until the tax year after the year of the destruction or damage to, or inability to plant, the crops, if he shows that under his practice, the income from the crops would be reported in a later year. To elect, check box in Part I on Schedule F and attach a statement to the return (or amended return) for the year payments are received. (Code Sec. 451(d); Reg § 1.451-6)[19]

One-year deferral also may be elected for income from livestock sold on account of a drought, flood or other weather-related condition so severe the sale had to take place in an earlier year than normal. Elect on a statement attached to the return for the sale year. (Code Sec. 451(e)(1); Reg § 1.451-7(g)) However, if the period for buying replacement property for such livestock under the involuntary conversion rules is extended to four years from the end of the year of sale (see ¶2438), the election of one-year deferral is valid if made during that replacement period. (Code Sec. 451(e)(3)) [20] (For involuntary conversions, see ¶2432.)

¶ 4508 Accrual method farmers.

Accrual farmers include farm income for the year earned, regardless of when payment is received, and deduct farm expenses for the year the "all events test" is met (¶2824 *et seq.*). Inventories must be used (¶4512). (Code Sec. 461(h); Reg § 1.61-4(b); Reg § 1.446-1(c))[21]

An accrual farmer's gross income for a tax year is the sum of: (1) the sales price of all livestock and other products held for sale that are sold during the year, (2) the inventory value of the livestock, etc. (i.e., the proceeds from the disposition of livestock, etc., during the

15. ¶614.054; TD ¶297,500
16. ¶N-1152.1; ¶4514.039
17. ¶s N-1021, N-1022; TD ¶118,007
18. ¶N-1022; TD ¶118,007

19. ¶N-1024 *et seq.*; ¶s 614.054, 4514.171; TD ¶118,005
20. ¶N-1031 *et seq.*; ¶4514.176; TD ¶118,003
21. ¶N-1017; ¶4614.15; TD ¶118,009

year, plus the inventory value of livestock, etc., not sold at the end of the year, reduced by the inventory value of livestock, etc., on hand at the start of the year, and by the cost of any livestock, etc., bought during the year and included in inventory), (3) miscellaneous farm receipts, e.g., fees from breeding or from renting teams, (4) all subsidy and conservation payments includible that year, plus (5) gross income from all other sources. Crop shares are included in the year they are reduced to money or its equivalent. (Reg § 1.61-4(b))[22]

¶ 4509   When accrual accounting is mandatory for farmers.

Corporations (except as noted below) and any partnership in which a corporation is a partner must use the accrual method of accounting to compute their taxable income from farming (as must tax shelters, which include farm syndicates, see ¶4510). Raisers and harvesters of nut and fruit trees are covered by this rule, but nurseries, sod farms and raisers and harvesters of other types of trees aren't. (Code Sec. 447(a))[23]

The mandatory accrual rule doesn't apply to:

(1) S corporations. (Code Sec. 447(c)(1))

(2) A "family corporation" (family members own at least 50% of (a) the total combined voting power of all voting stock, and (b) the total number of shares of all other classes of stock) other than one whose gross receipts exceed $25 million for any tax year. (Code Sec. 447(c)(2), Code Sec. 447(d)(2))[24] Two- or three-family corporations must meet special ownership tests, and must have been engaged in farming since Oct. 4, '76. (Code Sec. 447(h))[25]

(3) A corporation whose gross receipts (or any predecessor's) don't exceed $1 million for any tax year. (Code Sec. 447(c)(2), Code Sec. 447(d)(1))[26]

(4) Certain corporations (and partnerships having a corporate partner) engaged in growing sugar cane, that used "annual accrual" accounting methods for that business for a ten-year period ending with its first tax year starting after '75. (Code Sec. 447(g))[27]

¶ 4510   Tax shelters and farming syndicates.

All tax shelters, including farming syndicates, must use the accrual method. (Code Sec. 448(a)(3))[28] For pre-paid expenses, see ¶4516. For uniform capitalization rules, see ¶4518. For tax shelter losses for AMT purposes, see ¶3209.

A farming syndicate is any partnership (or other noncorporate enterprise) or S corporation engaged in the business of farming if:

. . . at any time, interests in the partnership, etc., have been offered for sale in an offering required to be registered with any federal or state agency having authority to regulate the offering of securities for sale; or

. . . more than 35% of the losses during any periods are allocable to limited partners or limited entrepreneurs (Code Sec. 464(c)); or

. . . it's a tax shelter. (Code Sec. 461(i)(3), Code Sec. 461(i)(4))[29]

¶ 4511   Crop method.

A farmer may, with IRS consent, use the crop method to report income from crops (other than timber) for which the process of planting, harvesting and sale isn't completed within the

---

22. ¶N-1014, N-1017; ¶614.051; TD ¶118,009
23. ¶N-1036 *et seq.*; ¶4474; TD ¶118,012
24. ¶s N-1036, N-1040; ¶4474; TD ¶118,012
25. ¶N-1056; ¶4474; TD ¶118,013

26. ¶N-1036; ¶4474; TD ¶118,012
27. ¶N-1049; ¶4474; TD ¶118,012
28. ¶G-2456; ¶4484; TD ¶118,001
29. ¶G-2456 *et seq.*; ¶4644; TD ¶442,023

same tax year. (Reg § 1.61-4(c))[30] Under this method, all expenses of the crop (including expenses of seed or young plants) are charged, and all crop receipts are credited, to a crop account. Profit (or loss) is realized and included in income (or loss deducted) only in the year the crop is harvested and disposed of. (Reg § 1.61-4(c), Reg § 1.162-12(a))[31]

¶ 4512   Farmers' inventories.

A farmer using inventories (¶4513) *must* inventory:

... all livestock and poultry, raised or purchased, held primarily for sale (Reg § 1.61-4(b));

... all harvested and purchased farm products held for sale, feed, or seed, such as grain, hay ensilage, concentrates, cotton, tobacco;

... supplies, unless only small amounts are on hand;

... if in the hatchery business, eggs in incubation and growing and pre-market chickens. (Inventories *may* be used for hens primarily held for egg production which are also held for sale after their egg-producing life.) [32]

Livestock held for dairy, breeding, sporting or draft purposes may be inventoried at the taxpayer's election. But raised livestock must be inventoried by farmers using the unit-livestock-price method. (Reg § 1.61-4(b), Reg § 1.471-6(f))[33]

¶ 4513   Inventory valuation methods for farmers.

Methods that farmers use to value inventory include:

... *Cost method* (¶2869). (Reg § 1.471-3)[34]

... *Lower-of-cost-or-market method* (¶2870). (Reg § 1.471-4)[35]

... *Farm price method.* Each item, raised or purchased, is valued at its market price less estimated direct cost of disposition. A farmer using this method must use it for all his inventory, but may use the unit-livestock-price method for livestock. (Reg § 1.471-6(d))[36]

... *Unit-livestock-price method.* Livestock is reasonably classified according to kind and age. A standard unit price is used for each animal within a class. Unit prices must reflect costs capitalized under the uniform capitalization rules, see ¶4518. Once established, the accounting methods used to determine unit prices and to classify animals must be consistently applied in all future tax years. Users of this method must annually reevaluate their unit prices and adjust them to reflect increases or decreases in the costs of raising livestock. IRS consent isn't required for these adjustments; however it is required for other changes in classification or unit prices. (Reg § 1.471-6(f))[37]

¶ 4514   Feed.

The cost of feed is a deductible business expense. (Reg § 1.162-12(a))[38] A cash method farmer may deduct in the year paid, the cost of feed his livestock will consume that year. Payments for feed to be used in the next tax year ("pre-paid feed") aren't deductible until the year of consumption, except the farmer may deduct pre-paid feed expenses in the payment year if: (1) the payment represents a purchase and not a deposit, (2) the advance payment is for a business purpose and not merely for tax avoidance, *and* (3) deduction in the payment year doesn't materially distort income. [39] For pre-paid farm expenses generally, see ¶4516.

---

30. ¶N-1018 *et seq.*; ¶614.056; TD ¶118,010
31. ¶N-1019; ¶614.056; TD ¶118,010
32. ¶N-1102; ¶614.057; TD ¶298,001
33. ¶s N-1109, N-1113; ¶s 614.057, 4714.73; TD ¶298,001
34. ¶N-1106; ¶s 614.057, 4714.41, 4714.73; TD ¶298,003

35. ¶N-1107; ¶s 614.057, 4714.51; TD ¶298,004
36. ¶N-1112; ¶s 614.057, 4714.73; TD ¶298,005
37. ¶N-1113; ¶s 614.057, 4714.73; TD ¶298,006
38. ¶N-1311; ¶1624.340; TD ¶297,514
39. ¶N-1312; ¶1624.340; TD ¶297,515

¶ 4515   Fertilizer.

The cost of acquiring fertilizer, lime, marl, and other materials used to enrich, neutralize, or condition farmland, and the costs of applying them, are deductible in the year the costs are paid or incurred if the benefit doesn't last beyond one year. If the benefit lasts substantially more than a year (so the costs would have to be capitalized), the farmer may either capitalize the costs or elect to deduct them in the year paid or incurred (Code Sec. 180(a))[40] by deducting them on his return for that year. (Code Sec. 180(c); Reg § 1.180-2)[41] The election to deduct isn't allowable for costs of preparing land not previously used for farming by the taxpayer or his tenant. (Code Sec. 180(b); Reg § 1.180-1(b))[42]

If fertilizer expenses are capitalized, the taxpayer may deduct a portion of the capitalized amounts for each year the benefits last. The portion deducted each year need not be the same if benefits are clearly greater in the early years. [43]

¶ 4516   Pre-paid farm expenses.

A cash method taxpayer's current deduction for pre-paid farm expenses (i.e., for feed, seed, fertilizer, and similar farm supplies that won't be used until a later tax year) is limited to one-half of his other deductible farming expenses for the year (for a special rule for feed, see ¶4514). The "excess" part (i.e., over that one-half amount) isn't deductible until the year the supplies are used. (Code Sec. 464(f)(1), Code Sec. 464(f)(2))[44] This rule also applies to farming syndicates (required to use the accrual method, see ¶4510). (Code Sec. 464(a))[45]

But this limit *doesn't apply* if the taxpayer's (or a family member's) principal home (within the meaning of Code Sec. 121, see ¶2442) is a farm or his principal business is farming, if: (1) for the three preceding tax years, his total pre-paid farm expenses are less than 50% of his total other deductible farm expenses, or (2) for the current year, his pre-paid farm expenses are more than 50% of his other farm expenses because of a change in business operations attributable to extraordinary circumstances. (Code Sec. 464(f)(3))[46]

¶ 4517   Pre-productive period expenses.

The taxpayer has the option to either deduct or capitalize certain costs of developing and operating his farm and crops (e.g., taxes, interest, upkeep) during its pre-productive period (Reg § 1.162-12(a))[47] (subject to the uniform capitalization rules, see ¶4518). But he can't deduct any capital expenditures. [48] The pre-productive period begins when the farmer first acquires the seed or plant, and ends when the plant produces marketable quantities or is reasonably expected to be sold or otherwise disposed of. (Code Sec. 263A(e)(3))[49]

¶ 4518   Application of uniform capitalization rules to farmers and ranchers.

Farmers and ranchers are subject to the uniform capitalization rules for taxpayers generally (¶1660) with respect to the production, growing, or raising of property that:

. . . is produced by a farmer required to use the accrual method (¶4509), (Code Sec. 263A(a), Code Sec. 263A(d)(1); Reg § 1.263A-4(a), Reg § 1.263A-4(b)) or

. . . has a pre-productive period (¶4517), of more than two years. (Code Sec. 263A(d)(1)(A)(ii))

---

40. ¶N-1306; ¶1804; TD ¶297,510
41. ¶N-1307; TD ¶297,511
42. ¶N-1306; TD ¶297,510
43. ¶N-1306; TD ¶297,510
44. ¶N-1319 *et seq.*; ¶4644; TD ¶297,519

45. ¶N-1319 *et seq.*; ¶4644; TD ¶297,519
46. ¶N-1319; ¶4644; TD ¶297,520
47. ¶N-1302; ¶1624.349; TD ¶298,009
48. ¶N-1303; ¶1624.349; TD ¶298,009
49. ¶N-1074; TD ¶298,009

For taxpayers not required to use the accrual method, the uniform capitalization rules *don't apply* to costs related to any animal, or plant with a pre-productive period of two years or less, which is produced by a taxpayer in a farming business. (Code Sec. 263A(d)(1)(A); Reg § 1.263A-4(a)(2))[50] The preproductive period is the period before the first marketable crop or yield, for plants that have more than one crop or yield (e.g., the orange tree); the period before a crop or yield is disposed of, for the crop or yield of a plant that will have more than one crop or yield (e.g., the orange); or, for any other plant, the period before it is disposed of. (Reg § 1.263A-4(b)(2)) IRS has published a noninclusive list of plants with preproductive periods in excess of 2 years. [1]

For exception for replanting because of casualties, see ¶4519. For election out of the uniform capitalization rules, see ¶4520.

¶ 4519   Exception to uniform capitalization rules for replanting because of casualties.

The uniform capitalization rules (¶4518) don't apply to costs incurred for the replanting, cultivation, maintenance and development of plants bearing an edible crop for human consumption (including citrus or almond) that were lost or damaged (while in the taxpayer's hands) by freezing temperatures, disease, drought, pests, or casualty (replanting costs). (Code Sec. 263A(d)(2)(A); Reg § 1.263A-4(e)(1), Reg § 1.263A-4(e)(4))[2]

This casualty exception generally applies to the costs of the person owning ("owner") the plants at the time of the loss or damage. But costs paid or incurred by another person (payor) in any tax year also may qualify if in that year: (1) the owner has a more-than-50% equity interest in the plants, and (2) the payor owns any of the remaining equity interest in them *and* materially participates in their planting, maintenance, cultivation or development. (Code Sec. 263A(d)(2)(B); Reg § 1.263A-4(e)(2))[3]

¶ 4520   Farmers' election to have uniform capitalization rules not apply.

Except as noted below, a farmer may elect to have the uniform capitalization rules at ¶4518 *not* apply to any plant produced in his farm business (Code Sec. 263A(d)(3)(A)), so he may currently deduct all otherwise deductible pre-productive costs. [4]

If the taxpayer or any related person (as specially defined) makes the election, he must use the Code Sec. 168(g)(2) alternative (i.e., straight-line) depreciation for all his property used predominantly in the farming business that was placed in service in any tax year during which the election is in effect (Code Sec. 263A(e)(2)(A); Reg § 1.263A-4(d)(4)(ii)) and follow other requirements in the regs. (Reg § 1.263A-4(d)(4))[5]

If the election is made, any plant with respect to which amounts would have been capitalized *but for* the election is treated as Code Sec. 1245 property (if it's not otherwise Code Sec. 1245 property). (Code Sec. 263A(e)(1)(A)(i); Reg § 1.263A-4(d)(4)(i)) Deductible amounts that *but for* the election would have been capitalized are treated as depreciation deductions for Code Sec. 1245 purposes (Code Sec. 263A(e)(1)(A)(ii), Code Sec. 263A(e)(1)(B)) so that they are recaptured as ordinary income when the product is disposed of, see ¶2695.[6]

The election can't be made with respect to any item attributable to the planting, maintenance or development of any citrus or almond grove (or part of a grove) that's incurred before the close of the fourth tax year beginning with the tax year the trees were planted. For this purpose, the portion of a grove planted in one tax year must be treated separately from the

50. ¶N-1071 et seq.; ¶263A4; TD ¶298,011
1. ¶N-1071.1; ¶263A4.15
2. ¶N-1081; ¶1624.339; TD ¶298,014
3. ¶N-1082; ¶263A4; TD ¶298,014

4. ¶N-1084; ¶263A4; TD ¶298,015
5. ¶N-1090; ¶263A4; TD ¶298,015
6. ¶N-1093; ¶263A4; TD ¶298,015

portion planted in another tax year. (Code Sec. 263A(d)(3)(C); Reg § 1.263A-4(d)(2))[7]

Elect out of UNICAP by not applying the rules of Code Sec. 263A to determine the capitalized costs of plants produced in a farming business and by applying the rules of Reg § 1.263A-4(d)(4) on original return for the first tax year capitalization of Code Sec. 263A costs is required. For partnerships or S corporations, the election is made by the partner, shareholder, or member. (Code Sec. 263A(d)(3)(D); Reg § 1.263A-4(d)(3)(i)) A taxpayer that does not make the automatic election described above must get IRS consent (¶2838) to change accounting methods. (Reg § 1.263A-4(d)(3)(ii))[8] The election can't be made by farmers who must use the accrual method of accounting, see ¶4509. (Code Sec. 263A(d)(3)(B))[9]

¶ 4521 Soil and water conservation and erosion prevention costs.

Farmers may deduct currently, as business expenses, certain outlays for soil and water conservation or erosion prevention that are incurred to maintain the farm and preserve its normal productivity, and not to increase its value or convert it to a new use. Costs that result in the acquisition of depreciable property must be capitalized. [10]

But a farmer may elect to deduct certain nondepreciable expenditures for conservation, etc., with respect to land he uses for farming (Code Sec. 175(a)) if the expenditures are consistent with a federal or state approved conservation plan. (Code Sec. 175(c)(3))[11] Qualifying expenditures include costs of: treating or moving earth (e.g., leveling, terracing or restoring fertility); constructing and protecting diversion channels, drainage ditches, earthen dams; eradicating brush; planting windbreaks; producing vegetation primarily to conserve soil or water, or prevent soil erosion. (Code Sec. 175(c); Reg § 1.175-2(a), Reg § 1.175-2(b)(2)) Costs of draining or filling wetlands or for center pivot irrigation systems don't qualify. (Code Sec. 175(c)(3)(B)) Nor does the election apply to depreciable assets. (Reg § 1.175-1)[12]

The amount of conservation, etc., expenses a farmer may deduct in any tax year under this election can't exceed 25% of his gross income from farming for the year. Any excess may be carried over to and deducted in the next tax year (subject to that year's 25% ceiling). (Code Sec. 175(b); Reg § 1.175-5(b))[13]

Elect by deducting the expenses on the return for the first tax year they are incurred. (Reg § 1.175-6(a))[14] IRS consent is needed to elect for a year other than that first year. (Code Sec. 175(d)(2))[15] Once the election is made, a farmer must continue to deduct all qualifying expenditures (subject to the 25% ceiling) unless IRS consents to a change. (Code Sec. 175(e))[16]

A farmer must recapture as ordinary income (use Form 4797) part of the conservation, etc., expenses if the farm land is disposed of after being held for less than 10 years. (Code Sec. 1252)[17]

¶ 4522 Depreciation for farm property—Form 4562.

A farmer may take depreciation deductions (on Form 4562) on property used in a farming business (Code Sec. 168(b)(2)(B)), including: buildings (except his dwelling); farm machinery; other physical property (not including land); orchards (trees and vines bearing fruits or nuts); and draft, breeding, sporting or dairy livestock (unless inventoried). (Reg § 1.167(a)-6(b))[18]

Most farm property is depreciated under MACRS using the 150% declining balance method (switching to straight-line for the first tax year for which that method would give a larger allowance). However, nonresidential real property, and trees or vines bearing fruits or nuts

7. ¶N-1089; ¶263A4; TD ¶298,015
8. ¶N-1087; ¶263A4; TD ¶298,016
9. ¶N-1085; ¶263A4; TD ¶298,015
10. ¶N-1401; ¶1754; TD ¶299,001
11. ¶N-1402; ¶1754.02; TD ¶299,002
12. ¶s N-1406, N-1407; ¶1754.02; TD ¶299,002

13. ¶N-1415; ¶1754.02; TD ¶299,015
14. ¶N-1420; TD ¶299,020
15. ¶N-1421; ¶1754; TD ¶299,021
16. ¶N-1422; TD ¶299,022
17. ¶N-1423; ¶12,524; TD ¶299,023
18. ¶N-1304; ¶1674.035; TD ¶298,501

are depreciated via straight-line. (Code Sec. 168(b)(1)(B), Code Sec. 168(b)(2)(B), Code Sec. 168(b)(3)(A), Code Sec. 168(b)(3)(B))[19]

The cost of *purchased* dairy, etc., livestock may be recovered under MACRS. The cost of *raised* livestock may be either deducted (but costs so deducted can't be included in depreciable basis) (Reg § 1.61-4(a), Reg § 1.162-12(a)) or capitalized as the taxpayer chooses. [20] But accrual method farmers using inventories can't depreciate any purchased dairy, etc., livestock that's inventoried. (Reg § 1.167(a)-6)[21]

¶ 4523   Unharvested crop sold with land.

Gain or loss on an unharvested crop sold, exchanged, or compulsorily or involuntarily converted with the underlying land qualifies under the capital gain-ordinary loss rule of Code Sec. 1231 (¶2684 *et seq.*), if: (1) the land was used in the taxpayer's trade or business and was held for the long-term capital gain holding period, *and* (2) the land and crops are sold at the same time and to the same person. (Code Sec. 1231(b)(4)) It doesn't matter how long the *crops* were held, or their state of maturity. (Reg § 1.1231-1(f))[22]

¶ 4524   Dispositions of converted wetlands or highly erodible croplands.

Gain on the disposition of land used for farming that is converted wetland or highly erodible cropland is ordinary income. Loss is long-term capital loss. (Code Sec. 1257)[23]

¶ 4525   Dispositions of breeding, dairy, sporting, draft livestock.

Gains and losses from the sale, exchange, or involuntary conversion of animals held for draft, breeding, dairy, or sporting purposes qualify for capital gain-ordinary loss treatment under Code Sec. 1231 (¶2684 *et seq.*) as follows:

. . . cattle and horses held for 24 months or more from the date of acquisition;

. . . other livestock (except poultry) held for 12 months or more from the date of acquisition. (Code Sec. 1231(a), Code Sec. 1231(b)(3); Reg § 1.1231-2(a))[24]

Inventorying the livestock doesn't preclude Code Sec. 1231 treatment if the animal is held for the required purposes and relevant period and not for sale to customers. [25]

¶ 4526   Like-kind exchange of livestock.

The trading of livestock may qualify as a tax-free like-kind exchange (¶2418 *et seq.*) if the exchanged animals are the same sex. (Code Sec. 1031(e); Reg § 1.1031(e)-1)[26]

¶ 4527   Special farm payments.

Conservation programs. Unless the taxpayer elects out (Code Sec. 126(c)), gross income doesn't include the excludable part of payments received under certain conservation programs specified in Code Sec. 126(a)(1) to Code Sec. 126(a)(8) or received under Code Sec. 126(a)(9) Agriculture Department programs affecting small watersheds found by IRS to be similar to those programs. (Code Sec. 126(b))[27]

Pledge of crops to secure CCC loan. Farmers who pledge part or all of their production to secure a Commodity Credit Corporation (CCC) loan can make a special election to treat the loan proceeds as income in the year received and obtain a basis in the commodity for the

---

19. ¶L-8912; ¶1684.01; TD ¶267,014
20. ¶s N-1020, N-1350 *et seq.*; ¶1624.339; TD ¶298,501
21. ¶N-1351; ¶1674.035; TD ¶298,501
22. ¶N-1206; ¶12,314.13; TD ¶117,012
23. ¶N-1424 *et seq.*; ¶12,574; TD ¶299,024

24. ¶s N-1209, N-1223; ¶s 12,314, 12,314.12; TD ¶117,001
25. ¶N-1209; TD ¶117,001
26. ¶N-1215; ¶10,314.04; TD ¶117,002
27. ¶N-1181; ¶1264; TD ¶116,002

amount reported as income. Thus, instead of a loan, the money advanced to the farmer may be treated as the sales price of the commodity pledged for the loan. This special election is made by reporting the CCC loan proceeds as income on Schedule F, Form 1040 for the year the loan is received and attaching a statement to the return showing the details of the CCC loan.[28]

Payments under the Tobacco Transition Payment Program. Eligible tobacco quota holders may receive total payments of $7 per pound of quota in 10 equal annual payments in fiscal years 2005 through 2014 in exchange for the termination of tobacco marketing quotas and related price support. Payments are proceeds from a sale of the owner's tobacco quota and may be reported on the installment method under Code Sec. 453 or deferred under the like-kind exchange rules of Code Sec. 1031 (if the owner otherwise qualifies). [29]

---

28. ¶N-1164; ¶774.03; TD ¶221,008   29. ¶N-1152.5

Chapter 23 Foreign Income—Foreign Taxpayers—Foreign Currency Transactions

¶ 4610 Foreign Income of U.S. Taxpayers. ████████████████████

U.S. taxpayers —U.S. citizens, U.S. residents, U.S. (domestic) corporations and other taxable U.S. entities —ordinarily are fully taxable on their income from outside the U.S., subject to special exemptions and other special treatment for particular taxpayers, and particular kinds and sources of income. Nonresident aliens, foreign corporations and other foreign entities, however, are taxed only on their income that is effectively connected with a U.S. trade or business, and certain passive income derived from U.S. sources. Nonresidents who gave up U.S. citizenship or terminated long-term U.S. residency are subject to special expatriation tax rules.

¶ 4611 Foreign income of U.S. citizens and resident aliens.

U.S. citizens, whether they reside in the U.S. or abroad, are generally subject to U.S. income tax on their income from sources outside the U.S. (Reg § 1.1-1(b))[1] with exemptions for foreign earned income and housing costs (¶4612), income from U.S. possessions (¶4621), and certain allowances for U.S. government employees (¶4624). For the foreign tax credit, see ¶2369 *et seq.* For when a foreign corporation's *undistributed* income is taxed to its U.S. shareholders, see ¶4628, ¶4636, and ¶4637. For a resident alien's U.S. income, see ¶4641.

Every person born or naturalized in the U.S. and subject to its jurisdiction is a U.S. citizen. A foreigner who has filed a declaration of intent to become a citizen but who hasn't yet been admitted to citizenship by a final order of a naturalization court is an alien. (Reg § 1.1-1(c))[2]

¶ 4612 Partial exclusion for foreign earned income.

For any tax year in which an individual "qualifies" (¶4617), he may elect (¶4619) to exclude from gross income $80,000 (as adjusted for inflation, see ¶4613) of foreign earned income. (Code Sec. 911(a), Code Sec. 911(b)(2))[3] For a *separate* exclusion for foreign housing costs, see ¶4614. For how the tax is calculated where the foreign earned income exclusion or foreign housing costs exclusion apply, see ¶4616.

An individual's "foreign earned income" is his earned income from foreign sources attributable to services he performed during the period he "qualifies." (Code Sec. 911(b)(1)(A))[4] Earned income means wages and other amounts received as compensation (i.e., not as a distribution of profits) for personal services actually rendered. This includes cash, the fair market value of property, and allowances or reimbursements (including taxable moving expense reimbursements) attributable to performing those services (Code Sec. 911(d)(2)(A); Reg § 1.911-3(e)(5)) and, where both personal services and capital are material income-producing factors in the taxpayer's noncorporate business, a reasonable allowance (up to 30% of his share of the net profits) as compensation for personal services. (Code Sec. 911(d)(2)(B))[5]

"Foreign earned income" doesn't include pensions or annuities, or certain amounts paid by the U.S. or a federal agency to its employees. (Code Sec. 911(b)(1)(B))[6]

---

1. ¶O-1001 *et seq.*; TD ¶190,501
2. ¶O-1003; TD ¶190,503
3. ¶O-1100 *et seq.*; ¶9114 *et seq.*; TD ¶191,000 *et seq.*
4. ¶O-1140 *et seq.*; ¶9114.01; TD ¶191,024

5. ¶O-1111, ¶O-1117 *et seq.*; ¶s 9114.01, 9114.06 *et seq.*; TD ¶191,019
6. ¶s O-1142, O-1143; ¶9114.10; TD ¶191,024

References beginning with a single letter are to paragraphs in RIA's Federal Tax Coordinator 2d and RIA's Analysis of Federal Taxes: Income. Those beginning with numbers are to paragraphs in RIA's United States Tax Reporter. Those beginning with TD are to paragraphs in RIA's Tax Desk.

¶ 4613 Ceiling on foreign earned income exclusion.

An individual's foreign earned income exclusion for a tax year can't exceed his foreign earned income (¶4612) for the year, as computed on a daily basis at an annual rate of $85,700 for 2007, as indexed for inflation ($87,600 for 2008). (Code Sec. 911(b)(2)(A), Code Sec. 911(b)(2)(D))[7]

The sum of an individual's foreign earned income exclusion (¶4612) and foreign housing costs exclusion (¶4614) and/or deduction (¶4615) for any tax year can't exceed his foreign earned income for the year. (Code Sec. 911(d)(7))[8]

Thus, if an individual elects both the foreign income exclusion and the housing costs exclusion (¶4614), his foreign earned income exclusion is the *lesser* of: (a) $80,000 (as indexed), multiplied by the number of days in the tax year on which he "qualified" (¶4617), and divided by the number of days in the year, or (b) his foreign earned income as reduced by the foreign housing costs exclusion for the year. (Reg § 1.911-3(d)(2), Reg § 1.911-4(d))[9]

For married couples, the exclusion (and ceiling) is computed separately for each spouse based on the income attributable to the spouse's services. If the spouses file separate returns, each may exclude the amount of his foreign earned income attributable to his services, subject to the ceilings. If the spouses file a joint return, the sum of those separate amounts may be excluded. (Reg § 1.911-5(a)(2))[10]

¶ 4614 Partial exclusion for foreign housing costs.

A qualified individual (¶4617) may elect (¶4619) to exclude from gross income a part of his housing costs paid or incurred as a result of his foreign employment. (Code Sec. 911(a)(2))[11] For deduction of nonemployer-provided housing expenses, see ¶4615.

A qualified individual who elects the housing costs exclusion may not claim less than the full amount of the allowable exclusion. (Reg § 1.911-4(d)(1))[12]

The amount of housing costs eligible for exclusion in a tax year is the excess of: (1) the individual's housing expenses for the year, over (2) 16% of the amount (computed on a daily basis) of the foreign earned income exclusion limitation (¶4613)—i.e., the base housing amount—*multiplied* by the number of days in the tax year within the individual's period of foreign residence or presence. (Code Sec. 911(c)(1)) The exclusion of foreign housing expenses in excess of the base housing amount is limited to 30% of the taxpayer's foreign earned income exclusion. IRS has used its authority to adjust this limit by listing high-cost areas in which taxpayers can deduct or exclude a higher portion of their housing costs. (Code Sec. 911(c)(2))[13]

> ***Illustration:*** Thus, the maximum amount of the foreign housing cost exclusion is $11,998 for 2007 ($85,700 × 30%) − ($85,700 × 16%). For 2008, it's $12,264 ($87,600 × 30%) − ($87,600 × 16%).

Where spouses reside together and both claim a foreign housing costs exclusion (or deduction), they may compute their exclusion separately or jointly. Spouses who file separate returns must make separate computations, but they may allocate the housing expenses between them. (Reg § 1.911-5(a)(3)(i)) Where spouses reside apart, they both may exclude (or deduct) their respective housing cost amounts if their tax homes (¶4617) aren't within reasonable commuting distance of each other and neither spouse's residence is within a reasonable commuting distance of the other spouse's tax home. If the spouses' tax homes or residences

---

7. ¶O-1102; ¶9114.12; TD ¶191,004
8. ¶O-1102, ¶O-1168; ¶9114.01; TD ¶191,004
9. ¶O-1102 *et seq.*; ¶s 9114.01, 9114.12; TD ¶191,004
10. ¶O-1115; ¶9114.09; TD ¶191,006

11. ¶O-1161 *et seq.*; ¶9114.02; TD ¶191,001
12. ¶O-1168; ¶9114.02; TD ¶191,001
13. ¶O-1166; ¶9114.02; TD ¶191,028

are within reasonable commuting distance, only one spouse may exclude (or deduct) his housing cost amount. In either case, and whether they file separately or jointly, the amount of the housing costs exclusion (or deduction) is determined separately for each spouse. (Code Sec. 911(d)(3); Reg § 1.911-5(a)(3)(ii))[14]

Also, only housing expenses for the abode bearing the closest relationship to the taxpayer's tax home, or to a second foreign household for his spouse and dependents who don't reside with him because of adverse living conditions, qualify for the exclusion. (Code Sec. 911(c)(2)(B); Reg § 1.911-4(b)(5)(i))[15]

¶ 4615   Deduction for foreign housing expenses not provided by employer.

A qualified individual (¶4617) may deduct foreign housing expenses that aren't attributable to employer-provided amounts. (Code Sec. 911(c)(3)(A))[16] The deduction is limited to the individual's foreign earned income for the tax year which isn't otherwise excluded from gross income under either the foreign earned income (¶4612) or foreign housing costs (¶4614) exclusions. (Code Sec. 911(c)(3)(B)) Any unused housing expenses may be carried over and deducted in the next tax year, subject to that year's limits. (Code Sec. 911(c)(4)(C))[17]

¶ 4616   Stacking rule applicable where taxpayer uses foreign earned income and housing costs exclusions.

A "stacking rule" limits the benefits of the earned income and housing costs exclusions by subjecting taxpayers using these exclusions to the same U.S. tax rates as individuals in the U.S. Any income in excess of the exclusion amount determined under Code Sec. 911 is taxed (under the regular tax and alternative minimum tax) by applying to that income the tax rates that would have applied had the individual not elected the Code Sec. 911 exclusions. (Code Sec. 911(f))

¶ 4617   Who qualifies for the foreign earned income/housing costs exclusions?

A taxpayer "qualifies" for the foreign earned income (¶4612) and housing costs (¶4614) exclusions for a tax year if his "tax home" (below) is in a foreign country *and* he is either:

. . . a U.S. citizen who meets a *foreign residence test.* To meet this test, the individual must be a bona fide *resident* of one or more foreign countries for an uninterrupted period including an entire tax year. (Code Sec. 911(d)(1)(A))[18] (A resident alien who's a national of a "treaty" country may qualify.) [19] or

. . . a U.S. citizen or resident who meets a *foreign presence test.* To meet this test, the individual must, in any period of 12 consecutive months, be *present* in one or more foreign countries during at least 330 full days. (Code Sec. 911(d)(1)(B)) This means *physically present*, including time while on vacation or unemployed. [20]

For married couples, if both spouses "qualify," each may elect the exclusion or deduction. (Reg § 1.911-5(a)(1))[21]

An individual's "tax home" is his home for purposes of deducting away-from-home travel expenses (¶1544). He has no "tax home" in a foreign country for any period his abode is in the U.S. (Code Sec. 911(d)(3)) But the fact that an individual is temporarily present in the U.S. or maintains a U.S. dwelling (even if used by his spouse or dependents) doesn't necessarily mean his abode is in the U.S. (Reg § 1.911-2(b))[22]

---

14. ¶s O-1174, O-1175; ¶9114.02; TD ¶191,032
15. ¶O-1164; ¶9114.02; TD ¶191,033
16. ¶O-1171; ¶9114.02; TD ¶191,030
17. ¶O-1173; ¶9114.02; TD ¶191,030
18. ¶O-1250 *et seq.*; ¶9114.04; TD ¶191,506

19. ¶O-1271; ¶9114.04; TD ¶191,509
20. ¶O-1300 *et seq.*; ¶9114.05; TD ¶191,501
21. ¶O-1351; ¶9114.09; TD ¶191,006
22. ¶s O-1202, O-1203, O-1250 *et seq.*

The foreign presence or residence time requirements may be waived where local unrest (war, civil disturbance, etc.) precludes the normal conduct of business, but only for taxpayers already present in, or bona fide residents of, the foreign country. (Code Sec. 911(d)(4)) IRS periodically issues revenue procedures listing when these requirements have been waived for various countries. [23]

The foreign earned income (¶4612) and housing costs exclusions (¶4614) are not available for a foreign country if U.S. law bars travel (or any related transactions) for that country. (Code Sec. 911(d)(8)) Cuba is the only country currently subject to these rules. [24]

¶ 4618   Denial of double deduction, exclusion or credit.

No deduction, exclusion or credit, including any credit or deduction for foreign or possessions taxes (¶2369 *et seq.*), is allowable to the extent the deduction, etc., is allocable to or chargeable against foreign income excluded from gross income under the foreign earned income (¶4612) or housing costs (¶4614) exclusions. (Code Sec. 911(d)(6))[25]

¶ 4619   Electing foreign earned income and housing costs exclusions— Form 2555 and Form 2555-EZ.

The foreign earned income (¶4612) and housing costs (¶4614) exclusions won't apply unless elected. (Code Sec. 911(a)) Each exclusion must be elected separately, on Form 2555 attached to the taxpayer's return for the first tax year it is to apply. (Reg § 1.911-7(a)(1), Reg § 1.911-7(a)(2)(i)) (Form 2555-EZ may be used for the foreign earned income exclusion if none of the individual's income was from self-employment, his total foreign earned income didn't exceed the $80,000 (see ¶4613) amount *and* he doesn't have business/moving expenses or claim the foreign housing costs exclusion or deduction.) [26]

Once either exclusion is elected for a year, it's effective for that year and all later years, unless revoked (Code Sec. 911(e))[27] or the taxpayer claims the foreign tax credit. [28]

¶ 4620   Exclusion for meals and lodging furnished at a foreign "camp."

If an individual is furnished lodging at a "camp" located in a foreign country by or for his employer, the camp is considered the employer's business premises for purposes of the exclusion for employer-provided meals and lodging (¶1268 *et seq.*). (Code Sec. 119(c)(1))[29]

¶ 4621   Income from certain U.S. possessions—exemption for individuals—Form 4563.

An individual who is a bona fide resident of American Samoa for the entire tax year is exempt from U.S. tax on his income (except for amounts earned as an employee of the U.S.) from sources within, or effectively connected with his conduct of a trade or business within American Samoa, Guam or the Commonwealth of the Northern Mariana Islands (CNMI). Form 4563 is used to claim the exemption. An individual who is a bona fide resident of Guam or CNMI for the entire tax year must file a return with the possession and is not subject to U.S. tax. (Code Sec. 931(a), Code Sec. 931(d); Reg § 1.931-1T; Former Code Sec. 935; Reg § 1.935-1T)

Special rules apply to determine if a person is a bona fide possessions resident and if income is possessions source income. (Code Sec. 937; Reg § 1.937-1; Reg § 1.937-2T)[30]

---

23. ¶O-1273; ¶9114.03; TD ¶191,511
24. ¶O-1148; ¶9114.06; TD ¶191,027
25. ¶O-1112; ¶9114.11; TD ¶191,002
26. ¶O-1351 *et seq.*; ¶9114.13; TD ¶191,036
27. ¶O-1351, O-1353; TD ¶191,039
28. ¶O-1354; TD ¶191,040
29. ¶H-1771; ¶1194.05; TD ¶191,033
30. ¶s O-1085 *et seq.*, O-10987 *et seq.*, O-1402 *et seq.*, O-1432 *et seq.*; ¶9374 *et seq.*

¶ 4622   Individuals with a bona fide Puerto Rican residence.

An individual (regardless of citizenship) who is a bona fide resident of Puerto Rico for the entire tax year is exempt from U.S. tax on income from Puerto Rican sources, *except* amounts received for services performed for the U.S. government. But no deductions (other than for personal exemptions) or credits are allowed (i.e., from *taxable* non-Puerto Rican source income) for items attributable to the excluded amounts. (Code Sec. 933(1))[31]

A U.S. citizen who gives up Puerto Rican residence after being a bona fide resident there for at least two years may exclude from gross income for the year of change in residence, any income from Puerto Rican sources attributable to the period before the change (including amounts received *after* that year), to the extent allowed above. (Code Sec. 933(2); Reg § 1.933-1(b))

Special rules apply to determine if a person is a bona fide possessions resident and if income is possessions source income. (Code Sec. 937; Reg § 1.937-1; Reg § 1.937-2T)[32]

¶ 4623   U.S. and Virgin Islands—taxation of individuals—Form 8689.

A U.S. citizen (or resident) who derives income from the Virgin Islands (VI) but is *not a bona fide resident* there for the entire tax year must file two identical returns, one with the U.S. and one with the VI (Form 8689). The individual's is taxed in the VI on the proportion of his adjusted gross income (AGI) from VI sources and the VI tax (if any) is credited against his total U.S. tax liability (¶2369 *et seq.*). (Code Sec. 932(a), Code Sec. 932(b); Reg § 1.937-1; Reg § 1.932-1T)[33]

An individual who is a *bona fide VI resident* for the entire tax year (or files a joint return with a person who is a VI resident for the entire tax year) files a VI return and pays VI tax on his worldwide income for that year. If the individual properly files and reports all his income from all sources on a VI tax return and pays the VI tax, he is not subject to tax in the U.S. (Code Sec. 932(c)(4); Reg § 1.932-1T)[34]

For a joint return, resident status is based on the residence of the spouse with the greater AGI for the year, without regard to community property laws. (Code Sec. 932(d))

Special rules apply to determine if a person is a bona fide possessions resident and if income is possessions source income. (Code Sec. 937; Reg § 1.937-1; Reg § 1.937-2T)[35]

¶ 4624   Exemption for certain U.S. government employees' allowances.

These allowances are exempt from U.S. tax:

. . . Cost-of-living allowances received by U.S. government civilian officers and employees (including judicial employees) stationed outside the continental U.S. (except Alaska). (Code Sec. 912(2))[36]

. . . Amounts received as allowances or otherwise under: Chapter 9 of Title I of the '80 Foreign Service Act; Section 4 of the '49 Central Intelligence Agency Act; Title II of the Overseas Differentials and Allowances Act; or Subsection (e) or (f) of the first section of, or Section 22 of, the '46 Administrative Expenses Act. (Code Sec. 912(1))[37]

. . . Allowances to a Peace Corps volunteer or volunteer leader and members of his family under Section 5 or 6 of the Peace Corps Act, *except:* termination payments, leave allowances, allowances to members of the family of a volunteer leader who is training in the

---

31. ¶O-1450 *et seq.*; ¶9314.04
32. ¶O-1452; ¶9314.04
33. ¶O-1471; ¶9314.05
34. ¶O-1472 *et seq.*; ¶9314.05

35. ¶O-1473; ¶9314.05
36. ¶H-3133; ¶9124.01; TD ¶138,034
37. ¶H-3135; TD ¶138,036

U.S. and the part of an allowance designated as basic compensation. (Code Sec. 912(3))[38]

The above exemptions don't apply to recruitment incentives given because of station location, foreign post or service differentials, or allowances that are part of a salary. [39]

¶ 4625 U.S. beneficiaries of foreign trusts.

A U.S. beneficiary is taxed on a foreign trust's foreign- and U.S.-source income, at the time it becomes distributable. (Code Sec. 643(a)(6), Code Sec. 652(a))[40] Distributions to the U.S. beneficiary of accumulated trust income are subject to the trust throwback rules (¶3953 *et seq.*)[41] and a nondeductible interest charge. (Code Sec. 668)[42] Post-Sept. 19, '95 loans to a U.S. beneficiary or related party generally are treated as distributions. (Code Sec. 643(i))[43]

¶ 4626 Domestic corporations—taxation of U.S. and foreign income.

A domestic corporation (i.e., created or organized in, or under the law of, the U.S. or any state) is subject to U.S. tax on its income from both foreign and U.S. sources (except for IC-DISCs, see ¶4627). (Code Sec. 63; Code Sec. 7701(a)(4))[44] It may also be taxed on the *undistributed* income of a controlled foreign corporation (¶4628) or certain types of PFICs (¶4636, ¶4637) in which it's a shareholder. [45]

¶ 4627 Interest charge domestic international sales corporations (IC-DISCs)

A qualifying corporation that elects (on Form 4876-A) to be an IC-DISC (also referred to as a "DISC") can defer income attributable to $10 million or less of qualified export receipts. However, the DISC's shareholders are subject to an interest charge (report on Form 8404) equal to the shareholder's DISC-related deferred tax liability for the year × the base period T-bill rate. (Code Sec. 995(f))[46]

Certain DISC income (e.g., taxable income attributable to qualified export receipts that exceed $10 million) for the year is treated as a dividend taxable to the DISC shareholders. So is an illegal (under U.S. law) bribe, kickback or other payment made, directly or indirectly, by or for an IC-DISC to an official, employee or agent-in-fact of a government. (Code Sec. 995(b)(1))[47]

An IC-DISC must file Form 1120-IC-DISC. [48]

¶ 4628 Tax on U.S. shareholders of controlled foreign corporations (CFCs).

If a foreign corporation is a CFC (¶4629) for an uninterrupted period of 30 days or more during its tax year, every person who is a "U.S. shareholder" (¶4629) of the CFC at any time that year, and who owns stock in the CFC on the last day of its tax year, must report (on Form 5471, see ¶4664) his pro rata share of the foreign corporation's undistributed earnings ("Subpart F income," see ¶4630) for that year. (Code Sec. 951(a)(1); Reg § 1.951-1(a)) A U.S. shareholder's pro rata share, which depends on his interest in the various classes of the corporation's stock, is determined under special rules. (Reg § 1.951-1(e))[49]

A CFC's "U.S. shareholders" are also taxed on their pro rata shares of the CFC's:

... increase during the tax year in earnings invested in U.S. property (to the extent not included as Subpart F income) (Code Sec. 951(a)(1)(B));[50]

38. ¶H-3136; ¶9124.02; TD ¶138,037
39. ¶H-3134; TD ¶138,035
40. ¶C-3021; ¶6524; TD ¶655,003
41. ¶C-4003; ¶s 6664, 6684; TD ¶656,002
42. ¶C-4107 *et seq.*; ¶6684; TD ¶656,009
43. ¶C-4107.1; ¶6684; TD ¶656,002
44. ¶O-1006

45. ¶s O-2600 *et seq.*, O-3600 *et seq.*; TD ¶601,516
46. ¶s O-2020 *et seq.*, O-2108 *et seq.*; ¶9914 *et seq.*
47. ¶O-2115 *et seq.*; ¶9954.01
48. ¶S-1917
49. ¶s O-2600 *et seq.*, O-2701; ¶9514.01
50. ¶O-2546 *et seq.*; ¶9564.01

. . . previously excluded income withdrawn from investment in less developed countries (under the rules in effect before the Tax Reduction Act of '75) (Code Sec. 951(a)(1)(A)(ii));[1]

. . . previously excluded Subpart F income withdrawn from foreign base company shipping operations for that year (Code Sec. 951(a)(1)(A)(iii));[2] and

. . . decrease in investments in export trade assets. (Code Sec. 970(b))[3]

¶ 4629 Controlled foreign corporation (CFC) defined.

A CFC is a foreign corporation more than 50% (25%, for insurance companies) of whose stock *by vote or value* is, on any day in the corporation's tax year, owned (directly or indirectly) by "U.S. shareholders." (Code Sec. 957(a), Code Sec. 957(b)) A "U.S. shareholder" is a U.S. citizen or resident, or a U.S. corporation, partnership, estate or trust, that owns, directly or indirectly, more than 10% of the corporation's voting stock. (Code Sec. 951(b))[4]

¶ 4630 What is Subpart F income?

A CFC's Subpart F income consists of:

(1) Income derived from insuring (or reinsuring) certain foreign risks. (Code Sec. 953)[5]

(2) Foreign base company income (FBCI), which is

. . . (a) Foreign personal holding company income (FPHCI). This includes investment income such as dividends, interest, rents, royalties and annuities; gains from certain property and commodities transactions, certain personal services income, and certain other passive type income. Exceptions apply for certain income received from related parties or as part of an active business. For tax years of foreign corporations beginning before Jan. 1, 2009, and tax years of U.S. shareholders with or within which such tax years of foreign corporations end, interest, rent, and royalties received or accrued from a CFC which is a related person will not be treated as FPHCI to the extent attributable or properly allocable to income of the related person which is not subpart F income or treated as effectively connected with a U.S. trade or business.

. . . (b) Foreign base company sales, services, and oil-related income. (Code Sec. 952(a)(2), Code Sec. 954(c)(6), Code Sec. 954; Reg § 1.954-1, Reg § 1.954-2)[6]

(3) Income from operations in compliance with an unsanctioned international boycott. (Code Sec. 952(a)(3))[7]

(4) The amount of any illegal (under the U.S. Foreign Corrupt Practices Act) payment made (directly or indirectly) by or for the CFC to a government official, employee or agent in fact. (Code Sec. 952(a)(4))[8]

(5) Income (reduced by allocable deductions and taxes) from a foreign country during any period that Code Sec. 901(j) (which denies any credit for taxes paid to certain foreign countries, see ¶2371) applies to that country. (Code Sec. 952(a)(5))[9]

Regs explain how CFCs treat their distributive share of partnership income. (Reg § 1.702-1(a)(8)(ii), Reg § 1.952-1(g))[10]

For tax years of foreign corporations beginning before 2009 (and for tax years of U.S. shareholders with or within which any such tax year of the foreign corporation ends), exceptions apply for certain income derived in the active conduct of a banking, financing, or similar

---

1. ¶O-3309; ¶s 9514.01, 9554
2. ¶O-2531; ¶s 9514.01, 9554.01
3. ¶O-2536 *et seq.*; ¶9704.01
4. ¶O-2300 *et seq.*; ¶9574.01
5. ¶O-2404 *et seq.*; ¶9534.01

6. ¶O-2424 *et seq.*; ¶9544 *et seq.*
7. ¶O-2528; ¶9524.02
8. ¶O-2529; ¶9524.03
9. ¶O-2530; ¶9524.04
10. ¶O-2401

business, or in the conduct of an insurance business. (Code Sec. 953(e)(10), Code Sec. 954(h)(9))[11]

Also, in any tax year when the sum of the CFC's FBCI and insurance income exceeds 70% of its gross income, *all* of its income for the year is treated as FBCI or insurance income (subject to the "high foreign tax" exception, below). (Reg § 1.954-1(d)(6)) If this sum is less than 5% of the CFC's gross income or $1,000,000 (whichever is less), *none* of the CFC's income is FBCI or insurance income. (Code Sec. 954(b)(3); Reg § 1.954-1(b))[12]

Any item of FBCI or insurance income that is subject to an effective rate of foreign tax which is greater than 90% of the maximum U.S. corporate rate may, at the election of the CFC's controlling U.S. shareholders, be excluded from Subpart F income. (Code Sec. 954(b)(4); Reg § 1.954-1(d))[13]

¶ 4631 Disposition of CFC stock.

Gain from the sale, exchange or redemption (under Code Sec. 302, see ¶3526 *et seq.*) of stock in, or from the liquidation of, a foreign corporation is (to the extent of its post-'62 earnings and profits attributable to that stock) taxable as ordinary dividend income *if*:

. . . the selling or exchanging shareholder is a U.S. citizen or resident, or a domestic partnership, corporation, trust or estate; *and*

. . . the shareholder was a "U.S. shareholder" (¶4629) of the corporation at some time during the five-year period ending on the date of the sale, etc.; *and*

. . . the foreign corporation was a CFC (¶4629) at some time during the period the shareholder was a "U.S. shareholder," during that five-year period. (Code Sec. 1248(a))[14]

This dividend treatment may also apply to certain distributions or dispositions with respect to a *domestic* corporation, e.g., where the domestic corporation was formed or availed of principally for holding (directly or indirectly) stock of one or more foreign corporations. (Code Sec. 1248(e), Code Sec. 1248(f))[15]

This dividend treatment doesn't apply to Code Sec. 303 redemptions, amounts otherwise treated as dividends, ordinary income, short-term capital gains, or gains from sales made by non-U.S. persons. (Code Sec. 1248(g)) Nor does it apply to gifts or other transfers that don't result in recognized gain. [16]

There is a ceiling on the tax on the "dividend" income for an individual shareholder who held the stock for the long-term holding period (¶2667). (Code Sec. 1248(b))[17]

¶ 4632 Sales of patents, etc, to a foreign corporation.

A U.S. citizen or resident, or a domestic partnership, corporation, trust or estate, that sells (or exchanges) a patent, invention, formula or process, or similar property right to a foreign corporation in which the seller owns (directly, indirectly or constructively) stock with over 50% of the combined voting power of all classes of stock must treat *as ordinary income* any gain recognized on that sale (exchange). (Code Sec. 1249)[18]

¶ 4633 U.S. shareholders in a passive foreign investment company— Form 8621.

A U.S. shareholder in a PFIC (¶4634) may defer the U.S. tax (with respect to that investment) until he disposes of the PFIC stock or receives an "excess distribution." At that time, the shareholder must pay U.S. tax, plus interest, based on the value of the tax deferral

---

11. ¶O-2423.1, O-2480.3
12. ¶O-2508 *et seq.*; ¶9544.01
13. ¶O-2520 *et seq.*; ¶9544.01
14. ¶s O-2801, O-2807; ¶12,484 *et seq.*

15. ¶O-2805
16. ¶O-2803; ¶12,484.01
17. ¶O-2811; ¶12,484.02
18. ¶O-2900 *et seq.*; ¶12,494

(unless the PFIC is a qualified electing fund, see ¶4636). (Code Sec. 1291(a)(1), Code Sec. 1291(a)(2)) All gain recognized and all distributions are ordinary income, allocated ratably to each day the shareholder held the stock. (Code Sec. 1291(a)(1)(A), Code Sec. 1291(a)(1)(B))[19] Report the distributions and dispositions on Form 8621. [20]

An "excess distribution" is a current year distribution received by a shareholder on PFIC stock, to the extent the distribution exceeds its ratable portion of 125% of the average amount so received during the three preceding years. (Code Sec. 1291(b))[21]

Portions of distributions that aren't "excess distributions" are taxed under the normal rules for corporate distributions, see ¶1285 *et seq.* (Code Sec. 1291(a)(1)(B))[22]

A transfer of stock on which gain otherwise wouldn't be recognized under these rules is nevertheless treated as gain on the sale or exchange of that stock. (Code Sec. 1291(f))[23]

A PFIC shareholder may claim both direct and indirect ("deemed") foreign tax credits (¶2369 *et seq.*) with respect to these dispositions and distributions. (Code Sec. 1291(g))[24]

For a special mark-to-market election, see ¶4637.

The CFC rules override the PFIC rules. Thus, amounts that could be included in gross income under the CFC rules (¶4628) are not included under the PFIC rules. (Code Sec. 951(c))[25]

¶ 4634   Passive foreign investment company (PFIC) defined.

A PFIC is any foreign corporation if: (1) at least 75% of its gross income for its tax year is passive, or (2) at least 50% of the assets it held during the year produce passive income. (Code Sec. 1297(a)) The 50% test is based on the adjusted basis of the corporation's assets if the corporation isn't publicly traded and is a controlled foreign corporation or elects to have the test based on the adjusted basis of the corporation's assets. The test is applied on the basis of the value of the corporation's assets if the corporation is publicly traded for the tax year or the test isn't required to be applied based on the adjusted basis of the corporation's assets. (Code Sec. 1297(f))[26] For treatment as a qualified electing fund, see ¶4636. For how the PFIC's shareholders are taxed, see ¶4633.

¶ 4635   Taxation of 10% U.S. shareholders of a controlled foreign corporation.

A passive foreign investment company (PFIC) isn't treated as a PFIC with respect to a U.S. shareholder who owns at least 10% of the stock, if the company is a controlled foreign corporation (CFC). (Code Sec. 1297(e))[27]

¶ 4636   Qualified electing fund (QEF) status avoids PFIC treatment—Form 8621.

A PFIC (¶4634) is treated as a qualified electing fund (QEF) with respect to a particular shareholder if he so elects (as explained below) and the PFIC complies with the requirements prescribed by regs for determining its ordinary earnings and net capital gain (under Reg § 1.1293-1(a)(2)(i)) and any other necessary information. (Code Sec. 1295)[28]

A U.S. investor in a PFIC makes the QEF election by attaching a completed Form 8621 to his timely filed income tax return (original or amended) for that year. (Code Sec. 1295(b)(2); Reg § 1.1295-1(e)) The investor must reflect in the Form 8621 the information provided by the PFIC in its annual information statement. (Reg § 1.1295-1(f)(1))

19. ¶s O-2200 *et seq.*, O-2218, O-2228; ¶12,914.01
20. ¶O-2228
21. ¶O-2225; ¶12,914.01
22. ¶O-2218
23. ¶O-2239; ¶12,914.01

24. ¶O-2253 *et seq.*; ¶12,914.01
25. ¶O-2605; ¶9514.03
26. ¶O-2202 *et seq.*; ¶12,974
27. ¶O-2219.1
28. ¶O-2268; ¶12,954

If the election is made, the shareholder's U.S. tax on disposition of the stock or receipt of an excess distribution won't be increased by any interest charge (that applies to PFICs, see ¶4633). (Code Sec. 1291(d)(1))[29] But the electing shareholder must currently include in income his share of the PFIC's earnings and profits (with appropriate basis adjustments for amounts not distributed and previously taxed distributions). The fund's ordinary income and net capital gain are passed through to the shareholder as ordinary income and long-term capital gain. (Code Sec. 1293) A 10% corporate shareholder is allowed a foreign tax credit on its share of the PFIC's earnings. (Code Sec. 1293(f))[30]

¶ 4637 Mark-to-market election for PFIC stock.

A shareholder of a passive foreign investment company (PFIC) may make a mark-to-market election for marketable PFIC stock and avoid the non-QEF rules described at ¶4633. (Code Sec. 1296; Code Sec. 1291(d)) Regs explain when stock is marketable PFIC stock. (Reg § 1.1296-2)

The election is made by filing Form 8621 with an annual original or amended return filed before the return due date (including extensions). Special rules apply for how the election is made by a controlled foreign corporation on behalf of its shareholders. (Reg § 1.1296-1(h)(1))[31] The election is effective for indirect shareholders who hold PFIC shares through a partnership, trust or estate and is effective only for the shareholder making the election, for all stock of the corporation for which the election is made. (Reg § 1.1296-1(b))[32]

If the election is made, the shareholder includes in income each year an amount equal to the excess, if any, of the fair market value of the PFIC stock as of the close of the tax year over the shareholder's adjusted basis in the stock. The shareholder is allowed a deduction for the lesser of the excess, if any, of the adjusted basis of the PFIC stock over its fair market value as of the close of the tax year, or the "unreversed inclusions" with respect to the PFIC stock—the excess, if any, of the mark-to-market gains for the stock included by the shareholder for earlier tax years, including any amount which would have been included for any earlier tax year but for the Code Sec. 1291 interest on tax deferral rules, over the mark-to-market losses for the stock that were allowed as deductions for earlier tax years. (Code Sec. 1296)[33]

Amounts included in income or deducted under the mark-to-market election, as well as gain or loss on the actual sale or other disposition of the PFIC stock, are treated as ordinary income or loss. (Code Sec. 1296(c)(1))[34]

¶ 4638 Recognition of gain on transfers to certain foreign entities.

Except as provided in regs, gain is recognized upon a transfer of appreciated property by a U.S. person to a foreign estate or trust to the extent its fair market value exceeds its basis in the hands of the transferor. (Code Sec. 684) Regs except transfers to the following from gain recognition:

. . . A foreign trust, to the extent the transferor is treated as the owner of the trust under Code Sec. 671. (Reg § 1.684-3(a))

. . . A charitable trust exempt from tax under Code Sec. 501(c)(3). (Reg § 1.684-3(b))

. . . A transfer of property by reason of death of the U.S. transferor if the basis of the property in the hands of the foreign trust is determined under Code Sec. 1014. (Reg § 1.684-3(c))

. . . An unrelated foreign trust to which property has been transferred for fair market value.

29. ¶O-2262 *et seq.*; ¶12,954
30. ¶O-2262; ¶12,934
31. ¶O-2217.7; ¶12,964
32. ¶O-2217.7; ¶12,964
33. ¶O-2217.1; ¶12,964
34. ¶O-2217.1; ¶12,964

(Reg § 1.684-3(d))

. . . A transfer of stock by a domestic corporation to a foreign trust if the domestic corporation doesn't recognize gain on the transfer under Code Sec. 1032. (Reg § 1.684-3(e))

Also, the general rule doesn't apply to a distribution to a trust with respect to an interest held by the trust in a corporation, partnership, investment trust, liquidating trust, or environmental remediation trust. (Reg § 1.684-3(f))

If a U.S. person transfers property to a domestic trust and for any reason the domestic trust becomes a foreign trust and neither is treated as owned by any person under the grantor trust rules, the domestic trust is deemed to have transferred all of its assets to a foreign trust. The domestic trust has to immediately recognize gain unless one of the above exceptions applies at that time. (Reg § 1.684-4)

For transfers after 2009, the gain recognition rule will also apply to transfers at death to a nonresident alien. (Code Sec. 684(a))[35]

For gain recognition on transfers to a foreign corporation, see ¶3586. For gain recognition on transfers to foreign partnerships, see ¶3710.

¶ 4639   Tax sanctions for international boycott activities— Form 5713.

Participation in or cooperation with an international boycott can result in: (1) reduction of the allowable foreign tax credit, ¶2369 *et seq.*, (Code Sec. 908), (2) reduced deferral under the DISC rules, ¶4627, (Code Sec. 995(b)(1)(F)), and (3) a CFC's undistributed earnings being currently taxed to its U.S. shareholders, ¶4630, (Code Sec. 952(a)(3)) Taxpayers must report (on Form 5713) boycott operations and requests to participate or cooperate. (Code Sec. 999)[36]

¶ 4640   Resident Aliens Taxed as U.S. Persons. ▬▬▬▬▬▬▬

A resident alien individual generally is subject to U.S. tax in the same manner as a U.S. citizen.

¶ 4641   Resident aliens as U.S. persons.

Resident aliens are generally taxed just like U.S. citizens on their U.S. and foreign source income. (Reg § 1.871-1(a))[37] An alien individual is treated as a U.S. resident for any calendar year in which he (1) meets a lawful permanent residence ("green card") test, (2) meets a "substantial presence" test (¶4642), or (3) makes the "first year election" (¶4643). (Code Sec. 7701(b)(1)(A))[38] For nonresident aliens, see ¶4644 *et seq.*

¶ 4642   Substantial presence test—Form 8843, Form 8840.

Subject to certain exceptions, an individual meets the substantial presence test (i.e., is a U.S. resident), for any calendar (current) year if:

(1) he is present in the U.S. on at least 31 days during the year, *and*

(2) the sum of the number of days he was present in the U.S. during the current year and the two preceding calendar years, when multiplied by the applicable multiplier (1 for the current year, ⅓ for the first preceding year, and ⅙ for the second preceding year), is at least 183. (Code Sec. 7701(b)(3)(A))[39]

⦿ *illustration:* A foreign citizen was present in the U.S. from Jan. 1 through Jan. 31 of Year 3, for all of Year 2, and from July 1 through Dec. 31 of Year 1. He will meet the

---

35. ¶C-1020; ¶6844
36. ¶O-3500 *et seq.*; ¶9994.01
37. ¶O-1008; ¶8714.01; TD ¶190,502

38. ¶O-1051; ¶8714; TD ¶190,509
39. ¶O-1057; ¶8714; TD ¶190,510

substantial presence test in Year 3, calculated as follows: 31 (31 days of Year 3 presence × 1) + 122 (365 days of Year 2 presence × ⅓) + 31 (184 days of Year 1 presence × ⅙) = 184.

An individual isn't present in the U.S. on any day on which he's exempt (e.g., foreign official, teacher) or his medical condition prevents him from leaving the U.S. (Code Sec. 7701(b)(3)(D), Code Sec. 7701(b)(5)) File Form 8843 to claim the exemption. (Reg § 301.7701(b)-8(b)(2)(i))[40]

An individual who otherwise meets the substantial presence test can avoid being treated as a U.S. resident that year if he: (1) is present in the U.S. on fewer than 183 days during the year, and (2) files a "closer connection statement" on Form 8840 which establishes that for the year, he has a tax home (¶1544) in a foreign country to which he has a closer connection than to the U.S. (Code Sec. 7701(b)(3)(B); Reg § 301.7701(b)-8(b)(1)(i)) If the individual is required to file Form 1040 or 1040NR, the statement must be attached to the return for the relevant tax year. An individual who doesn't have to file a return should send the form to the IRS center in Philadelphia, PA by the due date (including extensions) for filing an income tax return for the calendar year for which the statement applies. (Reg § 301.7701(b)-8(c))[41]

¶ 4643 "First year" election to be taxed as a U.S. resident.

A qualifying alien who arrives in the U.S. too late in a calendar year to meet the substantial presence test (¶4642) may elect (on a statement attached to the return) to be taxed as a U.S. resident for part of that first (election) year if he meets the substantial presence test in the next calendar year. (Code Sec. 7701(b)(4); Reg § 301.7701(b)-4(c)(3))[42] For joint return election where one spouse is a nonresident alien, see ¶4705.

¶ 4644 Taxation of Nonresident Aliens and Foreign Corporations. ▰▰▰▰▰

A nonresident alien or foreign corporation is taxed at a 30% (or lower treaty) rate on investment income from U.S. sources and, if engaged in a U.S. trade or business, at regular U.S. rates on income effectively connected with that business. Otherwise the nonresident alien or foreign corporation is exempt from U.S. tax. [43]

A foreign taxpayer also may be subject to the accumulated earnings tax (¶3316 *et seq.*), the personal holding company tax (¶3323 *et seq.*), (Reg § 1.881-1(e))[44] a branch profits tax (¶4650), a transportation tax (¶4652), and the alternative minimum tax (¶3200 *et seq.*).

For allowance of deductions and credits, see ¶4653.

¶ 4645 Nonresident alien individuals and foreign corporations.

A nonresident alien individual is an individual who isn't a U.S. citizen or resident. (Code Sec. 7701(b)(1)(B)) Aliens who are bona fide residents of Puerto Rico, Guam, American Samoa or the Northern Mariana Islands for the entire tax year are generally taxed like resident aliens (Code Sec. 876)[45] (except for income from these possessions, see ¶4621).

A foreign corporation is one that's organized outside the U.S. or under any law other than that of the U.S., a state or the District of Columbia. (Code Sec. 7701(a)(3), Code Sec. 7701(a)(4), Code Sec. 7701(a)(9))[46]

A corporation created or organized in or under the law of American Samoa or the Virgin Islands isn't treated as foreign for any tax year if: (1) at all times that year less than 25% (by value) of its stock is owned (directly or indirectly) by foreign persons; (2) at least 65% of its gross income for the last three tax years (or shorter period of existence) is shown to IRS's

---

40. ¶s O-1062, O-1080; ¶8714; TD ¶190,515 *et seq.*
41. ¶s O-1063, O-1081; ¶8714; TD ¶190,516
42. ¶O-1051, ¶O-1072 *et seq.*; ¶8714; TD ¶190,529
43. ¶s O-10101, O-10301; ¶s 8714.01, 8814 *et seq.*

44. ¶O-10300 *et seq.*; ¶8824; TD ¶641,002
45. ¶s O-1010, O-1086; ¶s 8714, 8764, 9314 *et seq.*; TD ¶630,110
46. ¶O-10360; ¶8814.01; TD ¶632,005

satisfaction to be effectively connected with a trade or business in either the possession or the U.S.; *and* (3) no substantial part of its income is used (directly or indirectly) to satisfy obligations to persons who are not bona fide residents of that possession or the U.S. (Code Sec. 881(b)(1); Reg § 1.881-5T(c))

A corporation formed in Guam or the Commonwealth of the Northern Mariana Islands (CNMI) is treated as foreign if: (a) at all times during the tax year, less than 25% in value of its stock is owned (directly or indirectly) by foreign persons and (b) at least 20% of its gross income is shown to IRS's satisfaction upon examination to have been derived from sources within the possession for the three-year period ending with the close of the preceding tax year of the corporation (or for such part of the period it was in existence). (Reg § 1.881-5T(d))[47]

¶ 4646   Tax on income "effectively connected" with a U.S. business.

A foreign corporation or nonresident alien engaged in a U.S. business (¶4647), at any time in the tax year is taxed at regular U.S. rates on taxable income "effectively connected" with that business —i.e., the gross income effectively connected with the U.S. business, less allowable deductions (¶4653). (Code Sec. 871(b), Code Sec. 882(a))[48] For tax on income that is not effectively connected with a U.S. trade or business, see ¶4648.

All *U.S.-source* income, gain, or loss (other than periodical income and capital gains and losses) derived by a nonresident alien or foreign corporation engaged in a U.S. business any time in the tax year is treated as "effectively connected." (Code Sec. 864(c)(3))[49]

Foreign-source income treated as "effectively connected" is limited to the items below to the extent the item is attributable to an office or other fixed place of business in the U.S.:

... Rents, royalties and gains on intangible personal property derived from an active licensing business.

... Dividends, interest or gain from stock or obligations derived from an active banking, financing or trading business.

... Certain inventory sales attributable to a U.S. sales office.

... Items that are economically similar to the above items on this list. (Code Sec. 864(c)(4))[50]

¶ 4647   What is "engaging in a U.S. business"?

A nonresident alien who performs personal services in the U.S. in the tax year engages in business in the U.S. that year (so he's taxed on the compensation income) *unless* his compensation for those services is $3,000 or less, he's in the U.S. for 90 days or less, *and* he works for a foreign person. (Code Sec. 864(b))[1] Special rules apply to foreign students, trainees, etc. (Code Sec. 871(c), Code Sec. 872(b)(3))[2]

An alien isn't subject to U.S. tax on compensation received for services as an employee of a foreign government or international organization, *except* where the services are primarily in connection with the foreign government's commercial activities, or where the alien is an employee of a "controlled commercial entity." (Code Sec. 893)[3]

If a partnership, estate or trust is engaged in a U.S. business, the entity's foreign partners or beneficiaries are considered so engaged. (Code Sec. 875)[4]

47. ¶O-10361; ¶s 8814.01, 8814.02; TD ¶632,005
48. ¶s O-10501, O-10601, O-10602; ¶8644 *et seq.*; TD ¶641,001
49. ¶O-10604; ¶8644 *et seq.*; TD ¶642,006
50. ¶O-10622; ¶8644.02; TD ¶642,011

1. ¶O-10502; ¶8644.01; TD ¶630,114
2. ¶O-10503; ¶s 8714.03, 8724.03; TD ¶630,116
3. ¶O-11829; ¶8934; TD ¶647,005
4. ¶s O-10504, O-10505; ¶8754; TD ¶641,510

¶ 4648 U.S.-source income not "effectively connected" with U.S. business—30% tax.

Nonresident aliens and foreign corporations are taxed at a flat 30% (or lower treaty rate) on this income, if U.S.-source and not "effectively connected" with a U.S. business:

. . . Interest (other than original issue discount (OID) and certain portfolio and bank account interest), dividends, rents, salaries, wages, premiums, annuities, compensations, remunerations, emoluments and other fixed or determinable annual or periodical gains, profits and income. (Code Sec. 871(a)(1)(A), Code Sec. 881(a)(1))

. . . Payments on bonds with OID, and amounts received on their disposition, that are ordinary income under the OID rules (¶¶1313 *et seq.*). (Code Sec. 871(a)(1)(C), Code Sec. 881(a)(3))

. . . Amounts includible in income of residual REMIC interest holders. (Code Sec. 860G(b)(1)) Special rules apply for this type of income, including rules regarding allocations by partnerships that hold residual REMIC interests where the first allocation of income to the foreign person takes place after July 31, 2006. (Reg § 1.860G-3T)

. . . 85% of Social Security benefits paid to nonresident aliens. (Code Sec. 871(a)(3))

. . . Gains on sale or exchange of patents, copyrights and the like, where payments are contingent on productivity, etc. (Code Sec. 871(a)(1)(D), Code Sec. 881(a)(4))

. . . Certain types of gambling winnings (but not winnings from blackjack, baccarat, craps, roulette or big six wheel, except to the extent provided in regs). (Code Sec. 871(j))

. . . Gains from the disposal, with a retained economic interest, of timber, coal or iron ore. (Code Sec. 871(a)(1)(B))[5]

The 30% tax does not apply to dividends paid by a foreign corporation with effectively connected income. (Code Sec. 871(i)(2)(D)) Also exempt are interest related RIC dividends that would not be subject to withholding and short-term capital gains. (Code Sec. 871(k); Code Sec. 881(e))

No deductions are allowed against this income. The 30% tax is on the *gross* amount. (Code Sec. 873, Code Sec. 882(c))[6] (But if a nonresident alien has a U.S. spouse, the couple can, effectively, elect to be taxed at regular rates, see ¶4705.)

Non-"effectively connected" long- and short-term capital gains (except as listed above) aren't taxed to foreign corporations (Code Sec. 881), and are taxed to nonresident aliens only if they are present in the U.S. for at least 183 days in the tax year. (Code Sec. 871(a)(2))[7]

¶ 4649 Election for investment income from U.S. real property.

A nonresident alien or foreign corporation may elect to treat certain income from U.S. real property held for investment as effectively connected with the conduct of a U.S. business. (Code Sec. 897(a), Code Sec. 871(d), Code Sec. 882(d)) The foreign taxpayer is thus taxed at regular U.S. rates (not 30%) on net rather than gross income, and can take depreciation deductions, etc., see ¶4646.[8] Elect on a statement attached to the income tax return for the election year. (Reg § 1.871-10(d)(1)(ii))[9]

---

5. ¶O-10201 *et seq.*; ¶s 8714.02, 8814.02; TD ¶632,001 *et seq.*
6. ¶O-10641, O-10648; ¶s 8734, 8814.02; TD ¶641,004
7. ¶O-10231; ¶s 8714.02, 8814.02; TD ¶630,132
8. ¶O-10615 *et seq.*; ¶8714.04; TD ¶642,016
9. ¶O-10619; TD ¶642,018

¶ 4650   Branch profits tax on foreign corporations— Form 1120F.

A foreign corporation engaged in a U.S. trade or business through a branch office in the tax year is liable for a branch profits tax (and regular income tax) equal to 30% of the year's "dividend equivalent amount" (pay on Form 1120F). (Code Sec. 884(a); Reg § 1.884-1(a)) The "dividend equivalent amount" is the corporation's effectively connected earnings and profits (E&P), *reduced* (not below zero) by any increase for the year in its U.S. net equity (i.e., amounts reinvested in the U.S. business), and *increased* (within limits) by any decrease for the year in its U.S. net equity (i.e., amounts remitted to the foreign head office). (Code Sec. 884(b); Reg § 1.884-1(b))[10]

If a foreign corporation is subject to the branch profits tax for any tax year (whether any branch profits tax is actually due), *income* tax withholding (see ¶4666 *et seq.*), isn't required on any dividends it pays out of its E&P for that year. (Code Sec. 884(e)(3))[11]

observation: The branch profits tax is the counterpart of the withholding tax, at the shareholder level, on dividends paid by a U.S. sub to its foreign parent, ¶4648.

The branch profits tax won't be imposed on a foreign corporation for the year it completely terminates its U.S. trade or business, except where there is a corporate liquidation or reorganization, or a Code Sec. 351 incorporation. The corporation must waive the statute of limitations for the year (on Form 8848 attached to the income tax return). (Reg § 1.884-2T; Reg § 1.884-2T(a)(2)(i))[12]

The branch profits tax doesn't apply if it's inconsistent with existing U.S. income tax treaties, if the foreign corporation is a qualified resident of the treaty country, except for treaty shopping situations. (Code Sec. 884(e)(1); Reg § 1.884-1(g))[13]

¶ 4651   Branch-level interest tax.

If a foreign corporation is engaged in a U.S. trade or business (or has gross income treated as "effectively connected"), interest (including original issue discount) paid by the corporation's U.S. trade or business (i.e., its U.S. branch) is treated as if it were paid by a U.S. corporation (i.e., the U.S. branch is treated as a sub) —i.e., it's subject to the 30% tax discussed at ¶4648. (Code Sec. 884(f)(1)(A); Reg § 1.884-4(a)(1), Reg § 1.884-4(b)(1)) To the extent the amount of interest allowable as a deduction in computing the foreign corporation's taxable "effectively connected" income exceeds the amount of interest paid by its U.S. branch, the foreign corporation is liable for the withholding tax discussed at ¶4667 (pay on Form 1120F) on "any interest" which is or is treated as "effectively connected" with a U. S. trade or business. (Code Sec. 884(f); Reg § 1.884-4(a)(2)) This treatment doesn't apply where the payor and recipient meet certain residency standards. (Code Sec. 884(f)(3))[14]

¶ 4652   4% tax on transportation income.

A 4% tax is imposed on the U.S.-source gross transportation income of foreign corporations and nonresident aliens. (Code Sec. 887(a)) Income subject to this 4% gross-basis tax isn't subject to the 30% tax (¶4648) or the regular U.S. tax on "effectively connected" income (¶4646). (Code Sec. 887(c))[15]

---

10. ¶O-11300 *et seq.*; ¶8844
11. ¶s O-11982, O-11454; ¶8844
12. ¶O-11356 *et seq.*; ¶8844
13. ¶O-11390 *et seq.*; ¶8844
14. ¶O-11376 *et seq.*; ¶8844
15. ¶O-11501; ¶8634.03; TD ¶644,501

¶ 4653   Deductions and credits of foreign corporations and nonresident aliens.

Foreign corporations and nonresident aliens generally may take deductions only to the extent related (under regs) to "effectively connected" income (¶4646). (Code Sec. 873(a), Code Sec. 882(c)(1)(A); Reg § 1.882-5) Regs provide rules for how interest deductions are allocated to effectively connected income. (Reg § 1.882-5; Reg § 1.882-5T)[16] But these deductions are allowed whether or not related to that income: for charitable contributions; and for nonresident aliens, for nonbusiness casualty and theft losses, and personal exemptions (limited). (Code Sec. 873(b), Code Sec. 882(c)(1)(B))[17]

Credits also generally are allowable only if attributable to "effectively connected" income, except for certain credits (e.g., for taxes withheld at source, earned income credit). (Code Sec. 874(b), Code Sec. 882(c)(2); Reg § 1.874-1)[18]

Generally, a return (see ¶4660 *et seq.*) must be filed in order to get the benefit of an otherwise allowable deduction or credit. (Code Sec. 874(a), Code Sec. 882(c)(2), Reg § 1.882-4(a)(2))[19] Regs require the return be timely filed; however, the Tax Court has invalidated this requirement. IRS may waive the deadlines in certain cases. (Reg § 1.874-1(b)(2), Reg § 1.882-4(a)(3)(ii))[20]

¶ 4654   Is income from U.S. or foreign sources?

Specific rules are used to determine the source of the following types of income:

Compensation — where the services were performed. (Code Sec. 861(a)(3); Code Sec. 862(a)(3); Reg § 1.861-4)[21]

Interest — where the debtor is located. (Code Sec. 861(a)(1); Code Sec. 862(a)(1))[22]

Dividends — where the corporation is incorporated. But dividends from a foreign corporation are U.S.-source unless less than 25% of all its income for the last three years is effectively connected with a U.S. business. (Code Sec. 861(a)(2); Code Sec. 862(a)(2))[23]

Rents and royalties — where the property is used. (Code Sec. 861(a)(4); Code Sec. 862(a)(4))[24]

Sales of personal property — where the seller resides. (Code Sec. 865(a)) Special rules apply to the sale of depreciable and intangible property (Code Sec. 865(c), Code Sec. 865(d)), and to inventory. (Code Sec. 865(b)) Income from the sale of any personal property (other than inventory sold for use or disposition outside the U.S.) that's attributable to a nonresident's U.S. office is U.S.-source income. Sales of certain property by a U.S. resident through a foreign office is foreign-source if at least a 10% foreign tax is paid on it. (Code Sec. 865(g))[25]

Sales of real property or natural resources — location of the property or resource. (Code Sec. 861(a)(5); Code Sec. 862(a)(8))[26]

Transportation income from transportation that either begins or ends in the U.S. (but not both) is half foreign- and half U.S.-source. (Code Sec. 863(c)(2)(A))[27]

International communications income of a U.S. person is half foreign- and half U.S.-source. (Code Sec. 863(e)(1)(A)) A foreign person's international communications income is foreign-source, except where it is attributable to an office or fixed place of business in the U.S. (Code Sec. 863(e)(1)(B))[28]

---

16. ¶O-10641, O-10648; ¶O-10649¶s 8734, 8824; TD ¶641,004
17. ¶O-10243, O-10648; ¶s 8734, 8824; TD ¶641,004
18. ¶s O-10643, O-10675; ¶8824; TD ¶641,006
19. ¶s O-10644, O-10676; TD ¶641,007
20. ¶O-10645.1, O-10676.1
21. ¶O-10931.1 *et seq.*; ¶8614.15 *et seq.*; TD ¶633,004
22. ¶O-10906 *et seq.*; ¶8614.01; TD ¶633,002

23. ¶O-10926 *et seq.*; ¶8614.10 *et seq.*; TD ¶633,003 *et seq.*
24. ¶O-10936; ¶8614.22; TD ¶633,005
25. ¶O-10948 *et seq.*; ¶8654 *et seq.*; TD ¶633,011
26. ¶O-10945; ¶s 8614.24, 8974; TD ¶633,023
27. ¶O-10941; ¶8634.03; TD ¶633,020
28. ¶O-10984; ¶8634.04

Space and ocean activity income of a U.S. person is U.S.-source, while that of a foreign person is foreign-source. (Code Sec. 863(d)(1))[29]

Insurance income from insuring U.S. risks is U.S.-source. (Code Sec. 861(a)(7))[30]

¶ 4655   Dispositions of U.S. real property—FIRPTA rules.

A gain or loss of a nonresident alien or foreign corporation from the disposition of a U.S. real property interest (USRPI) is treated as effectively connected with a U.S. trade or business. (Code Sec. 897(a)(1))[31] For reporting, see ¶4664, and withholding, see ¶4675.

A USRPI includes: (1) an interest in real property located in the U.S. or the Virgin Islands, and (2) any interest (other than solely as a creditor) in any U.S. corporation unless it's shown *not* to have been a U.S. real property holding corporation (USRPHC) during the five-year period ending on the date of disposition. (Code Sec. 897(c)(1)(A))[32]

Foreign taxpayers that hold USRPIs indirectly (e.g., as shareholders, partners or beneficiaries of a corporation, partnership, estate or trust that owns the property) are also, when they dispose of their interest in the entity, subject to U.S. tax on any gain attributable to the entity's USRPIs. (Code Sec. 897(g); Reg § 1.897-7T)[33]

Special rules apply to foreign taxpayers who hold interests in RICs and REITs that would otherwise be USRPIs. The special rules will not apply to RICs after Dec. 31, 2007 (although look-through and withholding rules will apply after this period). Code Sec. 897(h))[34]

Gain is recognized even if the disposition is a transfer to paid-in surplus or a capital contribution to a foreign corporation. (Code Sec. 897(j))[35] For exception, see ¶4656.

¶ 4656   Election by foreign corporation to be treated as a U.S. corporation.

A foreign corporation protected by treaty (with respect to USRPIs) may elect to be treated as a U.S. corporation for purposes of the FIRPTA rules (¶4655), including reporting and withholding (¶4675) (Code Sec. 897(i))[36] if the corporation: is a U.S. real property holding corporation (¶4655) (Reg § 1.897-8T(b)), holds the USRPI at the time of the election, and submits an election statement in proper form. (Reg § 1.897-3(b))[37]

¶ 4657   Tax treaties—Form 8833.

Tax treaties typically exempt or reduce U.S. tax on certain business, compensation and investment income. (Code Sec. 894(a))[38] Treaty partners appoint competent authorities to carry out the various provisions of treaties in force between them. For the U.S., the Assistant Commissioner (International) acts as "competent authority." [39]

The U.S. has income tax treaties with Australia, Austria, Barbados, Belgium, Canada, China (doesn't apply to Hong Kong), Commonwealth of Independent States (the U.S.-U.S.S.R. treaty applies to the countries of Armenia, Azerbaijan, Belarus, Georgia, Kyrgyzstan, Moldova, Tajikistan, Turkmenistan, and Uzbekistan), Cyprus, Czech Republic, Denmark, Egypt, Estonia, Finland, France, Germany, Greece, Hungary, Iceland, India, Indonesia, Ireland, Israel, Italy, Jamaica, Japan, Kazakstan, Korea (Republic of), Latvia, Lithuania, Luxembourg, Mexico, Morocco, Netherlands, New Zealand, Norway, Pakistan, Philippines, Poland, Portugal, Romania, Russia, Slovak Republic, Slovenia, South Africa, Spain, Sweden, Switzerland, Thailand, Trinidad & Tobago, Tunisia, Turkey, Ukraine, United Kingdom, and

29. ¶O-10976; ¶8634.04
30. ¶O-10985; ¶8614.27
31. ¶O-10700 *et seq.*; ¶8974; TD ¶643,001
32. ¶O-10735 *et seq.*; ¶8794; TD ¶643,016
33. ¶O-10733 *et seq.*; ¶8974; TD ¶643,014
34. ¶O-10734, O-10753; ¶8974; TD ¶643,015, 643,016

35. ¶O-10702; ¶8974; TD ¶643,006
36. ¶O-10810 *et seq.*; ¶8974.01; TD ¶643,029
37. ¶O-10812; ¶8974.01; TD ¶643,029
38. ¶O-15000 *et seq.*; ¶8944; TD ¶630,107
39. ¶O-15100 *et seq.*; ¶8944

Venezuela.[40]

Regs explain when tax treaty provisions apply to pass-through entities and their owners (e.g., partnership and its partners). (Reg § 1.894-1(d))[41]

A taxpayer who takes a return position that a treaty overrules or otherwise modifies the Code and thereby effects (or potentially effects) a reduction of any tax incurred at any time, must disclose that return position on Form 8833 attached to the return. (If a return wouldn't otherwise be required, the taxpayer must file one, signed, but need only include his name, address, TIN and disclosure statement.) Disclosure is waived for certain treaty-based return positions. (Code Sec. 6114(a); Reg § 301.6114-1)[42]

¶ 4658 Giving up U.S. citizenship or terminating long-term residency— Form 8854.

A nonresident alien individual described below, who within the 10-year period immediately preceding the close of the tax year lost U.S. citizenship, is subject to alternative expatriate income tax graduated rates for the year (if this alternative tax, after reducing it for the payment of foreign taxes, is greater than the ordinary tax on nonresident aliens to which he would be subject). (Code Sec. 877(a)(1)) The alternative expatriate income tax applies if:

(1) the individual's average annual net income tax for the period of five tax years ending before the date of the loss of U.S. citizenship is greater than $136,000 for 2007, as adjusted for inflation ($139,000 for 2008);

(2) the individual's net worth as of the date in (1) is $2,000,000 or more; or

(3) the individual: (i) fails to certify under penalty of perjury that he has met the requirements of the Code for the five preceding tax years, or (ii) fails to submit evidence of his compliance as IRS may require. (Code Sec. 877(a)(2)) The certification is made on Form 8854.

An expatriate subject to the alternative tax must provide an annual statement on Form 8854.[43]

The average income tax and net worth tests don't apply to certain individuals. (Code Sec. 877(c)) Individuals who are subject to the alternative tax must file information statements during the 10-year period. (Code Sec. 6039G)

In addition, individuals must provide notice of their expatriation on and file an information statement (using Form 8854) in order to expatriate. (Code Sec. 7701(n)) After expatriation, individuals may be taxed as U.S. citizens or residents if they satisfy a substantial presence test. (Code Sec. 877(g)(1))[44]

¶ 4659 Corporate and partnership expatriations (inversions)

Special rules apply where a domestic corporation or partnership is succeeded by a foreign corporation or partnership under a plan. These rules apply where (in the case of a corporation) substantially all of the domestic corporation's assets are transferred to a foreign entity and the former owners receive the following percentage interests in the transfer:

... Where the former owners own 80% or more of the interests, the successor entity is treated as a domestic entity

... Where the former owners own 60% or more of the interests, the taxable income of the expatriated entity cannot be less than the gain on the expatriation transaction. Similar rules apply to certain post-expatriation transactions with certain related entities. (Code Sec. 7874(a), Code Sec. 7874(b), Code Sec. 7874(e), Reg § 1.7874-1T, Reg § 1.7874-2T) Thus

40. ¶O-16500 *et seq.*; ¶8944; TD ¶192,010
41. ¶O-15025; ¶8944.01; TD ¶630,108
42. ¶O-15010 *et seq.*; ¶61,144; TD ¶192,006

43. ¶O-11701 *et seq.*; ¶8774; TD ¶644,701 *et seq.*
44. ¶O-11701.2 *et seq.*; ¶8774; TD ¶644,701.2 *et seq.*

these gains cannot be offset by losses or credits. (Code Sec. 7874(d))

An exception applies for where the entity (including certain related parties) has substantial activities in the country in which the successor entity is organized. (Code Sec. 7874(a))[45]

¶ 4660   Returns Relating to Foreign Taxpayers.

U.S. income tax returns must be filed by nonresident alien individuals and foreign corporations engaged in a U.S. business. Information returns are required for certain foreign transactions.

¶ 4661   Return of nonresident alien individual—Forms 1040NR and 1040NR-EZ.

A nonresident alien individual must file a U.S. tax return (Form 1040NR, or, for certain nonresident aliens with no dependents, Form 1040NR-EZ) for any tax year he was engaged in business in the U.S. (which includes most employees, see ¶4647), whether his income met the minimum (exemption amount); his tax was fully paid by withholding; or he claims tax treaty benefits. (Reg § 1.6012-1(b))[46] He must file to claim any deductions or to get a refund. (Reg § 1.6012-1(b)(2)(i))[47]

Form 1040NR and Form 1040NR-EZ are due by the 15th day of the sixth month (i.e., June 15), or fourth month (April 15, if the alien had wages subject to wage withholding) after the end of the year. (Reg § 1.6072-1(c))[48]

¶ 4662   Departing alien—"sailing permits" (Form 1040C, Form 2063).

An alien (resident or nonresident) leaving the U.S. generally must get a "certificate of [tax] compliance" ("sailing permit"), except for most tourists, students and foreign government personnel. (Code Sec. 6851(d)(1); Reg § 1.6851-2(a)(2)) The alien uses Form 1040C if he has income subject to U.S. tax (and Form 1040NR if required, see ¶4661), and Form 2063 if he has no taxable income. (Reg § 1.6851-2(b))[49]

¶ 4663   Return of foreign corporation—Form 1120F.

A foreign corporation must file a U.S. income tax return (Form 1120F) if it was engaged in business in the U.S., or its tax was not fully satisfied by withholding, or it claims tax treaty benefits (a statement claiming the benefits must be attached to the return) or a refund. Otherwise, no return is required. (Reg § 1.6012-2(g))[50]

A foreign corporation must file the return on or before the 15th day of the third month (sixth month if it has no U.S. office or place of business) following the close of the tax year. (Code Sec. 6072(b), Code Sec. 6072(c))[1] A foreign corporation that maintains an office in the U.S. may apply for both the automatic and the blanket filing extensions discussed at ¶4729.[2]

¶ 4664   Information returns—Form 5471; Form 5472; Form 926; Form 8865

A U.S. person who controls a foreign corporation for at least 30 consecutive days in his tax year must furnish IRS with certain information concerning the foreign corporation (on Form 5471). (Code Sec. 6038, Reg § 1.6038-2(a)) Similar reporting rules apply to U.S. partners that control foreign partnerships. (Code Sec. 6038, Reg § 1.6038-3)[3] "Control" means more than 50% ownership (by total vote or total value) of the corporation's stock. (Reg § 1.6038-2(b))[4] A person controls a partnership if the person owns, directly or indirectly, more than a 50%

---

45. ¶F-5700 *et seq.*; ¶78,744; TD ¶236,900 *et seq.*
46. ¶s S-1750, S-1752, S-1755; ¶60,124.02; TD ¶190,533
47. ¶S-1756; TD ¶630,104
48. ¶S-4703; ¶60,724; TD ¶630,104
49. ¶S-1760 *et seq.*; ¶68,514.04; TD ¶630,104

50. ¶S-1910; ¶s 8814, 60,124.03; TD ¶609,808
1. ¶S-4704
2. ¶S-5024
3. ¶S-3585; ¶60,384; TD ¶815,503
4. ¶S-3588; ¶60,384; TD ¶815,503

interest in the partnership. (Code Sec. 6038(e)(3)(A), Reg § 1.6038-3(b)) Use Form 8865 for partnership reporting. [5]

The organization or reorganization of, or acquisition of stock in, a foreign corporation must be reported (on Form 5471) by certain U.S. persons. (Code Sec. 6046; Reg § 1.6046-1)[6]

If a U.S. corporation, or a foreign corporation engaged in a U.S. trade or business, is controlled by a foreign person at any time in the tax year, it must maintain records and furnish IRS with certain information (on Form 5472) concerning specified transactions with related parties in that year. A separate form is required with respect to each related party. (Code Sec. 6038A(a), Code Sec. 6038C; Reg § 1.6038A-1, Reg § 1.6038A-2, Reg § 1.6038A-3)[7] To be in "control," the foreign person must own: (1) stock with at least 25% of the total combined voting power of all classes of voting stock, or (2) at least 25% of the total value of shares of all classes of stock. (Code Sec. 6038A(c)(1))[8]

Each U.S. person transferring property to a foreign corporation or partnership in specified tax-free exchanges or distributing property in complete liquidation to a non-U.S. person must report the transfer to IRS (on Form 926 for corporations, Form 8865 for partnerships) (Code Sec. 6038B; Reg § 1.6038B-1, Reg § 1.6038B-2)[9] A U.S. person must report (on Form 8865) an acquisition or disposition of an interest in a foreign partnership if he holds a 10% or greater interest in the partnership either before or after the event. (Code Sec. 6046A, Reg § 1.6046A-1)[10]

Foreign investors in U.S. real property must report their direct ownership interests to IRS. (Code Sec. 6039C)[11]

¶ 4665 Return of foreign partnership.

A foreign partnership isn't required to file a partnership return (Form 1065), if it doesn't have gross income that is (or is treated as) effectively connected with the conduct of a trade or business within the U.S. (ECI) and does not have gross income (including gains) derived from sources within the U.S.(U.S.-source income). Subject to exceptions, a foreign partnership that has ECI or has U.S.-source income that is not ECI must file a partnership return for its tax year. (Code Sec. 6031(e), Reg § 1.6031(a)-1(b)(1)) A foreign partnership (other than a withholding foreign partnership) that has $20,000 or less of U.S.-source income and has no ECI during its tax year need not file a partnership return if, at no time during the partnership tax year, 1% or more of any item of partnership income, gain, loss, deduction, or credit is allocable in the aggregate to direct U.S. partners. The U.S. partners must directly report their shares of the allocable items of partnership income, gain, loss, deduction, and credit. (Reg § 1.6031(a)-1(b)(2))

If a partnership is not a withholding foreign partnership and one or more withholding agents file the required Forms 1042 and 1042-S and pay the associated withholding tax, (1) a foreign partnership with U.S.-source income but no ECI and no U.S. partners is not required to file a partnership return, and (2) a foreign partnership with U.S.-source income and one or more U.S. partners but no ECI must file a partnership return. However, such a partnership need file Schedules K-1 only for its direct U.S.partners and for its passthrough partners through which U.S. partners hold an interest in the foreign partnership. (Reg § 1.6031(a)-1(b)(3))[12]

¶ 4666 Tax Withholding on Payments to Foreign Taxpayers. ▬▬▬▬▬▬▬

The payor or person controlling the amount subject to withholding (the withholding

---

5. ¶S-3585.3
6. ¶S-3602 *et seq.*; ¶60,464; TD ¶815,501
7. ¶S-3510 *et seq.*; ¶60,38A4; TD ¶815,504
8. ¶S-3580; ¶6038A4; TD ¶815,504

9. ¶S-3629 *et seq.*; ¶60,38B4; TD ¶815,506
10. ¶S-3643; ¶60,46A4, ¶60,38B4; TD ¶815,506
11. ¶S-3502 *et seq.*; ¶60,39C4; TD ¶815,508
12. ¶S-2717.1

agent), must withhold a 30% tax (or lower rates in certain cases) at source from certain U.S.-source amounts (e.g., interest and dividends) paid to nonresident aliens and foreign corporations.

¶ 4667   When withholding agent must withhold tax on payment to foreign payee.

Any person having the control, receipt, custody, disposal, or payment of specified items of income (¶4671) (a "withholding agent") must deduct and withhold U.S. income tax from those items, to the extent they are gross income from U.S. sources of foreigners subject to withholding (¶4669). (Code Sec. 1441(a))

The amount of tax to be deducted and withheld on an item is 30% unless a reduced rate applies by treaty (subject to an exception) or because the item is a scholarship or fellowship, or the item is specified compensation that's exempt from such withholding. (Code Sec. 1441(a)) In determining the withholding tax rate that applies to investment income earned in Guam by a nonresident alien, Guam is treated as part of the U.S. [13] Regs explain how to claim reduced withholding under a treaty. (Reg § 1.1441-6)[14]

The withholding agent is liable for the tax. (Code Sec. 1461)

A withholding agent must withhold the 30% tax on a payment made to a foreign payee, unless the agent can reliably associate the payment with documentation that the payment can be treated as made to a U.S. payee, or a foreign beneficial owner entitled to a reduced rate. (Reg § 1.1441-1(b)(1)) But the withholding agent need not withhold where the foreign person assumes responsibility for withholding on the payment as a (1) qualified intermediary (QI); (2) U.S. branch of a foreign person (or U.S. possessions financial institution treated as one); or (3) withholding foreign partnership or authorized foreign agent. (Reg § 1.1441-1(b)(2)) These persons provide a withholding agent with a withholding certificate Form W-8IMY.

Withholding by qualified intermediary . A QI is typically a foreign financial institution that enters into an agreement with IRS under which it acts as a withholding agent that determines the extent of its withholding obligation, as described above. (Reg § 1.1441-1(e)(5)) A QI is subject to the withholding and reporting provisions applicable to withholding agents and payors under the Code Sec. 1441 *et seq.* withholding, Code Sec. 6001 *et seq.* information reporting and the backup withholding and other withholding rules, except to the extent provided under the agreement. (Reg § 1.1441-1(e)(5)(iii))

However, the QI generally doesn't have to withhold if it doesn't assume primary withholding responsibility and has provided a valid withholding certificate and correct withholding statements to a withholding agent from which it receives an amount subject to that withholding. [15]

Withholding foreign trusts and partnerships may similarly enter into agreements with IRS under they may act as withholding agents, as described above. [16]

¶ 4668   Reporting withholding—Form 1042, Form 1042-S.

Form 1042 is an annual form that's used: (a) to report tax withheld and tax deposited that a withholding agent (¶4667) had to report on all Forms 1042-S (see below) for the preceding year; and (b) as a cover sheet for remitting Form 1042-S. It must be filed with IRS on or before Mar. 15 of the year following the year in which the income was paid, even though no tax was required to be withheld during a given year, if the withholding agent is required to file any Forms 1042-S for the year. (Reg § 1.1461-1(b)(1))

---

13. ¶O-1411
14. ¶O-12037

15. ¶O-11900 *et seq.*; ¶14,414 *et seq.*
16. ¶O-12005.8; ¶O-12014.2; ¶14,414 *et seq.*

A withholding agent (other than an individual who is not acting in the course of a trade or business with respect to a payment) must make an information return on Form 1042-S for each recipient of an amount subject to Code Sec. 1441 withholding (¶4667 *et seq.*), that was paid during the preceding year. But any person that withholds or is required to withhold under Code Sec. 1441 must file Form 1042-S for the payment withheld upon, whether or not that person is engaged in a trade or business, and whether or not the payment is an amount subject to reporting. (Reg § 1.1461-1(c)(1)(i))

One copy of Form 1042-S is filed with IRS on or before Mar. 15 of the year following the year in which the amount subject to reporting was paid, with a transmittal form. Another copy of Form 1042-S must be furnished to the recipient for whom the form is prepared on or before Mar. 15 of the year following the year in which the amount was paid. The withholding agent must retain a copy of each Form 1042-S. (Reg § 1.1461-1(c)(1)(i))[17]

¶ 4669   Which foreigners are subject to withholding

The following foreigners are subject to withholding at source on their U.S.-source income:

. . . nonresident alien individuals (Code Sec. 1441(a)) (even if an election is made to be treated as a U.S. resident for joint return purposes). (Reg § 1.1441-1(c)(3)(ii))

. . . a foreign corporation subject to U.S. income tax, other than a corporation created or organized in or under the laws of Guam, American Samoa, the Northern Mariana Islands, or the Virgin Islands if certain requirements are met. (Code Sec. 1442(c))

. . . a foreign partnership (but Reg § 1.1441-1(c)(6) applies concepts of payee and beneficial owner to determine if a payment is made to a foreign person). (Code Sec. 1441(a))

A withholding agent generally determines if a payee is a U.S. or foreign person on the basis of a withholding certificate (Form W-8) or a Form 8233 (indicating foreign status of the payee or beneficial owner) or a Form W-9 (indicating U.S. status of the payee). (Reg § 1.1441-1(b)(2)(i))

No withholding is required on payments to a foreign partnership or foreign corporation if IRS is satisfied that withholding would impose an undue administrative burden and that tax collection won't be jeopardized. (Code Sec. 1441(d); Code Sec. 1442(b))[18]

¶ 4670   How to claim exemption from withholding—Forms W-9, 8233, W-8, W-8EXP

Absent actual knowledge or reason to know otherwise, a withholding agent (¶4667) may treat a payee as a U.S. person, for whom withholding is not required, where the payee is required to furnish a Form W-9, and furnishes a Form W-9 under the backup withholding rules, which includes the payee's taxpayer identification number (TIN). A U.S. branch of a foreign person may establish its status as a foreign person exempt from Code Sec. 6001 information reporting rules and backup withholding by providing a withholding certificate on Form W-8. (Reg § 1.1441-1(d))

Where a payee is not required to furnish a Form W-9, the withholding agent may (absent knowledge or reason to know otherwise) rely on a certificate of U.S. status, i.e., an exemption certificate, or a Form W-9 (or a substitute form) that is signed under penalties of perjury by the payee and contains the name, residence address, and TIN of the payee. (Reg § 1.1441-1(d))

A withholding agent that makes a payment to an intermediary, a flow-through entity, or a U.S. branch, may treat the payment as made to a U.S. payee to the extent that, prior to the payment, the withholding agent can reliably associate the payment with: (a) a Form W-9 attached to a valid intermediary, flow-through, or U.S. branch withholding certificate, or (b) a

---

17. ¶S-3495.1; ¶14,414   18. ¶O-11900 *et seq.*; ¶14,414 *et seq.*

Form W-8 that evidences an agreement to treat a U.S. branch as a U.S. person. (Reg § 1.1441-1(d)(4))

To obtain an exemption from withholding on compensation for personal services of a nonresident alien individual by reason of a tax treaty, a separate withholding certificate must be submitted to each withholding agent from whom payments are to be received, for each of the nonresident's tax years. If the withholding agent is satisfied that an exemption from withholding is warranted, it accepts the certificate and forwards it to IRS within five days. The exemption from withholding becomes effective for payments made at least 10 days after a copy of the accepted withholding certificate is forwarded to IRS. (Reg § 1.1441-4(b)(2)(i))

The statement claiming exemption is made on Form 8233, an acceptable substitute for that form, or such other form as IRS may prescribe. (Reg § 1.1441-4(b)(2)(ii))

Foreign governments use Form W-8EXP to claim exemption from withholding. [19]

¶ 4671   What income items are subject to and exempt from withholding.

The gross amounts of these items of income (from U.S. sources) are subject to withholding:

. . . Interest (other than original issue discount (OID) and certain portfolio and bank account interest), dividends, rent, salary, wages, premiums, annuities, compensations, remunerations and emoluments.

. . . Other fixed or determinable annual or periodical gains, profits and income.

. . . Gains from lump-sum employee plan distributions.

. . . Original issue discount (OID) on sale, exchange, or retirement of corporate or governmental bonds.

. . . Gains from contingent payments with respect to patents and other intangibles sold or exchanged. (Code Sec. 1441(b); Code Sec. 1442(a))

. . . Gains from the disposal of timber, coal, or domestic iron ore with retained economic interests. (Code Sec. 1441(b); Reg § 1.1441-2(c))

. . . Social Security benefits paid to nonresident aliens, but only to the extent of 85% of those benefits. (Code Sec. 871(a)(3)(A))

. . . Amounts paid when a U.S. real property interest is acquired from a foreign person (¶4675). (Code Sec. 1445(a))

. . . Amounts includible in the gross income of the holder of a residual interest in a REMIC. (Code Sec. 860G(b)(1))

These items are exempt from withholding:

. . . The items listed above to the extent they are gross income from foreign sources. (Code Sec. 1441(b); Reg § 1.1441-3(a))

. . . Any item of income (other than compensation for personal services) which is effectively connected with the conduct of a U.S. business and taxed at regular U.S. tax rates. (Code Sec. 1441(c)(1); Code Sec. 1442(a)) Use Form W-8ECI to claim exemption.

. . . Amounts received as an annuity under a qualified employee benefit plan that are exempt from U.S. tax because they are attributable to the nonresident alien's foreign employment (including temporary U.S. employment for an employer located abroad) and at least 90% of the persons in the plan are U.S. citizens or residents. (Code Sec. 1441(c)(7)) Where the withholding agent is *not* the employer who established the plan, the recipient files a duplicate statement with the withholding agent, who must forward the duplicate with and attached to the Form 1042S filed by the withholding agent. (Reg § 1.1441-4(g))[20]

. . . RIC dividends that are paid out of interest that would not be subject to withholding and

---

19. ¶O-11964; ¶14,414.02   20. ¶O-11902; ¶14,414

short-term capital gains are exempt from withholding if certain requirements are satisfied. (Code Sec. 1441(c)(12))

¶ 4672 Wage withholding for compensation for personal services of a nonresident alien individual.

Compensation paid for personal services performed by a nonresident alien individual, which is otherwise "wages" and which is effectively connected with a U.S. trade or business, is subject to regular graduated income tax withholding under Code Sec. 3402. (Reg § 31.3401(a)(6)-1(a))[21]

Employers must (except for students and business apprentices from India) compute nonresident alien employees' wage withholding by adding an additional amount to their wages to offset an assumed standard deduction incorporated into withholding tables. For wages paid before Jan. 1, 2007, IRS won't assert employer's liability for underpayments of withholding (or interest and penalties), if the employer has made a good faith effort to implement these rules.[22]

The following aren't wages subject to regular wage withholding:

(1) wages paid for services performed outside the U.S. by a nonresident alien individual other than a resident of Puerto Rico; (Reg § 31.3401(a)(6)-1(b))

(2) remuneration paid to Canadian and Mexican residents who enter or leave the U.S. at frequent intervals and are engaged in transportation service or in service on international projects; (Reg § 31.3401(a)(6)-1(c))

(3) wages paid to Puerto Rican residents for services performed in Puerto Rico for an employer other than the U.S. government;

(4) wages paid for services performed outside the U.S., but not in Puerto Rico, by a Puerto Rican resident for an employer other than the U.S. government if the individual does not expect to be a Puerto Rican resident during the entire tax year;

(5) compensation paid for services performed outside the U.S. by a nonresident alien individual who is a resident of Puerto Rico as an employee of the U.S. government, if the individual does not expect to be a Puerto Rican resident during the entire tax year; (Reg § 31.3401(a)(6)-1(d)) or

(6) wages exempt from tax by law or treaty. (Reg § 31.3401(a)(6)-1(f))

To get exemptions under (2), (4) or (5) above, the employee must furnish a statement in duplicate to his employer confirming that he's entitled to it. The statement must be dated, identify the tax year to which it relates, be signed by the employee, and contain (or be verified by) a written declaration that it is made under penalty of perjury. (Reg § 31.3401(a)(6)-1)[23]

¶ 4673 Compensation subject to 30% withholding.

Although U.S. source compensation paid to a nonresident alien individual may be exempt from the definition of wages, and thus exempt from the regular graduated income tax withholding of Code Sec. 3402 (see ¶4672), the flat 30% withholding rate under Code Sec. 1441 (see ¶4667) applies to all forms of salaries, compensation, remuneration, etc. received by a nonresident alien individual to the extent these items of income are gross income from U.S. sources (Code Sec. 1441(a); Code Sec. 1441(b)), as well as to amounts paid as compensation for personal services that are effectively connected with the conduct of a U.S. trade or business. (Code Sec. 1441(c)(1)) Except that such Code Sec. 1441 withholding doesn't apply, if that compensation (Code Sec. 1441(c)(4)):

---

21. ¶O-11988 *et seq.*; ¶14,414.06
22. ¶H-4529.1

23. ¶O-11988 *et seq.*; ¶14,414.06

(1) is subject to withholding as "wages" under Code Sec. 3402 (see ¶4672).

(2) would be subject to graduated tax withholding as wages under Code Sec. 3402, except that it is specifically exempted from wages by Code Sec. 3401(a), with certain exceptions.

(3) is for services performed by Canadian or Mexican residents who enter or leave the U.S. at frequent intervals.

(4) is exempt from tax by law or treaty. (Reg § 1.1441-4(b)(1)) Where the exemption is by treaty the nonresident alien must submit a statement to each withholding agent from which amounts are to be received on Form 8233 (or an acceptable substitute); (Reg § 1.1441-4(b)(2))

(5) is paid as a commission or rebate by a ship supplier to a nonresident alien individual who is employed by a nonresident alien individual, foreign partnership or foreign corporation in the operation of ships of foreign registry, for placing orders for ship supplies; or

(6) is exempt from withholding under Code Sec. 3402 due to the Code Sec. 3402(e) "all-or-nothing rule," if the employee and employer enter into a voluntary nonwage withholding agreement. (Reg § 1.1441-4(b)(1))[24]

observation: Items (3) and (4) above are also exempt from regular wage withholding, see ¶4672.

¶ 4674   Withholding by partnerships with respect to foreign partners— Form 8813, Form 8804, Form 8805.

A partnership must pay a withholding tax if it has "effectively connected taxable income" for the tax year (whether or not the income is distributed), any part of which is allocable to a foreign partner. (Code Sec. 1446(a)) Unless the partner can show that the tax will be lower, the partnership must withhold at the highest rate of U.S. tax to which the foreign partner would be subject on the effectively connected taxable income allocable to the foreign corporate or noncorporate partner. (Code Sec. 1446(b); Reg § 1.1446-3; Reg § 1.1446-6T) The partnership must determine the status of its partners based on Forms W-8 or W-9 filed by the partners. In the absence of documentation of a partner's status, the partnership must follow the presumptions in the regs. (Code Sec. 1446(b); Reg § 1.1446-1) Special rules apply to publicly traded partnerships and tiered partnerships. (Reg § 1.1446-4; Reg § 1.1446-5)[25]

The partnership must pay the withheld amount in installments based on the estimated tax requirements (¶3349) together with a Form 8813. The partnership must also report the partnership's total withholding liability for its year on Form 8804 and notify each foreign partner of his share thereof on Form 8805. (Reg § 1.1446-3)[26]

A domestic partnership must withhold on amounts subject to withholding (¶4671) that are not effectively connected income and are includible in the gross income of a partner that is a foreign person. A U.S. partnership must withhold when any distributions (including guaranteed payments) that include amounts subject to withholding are made. To the extent a foreign partner's distributive share of income subject to withholding has not been actually distributed to the foreign partner, the partnership must withhold on the partner's distributive share of the income on the earlier of the date the Form K-1 is mailed or otherwise furnished to the partner, or the due date for furnishing the K-1. If a partnership withholds on a distributive share before the amount is actually distributed to the partner, then withholding is not required when the amount is later distributed. (Reg § 1.1441-5(b)(2))[27]

---

24. ¶O-11988 *et seq.*; ¶14,414.06
25. ¶O-12100 *et seq.*; ¶14,464; TD ¶634,030

26. ¶S-2718 *et seq.*; TD ¶634,031
27. ¶O-12010; ¶14,414

¶ 4675 U.S. real property dispositions—Form 8288, Form 8288-A, Form 8828-B.

U.S. tax must be withheld when a foreign investor disposes of a USRPI (¶4655) (Code Sec. 1445(a))[28] including certain interests in a partnership, trust, or estate that directly or indirectly owns a USRPI. (Code Sec. 1445(e)(5); Reg § 1.1445-11T(b))[29]

The amount to be withheld generally is 10% of the amount realized on the disposition. (Code Sec. 1445(a)) The amount realized is the sum of cash received (not including any stated or unstated interest or original issue discount), the fair market value of any other property received, and any liability assumed by the transferee (e.g., buyer) or to which the USRPI was subject. (Reg § 1.1445-1(g))[30]

The withholding obligation is generally imposed on the transferee, (Code Sec. 1445) who must report the amounts withheld and pay them over (to IRS) by the 20th day after transfer. (Reg § 1.1445-1(c)) Form 8288 and Form 8288-A are used for this purpose. Foreign transferees are required to include their taxpayer identification numbers (TINs) on withholding tax returns.[31]

Withholding isn't required if the transferor gives the transferee a sworn "nonforeign affidavit" showing the transferor's U.S. taxpayer identification number and stating that he isn't a foreign person (Code Sec. 1445(b)(2); Reg § 1.1445-2(b)), or a sworn "non-USRPHC affidavit" stating that it's not a U.S. real property holding corporation, [32] *unless* (in either case) the transferee knows the affidavit is false. (Code Sec. 1445(b)(7))[33]

Nor does withholding apply if the USRPI is acquired by the transferee as his residence, and the amount realized doesn't exceed $300,000. (Code Sec. 1445(b)(5))[34]

IRS will issue a certificate excusing or reducing withholding if the transferor is exempt from U.S. tax, or if either the transferor or transferee agrees to pay the tax and gives security for its payment. (Reg § 1.1445-3(e)) A certificate gotten before a transfer notifies the transferee that no withholding, or reduced withholding, is required. A certificate gotten after the transfer may authorize a normal or early refund. (Use Form 8288-B to request a certificate.) [35]

¶ 4676 Foreign Currency Rules. ▬▬▬▬▬▬▬▬▬▬▬▬▬

Transactions involving foreign currency must be expressed in U.S. dollars for U.S. tax purposes.

¶ 4677 Functional currency.

All U.S. taxpayers are required to make all federal income tax determinations in their "functional currency," (Code Sec. 985(a))[36] on a transaction-by-transaction basis. [37]

"Functional currency" generally means the U.S. dollar. (Code Sec. 985(b)(1)(A)) "Qualified business units" (QBUs) that conduct a significant part of their activities in an economic environment with a non-dollar currency in which they keep their books and records use that currency (Code Sec. 985(b)(1)(B))[38] unless the taxpayer elects (on Form 8819) to use the dollar as the QBU's functional currency. (Code Sec. 985(b)(3); Reg § 1.985-2)[39]

A QBU is any separate and clearly identified unit (or activity) of a trade or business of a taxpayer which maintains separate books and records. (Code Sec. 989(a); Reg § 1.989(a)-1(b)(2)(ii)) A corporation is a QBU. A partnership, trust or estate is a QBU of a partner or

28. ¶O-13001; ¶14,454; TD ¶644,002
29. ¶O-13035 *et seq.*; ¶14,454; TD ¶644,020
30. ¶O-13002; ¶14,454; TD ¶644,002
31. ¶S-5662; ¶14,454; TD ¶644,006
32. ¶O-13010 *et seq.*; ¶14,454; TD ¶644,007
33. ¶O-13013; TD ¶644,010

34. ¶O-13016; ¶14,454; TD ¶644,007
35. ¶O-13021 *et seq.*, S-5664; ¶14,454; TD ¶644,016
36. ¶G-6900 *et seq.*; ¶9854 *et seq.*
37. ¶G-6901
38. ¶G-6901 *et seq.*; ¶9854 *et seq.*
39. ¶G-6918 *et seq.*; ¶9854.01

beneficiary. An individual is not a QBU. (Reg §   1.989(a)-1(b)(2)(i))[40]

¶ 4678   Foreign currency gains and losses; section 988 transactions.

Foreign currency gain or loss attributable to a "Section 988 transaction" must generally be computed separately and be treated as interest income or expense, as the case may be. (Code Sec. 988(a)(1)(A), Code Sec. 988(a)(2))[41] However, a taxpayer may elect to treat the foreign currency gain or loss attributable to certain of these transactions as capital gain or loss. (Code Sec. 988(a)(1)(B); Reg § 1.988-3(b))[42]

Recognition of foreign currency gain or loss requires a closed and completed transaction, such as the payment of a liability. [43]

The source of these gains and losses is determined by reference to the residence of the taxpayer or QBU on whose books the relevant asset, liability or item of income or expense is properly reflected. (Code Sec. 988(a)(3); Reg § 1.988-4)[44] There are special rules for certain related corporations (Code Sec. 988(a)(3)(C))[45] currency swaps[46] and hedging transactions. (Code Sec. 988(d)(2))[47]

A "section 988 transaction" is any of specified transactions if the amount the taxpayer is entitled to receive, or is required to pay, by reason of the transaction is either: (1) denominated in terms of a nonfunctional currency; or (2) determined by reference to the value of one or more nonfunctional currencies. (Code Sec. 988(c)(1)(A))[48]

¶ 4679   Personal transactions.

The Code Sec. 988 rules apply to transactions entered into by an individual only to the extent the expenses properly allocable to them satisfy Code Sec. 162, Code Sec. 212(1) or Code Sec. 212(2). An individual who disposes of foreign currency in a personal transaction doesn't recognize gain by reason of fluctuations in exchange rates during the period the taxpayer held the currency, unless the gain the exceeds $200. [49]

¶ 4680   Recording and translating the results of foreign currency operations.

Any foreign business entity —whether a branch or a sub —that uses a nondollar functional currency must use a profit-and-loss method to translate the results of its operations into U.S. dollars, at the "appropriate exchange rate." (Code Sec. 987; Reg § 1.987-1)[50]

¶ 4681   Reporting Gifts from Foreign Persons. ▰▰▰▰▰▰▰▰▰▰▰▰▰▰

U.S. persons must report certain gifts from foreign persons.

¶ 4682   Reporting foreign gifts— Form 3520.

If the value of the aggregate "foreign gifts" (see below) received by a U.S. person (other than an exempt Code Sec. 501(c) organization) exceeds a threshold amount (see below), the U.S. person must report each "foreign gift" to IRS. (Code Sec. 6039F(a)) Form 3520 is used to report these gifts.

Different reporting thresholds apply for gifts received from (a) nonresident alien individuals or foreign estates, and (b) foreign partnerships or foreign corporations. For gifts from a nonresident alien or foreign estate, reporting of gifts over $5,000 is required only if the

40. ¶G-6912; ¶9854
41. ¶s G-7001 *et seq.*, G-7028; ¶9884 *et seq.*
42. ¶G-7024 *et seq.*; ¶9884.01
43. ¶G-7001
44. ¶G-7029; ¶9884.01
45. ¶O-4504; ¶9884.01

46. ¶G-7021 *et seq.*; ¶9884.01
47. ¶G-7027 *et seq.*; ¶s 9884.01, 9884.02
48. ¶G-6988 *et seq.*; ¶9884.01
49. ¶G-7047; ¶9884.01
50. ¶G-6966 *et seq.*; ¶9874 *et seq.*

aggregate amount of gifts from that person exceeds $100,000 during the tax year. For gifts from foreign corporations and foreign partnerships, the reporting threshold amount is an inflation adjusted aggregate amount of gifts of $13,258 for tax years beginning in 2007 ($13,561 for tax years beginning in 2008).

"Foreign gifts" include any amounts received from a person that isn't a U.S. person the recipient treats as a gift or bequest. The term doesn't include any qualified tuition or medical payments made on behalf of a U.S. person (under Code Sec. 2503(e)(2)) or any distribution that was properly disclosed under Code Sec. 6048(c)) (Code Sec. 6039F(b))[1]

1. ¶S-3649.1; ¶S-3649.5; ¶60,39F4; TD ¶746,002

Chapter 24   Returns and Payment of Tax

¶ 4700   Returns and Payment of Tax.   ▰▰▰▰▰▰▰▰▰▰▰▰▰▰▰▰▰▰▰▰▰

An individual taxpayer must file an income tax return if his gross income equals or exceeds a specified amount. Married taxpayers may file a joint return. Corporations, trusts and estates must also file income tax returns. A partnership files an information return of income. Payors and others must file information returns to report specified payments, sales, etc. Times, places and methods of paying tax are specified.

¶ 4701   Who must file individual income tax returns?

An income tax return must be filed by every individual U.S. citizen and resident alien (including an alien who is a bona fide resident of Puerto Rico during the entire tax year) (Reg § 1.1-1(b), Reg § 1.6012-1(a)(1)) and nonresident or dual-status alien married to a U.S. citizen or resident at year-end who has elected to be treated as a resident alien (Reg § 1.6013-6(a))[1] who has gross income (including excluded homesale gain and foreign earned income (Code Sec. 6012(c)) that equals or exceeds the following amounts:

	2008	2007
(1) Single (Code Sec. 6012(a)(1)(A)(i))	$8,950	$8,750
—65-or-over (Code Sec. 6012(a)(1)(B))	10,300	10,050
(2) Married filing joint return (Code Sec. 6012(a)(1)(A)(iv))	17,900	17,500
—one 65-or-over (Code Sec. 6012(a)(1)(B))	18,950	18,550
—both 65-or-over (Code Sec. 6012(a)(1)(B)).	20,000	19,600
(3) Married filing separate return (Code Sec. 6012(a)(1)(A))	3,500	3,400
(4) Head of Household (Code Sec. 6012(a)(1)(A)(ii))	11,500	11,250
—65-or-over (Code Sec. 6012(a)(1)(B))	12,850	12,550
(5) Surviving spouse (Code Sec. 6012(a)(1)(A)(iii))	14,400	14,100
—65-or-over (Code Sec. 6012(a)(1)(B))	15,450	15,150

The above rules don't apply to an individual who can be claimed as a dependent by another. That individual/dependent must file a return if (a) his unearned income is more than $850 for 2007 ($900 for 2008) plus any additional standard deduction for aged and blind (¶3112), or (b) his total gross income is more than the standard deduction (¶3112). (Code Sec. 6012(a)(1)(C)(i))[2] A married dependent whose spouse files a separate return and itemizes deductions must file if he has gross income of $5 or more. [3] However, no return is required for a child where the child's parent elects (¶3137) to include the child's income on the parent's return under the "kiddie tax" rules. For 2007, this election is available if the child's income is more than $850 ($900 for 2008) and less than $8,500 ($9,000 for 2008). (Code Sec. 1(g)(7)(A))[4]

The filing threshold in (2), above, applies only if the spouses, at the end of the tax year, had the same household as their home (Code Sec. 6012(a)(1)(A)(iv)) and no other taxpayer could claim an exemption for either spouse. (Code Sec. 6012(a)(1)(A))

An individual who has $400 or more net earnings from self-employment (¶3140) must file a return even though his gross income is less than the required amount. (Code Sec. 6017)[5]

---

1. ¶S-1701; ¶60,124.02; TD ¶570,201
2. ¶S-1705; ¶60,124; TD ¶570,204
3. ¶S-1705; TD ¶570,204
4. ¶S-1704.1; ¶14.11; TD ¶568,400
5. ¶S-1717; ¶60,174; TD ¶570,216

References beginning with a single letter are to paragraphs in RIA's Federal Tax Coordinator 2d and RIA's Analysis of Federal Taxes: Income. Those beginning with numbers are to paragraphs in RIA's United States Tax Reporter. Those beginning with TD are to paragraphs in RIA's Tax Desk.

Every individual who has received advance payments of earned income credit (¶2346) must file a return regardless of the amount of his income. (Code Sec. 6012(a)(8))[6]

Individuals required to file a short year return because of a change in accounting period must file a return if gross income received during the short year equals or exceeds $3,400 for 2007 ($3,500 for 2008), prorated in the ratio that the months of the short year bear to 12. (Reg § 1.6012-1(a)(2)(v))[7]

The following U.S. citizens or residents may have to file an income tax return even though they have gross income below the levels listed above:

. . . Individuals who received tips from which social security tax wasn't withheld. [8]

. . . Individuals receiving advance payment of the earned income credit.

. . . Individuals owing alternative minimum tax. [9]

. . . Employees of certain religious and other church-controlled organizations, if they receive more than $108.28 of compensation from the organization during the year. [10]

. . . Individuals receiving income from U.S. possessions. [11]

. . . Nonresident aliens (NRAs)[12] but not NRAs who earn less than the personal exemption amount.[13]

. . . Individuals who change their citizenship or country of residence during the year. [14]

. . . Individuals who must pay a tax with respect to an IRA, qualified retirement plan, Archer medical savings account, health savings account, Coverdell education savings account, or qualified tuition program. If filing only for this reason, use Form 5329 by itself. [15]

. . . Individuals who must pay a tax resulting from recapture of education credit, investment credit, low income housing credit, federal mortgage subsidy, qualified electric vehicle credit, new markets credit, or Indian employment credit. [16]

The filing thresholds that apply to a decedent's final return follow the rules for individuals, above; they aren't reduced or prorated. [17]

¶ 4702 Individual income tax return forms.

U.S. citizens and residents use Form 1040 (Reg § 1.6012-1(a)(6)), Form 1040A (Reg § 1.6012-1(a)(7)(i)) or Form 1040EZ.

Form 1040A may be used by a taxpayer in any filing status who has income only from wages, salaries, tips, IRA distributions, pension and annuities, taxable social security and railroad retirement benefits, mutual fund capital gain distributions, Alaska Fund dividends, taxable scholarships and fellowship grants, interest (other than from exempt private activity bonds), dividends, jury duty pay and unemployment compensation, who has only certain adjustments to gross income (educator expenses, IRA deduction, student loan interest deduction, tuition and fees deduction, and jury duty pay given to employer), who doesn't itemize, whose taxable income is less than $100,000, and who has only certain tax credits. Form 1040A may be used even if the taxpayer owes alternative minimum tax.

Single or married filing jointly taxpayers under 65 who aren't blind can use Form 1040EZ if they claim no dependents, have income only from wages, salaries, tips, taxable scholarships or fellowships, unemployment compensation, Alaska Permanent Fund Dividends, and interest (of $1,500 or less), no adjustments to gross income, no itemized deductions, taxable income of less than $100,000 and no tax credits other than the earned income credit (but no advance

6. ¶S-1710; ¶60,124; TD ¶570,209
7. ¶S-1707; ¶60,124; TD ¶570,206
8. ¶S-1709; ¶60,124; TD ¶570,208
9. ¶S-1716; ¶60,124; TD ¶570,215
10. ¶S-1718; ¶60,124; TD ¶570,217
11. ¶S-1704.3; ¶60,124.02; TD ¶570,207

12. ¶S-1750 *et seq.*; ¶60,124.02
13. ¶S-1755
14. ¶S-1758
15. ¶S-1708.1; ¶60,124; TD ¶570,203
16. ¶S-1708.1; ¶60,124; TD ¶570,203
17. ¶C-9602; ¶C-9603; ¶60,124.04; TD ¶579,501

payment of that credit).[18]

Rounding to the nearest dollar is permitted. (Code Sec. 6102(a)(2); Reg § 301.6102-1(a))[19]

¶ 4703 Electronic filing of individual returns.

Tax preparers can electronically file current year returns (Form 1040, Form 1040A and Form 1040EZ) (but not after Oct. 15 even with a filing extension) and Form 4868 automatic filing extensions for individual taxpayers, [20] including returns that show a balance due. [21] However an electronic return can't be filed for returns for years other than the current tax year, amended returns, returns that cover fiscal year tax periods, or in certain other situations. [22] Publication 1345A, published in December of each year, lists the forms and schedules associated with the Form 1040 series that can be electronically transmitted for the particular tax year. [23]

An electronic return is a composite return consisting of data transmitted to IRS electronically and of paper documents (filed later) that can't be electronically transmitted, such as an individual income tax declaration for an individual *e-file* return (use Form 8453), documents prepared by third parties, etc. [24] IRS has developed procedures for accepting signatures in digital or electronic form. (Code Sec. 6061(b))[25] Tax practitioners can e-file individual income tax returns only if the returns are signed electronically using one of two methods: either a Self-Select Personal Identification Number (PIN) or a Practitioner PIN. Practitioner PINs require the use of Form 8879, which is retained by the electronic return originator (ERO). [26] For how to submit payments for electronic returns on Form 1040-V, see ¶4721.

¶ 4704 Husband and wife—joint or separate returns.

Married persons have the choice of filing a joint return (one return reporting their combined incomes and deductions) (Code Sec. 6013(a))[27] or separate returns. (Code Sec. 1(d))[28] Neither a return prepared and executed by IRS nor a Form 870 waiver constitutes a valid election to file a joint return. [29]

observation: Filing separately may save taxes because of the 7.5% floor on medical expenses, the 2% floor on miscellaneous itemized deductions, and the 10% floor on casualty losses. Each floor is measured against adjusted gross income (AGI), so where either spouse has high amounts of these expenses, measuring them against the separate AGI can produce a larger deduction than if measured against the joint AGI. However, these advantages may be offset by the many restrictive rules for separate filers.

observation: Filing separately also avoids the joint and several liability that attaches to a joint return, see ¶4708.

¶ 4705 Qualifying for joint returns.

A husband and wife may file a joint return even if only one has income (Code Sec. 6013(a))[30] and even if they have different accounting *methods*. But they must be legally married as of the *end* of the tax year. (Code Sec. 6013(d))[31]

If the parties filed a joint return during their "marriage" and later get an annulment, they

18. ¶S-1715; ¶60,114.01; TD ¶570,213
19. ¶S-1006; ¶61,014; TD ¶570,105
20. ¶S-1601; ¶60,114.08; TD ¶572,010
21. ¶S-1617; ¶60,114.08; TD ¶572,029
22. ¶S-1604; TD ¶572,009
23. ¶S-1603; TD ¶572,008
24. ¶S-1601.2 *et seq.*; ¶60,114.08; TD ¶572,005

25. ¶S-4518; ¶60,614
26. ¶S-1617.3
27. ¶S-1801; ¶60,134 *et seq.*; TD ¶570,601
28. ¶A-1502; ¶14.01; TD ¶566,002
29. ¶S-1827
30. ¶S-1801; ¶60,134; TD ¶570,601
31. ¶S-1803; ¶60,134.03; TD ¶570,602

must refile as separate unmarried persons. [32]

A joint return *can't* be filed if:

... *either spouse was a nonresident alien* (NRA) at any time during the tax year (Code Sec. 6013(a)(1))[33] but where one spouse is an NRA for the entire year (Code Sec. 6013(g)) or where an NRA spouse becomes a U.S. resident during the tax year (Code Sec. 6013(h)), both spouses can *elect* to file a joint return by agreeing to subject their worldwide income to U.S. taxation;[34]

... *the spouses have different tax years,* except when one spouse dies, see ¶4707.

¶ 4706 Changing from joint to separate returns and vice versa.

Once a joint return has been filed spouses may revoke it by filing separate returns until the due date of the return. After the due date has passed, they can't switch from joint to separate. (Reg § 1.6013-1(a))[35]

🔷*observation:* The couple may file jointly in one year and separately in another.

A married couple who filed separate returns may switch to a joint return after the due date if: (a) the joint return is filed within 3 years from the original due date (without extension), and (b) neither spouse has, with respect to his previously filed separate return, petitioned the Tax Court, filed a suit for refund, or entered into a closing agreement or final compromise. (Code Sec. 6013(b); Reg § 1.6013-2(b))[36]

¶ 4707 Joint return for year spouse(s) dies.

A joint return may be filed for a husband and wife where their tax years start the same day and end on different days because of the death of either or both (unless the survivor remarries before the end of his tax year). The joint return must be made with respect to the tax year of each. (Code Sec. 6013(a)(2))[37] For when to file, see ¶4717.

🔷*recommendation:* File a joint return to get the benefits of the joint return rates, to use up decedent's net operating loss, capital loss, or charitable contribution carryforwards or other expiring deductions or credits, if the survivor has income or can generate income before the end of the survivor's tax year.

A surviving spouse may file a joint return for the deceased and surviving spouse if: the deceased spouse didn't previously file a return for the tax year; an executor/administrator hasn't been appointed by the time the joint return is made; and an executor/administrator hasn't been appointed before the due date for filing the return of the surviving spouse (including extensions). (Code Sec. 6013(a)(3))[38]

🔷*observation:* The return for the year before the year of death therefore also is subject to these rules if the decedent died before filing a return for that year.

If an executor or administrator is appointed on or before the filing due date, the surviving spouse *can't* file a joint return for the decedent. Only the fiduciary can act for the decedent, so both the fiduciary and the surviving spouse must sign the joint return. Even if the surviving spouse properly filed a joint return (because no fiduciary had been appointed by the due date), the fiduciary may disaffirm (revoke) the joint return by filing a *separate* return for the decedent within one year after the due date (including extensions). Any "joint" return improperly filed by the survivor or disaffirmed by the fiduciary is treated as a *separate* return of

---

32. ¶A-1609; ¶60,134.03; TD ¶566,509
33. ¶S-1802; ¶60,134; TD ¶570,601
34. ¶A-1800 *et seq.*; ¶60,134.01; TD ¶567,501
35. ¶S-1831; ¶60,134.01; TD ¶570,622

36. ¶S-1829; ¶60,134.01; TD ¶570,620
37. ¶S-1805; ¶60,134; TD ¶570,603
38. ¶S-1806; ¶60,134; TD ¶570,604

the survivor. (Code Sec. 6013(a)(3))[39]

For use of joint return *rates* where the survivor has a dependent child, see ¶3131.

¶ 4708 Liability for tax, penalties, and interest on spouses' returns.

Joint returns. Except as noted at ¶4709 to ¶4711, each spouse is jointly and severally liable for the full amount of the tax, penalties (other than civil fraud (¶4880)), and interest arising out of their joint return, regardless of the amount of his separate taxable income. (Code Sec. 6013(d)(3)) Only the spouse committing fraud can be subjected to fraud penalties. [40]

Separate returns. Each spouse is liable only for his own tax and penalties. [41]

¶ 4709 Elective relief from joint tax liability (innocent spouse rule)—Form 8857.

An individual who has filed a joint return may elect (use Form 8857) to seek relief from joint and several liability (¶4708) under innocent spouse procedures. (Code Sec. 6015(a)(1)) Under IRS procedures, an individual will be relieved of liability for tax (including interest, penalties, and other amounts) for a tax year to the extent the liability is due to an understatement if:

(a) a joint return was filed for the tax year;

(b) there's an understatement of tax on the return due to erroneous items of the other spouse;

(c) the individual establishes that, in signing the return, he didn't know *or have reason to know* of the understatement;

(d) taking into account all the facts and circumstances, it would be inequitable to hold the individual liable for the deficiency; and

(e) the individual elects the benefits of the innocent spouse provision, by filing Form 8857 (separately from the tax return) with specified attached statement, no later than two years after IRS has begun collection activities with respect to the individual. (Code Sec. 6015(b)(1))[42]

observation: Innocent spouse relief isn't available for liabilities that were properly reported on a joint return but weren't paid, because in that situation there's no understatement of tax. However, equitable relief (¶4711) may be available.

An individual who knew or had reason to know of the understatement, but establishes that he didn't know or have reason to know of its *extent,* is relieved of liability to the extent of the understatement of which he didn't know or have reason to know. (Code Sec. 6015(b)(2))[43]

Special innocent spouse relief applies to a spouse of a partner in a partnership subject to unified partnership audit procedures (¶4840) (Code Sec. 6230(a)(3), Code Sec. 6230(c)(5))[44] and to a spouse in a community property state who files a separate return and doesn't include the proper amount of community income on the return, unless it is inequitable to hold the other spouse liable. (Code Sec. 66)[45] In determining whether any innocent spouse relief is available, income, credits, and deductions are generally allocated to the spouses without regard to the operation of community property laws. (Reg § 1.6015-1(f)(1))[46]

For a spouse's separate liability election, see ¶4710. For equitable relief where other innocent spouse relief isn't available, see ¶4711. For exceptions to innocent spouse relief, see ¶4712.

---

39. ¶S-1806; ¶60,134; TD ¶570,605
40. ¶V-8502; ¶s 60,134.05, 66,534.11; TD ¶570,901
41. ¶V-8504; TD ¶570,903
42. ¶V-8506 *et seq.*; ¶60,154.01; TD ¶570,904

43. ¶V-8516; ¶60,154.01; TD ¶570,905
44. ¶T-2261.1; ¶62,304
45. ¶A-5016 *et seq.*; ¶664; TD ¶573,602
46. ¶V-8511

When IRS receives a request for relief (¶4710; ¶4711), it must send a notice to the nonrequesting spouse's last known address informing that spouse of the requesting spouse's claim for relief. (Reg § 1.6015-6(a)(1)) The nonrequesting spouse may file a protest and receive an IRS appeals conference regarding an innocent spouse determination. IRS's procedures protect domestic abuse victims who fear retaliation for applying for innocent spouse relief. [47] The nonrequesting spouse may also intervene to support the requesting spouse's innocent spouse claim. [48]

¶ 4710 Separate liability ("allocation of liability") election—Form 8857.

An individual who files a joint return and meets certain eligibility requirements can elect to limit his liability for any deficiency with respect to it. This "separate liability" (or "allocation of liability") election may be made in addition to the innocent spouse election (¶4709). (Code Sec. 6015(a)(2))[49] Separate liability relief is available only for unpaid liabilities resulting from understatements; refunds are not authorized. (Reg § 1.6015-3(c)(1))[50]

An individual is eligible to make the election only if, at the time the election is filed, he or she is no longer married to, or is legally separated from, the spouse with whom the joint return was filed, or wasn't a member of the same household as that spouse at any time during the previous 12-month period. If IRS demonstrates that assets were transferred between spouses in a fraudulent scheme joined in by both spouses, a separate liability election filed by either spouse will be invalid. (Code Sec. 6015(c)(3)(A))[1]

To elect, file Form 8857 (separately from the tax return) with specified attached statement no later than two years after IRS begins collection activity against the electing spouse. (Code Sec. 6015(c)(3)(B); Reg § 1.6015-5)[2]

Except as provided below, an electing spouse's liability for any deficiency that IRS assesses won't exceed the portion of the deficiency properly allocable to that spouse. (Code Sec. 6015(c)(1), Code Sec. 6015(d)(3)(A))[3] The liability is generally allocated between the spouses in proportion to the net items taken into account in determining the deficiency as if the spouses had filed separate returns. (Code Sec. 6015(d)(1))[4] However, the limitation on an electing spouse's tax liability is increased by the value of property transferred to that spouse by the nonelecting spouse principally to avoid tax, which is rebuttably presumed (except for divorce or separate maintenance transfers) to be the case for transfers made anytime after one year before the first letter of proposed deficiency is sent. (Code Sec. 6015(c)(4))[5] Also, except where a joint return was signed under duress, the election doesn't apply to the extent that IRS has evidence that the electing spouse had *actual* knowledge of an item giving rise to all or part of a deficiency allocable to the other spouse. (Code Sec. 6015(c)(3)(C))[6]

¶ 4711 Equitable relief for spouses—Form 8857.

If under all the facts and circumstances it's inequitable to hold a spouse liable for any portion of any unpaid tax or deficiency, and relief isn't available under the innocent spouse (¶4709) or separate liability election (¶4710) rules, IRS may relieve that spouse of liability for that unpaid tax or deficiency (Code Sec. 6015(f); Reg § 1.6015-4) and in limited cases may issue a refund. To request equitable relief, file Form 8857 (separately from the tax return) with specified attached statement. (Reg § 1.6015-5(a))

All of the following threshold conditions must be met to be considered for this relief:

(1) a joint return must have been filed for the tax year and the liability for which relief is

47. ¶V-8550
48. ¶U-2152
49. ¶V-8533; ¶60,154.02; TD ¶570,933
50. ¶T-5513
1. ¶V-8534; ¶60,154.02; TD ¶570,934

2. ¶V-8536; ¶60,154.02; TD ¶570,936
3. ¶V-8537; ¶60,154.02; TD ¶570,941
4. ¶V-8539; ¶60,154.02; TD ¶570,939
5. ¶V-8538; ¶60,154.02; TD ¶570,938
6. ¶V-8549; ¶60,154.02; TD ¶570,949

sought, subject to limited exceptions, must be attributable to the nonrequesting spouse;

(2) relief must not be available under Code Sec. 6015(b) or Code Sec. 6015(c);

(3) relief must be applied for no later than two years after IRS's first collection activity with respect to the individual;

(4) the liability must be unpaid when relief is requested. However, relief in the form of a refund of liabilities may be available for certain installment payments made after the claim for relief is requested;

(5) no assets were transferred between the individuals filing the joint return as part of a fraudulent scheme;

(6) there were no disqualified assets transferred to the individual by the nonrequesting spouse (if there were, relief will be available only to the extent the liability exceeds their value); and

(7) the individual didn't file the joint return with fraudulent intent. [7]

Equitable relief ordinarily will be granted to an individual who meets the above-listed threshold requirements where:

(1) the joint return liability was unpaid at the time the return was filed;

(2) at the time relief is requested, the individual is no longer married to, or is legally separated from, the spouse with whom the joint return was filed, or has not been a member of the same household as that spouse during the 12-month period ending on the date the relief is requested;

(3) when the return was signed, the individual didn't know, and had no reason to know, that the tax would not be paid. The individual must establish that it was reasonable for him to believe that the other spouse would pay the reported liability (partial relief may be available); and

(4) the individual will suffer economic hardship (determined by IRS under rules similar to those in Reg § 301.6343-1(b)(4)) if relief isn't granted.

Relief only applies to the tax liability shown on the return before any adjustment to the return, and is only available to the extent the unpaid tax is attributable to the spouse not requesting relief. IRS lists factors for and against granting relief. [8]

¶ 4712   Exceptions to innocent spouse relief.

Innocent spouse relief (¶4709, ¶4710, ¶4711) is not available:

... for liabilities other than income taxes, such as domestic service employment taxes (¶3029), that are required to be reported on a joint Federal income tax return (Reg § 1.6015-1(a)(3)); [9]

... for a tax year for which the spouse seeking relief has entered into an offer in compromise or a closing agreement with IRS that disposes of the liability (Reg § 1.6015-1(c)); [10] or

... if a spouse transferred assets to the other spouse as part of a fraudulent scheme to defraud IRS or another third party. (Reg § 1.6015-1(d)) [11]

¶ 4713   Returns for minors and incompetents.

Returns for minors and incompetents and others who are incapable of filing their own returns should be filed for them by their guardians or other fiduciaries. A minor may make his own return. (Reg § 1.6012-3(b)(3)) [12] For election to include a minor's income on a parent's

---

7. ¶V-8553; ¶60,154.04
8. ¶V-8554; ¶60,154.04; TD ¶570,954
9. ¶V-8501; ¶60,154

10. ¶V-8506.1A; ¶60,154
11. ¶V-8506.1A; ¶60,154; TD ¶570,935
12. ¶S-1704.1; ¶s 60,124, 60,124.04; TD ¶570,211

return, see ¶3137.

¶ 4714 Self-employment tax returns—Form 1040 Schedule SE.

Every individual (except a nonresident alien) who has self-employment income of $400 or more for the tax year must file a self-employment tax Form 1040, Schedule SE. (Code Sec. 6017) The self-employment tax (¶3138), which is in addition to the income tax, must also be reported on Form 1040 and paid as part of the income tax. [13]

¶ 4715 Decedent's final return.

A final income tax return must be filed for a deceased person who would be required to file if alive, for the part of the year up to the date of death. A decedent's final return is filed by the person entrusted with his property. Ordinarily, this would be the executor or administrator of his estate. (Code Sec. 6012(b)(1))[14] For where a refund is due, see ¶4847.[15]

For the surviving spouse filing a decedent's joint return, see ¶4707.

💡*recommendation:* Even though a final return may not otherwise be required, file one to claim any refund due for tax withheld from salary or for estimated tax paid.

The last tax year of a decedent ends with the day of his death. [16]

Personal exemptions (¶3116) and the standard deduction allowed on a decedent's final income tax return aren't reduced because the return is for a short year. [17]

A decedent's final return is due on the filing date that would have applied had the taxpayer lived. (Reg § 1.6072-1(b))[18]

For the income and deductions reportable on the decedent's final return, see ¶3964 *et seq.* For rules granting tax relief for a decedent who was a military or civilian U.S. employee who died in combat or a terrorist attack, see ¶4716.

¶ 4716 U.S. military and civilian employees dying in combat/ terrorist attacks.

If a military or civilian employee of the U.S. dies as a result of wounds or injury sustained in a terrorist or military action, income tax won't apply for the year of death and any earlier year beginning with the last year ending before the year in which the wounds or injury were sustained. (Code Sec. 692(c)(1)) IRS has outlined procedures for determining whether a terrorist or military action has occurred. Refund of withheld or estimated taxes may be claimed by filing Form 1040, or, if one had already been filed, Form 1040X. On joint returns, the tax liability must be allocated between the deceased and surviving spouses. [19]

¶ 4717 When and where to file individual returns.

Income tax returns (including self-employment tax returns) of U.S. citizens and resident aliens must be filed on or before the fifteenth day of the fourth month following the end of the tax year (Apr. 15 for calendar year taxpayers). (Code Sec. 6072(a); Reg § 1.6072-1(a)(1))

A "short period return" must be filed by the fifteenth day of the fourth month following the end of the short period. (Reg § 1.6071-1(b))[20]

For when a nonresident alien's return must be filed, see ¶4661.

File as specified on the return form (or instructions). For an individual, this usually is the

---

13. ¶S-1717; ¶s 14,024 *et seq.*, 60,174; TD ¶570,216
14. ¶C-9601, S-2003; ¶60,124.04; TD ¶570,212
15. ¶T-5710; ¶60,124.04; TD ¶802,039
16. ¶C-9601; ¶60,124.04; TD ¶579,501

17. ¶C-9602 *et seq.*; TD ¶579,507
18. ¶S-4702; ¶60,724; TD ¶570,220
19. ¶C-9660; ¶6924; TD ¶579,601
20. ¶S-4701; ¶60,724; TD ¶570,219

service center for the place where the individual lives. [21]

¶ 4718   Extensions of time for filing individual returns—Form 4868.

File Form 4868 to get an automatic extension of six months for filing (until Oct. 15 for a calendar year taxpayer). (Reg § 1.6081-4T)[22] The form must show the full amount properly estimated as tax for the year but it needn't be accompanied by payment of the balance of the tax estimated to be due. (Reg § 1.6081-4T(b))[23] (Failure to include the balance due won't affect the filing extension, but interest on the balance will still be charged, and a penalty for failure to pay may be imposed.) [24] IRS also accepts extension requests by e-filing. [25] For extension of time to pay, see ¶4722; for paying in installments, see ¶4723. IRS can terminate an automatic extension on 10 days' notice. (Reg § 1.6081-4T(d))[26]

Extensions can't exceed six months unless the taxpayer is abroad. (Code Sec. 6081(a))[27]

An automatic extension may be obtained without filing Form 4868 by making a payment by credit card, see ¶4721.

¶ 4719   Extensions for citizens or residents with tax homes outside the U.S.—Form 4868; Form 2350.

A U.S. citizen or resident whose tax home and abode is outside the U.S. and Puerto Rico (Reg § 1.6081-5(a)(5)) and a U.S. citizen or resident in military or naval service on duty outside the U.S. and Puerto Rico (Reg § 1.6081-5(a)(6)), get automatic extensions until the fifteenth day of the sixth month after the end of the tax year. A statement should be attached to the return which shows that the taxpayer qualified for this extension. (Reg § 1.6081-5T(b)) For these taxpayers, the automatic six-month extension for individuals (¶4718) runs concurrently with the two-month extension of time to file. (Reg § 1.6081-4T(a))

illustration: On Apr. 15, a U.S. citizen who is on the calendar year has a tax home outside the U.S. and Puerto Rico. His tax return and tax payment are due on June 15. By filing Form 4868 by June 15 and paying any estimated unpaid tax, he has until Oct. 15 to file.

U.S. citizens or resident aliens who expect to qualify for the foreign earned income exclusion (¶4612 *et seq.*) (and owe no tax), but not until more than two months after the regular return due date, should file extension request Form 2350 by that due date. (Reg § 1.911-7(c)(2))[28]

¶ 4720   Deadline and collection extensions for taxpayers serving in a combat zone or affected by a declared disaster, terrorist or military action.

Individuals serving in the U.S. armed forces in an area designated by the President as a "combat zone" (¶1224) or in a 10 USC 101(a)(13) "contingency operation" can suspend the period of time to perform various tax actions (e.g., tax return filing). (Code Sec. 7508) The suspension also applies to individuals serving in support of the Armed Forces in a combat zone, or acting under the Armed Forces' direction. These individuals are allowed extra time to perform tax acts (e.g., filing of any income, estate, gift, excise or employment tax return), or filing a claim for credit or refund) and the period is extended for the determination and assessment of their federal tax liability. (Code Sec. 7508(a)(1)) The suspension includes (1) any period of continuous hospitalization as a result of injury received while serving in the

---

21. ¶S-5100 *et seq.*; ¶60,914; TD ¶570,225
22. ¶S-5011; ¶60,814.03; TD ¶570,301
23. ¶S-5013; ¶60,814.03; TD ¶570,301
24. ¶s S-5010, S-5011; ¶60,814.03; TD ¶570,301

25. ¶S-1606; ¶60,814.03; TD ¶570,301
26. ¶S-5009; ¶60,814.03; TD ¶570,301
27. ¶S-5003; ¶60,814.04; TD ¶570,302
28. ¶S-5020; ¶9114.13; TD ¶570,305

combat zone, and (2) time in missing in action status plus a 180-day period after the termination of service or hospitalization. [29]

IRS may allow taxpayers affected by a Code Sec. 1033(h)(3) "Presidentially-declared" disaster or a Code Sec. 692(c)(2) terrorist or military action to extend for up to one year (1) the timely performance of acts under Code Sec. 7508(a)(1) (including filing any income, estate, gift, excise, or employment tax return); (2) the amount of any interest, penalty, additional amount, or addition to tax due for periods after the disaster date; and (3) the amount of any tax credit or refund. [30] (Code Sec. 7508A) IRS has specified acts subject to postponement, [31] (Reg § 301.7508A-1) including disasters occurring in 2007. [32]

On notice to IRS, the collection of income tax of a servicemember falling due before or during his military service is to be deferred for up to 180 days after termination of the taxpayer's service (or his release from it), if his ability to pay the tax is materially affected by the military service. No interest or penalty will accrue for this deferment period because of the nonpayment of any deferred amount. Also, the running of the statute of limitations against the collection of any deferred amount, by seizure or otherwise, is suspended for the period of service plus 270 days. [33]

For rules granting tax relief for a decedent who was a military or civilian U.S. employee who died in combat or a terrorist attack, see ¶4716.

¶ 4721 Payment of taxes due—Form 1040-V.

The tax is due on the original due date for filing the return despite any extensions of time for *filing* the return. (Code Sec. 6151(a); Reg § 1.6151-1(a)) [34] If IRS computes the tax, the tax due date is the later of the thirtieth day after the date IRS mails the tax bill or the tax return due date. (Reg § 1.6151-1(b)) [35] The automatic filing extension for taxpayers with a tax home and abode, or in military service, outside the U.S. (¶4719), also extends the time for payment. (Reg § 1.6081-5(a)) [36] For IRS acceptance of individuals' extension requests without full payment, see ¶4718.

Make tax payments by check or money order payable to the U.S. Treasury. Receipt of the check is payment, if the check is honored. IRS will accept personal checks or money orders drawn on any U.S. financial institution if the check or money order is payable in U.S. currency at par. Express, telegraphic, and similar money orders are also acceptable. (Reg § 301.6311-1) [37]

Taxes (including interest and penalties) also may be paid by any commercially acceptable means that IRS deems appropriate by regs, including credit or debit cards approved by IRS in the manner and in accordance with IRS forms, instructions, and procedures. (Code Sec. 6311(a); Code Sec. 6311(d)(1); Reg § 301.6311-2) Taxpayers can make credit card payments through tax software, by phone, or through the Internet. IRS doesn't set or collect any fees for credit card payments, but its private sector partners may impose convenience fees. IRS has authorized Official Payments Corporation (OPC) (1-800-2PAY-TAX; www.officialpayments.com) and Link2Gov Corporation (1-888-PAY-1040 or on the Web at www.pay1040.com) to accept credit card charges for federal taxes by phone. All individuals, whether filing on paper or electronically, may use this system to charge taxes to American Express, Discover Card, VISA, or MasterCard accounts. The option to pay taxes by credit card applies to payments with automatic extensions of time to file and to estimated tax payments. Taxpayers who charge a payment with an automatic extension request or who charge an estimated tax payment do not need to file the respective paper Form 4868 or Form 1040-ES. [38]

---

29. ¶S-8007; ¶75084; TD ¶138,018
30. ¶S-8502; ¶75,08A4; TD ¶868,531 *et seq.*
31. ¶S-8012; ¶75,08A4; TD ¶570,306
32. ¶S-8501.10; TD ¶570,316
33. ¶S-8001; ¶63,014.04; TD ¶904,001

34. ¶S-5451; ¶61,514; TD ¶570,226
35. ¶S-5454; ¶61,514
36. ¶S-5064; ¶60,814
37. ¶S-5752; ¶63,114; TD ¶559,802
38. ¶S-5756.1A *et seq.*; ¶63,114; TD ¶559,803

Tax payment by credit or debit card is deemed made when the issuer properly authorizes the transaction, provided payment is actually received by IRS in the ordinary course of business and isn't returned due to error resolution processing. (Reg § 301.6311-2(b))[39]

Where quarterly estimated tax payments (¶3149) aren't necessary, payments are generally made with the individual's return (¶4717).[40]

Taxpayers with a balance due on their returns can use a payment voucher Form 1040-V to make their payments, make a credit card payment by phone or by Internet, or make a payment using the electronic federal tax payment system (EFTPS). [41]

¶ 4722   Extension of time for paying individual income tax—Form 1127.

Apply on Form 1127 for a reasonable extension of time (not to exceed six months, unless taxpayer is abroad) to pay the tax. (Code Sec. 6161(a)(1)) File on or before the date prescribed for payment of the tax. (Reg § 1.6161-1(c)) IRS grants extensions only on a satisfactory showing that payment on the due date will result in undue hardship (more than an inconvenience), e.g., that taxpayer would have to sell property at a great financial sacrifice (i.e., below fair market value) to pay the tax. (Reg § 1.6161-1(b))[42]

¶ 4723   Installment payments of individual income tax— Form 9465.

To request an agreement to pay installments, attach Form 9465 to the front of the balance-due return. A fee of $105 ($52 if the fee is directly debited from the taxpayer's bank account; and $43 for certain low-income taxpayers), (Reg § 300.1(b)),[43] interest and a late-payment penalty of ½% per month apply, see ¶4873.

IRS must enter into an installment agreement requested by an *individual* whose aggregate tax liability (without interest, penalties, additions to tax, and additional amounts) isn't more than $10,000; and who (or whose spouse for joint return liability) hasn't failed to file or to pay income tax, or entered into another installment agreement, during any of the preceding five tax years, if IRS determines that the taxpayer is financially unable to pay the liability in full when due (and the taxpayer submits information that IRS may require to make this determination). The agreement must require full payment within three years, and the taxpayer must agree to comply with all Code provisions while it's in effect. (Code Sec. 6159(c)) IRS grants installment agreement requests to taxpayers who agree to pay a balance due of $25,000 or less within a five-year period, without requiring a collection manager's approval. [44]

IRS may (but isn't required to, except as noted above) enter into an agreement that allows a taxpayer to make payment of any tax in installments if it determines that the agreement will facilitate full or partial collection of the tax. (Code Sec. 6159(a)) IRS may disregard frivolous submissions of installment payment applications. (Code Sec. 7122(f))[45]

An individual who had an automatic six-month extension of time to file without paying the tax estimated to be due (¶4718), but can't pay by the extended due date, should use Form 9465 to arrange an installment agreement. [46]

¶ 4724   Amended income tax returns.

Amended income tax returns (on Form 1040X) may be filed to claim a refund after an original return has been filed if the period of limitations is open. (Reg § 301.6402-3(a)(2))[47]

---

39. ¶S-5756.4
40. ¶S-5200 *et seq.*
41. ¶S-5454.1
42. ¶S-5851; ¶61,614; TD ¶570,305
43. ¶T-10021; ¶61,594; TD ¶901,006

44. ¶V-5010 *et seq.*; ¶61,594; TD ¶901,006 *et seq.*
45. ¶V-5010; ¶61,594; TD ¶901,006
46. ¶s S-5020, V-5010 *et seq.*; ¶61,594; TD ¶570,227
47. ¶S-5151.5; ¶s 60,114.01, 64,024.15; TD ¶805,006

Amended returns can't be filed electronically. [48]

¶ 4725 Corporate returns.

Every corporation that is subject to federal income tax, and that's in existence during any portion of a tax year, must file an income tax return for that year (or portion), regardless of the amount of its gross income or whether it has taxable income. (Code Sec. 6012(a)(2); Reg § 1.6012-2(a))[49]

A corporation that has merely received a charter doesn't have to file if it furnishes a statement to IRS that it hasn't perfected its organization, has transacted no business, and has received no income from any source. (Reg § 1.6012-2(a)(2))[50]

After a corporation ceases business and dissolves, retaining no assets, it must make a return for that fractional part of the year during which it was in existence. But retention of even a small amount of cash keeps the corporation alive for filing purposes until the cash is distributed or paid. (Reg § 1.6012-2(a)(2))[1] A receiver, trustee in bankruptcy or dissolution, or assignee that has control and custody of all (or substantially all) of a corporation's business or property must make the return in the same manner and form as would the corporation. (Code Sec. 6012(b)(3))[2]

IRS may make a return for a corporation that is required to file a return but fails to do so. (Code Sec. 6020)[3]

¶ 4726 Who signs corporate returns.

The return and all related documents requiring a signature on behalf of the corporation, must be signed by the president, vice-president, treasurer, assistant treasurer, chief accounting officer (controller) or any other officer duly authorized to sign. If a return is made for the corporation by a trustee, receiver or assignee, that fiduciary must sign. (Code Sec. 6062)[4]

¶ 4727 Forms to file—Form 1120.

Most domestic corporations file Form 1120 as their income tax return. (Reg § 1.6012-2(a)) Form 1120, Schedule PH must be attached if the corporation is a personal holding company (¶3323 *et seq.*). (Reg § 1.6012-2(b))[5] (For foreign corporation returns, see ¶4663.)

A regulated investment company (mutual fund) uses Form 1120-RIC, [6] a real estate investment trust, Form 1120-REIT,[7] a political organization, Form 1120-POL, a homeowners association, Form 1120-H,[8] and a designated settlement fund, Form 1120-DF. [9] Insurance companies use Form 1120L (life) or Form 1120-PC (property and casualty). [10]

An S corporation uses Form 1120S, which must show information on actual and constructive distributions to shareholders. (Code Sec. 6037(a); Reg § 1.6012-2(h)) The corporation must, on or before the date it files the return, furnish this information to anyone who was a shareholder during the tax year. (Code Sec. 6037(b))[11]

Before the 2007 tax year, a corporation could have used a short Form 1120-A if its gross receipts, total income and total assets were each under $500,000, and it met certain ownership and other tests. [12]

48. ¶S-1604; TD ¶572,011
49. ¶s S-1900, S-1901, S-1908; ¶60,124.03; TD ¶609,801
50. ¶S-1908; ¶60,124.03; TD ¶609,801
1. ¶S-1909; ¶60,124.03; TD ¶609,803
2. ¶S-2014; ¶60,124.04; TD ¶803,056
3. ¶S-1004; ¶60,204; TD ¶570,104
4. ¶S-4508; ¶60,614; TD ¶609,801.1
5. ¶s S-1902, S-1903; ¶60,124.03; TD ¶609,801

6. ¶S-1920; ¶8514.09
7. ¶S-1919; ¶8564.10
8. ¶S-1921; ¶S-1922; ¶5284; ¶60,124; TD ¶609,811; TD ¶609,812
9. ¶S-1925; ¶468B4
10. ¶S-1904; ¶60,124.03; ¶8314
11. ¶s S-1905, S-1906; ¶60,374; TD ¶628,002
12. ¶S-1902; ¶60,124.03; TD ¶609,801

Small corporations (less than $250,000 in gross receipts and less than $250,000 in assets) don't have to complete Schedules L, M-1, and M-2 of Form 1120; or Schedules L and M-1 of Form 1120S.[13] Large corporations (reporting total assets of $10 million or more on Form 1120, Schedule L), must file Schedule M-3 instead of M-1. [14]

Electronic filing requirement. A corporation that files at least 250 returns of any kind in the aggregate, including information returns, during the calendar year ending with or within its tax year must file its income tax return electronically if it has assets of $10 million or more. Exemptions apply for (a) corporations not required to file for the preceding tax year or not in existence for at least one year before the original due date; (b) forms that can't be filed electronically, and (c) where IRS waives the requirement for undue hardship. All members of a controlled group of corporations must file electronically if the controlled group in the aggregate files at least 250 returns (including information returns). Failure to file electronically when required to do so is deemed to be a failure to file a return. (Reg § 301.6011-5T) Neither Form 7004 extension requests nor Form 940 series employment tax returns need to be filed electronically.[15]

¶ 4728   When and where to file corporate returns.

Domestic corporations (including RICs (mutual funds), REITs and S corporations) must file their income tax returns on or before the 15th day of the third month after the end of the tax year (Mar. 15 for a calendar year corporation). (Code Sec. 6072(b); Reg § 1.6037-1(b))[16] For filing extensions, see ¶4729.

"Short period" returns must be filed by the 15th day of the third month after the end of the short period. If a corporation dissolves and distributes all its assets, its final return is due by the 15th day of the third *full* month after the dissolution or liquidation. [17]

File as directed on the instructions for the returns. (Code Sec. 6091(b)(2)(A); Reg § 1.6091-2(c)) Hand-carried returns may be filed with any person assigned the responsibility to receive hand-carried returns in the local IRS office (i.e., the office that serves the corporation's principal place of business, etc.). (Code Sec. 6091(b)(4); Reg § 1.6091-2(d)(2))[18]

¶ 4729   Extensions for filing corporate returns—Form 7004.

Automatic sixth-month extensions —Form 7004. A corporation (including an S corporation, an affiliated group planning to file a consolidate return, see ¶3343, and a foreign corporation with a U.S. office) can get an automatic six-month extension by filing a Form 7004 that shows its estimated tax liability by the original due date. (Reg § 1.6081-3)[19] But this won't extend the time for *paying* the tax, see ¶4732. (Reg § 1.6081-3(c))[20] IRS can terminate the extension on ten days' notice. (Code Sec. 6081(b); Reg § 1.6081-3(d))[21]

Blanket extensions. A domestic corporation that transacts business and keeps its records outside the U.S. or Puerto Rico, or whose principal income is from sources within U.S. possessions, and a resident foreign corporation, may file its return up to the 15th day of the sixth month after the end of the tax year. A statement setting forth the qualifying facts must be attached to the return. (Reg § 1.6081-5(a)(2), Reg § 1.6081-5(a)(4), Reg § 1.6081-5T(b))[22]

---

13. ¶S-1902; TD ¶609,806
14. ¶S-1902.1; TD ¶609,801
15. ¶S-1941; ¶60,114.022
16. ¶S-4704; ¶s 60,374, 60,724
17. ¶S-4710; ¶60,724

18. ¶S-5104; ¶60,914
19. ¶S-5027 *et seq.*; ¶60,814.02; TD ¶609,802
20. ¶S-5027; ¶60,814.02; TD ¶609,802
21. ¶S-5009; ¶60,814.02
22. ¶S-5064; ¶60,814.01

¶ 4730 When to pay corporate tax.

Pay in full on or before the due date (without extension) for filing the return (¶4728). (Code Sec. 6151(a))[23] For extension of time to pay, see ¶4732. For corporate estimated tax, see ¶3346 *et seq.*

¶ 4731 Tax deposits—Form 8109.

Unless an exemption applies, a corporation has to make electronic deposits of all depository taxes using the Electronic Federal Tax Payment System (EFTPS) if the aggregate annual deposits of certain taxes by the corporation exceed $200,000 or if the corporation was required to use EFTPS in 2006. For EFTPS deposits to be timely, the corporation has to initiate the transaction at least one business day before the deposit is due. (Reg § 31.6302-1(h)(2)(ii))[24]

Corporations that aren't required to use EFTPS must make their income and estimated tax payments by depositing them with an authorized depositary by the return due date (¶4728) (Code Sec. 6302; Reg § 1.6302-1(a))[25] and report the deposits on the return. [26] For the requirement to make tax deposits by electronic funds transfer (EFT), see ¶3027. Deposits not made by electronic funds transfer must be accompanied by Form 8109 deposit coupons. [27] Deposits are timely if mailed (postmarked) at least two days before the due date. (Code Sec. 7502(e)(2))[28]

¶ 4732 Extensions of time for paying corporate tax—Form 1127, Form 1138.

Sixth-month extension for undue hardship —Form 1127. An extension (up to six months) for making a payment of corporate income tax may be granted by IRS at the taxpayer's request (on Form 1127) by the payment due date on a showing of undue hardship (¶4722). Late applications won't be considered. (Code Sec. 6161(a); Reg § 1.6161-1)[29]

Loss carryback expected —Form 1138. A corporation that expects a net operating loss in a current year can get an extension for paying the *preceding* year's tax based on the expected carryback (Code Sec. 6164(a)), by filing Form 1138. (Reg § 1.6164-1) The extension expires the last day of the month for filing the current year return or, if an application for a tentative carryback refund (Form 1139, see ¶4850) is filed before that date, on the date IRS sends notice that the refund is allowed or disallowed. (Code Sec. 6164(d))[30]

¶ 4733 Partnership return of income—Form 1065, Schedule K-1.

Partnerships (except foreign partnerships with no (or de minimis) gross income from sources within the U.S. and no gross income effectively connected with a U.S. trade or business (Reg § 1.6031(a)-1(b))) must file Form 1065 (Form 1065-B for electing large partnerships) to report gross income and deductions for their tax year. (Code Sec. 6031(a), Code Sec. 6031(e); Reg § 1.6031(a)-1(a))[31] Tax-exempt bond partnerships that meet certain conditions are exempt from this requirement. [32] (Reg § 1.6031(a)-1(a)(3)(ii)) A foreign partnership that is otherwise exempt from filing nonetheless must file a return to make any partnership election, (Reg § 1.6031(a)-1(b)) and a foreign or domestic partnership must file to elect to be excluded from the Code's partnership provisions. (Reg § 1.6031(a)-1(c))

A partnership needn't file a partnership return for any period before it receives taxable

---

23. ¶S-5451; ¶61,514
24. ¶S-5623; ¶63,014; TD ¶559,853
25. ¶s S-5601, S-5604, S-5607; ¶63,014; TD ¶609,202
26. ¶S-5601
27. ¶S-5601; ¶63,014; TD ¶609,202

28. ¶T-10777; ¶s 63,014, 75,024
29. ¶S-5850 *et seq.*; ¶61,614; TD ¶659,018
30. ¶S-5865 *et seq.*; ¶61,644; TD ¶804,016 *et seq.*
31. ¶S-2701; ¶60,314; TD ¶596,001
32. ¶S-2708

income or incurs deductible expenses. (Reg § 1.6031(a)-1(a)(3))[33] Nor does it file if it doesn't carry on a business in the U.S. and has no U.S. source income. (Reg § 1.6031(a)-1(b)(1))[34]

Form 1065 must be filed by the 15th day of the fourth month after the end of the partnership's tax year (Apr. 15 for a calendar year partnership). (Code Sec. 6072(a))[35]

Every partnership required to file a return must furnish (by its tax return due date, with extensions) Form 1065, Schedule K-1, containing information from the return to every person who was a partner (or who held an interest in the partnership as a nominee for another person) at any time during the partnership's tax year. An "electing large partnership" (¶3702) must provide this information by Mar. 15th following the end of its tax year. (Code Sec. 6031(b); Reg § 1.6031(b)-1T(a))[36] (The nominee must in turn give the information it gets to the other person (Code Sec. 6031(c)(2); Reg § 1.6031(c)-1T(h)) and furnish the partnership with specified information about that person.) (Code Sec. 6031(c)(1); Reg § 1.6031(c)-1T(a))[37]

Certain large partnerships have to file Form 1065, Schedule M-3 instead of Form 1065, Schedule M-1.[38]

Electronic filing requirement. Partnerships with more than 100 partners must file Form 1065 and schedule K-1 electronically, unless they are excluded from this filing method by IRS Pub 1524 (Procedures and Specifications for the 1065 e-file Program). Hardship waivers are available. (Reg § 301.6011-3) The Modernized e-File a platform using Extensible Markup Language (XML) format) is the only e-file platform available for partnership returns in 2008.[39]

¶ 4734   Extension for filing partnership return—Form 7004.

For an automatic six-month extension of time for filing a partnership return, use Form 7004. A partnership's automatic extension doesn't extend the time for filing a partner's return. (Reg § 1.6081-2T)[40]

¶ 4735   Returns of trusts and estates—Form 1041, Schedule K-1, Form 7004, etc.

Trusts and estates must file income tax returns (see ¶4736 and ¶4737, respectively) and a variety of information returns.[41]

If there are *joint* fiduciaries, a return by one will suffice if he states in the return that he has sufficient knowledge of the facts to make the return and that it is true to the best of his knowledge and belief. (Reg § 1.6012-3(c))[42]

The fiduciary who prepares the income tax return filed by the trust or estate must furnish to beneficiaries (or their nominees) receiving distributions or to whom an income item is allocated, a Form 1041, Schedule K-1 or a substitute that contains the same information. This must be furnished on or before a return is filed with IRS, and a copy must be filed with Form 1041. (Code Sec. 6034A(a)) (If a nominee is given this information, he must furnish it to his beneficiary, and he must furnish to the estate or trust specified information about the beneficiary.) (Code Sec. 6034A(b))[43]

Income tax returns that must be filed by estates, domestic trusts, and foreign trusts having an office or place of business in the U.S. must be filed on or before the 15th day of the fourth month following the end of the tax year. (Reg § 1.6072-1(a)(1)) Foreign trusts and estates of nonresident aliens that don't have an office or place of business in the U.S. must file on or

---

33. ¶S-2701; ¶60,314; TD ¶596,001
34. ¶S-2717.1; ¶60,314
35. ¶S-4923; ¶60,724; TD ¶596,016
36. ¶S-2710; ¶60,314; TD ¶596,008
37. ¶S-2740; ¶60,314; TD ¶596,014
38. ¶S-1902.1

39. ¶S-1350 *et seq.*; ¶60,114.065; TD ¶596,025
40. ¶S-5030; ¶60,814; TD ¶596,017
41. ¶s S-2004, S-2007; ¶60,124.04; TD ¶659,000
42. ¶S-2002; ¶60,124.04; TD ¶659,001
43. ¶s S-2019, S-2020; ¶60,34A4; TD ¶659,011

before the 15th day of the sixth month following the end of the tax year. (Reg § 1.6072-1(c))[44]

Trusts and estates get an automatic six-month extension to file Form 1041 (¶4736; ¶4737) by filing Form 7004 showing the full amount properly estimated as tax by the trust's return due date. A trust's or an estate's automatic extension doesn't extend the beneficiary's return due date. (Reg § 1.6081-6T)[45] IRS can terminate a trust's or an estate's automatic extension on 10 days' notice. (Reg § 1.6081-6T(e))[46] *Payment* extensions must be separately applied for under the rules at ¶4722.

¶ 4736 Income tax returns of trusts—Form 1041.

The trustee must file on Form 1041 if the trust isn't tax-exempt and if the trust has:

... any taxable income for the year;

... gross income of $600 or more; or

... any beneficiary who is a nonresident alien. (Code Sec. 6012(a)(4), Code Sec. 6012(a)(5))[47]

Trust income taxable to the grantor or other "owner" must be reported on a separate statement attached to Form 1041, except that alternative reporting methods are available, if certain requirements are met. The alternatives available depend on whether the trust is treated as owned by one grantor, or by two or more grantors (which in the latter case may require a Form 1099 to be provided by the trustee along with a statement showing trust income items, deductions and credits). (Reg § 1.671-4(b))[48]

Split-interest trusts must file Form 1041-A even if the trust must currently distribute all net income. (Code Sec. 6034(a))[49]

¶ 4737 Income tax returns of estates—Form 1041.

The executor or administrator must file Form 1041 if gross income for the estate's tax year is $600 or more (Code Sec. 6012(a)(3)) *or* if any beneficiary is a nonresident alien. (Code Sec. 6012(a); Reg § 1.6012-3(a)(1)(iii))[50]

A fiduciary doesn't have to file a copy of the will for income tax purposes unless IRS *requests* a copy. (Reg § 1.6012-3(a)(2))[1]

The executor who probates the entire will (in the state the decedent was domiciled) files Form 1041 reporting all the income. Any out-of-state or "ancillary" executor *also* files a Form 1041, but it shows only the gross income received by the ancillary fiduciary and the deductions attributable to that income. (Reg § 1.6012-3(a)(3))[2]

¶ 4738 Extension for making elections.

Two automatic extensions are available for taxpayer elections, if the taxpayer takes corrective action within the extension period:

(1) An automatic *12-month extension* for certain regulatory elections specified in Reg § 301.9100-2(a)(2). The more widely applicable ones are: the election to use a tax year other than the required tax year (¶2813); the election to use the LIFO inventory method (¶2874), and the election to adjust basis on partnership transfers and distributions (¶3780). The extension is available regardless of whether the taxpayer timely filed its return for the year the election should have been made. (Reg § 301.9100-2(a)(1))[3]

(2) An automatic *six-month extension* for regulatory elections and statutory elections

---

44. ¶S-4707; ¶60,724; TD ¶667,002; TD ¶659,013
45. ¶S-5032; ¶60,814.05; TD ¶659,014; TD ¶667,004
46. ¶S-5009; ¶60,814.05
47. ¶S-2007; ¶60,124.04; TD ¶659,003
48. ¶S-2009 *et seq.*; ¶6714; TD ¶659,004

49. ¶S-2806; ¶60,344
50. ¶S-2004; ¶60,124.04; TD ¶667,001
1. ¶S-2006; ¶60,124.04; TD ¶667,009
2. ¶S-2005; ¶60,124.04; TD ¶667,008
3. ¶S-4819; ¶78,054.02

which are required to be made by the due date of the return or the due date of the return *including extensions,* for taxpayers who timely filed the return for the year in which the election should have been made. (Reg § 301.9100-2(b))[4]

Nonautomatic extensions of time are available for regulatory elections that don't qualify for an automatic extension, if the taxpayer establishes to IRS that he acted reasonably and in good faith, and that granting relief won't prejudice IRS's interests. (Reg § 301.9100-3(a)) Generally, a request for a nonautomatic extension is a request for a letter ruling, and must be submitted under the procedures for letter ruling requests, with the applicable user fee. (Reg § 301.9100-3(e)(5))[5]

The grant of an extension of time to make an election isn't a determination that the taxpayer is otherwise eligible to make the election. (Reg § 301.9100-1(a))[6]

¶ 4739 Income tax returns of individual bankruptcy estates—Form 1041.

The debtor-in-possession or trustee, if one is appointed, for a bankruptcy estate for an individual under Chapter 7 or 11 must file an income tax return (Form 1041) if the estate's gross income equals at least the sum of the exemption amount plus the basic standard deduction for unmarried taxpayers who weren't surviving spouses or heads of household. (Code Sec. 6012(a)(9)) This amount is $8,750 for 2007 ($8,950 for 2008).[7]

¶ 4740 Information returns.

Taxpayers are required to report certain of their activities with third parties, on prescribed returns and statements, ¶4741. These "information returns" must be filed with IRS and in some cases furnished to the third parties.[8] For returns on magnetic media and electronic filing, see ¶4758.

¶ 4741 Information return forms and filing dates.

Payors (including nominees, see ¶4742) report their payments for a calendar year by filing an appropriate Form 1099 (or permitted substitute form) with respect to each payee (with a Form 1096 transmittal statement) after Sept. 30 of the calendar year of the payment (but not before the payor's final payments for the year) and on or before the next Feb. 28. (Reg § 1.6042-2(c), Reg § 1.6044-2(d), Reg § 1.6049-1(c))[9] However, returns filed electronically aren't due until Mar. 31 after the end of the calendar year to which they relate. (Code Sec. 6071(b); Reg § 31.6071(a)-1(a)(3)(i))[10] For filing extension, see ¶4751. For payee statements, see ¶4746.

¶ 4742 Nominees and middleman returns.

If reportable interest or dividends are paid to any person who, as middleman or nominee, then pays them over to the actual (or beneficial) owner, the original payor (corporation, bank, etc.) must file an information return (Form 1099) with respect to the nominee, who must file another Form 1099 with respect to the actual or beneficial owner. (Code Sec. 6042(a)(1)(B), Code Sec. 6049(a)(2); Reg § 1.6042-2(a)(1)(iii), Reg § 1.6049-4(b)(3))[11]

A nominee is any payee who isn't the actual owner of the dividend or interest, but who would be required to furnish his taxpayer identification number (¶4757) to the payor for inclusion on the *payor's* return. Nominees include banks, trust companies, etc., and, with

---

4. ¶S-4821; ¶78,054.02
5. ¶S-4823; ¶78,054.02
6. ¶S-4815.1; ¶78,054.02
7. ¶C-9700 *et seq.*, S-2016; ¶60,124; TD ¶578,021

8. ¶s S-2900 *et seq.*, S-4930; TD ¶811,000
9. ¶S-4930; ¶s 60,424, 60,494; TD ¶811,003
10. ¶S-4930; ¶60,414.06
11. ¶S-2904 *et seq.*; ¶s 60,424, 60,494; TD ¶811,007

respect to dividends, dealers and brokers. (Reg § 1.6042-2(a)(2), Reg § 1.6049-1(a)(2))[12]

Special reporting rules also apply for payments to joint payees (Reg § 1.6041-1(c)); and payments on behalf of another. (Reg § 1.6041-1(e))

¶ 4743 Dividend reporting—Form 1099-DIV, Form 5452, Form 1099-PATR.

A payor (including nominees, see ¶4742) must file a Form 1099-DIV for each person to whom it pays "reportable" dividends aggregating $10 or more during the calendar year. (Code Sec. 6042(a), Reg § 1.6042-2(a)(1)) Dividends that qualify for preferential tax rates must be differentiated from nonqualified dividends. [13] For payee statements, see ¶4746.

Reportable dividends are corporate "dividends" as defined at ¶1285 *et seq.*, and substitute dividends (e.g., payments in lieu of dividends that brokers pay on short sales). (Code Sec. 6042(b)(1))[14]

Corporations must file Form 5452 to report nontaxable dividends. [15] For liquidating dividends, see ¶4750.

Patronage dividends aggregating $10 or more to any payee in a calendar year are reported by payor cooperatives (¶4206) on Form 1099-PATR. (Code Sec. 6044(a)(1); Reg § 1.6044-2(b))[16]

¶ 4744 Reporting interest—Form 1099-INT.

Every person (including nominees, see ¶4742) who pays $10 or more of reportable interest to any person (except certain payees) in a calendar year must report the payments (Code Sec. 6049(a)(1), Code Sec. 6049(d)) on Form 1099-INT.[17] For payee statements, see ¶4746.

Reportable interest is interest on: (a) obligations issued publicly or in registered form (other than a short-term obligation held by a corporation), (b) deposits with banks or brokers, and (c) amounts held by insurance or investment companies. (Code Sec. 6049(b)(1))[18] Reportable interest also includes OID (¶4745); amounts includible in gross income with respect to regular REMIC interests (¶4204) (Code Sec. 6049(d)(6)(A)(i), Code Sec. 6049(d)(7)(A));[19] and interest paid on tax-exempt bonds. But interest on obligations issued by a natural person isn't "reportable." (Code Sec. 6049(b)(2))[20]

¶ 4745 Reporting original issue discount (OID)—Form 1099-OID, Form 8281.

Original issue discount (OID) of $10 or more on any obligation must be reported by the issuer (or nominee, see ¶4742) as a payment of interest. (Code Sec. 6049(d)(6)) Form 1099-OID is used to report the OID, and any interest actually paid on the obligation. [21]

In addition, an information return (Form 8281) must be filed by certain issuers of publicly-offered debt instruments having OID, within 30 days after issuance. (Code Sec. 1275(c)(2); Reg § 1.1275-3(c))[22]

🅡🅘🅐*observation:* The one-time reporting requirement on Form 8281 is in addition to the annual information reporting on Form 1099-OID.

---

12. ¶s S-2904 *et seq.*, S-3003 *et seq.*; ¶s 60,424, 60,494; TD ¶811,008
13. ¶S-2901; ¶60,424; TD ¶811,001
14. ¶S-2910; ¶S-3724; ¶60,424; TD ¶811,010
15. ¶S-2914; ¶60,424; TD ¶811,012
16. ¶S-2951; ¶60,444; TD ¶811,021

17. ¶S-3001 *et seq.*; ¶60,494; TD ¶811,501
18. ¶S-3011 *et seq.*, ¶S-3023 *et seq.*; ¶60,494; TD ¶811,512
19. ¶s S-3073, S-3087; ¶60,494; TD ¶811,537.
20. ¶s S-3040, S-3042; ¶60,494; TD ¶811,523
21. ¶s S-3073, S-3074; ¶60,494; TD ¶811,530
22. ¶S-3080 *et seq.*; ¶12,714.06; TD ¶811,536

¶ 4746   Statements to payees.

Payors of reportable dividends (and payments in lieu of dividends) and interest (including OID) must furnish the payee with a specified written statement of the amount reported to IRS (normally, Copy B of the Form 1099 sent to IRS). This generally must be done, either in person or in a "statement mailing," on or before Jan. 31 of the year following the calendar year for which the payor's Form 1099 was required. (Reg § 1.6042-4(d)(1), Reg § 1.6044-5(b), Reg § 1.6049-3(c)(1)) However, Form 1099 statements may be furnished electronically to recipients who consent to receive them in that way. [23]

¶ 4747   Business payments of $600 or more—Form 1099-MISC.

With limited exceptions, every person, corporate or otherwise, engaged in a trade or business who, in the course of that business, makes payments aggregating $600 or more to another person (e.g., an independent contractor) in a calendar year must file an information return (Form 1099-MISC) setting forth the name and address of the payee and the amount paid, and furnish a statement to the payee. Reportable payments are: rent, salaries, wages, premiums, annuities, compensations, remunerations, emoluments, or other fixed or determinable gains, profits and income. (Code Sec. 6041; Reg § 1.6041-1)[24]

This rule doesn't apply to transactions covered by other information return rules (e.g., for dividends, see ¶4743), or most payments to corporations. (Reg § 1.6041-3)[25]

IRS has issued guidance on how the above requirements may be met for payments made with credit cards or debit cards. [26]

¶ 4748   Mortgage interest (and points) received—Form 1098.

A person ("interest recipient") who receives interest, or reimburses interest overpayments, aggregating $600 or more for a calendar year on a mortgage must report (on Form 1098) those receipts or reimbursements, even if the interest is received on behalf of another. This applies to any person (including cooperative housing corporations) who, in the course of his trade or business (except governmental recipients), receives interest on a mortgage secured all or in part by real property, where the payor of record is an individual. (Code Sec. 6050H; Reg § 1.6050H-1, Reg § 1.6050H-2(a))[27] The return must also include any points received in the year that were paid directly by the buyer (including certain points paid by or charged to the seller). (Code Sec. 6050H(b)(2)(C); Reg § 1.6050H-1(f))[28]

¶ 4749   Mortgage insurance premiums.

IRS regs may prescribe that any person who, in the course of a trade or business, receives from any individual premiums for mortgage insurance aggregating $600 or more for any calendar year, must make a return with respect to that individual. (Code Sec. 6050H(h)(1))[29]

¶ 4750   Other information returns.

. . . *Abandonment or foreclosure of property held as security* for a business loan must be reported by the lender on Form 1099-A (Code Sec. 6050J; Reg § 1.6050J-1T) (unless related to a cancellation of debt reported on Form 1099-C, below). [30]

. . . *Accelerated death benefits* paid to any individual must be reported by the payor (Code

---

23. ¶S-2927 *et seq.*; ¶s 60,424, 60,444, 60,494; TD ¶811,015
24. ¶S-3655 *et seq.*; ¶s 60,414, 60,414.06; TD ¶814,001
25. ¶S-3676; ¶60,414.06; TD ¶814,001
26. ¶S-3656.1, J-9325; ¶34,064

27. ¶S-3901 *et seq.*; ¶60,50H4; TD ¶814,054
28. ¶S-3907 *et seq.*; TD ¶814,065
29. ¶S-3923; ¶60,50H4; TD ¶814,074.1
30. ¶S-4200 *et seq.*; ¶60,50J4; TD ¶816,001

Sec. 6050Q) on Form 1099-LTC.[31]

...*Acquiring corporation in taxable acquisition* must file an information return with IRS and furnish statements to shareholders if any shareholder of the acquired corporation recognizes gain or loss in whole or in part as a result of the acquisition. (Code Sec. 6043A(a))[32]

...*Alcohol and biodiesel fuel tax benefits, Code Sec. 34 credit for farming, off-highway and certain other nontaxable uses of fuel* —information return required by persons claiming alcohol or biodiesel fuel tax benefits or a Code Sec. 34 credit, providing information on the benefits or credit. (Code Sec. 4104(a))[33]

...*Applicable exempt organizations* that make a reportable acquisition of interests in a life insurance contract within the two years after Aug. 17, 2006 must report the acquisition. (Code Sec. 6050V)[34]

...*Attorney's fees* paid in the course of a trade or business that aren't reportable as wages or under Code Sec. 6041 (¶4747) (or would have to be reported under Code Sec. 6041 but for the $600 limitation), whether or not the services are performed for the payor (Code Sec. 6045(f); Reg § 1.6045-5) and whether or not the attorney is the exclusive payee, on Form 1099-MISC. (Reg § 1.6045-5)[35]

...*Barter exchanges* through which at least 100 exchanges of property or services are made during the calendar year must report each exchange on Form 1099-B. (Code Sec. 6045; Reg § 1.6045-1(e))[36]

...*Brokers* must report each sale of securities, commodities, and forwards or futures contracts the broker effects for its customers, on Form 1099-B. (Code Sec. 6045; Reg § 1.6045-1(c); Reg § 1.6045-2)[37] For real estate reporting persons, see below.

...*Cash of more than $10,000,* including certain cash equivalents (e.g., cashier's checks, foreign currency) received in connection with a trade or business must be reported by the recipient (Code Sec. 6050I(a), Code Sec. 6050I(d); Reg § 1.6050I-1(a)(1); Reg § 1.6050I-1(c)(1)) within 15 days after receipt. Use Form 8300 (Reg § 1.6050I-1(e)), except that banks file Form 4789 and casinos, under special rules (Reg § 1.6050I-1(d)(2)), file Form 8362 (certain Nevada casinos file Form 8852) to report cash from gaming activities. [38] Special rules apply if the cash is paid in installments. (Reg § 1.6050I-1(b))[39]

...*Change in control or recapitalization of a corporation* generally must be reported on Form 8806 showing the parties to the transaction, the fees involved, the changes in capital structure and any other information IRS requires. (Code Sec. 6043(c))[40]

...*Charitable organization required to acknowledge gift of auto, plane, or boat* (¶2139) must also provide the information to IRS in the manner it prescribes. (Code Sec. 170(f)(12)(D))[41]

...*Charitable property disposition* by the donee within three years of contribution must be reported on Form 8282 by the charity, if the deduction claimed for the property exceeds $5,000 (but disposition of items appraised for $500 or less doesn't have to be reported). (Code Sec. 6050L; Reg § 1.6050L-1)[42]

...*Direct sales of consumer goods* of $5,000 or more to any one buyer in a calendar year must be reported by the seller (Code Sec. 6041A) on Form 1099-MISC. [43]

...*Discharge of debt (including student loans) by banks, and certain other financial entities and organizations in the lending business* of $600 or more must be reported to IRS, on Form 1099-C. (Code Sec. 6050P; Reg § 1.6050P-1(a)(1); Reg § 1.6050P-2)[44]

31. ¶S-3440; ¶60,50Q4
32. ¶S-4317; ¶6043A4; TD ¶815,010
33. ¶S-4466; ¶41,044
34. ¶S-2896; ¶60,50V4
35. ¶S-3851; ¶60,454.06; TD ¶814,087
36. ¶S-3700 *et seq.*; ¶60,454; TD ¶814,037
37. ¶S-3700 *et seq.*; ¶60,454; TD ¶814,023

38. ¶S-4000 *et seq.*; ¶60,50I4 *et seq.*; TD ¶814,074
39. ¶S-4019 *et seq.*; ¶60,50I4.02; TD ¶814,084
40. ¶S-4308; ¶60,434; TD ¶815,006
41. ¶K-3948.1
42. ¶S-2873; ¶60,50L4; TD ¶688,033
43. ¶S-3677; ¶60,41A4; TD ¶814,020
44. ¶S-4251 *et seq.*; ¶60,50P4; TD ¶816,008

. . . Donee of qualified intellectual property ¶2106) must file annual information return (use Form 8899) of net income from property with respect to each specified tax year of the donee. (Code Sec. 6050L(b)(1))[45]

. . . Education-related payments received (or billed) by higher education institutions for qualified tuition and related expenses; qualified tuition refunded to an individual (Form 1098-T) (Reg § 1.6050S-1); and interest of $600 or more received from an individual for a calendar year on an educational loan (Form 1098-E) must be reported at such time as is prescribed by regs. (Code Sec. 6050S; Reg § 1.6050S-3)[46] In general, for educational loans, lenders must also report amounts (in addition to all other interest paid) attributable to capitalized interest and loan origination fees. [47] Statements to students and borrowers may be provided electronically if conditions are met. (Reg § 1.6050S-2(a)(1); Reg § 1.6050S-4(a))[48]

. . . Employer-owned life insurance contracts issued after Aug. 17, 2006, must be reported by applicable policyholders to IRS. (Code Sec. 6039I)[49]

. . . Education savings distributions (certain) from Coverdell ESAs[50] and qualified tuition programs or 529 plans are reported on Form 1099-Q. [1]

. . . Executors of estates of decedents dying after 2009 must report (with the decedent's final income tax return, or later as specified by regs (Code Sec. 6075(a))) information including the adjusted basis, decedents' holding period, and recipients of certain large property transfers at death. (Code Sec. 6018)[2]

. . . Fishing boat operators must report on Form 1099-MISC certain payments to their crewmen. (Code Sec. 6050A; Reg § 1.6050A-1)[3]

. . . Fish purchased for resale for cash must be reported on Form 1099-MISC with respect to each seller by every person engaged in the trade or business of purchasing fish for resale. (Code Sec. 6050R)[4]

. . . Foreign bank accounts must be reported on Form TDF 90-22.1 (FBAR) by any person with an interest in or signature authority over the account. [5]

. . . Gift tax return filers must furnish donees a written statement with identifying information about the return filer and the gift property, for post-2009 transfers. (Code Sec. 6019(b))[6]

. . . IRA (and Roth IRA) contributions and withdrawals must be reported by the IRA trustees or issuer (Code Sec. 408(i), Code Sec. 408A(d)(3)(D)), on Form 5498.[7] The trustee also must report on Form 5498 that a minimum distribution is required (but not the amount) for a calendar year. (Reg § 1.408-8, Q&10)[8] For required distributions, additional information must be provided to the IRA owner by Jan. 31 of the required distribution year. [9]

. . . Liquidating corporations report the adoption of the plan of liquidation on Form 966, [10] and liquidating distributions (Code Sec. 6043(a)) on Form 1099-DIV.[11]

. . . Long-term care payments made under a long-term care insurance contract to any individual must be reported by the payor (Code Sec. 6050Q) on Form 1099-LTC.[12]

. . . Medical savings account and health savings account contributions and distributions must be reported by the trustee on Form 5498-SA and Form 1099-SA, respectively. (Code Sec. 220(h))[13]

45. ¶S-2882.1; ¶60,50L4
46. ¶S-3430 *et seq.*; ¶60,50S4; TD ¶816,500 *et seq.*
47. ¶S-3436; ¶60,50S4.01
48. ¶S-1370; ¶60,50S4.01
49. ¶S-3246; ¶60,39I4
50. ¶S-3428
1. ¶S-3422; TD ¶147,110
2. ¶S-2310; ¶60,184.03
3. ¶S-3695; ¶60,50A4; TD ¶816,024
4. ¶S-3695.1; ¶60,50R4

5. ¶S-3650; ¶60,114.06
6. ¶S-2206; ¶60,194; TD ¶746,006.1
7. ¶S-3391; ¶4084.04; TD ¶813,032
8. ¶S-3392.1; ¶4084.04; TD ¶813,033.1
9. ¶S-3392.2; ¶4084.04; TD ¶813,033.1
10. ¶S-4314; ¶60,434; TD ¶815,009
11. ¶S-4315; ¶60,434; TD ¶815,009
12. ¶S-3440; ¶60,50Q4
13. ¶H-1328.1; ¶2204.02; TD ¶288,105

... *Mortgage credit certificate* (MCC) information must be reported (on Form 8329) by each person who makes a "certified indebtedness" loan under an MCC program. (Reg § 1.25-8T(a))[14] Each state or political subdivision with MCC programs must report (on Form 8330) the amount of MCCs issued each quarter. (Code Sec. 25(g); Reg § 1.25-4T)[15]

... *Outbound Code Sec. 355 distributions* (¶3557) and outbound Code Sec. 332 corporate liquidations (Reg § 1.6038B-1(e))[16] are reported on Form 926.

... *Parent tax-exempt organizations* that are controlling organizations (within the meaning of Code Sec. 512(b)(3)) have to report transactions with controlled entities on Form 990-T. (Code Sec. 6033(h))[17]

... *Partnership interest sales or exchanges* attributable to unrealized receivables, inventory, collectibles, or Code Sec. 1250 gain must be reported by the partnership on Form 8308. (Code Sec. 6050K; Reg § 1.1(h)-1(e), Reg § 1.6050K-1(a)(1))[18] But the partnership doesn't have to file until it's notified of the exchange (Code Sec. 6050K(c)(2)), i.e., when it either receives written notification required from the transferor, or has knowledge of the transfer. (Reg § 1.6050K-1)[19]

... *Pension, profit-sharing plans* file annual return/report forms in the Form 5500 series (Code Sec. 6058(a)),[20] file Form 5310A to notify IRS of a merger, consolidation or division of the plan, (Code Sec. 6057(b)(4))[21] and make returns and reports of designated Roth contributions. (Code Sec. 6047(f))[22] For plan years beginning after 2007, all annual reports — including any accompanying statements and schedules —must be filed electronically with DOL and in a format that can be displayed on the Internet. [23]

... *Political organizations* except for certain state and local committees under Code Sec. 527 must file an initial notice of status (Form 8871) (Code Sec. 527(i))[24], and periodic reports of contributions and expenditures (Form 8872) (Code Sec. 527(j)(2)), which can be filed on-line at www.irs.gov/polorgs with an IRS-supplied user ID and password). [25]

... *Prizes and awards* (taxable) of $600 or more (not paid for services rendered) must be reported by the payor on Form 1099-MISC. [26]

... *Qualified stock purchases* of a target must be reported on Form 8023, whether or not a Code Sec. 338 election is made. [27]

... *Real estate* reporting persons (as specially defined) must report real estate transactions on Form 1099-S, including the sale of a condominium unit or stock in a cooperative housing unit. For a transaction involving a residence, the return must include any portion of real property tax treated as imposed on the buyer. Reporting isn't required for sales of principal residences for $250,000 or less ($500,000 or less for married sellers) (IRS can authorize higher amounts by regulation) if the reporting person receives specified written assurances (IRS has provided a sample certification form) from the seller by Jan. 31 following the year of sale. (Code Sec. 6045(e); Reg § 1.6045-4)[28]

... *Refunds of state and local income tax* of $10 or more must be reported by the state or local tax authority/payor on Form 1099-G. (Code Sec. 6050E; Reg § 1.6050E-1)[29]

... *Royalty payments* that aggregate $10 or more per year per payee (including nominees) must be reported unless the payee is a corporation, exempt organization or government (Code Sec. 6050N), on Form 1099-MISC. Where a publisher pays royalties to an author's agent and the agent subtracts his commission and expenses, both parties must report the

14. ¶S-4206; ¶254.02; TD ¶816,011
15. ¶S-4207; ¶254.02; TD ¶816,012
16. ¶S-3640.1; ¶S-3640.1A
17. ¶S-2862.2; ¶60,334
18. ¶S-2725 *et seq.*; ¶60,50K4; TD ¶591,019
19. ¶S-2734 *et seq.*; ¶60,50K4; TD ¶591,022
20. ¶S-3351; ¶s 4014.01, 60,584; TD ¶813,001
21. ¶s S-3383, S-3384; ¶s 4014.01, 60,574; TD ¶813,028

22. ¶S-3400.1
23. ¶S-3400.1
24. ¶S-2858.7
25. ¶S-2858.9
26. ¶S-3658; TD ¶814,002
27. ¶S-4305
28. ¶S-3800 *et seq.*; ¶60,454.04; TD ¶814,040 *et seq.*
29. ¶S-3690; ¶60,50E4; TD ¶816,020

gross royalties on Form 1099-MISC, unreduced by the subtracted amounts. [30]

... *Sick pay* (nonwage) paid by a third party to an employee must be reported by the third party to the employee's employer. (Code Sec. 6051(f)(1); Reg § 31.6051-3(a))[31]

... *Simplified employee pension (SEP) contributions* must be reported by the SEP trustee or issuer of a SEP endowment contract (Code Sec. 408(l)) on Form 5498.[32]

... *Sponsoring organizations* (as defined in Code Sec. 4966(d)(1), see ¶4129), on their annual information returns filed for tax years ending after Aug. 17, 2006, must include information relating to donor advised funds (DAFs) owned by an organization at the end of the tax year. (Code Sec. 6033(k), see ¶4125)

... *Supporting organizations* (as defined in Code Sec. 509(a)(3)) must file annual information returns (for tax years ending after Aug. 17, 2006) listing supported organizations, what type of supporting organization it is, and a certification that the organization that it isn't controlled by one or more disqualified persons. (Code Sec. 6033(l))

... *Tips* must be reported by employees to employers on Form 4070. (Code Sec. 6053(a); Reg § 31.6053-1(b)(2))[33] Large food and beverage establishments (more than ten employees on a typical business day) must report to IRS (on Form 8027) and to employees, tips reported by the employees to the employer plus the excess (as specially allocated) of 8% of the establishment's gross receipts (as specially defined) over the amount of tips thus reported by the employees. The 8% can be reduced to not below 2%, on application to IRS. (Code Sec. 6053(c)(3); Reg § 31.6053-3)[34] For 2007-2009, employers meeting certain requirements may elect to participate in a voluntary tip reporting program (Attributed Tip Income Program or ATIP).[35]

... *Unemployment insurance benefit* payments of $10 or more must be reported by the payor on Form 1099-G. (Code Sec. 6050B; Reg § 1.6050B-1)[36]

¶ 4751   Extension of time for information returns—Form 8809.

Use Form 8809 to request a 30-day extension to file the following forms: W-2, -2G, 1042-S, 1098, 1099-A, -B, -C, -DIV, -G, -INT, -LTC, -MISC, -MSA, -OID, -PATR, -R, -S, 5498, 5498-ESA, 5498-SA, 8027. Approval is automatic for 30-day extension requests (no signature or explanation needed). Detailed explanation and signature are required for requests beyond the original 30-day extension. (Reg § 1.6081-8T(d))[37] Automatic extension is also available to file SSA's copy of Forms W-2 and W-3. (Reg § 31.6081(a)-1T)

Make a written application (don't use Form 8809) to request an extension of up to 30 days for furnishing the payee statement, see ¶4746.[38]

¶ 4752   Material advisors must disclose reportable transactions and maintain lists—Form 8264 or Form 8918.

Each material advisor with respect to any reportable transaction (as defined in Code Sec. 6707A(c), see ¶4890) must make a return setting out: information identifying and describing the transaction; information describing any potential tax benefits expected to result from the transaction; and any other information that IRS requests. (Code Sec. 6111(a); Reg § 301.6111-3(a)) The form should be filed by the last day of the month following the calendar quarter in which the person becomes a material adviser. On or before Oct. 31, 2007, either Form 8264 or Form 8918 may be used; for returns due after this date, only Form 8918 may be used.[39] For the penalty for failure to meet this requirement, see ¶4892.

---

30. ¶S-3684 *et seq.*; ¶60,50N4; TD ¶816,016

31. ¶S-3173; ¶60,514; TD ¶812,013

32. ¶S-3399 *et seq.*; ¶4084.05; TD ¶813,035

33. ¶H-4344; ¶60,534; TD ¶532,011

34. ¶S-3250 *et seq.*; ¶60,534; TD ¶812,054

35. ¶H-4344.3 *et seq.*

36. ¶S-3694; ¶60,50B4; TD ¶816,023

37. ¶S-5049; ¶60,814.07

38. ¶s S-5041, S-5042; ¶60,814.07; TD ¶811,015

39. ¶S-4401; ¶S-4401.4; ¶61,125.01(10); TD ¶817,005

A material advisor is any person who provides any material aid, assistance, or advice with respect to organizing, managing, promoting, selling, implementing, insuring, or carrying out any reportable transaction, and who directly or indirectly derives gross income in excess of a threshold amount (or such other amount prescribed by IRS) for that assistance or advice. (Code Sec. 6111(b)(1)(A); Reg § 301.6111-3(b)) A person becomes a material adviser when (1) he makes a tax statement, (2) he receives (or expects to receive) the minimum fees, and (3) the transaction is entered into by the taxpayer. [40]

The threshold amount is $50,000 for a reportable transaction substantially all of the tax benefits from which are provided to natural persons, and $250,000 in any other case. (Code Sec. 6111(b)(1)(B); Reg § 301.6111-3(b)(3))

Each material advisor must maintain a list with respect to any reportable transaction. The list must identify each person for whom the advisor acted as a material advisor for the transaction and contain any other information as IRS regs may require. (Code Sec. 6112(a); Reg § 301.6112-1) [41]

¶ 4753 Participation in confidential tax avoidance transactions—Form 8886.

Taxpayers must disclose (on Form 8886 due with an original or amended return reporting participation) their participation in "reportable transactions," by attaching an information statement to their income tax returns, including:

. . . listed transactions (i.e., transactions that have been specifically identified by IRS as tax avoidance transactions);

. . . confidential transactions offered under conditions of confidentiality and for which the taxpayer has paid an advisor a minimum fee;

. . . transactions with contractual protection;

. . . loss transactions resulting in a taxpayer claiming a tax loss exceeding specified amounts; and

. . . transactions of interest (i.e., transactions that are the same or substantially similar to transactions identified by IRS). (Reg § 1.6011-4) Transactions of interest include certain charitable contributions of property interests that involve inflated valuations, and "toggling" grantor trust transactions where grantor trusts are purportedly terminated and recreated to generate large losses. [42]

A copy of Form 8886 must be sent to the IRS Office of Tax Shelter Analysis (OTSA). For penalty for failure to disclose participation, see ¶4890.

Taxpayers also must disclose participation in listed transactions involving estate tax (Reg § 20.6011-4), gift tax (Reg § 25.6011-4), employment tax (Reg § 31.6011-4), excise tax related to private foundations and certain other tax exempts (Reg § 53.6011-4), excise taxes relating to qualified pension and other plans under Code Sec. 4971 through Code Sec. 4980F (Reg § 54.6011-4), and excise taxes relating to public charities. (Reg § 56.6011-4)

Confidential corporate tax shelters also are subject to the tax shelter registration rules of Code Sec. 6111. Affected transactions are listed transactions and other tax-structured transactions as specially defined. (Reg § 301.6111-2) [43]

¶ 4754 Reporting qualified residence interest on seller-provided financing.

A return on which taxpayer claims a deduction for qualified residence interest (¶1730) on seller-provided financing must show the name, address and taxpayer identification number (TIN) of the person (the seller) to whom the interest is paid or accrued. Any person who

---

40. ¶S-4401.2; ¶61,125.01(10); TD ¶817,003
41. ¶S-4408.1; ¶61,124

42. ¶S-4427.1; ¶S-4427.15; ¶61,114
43. ¶S-4419.1; ¶61,114; TD ¶817,002

receives or accrues interest from seller-provided financing must include on the return for the tax year in which the interest is so received or accrued the name, address and TIN of the person liable for the interest. (Code Sec. 6109(h))[44]

¶ 4755   Returns prepared by tax return preparers.

A tax return preparer (¶4756) must:

... *sign the return* in the manner prescribed by IRS in forms, instructions or other appropriate guidance (Code Sec. 6695(b)) after it is completed and before it is presented to the taxpayer for signature. If the preparer is unavailable for signature, another preparer must review the entire return and sign it. (Reg § 1.6695-1(b)(1)) If more than one return preparer is involved in preparation of a return, the individual with primary responsibility for the overall substantive accuracy is considered to be the return preparer. (Reg § 1.6695-1(b)(2)) Preparers may sign original or amended returns, or extension requests, as a return preparer with a rubber stamp, mechanical device, or computer software program. The method used must contain either a facsimile of the preparer's signature or the preparer's printed name. [45]

... *enter his (preparer's) taxpayer ID number (TIN) or preparer ID number (PTIN; apply on Form W-7P),* (Code Sec. 6109(a)(4))[46] *and address where the return was prepared* on any return he prepares; if there's a partnership or employment arrangement between two or more preparers, the identifying number of the partnership or employer must also appear on the return or claim for refund. The identifying number of a preparer (whether an individual, corporation, or partnership) who employs or engages one or more persons to prepare the return or claim for refund (other than for the preparer) is that preparer's employer identification number (EIN). (Reg § 1.6109-2(a))[47]

... *furnish the taxpayer with a completed copy of the return* (Code Sec. 6107(a)) in the form and manner IRS prescribes in forms, instructions, or other guidance. (Reg § 1.6107-1(a))[48]

... *retain for three years a completed copy of each return* or a list of the name and TIN of each taxpayer for whom a return was prepared (Code Sec. 6107(b));[49]

... *retain a record of the name, TIN, and principal place of work of each income tax return preparer* employed or engaged by the preparer/employer during each July 1 through June 30 period. (Reg § 1.6060-1(a)(1))[50]

¶ 4756   Tax return preparer defined.

A tax return preparer includes preparers of income, estate, gift, employment, excise tax, and exempt organization returns. (Code Sec. 7701(a)(36)(A))[1]

A person may also be a "preparer" of a related return if an entry on a return he actually prepared (e.g., partnership or S corporation return) is directly reflected on the related return (e.g., partner's or shareholder's return), and the entry is a substantial portion of the related return. (Reg § 301.7701-15(b)(3))[2]

A portion of a return prepared by any one of several persons won't be "substantial" if, aggregating all schedules, etc., he prepared, that portion involves amounts of gross income, deductions, or amounts on which credits are based that are: (1) less than $2,000, or (2) less than $100,000 *and* less than 20% of the gross income (adjusted gross income, for individuals) as shown on the return. (Reg § 301.7701-15(b)(2))[3]

---

44. ¶S-1524 *et seq.*; ¶61,094
45. ¶S-4603; ¶66,954; TD ¶867,010
46. ¶S-1522; ¶61,094; TD ¶867,012
47. ¶S-1523; ¶61,094; TD ¶867,012
48. ¶V-2674; ¶61,074; TD ¶867,015

49. ¶V-2675; ¶61,074; TD ¶867,014
50. ¶V-2676; ¶60,604; TD ¶867,013
1. ¶S-1107; ¶77,014.471; TD ¶867,002
2. ¶S-1117; TD ¶867,002
3. ¶S-1116; TD ¶867,006

A tax consultant is a "preparer" even though he may do no more than review a return already prepared by the taxpayer. [4]

A person is a "preparer" if he supplies enough information and advice to make the actual filling out of a return a mere mechanical or clerical matter (Reg § 301.7701-15(a)(1))[5] but not if he merely furnishes typing, reproducing or other mechanical assistance with respect to preparing a return. (Code Sec. 7701(a)(36)(B)(i))

A person who provides a computerized return preparation service is a preparer if his computer programs provide substantive tax determinations, but not if his services are limited to mechanical calculations and processing. [6]

¶ 4757 Taxpayer identification number (TIN)—Form SS-5.

Any person who files a return, statement, or other document must include his own TIN (Code Sec. 6109(a)(1))[7] and the TIN of any other person, as required by the form or instructions to the form. (Code Sec. 6109(a)(3); Reg § 301.6109-1(c))[8] Thus, an alimony payor's return must include the payee's TIN. (Use Form W-9 to request another person's TIN.) [9]

A child to whom the kiddie tax rules, ¶3134 *et seq.*, apply for any tax year must provide his parent's TIN on his (child's) tax return for that year. (Code Sec. 1(g)(6))[10]

Social security numbers (SSNs) are used to identify most individuals, sole proprietors not otherwise required to use employer identification numbers (EINs), and grantor trusts. (Code Sec. 6109(d); Reg § 301.6109-1(a))[11] To get an SSN, file Form SS-5 with the Social Security Administration. (Reg § 301.6109-1(d)(1))[12]

Aliens who aren't eligible for SSNs must use IRS individual taxpayer identification numbers (ITINs). (Reg § 301.6109-1(a)) Use Form W-7 to request an ITIN. [13]

Prospective adoptive parents who have had a child placed in their household by an authorized placement agency and meet certain other requirements may apply (use Form W-7A) for a temporary (two-year) adoption taxpayer identification number (ATIN) for the child (unless the child is an alien eligible to get an ITIN) to satisfy filing requirements (but not for earned income credit purposes (¶2341)). (Reg § 301.6109-3)[14]

Other entities use the EIN. (Reg § 301.6109-1(a)) Taxpayers can request an EIN instantly through http://www.irs.gov by entering the required information. Taxpayers may also apply for an EIN by phone, mail, or fax. (Reg § 301.6109-1(d))[15]

All employers, whether corporations, partnerships or sole proprietors, must get and use EINs for reporting employment and excise taxes. [16]

Large food and beverage establishments use a 15-digit identifying number for tip reporting. (Reg § 31.6053-3(a)(5))[17]

Buildings that have been or will be allocated a low-income housing credit must be assigned a building identification number (BIN) by the applicable state housing credit agency. [18]

Foreign transferors of U.S. real property interests (USRPIs) (and transferees where applicable) must provide their TINs on withholding tax returns, applications for withholding certificates, and other required notices and elections. Foreign persons must have TINs for placement on any return, statement, or other document required by the regs under Code

4. ¶S-1109; TD ¶867,004
5. ¶S-1109; ¶61,074; TD ¶867,004
6. ¶S-1110; ¶61,075; TD ¶867,005
7. ¶S-1502; ¶61,094; TD ¶570,106
8. ¶S-1531; ¶61,094; TD ¶861,050
9. ¶S-1535; ¶2154.03; TD ¶861,050
10. ¶S-1544
11. ¶S-1505; ¶61,094; TD ¶570,106

12. ¶S-1581; ¶61,094; TD ¶570,106
13. ¶S-1508.1; ¶61,094; TD ¶570,106
14. ¶S-1504.6 *et seq.*; ¶61,094.01; TD ¶570,110
15. ¶S-1582 *et seq.*; ¶61,094; TD ¶659,009
16. ¶S-1505; ¶61,094
17. ¶S-3289; TD ¶812,039
18. ¶S-1521; ¶424.70

Sec. 897 or Code Sec. 1445. (Reg § 301.6109-1(b)(2)(vi))[19]

¶ 4758   Magnetic media and electronic filing—Form 4419.

Certain information returns *must* be filed on magnetic media. (Code Sec. 6011(e)(2)(A))[20] There are exceptions for certain low-volume filers (fewer than 250 returns), but partnerships with more than 100 partners (counting any person who is a partner at any time during its tax year) must file on magnetic media. (Reg § 301.6011-3)[21] Electronic filing satisfies the magnetic media requirement. Hardship waivers (request on Form 8508) are available. (Code Sec. 6011(e)(2)(B))[22] For employee benefit reports (e.g., the Form 5500 series), magnetic media or electronic filing (under the EFAST program) is encouraged but not required until plan years beginning after 2007 (¶4750).[23]

Submit Form 4419 at least 30 days before the return due date to apply to transmit information returns electronically/magnetically.[24] The due dates for filing paper information returns with IRS also apply to magnetic media filings, but not to electronic filing. For magnetic media, Form 1098, forms in the Form 1099 series, and Form W-2G must be submitted to IRS postmarked by Feb. 28. For electronic filing, however, the due date for information returns is Mar. 31.[25] A transmittal statement on Form 4804 must accompany magnetic media; Form 4804 isn't required for electronic filers.[26]

For electronic filing of income tax returns, see ¶4703 for individuals, ¶4727 for corporations, and ¶4733 for partnerships.

¶ 4759   Timely mailing as timely filing and paying.

A return, claim, statement, document or payment (except a tax deposit) that must be filed or made by a certain date generally is considered timely filed or made if it has a timely postmark. (Code Sec. 7502(c)(1))[27] This also applies to claims for credit or refund made on a late-filed original return. (Reg § 301.7502-1(f))[28]

For the timely mailing rule to apply, the return, etc., must be: (1) deposited in the mail in the U.S. in a properly addressed envelope or wrapper with sufficient postage; (Code Sec. 7502(a)(2)(B)) (2) postmarked on or before the prescribed filing or payment date (Code Sec. 7502(a)(2)(A)) (returns postmarked after the due date are considered filed when received by IRS); and (3) actually delivered by U.S. mail to the proper place. (Code Sec. 7502(a)(1))[29]

Some courts permit delivery to be proven by the so-called common-law "mailbox rule" (i.e., when mail is properly addressed and deposited in the U.S. mails, with postage duly prepaid on it, there is a rebuttable presumption that it was received by the addressee in the ordinary course of the mail).[30]

Under authority to expand the timely-mailing rule to include certain private delivery services, (Code Sec. 7502(f)) IRS has designated the following as services for which the timely-mailing-as-timely filing rule also applies: *DHL* Same Day Service, DHL Next Day 10:30 am, DHL Next Day 12:00 PM, DHL Next Day 3:00 PM, and DHL 2nd Day Service; *FedEx* Priority Overnight, FedEx Standard Overnight, FedEx 2 Day, FedEx International Priority, and FedEx International First; *UPS* Next Day Air, UPS Next Day Air Saver, UPS 2nd Day Air, UPS 2nd Day Air A.M., UPS Worldwide Express Plus, and UPS Worldwide Express.[31]

The postmark stamp date on the mailing envelope overrides the postmark stamp date on a

19. ¶S-1508
20. ¶S-1301; ¶60,114.07; TD ¶861,061
21. ¶S-1350; ¶60,114.065; TD ¶596,025
22. ¶S-1314; ¶60,114.07
23. ¶S-1630 *et seq.*; ¶S-3361
24. ¶S-1311
25. ¶S-1305; TD ¶861,062

26. ¶S-1308; TD ¶861,062
27. ¶T-10751; ¶75,024; TD ¶570,237
28. ¶T-10752.1; ¶75,024
29. ¶T-10751 *et seq.*; ¶75,024; TD ¶570,237
30. ¶T-10774 *et seq.*
31. ¶T-10781; ¶75,024; TD ¶570,238

Certificate of Mailing (P.S. Form 3817). [32]

If a private postage meter is used, the postmark isn't enough. The document must actually be received by the proper office or officer not later than the time the postmark indicates it ordinarily would be received. If it is actually received later, taxpayer can prove timely mailing only by showing: (1) that the document was deposited in the mail before the last collection that was postmarked (by the U.S. Post Office) on the last day for filing; and (2) that the delay in receiving the document was due to delay in transmission of the mail; and (3) the cause of the delay. (Reg § 301.7502-1(c)(1)(iii)(B)) [33]

In general, an electronically filed tax return (¶4703) isn't considered filed until IRS acknowledges the electronic portion of the return as accepted and a signature has been received either electronically or on Form 8453 or Form 8453-OL. But, certain taxpayers can pick their own five-digit personal identification number (PIN) and don't have to file Form 8453. [34]

¶ 4760 Effect of registered or certified mail.

The date of registration is considered to be the postmark date, (Code Sec. 7502(c)(1)(B)) and registration is prima facie evidence the return, etc., was delivered to the agency, officer or office to which addressed. (Code Sec. 7502(c)(1)(A)) [35] The date of the U.S. postmark on the sender's receipt is treated as the postmark date of a document sent by certified mail (Reg § 301.7502-1(c)(2)), and proof that a properly postmarked certified mail sender's receipt was properly issued and that the envelope or wrapper was properly addressed is prima facie evidence that the document was properly delivered. (Reg § 301.7502-1(e)(1)) [36]

¶ 4761 Due date on Saturday, Sunday or holiday.

If a due date falls on Saturday, Sunday or legal holiday, there is an automatic extension of time to the next succeeding day that isn't a Saturday, Sunday or legal holiday. The rule applies to *all acts* required to be performed under the Code both by the *taxpayer* and IRS. "Legal holiday" includes: (1) the legal holidays throughout the state or possession where the office at which the act to be performed is located even if not a legal holiday in the state or possession where the taxpayer resides, and (2) all legal holidays in the District of Columbia (Code Sec. 7503), i.e.: New Year's Day —Jan. 1; Inauguration Day —Jan. 20 (every fourth year); Martin Luther King, Jr.'s birthday —third Monday in Jan.; President's Day —third Monday in Feb.; Emancipation Day —Apr. 16; Memorial Day —last Monday in May; Independence Day—July 4; Labor Day —first Monday in Sept.; Columbus Day —second Monday in Oct.; Veterans Day —Nov. 11; Thanksgiving Day —fourth Thursday in Nov.; Christmas Day—Dec. 25. If a holiday in the District of Columbia falls on Sunday, the next day is a holiday in the District of Columbia. When a legal holiday in the District of Columbia (other than Inauguration Day) falls on a Saturday, it's treated as falling on the preceding Friday. [37]

¶ 4762 How to get a copy of a previously filed tax return— Form 4506.

Use Form 4506. [38] IRS charges $39 for each tax period requested. There's *no* charge for a Form 4506-T Request for Transcript of Tax Return, which is used to request tax return transcripts, tax account transcripts, W-2 information, 1099 information, verification of non-filing, or a record of account. [39]

---

32. ¶T-10762
33. ¶T-10763; TD ¶570,237
34. ¶S-1609; ¶S-1617.3; ¶60,114.08; TD ¶572,018
35. ¶T-10762.3; ¶75,024; TD ¶570,237

36. ¶T-10776.1; TD ¶570,237
37. ¶T-10790 *et seq.*; ¶75,034; TD ¶570,240
38. ¶S-6407; ¶s 61,034, 61,034.09
39. ¶S-6409; ¶61,034

Chapter 25   Deficiencies—Refunds—Penalties

¶ 4800   Tax Audits, Deficiencies and Assessments.

IRS makes certain preliminary cursory checks of every return filed; it selects returns for audit based on various criteria. Once IRS finishes an audit, a taxpayer has various alternatives it can pursue to resolve any disputed items.

¶ 4801   Mathematical, etc., check of returns.

IRS checks every return for mathematical errors and computes the tax using the figures on the return. If the taxpayer made a computational error resulting in an underpayment of tax, IRS sends a corrected computation and a notice and demand for payment of any balance due (which doesn't entitle the taxpayer to go to Tax Court) (Code Sec. 6213(b)(1)) or reduces any refund. (Reg § 601.105(a)) Failure to include a correct TIN on the return, as required under Code Sec. 21 (child care credit), Code Sec. 24 (child credit), Code Sec. 25A (higher education credit), Code Sec. 32 (earned income credit), and Code Sec. 151 (personal exemptions), is treated as a mathematical or clerical error and assessed accordingly. If EIC is claimed on net earnings from self-employment, failure to pay the proper amount of self-employment tax is treated as a mathematical error. So is failing to provide IRS with certain information after improperly claiming EIC. (Code Sec. 6213(g)(2)) IRS may treat an earned income credit claim on a noncustodial parent's return as a math error. (Code Sec. 6213(g)(2)(M))[1] Adjustments to make an S corporation shareholder's return consistent with the corporation's return are treated as resulting from mathematical or clerical error. (Code Sec. 6037(c)(3))[2] Similar rules apply when beneficiaries of estates and trust file returns inconsistent with the entity's. (Code Sec. 6034A(c)(3))[3]

A taxpayer's federal income and estate tax returns may also be checked against his state or foreign tax returns. [4]

¶ 4802   Check against information returns.

IRS compares the taxpayers' income tax returns against information returns, such as wage, interest and dividend statements, under a document matching program (Information Returns Program). If there is a mismatch, IRS sends the taxpayer a computer-generated notice (CP-2000), which must describe the basis for, and identify, any amounts of taxes, additions, interest or penalties claimed to be due. (Code Sec. 7522) The notice, which isn't a demand for payment, can be challenged by the taxpayer, who has the burden of proof. IRS also matches information filed by pass-through entities (partnerships, S corporations, and trusts) to what the partners, shareholders, and beneficiaries report on their own returns. [5]

¶ 4803   Returns selected for examination.

IRS selects returns for examination, e.g., based on discrepancy with information returns (¶4802), history of deficiencies, random sampling (Taxpayer Compliance Measurement Program (TCMP)), questionable refunds, etc. IRS's computerized "discriminant function" (DIF) technique ranks and selects returns having the greatest audit potential. [6]

IRS has a comprehensive strategy for reducing the tax gap which includes reducing opportunities for evasion and improving technology and compliances.

---

1. ¶T-3628; TD ¶836,017
2. ¶D-1801; TD ¶614,724
3. ¶C-3081; ¶C-9081; ¶62,134.02; TD ¶655,501, 665,029

4. ¶T-1001; TD ¶655,501; TD ¶665,029
5. ¶s T-1003, T-1004; ¶75,224; TD ¶821,003
6. ¶T-1023, T-1060 et seq.; TD ¶821,004

References beginning with a single letter are to paragraphs in RIA's Federal Tax Coordinator 2d and RIA's Analysis of Federal Taxes: Income. Those beginning with numbers are to paragraphs in RIA's United States Tax Reporter. Those beginning with TD are to paragraphs in RIA's Tax Desk.

¶ 4804 Market Segment Specialization (MSSP) audit guidelines.

These provide revenue agents and tax examiners with a broad and detailed review of the way a particular industry (e.g., attorneys, taxicabs, air charters, trucking, bed and breakfasts) works and the things an agent should be looking for when reviewing a return from within that industry. The guides are available to practitioners and others. [7]

¶ 4805 Industry Issue Resolution and Pre-Filing Programs.

IRS's Industry Issue Resolution Program exists to provide guidance to resolve frequently disputed or burdensome issues common to any size business taxpayers. Issues most appropriate to the program generally will have two or more of the following characteristics: the proper tax treatment of a common factual situation is uncertain; the uncertainty results in frequent, and, often repetitive, examinations of the same issue; the uncertainty results in taxpayer burden; the issue is significant and impacts a large number of taxpayers, either within an industry or across industry lines; and the issue requires extensive factual development, and an understanding of industry practices and views concerning the issue would assist IRS in determining the proper tax treatment. [8]

Under IRS's Pre-Filing Agreement program, qualifying taxpayers under the jurisdiction of the Large and Mid-Size Business Division may request that IRS examine specific issues relating to tax returns before they are filed. [9]

¶ 4806 Settlement initiatives.

IRS periodically offers qualifying taxpayers who have participated in various tax shelters or who have otherwise taken tax positions that IRS considers abusive an opportunity to settle on terms that are more favorable than could result if the parties litigated. [10]

¶ 4807 Types of examinations (audits); time and place.

IRS fixes the time and method of examination, which must be reasonable under the circumstances. (Code Sec. 7605(a); Reg § 301.7605-1(a)) Depending on the amounts and sources of income and the nature of the taxpayer's business, an examination may be at: (1) an IRS office, with the taxpayer bringing (office audit) or mailing (correspondence audit) his records (Reg § 601.105(b)(2)(ii)), or (2) the office of the taxpayer (or his representative) (field audit). (Reg § 601.105(b)(3))[11]

IRS generally won't conduct the audit at the taxpayer's place of business if the business is so small that doing so essentially requires the taxpayer to close the business. [12]

The taxpayer may ask to have the audit transferred, e.g., to the district where his books and records are kept. IRS also may initiate a transfer, but the taxpayer may ask to keep the original site. (Reg § 301.7605-1(e), Reg § 301.7605-1(g))[13]

IRS can't use financial status or economic reality examination techniques (so-called "lifestyle" audits) to determine the existence of any unreported income unless it has a reasonable indication that there is a likelihood of unreported income. (Code Sec. 7602(e))[14]

7. ¶T-10161.1
8. ¶T-9974
9. ¶T-9552
10. ¶M-5977

11. ¶T-1090 *et seq.*; ¶76,054; TD ¶821,011
12. ¶T-1094; ¶75,214; TD ¶821,011
13. ¶T-1102; TD ¶821,015
14. ¶T-1076; ¶76,024; TD ¶821,010

¶ 4808   Taxpayer's rights in an examination.

Before or at an initial in-person interview (other than criminal investigations), IRS must give the taxpayer an explanation (written or oral) of the audit process (and assessment and collection) and his rights under that process. (Code Sec. 7521(b)(1))[15]

A taxpayer has the right to: be represented by an advisor (¶4809); make certain audio (but generally not videotape) recordings of meetings (on advance notice) with the IRS agent (Code Sec. 7521(a)(1)); claim additional deductions not claimed on the return; ask that a particular technical question raised in the examination be referred to IRS's National Office for technical advice; not be subjected to unnecessary examinations (¶4811); and claim constitutional rights if questioned about possible criminal violations. [16]

¶ 4809   Who can represent the taxpayer?

The taxpayer's representative may be an attorney, CPA, enrolled agent, enrolled actuary or any other person permitted (under Circular 230 Reg § 10.3) to represent taxpayers before IRS, who isn't disbarred or suspended from practice before IRS (IRS may censure (publicly reprimand), suspend, impose a monetary penalty (as explained in detailed IRS guidance), or disbar any practitioner from practice before IRS if he is shown to be incompetent or disreputable, refuses to comply with any of the Circular 230 requirements, or with intent to defraud, willfully and knowingly misleads or threatens a client or prospective client [17]), and who has a written power of attorney (on Form 2848) executed by the taxpayer. Absent a summons, IRS can't require the taxpayer to accompany the representative. (Code Sec. 7521(c))[18]

If, during an interview, the taxpayer clearly states a desire to consult with a representative, IRS must suspend the interview for that purpose. (Code Sec. 7521(b)(2))[19]

An attorney-client privilege of communications applies for other federally authorized tax practitioners with respect to tax advice (except for tax shelters) in any non-criminal tax matter or proceeding. (Code Sec. 7525)[20]

An individual can check a box on his return to authorize IRS to communicate with his paid preparer about math error notices and the status of a refund or payment but must sign a power of attorney for representation on examination matters, underreported income, appeals and collections notices.

¶ 4810   IRS's power to summon persons and records.

IRS can issue a summons for a taxpayer's testimony and records (Code Sec. 7602(a), Code Sec. 7602(b)) for a legitimate purpose, if IRS doesn't make unreasonable demands. [21] The summons (Form 2039) must describe with reasonable certainty the books and records sought (Code Sec. 7603), and set the time for examination —not less than ten days from the summons date. (Code Sec. 7605(a))[22]

If the taxpayer intentionally disregards the summons, IRS can apply to the district court (or U.S. Commissioner) for an order directing compliance. (Code Sec. 7604(b))[23]

IRS may issue a summons ("third-party summons") to a person other than the taxpayer (e.g., his employer, or a "third-party recordkeeper," such as his bank) for testimony and records bearing on its examination of the taxpayer. (Certain communications (see ¶4809) are privileged.) Subject to exceptions, within three days of the service of a summons on a third-

---

15. ¶T-1122 *et seq.*; ¶75,214; TD ¶821,016
16. ¶s T-1120 *et seq.*, T-1129 *et seq.*; ¶76,024.10; TD ¶821,017
    et seq.
17. ¶T-10930
18. ¶s T-1124, T-1127; ¶75,214; TD ¶821,018

19. ¶T-1127; ¶75,214; TD ¶821,017
20. ¶T-1334; ¶75,254
21. ¶s T-1201, T-1212 *et seq.*; ¶76,024 *et seq.*; TD ¶822,001
22. ¶s 76,024.04, 76,054; TD ¶822,002
23. ¶T-1357; ¶76,044; TD ¶822,012

party, but no later than the 23rd day before the day fixed in the summons as the day when the records are to be examined, IRS must send by registered or certified mail a notice of the summons, including a copy of the summons, and an explanation of the taxpayer's right to institute a suit to quash the summons. (Code Sec. 7609(a)(1)) If the taxpayer intervenes in a proceeding to enforce a third-party summons, the running of the assessment period with respect to the taxpayer is suspended for the period during which a proceeding, and any appeals, with respect to the enforcement of the summons is pending. (Code Sec. 7609(e)(1))

IRS generally can't contact any third parties without providing reasonable notice in advance to the taxpayer. (Code Sec. 7602(c)(1), Reg § 301.7602-1)[24]

With some exceptions, IRS may not issue, or begin any action to enforce, any summons to produce or analyze any tax-related computer software source code. (Code Sec. 7612)[25]

A summons can't be issued (or enforced) against a person for whom a Justice Department referral is in effect (i.e., criminal tax prosecution is recommended). (Code Sec. 7602(d))[26]

¶ 4811   One examination rule—unnecessary examinations.

Unnecessary examinations are barred. IRS may make only one inspection of a taxpayer's books and records for each tax year unless the taxpayer requests otherwise, or IRS notifies him *in writing* that an additional inspection is necessary (Code Sec. 7605(b)), or IRS suspects fraud. (Code Sec. 6212(c)) Re-examination also is permitted if the taxpayer doesn't file a timely Tax Court petition after receiving a 90-day letter (¶4825) for the year.[27]

¶ 4812   National Taxpayer Advocate—Taxpayer Assistance Orders (TAOs).

The Office of the Taxpayer Advocate is headed by the National Taxpayer Advocate, who reports directly to the Commissioner. (Code Sec. 7803(c)(1)) Its functions are to assist taxpayers in resolving problems with IRS, identify areas where taxpayers have problems dealing with IRS, propose changes in IRS administrative practices to mitigate these identified problems; and identify potential legislative changes that may do so. (Code Sec. 7803(c)(2)(A))

The National Taxpayer Advocate is responsible for the appointment of local taxpayer advocates. (Code Sec. 7803(c)(2)(D)) On taxpayer's application (on Form 911 or in a signed written statement containing the information prescribed in regs). (Reg § 301.7811-1(b)(1)) to the Office of the Taxpayer Advocate, the National Taxpayer Advocate (or his designee) can issue a Taxpayer Assistance Order (TAO) if he determines that the taxpayer is suffering (or will suffer) significant hardship because of IRS's administration of the tax laws, or if the taxpayer meets such other requirements provided in regs. (Code Sec. 7811(a)(1))[28]

¶ 4813   User fees for IRS rulings or determinations.

IRS charges taxpayers a separate user fee for each request for a ruling, determination letter, opinion letter, closing agreement, advance pricing agreement, installment agreement or similar service. (Code Sec. 7528)[29]

¶ 4814   Proposed deficiencies—revenue agent's report (RAR).

An IRS examiner may propose adjustments to a taxpayer's return before *determining* a deficiency (¶4824), (which generally doesn't exist until IRS issues a statutory notice of deficiency—"90-day letter," see ¶4825).[30] The agent will discuss the proposed adjustments with the taxpayer to settle the case informally. The taxpayer can agree to the adjustments or

---

24. ¶T-1250 *et seq.*; ¶76,094; TD ¶822,013
25. ¶T-1290; ¶76,124; TD ¶822,200
26. ¶s T-1205, T-1206; ¶76,024; TD ¶822,004
27. ¶T-1425 *et seq.*; ¶76,024.10; TD ¶822,022

28. ¶T-10200 *et seq.*; ¶78,114 *et seq.*; TD ¶821,023
29. ¶T-10000 *et seq.*; ¶76,557.401
30. ¶T-1550 *et seq.*; TD ¶823,502

argue they should be modified ("unagreed" case) before the examiner submits his report (revenue agent's report, or RAR). Once the RAR is submitted, the taxpayer can discuss and settle the case only in an Appeals Office conference (¶4817).[31]

In an unagreed field audit case, the agent prepares a report explaining the proposed adjustments. After review by the district review staff, the RAR is sent to the taxpayer with a transmittal letter ("30-day letter," see ¶4815). (Reg § 601.105(c)(2)(i))[32]

In an office audit, the taxpayer will usually be informed of the examiner's findings and given an opportunity to agree at the end of the interview. If he doesn't agree, he may request an immediate meeting with an appeals officer. If the taxpayer doesn't request an immediate conference, or it isn't practicable, the RAR (and 30-day letter) will be mailed to him. (Reg § 601.105(c)(1)(ii))[33]

¶ 4815   The 30-day letter.

The examiner's report that IRS sends, along with a transmittal ("30-day letter") to a taxpayer who rejects the examiner's findings from a field or office audit must show the basis for and amount of any proposed adjustments. (Code Sec. 7522(a), Code Sec. 7522(b)(3)) The letter also explains the appeal procedures and asks taxpayer to indicate, within 30 days, whether he will:

. . . accept the findings and sign a waiver of restrictions on assessment (Form 870), which allows IRS to collect the deficiency without issuing a 90-day letter (¶4825), and limits the taxpayer's appeal to a claim or suit for refund (no Tax Court petition);

. . . request an Appeals Office conference (¶4817); or

. . . do nothing and IRS will send a 90-day letter. (Reg § 601.105(d)(1))

IRS must include an explanation of the entire process from examination through collection with respect to a proposed deficiency (including the assistance available to the taxpayer from the National Taxpayer Advocate, ¶4812, at various points in the process) with any first letter of proposed deficiency that allows the taxpayer an opportunity for administrative review in the IRS Office of Appeals. [34]

¶ 4816   Early referral to Appeals.

Under procedures prescribed by IRS, any taxpayer may request early referral of one or more unresolved issues from either the examination or collection division, to the IRS Office of Appeals. (Code Sec. 7123(a))[35]

¶ 4817   Appeals Office conference.

The taxpayer can get an Appeals Office conference by sending a written request (in response to a 30-day letter, see ¶4815) and any required protest (¶4818) to the local district director.[36]

The Appeals Office proceedings are informal and testimony isn't under oath, although the taxpayer may be asked to submit affidavits. (Reg § 601.106(c))[37]

An Appeals Office conference still is available to a taxpayer even after IRS has issued a 90-day letter (¶4825), e.g., where the taxpayer ignored the 30-day letter or where the assessment period was about to expire (or the taxpayer requested the 90-day letter). If the taxpayer then files a Tax Court petition (income, estate or gift tax case) or pays the additional tax assessed

31. ¶T-1550 *et seq.*; TD ¶824,001
32. ¶T-1601; TD ¶823,502
33. ¶T-1604 *et seq.*; TD ¶823,505 *et seq.*
34. ¶T-1601 *et seq.*; TD ¶823,503

35. ¶T-1709; ¶71,234; TD ¶824,001
36. ¶T-1711; TD ¶824,002
37. ¶T-1720

(other taxes), he can get an Appeals conference. (Reg § 601.106(a)(1))[38]

¶ 4818 Protest.

An oral request is enough to get Appeals consideration in all office or correspondence audit cases. In a field audit case, a written protest is: *required* if the total amount of the proposed increase in tax (including penalties), proposed overassessment or claimed refund, or compromise offer, exceeds $10,000 for any tax period; *optional* (but a statement of issues is required) if that total amount is between $2,500 and $10,000; and *not required* if it is less than $2,500. (Reg § 601.106(a)(1)(iii)(a))[39] The 30-day letter (¶4815) contains instructions for the protest (Reg § 601.105(d)(2)) and spells out the required information. [40]

¶ 4819 Appeals Office settlement authority; nonbinding mediation and arbitration of unresolved issues.

The Appeals Office has authority to settle all factual and legal issues raised by the examiner's report (RAR, see ¶4814) or the taxpayer's protest (¶4818) (Reg § 601.106(f)(2))[41] as long as the case isn't docketed in the Tax Court. (Reg § 601.106(a)(2))[42]

If no settlement is reached, IRS will prepare a 90-day letter (¶4825).[43]

Under procedures prescribed by IRS, either the taxpayer or IRS Office of Appeals can request nonbinding mediation on any issue that is still unresolved after the conclusion of appeals procedures, or unsuccessful attempts to enter into a closing agreement or a compromise. (Code Sec. 7123(b)(1))[44] In addition, a taxpayer and IRS can jointly request binding arbitration of factual issues unresolved after the conclusion of appeals procedures, or unsuccessful attempts to enter into a closing agreement or a compromise. (Code Sec. 7123(b)(2))[45]

¶ 4820 Execution of Appeals Office settlement—Form 870, Form 890.

If the taxpayer accepts IRS's position in full, with no concessions, he signs a Form 870 (Form 890, in gift, estate or generation-skipping transfer tax cases), waiving restrictions on assessment (¶4830). (Reg § 601.106(d)(2))[46] For concessions, see ¶4821.

¶ 4821 Settlement with concessions—Form 870-AD, Form 890-AD.

If the Appeals Office makes any concessions, a Form 870-AD (Form 890-AD, in gift or estate tax cases) is executed stating that: the settlement is subject to acceptance by IRS; on acceptance it won't be reopened by IRS absent fraud, malfeasance, concealment or misrepresentation of a material fact, an important mathematical mistake, or an excessive tentative NOL carryback; *and* the taxpayer waives his right to file a claim for refund (other than from an NOL carryback) for any years covered by the agreement. [47]

¶ 4822 Final closing agreements—Form 866, Form 906.

The taxpayer and IRS may conclusively settle a tax dispute by entering into a final agreement to close either a tax year that has ended (use Form 866) (Code Sec. 7121(a); Reg § 301.7121-1(b)(2), Reg § 601.202(a)(2))[48] or a *specific transaction*, past or future (use

---

38. ¶s T-1710, T-1900 *et seq.*
39. TD ¶824,008
40. ¶T-1602 *et seq.*; TD ¶824,009
41. ¶T-1721; TD ¶824,003
42. ¶T-1725; TD ¶824,003
43. ¶T-1732; TD ¶824,003

44. ¶T-1733; ¶71,234; TD ¶824,003
45. ¶T-1756
46. ¶T-1731; TD ¶824,005
47. ¶T-3400 *et seq.*; TD ¶824,006
48. ¶T-9500; ¶71,214 *et seq.*; TD ¶841,011

Form 906). (Reg § 601.202(a)(2))[49] The agreement is irrevocable (except for fraud, malfea-sance or misrepresentation of a material fact) and binds *both* parties. (Code Sec. 7121(b))[50]

¶ 4823   Compromise—Form 656, Form 433-A, Form 433-B.

Civil or criminal tax cases can be compromised by IRS, after assessment, before referral to the Department of Justice (after referral, compromise can be only by the Attorney General). (Code Sec. 7122(a))[1]

IRS may compromise tax liabilities on any of these grounds: (1) doubt as to collectibility, (2) doubt as to liability, (3) economic hardship, and (4) extraordinary events beyond the tax-payer's control. (Reg § 301.7122-1(b)) To make an offer, file Form 656 (which has a box allowing a taxpayer to designate someone to assist while IRS is processing the offer) and, except for offers based solely on doubt as to liability, Form 433-A (individuals) or Form 433-B (businesses) (sole proprietors file must file both of the latter forms) and pay the $150 process-ing fee that generally applies. (Reg § 301.7122-1(d)(1)) IRS may disregard frivolous offer submissions. (Code Sec. 7122(f))[2]

¶ 4824   Deficiency defined.

A deficiency is the amount by which a taxpayer's correct tax liability is more than the excess of: (1) the tax shown on the return (mathematical or clerical errors corrected), plus (2) the amounts previously assessed (or collected without assessment) as a deficiency, over (3) the amount of any rebates (credits, refunds, or other repayments). (Code Sec. 6211(a), Code Sec. 6213(b)) The correct tax and the tax shown on the return are computed without regard to credits for estimated taxes and taxes withheld under Code Sec. 31 (i.e., on wages, including excess social security withholdings, and back-up withholding). (Code Sec. 6211(b)(1)) For pur-poses of determining a deficiency, any excess of the additional child tax credit for families with three or more children, the gasoline and special fuel tax credit under Code Sec. 34, the earned income credit, and the Code Sec. 53(e) alternative minimum tax refundable credit, over the tax imposed by subtitle A (without taking into account those credits) and any excess of those credits shown by the taxpayer on the return over the amount shown as tax on the return (without taking into account those credits) is taken into account as a negative amount of tax. (Code Sec. 6211(b)(4)) If no return was filed, or if a return doesn't show any tax, the deficiency equals the entire amount of the correct tax. Additional taxes reported on an amended return filed after its due date are treated as "tax shown" ((1) above), not deficien-cies. (Reg § 301.6211-1(a))[3]

If a taxpayer elects to have IRS compute the tax, IRS's computation of tax imposed is the "tax shown" on the return. (Code Sec. 6211(b)(3))[4]

Where a deficiency on a joint return is challenged by only one spouse, the deficiency as to that spouse is reduced by any tax collected from the other spouse. [5]

¶ 4825   Notice of deficiency—"90-day letter."

A statutory notice of deficiency ("90-day letter") tells a taxpayer that IRS has determined a deficiency (in income, estate or gift tax, or excise tax on private foundations or pension plans). This is the only notice IRS will issue for that determination. [6] It must describe the basis for and identify the amounts (if any) of tax, interest, additional amounts, additions to tax and assessable penalties (for exceptions, see ¶4827). (Code Sec. 7522(a))[7] and be sent by

49. ¶T-9524; ¶71,214; TD ¶841,012
50. ¶T-9507; ¶s 71,214.07, 71,214.08; TD ¶841,005
1. ¶T-9600 *et seq.*; ¶71,224 *et seq.*; TD ¶842,001
2. ¶T-9601; ¶71,224; TD ¶842,010
3. ¶T-1501 *et seq.*; ¶62,114 *et seq.*; TD ¶822,501

4. ¶T-1506; ¶62,114.01; TD ¶822,501
5. ¶T-1507; TD ¶822,501
6. ¶T-2701; ¶62,114; TD ¶831,001
7. ¶T-2714; ¶75,224; TD ¶831,004

certified or registered mail to the taxpayer at his last known address. [8]

After receiving the letter, the taxpayer can: pay the deficiency, not pay and seek to rescind it, pay and file a refund claim (¶4849), take no action (let tax be assessed) and then file a compromise offer (¶4823), or file a Tax Court petition (¶4858).[9]

©️ *observation:* The 90-day letter is a taxpayer's "ticket to Tax Court." It's only when (and if) IRS issues the letter that a taxpayer can go to Tax Court.

All 90-day letters must include the date determined by IRS as the last day on which the taxpayer may file a petition with the Tax Court, ¶4858. (Code Sec. 6213(a)) But the Tax Court says that failure to include the date doesn't necessarily invalidate the letter. [10] Notices must include information about interest (Code Sec. 6631) and penalties (Code Sec. 6751).[11]

¶ 4826 Time for making assessments.

Unless the taxpayer and IRS sign a closing agreement (¶4822), or the taxpayer voluntarily pays the deficiency or signs a Form 870 (¶4815), or IRS determines collection is in jeopardy (¶4828), IRS can't assess deficiencies in income, estate, and gift taxes, and the excise taxes on private foundations and qualified pension, etc., plans until after the taxpayer has had an opportunity to make a Tax Court appeal. (Code Sec. 6213(a))[12]

¶ 4827 Assessment of interest and penalties.

Interest may be assessed when the underlying tax is collectible. (Code Sec. 6601(g))[13]

For income, estate, gift and certain excise taxes, the negligence and fraud penalties are assessed like deficiencies (¶4826). So are the delinquency penalties (¶4872, ¶4873), but only if attributable to a deficiency and not if measured by the tax shown on the return. The penalty for estimated tax underpayments (¶3118, ¶3352) is assessed as a deficiency only if no return is filed. (Code Sec. 6665(b); Reg § 301.6659-1(c))[14]

The normal assessment and collection rules don't apply to the penalties for promoting an abusive tax shelter (¶4888) or for aiding and abetting a tax understatement (¶4883). A taxpayer may delay collection of these penalties by paying at least 15% of the penalty and filing a claim for refund of it, within 30 days of notice and demand for payment. If IRS denies the claim, the taxpayer has 30 days to sue for refund in a district court (where IRS may counterclaim for the unpaid penalty amount). The normal procedures also don't apply to the penalty for filing a frivolous return (¶4895). (Code Sec. 6703(b), Code Sec. 6703(c))[15]

¶ 4828 Jeopardy assessment and termination of a tax year.

If IRS believes assessment or collection of a deficiency will be jeopardized by delay, it can immediately assess the deficiency (plus any interest and penalties) and demand payment. (Code Sec. 6861(a); Reg § 301.6861-1(a)) However, within 60 days after making the assessment, IRS must issue the taxpayer a 90-day letter (¶4825) if it hasn't already done so. (Code Sec. 6861(b))[16] IRS Chief Counsel must pre-approve jeopardy assessments. (Code Sec. 7429(a)(1)(A))[17]

IRS can presume the collection of income tax is in jeopardy if an individual who has physical possession of more than $10,000 in cash or cash equivalents denies ownership of it and doesn't claim it belongs to another identifiable person who acknowledges ownership. (Code Sec. 6867(a), Code Sec. 6867(d); Reg § 301.6867-1(f)(2), Reg § 301.6867-1(f)(3)) The

---

8. ¶T-2801; ¶62,124; TD ¶831,004

9. ¶T-2738; TD ¶831,009

10. ¶T-2701.1; ¶62,134; TD ¶831,009

11. ¶T-2714.1; ¶T-2714.2; ¶67,514;-¶66,314

12. ¶T-3601; ¶62,134; TD ¶836,002

13. ¶T-3646; ¶66,014.01; TD ¶836,011

14. ¶T-3638 *et seq.*; ¶66,654; TD ¶836,012

15. ¶V-5650; ¶67,034

16. ¶T-3700 *et seq.*; ¶68,614 *et seq.*; TD ¶837,002

17. ¶T-3733.1; ¶74,294

entire amount of the cash is presumed to represent taxable income of the possessor for the year and is taxable at the highest individual tax rate. (Code Sec. 6867(b)) The possessor is treated as the taxpayer for assessment and collection purposes (unless the true owner comes forward), but not for purposes of administrative or judicial review of the assessment. (Code Sec. 6867(b), Code Sec. 6867(c); Reg § 301.6867-1(c), Reg § 301.6867-1(d), Reg § 301.6867-1(f)(4))[18]

IRS can also terminate a tax year and demand immediate payment of income taxes for the current and preceding year, if it finds that a taxpayer plans to leave (or remove his property from) the U.S. quickly, conceal himself or his property in the U.S., or do any other act that would prejudice the collection of those taxes ("termination assessment"). Within 60 days after the due date (with extensions) of the taxpayer's return for the full tax year or, if later, the date the return is actually filed, IRS must issue a 90-day letter to the taxpayer for the full year. (Code Sec. 6851(a), Code Sec. 6852(a))[19]

There are procedures for administrative and judicial review of jeopardy and termination assessments (Code Sec. 7429)[20] and for stay of collection. (Code Sec. 6863)[21]

observation: A jeopardy assessment is used only where IRS makes its determination *after* the end of the tax year to which it relates. In a termination assessment, the determination is made *before* the end of the tax year to which it relates or *before* the due date to file a return and pay the tax.

¶ 4829 Assessments in bankruptcy or receivership proceedings.

IRS may make an immediate assessment of any deficiency in income, estate and gift taxes, and certain excise taxes, whether or not a notice of deficiency (90-day letter, see ¶4825) has been issued in these situations:

. . . On the debtor's estate in a case under Title 11 of the U.S. Code (bankruptcy cases);

. . . On the debtor, but only if liability for the tax becomes res judicata under a determination in a Title 11 case; or

. . . On the appointment of a receiver for the taxpayer in any receivership proceeding. (Code Sec. 6871(a), Code Sec. 6871(b))[22]

¶ 4830 General three-year statute of limitations on assessments.

Generally (for exceptions, see ¶4832, ¶4835), all taxes must be assessed:

. . . within three years after the date the return was filed (below), or

. . . if the tax is payable by stamp, within three years after the date any part of the tax was paid. (Code Sec. 6501(a))[23]

A return filed before the filing deadline is considered filed on the due date. (Code Sec. 6501(b)(1))[24] But a return of tax withheld (from wages or at source) for any period ending with or within a calendar year is, if filed before Apr. 15 of the next calendar year, considered filed *on* Apr. 15. (Code Sec. 6501(b)(2); Reg § 301.6501(b)-1(b))[25]

The assessment period for items of a partnership, S corporation, trust or estate that are passed through to and reported by the partners, shareholders or beneficiaries, respectively, is based on their returns (not the partnership's, etc.), as specifically codified in Code Sec. 6501(a).[26]

18. ¶T-3726 *et seq.*; ¶68,674; TD ¶837,006
19. ¶T-3717 *et seq.*; ¶68,514
20. ¶T-3735 *et seq.*; ¶74,294; TD ¶837,009
21. ¶T-3757 *et seq.*; ¶68,634 *et seq.*; TD ¶903,002
22. ¶T-3802; ¶68,714; TD ¶837,007

23. ¶T-4001; ¶65,014;TD ¶838,001
24. ¶T-4002; ¶65,014.09; TD ¶838,002
25. ¶T-4010; ¶65,014.09; TD ¶838,002
26. ¶T-4020 *et seq.*; ¶65,014.04; TD ¶838,005

Subject to exceptions and special rules, the period for assessing tax attributable to a partnership item (or affected item), for a partnership tax year won't expire before the date that is three years after the later of: (1) the date the partnership return was filed, or (2) the last day for filing the return for that year (without regard to extensions). (Code Sec. 6229(a)) Courts have held that this special rule cannot shorten the general limitation period. [27]

The assessment period for a late-filed return starts on the day after the actual filing, whether the lateness is due to taxpayer's delinquency, or under a filing extension granted by IRS. (Code Sec. 6501(a))[28]

If within 60 days before the limitations period expires, IRS receives an amended return that shows an increase in tax liability, IRS has 60 days from the receipt to assess the additional tax. (Code Sec. 6501(c)(7))[29]

Failure to notify IRS of certain foreign transfers extends the assessment period to three years after the date IRS is notified. (Code Sec. 6501(c)(8))[30]

Failure to notify IRS of certain distributions in connection with a tax-free corporate division extends the assessment period to three years after the date IRS is notified. (Code Sec. 355(e)(4)(E)(i))[31]

Where the taxpayer makes (or revokes) an election to have the alcohol fuel credit, enhanced oil recovery credit, employer social security credit for taxes paid on employee tips, work opportunity credit, qualified electric vehicles credit, the alternative motor vehicle credit, the qualified alternative fuel vehicle refueling (QAFVR) property credit, or the "orphan drug" credit apply for any tax year, the limitations period for assessment of a deficiency attributable to the election (or revocation) won't expire until one year after the date that IRS is notified of the election or revocation. (Code Sec. 6501(m))[32]

¶ 4831 Expiration of the limitations period as a bar to assessment.

A taxpayer who claims that the assessment of a tax is barred by the expiration of the limitations period (¶4830) must raise the issue and has the burden of proof. [33]

¶ 4832 Six-year assessment period.

Over-25% omissions. The assessment period is six years for income tax (or estate, gift or excise tax) returns that omit from gross income (or gross estate, total gifts made in the return period, or excise tax) more than 25% of the gross income (or gross estate, total gifts or excise tax) that is reported. In applying these tests, capital gains and losses aren't netted; only gains are taken into account. These "omissions" don't include amounts for which adequate information is given on the return or attached statements. (Code Sec. 6501(e)) Courts have reached contrary results on whether a basis overstatement is an omission. [34]

Personal holding company tax on a personal holding company (PHC) that didn't file a PHC schedule with its income tax return may be assessed within six years after the income tax return was filed. (Code Sec. 6501(f))[35]

¶ 4833 Assessment period for carrybacks to and carryovers from closed years.

A deficiency attributable to a taxpayer's carryback of a net operating loss (NOL), capital loss, or business credit may be assessed at any time before expiration of the period applicable to the year the loss was sustained or the credit earned. (Code Sec. 6501(h), Code

---

27. ¶T-4018; ¶62,294; TD ¶838,003
28. ¶T-4003; ¶s 65,014.01, 65,014.02; TD ¶838,002
29. ¶T-4209.1; ¶65,014.28; TD ¶838,030
30. ¶T-4146;¶65,014.28
31. ¶F-5304; ¶3554

32. ¶T-4014.1; ¶65,014
33. ¶T-4030; ¶65,014.01; TD ¶838,007
34. ¶T-4201 *et seq.*; ¶65,014.15; TD ¶838,016
35. ¶T-4218; ¶65,014.29; TD ¶838,026

Sec. 6501(j))[36] A deficiency attributable to a foreign tax credit carryback may be assessed up to one year after the credit year's assessment period expires. (Code Sec. 6501(i))[37]

Where a credit carryback results from the carryback of an NOL, capital loss or other credit carryback from a later year, a deficiency for the carryback year can be assessed at any time before the expiration of the period for the later year. (Code Sec. 6501(j))[38]

¶ 4834 Assessment period for unreported listed transactions.

If a taxpayer fails to include on any return or statement for any tax year any information with respect to a listed transaction (as defined at ¶4890) that's required under Code Sec. 6011, the time for assessment of any tax with respect to that transaction won't expire before one year after the earlier of: (1) the date when the required information is furnished to IRS (an IRS procedure explains how to use Form 8886 to disclose, pending regs), or (2) the date that a material advisor meets the list-maintenance requirements of Code Sec. 6112 with respect to a request by IRS under Code Sec. 6112(b) relating to the transaction with respect to the taxpayer. (Code Sec. 6501(c)(10))[39]

¶ 4835 When the assessment period remains open.

The assessment period is open indefinitely where a taxpayer:

. . . fails to file a required return (Code Sec. 6501(c)(3)), but the assessment period starts to run if a trust or partnership return is filed by a taxpayer later held to be a corporation (Code Sec. 6501(g)(1)) or an exempt organization return is filed by an organization later held to be taxable (Code Sec. 6501(g)(2));[40]

. . . files a false or fraudulent income, gift or estate tax return with intent to evade tax. (Code Sec. 6501(c)(1)) The Tax Court has held that an income tax return preparer's fraud keeps a taxpayer's income tax return open indefinitely under this rule, even if the taxpayer had no intent to evade taxes. [41] Filing a later amended, nonfraudulent return won't starting the normal three-year assessment period running; [42]

. . . willfully attempts in any manner to defeat and evade taxes (Code Sec. 6501(c)(2));[43]

. . . fails to pay any part of a tax required to be paid by stamp (Code Sec. 6501(a); Reg § 301.6501(a)-1);[44]

. . . for gift tax, fails to show or adequately disclose (1) any gift of property (or increase in taxable gifts) whose value is determined under the special valuation rules or (2) any post-Aug. 5, '97 gift. (Code Sec. 6501(c)(9), Reg § 301.6501(c)-1(e), Reg § 301.6501(c)-1(f))[45] Filing an amended return with required information will get the limitation period running for a prior gift that wasn't adequately disclosed. [46]

. . . is subject to the tax for termination of private foundation status, see ¶4128.[47]

IRS says that a responsible person liable for the trust fund recovery penalty is subject to an unlimited assessment period where the employer has committed fraud, willfully attempted to evade tax, or failed to file an employment tax return. [48]

The penalties for promoting abusive tax shelters, or for aiding and abetting an understatement, can be assessed at any time, [49] as can the penalty (but not the tax) imposed on a return preparer for willful tax understatements. (Code Sec. 6696(d))[50]

36. ¶T-4034; ¶65,014.28; TD ¶838,008
37. ¶T-4042; ¶65,014.28; TD ¶838,009
38. ¶T-4039; ¶65,014.28; TD ¶838,009
39. ¶T-4163; ¶65,014.147; TD ¶838,051
40. ¶T-4101 *et seq.*; ¶s 65,014.05, 65,014.06, 65,014.14; TD ¶838,012 *et seq.*
41. ¶T-4127; ¶65,014.13; TD ¶838,014
42. ¶T-4209; ¶65,014.04; TD ¶838,014
43. ¶T-4141; ¶65,014.13; TD ¶838,015
44. ¶T-4122; TD ¶838,001
45. ¶T-4147; ¶65,014.28; TD ¶838,022
46. ¶T-4148
47. ¶T-4143
48. ¶T-4029.1
49. ¶s T-4125, T-4126; ¶67,034; TD ¶838,027
50. ¶T-4145; ¶66,964; TD ¶838,011

¶ 4836   Voluntary extension of the assessment period—Form 872.

At any time *before* expiration of the assessment period (¶4830), a taxpayer and IRS can agree in writing (usually on one of the Form 872 series) to extend the assessment period (except for estate taxes). They can also enter into successive agreements further extending the period. (Code Sec. 6501(c)(4))[1]

⊘ observation: Form 872 is generally referred to by IRS as a *"consent."* Tax practitioners sometimes refer to it as a *"waiver,"* which technically means a Form 870, ¶4820.

Restricted consent. A restricted consent postpones the close of the tax year with respect to an unsettled issue. It is used where some issues are resolved, but settlement of others must await the establishment of an IRS position through a court decision, etc., or where other equally meritorious circumstances exist. [2]

Indefinite consent—Form 872-A. A taxpayer whose case is before the Appeals Office (¶4817) can execute Form 872-A, which is an indefinite extension. [3] It expires 90 days after: (1) Appeals receives notice (on Form 872-T) of the taxpayer's desire to terminate the extension, (2) IRS mails Form 872-T to the taxpayer, or (3) IRS mails a 90-day letter. [4]

IRS must notify the taxpayer of the taxpayer's right to refuse to extend the period of limitations on assessment, or to limit the extension to particular issues or to a particular period of time, on each occasion when the taxpayer is requested to provide consent. (Code Sec. 6501(c)(4)(B))[5]

¶ 4837   Suspension of the assessment period.

A 90-day letter (¶4825) suspends the assessment period. It stops running on the date IRS mails the letter, and doesn't resume until 60 days after: (1) the 90-day period (150 days if the letter is addressed to a person outside the U.S.) if no petition is filed, or (2) the Tax Court's decision becomes final if a petition is filed. (Code Sec. 6503(a))[6]

A taxpayer's application for a Taxpayer Assistance Order (¶4812) also suspends the assessment period, up to the date the National Taxpayer Advocate makes a decision. (Code Sec. 7811(d))[7]

IRS's mailing of a notice of adjustment suspends the statute of limitations on the making of assessments for the longer of (1) the period during which IRS is prohibited from making the assessment, or (2) if a proceeding in respect of the notice of adjustment is placed on the docket of the Tax Court, until the decision of the Tax Court becomes final, and for 60 more days. (Code Sec. 6234(e)(2))[8]

The assessment period is suspended in Tax Court employment tax determinations. (Code Sec. 7436(d)(1))[9]

For returns of corporations being examined under the coordinated examination program or a successor program, the issuance of a "designated summons" to determine the amount of tax also suspends the assessment period, pending final resolution of its enforcement. (Code Sec. 6503(j))[10]

For effect of compromise, see ¶4823; summons intervention, see ¶4810. For suspension during bankruptcy or receivership proceedings, see ¶4912.

1. ¶T-4400 *et seq.*; ¶65,014.17 *et seq.*; TD ¶838,034
2. ¶T-4445; TD ¶838,034
3. ¶T-4402; TD ¶838,036
4. ¶T-4457 *et seq.*; TD ¶838,036
5. ¶T-4403; ¶65,014; TD ¶838,035

6. ¶T-4300 *et seq.*; ¶65,034.01; TD ¶838,043
7. ¶T-4324; ¶78,114.01; TD ¶838,045
8. ¶T-3554; ¶62,344
9. ¶T-4301.1; ¶74,364
10. ¶T-4333 *et seq.*; ¶65,034.04; TD ¶838,046

¶ 4838   Request for prompt assessment—Form 4810.

The normal three-year assessment period can be cut to 18 months *at the taxpayer's request* (use Form 4810) for an income tax return of a decedent or an estate, or for a return of a dissolved or dissolving corporation. (Code Sec. 6501(d))[11]

¶ 4839   Statutory (mitigation) and judicial relief for barred years.

Generally, after the period for assessment or refund has run, IRS can't make an assessment and a taxpayer can't get a refund. But an otherwise closed year may be reopened under the Code's "mitigation" provisions under certain circumstances. (Code Sec. 1311, Code Sec. 1312, Code Sec. 1313)[12]

Relief from the limitation periods may be available in the district court or Court of Federal Claims if the statutory mitigation conditions aren't met, under equitable recoupment (closed year's overpayment or underpayment used to offset open year's deficiency or refund, see ¶4858 for Tax Court's authority to do this)[13] estoppel[14] or election.[15]

¶ 4840   Unified Audit and Review for Partnerships.

IRS generally can't adjust partnership items on a partner's return except through a unified entity-level proceeding. A decision in the unified proceeding binds all of the partners and permits IRS to make the necessary corresponding adjustments on their individual returns. Simplified procedures apply for electing large partnerships.

¶ 4841   Unified audit and review procedure for partnerships and partners.

The tax treatment of any partnership item (¶4842), and the applicability of any penalty, addition to tax or additional amount which relates to an adjustment to a partnership item, is generally determined at the partnership level, in one unified proceeding. This applies at both the administrative and judicial levels. (Code Sec. 6221; Reg § 301.6221-1(c)) Partnership level determinations include all the legal and factual determinations that underlie the determination of any penalty, addition to tax, or additional amount (other than partner level defenses). (Reg § 301.6221-1(c))[16]

No assessment of a deficiency attributable to any partnership item may be made before the end of the 150th day after IRS issues a notice of final partnership administrative adjustment (FPAA, see ¶4844) to the tax matters partner (TMP, see ¶4843) or, if the TMP files a Tax Court petition in that 150-day period, before the Tax Court decision becomes final. (Code Sec. 6225(a))[17] However, IRS can make an earlier assessment in certain abusive tax shelter situations. (Reg § 301.6231(c)-1)[18]

These rules generally apply to any partnership (except certain small partnerships, see ¶4845) required to file a partnership return (Form 1065), and to any entity that, for the year it filed a partnership return, either wasn't a partnership or wasn't in existence for the full year. (Code Sec. 6231(a)(1), Code Sec. 6233; Reg § 301.6233-1)[19] A REMIC (¶4204) is treated as a partnership for these purposes. (Code Sec. 860F(e))[20] Special consistency and audit rules apply for electing large partnerships (¶3702) and their partners. (Code Sec. 6240 through Code Sec. 6255)[21]

IRS may rely on the partnership return in determining whether the unified audit rules

---

11. ¶T-4500 *et seq.*; ¶65,014.16; TD ¶838,032
12. ¶T-5000 *et seq.*; ¶13,134; TD ¶823,507
13. ¶T-5200 *et seq.*; ¶65,144; TD ¶444,531
14. ¶T-5300 *et seq.*; ¶74,338.400
15. ¶T-5400 *et seq.*; ¶74,338.424
16. ¶T-2100 *et seq.*; ¶62,214; TD ¶825,001

17. ¶T-4015;¶62,254; TD ¶838,003
18. ¶T-6517; ¶62,214; TD ¶804,012
19. ¶T-2101; ¶62,214; TD ¶825,005
20. ¶E-6927; ¶860A4.04; TD ¶825,004
21. ¶T-2300 *et seq.*; ¶62,404;TD ¶825,501 *et seq.*

apply. (Code Sec. 6231(g))[22]

The unified proceedings usually begin when IRS notifies the partnership that its return has been selected for audit. Or the TMP may file (use Form 8082) an "administrative adjustment request" (AAR) for the partnership. The AAR is treated as a substituted return (correcting errors) or a claim for refund. (Code Sec. 6227(a))[23]

Special deficiency procedures apply to a partner's "oversheltered return" (one that shows no taxable income and a net loss from a partnership). (Code Sec. 6234)[24]

¶ 4842   What are "partnership items"?

A "partnership item" is any item that must be taken into account for the partnership's tax year, to the extent regs provide the item is more appropriately determined at the partnership level than at the partner level (Code Sec. 6231(a)(3)), including: items of income, gain, loss, deduction or credit; expenditures not deductible in computing taxable income (e.g., charitable contributions); any partner's tax preference items; tax-exempt income; partnership liabilities; amounts needed to enable the partnership or the partners to compute the investment credit (or recapture), at-risk amounts or depletion; and items relating to contributions to or distributions from the partnership, and transactions between a partner and the partnership (e.g., guaranteed payments). (Reg § 301.6231(a)(3)-1(a))[25]

¶ 4843   Tax matters partner (TMP).

The tax matters partner (TMP) acts on behalf of the partners in the unified partnership proceedings. The TMP is: (a) the general partner the partnership designates as such on its return (Form 1065) (Form 1066, for a REMIC (Reg § 1.860F-4(d))) or (b) if no designation is made, the general partner with the largest profits interest in the partnership at the end of the tax year. (Code Sec. 6231(a)(7))

IRS may select a general partner (or limited partner, if no general partner is eligible) (Reg § 301.6231(a)(7)-1(p)) as TMP if no designation is made under (a), above, and it is impracticable (under regs) (Reg § 301.6231(a)(7)-1(o)) to use (b). (Code Sec. 6231(a)(7); Reg § 301.6231(a)(7)-1(n))[26]

The other partners generally must receive notice from the TMP of both IRS's and the TMP's actions. (Code Sec. 6223(g); Reg § 301.6223(g)-1)[27]

¶ 4844   Final partnership administrative adjustment (FPAA).

If after auditing the partnership IRS concludes that adjustments to the return are needed, it will issue a "final partnership administrative adjustment" (FPAA), which must be sent to the TMP and to "notice partners" IRS knows are eligible to receive notice. (Code Sec. 6223(a))[28] The TMP has 90 days from when the FPAA was mailed to file a petition for judicial review of the FPAA. (Code Sec. 6226(a)) If the TMP doesn't file within that time, any notice partner can file the partnership petition within the next 60 days. (Code Sec. 6226(b)(1)) Detailed procedures govern the conduct of the partnership-level proceeding (Code Sec. 6224; Reg § 301.6224(a)-1, Reg § 301.6224(c)-3)[29] assessments (Code Sec. 6225, Code Sec. 6229; Reg § 301.6229(b)-1), judicial review of FPAAs (Code Sec. 6226, Code Sec. 6228; Reg § 301.6226(f)-1) and other matters.[30]

observation: The notice of FPAA has the same effect as a 90-day letter, ¶4825.

---

22. ¶T-2108.1; ¶62,214.10; TD ¶825,002
23. ¶T-2002; ¶62,214; TD ¶825,021
24. ¶T-3551 *et seq.*; ¶62,344
25. ¶T-2110; ¶62,214; TD ¶825,009
26. ¶T-2121; TD ¶825,023

27. ¶T-2151; TD ¶825,056
28. ¶T-2156 *et seq.*; TD ¶825,217
29. ¶T-2156 *et seq.*; ¶62,214; TD ¶825,029
30. ¶T-2215 *et seq.*; TD ¶825,224

¶ 4845   Exception for certain small partnerships.

The unified audit rules at ¶4841 *et seq.* don't apply to a "small" partnership (unless it elects to have them apply under procedures set forth by regs). (Reg § 301.6231(a)(1)-1(b)(2)) A partnership is "small" for a tax year if it has ten or fewer partners, each of whom is an individual (other than a nonresident alien), a C corporation, or an estate of a deceased partner. (Code Sec. 6231(a)(1)(B)(i); Reg § 301.6231(a)(1)-1(a)(1), Reg § 301.6231(a)(1)-1(a)(3))[31]

¶ 4846   Refunds; Tax Litigation. ▬▬▬▬▬▬▬▬▬▬▬▬▬▬▬▬▬▬▬▬▬

A taxpayer can recover an overpayment as a credit or a refund by properly filing a claim and, if the claim is denied, bringing suit. A taxpayer who has been issued a 90-day letter can go to Tax Court without first paying the disputed tax.

¶ 4847   Overpayments—recovery by refund or credit.

An overpayment is the excess of the amount paid (or withheld) as tax over the taxpayer's correct tax liability. It includes the part of a correct tax paid after the applicable assessment period has run. (Code Sec. 6401)[32]

An overpayment can be recovered as a refund or credit, generally only by the taxpayer who paid the tax. But IRS may first credit the overpayment (including interest) against *any* of the taxpayer's past due tax liability (including interest, additions, penalties). (Code Sec. 6402(a), Reg § 301.6402-3(a)(5))[33] For offset against nontax debts, see ¶4848.

Electronic filers may elect (on Form 8453) to have their refunds deposited directly into their bank accounts. Paper filers elect direct deposit by filling in the appropriate blanks on the "Refund" lines of Form 1040. In either case, use Form 8888 to direct deposit a refund into two or three accounts including IRAs. [34]

A refund may be claimed for a deceased taxpayer. Attach Form 1310 (not needed for surviving spouse filing jointly with decedent) to the decedent's final return (¶4715).[35]

¶ 4848   Overpayments applied to child support and other nontax debts.

If a state notifies the Treasury that a taxpayer owes any child support payments, it must first apply the taxpayer's overpayment (including earned income amounts) to those past-due obligations, before making any refund or credit. (Code Sec. 6402(c))[36] If a federal agency notifies the Treasury of any past-due, legally enforceable nontax debt a taxpayer owes the agency, IRS must apply the balance (i.e., after the child support offset) of the taxpayer's overpayment to that nontax debt. (Code Sec. 6402(d))[37] Refunds can be offset by state income tax debts. (Code Sec. 6402(e))[38] Any overpayment remaining after these three permitted reductions can be reduced to recover overpayments made to the taxpayer under state family aid plans approved under part A of Title IV of the Social Security Act. (Code Sec. 6402(f))[39] A spouse should file Form 8379 to prevent her share of a joint return refund from being used to satisfy the other spouse's obligations.

---

31. ¶T-2104, T-2109; ¶62,214.10; TD ¶825,003, 825,008
32. ¶T-5500 *et seq.*; ¶64,014; TD ¶801,006
33. ¶T-5600 *et seq.* T-5700 *et seq.*; ¶64,024; TD ¶803,012
34. ¶T-5610; TD ¶802,011
35. ¶T-5710; TD ¶802,039

36. ¶T-6013 *et seq.*; ¶64,024.26; TD ¶803,022
37. ¶T-6023 *et seq.*; ¶64,024.23; TD ¶803,026
38. ¶T-6038; ¶64,024
39. ¶T-6037; TD ¶803,029

¶ 4849   Refund claim.

To get a refund, a taxpayer must file a timely (¶4854) written claim. For income, gift and federal unemployment taxes, a separate claim must be made for each tax year or period. (Reg § 301.6402-2(a), Reg § 301.6402-2(d))[40] Official forms are:

. . . Form 1040X (amended U.S. individual income tax return). (Use Form 1040, Form 1040A, or Form 1040-EZ *only* for refund of overwithheld taxes or excess estimated taxes.) (Reg § 301.6402-3(a)(2), Reg § 301.6402-4)

. . . Form 1120 or Form 1120X (original or amended corporate income tax return). (Reg § 301.6402-3(a)(2))

. . . Amended returns for taxpayers who filed a form other than Form 1040, Form 1040A, Form 1040-EZ or Form 1120 (e.g., a return for an estate or trust). (Reg § 301.6402-3(a)(4))

. . . Form 843 for refunds of non-income taxes (Reg § 601.105(e)(1)), except excise taxes reported on Form 720, Form 730, or Form 2290. Form 720X and Form 8849 are used for excise tax refund claims. [41]

IRS must explain disallowances of refund claims (Code Sec. 6402(j)) and it now notifies taxpayers whose refunds have been frozen under its questionable refund program.. [42]

For how a form in the 870 or 890 series (waiver of restrictions on assessment) affects a refund claim, see ¶4815 and ¶4821.

¶ 4850   Quick refund for carrybacks and claim of right— Form 1045; Form 1139.

A taxpayer who reports a carryback of a capital loss, net operating loss (NOL), business credit, or capital loss from a section 1256 contract under Code Sec. 1212(c) on his return can quickly recover a refund based on the carryback by filing Form 1045 (individuals) or Form 1139 (corporations) *on or after* the date the return for the loss or credit year is filed, and within 12 months after the end of the tax year *from which* the carryback is made. (Code Sec. 6411(a); Reg § 1.6411-1(b)(1))[43] This procedure also applies to overpayments attributable to a "claim of right" adjustment (¶2862), where the amount of repayment in any one year exceeds $3,000. (Code Sec. 6411(d))[44]

IRS has 90 days from the later of the date the claim is filed or the last day of the month the loss year return is due (with extensions), to make any credit or refund. (Code Sec. 6411(b); Reg § 1.6411-3)[45]

IRS's determination is tentative. If the claim is rejected, the taxpayer can't sue but must first file a standard refund claim. (Code Sec. 6411(a); Reg § 1.6411-3(c)) Even if IRS grants the refund, it can later examine the loss year return and the refund application. IRS may assess any part of the refund it finds excessive, without issuing a 90-day letter. (Code Sec. 6213(b)(3))[46]

¶ 4851   Quick refunds of corporate estimated tax overpayments— Form 4466.

A corporation that overpaid its estimated tax (¶3346 *et seq.*) can get a refund within 45 days after filing Form 4466. (Code Sec. 6425(b)(1), Code Sec. 6425(b)(2); Reg § 1.6425-1(b)) The form must be filed *after* the close of the corporation's tax year and *on or before* the 15th day of the third month after the end of the year (or before the corporation first files its income

---

40. ¶T-6702; ¶s 64,024, 64,024.08; TD ¶805,002
41. ¶T-6707 *et seq.*; ¶64,024 (Excise); TD ¶805,004 *et seq.*
42. ¶T-5618.1; ¶64,024; TD ¶802,018
43. ¶T-6501 *et seq.*; ¶64,114; TD ¶804,001

44. ¶T-6522; ¶64,114; TD ¶804,015
45. ¶T-6509; ¶64,114; TD ¶804,007
46. ¶T-6513; ¶62,134.02; TD ¶836,002

tax return for that year, if earlier). (Code Sec. 6425(a)(1); Reg § 1.6425-1(c)(1)) The corporation's estimated tax overpayment must be at least 10% of its revised expected annual tax, *and* at least $500. (Code Sec. 6425(b)(3)) If the refund is excessive, an addition to tax equal to the underpayment interest rate (¶4865), times the excessive amount is imposed. (Code Sec. 6655(h))[47]

¶ 4852   Protective refund claims.

A protective refund claim is a regular refund claim (on the regular form, see ¶4849) filed merely to keep a particular claim alive. It's generally used where IRS has a settled view adverse to a taxpayer on an issue being litigated by other taxpayers. A protective refund claim is usually filed just before the refund claim period expires. It will keep the taxpayer's claim alive (i.e., protect his right to sue) for the additional period from the date of filing to the date of rejection plus the refund suit period. [48]

¶ 4853   Interest on overpayments.

Interest on overpayments is allowed. (Code Sec. 6611(a)) The interest (compounded daily) runs from the date of the overpayment (below) to a date not more than 30 days before the refund is made (or to the (unextended) return due date for the amount against which the overpayment is credited). (Code Sec. 6611(b))[49]

But no interest is payable on a refund arising from an original income, employment, excise, estate or gift tax return made within 45 days after the later of the return due date (without extensions) or the date it was filed. (Code Sec. 6611(e)(1); Reg § 301.6611-1(g))[50] If a refund arising from an amended return or refund claim is issued within 45 days, no interest is payable for that up-to-45 day period. (Code Sec. 6611(e)(2))[1]

For refunds or credits arising from an adjustment initiated by IRS, the interest period is reduced by 45 days. (Code Sec. 6611(e)(3))[2]

With respect to returns filed after the due date (with extensions), no interest is payable for the period preceding the actual filing date. (Code Sec. 6611(b)(3))[3] And, no interest is payable on an estate's overpayment unless it shows that the interest (and refund) won't escheat to the state. (Code Sec. 6408)[4] IRS also won't pay interest when it refunds a conditional or advance payment of taxes. [5]

The overpayment rate for corporations except C corporations with large overpayments (see below) is the short-term AFR plus two percentage points. However, the overpayment rate for individuals is the short-term AFR plus 3 percentage points (i.e., the same as the underpayment rate, see ¶4865). (Code Sec. 6621(a)(1))[6] Recent overpayment rates for corporations are 7% (July 1, 2006 —Dec. 31, 2007). [7]

For C corporations, the rate is reduced to the short-term AFR plus 0.5 percentage points, to the extent the overpayment for any period exceeds $10,000. (Code Sec. 6621(a)(1))[8] Some of these recent rates are 5.5% (July 1, 2006 —Dec. 31, 2007). [9]

The overpayment date for taxes withheld or paid as estimated taxes is the unextended due date of the return. (Code Sec. 6513(b))[10]

A deposit that is returned to a taxpayer is treated as a payment of tax for any period to the extent (and only to the extent) attributable to a disputable tax for that period. (Code

47. ¶T-6600 *et seq.*; ¶s 64,254, 66,554; TD ¶804,500 *et seq.*
48. ¶T-6742; ¶64,024.17; TD ¶805,033
49. ¶s T-8008, T-8031, T-8034; ¶66,114; TD ¶807,006
50. ¶T-8024; ¶66,114; TD ¶807,012
1. ¶T-8027; ¶66,114; TD ¶807,015
2. ¶T-8028; ¶66,114; TD ¶807,016
3. ¶T-8008; ¶66,114; TD ¶807,006

4. ¶s T-8063, T-8065; ¶64,084; TD ¶807,044
5. ¶T-8046; ¶66,114
6. ¶T-8002; ¶66,214; TD ¶807,001
7. ¶T-8003.1; ¶66,214; TD ¶807,001
8. ¶T-8002; ¶66,214; TD ¶807,001
9. ¶T-8003.2; ¶66,214; TD ¶807,001
10. ¶T-7530; ¶s 66,114, 65,134; TD ¶806,026

Sec. 6603(d)(1)) However, the interest on the return of such a deposit is payable only at the short-term AFR rate compounded daily. (Code Sec. 6603(d)(4)) [11]

Overpayments resulting from the carryback of an NOL, net capital loss, business credit, or foreign tax credit, are considered not to have been made before the "filing date" for the tax year in which the loss or credit arose or the foreign tax was in fact paid or accrued. (Code Sec. 6611(f))[12] Similarly, where a business credit carryback is attributable to an NOL, etc., carryback from a later year, the overpayment is considered not to have been made before the filing date for that later year. (Code Sec. 6611(f)(3))[13]

¶ 4854 Deadline for refund claims.

A claim for credit or refund of a tax paid by *return* must be filed within the later of: (1) three years from the date the return was timely or untimely filed (or the due date if filed earlier), or (2) two years from the date the tax was paid. If the required return wasn't filed, the claim must be filed within two years from when the tax was paid. (Code Sec. 6511(a))[14] For the prohibited transaction excise tax (¶4347), the relevant return is the plan's annual Form 5500, not Form 5330 on which the tax is reported. [15] A remittance accompanying an automatic filing extension is a tax payment for this purpose. [16]

However, a longer refund claim period applies in these cases:

. . . If a taxpayer and IRS execute one of the Form 872 series extending the assessment period (see ¶4836), the claim can be filed within six months after the expiration of the extended assessment period. (Code Sec. 6511(c)(1))[17]

. . . For an overpayment resulting from carryback of an NOL, net capital loss, or business credit, the period expires three years after the time the return is due (including extensions) for the year the loss or credit arose, not the year to which it's carried back. The Federal Circuit has held that this exception does not apply to a year to which a net capital loss is carried over. (Code Sec. 6511(d)(2), Code Sec. 6511(d)(4))[18] If the overpayment is attributable to a carryback from a later year, the period expires three years after the time for filing the return (including extensions) for that later year. (Code Sec. 6511(d)(4))[19]

. . . For an overpayment resulting from the payment or accrual of foreign taxes for which a foreign tax credit is allowed, the claim period is ten years. (Code Sec. 6511(d)(3))[20]

. . . For an overpayment resulting from a bad debt or from worthless securities, the claim period is seven years. (Code Sec. 6511(d)(1))[21]

. . . For self-employment tax claims attributable to Tax Court employment status proceedings, the claim period is two years after the calendar year in which the Tax Court determination becomes final. (Code Sec. 6511(d)(7))[22]

. . . The two-year period for filing a refund suit is suspended where a declaratory judgment action is brought as to an estate's eligibility to make installment payments of estate tax under Code Sec. 6166, until the decision of the Tax Court has become final. (Code Sec. 7479(c))[23]

Also, under certain circumstances, the limitations period is suspended during any period an individual is unable to manage his financial affairs by reason of his medically-determinable physical or mental impairment. (Code Sec. 6511(h))[24]

---

11. ¶S-5804.3; ¶66,034.01; TD ¶807,006.1
12. ¶T-8049 *et seq.*; ¶66,114; TD ¶807,034
13. ¶T-8051; ¶66,114; TD ¶807,035
14. ¶T-7501 *et seq.*; ¶65,114; TD ¶806,001
15. ¶T-7524; ¶65,114.04; TD ¶806,022
16. ¶S-5801.4; TD ¶806,031
17. ¶T-7574; ¶65,114.09; TD ¶806,068

18. ¶T-7554; ¶s 65,114.11, 65,114.13; TD ¶806,050
19. ¶T-7563; ¶65,114.13; TD ¶806,058
20. ¶T-7569; ¶65,114.12; TD ¶806,063
21. ¶T-7552; ¶65,114.10; TD ¶806,049
22. ¶T-7573.1
23. ¶U-3855; ¶74,794
24. ¶T-7506; ¶65,114; TD ¶806,008

¶ 4855   Refund suit period.

A taxpayer *must* file a refund claim with IRS before starting a suit for refund (or credit). (Code Sec. 7422(a))[25] The refund suit can't be started *before* six months from filing the claim (unless IRS acts on the claim in that period), or *after* two years from the date IRS mails a notice of disallowance. (Code Sec. 6532(a)(1)) The taxpayer can waive (on Form 2297) issuance of this notice and the two-year period will start on the date the waiver is filed. (Code Sec. 6532(a)(3)) Also, the taxpayer and IRS can execute a Form 907 extending the two-year period. (Code Sec. 6532(a)(2))[26]

¶ 4856   Limits on amount of refund or credit.

If a claim is filed within three years from the time the return was filed, the refund or credit is limited to the portion of tax paid during the three years (plus the period of any filing extension) immediately preceding the filing of the claim. (Code Sec. 6511(b)(2)(A))[27]

If the claim wasn't filed within the three-year period, the refund or credit is limited to the portion of the tax paid during the two years immediately preceding the filing of the claim. (Code Sec. 6511(b)(2)(B)) This two-year limitation also applies if a claim, but no return, was filed. (Reg § 301.6511(b)-1(b)(1)(iii))[28]

Where no claim is filed and a refund or credit is allowed within three years from the time the return was filed, the refund or credit is limited to the portion of the tax paid during the three years immediately before the allowance. If the refund or credit is not allowed within that three-year period, it's limited to the portion of the tax paid during the two years immediately before the allowance. (Code Sec. 6511(b)(2)(C))[29]

The Tax Court cannot refund taxes that a non-filer paid more than two years before a deficiency notice was mailed. (Code Sec. 6512(b)(3))[30]

For purposes of determining the amount of an individual taxpayer's refund or credit under these rules, the refund claim periods described above are suspended during any period when the individual is unable to manage his financial affairs (see ¶4854). (Code Sec. 6511(h))[31]

¶ 4857   Tax litigation.

A taxpayer may go to:

. . . the Tax Court to set aside a deficiency determined by IRS (¶4858) (Code Sec. 6214(a));[32]

. . . a U.S. district court or the U.S. Court of Federal Claims to recover an overpayment of taxes (after filing a refund claim) (Code Sec. 6532(a));[33]

. . . a U.S. district court or the U.S. Court of Federal Claims to determine the correct amount of the estate's estate tax liability (or for any refund of the estate's estate tax liability) even if the full amount of that liability has not been paid by reason of an election under Code Sec. 6166. (Code Sec. 7422(j)(1))[34]

. . . the Tax Court, the district court for the DC Circuit or the U.S. Court of Federal Claims for a declaratory judgment on the tax status of a charity or foundation (Code Sec. 7428(a));[35]

. . . the Tax Court for a declaratory judgment on retirement plan qualification (Code Sec. 7476(a)),[36] eligibility for deferral of estate tax on a closely held business interest (Code

---

25. ¶T-6701; ¶74,224; TD ¶808,006
26. ¶T-9034; ¶65,324.01; TD ¶808,017
27. ¶T-7537; ¶65,114.07; TD ¶806,037
28. ¶s T-7546, T-7547; ¶65,114.07
29. ¶T-7548; ¶65,114.07; TD ¶806,045
30. ¶T-7578

31. ¶T-7537; ¶65,114; TD ¶806,008
32. ¶U-2100 *et seq.*; ¶s 62,144 *et seq.*, 74,414 *et seq.*
33. ¶s U-4000 *et seq.*, U-6000 *et seq.*; ¶74,224 *et seq.*; TD ¶802,019
34. ¶T-9007.1
35. ¶s U-3800 *et seq.*, U-4116, U-6005; ¶74,284
36. ¶U-3700 *et seq.*; ¶74,764

Sec. 7479),[37] or the value of certain gifts made (Code Sec. 7477);[38]

. . . the Tax Court for review of IRS's failure to abate interest (Code Sec. 6404(g));[39]

. . . the Tax Court for a worker classification determination in certain cases. (Code Sec. 7436)[40]

. . . a district court to enjoin IRS from assessing and collecting a tax in certain cases (¶4909), or to get damages for IRS's unauthorized collection activities or failure to release a lien. (Code Sec. 7432, Code Sec. 7433)[41]

. . . a bankruptcy court to sue for up to $1 million in damages for willful IRS violations of automatic stay or discharge in bankruptcy. (Code Sec. 7433(e))[42]

For taxpayers other than certain large partnerships, corporations, and trusts, IRS has the burden of proof in any court proceeding with respect to any factual issue relevant to ascertaining a taxpayer's liability for any tax imposed by subtitle A or B of the Code, e.g., income and self-employment, gift, estate, and generation-skipping transfer taxes, if the taxpayer: introduces credible evidence with respect to the issue; has complied with the substantiation requirements; has maintained all required records; and has cooperated with reasonable IRS requests for witnesses, information, documents, meetings, and interviews. (Code Sec. 7491(a))[43] IRS has the burden of production (i.e., to come forward initially with evidence) in any court proceeding with respect to the liability of any individual for any penalty imposed by the Code. (Code Sec. 7491(c))[44]

¶ 4858 The Tax Court.

To get Tax Court review of a deficiency, a taxpayer must file a petition with the Tax Court at Washington, D.C., in response to a notice of deficiency (90-day letter, see ¶4825) from IRS, within 90 days (150 days if the notice is addressed to a person outside the U.S.) after the notice is mailed (i.e., postmarked). A petition is treated as timely if it's filed with the Tax Court on or before the last date specified by IRS in the 90-day letter for filing it. (Code Sec. 6213(a))[45]

The Tax Court's jurisdiction generally is limited to the review (without a jury) of deficiencies asserted by IRS (and not paid when the 90-day letter is issued). It can order payment of a refund if it determines the taxpayer overpaid. (Code Sec. 6512(b)) But it can't grant equitable relief. The Tax Court has jurisdiction to order a refund of any amount collected while IRS was prohibited from collecting a deficiency by levy or court proceeding but only if a timely petition for a redetermination of the deficiency has been filed and only with respect to the deficiency at issue. (Code Sec. 6213(a))[46] The Tax Court has jurisdiction, which the Supreme Court has held is exclusive, to review IRS's failure to abate interest to taxpayers within certain net worth limits who bring an action within 180 days of IRS's final adverse determination, and to order abatement if IRS abused its discretion. (Code Sec. 6404(i))[47] It can also determine worker classification in certain cases and, according to it, the correct amount of employment taxes that relate to such determinations. (Code Sec. 7436)[48] It has jurisdiction to determine innocent spouse relief when a deficiency has been issued and the taxpayer elects regular or separate innocent spouse relief but it can't rule on the timeliness of an assessment in reviewing a denial of innocent spouse relief. It can review denials of equitable relief for taxes arising or remaining unpaid on or after Dec. 20, 2006. (Code Sec. 6015(e)) The Tax Court has held that it could adjudicate a taxpayer's claim for spousal relief even though her former spouse

---

37. ¶U-3851 *et seq.*; ¶74,794
38. ¶U-3880; ¶74,774
39. ¶U-2129.1; ¶64,044
40. ¶U-2143; ¶74,364
41. ¶s V-5801, V-6113; ¶s 74,324, 74,334; TD ¶903,010
42. ¶V-5809; ¶74,334

43. ¶U-1351; ¶74,914
44. ¶U-1331; ¶74,914
45. ¶U-2300 *et seq.*; ¶62,134 *et seq.*
46. ¶U-2134.1; ¶s 65,124, 74,424; TD ¶806,072
47. ¶U-2129.1; ¶64,044
48. ¶U-2143; ¶74,364

intervened and later filed for bankruptcy, triggering an automatic stay. [49] The Tax Court generally is barred from determining whether the tax for any period not before it has been overpaid or underpaid. However, for Tax Court actions or proceedings for which a decision has not become final as of Aug. 17, 2006, it may apply the doctrine of equitable recoupment. (Code Sec. 6214(b)) [50]

¶ 4859   Settlement after Tax Court petition is filed.

IRS District Counsel will refer all docketed Tax Court cases to the Appeals Office for consideration of settlement (unless Appeals issued the deficiency notice, in which case there will be no referral if there is little likelihood that all or part of the case can be settled in a reasonable period of time). Counsel and Appeals can agree otherwise, work together, or transfer the case back and forth to promote efficient disposition of the case. The taxpayer-petitioner and/or his representative will be notified as to who has the case and the settlement authority. [1]

If the taxpayer and IRS agree on a settlement, they enter into a written agreement stipulating the amount of any deficiency or overpayment. This stipulation is filed with the Tax Court which will enter a decision in accordance with it. (Reg § 601.106(d)(3)(i)) [2]

¶ 4860   Small tax claims in Tax Court.

Special informal procedures apply, at a taxpayer's election and with the Tax Court's concurrence, to any Tax Court case where neither the amount (including any additions to tax, additional amounts and penalties) of the deficiency disputed nor of any claimed overpayment exceeds $50,000 (the Tax Court has held that the limit includes tax, interest and penalties and applies to the total owed for all years in a single proceeding). The taxpayer thus gets the court's decision faster and more easily, but gives up the right to appeal. (Code Sec. 7463) [3]

¶ 4861   Appeals from Tax Court, district court and U.S. Court of Federal Claims.

Decisions of the Tax Court and U.S. district courts are appealable to the U.S. Court of Appeals. [4] The appeal is made generally in the circuit where the taxpayer's legal residence (for appeals from Tax Court) [5] or the trial court (for appeals from district courts) is located. [6] U.S. Court of Federal Claims decisions may be appealed to the Court of Appeals for the Federal Circuit. [7]

Appeals from the U.S. Courts of Appeals are heard by the U.S. Supreme Court. [8]

¶ 4862   Recovery of attorneys' fees and costs.

Taxpayers whose net worth doesn't exceed specified limits, who meet other requirements, and who prevail against the U.S. in court (or at the administrative level) may be awarded reasonable litigation and administrative costs (including the costs of recovering the award). (Code Sec. 7430) For 2007 (and 2008), the limit on attorney fee recoveries is $170 per hour. (Code Sec. 7430(c)(1)) To avoid an award of fees, IRS must establish that its position was substantially justified. (Code Sec. 7430(c)(4)(B)) Administrative costs can be awarded from the date IRS sends the "30-day letter." (Code Sec. 7430(c)(2)) IRS losses on similar issues in other circuits are taken into account in determining whether its position was substantially justified (Code Sec. 7430(c)(4)(B)(iii)), and costs can be awarded where a taxpayer makes an offer, IRS rejects it and later gets a judgment equal to or less than the offer. (Code

49. ¶U-2148; ¶75,214
50. ¶U-2138; ¶62,144.02
1. ¶T-1901 *et seq.*; TD ¶832,003
2. ¶T-1909; TD ¶832,004
3. ¶U-3600 *et seq.*

4. ¶s U-3417, U-5000 *et seq.*; ¶s 74,336.12, 74,824
5. ¶U-5202; ¶74,824
6. ¶U-5401
7. ¶U-6001; ¶74,336.10
8. ¶s U-5700 *et seq.*, U-7000 *et seq.*; ¶74,336.15

Sec. 7430(c)(4)(E)(i); Reg § 301.7430-7)[9]

¶ 4863 Interest and Penalties. ▄▄▄▄▄▄▄▄▄▄▄▄▄▄▄▄▄▄

Interest is charged on underpayments of tax. Various civil and criminal penalties are imposed on taxpayers (and/or return preparers) who violate the tax law.

¶ 4864 Interest on underpayments.

Interest is generally payable whenever any tax or civil penalty isn't paid when due (Code Sec. 6601(a)), even if the taxpayer has been granted an extension of time to pay the tax. (Code Sec. 6601(b)(1); Reg § 301.6601-1(a)) There's no interest on late payments of estimated tax (Code Sec. 6601(h)) (but for comparable penalty computations, see ¶3156 (individuals) and ¶3352 (corporations)) or unemployment tax. (Code Sec. 6601(i))[10]

Interest is payable on an erroneous refund or credit. (Code Sec. 6602)[11]

¶ 4865 Interest rate on underpayments.

The rate of interest on tax underpayments and penalties is keyed to the short-term applicable federal rate (AFR) for the first month of the previous calendar quarter (Code Sec. 6621(a)(2)), and is compounded daily. [12] Some of these recent rates (short-term AFR plus three percentage points) are 8% (July 1, 2006 —Dec. 31, 2007).[13]

If a C corporation's tax underpayment for any tax period exceeds $100,000, a higher interest rate (short-term AFR plus five percentage points) applies for the period after the 30th day after a notice (or proposed notice) of deficiency. Some of these recent rates are 10% (July 1, 2006—Dec. 31, 2007). (Code Sec. 6621(c)(3); Reg § 301.6621-3)[14]

A net interest rate of zero applies to equivalent amounts of underpayments and overpayments. (Code Sec. 6621(d)) Taxpayers must request interest netting under a procedure making use of Form 843. [15]

¶ 4866 Interest accrual period.

Interest on unpaid tax liabilities runs from the last day prescribed by the Code for payment (disregarding extensions or any installment payment agreement) (Code Sec. 6601(b)(1)), to the date paid. (Code Sec. 6601(a)) However, where the tax is paid within 21 days after notice and demand (10 business days if the amount is $100,000 or more), interest stops on the date of the notice and demand. (Code Sec. 6601(e)(3))[16] (For payments to stop interest, see ¶4867.)

Also, where a taxpayer consents to immediate assessment (by signing one of the Form 870 waiver of assessment series, see ¶4820) and IRS doesn't make notice and demand for payment within 30 days of the filing of that consent, interest stops running during the period beginning immediately after that 30th day and ending with the date of the notice and demand. (Code Sec. 6601(c))[17]

Interest on civil penalties runs from the date of notice and demand if not paid within 21 days after that date (10 business days for amounts of $100,000 or more). (Code Sec. 6601(e)(2)(A)) But for the penalties for failure to file, valuation misstatement (income tax) or understatement (estate or gift tax), substantial understatement, negligence, and (except for returns due (without extension) before '89) fraud, the interest period begins on the *return* due date (with extensions). In either case, the interest stops on the date the penalty is

9. ¶U-1240 *et seq.*; ¶74,304
10. ¶V-1000 *et seq.*; ¶66,014; TD ¶852,001
11. ¶T-9108; ¶66,024; TD ¶852,008
12. ¶s V-1101, V-1104; ¶66,214; TD ¶851,001
13. ¶V-1102; ¶66,214; TD ¶851,001

14. ¶V-1106 *et seq.*; ¶66,214; TD ¶851,005
15. ¶V-1301.1; ¶66,014; TD ¶851,008
16. ¶V-1200 *et seq.*, ¶V-1300; ¶66,014.02; TD ¶853,001
17. ¶V-1307; ¶66,014.02; TD ¶853,002

paid. (Code Sec. 6601(e)(2)(B))[18]

¶ 4867 "Advance payments" and deposits to prepay and/or stop the running of interest.

A cash deposit made in conformity with IRS rules may be used to pay income, gift, estate, or generation-skipping tax or certain excise taxes that have not yet been assessed at the time of the deposit. (Code Sec. 6603(a)) The amount of the deposit that is later used by IRS to pay tax is treated as a tax payment at the time of the deposit, for purposes of determining whether the taxpayer owes interest on an underpayment of tax. (Code Sec. 6603(b)) Interest may be allowed on the return of all or part of such a deposit, see ¶4853.[19]

¶ 4868 How other year's tax payments affect interest.

Interest on a deficiency isn't eliminated when the deficiency is eliminated by a net operating loss (NOL), net capital loss or business credit carryback (or a foreign tax credit carryback arising in a tax year beginning after Aug. 5, '97). It accrues from its original due date to the filing date for the tax year in which the carryback arose (or, with respect to any portion of a credit carryback attributable to a carryback from a later year, to the filing date for that later year). (Code Sec. 6601(d))[20]

An underpayment of tax in one year may be paid by crediting against it an overpayment of tax in another year. (Code Sec. 6402(a)) No interest accrues on any portion of the underpayment so paid for any period after the return due date (*without* extension) for the overpayment year or, if later, when the offsetting return is filed. This rule doesn't apply to the extent the zero rate (¶4865) applies. (Code Sec. 6601(f))[21]

When a taxpayer elects to apply an overpayment to the following year's estimated taxes, the overpayment will be applied to unpaid installments of estimated tax due on or after the date(s) the overpayment arose, in the order in which they are required to be paid to avoid an estimated tax penalty. IRS will assess interest on a later determined deficiency for the overpayment year only from the date(s) that the overpayment is applied to the following year's estimated taxes. [22]

¶ 4869 Abatement of interest, penalties and additions to tax—Form 843.

IRS has discretion to abate any interest that was assessed because of a deficiency attributable to any unreasonable error or delay by an IRS officer or employer acting in his official capacity when performing a managerial or ministerial act, or that is due on a notice of deficiency to the extent any error or delay in payment is attributable to an IRS employee or officer being erroneous or dilatory in performing a managerial or ministerial act, but only if no significant aspect of the error or delay can be attributed to the taxpayer involved. (Code Sec. 6404(e)(1); Reg § 301.6404-2)[23]

IRS must abate any portion of any penalty or addition to tax attributable to erroneous written advice (as specifically defined) (Reg § 301.6404-3(c)(1)) furnished to a taxpayer by an IRS officer or employee acting in an official capacity in response to a specific written request. The taxpayer must have reasonably relied on the advice (Code Sec. 6404(f)(1), Code Sec. 6404(f)(2)(A)), and the portion of the penalty or addition to tax must not have resulted from his failure to provide adequate or accurate information. (Code Sec. 6404(f)(2)(B))[24]

Make the abatement request on Form 843 (as annotated and with certain attachments as

18. ¶V-1225; ¶66,014.02; TD ¶853,018
19. ¶S-5804 *et seq.*; ¶66,034; TD ¶853,009 *et seq.*
20. ¶V-1302; ¶66,014.03; TD ¶853,015
21. ¶V-1301; ¶66,014.03

22. ¶V-1210; TD ¶853,013
23. ¶T-3919 *et seq.*; ¶64,044; TD ¶837,514
24. ¶T-3908 *et seq.*; ¶64,044; TD ¶837,504

required by the regs). (Reg § 301.6404-3(d))[25]

If IRS extends, for any period, the time for filing income tax returns and for paying income tax with respect to those returns, for any taxpayer located in an area that is Presidentially-declared a disaster area, IRS must also abate, for the same period, any interest that would otherwise be due on the extended income tax. (Code Sec. 6404(h)) If there's a postponement of tax-related deadlines under Code Sec. 7508A as well as an additional income tax return filing extension under Code Sec. 6081 and a tax payment extension under Code Sec. 6161, interest on an underpayment of income tax that arises during that period will be abated for the time period disregarded under the Code Sec. 7508A extension rules and the time periods covered by the filing and payment extensions. (Reg § 301.7508A-1(f))[26]

For Tax Court review of IRS's failure to abate interest, see ¶4858.

¶ 4870 Interest and penalties suspended where IRS fails to notify individual taxpayer of liability.

Subject to exceptions (including a gross misstatement such as a substantial omission of items to which the six-year statute of limitation applies (see ¶4832), a gross valuation misstatement (see ¶4878), undisclosed reportable transactions, and listed transactions (see ¶4890)), the imposition of interest and penalties with respect to any failure relating to a timely filed individual income tax return must be suspended if, before the end of the 18-month (36-month for post-Nov. 25, 2007 notices) period beginning on the date the return is filed or, if later, the date it's due (without regard to extensions), IRS fails to provide a notice to the taxpayer specifically stating the taxpayer's liability and the basis for the liability. The suspension period begins on the day after the end of the 18- or 36-month period and ends on the date that's 21 days after IRS provides the notice. Where a taxpayer files an amended return (or other written document) showing additional tax liability, the 18- or 36-month period for IRS to issue the required notice of liability (and avoid interest or penalty suspension) is restarted. (Code Sec. 6404(g)) For interest relating to listed transactions or undisclosed reportable transactions accruing before Oct. 4, 2004, the general rule for suspension applies to (1) a participant in a settlement initiative, (2) a taxpayer acting reasonably and in good faith, or (3) a closed transaction. (Code Sec. 301.6404-4T(b)(5))[27]

¶ 4871 When reasonable cause excuses civil penalties.

Certain civil penalties won't be imposed if the taxpayer's failure to perform the required act was due to reasonable cause —e.g., reliance on tax expert or IRS advice, irregularities in mail delivery, death or serious illness, unavoidable absence, casualty, disaster. Generally, a taxpayer who challenges IRS's imposition of a civil penalty has the burden of showing that his failure was due to reasonable cause and not willful neglect. [28]

No accuracy-related (¶4874 *et seq.*) or fraud (¶4880) penalty applies with respect to any portion of an underpayment for which the taxpayer shows reasonable cause and that he acted in good faith. (Code Sec. 6664(c)(1); Reg § 1.6664-4) A taxpayer's failure to disclose a reportable transaction (¶4753) is a strong indication that the taxpayer failed to act in good faith. (Reg § 1.6664-4(d))[29]

For returns filed after Aug. 17, 2006, the reasonable cause exception generally does not apply to an underpayment attributable to a substantial or gross valuation overstatement with respect to charitable deduction property. However, this bar doesn't apply to a substantial valuation overstatement if the claimed value of the property was based on a qualified appraisal made by a qualified appraiser, and the taxpayer made a good faith investigation of the

25. ¶T-3914 *et seq.*; TD ¶837,503
26. ¶T-3973; ¶64,044; TD ¶837,513
27. ¶V-1401, V-1601.2; ¶64,044; TD ¶s 837,509, 852,006

28. ¶V-1776 *et seq.*, ¶V-2750 *et seq.*; ¶66,644; TD ¶868,500 *et seq.*
29. ¶V-2060; TD ¶863,001

value of the contributed property. (Code Sec. 6664(c)(2))[30]

¶ 4872 Failure to file income, estate or gift tax returns when due.

The penalty is 5% of the amount of tax required to be shown on the return (less any earlier payments and credits) for the first month (Code Sec. 6651(b)(1)), plus an additional 5% for each month (or fraction of a month) that the failure continues without reasonable cause (¶4871), but not more than 25%. (Code Sec. 6651(a)(1))[31]

There's a minimum penalty for failure to file any income tax return within 60 days of the due date (including extensions), except if due to reasonable cause and not willful neglect. This minimum penalty is the lesser of $100 or the amount of tax required to be shown on the return. (Code Sec. 6651(a))[32]

The failure-to-file penalty (5%) is reduced (but not below the above minimum) by the amount of any failure-to-pay penalty (½%, see ¶4873) for that month. (Code Sec. 6651(c)(1)) The 25% ceiling is applied to each penalty before making this reduction. [33]

If the failure to file is fraudulent, the penalty is increased to 15% per month (or fraction), up to a 75% maximum. (Code Sec. 6651(f))[34]

For failure to file partnership returns or other information returns, see ¶4894 and ¶4895.

¶ 4873 Failure to pay tax.

A penalty is imposed on a taxpayer who, without reasonable cause (¶4871) fails to pay the tax shown on a return (including a substitute return) or an assessed deficiency of that tax by the prescribed date. The penalty is ½% of tax shown (or assessed) for each month (or fraction of a month) that it isn't paid (but not more than 25%). (Code Sec. 6651(a)(2); Code Sec. 6651(a)(3))[35] The penalty is increased to 1% per month or fraction (up to 25% penalty maximum) if the tax isn't paid within ten days after IRS serves notice of levy. (Code Sec. 6651(d))[36] The penalty is reduced to ¼% per month for individuals paying in installments. (Code Sec. 6651(h))[37]

An individual who gets an automatic extension of time for *filing* is subject to the penalty (absent reasonable cause) if any additional payment due with the extended return *either*: (1) exceeds 10% of the total shown on Form 1040, *or* (2) isn't paid by the extended filing date. (Reg § 301.6651-1(c)(3))[38]

For failure to pay estimated tax, see ¶3156 (individuals) and ¶3352 (corporations).

¶ 4874 Accuracy-related penalty.

A 20% "accuracy-related" civil penalty applies if any portion of an understatement of tax on a tax return is due (absent reasonable cause, see ¶4871) to:

. . . negligence (¶4875); or

. . . substantial income tax valuation misstatements (¶4876), income tax understatements (¶4877), estate or gift tax valuation understatements (¶4878), or pension liability overstatements (¶4879). (Code Sec. 6662(a), Code Sec. 6662(b), Code Sec. 6664(c)(1); Reg § 1.6662-2(a))[39]

The accuracy-related penalty doesn't apply to any portion of an underpayment for which

30. ¶V-2237; ¶66,644; TD ¶863,001
31. ¶V-1750 *et seq.*; ¶66,514.01; TD ¶861,001
32. ¶V-1752; ¶66,514.01; TD ¶861,001
33. ¶V-1791; ¶66,514.01; TD ¶861,001
34. ¶V-1753; ¶66,514.01

35. ¶V-1657 *et seq.*; ¶66,514.01; TD ¶862,001
36. ¶V-1683; ¶66,514.01; TD ¶862,003
37. ¶V-1684; ¶66,514; TD ¶862,514
38. ¶V-1681; ¶66,514
39. ¶V-2000 *et seq.*; ¶66,624; TD ¶863,000

the fraud penalty (¶4880) is imposed or to the portion of any underpayment which is attributable to a reportable transaction understatement on which the Code Sec. 6662A reportable transaction understatement penalty is imposed, except: (i) for purposes of determining whether an underpayment is substantial or (ii) where the 40% gross valuation misstatement penalty applies. (Code Sec. 6662(b))[40] Also, it only applies if a return is filed by the taxpayer (not by IRS). (Code Sec. 6664(b); Reg § 1.6662-2(a))[41]

¶ 4875 Negligence.

The "accuracy-related" penalty is imposed if any part of an underpayment of tax is due either to negligence or to disregard of rules or regs but without intent to defraud. The penalty is 20% of the portion of the underpayment attributable to the negligence, etc. (Code Sec. 6662(a), Code Sec. 6662(b)(1)) For rules common to all accuracy-related penalties, see ¶4874.

"Negligence" includes any failure to make a reasonable attempt to comply with the law or to exercise ordinary and reasonable care in preparing a tax return, as well as failure to keep adequate books and records or to substantiate items properly. "Disregard" includes any careless, reckless or intentional disregard. (Code Sec. 6662(c); Reg § 1.6662-3(b))[42]

The penalty won't be imposed with respect to income tax underpayments attributable to a position contrary to a revenue ruling or notice, if the position has a "realistic possibility" (¶4884) of being sustained on its merits. (Reg § 1.6662-3(a)) If contrary to a rule or reg, the disregard penalty, but not the negligence penalty, won't be imposed if the position is disclosed on Form 8275 (Form 8275-R, if contrary to a reg), has a reasonable basis (stricter than "realistic possibility") and represents a good faith challenge. (Reg § 1.6662-3(b)(3); Reg § 1.6662-7(b))[43]

¶ 4876 Misstating value or basis of property on income tax return.

The accuracy-related penalty is imposed on a taxpayer who makes any of these "substantial valuation misstatements": (Code Sec. 6662(b)(3))

. . . any value (or adjusted basis) claimed on an income tax return that is 150% or more of the correct figure (Code Sec. 6662(e)(1)(A));

. . . Code Sec. 482 transfer price adjustments where the price for any property (or its use) or services on an income tax return is 200% or more, or 50% or less, of the correct figure — transactional penalty (Code Sec. 6662(e)(1)(B)(i); Reg § 1.6662-6(b));

. . . a net increase in taxable income for a tax year (without regard to carryovers) resulting from all Code Sec. 482 adjustments in the transfer price of any property (or its use) or services, that (with certain adjustments) exceeds the lesser of $5 million or 10% of the taxpayer's gross receipts — net adjustment penalty. (Code Sec. 6662(e)(1)(B)(ii), Code Sec. 6662(e)(3); Reg § 1.6662-6(c))[44]

The penalty equals 20% of the portion of any income tax underpayment that results from the misstatement (except to the extent the fraud penalty is imposed) (Code Sec. 6662(a), Code Sec. 6662(b))—40% if the misstatement is gross (the above 200%, 150%, 50% and $5 million/10% figures are, respectively, 400%, 200%, 25% or $20 million/20%, or the correct value or basis is zero). (Code Sec. 6662(h); Reg § 1.6662-5(g))[45]

The penalty doesn't apply unless the amount of the underpayment for the tax year attributable to all these misstatements for the year exceeds $5,000 ($10,000 for corporations other

40. ¶V-2002; ¶66,624; TD ¶865,004
41. ¶V-2051; ¶66,624; TD ¶863,001
42. ¶V-2105; ¶66,624; TD ¶863,005.5

43. ¶V-2106 *et seq.*; ¶66,624.02; TD ¶863,009
44. ¶V-2200 *et seq.*; ¶66,624; TD ¶863,010
45. ¶V-2206 *et seq.*; ¶66,624; TD ¶863,010

than S corporations or personal holding companies). (Code Sec. 6662(e)(2))[46]

Reasonable cause (¶4871) excuses the penalty. There's no disclosure exception. (Code Sec. 6664(c)(1); Reg § 1.6662-5(a))[47] Strict appraisal requirements apply to overvalued charitable gifts. (Code Sec. 6664(c)(2), Code Sec. 6664(c)(3))[48]

For rules common to all accuracy-related penalties, see ¶4874.

¶ 4877   Penalty on substantial understatements of income tax.

The 20% accuracy-related penalty is imposed on any portion of an underpayment of tax that (absent reasonable cause, see ¶4871) is attributable to any substantial understatement of income tax, self-employment tax (¶3138 *et seq.*), (Code Sec. 6662(a), Code Sec. 6662(b)(1); Reg § 1.6662-4(b)(3))[49] or unrelated business income tax (¶4121).[50] For rules common to all accuracy-related penalties, see ¶4874.

An understatement is "substantial" if it exceeds the greater of: (1) 10% of the tax required to be shown on the return, or (2) $5,000 ($10,000 for corporations other than S corporations and personal holding companies). For corporate taxpayers (other than S corporations and personal holding companies), an understatement is substantial if the amount of the understatement exceeds the lesser of (a) 10% of the tax required to be shown on the return for that tax year (or $10,000 if that is greater), or (b) $10 million. (Code Sec. 6662(d)(1); Reg § 1.6662-4(b)(1))[1]

An understatement is the excess of (1) the amount of tax required to be shown on the return, over (2) the amount of tax that's shown (or withheld) reduced by any rebate. (Code Sec. 6662(d)(2)(A); Reg § 1.6662-4(b)(2), Reg § 1.6662-4(b)(3))[2] The understatement is reduced to the extent it is attributable to any item (other than tax shelter items, see below) for which:

(1) there is or was substantial authority for how the taxpayer treated it (Code Sec. 6662(d)(2)(B)(i)), or

(2) the relevant facts affecting the item's tax treatment are adequately disclosed either on the return (IRS each year lists which items on the return qualify) or on a Form 8275 (Form 8275-R if the taxpayer's position is contrary to a reg) attached to the return *and* there's a reasonable basis (¶4875) for the taxpayer's treatment of the item. (Code Sec. 6662(d)(2)(B)(ii); Reg § 1.6662-4(f)) A corporation doesn't have a reasonable basis for its tax treatment of an item attributable to a multi-party financing transaction if the treatment doesn't clearly reflect its income. (Code Sec. 6662(d)(2))[3]

For tax shelter items, a noncorporate taxpayer's understatement is reduced only to the extent there is or was substantial authority for that treatment *and* he reasonably believed his treatment was more likely than not proper. There's no disclosure exception. Corporate taxpayers get no reduction. (Code Sec. 6662(d)(2)(C); Reg § 1.6662-4(g))[4]

"Substantial authority" exists for the tax treatment of an item (only if the weight of the authorities supporting the treatment is substantial in relation to the weight of authorities supporting contrary positions (in light of the pertinent facts and circumstances). (Reg § 1.6662-4(d)(3)(i))[5]

46. ¶V-2205; ¶66,624; TD ¶863,010
47. ¶V-2234; ¶66,644; TD ¶863,001
48. ¶V-2237; ¶66,644; TD ¶863,011
49. ¶V-2150 *et seq.*; ¶66,624; TD ¶863,014
50. ¶V-2151

1. ¶V-2159; ¶66,624.03; TD ¶863,014
2. ¶V-2154; ¶66,624.03; TD ¶863,015
3. ¶s V-2154, V-2167 *et seq.*; ¶66,624.04; TD ¶863,017
4. ¶V-2154; ¶66,624.04
5. ¶V-2161, ¶V-2163; ¶66,624.04; TD ¶863,016

¶ 4878 Penalty for understating value of property on gift or estate tax return.

If the value of any property claimed on any gift or estate tax return is 65% or less of the correct value, the 20% accuracy-related penalty (¶4874) is imposed on an underpayment of tax that's attributable to that understatement. (Code Sec. 6662(a); Code Sec. 6662(b)(5); Code Sec. 6662(g)(1)) The penalty is increased to 40% for gross misstatements —i.e., the claimed value is 40% or less of the correct figure. (Code Sec. 6662(h)(1); Code Sec. 6662(h)(2)(C))[6] The penalty applies only if the portion of the underpayment attributable to all these undervaluations for the tax period exceeds $5,000. (Code Sec. 6662(g)(2))[7]

¶ 4879 Overstatement of pension liabilities.

A taxpayer who (absent reasonable cause, see ¶4871) substantially overstates pension liabilities for a tax year is subject to the accuracy-related penalty (¶4874) if the overstatement results in an income tax underpayment of $1,000 or more. (Code Sec. 6662(a), Code Sec. 6662(b)(4), Code Sec. 6662(f)(2))[8] The penalty equals 20% of the underpayment (40% for "gross" overstatements). (Code Sec. 6662(a), Code Sec. 6662(h)(1))[9]

Pension liabilities are substantially overstated if the actuarial determination of the liabilities taken into account in computing the contribution deduction (¶4333) is at least 200% of the correct amount. (Code Sec. 6662(f)(1)) The overstatement is "gross" if it's 400% or more of the correct figure. (Code Sec. 6662(h)(2)(B))[10]

¶ 4880 Fraud.

Fraudulent underpayment of tax required to be shown on a return results in a civil penalty of 75% of the portion of the underpayment attributable to fraud. (Code Sec. 6663(a))[11]

The fraud penalty can be imposed only if a return is filed (not by IRS). (Code Sec. 6664(b))[12] It won't be imposed where the taxpayer shows reasonable cause (¶4871) for the underpayment, and that he acted in good faith. (Code Sec. 6664(c)(1))[13]

Imposition of the fraud penalty on any part of an underpayment precludes imposition of any of the accuracy-related penalties (¶4874) on that same part. (Code Sec. 6662(b))[14]

If IRS establishes that any part of an underpayment is attributable to fraud, the entire underpayment is treated as attributable to fraud, except for any part the taxpayer establishes (by a preponderance of the evidence) isn't so attributable. (Code Sec. 6663(b))[15]

¶ 4881 "Responsible person's" willful failure to collect or account for and pay over a tax—trust fund recovery penalty.

Willful failure to collect or account for and pay over a tax or willful attempt to evade or defeat a tax, by a "responsible person" required to collect, account for, and pay over the tax carries a civil "trust fund recovery penalty" equal to 100% of the total tax evaded or not accounted for and paid over. (Code Sec. 6672) IRS can't assess the penalty without notifying a responsible person of its intent to do so at least 60 days before making notice and demand for the penalty (unless collection is in jeopardy). (Code Sec. 6672(b)) A "responsible person" is an officer or employee of the corporation, or a partner or employee of a partnership, who is under a duty to perform the act at issue. (Code Sec. 6671(b))[16] Unpaid volunteer board members of

6. ¶s V-2251, V-2252; ¶66,624 (Estate & Gift), ¶66,624.10; TD ¶863,013
7. ¶V-2251; ¶66,624 (Estate & Gift), ¶66,624.10; TD ¶863,013
8. ¶V-2270 *et seq.*; ¶66,624.09; TD ¶863,012
9. ¶V-2272; ¶66,624.09; TD ¶863,012
10. ¶V-2273; ¶s 66,624, 66,624.09; TD ¶863,012

11. ¶V-2300 *et seq.*; ¶s 66,634, 66,534; TD ¶865,001
12. ¶V-2051; ¶66,634; TD ¶865,001
13. ¶V-2060; ¶66,644; TD ¶865,001
14. ¶V-2002; ¶66,624; TD ¶865,004
15. ¶V-2302; ¶66,634; TD ¶865,001
16. ¶V-1700 *et seq.*; ¶66,724; TD ¶864,001

exempt organizations who aren't involved in day-to-day financial activities and don't know about the penalized failure are exempt from the penalty, unless that results in no one being liable for it. (Code Sec. 6672(e))[17]

IRS must disclose, at the written request of a responsible person, the names of other responsible persons and the collection activities related to them. (Code Sec. 6103(e)(9))[18] Responsible persons who pay more than their proportionate share of tax have the right to recover the excess from other responsible persons. (Code Sec. 6672(d))[19]

The penalty applies to an employer's failure to make advance earned income credit payments (see ¶2346) to an employee who has a valid certificate in effect (Code Sec. 3507(d)(4)) unless the employer has properly withheld and deposited all income and FICA taxes for the employee. (Reg § 31.3507-1(c)(4))[20]

¶ 4882   Penalty for filing erroneous refund claim.

If a post-May 25, 2007 claim for refund or credit of income tax (other than one relating to the earned income credit) is made for an "excessive amount," the person making the claim is liable for a penalty equal to 20% of the excessive amount. (Code Sec. 6676(a))

An "excessive amount" is the amount by which the claimed refund or credit exceeds the allowable amount. (Code Sec. 6676(b))

The penalty doesn't apply if it is shown that the claim for the excessive amount has a reasonable basis. (Code Sec. 6676(a))

The penalty doesn't apply to any portion of the excessive amount that's subject to an accuracy-related penalty imposed under Code Sec. 6662 (¶4874) or Code Sec. 6662A (¶4891) or under the Code Sec. 6663 fraud penalty (¶4880). (Code Sec. 6676(c))[21]

¶ 4883   Penalty for aiding and abetting understatement of tax liability.

A penalty of $1,000 ($10,000 for a corporation) (Code Sec. 6701(b))[22] is imposed on any person who:

. . . aids or assists, procures or advises with respect to the preparation or presentation of any portion of a return, affidavit, claim or other document connected with any matter arising under the internal revenue laws,

. . . knows (or has reason to believe) that the portion will be used in connection with any material matter arising under those laws, *and*

. . . knows that an understatement of another person's tax would result from that use (Code Sec. 6701(a)) even if there is no actual understatement. [23]

The penalty applies whether or not the taxpayer knew of or gave consent to the understatement. (Code Sec. 6701(d))[24]

The term "advises" includes the actions of lawyers and accountants who counsel a particular course of action[25] and appraisers who falsely or fraudulently overstate the value of property in a qualified appraisal (of property for which a charitable contribution is claimed, see ¶2138). (Reg § 1.170A-13(c)(3)(iii))[26]

𝕽𝖎*observation:* Unlike the return preparer penalties which apply only to "paid" preparers (¶4884), the aiding and abetting penalty applies regardless of whether a fee is charged.

---

17. ¶V-1703.1; TD ¶864,009
18. ¶S-6313.1; TD ¶864,024
19. ¶V-1730; TD ¶864,024
20. ¶V-1702
21. ¶V-2291; ¶66,764;

22. ¶V-2352; ¶67,104; TD ¶867,030
23. ¶V-2351 *et seq.*; ¶67,014; TD ¶867,027
24. ¶V-2354; ¶67,014; TD ¶867,027
25. ¶V-2353; ¶67,014; TD ¶867,027
26. ¶V-2351; TD ¶867,032

¶ **4884** **Understatements by income tax return preparers—"unrealistic position" ("one-in-three" test) and "willful or reckless conduct" penalties—for returns prepared before May 26, 2007.**

An income tax return preparer (¶4756) is subject to a "first tier" $250 civil penalty (and barred from practice), for each tax return or refund claim prepared if: (1) any part of any understatement of tax liability for the return or claim is due to a position that has no "realistic possibility" of being sustained on the merits, (2) the preparer knew (or should have known) of that "unrealistic position," *and* (3) the position wasn't disclosed as required or was frivolous. But the penalty won't apply to a preparer who shows both reasonable cause for the understatement *and* his good faith. (Former Code Sec. 6694(a); Reg § 1.6694-1(e)(1))[27]

A position meets the "realistic possibility" test if a reasonable and well informed analysis by a person knowledgeable in the tax law would lead him to conclude it has a one in three, or greater, chance of being sustained on the merits. [28]

A $1,000 penalty is imposed on the preparer for each return or claim prepared if any part of an understatement is due to the preparer's willful attempt to understate that tax or to his reckless or intentional disregard of rules or regs. But the amount of this penalty can be reduced by the amount of any "unrealistic position" penalty (above) the preparer pays for the same return or claim. (Former Code Sec. 6694(b)) [29]

¶ **4885** **Understatements by tax return preparers—"unrealistic position" and "unreasonable position" penalties—for returns prepared after May 25, 2007.**

A tax return preparer (see ¶4756) who prepares a return or refund claim for which any part of a tax liability understatement is due to an "unreasonable position" must pay a penalty for each return or claim equal to the greater of: (1) $1,000 or (2) 50% of the income derived (or to be derived) by the tax return preparer for preparing the return or claim. (Code Sec. 6694(a)(1)) A position is "unreasonable" if: the tax return preparer knew (or reasonably should have known) of the position; there was not a reasonable belief that the position would more likely than not be sustained on its merits; and the position was not disclosed as provided in Code Sec. 6662(d)(2)(B)(ii), or there was no reasonable basis for the position. (Code Sec. 6694(a)(2)) However, there's no penalty if it is shown that there is reasonable cause for the understatement and the tax return preparer acted in good faith. (Code Sec. 6694(a)(3)) Also, under IRS transitional relief, effective generally for original and amended returns and refund claims due before 2008, the standards in prior law's Code and regs (see ¶4884) apply in determining whether IRS will impose the "first tier" return preparer penalty under Code Sec. 6694(a).

A tax return preparer who prepares a return or refund claim for which any part of a tax liability understatement is due to "willful or reckless conduct" must pay a penalty for each return or claim equal to the greater of (1) $5,000 or (2) 50% of the income derived (or to be derived) by the tax return preparer for preparing the return or claim. (Code Sec. 6694(b)) "Willful or reckless conduct" is conduct by the tax return preparer which is a willful attempt to understate the tax liability on the return or claim, or a reckless or intentional disregard of rules or regulations. (Code Sec. 6694(b)(2)) A penalty payable by a person due to willful or reckless conduct in connection with a return or refund claim is reduced by the penalty paid by that person due to an unreasonable position. (Code Sec. 6694(b)(3))[30]

For other preparer penalties, see ¶4887.

---

27. ¶V-2631; ¶66,944; TD ¶867,019
28. ¶s T-10918 *et seq.*, V-2638; ¶66,944; TD ¶867,009

29. ¶s V-2659, V-2666; ¶66,944; TD ¶867,021
30. ¶V-2630; ¶66,944

¶ 4886　Penalty for valuation misstatements attributable to incorrect appraisals.

A penalty is imposed on any person who:

(A) prepares a property appraisal and knows, or reasonably should have known, that the appraisal would be used in connection with a return or a refund claim, and

(B) the claimed property value on the return or refund claim that is based on the appraisal results in a substantial valuation misstatement under Code Sec. 6662(e) or a gross valuation misstatement under Code Sec. 6662(h) (¶4876) for the property. (Code Sec. 6695A(a))[31]

No penalty, however, will be imposed if the person satisfies IRS that the value established in the appraisal was more likely than not the proper value. (Code Sec. 6695A(c))

The amount of the penalty equals the lesser of 125% of the gross income for preparing the appraisal received by the person who prepared it or an amount that is the greater of: (a) 10% of the underpayment attributable to the misstatement, or (b) $1,000. (Code Sec. 6695A(b))

¶ 4887　Other penalties on income tax return preparers.

An income tax return preparer who fails to perform the duties described at ¶4755 is subject to these civil penalties (up to a maximum $25,000 per calendar year for any single type of failure):

. . . $50 for each failure to sign a return as required. (Code Sec. 6695(b))[32]

. . . $50 for each failure to show his taxpayer ID number or PTIN as required. (Code Sec. 6695(e))[33]

. . . $50 for each failure to furnish completed copy of return to the taxpayer. (Code Sec. 6695(a))[34]

. . . $50 for each failure to retain a copy of a prepared return or to include it on a list of prepared returns. (Code Sec. 6695(d))[35]

. . . $50 for each failure to retain and make available a record of the preparers employed or engaged, plus $50 for each failure to include a required item in the record required to be retained and made available. (Code Sec. 6695(e))[36]

. . . $500 (with no annual maximum) for each income tax check issued to a taxpayer that the preparer endorses or otherwise negotiates, except where the preparer is a bank and deposits the check to the taxpayer's account in the bank. (Code Sec. 6695(f))[37]

. . . $100 for each failure to follow regulatory due diligence requirements as shown on Form 8867 in claiming the earned income credit. (Code Sec. 6695(g); Reg § 1.6695-2(b))[38]

Improper disclosure or use of information by return preparers is subject to a civil penalty of $250 for each improper disclosure or use ($10,000 maximum per calendar year), (Code Sec. 6713(a))[39] as well as a criminal penalty. (Code Sec. 7216)[40]

IRS may get a district court to enjoin a preparer from engaging in specific misconduct, but only if an injunction is appropriate to prevent recurrence of the misconduct. If the court finds that the preparer has continually or repeatedly engaged in this misconduct and an injunction isn't sufficient to prevent the preparer's interference with proper tax administration, it can enjoin him from practicing. (Code Sec. 7407(b))[41]

---

31. ¶V-2691; ¶66,95A4
32. ¶V-2673; ¶66,954; TD ¶867,016
33. ¶V-2677; ¶66,954; TD ¶867,016
34. ¶V-2674; ¶66,954; TD ¶867,016
35. ¶V-2675; ¶66,954; TD ¶867,016
36. ¶V-2676; ¶66,954; TD ¶867,016

37. ¶V-2671; ¶66,954; TD ¶867,018
38. ¶V-2677.1; ¶66,954
39. ¶V-2678; ¶67,134; TD ¶867,035
40. ¶V-3308; ¶72,164; TD ¶871,010
41. ¶V-2679 *et seq.*; ¶74,074; TD ¶867,033

¶ 4888   Abusive tax shelters and conduct.

A person who promotes an abusive tax shelter is subject to a penalty equal to the lesser of $1,000 or 100% of the gross income derived or to be derived from the activity. However, if an activity on which the penalty is imposed involves a false or fraudulent statement, the penalty equals 50% of the gross income derived or to be derived by that person from the activity. (Code Sec. 6700(a))[42] IRS may seek an injunction to stop any action or failure to take action:

(1) that is subject to penalty under Code Sec. 6700, Code Sec. 6701 (aiding or abetting an understatement, see ¶4883), Code Sec. 6707 (failure to furnish information regarding reportable transactions, see ¶4892), and Code Sec. 6708 (failure to provide list of advisees with respect to reportable transactions, see ¶4889) or

(2) in violation of any requirement imposed by regs issued under Section 330 of Title 31 of the U.S. Code (rules regulating the practice of taxpayer representatives before the Department of the Treasury), i.e., the Circular 230 rules. (Code Sec. 7408)[43]

¶ 4889   Penalty for failure to provide list of advisees with respect to reportable transactions.

Any person required under Code Sec. 6112 to maintain a list of advisees with respect to reportable transactions (see ¶4752) who fails to make that list available to IRS on its written request within 20 business days after the date of the request is liable for a $10,000 per day penalty for each day of that failure after the 20th day. This penalty isn't imposed, however, for any day that the failure to provide the list is due to reasonable cause. (Code Sec. 6708(a))[44]

¶ 4890   Penalty imposed for failure to report reportable transactions.

A penalty is imposed on any person who fails to include on any return or statement any information regarding a reportable transaction that's required under Code Sec. 6011 (see ¶4753) to be included with the return or statement. (Code Sec. 6707A(a)) The penalty is $10,000 for natural persons and $50,000 for others (increased to $100,000 and $200,000 if a listed transaction is involved. (Code Sec. 6707A(b)) A $200,000 penalty applies for failing to disclose certain penalties on SEC reports. (Code Sec. 6707A(e))

A reportable transaction is any transaction for which information must be included with a return or statement because it is of a type that IRS has determined under regs under Code Sec. 6011 as having a potential for tax avoidance or evasion. A listed transaction is a reportable transaction which is the same as, or substantially similar to, a transaction specifically identified by IRS as a tax avoidance transaction for Code Sec. 6011 purposes. (Code Sec. 6707A(c))

IRS can rescind all or a portion of a penalty imposed under Code Sec. 6707A if (a) the violation relates to a reportable transaction that is not a listed transaction and (b) rescission would promote compliance with the Code and effective tax administration. (Code Sec. 6707A(d)) The rescission also applies to any penalty imposed on a material advisor under Code Sec. 6707 (¶4892). (Code Sec. 6707(c)) IRS procedures establish how to request rescission.[45]

---

42. ¶V-2403; ¶67,004
43. ¶V-2451; ¶74,084

44. ¶V-2503; ¶67,084
45. ¶V-2531 *et seq.*; ¶67,07A4; TD ¶866,503

¶ 4891   Penalty for understatements regarding reportable transactions.

A 20% accuracy-related penalty applies for reportable transaction understatements. (Code Sec. 6662A(a)) The penalty is 30% for any portion of any reportable transaction understatement for which specified disclosure rules are not met. (Code Sec. 6662A(c))

A reportable transaction understatement is the sum of (1) the amount of the increase (if any) in taxable income resulting from a difference between (a) the proper tax treatment of an item subject to the penalty rules and (b) the taxpayer's treatment of the item (on the taxpayer's tax return), multiplied by the highest noncorporate rate (or corporate tax rate, in the case of a corporation), and (2) the amount of the decrease (if any) in the total amount of income tax credits which results from a difference between (a) the taxpayer's treatment of an item subject to the penalty rules (on the taxpayer's tax return) and (b) the proper tax treatment of the item. (Code Sec. 6662A(b)(1)(B))

For this purpose, any reduction in the excess of deductions allowed in the tax year over gross income for the year, and any reduction in the amount of capital losses which would (without regard to the capital loss carryover rules) be allowed for the year, is treated as an increase in taxable income. (Code Sec. 6662A(b)(1))

An item is subject to the penalty rules if the item is attributable to any listed transaction and any reportable transaction (other than a listed transaction) if a significant purpose of the transaction is federal income tax avoidance or evasion. (Code Sec. 6662A(b)(2)(B)) Listed and reportable transactions are defined under the Code Sec. 6707A penalty rules for reportable transactions for which disclosure is required (see ¶4890) (Code Sec. 6662A(d))

Except as provided in regs, no tax treatment included with an amendment or supplement to a tax return is taken into account in determining the amount of any reportable transaction understatement if the amendment or supplement is filed after the earlier of the date the taxpayer is first contacted by IRS regarding the examination of the return or any other date specified by IRS. (Code Sec. 6662A(e)(3))

The only exception to the penalty is a limited reasonable cause exception that applies only if certain disclosure, substantial authority and reasonable belief requirements are met. (Code Sec. 6662A(d))[46]

¶ 4892   Penalty for failure by material advisor to report reportable or listed transactions.

A material advisor who fails to file a timely information return required under Code Sec. 6111(a) (¶4752), or who files a false or incomplete information return, for a reportable transaction (including a listed transaction) is subject to a penalty of $50,000 for each failure. However, if the failure relates to a listed transaction, the penalty is increased to the greater of: (1) $200,000, or (2) 50% of the gross income received by the material advisor that is attributable to aid, assistance, or advice which is provided for the listed transaction before the date that the advisor files an information return that includes the transaction. If the reporting failure for a listed transaction is due to an intentional failure or act, the 50% of gross income penalty amount (item 2 above) is increased to 75% of gross income. (Code Sec. 6707(a), Code Sec. 6707(b)) Reportable and listed transactions are defined under Code Sec. 6707A(c) (see ¶4890). (Code Sec. 6707(d))[47]

---

46. ¶V-2281; ¶66,62A4; TD ¶868,101   47. ¶V-2500; ¶67,074

¶ 4893 Penalties for tax-exempts acting as accommodation parties in tax shelter transactions.

Certain tax-exempt entities are subject to penalties for participating in a prohibited tax-shelter transaction as accommodation parties, see ¶4113. An exempt organization that participates in a reportable transaction (including a listed transaction) in order to shelter from tax the organization's own tax liability is subject to disclosure rules. (Code Sec. 6033(a)(2), Code Sec. 6652(c)(3))

¶ 4894 Information return penalties.

A payor who, without reasonable cause, fails to timely file a required information return (¶4740 *et seq.*) in the required manner (e.g., on magnetic media), or fails to include all of the information required to be shown on the return, or includes incorrect information, is subject to a $50 penalty for each return, up to a $250,000 calendar year maximum ($100,000 if the payor's gross receipts for the year don't exceed $5 million). (Code Sec. 6721(a), Code Sec. 6721(d)(1)(A), Code Sec. 6724(a); Reg § 301.6721-1(a)(2)) The penalty and maximum are reduced to $15 per return ($75,000 maximum —$25,000 if gross receipts test is met) if corrected within 30 days from the required filing date, or to $30 per return ($150,000 maximum—$50,000 if gross receipts test is met) if corrected on or before Aug. 1 of the calendar year of the required filing date. (Code Sec. 6721(b), Code Sec. 6721(d)) For returns that are not due on Feb. 28 or Mar. 15 (for example, Forms 8300 reporting certain cash payments of $10,000 or more), if the failure is corrected within 30 days, the penalty is $15; if corrected after 30 days, the penalty is $50. (Reg § 301.6721-1(b)(6))[48]

A payor who, without reasonable cause, fails to timely furnish a payee statement to the person prescribed, fails to include all of the required information on the statement, or includes incorrect information, is subject to a penalty of $50 for each such statement, up to a $100,000 calendar year maximum. (Code Sec. 6722(a), Code Sec. 6722(b), Code Sec. 6724(a))[49]

However, subject to exceptions, the above penalties are increased *with no calendar year maximum* if the failure is due to intentional disregard. (Code Sec. 6721(e), Code Sec. 6722(c))[50]

The penalties won't apply to a de minimis number of information returns that don't include all the required information, or that include incorrect information, if the failure is corrected by Aug. 1 of the calendar year in which the required filing date occurs. This exception for any calendar year is limited to ten information returns or, if greater, ½% of the total number of information returns the payor is required to file that year (Code Sec. 6721(c)), and doesn't apply to returns that aren't due on Feb. 28 or Mar. 15. (Reg § 301.6721-1(d)(4))[1] Also, no penalty will be imposed solely by reason of any failure to comply with the rules requiring filing on magnetic media (¶4758) except (1) to the extent the failure is with respect to more than 250 returns or (2) in the case of a partnership having more than 100 partners, to the extent the failure occurs with respect to more than 100 information returns. (Code Sec. 6724(c), Reg § 301.6721-1(a)(2)(ii))[2]

The penalties described above apply to information returns required under:

. . . Code Sec. 110(d) (qualified lease construction allowances for short-term leases).

. . . Code Sec. 264(f)(5)(A)(iv) (natural-person-as-holder exception to the disallowance of the deduction of interest buildup on certain life insurance and annuity contracts).

. . . Code Sec. 338(h)(10)(C) (relating to elective recognition of gain or loss).

48. ¶V-1803 *et seq.*; ¶s 67,214, 67,244.01; TD ¶861,053 *et seq.*
49. ¶V-1814 *et seq.*; ¶s 67,224, 67,244.01; TD ¶861,066 *et seq.*
50. ¶s V-1811 *et seq.*, V-1816 *et seq.*; ¶s 67,214, 67,224;

TD ¶861,063
1. ¶V-1809; ¶67,214; TD ¶861,059
2. ¶V-1810

. . . Code Sec. 408(i) (individual retirement accounts (IRAs) or annuities).

. . . Code Sec. 1060(b) or Code Sec. 1060(e) (information required of transferors and transferees with respect to applicable asset acquisitions).

. . . Code Sec. 4101(d) (relating to fuels taxes).

. . . Code Sec. 6039(a) (transfers of stock from exercises of incentive stock options and certain purchases from employee stock purchase plans).

. . . Code Sec. 6041(a) (payments of $600 or more).

. . . Code Sec. 6041(b) (collection of foreign items).

. . . Code Sec. 6041A(a) (payments by recipients of services) or Code Sec. 6041A(b) (returns of direct sellers).

. . . Code Sec. 6042(a)(1) (corporate dividends).

. . . Code Sec. 6043A(a) (taxable mergers and acquisitions).

. . . Code Sec. 6044(a)(1) (patronage dividends).

. . . Code Sec. 6045(a) (transactions, including real estate transactions, reportable by brokers).

. . . Code Sec. 6045(d) (certain "substitute payments" made to brokers on behalf of customers in connection with short sales).

. . . Code Sec. 6047(d) (employers, plan administrators, etc.).

. . . Code Sec. 6049(a)(1) (payments of interest).

. . . Code Sec. 6050A(a) (payments made by certain fishing boat operators).

. . . Code Sec. 6050H(a) (payments of $600 or more in a calendar year of mortgage interest that is received in the course of a trade or business).

. . . Code Sec. 6050I(a) (receipts of more than $10,000 in cash in one transaction (or two or more related transactions) that are received in the course of a trade or business).

. . . Code Sec. 6050I(g)(1) (receipt of more than $10,000 in cash by criminal court clerks as bail).

. . . Code Sec. 6050J(a) (foreclosures and abandonments of property held as security for business loans).

. . . Code Sec. 6050K(a) (certain exchanges of partnership interests).

. . . Code Sec. 6050L(a) (certain dispositions of donated property).

. . . Code Sec. 6050N(a) (payments of royalties).

. . . Code Sec. 6050P(a) (discharges of indebtedness by certain financial entities and governmental agencies).

. . . Code Sec. 6050Q (relating to certain long-term care benefits).

. . . Code Sec. 6050R (cash payments by purchasers of fish for resale).

. . . Code Sec. 6050S (payments for qualified tuition and related expenses and deductible payments of interest on qualified education loans).

. . . Code Sec. 6050T (credit for health insurance costs of eligible individuals).

. . . Code Sec. 6050U (for post-2009 charges or payments for qualified long-term care insurance contracts, under combined arrangements).

. . . Code Sec. 6050V (applicable insurance contracts in which certain exempt organizations hold interests).

. . . Code Sec. 6051(d) (tax withheld).

. . . Code Sec. 6052(a) (wages paid in the form of group-term life insurance).

. . . Code Sec. 6053(c)(1) (certain tips from "large food or beverage establishments"). (Code Sec. 6724(d)(1))

¶ 4895   Other civil penalties relating to information reporting and other items.

Other civil penalties are provided for:

. . . failure to file information returns for dividend payments under $10 (Code Sec. 6652(a));

. . . failure to, file actuarial report of pension plan (¶4750), (Code Sec. 6692);[3]

. . . failure to file annual return for a pension plan (¶4750), (Code Sec. 6652(f));[4]

. . . failure to file annual return for an exempt organization or private foundation (¶4124), (Code Sec. 6652(c));[5]

. . . failure by split-interest trust to file an information return. (Code Sec. 6652(c)(2))[6]

. . . failure by an exempt organization to report excise tax on personal benefit contracts (Code Sec. 170(f)(10)(F)(iii));

. . . failure by any person, under a duty to comply with Code Sec. 6104(d) requirements relating to public inspection of, and provision of copies of, exempt organization annual returns or exempt status application materials, (Code Sec. 6652(c)(1)(C), Code Sec. 6652(c)(1)(D));[7]

. . . failure to file fringe benefit plan return (¶4750), (Code Sec. 6652(e));[8]

. . . failure to provide a written explanation to the recipient of a qualified rollover distribution, (Code Sec. 6652(i));[9]

. . . failure to file report on deductible employee contributions, (Code Sec. 6652(g));[10]

. . . failure to file notification of change of status of pension plan (¶4750), (Code Sec. 6652(d)(2));[11]

. . . failure to file registration statement of pension plan (¶4750), (Code Sec. 6652(d)(1))[12] or to give a plan participant a statement of the information in the statement, (Code Sec. 6690);[13]

. . . failure to file individual retirement account, simple retirement account reports, Archer MSA, HSA, Coverdell education savings account, and qualified tuition program, reports, (Code Sec. 6693);[14]

. . . overstatement reported on return by IRA participant of the amount of designated non-deductible contributions, (Code Sec. 6693(b));[15]

. . . failure to keep records for reporting on pension, annuity, etc., payments subject to withholding, (Code Sec. 6704(a));[16]

. . . failure to notify recipients of plan distributions of their option to elect out of withholding, (Code Sec. 6652(i));

. . . failure by a corporation that issues qualified small business stock to make prescribed reports to IRS, (Code Sec. 6652(k));[17]

. . . failure to file certain returns for foreign corporations, partnerships (Code Sec. 6679)[18] and trusts, (Code Sec. 6677);[19]

. . . failure to file information returns in connection with foreign corporations and partnerships (¶4664) (Code Sec. 6038(b), Code Sec. 6038(c); Code Sec. 6038A(d); Code Sec. 6038B(c); Code Sec. 6038C(c));

. . . failure to include tax information with passport or green card applications (Code

---

3. ¶V-1953; ¶66,924
4. ¶V-1953; ¶66,524
5. ¶V-1906; ¶66,524; TD ¶861,032
6. ¶V-2716; ¶66,524
7. ¶V-2718; ¶s 66,524, 66,854; TD ¶861,032
8. ¶V-1954; ¶66,524; TD ¶141,010
9. ¶V-1960; ¶66,524; TD ¶861,037
10. ¶V-1956; ¶66,524
11. ¶V-1953; ¶66,524; TD ¶861,037

12. ¶V-1953; ¶66,524; TD ¶861,037
13. ¶V-1953; ¶66,904
14. ¶V-1955; ¶66,934; TD ¶861,037
15. ¶V-1981; ¶66,934; TD ¶283,028
16. ¶V-1986; ¶67,044; TD ¶868,006
17. ¶V-1961; ¶66,524; TD ¶861,034
18. ¶V-1903; ¶66,794; TD ¶861,049
19. ¶V-1901; ¶66,774; TD ¶861,046

Sec. 6039E(c));

. . . failure to keep records, furnish information, or file DISC returns (¶4627), (Code Sec. 6686);[20]

. . . failure to keep records, furnish information or file returns for a FSC (or former FSC), (Code Sec. 6686);

. . . failure to meet FIRPTA reporting requirements, (Code Sec. 6652(f));[21]

. . . failure to file notice of redetermination of certain foreign taxes, (Code Sec. 6689);[22]

. . . failure to withhold tax on U.S. income of certain foreign persons (¶4666 *et seq.*), (Code Sec. 1463);[23]

. . . failure to disclose a treaty-based position taken on a return that overrules or otherwise modifies the tax law (¶4657), (Code Sec. 6712);[24]

. . . failure by individual who loses U.S. citizenship or terminates U.S. residency (¶4658) to file expatriate information statement. (Code Sec. 6039G(d));

. . . failure by an exempt organization to disclose that information it is offering to sell or soliciting money for is available free from the federal government, (Code Sec. 6711);[25]

. . . failure by an exempt organization to disclose that fund-raising solicitations are nondeductible as charitable contributions (¶4119), (Code Sec. 6710);[26]

. . . failure by an exempt organization to make the required disclosure for quid pro quo contributions of $75 or more (¶4119), (Code Sec. 6714);[27]

. . . willful failure to make available for inspection or provide copies of, a return or application for exemption of certain exempt organizations (Code Sec. 6685);[28]

. . . any repeated or willful and flagrant act or failure to act by any person who becomes liable for any excise tax on a private foundation by reason of the act or failure to act, (Code Sec. 6684);[29]

. . . making a negligent or fraudulent misstatement in connection with the issuance of a mortgage credit certificate or failing to file the required report (¶4750), (Code Sec. 6709);[30]

. . . failure to file partnership return (¶4733), (Code Sec. 6698), but certain domestic partnerships with ten or fewer partners (each of whom is a natural person or estate) meet a reasonable cause exception;[31]

. . . failure to file returns with respect to qualified rental housing projects, (Code Sec. 42(l)(2), Code Sec. 6652(j));[32]

. . . failure to deposit taxes (an IRS procedure explains how IRS applies deposits in determining the penalty when there is a shortfall) (Code Sec. 6656(a))[33] (including deposits required to be made by electronic funds transfer (EFT, see ¶3027);[34]

. . . use of bad checks or money orders to pay taxes, (Code Sec. 6657);[35]

. . . failure to pay stamp taxes, (Code Sec. 6653);[36]

. . . claiming excessive gasoline tax rebates, (Code Sec. 6675);[37]

. . . filing a frivolous income tax return or submitting a position identified as frivolous on IRS's list of frivolous positions, (Code Sec. 6702);[38]

. . . use of Tax Court primarily for delay or where: taxpayer's position is frivolous or groundless, he hasn't exhausted administrative remedies or he has instituted a frivolous or

20. ¶V-1910; ¶66,864
21. ¶V-1904; ¶66,524; TD ¶861,049
22. ¶V-1983; ¶66,894; TD ¶861,049
23. ¶O-11903; ¶14,614.01
24. ¶V-2722; ¶67,124; TD ¶868,011
25. ¶V-2704; ¶67,114; TD ¶861,032
26. ¶V-2701; ¶67,104; TD ¶861,032
27. ¶V-2703; ¶67,144; TD ¶861,032
28. ¶V-2801; ¶66,854
29. ¶V-2721; ¶66,844; TD ¶868,005
30. ¶V-1998; ¶67,094; TD ¶861,040
31. ¶V-1762 *et seq.*; ¶66,984; TD ¶861,041
32. ¶V-1996; ¶66,524; TD ¶861,039
33. ¶V-1652; ¶66,564; TD ¶862,005
34. ¶V-1658
35. ¶V-2713; ¶66,574; TD ¶868,001
36. ¶V-1651; ¶66,530.40
37. ¶V-2724; ¶ 66,754 (Excise); TD ¶868,012
38. ¶V-2551; ¶67,024; TD ¶866,001

groundless claim for damages against the U.S., (Code Sec. 6673);[39]

... failure to supply taxpayer identification numbers, (Reg § 301.6723-1(a));[40]

... failure to report tips (¶4750), (Code Sec. 6652(b));[41]

... failure by broker to provide back-up withholding notice, (Code Sec. 6705);[42]

... failure to file information return for change in control or recapitalization of corporation (¶4750), (Code Sec. 6652(l));[43]

... making a false statement that results in reduced amounts of withholding (Code Sec. 6682),[44] or relates to the applicability of backup withholding. (Code Sec. 6682)[45]

¶ 4896   Damages for filing fraudulent information return.

A person who is the subject of a fraudulent information return may sue the filer for damages (Code Sec. 7434(a)) of the greater of (1) $5,000, or (2) actual damages plus costs, and, in the court's discretion, reasonable attorney's fees. (Code Sec. 7434(b)) The court must specify the correct amount, if any, that should have been reported on the return. (Code Sec. 7434(e)) The person bringing the action must provide a copy of the complaint to IRS. (Code Sec. 7434(d))[46]

¶ 4897   Criminal tax evasion.

Tax evasion is a felony punishable by a fine of up to $100,000 ($500,000 for a corporation) and/or up to five years' imprisonment, plus costs of prosecution. The elements of the crime are willfulness, an attempt to evade tax and additional tax due. (Code Sec. 7201)[47]

¶ 4898   Criminal penalty for false or fraudulent tax advice.

Any person who willfully aids or assists in, or procures, counsels or advises the preparation or presentation of a materially false or fraudulent return, affidavit, claim or other document, is subject to a criminal penalty of up to $100,000 ($500,000 for a corporation) and/or up to three years' imprisonment, plus costs of prosecution. (Code Sec. 7206(2))[48]

¶ 4899   "Browsing" of tax returns by IRS employees and others.

Any federal officer or employee, IRS contractor or certain other persons with access to tax returns and return information who willfully inspects any tax return or return information without authorization is subject to a criminal fine of not more than $1,000 and imprisonment of not more than one year, or both. (Code Sec. 7213A)[49]

¶ 4900   Other criminal penalties.

Other criminal penalties (fines and/or imprisonment) are imposed for:

... willful failure to file a return (Code Sec. 7203);[50]

... willful filing of a false or fraudulent return (Code Sec. 7207);[1]

... willful failure to pay a tax (Code Sec. 7203);[2]

... willful failure to collect or pay over a tax as required (Code Sec. 7202);[3]

39. ¶V-2601; ¶66,734; TD ¶836,014
40. ¶V-1821 *et seq.*; ¶67,234; TD ¶861,050
41. ¶V-2721; ¶66,524; TD ¶861,038
42. ¶V-1842; ¶67,054; TD ¶861,079
43. ¶V-1911; ¶66,524; TD ¶861,031
44. ¶V-1741; ¶66,824; TD ¶868,002
45. ¶S-1743; ¶66,824; TD ¶868,004
46. ¶S-4470 *et seq.*; TD ¶810,501

47. ¶V-4100 *et seq.*; ¶72,014 *et seq.*; TD ¶871,001
48. ¶V-3110; ¶72,064; TD ¶871,009
49. ¶V-3305.1; ¶72,13A4
50. ¶V-3002; ¶72,034; TD ¶871,015
1. ¶V-3114; ¶72,074; TD ¶871,013
2. ¶V-3001; ¶72,034; TD ¶871,015
3. ¶V-3017; ¶72,024; TD ¶871,008

. . . willful failure to furnish a W-2 to employees in the manner, at the time or with the information required, or willful filing of a false or fraudulent W-2 (Code Sec. 7204);[4]

. . . willful failure to keep proper records (Code Sec. 7203);[5]

. . . willful failure to supply tax information (Code Sec. 7203);[6]

. . . failure to obey a summons (Code Sec. 7210);[7]

. . . various other offenses relating to returns, statements, stamp taxes, etc. [8]

¶ 4901   Tax Collection.

IRS has broad tax collection powers, including seizure and sale of a taxpayer's property (levy and distraint) and liens.

¶ 4902   Collection procedures.

Within 60 days after a tax has been assessed, IRS must send the taxpayer a notice of the amount assessed and a demand for payment, before it can start administrative collection proceedings. (Code Sec. 6303(a), Code Sec. 6331(a))[9] The taxpayer usually gets at least ten days from a date stated in the notice and demand to pay the tax, unless IRS finds that collection is in jeopardy. (Code Sec. 6331(a); Reg § 301.6331-1(a)(3))[10] Taxpayers suffering undue hardship can get an extension of time for paying the assessed taxes. For installment agreements, see ¶4903.[11] IRS must send delinquent taxpayers a written notice of the amount of the delinquency at least annually. (Code Sec. 7524)[12]

IRS has begun using private firms to collect tax debts, as authorized by Code Sec. 6306. [13]

¶ 4903   Agreements for installment payments of tax—Form 9465.

IRS may enter into a written agreement with a taxpayer for that taxpayer to satisfy liability for *any tax* in installment payments. (Code Sec. 6159(a); Reg § 301.6159-1(a))[14] An individual who owes $10,000 or less and meets other conditions can force IRS to enter into an installment agreement. (Code Sec. 6159(c))[15]

A taxpayer uses Form 9465 (attached to his balance due return) to request an installment agreement.[16] IRS may require the taxpayer to agree to certain terms and conditions. (Reg § 301.6159-1(b)(1))[17] Individuals can also apply online by completing an Online Payment Agreement on IRS's website.

A user fee is imposed for entering into, or restructuring or reinstating, an installment agreement. (Reg § 300.0, Reg § 300.1, Reg § 300.2)[18] See ¶4723.

observation: Submit the fee with the first installment payment, not with the Form 9465 request. A reminder notice (Form 521) sent to the taxpayer will reflect this.

The agreement remains in effect for its term unless the taxpayer fails to comply with it. (Code Sec. 6159(b)(2); Reg § 301.6159-1(b)(3)) However, IRS may modify or terminate the agreement under certain circumstances after 30 days' notice to the taxpayer. (Code Sec. 6159(b)(3); Reg § 301.6159-1(c)(2)(i); Reg § 301.6159-1(c)(4))[19]

---

4. ¶V-3013; ¶72,044
5. ¶V-3007; ¶72,034; TD ¶871,015
6. ¶V-3008; ¶72,034; TD ¶871,013
7. ¶V-3503; ¶72,104; TD ¶871,014
8. ¶V-3500 *et seq.*; TD ¶871,014
9. ¶s V-5003, V-5004; ¶s 63,014.03, 63,314.01; TD ¶901,013
10. ¶V-5007; ¶63,314.01; TD ¶901,014
11. ¶V-5009; TD ¶901,015

12. ¶V-5009.2; TD ¶901,002
13. ¶V-5000.2; ¶63,064; TD ¶901,031
14. ¶V-5010; ¶61,594; TD ¶901,006
15. ¶V-5011.2; ¶61,594; TD ¶901,007
16. ¶V-5010; ¶61,594; TD ¶901,006
17. ¶V-5011.1; ¶61,594; TD ¶901,006
18. ¶T-10020 *et seq.*; ¶61,594; TD ¶901,006
19. ¶V-5015 *et seq.*; ¶61,594; TD ¶901,006

¶ 4904   Seizure and sale of a delinquent taxpayer's property—levy and distraint.

IRS has power to collect taxes by levy and distraint. This means it may seize any property (unless it's exempt) of a delinquent taxpayer (whether held by the taxpayer or someone else), sell it, and apply the proceeds to pay the unpaid taxes. [20] The property seized may be real, personal, tangible, or intangible, including receivables, evidences of debt, securities (Code Sec. 6331(a)) and, to the extent they exceed a specified amount, present and future wages. (Reg § 301.6331-2(c)) There are exemptions for certain kinds of income (Code Sec. 6334(d)) and property (e.g., clothing, tools) (Code Sec. 6334(a); Reg § 301.6334-3(d)), and a complete exemption for a taxpayer's principal residence unless a judge or magistrate approves the levy in writing. (Code Sec. 6334(a)(13)(B)) There also is an exemption for real property used as a residence by a taxpayer, or any nonrental real property of the taxpayer used by any other individual as a residence, if the amount of the levy is $5,000 or less (Code Sec. 6334(a)(13)(A)), as well as an exemption for tangible personal property or real property (other than real property which is rented) used in a trade or business of an individual taxpayer, unless collection is in jeopardy, or the levy is approved in writing by an IRS district director or assistant district director. (Code Sec. 6334(a)(13)(B)) Levy is prohibited where an installment agreement is pending or in effect (Code Sec. 6331(k), Reg § 301.6331-4). Levy also is barred for unpaid divisible taxes (provided a portion of the taxes is paid and other conditions are met). (Code Sec. 6331(i)). (Code Sec. 6331(k)) Regs enumerate exemptions. (Reg § 301.6334-1)[21]

IRS must give the taxpayer 30 days' advance written notice before it can levy on any of his property, except where collection is in jeopardy. (Code Sec. 6331(d))[22]

Subject to exceptions, including one for employment tax levies issued after Sept. 21, 2007 (Code Sec. 6330(f)(3)), IRS may not levy against a person's property or right to property unless it gives the person a notification in writing of his right to, and the opportunity for, a pre-levy Collection Due Process hearing with IRS (a CDP hearing). (Code Sec. 6330(a)(1); Reg § 301.6330-1(a)(1)) The notice—the Collection Due Process Hearing Notice (CDP Notice)—must be given at least 30 days before the day of the first levy with respect to the unpaid tax for the tax period. (Code Sec. 6330(a)(2)) A person who receives a CDP Notice may request a hearing (use Form 12153) with the IRS Office of Appeals within the 30-day period beginning on the day after the date of the CDP Notice. (Code Sec. 6330(b)(1); Reg § 301.6330-1(b)(1), Reg § 301.6330-1(c)(1)) A person who requests a CDP hearing can, within 30 days of the date it was made, appeal the determination reached at the hearing. (Code Sec. 6330(d); Reg § 301.6330-1(f)) The Tax Court has sole jurisdiction over all CDP appeals. (Code Sec. 6330(d)(1)) IRS can disregard frivolous requests for a hearing before a levy is made. (Code Sec. 6330(g))[23]

A penalty (plus costs and interest) applies if the person fails or refuses to surrender the property. (Code Sec. 6332(d))[24]

If IRS is unable to sell the seized property for the minimum price it establishes, it can return the property to the taxpayer and add the cost of the unsuccessful sale to the unpaid tax liability. (Code Sec. 6335(e)(1)(D))[25]

Certain payments are subject to continuous levy under IRS's Federal Payment Levy Program. (Code Sec. 6331(h)(1))[26]

---

20. ¶V-5100 *et seq.*; ¶63,314 *et seq.*; TD ¶902,001
21. ¶V-5200 *et seq.*; ¶s 63,314.03, 63,314.05; TD ¶902,006
22. ¶V-5253 *et seq.*; ¶63,314.01; TD ¶902,505
23. ¶V-5271-*et seq.*; ¶63,304;TD ¶902,522

24. ¶V-5116; ¶63,314.04
25. ¶V-5437; ¶63,354.01
26. ¶V-5216; ¶63,314.01; TD ¶902,216

¶ 4905   Wrongful seizures.

If IRS has wrongfully levied on property, it may, on written request, return the specific property seized (or the proceeds from its sale) or the amount of money levied on (Code Sec. 6343(b)), with interest at the overpayment rate (Code Sec. 6343(c)). IRS may also return (without interest) property, including money deposited in the Treasury, that has been levied on if IRS determines that: (1) the levy was premature or otherwise was not in accordance with its administrative procedures (Code Sec. 6343(d)(2)(A)); (2) the taxpayer has agreed to pay off the underlying tax liability in installments, unless the agreement provides otherwise (Code Sec. 6343(d)(2)(B)); (3) the return of the property will make collection of the underlying tax liability easier (Code Sec. 6343(d)(2)(C)); or (4) the return of the property is in the taxpayer's best interests, as determined by the National Taxpayer Advocate (¶4812), and IRS, and the taxpayer or the National Taxpayer Advocate consent. (Code Sec. 6343(d)(2)(D); Reg § 301.6343-3)[27]

¶ 4906   Third-party remedies for wrongful IRS seizures.

If IRS wrongfully seizes property of a person other than the taxpayer, the third party may sue (in district court) for its return (or the sale proceeds, if it has been sold) (Code Sec. 7426), but must start the suit within nine months from the date of levy. (Code Sec. 6532(c)(1)) The Supreme Court has held that Code Sec. 7426(a)(1) is the exclusive remedy for third-party levy claims.[28] The third party may also recover damages (subject to limits, see ¶4907) if the action results in a finding that any IRS officer or employee recklessly, intentionally, or negligently disregarded any Code or reg provision. (Code Sec. 7426(h)). Regs spell out procedures for claiming damages. (Reg § 301.7426-2)[29]

The owner (or his heirs, etc.) of any real estate sold to satisfy a tax liability can redeem the property at any time within 180 days after the sale. (Code Sec. 6337(b)(1))[30]

¶ 4907   Damages for unauthorized IRS collection actions.

If any IRS officer or employee recklessly, intentionally or negligently disregards any Code or reg section in connection with any collection of tax, the taxpayer may bring a civil suit for damages against the U.S. in a district court. Damages are limited to the lesser of (1) $1 million ($100,000 for negligence) or (2) the actual, direct economic damages thus sustained plus the costs of the action. (Code Sec. 7433; Reg § 301.7433-1)[31]

A taxpayer may petition a bankruptcy court for damages (subject to the above limits) if, in connection with any collection of tax, an IRS officer or employee willfully violates any provision of 11 USCS 362 (relating to the automatic stay which arises when a debtor files a bankruptcy petition) or 11 USCS 524 (relating to the effect of a bankruptcy discharge, which operates as an injunction against the commencement or continuation of any action to collect a discharged debt as a personal liability of the debtor). (Code Sec. 7433(e)) Procedures for doing so are contained in regs. (Reg § 301.7433-2)[32]

¶ 4908   Collection period.

IRS must generally start distraint or court proceedings within ten years after assessment (Code Sec. 6502(a)). But if no return is filed, a collection suit may be brought at any time, without assessment. (Code Sec. 6501(c)(3))[33]

---

27. ¶V-5136; ¶V-5137; TD ¶902,005; TD ¶903,008
28. ¶s V-5120, V-5126; ¶s 65,324.04, 74,264; TD ¶903,007
29. ¶V-5135; ¶74,264; TD ¶903,007
30. ¶V-5424; ¶63,354.03; TD ¶903,007

31. ¶V-5800 *et seq.*; ¶74,334; TD ¶903,010
32. ¶V-5820; ¶74,334; TD ¶903,011
33. ¶V-5600 *et seq.*; ¶65,024 *et seq.*; TD ¶901,025

The collection period may be extended in connection with installment agreements. (Code Sec. 6502(a); Reg § 301.6502-1)[34]

The collection period is suspended under various circumstances. (Code Sec. 6330(e)(1); Reg § 301.6330-1(g))[35]

¶ 4909 Injunctions against tax collection.

Injunctions against collection of taxes are generally barred. But exceptions apply during the period allowed to file a Tax Court petition or, where a petition has been filed, before the Tax Court's decision becomes final, and where an individual other than the taxpayer sues to recover property wrongfully seized and in other cases. (Code Sec. 7421(a))[36]

¶ 4910 Federal tax liens.

Federal tax liens are claims against a taxpayer's property for payment of delinquent taxes (including any interest, additional amounts, additions to tax, assessable penalties, or accrued costs).[37] There are various federal tax liens, including:

... general tax lien, which applies to all property, both real and personal, tangible and intangible including a tenancy by the entirety and an heir's interest in an estate even though he later attempts to disclaim it (Code Sec. 6321; Reg § 301.6321-1);[38]

... gift tax lien (Code Sec. 6324(b); Reg § 301.6324-1(b));[39]

... estate tax lien (Code Sec. 6324(a); Reg § 301.6324-1(a));[40]

... special lien for deferred estate tax attributable to a farm or other closely held business (Code Sec. 6324A; Reg § 20.6324A-1, Reg § 301.6324A-1);[41]

... special lien for recapture of estate tax attributable to special use valuation of a farm or closely held business (Code Sec. 6324B; Reg § 20.6324B-1);[42]

... special lien for recapture of estate tax attributable to the deduction for family owned business interests for individuals dying before 2004. (Code Sec. 2057(i)(3)(P));[43]

... generation-skipping transfer tax lien. (Code Sec. 2661; Reg § 26.2662-1(f))[44]

IRS must give written notice of its filing of a notice of lien (NFTL), to the person whose property is to be subject to the lien, not more than five days after it files the notice of lien (Code Sec. 6320(a); Reg § 301.6320-1(a))[45] IRS must hold a Collection Due Process hearing with respect to the filing if the taxpayer timely requests one (use Form 12153). (Code Sec. 6320(b)(1); Reg § 301.6320-1(b)) But IRS can disregard frivolous requests for a hearing before a lien is filed. (Code Sec. 6320(c))[46]

Regs explain how a request for a withdrawal of a federal tax lien is made. (Reg § 301.6323(j)-1)[47]

¶ 4911 Priority of tax liens.

Priority of tax liens is governed by federal, not state, law. [48] The general rule is that a lien first in time is first in right. [49] But a tax lien is subordinated to certain later liens that arise either before notice of the tax lien (Form 668) is filed, or before the other lienor has actual knowledge of it. This protects purchasers for adequate consideration without actual notice,

34. ¶V-5604 *et seq.*; ¶65,024; TD ¶901,026
35. ¶V-5277; ¶63,304; TD ¶902,527
36. ¶V-5701; ¶74,214 *et seq.*
37. ¶V-6000 *et seq.*; TD ¶911,000 *et seq.*
38. ¶V-6002 *et seq.*; ¶63,214 *et seq.*; TD ¶911,023
39. ¶V-6042; ¶63,244 (Estate & Gift); TD ¶911,026
40. ¶V-6044; ¶63,244 (Estate & Gift); TD ¶911,027
41. ¶V-6046; ¶63,24A4 (Estate & Gift); TD ¶911,029

42. ¶V-6051; ¶63,24B4 (Estate & Gift); TD ¶911,031
43. ¶V-6054; ¶20,574
44. ¶V-6054; TD ¶911,033
45. ¶V-6001; ¶63,204
46. ¶V-6005; ¶63,204
47. ¶V-6134; ¶63,234.18
48. ¶V-6324; ¶63,234; TD ¶913,001
49. ¶V-6301; ¶63,214.04; TD ¶913,001

mortgagees, pledgees and other lienors whose rights arose before notice of the tax lien was filed. (Code Sec. 6323(a); Reg § 301.6323(a)-1)[50] It also protects certain interests arising even after the notice was filed, e.g., attorney's liens and certain security interests. (Code Sec. 6323(b); Reg § 301.6323(b)-1)[1]

The special gift and estate tax liens don't have to be filed to be superior to claims arising after the special lien arises. But certain later purchasers and creditors are protected, including holders of a security interest and holders of mechanics', repairmen's and attorney's liens. (Code Sec. 6324A(d)(3), Code Sec. 6324B(c)(1))[2]

IRS may withdraw a notice of lien if it was filed prematurely or otherwise not in accordance with its administrative procedures, and for certain other reasons. (Code Sec. 6323(j)(1)) At the taxpayer's request, IRS must make reasonable efforts to notify credit reporting agencies and creditors specified by the taxpayer of the withdrawal of the notice. (Code Sec. 6323(j)(2))[3]

¶ 4912   Taxes in bankruptcy or receivership proceedings.

A receiver in a receivership proceeding must give IRS notice of the receivership. (Code Sec. 6036) (Use Form 56) But a bankruptcy trustee, debtor-in-possession, or other like fiduciary in a bankruptcy proceeding needn't give notice (Reg § 301.6036-1(a)(1)(i)), because notice under the Bankruptcy Rules is sufficient. [4]

The filing of a federal bankruptcy petition (but not the start of a state receivership proceeding) automatically stays any tax proceedings against the taxpayer-debtor. [5] The running of the assessment period is suspended from the date a bankruptcy or receivership proceeding is instituted until 30 days after IRS has received notice of the proceeding, but the suspension may not exceed two years. (Code Sec. 6872; Reg § 301.6872-1)[6]

Although a taxpayer's bankruptcy triggers an immediate assessment (¶4829) collection of the tax is stayed while the taxpayer-debtor's assets are under the control of a federal or state court in bankruptcy or receivership proceedings. [7]

With some exceptions, debtor relief proceedings don't discharge the taxpayer's liability for taxes or interest (including certain post-petition interest). [8]

¶ 4913   Transferee's liability for transferor's unpaid taxes.

A transferee is liable for a taxpayer-transferor's unpaid taxes (and interest and penalties) where:

. . . the transfer is void or voidable under rules of equity, [9]

. . . transferee liability is imposed by statute, [10]

. . . transferee liability arises under contract. [11]

Transferees include a donee, heir, legatee, devisee or distributee of a decedent's estate, a shareholder of a dissolved corporation, the assignee or donee of an insolvent person, certain fiduciaries, a successor in a tax-free corporate reorganization, and various other classes of distributees. (Code Sec. 6901(h); Reg § 301.6901-1(b))[12]

IRS must assess the (first) transferee within one year after the limitations period against the transferor has run. (Code Sec. 6901(c)(1))[13]

---

50. ¶s V-6400 *et seq.*, V-6426 *et seq.*; ¶63,234 *et seq.*; TD ¶913,002
1. ¶V-6401; ¶63,234; TD ¶913,003
2. ¶s V-6455, V-6456; ¶63,244 (Estate & Gift); TD ¶911,028
3. ¶V-6134; TD ¶911,021
4. ¶S-4103; ¶60,364; TD ¶817,504
5. ¶U-1220; ¶68,714
6. ¶T-4323; ¶68,724; TD ¶838,050

7. ¶V-7301 *et seq.*; ¶68,714; TD ¶838,050
8. ¶V-7335 *et seq.*; ¶68,734
9. ¶s V-9100 *et seq.*, V-9200 *et seq.*; ¶69,014 *et seq.*
10. ¶V-9300 *et seq.*; ¶69,014 *et seq.*
11. ¶V-9400 *et seq.*; ¶69,014.02
12. ¶V-9001; ¶69,014.01
13. ¶V-9801; ¶69,014.10

¶ 4914   Early discharge of executor's personal liability.

An executor or administrator can be discharged from personal liability for estate tax as early as nine months after the estate tax return is due (or filed, if later) if he makes a written request to IRS to determine the estate tax liability, and any tax determined to be due is paid (or a bond is posted if the payment period was extended). (Code Sec. 2204(a))[14] A trustee or other fiduciary can get a similar discharge. (Code Sec. 2204(b))[15]

An executor or administrator can also request (on Form 5495) early discharge from personal liability for a decedent's income and gift taxes. (Code Sec. 6905(a))[16]

---

14. ¶s T-4511, T-4512; ¶22,044 (Estate & Gift)   16. ¶T-4518; ¶69,054
15. ¶T-4513; ¶22,044 (Estate & Gift)

Chapter 26 Estate, Gift and Generation-Skipping Transfer Taxes

¶ 5000 Estate Tax.

The federal estate tax is imposed on the transfer of an individual's property at death and on other transfers considered to be the equivalent of transfers at death. The tax is imposed on the "taxable estate," which is the value of the total property transferred or considered transferred at death (the "gross estate"), reduced by various deductions. The tax is computed under a unified rate schedule under which lifetime taxable gifts and transfers at death are taxed on a cumulative basis. The top rate is 45% (individuals dying in 2007 through 2009). For estates of individuals dying after 2009, the estate and generation-skipping transfer (GST) taxes will be repealed, and, subject to numerous exceptions, assets acquired from a decedent will receive a carryover basis, see ¶2523. The top gift tax rate will be 35% in 2010. After 2010, the estate and GST taxes will return under the sunset provision, see ¶1114.

In determining the tax on estates of individuals who at death were citizens or residents of the U.S., the entire estate is considered. (Code Sec. 2033)[1] For nonresident aliens, see ¶5036.

¶ 5001 Computation of estate tax—Form 706.

First, compute a tentative tax under the unified rate schedule at ¶1113 on the total of: (1) the amount of the taxable estate (¶5017), and (2) the total amount of taxable gifts made by the decedent after '76 that aren't includible in his gross estate. (Code Sec. 2001(b)(1)) Then reduce this amount by the amount of gift tax payable on the decedent's post-'76 gifts to get the gross estate tax payable (before credits). (Code Sec. 2001(b)(2))

The net estate tax payable is the gross estate tax minus the unified credit, and allowable credits for state death taxes, gift taxes on pre-'77 gifts, estate taxes on earlier transfers and foreign death taxes (¶5029 *et seq.*). (Code Sec. 2010, Code Sec. 2011, Code Sec. 2012, Code Sec. 2013, Code Sec. 2014)[2]

The estate of a "qualified decedent" who was an armed forces member or victim of terrorism, or an astronaut who died in the line of duty, is entitled to compute its estate tax liability under a special estate tax rate schedule containing lower rates, which in many cases results, in no tax being owed. (Code Sec. 2201)[3]

¶ 5002 Property owned by decedent.

The gross estate of a decedent includes the value of all property owned by him at his death. (Code Sec. 2033; Reg § 20.2033-1(a))[4]

¶ 5003 Gifts within three years of death—Form 706, Schedule G.

An individual who transferred an interest in, or relinquished a power over, any property, within three years of death, must include the value of the property in his gross estate to the extent it would have been included in his gross estate under Code Sec. 2036 (transfers with retained life estate, etc., ¶5005), Code Sec. 2037 (transfers taking effect at death, ¶5007), Code Sec. 2038 (revocable transfers, ¶5008), or Code Sec. 2042 (life insurance proceeds, ¶5015), if the interest or relinquished power had been retained. (Code Sec. 2035(a))[5] This rule

---

1. ¶R-1010 *et seq.*, ¶R-2000 *et seq.*; ¶20,314 *et seq.*, ¶20,334 *et seq.*; TD ¶761,001
2. ¶R-7001 *et seq.*; ¶20,014.02; TD ¶780,501
3. ¶R-7011; ¶22,014; TD ¶780,510
4. ¶R-2001; ¶20,334; TD ¶761,001
5. ¶R-2201 *et seq.*; ¶20,354; TD ¶763,001

References beginning with a single letter are to paragraphs in RIA's Federal Tax Coordinator 2d and RIA's Analysis of Federal Taxes: Income. Those beginning with numbers are to paragraphs in RIA's United States Tax Reporter. Those beginning with TD are to paragraphs in RIA's Tax Desk.

doesn't apply to any bona fide sale for full and adequate consideration. (Code Sec. 2035(d))

¶ 5004 Gift tax "gross-up"—Form 706, Schedule G.

Gift tax paid by the decedent, his estate or his donees on gifts made by decedent or his spouse within three years of decedent's death is included in his gross estate. But gift tax paid by the spouse on the spouse's share of decedent's gifts under the gift-splitting rules isn't included. (Code Sec. 2035(b))[6]

¶ 5005 Retained life estate—Form 706, Schedule G.

A decedent's gross estate includes transfers under which he retained the possession or enjoyment of, or the right to the income from, the transferred property. (Code Sec. 2036(a)(1); Reg § 20.2036-1)[7]

The decedent's gross estate also includes transfers where he retained the right to designate the person(s) to possess or enjoy the transferred property or its income. (Code Sec. 2036(a)(2))[8]

These rules don't apply to any bona fide sale for full and adequate consideration. (Code Sec. 2036(a))

IRS has had mixed results in getting assets transferred to family limited partnerships (FLPs) included in the transferor's gross estate under the foregoing rules. [9]

¶ 5006 Retention of voting rights in stock of a controlled corporation—Form 706, Schedule G.

Retention of voting rights in stock of a controlled corporation is a retention of the enjoyment of the transferred stock. The value of the transferred stock is included in the decedent's gross estate. (Code Sec. 2036(b))[10]

¶ 5007 Transfers taking effect at death—Form 706, Schedule G.

If a decedent transfers property during his lifetime, but the transferee cannot possess or enjoy the property except by surviving the decedent, and the decedent retained a significant reversionary interest (exceeding 5% of the value of the transferred property immediately before the decedent's death), then the value of the property is includible in decedent's gross estate. This rule doesn't apply to any bona fide sale for full and adequate consideration. (Code Sec. 2037)[11]

¶ 5008 Revocable transfers—Form 706, Schedule G.

The decedent's gross estate includes his lifetime transfers if the enjoyment of the transferred property was subject at his death to any change through the exercise by him of a power to *alter, amend, revoke or terminate.* This includes any power affecting the time or manner of enjoyment of property or its income. (Code Sec. 2038(a)(1)) This rule doesn't apply to any bona fide sale for full and adequate consideration. [12]

Includible revocable transfers include savings bank (Totten) trusts that are revocable in form,[13] and custodial accounts where the donor is custodian. [14]

---

6. ¶s R-2210, R-2211; ¶20,354; TD ¶763,010
7. ¶R-2400 *et seq.*; ¶20,364; TD ¶764,001
8. ¶R-2450; ¶20,364; TD ¶764,002
9. ¶R-2421.1
10. ¶R-2436; ¶20,364; TD ¶764,032

11. ¶R-2500 *et seq.*; ¶20,374; TD ¶765,000
12. ¶R-2600 *et seq.*; ¶20,384 *et seq.*; TD ¶765,501
13. ¶R-2621; TD ¶765,520
14. ¶R-2620; ¶20,384.03; TD ¶765,519

¶ 5009　Qualified terminable interest property (QTIP).

Qualified terminable interest property (QTIP) for which the estate tax (¶5022) or gift tax (¶5047) marital deduction was elected is includible in the estate of the donee spouse at its then fair market value unless the donee disposed of any part of the qualifying income interest for life. (Code Sec. 2044) The property is treated as passing from the surviving spouse. (Code Sec. 2044(c)) Where a predeceased spouse's estate made an unnecessary QTIP election that did not reduce its estate tax liability, steps may be taken so that the unneeded election will be treated as null and void for federal estate, gift, and generation-skipping transfer tax purposes. As a result, the property won't have to be included in the survivor's estate. [15]

The surviving spouse's executor may recover the estate taxes caused by the inclusion from the persons to whom the property passes at the surviving spouse's death, unless the surviving spouse's will specifically indicates an intent to waive the right of recovery. (Code Sec. 2207A(a))[16]

¶ 5010　Powers of appointment—Form 706, Schedule H.

If the decedent possessed a general power of appointment (created after Oct. 21, '42) at the time of his death, the property subject to the power is included in his gross estate. (Code Sec. 2041(a))[17] A "general" power is one exercisable in favor of the decedent, his estate, his creditors, or the creditors of his estate. (Code Sec. 2041(b)(1))[18]

¶ 5011　Jointly-held property—Form 706, Schedule E.

Joint ownership acquired through gift, bequest, devise, or inheritance from another. The decedent's fractional share of the property is included in the gross estate. (Reg § 20.2040-1(a)(1))[19]

Joint ownership created by co-owners. Except for husband-wife tenancies (¶5012), the *entire* value of the property is included in the co-owner's gross estate except the part, if any, attributable to the consideration in money or money's worth furnished by the other joint owner(s). Consideration furnished by the surviving joint owner(s) doesn't include money or property acquired from the decedent for less than a full and adequate consideration in money or money's worth. (Reg § 20.2040-1(a)(2))[20]

Tenancy in common. Only the value of decedent's undivided share of the property is included in his gross estate. [21]

¶ 5012　Spouses' jointly-held property—Form 706, Schedule E.

If an interest in property created after '76 is held by a decedent and his spouse as tenants by the entireties or as joint tenants with right of survivorship (if the decedent and his spouse are the only joint tenants), one half of the value of the jointly-owned interest will be included in the estate of the decedent spouse regardless of which spouse furnished the original consideration. (Code Sec. 2040(b)) Where the surviving spouse isn't a U.S. citizen, this rule applies only if the property passes in a qualified domestic trust (QDOT, ¶5025). (Code Sec. 2056(d)(1)(B), Code Sec. 2056(d)(2))[22]

Thus, the survivor gets a new basis for one-half of the property, see ¶2517.

---

15. ¶R-2900 *et seq.*; ¶20,444; TD ¶777,032
16. ¶R-6439 *et seq.*; ¶s 20,444, 20,564.08, 22,07A4, 25,194; TD ¶778,135
17. ¶R-3000 *et seq.*; ¶20,414; TD ¶767,301
18. ¶R-3006; ¶20,414; TD ¶767,319

19. ¶s R-2705, R-2709; ¶20,404; TD ¶766,005
20. ¶R-2700 *et seq.*; ¶20,404; TD ¶766,005
21. ¶R-2707; ¶20,334.15; TD ¶766,006
22. ¶R-2724 *et seq.*; ¶20,404; TD ¶766,019 *et seq.*

¶ 5013   Community property.

The value of the interest in community property vested in the decedent by state law — ordinarily, half of the community property — is included in the decedent spouse's estate. [23]

¶ 5014   Annuities—Form 706, Schedule I.

The value of an annuity or other payment receivable by a beneficiary is included in the decedent's gross estate if, under the contract or agreement, either:

(1) an annuity or other payment was payable to decedent, either alone or with another person(s), for decedent's life or for any period not ascertainable without reference to his death or for any period that doesn't in fact end before his death, or

(2) the decedent possessed, for one of the periods in (1), above, the right to receive such an annuity or other payment, either alone or with another. (Code Sec. 2039(a))

The amount included is an amount proportionate to the part of the purchase price contributed by the decedent. Contributions made by an employer are considered made by the employee if made by reason of his employment. (Code Sec. 2039(b))[24]

¶ 5015   Life insurance—Form 706, Schedule D.

Proceeds of insurance on the decedent's life receivable by the executor or administrator, or payable to the decedent's estate, are includible in his gross estate. (Code Sec. 2042(1)) The estate needn't be specifically named as the beneficiary. (Reg § 20.2042-1(b)(1))[25]

Proceeds of insurance on the decedent's life not receivable by or for the benefit of the estate are includible if the decedent possessed at his death any incidents of ownership in the policy, exercisable either alone or with any other person. (Code Sec. 2042(2)) "Incidents of ownership" include the power to change the beneficiary, to revoke an assignment, to pledge the policy for a loan, etc. (Reg § 20.2042-1(c)(2)), and certain reversionary interests. (Reg § 20.2042-1(c)(3))[26]

¶ 5016   Group term life insurance—Form 706, Schedule D.

An employee can prevent inclusion in his estate (under the rule at ¶5015) of the proceeds of group term life insurance furnished by his employer by transferring the insurance before his death, if:

(1) the group policy and applicable state law permit the employee to make an absolute assignment of all his incidents of ownership, and

(2) the employee irrevocably assigns all policy rights. [27]

¶ 5017   Computing the taxable estate.

To get the taxable estate, deduct the following from the gross estate: [28]

... Funeral expenses. (Code Sec. 2053(a)(1))

... Administration expenses, such as executors' and administrators' commissions, attorneys', accountants' and appraisers' fees, and court costs. (Code Sec. 2053(a)(2); Reg § 20.2053-3)

---

23. ¶R-2800 *et seq.*; ¶s 20,334.16, 20,334.17; TD ¶766,022
24. ¶R-4401 *et seq.*; ¶20,394; TD ¶768,054
25. ¶R-4002 *et seq.*; ¶20,424.01; TD ¶768,002
26. ¶R-4006 *et seq.*; ¶20,424 *et seq.*; TD ¶768,008

27. ¶R-4033; TD ¶768,032
28. ¶R-5400 *et seq.*; ¶s 20,514, 20,534, 20,544, 20,554, 20,564; TD ¶776,001

... Claims against the estate, including property taxes accrued before the decedent's death, unpaid income and gift taxes, and medical expenses of the decedent paid by his estate after his death (to the extent not claimed as an income tax deduction, see ¶2144). (Code Sec. 2053(a)(3); Reg § 20.2053-6)

... Transfers in satisfaction of claims by the decedent's former spouse. (Code Sec. 2043(b)(2))

... Indebtedness on property if the total value of the property is included in the gross estate. (Code Sec. 2053(a)(4))

... Casualty and theft losses. (Code Sec. 2054)

... Transfers to charitable and similar organizations (Code Sec. 2055), see ¶5019.

... Transfers to surviving spouse (marital deduction) (Code Sec. 2056), see ¶5020.

... State death taxes (Code Sec. 2058), see ¶5026.

For an item to be deductible as a debt, claim, or expense it must also be allowable by the jurisdiction under which the estate is being administered. (Code Sec. 2053(a))[29] If, at the time of filing the estate tax return, the exact amount of a deductible debt, claim or expense isn't known, an estimated amount may be used if that amount is ascertainable with reasonable certainty and it can be shown the item will be paid. (Reg § 20.2053-1(b)(3))[30]

¶ 5018   Income v. estate tax deduction.

Many estate administration expenses can qualify as an estate tax deduction on the estate tax return and as an income tax deduction, or an offset against the sales price of property in determining gain or loss, on the estate's income tax return. But the estate is entitled to an income tax deduction or offset only if an estate tax deduction for the item is waived. (Code Sec. 642(g))[31] For the election to take an income tax or estate tax deduction, see ¶3925.

¶ 5019   Deductions for charitable bequests—Form 706, Schedule O.

Deductions are allowed (on Form 706, Schedule O) for the value of property included in the gross estate and transferred by decedent during life or by will to or for the use of the U.S., any state, political subdivision thereof, or the District of Columbia, and to various types of charitable organizations (Code Sec. 2055(a)) including foreign ones.[32]

Strict requirements apply where the charitable bequest is of an income interest or a remainder interest. (Code Sec. 2055(e))[33]

¶ 5020   Marital deduction—Form 706, Schedule M.

A marital deduction is allowed (on Form 706, Schedule M) for the value of all property included in the gross estate that passes to the decedent's surviving spouse in a manner qualifying for the deduction. (Code Sec. 2056(a))[34] For terminable interests, see ¶5021. For where surviving spouse isn't a U.S. citizen, see ¶5025.

¶ 5021   Terminable interests and the marital deduction—Form 706, Schedule M.

With certain exceptions (see, e.g., ¶5022), a terminable interest doesn't qualify for the marital deduction if another interest in the same property passed from the decedent to some other person for less than adequate and full consideration in money or money's worth and by reason of its passing that other person or his heirs may enjoy part of the property after the termination of the surviving spouse's interest. (Code Sec. 2056(b)(1); Reg § 20.2056(b)-1(c)) A

29. ¶R-5404; ¶20,534 *et seq.*; TD ¶776,003
30. ¶R-5403; TD ¶776,002
31. ¶R-5507; ¶20,534; TD ¶776,082

32. ¶R-5700 *et seq.*; ¶20,554 *et seq.*; TD ¶777,000
33. ¶R-5735 *et seq.*; ¶s 20,554, 20,554.14, 20,554.16; TD ¶777,035
34. ¶R-6000 *et seq.*; ¶20,564 *et seq.*; TD ¶778,001

terminable interest is one that will terminate or fail after a certain period of time, the happening of some contingency, or the failure of some event to occur. (Reg § 20.2056(b)-1(b))[35]

¶ 5022 Qualified terminable interest property (QTIP) election—Form 706, Schedule M.

Property in which a spouse is given only a life estate may qualify for the marital deduction as an exception to the terminable interest rule (¶5021) if the executor elects (by listing the property on Form 706, Schedule M and deducting its value) to have all or part of the property so qualify and the surviving spouse has a "qualifying income interest for life." A surviving spouse has such an interest if:

(1) the surviving spouse is entitled for life to all the income from the property, payable at least annually, or the spouse has a usufruct interest for life in the property, and

(2) no person (including the spouse) has a power to appoint any part of the property to any person other than the surviving spouse during the surviving spouse's life. (Code Sec. 2056(b)(7))[36]

A surviving spouse's interest can meet the "all income" requirement if the spouse is entitled to income as determined by applicable local law that provides for a reasonable apportionment between the income and remainder beneficiaries of the trust's total return. (Reg § 20.2056(b)-5(f)(1), Reg § 20.2056(b)-7(d)(2))[37]

QTIP treatment isn't defeated merely because the spouse's income interest is contingent on the executor making a QTIP election. (Reg § 20.2056(b)-7(d)(3))[38]

An annuity, including one arising under community property law, where only the surviving spouse has the right to receive payments before the death of that surviving spouse qualifies and the QTIP election is treated as made with respect to it unless the executor otherwise elects. (Code Sec. 2056(b)(7)(C))[39]

Certain individual retirement accounts (IRAs) qualify. (Reg § 20.2056(b)-7(h), Ex 10) A revenue ruling explains how total return concepts affect QTIP deductions for IRAs. [40]

Partial QTIP elections that relate to a fractional or percentage share of the property are allowed. (Reg § 20.2056(b)-7(b)(2))[41] Protective QTIP elections are possible. (Reg § 20.2056(b)-7(c))[42]

For inclusion of the qualified terminable interest property in the surviving spouse's estate, see ¶5009.

¶ 5023 Effect of death taxes on amount of marital deduction.

Federal estate or other death taxes payable out of the marital share reduce the amount of the bequest that qualifies for the marital deduction. (Code Sec. 2056(b)(4)(A))

The spouse's interest can be completely absolved from the burden of the tax by a provision in decedent's will that is effective under local law. In such a case, death taxes won't affect the amount of the deduction. [43]

---

35. ¶R-6300 *et seq.*; ¶20,564; TD ¶778,049
36. ¶R-6393; ¶20,564.08; TD ¶778,100
37. ¶R-6355
38. ¶R-6400; ¶20,564.08; TD ¶778,115
39. ¶R-6413 *et seq.*; ¶20,564.08; TD ¶778,125

40. ¶R-6422; TD ¶778,129
41. ¶R-6431; ¶20,564.08; TD ¶778,106
42. ¶R-6430; TD ¶778,105
43. ¶R-6612 *et seq.*; ¶20,564.17; TD ¶778,145

¶ 5024 Effect of administration expenses on amount of marital deduction

The marital deduction is reduced by estate transmission expenses paid from the marital share (Reg § 20.2056(b)-4(d)(2)) but not by estate management expenses attributable to and paid from the marital share unless those expenses are deducted on the estate tax return under Code Sec. 2053. (Reg § 20.2056(b)-4(d)(3)) The marital deduction is reduced to the extent estate management expenses are paid from the marital share and are attributable to other property. (Reg § 20.2056(b)-4(d)(4)) Estate transmission expenses are expenses that wouldn't have been incurred but for the necessity of collecting the decedent's assets, paying his debts and death taxes, and distributing his property. They include any administration expense that is not a management expense. (Reg § 20.2056(b)-4(d)(1)(ii)) Management expenses are those incurred in connection with the investment of estate assets or with their preservation or maintenance during a reasonable period of administration. (Reg § 20.2056(b)-4(d)(1)(i))[44]

¶ 5025 Marital deduction where surviving spouse isn't a U.S. citizen—qualified domestic trust (QDOT) requirement.

No marital deduction is allowed if the surviving spouse isn't a U.S. citizen (Code Sec. 2056(d)(1)(A); Reg § 20.2056A-1(a)), unless the property passes (or is treated as passing) to the spouse in a QDOT (Code Sec. 2056(d)(2))—a trust that satisfies certain requirements (Code Sec. 2056A; Reg § 20.2056A-2) or the spouse timely becomes a citizen. (Code Sec. 2056(d)(4); Reg § 20.2056A-1(b))[45]

An estate tax is imposed (use Form 706-QDT) on any distribution (other than an income or a hardship distribution (Reg § 20.2056A-5(c))) from the trust before the date of the surviving spouse's death and on the value of the property remaining in the trust on the date of death of the surviving spouse (Code Sec. 2056A(b)(1)) (or the date the trust ceases to qualify). (Code Sec. 2056A(b)(3))[46]

¶ 5026 Deduction for state death taxes

The value of the taxable estate is determined by deducting from the gross estate any estate, inheritance, legacy, or succession taxes actually paid to any state or the District of Columbia for any property included in the gross estate, but not including any taxes paid for the estate of a person other than the decedent. (Code Sec. 2058)

¶ 5027 Value of property included in the gross estate.

The value of property included in the gross estate is the fair market value of the property at the date of the decedent's death (or at the alternate valuation date, see below). (Code Sec. 2031; Reg § 20.2031-1)[47]

Regs provide rules for valuing specific types of properties including: stocks and bonds (Reg § 20.2031-2); business interests (Reg § 20.2031-3); notes (Reg § 20.2031-4); household and personal effects (Reg § 20.2031-6); and life insurance and annuity contracts. (Reg § 20.2031-8)

An executor may elect (on Form 706, Schedule U) to exclude from the gross estate up to 40% of the value of land subject to a qualified conservation easement meeting certain requirements and subject to a dollar cap of $500,000. (Code Sec. 2031(c)) If a qualified conservation easement is granted after the decedent's death but on or before the due date (including

44. ¶R-6608; ¶20,564.05; TD ¶778,142
45. ¶R-6201 et seq.; ¶s 20,564, 20,56A4; TD ¶778,027
46. ¶R-7081 et seq.; ¶20,56A4.02; TD ¶781,501
47. ¶R-1006; ¶20,314; TD ¶751,005

extensions) for the estate tax return, an estate tax charitable deduction is allowed, but only if no income tax charitable deduction is allowed to any person with respect to the grant. (Code Sec. 2031(c)(9))[48]

The fair market value of annuities (other than commercial annuities), life estates, term of years, remainders, and reversions is their present value, as determined under IRS tables, which include an interest rate component and, if applicable, a mortality component. (Reg § 20.2031-7(a); 20.7520-1(a)(1))[49]

The executor can elect (irrevocably, on Form 706) to use an alternate valuation date rather than the decedent's date of death to value the property included in the gross estate. This alternate date is generally six months after decedent's death or earlier date of sale or distribution. (Code Sec. 2032(a))[50] Alternate valuation can be elected only if its use decreases both the value of the gross estate and the combined estate and generation-skipping transfer tax liability. (Code Sec. 2032(c); Reg § 20.2032-1(b)(1))[1]

✒️observation: The executor can't elect in order to step up the basis of assets that increase in value after death (for example, where there would otherwise be no estate tax cost to the increased valuation because the marital deduction eliminates any tax).

¶ 5028 Special-use valuation of farm or other business real property—Form 706, Schedule A-1.

If certain conditions are met, an executor may elect (irrevocably, on Form 706, Schedule A-1) to value qualified real property used for farming purposes or in a trade or business on the basis of the property's value for its actual use, rather than on its highest and best use. The total decrease in the value of all real property under this election may not exceed $940,000 for individuals dying in 2007 ($960,000 for 2008). (Code Sec. 2032A)[2] The resulting estate tax savings may be recaptured (use Form 706-A) under certain conditions. (Code Sec. 2032A(c))[3]

¶ 5029 Unified credit against estate tax.

The credit for estates of individuals dying in 2007 or 2008 is $780,800 (Code Sec. 2010(a)) but can't exceed the estate tax imposed. (Code Sec. 2010(c)) The effect is to exempt up to $2 million from estate taxation for individuals dying in 2007 or 2008. The gift tax effective exemption is $1 million and will remain at that level even when the estate tax exemption increases to $3.5 million in 2009 as a result of a credit of $1,455,800. There is no estate tax in 2010 but the estate tax returns in 2011 under the sunset provision, ¶1114.[4]

The credit is reduced by 20% of the amount of the pre-'77 $30,000 gift tax exemption allowed for gifts made before '77 and after Sept. 8, '76. (Code Sec. 2010(b))[5]

¶ 5030 Credit for tax on prior transfers—Form 706, Schedule Q.

Credit is allowed (on Form 706, Schedule Q) against the estate tax for federal estate tax paid by the estate of another decedent (the transferor) on the transfer of property to the present decedent from that transferor where the transferor died within ten years before, or within two years after, the present decedent's death. (Code Sec. 2013)[6]

Where a transferor decedent was denied a marital deduction because the surviving spouse wasn't a U.S. citizen or where the estate tax on qualified domestic trust distributions applied (see ¶5025), the surviving spouse decedent is allowed a credit for the estate tax paid by the

48. ¶R-4700 *et seq.*; ¶20,314.13; TD ¶773,400
49. ¶P-6615; ¶20,314.12; TD ¶521,501
50. ¶R-5002; ¶20,324; TD ¶773,001
1. ¶R-5001; ¶20,324; TD ¶773,001
2. ¶R-5200 *et seq.*; ¶20,32A4; TD ¶771,001

3. ¶R-5301; ¶20,32A4; TD ¶771,053
4. ¶R-7100 *et seq.*; ¶20,104; TD ¶781,801
5. ¶R-7103; ¶20,104; TD ¶781,804
6. ¶R-7300 *et seq.*; ¶20,134; TD ¶782,500 *et seq.*

transferor decedent, or by the trust, without regard to when the transferor decedent died. (Code Sec. 2056(d)(3))[7]

¶ 5031 Credit for gift taxes paid on pre-'77 gifts.

Credit for gift taxes paid on pre-'77 gifts is allowed against the estate tax where gifts were made by a decedent before '77 of property included in his gross estate. (Code Sec. 2012(a))[8]

¶ 5032 Credit for foreign death taxes—Form 706, Schedule P.

Credit is allowed (on Form 706, Schedule P), subject to certain limits, against the estate tax for estate, inheritance, legacy, or succession taxes actually paid to any foreign country or U.S. possession. (Code Sec. 2014)[9]

¶ 5033 Return requirements—Form 706.

An executor must file estate tax return Form 706 if the decedent's gross estate at death exceeds the amount effectively exempted by unified credit ($2 million for estates of individuals dying in 2007 and rising to $3.5 million in 2009, see ¶5029). This dollar amount is reduced by certain gifts made by the decedent. (Code Sec. 6018(a)(1), Code Sec. 6018(a)(3))[10]

¶ 5034 When to file estate tax return.

File within nine months after the date of death. (Code Sec. 6075(a))[11]

IRS will grant an automatic 6-month extension to file Form 706 and may grant a 6-month discretionary filing extension (1) for estates that didn't seek an automatic extension, (2) to file Form 706-NA for the estates of nonresident alien, and (3) to file specialized estate tax forms for various recapture estate taxes (e.g., Form 706-A for recapture of special use valuation). (use Form 4768 for all extensions). An executor who is abroad can request a longer discretionary extension. (Reg § 20.6081-1)[12]

¶ 5035 When to pay tax.

The estate tax must be paid at the time for filing the return. Filing extensions don't extend the time for payment, (Reg § 20.6151-1)[13] but extensions of time to pay can be granted (use Form 4768) for reasonable cause. (Code Sec. 6161(a)(1))[14]

Special extensions (elected on Form 706) are available where a future interest is included in the estate (Code Sec. 6163)[15] or where the estate consists largely of a closely-held business. (Code Sec. 6166)[16]

The estate tax on distributions made from qualified domestic trusts (QDOTs, see ¶5025), before the surviving spouse's death is due on Apr. 15 of the year following the calendar year the taxable event occurs. (Code Sec. 2056A(b)(5))[17]

¶ 5036 Estates of nonresident aliens—Form 706-NA.

Decedents who were neither U.S. citizens nor U.S. residents are taxed only on the transfer of property situated within the U.S. With that exception, the make-up of the gross estate is the same as that for a U.S. citizen or resident. (Code Sec. 2103)

---

7. ¶R-7301; ¶20,564; TD ¶782,515
8. ¶R-7501; ¶20,124; TD ¶783,001
9. ¶R-7400 et seq.; ¶20,144; TD ¶782,801
10. ¶S-2300 et seq.; ¶60,184; TD ¶751,015
11. ¶S-4902; ¶60,754; TD ¶783,508
12. ¶S-5035.1; ¶60,814; TD ¶783,509

13. ¶S-5851; ¶61,514; TD ¶783,513
14. ¶S-5900 et seq.; ¶61,614; TD ¶783,514
15. ¶S-5910; ¶61,634; TD ¶782,807
16. ¶S-6000 et seq.; ¶61,664 et seq.; TD ¶784,001
17. ¶R-7085 et seq.; ¶20,56A4.02; TD ¶781,506

The same rate schedule that applies to the estates of U.S. citizens (¶1113) applies to the estates of nonresident aliens. (Code Sec. 2101(b))

A marital deduction is allowed under the principles of the regular marital deduction rules (¶5020 *et seq.*), with respect to U.S. property. (Code Sec. 2106(a)(3)) Other deductions are also allowed, within limits. (Code Sec. 2106)

A unified credit of $13,000 is allowed against the estate tax of nonresident aliens, with an alternative credit computations for estates of certain residents of U.S. possessions (Code Sec. 2102(b)(1), Code Sec. 2102(b)(2)), and to the extent required under certain treaty obligations of the U.S. (Code Sec. 2102(b)(3)(A)) The $13,000 is reduced by any gift tax unified credit allowed. (Code Sec. 2102(b)(3)(B))

Credits are also allowed for estate tax on prior transfers and gift tax on certain pre-'77 gifts.(Code Sec. 2102(b)(5))[18]

An estate tax return on Form 706-NA must be filed for the estate of every nonresident not a U.S. citizen if the value of the part of the estate in the U.S. exceeds $60,000 (Code Sec. 6018(a)(2)), reduced by: (1) the amount of adjusted taxable gifts made by the decedent after '76, and (2) the amount of any pre-'77 specific exemption allowed for gifts made by the decedent after Sept. 8, '76. (Code Sec. 6018(a)(3))[19] The time for filing the return is the same as for U.S. citizens or residents, see ¶5034.

Expatriates and former long-term residents. A tougher expatriate estate tax is imposed on the transfer of a taxable estate of a decedent nonresident non-U.S. citizen who dies during the 10-year period that he is subject to the expatriate alternative tax described at ¶4658. (Code Sec. 2107(a))

¶ 5037   Gift Tax.

The gift tax is imposed on the transfer of money or other property by gift. The gift tax is integrated with the estate tax under a "unified" rate schedule that imposes a single tax on transfers during life and at death.

The tax is imposed on the transfer, not on the property transferred. It applies even though the property transferred may be exempt from income or other taxes. (Code Sec. 2501(a); Reg § 25.2501-1, Reg § 25.2511-1(a), Reg § 25.2511-2)[20]

Gifts made by a person who, in a tax year, makes no gift of a present interest with a value of over $12,000 in 2007 (and 2008) to any one person, and who makes no gifts of future interests, aren't subject to tax, see ¶5046 (and no gift tax return need be filed, see ¶5054).

¶ 5038   Who must pay gift tax?

The gift tax must be paid by the person (the donor) who makes the gift. (Code Sec. 2501(a); Reg § 25.2511-2(f)) It applies only to donors who are individuals (Reg § 25.2501-1(b)) but a gift by a corporation may be treated as a gift by the shareholders. (Reg § 25.2511-1(h)(1))[21]

If the donor fails to pay the tax when due, the donee is also liable for the tax to the extent of the value of his gift. (Code Sec. 6324(b); Reg § 25.2502-2, Reg § 301.6324-1(b))[22]

These rules apply to a U.S. citizen or resident no matter where the gift property (tangible or intangible) is situated. (Code Sec. 2501(a); Reg § 25.2501-1(a), Reg § 25.2511-3(a))[23]

A nonresident who's not a U.S. citizen is subject to gift tax only if the gift property is real estate or tangible personal property and is situated in the U.S. at the time of the gift. (Code

18. ¶R-8000 *et seq.*; ¶21,014.02; TD ¶786,000 *et seq.*
19. ¶S-2302; ¶60,184; TD ¶783,504
20. ¶Q-1000 *et seq.*; ¶s 25,009, 25,014; TD ¶701,002
21. ¶s Q-1000 *et seq.*, Q-2400 *et seq.*; ¶s 25,014, 25,114;

TD ¶714,000
22. ¶V-9301; ¶63,244; TD ¶702,001
23. ¶Q-1016; ¶s 25,014, 25,114 *et seq.*; TD ¶703,002

Sec. 2501(a); Code Sec. 2511(a); Reg § 25.2511-1(b); Reg § 25.2511-3(a)) A nonresident generally isn't subject to tax on a gift of intangible property. (Code Sec. 2501(a)(2))

However, the gift tax applies to transfers by an individual who is subject to the expatriate alternative tax discussed at ¶4658 for the tax year that includes the date of transfer of:

. . . U.S.-situated intangibles such as stock or securities (Code Sec. 2501(a)(3)(A)), and

. . . certain stock in a foreign corporation regardless of whether the stock is situated in the U.S. (Code Sec. 2501(a)(5)(A))

¶ 5039   What is a gift?

All transactions whereby property or property rights are gratuitously bestowed upon another are gifts. (Reg § 25.2511-1(c)) After 2009, a transfer to a trust is treated as a gift unless the trust is wholly owned by the transferor or his spouse. (Code Sec. 2511(c))

A gift isn't complete (i.e., taxable), until the donor parts with dominion or control over the transferred property or property interest. He must be left without power to change the disposition of the property either for his own benefit or for that of others. (Reg § 25.2511-2(b))[24]

There's no gift tax on a transfer to a political organization. (Code Sec. 2501(a)(5))[25]

¶ 5040   Educational or medical payment exclusion.

The gift tax doesn't apply to amounts paid by one individual:

(1) on behalf of another individual directly to a qualifying educational organization as tuition for that other individual. (Code Sec. 2503(e); Reg § 25.2503-6(b)(2))

(2) on behalf of another individual directly to a provider of medical care as payment for that medical care. (Code Sec. 2503(e); Reg § 25.2503-6(b)(3)) Payments for medical insurance qualify for this exclusion. (Reg § 25.2503-6(b)(3))

These exclusions are available in addition to the annual gift tax exclusion (¶5046). (Reg § 25.2503-6(a))[26] No gift tax return is required. (Code Sec. 6019)[27]

Contributions to qualified tuition programs (¶2209 *et seq.*) and Coverdell education savings accounts (¶2205 *et seq.*) don't qualify for the Code Sec. 2503(e) tuition exclusion but, instead, are treated as present gifts that can qualify for the gift tax annual exclusion including by electively spreading contributions in a single year over a five-year period. A contributor isn't subject to gift tax on distributions from qualified tuition programs and Coverdell education savings accounts. (Code Sec. 529(c), Code Sec. 530(d)(3)) A transfer by reason of a change in the designated beneficiary under a qualified tuition program, or a rollover to the account of a new beneficiary, is subject to gift and GST taxes unless the new beneficiary is: (1) assigned to the same generation as, or a higher generation than, the old beneficiary; and (2) a member of the old beneficiary's family. (Code Sec. 529(c)(5)(B))

¶ 5041   Below-market loans.

If a below-market (or interest-free) loan is a "gift loan" (that is, a below-market loan where the forgoing of interest is in the nature of a gift), it's treated as: (1) a loan to the borrower/donee in exchange for an interest-paying note, and (2) a gift to the borrower of the funds to pay the interest. The amount of the gift equals:

. . . the forgone interest—excess of interest payable at the applicable federal rate (¶1116)

---

24. ¶Q-3004; ¶25,114.01; TD ¶711,005   26. ¶Q-5250 *et seq.*; ¶25,034; TD ¶732,501
25. ¶Q-3201; ¶25,014; TD ¶716,015   27. ¶S-2201; ¶25,014; TD ¶746,001

over actual interest payable —if the loan is a demand loan, or

... the excess of the amount loaned over the present value (using a discount rate equal to the applicable federal rate) of all payments required under the terms of the loan, if the gift loan is a term loan. (Code Sec. 7872)[28]

For demand loans, the gift is treated as made on the last day of the calendar year. (Code Sec. 7872(a)) For term loans, the gift is treated as made on the date the loan was made. (Code Sec. 7872(b))[29]

These rules don't apply to certain gift loans between individuals that don't exceed $10,000. (Code Sec. 7872(c)(2))[30]

If the outstanding balance of a gift loan made between individuals is $100,000 or less, the amount of interest treated as retransferred by the borrower to the lender each year doesn't exceed the borrower's net investment income for that year. If the net investment income is $1,000 or less, the amount treated as retransferred is zero. (Code Sec. 7872(d)(1))[31]

¶ 5042 Joint ownership of property.

A gift may result where property is placed in joint ownership with someone other than a spouse or where joint ownership with someone other than a spouse ends. [32]

If an individual with his own funds buys property and has the title conveyed to himself and others as joint tenants, with rights of survivorship, but which rights may be defeated by any joint tenant severing his interest, there is an immediate gift to the other joint tenants of equal shares of the property. (Reg § 25.2511-1(h)(5))[33]

An individual doesn't make a gift when he opens a joint bank account with his own funds for himself and another but he can regain the entire fund without the other's consent. A gift is made only when the other person withdraws money for his own benefit. (Reg § 25.2511-1(h)(4)) Similar rules apply for joint brokerage accounts and U.S. savings bonds. [34]

¶ 5043 Qualified disclaimers.

A qualified disclaimer (an irrevocable and unqualified refusal to accept ownership, made in writing by a specified deadline) with respect to any interest in property has the effect of treating that interest, for gift (and estate and generation-skipping transfer tax) purposes, as if it had never been transferred to the disclaimant. (Code Sec. 2518) And the disclaimant isn't treated as having made a gift to the person to whom the interest passes by reason of the disclaimer. (Reg § 25.2518-1(b))[35]

¶ 5044 Amount of the gift.

The amount of the gift is the money given or, if property is given, the property's value as of the date of the gift. (Code Sec. 2512(a))[36]

The market value of annuities (other than commercial annuities), unitrust interests, life estates, term of years, remainders, and reversions transferred by gift is their present value (Reg § 25.2512-5(a); Reg § 25.7520-1(a)) determined by use of standard or special Code Sec. 7520 actuarial factors. These factors are derived by using the appropriate Code Sec. 7520 interest rate[37] and, if applicable, the mortality component for the valuation date of the interest that's being valued. These factors appear in IRS issued tables. (Reg § 25.2512-

28. ¶Q-2150 *et seq.*; ¶78,724; TD ¶155,001 *et seq.*
29. ¶Q-2150; ¶78,724; TD ¶155,003
30. ¶Q-2165; ¶78,724; TD ¶155,027
31. ¶J-2905; ¶78,724; TD ¶155,005
32. ¶Q-2900 *et seq.*; ¶25,114; TD ¶714,501

33. ¶Q-2906; ¶25,114; TD ¶714,507
34. ¶Q-2921 *et seq.*; TD ¶714,519
35. ¶Q-2350 *et seq.*; ¶25,184 *et seq.*; TD ¶713,012
36. ¶Q-1200; ¶25,124; TD ¶741,000
37. ¶P-6619

5(d)(1))[38]

¶ 5045   Taxable gifts.

Taxable gifts are the gifts made during the calendar year after the annual exclusion (¶5046), and reduced by allowable deductions (¶5047, ¶5048). (Code Sec. 2503(a), Code Sec. 2503(b))[39]

¶ 5046   Annual exclusion.

The first $12,000 of gifts of a present interest made by a donor *to each donee* in 2007 (or in 2008) is excluded from the amount of the donor's taxable gifts. (Code Sec. 2503(b))[40] For 2007, the first $125,000 ($128,000 for 2008) by a donor to a spouse who isn't a U.S. citizen is excluded. (Code Sec. 2523(i)(2))[41]

No annual exclusion is allowed for gifts of future interests (Code Sec. 2503(b); Reg § 25.2503-2), e.g., reversions or remainders. (Reg § 25.2503-3)[42]

A "Crummey" power (in general, a trust beneficiary's noncumulative right to withdraw a specified amount of trust principal within a limited period) makes a transfer to the trust a gift of a present interest. [43]

A transfer for the benefit of a *minor* isn't considered a gift of a future interest if the property and its income:

(1) may be expended by or for the benefit of the minor before he reaches 21, and

(2) any balance not so expended *will pass to the minor* when he reaches 21, or if he dies before 21 will go either to his *estate* or as he may appoint under a general power of appointment. (Code Sec. 2503(c); Reg § 25.2503-4(a))[44]

Gifts to minors made through custodians designated under Uniform Acts for gifts or transfers to minors qualify for the annual exclusion. [45]

¶ 5047   Marital deduction.

A marital deduction is allowed for the value of all qualifying gifts made by one spouse to the other if the donee spouse is a U.S. citizen (with some exceptions) and the gift isn't a nondeductible "terminable interest." (Code Sec. 2523)[46]

Qualified terminable interest property (QTIP) qualifies for the deduction if the donee spouse receives income payments for life and no person has a power to appoint any part of the property to anyone other than the donee spouse during that spouse's life. (Code Sec. 2523(f))[47]

For an increased exclusion for transfers to noncitizen spouses, see ¶5046.

¶ 5048   Charitable gifts.

Charitable gifts and certain similar gifts are deducted in arriving at taxable gifts for the calendar year. (Code Sec. 2522)[48]

---

38. ¶P-6615; ¶25,124; TD ¶521,501
39. ¶Q-1000; ¶25,034; TD ¶744,008
40. ¶Q-5000 *et seq.*; ¶25,034; TD ¶731,002
41. ¶Q-5003; ¶25,034; TD ¶731,003
42. ¶Q-5100 *et seq.*; ¶25,034; TD ¶731,008
43. ¶Q-5112; ¶25,034; TD ¶731,022

44. ¶Q-5201 *et seq.*; ¶25,034; TD ¶732,001
45. ¶Q-5212; ¶25,034; TD ¶732,014
46. ¶Q-6100 *et seq.*; ¶25,234; TD ¶734,001
47. ¶Q-6300 *et seq.*; ¶25,234; TD ¶736,001
48. ¶Q-6000 *et seq.*; ¶25,224; TD ¶733,001

¶ 5049   Split gifts to third parties by married donors.

A husband and wife may consent to have their gifts to others treated as if made one-half by each (Code Sec. 2513(a); Reg § 25.2513-1) if:

... both spouses are U.S. citizens or residents on the date of the gift (Code Sec. 2513(a));

... both spouses consent (on Form 709) to have all gifts made to others in the calendar year treated as split gifts (Code Sec. 2513(a), Code Sec. 2513(b), Code Sec. 2513(c); Reg § 25.2513-1(b)(5));

... the consenting spouses are married to each other on the date of the gift and don't remarry during the remainder of the calendar year. (Code Sec. 2513(a))[49]

Each spouse is liable, jointly and severally, for the *entire* gift tax for the period in which he or she consents to split gifts. (Code Sec. 2513(d); Reg § 25.2513-4)[50]

Gifts of community property to a third party are generally considered to have been made one half by each spouse.[1]

¶ 5050   Gift tax on "estate freeze" transfers (Chapter 14 rules).

For gift tax valuation purposes, certain interests retained by the transferor after a transfer to a family member are disregarded. (This insures that a high gift tax will be imposed on the transferred interest at the time of the transfer.) These Chapter 14 (of the Code) rules apply to:[2]

... transfers of interests in corporations and partnerships;

... transfers of interests in trusts (other than certain trusts known as GRATs, GRUTs, and qualified personal residence trusts);

... buy-sell agreements and options; and

... lapsing rights.

¶ 5051   Unified credit against gift tax.

A "unified" credit of $345,800 is allowed against gift tax on gifts made by a U.S. citizen or resident. The credit effectively exempts the first $1,000,000 of transfers and remains at that level even though the unified credit against estate tax exempts $2 million in 2007 and 2008 and increases in 2009, see ¶5029. The credit against tax on gifts in a calendar period is reduced by the sum of all amounts allowable as a credit in preceding calendar periods. (Code Sec. 2505)[3]

¶ 5052   How to compute gift tax if no gifts made before current year.

If a person has *not* made any taxable gifts (in excess of annual exclusions and deductions and the pre-'77 specific lifetime exemption) before the calendar year for which the tax is being computed, the gift tax is computed as follows:[4]

(1) Determine the aggregate value of the total gifts made during the calendar year for which the tax is being computed. If the donor is married, and he and his wife have consented to split their gifts to third parties, only half of the gifts he made to third parties plus half of the gifts, if any, she made to third parties are included in computing his total gifts. (A separate gift tax computation is made for the wife, and the other half of the husband's

49. ¶Q-7000 *et seq.*; ¶25,134; TD ¶743,001
50. ¶V-8505 *et seq.*; ¶25,134; TD ¶746,007
1. ¶Q-2929 *et seq.*; ¶25,134.01; TD ¶743,001

2. ¶Q-3350; ¶s 27,014, 27,024, 27,034, 27,044; TD ¶721,002
3. ¶Q-8005; ¶25,054; TD ¶744,004
4. ¶Q-8010 *et seq.*; ¶25,009 *et seq.*; TD ¶744,008

gifts to third parties plus the other half of the wife's gifts to third parties are included in computing the wife's total gifts.)

(2) Deduct from the amount in (1), above, any amounts qualifying for the year's annual exclusion (¶5046).

(3) From the excess of (1) over (2), above, subtract the amount of charitable (¶5048) and marital (¶5047) gifts.

(4) Compute a gift tax on the excess of (1) over the sum of (2) and (3), using the unified rate schedule (¶1113).

(5) Subtract from the gift tax computed in (4), the allowable unified credit.

¶ 5053   Cumulative computation where gifts were made before current year.

Previous taxable gifts affect the amount of gift tax imposed on gifts made in the current year. These taxable gifts are taken into account whether they were made before '77 or after '76. (Code Sec. 2502) In general the gift tax (before unified credit) is the excess of: (1) a tentative tax computed under the unified rate schedules on the aggregate sum of taxable gifts for the current calendar year for which the tax is being computed *and* taxable gifts (made after June 6, '32) for all preceding years, over (2) a tentative tax computed under the unified rate schedule on the aggregate sum of the taxable gifts (made after June 6, '32) for all of the years preceding the current calendar year for which the tax is being computed. (Code Sec. 2502(a)) The gift tax payable is the excess of the tentative tax in (1) over the tentative tax in (2) reduced by the unified credit allowable.

¶ 5054   Gift tax returns—Form 709.

Any individual who makes gifts to any one donee during a calendar year which aren't fully excluded under the $12,000 annual exclusion for 2007 (and 2008) must file a gift tax return (Form 709). A return must be filed even if no tax is payable. (Reg § 25.6019-1(f)) But no return is required to report a qualified transfer for educational or medical costs (¶5040), most charitable transfers, or a transfer that qualifies for the marital deduction (¶5047) (Code Sec. 6019), except that a return must be filed to make a QTIP (¶5047) election. (Reg § 25.6019-1(a))[5] The return is due on Apr. 15 of the year following the year the gifts were made. (Code Sec. 6075) A different rule applies if the donor has died. [6] An extension for filing the income tax return automatically extends the time for filing the gift tax return for the same calendar year. (Code Sec. 6075(b)(2)) Use Form 8892 to request an extension of time to file Form 709 when not applying for an extension to file an income tax return or to make a payment of gift (or GST) tax when applying for an extension of time to file Form 709. (Reg § 25.6081-1T)[7]

¶ 5055   Generation-Skipping Transfer Tax. ▪▪▪▪▪▪▪▪▪▪▪▪▪▪▪▪▪▪▪

A "generation-skipping" transfer (GST) tax is imposed on transfers outright or in trust to beneficiaries more than one generation below the transferor's generation at a flat rate, equal to the maximum gift and estate tax rate (45% for individuals dying in 2007 through 2009). The GST tax is repealed in 2010, see ¶5000.

¶ 5056   Transfers subject to tax.

The generation-skipping tax is imposed on every generation-skipping transfer. (Code Sec. 2601) A generation-skipping transfer is any one of three taxable events: (1) a *taxable termination* of an interest in a trust if, after the termination, all interests in the trust are

---

5. ¶S-2200 *et seq.*; ¶s 25,014, 60,194; TD ¶746,001   7. ¶S-5035; ¶s 60,754, 60,814; TD ¶746,010
6. ¶S-4901; ¶60,754; TD ¶746,009

held by or for the benefit of persons two or more generations below that of the transferor (trustee pays the GST tax on taxable terminations on Form 706GS(T)), (2) a *taxable distribution* of income or principal from a trust to or for the benefit of a person two or more generations below that of the transferor (transferee pays the tax on Form 706GS(D), the trustee must file Form 706GS(D-1)), and (3) a *direct skip,* which is a transfer of an interest in property to or for the benefit of a person two or more generations below that of the transferor (transferor pays tax with Form 709 for lifetime direct skips, executor pays with Form 706 and attached Form 706, Schedule R or Form 706, Schedule R-1, for direct skips occurring at death). (Code Sec. 2611(a); Code Sec. 2612) (Use Form 8892 to request an extension of time to file Form 709 when not applying for an extension to file an income tax return or to make a payment of GST tax when applying for an extension of time to file Form 709.) In determining whether there is a generation-skipping transfer, a special rule "steps up" the generation of an individual (or the descendants of an individual) with a deceased parent that's a descendant of the transferor's parent. (Code Sec. 2651(e)(1); Reg § 26.2651-1)[8]

¶ 5057 Exemptions from tax.

Every individual is allowed a $2 million exemption (for transfers in 2007 and 2008) which may be allocated to any property transferred. (Code Sec. 2631) Married couples may treat transfers as made one-half by each spouse, in effect giving them a combined $4 million exemption (for transfers in 2007 and 2008). The GST exemption rises to $3.5 million in 2009. (Code Sec. 2652(a)(2))[9] Once a transfer is designated as exempt, all later appreciation in the value of the exempt property is also exempt. [10] The tax doesn't apply to lifetime transfers (except for certain transfers in trust) that are exempt from gift tax because of the annual exclusion (¶5046) or the exclusion for certain tuition and medical expense payments (¶5040). (Code Sec. 2642(c)(3)) For lifetime transfers, the available GST exemption is automatically allocated to a direct skip under Code Sec. 2632(b), and to indirect skips made after Dec. 31, 2000 under Code Sec. 2632(c), unless the individual elects out of the automatic allocation under Code Sec. 2632(b)(3) and Code Sec. 2632(c)(5), respectively. The automatic allocation under Code Sec. 2632(c) also applies to an indirect skip occurring upon the post-2000 termination of an estate tax inclusion period. (Code Sec. 2632(c)(4)) Regs provide details about these elections. (Reg § 26.2632-1)[11]

8. ¶R-9500 *et seq.*; ¶s 26,014, 26,114, 26,124 *et seq.*; TD ¶791,001
9. ¶R-9551; ¶s 26,014, 26,314; TD ¶791,004

10. ¶R-9557; ¶26,324; TD ¶791,004
11. ¶R-9501 *et seq.*; ¶26,424; TD ¶791,001

INDEX

References are to paragraph [¶] numbers.

A

Abandonment
. loss
    generally 1784
. . deductible loss, defined 1774
. . fruitless searches 1504
. . mortgaged property 1788
. reporting of, for secured property 4750
. U.S. citizenship 4658
Abatement of interest
    generally 4869
. failure to abate 4857, 4858
Abortion as medical expense 2145
**Above-the-line deductions (adjustments
    to income)**
. alimony paid 2155
. Archer medical savings accounts (MSAs) 1528
. educators, limited deduction for expenses
    of 2232
. higher education expenses . . . . 2222 et seq.
. IRAs 4352
. military reservists, overnight travel ex-
    penses 1554
. moving expenses 1647
. performing artists, expenses of 3105
. self-employed health insurance 1533
. self-employed retirement plans 4351
. student loan interest . . . . 2225 et seq.
. taxes 1757
Abusive tax shelters
. penalties 4827, 4835,
    4888
. potentially abusive 1319
Accelerated depreciation
    See "Depreciation"
Accident and health insurance plans
    *See "Health and accident insurance
    plans"*
Accountants
. audits by IRS, representing taxpayer at 4809
. expenses of 1633
. fees for 1603, 1605,
    5017
. . corporate dissolution and liquidation 3578
Accounting expenses, deductibility 1603, 1605
Accounting income 3938
Accounting methods
    generally . . . . 2816 et seq.
. accrual method
    See "Accrual basis"
. advance payments, accrual method of ac-
    counting 2829
. Advance Trade Discount Method 2826
. carryover by successor corporation 3562
. cash method
    See "Cash basis"
. changes of
    generally . . . . 2837 et seq.
. . adjustments required . . . . 2841 et seq.

Accounting methods — Cont'd
. changes of — Cont'd
. . allocations, relief for high-impact adjust-
    ments 2844
. . application for 2840
. . automatic consent procedure 2840, 2845
. . definition 2839
. . depreciation, accounting for 1901, 2839
. . four-year/one-year rule, adjustment inclu-
    sion periods 2843
. . inclusion period, adjustment 2843
. . inventories 2868, 2881
. . IRS permission to change 2838
. . Sec. 481(a) adjustments . . . . 2841 et seq.
. establishing method 2817
. farmers . . . . 4504 et seq.
. hybrid methods 2818
. inventories
    See "Inventories"
. limits on choice of 2818
. long-term contracts . . . . 2848 et seq.
. records to substantiate 2817
Accounting period
    See also "Taxable year"
    generally . . . . 2800 et seq.
. change of 2805, 2814,
    2815
Accounting reserves, deductibility 2846, 2847
Accounts receivable
. amortization 1980
. capital assets 2617
. intangible assets 2471
Accrual basis
    generally . . . . 2824 et seq.
. acquisition discount 1328
. advance payments . . . . 2829 et seq.
. all-events test 2832
. charitable contributions, 2 1/2 month rule 2134
. compensation for personal services
. . time for deduction . . . . 1538 et seq.
. . time to report 1274
. contested liability 2834
. contingent rights to income 2826
. dealers' reserves 2828
. decedents 3965
. discounts on purchases 2869
. disputed liability for goods, income accrual
    for 2827
. economic performance 2833
. expense deductions, timing of . . . . 1538 et seq.,
    2832
. farmers . . . . 4508 et seq.,
    4518
. gain or loss on sale or exchange 2408
. interest income, time to report 1335, 1337
. interest paid, time to deduct 1748, 1750
. payments to related cash basis taxpayer 2836
. payroll tax liability 1539
. prepaid insurance 1609
. previously reported income, repayments of,
    time for deduction of repayment 2861

References are to paragraph [¶] numbers.   **I-13**

References are to paragraph [¶] numbers.

    References are to paragraph [¶] numbers.

References are to paragraph [¶] numbers.

References are to paragraph [¶] numbers.

References are to paragraph [¶] numbers.

References are to paragraph [¶] numbers.

References are to paragraph [¶] numbers.

MARGIN INDEX

To use, bend book in half and follow margin index to page with black edge marker.

The left index column refers to the left bank of markers; the right index column to the right bank of markers.